BUSINESS MATHEMATICS

Annotated Instructor's Edition

BUSINESS MATHEMATICS

WILLIAM L. KINDSFATHER

W. ALTON PARISH

Prentice Hall Upper Saddle River, New Jersey 07458

The Library of Congress has cataloged the full edition as follows:

Kindsfather, William L.
  Business mathematics / William L. Kinsfather, W. Alton Parish.
    p. cm.
  Includes index.
  ISBN 0-13-086699-7
    1. Business mathematics.   I. Parish, W. Alton.   II. Title.
HF5691 .K625 2003
650′.01′51--dc21

2002020792

Publisher: Stephen Helba
Executive Editor: Frank Mortimer, Jr.
Editorial Assistant: Barbara Rosenberg
Managing Editor: Mary Carnis
Production Management: Ann Mohan, WordCrafters Editorial Services, Inc.
Production Liaison: Brian Hyland
Director of Manufacturing and Production: Bruce Johnson
Manufacturing Manager: Ilene Sanford
Creative Director: Cheryl Asherman
Senior Design Coordinator: Miguel Ortiz
Marketing Manager: Tim Peyton
Composition: The Clarinda Company
Printer/Binder: Banta Menasha
Copyeditor: Patsy Fortney
Proofreader: Shirley Ratliff
Interior Design: Lee Goldstein
Cover Design: Wanda España
Cover Printer: Phoenix Color Corp.

Pearson Education Ltd.
Pearson Education Australia Pty. Limited
Pearson Education Singapore Pte.Ltd.
Pearson Education North Asia Ltd.
Pearson Education Canada Ltd.
Pearson Educación de Mexico, S.A. de C.V.
Pearson Education—Japan
Pearson Education Malaysia, Pte. Ltd.
Pearson Education, Upper Saddle River, New Jersey

10 9 8 7 6 5 4 3 2 1
ISBN 0-13-086707-1

CONTENTS

2 FUNDAMENTAL OPERATIONS WITH DECIMAL FRACTIONS   34

UNIT 2

FUNDAMENTALS FOR DOING BUSINESS

6 PAYROLL APPLICATIONS — 166

7 MARKETING APPLICATIONS: BUYING — 222

UNIT 3

BANKING AND FINANCE IN BUSINESS

9 DEMAND DEPOSITS (CHECKING ACCOUNTS) AND BANK RECONCILIATION   300

10 BANKING APPLICATIONS: SIMPLE INTEREST   338

UNIT 5

BUSINESS TOOLS

23 INTERNATIONAL BUSINESS MATH   798

PREFACE

Business Mathematics was written with the student in mind. Some textbooks present concepts in skeletal form, either because the authors believe that the student already knows the concepts or because they are attempting to conserve space. While it is necessary to present the mathematical concepts in as clear and understandable a manner as possible, the business uses of mathematics should not be overlooked. Business math is one of the first business courses taken by many students. These students, new to the discipline, still do not know business terminology. They certainly do not know much about the functional areas of business or the environment within which business firms operate. Thus, a business math course must fulfill a dual role to be successful. It is much easier for students to understand how to do the math if they also understand why business firms use it.

Business Mathematics provides students with practical concepts and skills that are useful in a business career. Those same skills are also useful in related business courses and for functioning in consumer markets. Students who develop an understanding of this book will have a head start in such courses as introduction to business, accounting, marketing, management, finance, and economics. In those classes they can devote their study time to understanding the concepts of the discipline rather than having to learn the mathematics associated with it. Business majors should find the chapters Marketing Applications, Financial Applications, Accounting Applications, and Management Applications especially useful.

Business Mathematics is constructed in such a way that any chapter can be omitted without sacrificing continuity or logical progression. The five-unit, twenty-three-chapter format is intended to fit a typical 16-week semester with one unit covered every three weeks and a 16th week for review and final exams.

UNIT ONE, Basic Mathematics for Business (Chapters 1 through 5), is intended entirely for review, and some instructors may choose to move through it quickly. The only chapter the authors consider an absolute necessity for background is Chapter 5, Percentage Applications.

UNIT TWO, Fundamentals for Doing Business (Chapters 6 through 8), exposes students to the fundamental activities of carrying on a day-to-day enterprise, such as taking care of their employees' payroll, buying goods, and selling goods.

UNIT THREE, Banking and Finance in Business (Chapters, 9 through 15), reviews the uses of checking accounts and how to maintain them, the various methods of calculating interest, including compound interest, present value, future value, and annuities. It also discusses installment buying and mortgages.

UNIT FOUR, Record Keeping and Analysis (Chapters 16 through 21), is significant not only for people who major in business hoping to work for large business firms, but also for people who hope to succeed as independent business entrepreneurs. Understanding the basics of accounting principles, interpreting financial statements, calculating depreciation, keeping accurate records of inventory and overhead, keeping up with taxes, and maintaining adequate insurance coverage are essential skills for independent businesspeople. For others, especially those involved with corporate business, a look at buying and selling corporate securities (stocks and bonds) is important.

UNIT FIVE, Business Tools (Chapters 22 and 23), introduces students to the uses of statistics and to reading and designing graphs. Chapter 23 completes the course with a discussion of foreign currencies, including the new euro.

The authors of *Business Mathematics* have provided the best possible text and supporting package so that instructors can devote all of their energies to providing educational classroom experiences. The textbook includes the following features:

Using the Electronic Calculator The inside cover of *Business Mathematics* describes the proper use of a hand-held electronic calculator. Calculators are valuable tools when all of their features are understood and used. Students can refer to this feature to learn how to use common calculator functions. Some instructors may want to review this material with their students at some point in the course, or they may just want to make the students aware of the feature and its potential usefulness.

Chapter Vignettes Each chapter begins with a kind of short story to "break the ice." Although a few are purely fictional, most are based on actual happenings, history, or situations. Each opens the door to the chapter topic in a light way intended to put students at ease.

Objectives Each chapter includes a list of objectives students should meet. If a student accomplishes those objectives, it can be assumed that the student and the chapter both have succeeded.

Glossary A list of key words, terms, and expressions is provided, with accompanying definitions. Placing the glossary at the beginning of the chapter introduces students to terminology at a point where it is easily accessible and makes a strong first impression.

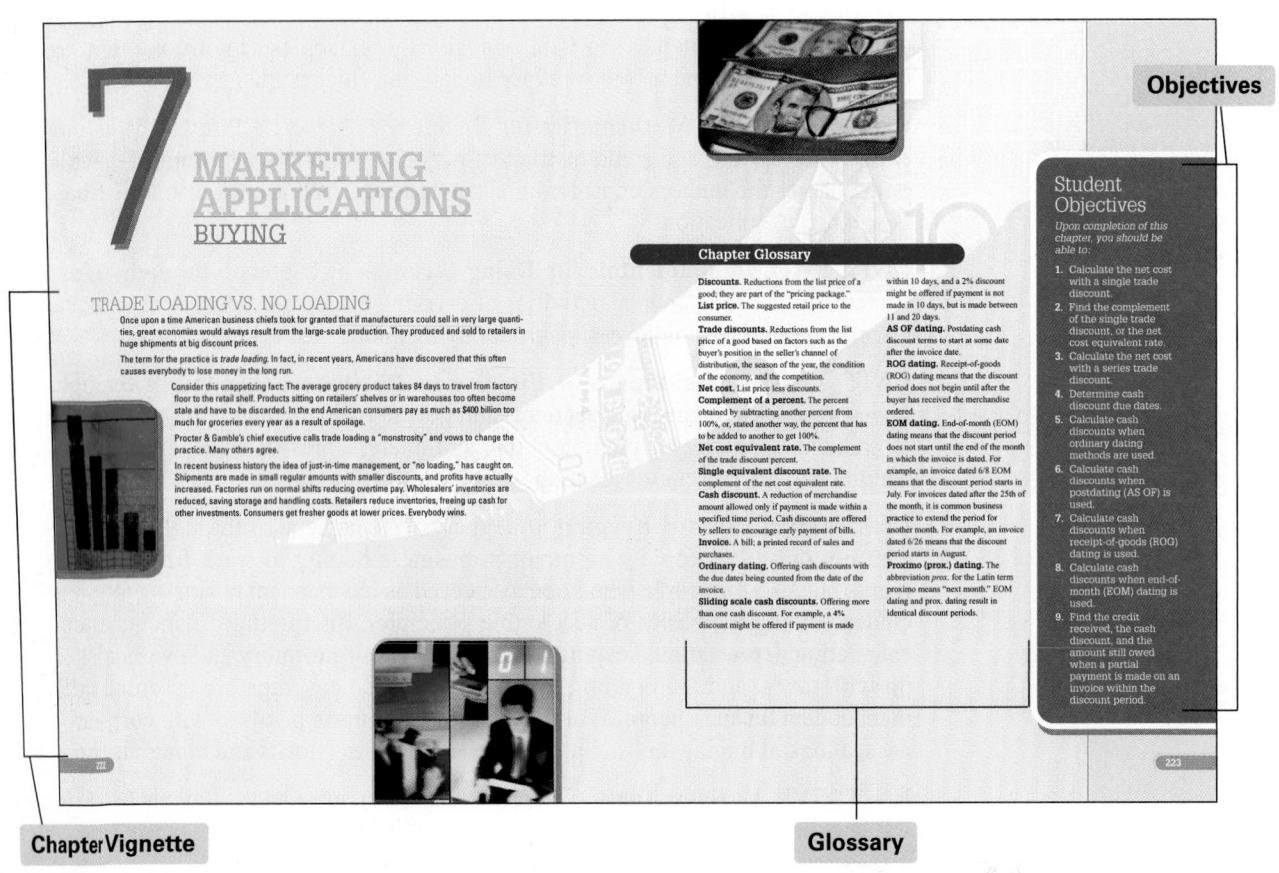

Objectives

Chapter Vignette

Glossary

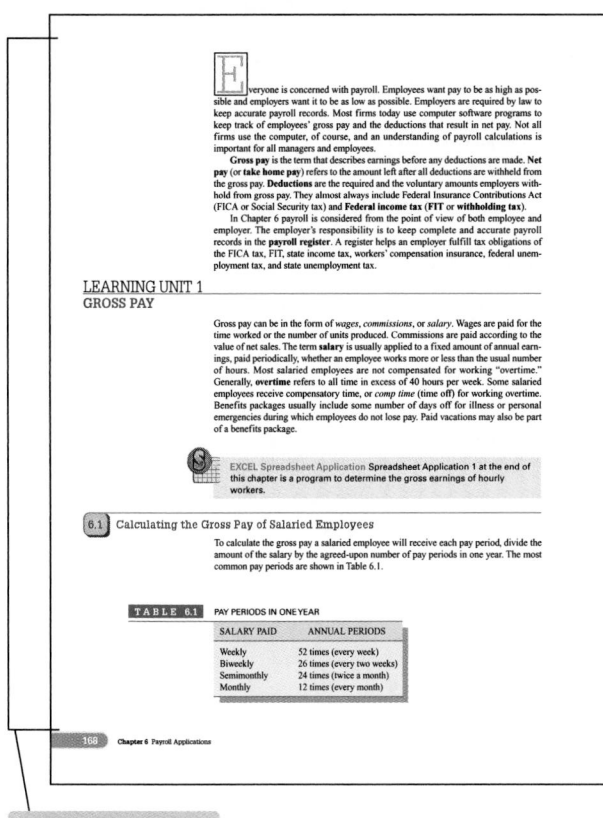

Logical Layout

Logical Layout Each section of *Business Mathematics* opens with an explanation of a concept, an example of a problem illustrating that concept, and a solution to the problem. The section concludes with four practice problems and their solutions so that students can check their understanding of the section's content. This feature is unique. Other texts provide practice problems and give the correct answer, but not the solution. The solution is a tremendous learning tool, giving students the opportunity to attempt the problems, check the answers, and, if their answers are incorrect, discover where they went wrong.

Calculator Solution

Practice Problems

Solutions

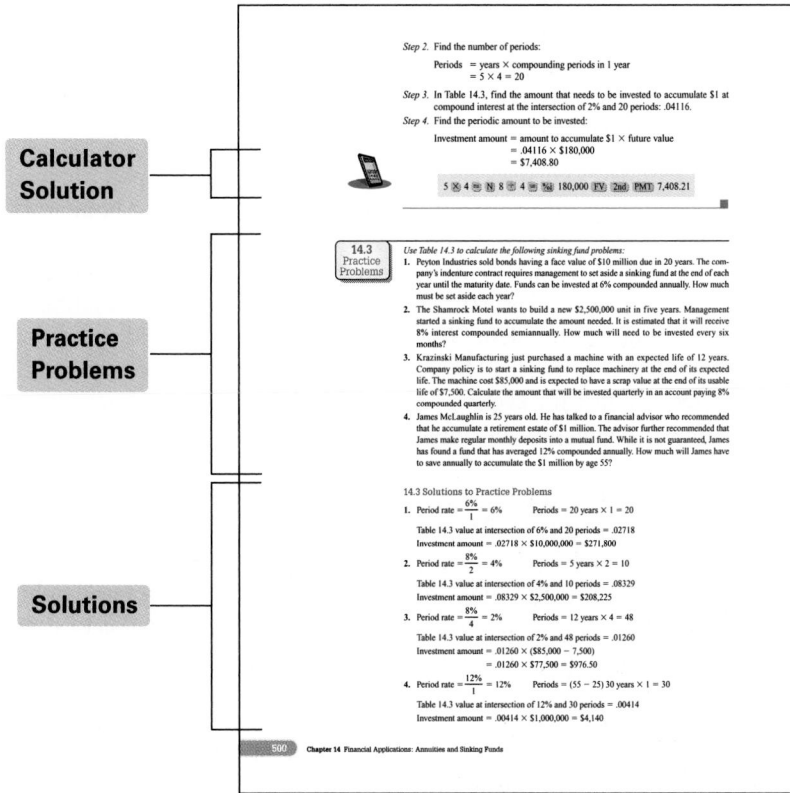

Calculator Solutions Calculator solutions are included for each example in which the authors have determined that an electronic calculator might be most useful. Of course a calculator can help with almost any math problem, but specialized features can be especially helpful in some instances. The problems are worked as they would be with a calculator, with the necessary keystrokes indicated.

Quick Reference Summary and Review *Business Mathematics* furnishes, at the completion of the material in each chapter, a reinforcement section that reviews every topic in the chapter, with an explanation and an example problem and solution.

End-of-Chapter Materials The end-of-chapter material begins with a feature called Surfing the Internet. Students who have access to computers are encouraged to check out Internet sites to further enhance their understanding of chapter materials.

Business Mathematics contains more problems than most instructors would probably require their students to work.

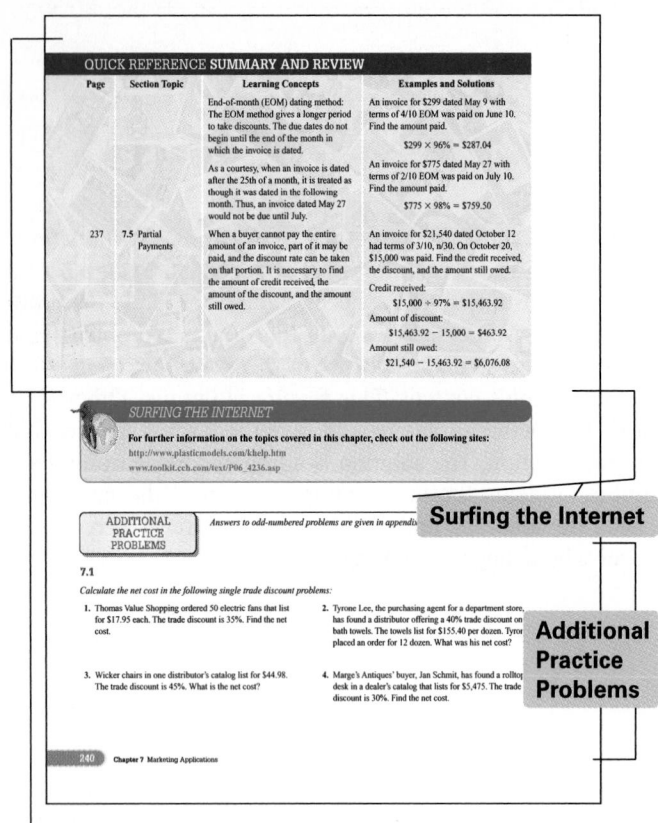

Quick Reference Summary and Review

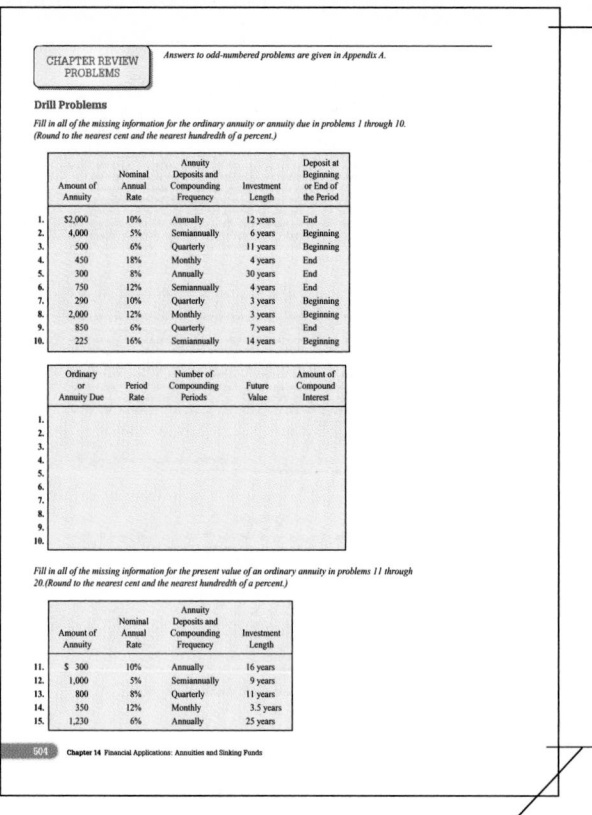

Surfing the Internet

Additional Practice Problems

Chapter Review Problems

This is intentional. With so many problems from which to choose, instructors can fashion the course to satisfy the requirements of the skill level of any particular class. Some students will need more practice than others. The amount required should be for the skilled instructor, not the authors, to determine. Problems are divided into Additional Practice Problems, Chapter Review Problems, Enrichment Problems, Critical Thinking Group Project, and Self-Testing Exercises and are followed by Excel Spreadsheet Applications and Group Reports.

- **Additional Practice Problems** correspond with each section in the chapter's textual material, which makes it easy for instructors to assign in-class work or homework according to the material that has been covered.
- **Chapter Review Problems** consist of drill problems and word problems. Drill problems give students practice using specific procedures without having to delineate specifics from the wording of a problem. Word problems must be solved by using a conceptual problem-solving approach. These problems are different from the additional practice problems in that the section from which they are taken is not identified, and thus require more thought and a more thorough understanding of the chapter materials.
- **Enrichment Problems** are designed to be a little more difficult and thought provoking and will stretch the abilities of most students. They can also be used in a group problem-solving situation.
- **Critical Thinking Group Project** These projects are designed to be considerably more involved and taxing than the other problems in the chapter. The goal is to stimulate and encourage problem analysis as well as problem solving through group interaction.
- **Self-Testing Exercises** are a group of problems assembled much like a test for the material in the chapter. The purpose is to inform students about what to expect at exam time. To promote an all-inclusive educational process, each Self-Testing Exercise

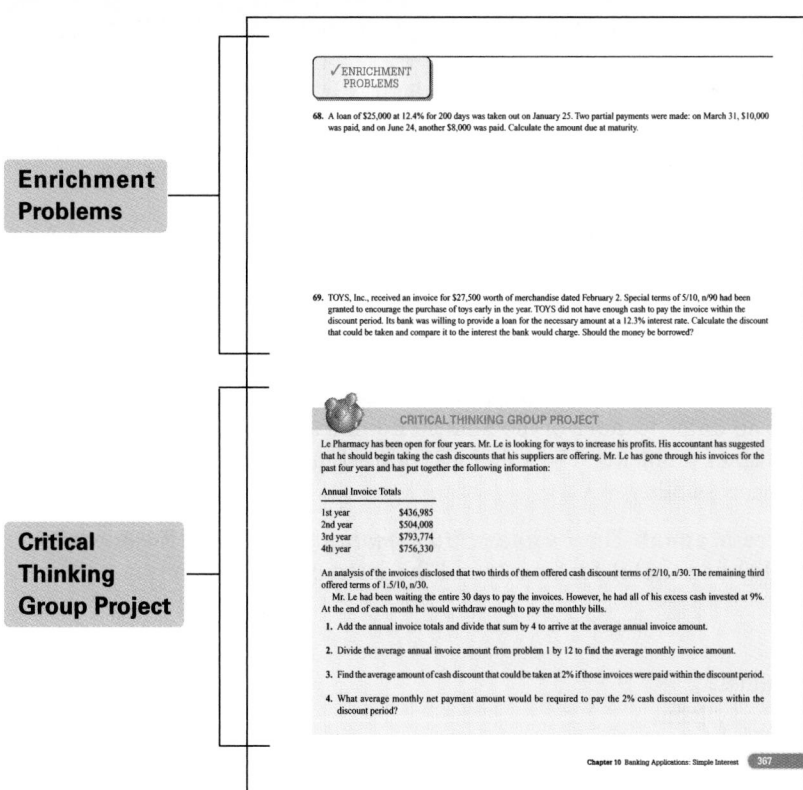

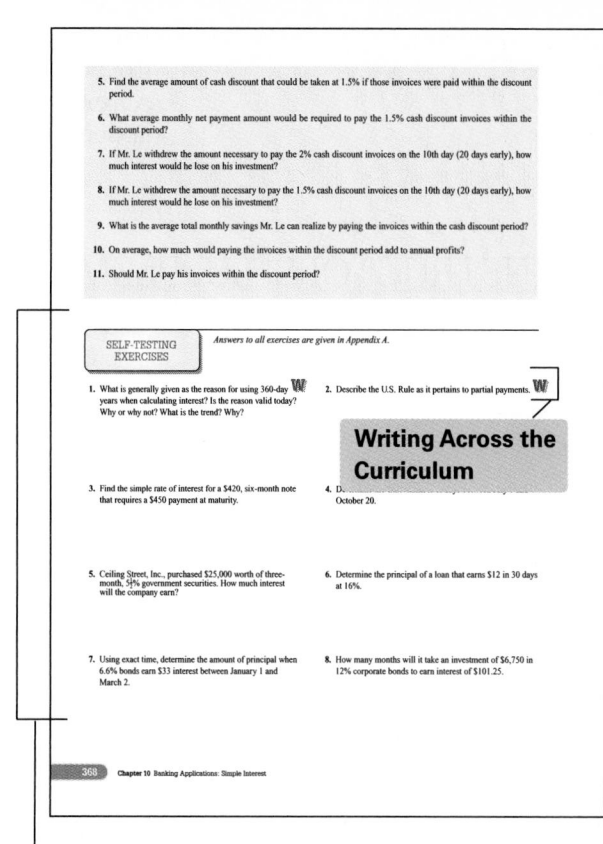

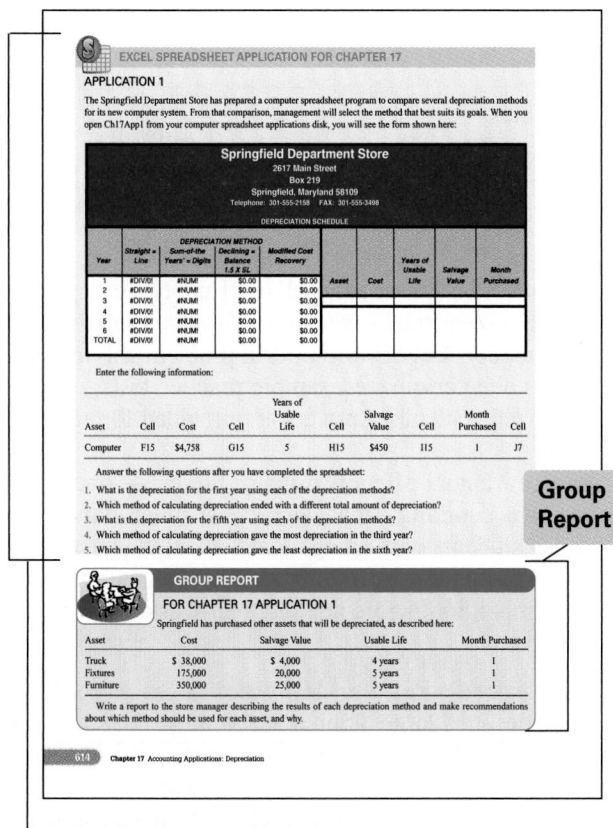

section begins with one or two problems for "Writing Across the Curriculum." These problems require written answers to questions. Their purpose is to incorporate business mathematics with written expression. Writing Across the Curriculum problems are indicated by a **W** icon.

- **Excel Spreadsheet Applications** are provided in most chapters, and, for continuity, all use the fictitious Springfield Department Store as the example. These applications exemplify the originality of the text. Each application is relevant to the material in the chapter and can enhance student interest in the subject. In our technological age, these exercises provide a reason to practice and learn more about computer usage. An icon and boxed reference is placed within the text to identify the chapter material to which the Excel Spreadsheet Application relates.

- **Group Report** After the Excel Spreadsheet Application, a Group Report activity is presented to stimulate individual and group interest and insight. Students are asked to prepare a report to the management of Springfield Department Store.

APPENDIXES The textbook concludes with the following appendixes:

- Appendix A provides answers to the odd-numbered Additional Practice Problems and Chapter

Review Problems, and all answers to Enrichment Problems and Self-Testing Exercises.
- Appendix B teaches students how to calculate federal (FUTA) and state (SUTA) unemployment taxes.

INSTRUCTORS' SUPPLEMENTS

In addition to the textbook, *Business Mathematics* provides an extensive package of supplements to aid instructors and enhance the teaching and learning experience.

Annotated Instructor's Edition The Annotated Instructor's Edition of *Business Mathematics* contains all of the features of the Student Edition as well as the solutions to all of the end-of-chapter problems. The solutions, printed in color, are adjacent to the problems for easy accessibility.

Instructor's Resource Manual The *Business Mathematics* Instructor's Resource Manual offers the following useful features to aid the instructor in structuring and teaching the course:

- *Course Structure*
  - Scheduling guidelines.
  - A suggested course syllabus.
  - Suggestions for incorporating use of the electronic calculator.
  - Suggestions for using the Spreadsheet Applications.
  - Suggestions for assigning and grading the projects on the stock and bond markets and accounting.

- *Teaching Aids*
  - Chapter overview.
  - Teaching tips.
  - Student objectives.
  - Chapter glossary.
  - Lecture outline with space for notes.
  - Quick reference summary and review.
  - Answers to even-numbered end-of-chapter problems.
  - Solutions to the Spreadsheet Applications.

- *Exams* A series of exams are provided in the Instructor's Resource Manual, including two short exams for each chapter, two exams for each unit, and two comprehensive final exams. In each of these categories, one exam is objective and can be scored electronically, while the other consists of word or drill problem-solving exercises. These exams can be used as chapter quizzes, sample practice tests, or questions to be added to the computerized testbank. Answers are provided for all of the exam questions.
- *Projects* The Instructor's Resource Manual offers two major projects—one on the stock and bond markets and one on accounting—that can be used either individually or in teams. These projects furnish students with an up-close look at the major principles at work in financial markets. Using these projects, students can gain from the valuable experience of friendly competition before tackling real-world competition, which often is not so friendly.

Testbank (Hardcopy and Computerized) *Business Mathematics* has an extensive testbank from which instructors can design a large number and variety of tests. It contains almost 2,500 test questions, including fill-in-the-blank questions (which can easily be changed to matching questions if preferred), true/false questions, multiple-choice questions, drill problems, and word problems. This testbank is available both in hard copy and as the computerized *Prentice Hall Test Manager.*

PowerPoint Presentation *Business Mathematics* makes this innovative package available for use when students need additional help. The package provides opportunities to review and practice problem solving.

Transparencies Two types of transparencies are available as part of the *Business Mathematics* package:

- *Problem Transparencies* Solutions for all example problems in the text, as well as for representative end-of-chapter problems. These are provided as transparency masters in the Instructor's Resource Manual.
- *Teaching Transparencies* Color transparencies available on PowerPoint to adopters of the text. These transparencies help illustrate and dramatize material presented in the chapters.

STUDENT SUPPLEMENTS

Study Wizard with Excel Spreadsheet Applications A CD is provided free of charge with each *Business Mathematics* textbook to enhance and enrich the student's learning experience. The instructor can use this CD to assign additional homework or study assignments, or students may use it as a study guide for exams. It provides a multitude of additional practice problems for each chapter in different formats, including vocabulary terms, true/false questions, and multiple-choice questions.

Student Solutions Manual *Business Mathematics* provides solutions for student use as follows:

- *Additional Practice Problems* Solutions to all odd-numbered problems.
- *Chapter Review Problems*
  - Drill Problems Answers to all odd-numbered problems, and solutions to the first odd-numbered problem that is representative of a section of problems.
  - Word Problems Solutions to all odd-numbered problems.
- *Enrichment Problems* Solutions to all problems.
- *Self-Testing Exercises* Solutions to all problems.

Companion Website The Companion Website acts as an electronic study guide providing students with additional exercises and resources. It can be found at **www. prenhall.com/kindsfather.**

Handbook of Tables and Using the Electronic Calculator This supplement contains all of the tables used in the textbook, most of them in a more complete form. These can be used by instructors and students alike. Instructors can use better examples not limited by a partial table. Test questions can refer students to the Handbook when tables are necessary to solve the test questions. It also provides instruction in the 10-key calculator and computer keypad, helping students apply new skills in the world of business math. Additional practice problems are provided so students can practice solving problems using various features of the electronic calculator.

ACKNOWLEDGMENTS

We are grateful to the following reviewers for their insight and advice:

Russell Baker, Howard Community College, Columbia, MD

James Abbott, Broome Community College, Binghamton, NY

Erwin Zweifel, Madison Area Technical College, Madison, WI

Dr. Robert Smits, Towson University, Towson, MD

Susan Pfeifer, Butler County Community College, Andover, KS

In addition, we are thankful to David Cook and Robbie Sheffy for their help in ensuring the accuracy of the text.

The following editors and support people have given long hours, inspired help, and significant recommendations toward making this book and supplement package the best it could be: Frank Mortimer, Brian Hyland, and Mary Carnis at Prentice Hall; Carey Davies at Pearson Education; Mickey Orcutt and Jeffrey Rahman at Tamarack; and Ann Mohan at WordCrafters.

Most of all, to those two who had to sacrifice companionship while we were at the computer and weather temper tantrums when things did not go as planned, yet continued to offer support, aid, and love, we want to thank Vivian Kindsfather and Juanita Parish.

While we take responsibility for any errors that may appear, we must share any success this book might enjoy with all of the people listed above and many others who made contributions. Thank you one and all.

William L. Kindsfather

W. Alton Parish

ABOUT THE AUTHORS

William L. Kindsfather is Professor of Marketing, Emeritus, Tarrant County College. He earned his B.B.A. from the University of New Mexico and his M.B.A. from the University of Texas at Arlington. Professor Kindsfather spent several years as a sales representative for the American Hospital Supply Company, a marketing research manager for Lone Star Gas, and an instructor of marketing and management at the University of Texas at Arlington before joining the faculty of Tarrant County College in 1972. He is coauthor of *Today's Business World* and author of articles on the state of marketing education in the United States in the *Journal of Expression.*

W. Alton Parish is Professor of Economics, Emeritus, Tarrant County College. He earned his B.S. and M.S. from the University of North Texas and his Ed.D. from the University of Arkansas, Fayetteville. Dr. Parish taught macro and microeconomics at Paris Junior College, the University of Indianapolis, and the University of Arkansas before joining the faculty of Tarrant County College in 1972. He has written more than 57 economic and political editorials for the *Dallas Morning News, Fort Worth Star-Telegram, Illinois Farm Alliance, Arkansas Times, Arkansas Gazette, Journal of Expression, Texas Community College Teachers' Journal,* and *Granbury Gazette.* He founded the *Journal of Expression* and served as political editor for *The Granbury Gazette.*

BUSINESS MATHEMATICS

1 FUNDAMENTAL OPERATIONS WITH WHOLE NUMBERS

HOW BIG IS A BIG NUMBER?

The late U.S. Senator Everett Dirksen (R of Illinois) used a line that went "a billion here a billion there, a billion here a billion there, and after a while we are talking about some real money." Numbers used to describe societal functions today are commonly so large that people cannot identify with them.

A recent newspaper article reports that the U.S. government will spend $400 billion for national defense this year. Does that mean exactly $400,000,000,000, or might it have been $391,538,253,198.17? Would anybody read a story about the government spending three hundred ninety-one billion, five hundred thirty-eight million, two hundred fifty-three thousand, one hundred ninety-eight dollars, and seventeen cents? A real question that might be raised is, what was the seventeen cents for? The 400 billion figure is rounded to the 100 billions place, but what became of $8,461,746,801.83 (eight billion, four hundred sixty-one million, seven hundred forty-six thousand, eight hundred one dollars, and eighty-three cents)? The number was rounded.

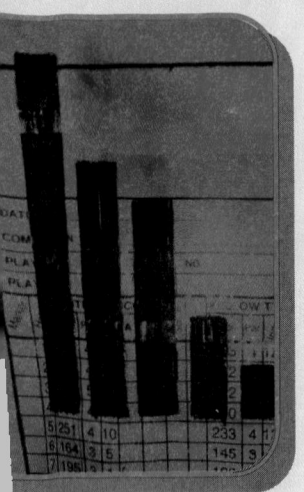

In macroeconomics courses, professors point out that there are two ways to add up the total production of the nation. Either add all the spending or add all the earnings. The figures will be exactly equal, give or take a few billion dollars. That few-billion-dollar error is called a statistical error, the result of rounding two series of numbers in the billions.

Chapter Glossary

Eras. Three-digit intervals in a decimal whole number separated by commas to simplify reading.

Addend. Numbers to be added.

Sum (or Total). The result of addition.

Estimation. A ballpark figure that helps verify an answer.

Rounding all the way. Rounding numbers until only the leftmost number is a nonzero.

Minuend. The number from which another number is subtracted.

Subtrahend. The number to be subtracted from another number.

Difference. The distance between two numbers (the result of subtraction).

Factors. Numbers being multiplied together.

Multiplicand. The number being multiplied.

Multiplier. The number multiplying.

Product. The result of a multiplication problem.

Partial product. The numbers between the bottom factor and the product. The result of multiplying the top factor by one of the digits in the bottom factor.

Quotient. The answer in a division problem. The number of times one number, the divisor, is contained in another number, the dividend.

Divisor. The number dividing by.

Dividend. The number being divided.

Remainder. The number left as a result of uneven division (when the divisor will not divide evenly into the dividend).

Student Objectives

Upon completion of this chapter, you should be able to:

1. Read and write whole numbers.
2. Round whole numbers.
3. Add, subtract, multiply, and divide whole numbers.
4. Estimate answers in addition, subtraction, multiplication, and division.
5. Recite the multiplication table through 12.
6. Multiply and divide whole numbers by 10, powers of 10, and other zeros.
7. Prove answers in addition, subtraction, multiplication, and division of whole numbers.

LEARNING UNIT 1
REVIEW OF FUNDAMENTAL ARITHMETIC OPERATIONS

The yearly output of the United States is well over $7 trillion. World businesses and governments annually buy and sell goods and services valued in hundreds of billions of dollars. The use of very large numbers has become common, so the ability of individuals to read, write, and understand them is essential.

1.1 Reading and Writing Whole Numbers

Decimal numbering is a positional system. That means numbers take on different *values* when they occupy different positions. To simplify reading and writing numbers, commas are placed at three-digit intervals, called *eras*, starting at the right and moving to the left. When writing numbers, you must hyphenate the numbers twenty-one (21) to ninety-nine (99). Study Table 1.1 to learn decimal positional value names.

EXAMPLE   Write the whole number two million, eight hundred sixty-seven thousand, three hundred ten with the commas in the proper positions.

Solution   2,867,310

EXAMPLE   Read the whole number 7,194,295,368 in verbal form.

Solution   7, 1 9 4, 2 9 5, 3 6 8

From the illustration, read the number as seven billion, one hundred ninety-four million, two hundred ninety-five thousand, three hundred sixty-eight. (*Note:* The word *and* was not used in the verbal reading or writing of the whole number. The word *and* designates the position of a decimal point when one is necessary.)

1.1 Practice Problems

Write the following in verbal form:
1. 3,582
2. 938
3. 104,523,678
4. 948,195

1.1 Solutions to Practice Problems
1. three thousand, five hundred eighty-two
2. nine hundred thirty-eight
3. one hundred four million, five hundred twenty-three thousand, six hundred seventy-eight
4. nine hundred forty-eight thousand, one hundred ninety-five

TABLE 1.1   DECIMAL POSITIONAL VALUE NAMES

Trillions	Billions	Millions	Thousands	Units
0 0 0,	0 0 0,	0 0 0,	0 0 0,	0 0 0

1.1 Practice Problems

Write the following as numerals:
1. Two thousand, nine hundred fifty-five
2. Four billion, three hundred five thousand, eight hundred
3. One million, five hundred fifty-seven thousand, sixty-one
4. Five hundred sixty million, four hundred thirty-five

1.1 Solutions to Practice Problems
1. 2,955   **2.** 4,000,305,800   **3.** 1,557,061   **4.** 560,000,435

1.2 Rounding Whole Numbers

A number is often rounded off because either it is unnecessary to be perfectly accurate or it is not feasible or convenient to determine the exact number. The following rules should be followed in rounding:*

1. Identify the digit occupying the position to be rounded.
2. If the first digit to the right of the number to be rounded is 5 or greater, the digit identified to be rounded should be increased by 1, and all digits to the right of it should be replaced by zeros.
3. If the first digit to the right of the digit to be rounded is 4 or less, it and all digits to the right of it are replaced by zeros. Do not change the identified digit.

EXAMPLE   Round 653,729 to the nearest thousand.

Solution   654,000   3 is in the thousands position and is the identified digit to be rounded. The first digit to its right is 7, which is greater than 4. Thus, the 3 is raised to 4, and the 7, 2, and 9 should be replaced by zeros.

EXAMPLE   Round 653,729 to the nearest hundred.

Solution   653,700   7 is in the hundreds position and is the identified digit to be rounded. The first digit to its right is 2, which is less than 4. Therefore, the identified digit is not changed, and the 2 and 9 are replaced by zeros.

> *In this text, unless otherwise stated, all answers will be rounded to the nearest thousandth, except dollar amounts. They will be rounded to the nearest cent (hundredth).*

1.2 Practice Problems

Round the following problems as indicated:
1. 738 to the nearest hundred
2. 8,376 to the nearest ten
3. 764,038,365 to the nearest ten thousand
4. 56,476,287 to the nearest million

1.2 Solutions to Practice Problems
1. 700   7 is the identified digit. To its right, the 3 is less than 5. Thus, the 7 is unchanged, and the 3 and 8 are changed to zeros.
2. 8,380   7 is the identified digit. To its right, the 6 is greater than 5. Thus, the 7 is changed to an 8, and the 6 is changed to a zero.

3. 764,040,000   3 (in the ten thousands position) is the identified digit. To its right, the 8 is greater than 5. Thus, the 3 is changed to 4, and the 8, 3, 6, and 5 are all changed to zeros.

4. 56,000,000   6 (in the millions position) is the identified digit. To its right, the 4 is less than 5. Thus, the 6 is unchanged, and the 4, 7, 6, 2, 8, and 7 are all changed to zeros.

LEARNING UNIT 2
ADDITION

All numbers to be added are called **addends**. The result of addition is called the **sum**, or **total**.

1.3 Adding Whole Numbers

When aligning whole numbers to be added, be certain the units are under each other. That means they should be *justified* on the right. You can add from the top down or the bottom up. To check your work, reverse the process. While not necessary for a correct answer, for clarity the number with the most digits is generally written first, then the number with the second most digits, and so on.

EXAMPLE   Find the sum of 52 + 389 + 12 + 23,385 + 7,214.

Solution

			Proof:	
23,385	Addend			12
7,214	Addend			52
389	Addend			389
52	Addend			7,214
12	Addend			23,385
31,052	Sum or total			31,052

1.3 Practice Problems

Find the sum for the following problems:

1. 27 + 64 + 8

2. 8,174 + 147 + 10,250

3. 98,472 + 906,452 + 9,846

4. 115,038 + 12,763 + 1,236

1.3 Solutions to Practice Problems

1.	**2.**	**3.**	**4.**
27	10,250	906,452	115,038
64	8,174	98,472	12,763
8	147	9,846	1,236
99	18,571	1,014,770	129,037

1.4 Estimating Addition Problems

Common sense is often the best tool available when solving business mathematics problems. Everyone makes an occasional mistake, such as hitting the wrong key on a calculator. It stands to reason that everyone should develop a way to estimate mathematical solutions to which actual calculations can be compared. **Estimations** will verify that the calculation is in the "ballpark."

Solutions to addition problems can be estimated by a process called **rounding all the way**. Rounding all the way means that there will be only one non-zero digit. The estimate may not be very close to exact when rounded all the way. If greater accuracy is necessary, round to a specific digit, for example, the nearest thousand. Rounding to a specific digit depends on the accuracy being sought. If, for example, the number 54,999 is rounded to the nearest thousand, the resulting number will be 55,000, which is only 1 from the actual value. If rounding all the way is used, the resulting number would be 50,000. (The leftmost digit is 5, and the number to its right is 4. Therefore, the 5 is left unchanged, and the 4, 9, 9, and 9 are all changed to zeros.) That answer is 4,999 less than the original number.

E X A M P L E Add 1,416 + 2,189 + 104 + 36,429. Find both the actual and estimated figures by rounding all the way.

Solution

Actual	Estimated
36,429	40,000
1,416	1,000
2,189	2,000
+ 104	+ 100
40,138	43,100

1.4
Practice
Problems

Add the following decimal numbers and estimate the solution using rounding all the way:
1. 56 + 23 + 76
2. 376 + 847 + 198 + 79
3. 2,856 + 164,274 + 29,461
4. 92,957 + 271,276 + 2,723

1.4 Solutions to Practice Problems

	Actual	Estimated		Actual	Estimated
1.	56	60	**2.**	376	400
	23	20		847	800
	+ 76	+ 80		198	200
	155	160		+ 79	+ 80
				1,500	1,480
3.	164,274	200,000	**4.**	271,276	300,000
	29,461	30,000		92,957	90,000
	+ 2,856	+ 3,000		+ 2,723	+ 3,000
	196,591	233,000		366,956	393,000

LEARNING UNIT 3
SUBTRACTION

Subtraction involves finding the difference between two numbers.

1.5 **Subtracting Whole Numbers**

Finding the **difference** or **remainder** between two numbers involves subtracting a number called the **subtrahend** from another number called the **minuend**. Typically, the minuend is placed on the top and the subtrahend on the bottom in a set-up problem.

E X A M P L E Subtract 2,893 from 9,928

Solution

9,928	*Minuend*	Proof:	7,035	*Difference*
−2,893	*Subtrahend*		+2,893	*Subtrahend*
7,035	*Difference*		9,928	*Minuend*

Subtraction is begun with the rightmost digit. First subtract 3 from 8 in the units position and get a difference of 5 (8 − 3 = 5). The next column to the left is the tens position. Subtract 9 tens (90) from 2 tens (20). Since that cannot be done, 1 hundred must be borrowed from the 9 in the hundreds position in the minuend.

The 9 is reduced to an 8 (9 hundreds − 1 hundred = 8 hundreds). The borrowed hundred is turned into 10 tens. Add the 2 tens and the 10 tens together, and we have 12 tens in the minuend. Subtract the 9 tens in the subtrahend from the 12 tens in the minuend. That results in a difference of 3 tens (12 − 9 = 3). In the hundreds column subtract the 8 hundreds in the subtrahend from the 8 hundreds left in the minuend and get a difference of 0 hundreds (8 − 8 = 0). The last operation is to subtract the 2 in the thousands position in the subtrahend from the 9 in the thousands position in the minuend and get a difference of 7 (9 − 2 = 7). Thus, the final difference is 7,035. The correctness of the answer can be proved by adding the difference and the subtrahend together. If the sum is the minuend of the original problem, the answer is correct.

1.5 Practice Problems

Solve for the difference in each of the following subtraction problems:

1. 435 − 124
2. 2,750 − 371
3. 28,563 − 4,875
4. 370,472 − 318,936

1.5 Solutions to Practice Problems

1.	435	2.	2,750	3.	28,563	4.	370,472
	−124		− 371		− 4,875		−318,936
	311		2,379		23,688		51,536

1.6 Estimating Subtraction Problems

As in addition, the digit to be rounded in subtraction will be dictated by the need for estimating accuracy. For ballpark figures, however, rounding all the way is recommended.

EXAMPLE Subtract 3,850 from 47,389. Find both the actual and the estimated figures by rounding all the way.

Solution

	Actual	Estimated
	47,389	50,000
	− 3,850	− 4,000
	43,539	46,000

1.6 Practice Problems

Subtract the following decimal numbers and estimate the solution using rounding all the way.

1. 479 − 383
2. 17,349 − 4,985
3. 9,351 − 936
4. 389,193 − 327,120

1.6 Solutions to Practice Problems

	Actual	Estimated		Actual	Estimated
1.	479	500	2.	17,349	20,000
	−383	−400		− 4,985	− 5,000
	96	100		12,364	15,000
3.	9,351	9,000	4.	389,193	400,000
	− 936	− 900		−327,120	−300,000
	8,415	8,100		62,073	100,000

LEARNING UNIT 4
MULTIPLICATION

Multiplication is essentially a shortcut method of addition that is used when a series of addends have the same value.

$$5 + 5 + 5 + 5 + 5 = 25, \text{ just as } 5 \times 5 = 25.$$

1.7 Multiplying Whole Numbers

If you have not done so already, you should memorize the multiplication table provided on the inside cover. The numbers being multiplied in a multiplication problem are referred to as **factors**. (Another name for the top number in multiplication is the **multiplicand**, which is the number being multiplied, and the bottom number is sometimes called the **multiplier**, which is the number you are multiplying by. The answer is referred to as the **product**, and the numbers between the bottom factor and the product are **partial products**.

In multiplication, the order of the factors can be reversed; for example, 4×5 will result in the same product as 5×4.

EXAMPLE Multiply 4,132 by 24

Solution

4,132	*Factor*	
$\times$ 24	*Factor*	
16 528	*Partial product*	
82 64	*Partial product*	
99,168	*Product*	

Proof: 24
          $\times$ 4,132
              48
              72
            2 4
            96
          99,168

The process can be illustrated as shown here:

$$4,132 \times 4 \;=\; 16,528 \quad \textit{Partial product}$$
$$4,132 \times 20 = +\ 82,640 \quad \textit{Partial product}$$
$$\ 99,168 \quad \textit{Product}$$

For the first partial product, 4,132 is multiplied by 4 (the 4 occupies the units position, and $4 \times 1 = 4$). The result is 16,528. Next, 4,132 is multiplied by 20 (the 2 in 24 occupies the tens position, and $2 \times 10 = 20$). The result is 82,640 for the second partial product. The two partial products are then added together to arrive at the final product ($4,132 + 82,640 = 99,168$). The location of the partial products is important. On each partial product line, the rightmost digit of each partial product is placed directly below the digit we are multiplying by in the multiplication process. While multiplication can be proved by reversing the factors as illustrated, it is more common to prove multiplication by division. That process will be illustrated later.

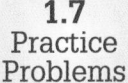

1.7 Practice Problems

Find the product in the following multiplication problems.

1. 27×74
2. 245×934
3. $3,025 \times 1,032$
4. 280×25

1.7 Solutions to Practice Problems

1.
$$\begin{array}{r} 27 \\ \times\,74 \\ \hline 108 \\ 1\,89 \\ \hline 1,998 \end{array}$$

2.
$$\begin{array}{r} 245 \\ \times\,934 \\ \hline 980 \\ 7\,35 \\ 220\,5 \\ \hline 228,830 \end{array}$$

3.
$$\begin{array}{r} 3,025 \\ \times\,1,032 \\ \hline 6\,050 \\ 90\,75 \\ 000\,0 \longleftarrow \\ 3\,025 \\ \hline 3,121,800 \end{array}$$

Unnecessary, except to remind you to properly position 3,025.

4.
$$\begin{array}{r} 280 \\ \times\,25 \\ \hline 1\,400 \\ 5\,60 \\ \hline 7,000 \end{array}$$

1.8 Multiplying Whole Numbers by 10, Powers of 10, and Other Zeros

To multiply any number by 10, you merely add the number of zeros in the 10-multiple factor to the number being multiplied. That means it is unnecessary to multiply rows of zeros.

EXAMPLE Multiply 410 by 10, 100, 1,000, and 10,000.

Solution

$$410 \times 10 = 4,10\mathit{0} \qquad \text{Add 1 zero to 410.}$$
$$410 \times 100 = 41,0\mathit{00} \qquad \text{Add 2 zeros to 410.}$$
$$410 \times 1,000 = 410,\mathit{000} \qquad \text{Add 3 zeros to 410.}$$
$$410 \times 10,000 = 4,100,\mathit{000} \qquad \text{Add 4 zeros to 410.}$$

When either or both factors end in one or more zeros, merely multiply all the other digits together and add the total number of zeros in all the factors combined.

EXAMPLE Multiply 4,200 by 50 and 140.

Solution

4,200	would be	42	(+ 2 zeros)
× 50		× 5	(+ 1 zero)
		210,*000*	(+ 3 zeros)

4,200	would be	42	(+ 2 zeros)
× 140		× 14	(+ 1 zero)
		168	
		42	
		588,*000*	(+ 3 zeros)

When a zero or zeros are in the middle of a factor, you do not need to have a row of zeros. Instead, you can leave a space for it in the partial product and multiply by the number to the left of the zero in the factor you are multiplying by.

Remember to write the rightmost digit of the partial product below the number you are multiplying by.

EXAMPLE Multiply 469 by 108.

Solution

$$\begin{array}{r} 469 \\ \times\,108 \\ \hline 3\,752 \\ 0\,00 \\ 46\,9 \\ \hline 50,652 \end{array} \qquad \begin{array}{r} 469 \\ \times\,108 \\ \hline 3\,752 \\ 46\,9 \\ \hline 50,652 \end{array}$$

Multiply the following:

1.	673	**2.**	210	**3.**	1,000	**4.**	7,200
	× 100		× 10		× 322		× 3,008

1.8 Solutions to Practice Problems

1. 673 × 1 = 673 (+ 2 zeros) = 67,3*00*   **2.** 210 × 1 = 210 (+ 1 zero) = 2,10*0*

3. 322 × 1 = 322 (+ 3 zeros) = 322,*000*   **4.**
$$\begin{array}{r} 3{,}008 \\ \times\ 72 \quad \text{(+ \textbf{2 zeros})} \\ \hline 6\,016 \\ 210\,56\ \\ \hline 21{,}657{,}6\textit{00} \quad \text{(with 2 zeros)} \end{array}$$

1.9 Estimating Multiplication Problems

Estimating multiplication problems is usually a good idea because of the potential for sizable errors. Rounding all the way is recommended. The result of rounding all the way may not be very accurate, but remember, you want a ballpark estimate so that you know your answer is approximately correct, say 3,000 and not 300 or 30,000.

E X A M P L E   Multiply 56 × 193 × 32. Find both the actual and estimated products by rounding all the way.

Solution

	Actual		*Estimated*	
193	10,808	200	10,000	
× 56	× 32	× 60	× 30	
1 158	21 616	12,000	300,000	
9 65	324 24			
10,808	345,856			

Multiply the following problems and estimate the solutions by rounding all the way.

1. 12 × 35   **2.** 48 × 47   **3.** 340 × 1,600   **4.** 205 × 700

1.9 Solutions to Practice Problems

	Actual	*Estimated*
1.	12	10
	× 35	× 40
	60	400
	36	
	420	
2.	48	50
	× 47	× 50
	336	2,500
	1 92	
	2,256	
3.	34 (+ 1 zero)	300
	× 16 (+ 2 zeros)	× 2,000
	204	600,000
	34	
	544,*000* (with 3 zeros)	
4.	205	200
	× 7 (+ 2 zeros)	× 700
	143,5*00* (with 2 zeros)	140,000

Division is the reverse of multiplication.

1.10 Dividing Whole Numbers

In division a quantity (the **quotient**), is found when a given quantity (the **dividend**) is divided by another quantity (the **divisor**). For example, $28 \div 7 = 4$ and $4 \times 7 = 28$. This determines how many times one number or quantity is contained in another. If a divisor does not divide evenly into the dividend, there will be *uneven division*. That means there is a **remainder**.

Several symbols are used to indicate division such as: $\div$, $\overline{)}$, $\dfrac{n}{n}$ and $/$. These symbols are used interchangeably throughout this book.

EXAMPLE   Divide 468 by 6.

Solution

$$\begin{array}{r} 78 \\ \text{Divisor} \quad 6\overline{)468} \end{array}$$

Quotient
Dividend

This example illustrates even, short division. It is even division because there is no remainder. It is short division because the divisor has only one digit.

EXAMPLE   Divide 9,456 by 54.

Solution

$$\begin{array}{r} 175 \\ 54\overline{)9{,}456} \\ \underline{54} \\ 405 \\ \underline{378} \\ 276 \\ \underline{270} \\ 6 \end{array}$$

This example illustrates uneven, long division. It is uneven division because there is a remainder. It is long division because the divisor has more than one digit.

1.10 Practice Problems

Divide the following numbers:

1. Even, short division
   a. Divide 55 by 5.
   b. Divide 64 by 4.
   c. Divide 2,328 by 8.

2. Even, long division
   a. Divide 55 by 11.
   b. Divide 64 by 16.
   c. Divide 2,328 by 291.

3. Uneven, short division
   a. Divide 77 by 9.
   b. Divide 83 by 3.
   c. Divide 3,219 by 7.

4. Uneven, long division
   a. Divide 612 by 52.
   b. Divide 97 by 12.
   c. Divide 27,173 by 264.

1.10 Solutions to Practice Problems

1. a.
$$\begin{array}{r} 11 \\ 5\overline{)55} \\ \underline{55} \end{array}$$

b.
$$\begin{array}{r} 16 \\ 4\overline{)64} \\ \underline{64} \end{array}$$

c.
$$\begin{array}{r} 291 \\ 8\overline{)2,328} \\ \underline{2,328} \end{array}$$

2. a.
$$\begin{array}{r} 5 \\ 11\overline{)55} \\ \underline{55} \end{array}$$

b.
$$\begin{array}{r} 4 \\ 16\overline{)64} \\ \underline{64} \end{array}$$

c.
$$\begin{array}{r} 8 \\ 291\overline{)2,328} \\ \underline{2,328} \end{array}$$

3. a.
$$\begin{array}{r} 8 \ \text{R5} \\ 9\overline{)77} \\ \underline{72} \\ 5 \end{array}$$

b.
$$\begin{array}{r} 27 \ \text{R2} \\ 3\overline{)83} \\ \underline{6} \\ 23 \\ \underline{21} \\ 2 \end{array}$$

c.
$$\begin{array}{r} 459 \ \text{R6} \\ 7\overline{)3,219} \\ \underline{2\,8} \\ 41 \\ \underline{35} \\ 69 \\ \underline{63} \\ 6 \end{array}$$

4. a.
$$\begin{array}{r} 11 \ \text{R40} \\ 52\overline{)612} \\ \underline{52} \\ 92 \\ \underline{52} \\ 40 \end{array}$$

b.
$$\begin{array}{r} 8 \ \text{R1} \\ 12\overline{)97} \\ \underline{96} \\ 1 \end{array}$$

c.
$$\begin{array}{r} 102 \ \text{R245} \\ 264\overline{)27,173} \\ \underline{26\,4} \\ 77 \\ \underline{0} \\ 773 \\ \underline{528} \\ 245 \end{array}$$

1.11 Dividing Whole Numbers by 10, Powers of 10, and Other Zeros

When the divisor is 10 or any multiple of 10, and the dividend also ends with a zero or zeros, the division process can be shortened. Drop the same number of zeros from the end of both the dividend and the divisor, beginning on the right and moving to the left.

The same process can be used when both the divisor and the dividend end in zeros even when the divisor does not begin with a 1. However, the division process is still necessary. It is only shortened.

EXAMPLE   Divide 40,000 by 10, 100, and 1,000.

Solution
$40,000 \div 10 = 4,000$ *Drop 1 zero.*
$40,000 \div 100 = 400$ *Drop 2 zeros.*
$40,000 \div 1,000 = 40$ *Drop 3 zeros.*

EXAMPLE   Divide 34,000 by 1,700.

Solution $34,000 \div 1,700 = 340 \div 17$ *Drop 2 zeros.*

$$\begin{array}{r} 20 \\ 17\overline{)340} \\ \underline{34} \\ 0 \\ \underline{0} \end{array}$$

Since 1,700 contains two zeros and the dividend, 34,000, contains as many (or more) zeros, drop two zeros from both numbers. Then complete the division process.

1.11 Practice Problems

Divide the following numbers by 10 or powers of 10 and other zeros:

1. $50,000 \div 10$

2. $35,000 \div 1,000$

3. $14,000 \div 700$

4. $6,300 \div 210$

1. $50,000 \div 10$ (drop 1 zero) $5,000 \div 1 = 5,000$
2. $35,000 \div 1,000$ (drop 3 zeros) $35 \div 1 = 35$
3. $14,000 \div 700$ (drop 2 zeros) $140 \div 7 = 20$
4. $6,300 \div 210$ (drop 1 zero) $630 \div 21 = 30$

1.12 Estimating Division Problems

Before division problems are worked, it is useful to estimate the answer by rounding. Unless more accuracy is necessary, rounding all the way is recommended to provide rough figures.

EXAMPLE   Divide 428 by 64. Find both the actual and the estimated figures.

Solution

Actual	*Estimated*
6 R44	$400 \div 60 = 40 \div 6$ (drop 1 zero)
64)428	6 *Since we are only interested in*
384	6)40 *approximations, we do not need to*
44	36 *be concerned about the remainder.*

1.12 Practice Problems

Divide the following. Find both the actual and the estimated quotient.
1. $448 \div 14$
2. $2,268 \div 18$
3. $632 \div 79$
4. $756 \div 12$

1.12 Solutions to Practice Problems

	Actual	*Estimated*		*Actual*	*Estimated*
1.	32	$400 \div 10 = 40$	2.	126	$2000 \div 20 = 100$
	14)448			18)2,268	
	42			1 8	
	28			46	
	28			36	
				108	
				108	
3.	8	$600 \div 80 = 60 \div 8 = 7$	4.	63	$800 \div 10 = 80$
	79)632			12)756	
	632			72	
				36	
				36	

LEARNING UNIT 6
PROVING MULTIPLICATION AND DIVISION PROBLEMS

Since multiplication is the reverse of division, multiplication can be proved by division, and division can be proved by multiplication.

1.13 Proving Multiplication and Division Problems

Prove multiplication by *dividing the product by one of the factors*. If the answer is correct, the *quotient* will be *the other factor* of the original problem.

If the division is correct and the answer is *even, multiplying the quotient by the divisor* will render a product that is the *dividend*. If the answer to the problem is *uneven, multiply the quotient by the divisor, and add the remainder*. The sum will be the *dividend*.

EXAMPLE Multiply and prove 312 × 38.

Solution

$$\begin{array}{r} 312 \\ \times\ 38 \\ \hline 2\ 496 \\ 9\ 36\ \\ \hline 11,856 \end{array}$$

Proof:
$$\begin{array}{r} 312 \\ 38\overline{)11,856} \\ \underline{11\ 4} \\ 45 \\ \underline{38} \\ 76 \\ \underline{76} \end{array}$$

EXAMPLE Divide and prove 962 ÷ 26.

Solution

$$\begin{array}{r} 37 \\ 26\overline{)962} \\ \underline{78} \\ 182 \\ \underline{182} \end{array}$$

Proof:
$$\begin{array}{r} 37 \\ \times\ 26 \\ \hline 222 \\ 74\ \\ \hline 962 \end{array}$$

EXAMPLE Divide and prove 4,965 ÷ 47.

Solution

$$\begin{array}{r} 105\ \text{R30} \\ 47\overline{)4,965} \\ \underline{4\ 7} \\ 26 \\ \underline{0} \\ 265 \\ \underline{235} \\ 30 \end{array}$$

Proof:
$$\begin{array}{r} 105 \\ \times\ 47 \\ \hline 735 \\ 4\ 20\ \\ \hline 4,935 \\ +\ 30 \quad \text{Remainder} \\ \hline 4,965 \end{array}$$

1.13 Practice Problems

Perform the indicated operations and prove your answer.
1. 12)38,412
2. 414 × 89
3. 57)1,433
4. 99 × 60

1.13 Solutions to Practice Problems

Solution	*Proof*		*Solution*	*Proof*

1.
$$\begin{array}{r} 3,201 \\ 12\overline{)38,412} \\ \underline{36} \\ 2\ 4 \\ \underline{2\ 4} \\ 1 \\ \underline{0} \\ 12 \\ \underline{12} \end{array}$$

$$\begin{array}{r} 3,201 \\ \times\ 12 \\ \hline 6\ 402 \\ 32\ 01\ \\ \hline 38,412 \end{array}$$

2.
$$\begin{array}{r} 414 \\ \times\ 89 \\ \hline 3\ 726 \\ 33\ 12\ \\ \hline 36,846 \end{array}$$

$$\begin{array}{r} 414 \\ 89\overline{)36,846} \\ \underline{35\ 6} \\ 1\ 24 \\ \underline{89} \\ 356 \\ \underline{356} \end{array}$$

	Solution	Proof		Solution	Proof

3.

```
       25 R8        57
57)1,433          × 25
   1 14           285
   293          1 14
   285          1,425
     8          +  8
                1,493
```

4.

```
    99                99
  × 6(0)        6(0))5,94(0)
    54                5 4
    5 4               54
  5,940               54
```

 **EXCEL Spreadsheet Application** The spreadsheet application at the end of this chapter determines the salaries for the employees of the Springfield Department Store, and the total salary expense for the store.

LEARNING UNIT 7
FORMATTING: A BLUEPRINT TO SUCCESS

Guidelines are helpful in problem solving. Just as a builder must have a plan, as a math student you need a format to help solve problems. The format forces you to search for particular concepts to help find solutions through a workable structure. As you learn to use formatting properly, you should find that your errors will be fewer and fewer.

 ## 1.14 Using Formatting to Solve Problems in Addition, Subtraction, Multiplication, and Division

The recommended format for solving equations is shown in Figure 1.1. There are three parts to the format.

Question or Unknown
What are you trying to find? Ultimately, a problem will either ask a specific question or tell you to find something. If the problem ends in a question mark (?), it is almost always a question. If there is no question mark, be aware of a sentence that sounds like an order.

Key Words or Phrases
Certain words tip you off as to which type of problem you have encountered. If you find one of the following words, you might be able to assume which kind of problem it is:

Addition	sum, plus, more, total
Subtraction	difference, minus, less, fewer
Multiplication	product, times, of
Division	quotient, by, per, into
Solution	statement that constructs a solvable mathematical problem

Figure 1.1.
Format For Solving Basic Arithmetic Problems

Question or Unknown	Key Word or Phrase	Mathematical Operation

Addition Problems

EXAMPLE

Jan is now 18. Harold is 13. What is their total age?

Solution

Question or Unknown	Key Word or Phrase	Mathematical Operation
What is their total age?	total	Addition

18	*Jan's age*
+ 13	*Harold's age*
31	*Total age*

Subtraction Problems

EXAMPLE

Profit is $2,000 less this year than last year at Buckhorn Cowboy Supplies. Last year's profit was $47,000. How much is this year's profit?

Solution

Question or Unknown	Key Word or Phrase	Mathematical Operation
How much is this year's profit?	less	Subtraction

$47,000	*Last year's profit*
− 2,000	*Amount of decrease in profit*
$45,000	*This year's profit*

Multiplication Problems

EXAMPLE

A machine can produce 146 books in 1 hour. What would be the product if the machine was operated 14 hours?

Solution

Question or Unknown	Key Word or Phrase	Mathematical Operation
What would be the product?	product	Multiplication

146	*Number of books a machine can produce in one hour*
×14	*Number of hours machine is operated*
2,044	*Product (number of books produced)*

Division Problems

EXAMPLE

A car gets 31 miles per gallon of gasoline. On a 1,147-mile trip, how many gallons of gasoline were required?

Solution

Question or Unknown	Key Word or Phrase	Mathematical Operation
How many gallons of gasoline?	per	Division

$$31 \text{ miles per gallon } \overline{)1,147 \text{ miles}} \quad 37 \text{ gallons}$$

1. Last week Charlie Jones jogged 14 miles, his wife, Clara Belle, jogged 21 miles, and his daughter Elsie jogged 27 miles. How many total miles did the Jones family jog?

2. Ngumu Btumo drank 14 cups of coffee yesterday. She drank 5 cups today. How many fewer did she drink today than yesterday?

3. Jesse Pate bought 4 tires for his car at $72 each and 5 quarts of oil at $2 each. How much was his total bill?

4. June January is making stew for a family of four. Her recipe called for 12 ounces of diced onions per 12 people. How many ounces should June use?

1.14 Solutions to Practice Problems

1.

Question or Unknown	Key Word or Phrase	Mathematical Operation
How many total miles did the Jones family jog?	total	Addition

$$
\begin{array}{r}
14 \\
21 \\
+\ 27 \\
\hline
62
\end{array}
\quad
\begin{array}{l}
\textit{Charlie's miles} \\
\textit{Clara Belle's miles} \\
\textit{Elsie's miles} \\
\textit{Total miles}
\end{array}
$$

2.

Question or Unknown	Key Word or Phrase	Mathematical Operation
How many fewer did Nguma drink yesterday?	fewer	Subtraction

$$
\begin{array}{r}
14 \\
-\ 5 \\
\hline
9
\end{array}
\quad
\begin{array}{l}
\textit{Cups drunk yesterday} \\
\textit{Cups drunk today} \\
\textit{Fewer today than yesterday}
\end{array}
$$

3.

Question or Unknown	Key Word or Phrase	Mathematical Operation
Tires as part of the total bill	How much	Multiplication

$$
\begin{array}{r}
\$\ 72 \\
\times\ 4 \\
\hline
\$\ 288
\end{array}
\quad
\begin{array}{l}
\textit{Price per tire} \\
\textit{Number of tires bought} \\
\textit{Total bill for tires}
\end{array}
$$

Question or Unknown	Key Word or Phrase	Mathematical Operation
Oil as part of the total bill	How much	Multiplication

$$
\begin{array}{r}
\$\ 2 \\
\times\ 5 \\
\hline
\$\ 10
\end{array}
\quad
\begin{array}{l}
\textit{Price per quart} \\
\textit{Number of quarts bought} \\
\textit{Total bill for oil}
\end{array}
$$

Question or Unknown	Key Word or Phrase	Mathematical Operation
How much was his total bill?	total	Addition

$$\begin{array}{r} \$288 \\ +\ 10 \\ \hline 298 \end{array}$$ *Total bill for tires*
Total bill for oil
Total bill

4.

Question or Unknown	Key Word or Phrase	Mathematical Operation
How many ounces of diced onions?	per	Division

Size of group to be served $4\overline{)12}$ to serve 12 people

3 ounces to serve 4 people

QUICK REFERENCE SUMMARY AND REVIEW

Page	Section Topic	Learning Concepts	Examples and Solutions
4	**1.1** Reading and Writing Whole Numbers	Place commas at three-digit intervals called eras. Learn decimal place values. Do not use the word *and* when reading numbers. Hyphenate numbers 21 through 99.	1. 128 is read and written, one hundred twenty-eight. 2. 1,498,765 is read one million, four hundred ninety-eight thousand, seven hundred sixty-five.
5	**1.2.** Rounding Whole Numbers	1. Identify digit to be rounded. 2. Round up if digit to the right of the identified digit is 5 or more. Do not change the identified digit if digit is 4 or less. 3. Replace numbers to the right of the identified digit with zeros.	Round 128 to the nearest ten. 130. 2 is the identified digit. The number to its right is 8, which is greater than 5. 2 is rounded up to 3, and the number to its right is replaced with a zero.
6	**1.3** Adding Whole Numbers	Numbers to be added are addends. Answers are a sum or total. Adding a column can be done by adding up or down. Reverse the direction to prove your answer.	$\begin{array}{rl} 956 & \text{Addend} \\ +\ 317 & \text{Addend} \\ \hline 1,273 & \text{Sum} \end{array}$
6	**1.4** Estimating Addition Problems	Use rounding all the way. The leftmost digit is the only nonzero digit.	$\begin{array}{rcr} 956 & \to & 1,000 \\ +\ 317 & \to & +\ 300 \\ \hline 1,273 & \to & 1,300 \end{array}$
7	**1.5** Subtracting Whole Numbers	Finding the difference between the larger number, the minuend, and the smaller number, the subtrahend. Add the difference and subtrahend to prove. The sum will be the minuend.	$\begin{array}{rl} 417 & \text{Minuend} \\ -\ 329 & \text{Subtrahend} \\ \hline 88 & \text{Difference} \end{array}$ Proof: $\begin{array}{r} 329 \\ +\ 88 \\ \hline 417 \end{array}$

Page	Section Topic	Learning Concepts	Examples and Solutions
8	**1.6** Estimating Subtraction Problems	Use rounding all the way.	$\begin{array}{rcr} 417 & \rightarrow & 400 \\ -329 & \rightarrow & -300 \\ \hline 88 & \rightarrow & 100 \end{array}$
9	**1.7** Multiplying Whole Numbers	A shortcut method of addition. Numbers being multiplied are factors. The answer is the product. The numbers between the bottom factor and the product are partial products.	$\begin{array}{rl} 78 & \text{Factor} \\ \times\,21 & \text{Factor} \\ \hline 78 & \rceil\ \textit{Partial} \\ 1\,56 & \rfloor\ \textit{Products} \\ \hline 1{,}638 & \text{Product} \end{array}$
10	**1.8** Multiplying by 10, Powers of 10, and Other Zeros	Count ending zeros, but do not multiply by them. Multiply remaining digits and, after finding the product, place counted zeros on the right of the product.	$217 \times 100 = 21{,}700$ (Count two zeros. Multiply 217 by 1. Place the two counted zeros to the right of the product.) $\begin{aligned} & 700 \times 140 \\ =\ & 7 \times 14\ (+\ 3\ \text{zeros}) \\ =\ & 98\ (+\ 3\ \text{zeros}) \\ =\ & 98{,}000 \end{aligned}$
11	**1.9** Estimating Multiplication Problems	Use rounding all the way.	$\begin{array}{rclr} 78 & \rightarrow & & 80 \\ \times\,21 & \rightarrow & & \times\,20 \\ \hline 78 & & & 1{,}600 \\ 1\,56 & & & \\ \hline 1{,}638 & & & \end{array}$
12	**1.10** Dividing Whole Numbers	Division is the reverse of multiplication. The result (the quotient) is the number of times one number (divisor) is contained in another (dividend). The divisor can go an even number of times or uneven number of times into the dividend. If uneven, there there will be a remainder.	$\begin{array}{r} 15 \quad \text{even} \\ 25\overline{)375} \\ \underline{25} \\ 125 \\ \underline{125} \end{array}$ $\begin{array}{r} 65 \quad \text{R15} \\ 76\overline{)4{,}955} \\ \underline{4\,56} \\ 395 \\ \underline{380} \\ 15 \end{array}$
13	**1.11** Dividing by 10, Powers of 10, and Other Zeros	Drop the same number of zeros from the end of the dividend and the divisor. Then, divide as usual.	$\begin{aligned} 76{,}000 \div 100 &= \\ 760 \div 1 &= 760 \\ 2{,}500 \div 50 &= \\ 250 \div 5 &= 50 \end{aligned}$
14	**1.12** Estimating Division Problems	Use rounding all the way.	$\begin{aligned} & 4{,}955 \div 76 \\ =\ & 5{,}000 \div 80 \\ =\ & 500 \div 8 \\ =\ & 62 \end{aligned}$

Page	Section Topic	Learning Concepts	Examples and Solutions
14	**1.13** Proving Multiplication and Division Problems	**1.** Prove multiplication by dividing the product by one of the factors. The quotient should be the other factor. **2.** Prove division by multiplying the quotient by the divisor. If the division is even, the product will be the dividend. **3.** If the division is uneven, add the remainder to the product. The sum will be the dividend.	Proof:

$$\begin{array}{rr} 78 & 78 \\ \times\,21 & 21\overline{)1{,}638} \\ \hline 78 & \underline{1\,47} \\ \underline{1\,56} & 168 \\ 1{,}638 & \underline{168} \end{array}$$

$$\begin{array}{rr} 15 & 15 \\ 25\overline{)375} & \times\,25 \\ \underline{25} & 75 \\ 125 & \underline{30} \\ \underline{125} & 375 \end{array}$$

$$\begin{array}{rr} 65 \text{ R15} & \\ 76\overline{)4{,}955} & 76 \\ \underline{4\,56} & \times\,65 \\ 395 & 380 \\ \underline{380} & \underline{4\,56} \\ 15 & 4{,}940 \\ & \underline{+\;15} \\ & 4{,}955 \end{array}$$

Page	Section Topic	Learning Concepts	Examples and Solutions
16	**1.14** Using Formatting to Solve Problems in Addition, Subtraction, Multiplication, and Division	Use certain key words to determine the kind of problem. *Addition*—sum, plus, more, total. *Subtraction*—difference, minus, less. *Multiplication*—product, times, of. *Division*—quotient, by, per.	Roy gathered 87 pounds of pecans, and Al gathered 73 pounds more than Roy. How many total pounds did they gather?

Question or Unknown	Key Word or Phrase	Mathematical Operation
How many total pounds?	total	Addition

$$\begin{array}{rl} 87 & Roy \\ \underline{+\;73} & Al \\ 160 & Total \end{array}$$

For examples of subtraction, multiplication, and division, see p. 17.

SURFING THE INTERNET

For further information on the topics covered in this chapter, check out the following sites:

http://www.mathbuilder.com/cgi-bin/math2.cgi

http://www.hbcollege.com/businessmath/brechner/students/mathgames.htm

1.1

Write the following numbers in proper form with the commas in the correct positions:

1. Eight thousand, seven hundred sixty-three
8,763

2. Four hundred thirty-five thousand, two hundred six.
435,206

3. Forty-nine trillion, four hundred twelve million, twenty-seven
49,000,412,000,027

4. Five hundred two
502

Read the following numbers and write them in verbal form with the commas in the correct positions:

5. 14
Fourteen

6. 8,765
Eight thousand, seven hundred sixty-five

7. 120
One hundred twenty

8. 72,341
Seventy-two thousand, three hundred forty-one

1.2

Round off the following numbers as indicated:

9. 5,412 to the nearest thousand
5,000

10. 16,124 to the nearest ten thousand
20,000

11. 576,942,318,731,673 to the nearest trillion
577,000,000,000,000

12. 572,135 to the nearest hundred
572,100

1.3

Add the following whole numbers by placing them in columns:

13. 87 + 168 + 23 + 44
```
  87
 168
  23
+ 44
 322
```

14. 4 + 25 + 246 + 57 + 217 + 18
```
   4
  25
 246
  57
 217
+ 18
 567
```

15. 72,168 + 3,728,107 + 30,062
```
   72,168
3,728,107
+  30,062
3,830,337
```

16. 86,271 + 93,170 + 8,627 + 96
```
 86,271
 93,170
  8,627
+    96
188,164
```

1.4

Add the following whole numbers and estimate the solution using rounding all the way:

	Estimated	Actual		Estimated	Actual
17. 14 + 98 + 731	10 / 100 / + 700 / 810	14 / 98 / + 731 / 843	18. 125 + 179 + 1,382	100 / 200 / + 1,000 / 1,300	125 / 179 / + 1,382 / 1,686
19. 17,836 + 18,567 + 572,038	20,000 / 20,000 / + 600,000 / 640,000	17,836 / 18,567 / + 572,038 / 608,441	20. 2,854,017 + 385,902	3,000,000 / + 400,000 / 3,400,000	2,854,017 / + 385,902 / 3,239,919

1.5

Solve the following subtraction problems:

21. 3,612 − 315
```
 3,612
 − 315
 3,297
```

22. 8,721 − 7,635
```
  8,721
 − 7,635
  1,086
```

23. 253,583 − 164,251
```
 253,583
− 164,251
  89,332
```

24. 47,693 − 6,937
```
 47,693
 − 6,937
 40,756
```

1.6

Subtract the following whole numbers and estimate the solution using rounding all the way:

	Estimated	Actual			Estimated	Actual

25. 14,321 − 4,896

$$\begin{array}{r} 10{,}000 \\ -\,5{,}000 \\ \hline 5{,}000 \end{array} \qquad \begin{array}{r} 14{,}321 \\ -\,4{,}896 \\ \hline 9{,}425 \end{array}$$

26. 1,498 − 746

$$\begin{array}{r} 1{,}000 \\ -\,700 \\ \hline 300 \end{array} \qquad \begin{array}{r} 1{,}498 \\ -\,746 \\ \hline 752 \end{array}$$

27. 7,798 − 2,349

$$\begin{array}{r} 8{,}000 \\ -\,2{,}000 \\ \hline 6{,}000 \end{array} \qquad \begin{array}{r} 7{,}798 \\ -\,2{,}349 \\ \hline 5{,}449 \end{array}$$

28. 4,967,105 − 564,856

$$\begin{array}{r} 5{,}000{,}000 \\ -\,600{,}000 \\ \hline 4{,}400{,}000 \end{array} \qquad \begin{array}{r} 4{,}967{,}105 \\ -\,564{,}856 \\ \hline 4{,}402{,}249 \end{array}$$

1.7

Find the product in the following multiplication problems:

29. 37 × 326

$$\begin{array}{r} 326 \\ \times\,37 \\ \hline 2\,282 \\ 9\,78 \\ \hline 12{,}062 \end{array}$$

30. 94 × 129

$$\begin{array}{r} 129 \\ \times\,94 \\ \hline 516 \\ 11\,61 \\ \hline 12{,}126 \end{array}$$

31. 7,518 × 9,836

$$\begin{array}{r} 9{,}836 \\ \times\,7{,}518 \\ \hline 78\,688 \\ 98\,36 \\ 4\,918\,0 \\ 68\,852 \\ \hline 73{,}947{,}048 \end{array}$$

32. 2,716 × 382

$$\begin{array}{r} 2{,}716 \\ \times\,382 \\ \hline 5\,432 \\ 217\,28 \\ 814\,8 \\ \hline 1{,}037{,}512 \end{array}$$

1.8

Multiply the following problems using the rules for multiplying by 10, powers of 10, or other zeros:

33. 295 × 10

$$\begin{array}{r} 295 \\ \times\,1 \\ \hline 2{,}950 \end{array}$$

34. 462 × 10,000

$$\begin{array}{r} 462 \\ \times\,1 \\ \hline 4{,}620{,}000 \end{array}$$

35. 736,000 × 12,700

$$\begin{array}{r} 736 \\ \times\,127 \\ \hline 515\,2 \\ 1\,472 \\ 7\,36 \\ \hline 9{,}347{,}200{,}000 \end{array}$$

36. 47,050 × 2,000

$$\begin{array}{r} 4705 \\ \times\,2 \\ \hline 94{,}100{,}000 \end{array}$$

1.9

Multiply the following problems and estimate the solutions by rounding all the way:

	Estimated	Actual			Estimated	Actual

37. 36 × 72

$$\begin{array}{r} 40 \\ \times\,70 \\ \hline 2{,}800 \end{array} \qquad \begin{array}{r} 36 \\ \times\,72 \\ \hline 72 \\ 2\,52 \\ \hline 2{,}592 \end{array}$$

38. 14 × 45

$$\begin{array}{r} 10 \\ \times\,50 \\ \hline 500 \end{array} \qquad \begin{array}{r} 14 \\ \times\,45 \\ \hline 70 \\ 56 \\ \hline 630 \end{array}$$

39. 12 × 305

$$\begin{array}{r} 300 \\ \times\,10 \\ \hline 3{,}000 \end{array} \qquad \begin{array}{r} 305 \\ \times\,12 \\ \hline 610 \\ 3\,05 \\ \hline 3{,}660 \end{array}$$

40. 295 × 280

$$\begin{array}{r} 300 \\ \times\,300 \\ \hline 90{,}000 \end{array} \qquad \begin{array}{r} 295 \\ \times\,28 \\ \hline 23\,60 \\ 59\,0 \\ \hline 82{,}600 \end{array}$$

1.10

Find the quotient in the following division problems:

41. 35)630

$$\begin{array}{r} 18 \\ 35\overline{)630} \\ 35 \\ \hline 280 \\ 280 \end{array}$$

42. 379 ÷ 3

$$\begin{array}{r} 126\ \ \text{R1} \\ 3\overline{)379} \\ 3 \\ \hline 7 \\ 6 \\ \hline 19 \\ 18 \\ \hline 1 \end{array}$$

43. 173/94

$$\begin{array}{r} 1\ \ \text{R79} \\ 94\overline{)173} \\ 94 \\ \hline 79 \end{array}$$

44. 785 ÷ 9

$$\begin{array}{r} 87\ \ \text{R2} \\ 9\overline{)785} \\ 72 \\ \hline 65 \\ 63 \\ \hline 2 \end{array}$$

1.11

Divide the following problems and use the rules for dividing by 10, powers of 10, and other zeros:

45. 2,480 ÷ 10

$$\begin{array}{r} 248 \\ 1\overline{)248} \\ 248 \end{array}$$

46. 36,200 ÷ 100

$$\begin{array}{r} 362 \\ 1\overline{)362} \\ 362 \end{array}$$

47. $907,200 \div 2,100$

$$
\begin{array}{r}
432 \\
21\overline{)9,072} \\
\underline{8\,4} \\
67 \\
\underline{63} \\
42 \\
\underline{42}
\end{array}
$$

48. $140,000 \div 3,800$

$$
\begin{array}{r}
36 \text{ R32} \\
38\overline{)1,400} \\
\underline{1\,14} \\
260 \\
\underline{228} \\
32
\end{array}
$$

1.12

Find the quotient in the following problems and use rounding all the way to estimate your answer:

	Estimated	*Actual*
49. $6\overline{)372}$	$\begin{array}{r} 66 \\ 6\overline{)400} \\ \underline{36} \\ 40 \\ \underline{36} \\ 4 \end{array}$	$\begin{array}{r} 62 \\ 6\overline{)372} \\ \underline{36} \\ 12 \\ \underline{12} \end{array}$

	Estimated	*Actual*
50. $47\overline{)1,222}$	$\begin{array}{r} 1,000 \div 50 \\ 20 \\ 5\overline{)100} \\ \underline{100} \end{array}$	$\begin{array}{r} 26 \\ 47\overline{)1,222} \\ \underline{94} \\ 282 \\ \underline{282} \end{array}$

| **51.** $792\overline{)56,856}$ | $\begin{array}{r} 60,000 \div 800 \\ 75 \\ 8\overline{)600} \\ \underline{56} \\ 40 \\ \underline{40} \end{array}$ | $\begin{array}{r} 71 \text{ R624} \\ 792\overline{)56,856} \\ \underline{55\,44} \\ 1\,416 \\ \underline{792} \\ 624 \end{array}$ |

| **52.** $38\overline{)238}$ | $\begin{array}{r} 200 \div 40 \\ 5 \\ 4\overline{)20} \\ \underline{20} \end{array}$ | $\begin{array}{r} 6 \text{ R10} \\ 38\overline{)238} \\ \underline{228} \\ 10 \end{array}$ |

1.13

Perform the indicated operations and prove your answer in the following problems:

	Actual	*Proof*
53. 239×29	$\begin{array}{r} 239 \\ \underline{29} \\ 2\,151 \\ \underline{4\,78} \\ 6,931 \end{array}$	$\begin{array}{r} 239 \\ 29\overline{)6,931} \\ \underline{5\,8} \\ 1\,13 \\ \underline{87} \\ 261 \\ \underline{261} \end{array}$

	Actual	*Proof*
54. $1,800 \times 460$	$\begin{array}{r} 18 \\ \underline{46} \\ 108 \\ \underline{72} \\ 828,000 \end{array}$	$\begin{array}{r} 1,800 \\ 46\overline{)82,800} \\ \underline{46} \\ 368 \\ \underline{368} \end{array}$

| **55.** $2,100 \div 70$ | $\begin{array}{r} 30 \\ 7\overline{)210} \\ \underline{210} \end{array}$ | $\begin{array}{r} 30 \times 70 \\ 3 \\ \underline{\times 7} \\ 2,100 \end{array}$ |

| **56.** $23\overline{)487}$ | $\begin{array}{r} 21 \text{ R4} \\ 23\overline{)487} \\ \underline{46} \\ 27 \\ \underline{23} \\ 4 \end{array}$ | $\begin{array}{r} 21 \\ \underline{23} \\ 63 \\ \underline{42} \\ 483 \\ \underline{+4} \\ 487 \end{array}$ |

1.14

57. Last week Charlene Jacks worked 9 hours Monday, 5 hours Tuesday, 7 hours Wednesday, 4 hours Thursday, and 9 hours Friday. How many total hours did Charlene work last week?

Question or Unknown	Key Word or Phrase	Mathematical Operation
How many hours did Charlene work?	total	Addition

$$
\begin{array}{rl}
9 & \text{Monday hours} \\
5 & \text{Tuesday hours} \\
7 & \text{Wednesday hours} \\
4 & \text{Thursday hours} \\
\underline{+\,9} & \text{Friday hours} \\
34 & \text{Total hours}
\end{array}
$$

58. Sunday Adibayo hit 37 home runs last year and 19 this year. How many more home runs did he hit last year than this year?

Question or Unknown	Key Word or Phrase	Mathematical Operation
How many more home runs?	more	Subtraction

$$
\begin{array}{rl}
37 & \text{Home runs last year} \\
\underline{-\,19} & \text{Home runs this year} \\
18 & \text{More last year than this year}
\end{array}
$$

59. Jean Morales bought 15 Snickers candy bars, which were priced 3 for $1. How much was the cost for all the candy bars?

Question or Unknown	Key Word or Phrase	Mathematical Operation
How much was the cost for all the candy bars?	all	Multiplication

$$\frac{\text{Snickers}}{\text{Pricing group}} \quad \frac{15}{3} = 5 \text{ groups}$$

$1	Price for 3 Snickers candy bars
× 5	Groups of 3 Snickers candy bars

60. George Meany has been collecting dues for a labor organization. The organization has 250 members. Dues are $12 per month. How much will George collect if everybody pays?

Question or Unknown	Key Word or Phrase	Mathematical Operation
How much will George collect?	How much	Multiplication

$12	Cost of dues each
× 250	Number of members
$3,000	Total collection for dues

CHAPTER REVIEW PROBLEMS

Answers to odd-numbered problems are given in Appendix A.

Drill Problems

Add the following:

1. 265
   109
+ 45
419

2. 428
  156
+ 850
1,434

3. 195,871
195,572
+ 2,830
394,273

Subtract the following:

4. 239
− 72
167

5. 903
− 296
607

6. 387,276
− 29,079
358,197

Multiply the following:

7. 18
× 7
126

8. 387
× 15
1 935
3 87
5,805

9. 42,000
× 5,200
8 4
210
218,400,000

Divide the following (quotients are even):

10. $24\overline{)312}$
  13
  24
  72
  72

11. $9\overline{)207}$
  23
  18
  27
  27

12. $100\overline{)2,100}$
  21
  2 00
  100
  100

Divide the following (quotients are uneven):

13. $7\overline{)146}$ 20 R6
  14
  6
  0
  6

14. $3,895\overline{)183,288}$ 47 R223
  155 80
  27 488
  27 265
  223

Round all the way to estimate the following addition problems:

15. 9,286
+ 129
9,000
  100
9,100

16. 390
  18
  25
+ 76
400
 20
 30
 80
530

17. 36,904
22,750
+ 1,058
40,000
20,000
 1,000
61,000

Round all the way to estimate the following subtraction problems:

18. 299,274
− 29,385
300,000
− 30,000
270,000

19. 33,261
− 4,317
30,000
− 4,000
26,000

20. 10,027
− 792
10,000
− 800
9,200

Round all the way to estimate the following multiplication problems:

21. 118
× 7
100
× 7
700

22. 39
× 93
40
× 90
3,600

23. 387
× 14
400
× 10
4,000

Round all the way to estimate the following division problems:

24. $37\overline{)377}$
  10
$4\overline{)40}$
  4

25. $1,998\overline{)28,376}$
  15
$2\overline{)30}$
  20
  10
  10

Round the following problems as indicated:

26. 381 to the nearest hundred
400

27. 228,937 to the nearest ten thousand
230,000
230,000

28. 288 to the nearest ten
290

Solve and prove the following multiplication and division problems using the methods for 10, powers of 10, and other zeros:

29. 90 × 3,500

Solution	Proof
35	350
× 9	9)3,150
315,*000*	2 7
	45
	45

30. 25,000 ÷ 500

Solution	Proof
50	50 × 500
5)250	
250	5
	× 5
	25,*000*

31. 6,200,000 ÷ 3,100

Solution	Proof
2,000	31
31)62,000	2
62	6,200,*000*

32. 100,000 × 3,498

Solution	Proof
3,498	3,498
1	1)3,498
349,800,*000*	3,498

33. 3,000,300 × 2,000

Solution	Proof
30,003	30,003
× 2	2)60,006
6,000,600,*000*	

34. 200,700 ÷ 800

Solution	Proof
250 R7	250
8)2,007	× 8
16	200 0
40	+ 7
40	200,*700*
7	
0	
7	

Word Problems

35. Susan held a garage sale. After the first hour, she had sold a painting for $14, a sofa for $75, and a golf cart for $425. Calculate Susan's actual and estimated total sales receipts. (Use rounding all the way to estimate your answer.)

Estimated	Actual
$ 10	$ 14
80	75
+ 400	+ 425
$490	$514

36. Speedy's Print Shop has a production capacity of 50,000 units per week. The daily production last week was as follows: Monday, 3,274; Tuesday, 2,492; Wednesday, 3,194; Thursday, 6,436; and Friday, 5,432. Determine the difference between actual production and production capacity.

3,274	
2,492	50,000
3,194	− 20,828
6,436	29,172
5,432	
20,828	

37. O'Casey's Bookstore begins each day with $240 in petty cash. One busy day, $4,943 was added and $3,348 was taken out. Calculate the amount of cash that would be deposited in the bank to maintain the desired petty cash level.

$4,943	$5,183	$1,835
+ 240	− 3,348	− 240
$5,183	$1,835	$1,595

38. IBM stock trades over domestic and foreign exchanges. One trading day, 27,450,400 shares traded in the United States; 3,438,173 traded in Japan; 727,281 traded in London; 4,289,300 traded in Canada; and 11,466,500 traded over the remaining foreign exchanges. Find the total number of shares traded.

27,450,400
3,438,173
727,281
4,289,300
11,466,500
47,371,654

39. Tony Chen sold a business for $47 per square foot. It measured 23,512 square feet. Find the selling price.

23,512	
$ 47	
164 584	
940 48	
$1,105,064	

40. Todd King bought a lawnmower for $547 plus $65 interest. Assuming Todd paid for the mower monthly for one year, how much was each payment?

$547	$51
+ 65	12)612
$612	60
	12
	12

41. A tire dealer pays $44 each for Sayana Tires. He sells them to customers for $79. If 40 tires were sold, what was the amount of gross profit earned? (Gross profit = selling price minus cost)

$44	$79	$3,160		$79	$35
× 40	× 40	− 1,760	or	− 44	× 40
$1,760	$3,160	$1,400		$35	$1,400

42. Liederkranz, Inc., purchased 20 cars for its sales force. Peugeot Auto Sales sent a bill for $296,000. Find the average price for each car.

$296,000 ÷ 20

$14,800
2)29,600

43. The Office of Business Statistics has just released information that shows that, on average, each American consumes 24 pounds of peanuts each year. If there are 250,000,000 Americans, how many total pounds of peanuts are consumed?

250,000,000 × 24

```
    25
  × 24
   100
    50
6,000,000,000
```

44. Maria Munoz is buying a new truck to use in her landscaping business. The total purchase price is $22,500. She will receive a $7,000 trade-in for her old truck. Maria will have to pay $3,520 interest if she finances the balance through the dealer. Assuming she will borrow the money for 60 months, how much will Maria's monthly payments be?

```
 $22,500      $15,500      $19,020 ÷ 60        $317
 − 7,000      + 3,520                        6)1,902
 $15,500      $19,020                           1 8
                                                 10
                                                  6
                                                 42
                                                 42
```

45. A textile mill makes and sells towels. Its price list is for a gross (144 = a dozen dozen). The top-of-the-line bath towel lists for $432. James Bros. buys the towels and sells them in its retail mall outlets for $5 each. Does James Bros. sell the towels for more than its costs? If so, how much for a gross?

```
   144        $720       Selling price
 × $5       − 432        Cost
 $720        $288        Profit per gross
```

46. June Voorhies owns a shop that sells leather products. Lately business has been down. Sales figures for the month of May, this year and last, are as follows:

	Last Year	This Year
Purses	$128,000	$124,000
Coats	225,000	215,000
Wallets	53,000	44,000
Belts	67,000	75,000
Other	33,000	29,000

Calculate the estimated and the actual amount of each year's sales. How much are actual sales down this year?

Last Year		This Year		
Estimated	*Actual*	*Estimated*	*Actual*	
$100,000	$128,000	$100,000	$124,000	$506,000
200,000	225,000	200,000	215,000	− 487,000
50,000	53,000	40,000	44,000	$ 19,000
70,000	67,000	80,000	75,000	**down from**
30,000	33,000	30,000	29,000	**last year**
$450,000	$506,000	$450,000	$487,000	

47. Tommy Yee owns a small grocery store. He is shopping at a Cash and Carry Wholesalers and needs to make certain he doesn't exceed his budgeted amount for groceries. Use rounding all the way to estimate his purchases so far. His purchases are as follows:

Fruit	$ 75	Laundry detergent	$ 94
Vegetables	114	Cleaning products	218
Bread	198	Soft drinks	121
Meat	449	Candy and gum	368
Milk	53	Cheese	84

His budget is $2,000. Approximately how much more can he spend?

```
Estimated      $2,000
    80        − 1,700
   100           $300
   200
   400
    50
    90
   200
   100
   400
    80
 1,700
```

48. Jabia Semanski, a custom decorator, is going to cover a wall with vinyl. The wall measures 24 feet long and 8 feet high. The vinyl costs $3.67 per square foot (height × length). How much will the paper cost if there is no waste?

```
   24                  $3.67
  × 8                × 192
  192  square feet      7 34
                      330 3
                       367
                    $704.64
```

49. Mike Redd's company reimburses him for his expenses. On a trip Mike spent the following: gas for automobile, $24; breakfast, $6; lunch, $8; dinner and entertainment, $78; motel, $65; telephone, $13. How much can he claim?

```
  $24
    6
    8
   78
   65
 + 13
 $194
```

50. Jackie Wu, a financial consultant, recommended that a client company buy three different securities. They are:

Company	Type of Security	Price Per Unit
Royal Dutch Shell Co.	Common stock	$ 54
Mitsubishi, Inc.	Common stock	28
Kodak	Bond	980

Her client bought 500 shares of Royal Dutch Shell, 250 shares of Mitsubishi, and 75 Kodak bonds. What was the total cost for each company's securities, and the total overall cost for all securities?

$$500 \times \$54 = \$ 27,000$$
$$250 \times 28 = 7,000$$
$$75 \times 980 = \underline{73,500}$$
$$\$107,500$$

52. Cecil Anderson keeps track of his gas mileage. Before beginning a 360-mile trip, he filled his tank. Upon arrival, Cecil refilled the tank. It required 12 gallons. Determine the miles per gallon Cecil's car got on this trip.

$$\begin{array}{r} 30 \\ 12\overline{)360} \\ \underline{360} \end{array}$$

51. The Hogan company produces golf balls. The employees work three shifts. Shifts 1 and 2 produce balls with customized names or logos on them, and colored balls. Shift 3, which produces only standard white balls, can produce three times as many balls as shift 1. Shifts 1 and 2 produce 200 dozen balls per shift. How many dozen balls are produced on shift 3? How many dozen balls are produced on all shifts in one five-day week? How many balls are produced in one year?

$$\begin{array}{r} 200 \\ \times 3 \\ \hline 600 \end{array} \text{ dozen on shift 3}$$

$$\begin{array}{r} 600 \\ 200 \\ +200 \\ \hline 1,000 \end{array} \text{ dozen per day}$$

$$\begin{array}{r} 1,000 \\ \times 5 \\ \hline 5,000 \end{array} \text{ dozen per week}$$

$$\begin{array}{r} 5,000 \\ \times 52 \\ \hline 260,000 \end{array} \text{ dozen per year}$$

53. A small hospital in Hot Springs has a capacity of 100 beds. During the past year, the hospital was filled to capacity on 71 occasions. On 80 other days, 75 beds were occupied. For the remainder of the year (365 days) the average occupancy was 68. During the year, how many additional patients could have been admitted?

$$\begin{array}{r} 100 \\ \times 71 \\ \hline 7,100 \end{array} \quad \begin{array}{r} 75 \\ \times 80 \\ \hline 6,000 \end{array} \quad \begin{array}{r} 80 \\ +71 \\ \hline 151 \end{array} \quad \begin{array}{r} 365 \\ -151 \\ \hline 214 \end{array} \quad \begin{array}{r} 214 \\ \times 68 \\ \hline 14,552 \end{array} \quad \begin{array}{r} 7,100 \\ 6,000 \\ +14,552 \\ \hline 27,652 \end{array}$$

$$\begin{array}{r} 365 \\ \times 100 \\ \hline 36,500 \end{array} \quad \begin{array}{r} 36,500 \\ -27,652 \\ \hline 8,848 \end{array} \quad \text{or}$$

For 71 days—0 more per day
For 80 days—25 more per day
For 214 days—32 more per day
(365 − 151)

$$80 \times 25 = 2,000$$
$$+ 214 \times 32 = \underline{6,848}$$
$$8,848$$

✓ ENRICHMENT PROBLEMS

54. Johnson & Sons made a chart of a salesperson's weekly travel expenses. Add each day's expenses for a total daily record and find the total for each expense. The final totals should be the same adding either vertically or horizontally. Fill in the following chart:

Weekly Travel Expenditures

	Monday	Tuesday	Wednesday	Thursday	Friday	Totals
Room	$ 74	$ 63	$ 128	$ 74	$ 88	$ 427
Transportation	179	0	57	215	176	627
Meals	53	38	44	19	73	227
Entertainment	0	25	6	218	175	+ 424
Totals	$306 +	$126 +	$ 235 +	$526 +	$512	= $1,705

55. Bill keeps a continuous record of the results from playing a computer game. In the game, he can acquire squares of land, knights, servants, peasants, and nomads. The first five games played after record-keeping began yielded the following results:

	Squares	Knights	Servants	Peasants	Nomads	Total
Game 1	635	136	942	6,423	19,094	27,230
Game 2	730	148	699	4,627	3,011	9,215
Game 3	515	135	473	3,321	1,814	6,258
Game 4	569	140	969	3,096	300	5,074
Game 5	640	140	532	1,494	41,769	+ 44,575
Totals	3,089 +	699 +	3,615 +	18,961 +	65,988	= 92,352

Total all of the results.

56. Village Estates Country Club golf shop is taking and valuing its inventory. Following are the items, the number of units, and the value of each unit in the inventory. Calculate the total value of the inventory.

Item	# of Units	Value	Total Value
Golf clubs	20 sets	$ 325 per set	$ 6,500
Golf balls	215 dozen	10 per dozen	2,150
Golf bags	25	75	1,875
Pull carts	60	54	3,240
Shirts	80	10	800
Sweaters	25	35	875
Trousers	20	18	360
Blouses	55	15	825
Shorts	70	8	560
Caps	100	3	300
Shoes	50	36	1,800
		Total value of the inventory	$19,285

57. Murdock Inc. management knew bad times were coming for the company because of an upcoming congressional investigation. They sold their 228,562 shares of stock for $96 per share, which was $7 below the price Michael Schmaltz had paid for his 375 shares. How much did the managers receive, and how much will Michael lose if he sells his stock also?

$$
\begin{array}{rl}
228,562 & \text{Number of shares} \\
\times \quad \$\ 96 & \text{Price per share} \\
\hline
\$21,941,952 & \text{Amount managers received}
\end{array}
$$

$$
\begin{array}{rl}
375 & \text{Number of shares Michael Schmaltz owns} \\
\times \quad \$7 & \text{Loss per share} \\
\hline
\$\ 2,625 & \text{Loss to Michael Schmaltz if he sells his stock}
\end{array}
$$

CRITICAL THINKING GROUP PROJECT

The United States' national debt is approximately $5 trillion. Everyone knows that's a sizable amount of money. Most of us, however, don't have a frame of reference for such an immense number. Thus, most of us have very little reaction to the economic news telling us about our national debt.

You should remember that when the federal government spends more than it earns in revenue, it has to borrow the difference. The amount borrowed plus interest must be repaid. Repayment is primarily made by you and me in the form of taxes. The population in the United States is approximately 250 million.

a. Change the numbers $5 trillion and 250 million to their numerical equivalents. (For example, 5 hundred would be written as 500.)

a. $5,000,000,000,000   250,000,000

b. Determine how much each man, woman, and child in the United States owes in taxes at this time to pay off the debt.

b. 250,000,000)$5,000,000,000,000

25)$500,000   eliminate seven zeros in both the numerator and the denominator.

$ 20,000
25)$500,000

Of course, not every man, woman, and child is a taxpayer. Those people who are too young to work, too old to work, physically or mentally unable to work, or who lack the skills or ambition to work don't pay taxes on their labor. Some pay taxes on investment income. Approximately 125 million people in the United States pay taxes.

c. Determine each taxpayer's share of the national debt.
When are you going to pay your share?

c. 125,000,000)$5,000,000,000,000

125)$5,000,000   eliminate six zeros in both the numerator and the denominator.

$ 40,000
125)$5,000,000

1. Why is it useful to have memorized the multiplication **W** table through 12?

Multiplication is essentially a shortcut method of addition. If you have memorized the table, you can avoid cumbersome addition of a series of addends that have the same value.

2. Why would you choose to round off a number? **W**

A number is often rounded off because either it is unnecessary to be perfectly accurate or it is not feasible or convenient to determine the exact number.

Express the following as numerals with commas inserted:

3. Sixty-two billion, five hundred thousand, eight hundred twenty-six
62,000,500,826

4. Thirty-seven million, one hundred twenty-three thousand
37,123,000

5. Eight hundred seventy-one thousand, one hundred
871,100

6. Four hundred million, one thousand, one
400,001,001

7. Fourteen thousand, three hundred ninety-seven
14,397

Round off the following to the place indicated:

8. 36,826 to the nearest thousand
37,000

9. 87,536,598 to the nearest hundred thousand
87,500,000

10. 69,431 to the nearest ten
69,430

11. 8,964,328 to the nearest million
9,000,000

12. 867,435 to the nearest ten thousand
870,000

Add the following decimal numbers. Find the actual and the estimated solutions and prove your answer (by reversing the direction of adding).

	Actual	Estimated	Proof		Actual	Estimated	Proof		Actual	Estimated	Proof
13.	873	900	239	**14.**	428	400	1	**15.**	84,312	84,000	181
	457	500	913		60	60	6		41	40	12
	415	400	771		0	0	495		18,974	20,000	9
	771	800	415		495	500	0		9	9	18,974
	913	900	457		6	6	60		12	10	41
	239	200	873		1	1	428		181	200	84,312
	3,668	3,700	3,668		990	967	990		103,529	104,259	103,529

Subtract the following decimal numbers. Find the actual and the estimated solutions and prove your answers.

	Actual	Estimated	Proof		Actual	Estimated	Proof		Actual	Estimated	Proof
16.	392	400	325	**17.**	5,738	6,000	5,265	**18.**	25,194	25,000	19,473
	− 67	− 70	+ 67		− 473	− 500	+ 473		− 19,473	− 20,000	+ 5,721
	325	330	392		5,265	5,500	5,738		5,721	5,000	25,194

Multiply the following decimal numbers. Find the actual and the estimated solutions and prove your answers.

	Actual	Estimated	Proof		Actual	Estimated	Proof
19.	732	700	732	**20.**	21,000	20,000	12,180,000 ÷ 580
	× 6	× 6	6)4,392		× 580	× 600	

19.
```
  732        700         732
 × 6        × 6       6)4,392
4,392      4,200        4 2
                         19
                         18
                         12
                         12
```

20.
```
21,000     20,000     12,180,000 ÷ 580
× 580      × 600          21,000
                      58)1,218,000
            21            1 16
           ×58             58
           168            58
          ×6
       12,000,000
       168
       1 05
       12,180,000
```

	Actual	Estimated	Proof
21.	725,000	700,000	725,000

21.
```
  725,000       700,000        725,000
 × 600         × 600        6)4,350,000
435,000,000   420,000,000       4 2
                                 15
                                 12
                                 30
                                 30
```

Divide the following decimal numbers. Find the actual and the estimated solutions and prove your answers.

	Actual	*Estimated*	*Proof*		*Actual*	*Estimated*	*Proof*

22.
```
      11 R3        11         11
   6)69          6)70        × 6
     6             6          66
     9            10         + 3
     6             6          69
     3             4
```

23.
```
         34          30        182
   182)6,188       2)60        × 34
       5 46          6         728
         728         0         5 46
         728         0        6,188
```

	Actual	*Estimated*	*Proof*

24.
```
           40      300,000 ÷ 7,000    6,500 × 40
   6,500)260,000
         260,00          42            65
                      7)300             4
                        280          260,000
                         20
                         14
                          6
```

25. Percy had trouble keeping a job and was employed by six different firms last year. His W-2 forms revealed that he had the following earnings: $319; $2,418; $652; $129; $1,847; and $11,860. What were his total earnings for the year?
```
   $  319
    2,418
      652
      129
    1,847
 + 11,860
  $17,225
```

26. Sandra owns an apartment building that she cannot keep leased since she is such a disagreeable landlord. The vacant apartments are of the following sizes: 632 square feet, 1,430 square feet, 982 square feet, and 896 square feet. How much space is vacant?
```
     632
   1,430
     982
  +  896
   3,940    Square feet
```

27. Honest John's Used Cars paid $1,500 for an old car. The cost to deliver it from another state was $125. Upon receipt of the car, it was discovered that the engine block was cracked. Honest John's did superficial repairs for $65. How much gross profit did the company make if the car was sold for $2,400.
```
  $1,500      $2,400
     125     − 1,690
   + 65       $  710
  $1,690
```

28. The college library had 87,000 volumes at the beginning of the year. In the first quarter, the library purchased 472 more volumes; during the second quarter, 731; during the third quarter, 1,241; and during the fourth quarter, 216. During the year, students and faculty either lost, stole, or destroyed 261 of them. How many volumes did the library contain at the end of the year?
```
  87,000
     472       89,660
     731      −  261
   1,241       89,399
   + 216
  89,660
```

29. A machine produces 124 Frisbees per hour. How many units can it produce in 40 hours?
```
    124
  ×   4
  4,960
```

30. A customer made the following purchases:

12	baseball bats	@	$ 28 ea.
32	baseball gloves	@	53 ea.
20	dozen baseballs	@	30 dz.
24	sets of bases	@	73 set

Unfortunately, three bats, one glove, and two sets of bases were unacceptable upon delivery and were returned for credit (a refund). Calculate the amount the customer owes.
```
  12  −  3  =   9  × $28  =  $ 252
  32  −  1  =  31  ×  53  =   1,643
  20                ×  30  =     600
  24  −  2  =  22  ×  73  =   1,606
                             $4,101
```

31. Harry received a paycheck for $960. Maria's check was for $840. If Harry worked an average of 40 hours per week for four weeks and Maria worked an average of 30 hours per week during the four-week period, which employee is paid more per hour and how much more?

Harry
$$\begin{array}{cc} & \$6 \\ 40 & 160\overline{)960} \\ \times 4 & \underline{960} \\ \hline 160 & \end{array}$$

Maria
$$\begin{array}{ccc} & \$7 & \$7 \\ 30 & 120\overline{)840} & \underline{-6} \\ \times 4 & \underline{840} & \$1 \\ \hline 120 & & \end{array}$$

Maria is paid $1 more per hour

32. If three cups of molasses are required to make a pecan pie, how many pies can be made with 96 cups of molasses?

$$\begin{array}{r} 32 \\ 3\overline{)96} \\ \underline{9} \\ 6 \\ \underline{6} \end{array}$$

33. A pharmacist uses 132 mg of pseudephedrine in each decongestant capsule. Each prescription contains 50 pills. The druggist has 396,000 mg on hand. How many prescriptions of the medication can be filled?

$$396,000 \div 6,600$$
$$\begin{array}{cc} 132 & 60 \\ \times 50 & 66\overline{)3,960} \\ \hline 6,600 & \underline{3\,96} \end{array}$$

34. Su Tong wants to buy a convertible for a prize to be given to the winner of the beauty pageant he sponsors. So far, his best deal for the model he wants is $23,000. Su wants to make monthly payments for 48 months. The finance company will lend him the money for the car and will charge $6,040 interest. What will be the size of the monthly payments?

$$\begin{array}{cc} \$23,000 & \$605 \\ \underline{+\,6,040} & 48\overline{)29,040} \\ \$29,040 & \underline{28\,8} \\ & 240 \\ & \underline{240} \end{array}$$

35. Krystal Stallings went to Office Depot to purchase office supplies. She bought the following:

50 notepads @ $3 each

6 boxes of computer paper @ $28 each

8 boxes of 3 1/2″ computer microdisks @ $20 each

60 boxes of pencils @ $2 each

Krystal gave the clerk a $750 check. How much change should she receive?

$$\begin{array}{ccccccc} 50 & \$28 & \$20 & 60 & & \$750 \\ \times\,\$3 & \times\,6 & \times\,8 & \times\,\$2 & & \underline{-598} \\ \hline \$150 & +\ 168 & +\ 160 & +\ 120 & =\ \$598 & \$152 \end{array}$$

36. A printing press can process 30,000 pages per hour. A magazine contains 150 pages. How many magazines can be run in an eight-hour day?

$$\begin{array}{cc} 30,000 & 1,600 \\ \underline{\times\,8} & 15\overline{)24,000} \\ 240,000 & \underline{15\,0} \\ & 9\,00 \\ & \underline{9\,00} \end{array}$$

$$240,000 \div 150$$

37. Linda Johnson placed an order for the following supplies:

Quantity	Description	Unit Price	Total
6 ea.	Pocket calculators	$ 24	
20 ea.	Desk calendars	2	
15 ea.	Staplers	8	
12 ea.	File boxes	10	
2 ea.	File cabinets	147	

How much is the total owed? Upon receipt of the shipment, two staplers and one file cabinet were backordered (will be delivered later). What is the price of the merchandise received?

$$\begin{array}{ccccc} \$24 & 20 & 15 & 12 & \$147 \\ \underline{\times\,6} & \underline{\times\,\$2} & \underline{\times\,\$8} & \underline{\times\,\$10} & \underline{\times\,2} \\ 144\ + & 40\ + & 120\ + & 120\ + & 294 \end{array}$$

$$= \$718 \quad \text{Total owed}$$
$$\underline{-\ 163} \quad \text{Backordered merchandise}$$
$$\$555 \quad \text{Price of merchandise received}$$

$$\begin{array}{c} \$8 \\ \underline{\times\,2} \\ \$16\ +\ \$147\ =\ \$163 \end{array}$$

38. The Asteroid Company has not had the expected impact on the market. In fact, information was just released that insiders (in this case middle managers) who had received stock options in the past had just sold 340,000 shares of the company's stock at the market price of $140 per share. What is the value of the stock sold?

$$340,000 \times \$140$$
$$\begin{array}{c} 34 \\ \underline{\times\,14} \\ 13\,6 \\ \underline{34} \\ \$47,600,000 \end{array}$$

EXCEL SPREADSHEET APPLICATION FOR CHAPTER 1

This spreadsheet application is to determine the total salaries for each position in the department store, and the total salaries for the store. Remember to use the arrow keys to move the cursor to the proper cell. You do not need to enter signs (such as the $ sign) or commas. The spreadsheet format will automatically take care of those for you. Reread the General Information if necessary to get started. When you open Ch1App1 from your disk, you will see a screen like the one shown here:

Springfield Department Store

2617 Main Street
Box 219
Springfield, Maryland 58109
Telephone: 301-555-2158   FAX: 301-555-3498

SALARY COMPARISON

POSITION	NUMBER	PER PERSON SALARY	TOTALS
			$0
			$0
			$0
			$0
TOTALS	0		$0

Enter the following information:

In the cell for number of store managers, enter 1

In the cell for per person salary, enter 88500

In the cell for number of department managers, enter 7

In the cell for per person salary for department managers, enter 58000

In the cell for number of assistant department managers, enter 7

In the cell for per person salary for assistant department managers, enter 24960

In the cell for number of sales clerks, enter 125

In the cell for per person salary for sales clerks, enter 15080

Answer the following questions after you have completed the spreadsheet:

1. What is the total salary for the department managers? $_____
2. What is the total salary for the assistant department managers? $_____
3. What is the total salary for sales clerks? $_____
4. What are the total store salaries for the year? $_____

GROUP REPORT

1. Write a memo to the CEO (Chief Executive Officer) of the Springfield Department Store reporting the information contained in the salary comparison spreadsheet.

2. Ask other members of your group how their salaries compare to those of the Springfield employees.

3. Interview a manager at a local department store in your area. Ask the manager how the Springfield salaries compare to those in his/her store.

Chapter 1 Fundamental Operations with Whole Numbers   33

2 FUNDAMENTAL OPERATIONS WITH DECIMAL FRACTIONS

TALKING TO NEIGHBORS FROM OTHER PLANETS

Some people believe we will encounter intelligent beings from other planets someday. If this does happen, how could we communicate with them since they certainly would not speak Chinese, English, Spanish, Japanese, Arabic, French, Hebrew, German, or any other language known to earthlings.

Since mathematics is a universal language, we are told, one suggestion has been to communicate with math formulas.

But what if these beings have only, say, three fingers on each hand instead of five? Certainly they would not use the same mathematical notation as earthbound people do.

Our numbering system is called decimal, from "deci," which means ten. While decimal numbering seems to comes naturally to all of us, there is really nothing "natural" about 10. All earthlings use 10 because all human beings are born with 10 fingers and 10 toes. The nonearthlings with six fingers would probably use a base 6 numbering system—as foreign and difficult for us to understand as a base 10 system (or any earthly spoken language) would be for them.

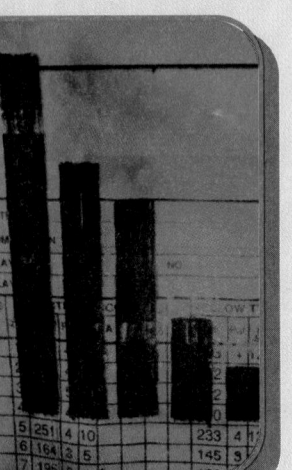

Chapter Glossary

Decimal fraction. A fraction expressed as a part of a whole in the base 10 system. Thus, the value is stated in ten*ths*, hundred*ths*, thousand*ths*, etc.

Decimal point. A period placed to the left of a decimal fraction.

"th" The ending on a proportional value that is a decimal.

Mixed decimal. A whole number combined with a decimal fraction.

REVIEW OF FUNDAMENTAL ARITHMETIC OPERATIONS

The decimal numbering system provides for writing fractions. As in writing whole numbers, **decimal fractions** are positional. Their value depends on the position they occupy to the *right* of the **decimal point**.

2.1 Reading and Writing Decimal Fractions

Table 2.1 illustrates the values of the decimal positions. Observe that the positional values to the right of the decimal point (fractional positions) are very similar to the positional values studied in Chapter 1 for whole numbers. The difference is that instead of being the tens position, they are in the ten**ths** position. If a positional value ends with *th* or *ths*, it represents a decimal fraction.

EXAMPLE Write the decimal fraction one hundred five ten thousandths properly in numerical form.

Solution

.0	1	0	5
t	h	t	t
e	u	h	e
n	n	o	n
t	d	u	
h	r	s	t
s	e	a	h
	d	n	o
	t	d	u
	h	t	s
	s	h	a
		s	n
			d
			t
			h
			s

TABLE 2.1 DECIMAL FRACTION POSITIONAL VALUE NAMES

$\dfrac{1}{10}$	$\dfrac{1}{100}$	$\dfrac{1}{1,000}$	$\dfrac{1}{10,000}$	$\dfrac{1}{100,000}$	$\dfrac{1}{1,000,000}$	$\dfrac{1}{10,000,000}$
t	h	t	t t	h t	m	t m
e	u	h	e h	u h	i	e i
n	n	o	n o	n o	l	n l
t	d	u	o u	d u	l	l
h	r	s	u s	r s	i	i
s	e	a	s a	e a	o	o
	d	n	a n	d n	n	n
	t	d	n d	d	t	t
	h	t	d t	t	h	h
	s	h	t h	h	s	s
		s	h s	s		
			s			

EXAMPLE   Read .163 and write it properly in verbal form as it is read.

Solution   The number is read "one hundred sixty-three thousandths." Read decimal numbers using the following rules:

1. Read the number without regard to the decimal point (in this example, one hundred sixty-three).
2. Attach the positional value of the rightmost number (in this example, thousandths).

```
.1   6   3
 t   h   t
 e   u   h
 n   n   o
 t   d   u
 s   r   s
     e   a
     d   n
     t   d
     h   t
     s   h
         s
```

2.1 Practice Problems

Write the following decimal fractions in verbal form:
1. .24
2. .639
3. .0371
4. .00267

2.1 Solutions to Practice Problems
1. Twenty-four hundredths
2. Six hundred thirty-nine thousandths
3. Three hundred seventy-one ten thousandths
4. Two hundred sixty-seven hundred thousandths

2.1 Practice Problems

Write the following decimal fraction in numerical form:
1. Seven tenths
2. Three hundred five ten thousandths
3. One hundred forty-eight thousand, nine hundred fifty-six ten millionths
4. Thirty-nine hundredths

2.1 Solutions to Practice Problems
1. .7
2. .0305
3. .0148956
4. .39

2.2 Reading and Writing Combinations of Whole Numbers and Decimal Fractions: the Mixed Decimal

Whole numbers are often combined with decimal fractions. This is frequently referred to as a **mixed decimal**. Since the decimal system is based on 10, each position has a value of 10 or a power of 10. Each move to the left increases the value of the number 10 times. Each move to the right decreases the value of the number 10 times. The decimal point is read "and." Table 2.2 illustrates the values of mixed decimal positions.

Write fifteen thousand, five and thirty-eight thousandths in proper mixed decimal number form.

Solution

1	5,	0	0	5	.	0	3	8
ten thousands	thousands	hundreds	tens	units	and	tenths	hundredths	thousandths

The word "and" tells us that this is a mixed decimal number. If "and" is not a part of the number statement, it is either a decimal whole number, or a decimal fraction.

EXAMPLE

Read 398,156.1325 and write it properly as read.

Solution

The number is read "three hundred ninety-eight thousand, one hundred fifty-six and one thousand three hundred twenty-five ten thousandths."

3	9	8,	1	5	6	.	1	3	2	5
hundred thousands	ten thousands	thousands	hundreds	tens	units	and	tenths	hundredths	thousandths	ten thousandths

---

2.2 Practice Problems

Write the following mixed decimal numbers in verbal form:

1. 15.6
2. 2,129.683
3. 684,386.00945
4. 3,000,025.47

2.2 Solutions to Practice Problems

1. Fifteen and six tenths
2. Two thousand one hundred twenty-nine and six hundred eighty-three thousandths
3. Six hundred eighty-four thousand, three hundred eighty-six and nine hundred forty-five hundred thousandths
4. Three million twenty-five and forty-seven hundredths

TABLE 2.2 MIXED DECIMAL NUMBER POSITIONAL VALUE NAMES

|,			|,			|,				.								
billions	hundred millions	ten millions	millions	hundred thousands	ten thousands	thousands	hundreds	tens	units	.	tenths	hundredths	thousandths	ten thousandths	hundred thousandths	millionths	ten millionths	hundred millionths

---

2.2 Practice Problems

Write the following mixed decimal numbers in numerical form:
1. Twenty-one thousand, nine hundred five and thirty-one hundredths
2. Four million, two hundred and sixty-eight thousand, four hundred nineteen millionths
3. Five hundred seventy-seven and twenty-five hundredths
4. Eighty-six thousand, four hundred two and two hundred two ten thousands

2.2 Solutions to Practice Problems

1. 21,905.31
2. 4,000,200.068419
3. 577.25
4. 86,402.0202

2.3 Rounding Decimal Numbers

In business operations a number is often rounded off because either it is unnecessary to be perfectly accurate or it is not feasible to determine the exact number. Rounding whole numbers was discussed in Chapter 1. The same operation would be used if a mixed decimal number were to be rounded to a whole number. If the fractional portion of a mixed decimal number is to be rounded, follow these steps:

1. Identify the digit to be rounded.[*]
2. If the number to the right of the identified digit is 5 or greater, round the identified digit up one number. If the number to the right of the identified digit is less than 5, do not change the identified digit.
3. Drop all digits to the right of the identified digit.

EXAMPLE Round 482.57 to the nearest hundred.

Solution 500 The identified digit is the 4 in the hundreds position. The number to its right is an 8, which is greater than 5. Round the 4 to a 5. Change the remaining whole

---

[*]*In this text, unless otherwise stated, all answers will be rounded to the nearest thousandth, except dollar amounts. Dollar amounts will be rounded to the nearest cent (hundredth).*

numbers (the 8 and the 2) to zeros. Drop the decimal fraction's digits (the 5 and 7).

EXAMPLE   Round 14.761 to the nearest tenth.

Solution   14.8   7 is in the tenths position and is the identified digit. The number to its right is 6 (which is greater than 5). 7 should be rounded up one number to 8. The digits to the right of the identified digit (the 6 and 1) should be dropped.

EXAMPLE   Round 74.538 to the nearest tenth.

Solution   74.5   5 is in the tenths position and is the identified digit. The number to its right is 3 (which is less than 5). The identified digit should not be changed. The numbers to the right of the identified digit (3 and 8) should be dropped.

2.3
Practice
Problems

Round the following decimal fraction numbers as indicated:
1. .47 to the nearest tenth
2. .29234 to the nearest ten thousandth
3. .49823 to the nearest hundredth
4. .6835 to the nearest thousandth

2.3 Solutions to Practice Problems
1. .5 The identified digit is 4. To its right is a 7, which is greater than 5. Four is raised to 5, and the number to its right, the 7, is dropped.
2. .2923 The identified digit is 3. To its right is 4, which is less than 5. Three is not changed, and the number to its right, 4, is dropped.
3. .50 The identified digit is 9. The number to its right is 8, which is greater than 5. Nine is rounded up to 10, and .4 + 10 = .50. The zero in .50 is left to indicate that rounding to the hundredth has been done. The numbers to the right of the zero (8, 2, and 3) are dropped.
4. .684 The identified digit is 3. The number to its right is 5. Three is raised to 4, and 5 is dropped.

2.3
Practice
Problems

Round the following mixed decimal numbers as indicated:
1. 5.48 to the nearest tenth
2. 67.428 to the nearest hundredth
3. 3,856.51967 to the nearest thousand
4. 582.230845 to the nearest thousandth

2.3 Solutions to Practice Problems
1. 5.5 The identified digit is 4. To its right is 8, which is greater than 5. Four is raised to 5, and 8 is dropped.
2. 67.43 The identified digit is 2. The number to its right is 8, which is greater than 5. Two is raised to 3, and 8 is dropped.
3. 4,000 The identified digit is 3. To its right is 8, which is greater than 5. Three is raised to 4. The other whole numbers, 8, 5, and 6, are changed to zeros. The decimal fraction numbers 5, 1, 9, 6, and 7 are dropped.
4. 582.231 The identified digit is 0. The number to its right is 8, which is greater than 5. Zero is increased to 1, and the numbers to its right, 8, 4, and 5, are dropped.

LEARNING UNIT 2
ADDITION

2.4 Adding Decimal Numbers

 **EXCEL Spreadsheet Application** The spreadsheet application at the end of this chapter is a record of daily departmental sales submitted weekly to the Springfield Department Store's management.

Since the decimal system is positional, the value of a digit depends on its position as well as on its numeric value. When adding, you first align the decimal points in the addends. *If no decimal point appears in the addend, it is understood to be at the right end of the addend.* For example, 4 is understood to be 4. even though the decimal point does not appear. When the decimal points are aligned, they are lined up in their place values.

EXAMPLE Find the sum of 4.36 + 27 + 72.893 + 632.01 + 102.

Solution

4.36		4.36<u>0</u>
27.	*While it is not*	27.<u>000</u>
72.893 >	*necessary, it adds clarity to add enough zeros to some digits* >	72.893
632.01	*so that the number of*	632.01<u>0</u>
102.	*decimal positions is*	102.<u>000</u>
838.263	*the same in all numbers.*	838.263

2.4 Practice Problems

Add the following decimal numbers by placing them in columns with the decimal points aligned. Do not round answers.

1. 12.785 + 4 + 340.5349
2. 3.45 + 805.213 + 334,456
3. .435 + 324.5 + 9,803.5408
4. 653.438 + 45.13 + 6.34603

2.4 Solutions to Practice Problems

1.	12.785	**2.**	3.45	**3.**	0.435	**4.**	653.438
	4		805.213		324.5		45.13
	+ 340.5349		+ 334,456		+ 9,803.5408		+ 6.34603
	357.3199		335,264.663		10,128.4758		704.91403

2.5 Estimating Decimal Addition Problems

As in addition of whole numbers, solutions can be estimated by rounding all the way if it is desirable to verify that the calculation is reasonable. When adding decimal fractions or mixed decimals, only the leftmost digit is a nonzero digit.

EXAMPLE Add .375 + .239 + .2 + .3923. Find both the actual and the estimated sums by rounding all the way.

Solution

Actual	Estimated
.375	.4
.239	.2
.2	.2
.3923	.4
1.2063	1.2

EXAMPLE Add 57.27 + 4.9 + 34.92 + .382. Find both the actual and estimated sums by rounding all the way.

Solution

Actual	Estimated
57.27	60
4.9	5
34.92	30
+ .382	+ .4
97.472	95.4

2.5 Practice Problems

Add the following problems. Find both the actual and estimated sums using rounding all the way. Do not round the actual sum.

1. 48.59 + 2,875 + 345.38

2. .3402 + 3.48 + .49

3. 347,593.80943 + 57,457.482

4. 95.38 + 456.405 + 354

2.5 Solutions to Practice Problems

1.			
48.59	50		
2,875	3,000		
+ 345.38	+ 300		
3,268.97	3,350		

2.		
.3402	.3
3.48	3
+ .49	+ .5
4.3102	3.8

3.	
347,593.80943	300,000
+ 57,457.482	+ 60,000
405,051.29143	360,000

4.	
95.38	100
456.405	500
+ 354	+ 400
905.785	1,000

LEARNING UNIT 3
SUBTRACTION

Subtraction requires that the decimal points be aligned. The rules are exactly the same as with addition.

2.6 Subtracting Decimal Numbers

When the minuend contains fewer positions to the right of the decimal point than does the subtrahend, zeros are usually added in the minuend. They are placed to the immediate right of the minuend, and as many zeros as necessary are added until the same number of positions are occupied to the right of the decimal point in the minuend as in the subtrahend. This enhances clarity and should aid your understanding.

To prove answers in subtraction, add the difference to the subtrahend. The sum is the minuend.

EXAMPLE Subtract 41.31242 from 5,628.23. Prove your answer.

Solution

5,628.23*000*	Proof:	5,586.91758
− 41.31242		+ 41.31242
5,586.91758		5,628.23___
		↑↑↑
		Drop the zeros.

2.6 Practice Problems

Find the difference in the following subtraction problems and prove the answers (do not round answers):

1. .356 − .193   **2.** 1.45 − .9346

3. 3,876.46 − 371.398   **4.** 290.39 − 48.2734

2.6 Solutions to Practice Problems

	Actual	*Proof*		*Actual*	*Proof*
1.	.356	.163	**2.**	1.4500	.5154
	− .193	+ .193		− .9346	+ .9346
	.163	.356		.5154	1.45
3.	3,876.460	3,505.062	**4.**	290.3900	242.1166
	− 371.398	+ 371.398		− 48.2734	+ 48.2734
	3,505.062	3,876.46		242.1166	290.39

2.7 Estimating Decimal Subtraction Problems

Rounding all the way is the recommended method for estimating answers when subtracting, unless greater accuracy is needed. As in addition, rounding is to the leftmost digit. All other digits are changed to zeros.

E X A M P L E

Find the actual and the estimated difference between .3309 and .385. (The larger number is the minuend; the smaller number is the subtrahend.)

Solution

Actual	*Estimated*
.3850	.4
− .3309	− .3
.0541	.1

E X A M P L E

Subtract 23.687 from 573.39. Find the actual and the estimated differences.

Solution

Actual	*Estimated*
573.390	600
− 23.687	− 20
549.703	580

2.7 Practice Problems

Solve the following subtraction problems. Find both the actual and the estimated differences. (Do not round the actual differences.)

1. .187 − .09932   **2.** 6,012.728 − 428.574

3. 784.0439 − 435.317   **4.** 158.2 − 19.608

2.7 Solutions to Practice Problems

	Actual	*Estimated*		*Actual*	*Estimated*
1.	.18700	.2	**2.**	6,012.728	6,000
	− .09932	− .1		− 428.574	− 400
	.08768	.1		5,584.154	5,600
3.	784.0439	800	**4.**	158.200	200
	− 435.317	− 400		− 19.608	− 20
	348.7269	400		138.592	180

LEARNING UNIT 4
MULTIPLICATION

As shown in Chapter 1, multiplication is merely a shortcut method of addition.

2.8 | **Multiplying Decimal Numbers**

When multiplying decimal numbers, multiply one factor by the other while disregarding the decimal points. Once a product has been determined, the number of decimal places equals the sum of the decimal places in the factors.

E X A M P L E   Multiply 3.251 by 21.36.

Solution

$$
\begin{array}{r}
3.251 \\
\times\ 21.36 \\
\hline
19506 \\
9753 \\
3251 \\
6502 \\
\hline
69.44136
\end{array}
$$

3 decimal positions
+ 2 decimal positions

= 5 decimal positions

Step 1. Multiply the factors together while ignoring the decimal points.

Step 2. Count the number of decimal positions to the right of the decimal point in each of the factors. (3.251 has three decimal positions occupied, and 21.36 has two decimal positions occupied.) Thus, five decimal positions are occupied.

Step 3. Starting from the right side of the product, count five spaces to the left. Place the decimal point in that position.

2.8 Practice Problems

Find the product in the following multiplication problems. (Do not round your answers.)

1. 29.674×2.57
2. $.45 \times .051$
3. 58.901×3.08
4. $300 \times .429$

2.8 Solutions to Practice Problems

1.
$$
\begin{array}{r}
29.674 \\
\times\ 2.57 \\
\hline
207718 \\
148370 \\
59348 \\
\hline
76.26218
\end{array}
$$

2.
$$
\begin{array}{r}
.45 \\
\times\ .051 \\
\hline
45 \\
225 \\
\hline
.02295
\end{array}
$$

3.
$$
\begin{array}{r}
58.901 \\
\times\ 3.08 \\
\hline
471208 \\
1767030 \\
\hline
181.41508
\end{array}
$$

4.
$$
\begin{array}{r}
.429 \\
\times\ 300 \\
\hline
128.700 = 128.7
\end{array}
$$

2.9 | **Multiplying Decimal Numbers by 10, Powers of 10, and Other Zeros**

When multiplying by any multiple of 10, you need only move the decimal point in the factor being multiplied one place to the right for every zero in the 10-multiple factor.

E X A M P L E   Multiply 3.87 by 10, 100, and 1,000.

Solution $3.87 \times 10 = 38.7$ *Move the decimal point one place to the right because 10 contains one zero.*

$3.87 \times 100 = 387$ *Move the decimal point two places to the right because 100 contains two zeros.*

Chapter 2 Fundamental Operations with Decimal Fractions

$3.87 \times 1,000 = 3,870$ *Move the decimal point three places to the right because 1,000 contains three zeros.*

When multiplying a decimal number by a whole number ending with one or more zeros, you may find it faster to move the decimal point to the right as many places as there are zeros in the whole number. The resulting number would then be multiplied by the remaining whole number (without the zeros).

EXAMPLE Multiply 9.456 by 70, 700, and 7,000.

Solution

$$9.456 \times 70 = 94.56 \times 7 = 661.92$$
$$9.456 \times 700 = 945.6 \times 7 = 6,619.2$$
$$9.456 \times 7,000 = 9,456 \times 7 = 66,192$$

2.9 Practice Problems

Multiply the following:
1. 3.98×100
2. 3.98×500
3. $.024 \times 1,000$
4. $.024 \times 8,000$

2.9 Solutions to Practice Problems
1. $3.98 \times 100 = 398$
2. $3.98 \times 500 = 398 \times 5 = 1,990$
3. $.024 \times 1,000 = 24$
4. $.024 \times 8,000 = 24 \times 8 = 192$

2.10 Estimating Decimal Multiplication Problems

Estimating decimal multiplication problems is especially useful because of the potential for large errors. Rounding all the way is recommended.

2.10 Practice Problems

Multiply the following and find the estimated as well as the actual solutions by rounding all the way. (Do not round the actual solutions.)
1. 446.4×3.47
2. $677.012 \times .36$
3. $11.71 \times .519$
4. 38.09×8.5

2.10 Solutions to Practice Problems

	Actual	*Estimated*		*Actual*	*Estimated*
1.	446.4	400	**2.**	677.012	700
	× 3.47	× 3		× .36	× .4
	31248	1,200		4062072	280
	17856			203 1036	
	13392			243.72432	
	1,549.008				
3.	11.71	10	**4.**	38.09	40
	× .519	× .5		× 8.5	× 9
	10539	5		19045	360
	1171			30472	
	5855			323.765	
	6.07749				

LEARNING UNIT 5
DIVISION

As shown in Chapter 1, division is the reverse of multiplication.

Dividing Decimal Numbers

When the divisor (the number you are dividing by) is a whole number, place the decimal point in the quotient (the answer) directly above the decimal point in the dividend (the number being divided). Then divide as usual.

E X A M P L E   Divide 43.5132 by 6.

Solution

$$6)\overline{43.5132}$$

Place the decimal point directly above the decimal point in the dividend.

$$\begin{array}{r} 7.2522 \\ \hline 6)43.5132 \end{array}$$

Divide as usual.

When the divisor contains a decimal fraction, it must be cleared before performing the calculation. The decimal point in the divisor is moved to the far right end of the divisor, making it a whole number. Then the decimal point in the dividend must be moved to the right the same number of spaces. If needed, add enough zeros in the dividend to occupy the number of spaces required in moving the decimal. Place the decimal point in the quotient above where it is in the dividend after the move. Divide as usual.

E X A M P L E   Divide 83.22 by 3.8.

Solution $3.8)\overline{83.22}$

Move the decimal point in the dividend and the divisor one place to the right (that is, as many places as needed to make 3.8 the whole number 38). Place the decimal point in the quotient directly above the decimal point in the dividend.

$$38)\overline{832.2}$$

$$\begin{array}{r} 21.9 \\ \hline 38)832.2 \end{array}$$

Divide as usual.

2.11 Practice Problems

Divide the following decimal numbers. (Do not round your answers.)

1. Divide 1,840.8 by 472.
2. Divide 63.2341 by 3.67.
3. Divide 18.82795 by 42.31.
4. Divide 26.98 by 1.42.

2.11 Solutions to Practice Problems

1.
$$\begin{array}{r} 3.9 \\ \hline 472)1,840.8 \\ \underline{1,416} \\ 424\ 8 \\ \underline{424\ 8} \end{array}$$

2. $3.67)\overline{63.2341}$
$$\begin{array}{r} 17.23 \\ \hline 367)6323.41 \\ \underline{367} \\ 2653 \\ \underline{2569} \\ 84\ 4 \\ \underline{73\ 4} \\ 11\ 01 \\ \underline{11\ 01} \end{array}$$

3. $42.31)\overline{18.82795}$
$$\begin{array}{r} .445 \\ \hline 4231)1,882.795 \\ \underline{1\ 692\ 4} \\ 190\ 39 \\ \underline{169\ 24} \\ 21\ 155 \\ \underline{21\ 155} \end{array}$$

4. $1.42)\overline{26.98}$
$$\begin{array}{r} 19 \\ \hline 142)2,698 \\ \underline{1\ 42} \\ 1\ 278 \\ \underline{1\ 278} \end{array}$$

Dividing Decimal Numbers by 10, Powers of 10, and Other Zeros

When the divisor is 10 or any multiple of 10, you can divide by moving the decimal point in the dividend *to the left* as many places as there are zeros in the divisor.

EXAMPLE   Divide 2,816 by 10, 100, and 1,000.

Solution
$$2{,}816 \div 10 = 281.6 \qquad \textit{(1 zero, 1 place)}$$
$$2{,}816 \div 100 = 28.16 \qquad \textit{(2 zeros, 2 places)}$$
$$2{,}816 \div 1{,}000 = 2.816 \qquad \textit{(3 zeros, 3 places)}$$

EXAMPLE   Divide 38.25 by 10, 100, and 1,000.

Solution
$$38.25 \div 10 = 3.825 \qquad \textit{(1 zero, 1 place)}$$
$$38.25 \div 100 = .3825 \qquad \textit{(2 zeros, 2 places)}$$
$$38.25 \div 1{,}000 = .03825 \qquad \textit{(3 zeros, 3 places)}$$

When the divisor ends with a zero or zeros (other than 10 or multiples of 10), move the decimal point in the dividend *and in the divisor* to the left as many places as there are zeros in the divisor. Then divide as usual.

EXAMPLE   Divide 4,632.24 by 60, 600, and 6,000.

Solution
$$4{,}632.24 \div 60 = 463.224 \div 6 = 77.204$$
$$4{,}632.24 \div 600 = 46.3224 \div 6 = 7.7204$$
$$4{,}632.24 \div 6{,}000 = 4.63224 \div 6 = .77204$$

2.12 Practice Problems

Divide the following problems. (Do not round your answers.)
1. Divide 11.34 by 100.
2. Divide 409.347 by 300.
3. Divide 487 by 1,000.
4. Divide 28,435 by 55,000.

2.12 Solutions to Practice Problems
1. $11.34 \div 100 = .1134$
2. $409.347 \div 300 = 4.09347 \div 3 = 1.36449$
3. $487 \div 1{,}000 = .487$
4. $28{,}435 \div 55{,}000 = 28.435 \div 55 = .517$

2.13 Estimating Decimal Division Problems

Estimating the results of division when decimal numbers are involved can be very useful, especially if decimal points are being moved around as a part of the actual division. Unless there is a need for more accuracy, rounding all the way is recommended. *When estimating an answer, if there are whole numbers in the solution, it is not necessary to carry the quotient to fractional form. Just round it off to the nearest whole number. If there are no whole numbers in the solution, round the estimated answer to the leftmost significant (nonzero) fractional digit.* That is, the quotient 7.832 would be rounded to 8, and the quotient .0035 would be rounded to .004.

EXAMPLE   Divide 345.38 by 300. Use rounding all the way to estimate the answer. Then find the actual quotient. (Round to the nearest thousandth.)

Solution   *Estimated*   *Actual*

$$300\overline{)300} = 1 \qquad \begin{array}{r} 1.1512 \\ 3\overline{)3.4538} \end{array}$$

$$= 1.151$$

Since the division was by a number ending in two zeros, the decimal point was moved two places to the left in both the dividend and in the divisor.

The quotient was carried to the ten thousandth position and rounded to the nearest thousandth.

Find the estimated and the actual solutions in each of the following problems. (Round your answers to the nearest thousandth if necessary.)

1. $.98765\overline{)3.923}$

2. $1.04\overline{)7.86}$

3. $5,000\overline{)4,820}$

4. $10.48\overline{)59.26}$

2.13 Solutions to Practice Problems

1. *Estimated*   *Actual*

$$\frac{4}{1\overline{)4}}$$

$$.98765\overline{)3.923}$$

$$3.9720 = 3.972$$
$$= 98765\overline{)392300.0000}$$
$$\underline{296295}$$
$$96005\ 0$$
$$\underline{88888\ 5}$$
$$7116\ 50$$
$$\underline{6913\ 55}$$
$$202\ 950$$
$$\underline{197\ 530}$$
$$5\ 4200$$

2. *Estimated*   *Actual*

$$\frac{8}{1\overline{)8}}$$

$$1.04\overline{)7.86}$$

$$7.5576 = 7.558$$
$$= 104\overline{)786.0000}$$
$$\underline{728}$$
$$58\ 0$$
$$\underline{52\ 0}$$
$$6\ 00$$
$$\underline{5\ 20}$$
$$800$$
$$\underline{728}$$
$$720$$
$$\underline{624}$$
$$96$$

3. $5,000\overline{)5,000}$ $5,000\overline{)4,820}$

$$\frac{1}{= 5\overline{)5}}$$

$$.964$$
$$= 5\overline{)4.820}$$
$$\underline{4\ 5}$$
$$32$$
$$\underline{30}$$
$$20$$
$$\underline{20}$$

4.

$$\frac{6}{10\overline{)60}} = 1\overline{)6}$$

$$10.48\overline{)59.26}$$

$$5.6545 = 5.655$$
$$= 1048\overline{)5926.0000}$$
$$\underline{5240}$$
$$686\ 0$$
$$\underline{628\ 8}$$
$$57\ 20$$
$$\underline{52\ 40}$$
$$4\ 800$$
$$\underline{4\ 192}$$
$$6080$$
$$\underline{5240}$$
$$840$$

QUICK REFERENCE SUMMARY AND REVIEW

Page	Section Topic	Learning Concepts	Examples and Solutions
36	**2.1** Reading and Writing Decimal Fractions	The value of decimal fractions depends on the numerical value of the digit and its position to the right of the decimal point. A decimal position is read and written with a "th," for example, ten*th*.	.156 is read, "one hundred fifty-six thousandths."
37	**2.2** Reading and Writing Combinations of Whole Numbers and Decimal Fractions: the Mixed Decimal	A mixed decimal is a whole number and a decimal fraction combined. The decimal point is read "and."	15.615 is read, "fifteen and six hundred fifteen thousandths."

Page	Section Topic	Learning Concepts	Examples and Solutions
39	**2.3** Rounding Decimal Numbers	**1.** Identify the digit to be rounded. **2.** If the number to the right of the identified digit is 5 or greater, round up. If it is less than 5, do not change the identified digit. **3.** Drop the decimal digits to the right of the identified digit.	18.925 rounded to the nearest tenth is 18.9. (Do not change the identified digit.) 18.925 rounded to the nearest hundredth is 18.93. (Round the 2 up to 3.)
41	**2.4** Adding Decimal Numbers	Align the decimal points and the place values will be properly aligned.	$21.74 + 7.219$ 21.74 $\underline{+\ 7.219}$ 28.959
41	**2.5** Estimating Decimal Addition Problems	Use rounding all the way.	$.832 + 1.6 + .0498$ .8 2.0 $\underline{+\ .05}$ 2.85
42	**2.6** Subtracting Decimal Numbers	Align the decimal points. When the minuend contains fewer digits than the subtrahend, zeros are placed to the right of the last decimal digit until there are as many digits in the minuend as in the subtrahend.	$8.41 - 2.893$ 8.41*0* $\underline{-\ 2.893}$ 5.517
43	**2.7** Estimating Decimal Subtraction Problems	Use rounding all the way.	$2.159 - .785$ 2.0 $\underline{-\ .8}$ 1.2
44	**2.8** Multiplying Decimal Numbers	Multiply ignoring the decimal point. Once the product is determined, add the number of decimal positions in the factors to be multiplied, count from right to left in the product the number of places found in the sum above, and place the decimal point at this position.	1.*31* 2 places $\underline{\times\ 2.05}$ + 2 places 6 55 $\underline{262\ 0}$ 2.*6855* = 4 places
44	**2.9** Multiplying Decimal Numbers by 10, Powers of 10, and Other Zeros	When multiplying by 10 or a multiple of 10, move the decimal point in the factor being multiplied one place to the right for each zero in the 10-multiple factor. When multiplying by a whole number ending in one or more zeros, move the decimal point to the right as many places as there are zeros in the whole number. Multiply by the whole number *without the zeros*.	**1.** $6.41 \times 100 = 641$ (2 zeros, 2 decimal places) **2.** $6.41 \times 300 = 641 \times 3 = 1{,}923$ (2 zeros, 2 decimal places—then multiply by 3)
45	**2.10** Estimating Decimal Multiplication Problems	Use rounding all the way.	15.12×7.49 20 $\underline{\times\ 7}$ 140

Page	Section Topic	Learning Concepts	Examples and Solutions
46	**2.11** Dividing Decimal Numbers	**1.** If the divisor is a whole number, place the decimal point in the quotient directly above the decimal point in the dividend. **2.** If the divisor is a decimal number, move the decimal point in the divisor to the right enough places so that it is a whole number. Move the decimal point in the dividend the same number of places. Then, place the decimal point in the quotient directly above the decimal point in the dividend.	$$\begin{array}{r} .301 \\ 17\overline{)5.117} \\ \underline{5\,1} \\ 1 \\ \underline{0} \\ 17 \\ \underline{17} \end{array}$$ $$.17\overline{)5.117}$$ $$\begin{array}{r} 30.1 \\ 17\overline{)511.7} \\ \underline{51} \\ 1 \\ \underline{0} \\ 1\,7 \\ \underline{1\,7} \end{array}$$
46	**2.12** Dividing Decimal Numbers by 10, Powers of 10, and Other Zeros	**1.** When the divisor is 10 or a multiple of 10, move the decimal point to the left in the dividend as many places as there are zeros in the divisor. **2.** When the divisor is a whole number that ends in a zero or zeros, move the decimal point in both the dividend and the divisor as many places to the left as there are zeros in the divisor. Then divide as usual.	$8.91 \div 100$ $= .0891$ (2 places to the left) $12.24 \div 600$ $= .1224 \div 6$ $= .204$
47	**2.13** Estimating Decimal Division Problems	Use rounding all the way.	$7.14 \div 6.9$ $7 \div 7 = 1$

SURFING THE INTERNET

For further information on the topics covered in this chapter, check out the following sites:

http://www.math.com/school/subject1/lessons/S1U1L2GL.html

http://www.gomath.com/algebra/decimal.asp

ADDITIONAL PRACTICE PROBLEMS

Answers to odd-numbered problems are given in Appendix A.

2.1

Write the following numbers in verbal form as they would be read:

1. .9
nine tenths

2. .307
three hundred seven thousandths

3. .051
fifty-one thousandths

4. .5078
five thousand, seventy-eight ten thousandths

Write the following numbers in decimal form:

5. Seventy-six hundredths
.76

6. Two thousand, eight hundred ninety-three millionths
.002893

7. Six hundred twelve thousandths
.612

8. Eleven ten thousandths
.0011

2.2

Write the following numbers in verbal form as they would be read:

9. 15.69
Fifteen and sixty-nine hundredths

10. 4.0723
Four and seven hundred twenty-three ten thousandths

11. 2,572.231
Two thousand, five hundred seventy-two and two hundred thirty-one thousandths

12. 184.8
One hundred eighty-four and eight tenths

Write the following numbers in decimal form:

13. One and sixteen thousandths
1.016

14. Two hundred thirty-seven and eight tenths
237.8

15. Five thousand, four hundred sixty-nine and one hundred seventy-four ten thousandths
5,469.0174

16. Four trillion, fifty-six million, three hundred seventy thousand, two hundred ten and twenty-one hundredths
4,000,056,370,210.21

2.3

Round the following decimal numbers as indicated:

17. 284.68 to the nearest ten
280

18. .2475 to the nearest thousandth
.248

19. 534.934 to the nearest tenth
534.9

20. 58,074.454 to the nearest hundredth
58,074.45

2.4

Add the following decimal numbers by placing them in columns (be sure to align the decimal points):

21. .45 + .5987 + .0048

```
  .45
  .5987
+ .0048
 1.0535
```

22. .4597 + .334 + .22 + .018

```
  .4597
  .334
  .22
+ .018
 1.0317
```

23. 39.560 + .24 + 348.205

```
  39.560
    .24
+ 348.205
 388.005
```

24. 32.872 + 10,089.48 + 4,358.9201

```
    32.872
 10,089.48
+ 4,358.9201
 14,481.2721
```

2.5

Add the following decimal numbers. Estimate the solution using rounding all the way, and then find the actual sum.

	Estimated	Actual		Estimated	Actual

25. 449.06 + 8,391.6021 + 378.208

```
   400      449.06
 8,000    8,391.6021
+ 400    + 378.208
 8,800    9,218.8701
```

26. .67925 + .56983 + .047

```
   .7       .67925
   .6       .56983
+ .05     + .047
 1.35     1.29608
```

27. 2.88 + .239 + 48.106

```
   3        2.88
   .2        .239
+ 50       48.106
 53.2      51.225
```

28. 220.26 + 198.05 + 3.87 + 43.98

```
 200      220.26
 200      198.05
   4        3.87
+ 40     + 43.98
 444      466.16
```

2.6

Find the difference in the following problems (be certain to align the decimal points):

29. .4401 − .1763

```
  .4401
− .1763
  .2638
```

30. .873 − .43205

```
  .87300
− .43205
  .44095
```

31. 283.793 − 109.93276

```
 283.79300
− 109.93276
 173.86024
```

32. 1.58654 − .3923

```
 1.58654
−  .3923
 1.19424
```

2.7

Find the difference in the following decimal numbers. Estimate your answer using rounding all the way, and then find the actual difference.

	Estimated	Actual		Estimated	Actual

33. .56 − .149

```
   .6       .56
  − .1     − .149
   .5       .411
```

34. 22.09 − 5.722

```
   20      22.090
  − 6     − 5.722
   14      16.368
```

35. 4,978 − 478.287

```
  5,000     4,978.000
  − 500    − 478.287
  4,500     4,499.713
```

36. 39.548 − 4.29

```
   40       39.548
  − 4      − 4.290
   36       35.258
```

2.8

Multiply the following decimal numbers. (Do not round your answers.)

37. .38 × .291
```
   .291
  × .38
  2328
   873
  .11058
```

38. 48.09 × 1.3
```
  48.09
  × 1.3
  14427
  4809
  62.517
```

39. 2.8 × .009
```
    2.8
  × .009
  .0252
```

40. 23.34 × 9.012
```
    23.34
  × 9.012
    4668
    2334
  210060
  210.34008
```

2.9

Multiply the following problems using rules for multiplying by 10, powers of 10, or other zeros. (Do not round your answers.)

41. .0349 × 1,000
```
.0349 × 1000 = 34.9
```

42. 3.98 × 10
```
   3.98
  × 10
  39.8
```

43. 28.274 × 500
```
  28.274
  ×  500
  14,137
```

44. 2.0298 × 6,000
```
   2.0298
  × 6,000
  12,178.8
```

2.10

Multiply the following problems. Estimate your answer by using rounding all the way. Find the actual product (round it to the nearest thousandth if necessary).

	Estimated	Actual		Estimated	Actual

45. 9.91 × 3.6
```
   10       9.91
  × 4      × 3.6
   40      35.676
```

46. .10129 × .57
```
    .1      .10129
  × .6      × .57
   .06     .0577353
```

47. 25.109 × 4.78
```
    30      25.109
  × 5      ×  4.78
   150     120.02102
```

48. 440 × .29
```
   400      440
  × .3     × .29
   120     127.6
```

2.11

Find the quotient in the following division problems. (Round your answer to the nearest thousandth if necessary.)

49. .5)‾.75
```
    1.5
  5)7.5
    5
    2 5
    2 5
```

50. .231)‾.247
```
            1.0692 = 1.069
  231)247.0000
      231
      16 00
      13 86
       2 140
       2 079
         610
         462
```

51. 4.5)‾1.3901
```
          .3089 = .309
  45)13.9010
     13 5
      401
      360
      410
      405
```

52. 45.03)‾1,098
```
                24.3837 = 24.384
  4503)109,800.0000
        90 06
        19 740
        18 012
         1 728 0
         1 350 9
           377 10
           360 24
            16 860
            13 509
             3 3510
             3 1521
```

2.12

Use the rules for dividing by 10, powers of 10, and other zeros to find the quotients in the following problems (Round your answers to the nearest thousandth if necessary.)

53. 2.8 ÷ 10
```
.28
```

54. 4.75 ÷ 1,000
```
.005
```

55. 68.104 ÷ 2,000
```
.034
```

56. 3.87 ÷ 300 .
```
.013
```

2.13

Find the quotients in the following problems. Round all the way to estimate your answer. Find the actual solution and round to the nearest thousandth.

	Estimated	*Actual*		*Estimated*	*Actual*

57. $.645\overline{)389}$

Estimated:
```
  667
6)4,000
  3 6
   40
   36
   40
   36
```

Actual: $603.1007 = 603.101$
```
645)389,000.0000
    387 0
      2 000
      1 935
        65 0
        64 5
         5000
         4515
          485
```

58. $.35\overline{).2409}$

Estimated: $.4\overline{).2} = 4\overline{)2.0}$ result $.5$

Actual:
```
    .688
35)24.0900
   21 0
    3 09
    2 80
      290
      280
       10
```

59. $6.09\overline{)3.61}$

Estimated:
```
  .667
6)4.0000
  3 6
   40
   36
   40
   36
   40
   36
```

Actual: $.5927 = .593$
```
609)361.0000
    304 5
     56 50
     54 81
      1 690
      1 218
       4720
       4263
```

60. $2.7\overline{)3,091.9}$

Estimated:
```
     1,000
3)3,000
```

Actual:
```
       1,145.148
27)30,919.0000
   27
    3 9
    2 7
    1 21
    1 08
      139
      135
       4 0
       2 7
       1 30
       1 08
         220
         216
```

> **CHAPTER REVIEW PROBLEMS**

Answers to odd-numbered problems are given in Appendix A.

Drill Problems

Write the following decimal fractions in proper form:

1. Two tenths
.2

2. Thirty-six hundredths
.36

3. Five ten thousandths
.0005

4. Fifty-four thousand, six hundred five millionths
.054605

Write the following decimal fractions in verbal form as they are read:

5. .014
Fourteen thousandths

6. .15
Fifteen hundredths

7. .8765
Eight thousand, seven hundred sixty-five ten thousandths

8. .00012
Twelve hundred thousandths

Write the following numbers in proper decimal form:

9. One and six hundredths
1.06

10. Five hundred fifteen and thirty-three hundredths
515.33

11. Three million, twenty-five and two hundred one ten thousandths
3,000,025.0201

12. Eight thousand three hundred twenty and four tenths
8,320.4

Write the following decimal numbers verbally as they are read:

13. 23.41
Twenty-three and forty-one hundredths

14. 1,215.003
One thousand, two hundred fifteen and three thousandths

15. 78,046.91385
Seventy-eight thousand, forty-six and ninety-one thousand, three hundred eighty-five hundred thousandths

16. 167.9
One hundred sixty-seven and nine tenths

Round the following decimal numbers as indicated:

17. .102 to the nearest hundredth
.10

18. .0658 to the nearest thousandth
.066

19. 16.05 to the nearest tenth
16.1

20. 2,384.87648 to the nearest thousandth
2,384.876

21. $18.087 to the nearest hundredth
$18.09

22. 12.583 to the nearest unit
13

23. $38.2832 to the nearest cent
$38.28

24. 215,024.68 to the nearest hundred
215,000

25. 15.9004 to the nearest tenth
15.9

Add the following decimal numbers by placing them in columns with the decimal points aligned:

26. 8.2568 + 28.107 + 30.06

    8.2568
   28.107
 + 30.06
   66.4238

27. .7216 + 3.8903 + 3.0062

    .7216
   3.8903
 + 3.0062
   7.6181

28. 2.71 + 9.317 + 86.27

    2.71
    9.317
 + 86.27
   98.297

29. 496.22 + 17.3543 + .27 + .1

   496.22
    17.3543
      .27
 +   .1
   513.9443

Use rounding all the way to estimate the solutions to the following addition problems, and then find the actual sum:

	Estimated	Actual			Estimated	Actual
30. 25.6 + 7.304 + 1,382.97	30 7 + 1,000 1,037	25.6 7.304 + 1,382.97 1,415.874	**31.** .14 + .98 + .731		.1 1. + .7 1.8	.14 .98 + .731 1.851
32. 3,982.03 + 29,298.0037	4,000 + 30,000 34,000	3,982.03 + 29,298.0037 33,280.0337	**33.** .387 + 3.09 + 12.095		.4 3 + 10 13.4	.387 3.09 + 12.095 15.572

Solve the following subtraction problems. Be certain to align the decimal points and add zeros in the minuend when necessary.

34. 15.3 − 3.2

   15.3
 − 3.2
   12.1

35. 253.5834 − 1.642513

   253.583400
 −   1.642513
   251.940887

36. 47.6938 − 47.6937

   47.6938
 − 47.6937
    .0001

37. 164.2513 − 25.35824

   164.25130
 − 25.35824
   138.89306

Use rounding all the way to estimate the solutions to the following subtraction problems, and then find the actual difference:

	Estimated	Actual		Estimated	Actual
38. 14,321.89 − 4,896.215	10,000 − 5,000 5,000	14,321.890 − 4,896.215 9,425.675	**39.** 1,598 − 346.41	2,000 − 300 1,700	1,598.00 − 346.41 1,251.59
40. 7,798.42 − 2,344.2856	8,000 − 2,000 6,000	7,798.4200 − 2,344.2856 5,454.1344	**41.** 393.09 − 2.9501	400 − 3 397	393.0900 − 2.9501 390.1399

Find the product in the following multiplication problems. (Do not round your answers.)

42. 2.716 × 3

   2.716
 ×   3
   8.148

43. 47.352 × 6.3

   47.352
 ×   6.3
   142 056
   2841 12
   298.3176

44. 511.23 × 5.31

   511.23
 × 5.31
   511 23
   15336 9
   25561 5
   2,714.6313

45. .6453 × .27

   .6453
 × .27
   45171
   12906
   .174231

46. 2.95 × 1,000

   2.95
 × 1,000
   2,950

47. 46.2 × 10,000

   46.2
 × 10,000
   462,000

48. .678 × 4,000

   .678
 × 4,000
   2,712

49. 73.6 × 1,200

   73.6
 × 1,200
   147 2
   736
   88,320

Chapter 2 Fundamental Operations with Decimal Fractions

Multiply the following problems. Use rounding all the way to estimate the solutions before you find the actual product. (Do not round the actual products.)

	Estimated	*Actual*		*Estimated*	*Actual*

50. 14.9×45.15

Estimated:
$$\begin{array}{r} 10 \\ \times\ 50 \\ \hline 500 \end{array}$$

Actual:
$$\begin{array}{r} 45.15 \\ \times\ 14.9 \\ \hline 4063\ 5 \\ 18060 \\ 4515\ \ \\ \hline 672.735 \end{array}$$

51. $12 \times 30.5 \times .7$

Estimated:
$$\begin{array}{r} 10 \\ \times\ 30 \\ \hline 300 \\ \times\ .7 \\ \hline 210 \end{array}$$

Actual:
$$\begin{array}{r} 12 \\ \times\ 30.5 \\ \hline 6\ 0 \\ 360\ \ \\ \hline 366 \\ \times\ .7 \\ \hline 256.2 \end{array}$$

52. $.36 \times .072$

Estimated:
$$\begin{array}{r} .4 \\ \times\ .1 \\ \hline .04 \end{array}$$

Actual:
$$\begin{array}{r} .36 \\ \times\ .072 \\ \hline 72 \\ 252\ \ \\ \hline .02592 \end{array}$$

53. $3.781 \times 6,000$

Estimated:
$$\begin{array}{r} 4 \\ \times\ 6,000 \\ \hline 24,000 \end{array}$$

Actual:
$$\begin{array}{r} 3.781 \\ \times\ 6,000 \\ \hline 22,686 \end{array}$$

Divide and round your answers to the nearest thousandth.

54. $2.8\overline{)237}$

$$\begin{array}{r} 84.6428 = 84.643 \\ 28\overline{)2370.0000} \\ 224\ \ \ \ \ \ \ \ \ \\ \hline 130\ \ \ \ \ \ \ \\ 112\ \ \ \ \ \ \ \\ \hline 18\ 0\ \ \ \ \ \\ 16\ 8\ \ \ \ \ \\ \hline 1\ 20\ \ \ \ \\ 1\ 12\ \ \ \ \\ \hline 80\ \ \\ 56\ \ \\ \hline 240 \\ 224 \end{array}$$

55. $301\overline{)22.5}$

$$\begin{array}{r} .0747 = .075 \\ 301\overline{)22.5000} \\ 21\ 07\ \ \ \\ \hline 1\ 430\ \ \\ 1\ 204\ \ \\ \hline 2260 \\ 2107 \end{array}$$

56. $5.36\overline{).736}$

$$\begin{array}{r} .1373 = .137 \\ 536\overline{)73.6000} \\ 53\ 6\ \ \ \ \\ \hline 20\ 00\ \ \\ 16\ 08\ \ \\ \hline 3\ 920 \\ 3\ 752 \\ \hline 1680 \\ 1608 \end{array}$$

57. $.473\overline{).653}$

$$\begin{array}{r} 1.3805 = 1.381 \\ 473\overline{)653.0000} \\ 473\ \ \ \ \ \\ \hline 180\ 0\ \ \\ 141\ 9\ \ \\ \hline 38\ 10 \\ 37\ 84 \\ \hline 2600 \\ 2365 \end{array}$$

Divide the following decimal numbers using the rules for division by 10, powers of 10, and other zeros. (Do not round your answers.)

58. $.263 \div 100$
.00263

59. $37.82 \div 1,000$
.03782

60. $93.6 \div 3900$

$$\begin{array}{r} .024 \\ 39\overline{).936} \\ 78\ \ \\ \hline 156 \\ 156 \end{array}$$

61. $.9072 \div 2100$

$$\begin{array}{r} .000432 \\ 21\overline{).009072} \end{array}$$

Use rounding all the way to estimate the solutions to the following division problems. (When estimating, you do not need to carry a solution to fractional form.) Then find the actual quotient. (Round the actual solution to the nearest thousandth if necessary.)

	Estimated	*Actual*		*Estimated*	*Actual*

62. $1.5\overline{)1.845}$

Estimated:
$$\begin{array}{r} 1 \\ 2\overline{)2} \end{array}$$

Actual:
$$\begin{array}{r} 1.23 \\ 15\overline{)18.45} \\ 15\ \ \ \\ \hline 3\ 4\ \\ 3\ 0\ \\ \hline 45 \\ 45 \end{array}$$

63. $.66\overline{)14.22}$

Estimated:
$$\begin{array}{r} 14 \\ 7\overline{)100} \end{array}$$

Actual:
$$\begin{array}{r} 21.5454 = 21.545 \\ 66\overline{)1422.0000} \\ 132\ \ \ \ \ \ \ \\ \hline 102\ \ \ \ \ \ \\ 66\ \ \ \ \ \ \\ \hline 36\ 0\ \ \ \ \\ 33\ 0\ \ \ \ \\ \hline 3\ 00\ \ \\ 2\ 64\ \ \\ \hline 360 \\ 330 \\ \hline 300 \\ 264 \end{array}$$

	Estimated	Actual		Estimated	Actual

64. $.105\overline{)1,062.6}$

$10,000 \div 1 = 10,000$

$105\overline{)1,062,600}$
$\underline{1\ 05}$
$12\ 6$
$\underline{10\ 5}$
$2\ 10$
$\underline{2\ 10}$

Actual: 10,120

65. $1.2\overline{)58.74}$

$60 \div 1 = 60$

$12\overline{)587.40}$
$\underline{48}$
107
$\underline{96}$
$11\ 4$
$\underline{10\ 8}$
60
$\underline{60}$

Actual: 48.95

Word Problems

66. Cecil Brown owns four restaurants. Last week, profits were $3,619.44, $326.50, $4,142.96, and $57.31. How much were the total estimated and actual profits?

Estimated	Actual
$4,000	$3,619.44
300	326.50
4,000	4,142.96
60	57.31
$8,360	$8,146.21

67. The Friendly Bank and Trust had a cash balance of $24,926,375.18 one morning. During the day, the bank received deposits of $2,758,548.36 and paid out $3,944,729.56. Find the closing balance at the end of the day.

$24,926,375.18
$+\ 2,758,548.36$
27,684,923.54
$-\ 3,944,729.56$
$23,740,193.98

68. Alan's earnings are subject to a state income tax of .052 times earnings. Calculate his state income tax if his earnings are $9,447.30.

$9,447.30
$\times .052$
1889460
4723650
$491.25960 = $491.26

69. Robin Cole Enterprises tries to keep an inventory of 325 pipes on hand. At the end of business on Friday, there were 86 pipes on display and 128 pipes in the storage room. How many pipes would have to be ordered to adjust the inventory to the desired level?

128   325
$+\ 86$ $-\ 214$
214   111

70. Tony Pear sold a business building for $47.25 per square foot. The building measured 23,512.9 square feet. Estimate the selling price and find the actual price.

Estimated	Actual
20,000	23,512.9
$\times 50	$\times\ 47.25
$1,000,000	1175645
	470258
	1645903
	940516
	$1,110,984.53

71. McDonald Incorporated has a computerized payroll department. The computer has the capacity of processing 168.5 payroll checks per minute. Calculate the computer time necessary to process 26,960 employee checks. Estimate and then calculate the actual number of minutes, and then the number of hours. (Round your answer to the nearest tenth if necessary.)

Estimated	Actual
150 mins.	160 mins.
$200\overline{)30,000}$	$1,685\overline{)269,600}$
$\underline{20\ 0}$	$\underline{168\ 5}$
$10\ 00$	$101\ 10$
$\underline{10\ 00}$	$\underline{101\ 10}$
2.5 hrs.	2.66 = 2.7 hrs.
$60\overline{)150.}$	$60\overline{)160.00}$
$\underline{120}$	$\underline{120}$
300	$40\ 0$
$\underline{300}$	$\underline{36\ 0}$
	$4\ 00$
	$\underline{3\ 60}$

72. J. P. Morgan Incorporated pays the following monthly salaries: $2,768.13, $5,236.07, $3,258.33, $6,755.26, $8,157.61, $9,946.15, $1,678.42, $7,785.23, $5,587.20, $746.88, $237.80, $2,344.28. Calculate the monthly payroll.

$ 2,768.13
5,236.07
3,258.33
6,755.26
8,157.61
9,946.15
1,678.42
7,785.23
5,587.20
746.88
237.80
$+\ 2,344.28$
$ 54,501.36

73. Stan and Joan operate S & J Stamp Redemption Center. The previous five customers traded for merchandise costing 8.25 books, 17.5 books, 12 books, 115.25 books, and 24.5 books. What is the total number of books of stamps that have been redeemed? Give the actual and estimated figures.

Estimated	Actual
8	8.25
20	17.5
10	12
100	115.25
$+\ 20$	$+\ 24.5$
158	177.5

74. Chou Lai owns land that he leases for grazing. Chou owns a total of 85.67 acres. The sizes of three of his pastures are: 21.35 acres 19.24 acres, and 24.82 acres. How many acres are there in the fourth pasture?

```
  21.35        85.67
  19.24      − 65.41
+ 24.82        20.26
  65.41
```

75. Argyle socks cost $1.863 per pair to produce and sell to wholesalers for $2.631 per pair in lots of 100 pairs. Determine the amount of markup on 200 pairs. (Markup is the difference between the selling price and the cost of merchandise.)

```
$ 2.631      $  .768
− 1.863      ×   200
$  .768      $153.60
```

76. Snake Thompson placed the following order for his company:

Quantity	Item Description	Unit Price
10 boxes	Stationary	$12.49
5 cases	12 oz. glasses	15.50
2 cartons	Flatware—spoons	8.95
3 cartons	Flatware—knives	8.95
5 cartons	Flatware—forks	10.29

Estimate the total amount of the order and then determine the actual cost to Snake's company.

Estimated	Actual
10 × $10 = $100	10 × $12.49 = 124.90
5 × 20 = 100	5 × 15.50 = 77.50
2 × 9 = 18	2 × 8.95 = 17.90
3 × 9 = 27	3 × 8.95 = 26.85
5 × 10 = 50	5 × 10.29 = 51.45
$295	$298.60

77. The new Burbank school system consumes 22,275 pounds of milk each year. If one gallon of milk weighs 5.75 pounds, how many gallons of milk does the school system consume? (Round your answer to the nearest gallon.)

```
        3,873.9 = 3,874 gallons
575)2,227,500.0
    1 725
      502 5
      460 0
       42 50
       40 25
        2 250
        1 725
          525 0
          517 5
```

78. Muhammad Haque rented an automobile at the airport upon arrival in Chicago. The rate was $24.95 per day plus $.165 (16.5 cents) per mile. Muhammad kept the car for three days and drove it 257 miles. What is the total automobile rental fee?

```
$24.95             257
×   3           × $.165
$74.85            1285
                  1542
                   257
        $74.85 + $42.41 = $117.26
```

79. It is the 14th of June. It has rained for 6 of the 14 days. The official weather bureau rainfall amounts of those 6 days are:

June 2	2.27 inches	June 9	3.321 inches
June 3	1.94 inches	June 12	2.5 inches
June 7	4.1 inches	June 14	1.78 inches

If the average monthly rainfall for June is 12.34 inches, by how many inches is this month's rain exceeding the average?

```
  2.27
  1.94
  4.1        15.911
  3.321    − 12.34
  2.5        3.571
+ 1.78
 15.911
```

✓ ENRICHMENT PROBLEMS

80. In baseball on-base average is calculated by dividing the total number of times a player reached base by the total number of times the player batted. Kinky Callaway has been up 235 times. In his plate appearances, he has made it to base in the following ways:

55 times as a result of base hits

27 times as a result of walks

3 times as a result of being hit by a pitch

1 time as a result of catcher interference

Calculate Kinky's on-base average.

```
  55            .3659 = .366
  27         235)86.0000
   3            70 5
+  1            15 50
  86            14 10
                 1 400
                 1 175
                  2250
                  2115
```

81. Stella Green is a hog buyer. The price for hogs fluctuates regularly. Stella has made the following purchases today:

4 hogs @ $50.00

3 hogs @ $51.75

5 hogs @ $52.25

2 hogs @ $53.50

What was Stella's total expense? A weighted average can be calculated by dividing the *total cost* by the *total number* of hogs purchased (total cost/total number). What was the weighted average cost of Stella's hogs?

```
4 × $50.00 = $200.00          $ 51.678 = $51.68
3 ×  51.75 =  155.25      14)$723.500
5 ×  52.25 =  261.25          70
2 ×  53.50 =  107.00          23
14            $723.50         14
                 ↑            9 5
              Total           8 4
              expense         1 10
                              98
                              120
                              112
```

82. Jonathan Marcos's home office measures 20 feet wide by 30 feet long. He has been saving in his company's piggy bank to have new carpet installed. He paid the carpet company with 17 pennies, 12 nickels, 30 dimes, 7 quarters, 45 one-dollar bills, 7 five-dollar bills, 4 ten-dollar bills, 6 twenty-dollar bills, 3 fifty-dollar bills, and 5 hundred-dollar bills. He still owed $73.65. Find the average cost per square foot. (Square feet can be found by multiplying length by width. The average cost per square foot can be found by dividing the total cost by the total square footage.)

```
   20        17 × $  .01 = $   .17              $ 1.615 = $1.62   Average cost per square foot
 × 30        12 × $  .05 = $   .60          600)$969.170
 600 square feet  30 × $  .10 = $  3.00          600
              7 × $  .25 = $  1.75          369 1
             45 × $ 1.00 = $ 45.00          360 0
              7 × $ 5.00 = $ 35.00          9 17
              4 × $10.00 = $ 40.00          6 00
              6 × $20.00 = $120.00          3 170
              3 × $50.00 = $150.00          3 000
              5 × $100.00 = $500.00
                            $895.52
                          + $ 73.65
                            $969.17   Total cost
```

CRITICAL THINKING GROUP PROJECT

The federal government did not start out with $5 trillion in debt. The debt was incurred year after year. When a government spends more than it earns in revenue, it incurs a deficit. For several years, the deficit was in excess of $300 billion. Once again, however, most Americans do not have a frame of reference for such large amounts. Let's see if we can provide a frame of reference. Assuming that the debt was $300 billion in one year, calculate the following (round your answers to the nearest cent if necessary):

a. Debt per day (Divide the annual debt by the number of days in one year.)
   $300,000,000,000 ÷ 365 = $821,917,808.20 per day

b. Debt per hour (Divide the amount from the calculation in question (a) by the number of hours in a day.)
   $821,917,808.20 ÷ 24 = $34,246,575.34 per hour

c. Debt per minute (Divide the amount from the calculation in question (b) by the number of minutes in an hour.)
   $34,246,575.34 ÷ 60 = $570,776.25 per minute

d. Debt per second (Divide the amount from the calculation in question (c) by the number of seconds in a minute.)
   $570,776.25 ÷ 60 = $9,512.94 per second 24/7/365

The result is the additional amount of debt the federal government incurred each and every second of every day in a year. Think of how much the government spends every second.

Chapter 2 Fundamental Operations with Decimal Fractions

1. Define a mixed decimal.
A mixed decimal is a whole number combined with a decimal
fraction.

2. What is a decimal fraction?
A decimal fraction is a fraction expressed as a part of a whole in the
base 10 system. Thus, the value is stated in ten*ths*, hundred*ths*, thousand*ths*, and so on, depending on the position occupied.

Express the following as numerals:

3. Twenty-six thousandths
.026

4. Three thousand, four hundred seventy-nine ten thousandths
.3479

5. Forty-three billion, three hundred thousand, two hundred
fifty-seven and forty-one hundredths
43,000,300,257.41

6. Three hundred sixty-two thousand, three hundred and
thirty-three thousandths
362,300.033

7. Twenty-two million, nine hundred seventy-six thousand
and five hundred twenty-seven thousandths
22,976,000.527

Round the following to the place indicated:

8. 1.1235 to the nearest tenth
1.1

9. 6,286.24938 to the nearest thousandth
6,286.249

10. 14.9853 to the nearest hundredth
14.99

11. 12,976.58 to the nearest unit
12,977

12. 38.549365 to the nearest hundred thousandth
38.54937

*Add the following decimal numbers. Find the actual and the estimated solutions. Be certain that all decimal
points are aligned before completing your calculations.*

		Estimated	*Actual*				*Estimated*	*Actual*
13.	87.3	90	87.3		**14.**	428.6	400	428.6
	4.57	5	4.57			60.63	60	60.63
	41.5	40	41.5			9.207	9	9.207
	7.71	8	7.71			495.4	500	495.4
	9.13	9	9.13			6.806	7	6.806
	+ 23.9	+ 20	+ 23.9			+ 1.003	+ 1	+ 1.003
		172	174.11				977	1,001.646
15.	84,312.6	80,000	84,312.6		**16.**	101.5	100	101.5
	41.836	40	41.836			2,728	3,000	2,728
	18,974	20,000	18,974.			31.382	30	31.382
	9.101	9	9.101			5.87	6	5.87
	12.8	10	12.8			1.899	2	1.899
	+ 181.666	+ 200	+ 181.666			+ 987	+ 1,000	+ 987
		100,259	103,532.003				4,138	3,855.651

*Subtract the following decimal numbers. Find the actual and the estimated solutions. Be certain you align
the decimal points before you complete the calculations.*

		Estimated	*Actual*				*Estimated*	*Actual*
17.	392.86	400	392.86*0*		**18.**	5,738.6	6,000	5,738.6*0*
	− 67.055	− 70	− 67.055			− 473.24	− 500	− 473.24
		330	325.805				5,500	5,265.36
19.	48.934	50	48.934*00*		**20.**	298.2	300	298.2*000*
	− 28.40415	− 30	− 28.40415			− 28.0879	− 30	− 28.0879
		20	20.52985				270	270.1121

Multiply the following decimal numbers. Find the actual and the estimated solutions.

	Estimated	*Actual*

21. 732.1
×6.35

700
× 6
4,200

732.1
× 6.35
36605
21963
43926
4,648.835

22. 87.612
× 9.37

90
× 9
810

87.612
× 9.37
6 13284
26 2836
788 508
820.92444

23. 7.25
×600

7
× 600
4,200

7.25
× 600
4,350

24. 28.093
× 1,000

30
× 1,000
30,000

28.093
× 1,000
28,093

Divide the following decimal numbers. Find the actual and the estimated solutions.

25. 6.5)69.465

10
7)70

10.6869 = 10.687
65)694.6500
65
44 6
39 0
5 65
5 20
450
390
600
585

26. .182)57

300
2)600

313.187
182)57,000.0000
54 6
2 40
1 82
580
546
34 0
18 2
15 80
14 56
1 240
1 092
1480
1456

27. 6,500)7,800

1
7)8

1.2
65)78.0
65
13 0
13 0

28. 2100)63

.03
200)6.00

.03
21).63
63

29. Paul Hernandez had several jobs last year. He was employed by six different firms. His W-2 forms showed the following earnings: $319.41, $2,418.35, $652.28, $129, $1,847.28, and $11,860. How much were his total earnings for the year?

$ 319.41
2,418.35
652.28
129
1,847.28
+ 11,860
$17,227.32

30. An enterprising student at Atlantic U. tried to earn some money by importing piñatas from Mexico and selling them at a profit during the Easter holidays. Since piñatas are for Christmas celebrations rather than Easter, she lost money. She paid $140.60 for 200 piñatas, $16.25 for import duties, and $31.80 for transportation charges. She sold them in town for $182.50, but had to pay a $4.12 delivery charge to one customer. How much did the student lose?

$140.60
16.25
+ 31.80
$188.65

$182.50
− 4.12
$178.38

$188.65
− 178.38
$ 10.27

31. At the pawn shop, a customer gave the clerk a five-dollar bill to pay for purchases of $.33, $1.29, $.88, and $.45. How much change should the customer receive?

$ .33
1.29
.88
+ .45
$2.95

$ 5.00
− 2.95
$ 2.05

32. Maria received a paycheck for $928.74. Harry's check was for $672.12. If Maria worked an average of 40 hours per week for four weeks and Harry worked an average of 30 hours per week during one four-week pay period, who made more per hour and how much more?

Maria

4 × 40 = 160

$ 5.80
160)$928.74
800
128 7
128 0
74

Harry

4 × 30 = 120

$ 5.60
120)$672.12
600
72 1
72 0
12

$5.80
− 5.60
$ .20
Maria earned $.20 per hour more than Harry.

33. The total cost for 206 cartons of sugarless bubble gum was $494.40. What was the cost per carton?

```
        $2.40
206)$494.40
     412
      82 4
      82 4
```

34. A recipe calls for 2.5 cups of sugar and 2 tablespoons of malt, among other ingredients. If this recipe will serve 4, how many cups of sugar and tablespoons of malt would be necessary to serve 2? to serve 16?

```
4 ÷ 2 = 2                      16 ÷ 4 = 4
   1.25 cups sugar          2.5 × 4 = 10 cups sugar
2)2.50

2
― = 1 tablespoon malt      2 × 4 = 8 tablespoons malt
2
```

35. Miles Friedman is thinking of purchasing a new lakeside cabin. The developer will finance the cabin for $637.65 per month for 20 years. The asking price for the cabin is $72,850. All payments above that price are interest. How much interest will Miles end up paying if he concludes the transaction as stated?

```
    20          $637.65       $153,036
  × 12          × 240        − 72,850
 240 months     2550600      $80,186 interest
                127530
                $153,036
```

36. Malcolm Kennedy took his car to a repair shop for a tune-up. The tune-up was a specialty of the shop, and it charged $44.44 for a four-cylinder car. When Malcolm picked his car up, he found that his wife has authorized other repairs over the phone. Those were:

New distributor cap	$ 14.95
New sparkplug wires	23.50
New alternator	123.42
New battery	82.67
New battery mounting bracket	36.06

In addition, Malcolm's city has a sales tax of $.075 on each dollar of repair work done. Calculate his total bill.

```
$ 44.44
  14.95        $325.04       $325.04
  23.50        × .075       + 24.38
 123.42        162520        $349.42
  82.67        227528
+ 36.06        $24.378
$325.04
```

37. A major indoor soccer league franchise offers a block of season tickets to home games. There are 64 home games next season. The block of tickets sell for $608. Dominick wants to have tickets to some of the games, but he cannot attend all of them. His friends, Sushi and Duc Tram, have offered to buy a total of 12 tickets from him. How much should they pay Dominick? How much is Dominick's share of the season ticket price?

```
      $9.50       $9.50        $608
64)$608.00       × 12         − 114
    576          1900         $494
    32 0          950
    32 0         $114.00
```

38. Under a licensing agreement with a business firm in Hong Kong, Michelle Pipper will pay $.05 for every $1 of sales to her dress seamstress. Last year's sales totaled $93,739.18. How much did Michelle pay her seamstress?

```
$93,739.18
   × .05
$ 4,686.96
```

39. Mario's lawn measures 75.7 feet by 127.5 feet. He is shopping for fertilizer. One bag's label claims it will cover 2,500 square feet of lawn. How many bags should Mario buy? (Square footage is determined by multiplying the length by the width.)

```
   127.5 ft.
 × 75.7 ft.      2,500)9,651.75
   89 25
   637 5          3.8   = 4 bags
 8 925          25)96.5175
 9,651.75          75
                   21 5
                   20 0
```

40. Father Flanigan just opened his collection box. He has separated the money into groups as follows:

28 pennies	23 one-dollar bills
17 nickels	5 five-dollar bills
44 dimes	1 ten-dollar bill
18 quarters	

How much money was in the box?

```
28 ×   .01 = $   .28
17 ×   .05 =     .85
44 ×   .10 =    4.40
18 ×   .25 =    4.50
23 ×  1.00 =   23.00
 5 ×  5.00 =   25.00
 1 × 10.00 =   10.00
               $68.03
```

41. Dora still owes $522 on her tuition at Prince Hill College. She has already paid $2,186 for this semester in which she registered for 16 hours. How much does the college charge per semester hour?

```
  $2,186          $169.25
+   522       16)$2,708.00
  $2,708          1 6
                  1 10
                    96
                   148
                   144
                     4 0
                     3 2
                      80
                      80
```

42. Washington Wallace had a great year in basketball at the U. of Indianapolis. In the last 10 games of the 2002 season he scored 28 points, 31 points, 16 points, 23 points, 32 points, 27 points, 18 points, 29 points, 15 points, and 25 points. What was Wallace's average score per game? (The average is the total number of points divided by the total number of games.)

```
    28
    31
    16
    23
    32
    27              24.4
    18          10)244
    29              20
    15              44
+   25              40
   244              40
                    40
                    40
```

EXCEL SPREADSHEET APPLICATION FOR CHAPTER 2

The Springfield Department Store management keeps a record of the sales by department. Each department's sales form is submitted weekly and recorded. From the daily sales the store's total daily and total weekly sales are reported. When you open Ch2App1 from your spreadsheet disk, it will look like the one shown here:

Springfield Department Store
2617 Main Street
Box 219
Springfield, Maryland 58109
Telephone: 301-555-2158   FAX: 301-555-3498

DEPARTMENTAL SALES

Day of Week	Men's Clothing	Women's Clothing	Children's Clothing	Household Linens	Home Furnishings	Appliances	Automotive	TOTALS
Sunday								$0.00
Monday								$0.00
Tuesday								$0.00
Wednesday								$0.00
Thursday								$0.00
Friday								$0.00
Saturday								$0.00
TOTALS	$0.00	$0.00	$0.00	$0.00	$0.00	$0.00	$0.00	$0.00

Enter the following departmental sales data. (Remember, do not enter signs or commas.)

	Men's Clothing	Women's Clothing	Children's Clothing	Household Linens	Home Furnishings	Appliances	Automotive
Sunday	3,339.20	8,210.73	4,299.39	2,394.29	4,560.45	2,283.29	2,394.46
Monday	7,914.59	7,302.49	4,338.20	4,285.10	3,949.20	3,293.48	2,394.98
Tuesday	5,294.02	8,339.02	3,293.59	2,194.93	3,242.49	4,394.10	4,405.91
Wednesday	4,392.33	9,293.12	4,294.73	3,989.01	4,302.45	4,592.10	4,392.09
Thursday	4,375.24	8,289.07	3,381.39	3,392.28	3,472.36	5,230.02	3,937.65
Friday	5,928.78	12,329.30	3,992.06	3,873.21	5,452.31	5,439.39	5,991.32
Saturday	9,224.83	18,382.31	4,291.03	3,478.93	7,309.27	9,300.32	8,003.26

Answer the following questions after you have completed the spreadsheet:

1. What is the weekly sales total for the Men's Clothing Department? $_____

2. What are the total store sales for Sunday? $_____

3. What are the weekly sales for Home Furnishings? $_____

4. What are the weekly sales for the Automotive Department? $_____

5. What are the total store sales for Saturday? $_____

6. Which department has the highest weekly sales, and what is the amount? $_____

7. Which department has the lowest weekly sales, and what is the amount? $_____

8. Which day's total sales were the highest, and what is the amount? $_____

9. Which day's total sales were the lowest, and what is the amount? $_____

10. What are the total store sales for the week? $_____

GROUP REPORT

The next week, Springfield had a "Green Tag" sale. Every item with a green tag was on sale at 20% off. Enter the following departmental sales from that week:

	Men's Clothing	Women's Clothing	Children's Clothing	Household Linens
Sunday	4,847.19	10,138.10	5,019.31	2,288.15
Monday	9,029.70	8,413.60	5,449.31	4,277.64
Tuesday	6,405.13	9,450.13	4,404.70	2,244.65
Wednesday	5,626.89	9,725.22	4,472.00	2,901.53
Thursday	4,388.91	8,193.45	3,401.33	3,729.11
Friday	5,937.86	12,917.43	4,229.38	3,993.57
Saturday	11,128.87	18,381.39	6,239.91	4,100.75

	Home Furnishings	Appliances	Automotive
Sunday	4,661.46	3,415.41	1,405.56
Monday	5,171.42	3,626.81	4,010.45
Tuesday	3,152.65	4,771.53	3,452.05
Wednesday	4,443.17	5,226.81	4,773.13
Thursday	5,132.58	5,811.30	4,173.00
Friday	8,302.10	4,994.01	7,105.79
Saturday	7,999.21	10,308.63	10,104.68

Write a report to the store manager that addresses the success (or failure) of the sale. Your group report should include, but not be limited to, all of the following:

1. Compare this week's sales with last week's sales by department and in total.

2. Identify the departments that were most affected by the sale.

3. Identify the departments that were least affected by the sale.

4. Make recommendations on future sales based on the results of this "Green Tag" sale.

3 COMMON FRACTIONS AND COMMON/DECIMAL FRACTION CONVERSION

WHITHER FRACTIONS

"Half a league, half a league, half a league onward . . . ., wrote Alfred Lord Tennyson. How far is half a league? According to Webster, a league is about three miles. So if the 600 in the light brigade rode half a league, they must have ridden their horses about one and a half miles "into the valley of death."

Are you an optimist or a pessimist? Do you see a glass half full or half empty?

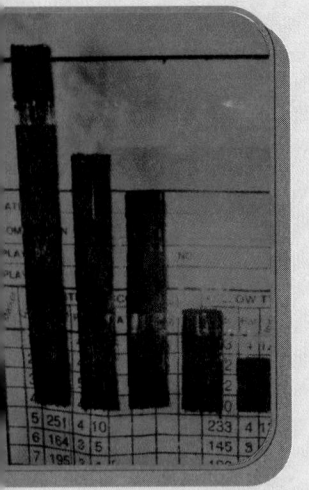

What is a foot measure? Some sources say it is the length of the medieval emperor (742–814 A.D.) Charlemagne's foot (more likely the boot of his armor). Another says it is one third of a yard, which is one third of the distance from the center of English King (1068–1135) Henry I's chest to the end of his index finger. Whatever a foot is, we know that one twelfth of it is an inch, each of which is divided into sixteen equal parts.

A pound is supposedly the weight of 7,000 grains of wheat. The trouble is—which kind of wheat, in which country, and during a good year or a bad year for wheat? Pounds are divided into sixteen equal parts called ounces.

All of the preceding measurements are broken down into fractions, which are parts of the whole.

Chapter Glossary

Fraction. A part of a whole number.

Numerator. The top number in a common fraction.

Denominator. The bottom number in a common fraction.

Proper fraction. A common fraction in which the numerator is less than the denominator.

Improper fraction. A common fraction in which the numerator is greater than, or equal to, the denominator.

Mixed number. A common fraction that is a combination of a whole number and a proper fraction.

Greatest common divisor. The largest number that will divide evenly into both the numerator and the denominator of a fraction.

Prime number. A whole number that is evenly divisible by itself and by 1.

Equivalent fractions. Fractions that are equal in value although the numerators and denominators are different.

Least common denominator (LCD). The smallest nonzero whole number into which all problem denominators will divide evenly.

Cancellation. The act of dividing the numerator of one fraction and the denominator of another fraction by the same number to reduce a product to lowest terms before multiplication takes place.

Reciprocal. The inverse of a number.

Aliquot part. Any number that will divide evenly into another number.

Common **fractions** and decimal fractions are used every day by many millions of people in thousands of business situations. A glance at a daily newspaper illustrates these common examples:

Wool plaid jackets–broken sizes. Were $24 and $38. One-third off!!!

Cash specials, 4′ × 8′ × 3/8″ particle board, 4′ × 8′ × 5/8″ exterior plywood.

2.56 acres, high on a hill. Great view. $91,950, owner financed, $3,950 down, $491.80 monthly.

What all such ads have in common is that they refer to numbers that are parts of a whole. You need a clear understanding of fractions to function, because whole numbers are so often divided into parts. Fractions indicate that division. The line, or bar, between the top number and the bottom number means "divided by." The top number is called the **numerator**, and the bottom number is called the **denominator**. For example,

$$\frac{38}{65} \begin{array}{l} \longleftarrow \textit{Numerator} \\ \textit{Divided by} \\ \longleftarrow \textit{Denominator} \end{array}$$

The bar, signifying division, is sometimes drawn diagonally, /, but it still means "divided by." Therefore, 38/65 is the same as $\frac{38}{65}$.

3.1 | Types of Common Fractions

There are three types of common fractions: proper fractions, improper fractions, and mixed numbers.

Proper Fractions
A **proper fraction** is one in which the numerator, the number on top, is less than the denominator, the number on the bottom. Therefore, 5/6, 2/21, 1/2, and 61/123 are all examples of proper fractions.

Improper Fractions
Fractions in which the numerator is greater than, or equal to, the denominator are called **improper fractions.** Examples are 16/3, 3/2, 146/31, 2/2, and 9/8.

Mixed Numbers
Mixed numbers are combinations of a whole number and a proper fraction, such as 1 3/5, 16 3/8, 126 7/8, 6 5/6, and 3 1/9.

3.1 Practice Problems

Identify the following fractions as proper, improper, or mixed numbers (write P for proper, I for improper, or M for a mixed number):

1. $\frac{6}{5}$
2. $\frac{3}{5}$
3. $\frac{5}{5}$
4. $34\frac{9}{26}$

3.1 Solutions to Practice Problems

1. I (The numerator is larger than the denominator.)
2. P (The numerator is smaller than the denominator.)
3. I (The numerator is the same value as the denominator.)
4. M (A combination of a whole number and a proper fraction.)

You may find it easier to work with common fractions by changing their form, without changing their value. This section is important to anyone who has ever had difficulties with common fractions. A thorough understanding of how to convert common fractions make the other operations performed with common fractions much easier.

3.2 Converting Mixed Numbers to Improper Fractions

A mixed number can be changed into an improper fraction as follows:

1. Multiply the whole number by the denominator of the fraction.
2. Add the numerator to that product. The resulting sum becomes the new fraction's numerator.
3. Put that sum (the new numerator) over the original fraction's denominator.

EXAMPLE Convert $3\frac{5}{9}$ to an improper fraction.

Solution *Step 1.* Multiply the whole number, 3, by the denominator of the fraction, 9: $3 \times 9 = 27$.

Step 2. Add the numerator of the fraction, 5, to the product from the first step: $27 + 5 = 32$

Step 3. Place the sum, 32, over the original fraction's denominator, 9: $\frac{32}{9}$.

3.2 Practice Problems

Convert the following mixed numbers to improper fractions:

1. $4\frac{5}{19}$ 2. $1\frac{9}{22}$ 3. $35\frac{1}{7}$ 4. $9\frac{20}{31}$

3.2 Solutions to Practice Problems

1. $\frac{81}{19}$ Multiply the whole number, 4, by the fraction denominator, 19 ($4 \times 19 = 76$). Add the numerator, 5, to that product ($76 + 5 = 81$). Place that sum over the original fraction's denominator, 19.

2. $\frac{31}{22}$ Multiply 1 by 22 ($1 \times 22 = 22$). Add 9 to that product ($22 + 9 = 31$). Place 31 over 22, the original fraction's denominator.

3. $\frac{246}{7}$ Multiply: $35 \times 7 = 245$. Add: $1 + 245 = 246$. Place 246 over 7.

4. $\frac{299}{31}$ Multiply: $9 \times 31 = 279$. Add: $20 + 279 = 299$. Place the 299 over 31.

3.3 Converting Improper Fractions to Mixed Numbers

Improper fractions are converted to mixed numbers by dividing the numerator by the denominator and placing the remainder (if any) over the original denominator (the divisor).

EXAMPLE Convert $\frac{121}{14}$ to a mixed number.

Solution

$$14\overline{)121}^{\,8\frac{9}{14}}$$
$$\underline{112}$$
$$9$$

Divide the numerator, 121, by the denominator, 14, and place the remainder, 9, over the orginal fraction denominator, 14.

3.3 Practice Problems

Convert the following improper fractions to mixed numbers:

1. $\frac{23}{16}$ 2. $\frac{38}{15}$ 3. $\frac{121}{9}$ 4. $\frac{47}{18}$

3.3 Solutions to Practice Problems

1. $1\frac{7}{16}$
$16\overline{)23}$
$\underline{16}$
7

2. $2\frac{8}{15}$
$15\overline{)38}$
$\underline{30}$
8

3. $13\frac{4}{9}$
$9\overline{)121}$
$\underline{9}$
31
$\underline{27}$
4

4. $2\frac{11}{18}$
$18\overline{)47}$
$\underline{36}$
11

LEARNING UNIT 3
REDUCING FRACTIONS

Fractions should always be reduced to *lowest terms*. A fraction is in lowest terms *when no whole number except the number one (1) will divide evenly into the numerator and the denominator of the fraction.*

3.4   Reducing Fractions: Trial-and-Error Method

The numerator and the denominator must be divided by the largest number that will divide evenly into both. That number is called the **greatest common divisor**.

Often, you can reduce by simple inspection because you have probably memorized the multiplication table through 12.

Certain aids are available to help speed up the process of trial-and-error reduction. Table 3.1 illustrates those aids.

TABLE 3.1   AIDS FOR TRIAL-AND-ERROR REDUCTION

1. If the numerator will divide evenly into the denominator, the numerator is the greatest common divisor.
2. If both the numerator and the denominator are even numbers, both can be divided by 2.
3. If both the numerator and the denominator end with 0, they can be divided by 10.
4. If both the numerator and the denominator end with 5 or one ends with 5 and the other ends with 0, they can be divided by 5.
5. If the sums of the digits in both the numerator and the denominator are multiples of 3 (that is, 6, 9, 12, 15, 18, and so on), they can be divided by 3.

EXAMPLE   Reduce $\frac{18}{48}$ to lowest terms.

Solution   The numbers 18 and 48 satisfy the requirements of both the second and the fifth aid given in Table 3-1. Both are even numbers, and the sums of the digits of both numbers are multiples of 3. (The sum of the digits of 18 [1 + 8 = 9] is a multiple of 3. The sum of the digits of 48 [4 + 8 = 12] is also a multiple of 3.)

Both 18 and 48 are, therefore, evenly divisible by both 2 and 3. Thus, they are also evenly divisible by 6 because $2 \times 3 = 6$.

$$\frac{18 \div 6 = 3}{48 \div 6 = 8}$$

Note: To reduce a fraction to lowest terms, divide the numerator and the denominator by the largest factor possible. We could have divided by both 2 and then by 3, but it is easier and faster to combine the two factors into 2×3, the greatest common factor.

3.4
Practice
Problems

Using the trial-and-error method, reduce the following fractions to lowest terms:

1. $\dfrac{24}{36}$ **2.** $\dfrac{4}{18}$ **3.** $\dfrac{45}{60}$ **4.** $\dfrac{19}{57}$

3.4 Solutions to Practice Problems

1. $\dfrac{24}{36} = \dfrac{2}{3}$ Both 24 and 36 are even numbers, and both have digits that, when added together, are multiples of 3. Both are evenly divisible by 6 ($2 \times 3 = 6$):

$$\frac{24 \div 6 = 4}{36 \div 6 = 6}$$

However, $\dfrac{4}{6}$ is not lowest terms. Both 4 and 6 are even numbers so each can be divided by 2:

$$\frac{4 \div 2 = 2}{6 \div 2 = 3}$$

2. $\dfrac{4}{18} = \dfrac{2}{9}$ Both 4 and 18 are even numbers. Thus each is evenly divisible by 2:

$$\frac{4 \div 2 = 2}{18 \div 2 = 9}$$

3. $\dfrac{45}{60} = \dfrac{3}{4}$ 45 ends with a 5, and 60 ends with a 0. That means both the numerator and the denominator are evenly divisible by 5. Adding the digits of both results in multiples of 3 ($4 + 5 = 9$ and $6 + 0 = 6$). Both are evenly divisible by 15 ($5 \times 3 = 15$):

$$\frac{45 \div 15 = 3}{60 \div 15 = 4}$$

4. $\dfrac{19}{57} = \dfrac{1}{3}$ If the denominator, 57, is divided by the numerator, 19, the result is 3. Hence, 19 is the greatest common divisor.

$$\frac{19 \div 19 = 1}{57 \div 19 = 3}$$

3.5 | **Reducing Fractions: Greatest Common Divisor**

Trial-and-error reduction works well enough when numbers are small and when numbers end in zeros. But if a common fraction is made up of a numerator and a denominator that are large, another method is necessary. Even if one or more of the trial-and-error aids can be used, the result is often large, and it is not always clear if the numerator and denominator can be reduced further.

Prime Numbers
One of the reasons for the difficulty is that there are some numbers that can be divided evenly only by themselves and by the number 1. These numbers are called

prime numbers. There is an infinite number of prime numbers. Some examples are 2, 3, 5, 7, 11, 13, 17, 19, 23, 29, and 31.

Greatest Common Divisor

Since the number being sought is the largest number that will divide evenly into the numerator and denominator, that number is called the *greatest common divisor*. To find the greatest common divisor, follow these steps:

1. Divide the larger number (usually the denominator) by the smaller number (usually the numerator).
2. If there is a remainder from step 1, divide it into the previous divisor.
3. Continue this process until there is no remainder or until there is a remainder of 1.
4. If there is no remainder, the last divisor is the greatest common divisor.
5. Divide both the numerator and the denominator by the greatest common divisor. The result will be the reduction of the fraction to lowest terms.
6. If there is a remainder of 1, the fraction is already in lowest terms.

EXAMPLE   Reduce $\dfrac{187}{357}$ to lowest terms.

Solution   *Step 1.* Divide the larger number by the smaller number:

$$\begin{array}{r} 1 \\ 187\overline{)357} \\ \underline{187} \\ 170 \end{array}$$

Step 2. Divide the divisor used in step 1 by the remainder in step 1:

$$\begin{array}{r} 1 \\ 170\overline{)187} \\ \underline{170} \\ 17 \end{array}$$

Step 3. Continue the process until there is no remainder:

$$\begin{array}{r} 10 \\ 17\overline{)170} \\ \underline{17} \\ 0 \\ \underline{0} \end{array}$$

The greatest common divisor is 17 since it is the divisor when the remainder is 0.

Had there been a remainder in the previous division, the process would have continued. It may take several divisions before we get either a remainder of 0 or 1.

Step 4. Divide both the numerator and the denominator by the greatest common divisor, 17.

$$\begin{array}{l} 187 \div 17 = 11 \\ 357 \div 17 = 21 \end{array} \qquad \textit{Lowest terms}$$

3.5 Practice Problems

Using the greatest common divisor method, reduce the following fractions to lowest terms:

1. $\dfrac{99}{176}$
2. $\dfrac{161}{345}$
3. $\dfrac{406}{638}$
4. $\dfrac{407}{925}$

3.5 Solutions to Practice Problems

1.

$$99\overline{)176}$$
$$\underline{99}$$
$$77$$

$$77\overline{)99}$$
$$\underline{77}$$
$$22$$

$$22\overline{)77}$$
$$\underline{66}$$
$$11$$

$$11\overline{)22} \quad \text{11 is the}$$
$$\underline{22} \quad \text{greatest common divisor.}$$

$$\frac{99 \div 11 = 9}{176 \div 11 = 16}$$

2.

$$161\overline{)345}$$
$$\underline{322}$$
$$23$$

$$23\overline{)161} \quad \text{23 is the greatest common divisor.}$$
$$\underline{161}$$

$$\frac{161 \div 23 = 7}{345 \div 23 = 15}$$

3.

$$406\overline{)638}$$
$$\underline{406}$$
$$232$$

$$232\overline{)406}$$
$$\underline{232}$$
$$174$$

$$174\overline{)232}$$
$$\underline{174}$$
$$58$$

$$58\overline{)174}$$
$$\underline{116}$$
$$58$$

$$58\overline{)58} \quad \text{58 is the greatest common divisor.}$$
$$\underline{58}$$

$$\frac{406 \div 58 = 7}{638 \div 58 = 11}$$

4.

$$407\overline{)925}$$
$$\underline{814}$$
$$111$$

$$111\overline{)407}$$
$$\underline{333}$$
$$74$$

$$74\overline{)111}$$
$$\underline{74}$$
$$37$$

$$37\overline{)74} \quad \text{37 is the greatest common divisor.}$$
$$\underline{74}$$

$$\frac{407 \div 37 = 11}{925 \div 37 = 25}$$

LEARNING UNIT 4
ADDITION AND SUBTRACTION OF COMMON FRACTIONS

Just as whole numbers can be added or subtracted, so can common fractions. But the process is more involved.

3.6 Raising Fractions

Just as fractions can be reduced by *dividing* both the numerator and the denominator by the same number, they can also be raised by *multiplying* both the numerator and the denominator by the same number. Raising fractions may be necessary to obtain a denominator common to all the fractions in the problem. This is often a necessary step when adding or subtracting common fractions.

To determine the number to multiply the numerator by to maintain the original value of the fraction, the desired denominator is divided by the original denominator and the quotient is then multiplied by the numerator. The resulting fraction is called the **equivalent fraction**, and its value is the same as that of the original fraction.

EXAMPLE   Raise $\dfrac{7}{8}$ to a fraction with a denominator of 32.

Solution $\dfrac{7}{8} = \dfrac{?}{32}$

$$32 \div 8 = 4$$
$$7 \times 4 = 28$$
$$\overline{8 \times 4 = 32}$$

Divide the desired denominator by the original denominator. Multiply the numerator by the resultant quotient to determine the equivalent fraction.

3.6 Practice Problems

Raise the following fractions to equivalent fractions with the indicated denominator:

1. $\dfrac{4}{5} = \dfrac{}{30}$ **2.** $\dfrac{8}{9} = \dfrac{}{63}$ **3.** $\dfrac{9}{14} = \dfrac{}{70}$ **4.** $\dfrac{21}{25} = \dfrac{}{100}$

1. $\begin{array}{r} 6 \\ \hline 5\overline{)30} \end{array}$ $\qquad 4 \times 6 = \dfrac{24}{30}$ **2.** $\begin{array}{r} 7 \\ \hline 9\overline{)63} \end{array}$ $\qquad 8 \times 7 = \dfrac{56}{63}$

3. $\begin{array}{r} 5 \\ \hline 14\overline{)70} \end{array}$ $\qquad 9 \times 5 = \dfrac{45}{70}$ **4.** $\begin{array}{r} 4 \\ \hline 25\overline{)100} \end{array}$ $\qquad 21 \times 4 = \dfrac{84}{100}$

3.7 Least Common Denominator (LCD)

To add or subtract fractions, they must all have the same denominator. It is always wise to raise all fractions to be added or subtracted to the *smallest nonzero whole number into which all denominators will divide evenly*. With some fractions the lowest (or least) common denominator can be found by simple observation. Another method, called the **least common denominator (LCD)** method, is used when observation will not work. It is done as follows:

1. Copy the denominators to be added or subtracted in a row.
2. Determine a prime number that will divide evenly into at least two of the denominators. If more than one prime number could be chosen, the selection is up to your individual preference. However, the best method is to be consistent in your choices. For example, always choose the smallest of the prime numbers, or always start with a prime number that will divide evenly into the leftmost denominator listed.
3. Divide the prime number into all the denominators into which it will divide evenly, and place the quotient directly below the denominator being divided.
4. If the prime number will not divide evenly into a denominator, place the denominator directly below itself in the new row.
5. Continue dividing each row of numbers by a prime number that will divide evenly into two or more of the numbers in the row. When no prime number will divide evenly into at least two numbers, the prime factors of the least common denominator have been determined.
6. Multiply all the numbers in the divisors (the prime numbers used) and all of the numbers in the last row that are not the number 1. You have now found the LCD.

E X A M P L E   Find the least common denominator for the fractions 1/3, 1/9, 1/8, and 1/6.

Solution   3 9 8 6   *Copy the denominators into a row.*

$3\overline{)3\ 9\ 8\ 6}$ *Divide the denominators by a prime number that will divide evenly into at least two of the denominators.*

$\underline{/1\ 3\ 8\ 2}$ *Place the quotients of the division into a new row. If the prime number will not divide evenly into a number, bring the original number down into the new row.*

$2\overline{)1\ 3\ 8\ 2}$ *Continue finding prime numbers that will divide evenly into two or more of the numbers in the row.*

$\underline{/1\ 3\ 4\ 1}$ *When no prime number can be found that will divide evenly into two or more numbers, the LCD factors have been determined. They include prime numbers that have been used (in this example, 3 and 2), plus the numbers in the last row other than 1 (3 and 4). Thus, the factors of the LCD in this problem are 3, 2, 3, and 4.*

The process would be as follows:

$3\overline{)3\ 9\ 8\ 6}$
$2\overline{)1\ 3\ 8\ 2}$
$\quad\ 1\ 3\ 4\ 1$
$3 \times 2 \times 3 \times 4 = 72$ *Multiply the factors together. This is the LCD.*

Find the least common denominator for the following sets of fractions:

1. $\dfrac{1}{4}, \dfrac{1}{6}, \dfrac{1}{9}, \dfrac{1}{15}$

2. $\dfrac{1}{3}, \dfrac{1}{7}, \dfrac{1}{9}, \dfrac{1}{14}$

3. $\dfrac{1}{12}, \dfrac{1}{14}, \dfrac{1}{15}, \dfrac{1}{16}$

4. $\dfrac{1}{2}, \dfrac{1}{4}, \dfrac{1}{6}, \dfrac{1}{8}, \dfrac{1}{10}$

3.7 Solutions to Practice Problems

1.
$$2\underline{/4\ \ 6\ \ 9\ \ 15}$$
$$3\underline{/2\ \ 3\ \ 9\ \ 15}$$
$$\ \ \ 2\ \ 1\ \ 3\ \ \ 5$$
$$2 \times 3 \times 2 \times 3 \times 5 = 180 \text{ (LCD)}$$

2.
$$3\underline{/3\ \ 7\ \ 9\ \ 14}$$
$$7\underline{/1\ \ 7\ \ 3\ \ 14}$$
$$\ \ \ 1\ \ 1\ \ 3\ \ \ 2$$
$$3 \times 7 \times 3 \times 2 = 126 \text{ (LCD)}$$

3.
$$2\underline{/12\ \ 14\ \ 15\ \ 16}$$
$$2\underline{/\ 6\ \ \ 7\ \ 15\ \ \ 8}$$
$$3\underline{/\ 3\ \ \ 7\ \ 15\ \ \ 4}$$
$$\ \ \ 1\ \ \ 7\ \ \ 5\ \ \ 4$$
$$2 \times 2 \times 3 \times 2 \times 5 = 120 \text{ (LCD)}$$

4.
$$2\underline{/2\ \ 4\ \ 6\ \ 8\ \ 10}$$
$$2\underline{/1\ \ 2\ \ 3\ \ 4\ \ \ 5}$$
$$\ \ \ 1\ \ 1\ \ 3\ \ 2\ \ \ 5$$
$$2 \times 2 \times 3 \times 7 \times 5 \times 4 = 1,680 \text{ (LCD)}$$

Having reviewed common fraction types and the methods of converting them from one form to another, you can put those concepts to use in adding, subtracting, multiplying, and dividing common fractions.

3.8 Adding Common Fractions

Adding Proper Fractions

Adding proper fractions requires a combination of finding the least common denominator and converting each fraction being added to an equivalent fraction with that same denominator. Then you add the numerators and place the sum over the LCD. If necessary, convert the resulting fraction to a mixed number and/or reduce to lowest terms.

EXAMPLE

Add the following proper fractions: $\dfrac{1}{3} + \dfrac{6}{7} + \dfrac{3}{4} + \dfrac{3}{8}$

Solution **Step 1.** Find the least common denominator:

$$2\underline{/3\ \ 7\ \ 4\ \ 8}$$
$$2\underline{/3\ \ 7\ \ 2\ \ 4}$$
$$\ \ \ 3\ \ 7\ \ 1\ \ 2$$

$$2 \times 2 \times 3 \times 7 \times 2 = 168 \text{ LCD}$$

Step 2. Raise all fractions to equivalent fractions with denominators of 168:

$\dfrac{1}{3} = \dfrac{}{168}$	$168 \div 3 = 56$	$56 \times 1 = 56$	$\dfrac{56}{168}$
$\dfrac{6}{7} = \dfrac{}{168}$	$168 \div 7 = 24$	$24 \times 6 = 144$	$\dfrac{144}{168}$
$\dfrac{3}{4} = \dfrac{}{168}$	$168 \div 4 = 42$	$42 \times 3 = 126$	$\dfrac{126}{168}$
$\dfrac{3}{8} = \dfrac{}{168}$	$168 \div 8 = 21$	$21 \times 3 = 63$	$\dfrac{63}{168}$

Step 3. Place the numerators over 168 and add:

$$\frac{56 + 144 + 126 + 63}{168} = \frac{389}{168} = 2\frac{53}{168} \qquad \left(\frac{53}{168} \text{ is in lowest terms}\right)$$

Adding Mixed Numbers

To add mixed numbers, follow these steps:

1. Add the whole numbers.
2. Add the fractions. Find the LCD as was done when adding proper fractions.
3. Add the sums found in step 1 and step 2. Be certain there are no improper fractions in the total.
4. Reduce the proper fraction portion of your answer to lowest terms if necessary.

EXAMPLE

Add the following mixed numbers: $13\frac{1}{4} + 16\frac{3}{8} + 3\frac{5}{6}$

Solution *Step 1.* Find the least common denominator:

$$\begin{array}{l} 2\overline{)4\ 8\ 6} \\ 2\overline{)2\ 4\ 3} \\ 1\ 2\ 3 \end{array} \quad 2 \times 2 \times 2 \times 3 = 24\ \text{LCD}$$

Step 2. Place the fractions in a column and change the proper fraction portion to equivalent fractions with 24 (the LCD) as the denominator. Then, add the whole numbers. Next, add the proper fraction numerators and place the sum over 24 (the LCD):

$$13\frac{1}{4} = 13\frac{6}{24}$$
$$16\frac{3}{8} = 16\frac{9}{24}$$
$$3\frac{5}{6} = 3\frac{20}{24}$$
$$\rule{3cm}{0.4pt}$$
$$32\frac{35}{24}$$

Step 3. Add (or combine) the whole numbers sum and the proper fraction sum. Then, convert the improper fraction 35/24 to a mixed number and add it to the whole number, 32:

$$\frac{35}{24} = 1\frac{11}{24} \qquad 32 + 1\frac{11}{24} = 33\frac{11}{24} \qquad \textit{Final answer}$$

3.8 Practice Problems

Add the following fractions:

1. $\dfrac{3}{10} + \dfrac{4}{15} + \dfrac{5}{6}$

2. $\dfrac{9}{20} + \dfrac{3}{8} + \dfrac{5}{9}$

3. $4\dfrac{2}{7} + 8\dfrac{4}{21} + 2\dfrac{9}{14}$

4. $37\dfrac{1}{18} + 58\dfrac{7}{15} + 8\dfrac{5}{12}$

3.8 Solutions to Practice Problems

1.

$$\begin{array}{l} 2\overline{)10\ 15\ 6} \\ 5\overline{)\ 5\ 15\ 3} \\ 3\overline{)\ 1\ \ 3\ 3} \\ 1\ \ \ 1\ 1 \end{array} \quad 2 \times 5 \times 3 = 30\ \text{LCD}$$

$$\frac{3}{10} = \frac{10}{30}$$
$$\frac{4}{15} = \frac{8}{30}$$
$$\frac{5}{6} = \frac{25}{30}$$

$$\frac{10 + 8 + 25}{30} = \frac{43}{30}$$
$$= 1\frac{13}{50} \qquad \textit{Final answer}$$

2. $2\underline{/20\ 8\ 9}$
$\quad\ 2\underline{/10\ 4\ 9}$ $\quad 2 \times 2 \times 5 \times 2 \times 9 = 360$ LCD $\quad \dfrac{9}{20} = \dfrac{162}{360}, \dfrac{3}{8} = \dfrac{135}{360}, \dfrac{5}{9} = \dfrac{200}{360}$
$\quad\quad\ 5\ 2\ 9$

$$\frac{162 + 135 + 200}{360} = \frac{497}{360} = 1\frac{137}{360} \quad \textit{Final answer}$$

3. $7\underline{/7\ 21\ 14}$ $\quad 7 \times 3 \times 2 = 42$ LCD $\quad\quad\quad 4\dfrac{2}{7} = 4\dfrac{12}{42}$
$\quad\quad\ 1\ \ 3\ \ 2$

$$\frac{12 + 8 + 27}{42} = \frac{47}{42} = 1\frac{5}{42} \quad\quad\quad 8\frac{4}{21} = 8\frac{8}{42}$$

$$2\frac{9}{14} = 2\frac{27}{42}$$

$$14\frac{47}{42} = 15\frac{5}{42} \quad \textit{Final answer}$$

4.
$$37\frac{1}{18} = 37\frac{10}{180}$$

$2\underline{/18\ 15\ 12}$
$3\underline{/\ 9\ 15\ \ 6}$ $\quad 2 \times 3 \times 3 \times 5 \times 2 = 180$ LCD $\quad\quad 58\dfrac{7}{15} = 58\dfrac{84}{180}$
$\quad\quad\ 3\ \ 5\ \ 2$

$$8\frac{5}{12} = 8\frac{75}{180}$$

$$103\frac{169}{180} \quad \textit{Final answer}$$

3.9 ## Subtracting Common Fractions

As with the addition of fractions, subtraction of fractions can be done only when the fractions have a common denominator.

Subtraction of Proper Fractions
The procedure for subtracting proper fractions is as follows:

1. Find the least common denominator for the fractions.
2. Change the fractions to equivalent fractions with the LCD.
3. Subtract the numerators.
4. Write the difference over the LCD.
5. Reduce to lowest terms if necessary.

E X A M P L E Subtract the proper fractions: $5/6 - 3/32$

Solution $2\underline{/6\ 32}$ $\quad 2 \times 3 \times 16 = 96$
$\quad\quad\quad\ \ 3\ 16$

$$\frac{5}{6} = \frac{80}{96}$$
$$-\frac{3}{32} = \frac{9}{96}$$
$$\frac{71}{96}$$

Subtracting Mixed Numbers When Borrowing Is Not Needed
If no borrowing is necessary in the proper fraction portion of the mixed number, then merely do the following:

1. Subtract the whole numbers.
2. Follow the procedure for the subtraction of proper fractions.
3. Combine the answers found in step 1 and step 2.

EXAMPLE

Subtract the mixed numbers: $4\frac{3}{5} - 1\frac{7}{15}$

Inspection is all that is required to see that the LCD is 15.

$$4\frac{3}{5} = 4\frac{9}{15}$$
$$1\frac{7}{15} = 1\frac{7}{15} \qquad \textit{No borrowing is required.}$$
$$\overline{\phantom{4\frac{3}{5}} 3\frac{2}{15}}$$

Subtracting Mixed Numbers When Borrowing Is Needed

When the value of the proper fraction in the subtrahend is greater than the value of the proper fraction in the minuend, borrow from the whole number portion of the mixed number in the minuend using the following steps:

1. Find the least common denominator (if necessary) for the proper fraction portions of the mixed numbers.
2. Convert the proper fraction portions to equivalent fractions having the LCD.
3. Borrow one unit from the whole number in the minuend, and convert it to an improper fraction with the LCD.
4. Subtract the whole numbers.
5. Subtract the fractions and reduce to lowest terms.

EXAMPLE

Subtract the mixed numbers: $20\frac{1}{4} - 13\frac{5}{8}$

Solution   Inspection is all that is required to see that the LCD is 8.

$$20\frac{1}{4} = 20\frac{2}{8}$$

Since 5/8 is larger than 2/8, borrowing is required, so:

$$13\frac{5}{8} = 13\frac{5}{8} \qquad 20 = 19\frac{8}{8} \qquad \text{and} \qquad 19\frac{8}{8} + \frac{2}{8} = 19\frac{10}{8}$$

Thus,

$$
\begin{array}{r}
19\frac{10}{8} \\
- \ 13\frac{5}{8} \\
\hline
6\frac{5}{8}
\end{array}
$$

3.9 Practice Problems

Subtract the following common fractions:

1. $\dfrac{15}{16} - \dfrac{5}{8}$ **2.** $8\dfrac{5}{9} - 3\dfrac{1}{3}$ **3.** $65\dfrac{3}{15} - 38\dfrac{4}{5}$ **4.** $4\dfrac{10}{21} - 3\dfrac{1}{6}$

Chapter 3 Common Fractions and Common/Decimal Fraction Conversion

3.9 Solutions to Practice Problems

1.
$$\frac{15}{16} = \frac{15}{16}$$
$$\frac{5}{8} = \frac{10}{16}$$
$$\frac{5}{16}$$

2.
$$8\frac{5}{9} = 8\frac{5}{9}$$
$$3\frac{1}{3} = 3\frac{3}{9}$$
$$5\frac{2}{9}$$

3.
$$65\frac{3}{15} = 65\frac{3}{15} = 64\frac{18}{15}$$
$$38\frac{4}{5} = 38\frac{12}{15} = 38\frac{12}{15}$$
$$26\frac{6}{15} = 26\frac{2}{5}$$

4.
$$4\frac{10}{21} = 4\frac{20}{42}$$
$$3\frac{1}{6} = 3\frac{7}{42}$$
$$1\frac{13}{42}$$

LEARNING UNIT 5
MULTIPLICATION AND DIVISION OF COMMON FRACTIONS

Common fractions are multiplied in business and life every day. When a retailer advertises a sale in which everything is 1/3 off, someone at the store must multiply by common fractions to price the goods. If a recipe that serves four calls for 3/4 cup of milk, you must multiply a fraction to serve 12.

 Multiplying Common Fractions

Multiplying Proper (or Improper) Fractions
There are three steps in multiplying proper or improper fractions:

1. Multiply the numerators.
2. Multiply the denominators.
3. Reduce to lowest terms if necessary.

Cancellation
Cancellation is a shortcut to reducing fractions to lowest terms before multiplying. If cancellation is done before multiplication, the product will be in lowest terms and the fraction will not need to be reduced. Canceling is accomplished in almost the same way as trial-and-error reduction. The difference is that *cancellation involves "reducing" the numerator of one fraction with the denominator of another*. The steps are as follows:

1. Select a number that will divide evenly into both the numerator and the denominator.
2. Divide the numerator and the denominator by that number.
3. Continue canceling numerators and denominators as long as a number can be found that will divide evenly into both.
4. Multiply the numerators.
5. Multiply the denominators.

E X A M P L E   Multiply: $\dfrac{2}{3} \times \dfrac{3}{4} \times \dfrac{8}{9}$

Solution   Without cancellation: $\dfrac{2 \times 3 \times 8}{3 \times 4 \times 9} = \dfrac{48}{108} = \dfrac{4}{9}$

With cancellation: $\dfrac{\overset{1}{\cancel{2}}}{\underset{1}{\cancel{3}}} \times \dfrac{\overset{1}{\cancel{3}}}{\underset{1}{\cancel{4}}} \times \dfrac{\overset{4}{\cancel{8}}}{9} = \dfrac{4}{9}$

Multiplying Proper Fractions and Whole Numbers

To multiply a fraction and a whole number, follow these steps:

1. Put the whole number over a denominator of 1. For example, the whole number 3 would be written $\dfrac{3}{1}$.
2. Cancel if possible.
3. Multiply the numerators.
4. Multiply the denominators.
5. Convert an improper fraction to a mixed number if necessary.

EXAMPLE

Multiply: $8 \times \dfrac{7}{16}$

Solution $\dfrac{\overset{1}{\cancel{8}}}{1} \times \dfrac{7}{\underset{2}{\cancel{16}}} = \dfrac{7}{2} = 3\dfrac{1}{2}$

Multiplying Mixed Numbers

To multiply mixed numbers, first convert them into improper fractions. Then proceed as with multiplication of proper fractions.

EXAMPLE $6\dfrac{2}{5} \times 3\dfrac{4}{7} \times 2$

Solution

$\dfrac{32}{5} \times \dfrac{25}{7} \times \dfrac{2}{1}$ *Convert to improper fractions, and put 2 over 1 for clarity.*

$\dfrac{32}{\underset{1}{\cancel{5}}} \times \dfrac{\overset{5}{\cancel{25}}}{7} \times \dfrac{2}{1}$ *Cancel.*

$\dfrac{32 \times 5 \times 2}{1 \times 7 \times 1} = \dfrac{320}{7}$ *Multiply numerators. Multiply denominators.*

$\dfrac{320}{7} = 45\dfrac{5}{7}$ *Convert to a mixed number.*

3.10 Practice Problems

Multiply the following fractions:

1. $\dfrac{6}{7} \times \dfrac{7}{15}$ 2. $4 \times \dfrac{7}{8}$ 3. $6\dfrac{2}{9} \times 2\dfrac{4}{7}$ 4. $\dfrac{3}{5} \times 15 \times 2\dfrac{8}{9}$

3.10 Solutions to Practice Problems

1. $\dfrac{\overset{2}{\cancel{6}}}{\underset{1}{\cancel{7}}} \times \dfrac{\overset{1}{\cancel{7}}}{\underset{5}{\cancel{15}}} = \dfrac{2}{5}$ 2. $\dfrac{\overset{1}{\cancel{4}}}{1} \times \dfrac{7}{\underset{2}{\cancel{8}}} = \dfrac{7}{2} = 3\dfrac{1}{2}$ 3. $\dfrac{\overset{8}{\cancel{56}}}{\underset{1}{\cancel{9}}} \times \dfrac{\overset{2}{\cancel{18}}}{\underset{1}{\cancel{7}}} = 16$

$$4. \quad \frac{\overset{1}{\cancel{3}}}{\underset{1}{\cancel{5}}} \times \frac{\overset{\overset{1}{\cancel{3}}}{\cancel{15}}}{1} \times \frac{26}{\underset{\underset{1}{\cancel{3}}}{\cancel{9}}} = 26$$

3.11 Dividing Common Fractions

In the explanation of multiplication of common fractions, there was an example of a recipe that would serve four calling for 3/4 cup of milk. How much milk is needed to serve two? The answer requires division.

Dividing Proper (or Improper) Fractions

To divide proper or improper fractions, invert the divisor or divisors and proceed as in multiplication. The following description provides more detail on the process.

The *divisor* is the number by which we are dividing. To divide, the divisor(s) must first be inverted (turned upside down). That is, make the numerator the denominator and make the denominator the numerator. More properly, the inverse of a number is referred to as its **reciprocal**. Then, proceed as with multiplication, canceling when possible.

EXAMPLE   Divide 3/8 by 3/4.

Solution
$$\frac{3}{8} \div \frac{3}{4}$$

$$\frac{3}{8} \times \frac{4}{3} \qquad \textit{Invert the divisor and change signs from division to multiplication.}$$

$$\frac{\overset{1}{\cancel{3}}}{\underset{2}{\cancel{8}}} \times \frac{\overset{1}{\cancel{4}}}{\underset{1}{\cancel{3}}} = \frac{1}{2} \qquad \textit{Cancel and multiply.}$$

Dividing Proper (or Improper) Fractions by Whole Numbers

When dividing by a whole number, the whole number is the divisor and must be inverted. First, place the whole number over 1 for clarity, and then invert and proceed as in multiplication, canceling when possible.

EXAMPLE   Divide $\frac{3}{25}$ by 5.

Solution
$$\frac{3}{25} \div \frac{5}{1} \qquad \textit{Put the whole number over 1.}$$

$$\frac{3}{25} \times \frac{1}{5} = \frac{3}{125} \qquad \textit{Invert divisor and multiply.}$$

Dividing Mixed Numbers

Division of mixed numbers is accomplished in three steps.

1. Convert all mixed numbers to improper fractions.
2. Invert the divisor or divisors and change signs from division to multiplication.
3. Proceed as in multiplication.

EXAMPLE   Divide $6\frac{3}{8}$ by $3\frac{9}{10}$.

Solution $\dfrac{51}{8} \div \dfrac{39}{10}$ *Convert to improper fractions.*

$\dfrac{51}{8} \times \dfrac{10}{39}$ *Invert the divisor.*

$\dfrac{\overset{17}{\cancel{51}}}{\underset{4}{\cancel{8}}} \times \dfrac{\overset{5}{\cancel{10}}}{\underset{13}{\cancel{39}}} = \dfrac{85}{52}$ *Cancel and multiply.*

$\dfrac{85}{52} = 1\dfrac{33}{52}$ *Convert to a mixed number.*

3.11 Practice Problems

Divide the following common fractions:

1. $64 \div \dfrac{2}{3}$ **2.** $\dfrac{2}{3} \div 64$ **3.** $\dfrac{7}{15} \div 2\dfrac{4}{5}$ **4.** $\dfrac{2}{3} \div \dfrac{8}{21}$

3.11 Solutions to Practice Problems

1. $\dfrac{64}{1} \div \dfrac{2}{3}$ $\dfrac{\overset{32}{\cancel{64}}}{1} \times \dfrac{3}{\underset{1}{\cancel{2}}} = 96$ **2.** $\dfrac{2}{3} \div \dfrac{64}{1}$ $\dfrac{\overset{1}{\cancel{2}}}{3} \times \dfrac{1}{\underset{32}{\cancel{64}}} = \dfrac{1}{96}$

3. $\dfrac{7}{15} \div \dfrac{14}{5}$ $\dfrac{\overset{1}{\cancel{7}}}{\underset{3}{\cancel{15}}} \times \dfrac{\overset{1}{\cancel{5}}}{\underset{2}{\cancel{14}}} = \dfrac{1}{6}$ **4.** $\dfrac{2}{3} \div \dfrac{8}{21}$ $\dfrac{\overset{1}{\cancel{2}}}{\underset{1}{\cancel{3}}} \times \dfrac{\overset{7}{\cancel{21}}}{\underset{4}{\cancel{8}}} = \dfrac{7}{4} = 1\dfrac{3}{4}$

LEARNING UNIT 6
CONVERSIONS OF DECIMAL FRACTIONS TO COMMON FRACTIONS AND COMMON FRACTIONS TO DECIMAL FRACTIONS

Often, for clarity or convenience or to make problem-solving simpler in a business situation, fraction conversion is necessary. With the widespread use of calculators and computers, decimal fractions are used most often. However, many problems can be solved quickly and/or more accurately with common fractions, especially as shown in the section on aliquot parts (Section 3.14).

3.12 Converting Common Fractions to Decimal Fractions

Converting Proper Fractions to Decimal Fractions
Conversion of proper fractions into decimal fractions is done by dividing the numerator by the denominator. Unless otherwise specifically indicated, round the answer to the nearest thousandth.

EXAMPLE   Convert $\dfrac{6}{7}$ to a decimal fraction. Round to the nearest thousandth.

Solution $\dfrac{6}{7} =$

$$\begin{array}{r} .8571 = .857 \\ 7\overline{)6.0000} \\ \underline{5\ 6} \\ 40 \\ \underline{35} \\ 50 \\ \underline{49} \\ 10 \\ \underline{\ 7} \end{array}$$

When converting proper fractions with 10 or multiples of 10 as the denominator, use the process of simply moving the decimal point one place to the left for each zero in the 10-multiple.

EXAMPLE

Convert $\dfrac{39}{100}$ to a decimal fraction.

Solution $39/100 = .39$ *Move the decimal point one position to the left for each zero (100 has two zeros—move the decimal point two places to the left).*

Converting Mixed Numbers to Mixed Decimals

A mixed number is a combination of a whole number and a proper fraction. A mixed decimal is a combination of a whole number and a decimal fraction. Converting mixed numbers to mixed decimals can be done in two steps:

1. Convert the fractional part of the mixed number to its decimal fraction equivalent by dividing the numerator by the denominator. Unless otherwise specifically indicated, round the answer to the nearest thousandth.
2. Add the decimal fraction to the whole number.

EXAMPLE

Convert $6\dfrac{3}{8}$ to a decimal fraction.

Solution

$$\begin{array}{r} .375 \\ 8\overline{)3.000} \\ 2\,4 \\ \hline 60 \\ 56 \\ \hline 40 \\ 40 \\ \hline \end{array}$$

Convert $\dfrac{3}{8}$ to its decimal fraction equivalent. Then, add the whole number to it:

$6 + .375 = 6.375$

3.12 Practice Problems

Convert the following common fractions to their decimal fraction equivalents:

1. $\dfrac{4}{9}$ **2.** $4\dfrac{3}{5}$ **3.** $8\dfrac{21}{25}$ **4.** $\dfrac{114}{329}$

3.12 Solutions to Practice Problems

1. $\begin{array}{r} .4444 = .444 \\ 9\overline{)4.0000} \end{array}$

2. $\begin{array}{r} .6 \quad .6 + 4 = 4.6 \\ 5\overline{)3.0} \end{array}$

3. $\begin{array}{r} .84 \quad .84 + 8 = 8.84 \\ 25\overline{)21.00} \\ 20\,0 \\ \hline 1\,00 \\ 1\,00 \\ \hline \end{array}$

4. $\begin{array}{r} .3465 = .347 \\ 329\overline{)114.0000} \\ 98\,7 \\ \hline 15\,30 \\ 13\,16 \\ \hline 2\,140 \\ 1\,974 \\ \hline 1660 \\ 1645 \\ \hline 15 \end{array}$

3.13 Converting Decimal Fractions to Common Fractions

When a decimal fraction is correctly read, it is simple to convert it into a common fraction. For example, .35 is properly read "thirty-five hundredths," which is the same as $\dfrac{35}{100}$. The following steps can also be used:

1. Place the decimal number to be converted in the numerator position of a common fraction.
2. Count the digits to the right of the decimal point. Place that many zeros in the denominator of the common fraction.
3. Remove the decimal point from the number in the numerator position.
4. Place a 1 in front of the zeros in the denominator position.
5. Convert to a mixed number and/or reduce to lowest terms if necessary.

EXAMPLE   Convert .875 into a common fraction.

Solution   *Step 1.* $\dfrac{.875}{}$ *Place .875 in the numerator position.*

Step 2. $\dfrac{.875}{000}$ *Count the digits to the right of .875 (3). Place three zeros in the denominator position.*

Step 3. $\dfrac{875}{000}$ *Remove the decimal point from the .875.*

Step 4. $\dfrac{875}{1,000}$ *Place a 1 in front of the zeros.*

Step 5. $\dfrac{875}{1,000} = \dfrac{7}{8}$ *Reduce to lowest terms.*

EXAMPLE   Convert 5.32 into a common fraction.

Solution   *Step 1.* $\dfrac{5.32}{}$ *Place 5.32 in the numerator position.*

Step 2. $\dfrac{5.32}{00}$ *There are two digits to the right of the decimal point. Place two zeros in the denominator position.*

Step 3. $\dfrac{532}{00}$ *Remove the decimal point from the 5.32.*

Step 4. $\dfrac{532}{100}$ *Place a 1 in front of the zeros.*

Step 5.
$$\begin{array}{r} 5 \\ 100\overline{)532} \\ \underline{500} \\ 32 \end{array} \quad \dfrac{32}{100}$$
Convert to a mixed number.

$$5\dfrac{32}{100} = 5\dfrac{8}{25}$$ *Reduce to lowest terms.*

Sometimes a decimal fraction contains a common fraction. An interest rate, for example, might be stated as 18 1/2%, and you face a situation that requires you to change the decimal to a common fraction. The topic of percents has not been covered, but for now, just accept that 18 1/2% = .18½

To convert .18 1/2 to its common fraction equivalent, put it over 1.00 $\left(\frac{.18\frac{1}{2}}{1.00}\right)$. Then, decimal points in both the numerator and the denominator can be moved two places to the right $\left(\frac{18\frac{1}{2}}{100}\right)$. The remainder of the conversion is shown here:

$$18\frac{1}{2} \div 100$$
$$= \frac{37}{2} \div \frac{100}{1}$$
$$= \frac{37}{2} \times \frac{1}{100}$$
$$= \frac{37}{200} \qquad \text{as a common fraction}$$

EXAMPLE   Convert $13.35\frac{1}{3}$ to its common fraction equivalent.

Solution $\dfrac{13.35\frac{1}{3}}{1.00} = \dfrac{1,335\frac{1}{3}}{100}$

$= 1,335\dfrac{1}{3} \div 100$

$= \dfrac{4,006}{3} \div \dfrac{100}{1}$

$= \dfrac{4,006}{3} \times \dfrac{1}{100}$

$= \dfrac{4,006}{300} = 13\dfrac{106}{300} = 13\dfrac{53}{150}$ *as a common fraction*

3.13 Practice Problems

Convert the following decimal fractions into common fractions:

1. .25   **2.** .65   **3.** $.2\dfrac{1}{5}$ **4.** 31.48

3.13 Solutions to Practice Problems

1. $\dfrac{25}{100} = \dfrac{1}{4}$ **2.** $\dfrac{65}{100} = \dfrac{13}{20}$

3. $\dfrac{.2\frac{1}{5}}{1.0}$ $2\dfrac{1}{5} \div \dfrac{10}{1} = \dfrac{11}{5} \times \dfrac{1}{10} = \dfrac{11}{50}$ **4.** $\dfrac{3,148}{100} = 31\dfrac{48}{100} = 31\dfrac{12}{25}$

3.14 Aliquot Parts: A Mathematical Shortcut

An **aliquot part** is any number that will divide evenly into another number. For example, 25 is contained 4 times in 100. Twenty-five is, therefore, an aliquot part of 100.

Aliquot parts are used by business people to simplify calculations and save time whenever they are applicable. Table 3.2 contains the most frequently used aliquot parts of 1.

This table should be memorized so that any number in it is immediately recognizable.

TABLE 3.2   ALIQUOT PARTS OF 1

Name	Common Fraction	Decimal Fraction Equivalent	Name	Common Fraction	Decimal Fraction Equivalent
Half	$\frac{1}{2}$	.50	Eighths	$\frac{1}{8}$	.125
Thirds	$\frac{1}{3}$	$.33\frac{1}{3}$ $(.3\overline{3})$		$\frac{3}{8}$	.375
	$\frac{2}{3}$	$.66\frac{2}{3}$ $(.6\overline{6})$		$\frac{5}{8}$	.625
Fourths	$\frac{1}{4}$	.25		$\frac{7}{8}$	.875
	$\frac{3}{4}$	.75	Tenths	$\frac{1}{10}$	.10
Fifths	$\frac{1}{5}$	.20		$\frac{3}{10}$	.30
	$\frac{2}{5}$	.40		$\frac{7}{10}$	.70
	$\frac{3}{5}$	.60			
	$\frac{4}{5}$	.80			

Aliquot Parts of 1

In making aliquot part calculations, the common fraction is used instead of the decimal fraction. Follow these steps:

1. Recognize that one of the numbers in a multiplication or a division problem is an aliquot part.
2. Substitute the common fraction equivalent for the decimal fraction.
3. Perform the indicated operation.

E X A M P L E   Multiply 24 by .125.

Solution $24 \times .125$

$$24 \times \frac{1}{8} \qquad \text{\textit{Substitute the common fraction equivalent for the decimal fraction.}}$$

$$\overset{3}{\cancel{24}} \times \frac{1}{\underset{1}{\cancel{8}}} = 3 \qquad \text{\textit{Cancel and multiply.}}$$

E X A M P L E   Divide 12 by .25.

Solution $12 \div .25$

$$12 \div \frac{1}{4} \qquad \text{\textit{Substitute the common fraction equivalent for the decimal fraction.}}$$

$$\frac{12}{1} \times \frac{4}{1} = 48 \qquad \text{\textit{Invert and multiply.}}$$

The preceeding examples illustrate how easy the use of aliquot parts can be. You will also find that their use is extremely fast once you have had practice using them. Many, in fact, can be done in your head.

Using Aliquot Parts with Repeating Decimals

Not only is the use of aliquot parts fast, it is also more accurate when their equivalent is a repeating decimal.

E X A M P L E   Multiply 27 by $.33\frac{1}{3}$.

Solution $27 \times .33\frac{1}{3}$

$$27 \times \frac{1}{3} \qquad \text{\textit{Substitute the common fraction equivalent for the decimal fraction.}}$$

$$\frac{\overset{9}{\cancel{27}}}{1} \times \frac{1}{\underset{1}{\cancel{3}}} = 9 \qquad \text{\textit{Cancel and multiply.}}$$

E X A M P L E   Divide 70 by $.33\frac{1}{3}$

Solution $70 \div .33\frac{1}{3}$

$70 \div \frac{1}{3}$ *Substitute the common fraction equivalent for the decimal fraction.*

$70 \times 3 = 210$ *Invert and multiply.*

Aliquot Parts of 10 and Powers of 10

Table 3.2 illustrated aliquot parts of 1, and all of the examples so far have used aliquot parts of 1. However, aliquot parts exist for all numbers. It is just easier to use them for numbers like 1, 10, 100, 1,000, and so on. To find the aliquot parts of 10, just multiply those for 1 by 10; to find the aliquot parts of 100, multiply those for 1 by 100, and so forth. For example:

$$\frac{1}{4} \times 1 \quad = .25$$

$$\frac{1}{4} \times 10 \quad = 2.5$$

$$\frac{1}{4} \times 100 \quad = 25$$

$$\frac{1}{4} \times 1,000 = 250$$

To multiply 25 by 64, recognize that 25 is an aliquot part (as is .25). Solve problems as in the previous examples. However, since 25 is 100 times as large as .25, move the decimal point in the answer two places to the right. (Recall the section on multiplying by 10, powers of 10, and other zeros.)

E X A M P L E   Multiply 64 by .25, 2.5, 25, and 250.

Solution

$64 \times .25$ $\quad$ $64 \times \frac{1}{4}$ (of 1) $\quad = 16$

64×2.5 $\quad$ $64 \times \frac{1}{4}$ (of 10) $\quad = 160$

64×25 $\quad$ $64 \times \frac{1}{4}$ (of 100) $\quad = 1{,}600$

64×250 $\quad$ $64 \times \frac{1}{4}$ (of 1,000) $= 16{,}000$

E X A M P L E   Divide 240 by $33\frac{1}{3}$ and $666\frac{2}{3}$.

Solution

$240 \div \frac{1}{3}$ (of 100)   *Replace decimal fraction with common fraction.*

$240 \times \frac{3}{1} = 720 \ (\div 100)$ *Invert and multiply—ignore zeros for now.*

$= 7.20$ *Move decimal point.*

$$240 \div \frac{2}{3} \ (\text{of } 1{,}000) \quad \frac{\overset{120}{\cancel{240}}}{1} \times \frac{3}{\underset{1}{\cancel{2}}} = 360 \ (\div 1{,}000) = .360$$

3.14 Practice Problems

Use aliquot parts to solve the following multiplication problems:

1. $35 \times .4$
2. $81 \times .66\frac{2}{3}$
3. $.125 \times 816$
4. $.25 \times 404$

3.14 Solutions to Practice Problems

1. $\dfrac{\overset{7}{\cancel{35}}}{1} \times \dfrac{2}{\underset{1}{\cancel{5}}} = 14$

2. $\dfrac{\overset{27}{\cancel{81}}}{1} \times \dfrac{2}{\underset{1}{\cancel{3}}} = 54$

3. $\dfrac{1}{\underset{1}{\cancel{8}}} \times \dfrac{\overset{102}{\cancel{816}}}{1} = 102$

4. $\dfrac{1}{\underset{1}{\cancel{4}}} \times \dfrac{\overset{101}{\cancel{404}}}{1} = 101$

3.14 Practice Problems

Use aliquot parts to solve the following division problems:

1. $\dfrac{3}{4} \div .375$
2. $8 \div .66\frac{2}{3}$
3. $15 \div .625$
4. $76 \div .5$

3.14 Solutions to Practice Problems

1. $\dfrac{3}{4} \div \dfrac{3}{8}$ $\dfrac{\overset{1}{\cancel{3}}}{\underset{1}{\cancel{4}}} \times \dfrac{\overset{2}{\cancel{8}}}{\underset{1}{\cancel{3}}} = 2$

2. $8 \div \dfrac{2}{3}$ $\dfrac{\overset{4}{\cancel{8}}}{1} \times \dfrac{3}{\underset{1}{\cancel{2}}} = 12$

3. $15 \div \dfrac{5}{8}$ $\dfrac{\overset{3}{\cancel{15}}}{1} \times \dfrac{8}{\underset{1}{\cancel{5}}} = 24$

4. $76 \div \dfrac{1}{2}$ $76 \times 2 = 152$

3.14 Practice Problems

Use aliquot parts to solve the following problems:

1. 875×16
2. 50×272
3. $72 \times 33\frac{1}{3}$
4. $12 \div 75$

3.14 Solutions to Practice Problems

1. $\dfrac{7}{\underset{1}{\cancel{8}}} \text{ (of 1,000)} \times \dfrac{\overset{2}{\cancel{16}}}{1} = 14 \; (+ 3 \text{ zeros}) = 14,000$

2. $\dfrac{1}{\underset{1}{\cancel{2}}} \text{ (of 100)} \times \dfrac{\overset{136}{\cancel{272}}}{1} = 136 \; (+ 2 \text{ zeros}) = 13,600$

3. $\dfrac{\overset{24}{\cancel{72}}}{1} \times \dfrac{1}{\underset{1}{\cancel{3}}} \text{ (of 100)} = 24 \; (+ 2 \text{ zeros}) = 2,400$

4. $12 \div \dfrac{3}{4} \text{ (of 100)}$ $\dfrac{\overset{4}{\cancel{12}}}{1} \times \dfrac{4}{\underset{1}{\cancel{3}}} \text{ (left 2 zeros)} = 16 \text{ (left 2 zeros)} = .16$

*Estimating the solution to this problem would be very beneficial (*not *required as part of the solution).*

$$12 \div 75 = \dfrac{12}{75}$$

Then, $\dfrac{10}{80} = \dfrac{1}{8} = .125$ (from aliquot memorization)

QUICK REFERENCE SUMMARY AND REVIEW

Page	Section Topic	Learning Concepts	Examples and Solutions
66	3.1 Types of Common Fractions	The three types of common fractions are proper fractions, improper fractions, and mixed numbers.	3/7 is a proper fraction: the numerator is smaller than the denominator. 7/3 is an improper fraction: the numerator is larger than the denominator. 2 1/3 is a mixed number: a combination of a whole number and a proper fraction.
67	3.2 Converting Mixed Numbers to Improper Fractions	Use the following procedure: 1. Multiply the whole number by the denominator. 2. Add the numerator to the product. 3. Put the sum over the denominator.	Convert 8 2/5 to an improper fraction: Multiply 8 by 5 = 40. Add 40 and 2 = 42. Put 42 over 5 = 42/5.
67	3.3 Converting Improper Fractions to Mixed Numbers	Divide the numerator by the denominator and place the remainder over the original denominator. Reduce to lowest terms.	Convert 147/9 to a mixed number: $$16\frac{3}{9} = 16\frac{1}{3}$$ $9)\overline{147}$
68	3.4 Reducing Fractions: Trial-and-Error Method	Reduce fractions to lowest terms by the process of inspection.	Reduce 15/55 to lowest terms: Both 15 and 55 can be divided evenly by 5: $$\frac{15 \div 5}{55 \div 5} = \frac{3}{11}$$
69	3.5 Reducing Fractions: Greatest Common Divisor	Follow these steps: 1. Divide the larger number by the smaller number. 2. Divide any remainder into the previous divisor. 3. Continue dividing remainders into previous divisors until there is no remainder. 4. The last divisor used to get a remainder of zero is the greatest common divisor. 5. Divide both the numerator and the denominator by the greatest common divisor.	Reduce $\frac{91}{169}$ to lowest terms: $$\begin{array}{ccc} 1 & 1 & 6 \\ 91)\overline{169} & 78)\overline{91} & 13)\overline{78} \\ \underline{91} & \underline{78} & \underline{78} \\ 78 & 13 & \end{array}$$ 13 is the greatest common divisor. $$\frac{91 \div 13}{169 \div 13} = \frac{7}{13}$$
71	3.6 Raising Fractions	Divide the desired denominator by the original denominator. Multiply the numerator by the quotient. Place that product in the numerator position of the desired equivalent fraction.	Raise $\frac{5}{9}$ to an equivalent fraction with 27 as the denominator: $$\frac{5}{9} = \frac{}{27}$$ $9)\overline{27}$ $\frac{3 \times 5}{3 \times 9} = \frac{15}{27}$

Page	Section Topic	Learning Concepts	Examples and Solutions
72	**3.7** Least Common Denominator (LCD)	Also frequently called the lowest common denominator. Follow these steps: 1. Copy the denominators to be added or subtracted in a row. 2. Find a prime number that will divide evenly into at least two of the denominators. 3. Divide the prime number into all denominators into which it goes evenly. 4. If the prime number will not go into a number evenly, place that number below itself in the new row. 5. Continue that process until there is no prime number that will divide evenly into at least two numbers in a row. 6. Multiply all prime numbers and all numbers other than 1 left in the final row. The product is the LCD.	Find the LCD for $\frac{1}{2}, \frac{1}{4}, \frac{1}{6}$: Put the denominators in a row: 2 4 6 Find a prime number that will divide evenly into at least two of the denominators: $\frac{2\,/\,4\ \ 2\ \ 6}{2\ \ 1\ \ 3}$ When no prime number will divide evenly into at least two of the numbers remaining in a row, multiply the prime numbers used and the numbers remaining in a row (other than 1) together: $2 \times 2 \times 3 = 12$ The product is the LCD.
73	**3.8** Adding Common Fractions	When adding proper fractions, find the LCD; raise fractions to equivalent fractions with the LCD as the denominator. Add the numerators and put them over the LCD. Reduce if necessary. Mixed numbers are handled the same way for the proper fraction portion. Then add the whole numbers together and combine with the sum of the proper fraction portion.	Add $\frac{3}{4} + \frac{5}{6}$: $\frac{3}{4} = \frac{9}{12}$ $+\frac{5}{6} = \frac{10}{12}$ $\frac{19}{12} = 1\frac{7}{12}$ Add $2\frac{8}{15} + 6\frac{4}{5}$: $2\frac{8}{15} = 2\frac{8}{15}$ $+6\frac{4}{5} = 6\frac{12}{15}$ $8\frac{20}{15} = 9\frac{1}{3}$
75	**3.9** Subtracting Common Fractions	To subtract proper fractions, find the LCD and raise fractions to equivalent fractions. Subtract the numerator of the subtrahend from the numerator of the minuend and place the difference over the LCD.	Subtract $\frac{1}{2} - \frac{3}{8}$: $\frac{1}{2} = \frac{4}{8}$ $-\frac{3}{8} = \frac{3}{8}$ $\frac{1}{8}$

Page	Section Topic	Learning Concepts	Examples and Solutions
		When subtracting mixed numbers, use the previous procedure, but also subtract the whole numbers. If borrowing is necessary, borrow 1 from the minuend. Change that 1 to an improper equivalent fraction with the LCD as the denominator. Add it to the proper fraction. Subtract the proper fractions. Subtract the whole numbers. Reduce if necessary.	Subtracts $4\frac{2}{3} - 1\frac{2}{9}$: $$4\frac{2}{3} = 4\frac{6}{9}$$ $$1\frac{2}{9} = 1\frac{2}{9}$$ $$3\frac{4}{9}$$ Subtract $7\frac{3}{20} - 4\frac{5}{8}$: $$7\frac{3}{20} = 7\frac{6}{40} = 6\frac{46}{40}$$ $$-4\frac{5}{8} = 4\frac{25}{40} = 4\frac{25}{40}$$ $$2\frac{21}{40}$$
77	**3.10** Multiplying Common Fractions	Multiply the numerators. Multiply the denominators. Reduce to lowest terms. Cancellation can allow for reduction of a product before multiplying. Mixed numbers must be converted to improper fractions before cancellation and/or multiplication.	Multiply $\frac{4}{15}$ by $\frac{3}{8}$: $$\frac{4}{15} \times \frac{3}{8} = \frac{12}{120} = \frac{1}{10}$$ OR, $$\frac{\overset{1}{\cancel{4}}}{\underset{5}{\cancel{15}}} \times \frac{\overset{1}{\cancel{3}}}{\underset{2}{\cancel{8}}} = \frac{1}{10}$$ Multiply $7\frac{3}{4}$ by $1\frac{19}{31}$: $$7\frac{3}{4} \times 1\frac{19}{31} = \frac{31}{4} \times \frac{50}{31}$$ $$= \frac{\overset{1}{\cancel{31}}}{\underset{2}{\cancel{4}}} \times \frac{\overset{25}{\cancel{50}}}{\underset{1}{\cancel{31}}} = \frac{25}{2} = 12\frac{1}{2}$$
79	**3.11** Dividing Common Fractions	Invert the divisors and proceed as in multiplication. Mixed numbers must be converted to improper fractions before inverting takes place.	Divide $\frac{3}{10}$ by $1\frac{4}{5}$: $$\frac{3}{10} \div 1\frac{4}{5} = \frac{3}{10} \div \frac{9}{5}$$ $$= \frac{\overset{1}{\cancel{3}}}{\underset{2}{\cancel{10}}} \times \frac{\overset{1}{\cancel{5}}}{\underset{3}{\cancel{9}}} = \frac{1}{6}$$
80	**3.12** Converting Common Fractions to Decimal Fractions	Divide the numerator of the common fraction by its denominator.	Convert $\frac{2}{11}$ to a decimal fraction: $$.1818 = .182$$ $$11\overline{)2.0000}$$

Page	Section Topic	Learning Concepts	Examples and Solutions
		If the common fraction is a mixed number, proceed as above for the proper fraction portion and add the whole number to obtain the mixed decimal equivalent.	Convert $5\frac{2}{11}$ to a mixed decimal. (Proceed as above for the $\frac{2}{11}$. Then add the whole number.) $$5 + .182 = 5.182$$
81	**3.13** Converting Decimal Fractions to Common Fractions	Follow these steps: 1. Place the decimal number in the numerator position. 2. Count the number of digits to the right of the decimal point. Place that many zeros in the denominator. 3. Remove the decimal point. 4. Place a 1 in front of the zeros in the denominator. 5. Convert to a mixed number and/or reduce to lowest terms.	Convert .75 to a common fraction: Step 1: $\underline{.75}$ Step 2: $\frac{.75}{00}$ Step 3: $\frac{75}{00}$ Step 4: $\frac{75}{100}$ Step 5: $\frac{3}{4}$
83	**3.14** Aliquot Parts: A Mathematical Shortcut	An aliquot part is any number that will divide evenly into another number. 1. Recognize that one of the numbers in a multiplication or division problem is an aliquot part. 2. Substitute the common fraction equivalent for the decimal fraction. 3. Perform the indicated operation.	Multiply $.33\frac{1}{3}$ by 9: $$.33\frac{1}{3} = \frac{1}{3}$$ $$\frac{1}{3} \times 9 = \frac{1}{\overset{}{\underset{1}{3}}} \times \frac{\overset{3}{\cancel{9}}}{1} = 3$$

SURFING THE INTERNET

For further information on the topics covered in this chapter, check out the following sites:

http://www.infoplease.com/ipa/A0001727.html

http://www.vpcalendar.net/utopia/Reference/Fractions.html

http://www.aaamath.com/fra.html

ADDITIONAL PRACTICE PROBLEMS

Answers to odd-numbered problems are given in Appendix A.

3.1

Identify whether the following fractions are proper, improper, or mixed numbers. Write P *for proper,* I *for improper, or* M *for mixed numbers.*

1. $\frac{6}{5}$
1. I (The numerator is larger than the denominator.)

2. $1\frac{2}{3}$
2. M (A combination of a whole number and a proper fraction.)

3. $\frac{5}{4}$
3. I (The numerator is larger than the denominator.)

4. $\frac{2}{31}$
4. P (The numerator is smaller than the denominator.)

3.2

Convert the following mixed numbers to improper fractions:

5. $2\dfrac{5}{6}$ **6.** $6\dfrac{11}{12}$ **7.** $4\dfrac{1}{3}$ **8.** $121\dfrac{14}{23}$

  5. $2 \times 6 = 12$ $12 + 5 = 17$ (17/6)   7. $4 \times 3 = 12$ $12 + 1 = 13$ (13/3)
  6. $6 \times 12 = 72$ $72 + 11 = 83$ (83/12)   8. $121 \times 23 = 2{,}783$ $2{,}783 + 14 = 2{,}797$ (2,797/23)

3.3

Convert the following improper fractions to mixed numbers:

9. $\dfrac{16}{5}$ **10.** $\dfrac{11}{4}$ **11.** $\dfrac{58}{3}$ **12.** $\dfrac{256}{27}$

9. $3\frac{1}{5}$ $5\overline{)16}$ $\underline{15}$ 1

10. $2\frac{3}{4}$ $4\overline{)11}$ $\underline{8}$ 3

11. $19\frac{1}{3}$ $3\overline{)58}$ $\underline{3}$ 28 $\underline{27}$ 1

12. $9\frac{13}{27}$ $27\overline{)256}$ $\underline{243}$ 13

3.4.

Using the trial-and-error method, reduce the following fractions to lowest terms:

13. $\dfrac{16}{32}$ **14.** $\dfrac{82}{100}$ **15.** $\dfrac{16}{56}$

13. The numerator will divide evenly into the denominator.
$\dfrac{16 \div 16 = 1}{32 \div 16 = 2}$

14. Both are even numbers.
$\dfrac{82 \div 2 = 41}{100 \div 2 = 50}$

15. Both are even numbers.
$\dfrac{16 \div 2 = 8 \div 2 = 4 \div 2 = 2}{56 \div 2 = 28 \div 2 = 14 \div 2 = 7}$
Inspection should be sufficient to find 8 as the greatest common divisor.

16. $\dfrac{7}{49}$ The numerator will divide evenly into the denominator. $\dfrac{7 \div 7 = 1}{49 \div 7 = 7}$

3.5

Using the greatest-common-divisor method, reduce the following fractions to lowest terms:

17. $\dfrac{26}{91}$ **18.** $\dfrac{57}{76}$ **19.** $\dfrac{43}{172}$ **20.** $\dfrac{93}{248}$

17. 3 $26\overline{)91}$ $\underline{78}$ 13

18. 1 $57\overline{)76}$ $\underline{57}$ 19

19. 4 $43\overline{)172}$ $\underline{172}$ 43 is the greatest common divisor

20. 2 $93\overline{)248}$ $\underline{186}$ 62 1 $62\overline{)93}$ $\underline{62}$ 31

17. 2 $13\overline{)26}$ $\underline{26}$ 13 is the greatest common divisor.
$\dfrac{26 \div 13 = 2}{91 \div 13 = 7}$

18. 3 $19\overline{)57}$ $\underline{57}$ 19 is the greatest common divisor.
$\dfrac{57 \div 19 = 3}{76 \div 19 = 4}$

19. $\dfrac{43 \div 43 = 1}{172 \div 43 = 4}$

20. 2 $31\overline{)62}$ $\underline{62}$ 31 is the greatest common divisor.
$\dfrac{93 \div 31 = 3}{248 \div 31 = 8}$

3.6

Raise the following fractions to equivalent fractions with the indicated denominator:

21. $\dfrac{3}{5} = \dfrac{}{20}$ **22.** $\dfrac{1}{2} = \dfrac{}{40}$ **23.** $\dfrac{13}{22} = \dfrac{}{66}$ **24.** $\dfrac{2}{17} = \dfrac{}{136}$

21. 4 $5\overline{)20}$ $\underline{20}$ $3 \times 4 = \dfrac{12}{20}$

22. 20 $2\overline{)40}$ $\underline{40}$ $1 \times 20 = \dfrac{20}{40}$

23. 3 $22\overline{)66}$ $\underline{66}$ $13 \times 3 = \dfrac{39}{66}$

24. 8 $17\overline{)136}$ $\underline{136}$ $2 \times 8 = \dfrac{16}{136}$

3.7

Find the least common denominator for the following sets of fractions:

25. $\dfrac{1}{5}, \dfrac{1}{8}, \dfrac{1}{6}$ **26.** $\dfrac{3}{4}, \dfrac{2}{7}, \dfrac{1}{8}$ **27.** $\dfrac{1}{9}, \dfrac{2}{15}, \dfrac{5}{18}$ **28.** $\dfrac{4}{5}, \dfrac{8}{9}, \dfrac{2}{3}, \dfrac{8}{21}$

25. $2\underline{)5\ 8\ 6}$
   $5\ 4\ 3$
$2 \times 5 \times 4 \times 3 = 120$ LCD

26. $2\underline{)4\ 7\ 8}$
   $2\underline{)2\ 7\ 4}$
     $1\ 7\ 2$
$2 \times 2 \times 7 \times 2 = 56$ LCD

27. $3\underline{)9\ 15\ 18}$
   $3\underline{)3\ \ 5\ \ 6}$
     $1\ \ 5\ \ 2$
$3 \times 3 \times 5 \times 2 = 90$ LCD

28. $3\underline{)5\ 9\ 3\ 21}$
    $5\ 3\ 1\ \ 7$
$3 \times 5 \times 3 \times 7 = 315$ LCD

3.8

Add the following fractions:

29. $\dfrac{1}{2} + \dfrac{3}{8}$

$$\begin{array}{r} 2\big/\;2\;\;8 \\ 1\;\;4 \end{array}$$

$2 \times 4 = 8$ LCD

$$\dfrac{1}{2} = \dfrac{4}{8}$$
$$\dfrac{3}{8} = \dfrac{3}{8}$$
$$\dfrac{7}{8}$$

30. $1\dfrac{1}{3} + 2\dfrac{1}{4} + 6\dfrac{1}{6}$ $\quad 1\dfrac{1}{3} = 1\dfrac{4}{12}, 2\dfrac{1}{4} = 2\dfrac{3}{12}, 6\dfrac{1}{6} = 6\dfrac{2}{12}$

$$\begin{array}{r} 3\big/\;3\;\;4\;\;6 \\ 2\big/\;1\;\;4\;\;2 \\ 2\;\;1 \end{array}$$

$1\dfrac{4}{12} + 2\dfrac{3}{12} + 6\dfrac{2}{12} = 9\dfrac{9}{12} = 9\dfrac{3}{4}$

$3 \times 2 \times 2 = 12$ LCD

31. $\dfrac{5}{6} + \dfrac{1}{4} + \dfrac{2}{3}$ $\quad \dfrac{5}{6} = \dfrac{10}{12}, \dfrac{1}{4} = \dfrac{3}{12}, \dfrac{2}{3} = \dfrac{8}{12}$

$$\begin{array}{r} 2\big/\;6\;\;4\;\;3 \\ 3\big/\;3\;\;2\;\;3 \\ 1\;\;2\;\;1 \end{array}$$

$\dfrac{10 + 3 + 8}{12} = \dfrac{21}{12} = 1\dfrac{9}{12} = 1\dfrac{3}{4}$

$2 \times 3 \times 2 = 12$ LCD

32. $14\dfrac{2}{3} + 1\dfrac{4}{9}$ $\quad$ 9 divides evenly by 3. 9 LCD

$14\dfrac{2}{3} = 14\dfrac{6}{9}, \quad 14\dfrac{6}{9} + 1\dfrac{4}{9} = 15\dfrac{10}{9} = 16\dfrac{1}{9}$

3.9

Subtract the following fractions:

33. $\dfrac{4}{5} - \dfrac{1}{3}$

$$\dfrac{4}{5} = \dfrac{12}{15}$$
$$-\dfrac{1}{3} = \dfrac{5}{15}$$
$$\dfrac{7}{15}$$

34. $22\dfrac{7}{9} - 12\dfrac{2}{15}$

$$22\dfrac{7}{9} = 22\dfrac{35}{45}$$
$$-12\dfrac{2}{15} = 12\dfrac{6}{45}$$
$$10\dfrac{29}{45}$$

35. $\dfrac{2}{9} - \dfrac{2}{21}$

$$\dfrac{2}{9} = \dfrac{14}{63}$$
$$-\dfrac{2}{21} = \dfrac{6}{63}$$
$$\dfrac{8}{63}$$

36. $3\dfrac{3}{4} = \quad - \dfrac{4}{5}$

$$3\dfrac{3}{4} = 3\dfrac{15}{20} = 2\dfrac{35}{20}$$
$$-\dfrac{4}{5} = \dfrac{16}{20} = \dfrac{16}{20}$$
$$2\dfrac{19}{20}$$

37. $113\dfrac{1}{2} - 14\dfrac{5}{16}$

$$113\dfrac{1}{2} = 113\dfrac{8}{16}$$
$$-14\dfrac{5}{16} = 14\dfrac{5}{16}$$
$$99\dfrac{3}{16}$$

3.10

Multiply the following:

38. $\dfrac{2}{3} \times \dfrac{3}{4}$

$\dfrac{\cancel{2}^1}{\cancel{3}_1} \times \dfrac{\cancel{3}^1}{\cancel{4}_2} = \dfrac{1}{2}$

39. $4\dfrac{4}{9} \times 6\dfrac{3}{4}$

$\dfrac{\cancel{40}^{10}}{\cancel{9}_1} \times \dfrac{\cancel{27}^3}{\cancel{4}_1} = 30$

40. $\dfrac{1}{12} \times \dfrac{3}{20}$

$\dfrac{1}{\cancel{12}_4} \times \dfrac{\cancel{3}^1}{20} = \dfrac{1}{80}$

41. $5\dfrac{5}{6} \times 3\dfrac{2}{3}$

$\dfrac{35}{6} \times \dfrac{11}{3} = \dfrac{385}{18} = 21\dfrac{7}{18}$

3.11

Solve the following division problems:

42. $\dfrac{3}{5} \div \dfrac{5}{21}$

$\dfrac{3}{5} \times \dfrac{21}{5} = \dfrac{63}{25} = 2\dfrac{13}{25}$

43. $\dfrac{9}{16} \div \dfrac{3}{4}$

$\dfrac{\cancel{9}^3}{\cancel{16}_4} \times \dfrac{\cancel{4}^1}{\cancel{3}_1} = \dfrac{3}{4}$

44. $15 \div 3\dfrac{4}{7}$

 $\dfrac{\cancel{15}^3}{1} \times \dfrac{7}{\cancel{25}_5} = \dfrac{21}{5} = 4\dfrac{1}{5}$

45. $4\dfrac{2}{3} \div 7\dfrac{3}{5}$

$\dfrac{\cancel{14}^7}{3} \times \dfrac{5}{\cancel{38}_{19}} = \dfrac{35}{57}$

3.12

Convert the following common fractions to decimal fractions. (Round to the thousandth position if necessary.)

46. $\dfrac{2}{5}$

$$\begin{array}{r} .4 \\ 5\overline{)2.0} \end{array}$$

47. $\dfrac{5}{9}$

$.5555 = .556$
$$9\overline{)5.0000}$$

48. $\dfrac{6}{11}$

$.5454 = .545$
$$11\overline{)6.0000}$$

49. $\dfrac{29}{1,000}$

$.029$
$$1000\overline{)29.000}$$

3.13

Convert the following decimal fractions to common fractions:

50. .26

$$\frac{26}{100} = \frac{13}{50}$$

51. .305

$$\frac{305}{1,000} = \frac{61}{200}$$

52. .375

$$\frac{375}{1,000} = \frac{3}{8}$$

53. 1.8

$$1\frac{8}{10} = 1\frac{4}{5}$$

3.14

Use aliquot parts to solve the following multiplication problems:

54. .875 × 16

$$\frac{7}{\cancel{8}} \times \cancel{16}^{\,2} = 14$$

55. $.33\frac{1}{3} \times 18$

$$\frac{1}{\cancel{3}} \times \cancel{18}^{\,6} = 6$$

56. 24 × 12.5

$$.125 = \frac{1}{8}$$
$$12.5 = \frac{1}{8} \times 100$$
$$\cancel{24}^{\,3} \times \frac{1}{\cancel{8}} \times 100 = 300$$

57. .2 × 55

$$\frac{1}{\cancel{5}} \times \cancel{55}^{\,11} = 11$$

58. 750 × 124

$$\frac{3}{\cancel{4}} \, (\text{of } 1,000) \times \frac{\cancel{124}^{\,31}}{1} = 43,000$$

Use aliquot parts to solve the following division problems:

59. $30 \div .33\frac{1}{3}$

$$30 \times 3 = 90$$

60. 12 ÷ .25

$$12 \times 4 = 48$$

61. $.625 \div \frac{5}{24}$

$$\frac{\cancel{5}}{\cancel{8}} \div \frac{\cancel{24}^{\,3}}{\cancel{5}} = 3$$

62. $.75 \div 2\frac{1}{4}$

$$\frac{\cancel{3}}{\cancel{4}} \times \frac{\cancel{4}}{\cancel{9}}^{\,3} = \frac{1}{3}$$

63. $720 \div 66\frac{2}{3}$

$$\frac{\cancel{720}^{\,360}}{1} \times \frac{3}{\cancel{2}} \; (\text{left 2 zeros}) = 10.8$$

64. $\frac{1}{48} \div .125$

$$\frac{1}{\cancel{48}_{\,6}} \times \frac{\cancel{8}}{1} = \frac{1}{6}$$

CHAPTER REVIEW PROBLEMS

Answers to odd-numbered problems are given in Appendix A.

Drill Problems

Identify the following as proper fractions, improper fractions, or mixed numbers:

1. $4\frac{1}{2}$ M

2. $\frac{19}{19}$ I

3. $\frac{263}{142}$ I

4. $\frac{6}{7}$ P

Convert the following to improper fractions:

5. $4\frac{9}{25}$ $\frac{109}{25}$

6. $6\frac{3}{7}$ $\frac{45}{7}$

7. $45\frac{2}{3}$ $\frac{137}{3}$

8. $10\frac{21}{100}$ $\frac{1,021}{100}$

Convert the following to mixed numbers:

9. $\frac{12}{7}$

$$1\frac{5}{7}$$

10. $\frac{56}{21}$

$$2\frac{14}{21} = 2\frac{2}{3}$$

11. $\frac{325}{122}$

$$2\frac{81}{122}$$

12. $\frac{82}{5}$

$$16\frac{2}{5}$$

13. $\frac{1,732}{9}$

$$192\frac{4}{9}$$

Convert the following decimal fractions to common fractions:

14. .25

$$\frac{25}{100} = \frac{1}{4}$$

15. .125

$$\frac{125}{1,000} = \frac{1}{8}$$

16. .3357

$$\frac{3,357}{10,000}$$

17. .18725

$$\frac{18,725}{100,000} = \frac{749}{4,000}$$

Convert the following common fractions to decimal fractions:

18. $3\frac{8}{9}$

$$9\overline{)8.0000}^{\,.8888} = 3.889$$

19. $212\frac{1}{12}$

$$12\overline{)1.0000}^{\,.0833} = 212.083$$

20. $15\frac{5}{8}$

$$8\overline{)5.000}^{\,.625} = 15.625$$

21. $2\frac{1}{7}$

$$7\overline{)1.0000}^{\,.1428} = 2.143$$

Reduce the following fractions to lowest terms:

22. $\dfrac{65}{200}$

$\dfrac{65 \div 5 = 13}{200 \div 5 = 40}$

23. $\dfrac{105}{126}$

$\dfrac{105 \div 21 = 5}{126 \div 21 = 6}$

24. $\dfrac{80}{90}$

$\dfrac{80 \div 10 = 8}{90 \div 10 = 9}$

25. $\dfrac{1{,}441}{2{,}992}$

$$\begin{array}{r} 2 \\ 1{,}441\overline{)2{,}992} \\ 2{,}882 \\ \hline 110 \end{array} \qquad \begin{array}{r} 13 \\ 110\overline{)1{,}441} \\ 1\ 10 \\ \hline 341 \\ 330 \\ \hline 11 \end{array}$$

$$\begin{array}{r} 10 \\ 11\overline{)110} \end{array}$$

$\dfrac{1{,}441 \div 11 = 131}{2{,}992 \div 11 = 272}$

26. $\dfrac{153}{170}$

$$\begin{array}{r} 1 \\ 153\overline{)170} \\ 153 \\ \hline 17 \end{array}$$
$$\begin{array}{r} 9 \\ 17\overline{)153} \\ 153 \end{array}$$

$\dfrac{153 \div 17 = 9}{170 \div 17 = 10}$

27. $\dfrac{323}{589}$

$$\begin{array}{r} 1 \\ 323\overline{)589} \\ 323 \\ \hline 266 \end{array}$$
$$\begin{array}{r} 1 \\ 266\overline{)323} \\ 266 \\ \hline 57 \end{array}$$
$$\begin{array}{r} 4 \\ 57\overline{)266} \\ 228 \\ \hline 38 \end{array}$$
$$\begin{array}{r} 1 \\ 38\overline{)57} \\ 38 \\ \hline 19 \end{array}$$
$$\begin{array}{r} 2 \\ 19\overline{)38} \quad \text{LCD} \\ 38 \end{array}$$

$\dfrac{323 \div 19 = 17}{589 \div 19 = 31}$

28. $\dfrac{161}{253}$

$$\begin{array}{r} 1 \\ 161\overline{)253} \\ 161 \\ \hline 92 \end{array}$$
$$\begin{array}{r} 1 \\ 92\overline{)161} \\ 92 \\ \hline 69 \end{array}$$
$$\begin{array}{r} 1 \\ 69\overline{)92} \\ 69 \\ \hline 23 \end{array}$$
$$\begin{array}{r} 3 \\ 23\overline{)69} \quad \text{LCD} \end{array}$$

$\dfrac{161 \div 23 = 7}{253 \div 23 = 11}$

29. $\dfrac{145}{203}$

$$\begin{array}{r} 1 \\ 145\overline{)203} \\ 145 \\ \hline 58 \end{array}$$
$$\begin{array}{r} 2 \\ 58\overline{)145} \\ 116 \\ \hline 29 \end{array}$$
$$\begin{array}{r} 2 \\ 29\overline{)58} \quad \text{LCD} \end{array}$$

$\dfrac{145 \div 29 = 5}{203 \div 29 = 7}$

Raise the following fractions to equivalent fractions having the indicated denominators:

30. $\dfrac{7}{8} = \dfrac{}{72}$

$9 \times 7 = 63$
$8\overline{)72}$

31. $\dfrac{2}{127} = \dfrac{}{762}$

$6 \times 2 = 12$
$127\overline{)762}$

32. $\dfrac{9}{17} = \dfrac{}{51}$

$3 \times 9 = 27$
$17\overline{)51}$

33. $\dfrac{123}{311} = \dfrac{}{1{,}555}$

$5 \times 123 = 615$
$311\overline{)1{,}555}$

Find the LCD for the following sets of fractions and raise each fraction to an equivalent fraction with the LCD:

34. $\dfrac{5}{8}, \dfrac{7}{12}, \dfrac{47}{60}, \dfrac{3}{5}$

$$\begin{array}{r} 2\,\underline{/\,8 \quad 12 \quad 60 \quad 5} \\ 2\,\underline{/\,4 \quad 6 \quad 30 \quad 5} \\ 5\,\underline{/\,2 \quad 3 \quad 15 \quad 5} \\ 3\,\underline{/\,2 \quad 3 \quad 3 \quad 1} \\ 2 \quad 1 \quad 1 \quad 1 \end{array}$$

$2 \times 2 \times 5 \times 3 \times 2 = 120$ LCD

$\dfrac{75}{120}, \dfrac{70}{120}, \dfrac{94}{120}, \dfrac{72}{120}$

35. $\dfrac{3}{4}, \dfrac{7}{8}, \dfrac{2}{9}, \dfrac{5}{6}$

$$\begin{array}{r} 2\,\underline{/\,4 \quad 8 \quad 9 \quad 6} \\ 2\,\underline{/\,2 \quad 4 \quad 9 \quad 3} \\ 3\,\underline{/\,1 \quad 2 \quad 9 \quad 3} \\ 2 \quad 3 \quad 1 \end{array}$$

$2 \times 2 \times 3 \times 2 \times 3 = 72$ LCD

$\dfrac{54}{72}, \dfrac{63}{72}, \dfrac{16}{72}, \dfrac{60}{72}$

36. $\dfrac{4}{15}, \dfrac{3}{10}, \dfrac{5}{24}$

$$\begin{array}{r} 5\,\underline{/\,15 \quad 10 \quad 24} \\ 3\,\underline{/\,3 \quad 2 \quad 24} \\ 2\,\underline{/\,1 \quad 2 \quad 8} \\ 1 \quad 1 \quad 4 \end{array}$$

$5 \times 3 \times 2 \times 4 = 120$ LCD

$\dfrac{32}{120}, \dfrac{36}{120}, \dfrac{25}{120}$

37. $\dfrac{8}{21}, \dfrac{1}{9}, \dfrac{3}{15}, \dfrac{2}{35}$

$$\begin{array}{r} 3\,\underline{/\,21 \quad 9 \quad 15 \quad 35} \\ 5\,\underline{/\,7 \quad 3 \quad 5 \quad 35} \\ 7\,\underline{/\,7 \quad 3 \quad 1 \quad 7} \\ 1 \quad 3 \quad 1 \quad 1 \end{array}$$

$3 \times 5 \times 7 \times 3 = 315$ LCD

$\dfrac{120}{315}, \dfrac{35}{315}, \dfrac{63}{315}, \dfrac{18}{315}$

Add the following fractions:

38. $\dfrac{2}{5} + \dfrac{8}{15} + \dfrac{24}{35}$

$$\begin{array}{r} 5\,\underline{/\,5 \quad 15 \quad 35} \\ 1 \quad 3 \quad 7 \end{array}$$

$5 \times 3 \times 7 = 105$ LCD

$\dfrac{42}{105} + \dfrac{56}{105} + \dfrac{72}{105} = \dfrac{170}{105} = 1\dfrac{65}{105} = 1\dfrac{13}{21}$

39. $\dfrac{5}{64} + \dfrac{3}{32} + \dfrac{7}{16}$

64 is evenly divisable by 32 and by 16. 64 LCD

$\dfrac{5}{64} + \dfrac{6}{64} + \dfrac{28}{64} = \dfrac{39}{64}$

40. $\dfrac{3}{7} + \dfrac{3}{28} + \dfrac{5}{8}$

$\dfrac{24}{56} + \dfrac{6}{56} + \dfrac{35}{56} = \dfrac{65}{56} = 1\dfrac{9}{56}$

41. $3\dfrac{1}{8} + 5\dfrac{6}{7} + 9\dfrac{1}{4}$

$3\dfrac{7}{56} + 5\dfrac{48}{56} + 9\dfrac{14}{56} = 17\dfrac{69}{56} = 18\dfrac{13}{56}$

Chapter 3 Common Fractions and Common/Decimal Fraction Conversion

Subtract the following fractions:

42. $\dfrac{7}{12} - \dfrac{2}{5}$

$\dfrac{35}{60} - \dfrac{24}{60} = \dfrac{11}{60}$

43. $\dfrac{3}{4} - \dfrac{2}{3}$

$\dfrac{9}{12} - \dfrac{8}{12} = \dfrac{1}{12}$

44. $\dfrac{7}{10} - \dfrac{8}{15}$

$\dfrac{21}{30} - \dfrac{16}{30} = \dfrac{5}{30} = \dfrac{1}{6}$

45. $1\dfrac{1}{10} - \dfrac{1}{2}$

$\dfrac{11}{10} - \dfrac{5}{10} = \dfrac{6}{10} = \dfrac{3}{5}$

Multiply the following fractions:

46. $\dfrac{4}{15} \times \dfrac{7}{10} \times \dfrac{3}{4}$

$\dfrac{\cancel{4}}{\cancel{15}_5} \times \dfrac{7}{10} \times \dfrac{\cancel{3}}{\cancel{4}_1} = \dfrac{7}{50}$

47. $\dfrac{5}{6} \times \dfrac{5}{16} \times \dfrac{2}{5}$

$\dfrac{\cancel{5}}{\cancel{6}_3} \times \dfrac{5}{16} \times \dfrac{\cancel{2}}{\cancel{5}_1} = \dfrac{5}{48}$

48. $\dfrac{3}{20} \times \dfrac{5}{36} \times \dfrac{7}{12} \times \dfrac{1}{21}$

$\dfrac{\cancel{3}}{20}_4 \times \dfrac{\cancel{5}}{\cancel{36}}_{12} \times \dfrac{\cancel{7}}{12} \times \dfrac{1}{\cancel{21}}_3 = \dfrac{1}{1{,}728}$

49. $2\dfrac{1}{4} \times 1\dfrac{2}{7} \times \dfrac{4}{27}$

$\dfrac{\cancel{9}}{\cancel{4}}_1 \times \dfrac{\cancel{9}}{7}^3 \times \dfrac{\cancel{4}}{\cancel{27}}_{\cancel{3}}^1 = \dfrac{3}{7}$

Use aliquot parts to multiply the following:

50. $.4 \times 25$

$\dfrac{2}{\cancel{5}}_1 \times \dfrac{\cancel{25}^5}{1} = 10$

51. $.75 \times 20$

$\dfrac{3}{\cancel{4}}_1 \times \cancel{20}^5 = 15$

52. $348 \times .5$

$\cancel{348}^{174} \times \dfrac{1}{\cancel{2}}_1 = 174$

53. $.875 \times 8$

$\dfrac{7}{\cancel{8}}_1 \times \cancel{8}^1 = 7$

54. $.33\dfrac{1}{3} \times 210$

$\dfrac{1}{\cancel{3}}_1 \times \cancel{210}^{70} = 70$

55. $12 \times 6.6\dfrac{2}{3}$

$\cancel{12}^4 \times \dfrac{2}{\cancel{3}}_1 = 80$ (one zero right)

56. $48 \times .33\dfrac{1}{3} \times 125$

$\cancel{48}^{16}_2 \times \dfrac{1}{\cancel{3}}_1 \times \dfrac{1}{\cancel{8}}_1 = 2{,}000$ (3 zeros right)

57. 200×555

$\dfrac{1}{\cancel{5}}_1 \times \cancel{555}^{111} = 111{,}000$ (3 zeros right)

Divide the following fractions:

58. $\dfrac{21}{31} \div \dfrac{7}{9}$

$\dfrac{\cancel{21}^3}{31} \times \dfrac{9}{\cancel{7}_1} = \dfrac{27}{31}$

59. $\dfrac{2}{5} \div \dfrac{1}{8} \div \dfrac{3}{5}$

$\dfrac{2}{\cancel{5}} \times \dfrac{8}{1} \times \dfrac{\cancel{5}}{3}_1 = \dfrac{16}{3} = 5\dfrac{1}{3}$

60. $\dfrac{4}{7} \div \dfrac{9}{10} \div \dfrac{3}{16}$

$\dfrac{4}{7} \times \dfrac{10}{9} \times \dfrac{16}{3} = \dfrac{640}{189} = 3\dfrac{73}{189}$

61. $\dfrac{2}{3} \div 76$

$\dfrac{\cancel{2}^1}{3} \times \dfrac{1}{\cancel{76}_{38}} = \dfrac{1}{114}$

Use aliquot parts to divide the following:

62. $.3 \div 2\dfrac{7}{10}$

$\dfrac{\cancel{3}^1}{\cancel{10}_1} \times \dfrac{\cancel{10}^1}{\cancel{27}_9} = \dfrac{1}{9}$

63. $105 \div 87.5$

$105 \div \dfrac{7}{8}$

$\cancel{105}^{15} \times \dfrac{8}{\cancel{7}_1} = 120 = 1.2$ (left 2 places)

64. $\dfrac{1}{5} \div .6$

$\dfrac{1}{\cancel{5}} \times \dfrac{\cancel{5}}{3}_1 = \dfrac{1}{3}$

65. $125 \div 375$

$\dfrac{1}{\cancel{8}} \times \dfrac{\cancel{8}}{3}_1 = \dfrac{1}{3}$

Word Problems

66. Three bins have capacities of $24\dfrac{1}{2}$ pounds, $13\dfrac{1}{8}$ pounds, and $18\dfrac{3}{4}$ pounds. What is the total capacity of the three bins?

$24\dfrac{1}{2} = 24\dfrac{4}{8}$
$13\dfrac{1}{8} = 13\dfrac{1}{8}$
$18\dfrac{3}{4} = 18\dfrac{6}{8}$
$\overline{55\dfrac{11}{8} = 56\dfrac{3}{8}}$

67. A wall measures $24\dfrac{3}{16}$ feet in length. A remodeling project would move the wall in $2\dfrac{1}{8}$ feet from *each* end. How long would the wall be after remodeling?

$2\dfrac{1}{8} \times 2 = \dfrac{17}{\cancel{8}}_4 \times \cancel{2}^1 = \dfrac{17}{4} = 4\dfrac{1}{4}$

$24\dfrac{3}{16} = 24\dfrac{3}{16} = 23\dfrac{19}{16}$
$-\ 4\dfrac{1}{4} = 4\dfrac{4}{16} = 4\dfrac{4}{16}$
$\overline{19\dfrac{15}{16}}$

68. Sam owns $\dfrac{1}{3}$ of the ABT Corporation. If he sells $\dfrac{1}{4}$ of his ownership interest in the firm to Joe, how much of ABT will Joe own?

$\dfrac{1}{3} \times \dfrac{1}{4} = \dfrac{1}{12}$

69. A recipe calls for $\dfrac{2}{3}$ cup of flour. Once thoroughly mixed, the recipe is divided into portions containing $\dfrac{1}{6}$ cup of flour each. How many portions are there?

$\dfrac{2}{3} \div \dfrac{1}{6} = \dfrac{2}{\cancel{3}} \times \dfrac{\cancel{6}^2}{1} = 4$

70. A carpet that is $\frac{5}{8}$ inch thick is laid on top of a mat that is $\frac{3}{16}$ inch thick. What is the total thickness?

$$\frac{5}{8} = \frac{10}{16}$$
$$+\frac{3}{16}$$
$$\frac{13}{16}$$

71. In a college economics class, the average grade on an exam was $74\frac{3}{10}$. One student received a grade of $85\frac{1}{2}$. What was the difference between the average grade and the student's grade?

$$85\frac{1}{2} = 85\frac{5}{10}$$
$$-74\frac{3}{10}$$
$$6\frac{2}{10} = 6\frac{1}{5}$$

72. Grace invested $1,500 last year. Her investment is now worth $\frac{2}{3}$ more. How much has it increased in value?

$$\$1,500 \times \frac{2}{3} = \$1,000$$

73. A can contains $\frac{7}{8}$ gallon of gasoline. How many times can a lawnmower be filled if it has a tank capacity of $\frac{1}{4}$ gallon?

$$\frac{7}{8} \div \frac{1}{4} = \frac{7}{\underset{2}{8}} \times \frac{\overset{1}{4}}{1} = \frac{7}{2} = 3\frac{1}{2}$$

74. Statistics show that $.66\frac{2}{3}$ of the people in the United States earn in excess of $12,500 annually. If we gathered 47,400 people at random from the population, how many would we expect to earn *less* than $12,500 annually?

$$\begin{array}{r} 1.00 \\ -.66\frac{2}{3} \\ \hline .33\frac{1}{3} \end{array} \qquad 47,400 \times \frac{1}{3} = 15,800$$

75. Three component parts used in the manufacture of a stereo set weigh $\frac{7}{8}$ pound, $\frac{3}{16}$ pound, and $\frac{3}{4}$ pound. How much is the total weight of the three components?

$$\frac{7}{8} + \frac{3}{16} + \frac{3}{4} = \frac{14}{16} + \frac{3}{16} + \frac{12}{16} = \frac{29}{16} = 1\frac{13}{16}$$

76. The length of the walls in a rectangular office is $18\frac{5}{8}$ feet. The width is $12\frac{3}{32}$ feet. What is the perimeter of the room? (The perimeter is the distance around.)

$$18\frac{5}{8} = 18\frac{20}{32} + 12\frac{3}{32} = 30\frac{23}{32} \qquad \frac{983}{\underset{16}{32}} \times \frac{\overset{1}{2}}{1} = \frac{983}{16} = 61\frac{7}{16}$$

77. Workers in a machine shop have to complete a job by tomorrow. When they began work this morning, they had $\frac{3}{4}$ of the job remaining. Today they completed $\frac{1}{3}$ of the job. What portion must be completed tomorrow?

$$\frac{3}{4} - \frac{1}{3} = \frac{9}{12} - \frac{4}{12} = \frac{5}{12}$$

78. A used Ford cost $12,000 last year. This year, the same Ford model sells for .125 more. How much was the price increase?

$$\$12,000 \times \frac{1}{8} = \$1,500$$

79. The average family size in Tulok County is $4\frac{3}{5}$ people. If the total population is 46,000, determine the number of families living there.

$$46,000 \div 4\frac{3}{5} = \overset{2,000}{46,000} \times \frac{5}{\underset{1}{23}} = 10,000$$

80. The total invoice price for an industrial cleaning compound is $450. If each case costs $37.50, how many cases were purchased?

$$\$450 \div \$37.50 = \$450 \div \frac{3}{8}$$
$$= \text{(left 2 places)}\ \frac{\overset{150}{450}}{1} \times \frac{8}{\underset{1}{3}} = 1200\ \text{(left 2 places)} = 12$$

81. A metal pipe $16\frac{3}{8}$ inches long was cut into two pieces. One was $6\frac{7}{16}$ inches long. What was the length of the second piece?

$$16\frac{3}{8} - 6\frac{7}{16} = 16\frac{6}{16} - 6\frac{7}{16} = 15\frac{22}{16} - 6\frac{7}{16} = 9\frac{15}{16}$$

82. On the average, of every 87.5 units produced, 1 unit is defective. If an average daily run results in 32 defective units, determine the total average daily production.

$$\begin{array}{r} 87.5 \\ \times\ 32 \\ \hline 2,800 \end{array} \quad \text{or,} \quad \text{using aliquot parts,}\ \frac{7}{8}\ (+\ 2\ \text{zeroes}) \times \frac{\overset{4}{32}}{1} = 2,800$$

✓ ENRICHMENT PROBLEMS

83. Joan is paid $\frac{5}{6}$ as much as Ann. Joan's salary is $825 per month. Find Ann's salary.

$$\$825 \div \frac{5}{6} = \$\overset{165}{825} \times \frac{6}{\underset{1}{5}} = \$990$$

84. Three business partners share profits as follows: Robert, $\frac{1}{2}$; John, $\frac{1}{3}$; and Mike, $\frac{1}{6}$. If the firm's profits this year were $150,000, how much will each partner receive?

$$\frac{1}{\underset{1}{2}} \times \$\overset{75,000}{150,000} = \$75,000\ \text{(Robert)}$$

$$\frac{1}{\underset{1}{3}} \times \$\overset{50,000}{150,000} = \$50,000\ \text{(John)} \qquad \frac{1}{\underset{1}{6}} \times \$\overset{25,000}{150,000} = \$25,000\ \text{(Mike)}$$

CRITICAL THINKING GROUP PROJECT

Next fall, a community college is opening a fourth campus in the Southeast section of the county. The Southwest campus was the first to open and presently has an enrollment of 12,250 students. The Northeast campus was opened five years later and has a current enrollment of 12,580. Ten years ago, the Northwest campus opened. It never reached the expected enrollment because an air force base located nearby was closed due to military downsizing. Its current enrollment is 4,500.

Projected enrollment figures for the next term are based on the following assumptions:

1. Due to economic conditions and current declines in area high school graduates, without the addition of the new campus, the existing campuses' enrollments would decline.

    a. The Southwest campus enrollment would have a decline of $\frac{1}{20}$.

    b. The Northeast campus enrollment would decline by $\frac{2}{25}$.

    c. The Northwest campus would decline by $\frac{3}{80}$.

2. The addition of the new campus will cannibalize enrollments from the Southwest and the Northeast campuses. It is not expected to draw students from the Northwest campus. These figures are calculated after the expected declines in enrollments in 1 (above) have been considered.

    a. One-fifth of the enrollment at the Southwest campus will go to the new Southeast campus.

    b. Two-fifteenths of the enrollment at the Northeast campus will go to the new campus.

    c. One thousand, eight hundred seventy-five students that would not otherwise have attended the community college without the addition of the Southeast campus will attend that campus.

Based on the previous information above, answer the following questions:

1. What would have been the projected enrollment for the three existing campuses without the addition of the fourth campus? Round to the nearest student.
   Southwest: 12,250 × 1/20 = 613 12,250 − 613 = 11,637   Northeast: 12,580 × 2/25 = 1,006   12,580 − 1,006 = 11,574
   Northwest: 4,500 × 3/80 = 169   4,500 − 169 = 4,331

2. What will be the new projected enrollments at the four campuses? Round to the nearest student.
   Southwest: 11,637 × 1/5 = 2,327   11,637 − 2,327 = 9,310   Northeast: 11,574 × 2/15 = 1,543   11,574 − 1,543 = 10,031
   Northwest: 4,331   Southeast: 1,875 + 2,327 + 1,543 = 5,745

3. What is the total difference in the current enrollment and the projected enrollment after the addition of the new campus?
   Current enrollment: 12,250 + 12,580 + 4,500 = 29,330   Projected enrollment: 9,310 + 10,031 + 4,331 + 5,745 = 29,417
   29,417 − 29,330 = 87 additional students after the opening of the new campus

4. What would you recommend to the college administration about the advisability of opening the new campus? What other information would you like to have to make a better decision?
   Student answers will vary, but most will probably say that based on the current information, the addition of a new campus will not add enough new students to justify its expenses. Other needed information could include student enrollment projections for several more years, additional costs incurred to operate the new campus, community attitude toward the addition of the new campus, state and local government funding intentions, etc.

SELF-TESTING EXERCISES

Answers to all exercises are given in Appendix A.

1. Differentiate between the greatest common divisor and the least common denominator. **W**

   The greatest common divisor is the largest number that will divide evenly into both the numerator and denominator of a fraction, while the least common denominator is the smallest number that is evenly divisible by each denominator of common fractions being added or subtracted.

2. What is a prime number? **W**

   A prime number is a number that can be divided evenly only by itself and 1.

Perform the indicated operations with proper fractions:

3. $\dfrac{5}{6} + \dfrac{2}{3}$

$\dfrac{5}{6} + \dfrac{4}{6} = \dfrac{9}{6} = 1\dfrac{3}{6} = 1\dfrac{1}{2}$

4. $\dfrac{3}{16} - \dfrac{1}{8}$

$\dfrac{3}{16} - \dfrac{2}{16} = \dfrac{1}{16}$

5. $\dfrac{1}{3} + \dfrac{2}{5} + \dfrac{4}{15} - \dfrac{1}{5}$

$\dfrac{5}{15} + \dfrac{6}{15} + \dfrac{4}{15} - \dfrac{3}{15} = \dfrac{12}{15} = \dfrac{4}{5}$

6. $\dfrac{1}{4} \div \dfrac{2}{3}$

$\dfrac{1}{4} \times \dfrac{3}{2} = \dfrac{3}{8}$

7. $\dfrac{1}{12} \times \dfrac{7}{8}$

$\dfrac{7}{96}$

8. $\dfrac{1}{9} \times \dfrac{3}{4} \div \dfrac{5}{6} \div \dfrac{1}{8}$

$\dfrac{1}{\cancel{9}} \times \dfrac{\cancel{3}}{\cancel{4}} \times \dfrac{\cancel{6}}{5} \times \dfrac{\cancel{8}}{1} = \dfrac{4}{5}$

Perform the indicated operations with mixed numbers:

9. $115\dfrac{3}{8} - 109\dfrac{1}{2}$

$\begin{array}{r} 115\dfrac{3}{8} = 114\dfrac{11}{8} \\ -109\dfrac{4}{8} \\ \hline 5\dfrac{7}{8} \end{array}$

10. $4\dfrac{16}{19} \div 3\dfrac{3}{13}$

$\dfrac{92}{19} \div \dfrac{42}{13} = \dfrac{598}{399} = 1\dfrac{199}{399}$

11. $37\dfrac{15}{16} + 18\dfrac{3}{4}$

$\begin{array}{r} 37\dfrac{15}{16} \\ +18\dfrac{12}{16} \\ \hline 55\dfrac{27}{16} = 56\dfrac{11}{16} \end{array}$

12. $6\dfrac{5}{18} \times 2\dfrac{4}{7}$

$\dfrac{113}{\cancel{18}} \times \dfrac{\cancel{18}}{7} = \dfrac{113}{7} = 16\dfrac{1}{7}$

13. $3\dfrac{2}{7} + 4\dfrac{9}{14} + 8\dfrac{5}{6}$

$3\dfrac{12}{42} + 4\dfrac{27}{42} + 8\dfrac{35}{42} = 15\dfrac{74}{42} = 16\dfrac{32}{42} = 16\dfrac{16}{21}$

14. $1\dfrac{5}{9} \times 1\dfrac{2}{7} \div 1\dfrac{1}{7}$

$\dfrac{\cancel{14}}{\cancel{9}} \times \dfrac{\cancel{9}}{\cancel{7}} \times \dfrac{7}{\cancel{8}} = \dfrac{7}{4} = 1\dfrac{3}{4}$

Convert the following common fractions to decimal fractions:

15. $\dfrac{3}{8}$

$\begin{array}{r} .375 \\ 8)\overline{3.000} \end{array}$

16. $\dfrac{2}{3}$

$\begin{array}{r} .66\overline{66} = .667 \\ 3)\overline{2.0000} \end{array}$

17. $\dfrac{15}{16}$

$\begin{array}{r} .9375 = .938 \\ 16)\overline{15.0000} \end{array}$

18. $13\dfrac{5}{6}$

$\begin{array}{r} .8333 \quad 13.833 \\ 6)\overline{5.0000} \end{array}$

19. $216\dfrac{3}{5}$

$\begin{array}{r} .6 \quad 216.6 \\ 5)\overline{3.0} \end{array}$

Reduce the following to lowest terms:

20. $\dfrac{48}{72}$

$\dfrac{48}{72} \div \dfrac{24}{24} = \dfrac{2}{3}$

21. $\dfrac{135}{216}$

$\dfrac{135}{216} \div \dfrac{27}{27} = \dfrac{5}{8}$

22. $\dfrac{45}{54}$

$\dfrac{45}{54} \div \dfrac{9}{9} = \dfrac{5}{6}$

23. $\dfrac{189}{504}$

$\dfrac{189}{504} \div \dfrac{63}{63} = \dfrac{3}{8}$

Convert the following decimal fractions to common fractions:

24. .23

$\dfrac{23}{100}$

25. 1.2

$1\dfrac{2}{10} = 1\dfrac{1}{5}$

26. .375

$\dfrac{375}{1,000} = \dfrac{3}{8}$

27. 2.138

$2\dfrac{138}{1,000} = 2\dfrac{69}{500}$

Use aliquot parts to solve the following problems:

28. $.5 \times 250$

$\dfrac{1}{\cancel{2}} \times \overset{125}{\cancel{250}} = 125$

29. $.25 \times 804$

$\dfrac{1}{\cancel{4}} \times \overset{201}{\cancel{804}} = 201$

30. $12 \div .33\dfrac{1}{3}$

$12 \times \dfrac{3}{1} = 36$

31. $40 \div .2$

$\overset{20}{\cancel{40}} \times \dfrac{10}{\cancel{2}} = 200$

32. 48×12.5

$\overset{6}{\cancel{48}} \times \dfrac{1}{\cancel{8}} = (+ 2 \text{ zeros}) = 600$

33. A car can be driven for 14 hours on a tank of gas. If it gets $25\dfrac{9}{10}$ miles per gallon of gas and is driven at an average rate of speed of $55\dfrac{1}{2}$ miles per hour, determine the gasoline tank capacity.

$14 \times 55\dfrac{1}{2} = \dfrac{\overset{7}{\cancel{14}}}{1} \times \dfrac{111}{\cancel{2}} = 777$

$\dfrac{777}{1} \div 25\dfrac{9}{10} = \dfrac{\overset{3}{\cancel{777}}}{1} \times \dfrac{10}{\cancel{259}} = 30 \text{ gallons}$

34. A length of pipe measuring $72\dfrac{3}{4}$ inches was cut into five pieces. Four of the cuts were as follows: $5\dfrac{1}{2}$ inches, $12\dfrac{3}{32}$ inches, $16\dfrac{5}{6}$ inches, and $15\dfrac{7}{8}$ inches. Calculate the length of the remaining piece.

$5\dfrac{1}{2} + 12\dfrac{3}{32} + 16\dfrac{5}{6} + 15\dfrac{7}{8}$

$5\dfrac{48}{96} + 12\dfrac{9}{96} + 16\dfrac{80}{96} + 15\dfrac{84}{96} = 48\dfrac{221}{96} = 50\dfrac{29}{96}$

$72\dfrac{3}{4} - 50\dfrac{29}{96} = 72\dfrac{72}{96} - 50\dfrac{29}{96} = 22\dfrac{43}{96}$

35. The area of a rectangle is found by multiplying the length of two adjacent sides (length × width). If a rectangle has adjacent sides measuring $12\frac{3}{4}$ inches and $6\frac{2}{3}$ inches, what is the area? (Your answer will be in square inches.)

$$12\frac{3}{4} \times 6\frac{2}{3} = \frac{\overset{17}{\cancel{51}}}{\underset{1}{\cancel{4}}} \times \frac{\overset{5}{\cancel{20}}}{\underset{1}{\cancel{3}}} = 85 \text{ square inches}$$

36. If molding strips necessary for a job are to be $3\frac{1}{2}$ feet long, how many will we get from a strip 28 feet long?

$$28 \div 3\frac{1}{2} = \overset{4}{\cancel{28}} \times \frac{2}{\underset{1}{\cancel{7}}} = 8$$

37. What is the total capacity of a bus if seven people represent .125 of it?

$$7 \div .125 = 7 \div \frac{1}{8} \qquad 7 \times 8 = 56$$

38. A machine that a company uses only during peak periods operates, on the average, $\frac{1}{4}$ of the year. Its average output when in operation is $22\frac{1}{2}$ units per week. How many units will this machine contribute to the company's output in a year?

$$52 \times \frac{1}{4} \times 22\frac{1}{2} = \frac{\overset{13}{\cancel{52}}}{1} \times \frac{1}{\underset{1}{\cancel{4}}} \times \frac{45}{2} = \frac{585}{2} = 292\frac{1}{2} \text{ units}$$

39. A metal worker has 360 sheets of steel stacked together. If each sheet is $.66\frac{2}{3}$ inch thick, compute the total thickness of the stack.

$$360 \times \frac{2}{3} = 240$$

40. For every yard of material used in an industrial process, $\frac{1}{10}$ is lost to shrinkage and waste. If the total amount of material available for a job is 270 yards, how much *usable* material will be available?

$$270 \times \frac{1}{10} = 27 \qquad 270 - 27 = 243 \text{ yards}$$

41. Roland Finestein is paid $7.25 per hour. One week he worked the following schedule:

Monday	7 1/2 hrs.	Thursday	8.875 hrs.
Tuesday	9.25 hrs.	Friday	$10\frac{3}{5}$ hrs.
Wednesday	1.4 hrs.	Saturday	4.375 hrs.

Overtime pay does not begin until an employee has worked 44 hours in a week. Determine Roland's total pay for the week.

$$7\frac{1}{2} + 9\frac{1}{4} + 1\frac{2}{5} + 8\frac{7}{8} + 10\frac{3}{5} + 4\frac{3}{8} =$$

$$7\frac{20}{40} + 9\frac{10}{40} + 1\frac{16}{40} + 8\frac{35}{40} + 10\frac{24}{40} + 4\frac{10}{40} = 39\frac{120}{40} = 42$$

$$42 \times \$7.25 = \$304.50$$

42. Chou, Tran, and Phan went into business together. Chou owns $\frac{1}{6}$ of the business. Tran has $\frac{1}{9}$ of the partnership. What is Phan's ownership share?

$$\frac{1}{6} + \frac{1}{9} = \frac{3}{18} + \frac{2}{18} = \frac{5}{18} \qquad \frac{18}{18} - \frac{5}{18} = \frac{13}{18}$$

43. A data disk holds 1.44 MB of information in memory. If $.33\frac{1}{3}$ of the memory has been used, how many *more* MB of memory are available for use?

$$1.44 \times \frac{1}{3} = .48 \qquad 1.44 - .48 = .96$$

4

SOLVING FOR THE UNKNOWNS IN FORMULAS AND EQUATIONS

DESCARTES "WAS" BECAUSE OF ALGEBRA

Cogito, ergo sum, "I think, therefore I am," said French philosopher René Descartes (1596–1650).

The root for the word *algebra* is actually the Arabic word *al-jabru*, meaning "restoration." Algebra was already an ancient study when Descartes began his inquiry through a method called Cartesianism. Thousands of years earlier, Chinese, Persians, Indians, and Egyptians made practical use of the science in constructing roads and buildings.

But Descartes, who could not "doubt that he doubted," was the first to use the last letters of the alphabet to designate unknown quantities and the first letters to designate known ones.

He invented the method of indices (as in X^2) to express powers of numbers. Through his efforts Descartes raised the level of awareness of using decimal-based mathematical formulas and, in the end, ushered a change in the way European people would think ever after. By reducing the solutions of geometric problems to the solutions of algebraic ones, Descartes effectively caused people to reason algebraically instead of geometrically. By causing the shift toward and appreciation of a mathematics operating from base 10, Descartes set the stage for developing, among other things, a more rational system of weights and measures called the metric system.

Chapter Glossary

Infinite numbers. Both positive and negative numbers that continue without end.

Absolute value. The value of a number without regard to its sign. (The absolute value of both $+5$ and -5 is 5.)

Equation. An expression of an equal relationship that exists between two or more numbers.

Variables. Mathematical symbols or letters used to represent numbers.

Constants. Known numbers or values in formulas and equations.

Cross multiplication. Multiplying the numerator on one side of the equation by the denominator on the other side of the equation.

Formatting. Providing a guideline for solving word problems; a blueprint that aids in the search for particular concepts to solve formulas and equations.

LEARNING UNIT 1
POSITIVE AND NEGATIVE (SIGNED) NUMBERS

Almost daily we are confronted with both positive and negative numbers. A weather report may give you a winter temperature in one locale as 20° below zero and in another as 40° above zero. This could just as easily be expressed as a negative 20° and a positive 40°. Some businesses make money one month and lose money the next. It is then both convenient and necessary to understand that numbers can be expressed as either negative or positive.

On a straight line, a continuum, both positive and negative numbers can be illustrated as in Figure 4.1.

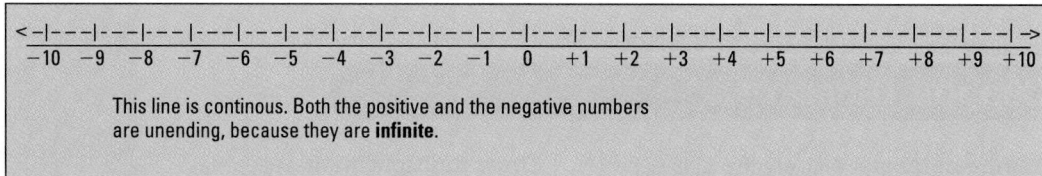

```
<-|---|---|---|---|---|---|---|---|---|---|---|---|---|---|---|---|---|---|---|---|->
 -10  -9  -8  -7  -6  -5  -4  -3  -2  -1   0  +1  +2  +3  +4  +5  +6  +7  +8  +9 +10
```

This line is continous. Both the positive and the negative numbers are unending, because they are **infinite**.

Figure 4.1
Positive and Negative Number Continuum

4.1 Adding Positive and Negative Numbers

Adding two positive numbers results in a positive sum (+5 added to +7 results in a sum of +12). Adding two negative numbers results in a negative sum (−5 added to −7 results in a sum of −12).

Adding numbers with mixed, or unlike, signs can result in a positive sum (as in example 1 below), a negative sum (as in example 2 below), or zero (as in example 3 below). Simply find the difference between the numbers and prefix the difference with the sign of the larger number. If several numbers are to be added, some with positive signs (*an unsigned number is always positive*) and some with negative signs, it may be necessary to add the numbers with like signs independently and then determine the difference between the two sums, prefixing the difference with the sign of the larger absolute value. The **absolute value** is the number itself without regard to its sign. The absolute value of both −5 and +5 is 5.

E X A M P L E 1   Add −2, +8, −16, −3, and +15.

Solution   Add numbers with like signs:

$$
\begin{array}{rr}
-\ 2 & +\ 8 \\
-16 & +\ 15 \\
\underline{-\ 3} & +\ 23 \\
-21 &
\end{array}
$$

Find the difference between the two sums and prefix the difference with the sign of the larger absolute value:

$$
\begin{array}{r}
+\ 23 \\
\underline{-\ 21} \\
+\ 2
\end{array}
$$

EXAMPLE 2   Add +28, −17, +3, −21, and −7.

Solution   Add numbers with like signs. Then find the difference between the two sums and prefix the difference with the sign of the larger absolute value:

$$
\begin{array}{rr}
+\,28 & -\,17 \\
+\,\ 3 & -\,21 \\
\hline
+\,31 & -\,\ 7 \\
& \hline
& -\,45 \\
\end{array}
\qquad
\begin{array}{r}
-\,45 \\
+\,31 \\
\hline
-\,14 \\
\end{array}
$$

Notice that the larger absolute value is placed in the top position regardless of its sign.

EXAMPLE 3   Add 47, −2, +20, −56, and −9.

Solution   Add numbers with like signs. Then find the difference between the two sums:

$$
\begin{array}{rr}
47 & -\,\ 2 \\
+20 & -56 \\
\hline
67 & -\,\ 9 \\
& \hline
& -67 \\
\end{array}
\qquad
\begin{array}{r}
67 \\
-67 \\
\hline
0 \\
\end{array}
$$

Zero is neither + nor − so it is left unsigned.

4.1 Practice Problems

Add the following:

1. −4, +6, −8
2. +3, −9, +10
3. −4, −5, −6, +4, −18, +3
4. 21, −65, +78, −99

4.1 Solutions to Practice Problems

$$
\textbf{1.}\quad
\begin{array}{r}
-\,4 \\
-\,8 \\
\hline
-12 \\
\end{array}
\quad
\begin{array}{r}
-12 \\
+\,6 \\
\hline
-\,6 \\
\end{array}
\qquad
\textbf{2.}\quad
\begin{array}{r}
+\,3 \\
+10 \\
\hline
+13 \\
\end{array}
\quad
\begin{array}{r}
+13 \\
-\,9 \\
\hline
+\,4 \\
\end{array}
\qquad
\textbf{3.}\quad
\begin{array}{r}
-\,4 \\
-\,5 \\
-\,6 \\
-18 \\
\hline
-33 \\
\end{array}
\quad
\begin{array}{r}
+4 \\
+3 \\
+7 \\
\end{array}
\quad
\begin{array}{r}
-33 \\
+\,7 \\
\hline
-26 \\
\end{array}
$$

$$
\textbf{4.}\quad
\begin{array}{r}
21 \\
+78 \\
\hline
+\,99 \\
\end{array}
\quad
\begin{array}{r}
-\,65 \\
-\,99 \\
\hline
-164 \\
\end{array}
\quad
\begin{array}{r}
-164 \\
+\,99 \\
\hline
-\,65 \\
\end{array}
$$

4.2 Multiplying Signed Numbers

Multiplying positive and negative numbers is not difficult if you remember the basic rules:

1. Numbers with like signs multiplied together result in a positive product (+ × + = + and − × − = +).
2. Numbers with unlike signs multiplied together result in a negative product (+ × − = − and − × + = −).

When multiplying signed numbers, they are often written without the times sign (×) because × is used as a symbol for a numeric value. Thus, for example, we might write (+6)(+8) or 6 · 8.

EXAMPLE   Multiply +6 by +8.

Solution $(+6)(+8) = +48$ *Like signs yield a positive product.*

EXAMPLE   Multiply −6 by −8.

Solution $(-6)(-8) = +48$ *Like signs yield a positive product.*

EXAMPLE   Multiply −6 by +8.

Solution $(-6)(+8) = -48$ *Unlike signs yield a negative product.*

EXAMPLE   Multiply +6 by −8.

Solution $(+6)(-8) = -48$ *Unlike signs yield a negative product.*

4.2 Practice Problems

Multiply the following (remember that an unsigned number is assumed to be positive):

1. (6)(7)   **2.** (6)(−7)
3. (−6)(7)   **4.** (−6)(−7)

4.2 Solutions to Practice Problems

1. $6 \cdot 7 = 42$ **2.** $6 \cdot -7 = -42$ **3.** $-6 \cdot 7 = -42$ **4.** $-6 \cdot -7 = 42$

4.3 Dividing Signed Numbers

Division follows exactly the same rules of signs as multiplication, since it is the opposite process:

1. Dividing like signed numbers results in a positive quotient ($+ \div + = +$ and $- \div - = +$).
2. Dividing unlike signed numbers results in a negative quotient ($+ \div - = -$ and $- \div + = -$).

EXAMPLE   Divide +6 by +2, which can be written $2\overline{)6}$, $6 \div 2$, 6/2, or $\dfrac{6}{2}$.

Solution $$\dfrac{6}{2} = +3$$ *Like signs yield positive quotients.*

EXAMPLE   Divide −6 by 2.

Solution $$\dfrac{-6}{2} = -3$$ *Unlike signs yield negative quotients.*

EXAMPLE   Divide −6 by −2.

Solution $$\dfrac{-6}{-2} = +3$$ *Like signs yield positive quotients.*

Chapter 4 Solving for the Unknowns in Formulas and Equations

EXAMPLE   Divide 6 by −2.

Solution $\dfrac{6}{-2} = -3$ *Unlike signs yield negative quotients.*

4.3 Practice Problems

1. $\dfrac{+18}{-3}$ 2. $-3\overline{)-18}$ 3. $18 \div 3$ 4. $\dfrac{-18}{+3}$

4.3 Solutions to Practice Problems
1. −6   2. 6   3. 6   4. −6

LEARNING UNIT 2
FORMULA AND EQUATION CONVERSION: SOLVING FOR THE UNKNOWN

Many business problems are solved with the aid of a formula or equation. Formulas or **equations** are ways of expressing equal relationships that always exist between two or more numbers. Therefore, an equation might state that $3 + 9 = 12$. It is entirely possible, however, that any of the "ingredients" of the equation could be unknown. That could be symbolized by:

$3 + 9 = ?$ *We would normally substitute* $3 + 9 = N$
$3 + ? = 12$ *a letter to represent the* $3 + N = 12$
$? + 9 = 12$ *unknown value* ⟶ $N + 9 = 12$

Instead of words, mathematical symbols or letters are frequently used to represent one or more numbers. These letters or symbols are **variables**. They represent the unknowns in formulas or equations. In the previous equations, for example, the unknown numbers represented by the letter N are variables. The known numbers (in the first equation, 3 and 9) are called **constants**. Unknown values are variables, and known values are constants.

A formula is often stated only in terms of variables. For example, the formula for computing simple interest is

$$I = P \times R \times T$$

This formula states that the interest (I) can always be determined by multiplying principal (P) by rate (R) and time (T). Any of the "ingredients" (I, P, R, or T) could be the unknown, or the variable. So long as the other three "ingredients" are known (that is, given in a problem statement as constants), the unknown value can be calculated.

Solving for Unknowns in Equations
To determine the unknown in any equation, the letter representing that variable must be *isolated* (left by itself) on one side of the equal sign, usually the left side. To isolate the unknown on one side of the equation, one or a series of operations (addition, subtraction, multiplication, division, inversion, and/or cross multiplication) may have to be done. *The equality of the equation must be maintained at all times*, meaning that *whatever is done to one side of the equation must also be done to the other side*. Maintaining the equality of an equation is possible by always doing the same thing to both sides of an equation. However, that process will not always solve the problem. *When an equation indicates a mathematical operation, the variable can be found by using the opposite mathematical process*. If the equation indicates addition, solve for the unknown by subtracting from both sides of the equation. If the equation process is multiplication, solve by using division.

4.4 | Equation Conversion Using Addition or Subtraction

If the same number is added to or subtracted from both sides of an equation, the equality is maintained.

EXAMPLE $8 + N = 29$

Solution N is our variable or unknown that is to be found. Addition is the equation process. The opposite mathematical process is subtraction. Thus, we need to subtract 8 from each side of the equation. (Remember, you want the unknown on one side of the equation— usually the left side—by itself. Thus, you must get rid of the 8 on the left of the equation and still maintain equality.)

$$\begin{array}{r} 8 + N = 29 \\ \underline{-\,8 \qquad\quad -8} \\ 0 + N = 21 \\ N = 21 \end{array}$$

Proof: Substitute the answer into the original equation: 8 + 21 = 29.

EXAMPLE $N - 8 = 29$

Solution We must find N. The equation process is subtraction. The opposite mathematical operation is addition.

$$\begin{array}{r} N - 8 = 29 \\ \underline{+\,8 \quad +8} \\ N \qquad = 37 \end{array}$$

Proof: 37 − 8 = 29

EXAMPLE Net sales of a business equal its gross sales minus sales returns. What were the gross sales of the Stephen Corporation if net sales were $125,000 and sales returns were $2,500?

Solution Using N for net sales, G for gross sales, and R for sales returns, the problem states that: $N = G - R$. (The actual letters selected to represent the parts of the problem are a matter of choice. One letter is not better than another, but it is helpful if the selection is easy to remember.) Our variable is gross sales (the unknown). By substituting the known values into the equation, we have

$$\$125{,}000 = G - \$2{,}500.$$

The equation process is subtraction. The opposite of subtraction is addition.

$$\begin{array}{l} \$125{,}000 = G - \$2{,}500 \\ \underline{+\;2{,}500 \qquad\; +\;2{,}500} \\ \$127{,}500 = G \end{array}$$

Since the variable is usually written on the left, we can now simply reverse the order and write the answer as $G = \$127{,}500$.

$$\text{Proof: } \$125{,}000 = \$127{,}500 - \$2{,}500$$

EXAMPLE Assets equal liabilities plus ownership equity. Determine the ownership equity if assets are $27,500 and liabilities are $18,750.

Solution Let : A = assets
L = liabilities
E = ownership equity
Then, $A = L + E$.

Chapter 4 Solving for the Unknowns in Formulas and Equations

Substitute the given numbers into the equation:

$$\$27,500 = \$18,750 + E$$

The equation process is addition. The opposite of addition is subtraction:

$$
\begin{array}{rl}
\$27,500 = & \$18,750 + E \\
-18,750 & -18,750 \\
\hline
\$\ \ 8,750 = & E
\end{array}
$$

$$E = \$8,750$$

Proof: $\$27,500 = \$18,750 + \$8,750$

4.4 Practice Problems

Find the unknowns in the following:

1. $A + 12 = 21$
2. $X - 5 = 82$
3. $N + 14 = 41$
4. $P + 36 - 10 = 43$

4.4 Solutions to Practice Problems

1.
$$
\begin{array}{rl}
A + 12 = & 21 \\
-12 & -12 \\
\hline
A\ \ \ = & 9
\end{array}
$$

2.
$$
\begin{array}{rl}
X - 5 = & 82 \\
+5 & +\ 5 \\
\hline
X\ \ \ = & 87
\end{array}
$$

3.
$$
\begin{array}{rl}
N + 14 = & 41 \\
-14 & -14 \\
\hline
N\ \ \ = & 27
\end{array}
$$

4.
$$
\begin{array}{rl}
P + 36 - 10 = & 43 \\
-36 + 10 = & -36 + 10 \\
\hline
P\ \ \ \ \ \ \ \ \ \ = & 7 + 10 \\
P\ \ \ \ \ \ \ \ \ \ = & 17
\end{array}
$$

4.5 Equation Conversion Using Multiplication or Division

If both sides of an equation are multiplied by or divided by the same number, equality is maintained. Remember that *when an equation indicates a mathematical operation, the variable can be found by using the opposite mathematical process.* If the equation process is multiplication, you must divide both sides of the equation. If the equation process is division, you must multiply both sides of the equation.

If you want to multiply 5 by N, you can so indicate by the following methods:

1. $5 \times N$ (This method can be confusing since the X could be a variable.)
2. $5 \cdot N$
3. $5(N)$
4. $(5)N$
5. $(5)(N)$
6. $5N$ (because of its simplicity this method is the one most often used)

EXAMPLE $5N = 35$. Find N.

Solution
$$\frac{\overset{1}{\cancel{5}}N}{\cancel{5}_1} = \frac{\overset{7}{\cancel{35}}}{\cancel{5}_1}$$

N *is being multiplied by 5. To remove the 5 from the left side of the equation, divide both sides by 5 and cancel.*

$$1N = 7 \qquad \textit{Perform the indicated operations.}$$
$$N = 7 \qquad \textit{1} \cdot N \textit{ is } N$$

Proof: $5 \cdot 7 = 35$ *Substitute 7 for* N *in the original equation.*

EXAMPLE $\dfrac{N}{5} = 35$. Find N.

Solution $\dfrac{N}{\cancel{5}} \cdot \dfrac{\overset{1}{\cancel{5}}}{1} = 35 \cdot 5$

N *is being divided by 5 in the original equation. To remove the 5 from the left side of the equation, multiply both sides by 5 and cancel.*

$N = 175$

Perform the indicated operations.

Proof: $\dfrac{175}{5} = 35$

Substitute 175 for N in the original equation.

EXAMPLE $P = BR$. Find R.

Solution R is the unknown we want to isolate. Since R is being multiplied by B in the original equation, then to remove B from the right side of the equation, divide both sides of the equation by B:

$$\dfrac{P}{B} = \dfrac{\overset{1}{\cancel{B}}R}{\underset{1}{\cancel{B}}}$$

Divide both sides by B and cancel.

$$\dfrac{P}{B} = R$$

Show result after cancellation.

$$R = \dfrac{P}{B}$$

Rewrite with the R on the left side of the equation.

Proof: $P = BR$

$$P = \dfrac{\overset{1}{\cancel{B}}}{1} \cdot \dfrac{P}{\underset{1}{\cancel{B}}}$$

Substitute $\dfrac{P}{B}$ for R in the original equation.

$$P = P$$

After cancellation.

EXAMPLE $T = \dfrac{D}{S}$. Find D.

Solution D is the unknown we want to isolate. It is divided by S in the original equation. To remove S from the right side of the equation, multiply both sides of the equation by S:

$$T = \dfrac{D}{S}$$

$$TS = \dfrac{D\overset{1}{\cancel{S}}}{\underset{1}{\cancel{S}}}$$

Multiply both sides by S and cancel.

$$TS = D$$

Perform indicated operations.

$$D = TS$$

Rewrite with the variable, D, on the left.

Proof: $T = \dfrac{D}{S}$

$$T = \frac{T\cancel{S}^{\,1}}{\cancel{S}_{\,1}}$$ *Substitute* TS *for* D *in the original equation and cancel.*

$$T = T$$ *After cancellation*

4.5 Practice Problems

Find the indicated unknowns:

1. $20N = 240$

2. $66 = \dfrac{Y}{96}$

3. $52Z = 416$

4. $NM = G$. Find M.

4.5 Solutions to Practice Problems

1. $\dfrac{\cancel{20}^{\,1} N}{\cancel{20}_{\,1}} = \dfrac{\cancel{240}^{\,12}}{\cancel{20}_{\,1}}$

$N = 12$

2. $66 \cdot 96 = \dfrac{Y}{\cancel{96}_{\,1}} \cdot \dfrac{\cancel{96}^{\,1}}{1}$

$Y = 6{,}336$

3. $\dfrac{\cancel{52}^{\,1} Z}{\cancel{52}_{\,1}} = \dfrac{\cancel{416}^{\,8}}{\cancel{52}_{\,1}}$

$Z = 8$

4. $\dfrac{\cancel{N}^{\,1} M}{\cancel{N}_{\,1}} = \dfrac{G}{N}$

$M = \dfrac{G}{N}$

4.6 Equation Conversion Using Inversion

Sometimes the unknown to be isolated is in the denominator of a fraction. For example, $\dfrac{1}{N} = \dfrac{1}{8}$. To find N we need to *invert* the equation (turn it upside down). Remember, what we do to one side of the equation we must do to both sides to maintain equality. Thus, when we invert, we get $\dfrac{N}{1} = \dfrac{8}{1}$, or $N = 8$. To prove our answer, we can substitute 8 for N in our original equation. We then have $\dfrac{1}{8} = \dfrac{1}{8}$. The important thing to keep in mind is that inversion is necessary only when the unknown variable is in the denominator of a fraction.

EXAMPLE $T = \dfrac{D}{S}$. Find S.

Solution Since S is in the denominator of the fraction, we can invert both sides of the equation. We will first put T over 1 and then proceed:

$$\frac{T}{1} = \frac{D}{S}$$ *Place* T *over 1 for clarity.*

$$\frac{1}{T} = \frac{S}{D}$$ *Invert both sides of the equation.* S *is still not isolated. To remove* D *from the right side of the equation, we must multiply both sides by* D.

$$\frac{1}{T} \cdot \frac{D}{1} = \frac{S}{\cancel{D}_{\,1}} \cdot \frac{\cancel{D}^{\,1}}{1}$$ *Multiply both sides of the equation by* D *and cancel.*

$$\frac{D}{T} = S$$ *Perform the indicated operations.*

$$S = \frac{D}{T}$$ *Rewrite so that the desired variable is on the left side of the equation.*

Find the indicated unknowns:

1. $\dfrac{270}{X} = 18$ **2.** $\dfrac{450}{N} = 18$ **3.** $\dfrac{527}{Y} = 17$ **4.** $\dfrac{R}{S} = T$. Find S.

4.6. Solutions to Practice Problems

1. $\dfrac{X}{270} = \dfrac{1}{18}$

$$\dfrac{X}{\cancel{270}^{\,1}} \cdot \dfrac{\cancel{270}^{\,1}}{1} = \dfrac{1}{\cancel{18}^{\,1}} \cdot \dfrac{\cancel{270}^{\,15}}{1}$$

$$X = 15$$

2. $\dfrac{N}{450} = \dfrac{1}{18}$

$$\dfrac{N}{\cancel{450}^{\,1}} \cdot \dfrac{\cancel{450}^{\,1}}{1} = \dfrac{1}{\cancel{18}^{\,1}} \cdot \dfrac{\cancel{450}^{\,25}}{1}$$

$$N = 25$$

3. $\dfrac{Y}{527} = \dfrac{1}{17}$

$$\dfrac{Y}{\cancel{527}^{\,1}} \cdot \dfrac{\cancel{527}^{\,1}}{1} = \dfrac{1}{\cancel{17}^{\,1}} \cdot \dfrac{\cancel{527}^{\,31}}{1}$$

$$Y = 31$$

4. $\dfrac{S}{R} = \dfrac{1}{T}$

$$\dfrac{S}{\cancel{R}^{\,1}} \cdot \dfrac{\cancel{R}^{\,1}}{1} = \dfrac{1}{T} \cdot \dfrac{R}{1}$$

$$S = \dfrac{R}{T}$$

4.7 | Equation Conversion Using Cross Multiplication

Finding the reciprocal sometimes can become a complicated procedure, especially if the equation involves several operations. An alternative method to solve for unknown variables when they appear as denominators in an equation is **cross multiplication**. Cross multiplication means multiplying the numerator on one side of the equation by the denominator on the other side of the equation.

EXAMPLE $\dfrac{1}{N} = \dfrac{1}{8}$. Find N.

Solution   To cross multiply:

Step 1. Multiply the denominator on the left side of the equation by the numerator on the right side (that will keep the unknown N on the left side of the equation).

Step 2. Then, multiply the numerator on the right by the denominator on the left:

Step 1	*Step 2*
$\dfrac{1}{N} \nearrow \dfrac{1}{8}$	$\dfrac{1}{N} \searrow \dfrac{1}{8}$

$$N \times 1 \quad = \quad 1 \times 8$$

$$N = 8$$

EXAMPLE $T = \dfrac{D}{S}$. Find S.

Solution S is the unknown and is a denominator. Therefore, cross multiply:

$$\dfrac{T}{1} \,\times\, \dfrac{D}{S} \qquad \textit{Multiply T} \times \textit{S and 1} \times \textit{D.}$$

$$TS = D$$

S has to be isolated:

$$\frac{\overset{1}{\cancel{T}} S}{\underset{1}{\cancel{T}}} = \frac{D}{T} \qquad \textit{Divide both sides by T and cancel.}$$

$$S = \frac{D}{T}$$

4.7 Practice Problems

1. $\dfrac{21}{N} = 7$ 2. $\dfrac{432}{B} = 36$ 3. $\dfrac{121}{V} = 11$ 4. $\dfrac{P}{B} = R$. Find B.

4.7 Solutions to Practice Problems

1. $\dfrac{21}{N} = \dfrac{7}{1}$

$7N = 21$

$$\frac{\overset{1}{\cancel{7}}N}{\underset{1}{\cancel{7}}} = \frac{\overset{3}{\cancel{21}}}{\underset{1}{\cancel{7}}}$$

$N = 3$

2. $\dfrac{432}{B} = \dfrac{36}{1}$

$36B = 432$

$$\frac{\overset{1}{\cancel{36}} B}{\underset{1}{\cancel{36}}} = \frac{\overset{12}{\cancel{432}}}{\underset{1}{\cancel{36}}}$$

$B = 12$

3. $\dfrac{121}{V} = \dfrac{11}{1}$

$11V = 121$

$$\frac{\overset{1}{\cancel{11}} V}{\underset{1}{\cancel{11}}} = \frac{\overset{11}{\cancel{121}}}{\underset{1}{\cancel{11}}}$$

$V = 11$

4. $\dfrac{P}{B} = \dfrac{R}{1}$

$BR = P$

$$\frac{B\overset{1}{\cancel{R}}}{\underset{1}{\cancel{R}}} = \frac{P}{R}$$

$B = \dfrac{P}{R}$

4.8   Solving Equations Using Multiple Arithmetic Operations

When solving equations requires several steps, perform addition and subtraction before multiplication and division.

E X A M P L E $5N + 18 = 43$. Find N.

Solution

$$
\begin{array}{rr}
5N + 18 = & 43 \\
- 18 & - 18 \\
\hline
5N \quad = & 25
\end{array}
$$
    Subtract 18 from both sides of the equation.

$$\frac{\overset{1}{\cancel{5}}N}{\underset{1}{\cancel{5}}} = \frac{\overset{5}{\cancel{25}}}{\underset{1}{\cancel{5}}}$$
    Next, divide both sides of the equation by 5 and cancel.

$N = 5$

Proof:

$5 \cdot 5 + 18 = 43$
$25 + 18 = 43$
$43 = 43$
    Substitute 5 for N in the original equation. When performing multiple arithmetic operations with known values, perform multiplication and division before addition and subtraction.

E X A M P L E $\dfrac{N}{228} - 12 = 7$

Solution

$$
\begin{array}{rr}
\dfrac{N}{228} - 12 = & 17 \\
+ 12 & + 12 \\
\hline
\dfrac{N}{228} \quad = & 19
\end{array}
$$
    Add 12 to both sides of the equation

$$\frac{N}{\cancel{228}_1} \cdot \frac{\cancel{228}^1}{1} = 19 \cdot 228$$ *Then, multiply both sides of the equation by 228 and cancel.*

$N = 4{,}332$

Proof:

$$\frac{4{,}332}{228} - 12 = 7$$ *Perform the indicated operations: divide 4,332 by 228 (= 19) and subtract 12 (19 − 12 = 7).*

$7 = 7$

Find the unknown variable in the following problems:

1. $2H - 17 = 89$ **2.** $9N + 48 = 102$ **3.** $\dfrac{N}{8} - 5 = 2$ **4.** $\dfrac{R}{12} + 34 = 286$

4.8 Solutions to Practice Problems

1.
$$\begin{array}{rl} 2H - 17 = & 89 \\ + 17 + & 17 \\ \hline 2H \quad = & 106 \end{array}$$

$$\frac{\cancel{2}^1 H}{\cancel{2}_1} = \frac{\cancel{106}^{53}}{\cancel{2}_1}$$

$H = 53$

2.
$$\begin{array}{rl} 9N + 48 = & 102 \\ - 48 \ - & 48 \\ \hline 9N \quad = & 54 \end{array}$$

$$\frac{\cancel{9}^1 N}{\cancel{9}_1} = \frac{\cancel{54}^6}{\cancel{9}_1}$$

$N = 6$

3.
$$\begin{array}{rl} \dfrac{N}{8} - 5 = & 2 \\ + 5 + & 5 \\ \hline \dfrac{N}{8} \quad = & 7 \end{array}$$

$$\frac{N}{\cancel{8}_1} \cdot \frac{\cancel{8}^1}{1} = 7 \cdot 8$$

$N = 56$

4.
$$\begin{array}{rl} \dfrac{R}{12} + 34 = & 286 \\ - 34 \ - & 34 \\ \hline \dfrac{R}{12} \quad = & 252 \end{array}$$

$$\frac{R}{\cancel{12}_1} \cdot \frac{\cancel{12}^1}{1} = 252 \cdot 12$$

$R = 3{,}024$

4.9 Solving Equations by Combining Like Unknowns

To solve equations with like unknowns, you first combine them and then solve the equation by performing the opposite arithmetic process.

EXAMPLE $4A + 8 - A = 38$. Find A.

Solution   First, combine unknowns:

$$\begin{array}{r} 4A \\ - 1A \\ \hline 3A \end{array}$$ *Note that A is 1A. If there is no number in front of a letter, it is a 1.*

$3A + 8 = 38$

Next, perform the necessary operations to isolate the variable unknown as in previous sections.

$$\begin{array}{rl} 3A + 8 = & 38 \\ - 8 \ - & 8 \\ \hline 3A \quad = & 30 \end{array}$$ *Subtract 8 from both sides of the equation.*

$$\frac{\cancel{3}^1 A}{\cancel{3}_1} = \frac{\cancel{30}^{10}}{\cancel{3}_1}$$ *Divide both sides of the equation by 3 and cancel.*

$A = 10$

Proof:

$$4A + 8 - A = 38$$ *Substitute the answer into the original equation.*
$$4 \cdot 10 + 8 - 10 = 38$$
$$40 + 8 - 10 = 38$$
$$38 = 38$$

Remember that when you have a combination of mathematical operations with numbers, perform the multiplication and division before you do the addition and subtraction.

4.9 Practice Problems

1. $3N + N = 20$ **2.** $6N - 2N = 36$ **3.** $12A - A + 3A = 56$ **4.** $8G = 4G + 12$

4.9 Solutions to Practice Problems

1. $4N = 20$

2. $4N = 36$

3. $14A = 56$

4. $8G = 4G + 12$
$$\underline{-4G \quad -4G}$$
$$4G = \qquad 12$$

1.
$$\frac{\overset{1}{\cancel{4}}N}{\underset{1}{\cancel{4}}} = \frac{\overset{5}{\cancel{20}}}{\underset{1}{\cancel{4}}}$$
$$N = 5$$

2.
$$\frac{\overset{1}{\cancel{4}}N}{\underset{1}{\cancel{4}}} = \frac{\overset{9}{\cancel{36}}}{\underset{1}{\cancel{4}}}$$
$$N = 9$$

3.
$$\frac{\overset{1}{\cancel{14}}A}{\underset{1}{\cancel{14}}} = \frac{\overset{4}{\cancel{56}}}{\underset{1}{\cancel{14}}}$$
$$A = 4$$

4.
$$\frac{\overset{1}{\cancel{4}}G}{\underset{1}{\cancel{4}}} = \frac{\overset{3}{\cancel{12}}}{\underset{1}{\cancel{4}}}$$
$$G = 3$$

4.10 Parentheses and Brackets

Some problems have problems within the problem. Such problems are set apart by parentheses ( ) or by brackets [ ]. The purpose of the parentheses or brackets is to guide you toward the order of the solution to the problem. If included, the order of operation should be as follows:

1. Solve the portion of the problem within the parentheses.
2. Solve the portion within the brackets.
3. Finally, solve the portion outside the brackets and/or parentheses.

EXAMPLE $N = 3[(4 + 5)(7 + 1)]$. Find N.

Solotion
$$N = 3[(9)(8)]$$
$$N = 3[72]$$
$$N = 216$$

With some problems, the portion of the problem inside the parentheses or brackets cannot be fully solved before a mathematical operation must be performed to solve an equation.

EXAMPLE $5(N - 3) = 90$

Solution The portion $N - 3$, which is inside the parentheses, cannot be further solved. Thus, we will multiply each item in the parentheses by the 5. That would result in $5N - 15$, and it still equals 90. Thus, $5N - 15 = 90$. Now the problem can be solved using the processes from previous sections of this chapter:

$$5N - 15 = \qquad 90$$
$$\underline{+ 15 \quad + \ 15}$$
$$5N \qquad = \qquad 105$$

$$\frac{\overset{1}{\cancel{5}N}}{\underset{1}{\cancel{5}}} = \frac{\overset{21}{\cancel{105}}}{\underset{1}{\cancel{5}}}$$

$$N = 21$$

Proof:

$$5(21 - 3) = 90 \qquad \textit{Substitute 21 for N in the original equation and solve.}$$

$$5(18) = 90$$

$$90 = 90$$

4.10 Practice Problems

Solve for the unknown in the following problems:

1. $8(H + 20) = 200$
2. $4[2(X - 3) + (4X - 4)] = 56$
3. $3(M - 7) = (4M - 47)(3 \cdot 5)$
4. $2R = 2(3 - 4R) + 2(R + 5)$

4.10 Solutions to Practice Problems

1. $8H + 160 = 200$

$$\underline{ -160 \quad -160}$$

$$8H \quad = \quad 40$$

$$\frac{\overset{1}{\cancel{8}}H}{\underset{1}{\cancel{8}}} = \frac{\overset{5}{\cancel{40}}}{\underset{1}{\cancel{8}}}$$

$$H = 5$$

2. $4[2X - 6 + 4X - 4] = 56$

$$8X - 24 + 16X - 16 = 56$$

$$24X - 40 = 56$$

$$\underline{ +40 \quad +40}$$

$$24X \quad = \quad 96$$

$$\frac{\overset{1}{\cancel{24}}X}{\underset{1}{\cancel{24}}} = \frac{\overset{4}{\cancel{96}}}{\underset{1}{\cancel{24}}}$$

$$X = 4$$

3. $3M - 21 = (4M - 47)(15)$

$$3M - 21 = 60M - 705$$

$$\underline{-3M -3M}$$

$$-21 = 57M - 705$$

$$\underline{+705 +705}$$

$$684 = 57M$$

$$\frac{\overset{12}{\cancel{684}}}{\underset{1}{\cancel{57}}} = \frac{\overset{1}{\cancel{57}}M}{\underset{1}{\cancel{57}}}$$

$$M = 12$$

4. $2R = 6 - 8R + 2R + 10$

$$2R = 16 - 8R + 2R$$

$$2R = 16 - 6R$$

$$\underline{+6R +6R}$$

$$8R = 16$$

$$\frac{\overset{1}{\cancel{8}}R}{\underset{1}{\cancel{8}}} = \frac{\overset{2}{\cancel{16}}}{\underset{1}{\cancel{8}}}$$

$$R = 2$$

4.11 Writing Equations

Now that you have learned to solve for the unknown variable in an equation, you should learn to write equations. The best way to learn this is through repetition. With effort the concepts become clear. With confidence successes will be more frequent, and before you know it, you will be able to write and solve equations consistently.

This section is somewhat different from others in this chapter. Instead of solving problems, you will write equations. You are urged to cover the answers, write your answers, and then compare. Remember, repetition and perseverance are the keys to success.

4.11 Practice Problems

Problems Without Final Solutions. *You need only write the equations for the following statements, although you may want to solve them for practice. Use N to represent the unknown variable.*

1. What number increased by 60 gives 90?
2. What number decreased by 14 gives 27?
3. What number multiplied by 8 gives 56?
4. What number divided by 90 gives 40?

Chapter 4 Solving for the Unknowns in Formulas and Equations

4.11 Solutions to Practice Problems

1. $N + 60 = 90$ 2. $N - 14 = 27$ 3. $8N = 56$ 4. $\dfrac{N}{90} = 40$

4.11
Practice
Problems

Problems with Final Solutions. *You need to write the equations and solve the following problems.*

1. What number less 40 equals 49?
2. What number added to 31 is 57?
3. Some number times 13 is 39.
4. A number divided by 7 is 5.

4.11 Solutions to Practice Problems

1. $N - 40 = 49$ $N - 40 + 40 = 49 + 40$ $N = 89$
2. $N + 31 = 57$ $N + 31 - 31 = 57 - 31$ $N = 26$
3. $13N = 39$ $13\dfrac{N}{13} = \dfrac{39}{13}$ $N = 3$
4. $\dfrac{N}{7} = 5$ $\dfrac{N}{7} \cdot \dfrac{7}{1} = 5 \cdot 7$ $N = 35$

LEARNING UNIT 3
FORMATTING

As you learned in Chapter 1, a format is a useful tool for gaining an understanding of mathematics. When searching for an unknown in an equation, you will find formatting even more valuable than with the more basic material.

4.12 Using Formatting to Solve for the Unknowns in Equations

The recommended format for solving equations is in Figure 4.2. Of the four parts to the format, one may not be used in any given problem. The inclusion of price as one of the parts to the format, even though it is not used in all problems, is easier than having to memorize two formats and when to use which. If price is not used, then that column will be blank.

Figure 4.2.
Format for Solving Equations

Unknown(s)	Variable(s)	Price	Formula or Equation

Unknowns
What are we trying to find? Generally, the final question in a problem will ask for a certain item or items and thus reveal the unknown or unknowns.

Variables
The unknown or unknowns are assigned a letter to designate them. We usually choose a letter that will remind us of the unknown. For example, if we are trying to find profits, we would probably choose the letter P. The letter chosen is a matter of individual choice and is not right or wrong. When more than one unknown has to be designated by a variable, we use a single letter variable for the unknown being used as a reference. The other unknown is then set up using the same letter. For example if Becky is twice

as old as Todd, Todd's age could be set up as A (for age). That is because Becky's age is in reference to Todd's age. Becky's age would then be set up as $2A$ (for twice as old).

Price

Frequently, unknowns are stated as the number of units of a product being sold. For example, we might have a problem that states that a movie theater sold twice as many colas as bags of popcorn. The word *many* indicates units. In the next sentence of the problem, the prices of each product may be given, and the final question may be stated in dollar (price) terms. For example, the problem might go on to say: The price of colas was $.50 per cup and the popcorn sold for $.75 per bag. If total sales were $687.50, how many bags of popcorn were sold? We will get to the solution of the problem later. What is important now is to notice that price times quantity must be used to obtain total sales. Price, therefore, must become part of the format.

Formula or Equation

Last comes the tricky part. You need to write the equation to solve the problem. You must pay attention to certain key words in the problem. *Total*, for example, means that addition is to take place. *Difference* would indicate subtraction. The word *per* almost always indicates division, and the word *of* when used in a problem statement such as "nine-tenths of the students," indicates multiplication. The important thing is to set up an equality that contains only one unknown letter. Let us now look at several examples of problems that can be solved using the format.

Problems Using Addition

EXAMPLE   In 7 years, Jan will be 18. How old is she now?

Solution

Unknown(s)	Variable(s)	Price	Formula or Equation
Jan's current age	A		$A + 7 = 18$

Jan's age now is A. In 7 years, she will be $A + 7$. According to the information in the problem she will be 18 in 7 years, so $A + 7 = 18$.

$$\begin{array}{rcl} A + 7 &=& 18 \\ -7 & & -7 \\ \hline A &=& 11 \end{array}$$ *Jan's age now*

Problems Using Subtraction

EXAMPLE   Halverson's Hardware is experiencing difficulties this year. Profits are $12,000 less this year than they were last year. This year's profits are $45,000. What were they last year?

Solution

Unknown(s)	Variable(s)	Price	Formula or Equation
Last year's profits	P		$P - \$12,000 = \$45,000$

Our desired unknown is last year's profits, P.
This year's profits are given in two ways: $12,000 less than last year's and $45,000. Since they represent the same thing, they must be equal:

$$P - \$12,000 = \$45,000$$
$$\underline{+ \$12,000 \quad + \$12,000} \quad \text{\textit{Add \$12,000 to each side.}}$$
$$P \quad\quad = \$57,000 \quad \text{\textit{Last year's profits}}$$

Problems Using Multiplication

E X A M P L E   Nine-tenths of the students in business math find that formatting problems helps them to get correct answers to problems on formulas and equations. If a class has 50 students in it, how many will be helped by formatting?

Solution

Unknown(s)	Variable(s)	Price	Formula or Equation
Students Helped	H		$H = \dfrac{9}{10} \cdot 50$

$$H = \frac{9}{\cancel{10}_{1}} \cdot \frac{\cancel{50}^{5}}{1} \quad \text{\textit{Cancel.}}$$

$$H = 45 \quad \text{\textit{Students helped}}$$

Problems Using Division

E X A M P L E   A car gets 26 miles per gallon of gasoline. If a trip covered 780 miles, how many gallons of gasoline were required?

Solution

Unknown(s)	Variable(s)	Price	Formula or Equation
Gallons of gas	G		$G = \dfrac{780}{26}$

$$G = \frac{780}{26} \quad \text{\textit{Divide.}}$$
$$G = 30 \text{ gallons of gasoline}$$

Problems Finding the Whole When Part Is Known

E X A M P L E   Martin received his paycheck today. His deductions were $.33\frac{1}{3}$ of his total pay. If the deductions were $423, what was Martin's gross pay?

Solution

Unknown(s)	Variable(s)	Price	Formula or Equation
Martin's gross pay	P		$.33\frac{1}{3} P = \$423$

$$.33\tfrac{1}{3} = \frac{1}{3} \quad \text{\textit{Remember aliquot parts.}}$$

thus, $\frac{1}{3}P = \$423$ *Substitute aliquot part.*

$$\frac{\cancel{3}^{1}}{1} \cdot \frac{P}{\cancel{3}_{1}} = \$423 \cdot 3$$ *Multiply both sides of the equation by 3 and cancel.*

$P = \$1,269$ *Martin's gross pay*

Problems With Two or More Unknowns

E X A M P L E   Schlosky's Inc. had utility bills totaling $17,300 this month. The gas bill was three times as much as the electric bill, and the water bill was $2,300 less than the gas bill. Calculate the amount of each utility bill.

Solution

Unknown(s)	Variable(s)	Price	Formula or Equation
Electric bill	E		$1E$
Gas bill	$3E$		$3E$
Water bill	$3E - \$2,300$		$+ \quad 3E - \$2,300$
			$\$17,300$

$$1E + 3E + 3E - \$2,300 = \$17,300$$

$7E - \$2,300 = \quad \$17,300$ *Combine like terms.*
$\underline{+ \$2,300 \quad + \quad 2,300}$ *Add $2,300 to both sides.*
$7E \qquad = \quad \$19,600$

$$\frac{\cancel{7}^{1}E}{\cancel{7}_{1}} = \frac{\overset{2,800}{\cancel{\$19,600}}}{\cancel{7}}$$ *Divide both sides by 7 and cancel.*

$E = \qquad\qquad \$\;2,800$ *Electric bill*
$3E = \qquad\qquad \$\;8,400$ *Gas bill*
$3E - \$\;2,300 = \underline{\$\;6,100}$ *Water bill*
Total $\qquad\qquad \$17,300$

Problems Calculating Unit and Dollar Values When Total Units Are Not Given

E X A M P L E   A theater sold four times as many colas as bags of popcorn. Each cup of cola sells for $ .50 and popcorn sells for $ .75 a box. Total sales amounted to $687.50. Determine the unit and dollar amount of sales for each product.

Solution

Unknown(s)	Variable(s)	Price	Formula or Equation
Popcorn	P	$ .75	$\$ \qquad .75P$
Colas	$4P$	$ .50	$+ \; 4P (\$ .50)$
			$\$ \; 687.50$

$$\$ .75P + 4P(\$ .50) = \$687.50$$

$\$ .75P + \$2P = \$687.50$ *Multiply $4P \cdot \$ .50$.*

$\$ 2.75P = \$687.50$ *Combine like terms.*

Chapter 4 Solving for the Unknowns in Formulas and Equations

$$\frac{\overset{1}{\cancel{\$2.75}P}}{\underset{1}{\cancel{\$2.75}}} = \frac{\overset{250}{\cancel{\$687.50}}}{\underset{1}{\cancel{2.75}}}$$ *Divide both sides by $2.75 and cancel.*

$P = 250$ *bags of popcorn (unit sales)*

$4P = 1{,}000$ *cups of cola (unit sales)*

$250 \cdot \$.75 = \$187.50$ *(popcorn dollar sales)*
$1{,}000 \cdot \$.50 = \underline{\$500.00}$ *(cola dollar sales)*
Total $\$687.50$

Problems Calculating Unit and Dollar Values When Total Units Are Given

EXAMPLE   A theater sold 1,250 total cups of cola and bags of popcorn. Each cup of cola sells for $.50 and popcorn sells for $.75 a box. Total sales amounted to $687.50. Determine the unit and dollar amount of sales for each product.

Solution   When the total units are known, but not the exact relationship of one product's units to the units of the other product, either can be set up as the single unknown variable. However, in order to keep calculations in positive numbers, you should always set the higher value item up as the single letter variable. Thus, in this problem, popcorn is set up as the variable to which cola will be referenced.

The total number of units sold were 1,250. If P of them are bags of popcorn, then the remainder (or $1{,}250 - P$) must be cups of cola.

Unknown(s)	Variable(s)	Price	Formula or Equation
Popcorn	P	$ .75	$ .75P
Cola	$1{,}250 - P$	$ .50	$ .50(1{,}250 - P)
			$\overline{\$687.50}$

$$\$.75P + \$.50(1{,}250 - P) = \$687.50$$

$\$.75P + \$625 - \$.50P = \$687.50$ *Multiply $.50 · 1,250 and $.50 · P.*

$\$.25P + \$625 = \$687.50$ *Combine like terms.*
$\underline{\quad\quad - \$625 - \$625.00}$ *Subtract $625 from both sides.*
$\$.25P \quad\quad = \$\ \ 62.50$

$$\frac{\overset{1}{\cancel{\$25}P}}{\underset{1}{\cancel{\$25}}} = \frac{\overset{250}{\cancel{\$62.50}}}{\underset{1}{\cancel{\$25}}}$$ *Divide both sides by $.25 and cancel.*

$P = 250$ *bags of popcorn (unit sales)*

$1{,}250 - 250 = 1{,}000$ *cups of cola (unit sales)*

$250 \cdot \$.75 = \$187.50$ *(popcorn dollar sales)*
$1{,}000 \cdot \$.50 = \underline{\$500.00}$ *(cola dollar sales)*
Total $\$687.50$

4.12 Practice Problems

1. Michelle is 12 years older than her friend Joan. She is 57; how old is Joan?
2. Sales have increased by $22,500 over last year. Last year's sales were $158,050. Find this year's sales.

3. Drvnkoy's Jewelry Store changed inventory valuation methods. It resulted in the inventory being valued at .85 of the original value. If the original valuation was for $3,234,000, what is the new valuation?

4. What number divided by 27 equals 243?

4.12 Solutions to Practice Problems

1.

Unknown(s)	Variable(s)	Price	Formula or Equation
Joan's age	A		
Michelle's age	$A + 12$		$A + 12 = 57$

$$
\begin{array}{rl}
A + 12 = & 57 \\
-12 & -12 \\
\hline
A \quad\; = & 45 \quad \textit{Joan's age}
\end{array}
$$

2.

Unknown(s)	Variable(s)	Price	Formula or Equation
Last year's sales	S		$S = \$158{,}050$
This year's sales	$S + \$22{,}500$		

$$S + \$22{,}500 = \qquad \textit{This year's sales}$$
$$\$158{,}050 + \$22{,}500 = \$180{,}550 \qquad \textit{This year's sales}$$

3.

Unknown(s)	Variable(s)	Price	Formula or Equation
Original value	V		$V = \$3{,}234{,}000$
New value	$.85V$		

$$.85V = \qquad \textit{New value}$$
$$.85 \cdot \$3{,}234{,}000 = \$2{,}748{,}900 \qquad \textit{New valuation}$$

4.

Unknown(s)	Variable(s)	Price	Formula or Equation
Some number	N		
New number	$N/27$		$N/27 = 243$

$$\frac{N}{27} = 243$$

$$\frac{N}{\cancel{27}} \cdot \frac{\cancel{27}^{\,1}}{1} = 243 \cdot 27$$

$$N = 6{,}561$$

Page	Section Topic	Learning Concepts	Examples and Solutions
102	**4.1** Adding Positive and Negative Numbers	**1.** Adding positive numbers results in sums that are positive. **2.** Adding negative numbers results in sums that are negative. **3.** Adding numbers with mixed signs can result in either a positive or a negative sum, or zero.	**1.** $\begin{array}{r} +\ 21 \\ +\ 39 \\ \underline{+\ \ 4} \\ +\ 64 \end{array}$ **2.** $\begin{array}{r} -\ 19 \\ -\ 58 \\ \underline{-\ \ 7} \\ -\ 84 \end{array}$ **3.** $\begin{array}{rr} -\ 30 & +\ 30 \\ \underline{+\ 21} & \underline{-\ 21} \\ -\ \ 9 & +\ \ 9 \end{array}$ $\begin{array}{r} 12 \\ \underline{-\ 12} \\ 0 \end{array}$
103	**4.2** Multipliying Signed Numbers	**1.** Numbers with like signs multiplied together result in a positive product. **2.** Numbers with unlike signs multiplied together result in negative product.	**1.** $\begin{array}{rr} +\ 5 & -\ 5 \\ \underline{\times +\ 8} & \underline{\times -\ 8} \\ +\ 40 & +\ 40 \end{array}$ **2.** $\begin{array}{rr} +\ 5 & -\ 5 \\ \underline{\times -\ 8} & \underline{\times +\ 8} \\ -\ 40 & -\ 40 \end{array}$
104	**4.3** Dividing Signed Numbers	**1.** Dividing like signed numbers results in a positive quotient. **2.** Dividing unlike signed numbers result in a negative quotient.	**1.** $\dfrac{+\ 40}{+\ 8} = +5 \qquad \dfrac{-\ 40}{-\ 8} = +5$ **2.** $\dfrac{+\ 40}{-\ 8} = -5 \qquad \dfrac{-\ 40}{+\ 8} = -5$
106	**4.4** Equation Conversion Using Addition or Subtraction	If the same number is added to or subtracted from both sides of an equation, the equality is maintained.	$\begin{array}{rr} N + 231 = & 387 \\ \underline{-\ 231\quad} & \underline{-\ 231} \\ N\qquad = & 156 \end{array}$ $\qquad$ $\begin{array}{rr} N - 231 = & 156 \\ \underline{+\ 231\quad} & \underline{+231} \\ N\qquad = & 387 \end{array}$
107	**4.5** Equation Conversion Using Multiplication or Division	If both sides of an equation are multiplied or divided by the same number, equality is maintained.	$8N = 40$ $\dfrac{\overset{1}{\cancel{8}}\,N}{\underset{1}{\cancel{8}}} = \dfrac{\overset{5}{\cancel{40}}}{\underset{1}{\cancel{8}}}$ $N = 5$ $\dfrac{N}{8} = 5$ $\dfrac{\overset{1}{\cancel{8}}\,N}{\underset{1}{\cancel{8}}} = 5 \cdot 8$ $N = 40$	*Divide both sides of the equation by 8 to isolate the unknown and solve the equation.* *Multiply both sides of the equation by 8 to isolate the unknown and solve the equation.*

Page	Section Topic	Learning Concepts	Examples and Solutions	
109	**4.6** Equation Conversion Using Inversion	If the unknown variable is in the denominator of a fraction, we can use inversion as the first step toward solving the equation.	$\dfrac{14}{N} = 7$ $\dfrac{N}{14} = \dfrac{1}{7}$	*Invert both sides. Multiply both sides by 14 and cancel:*
			$\dfrac{\overset{1}{\cancel{14}}}{1} \cdot \dfrac{N}{\underset{1}{\cancel{14}}} = \dfrac{1}{\underset{1}{\cancel{7}}} \cdot \dfrac{\overset{2}{\cancel{14}}}{1}$	
			$N = 2$	
110	**4.7** Equation Conversion Using Cross Multiplication	Solving for unknown variables in the denominator of an equation can also be accomplished by cross multiplication.	$\dfrac{14}{N} = 2$	*Put the 2 over the 1.*
			$\dfrac{14}{N} = \dfrac{2}{1}$	
			$2N = 14$	*Cross Multiply.*
			$\dfrac{\overset{1}{\cancel{2}}N}{\underset{1}{\cancel{2}}} = \dfrac{\overset{7}{\cancel{14}}}{\underset{1}{\cancel{2}}}$	*Divide both sides by 2 and cancel.*
			$N = 7$	
111	**4.8** Solving Equations Using Multiple Arithmetic Operations	When several steps are required to isolate an unknown, perform addition and subtraction before multiplication and division.	$4N - 32 = 16$ $\begin{aligned} 4N - 32 &= 16 \\ \underline{+32} \quad & \underline{+32} \\ 4N &= 48 \end{aligned}$	
			$\dfrac{\overset{1}{\cancel{4}}N}{\underset{1}{\cancel{4}}} = \dfrac{\overset{12}{\cancel{48}}}{\underset{1}{\cancel{4}}}$	
			$N = 12$	
112	**4.9** Solving Equations by Combining Like Unknowns	When equations contain several like unknowns, combine them first and then solve the equation.	$5N + N = 36$ $6N = 36$	
			$\dfrac{\overset{1}{\cancel{6}}N}{\underset{1}{\cancel{6}}} = \dfrac{\overset{6}{\cancel{36}}}{\underset{1}{\cancel{6}}}$	
			$N = 6$	
113	**4.10** Parentheses and Brackets	Parentheses or brackets guide you toward the order of the solution to the problem. The order of operation is: 1. Solve the portion of the problem within the parentheses. 2. Solve the portion within the brackets. 3. Solve the portion outside the brackets and/or the parentheses.	$N = [(2 + 8) - 3]$ $N = [10 - 3]$ $N = 7$ $N = 6(5 + 3)(6 - 2)$ $N = 6(8)(4)$ $N = 6 \cdot 8 \cdot 4$ $N = 192$	

Page	Section Topic	Learning Concepts	Examples and Solutions
114	**4.11** Writing Equations	When writing equations, repetition and perseverance are the keys to success.	What number added to 19 totals 75? What number (N) added to ($+$) 19 totals 75? $$\begin{aligned} N + 19 &= 75 \\ -19 &\ -19 \\ N &= 56 \end{aligned}$$
115	**4.12** Using Formatting to Solve for the Unknowns in Equations	Formatting is a concept that aids in problem solution. The recommended format is:	

Unknown(s)	Variable(s)	Price	Formula or Equation

Unknown(s)	Variable(s)	Price	Formula or Equation
Al's age	A		$A + 7 = 21$

Problems Using Addition
In seven years Al will be 21. How old is he now?

$$\begin{aligned} A + 7 &= 21 \\ -7 &\ -7 \\ A &= 14 \end{aligned}$$

Unknown(s)	Variable(s)	Price	Formula or Equation
Lake depth	D		$D - 12 = 22$

Problems Using Subtraction
The water level in a lake is down 12 feet from its average depth. Now it is 22 feet deep. Find average depth.

$$\begin{aligned} D - 12 &= 22 \\ +12 &\ +12 \\ D &= 34 \end{aligned}$$

Unknown(s)	Variable(s)	Price	Formula or Equation
Last year's profit's	P		$2P = \$40,000$

Problems Using Multiplication
Sally's profits are double last year's. This year's profits are $40,000. Calculate last year's.

$$2P = \$40,000$$

$$\frac{\overset{1}{2}P}{\underset{1}{\cancel{2}}} = \frac{\overset{\$20,000}{\cancel{\$40,000}}}{\underset{1}{\cancel{2}}}$$

$$P = \$\,20,000$$

Page	Section Topic	Learning Concepts	Examples and Solutions

Unknown(s)	Variable(s)	Price	Formula or Equation
Points earned	P		$\dfrac{P}{500} = .87$

Problems Using Division A student's final course average was determined by dividing the points earned on exams by the total points possible. If Sam had a final average of .87 and the total points possible were 500, how many points did he earn on exams?

$$\frac{P}{\overset{1}{\cancel{500}}} \cdot \frac{\overset{1}{\cancel{500}}}{1} = .87 \cdot 500$$

$$P = 435$$

Unknown(s)	Variable(s)	Price	Formula or Equation
List Price	L		$\dfrac{3L}{4} = \$210$

Problems Finding the Whole When Part Is Known

A wholesaler is required to pay $\frac{3}{4}$ of the list price of a table. It receives a bill for $210. What is the amount of the list price?

$$\frac{3L}{4} = \$210$$

$$\frac{\overset{1}{\cancel{4}}}{\cancel{3}} \times \frac{\overset{1}{\cancel{3}}L}{\cancel{4}} = \frac{\overset{70}{\cancel{\$210}}}{1} \cdot \frac{4}{\cancel{3}}$$

$$L = \$280$$

Unknown(s)	Variable(s)	Price	Formula or Equation
Steve's inv.	I		I
Jon's inv.	$2I$		$2I$
Karen's Inv.	$2I + \$15,000$		$\underline{+\ 2I + \$15,000}$
			$\$300,000$

Problems With Two or More Unknowns
Jon, Karen, and Steve are partners in a business. Jon has invested twice as much as Steve, and Karen has invested $15,000 more than Jon. The total investment is $300,000. Determine the investment amount for each partner.

$$I + 2I + 2I + \$15,000 = \$300,000$$

$$
\begin{array}{rcr}
5I + \$15,000 & = & \$300,000 \\
-\ \$15,000 & & -\ \$15,000 \\
\hline
5I & = & \$285,000
\end{array}
$$

$$\frac{\overset{1}{\cancel{5}}I}{\underset{1}{\cancel{5}}} = \frac{\overset{57,000}{\cancel{\$285,000}}}{\underset{1}{\cancel{5}}}$$

$I =$	$\$57,000$	Steve's investment
$2I =$	$\$114,000$	Jon's investment
$2I + \$15,000 =$	$\underline{\$129,000}$	Karen's investment
	$\$300,000$	Total

Page	Section Topic	Learning Concepts	Examples and Solutions

Unknown(s)	Variable(s)	Price	Formula or Equation
Egg dish	E	$5	$ 5E
Pancakes	$3E$	$4	+ $12E
			$23,800

Problems Calculating Unit and Dollar Values When Total Units Are Not Given
Julio Orancha's Diner serves two breakfast specialties. The egg dish costs $5, and the pancake speciality is $4. Julio's sold 3 times as many pancake specialties as egg specialties. Total sales revenue for the two dishes for the week were $23,800. Calculate both the number of each dish sold and the dollar value of each dish.

$$\$5E + \$12E = \$23,800$$

$$\$17E = \$23,800$$

$$\frac{\cancel{\$17}^{1}E}{\cancel{\$17}_{1}} = \frac{\cancel{\$23,800}^{1,400}}{\cancel{\$17}_{1}}$$

$$E = 1,400 \text{ egg orders}$$

$$3E = 4,200 \text{ pancake orders}$$

$$1,400 \cdot \$5 = \$ 7,000$$

$$4,200 \cdot \$4 = \$16,800$$

Unknown(s)	Variable(s)	Price	Formula or Equation
Egg dish	E	$5	$5E
Pancakes	$5,600 - E$	$4	+ $4(5,600 − E)
			$23,800

Problems Calculating Unit and Dollar Values When Total Units Are Given
Julio Orancha's Diner serves two breakfast specialties. The egg dish costs $5, and the pancake speciality is $4. Julio's sold a total of 5,600 specialty dishes. Total sales revenue for the two dishes for the week were $23,800. Calculate both the number of each dish sold and the dollar value of each dish.

$$\$5E + \$4(5,600 - E) = \$23,800$$

$$\$5E + \$22,400 - \$4E = \$23,800$$

$$\$1E + \$22,400 = \$23,800$$
$$\underline{\quad - \$22,400 \quad -\$22,400}$$
$$E \qquad = \$ 1,400$$

$$E = 1,400 \text{ egg orders}$$

$$5,600 - 1,400 = 4,200 \text{ pancake orders}$$

$$1,400 \cdot \$5 = \$7,000$$

$$4,200 \cdot \$4 = \$16,800$$

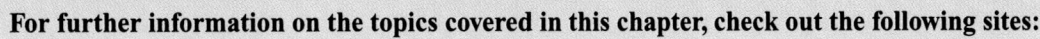

SURFING THE INTERNET

For further information on the topics covered in this chapter, check out the following sites:

http://www.frontiernet.net/~ jlkeefer/probsolv.html

http:// library.thinkquest.org/20991/prealg/eq.html

http://www.geocities.com/CollegePark/Classroom/7545/Part12.html

Answers to odd-numbered problems are given in Appendix A.

4.1

Add the following signed numbers:

1. $+4, +19$

$$\begin{array}{r} 19 \\ \underline{4} \\ 23 \end{array}$$

2. $-9, -18$

$$\begin{array}{r} -18 \\ \underline{-9} \\ -27 \end{array}$$

3. $+6, -55, +182, -4$

$$\begin{array}{rr} -55 & 182 & 188 \\ \underline{-4} & \underline{6} & \underline{-59} \\ -59 & 188 & 129 \end{array}$$

4. $-488, -674, +4,615, -123$

$$\begin{array}{rr} -488 & 4,615 \\ -674 & \underline{-1,285} \\ \underline{-123} & 3,330 \\ -1,285 \end{array}$$

4.2

Multiply the following signed numbers:

5. $(-18)(-7)$

$$\begin{array}{r} -18 \\ \underline{\times -7} \\ 126 \end{array}$$

6. $(21)(-7)$

$$\begin{array}{r} 21 \\ \underline{\times -7} \\ -147 \end{array}$$

7. $(-24)(-4)$

$$\begin{array}{r} -24 \\ \underline{\times -4} \\ 96 \end{array}$$

8. $(9)(7)$

$$\begin{array}{r} 9 \\ \underline{\times 7} \\ 63 \end{array}$$

4.3

Divide the following signed numbers:

9. $\dfrac{-62}{-31} = 2$

10. $15)\overline{-75}^{\,-5}$

11. $72 \div -8 = -9$

12. $\dfrac{+72}{+9} = 8$

Solve for the unknown in the following:

13. $Y + 48 = 72$

$Y = 72 - 48 = 24$

14. $P - 10 + 18 = 0$

$P = 10 - 18 = -8$

15. What number increased by 60 gives 90?

$N + 60 = 90$

$N = 90 - 60 = 30$

16. The net invoice payment due equals the total cost of merchandise purchased, plus freight charges, less sales returns, less sales allowance. Given the following information, determine the freight charges:

Net invoice payment due: $150
Four tables: $50 each
One table damaged and returned for full credit
Sales allowance: $50

$I = C + F - R - A; F = I - C + R + A; F = \$150 - (4 \times \$50) + \$50 + \$50; F = \$150 - \$200 + \$50 + \$50; F = \$50$

4.5

17. $40A = 720$

$A = \dfrac{720}{40} = 18$

18. $AR = N$. Find R.

$R = \dfrac{N}{A}$

19. What number multiplied by 8 gives 56?

$8N = 56 \qquad N = \dfrac{56}{8} = 7$

20. What number divided by 90 gives 40?

$\dfrac{N}{90} = 40 \qquad N = 90 \cdot 40 = 3,600$

4.6

Use inversion to solve the following problems:

21. $\dfrac{30}{B} = 5$

$\dfrac{B}{30} = \dfrac{1}{5}$

$B = \dfrac{1}{5} \cdot 30 = 6$

22. $\dfrac{9}{X} = \dfrac{1}{3}$

$\dfrac{X}{9} = \dfrac{3}{1}$

$X = 3 \cdot 9 = 27$

23. $\dfrac{M}{X} = T$. Find X.

$\dfrac{X}{M} = \dfrac{1}{T}$

$X = \dfrac{1}{T} \cdot M = \dfrac{M}{T}$

24. 75 divided by what number gives 15?

$\dfrac{75}{N} = 15 \qquad \dfrac{N}{75} = \dfrac{1}{15} \qquad N = \dfrac{1}{\cancel{15}} \cdot \cancel{75}^{\,5} = 5$

4.7

Use cross multiplication to solve the following problems:

25. $\dfrac{45}{R} = 5 \qquad 5R = 45 \qquad R = \dfrac{45}{5} = 9$

26. $\dfrac{W}{Q} = V$. Find Q. $\qquad QV = W \qquad Q = \dfrac{W}{V}$

27. 594 divided by what number gives 12?

$$\frac{594}{N} = 12 \qquad 12N = 594 \qquad N = \frac{594}{12} = 49.5$$

28. The tax rate is determined by dividing the tax by the assessed valuation. Calculate the assessed valuation if the tax is $600 and the tax rate is .03.

$$R = \frac{T}{V} \qquad VR = T \qquad V = \frac{T}{R} \qquad V = \frac{\$600}{.03} \qquad V = \$20,000$$

4.8

Solve for the unknown in the following problems:

29. $8G - 42 = 30$
$8G = 30 + 42$
$8G = 72$
$G = \frac{72}{8} = 9$

30. $8P + 35 = 683$
$8P = 683 - 35$
$8P = 648$
$P = \frac{648}{8} = 81$

31. 17 times what number less 8 gives 43?

$$17N - 8 = 43 \qquad 17N = 43 + 8 \qquad 17N = 51 \qquad N = \frac{51}{17} = 3$$

32. $ZP + Y = X$ Solve for Z.
$ZP = X - Y \qquad Z = \frac{X - Y}{P}$

4.9

Solve for the unknown in the following:

33. $17D - 8D = 27$
$9D = 27$
$D = \frac{27}{9} = 3$

34. $A + 9 + 3A = 33$
$4A + 9 = 33$
$4A = 33 - 9$
$A = \frac{24}{4} = 6$

35. $5T - 7 = T + 9$
$5T - T = 9 + 7$
$4T = 16$
$T = \frac{16}{4} = 4$

36. $3K + 87 = 102 - 12K$
$3K + 12K = 102 - 87$
$15K = 15$
$K = \frac{15}{15} = 1$

4.10

Solve for the unknown in the following:

37. $5(H - 3) = 0$
$5H - 15 = 0$
$5H = 15$
$H = \frac{15}{5} = 3$

38. $2[(3 - H) + 3(H + 8)] = 74$
$2[3 - H + 3H + 24] = 74$
$2[27 + 2H] = 74$
$54 + 4H = 74$
$4H = 20$
$H = \frac{20}{4} = 5$

39. $\dfrac{R(3 \times 4)}{(4 + 2)} = 5(R - 9)$
$\frac{12R}{6} = 5R - 45$
$2R = 5R - 45$
$45 = 3R$
$R = \frac{45}{3} = 15$

40. $R[5(3 + 5) - 9(4 - 2)] = 112$

$R[5(8) - 10(2)] = 120$
$R[40 - 20] = 120$
$R[20] = 120$
$20R = 120$
$R = \frac{120}{20} = 6$

4.11 and 4.12

Write equations for the following problems using formatting when appropriate and then solve for the unknown(s):

41. What number decreased by 14 gives 27?
$N - 14 = 27$
$N = 27 + 14 = 41$

42. Interest equals principal times rate times time. Find the principal if interest on a loan is $360, the rate is .09, and the time is 2 years.

$I = PRT \qquad P = \frac{I}{RT}$

$P = \frac{\$360}{.09 \times 2} \qquad P = \frac{\$360}{.18}$

$P = \$2,000$

43. Stan Wright and Carla Rong sell real estate. Together they sold 44 lots. Carla sold three times as many lots as Stan. How many did each sell?

Unknown(s)	Variable(s)	Price	Formula or Equation
Stan's sales	S		S
Carla's sales	$3S$		$+\,3S$
Total sales			44

$S + 3S = 44$ $4S = 44$ $S = 11$ lots (Stan's Sales)
$3S = 33$ lots (Carla's sales)

44. Rusty ran twice as many pages of photocopy as Bill. Sorita ran 6 more pages than Bill. The total number of pages of photocopy was 366. Calculate the number each person ran.

Unknown(s)	Variable(s)	Price	Formula or Equation
Bill's copies	P		P
Rusty's copies	$2P$		$+\,2P$
Sorita's copies	$P + 6$		$+\,P + 6$
Total copies			366

$P + 2P + P + 6 = 366$ $4P + 6 = 366$ $4P = 360$ $P = \dfrac{360}{4} = 90$

Bill ran 90 copies (P)
Rusty ran 180 copies $(2P)$
Sorita ran 96 copies $(P + 6)$

45. One case of disposable syringes costs $150. Disposable needles cost $60 per case. If an order of 24 cases of needles and syringes totals $3,150, determine the number of cases and the total cost for each.

Unknown(s)	Variable(s)	Price	Formula or Equation
Case cost of:			
Syringes	S	$150	$150S$
Needles	$24 - S$	$ 60	$+\,\$60\,(24 - S)$
			$3,150

$150S + \$1,440 - \$60S = \$3,150$ $90S = \$3,150 - \$1,440$
$ 90S = \$1,710$
$S = \dfrac{\$1,790}{\$90} = 19$ cases of syringes
$24 - S = 24 - 19 = 5$ cases of needles
19 cases at $150 per case = $2,850
5 cases at $60 per case = $ 300

46. A soup manufacturer has shift production as follows:
  Five times as many cans of soup were produced on shift 1 as on shift 2.
  Shift 3 produces 47 fewer cans than shift 2.
  A total of 4,153 cans was produced.
How many cans were produced on each shift?

Unknown(s)	Variable(s)	Price	Formula or Equation
Shift 1	$5P$		$5P$
Shift 2	P		P
Shift 3	$P - 47$		$+\,P - 47$
Total			4,153

$7P - 47 = 4,153$ $7P = 4,153 + 47$ $7P = 4,200$
$P = \dfrac{4,200}{7} = 600$ (shift 2)

$5P = 3,000$ (shift 1) $600 - 47 = 553$ (shift 3)

47. Tables sell for $80 and chairs for $30. Stratten Furniture Co. sold five times as many chairs as tables. During June, total sales for tables and chairs were $41,400. How many chairs and tables were sold, and what was the sales amount for each?

Unknown(s)	Variable(s)	Price	Formula or Equation
Tables	T	$80	$80T
Chairs	$5T$	$30	$+\,\$30 \cdot 5T$
Total			$41,400

$\$80T + \$150T = \$41,400$ $\$230T = \$ 41,400$
$T = \dfrac{\$41,400}{\$230} = 180$ tables $5T = 900$ chairs
$\$80 \times 180 = \$14,400$ for tables
$\$30 \times 900 = \$27,000$ for chairs

48. Fergamo & Mao Carpet Cleaners provides credit to some customers. All others must pay cash. Last month, credit customers accounted for $\frac{1}{5}$ of total sales. If credit sales totaled $11,000, what were total sales?

Unknown(s)	Variable(s)	Price	Formula or Equation
Total Sales	T		$\frac{1}{5}\,T$ = Credit sales
			$\frac{1}{5}\,T = \$11,000$

$\frac{1}{5} = .2$ $.2T = \$11,000$ $T = \dfrac{\$11,000}{.2}$ $T = \$55,000$

Drill Problems

Add the following:

1. $+5, +4 = 9$ **2.** $-2, -9 = -11$ **3.** $+6, -1 = 5$

4. $+93, -193, -58, -292, +357$

$$\begin{array}{r} +357 \\ +\ 93 \\ \hline 450 \end{array} \qquad \begin{array}{r} -193 \\ -\ 58 \\ -292 \\ \hline -543 \end{array} \qquad \begin{array}{r} -543 \\ +450 \\ \hline -93 \end{array}$$

Multiply the following:

5. $+4 \cdot +39$

$$\begin{array}{r} 39 \\ \times\ 4 \\ \hline 156 \end{array}$$

6. $-4 \cdot -24$

$$\begin{array}{r} -24 \\ \times -4 \\ \hline 96 \end{array}$$

7. $-2 \cdot +26$

$$\begin{array}{r} 26 \\ \times -2 \\ \hline -52 \end{array}$$

8. $-27 \cdot -21$

$$\begin{array}{r} -27 \\ \times -21 \\ \hline 567 \end{array}$$

Divide the following:

9. $42 \div -7$

$$-7\overline{)42} \quad -6$$

10. $\dfrac{-56}{28}$

$$28\overline{)-56} \quad -2$$

11. $\dfrac{-345}{-15}$

$$-15\overline{)-345} \quad 23$$

12. $-2/-5$

$$-5\overline{)-2.0} \quad .4$$

Find N in each of the following addition problems:

13. $N + 17 = 32$
$N = 32 - 17 = 15$

14. $N + 3 = 19$
$N = 19 - 3 = 16$

15. $N + 29 = 54$
$N = 54 - 29 = 25$

16. $N + 483 - 2{,}893$
$N = 2{,}893 - 483 = 2{,}410$

Find N in each of the following multiplication problems:

17. $25N = 125$
$N = \dfrac{125}{25} = 5$

18. $23N = 253$
$N = \dfrac{253}{23} = 11$

19. $4N = 496$
$N = \dfrac{496}{4} = 124$

20. $489N = 174{,}573$
$N = \dfrac{174{,}573}{489} = 357$

Find N in each of the following division problems:

21. $\dfrac{N}{5} = 27$
$N = 27 \times 5 = 135$

22. $\dfrac{N}{23} = 7$
$N = 23 \times 7 = 161$

23. $\dfrac{N}{119} = 12$
$N = 119 \times 12 = 1{,}428$

24. $\dfrac{N}{734} = 20$
$N = 734 \times 20 = 14{,}680$

Find N in each of the following:

25. $N - Q = R$
$N = R + Q$

26. $QN = R$
$N = \dfrac{R}{Q}$

27. $\dfrac{N}{Q} = R$
$N = RQ$

28. $\dfrac{Q}{N} = R$
$NR = Q \qquad N = \dfrac{Q}{R}$

Find N in each of the following:

29. $5N + 33 = 53$
$5N = 53 - 33$
$5N = 20$
$N = \dfrac{20}{5} = 4$

30. $12N - 17 = 19$
$12N = 19 + 17$
$12N = 36$
$N = \dfrac{36}{12} = 3$

31. $\dfrac{6N}{17} - 11 = 25$
$\dfrac{6N}{17} = 25 + 11$
$6N = 36 \cdot 17$
$N = \dfrac{612}{6} = 102$

32. $\dfrac{18N}{132} + 57 = 111$
$\dfrac{18N}{132} = 111 - 57$
$18N = 54 \cdot 132$
$N = \dfrac{7{,}128}{18} = 396$

Find N in each of the following:

33. $7N + 3 = 15N - 13$
$7N + 3 + 13 = 15N$
$3 + 13 = 15N - 7N$
$16 = 8N$
$\dfrac{16}{8} = N$
$N = 2$

34. $2(N - 3) = (N - 1)(3 + 7)$
$2N - 6 = (N - 1)(10)$
$2N - 6 = 10N - 10$
$2N + 10 - 6 = 10N$
$10 - 6 = 10N - 2N$
$4 = 8N$
$\dfrac{4}{8} = N$
$N = .5$

35. $4(3N + 25) = 21N - 8$
$12N + 100 = 21N - 8$
$12N + 100 + 8 = 21N$
$108 = 21N - 12N$
$108 = 9N$
$\dfrac{108}{9} = N$
$N = 12$

36. $9[(3N - 4) - (23 - 9)] = 0$
$9[(3N - 4) - (14)] = 0$
$9[3N - 4 - 14] = 0$
$9[3N - 18] = 0$
$27N - 162 = 0$
$27N = 0 + 162$
$N = \dfrac{162}{27}$
$N = 6$

Word Problems

37. What number added to 6 gives 84?
$N + 6 = 84 \qquad N = 84 - 6 \qquad N = 78$

38. What number less 9 gives 29?
$N - 9 = 29 \qquad N = 29 + 9 \qquad N = 38$

39. What number multiplied by 36 gives 288?
$36N = 288 \qquad N = \dfrac{288}{36} \qquad N = 8$

40. What number divided by 44 gives 5?

$$\frac{N}{44} = 5 \qquad N = 5 \cdot 44 \qquad N = 220$$

41. Stankowsky's, Inc., budgets $\frac{2}{9}$ of its total budget for salaries. If salaries are budgeted at \$270,000, what is the total budget for Stankowsky's?

$$\frac{2}{9}B = S \qquad \frac{2}{9}B = \$270,000 \qquad B = \$270,000 \cdot \frac{9}{2} \qquad B = \$1,215,000$$

42. Shawna is eight years younger than Miranda. Miranda is 44. How old is Shawna?

$$S = M - 8 \qquad S = 44 - 8 \qquad S = 36$$

43. Dale is seven times as old as Yvonne. The difference in their ages is 24 years. How old is each person?

Unknown(s)	Variable(s)	Price	Formula or Equation
Yvonne's age	A		$7A - A = 24$
Dale's age	$7A$		

$$6A = 24 \qquad A = \frac{24}{6} \qquad A = 4 \text{ Yvonne's age} \qquad 7A = 28 \text{ Dale's age}$$

44. Sue is three times as old as Bruce. The sum of their ages is 96. How old are they?

Unknown(s)	Variable(s)	Price	Formula or Equation
Bruce's age	A		$A + 3A = 96$
Sue's age	$3A$		

$$4A = 96 \qquad A = \frac{96}{4} \qquad A = 24 \text{ Bruce's age} \qquad 3A = 72 \text{ Sue's age}$$

45. An automobile parts manufacturer, Auto Bright, has four times the gross sales as its competitor. Together they have gross sales of \$9,000,000. Determine the gross sales of each.

Unknown(s)	Variable(s)	Price	Formula or Equation
Sales for:			
Competitor	S		S
Auto Bright	$4S$		$+ 4S$
Total			$\$9,000,000$

$$5S = \$9,000,000 \qquad S = \frac{9,000,000}{5} \qquad S = \$1,800,000$$
$$4S = \$7,200,000 \text{ Auto Bright's sales}$$

46. A department store keeps track of sales in its hard goods and soft goods lines. Sales in soft goods average \$40 per customer while sales per customer for hard goods average \$120. Soft goods' sales volume is five times that of hard goods. Together sales last year were \$248,000. What were the dollar sales for each category?

Unknown(s)	Variable(s)	Price	Formula or Equation
Sales of:			
Hard goods	S	\$120	$\$120S$
Soft goods	$5S$	\$40	$+ \$40 \cdot 5S$
			$\$ 248,000$

$$\$120S + \$200S = \$248,000 \qquad \$320S = \$248,000 \qquad S = \frac{\$248,000}{\$320} = 775$$

$S = 775$ sales volume for hard goods
$5S = 3,875$ sales volume for soft goods
$775 \times \$120 = \$93,000$ hard good sales
$3,875 \times \$40 = \$155,000$ soft good sales

47. Sampson's Beauty Supply sells combs for \$2.50 and brushes for \$8. Together, 300 combs and brushes were sold one week. Total realized revenue from the sale of both products was \$1,465. How many of each were sold, and what was the dollar sales for each product?

Unknown(s)	Variable(s)	Price	Formula or Equation
Brush sales	B	\$8	$\$8B$
Comb sales	$300 - B$	\$2.50	$+ \$2.50(300 - B)$
			$\$1,465$

$$\$8B + \$750 - \$2.5B = \$1,465 \qquad \$5.5B = \$1,465 - \$750$$
$$\$5.5B = \$715 \qquad B = \frac{\$715}{\$5.5} = 130$$

$B = 130$ brushes sold
$300 - B = 170$ combs sold
$130 \times \$8 = \$1,040$ brush sales
$170 \times \$2.50 = \$425$ comb sales

48. This year's expenses are $40,000 less than last year's due to cost-cutting moves. This year, expenses are $229,500. What were the expenses last year?

Unknown(s)	Variable(s)	Price	Formula or Equation
Expenses:			
Last year	L		
This year	$L - \$40,000$		$L - \$40,000 = \$229,000$

$L = \$229,500 + 40,000$ $L = \$269,500$

49. Alan Shipiro and Craig Sustaire wait tables in an exclusive night club. Alan earned $59.50 more in tips than Craig. Together the tips totaled $849.20. Calculate the tips earned by each waiter.

Unknown(s)	Variable(s)	Price	Formula or Equation
Craig's tips	T		T
Alan's tips	$T + \$59.50$		$+\ T + \$59.50$
			$\$849.20$

$2T + \$59.50 = \$849.20$
$2T = \$849.20 - 59.50$
$2T = \$789.70$
$T = \dfrac{\$789.70}{2} = \$394.85$ Craig's tips
$T + \$59.50 = \$454.35$ Alan's tips

50. Lu Yung has determined that .3 of her gross earnings are deducted from her paycheck. Her deductions this week are $360. What are Lu's gross earnings?

$.3G = D$ $.3G = \$360$ $G = \dfrac{\$360}{.3}$ $G = \$1,200$

51. Apex Floor Covering sells tile and carpet floor coverings. Last month it sold 2.5 times as many square feet of carpeting as tile. The carpet averages $20 per square foot; the tile averages $12 per square foot. The total floor covering sales were $240,250 for the month. Calculate the square footage and the dollar sales of each.

Unknown(s)	Variable(s)	Price	Formula or Equation
Tile	T	$\$12$	$\$12T$
Carpet	$2.5T$	$\$20$	$+\ \$20 \cdot 2.5T$
Total			$\$240,250$

$\$12T + \$50T = \$240,250$ $\$62T = \$240,250$
$T = \dfrac{\$240,250}{\$62} = 3,875$ sq. ft. of tile $3,875 \times \$12 = \$46,500$ tile
$2.5T = 9,687.5$ sq. ft. of carpet $9,687.5 \times \$20 = \$193,750$ carpet

52. St. Paul Realty separates its sales among industrial real estate, commercial real estate, and residential real estate. This year total sales of all property came to $24,300,000. The number of residential property sales (which averaged $75,000 per unit) were 12 times those of industrial property (which averaged $500,000 per unit). Unit sales of commercial property (which averaged $150,000) were two more than four times as many as industrial property. Determine the number and dollar value of all three classifications of property.

Unknown(s)	Variable(s)	Price	Formula or Equation
Industrial	I	$\$500,000$	$\$500,000I$
Residential	$12I$	$\$75,000$	$\$75,000 \times 12I$
Commercial	$4I + 2$	$\$150,000$	$+\ \$150,000\,(4I + 2)$
Total			$\$24,300,000$

$\$500,000I + \$900,000I + \$600,000I + \$300,000 = \$24,300,000$
$\$2,000,000I = \$24,300,000 - \$300,000$
$\$2,000,000I = \$24,000,000$
$I = \dfrac{\$24,000,000}{\$2,000,000} = 12$ industrial sales $\times \$500,000 = \$6,000,000$
$12I = 12 \cdot 12 = 144$ residential sales $\times \$75,000 = \$10,800,000$
$4I + 2 = 4 \cdot 12 + 2 = 50$ commercial sales $\times \$150,000 = \$7,500,000$

53. Red Tree Shoes sells both men's and women's shoes at discount prices. Women's shoes averaged $30 per pair; men's averaged $40. Total unit sales were 6,000 pair. Total dollar sales were $192,000. Calculate the unit and dollar value of each.

Unknown(s)	Variable(s)	Price	Formula or Equation
Men's Shoes	M	$40	$40M$
Women's Shoes	$6{,}000 - M$	$30	$+ \$30(6{,}000 - M)$
Total			$192,000

$\$40M + \$180{,}000 - \$30M = \$192{,}000$
$\$10M = \$192{,}000 - \$180{,}000$
$M = \dfrac{\$12{,}000}{\$10} = 1{,}200$ men's shoes sold $\times \$40 = \$48{,}000$
$6{,}000 - M = 4{,}800$ women's shoes sold $\times \$30 = \$144{,}000$

54. Julie is $\frac{1}{2}$ Wade's present age. Six years ago, Julie was $\frac{1}{8}$ Wade's age. How old is each now?

Unknown(s)	Variable(s)	Price	Formula or Equation
Wade's present age	$2A$		
Julie's present age	A		
Wade's age 6 years ago	$2A - 6$		
Julie's age 6 years ago	$A - 6$		
6 years ago Wade was 8 times Julie's age.			$2A - 6 = 8(A - 6)$

$2A - 6 = 8A - 48 \qquad 2A + 48 - 6 = 8A \qquad 42 = 8A - 2A \qquad 6A = 42 \qquad A = \dfrac{42}{6} \qquad A = 7 \text{ Julie's age now} \qquad 2A = 14 \text{ Wade's age now}$

55. A department store sells shirts for $25 and shorts for $15. During May it sold five times as many pairs of shorts as shirts. Total sales were $25,000. Determine the number of shirts and shorts sold and the dollar value of each.

Unknown(s)	Variable(s)	Price	Formula or Equation
Shirt sales	S	$25	$25S$
Short Sales	$5S$	$15	$+ \$15 \cdot 5S$
Total			$25,000

$\$25S + \$75S = \$25{,}000$
$\$100S = \$25{,}000$
$S = \dfrac{\$25{,}000}{\$100} = 250$ shirts were sold $\times \$25 = \$6{,}250$
$5S = 1{,}250$ shorts were sold $\times \$15 = \$18{,}750$

CRITICAL THINKING GROUP PROJECT

Mapleleaf Real Estate had $785,558 total revenue from sales commissions and for property rentals. Management just completed analyzing its financial records for the past year. Some of the information from that analysis follows:

1. Commissions on the sale of property were $2,944 less than 5 times as great as income from rental property.

2. Receipts from the rental property were further broken down as follows:

   a. Commercial rental property income was $1,500 more than 2.5 times as much as industrial rental property income.

   b. Residential rental property income was 4.25 times commercial rental property income.

3. Commissions from the sale of property were further broken down as follows:

   a. Commissions from sales of industrial property were $7,290 less than 6 times as much as commissions from residential property sales.

   b. Residential property commissions were $954 more than twice as much as commercial property commissions.

Answer the following questions and round your final answers to the nearest dollar if necessary: (Do not round the intermediate answers.)

1. What were the total receipts for rental property?

Unknown (s)	Variable (s)	Price	Formula or Equation
Rental income	R		R
Commissions	5R − $2,944		+ 5R − $2,944
Total Revenue			$785,558

$$R + 5R - \$2,944 = \$785,558$$
$$6R = \$785,558 + 2,944$$
$$R = \frac{\$788,502}{6}$$
$$R = \$131,417$$

2. What were the total commissions from sales of property?

$$C + 5B - \$2,944$$
$$C = 5 \cdot \$131,417 - \$2,944$$
$$= \$654,141$$

3. What was the income from the rental of industrial property?

Unknown(s)	Variable(s)	Price	Formula or Equation
Industrial rental income	I		I
Commercial rental income	$\$1,500 + 2.5I$		$\$1,500 + 2.5I$
Residential rental income	$4.25\,(\$1,500 + 2.5I)$		$+ 4.25(\$1,500 + 2.5I)$
Total rental income			$\$131,417$

$$I + \$1,500 + 2.5I + 4.25(\$1,500 + 2.5I) = \$131,417$$
$$I + {-}\$1,500 + 2.5I + \$6,375 + 10.625I = \$131,417$$
$$14.125I + \$7,875 = \$131,417$$
$$14.125I = \$131,417 - 7,875$$
$$I = \frac{\$123,542}{14.125}$$
$$I = \$8,746$$

4. What was the income from the rental of commercial property?

$$\text{Commercial rental property} = \$1,500 + 2.5I$$
$$= \$1,500 + (2.5 \times \$8,746)$$
$$= \$1,500 + 21,865$$
$$= \$23,365$$

5. What was the income from the rental of residential property?

$$\text{Residential rental income} = 4.25(\$1,500 + 2.5I)$$
$$= \$6,375 + (10.625 \times \$8,746)$$
$$= \$6,375 + 92,926$$
$$= \$99,301$$

6. What were the commissions from the sale of commercial property?

Unknown(s)	Variable(s)	Price	Formula or Equation
Commercial sales commissions	C		C
Residential sales commissions	2C + $954		2C + $954
Industrial sales commissions	6(2C + $954) − $7,290		+ 6(2C + $954) − $7,290
Total sales commissions			$654,141

$$C + 2C + \$954 + 6(2C + \$954) - \$7,290 = \$654,141$$
$$C + 2C + \$954 + 12C + \$5,724 - \$7,290 = \$654,141$$
$$15C - \$612 = \$654,141$$
$$15C = \$654,141 + \$612$$
$$C = \frac{\$654,753}{15}$$
$$\$43,650$$

7. What were the commissions from the sale of industrial property?

$$6(2C + \$954) - \$7,290$$
$$12C + \$5,724 - \$7,290$$
$$(12 \times \$43,650) - \$1,566$$
$$\$522,234$$

8. What were the commissions from the sale of residential property?

$$2C + \$954$$
$$(2 \times \$43,650) + 954$$
$$\$88,254$$

1. What is meant by "absolute value"? **W**
Absolute value refers to the value of a number itself without regard to its positive or negative sign.

Perform the indicated operations in the following:

3. $(-4)(18)$

$$\begin{array}{r} 18 \\ \times \ -4 \\ \hline -72 \end{array}$$

4. $-30 \div -6$

$$\begin{array}{r} 5 \\ -6\overline{)-30} \end{array}$$

5. $-4 + 8 - 5$

$$\begin{array}{rr} -4 & -9 \\ -5 & 8 \\ \hline -9 & -1 \end{array}$$

6. $48 \div -6$

$$\begin{array}{r} -8 \\ -6\overline{)48} \end{array}$$

2. What does an equation represent? **W**
An equation represents the equality between two quantities.

Find the value of the unknown:

7. $6N = 18$

$N = \dfrac{18}{6}$

$N = 3$

8. $G + 16 = 27$

$G = 27 - 16 = 11$

9. $\dfrac{15}{N} = 3$

$3N = 15$

$N = \dfrac{15}{3} = 5$

10. $5R = \dfrac{3}{5}$

$R = \dfrac{3}{5} \div 5 \qquad R = \dfrac{3}{5} \cdot \dfrac{1}{5} = \dfrac{3}{25}$

Find T *in each of the following:*

11. $T - Z = P$

$T = P + Z$

12. $\dfrac{T}{H} = Z$

$T = ZH$

13. $TU = RS$

$T = \dfrac{RS}{U}$

14. $\dfrac{TZ}{B} = C$

$TZ = C \cdot B$

$T = \dfrac{CB}{Z}$

15. $4T + 5 = T + 20$

$4T - T = 20 - 5$

$3T = 15$

$T = \dfrac{15}{3} = 5$

16. $-8 + T = 3T + 16$

$-8 - 16 = 3T - T$

$-24 = 2T$

$T = \dfrac{-24}{2} = -12$

17. Abe sold twice as much as Judy. Together they sold $7,155 worth of merchandise. What were Abe's sales?

Unknown(s)	Variable(s)	Price	Formula or Equation
Judy's Sales	J		J
Abe's Sales	$2J$		$+ 2J$
Total			$7,155

$3J = \$7,155 \quad J = \dfrac{\$7,155}{3} = \$2,385$ Judy's sales

$2J = \$4,770$ Abe's sales

18. What number divided by 5 gives $\dfrac{5}{43}$?

$\dfrac{N}{5} = \dfrac{5}{43} \qquad N = \dfrac{5}{43} \cdot 5 = \dfrac{25}{43}$

19. Sally Stewart's batting average went down .120 points after a particularly bad week at the plate. Her new average is .294. What was her batting average at the beginning of the week?

Unknown(s)	Variable(s)	Price	Formula or Equation
Old batting average	A		
New batting average	$A - .120$		$A - .120 = .294$

$A = .294 + .120 \qquad A = .414$

20. Stuart is six years younger than twice as old as Dave. Coreena is four years older than half Stuart's age. The sum of their ages is 55. How old is Coreena?

Unknown(s)	Variable(s)	Price	Formula or Equation
Dave's age	A		A
Stuart's age	$2A - 6$		$2A - 6$
Coreena's age	$\frac{1}{2}(2A - 6) + 4$		$+ \frac{1}{2}(2A - 6) + 4$
			55

$A + 2A - 6 + A - 3 + 4 = 55$
$4A - 5 = 55$
$4A = 55 + 5$
$A = \dfrac{60}{4} = 15$ Dave's age

$\frac{1}{2}(2 \cdot 15 - 6) + 4 = \frac{1}{2}(24) + 4 = 16$ Coreena's age

21. Max's Quality Discount Bookstore sells both hardback and paperback books. The hardback books sell for an average price of $17.50, and the paperback books sell for an average price of $5.75. Paperback books sell seven times more than hardbacks. Last month, sales of all books totaled $11,550. Determine the number and dollar value of sales of both types of books.

Unknown(s)	Variable(s)	Price	Formula or Equation
Hardback books	H	$17.50	$17.50H$
Paperback books	$7H$	$ 5.75	$+ $ 5.75 \cdot 7H$
Total			$11,550

$17.50H + $40.25H = $11,550$
$57.75H = $11,550$
$H = \dfrac{\$11,550}{\$57.75} = 200$ hardback book sales $\times$ $17.50 = $ 3,500
$7H = 1,400$ paperback book sales $\times$ $ 5.75 = $ 8,050

22. The BU bookstore purchased a total of 70 dozen pencils and pens for the beginning of the fall semester. Pencils cost $.72 per dozen and the pens cost $8.50 per dozen. The total cost to the bookstore was $439.40. Find the total number of pencils and pens and the total cost of each. (Your answer should be in dozens, that is, how many dozen pencils and how many dozen pens were bought and what was the cost per dozen of each.)

Unknown(s)	Variable(s)	Price	Formula or Equation
Pens	P	$8.50	$8.50P$
Pencils	$70 - P$	$ .72	$+ $.72 (70 - P)$
Total			$439.40

$8.50P + $50.40 - $.72P = 439.40
$7.78P = $439.40 - 50.40
$7.78P = 389
$P = \dfrac{\$389}{\$7.78} = 50$ dozen pens were bought $\times$ $8.50 = $425
$70 - P = 20$ dozen pencils were bought $\times$ $ .72 = $ 14.40

Write equations for exercises 23 – 27:

23. A number less 25, multiplied by 12 is 72.
$12(N - 25) = 72$

24. 15 less than one fourth of a number is 10.
$\dfrac{1}{4}N - 15 = 10$

25. 200 decreased by 8 times a number is 80.
$200 - 8N = 80$

26. 6 added to twice a number is the same as that number plus 14.
$6 + 2N = N + 14$

27. A number less 6, multiplied by 5 equals the number plus 2, multiplied by 3.
$5(N - 6) = 3(N + 2)$

28. Liz had real estate sales that were $4,000 less than twice as much as Jim's sales. Together they sold $146,000 worth of property last month. What were both Jim's and Liz's sales?

Unknown(s)	Variable(s)	Price	Formula or Equation
Jim's sales	S		S
Liz's sales	$2S - $4,000$		$+ 2S - $4,000$
Total			$146,000

$3S - $4,000 = $146,000$
$3S = $146,000 + $4,000$
$S = \dfrac{\$150,000}{3} = $50,000$ Jim's sales
$2S - $4,000 = $96,000$ Liz's sales

5 PERCENTAGE APPLICATIONS

A BETTER WAY TO EXPRESS
THE WAY IT IS

Nike makes athletic shoes. Everybody who knows who Tiger Woods is (which is just about everybody) knows that. But the great golfer is a tool used by the Nike company for its real goal—making money.

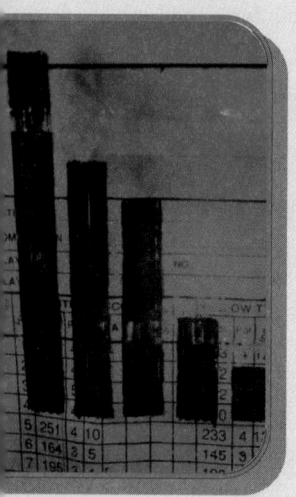

Nike was incorporated in 1968 in Oregon with about $1 billion in sales the first year. In the 1980s and 1990s the company enjoyed enormous growth. It now produces annual sales of about $5 billion. Almost one out of three athletic shoes sold are made by Nike, and it sells four times as many products in the United States as it does in the combined other 60 countries in which it sells its products. In its earliest years Nike's sales increased by almost one sixth each year, but recently that growth has slowed to about one twentieth. To increase its profit margin, management has reduced the workforce by about one fourteenth.

All of the above may be true, but appreciating such data is simpler for most of us if we say something more like: Since its inception in 1968 Nike's sales have increased 500%. It now produces 30% of all the athletic shoes sold in the United States, and 80% of its products are sold here. In its early years Nike's sales increased about 15% per year, but that growth has since slowed to about 5%. To protect its profit margin, management has recently reduced the workforce by 7%.

Chapter Glossary

Percent. A mathematical symbol (%) with the value of one hundredth.

Base. The starting or reference point to which comparisons are made. The base is always represented by 100%.

Rate. A percent, decimal fraction, or common fraction representing the relationship between the percentage and the base.

Percentage. A portion or a part of the base.

Student Objectives

Upon completion of this chapter, you should be able to:

1. Convert percents to decimal fractions.
2. Convert decimal fractions to percents.
3. Convert percents to common fractions.
4. Convert common fractions to percents.
5. Write the percentage (portion) formula.
6. Define the components of the percentage (portion) formula.
7. Calculate any component of the percentage (portion) formula when given the other two components.
8. Calculate the value after an increase given a base and rate.
9. Calculate the value after a decrease given a base and rate.
10. Calculate the rate of increase given a base and increased amount.
11. Calculate the rate of decrease given a base and decreased amount.

$\boxed{\text{T}}$he percent sign (%) has the mathematical value of one hundredth (.01 or 1/100). When you write a percent, the number is followed by a percent sign (%). Percents, then, are the result of expressing numbers as a part of 100. That means the number is being multiplied by .01 (or by 1/100). For example, 13% represents 13 parts of 100 and can be expressed in decimal fraction form as .13 (13 × .01 = .13) or in common fraction form as 13/100 (13 × 1/100 = 13/100).

LEARNING UNIT 1
CONVERSIONS

In business, percents are frequently used to illustrate relationships between two or more numbers. Percents are common, but to use them in arithmetic applications you must convert them into decimal or common fractions. Conversions are crucial in solving a large variety of problems and should be clearly understood.

5.1 Converting Percents to Decimal Fractions

To convert a percent to a decimal fraction, remove the percent sign and move the decimal point two places to the left. This is the same as multiplying a number by .01.

When the decimal point is not shown in a value expressed as a percent, the decimal point is always understood to be at the right of the last whole number.

EXAMPLE Convert 82% to a decimal fraction.

Solution 82% = .82   *Remove the percent sign and move the decimal point, which is assumed to be at the right of the 2 in 82, two places to the left: 82 × .01 = .82.*

When there are fewer than two places to the left of the decimal point in the number being converted, a zero or zeros must be placed to the left of the decimal point to total two positions.

EXAMPLE a. Convert 7% to a decimal fraction.
b. Convert .25% to a decimal fraction.

Solution a. 7% = 07% = .07   *It is not necessary to show these intermediate steps in the solution; they are shown here only to illustrate the principle.*
b. .25% = 00.25% = .0025

When the percent contains a common fraction, the fractional part must first be converted into a decimal fraction. Then, the decimal point can be moved two places to the left.

EXAMPLE Convert $8\frac{1}{8}\%$ to a decimal fraction.

Solution $8\frac{1}{8}\% = 8.125\% = 08.125\% = .08125$

5.1 Practice Problems

Convert the following percents to decimal fractions. (Do not round off your answers.)

1. 8%   **2.** 26%   **3.** 1/2%   **4.** .4%

5.1 Solutions to Practice Problems

1. .08   **2.** .26   **3.** .5% = .005   **4.** .004

5.2 Converting Decimal Fractions to Percents

To convert a decimal fraction to a percent, move the decimal point two places to the right and add a percent sign. That divides the number by .01, which is the opposite of multiplying by .01.

E X A M P L E   Convert the decimal fraction .03 to a percent.

Solution   .03 = 3%   *Move the decimal point two places to the right and add a percent sign (.03 ÷ .01=3%).*

When there are not two numbers to the right of the decimal point in the number being converted, a zero or zeros must be placed to the right of the decimal point to total two positions.

E X A M P L E   a. Convert .2 to a percent.
b. Convert 5 to a percent.

Solution   a. .2 = .20 = 20%   *In both numbers, add enough zeros to total two places to the*
b. 5 = 5.00 = 500%   *right of the decimal point. Then, move the decimal point two places to the right and add the percent sign.*

If the decimal fraction contains a common fraction remainder, it must be converted to a decimal fraction if there are fewer than two spaces to the right of the decimal point in the decimal fraction.

E X A M P L E   a. Convert $.6\frac{1}{4}$ to a percent.
b. Convert $.41\frac{2}{3}$ to a percent.

Solution   a. $.6\frac{1}{4} = .625 = 62.5\%$ *Convert 1/4 to its decimal fraction equivalent, .25. Note that the 1/4 occupies the hundredths position in the original fraction. Thus, the 2 occupies the hundredths position and the 5 occupies the thousandths position. Next, move the decimal point two places to the right and add the percent sign.*

b. $.41\frac{2}{3} = 41\frac{2}{3}\%$ *Unless the instructor indicates differently, it is unnecessary to convert the common fraction into its decimal fraction equivalent when there are two places to the right of the decimal point in the original fraction. Hence, move the decimal point two places to the right of the decimal point and add the percent sign.*

5.2 Practice Problems

Convert the following decimal fractions to percents:

1. .19   **2.** .01   **3.** $.5\frac{1}{5}$ **4.** $4.2\frac{5}{6}$

5.2 Solutions to Practice Problems

1. 19%   **2.** 1%   **3.** $.5\frac{1}{5} = .52 = 52\%$ **4.** $4.2\frac{5}{6} = 4.283 = 428.3\%$

5.3 Converting Percents to Common Fractions

To convert whole number percents and proper common fraction percents to common fractions, remove the percent sign, multiply by 1/100 and reduce to lowest terms (remember that you can often reduce to lowest terms by using cancellation).

E X A M P L E Convert the following to common fractions:

a. 25% b. $\dfrac{3}{5}\%$ c. $\dfrac{5}{8}\%$

Solution a. $\overset{1}{\cancel{25}} \times \dfrac{1}{\underset{4}{\cancel{100}}} = \dfrac{1}{4}$ *Remove the percent sign, and multiply 25 by 1/100 and cancel.*

b. $\dfrac{3}{5} \times \dfrac{1}{100} = \dfrac{3}{500}$ *Remove the percent sign and multiply $\dfrac{3}{5}$ by $\dfrac{1}{100}$.*

c. $\dfrac{\overset{1}{\cancel{5}}}{8} \times \dfrac{1}{\underset{20}{\cancel{100}}} = \dfrac{1}{160}$ *Remove the percent sign, multiply $\dfrac{5}{8}$ by $\dfrac{1}{100}$, and cancel.*

To convert mixed number common fraction percents to common fractions:

1. Remove the percent sign.
2. Convert the mixed number to an improper fraction.
3. Multiply by 1/100.
4. If necessary, reduce to lowest terms.

If the percent is a mixed decimal percent (such as 3.125%), convert the fractional portion to a proper common fraction and then follow the previous steps.
An alternative method is as follows:

1. Convert the mixed number percent to a decimal number percent.
2. Remove the percent sign and put the mixed number over 100.
3. Clear any decimal points.
4. Reduce to lowest terms.

The following examples will show the two methods. Work with both methods until you become proficient using both. Then, select the method you find easier and more accurate for you.

E X A M P L E Convert the following percents to common fractions:

a. $3\dfrac{1}{5}\%$ b. $12\dfrac{12}{25}\%$ c. $2\dfrac{8}{9}\%$ d. 3.125%

Solution *Suggested Method* *Alternative Method*

a. $3\dfrac{1}{5}\% = \dfrac{16}{5}\%$ *Convert to improper fraction and reduce by cancellation.* *Convert to decimal fraction, clear decimal, and reduce.* a. $3\dfrac{1}{5}\% = 3.2\%$

$\dfrac{\overset{4}{\cancel{16}}}{5} \times \dfrac{1}{\underset{25}{\cancel{100}}} = \dfrac{4}{125}$ $\dfrac{3.2}{100} = \dfrac{32}{1000} = \dfrac{4}{125}$

b. $12\dfrac{12}{25}\% = \dfrac{312}{25}\%$ b. $12\dfrac{12}{25}\% = 12.48\%$

$\dfrac{\overset{78}{\cancel{312}}}{25} \times \dfrac{1}{\underset{25}{\cancel{100}}} = \dfrac{78}{625}$ *Notice how much easier fraction reduction is with the suggested method.* $\dfrac{12.48}{100} = \dfrac{1248}{10,000} = \dfrac{78}{625}$

c. $2\dfrac{8}{9}\% = \dfrac{26}{9}\%$ *The final answer in this example is different when using the two methods due to the inaccuracy caused by rounding in the alternative method.* c. $2\dfrac{8}{9}\% = 2.889\%$
(rounded)

$$\frac{\overset{13}{\cancel{26}}}{9} \times \frac{1}{\underset{50}{\cancel{100}}} = \frac{13}{450}$$

$$\frac{2.889}{100} = \frac{2,889}{100,000}$$

d. $3.125\% = 3\frac{1}{8}\%$ *If you have memorized the decimal fraction equivalents of the eighths, the suggested method is much easier than the alternative method. Otherwise, it is a matter of preference. Note, however, the difficult reduction required using the alternative method.*

d. 3.125%

$$3\frac{1}{8}\% = \frac{25}{8}\%$$

$$\frac{3.125}{100} = \frac{3,125}{100,000}$$

$$\frac{\overset{1}{\cancel{25}}}{8} \times \frac{1}{\underset{4}{\cancel{100}}} = \frac{1}{32}$$

$$= \frac{1}{32}$$

5.3 Practice Problems

Convert the following percents to common fractions:

1. 35%
2. $3\frac{1}{2}\%$
3. 4.25%
4. $9\frac{3}{5}\%$

5.3. Answers to Practice Problems

1. $\dfrac{35}{100} = \dfrac{7}{20}$

2. $\dfrac{7}{2} \times \dfrac{1}{100} = \dfrac{7}{200}$

3. $4\dfrac{1}{4}\% = \dfrac{17}{4} \times \dfrac{1}{100} = \dfrac{17}{400}$

4. $\dfrac{\overset{12}{\cancel{48}}}{5} \times \dfrac{1}{\underset{25}{\cancel{100}}} = \dfrac{12}{125}$

5.4   Converting Common Fractions to Percents

To convert a common fraction to a percent, convert the common fraction to its decimal fraction equivalent (divide the numerator by the denominator), move the decimal point two places to the right, and add the percent sign.

EXAMPLE   Convert $\frac{7}{25}$ to a percent.

Solution

$$\begin{array}{r} .28 = 28\% \\ 25\overline{)7.00} \\ .28 \end{array}$$

     Divide the numerator, 7, by the denominator, 25. The quotient is .28.
     Move the decimal point two places to the right and add the percent sign.

When the common fraction to be converted is one that can be raised or lowered to an equivalent fraction with a denominator of 100, a shortcut can be used to convert it to a percent. Simply raise (or lower) the fraction to an equivalent fraction with a denominator of 100, remove the 100, and add a percent sign to the numerator.

EXAMPLE   Convert the following to percents: a. $\frac{7}{25}$ b. $\frac{36}{300}$

Solution   a. $\dfrac{7}{25} = \dfrac{28}{100} = 28\%$

     25 divides into 100 4 times; 4 times 7 = 28. Thus, the equivalent fraction with a denominator of 100 is 28/100. Remove the 100 and add the percent sign to 28 making the answer 28%.

b. $\dfrac{36}{300} = \dfrac{12}{100} = 12\%$

     In this problem, the denominator, 300, must be lowered by dividing it by 3 to find an equivalent fraction with a denominator of 100. Dividing the numerator, 36, by 3 provides a quotient of 12. Remove the 100 and add a percent sign to 12 for a conversion to 12%.

Convert the following common fractions to percents:

1. $\dfrac{5}{6}$ **2.** $3\dfrac{1}{2}$ **3.** $\dfrac{3}{50}$ **4.** $\dfrac{25}{500}$

5.4 Solutions to Practice Problems

1. $6\overline{)5.0000}$ $.8333 = 83.3\%$ **2.** $3.50 = 350\%$

3. $\dfrac{6}{100} = 6\% = 6\%$ **4.** $\dfrac{5}{100} = 5\%$

LEARNING UNIT 2
USING FORMULAS TO SOLVE PERCENTAGE, RATE, AND BASE PROBLEMS

Each percentage problem will have three main components. They are the base, the rate, and the percentage. You must be able to identify each of these elements in order to solve a problem.

Definitions

Base. The **base** represents the starting point. It may be the sales at the beginning of a year, or it may be the amount of material a tailor started with before cutting it to make a suit of clothes.

Other numbers are compared to the base, so it is a reference point. The base is the total of several items, or it is the whole amount of something. All totals include all of the parts and, therefore, can be represented by 100%. For example, the base might be the total (whole amount, 100%) of your earnings for the month. From that total, taxes and other deductions are taken. You spend your earnings after taxes on such things as food, clothing, shelter, and medical care. Maybe you are even able to save some. The base can be identified in three ways:

1. The base represents the starting point.
2. The base is the number to which comparisons are made.
3. The base is the total or whole amount and is always 100%.

Rate. The **rate** is a percent, decimal fraction, or common fraction representing the relationship between the percentage and the base. The rate is usually stated as a percent. Thus the percent symbol can help identify the rate. For example, taxes withheld from your total earnings may be 28%. *Notice that taxes and rate represent the same thing.* However, taxes are the dollar amount withheld, and 28% (the rate) is the percent withheld.

Percentage. The **percentage** is sometimes called the portion or the part. Percentage and percent are easily confused and they are frequently misused. You must use them correctly. A percentage is a part of the base. A **percent** is a numerical comparison between a percentage and a base. For example, taxes are 28% of your total earnings. The amount of tax is the part of the base to be determined by multiplying the base by the rate. The other part or parts of the base could be net earnings, food expenditures, clothing expenditures, and so forth.

Three formulas are possible for finding each of the components. The unknown you are solving for can be found by using the pie chart shown in Figure 5.1. It shows that the basic formula is

$$\text{percentage} = base \times rate.$$

Figure 5.1
Basic Formula for Finding a Percentage

If you need to solve for the rate, cover R and your formula is $R = \frac{P}{B}$. If you need to solve for the base, cover B and your formula is $\frac{P}{R}$.

Therefore, the three formulas are

$$P = B \times R, \quad R = \frac{P}{B}, \quad \text{and } B = \frac{P}{R}.$$

5.5 Finding the Percentage

Percentage problems involve finding one or more parts of the base. The base is the whole thing and, like the whole pie, it can be split into parts. In these problems, the rate and the base will be known or given in the problem. The formula is

$$\text{percentage } (P) = \text{base } (B) \times \text{rate } (R).$$

E X A M P L E   How much is 40% of 380?

Solution $P = B \times R$ The base comes after the word of. The word of indicates that
$P = 380 \times 40\%$ multiplication is to take place. The base frequently will be given in
$P = 152$ words or numbers immediately after the word of.

E X A M P L E   A capping machine caps 3,000 soft drink bottles each hour of operation. Records show 3% of the bottles' tops are chipped during capping. How many are expected to be chipped each hour?

Solution $P = B \times R$

Chipped tops (P) = bottles capped each hour $(B) \times$ % chipped tops (R)
$\uparrow$ $\qquad\qquad\qquad\qquad\uparrow\qquad\qquad\qquad\qquad\uparrow$
$\quad P \qquad = \qquad\qquad\quad 3,000 \qquad\times\qquad 3\%$

$P = 3,000 \times .03$ Note that the percentage and the rate represent the same
$P = 90$ chipped tops   thing—chipped tops.

The two previous examples illustrate typical percentage problems.

However, while the base is sometimes larger than the percentage, it is not always. The percentage is larger than the base when the rate is greater than 100%.

E X A M P L E   Ms. Rodriguez placed $1,000 in her savings account 20 years ago. It contains 150% as much now as it did then. How much does it contain now?

Solution $P = B \times R$

Amount *more* in savings account = original amount in savings $\times$ % *more*
$\uparrow$ $\qquad\qquad\qquad\qquad\qquad\uparrow\qquad\qquad\qquad\uparrow$
$\quad P \qquad\qquad = \qquad\qquad \$1,000 \qquad\times\quad 150\%$

$P = \$1,000 \times 1.5$ Note that the percentage and the rate are representations of the
$P = \$1,500$ same thing (more in the account).

5.5 Practice Problems

1. How much is 80% of 750?
2. How much is 124% of 25?
3. Twenty percent of a college's total student body of 18,450 is over the age of 40. How many students are over 40?

4. Sam purchased three items totaling $63. One item, a purse, was 30% of the total. How much did the purse cost?

5.5 Solutions to Practice Problems

1. $P = B \times R$
   $P = 750 \times 80\,\%$
   $P = 750 \times .8$
   $P = 600$

2. $P = B \times R$
   $P = 25 \times 124\,\%$
   $P = 25 \times 1.24$
   $P = 31$

3. $P = B \times R$

   Students over 40 (P) = total students (B) × % over 40 (R)
   $\uparrow$ $\uparrow$ $\uparrow$

   $P \quad\quad = \quad 18{,}450 \quad\times\quad 20\%$
   $P = 18{,}450 \times .2$
   $P = 3{,}690$

4. $P = B \times R$

   Amount spent on purse (P) = total cost (B) × % spent on purse (R)
   $\uparrow$ $\uparrow$ $\uparrow$

   $P \quad\quad = \quad \$63 \quad\times\quad 30\%$
   $P = \$63 \times .3$
   $P = \$18.90$

5.6 Finding the Rate

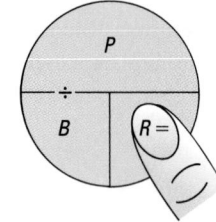

Figure 5.2

Rates (or percents) are tools for showing the relationship between a percentage and a base (Figure 5.2). The rate is found by dividing the percentage by the base.

$$R = \frac{P}{B}$$

Remember that the rate for which you are solving and the percentage you are dividing represent the same thing.

EXAMPLE   Twenty-six is what percent of 104?

Solution

$$R = \frac{P}{B}$$

$$R = \frac{26}{104}$$

$$R = .25 = 25\%$$

EXAMPLE   A quarterback completed 24 of 40 pass attempts. What was his completion rate?

Solution   Percent of completions $(R) = \dfrac{\text{number of completions } (P)}{\text{pass attempts } (B)}$

$$R = \frac{24}{40}$$

$$R = .6 = 60\%$$

EXAMPLE   Standard Auto Glass has an old machine that can cut 40 sheets of glass every minute. A new machine will result in an increase of 64 sheets per minute. Determine the rate of increase.

Solution % of increase $(R) = \dfrac{\text{amount of increase } (P)}{\text{old machine cuts } (B)}$

$$R = \dfrac{64}{40}$$

$$R = 1.6 = 160\%$$

5.6 Practice Problems

1. $2 is what percent of $8?
2. $2,494 is what percent of $1,247?
3. The cost of a textbook increased by $14 over its $28 price three years ago. Determine the rate of increase.
4. Of 30 million new television sets sold worldwide by U.S. manufacturers last year, 25.5 million were color sets. Calculate the rate of color set sales.

5.6 Solutions to Practice Problems

1. $R = \dfrac{P}{B}$

   $R = \dfrac{\$2}{\$8}$

   $R = .25 = 25\%$

2. $R = \dfrac{P}{B}$

   $R = \dfrac{\$2,494}{\$1,247}$

   $R = 2 = 200\%$

3. $R = \dfrac{P}{B}$

   % of increase $(R) = \dfrac{\text{amount of increase } (P)}{\text{original cost } (B)}$

   $R = \dfrac{\$14}{\$28}$

   $R = .5 = 50\%$

4. $R = \dfrac{P}{B}$

   % of color set sales $(R) = \dfrac{\text{number of color set sales } (P)}{\text{total set sales } (B)}$

   $R = \dfrac{25.5 \text{ million}}{30 \text{ million}}$

   $R = .85 = 85\%$

5.7 Finding the Base

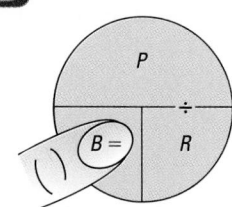

Figure 5.3

When the percentage and the rate are known, the base can be calculated (Figure 5.3). The formula is:

$$B = \dfrac{P}{R}$$

EXAMPLE Eighteen is 3% of what number?

Solution $B = \dfrac{18}{3\%} = \dfrac{18}{.03} = 600$

EXAMPLE Barbara Schrub administers penicillin shots. At the end of one day, she had used 12% of the penicillin available. She had used 24cc. How much penicillin was available at the beginning of the day?

Solution $B = \dfrac{P}{R}$

$$\text{Penicillin available } (B) = \frac{\text{amount of penicillin used } (P)}{\text{percent of penicillin used } (R)}$$

$$B = \frac{24cc}{12\%} = \frac{24cc}{.12} = 200cc$$

Remember that the percentage and the rate must refer to the same part of the base. That is especially important when the information in a problem refers to different parts of the base.

The following format could be used for any of these problems involving percents. However, it is most helpful for problems in which the percentage and the rate represent different parts of the base.

	Amount	%
Base		
+/− Percentage		
= Percentage		

The base is represented by 100%. All the parts of the base must add up to 100%. Only when a percentage and a rate represent the same thing can the problem be solved.

EXAMPLE At one car/truck dealership, new truck sales were 18% of total sales last month. New car sales were $369,000.

What are the total car and truck sales?

Solution

	Amount	%
Base		
+/− Percentage		
= Percentage		

In this problem, total sales are the base. New car sales are one percentage, and new truck sales are the other percentage. The rate for new truck sales is given. With that information and the previous format, the problem can be solved. The general format will be turned into a specific format for this problem (shown here):

	Amount	%
Total sales	[$450,000]	100%
− New truck sales		18%
= New car sales	$369,000	[82%]

Numbers in brackets represent answers after calculations (shown below) have been made.

Now the formula can be used. The amount and the % are both known for the "new car sales" percentage. The formula is

$$B = \frac{P}{R} \quad \text{total sales } B = \frac{\text{amount of new car sales } (P)}{\text{% of new car sales } (R)}$$

$$B = \frac{\$369,000}{82} = \frac{\$369,000}{.82} = \$450,000$$

1. Six percent of what number equals $25.20?
2. Two hundred percent of what number equals $6,142?
3. Sixteen percent of the original cost of a machine owned by A. D. Machine Shop will be depreciated this year. The depreciation will be $3,200. How much did the machine cost?
4. A collection agency collected $1,500, which was 75% of a delinquent account. How much was the total amount of the delinquent account?

5.7 Solutions to Practice Problems

1. $B = \dfrac{P}{R}$

    $B = \dfrac{\$25.20}{6\%}$

    $B = \dfrac{\$25.20}{.06} = \$420$

2. $B = \dfrac{P}{R}$

    $B = \dfrac{\$6,142}{200\%}$

    $B = \dfrac{\$6,142}{2} = \$3,071$

3. $B = \dfrac{P}{R}$ Original cost $(B) = \dfrac{\text{amount of depreciation } (P)}{\% \text{ of depreciation } (R)}$

    $B = \dfrac{\$3,200}{16\%} = \dfrac{\$3,200}{.16} = \$20,000$

4. $B = \dfrac{P}{R}$ Delinquent account $B = \dfrac{\text{amount collected } (P)}{\% \text{ collected } (R)}$

    $B = \dfrac{\$1,500}{75\%} = \dfrac{\$1,500}{.75} = \$2,000$

LEARNING UNIT 3
FINDING INCREASES AND DECREASES

EXCEL SPREADSHEET APPLICATION

The spreadsheet application at the end of this chapter will calculate a percent of change in department sales before and after a sale's promotion by the Springfield Department Store.

People in business often need to determine the result following an increase or decrease of something. For example, the value of an investment in a piece of land may have increased in value over the past five years. How much is the land now worth? When paying wages, employers must withhold certain deductions. Paychecks are written for the amount after those deductions have been subtracted.

Other times the original value (base) and the value after an increase or a decrease (percentage) are known. The rate of increase or decrease needs to be determined. For example, you know how much you earn, and you know how much your paycheck is. You want to calculate the percent of the deductions. You know how much you paid for your home. Someone offered you more. You want to know the percent increase of the offer.

The format used to solve problems using the percentage formulas can be used to solve these problems also.

5.8   Finding the Value after an Increase

EXAMPLE   The original cost of a piece of land was $240,000. Its market value has increased 28% over five years. How much is it worth now?

Solution

	Amount	%
Cost 5 years ago	$240,000	100%
+ Increase in value		28%
= Value of land now	[$307,200]	[128%]

$$P = B \times R$$

Value of land now (P) = cost of land 5 years ago (B) $\times$ % value of land now (R)

$P = \$240,000 \times 128\%$

$P = \$240,000 \times 1.28 = \$307,200$

In determining the value of the land now, the percentage and the rate are of the same part.

The use of the format can be time consuming. The process used was to add the percent of increase to 100% (100% represents the base), and then multiply the base by the resulting percent:

Base percent	100%
+ percent of increase	28%
= percent for new value	128% $\times$ $240,000 ($B$) = $307,200

Another way of solving this problem would be to solve for the amount of increase and then add it to the original cost:

$$P = B \times R$$

Increase in value (P) = cost of land 5 years ago (B) $\times$ % increase in value (R)

$P = \$240,000 \times 28\%$

$P = \$240,000 \times .28 = \$67,200$

$\$240,000$
$+ \ 67,200$
$\$307,200$

Both methods produce the same results. The choice of method is usually a matter of individual preference. However, occasionally, one of the methods is the only way the problem can be solved and choice is eliminated. Therefore, it is important to understand both methods and to be certain that the rate and the percentage represent the same part of the base.

5.8 Practice Problems

1. Jane Lauflin purchased some stock for $2,100. Two years later the stock had increased in market value by 24%. How much was the stock then worth?

2. Sam's sales were up 10% this year. Last year he sold $43,000 worth of goods. How much did he sell this year?

3. Enrollment at ASU is 16,450. Enrollment is expected to increase 42% in three years. What will the expected enrollment be at that time?

4. The price of gasoline has gone up 220% since 1956. Lui paid $.39 per gallon before the increase. Determine the price per gallon now. (Round your answer to the nearest cent.)

5.8 Solutions to Practice Problems

1.
Base percent	100%	$2,100
+ % of increase	+ 24%	$\times$ 1.24
% for stock worth now	124%	$2,604

2.
Base percent	100%	$43,000
+ % sales were up	+ 10%	$\times$ 1.10
% for sales this year	110%	$47,300

3.
Base percent	100%	16,450
+ % enrollment was up	+ 42%	$\times$ 1.42
% for enrollment in 3 years	142%	23,359

4.
Base percent	100%	$ .39
+ % gasoline price was up	+ 220%	$\times$ 3.20
% for gasoline price now	320%	$ 1.25

EXAMPLE Jorg Kievski earns $2,350 each month. The income tax rate for his bracket is 28%. What is the amount of Jorg's paycheck?

Solution

	Amount	%
Earnings	$2,350	100%
− Income tax deduction		28%
= Amount of paycheck	[$1,692]	[72%]

$$P = B \times R$$
Amount of paycheck (P) = earnings (B) × % of paycheck (R)
$$P = \$2,350 \times 72\% = \$2,350 \times .72 = \$1,692$$

The process is to subtract the percent of decrease from 100% (100% percent represents the base), and then multiply by the resulting percent:

Base percent	100%
− percent of decrease	28%
= percent for new value	72 % × $2,350 (B) = $1,692

The alternative method is to multiply the earnings by the % of deductions to find the amount of deductions and subtract them from the total earnings.

$$P = B \times R$$
Deductions (P) = earnings (B) × % of deductions (R)
$$P = \$2,350 \times 28\% = \$2,350 \times .28 = \$658$$

$$\begin{array}{r} \$2,350 \\ -\ \ 658 \\ \hline \$1,692 \end{array}$$

5.9 Practice Problems

1. The population of a city of 250,000 declined 18%. How large was the city after the decline?
2. Twenty-five percent of the cloth used in producing men's suits is lost in cutting. If a suit requires four yards of fabric before cutting begins, how many yards of cloth do finished suits actually contain?
3. Bobbin Pools, Inc., installed a swimming pool for $20,000. After a down payment of 16%, how much was still owed?
4. Fabric Emporium bought a new sewing machine that was on sale for 20% off the original selling price of $1,600. How much had to be paid?

5.9 Solutions to Practice Problems

1. | Base percent | 100% | $250,000 |
   |---|---|---|
   | − % of population decline | − 18% | × 82% |
   | % population after decline | 82% | $205,000 |

2. | Base percent | 100% | 4 |
   |---|---|---|
   | − % of lost cloth | − 25% | × 75% |
   | % of cloth in suit | 75% | 3 |

3. | Base percent | 100% | $20,000 |
   |---|---|---|
   | − % down | − 16% | × 84% |
   | % still owed | 84% | $16,800 |

4. | Base percent | 100% | $1,600 |
   |---|---|---|
   | − % off | − 20% | × 80% |
   | % paid | 80% | $1,280 |

EXAMPLE Profits at the Gossage Garage have increased from $24,000 last year to $30,000 this year. Calculate the rate of increase.

Solution

	Amount	%
Last year's profits	$24,000	100%
+ Amount of increase	[$ 6,000]	[25%]
= This year's profits	$30,000	

The information given in the problem has now been entered in the format. The problem calls for finding the rate of increase. That means we must have the amount of increase as our percentage so that *the rate and the percentage will be representations of the same part of the base*. The calculation to find the amount of increase is done by subtracting last year's profits from this year's profits.

$$\text{This year's profits} - \text{last year's profits} = \text{increase in profits}$$
$$\quad\quad \uparrow \quad\quad\quad\quad\quad\quad \uparrow \quad\quad\quad\quad\quad\quad \uparrow$$
$$\quad \$30,000 \quad\quad - \quad\quad \$24,000 \quad\quad = \quad\quad \$6,000$$

The base (last year's profits) and the percentage that matches its rate can be determined. Calculate the rate of increase by using the formula for finding the rate:

$$R = \frac{P}{B} \quad\quad R = \frac{\$6,000}{\$24,000} \begin{matrix} \longleftarrow \text{Amount of increase } (P) \\ \longleftarrow \text{Last year's sales } (B) \end{matrix}$$
$$R = .25 = 25\%$$

5.10 Practice Problems

1. Sale of air conditioners is forecast to increase from 2,400,000 to 3,200,000 units next summer. Determine the rate of increase.

2. A veterinarian is concerned because known rabies cases have increased from an average of two each month to nine this month. What is the rate of increase?

3. To improve its customer image, a supermarket chain has increased its advertising expenditures from $34 million to $51 million. Calculate the rate of increase.

4. A major wholesaler has increased its hours of operation. It used to be open 8 hours a day, 5 days per week. Now, it is open 10 hours a day, Monday through Friday, and 5 hours on Saturday. Determine the rate of increase in total hours per week.

5.10 Solutions to Practice Problems

1. $R = \dfrac{P}{B}$ Rate of increase $(R) = \dfrac{\text{amount of increase } (P)}{\text{original demand for A/C } (B)}$

   Amount of increase = 3,200,000 − 2,400,000 = 800,000

   $R = \dfrac{800,000}{2,400,000} = .33\dfrac{1}{3} = 33\dfrac{1}{3}\%$

2. $R = \dfrac{P}{B}$ Rate of increase $R = \dfrac{\text{amount of increase } (P)}{\text{original avg. rabies cases } (B)}$

   Amount of increase = 9 − 2 = 7

   $R = \dfrac{7}{2} = 3.50 = 350\%$

3. $R = \dfrac{P}{B}$ Rate of increase $(R) = \dfrac{\text{amount of increase }(P)}{\text{original hrs. of operation }(B)}$

Amount of increase = $51 million − $34 million = $17 million

$R = \dfrac{\$17}{\$34} = .50 = 50\%$

4. $R = \dfrac{P}{B}$ Rate of increase $(R) = \dfrac{\text{amount of increase }(P)}{\text{original adv. expenditures }(B)}$

Amount of increase = $[(10 \times 5) + 5] − (8 \times 5) = 55 − 40 = 15$

$R = \dfrac{15}{40} = .375 = 37.5\%$

5.11 Finding the Rate after a Decrease

EXAMPLE   The manufacturer's suggested retail price for one of the calculators in its line has decreased from $20 to $16. What is the rate of decrease?

Solution

	Amount	%
Last year's price	$20	100%
+ Amount of decrease	[$ 4]	[20%]
= This year's price	$16	

The information given in the problem has now been entered into the format. The problem calls for finding the rate of decrease. That means we must have the amount of decrease as our percentage so that *the rate and the percentage will be representations of the same part of the base*. The calculation to find the amount of decrease is to subtract this year's price from last year's price:

$$\begin{array}{ccccc}
\text{Last year's price} & - & \text{this year's price} & = & \text{decrease in price} \\
\uparrow & & \uparrow & & \uparrow \\
\$20 & - & \$16 & = & \$4
\end{array}$$

The base (last year's price) and the percentage that matches the desired rate can be calculated. Calculate the rate of decrease by using the formula for finding the rate:

$$R = \dfrac{P}{B} \qquad R = \dfrac{\$4 \longleftarrow \text{Amount of decrease }(P)}{\$20 \longleftarrow \text{Last year's price }(B)}$$

$$R = .20 = 20\%$$

5.11 Practice Problems

1. High photocopying costs forced Stanham's Secretarial Service to use alternate reproduction methods. In the past month photocopying costs have declined from $2,000 to $1,500. Calculate the rate of decline.

2. The water level in a lake has declined from 27 feet to 18 feet in the last six months. What is the rate of decline?

3. Jones and Company reduced its inventory from $45,000 to $41,625. What was the percent of reduction?

4. Sales have declined from $88,000 to $80,000. What is the rate of decline?

5.11 Solutions to Practice Problems

1. Last year's costs − this year's costs = amount of decline
   $2,000 − $1,500 = $500

   $$R = \dfrac{P}{B} \qquad R = \dfrac{\$500 \longleftarrow \text{Amount of decline }(P)}{\$2,000 \longleftarrow \text{Last year's costs }(B)}$$

   $$R = .25 = 25\%$$

2. Last year's level − this year's level = amount of decline

27 − 18 = 9

$$R = \frac{P}{B} \qquad R = \frac{9}{27} \longleftarrow \text{Amount of decline } (P) \\ \phantom{R = \frac{9}{27}} \longleftarrow \text{Last year's level } (B)$$

$$R = .33\frac{1}{3} = 33\frac{1}{3}\%$$

3. Last year's inventory − this year's inventory = amount of reduction

$45,000 − $41,625 = $3,375

$$R = \frac{P}{B} \qquad R = \frac{\$3,375}{\$45,000} \longleftarrow \text{Amount of reduction } (P) \\ \phantom{R = \frac{\$3,375}{\$45,000}} \longleftarrow \text{Last year's inventory } (B)$$

$$R = .075 = 7.5\%$$

4. Last year's sales − this year's sales = amount of decline

$88,000 − $80,000 = $8,000

$$R = \frac{P}{B} \qquad R = \frac{\$8,000}{\$88,000} \longleftarrow \text{Amount of decline } (P) \\ \phantom{R = \frac{\$8,000}{\$88,000}} \longleftarrow \text{Last year's sales } (B)$$

$$R = .0909 = 9.1\%$$

QUICK REFERENCE SUMMARY AND REVIEW

Page	Section Topic	Learning Concepts	Examples and Solutions
138	**5.1** Converting Percents to Decimal Fractions	Remove the percent sign and move the decimal point two places to the left.	Convert 13% to a decimal fraction: $13\% = .13. = .13$
139	**5.2** Converting Decimal Fractions to Percents	Move the decimal point two places to the right and add a percent sign.	Convert .034 to a percent: $.034 = .03.4\% = 3.4\%$
139	**5.3** Converting Percents to Common Fractions	Remove the percent sign, multiply by 1/100, and reduce to lowest terms.	Convert 48% to a common fraction: $48\% = 48 \times \frac{1}{100} = \frac{48}{100}$ $= \frac{12}{25}$
141	**5.4** Converting Common Fractions to Percents	Convert the common fraction to a decimal fraction and then move the decimal point two places to the right and add the percent sign.	Convert $\frac{32}{75}$ to a percent: $\frac{32}{75} = .427 = 42.7\%$
143	**5.5** Finding the Percentage	The percentage, often called the portion or the part, is found by multiplying the base by the rate.	If the rate is 18% and the base is $900, find the percentage: $P = B \times R$ $P = \$900 \times 18\%$ $P = \$162$
144	**5.6** Finding the Rate	The rate is found by dividing the percentage by the base.	If the base is $3,000 and the percentage is $1,800, find the rate: $R = \frac{P}{B} = \frac{\$1,800}{\$3,000} = 60\%$

Page	Section Topic	Learning Concepts	Examples and Solutions
145	**5.7** Finding the Base	The base is found by dividing the percentage by the rate.	If the rate is 44% and the percentage is 19,800, find the base: $B = \dfrac{P}{R} = \dfrac{19,800}{44\%} = \dfrac{19,800}{.44} = 45,000$
147	**5.8** Finding the Value after an Increase	The percentage to be found is the resulting value after a base has been increased by some amount.	If sales increased by 25% this year over last year's sales of $127,500, what are this year's sales? $127,500 100% + increase 25% = this year's sales 125% $B \times R = P$ $\$127,500 \times 125\% = \$159,375$
149	**5.9** Finding the Value after a Decrease	The percentage to be found is the resulting value after a base has been decreased by some amount.	If sales decreased by 25% from last year's $127,500, what are this year's sales? $127,500 100% − decrease 25% = this year's sales 75% $B \times R = P$ $\$127,500 \times 75\% = \$95,625$
150	**5.10** Finding the Rate after an Increase	The rate to be found is the rate of increase, given the original amount and the amount after the increase.	Costs have increased from $20,000 to $24,000. Find the rate of increase. R = % of increase; thus, P has to be the amount of increase. $P = \$24,000 - \$20,000 = \$4,000$ $R = \dfrac{P}{B} \quad R = \dfrac{\$4,000}{\$20,000} = 20\%$
151	**5.11** Finding the Rate after a Decrease	The rate to be found is the rate of decrease, given the original amount and the amount after the decrease.	Costs have declined from $24,000 to $20,000. Find the rate of decline. R = % of decline; thus, P has to be the amount of decline. $P = \$24,000 - \$20,000 = \$4,000$ $R = \dfrac{P}{B} \quad R = \dfrac{\$4,000}{\$24,000} = 16.7\%$

SURFING THE INTERNET

For further information on the topics covered in this chapter, check the following sites:

http://www.eduplace.com/math/mathsteps/6/c/index.html

http://www.mathleague.com/help/percent/percent.htm

5.1

Convert the following percents to decimal fractions:

1. 12%
.12

2. 165%
1.65

3. .035%
.00035

4. $5\frac{4}{5}$%

$5.8\% = .058$

5.2

Convert the following decimal fractions to percents:

5. .8
80%

6. .284
28.4%

7. $.8\frac{8}{9}$
$.889 = 88.9\%$

8. $.03\frac{1}{8}$
$.03125 = 3.125\%$

5.3

Convert the following percents to common fractions:

9. $9\frac{3}{5}$%

$\dfrac{48}{5}\% = \dfrac{\overset{12}{\cancel{48}}}{5} \times \dfrac{1}{\underset{25}{\cancel{100}}} = \dfrac{12}{125}$

10. $\dfrac{6}{25}$%

$\dfrac{\overset{3}{\cancel{6}}}{25} \times \dfrac{1}{\underset{50}{\cancel{100}}} = \dfrac{3}{1,250}$

11. .055%

$\dfrac{\overset{11}{\cancel{55}}}{1,000} \times \dfrac{1}{\underset{20}{\cancel{100}}} = \dfrac{11}{20,000}$

12. 11.2%

$\dfrac{112}{1,000} = \dfrac{14}{125}$

5.4

Convert the following common fractions to percents:

13. $\dfrac{7}{8}$

$\dfrac{.875}{8)7.000} = 87.5\%$

14. $\dfrac{16}{50}$

$\dfrac{.32}{50)16.00} = 32\%$

15. $.5\dfrac{2}{25}$

$.508 = 50.8\%$

16. $18\dfrac{2}{3}$

$\dfrac{56}{3} = 18.667 = 1,866.7\%$

5.5

Find the percentage in each of the following:

17. P = ?
B = 39
R = 32%
$P = B \times R$
$P = 39 \times .32$
$P = 12.48$

18. P = ?
B = 14
R = 215%
$P = B \times R$
$P = 14 \times 2.15$
$P = 30.1$

19. An employee has sales of $120,000. Find her earnings if she earns 9% of her total sales in commissions.
$P = B \times R$
$P = \$120,000 \times .09$
$P = \$10,800$

20. Zeke's computer proficiency has increased 28% since he attended a computer usage workshop. Before he attended, he averaged 22 pages of output per day. What is the number of additional pages Zeke now produces?
$P = B \times R$
$P = 22 \times .28$
$P = 6.16$

5.6

Find the rate in each of the following problems:

21. P = $9.80
B = $28
R = ?
$R = \dfrac{P}{B}$
$R = \dfrac{\$9.80}{\$28}$
$R = .35$
$R = 35\%$

22. P = $7.75
B = $125
R = ?
$R = \dfrac{P}{B}$
$R = \dfrac{\$7.75}{\$125}$
$R = .062$
$R = 6.2\%$

23. Calculate the percent of tax Joan pays if she must pay $2,850 on earnings of $19,000.
$R = \dfrac{P}{B}$ $R = \dfrac{\$2,850}{\$19,000} = .15 = 15\%$

24. During the Christmas selling season the Torburg Toy Store had sales of $136,500. Torburg's total sales for the year were $210,000. What percent of the total sales were made during the Christmas season?
$R = \dfrac{P}{B}$ $R = \dfrac{\$136,500}{\$210,000} = .65 = 65\%$

5.7

Find the base in each of the following problems:

25. $P = 430$

$B = ?$

$R = 25\%$

$B = \dfrac{P}{R}$

$B = \dfrac{430}{.25}$

$B = 1{,}720$

26. $P = \$9.50$

$B = ?$

$R = 2\frac{3}{8}\%$

$B = \dfrac{P}{R}$

$B = \dfrac{\$9.50}{.02375}$

$B = \$400$

27. Bowling Green State Bank pays an interest rate of $4\frac{1}{4}\%$ on savings. Suki earned \$2,125. How much was in her account before the interest was paid?

$B = \dfrac{P}{R}$ $B = \dfrac{\$2{,}125}{.0425}$ $B = \$50{,}000$

28. The state and city sales tax rate is $7\frac{1}{2}\%$. The waiter has added \$1.60 tax. What is the total food and drink bill?

$B = \dfrac{P}{R}$ $B = \dfrac{\$1.60}{.075}$ $B = \$21.33$

5.8

Find the value after an increase in each of the following problems:

29. $P = ?$ (amount of increase)

$B = \$35{,}000$

$R = 22\%$ increase

$V = ?$

100%	\$35,000
+ 22%	× 1.22
122%	\$42,700

30. $P = ?$ (amount of increase)

$B = 14.8$

$R = 5\frac{1}{4}\%$ increase

$V = ?$

100%	14.8
+ 5.25%	× 1.0525
105.25%	15.577

31. Sylvia joined a power lifting gym to increase her strength and fitness. After two weeks she was able to power lift 30% more than the 55 pounds she could lift when she started. How much can she now lift?

100%	55
+ 30%	× 1.3
130%	71.5

32. Glamour Poodles Grooming has had to increase its fees 12.5% across the board. If boarding had cost \$35 per day, how much does it cost now?

100%	\$35.00
+12.5%	×1.125
112.5%	\$39.38

5.9

Find the value after a decrease in each of the following problems:

33. $P = ?$ (amount of decrease)

$B = \$125$

$R = 60\%$ decrease

$V = ?$

100%	\$125
− 60%	× .4
40%	\$50

34. $P = ?$ (amount of decrease)

$B = 2\frac{3}{8}$

$R = 44.5\%$ decrease

$V = ?$

100%	2.375
− 44.5%	× .555
55.5%	1.318 (rounded)

35. The price of a computer work station has been reduced 27%. It previously sold for \$399. Find the current selling price.

100%	\$399
− 27%	× .73
73%	\$291.27

36. The advertising cost for spot commercials during one specific time frame has been reduced 7.5%. Last year each spot cost \$32,750. How much would the spots be now?

100%	\$32,750.00
−7.5%	× .925
92.5%	\$30,293.75

5.10

Find the rate after an increase in each of the following problems:

37. $P = \$56$ (amount after increase)

$B = \$42$

Amount of increase = ?

$R = ?$ (rate of increase)

$\begin{array}{l} \$56 \\ -42 \\ \hline \$14 \end{array}$ $R = \dfrac{P}{B} = \dfrac{14}{42} = 33\frac{1}{3}\%$

38. $P = 16{,}000$ (amount after increase)

$B = 12{,}000$

Amount of increase = ?

$R = ?$ (rate of increase)

$\begin{array}{l} 16{,}000 \\ -12{,}000 \\ \hline 4{,}000 \end{array}$ $R = \dfrac{P}{B} = \dfrac{4{,}000}{12{,}000} = 33\frac{1}{3}\%$

39. Profit increased from \$35,000 to \$42,700. Find the rate of increase.

$\begin{array}{l} 42{,}000 \\ -35{,}000 \\ \hline 7{,}700 \end{array}$ $R = \dfrac{P}{B} = \dfrac{7{,}700}{35{,}000} = 22\%$

40. Giving residents of the city collection bins has resulted in increased average collection poundage as follows:

Before Bin Giveaway	*After Bin Giveaway*
22 tons of newspapers	27 tons of newspapers
8 tons of plastic containers	10 tons of plastic containers
10 tons of aluminum containers	15 tons of aluminum containers

Calculate the percent increase in each of the three items, and the percent increase in the total tonnage.

$$\begin{array}{r} 27 \\ -22 \\ \hline 5 \end{array} \quad \frac{5}{22} = 22.72\% \text{ newspapers} \qquad \begin{array}{r} 10 \\ -8 \\ \hline 2 \end{array} \quad \frac{2}{8} = 25\% \text{ plactic containers} \qquad \begin{array}{r} 15 \\ -10 \\ \hline 5 \end{array} \quad \frac{5}{10} = 50\% \text{ aluminum containers}$$

Total tonnage

From	To		
22	27	52	$\frac{12}{40} = 30\%$
8	10	-40	
10	15	12	
40	52		

5.11

41. $P = 5,250$ (amount after decrease)
$B = 7,000$
Amount of decrease = ?
$R = ?$ (rate of decrease)

$$\begin{array}{r} 7,000 \\ -5,250 \\ \hline 1,750 \end{array} \quad \frac{1,750}{7,000} = 25\%$$

42. $P = \$12$ (amount after decrease)
$B = \$18$
Amount of decrease = ?
$R = ?$ (rate of decrease)

$$\begin{array}{r} \$18 \\ -12 \\ \hline \$\,6 \end{array} \quad \frac{\$6}{\$18} = 33\frac{1}{3}\%$$

43. One hundred fifty square yards of carpet were needed for a house that measured 147 square yards of floor space. Find the rate of loss from cutting.

$$\begin{array}{r} 150 \\ -147 \\ \hline 3 \end{array} \quad \frac{3}{150} = 2\%$$

44. Last year John "Stretch" Zukurski averaged 9 points per game. This year he averaged 7.875 points per game. Calculate the rate of decline.

$$\begin{array}{r} 9.000 \\ -7.875 \\ \hline 1.125 \end{array} \quad \frac{1.125}{9} = .125 = 12.5\%$$

CHAPTER REVIEW PROBLEMS

Answers to odd-numbered problems are given in Appendix A.

Drill Problems

Fill in all the blanks in conversion problems 1 through 12.

	Common Fraction	Decimal Fraction	Percent
1.	1/25	.04	4%
2.	9/1,000	.009	.9%
3.	3 9/10	3.9	390%
4.	1/10	.1	10%
5.	$\frac{4}{5}$	.8	80%
6.	$2\frac{13}{40}$	2.325	232.5%
7.	$\frac{4}{33}$	.121	12.1%
8.	$\frac{218}{500}$	.436	43.6%
9.	1/8	.125	12.5%
10.	29/800	.03625	$3\frac{5}{8}\%$
11.	$\frac{3}{400}$	.0075	$\frac{3}{4}\%$
12.	1 41/90	1.456	145.6%

Fill in the blank in problems 13 through 24.

	Base	Rate	Percentage
13.	$ 500	25%	$ 125
14.	$ 15	4%	$ .60
15.	$ 2,000	12%	$ 240
16.	$ 16	$4\frac{5}{8}\%$	$ .74
17.	$ 4	36%	$ 1.44
18.	$ 284	15%	$ 42.60
19.	$ 33	125%	$ 41.25
20.	$ 475,000	3.6%	$ 17,100
21.	$ 650	18%	$ 117
22.	$ 500	22.5%	$ 112.50
23.	$ 16,000	94%	$ 15,040
24.	$ 36	325%	$ 117

Chapter 5 Percentage Applications

Fill in the blanks in problems 25 through 32.

	Base	Percentage (Amount after an Increase)	Percentage (Amount of Increase)	% of Increase
25.	$ 1,250	$ 2,062.50	$ 812.50	65%
26.	$ 8.50	$ 11.22	$ 2.72	32%
27.	$ 342	$ 364.23	$ 22.23	6.5%
28.	$ 50,000	$ 116,500	$ 66,500	133%
29.	$ 2,875	$ 4,456.25	$ 1,581.25	55 %
30.	$ 514	$ 585.96	$ 71.96	14 %
31.	$ 250	$ 275	$ 25	10 %
32.	$ 2,222	$ 3,221.90	$ 999.90	45 %

Fill in the blanks in each of the problems 33 through 40 below:

	Base	Percentage (Amount after a Decrease)	Percentage (Amount of Decrease)	% of Decrease
33.	$ 4,000	$ 3,080	$ 920	23%
34.	$ 28.70	$ 19.80	$ 8.90	31%
35.	$ 25,950	$ 22,498.65	$ 3,451.35	13.3%
36.	$750,000	$ 745,078.12	$ 4,921.88	.656 %
37.	$ 475	$ 123.50	$ 351.50	74%
38.	$ 7,800	$ 6,942	$ 858	11%
39.	$ 6.29	$ 5.98	$ .31	4.9%
40.	$ 84	$ 19.74	$ 64.26	76.5%

Word Problems

41. Ralph Sterling earned $8.25 per hour. He worked 40 hours per week. Total payroll deductions were 35%. How much was deducted from each week's pay?

$8.25
× 40
$ 330

$330.00
× .35
$115.50

42. Due to a forklift mishap a container of goods valued at $1,640 was dropped. The resulting damage required reducing the price by 32%. How much was the price reduction?

$ 1,640
× .32
$524.80

43. A vegetable bin in a supermarket held 36 pounds of tomatoes. Before they could be sold, 5% were ruined or spoiled. How many pounds were lost?

36
× .05
1.8

44. New foreign car prices increased an average of 3% this year due to changes in currency valuation. If last year's average price was $18,000, how much was the price increase?

$18,000
× .03
$ 540

45. "Boomer" Bartholomew drives to the golf course every day to practice. His gas tank holds 14.8 gallons of gas. The price of gasoline averages $1.099 per gallon. The drive to the course takes 30% of the gas in the tank. How much is the gasoline cost for the trip to the course?

14.8
× .3
4.44

4.44
× $1.099
$ 4.88

46. Jefferson's Printing offered a 15% discount for custom Christmas cards ordered by September 1. Cards were packaged 25 to a box. Stan Johnson had 212 customers to whom he wanted to send cards. The cards he ordered August 28th were originally priced at $33.25 per box. What was Stan's total discount? (Cards are sold in full boxes only.)

$\frac{212}{25}$ = 8.48 (9 boxes must be bought)

$ 33.25
× 9
$299.25

$299.25
× 15%
$ 44.89

47. Sales for Howard Publications have increased by 225% in the past 10 years. Sales 10 years ago were $180,000. Calculate the amount of increase.

$180,000
× 2.25
$405,000

48. The NASDAQ stock index fell $1\frac{2}{3}$ % last week. At the beginning of the week, it was 792. How many points did it decline? (Round to nearest whole number.)

1,792
× .0167
29.93 = 30

or, $1\frac{2}{3}\% = \frac{5}{3}\% = \frac{\frac{5}{3}}{1} \times \frac{1}{100} = \frac{1}{60}$ $792 \times \frac{1}{60} = 30$

49. Susan uses her automobile to deliver fresh flowers. She anticipates that the car will lose 20% of its original value every year. If the automobile cost $14,365 new, how much value will it lose each year?

$14,365
× .2
$ 2,873

50. Executive Fashions, Inc., has decided to reduce the price of its $400 line of suits by 25%. Calculate the amount of reduction.

$ 400
× .25
$ 100

51. Toys Galore takes pride in offering a very deep line of toy products for all ages. It stocks a large number of boy and girl dolls. Seven and one-half percent of all dolls sold are male dolls. Last month 800 dolls were sold. How many were male dolls?

800
× .075
60

52. When a refrigerator malfunctioned, 114 pounds of fruit spoiled. The original truckload contained 1,425 pounds of fruit. What percent spoiled?

$\frac{114}{1,425}$ = .08 = 8%

53. Skinner, Inc., has the following office expenses each month:

Rent	$ 2,500
Utilities	760
Coffee	190
Salaries	7,150
Miscellaneous	5,400

What percent of the total budget does each expenditure represent? (Round to the nearest hundredth of a percent.)

$$\begin{array}{l} \$ 2,500 \\ 760 \\ 190 \\ 7,150 \\ 5,400 \\ \hline \$16,000 \end{array}$$

$\dfrac{\$2,500}{\$16,000} = 15.63\%$ $\dfrac{\$190}{\$16,00} = 1.19\%$ $\dfrac{\$5,400}{\$16,00} = 33.75\%$

$\dfrac{\$760}{\$16,000} = 4.75\%$ $\dfrac{\$7,150}{\$16,000} = 44.69\%$

54. A lawsuit for discrimination on the basis of sex was filed by the Equal Employment Opportunity Commission when an investigation found that an office employed 40 people, of whom 32 were male. What percent were male?

$\dfrac{32}{40} = 80\%$

55. In the last presidential election, approximately 70 million votes were cast. Close to 100 million Americans were registered to vote. What percent voted?

$\dfrac{70}{100} = 70\%$

56. Blaine Shinto purchased 8 computers at $3,500 each, 8 color printers at $1,395 each, and 6 computer workdesks at $445 each. His company was granted a cumulative quantity discount on the purchase amounting to $2,509.80. Calculate the quantity discount percent.

$$\begin{array}{l} \$3,500 \\ \underline{\times \quad 8} \\ \$28,000 \end{array} \quad \begin{array}{l} \$1,395 \\ \underline{\times \quad 8} \\ \$11,160 \end{array} \quad \begin{array}{l} \$445 \\ \underline{\times \quad 6} \\ \$2,670 \end{array} \quad \begin{array}{l} \$28,000 \\ 11,160 \\ \underline{2,670} \\ \$41,830 \end{array}$$

$\dfrac{\$ 2,509.80}{\$ 41,830.00} = 6\%$

57. The cost of a major economics textbook has increased $8 over its price last year of $48. Determine the rate of increase.

$\dfrac{\$8}{\$48} = .167 = 16.7\%$

58. An inspection of the radar equipment in an airline fleet disclosed that 8 of the 40 units were defective. What percent were defective?

$\dfrac{8}{40} = .2 = 20\%$

59. Business is improving dramatically. Consequently, employees are being asked to work overtime. Hourly employees are averaging $5 per hour more because of the overtime pay. They previously earned an average of $12.50 per hour. What is the rate of increase?

$\dfrac{\$ 5.00}{\$12.50} = .4 = 40\%$

60. In a recent survey, a hair products company found that 1 in 30 women used a hair color product. What percent of the women colored their hair?

$\dfrac{1}{30} = .0333 = 3.33\%$

61. A welder uses welding rods in which 7% of the total weight is brass. The rods used last month contained a total of 6.72 ounces of brass. How many pounds did the welding rods weigh? (There are 16 ounces in a pound.)

$\dfrac{6.72}{.07} = 96$ ounces $\dfrac{96}{16} = 6$ pounds

62. An employee had $101.25 withheld for federal income tax, $10.13 withheld for state income tax, $51.64 for FICA, $23.63 for union dues, and $48.25 for insurance. That totaled 34.8% of the employee's total earnings. What were her total earnings?

$$\begin{array}{l} \$101.25 \\ 10.13 \\ 51.64 \\ 23.63 \\ \underline{+ 48.25} \\ \$234.90 \end{array}$$

$\dfrac{\$234.90}{.348} = \$675$

63. The price of a new car increased $\frac{1}{2}\%$ over last year. The increase was $91.80. What was the price of last year's model?

$\dfrac{\$91.90}{.005} = \$18,360$

64. Richard owns a plumbing business. He paid income tax of $12,900 last year. That was 28% of his total income. What was his total income last year?

$\dfrac{\$12,900}{.28} = \$46,071.43$

65. Thirteen thousand students at ESU are women. That is 52% of the student body. How many students attend ESU?

$\dfrac{13,000}{.52} = 25,000$

66. Fifteen percent of the purchase price of machinery owned by A. D. Machine Shop will be depreciated this year. The depreciation will be $39,600. What was the purchase price of the machinery?

$\dfrac{\$39,600}{.15} = \$264,000$

67. A mutual fund company purchased 3 million shares of Shannon Products Inc. The purchase gave the mutual fund company $2\frac{7}{8}$ of the total outstanding stock. How many shares are outstanding? (Round your answer to the nearest thousand shares.)

$\dfrac{3,000,000}{.02875} = 104,348,000$

68. Three thousand square feet of floor space at Save-More Fashions is devoted to selling and display of merchandise. That is 60% of the total floor space. Calculate the total amount of floor space.

$$\frac{3,000}{.6} = 5,000$$

69. *Universal News* magazine has reached 64% of its annual subscription goal. So far, 256,000 copies have been subscribed. What is Universal's subscription goal?

$$\frac{256,000}{.64} = 400,000$$

70. Ms. Browning, owner of Rene's Pet Supplies, keeps track of parakeet sales by color. She sold 35 green birds last week, which accounted for 70% of all parakeet sales. How many parakeets were sold last week?

$$\frac{35}{.7} = 50$$

71. Smoke and water damage sustained during a fire required a sale of merchandise that brought only 55% of its original value. The auction company handling the sale received $330,000 for the merchandise. What was the original value of the merchandise?

$$\frac{\$330,000}{.55} = \$600,000$$

72. The consumer price index rose $7\frac{7}{10}$% this year. At the beginning of the year it was 137. What was it at the end of the year? (Round your answer to the nearest tenth).

100.0%	137
+ 7.7%	× 1.077
107.7%	147.549 = 147.5

73. Utility rates were increased by 8% two years ago, 6% last year, and another 12% at the beginning of this year. If the average commercial utility bill averaged $576 two years ago, how much more is the average bill this year?

100%	$576.00	100%	$622.08	100%	$659.40
+ 8%	× 1.08	+ 6%	× 1.06	+12%	× 1.12
108%	$622.08	106%	$659.40	112%	$738.53

74. A sales forecast indicated significantly higher sales for the coming year. Carra's Electronics Corp. will need to increase its $200,000 inventory 32%. What will the new inventory level be?

100%	$200,000
+ 32%	× 1.32
132%	$264,000

75. An incentive clause in "Slamming Sammy"" Aragon's baseball contract calls for an 8.5% bonus if he hits 40 home runs in a season. Sammy hit number 38 last night. His base contract figure is $3,575,900. What will Sammy's total earnings be after he hits number 40? (Round your answer to the nearest thousand dollars.)

100.0%	$3,575,900.00
+ 8.5%	× 1.085
108.5%	$3,879,851.50 = $3,880,000

76. Renner Department Stores wants to increase catalog sales. Last year it mailed 34,000 catalogs to residents of Oak Park. This year 15% more will be mailed. How many catalogs will be mailed this year?

100%	34,000
+ 15%	× 1.15
115%	39,100

77. Computer home video game sales are booming. Ideal Games, Inc., presently has 28 game diskettes. This year, 18% more new games will be marketed by Ideal. How many games will be available then?

100%	28
+ 18%	× 1.18
118%	33

78. During the Super Bowl, the Desert Mirage Country Inn raised its rate 210% for double-occupancy rooms. The normal rate was $112 per night. What was the rate during the Super Bowl?

100%	$112.00
+ 210%	× 3.1
310%	$347.20

79. Alpine Ski Resort owners were happy when new snow began to fall the day before yesterday. The base snow at the beginning of the snowfall was six feet. It increased 16% yesterday and another 7% on top of that today. What is the base snow now? (Round your final answer to the nearest tenth of a foot.)

100%	6	100%	6.96
+ 16%	× 1.16	+ 7%	× 1.07
116%	6.96	107%	7.4

80. Myrtle Wagner-Combes purchased 200 shares of American Fidelity stock at 20 dollars per share. After four months, the market price of the stock declined by 14%. What is the total value of the investment?

$ 20	100%	$4,000
× 200	−14%	× .86
$ 4,000	86%	$3.440

81. Medcare Corp. is offering special room rates to persons who opt to have elective surgery on Friday after a record check revealed that hospital check-ins on Fridays averaged 41% less than the Monday-through-Thursday average of 470 persons per day. On average, how many people checked in on an average Friday?

100%	470
−41%	× .59
59%	277

82. A shift in the demographics of the neighborhood has resulted in an 11% sales decline for a chain store. If its sales last year were $850,000, how much are they this year?

100%	$850,000
−11%	× .89
89%	$756,500

83. Recent interest rate increases have delayed new office building construction. This month's starts were down 5.8% from last year's same-month starts of 17,500. How many office buildings starts were made this month?

100.0%	17,500
− 5.8%	× .942
94.2%	16,485

84. Downtime for machine maintenance has been reduced 40% after a newly instituted employee training program. The average weekly downtime for all machines was 12 hours. What is it after training?

$$
\begin{array}{cc}
100\% & 12 \\
-40\% & \times .6 \\
\hline
60\% & 7.2
\end{array}
$$

85. Henry's Designer Shirts reduced the price of short-sleeved shirts 20%. One style previously sold for $39.95. Calculate the price after the reduction.

$$
\begin{array}{cc}
100\% & \$39.95 \\
-20\% & \times .80 \\
\hline
80\% & \$31.96
\end{array}
$$

86. Tax deductions for contributions to the Homeless Food and Shelter Center are no longer allowed. Two years ago contributions declined by 15%. Last year the decline was 12%. This year it was 10%. Before the declines began, contributions had reached a high of $228,500 for the year. How much were the amount of contributions this year?

$$
\begin{array}{cccccc}
100\% & \$228,500 & 100\% & \$194,225 & 100\% & \$170,918 \\
-15\% & \times \quad .85 & -12\% & \times \quad .88 & -10\% & \times \quad .90 \\
\hline
85\% & \$194,225 & 88\% & \$170,918 & 90\% & \$153,826.20
\end{array}
$$

87. Franz-Jones Bros. Trucking increased its tonnage 12% this month over last. The increase amounted to 44 tons. What was the end-of-the-month tonnage? (Round your answer to the nearest ton.)

$$\frac{44}{.12} = 367$$

88. The down payment for a new car was 8% of the purchase price. The buyer still owes $13,850. What was the purchase price?

$$
\begin{array}{c}
100\% \\
-8\% \\
\hline
92\%
\end{array}
\qquad
\frac{\$13,850}{.92} = \$15,054.35
$$

89. Eighty-eight new customers placed orders yesterday. Today there were 96. What was the rate of increase?

$$
\begin{array}{c}
96 \\
-88 \\
\hline
8
\end{array}
\qquad
\frac{8}{88} = .0909 = 9.1\%
$$

90. An old machine was replaced recently. It consistently stamped 36 molds per minute. The new machine stamps 90 per minute. What is the rate of improvement?

$$
\begin{array}{c}
90 \\
-36 \\
\hline
54
\end{array}
\qquad
\frac{54}{36} = 1.5 = 150\%
$$

91. A mutual fund received $155 million from investors this month. Last month $144.15 million was received. What is the rate of increase?

$$
\begin{array}{c}
\$155.00 \text{ m} \\
-144.15 \\
\hline
\$ \ 10.85
\end{array}
\qquad
\frac{\$10.85 \text{ m}}{\$144.15} = .07526 = 7.5\%
$$

92. Wholesale Auto Parts, Ltd., specializing in parts for limited edition foreign cars, has had sales go from $275,000 last year to $325,000 this year. What is the rate of increase?

$$
\begin{array}{c}
\$325,000 \\
-275,000 \\
\hline
\$ \ 50,000
\end{array}
\qquad
\frac{\$50,000}{\$275,000} = .1818 = 18.2\%
$$

93. This year's expense budget will be increased from $63,027 to $94,872. Find the rate of increase.

$$
\begin{array}{c}
\$94,872 \\
-63,027 \\
\hline
\$31,845
\end{array}
\qquad
\frac{\$31,845}{\$63,027} = .5052 = 50.5\%
$$

94. A local golf course has announced that beginning in May the 18-hole fee will go from $24 to $30. Calculate the rate of increase.

$$
\begin{array}{c}
\$30 \\
-24 \\
\hline
\$ \ 6
\end{array}
\qquad
\frac{\$6}{\$24} = .25 = 25\%
$$

95. Money put into an investment account grew at the rate of 5% each year. Trans World Trucking put $3,000,000 into the account. How much would be in the account at the end of the first three years if no money was withdrawn before then?

$$
\begin{array}{cccc}
100\% & \$3,000,000 & \$3,150,000 & \$3,307,500 \\
+ \ 5\% & \times \quad 1.05 & \times \quad 1.05 & \times \quad 1.05 \\
\hline
105\% & \$3,150,000 & \$3,307,500 & \$3,472,875
\end{array}
$$

96. Sales increased 22% last year and $12\frac{1}{4}\%$ this year. Two years ago sales were $138,000. What were they at the end of this year?

$$
\begin{array}{cccc}
100\% & \$138,000 & 100.00\% & \$168,360.00 \\
+ \ 22\% & \times \quad 1.22 & + \ 12.25\% & \times \quad 1.1225 \\
\hline
122\% & \$168,360 & 112.25\% & \$188,984.10
\end{array}
$$

97. Backorders have been reduced from an average of 37 per day to an average of 6.66 per day after buying a new computer inventory software program. What is the rate of reduction?

$$
\begin{array}{c}
37.00 \\
-6.66 \\
\hline
30.34
\end{array}
\qquad
\frac{30.34}{37} = .82 = 82\%
$$

98. The IBC Corporation has been downsizing. One method of doing that is to reduce the number of middle managers from 12,250 to 10,045. What is the rate of reduction?

$$
\begin{array}{c}
12,250 \\
-10,045 \\
\hline
2,205
\end{array}
\qquad
\frac{2,205}{12,250} = .18 = 18\%
$$

99. New computer chips have decreased down-loading time for end-of-day reports from subsidiaries to 18 minutes from the previous 27 minutes. What is the rate of decrease?

$$
\begin{array}{c}
27 \\
-18 \\
\hline
9
\end{array}
\qquad
\frac{9}{27} = .33\overline{3} = 33.3\% \text{ or } 33\frac{1}{3}\%
$$

100. Foreign cars are beginning to lose some of their market share. One model went from selling 23,275 units last year to 20,910 units this year. Determine the rate of decline.

$$\begin{array}{r} 23,275 \\ -\ 20,910 \\ \hline 2,365 \end{array}$$

$$\frac{2,365}{23,275} = .1016 = 10.2\%$$

101. Last year Juan Hernandez batted .327 for the Flyers. This year his average has dropped to .298. What is the percent of decline?

$$\begin{array}{r} .327 \\ -.298 \\ \hline .029 \end{array}$$

$$\frac{.029}{.327} = .0886 = 8.9\%$$

102. Weiberling Stereo Sales and Supplies is going out of business. Everything has been reduced for a quick sale. One stereo is on sale for $899 from $1,245.95. What is the rate of reduction?

$$\begin{array}{r} \$1,245.95 \\ -\ \ 899.00 \\ \hline \$\ 346.95 \end{array}$$

$$\frac{\$346.95}{\$1,245.95} = .2784 = 27.8\%$$

103. A successful environmental program has reduced the contaminants from 234 grains to 159 grains per 10,000 cubic centimeters. Find the rate of improvement.

$$\begin{array}{r} 234 \\ -\ 159 \\ \hline 75 \end{array}$$

$$\frac{75}{234} = .3205 = 32.1\%$$

104. Jason's pension fund invests in a mixture of bonds, common stock, and money market funds. Recently he has noted that the amount of funds invested in common stock has been decreasing. Last month $37.7 million was in common stock. This month it declined to $31.4 million. Find the rate of decline.

$$\begin{array}{r} \$37.7\ m \\ -\ 31.4 \\ \hline \$\ 6.3 \end{array}$$

$$\frac{\$6.3\ m}{\$37.7} = .1671 = 16.7\%$$

✓ENRICHMENT PROBLEMS

105. You and your significant other are considering a romantic dinner for two that costs $55. If the sales tax rate is 7% and you wish to leave a 15% tip including the cost of the meal plus tax, should you order the $55 meal if you only have $65? What would be the result if you did?

$$\begin{array}{r} 100\% \\ +\ 7\% \\ \hline 107\% \end{array} \quad \begin{array}{r} \$\ 55 \\ \times\ 1.07 \\ \hline \$58.85 \end{array} \quad \begin{array}{r} 100\% \\ +\ 15\% \\ \hline 115\% \end{array} \quad \begin{array}{r} \$58.85 \\ \times\ 1.15 \\ \hline \$67.68 \end{array}$$

The meal plus tax plus tip would come to $67.68. Thus, with only $65 the tip amount would be $6.15:

$$\begin{array}{r} \$65.00 \\ -\ 58.85 \\ \hline \$\ 6.15 \end{array} \quad \text{which is a tip of:} \quad \frac{\$\ 6.15}{\$58.85} = .1045 = 10.5\%$$

106. A car was purchased with a 12% down payment. The buyer still owes $9,386. What was the total purchase price?

	Amount	Percent
Purchase price		100%
− down payment		12%
amt still owed	$9,386.00	88%

$$\frac{\$9,386}{88\%} = \$10,665.91$$

107. Sales increased 15% each year for the past three years. What were the sales three years ago if sales this year are $304,175.

	Amount	Percent
Last year's sales		100%
+ increase		15%
this year's sales	$304,175	115%

$$\frac{\$304,175}{115\%} = \$264,500$$

Sales 1 year ago

	Amount	Percent
Sales 2 years ago		100%
+ increase		15%
last year's sales	$264,500	115%

$$\frac{\$264,500}{115\%} = \$230,000$$

Sales 2 years ago

	Amount	Percent
Sales 3 year's ago		100%
+ increase		15%
sales 2 years ago	$230,000	115%

$$\frac{\$230,000}{115\%} = \$200,000$$

Sales 3 years ago

John Trenton Electronics bases its buying budget estimates for each year on past history, economic trends and projections, and marketing research on community activity and population projections. Last year's buying budget is shown here:

Software		Printers	
IBM and compatibles	$ 157,000	IBM and compatibles	$438,000
Macintosh	44,500	Macintosh	85,500
Computers		Modems	59,000
IBM and compatibles	1,750,000	Fax Machines	105,000
Macintosh	225,000	Photocopying Machines	335,000
		Parts and Supplies	172,000

Projected costs this year will change from last to this year as follows:

1. The cost of all software is expected to increase by 4.75%.
2. IBM and compatible computers' costs will increase by 6%.
3. Costs for Macintosh computers will decline by 1.8%.
4. The average cost of all printers will decline by 5.3%.
5. Modem costs will remain constant.
6. Fax machine costs will increase by 2.33%.
7. Photocopying machine costs will decline by 1.15%.
8. Parts and supplies will experience an average cost increase of 4%.

Sales projections for the coming year are as follows:

1. IBM and compatibles software will increase in popularity by 8%.
2. Macintosh sales are under pressure because of the negative publicity on the state of the company's finances. Software purchases will decline by 3.5%.
3. IBM and compatibles computer sales will increase by 11%.
4. Macintosh computer sales will decrease by 7.6%.
5. Printer sales will increase by 12%.
6. Modem sales will increase by 3.25%.
7. Fax machine sales will increase by 8.75%.
8. Photocopying sales will decline by 4.9%.
9. Parts and supplies sales will decline by .5%.

Determine the dollar amount that should be budgeted for this year's purchases in each category. (Round to the nearest hundred dollars.)

Software	
IBM and compatibles	$ 177,600
Macintosh	45,000
Computers	
IBM and compatibles	2,059,100
Macintosh	204,200
Printers	
IBM and compatibles	464,600
Macintosh	90,700
Modems	60,900
Fax Machines	116,800
Photocopying Machines	314,900
Parts and Supplies	178,000

1. Identify the three main components of percentage
   problems and define each of them.
   The three main components are the base, the rate, and the percentage.
   Base can be defined as the starting point, the number to which comparisons are made, or the total amount. Rate can be defined as the
   percent relationship determined by dividing the percentage by the
   base. Percentage can be defined as a part of the base.

2. Describe the arithmetic operation that must be done to
   convert a percent to a decimal fraction.
   To convert a percent to a decimal fraction, move the decimal point
   two places to the left and remove the percent sign.

3. Convert $\frac{5}{8}$ to a percent.
   $$\frac{5}{8} = .625 = 62.5\%$$

4. Convert .056 to a percent.
   5.6%

5. Convert $5\frac{3}{4}\%$ to a decimal fraction.
   .575 % = .00575

6. Convert $33\frac{1}{3}\%$ to a common fraction.
   $$.33\frac{1}{3}\% = 33\frac{1}{3} \times \frac{1}{100} = \frac{\overset{1}{\cancel{100}}}{3} \times \frac{1}{\underset{1}{\cancel{100}}} = \frac{1}{3}$$

7. Shultz, Inc., withholds 7.3% from the gross pay of all
   employees for the retirement fund. If $33,945 was
   withheld one week, what was the gross payroll?
   $$\frac{\$33,945}{.073} = \$465,000$$

8. Sara has found that if she drives slowly, her classic Pierce-
   Arrow automobile gets 15 miles per gallon of gasoline.
   When she drives faster, it gets 10 miles per gallon. What
   percent of gasoline savings does she realize when she
   drives slowly?

   $$\begin{array}{r} 15 \\ -10 \\ \hline 5 \end{array} \qquad \frac{5}{15} = 33\frac{1}{3}\%$$

9. Havenview Savings and Loan pays a $5\frac{1}{2}\%$ simple annual
   rate of interest. If $550 interest was paid one year to
   Shawna Grey Consulting, what was the amount of the
   balance before the interest was earned?
   $$\frac{\$550}{.055} = \$10,000$$

10. Gas Equipment Testing Service offers a 2% discount to
    customers who pay promptly. Joyce Construction paid a
    bill for merchandise totaling $58,000 in time to take the
    discount. What amount will have to be paid?

    $$\begin{array}{r} 100\% \\ -\ 2\% \\ \hline 98\% \end{array} \qquad \begin{array}{r} \$58,000 \\ \times\quad .98 \\ \hline \$56,840 \end{array}$$

11. Of 1,500 marketing questionnaires mailed, 330 were
    returned. What was the rate of return?
    $$\frac{330}{1,500} = .22 = 22\%$$

12. Automobile insurance rates have increased $33\frac{1}{3}\%$ in the
    past 10 years. If the cost of a policy 10 years ago was
    $240, what is the cost of the same policy today?

    $$\begin{array}{r} 100.0\% \\ +\ 33.3\% \\ \hline 133.3\% \end{array} \qquad \begin{array}{r} \$240.00 \\ \times\ 1.333 \\ \hline \$319.92 \end{array} \quad \text{OR,} \quad 33\frac{1}{3}\% = .33\frac{1}{3} = \frac{1}{3} \qquad \$240 \times \frac{1}{3} = \$80$$
    $$\$240 + \$80 = \$320$$

13. An investor in the stock market found that a $2,500
    investment had declined 15% in value. How much is the
    investment worth now?

    $$\begin{array}{r} 100\% \\ -\ 15\% \\ \hline 85\% \end{array} \qquad \begin{array}{r} \$2,500 \\ \times\quad .85 \\ \hline \$2,125 \end{array}$$

14. Seagorshi and Company reduced its inventory from
    $45,000 to $41,625. What was the percent of reduction?

    $$\begin{array}{r} \$45,000 \\ -\ 41,625 \\ \hline \$\ 3,375 \end{array} \qquad \frac{\$3,375}{\$45,000} = .075 = 7.5\%$$

15. A store adds 40% to the cost of merchandise. If the cost
    for an electric hairbrush is $17.50, what is the amount that
    will be added?

    $$\begin{array}{r} \$17.50 \\ \times\ .4 \\ \hline \$\ 7.00 \end{array}$$

16. A chemical formula consists of 2 liters of sulfuric acid for
    every 24 liters of the compound. What percent of the
    compound is sulfuric acid?
    $$\frac{2}{24} = .0833 = 8.3\%$$

17. A dance studio's management is planning an advertising
    campaign to attract men to take lessons. Only 18% of the
    200 students presently enrolled are men. How many are
    men?

    $$\begin{array}{r} 200 \\ \times .18 \\ \hline 36 \end{array}$$

18. Twenty-five of every 40 people entering Johnson's Curio
    Shop to browse make purchases. What percent do not
    make purchases?

    $$\begin{array}{r} 40 \\ -\ 25 \\ \hline 15 \end{array} \qquad \frac{15}{40} = .375 = 37.5\%$$

19. Country Girl Cosmetics sold $82,000 worth of nail polish. Total company sales were $656,000. What percent of total sales was nail polish?

$$\frac{\$82,000}{\$625,000} = .125 = 12.5\%$$

20. Leslie Steel earned $3,705 one year cutting lawns. This accounted for 28.5% of her total lawn care income. Calculate Leslie's gross income.

$$\frac{\$3,705}{.285} = \$13,000$$

21. Sales Boosters, Inc., earned net income of $43,000 last year. This year's net income is $61,060. Determine the rate of increase.

$$\begin{array}{r} \$61,060 \\ - 43,000 \\ \hline \$18,060 \end{array}$$

$$\frac{\$18,060}{\$43,000} = .42 = 42\%$$

22. A customer made these purchases: $348.79 for a television set, $299.95 for a VCR, and $1,343.49 for a camcorder. A down payment of $150 was required. What percent of the total purchase price remains to be made?

$$\begin{array}{r} \$348.79 \\ 299.95 \\ + 1,343.49 \\ \hline \$1,992.23 \end{array}$$

$$\begin{array}{r} \$1,992.23 \\ - 150.00 \\ \hline \$1,842.23 \end{array}$$

$$\frac{\$1,842.23}{\$1,992.23} = .9247 = 92.5\%$$

EXCEL SPREADSHEET APPLICATION FOR CHAPTER 5

You have been asked to calculate the result of a recent store promotion by calculating a percent of change from the average department sales for the week before the promotion to the department sales at the end of the week of the sale. When you open Ch5App1 in your spreadsheet applications disk, it will appear as shown here:

Springfield Department Store

2617 Main Street

Box 219

Springfield, Maryland 58109

Telephone: 301-555-2158   FAX: 301-555-3498

RESULTS OF PROMOTION

Departments	Average Weekly Sales	Sales After Promotion	Amount of Increase	Percent of Increase
Men's Clothing				#DIV/0!
Women's Clothing				#DIV/0!
Children's Clothing				#DIV/0!
Household Linens				#DIV/0!
Home Furnishings				#DIV/0!
Appliances				#DIV/0!
Automotive				#DIV/0!
TOTALS	$0.00	$0.00	$0.00	#DIV/0!

Enter the following information:

	Average Weekly Sales	Sales after Promotion
Men's Clothing	$ 4,826.29	$ 5,285.98
Women's Clothing	9,576.91	12,377.22
Children's Clothing	4,119.35	4,342.47
Household Linens	3,370.32	3,432.12
Home Furnishings	4,121.48	4,193.11
Appliances	3,229.57	4,392.00
Automotive	4,392.76	6,392.47

Answer the following questions after completing the spreadsheet:

1. Which department had the greatest percent increase?
2. Which department had the greatest amount increase?
3. What was the percent increase for the Household Linens department?
4. What was the percent increase for the store?
5. Which department had the smallest percent increase?
6. Which department had the smallest amount increase?

GROUP REPORT

Write a report to the store manager describing the results of the promotion in each department and storewide. Based on the results, would your group consider the promotion successful? If so, why? If not, why not? Is any further information needed to make such a decision? If so, what information would be needed, and how would your group go about gathering it?

6 PAYROLL APPLICATIONS

SPANISH SIESTAS MAKE BETTER WORKERS—BUT DON'T SLEEP TOO LONG

The idea that tireless toil while in constant fear of unemployment is the best avenue to high productivity was rejected long ago by most American managers. Instead, Americans now believe that happy workers are more productive.

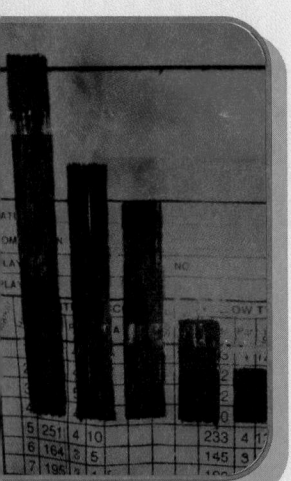

Today Americans are recognized as some of the most productive workers on earth. Much of the recent gains in productivity have been accomplished by working harder for longer hours. We have even recently passed the Japanese in numbers of hours worked per year. But are we happy? Numerous suggestions have been presented for changes in our work habits to make us happier. For example, there has been some talk that we might be happier if we emulated most Western Europeans by taking more vacation time. The Dutch, French, and Germans commonly take eight to ten weeks off per year.

However, the Latin custom of taking a short rest in the afternoon has rarely been seriously considered in the United States. In fact, with globalization, many firms in Spain have become Americanized, and their managers have required workers to work more as their American counterparts do.

New research at the College of Psychology in Seville, Spain, has determined that the Spanish siesta encourages worker productivity, lowers stress, and reduces mental saturation. According to the study a 10- to 40-minute nap gives your brain and muscles time to rest.

"In reinforcing memory and concentration, the siesta gives way to new cycles of cerebral activity in a more relaxed way," says the study's main author, Cesar Escalante. Professor Escalante warned, however, that one must not nap for too long, as "excessive rest can alter normal sleep patterns." Noting that the Spanish siesta tradition is gathering favor in Anglo–Saxon and Asian societies, he recommends that the naps last no longer than 40 minutes. A longer siesta, he says, can produce certain undesired effects in workers, such as "the feeling that they lack rest, a bad mood, and difficulty in waking up."

Chapter Glossary

Gross pay. Earnings before any deductions are made.

Net pay. Amount left after deductions are withheld from gross pay.

Deductions. Required and voluntary amounts withheld from the gross pay.

Salary. A typically contractual amount of money paid to an employee usually on an annual basis.

Overtime pay. Extra pay for working in excess of a stipulated amount of time per day or week, on weekends or holidays, or undesirable shifts.

Hourly wage. The most commonly used method for calculating earnings; based on the amount of time on the job.

Payroll register. An accurate record of salaries showing employees' number of regular and overtime hours, hourly rate of pay, gross income, involuntary deductions required by law, voluntary deductions authorized by the employees, and net income.

Piecework wages. Payment to workers according to the number of units they produce.

Differential piecework wages. Piecework wage rate that increases per unit as higher levels of productivity are reached.

Single-rate straight commissions. Salespersons' entire earnings calculated as a percent of net sales.

Draw. An advance payment of a salesperson's commissions.

Variable-rate straight commission. A commission rate that increases as higher sales levels are reached.

FICA. Passed by Congress in 1937 originally as a retirement supplement, now a federally supported retirement system with many other benefits for support of Americans.

Social Security tax. See FICA.

Medicare. A federal government system to pay a portion of the medical costs for senior citizens.

Federal income tax (FIT). Tax based on gross earnings an employer must withhold from each wage payment according to an employee's Form W-4 and the correct withholding rate.

Student Objectives

Upon completion of this chapter, you should be able to:

1. Calculate employees' gross pay using all of the following methods: salary, hourly wages, piecework wages, differential piecework wages, single-rate straight commissions, commissions with draw, variable-rate straight commissions, and salary plus commission.

2. Differentiate among various pay periods.

3. Calculate overtime pay on the basis of time.

4. Calculate Federal Insurance Contributions Act (FICA), Social Security tax, and deductions.

5. Calculate Medicare tax deductions.

6. Find the federal withholding tax (FIT) using the wage bracket method.

7. Find the federal withholding tax (FIT) using the percentage method.

Everyone is concerned with payroll. Employees want pay to be as high as possible and employers want it to be as low as possible. Employers are required by law to keep accurate payroll records. Most firms today use computer software programs to keep track of employees' gross pay and the deductions that result in net pay. Not all firms use the computer, of course, and an understanding of payroll calculations is important for all managers and employees.

Gross pay is the term that describes earnings before any deductions are made. **Net pay** (or **take home pay**) refers to the amount left after all deductions are withheld from the gross pay. **Deductions** are the required and the voluntary amounts employers withhold from gross pay. They almost always include Federal Insurance Contributions Act (FICA or Social Security tax) and **Federal income tax** (**FIT** or **withholding tax**).

In Chapter 6 payroll is considered from the point of view of both employee and employer. The employer's responsibility is to keep complete and accurate payroll records in the **payroll register**. A register helps an employer fulfill tax obligations of the FICA tax, FIT, state income tax, workers' compensation insurance, federal unemployment tax, and state unemployment tax.

LEARNING UNIT 1
GROSS PAY

Gross pay can be in the form of *wages*, *commissions*, or *salary*. Wages are paid for the time worked or the number of units produced. Commissions are paid according to the value of net sales. The term **salary** is usually applied to a fixed amount of annual earnings, paid periodically, whether an employee works more or less than the usual number of hours. Most salaried employees are not compensated for working "overtime." Generally, **overtime** refers to all time in excess of 40 hours per week. Some salaried employees receive compensatory time, or *comp time* (time off) for working overtime. Benefits packages usually include some number of days off for illness or personal emergencies during which employees do not lose pay. Paid vacations may also be part of a benefits package.

 **EXCEL Spreadsheet Application** Spreadsheet Application 1 at the end of this chapter is a program to determine the gross earnings of hourly workers.

6.1 Calculating the Gross Pay of Salaried Employees

To calculate the gross pay a salaried employee will receive each pay period, divide the amount of the salary by the agreed-upon number of pay periods in one year. The most common pay periods are shown in Table 6.1.

TABLE 6.1   PAY PERIODS IN ONE YEAR

SALARY PAID	ANNUAL PERIODS
Weekly	52 times (every week)
Biweekly	26 times (every two weeks)
Semimonthly	24 times (twice a month)
Monthly	12 times (every month)

EXAMPLE Joyce Goodyear is paid an annual salary of $27,950. Find her gross pay under each of the pay period alternatives.

Solution

$$\text{Weekly pay} = \frac{\$27,950}{52} = \$537.50$$

$$\text{Biweekly pay} = \frac{\$27,950}{26} = \$1,075$$

$$\text{Semimonthly pay} = \frac{\$27,950}{24} = \$1,164.58$$

$$\text{Monthly pay} = \frac{\$27,950}{12} = \$2,329.17$$

6.1 Practice Problems

Calculate the gross pay per period in the following problems:

1. Marie Alvarez's annual salary is $17,520. Marie is paid monthly. How much is her monthly gross pay?
2. A computer programmer is paid $42,900 yearly. How much is her gross pay per week?
3. Gerald "Mac" McDuff is paid twice a month, on the 15th and the last day of the month. His salary is $16,680 annually. Find his semimonthly gross pay.
4. Lana Winfrey is paid every two weeks. Her salary as a tax accountant is $75,000 annually. How much is her check each payday?

6.1 Solutions to Practice Problems

1. $\dfrac{\$17,520}{12} = \$1,460$

2. $\dfrac{\$42,900}{52} = \$825$

3. $\dfrac{\$16,680}{24} = \$695$

4. $\dfrac{\$75,000}{26} = \$2,884.62$

The most common method for calculating earnings is on the basis of the amount of time spent on the job. That is called an **hourly wage**. A **payroll register** is an accurate record of salaries showing employees' number of regular and overtime hours, hourly rate of pay, their gross income, involuntary deductions required by law, voluntary deductions authorized by the employees, and net income (Table 6.2). Today it is usually kept on a computer and shows deductions and net pay. Most hourly workers are covered by the federal Fair Labor Standards Act, which sets minimum wages and overtime standards and requires wages to be paid at a minimum rate of time-and-one-half for all hours worked in excess of 40 hours per week. Managerial workers are often exempt from the law.

TABLE 6.2 PAYROLL REGISTER

	Hours Worked	Total Hours		Reg	Gross Earnings		
Employee	S M T W H F S	Reg.	O.T.	Rate	Reg.	O.T.	Total
Martin, P.	– 8 8 9 8 6 4	40	3	$7.25	$290.00	$ 32.63	$322.63
Stans, M.	6 – 9 8 8 8 9	40	8	$9.14	$365.60	$109.68	$475.28

6.2 Calculating the Gross Pay for Employees Paid an Hourly Wage: Overtime for Over 40 Hours per Week

Gross pay can be calculated in either of two ways:

1. The standard method for the calculation is as follows:
   a. Multiply the regular rate of pay by 40 hours or less.
   b. Multiply the regular rate of pay by 1.5 and multiply that number by the overtime hours (all hours in excess of 40 per week).
   c. Add steps (a) and (b).

> Hourly rate × regular hours
> + Hourly rate × (1.5 × overtime hours)
> = Gross pay

2. The overtime premium method is favored by some businesses because it readily identifies the extra cost of overtime labor, which can point to inefficiencies. Also, workers' compensation insurance premiums are based on a worker's regular rate earnings.
   a. Multiply the regular rate of pay by all hours worked.
   b. Multiply the regular rate of pay by .5 and multiply that number by the overtime hours. The product is the overtime premium.
   c. Add steps (a) and (b).

> Hourly rate × all hours worked ← *Straight-time pay*
> + .5 × hourly rate (overtime hours) ← *Overtime premium*
> = Gross pay

Note. Do *not* round the intermediate calculations if they have more than two decimal positions. Round only the final answer to the nearest cent.

EXAMPLE   Calculate the gross pay for Zelda, who worked 47 hours one week. She is paid $8.45 per hour and time-and-one-half for all hours over 40 in one week.

Solution

Standard Method:

$8.45 × 40   = $338.00
$8.45 (1.5 × 7) = __88.73__
                  $426.73 ← *Gross pay*

8.45 ✕ 40 ▱ STO 8.45 ✕ 1.5 ✕ 7 ⊞ RCL ▱ 426.73

Overtime Premium Method:

$8.45 × 47   = $397.15
$8.45 (.5 × 7) = $_29.58_ ← *Overtime premium*
                 $426.73 ← *Gross pay*

8.45 ✕ 47 ▱ STO 8.45 ✕ .5 ✕ 7 ⊞ RCL ▱ 426.73

Calculate the following hourly wage problems assuming they all are paid time-and-one-half for all time over 40 hours per week:

1. Samuel Bowie is paid $6.95 per hour. He works part-time while going to school. Last week he worked 25 hours. Calculate his gross pay.

2. Sharon Hughes payroll register for the week follows:

	Hours Worked		Total Hours		Reg	Gross Earnings		
Employee	S M T W H F S		Reg.	O.T.	Rate	Reg.	O.T.	Total
Hughes, S.	– 9 8 8 7 8 6				$9.50			

Calculate her gross pay, and fill out the payroll register.

3. Phan Dun works in a convenience store for $5.65 per hour. One week she worked 52 hours. Calculate her gross pay using both methods.

4. Jabal Jefferson is paid $12.75 per hour on a GM production line. He just finished a work-week in which he put in $44\frac{3}{4}$ hours. Calculate his gross pay using both methods.

6.2 Solutions to Practice Problems

1. $6.95 × 25 = $173.75.

2.

	Hours Worked		Total Hours		Reg	Gross Earnings		
Employee	S M T W H F S		Reg.	O.T.	Rate	Reg.	O.T.	Total
Hughes, S.	– 9 8 8 7 8 6		40	6	$9.50	$380	$85.50	$465.50

$$
\begin{aligned}
\$9.50 × 40 &= \$380.00 \\
\$9.50\,(1.5 × 6) &= \underline{\ \ 85.50} \\
&\ \$465.50
\end{aligned}
$$

3. *Standard Method*

$$
\begin{aligned}
\$5.65 × 40 &= \$226.00 \\
\$5.65\,(1.5 × 12) &= \underline{101.70} \\
&\ \$327.70
\end{aligned}
$$

Overtime Premium Method

$$
\begin{aligned}
\$5.65 × 52 &= \$293.80 \\
\$5.65\,(.5 × 12) &= \underline{\ 33.90} \\
&\ \$327.70
\end{aligned}
$$

4. *Standard Method*

$$
\begin{aligned}
\$12.75 × 40 &= \$510.00 \\
\$12.75\,(1.5 × 4.75) &= \underline{\ 90.84} \\
&\ \$600.84
\end{aligned}
$$

Overtime Premium Method

$$
\begin{aligned}
\$12.75 × 44.75 &= \$570.56 \\
\$12.75\,(.5 × 4.75) &= \underline{\ 30.28} \\
&\ \$600.84
\end{aligned}
$$

6.3 Calculating the Gross Pay for Employees Paid an Hourly Wage: Other Methods of Computing Overtime

The Fair Labor Standards Act only sets a required minimum for pay. Overtime pay methods negotiated between labor unions and management are often more favorable to employees than is required by the law. Overtime is frequently paid for any hours in excess of eight hours per day instead of on an excess over 40 hour per week. Double time may be paid for weekends and holidays. A shift differential is often paid for the swing shift (3 P.M.–11 P.M. or 4 P.M.–midnight) and for the graveyard shift (11 P.M.–7 A.M. or midnight–8 A.M.). Split-shift premiums are for working the busiest times of a day such as a waiter who works the lunch shift, leaves, and then returns for the dinner shift.

A union has negotiated a contract that calls for overtime at time-and-one-half to be paid for all hours in excess of eight hours per day and double time for weekends and holidays. Joan Iberson's payroll ledger showed that she had worked the following schedule one week:

	Hours Worked		Total Hours		Reg	Gross Earnings		
Employee	S M T W H F S		Reg.	O.T.	Rate	Reg.	O.T.	Total
				1.5 2				
Iberson, J	– 7 9 9 6 5 4				$6.76			

Friday was July 4th and a holiday. Calculate Joan's gross pay.

Solution

	Hours Worked		Total Hours		Reg	Gross Earnings		
Employee	S M T W H F S		Reg.	O.T.	Rate	Reg.	O.T.	Total
				1.5 2				
Iberson, J	– 7 9 9 6 5 4		29	2 9	$6.76	$196.04	$141.96	$338.00

Standard Method:

$6.76 \times 29 =$ $196.04
$6.76 (1.5 \times 2) =$ 20.28
$6.76 (2 \times 9) =$ 121.68
                  $338.00

Overtime Premium Method:

$6.76 \times 40 =$ $270.40
$6.76 (.5 \times 2) =$ 6.76
$6.76 (1 \times 9) =$ 60.84
                  $338.00

The premium pay for double time is the same as regular pay—normally, the 1 need not be written.

Standard Method

6.76 ✕ 29 ▭ STO 6.76 ✕ 1.5 ✕ 2 ▭ RCL ▭ STO 6.76 ✕ 2 ✕ 9 ▭ RCL ▭ 338

Overtime Premium Method

6.76 ✕ 40 ▭ STO 6.76 ✕ .5 ✕ 2 ▭ RCL ▭ STO 6.76 ✕ 9 ▭ RCL ▭ 338

6.3 Practice Problems

Calculate the following gross payroll problems using both the standard method and the overtime premium method:

1. Michael Urestes works on a furniture assembly line. He is paid $5.95 per hour. Overtime at time-and-one-half is anything in excess of eight hours per day. One week he worked the following schedule:

   M 7:00 A.M.–5:30 P.M.

   T 7:00 A.M.–4:15 P.M.

   W 7:00 A.M.–5:00 P.M.　　　　*Michael is allowed a half hour for lunch at no pay.*

   H 6:45 A.M.–4:30 P.M.

   F 7:00 A.M.–4:45 P.M.

2. Eric Brewer worked the following hours last week:

   M 8:00 A.M.–5:30 P.M.

   T 8:00 A.M.–6:00 P.M.

W 7:00 A.M.–5:30 P.M.

H 8:00 A.M.–7:15 P.M.

F 7:30 A.M.–3:30 P.M.

Eric is paid $6.60 per hour. Overtime at $1\frac{1}{2}$ times the regular rate is any time before 8:00 A.M. and any time after 5:00 P.M. Lunch is one hour at no pay.

3. Kiki Vandameer works as a window dresser. She is paid $8.90 per hour. Overtime at $1\frac{1}{2}$ times the regular rate is for any time in excess of eight hours per day. Kiki sometimes has to work the midnight shift. She is paid double time for that. Last week Kiki worked the following schedule:

M 8:00 A.M.–5:00 p.m.

T 8:00 A.M.–6:30 P.M.

W 7:30 A.M.–5:30 P.M.

H off

F 12:00 midnight– 9:00 A.M.

S 6:30 A.M.–12:00 noon

Kiki takes one hour for lunch (for which she is not paid) when she works over four consecutive hours.

4. James Mahafey works as a waiter. His regular pay rate is $6.25 per hour. James frequently must work a split shift for which he is paid time-and-one-half. He is also paid time-and-one-half for any time over eight hours per day. If a holiday falls on a weekend that James works, he is paid double time. It is expected that he will snack during slack periods, so no time is provided for lunch or dinner. During one week, James had the following schedule:

S off

M 10:30 A.M.–2:30 P.M. & 6:30 P.M.–10:30 P.M.

T 12:30 P.M.–8:30 P.M.

W off

H off

F 11:00 A.M.–3:00 P.M. & 6:30 P.M.–11:00 P.M.

S 12:00 noon–8:00 P.M. (December 25th, a holiday)

6.3 Solutions Practice Problems

1. *Total Hours Worked*

		Regular Hours	O.T. Hours
M	10 hours	8	2
T	8 hours 45 minutes	8	.75
W	9 hours 30 minutes	8	1.5
H	9 hours 15 minutes	8	1.25
F	9 hours 15 minutes	8	1.25
	46 hours 45 minutes	40	6.75

Standard Method

$5.95 × 40 = $238.00
$5.95 (1.5 × 6.75) =   60.24
                   $298.24

Overtime Premium Method

$5.95 × 46.75 = $278.16
$5.95 (.5 × 6.75) =   20.08
                   $298.24

2. *Total Hours Worked*

		Regular Hours	O.T. Hours
M	8 hours 30 minutes	8	.5
T	9 hours	8	1
W	9 hours 30 minutes	8	1.5
H	10 hours 15 minutes	8	2.25
F	7 hours	6.5	.5
	44 hours 15 minutes	38.5	5.75

Note the difference here because of the way overtime is defined.

Standard Method

$6.60 × 38.5 = $254.10
$6.60 (1.5 × 5.75) =   56.93
                   $311.03

Overtime Premium Method

$6.60 × 44.25 = $292.05
$6.60 (.5 × 5.75) =   18.98
                   $311.03

3.

Total Hours Worked		Regular Hours	O.T. Hours 1.5×	2×
M	8 hours	8		
T	9 hours 30 minutes	8	1.5	
W	9 hours	8	1	
H				
F	8 hours			8
S	4 hours 30 minutes	4.5	___	_
	39 hours	28.5	2.5	8

Standard Method

$8.90 × 28.5 = $253.65
$8.90 (1.5 × 2.5) = 33.38
$8.90 × 2 × 8 = 142.40
$429.43

Overtime Premium Method

$8.90 × 39 = $347.10
$8.90 (.5 × 2.5) = 11.13
$8.90 × 1 × 8 = 71.20
$429.43

4.

Total Hours Worked		Regular Hours	O.T. Hours 1.5×	2×
M	8 hours		8	
T	8 hours	8		
W				
H				
F	8 hours 30 minutes		8.5	
S	8 hours	_	___	8
	32 hours 30 minutes	8	16.5	8

Standard Method

$6.25 × 8 = $ 50.00
$6.25 (1.5 × 16.5) = 154.69
$6.25 × 2 × 8 = 100.00
$304.69

Overtime Premium Method

$6.25 × 32.5 = $203.13
$6.25 (.5 × 16.5) = 51.56
$6.25 × 1 × 8 = 50.00
$304.69

At the turn of the century Frederick Taylor, the Father of Scientific Management, recommended that when the output of a worker was measurable, pay should be based on it. In that way, the better, more productive worker would be paid more, in accordance with his or her contribution to the organization's success.

In a **piecework wage** system workers are paid according to the number of units produced. The objective is to increase worker productivity by providing an incentive to reach higher levels of productivity for higher gross pay. Manufacturers in some industries such as garment making and agriculture pay on a piecework basis.

6.4 Calculating Straight Piecework Wages

One good characteristic of straight piecework is the simplicity of calculating gross earnings. This is done by adding the units produced in the pay period and multiplying the resulting sum by the piecework rate.

EXAMPLE Trina sews garments. She receives $.44 for each pocket, $.33 for each zipper, $.15 for each cuff, and $.05 for each belt loop she sews on men's trousers. How much would her gross pay be if she sewed 110 pockets, 55 zippers, 110 cuffs, and 330 belt loops during one pay period?

Solution

110 × $.44 = $48.40
55 × $.33 = 18.15
110 × $.15 = 16.50
330 × $.05 = 16.50
$99.55

110 ✕ .44 = STO 55 ✕ .33 + RCL = STO 110 ✕ .15 + RCL = STO 330 ✕ .05 + RCL = 99.55.

6.4 Practice Problems

Solve the following straight piecework problems:

1. Dennis machines handlebars for motorcycles. He is paid $1.15 per set. One week he produced 493 sets. How much did he earn?

2. Mortavia is paid $6.35 per hour or $.55 for each completed hand-blown glass, whichever is higher. Last week she worked 40 hours and completed 480 glasses. How much was her gross pay?

3. The minimum hourly wage set by federal law is $5.15 (the minimum is set by Congress and may vary). The Janis Corporation daily pays production workers $.84 for each lamp assembled, or the minimum wage, whichever is higher. Hugh Johnson assembled 45 lamps today in eight hours. How much is his gross pay?

4. Yesterday Jesus Rodriquez had the following production results: He sanded 30 cabinet doors, painted 18 doors, attached 45 doors, and crated and shipped 28 units. He is paid on the following per unit basis: $.25 for sanding, $.88 for painting, $.15 for assembly, and $.40 for crating. How much did he earn?

6.4 Solutions to Practice Problems

1. 493 × $1.15 = $566.95

2. 480 × $ .55 = $264   for piecework wage
   40 × $6.35 = $254   for hourly wage   Her gross pay is $264.

3. 8 × $5.15 = $41.20   hourly wage
   45 × $ .84 = $37.80   piecework wage   His gross pay is $41.20.

4. 30 × $.25 = $ 7.50
   18 × $.88 =   15.84
   45 × $.15 =   6.75
   28 × $.40 = +11.20
             $41.29

6.5 Calculating Differential Piecework Wages

The purpose of all piecework pay systems is to provide employees incentives to reach higher levels of production. A **differential piecework wage** system offers even more incentives because the wage rate increases per item as higher levels of productivity are reached.

EXAMPLE   The Aldolphus Corporation has the following differential piecework schedule:

0–50 units	$.59 each
51–100 units	.75 each
101–200 units	.92 each
all units over 200	1.10 each

Abe Ross produced 323 units. How much was his gross pay?

Solution

50 units × $ .59 = $ 29.50
50 units × $ .75 =   37.50
100 units × $ .92 =   92.00
123 units × $1.10 = 135.30
              $294.30

Multiply each pay rate by the number of units produced at that rate and add them all together to find the gross pay.

Note two things: 1. Do not skip categories
2. Subtract the ending number in a category from the next category's ending number to find the number of units in a category. The last category is all units left to calculate.

50 ✕ .59 ═ STO 50 ✕ .75 ╋ RCL ═ STO 100 ✕ .92 ╋ RCL ═

STO 123 ✕ 1.10 ╋ RCL ═ 294.30

6.5 Practice Problems

1. Strawberry pickers are paid daily for their production on the following differential piecwork schedule:

0–25 boxes	$.19 each
26–75 boxes	.25 each
all boxes over 75	.32 each

Calvin picked enough to fill 83 boxes. How much did he earn?

2. Tomasco Valdez produced plastic inserts for a machine. He was paid on the the following basis:

0–100 units	$.44 each
101–250 units	.55 each
251–500 units	.68 each
all units over 500	.80 each

Tomasco produced 607 units this week. What is his gross pay?

3. Jeremy Hass makes hand-tooled belts. He is paid on the following differential piecework schedule:

0–20 belts	$3.00 each
21–50 belts	5.00 each
all belts over 50	7.50 each

Jeremy completed 48 belts. How much is his gross pay?

4. Mi Kua does ornamental stitching on shirts and blouses. She is paid on the following schedule:

0–40 units	$1.00 each
41–100 units	1.25 each
all units over 100	1.50 each

Mi stitched a total of 143 shirts and blouses. How much did she earn?

6.5 Solutions to Practice Problems

1. 25 ✕ $ .19 = $ 4.75
   50 ✕   .25 = 12.50
    8 ✕   .32 =   2.56
                $19.81

2. 100 ✕ $.44 = $ 44.00
   150 ✕ .55 =   82.50
   250 ✕ .68 = 170.00
   107 ✕ .80 =   85.60
               $382.10

3. 20 ✕ $3.00 = $ 60.00
   28 ✕ $5.00 = 140.00
              $200.00

4. 40 ✕ $1.00 = $ 40.00
   60 ✕ 1.25 =   75.00
   43 ✕ 1.50 =   64.50
              $179.50

Commissions and piecework are both incentive pay systems. **Commissions** are paid to salespeople to reward them for their contribution to overall company sales and profits. There are several variations of commissions in practice.

6.6 Calculating Single-Rate Straight Commissions

A **single-rate straight commission** is being paid when a salesperson's entire earnings are from commissions, which can be a set amount per item sold or, more commonly, a percent of the net sales. Net sales are found by subtracting any sales returns or allowances from total, or gross, sales. The formula for finding commissions is an application of the percentage formula you studied in the last chapter.

EXAMPLE   Jim Lone Wolf sells medical supplies. He receives a commission rate of 6.5% on net sales. During September he sold merchandise worth $45,800. Customers returned $584 worth. Find Jim's gross earnings.

	$45,800	Gross sales
	− 584	Sales returns
	$45,216	Net sales

Solution

Net sales (*B*) × commission rate (*R*) = commission (*P*)

$45,216 × 6.5% = $2,939.04

A **draw** is an advance payment of a salesperson's commission and is commonly paid to the salesperson on a weekly basis. Commissions earned during the month are calculated and paid on the last day of the month after the total draw has been deducted.

EXAMPLE   Nicholas Stewart works on commission with a draw. On Friday of each week, except the last Friday of the month, he is paid $300. On the last Friday his commissions are calculated, and the difference between them and his draw is paid to him. In June the Fridays come on the 6th, 13th, 20th, and 27th. If Nicholas's net sales were $24,945 and he has a commission rate of 5%, how much was he paid on each of the June paydays?

Solution

June 6: $ 300.00 draw $24,945 × 5% = $1,247.25
June 13:   300.00 draw
June 20:   300.00 draw $ 1,247.25   *Commission*
June 27: + 347.25 ←   − 900.00   *Total draw*
          $1,247.25   ↘ $ 347.25   *Final check*

6.6 Practice Problems

Calculate the commission earned in each of the following problems:

1. Net sales = $23,500
   Commission rate = 8%
   Commissions = ?

2. Net sales = $16,592
   Commission rate = 4.2%
   Commissions = ?

3. Shelia Walker sells encyclopedias door-to-door. She receives a 17.5% commission rate. Last week she sold nine sets of encyclopedias at $435 each. One set was returned by the customer. How much did Shelia earn?

4. Mustaf Ishmil sells small appliances. He receives a draw against commissions. His draw is $1,000 semimonthly. His commissions are calculated and paid at the end of each quarter (at the end of every three months). His gross sales for the quarter were $94,934. Mustaf's commission rate is 7.5%. During the quarter, $1,945 worth of merchandise was returned. Calculate his commission check at the end of the quarter.

6.6 Solutions to Practice Problems

1. $23,500 × 8% = $1,880

2. $16,592 × 4.2% = $696.86

3. 9 − 1 = 8

   $ 435 $3,480
   ×   8   × 17.5%
   $3,480 $609

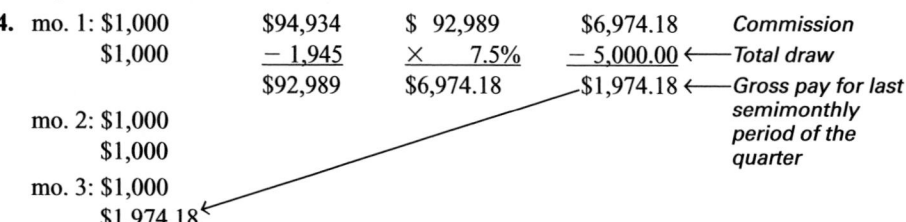

4. mo. 1: $1,000 $94,934 $ 92,989 $6,974.18   *Commission*
           $1,000   − 1,945   ×   7.5%   − 5,000.00 ←── *Total draw*
                        $92,989 $6,974.18 $1,974.18 ←── *Gross pay for last semimonthly period of the quarter*
   mo. 2: $1,000
           $1,000
   mo. 3: $1,000
           $1,974.18 ←

Commission

6.7 Calculating Variable-Rate Straight Commissions

Variable-rate, sliding-scale, or graduated commissions are the same thing. This type of commission provides greater incentives for salespeople to reach higher sales levels and helps companies retain the top producers. A variable rate is similar in many respects to a differential piecework system. A variable-rate straight commission increases as higher sales levels are reached.

EXAMPLE The Boron Corporation pays its salespeople on the following variable commission schedule:

0 – $5,000	3%
$5,000.01 – $7,000	5%
$7,000.01 – $10,000	8%
$10,000.01 – $15,000	10%
All over $15,000	15%

Boron's top salesperson had net sales of $21,750. How much did she earn?

Solution

$$\$ 5,000 \times 3\% = \$ 150$$
$$\$ 2,000 \times 5\% = \$ 100$$
$$\$ 3,000 \times 8\% = \$ 240$$
$$\$ 5,000 \times 10\% = \$ 500$$
$$\underline{\$ 6,750} \times 15\% = \underline{\$1,012.50}$$
$$\$21,750 \qquad \$2,002.50$$

Each level of sales must be calculated. You cannot skip categories. Be sure to subtract the last number at one level from the last number at the next higher level to find the amount of sales at that rate.

It is not necessary to add this column, but if you do, it provides a check figure for the net sales amount.

5,000 ✕ 3% 🟰 STO 2,000 ✕ 5% ➕ RCL 🟰 STO 3,000 ✕ 8% ➕ RCL 🟰 STO 5,000 ✕ 10% ➕ RCL 🟰 STO 6,750 ✕ 15% ➕ RCL 🟰 2,002.50

6.7 Practice Problems

1. Calculate the commissions for a salesperson who had net sales of $22,005 using the following variable schedule below:

$0–$10,000	5%
$10,000.01–$20,000	8%
$20,000.01 and over	12%

2. Marcus Quintana sells cleaning products. He had sales of $44,000, but $3,110 was returned. The company's variable schedule is as follows:

0–$10,000	4%
$10,000.01–$20,000	7%
$20,000.01 and over	10%

3. Ronald Williams works in a company that has a variable commission schedule. He had sales of $17,350, and customers returned $385 worth of merchandise. Determine his commissions using the following schedule :

the first $7,000	7.5%
over $7,000 to $12,000	10.0%
over $12,000 to $20,000	12.5%
all over $20,000	15.0%

4. Nancy Chang sells fashion clothing. She works on straight commission for a large wholesaler that has a variable commission structure. Nancy's sales were $28,957. Returns and allowances from customers amounted to $1,122. Calculate her commissions based on the following schedule:

the first $10,000	4%
over $10,000 to $17,500	7%

over $17,500 to $25,000   10%
all over $25,000   14%

6.7 Solutions to Practice Problems

1. $10,000 × 5% = $ 500
   $10,000 × 8% = $ 800
   $ 2,005 × 12% = $ 240.60
   $22,005 $1,540.60

2. $44,000 Total sales $10,000 × 4% = $ 400
   − 3,110 Sales returns $10,000 × 7% = $ 700
   $40,890 Net sales $20,890 × 10% = $2,089
                                $40,890 $3,189

3. $17,350 Total sales $ 7,000 × 7.5% = $ 525
   − 385 Sales returns $ 5,000 × 10.0% = $ 500
   $16,965 Net sales $ 4,965 × 12.5% = $ 620.63
                                $16,965 $1,645.63

4. $28,957 Total sales $10,000 × 4% = $ 400
   − 1,122 Returns & Allowances $ 7,500 × 7% = $ 525
   $27,835 Net sales $ 7,500 × 10% = $ 750
                                $ 2,835 × 14% = $ 396.90
                                $27,835 $2,071.90

6.8 Calculating Salary Plus Commissions

Many firms, especially retailers, offer a salary plus commission. The salary is to provide a stable income employees can depend on and compensates them for performing nonselling activities. The commission provides an incentive to sell and earn more without an upper limit on earnings.

EXAMPLE

Sally May Washington works in a department store that pays her $700 per month plus 4% on net sales. Last month she had net sales of $14,458. How much was her gross pay?

Solution

$14,458 × 4% = $ 578.32   *Commission*
              +   700.00   *Salary*
              $ 1,278.32   *Gross pay*

6.8 Practice Problems

1. June Langley is paid $150 per week plus a 7% commission rate for sales. At the end of this week June had sold $4,300 worth of merchandise. Calculate her gross pay.

2. Jim's sales were $39,994 this month. He receives a salary of $225 per month to compensate him for nonselling duties that are required of him. In addition, he receives a 4.5% commission. How much did he earn this month?

3. Winifred O'Brian sold $16,450 worth of VCRs and TVs in December. She receives a salary of $350 plus 6% of all sales over $4,500. How much was her gross pay?

4. Elton Marsh works in a sporting goods shop. He is paid $100 plus 3.5% for sales in clothing and other soft goods, 5.0% for sales of athletic shoes, 5.5% for sales of athletic equipment, and 4.0% for sales of all other merchandise. His sales for the week were as follows: clothes and soft goods, $1,473; athletic shoes, $877; athletic equipment, $1,943; and other merchandise, $195. Determine his total gross pay.

6.8 Solutions to Practice Problems

1. $4,300 × 7% = $301 Commission
              + 150 Salary
                $451 Gross pay

2. $39,994 \times 4.5\% = \$1,799.73$ Commission
$$\underline{+\ \ 225.00}\ \text{Salary}$$
$$\$2,024.73\ \text{Gross pay}$$

3. $16,450 \qquad \$11,950 \times 6\% = \$\ \ 717$ Commission
$$\underline{-4,500} \qquad\qquad\qquad \underline{+\ 350}\ \text{Salary}$$
$$\$11,950 \qquad\qquad\qquad \$1,067\ \text{Gross pay}$$

4. $\ \$1,473 \times 3.5\% = \$\ \ 51.56 \qquad\qquad \$\ 210.08$ Commission
$$877 \times 5\% \quad=\quad 43.85 \qquad\qquad \underline{+100.00}\ \text{Salary}$$
$$1,943 \times 5.5\% = \quad 106.87 \qquad\qquad \$\ 310.08\ \text{Gross pay}$$
$$\underline{195 \times 4\% \quad=\quad \ \ \ 7.80}$$
$$\$210.08\ \text{Commission}$$

LEARNING UNIT 2
CALCULATING PAYROLL DEDUCTIONS

Most employees have deductions subtracted from their gross pay. What is left over is net pay or take-home pay.

$$\text{Net pay} = \text{gross pay} - \text{deductions}$$

For most employees, the largest deductions are those required by law. Examples include federal income tax, Social Security tax, Medicare tax, and state income tax in most states. These are involuntary deductions. Other deductions may be voluntary, such as deductions for retirement, health and life insurance, and union dues. Table 6.3 shows a list of some of the more common deductions. While all of these deductions are important, and everyone should be aware of all of them, most vary so widely that a detailed discussion of them is beyond the scope of this text. The FICA and federal income tax deductions are discussed in this unit.

6.9 **Calculating the FICA Deduction**

The **Federal Insurance Contributions Act (FICA)** (also referred to as Social Security) was created by Congress in 1937 as a retirement supplement. The purpose of the act was to provide minimum benefits for people who were past their productive employment age and had no means of support. Since its modest beginnings, Social Security has grown into a federally supported retirement system with many other benefits for support of Americans who may or may not be in a position to

TABLE 6.3 COMMON DEDUCTIONS FROM GROSS PAY

Taxes	Retirement Plans	Insurance
Federal income tax	FICA (Social Security & Medicare)	Life insurance
State income tax		Health insurance
County and city income tax	State retirement plans	Disability insurance
	Company retirement plans	Dental insurance
	Private retirement plans	
Savings and Investments	**Professional Dues**	**Charitable Contributions**
Savings bonds	Union dues	Contributions to United Way
Tax-sheltered annuities	Professional associations	
Company stock plans (ESOP)		
Savings in credit unions		

support themselves effectively. These are the major benefits received by Americans covered by Social Security:

1. *Retirement benefits*: Monthly benefits made to retired citizens.
2. *Disability benefits*: Monthly payment made to those who are unable to work because of physical or mental disability.
3. *Survivor benefits*: Burial payments and monthly benefits made to the family of a deceased worker.
4. *Medical care for older citizens*: Payments to cover all or a portion of the medical costs for senior citizens. This program is called **Medicare.**

Almost 120 million workers in the United States pay Social Security taxes, and nearly one of every seven in the population receives a Social Security check. This heavy usage has compelled Congress to increase continually both the tax rate and the maximum earnings from which taxes are taken. Until 1991 the Social Security tax and the Medicare tax were combined. Since 1991, however, these tax rates have been expressed separately. The employer is legally required to withhold the tax from an employee's gross earnings, and must also match (pay dollar for dollar) all employee contributions.

As illustrated in Table 6.4, the Social Security tax was 6.2% in 2001 on a maximum of $80,400 of earnings. The Medicare tax was 1.45% on all earnings.

EXAMPLE Samuel Kress earns $8,750 each month. Calculate his Social Security and Medicare taxes for January.

Solution

Social Security Tax		Medicare Tax	
$8,750.00	Gross earnings	$8,750.00	Gross earnings
× 6.2%	SS tax rate	× 1.45%	Medicare tax rate
$ 542.50	SS tax withheld	$ 126.88	Medicare tax withheld

8750 ⊠ 6.2% ⊟ 542.50   1.45% ⊟ 126.875

Since it was the first month of the year, the employee had no previous annual earnings. In any month except January the employee's previous earnings during the

TABLE 6.4 SOCIAL SECURITY AND MEDICARE TAX INFORMATION FOR SELECTED PERIODS

	Social Security Tax		Medicare Tax	
Year	Social Security Tax Rate	Employee Earnings Subject to the Tax	Medicare Tax Rate	Employee Earnings Subject to Tax
1937	1.00%	$ 3,000		
.	.	.		
.	.	.		
.	.	.		
1949	1.00%	$ 3,000		
1985	7.05%	$ 39,600		
1990	7.65%	$ 51,300		
1995	6.20%	$ 61,200	1.45%	All wages
1998	6.20%	$ 68,400	1.45%	All wages
1999	6.20%	$ 72,600	1.45%	All wages
2000	6.20%	$ 76,200	1.45%	All wages
2001	6.20%	$ 80,400	1.45%	All wages

calendar year need to be known to assure that the tax is not withheld after the maximum has been reached.

EXAMPLE   Calculate the Social Security and Medicare taxes for Mr. Kress for the month of October. Assume he still earns $8,750 each month.

Solution   *Step 1.*   Find the previous calendar year earnings:

$ 8,750 ⟵ *Gross earnings per month*
× 9 ⟵ *October is the tenth month of the year and we need to calculate*
$78,750   *the earnings for the previous nine months.*

Step 2.   Subtract previous earnings this calendar year from the maximum earnings subject to the Social Security tax:

$ 80,400   *Maximum earnings subject to SS tax*
− 78,750   *Previous earnings this calendar year*
$ 2,094   *Gross monthly earnings subject to SS tax*

Step 3.   Multiply the Social Security tax rate by the smaller of the difference found in step 2 or the employee's gross earnings for the pay period (monthly in this example). The $2,094 difference found in step 2 is smaller than the gross monthly earnings of $8,750.

Social Security Tax

$2,094.00   *Earnings subject to SS tax*
× 6.2%   *SS tax rate*
$ 129.83   *SS tax withheld*

Step 4.   Medicare tax is always calculated on gross earnings for the pay period since there is no ceiling on earnings subject to it:

Medicare Tax

$ 8,750.00   *Gross earnings per month*
× 1.45%   *Medicare tax rate*
$ 126.88   *Medicare tax withheld*

Persons who are self-employed must pay both the employee's portion and the employer' matching contribution. This means they pay double the rates for the social security tax (6.20% × 2 = 12.40%) on the first $80,400, and for the Medicare tax (1.45% × 2 = 2.90%) on all earnings.

EXAMPLE   John Starkovic owns John's Gallery. He pays himself a weekly salary of $1,500. Calculate his Social Security and his Medicare deductions for the first week of July.

Solution   July is the seventh month of the year. The earnings from January 1 through the sixth month, June, need to be known. June ends the first half of the year: $\frac{1}{2}$ year × 52 weeks in one year equals 26 weeks.

$ 1,500   *Gross weekly earnings*
× 26   *Number of weeks in previous calendar year*
$39,000   *Previous annual earnings*

$ 80,400   *Maximum earnings subject to SS tax*
− 39,000   *Pevious earnings*
$ 41,400   *Earnings still subject to SS tax*

$1,500 is smaller than $41,400, so:

Social Security Tax

$1,500.00   *Gross earnings*
×   12.4%   *SS tax rate*
$ 186.00   *SS tax withheld*

Medicare Tax

$1,500.00   *Gross earnings*
×   2.9%   *Medicare tax rate*
$ 43.50   *Medicare tax withheld*

1,500 ⊠ 12.4% ⊜ 186   2.9% ⊜ 43.50

(This assumes use of the calculator constant functions.)

6.9 Practice Problems

Calculate the Social Security and Medicare deductions for the following problems:

1. Gerald Childress had earned $28,385 prior to this week's paycheck. The check is for $443. Determine the deduction for Social Security and Medicare.

2. If $39,000 has been earned before the current monthly paycheck for $3,498 is paid, how much will be withheld for Social Security and Medicare?

3. Suzanne Peters is paid $9.75 per hour. She is paid biweekly. The week before last she worked 40 hours. This week she worked 46 hours. She is paid time-and-one-half for all hours over 40 per week. Her previous earnings were $12,599. How much will be deducted from her check this payday for Social Security and for Medicare?

4. Bobbie Linstrum is paid $7,750 monthly. She wants to calculate how much will be withheld for Medicare and Social Security in November. Make the calculations for her.

6.9 Solutions to Practice Problems

1. $ 80,400 Maximum earnings subject to SS tax
   − 28,385 Previous earnings
   $ 52,015 Earnings still subject to SS tax
   $443 is smaller than $52,015.

Social Security Tax	Medicare Tax
$ 443.00 Gross earnings	$ 443.00 Gross earnings
× 6.2% SS tax rate	× 1.45% Medicare tax rate
$ 27.47 SS tax withheld	$ 6.42 Medicare tax withheld

2. $ 80,400 Maximum earnings subject to SS tax
   − 39,000 Previous earnings
   $ 41,400 Earnings still subject to SS tax
   $ 3,498 is smaller than $41,400.

Social Security Tax	Medicare Tax
$3,498.00 Gross earnings	$ 3,498.00 Gross earnings
× 6.2% SS tax rate	× 1.45% Medicare tax rate
$ 216.88 SS tax withheld	$ 50.72 Medicare tax withheld

3. $9.75 × 40 = $390.00
   $9.75 × 40 =   390.00
   $9.75 × 1.5 × 6 =   87.75
                  $867.75

   $ 80,400 Maximum earnings subject to SS tax
   − 12,599 Previous earnings
   $ 67,801 Earnings still subject to SS tax
   $867.75 is smaller than $67,801.

Social Security Tax	Medicare Tax
$867.75 Gross earnings	$ 867.75 Gross earnings
× 6.2% SS tax rate	× 1.45% Medicare tax rate
$ 53.80 SS tax withheld	$ 12.58 Medicare tax withheld

4. $ 7,750 Monthly earnings
   ×   10 Earnings for previous 10 months (Nov. is 11th month).
   $77,500 Previous earnings

$ 80,400 Maximum earnings subject to SS tax
−77,500 Previous earnings
$ 2,900 Earnings still subject to SS tax
$ 2,900 is smaller than $7,750.

Social Security Tax	Medicare Tax
$ 2,900.00 Earnings subject to SS tax	$ 7,750.00 Gross earnings
× 6.2% SS tax rate	× 1.45% Medicare tax rate
$ 179.80 SS tax withheld	$ 112.38 Medicare tax wthld

6.10 Calculating the Federal Income Tax Withholding

The **Federal Income Tax (FIT)**, also known as the *personal income tax*, is usually the largest deduction made from gross pay. It is also the single largest source of revenue to the federal government. The law states that an employer must "withhold tax from each wage payment . . . according to the employee's Form W-4 and the correct withholding rate." A sample Form W-4, the Employee's Withholding Allowance Certificate, is shown in Table 6.5. Each employee completes a Form W-4 when hired. The tax becomes effective with the first wage payment. To determine the income tax withholding, several considerations must be made:

1. *Wages paid*, including tips reported.
2. *Marital status*. The withholding tables are different for single and for married employees.
3. *Withholding allowances*. The process to determine the correct number of withholding allowances claimed on Form W-4 begins with the number of personal exemptions the employee expects to claim on her or his tax return. Generally, the employee is allowed to claim one allowance for each person who depends on the income. However, the number of allowances claimed may be adjusted by nonwage income on which tax has not been withheld, large amounts of itemized deductions, and more than one wage earned in the family. This

TABLE 6.5

- - - - - - - - - - - Cut here and give Form W-4 to your employer. Keep the top part for your records. - - - - - - - - - - -

Form **W-4** Department of the Treasury Internal Revenue Service	**Employee's Withholding Allowance Certificate** ► **For Privacy Act and Paperwork Reduction Act Notice, see page 2.**	OMB No. 1545-0010 2001
1 Type or print your first name and middle initial Last name		2 Your social security number
Home address (number and street or rural route)	3 ☐ Single ☐ Married ☐ Married, but withhold at higher Single rate. **Note:** *If married, but legally separated, or spouse is a nonresident alien, check the Single box.*	
City or town, state, and ZIP code	4 If your last name differs from that on your social security card, check here. You must call 1-800-772-1213 for a new card. ► ☐	

5   Total number of allowances you are claiming (from line **H** above **or** from the applicable worksheet on page 2) · · · · · · | **5** |
6   Additional amount, if any, you want withheld from each paycheck . . . . | **6** | $ |
7   I claim exemption from withholding for 2001, and I certify that I meet **both** of the following conditions for exemption:
 • Last year I had a right to a refund of **all** Federal income tax withheld because I had **no** tax liability **and**
 • This year I expect a refund of **all** Federal income tax withheld because I expect to have **no** tax liability.
 If you meet both conditions, write "Exempt" here . . . . ► | **7** |

Under penalties of perjury, I certify that I am entitled to the number of withholding allowances claimed on this certificate, or I am entitled to claim exempt status.
Employee's signature
(Form is not valid
unless you sign it.) ►   Date ►

8 Employer's name and address (Employer: Complete lines 8 and 10 only if sending to the IRS.)	9 Office code (optional)	10 Employer identification number

Cat. No. 10220Q

increase or decrease is based on the employee's financial situation, as outlined on the Form W-4 worksheets. Employees may claim *fewer* withholding allowances than they are entitled to claim. Fewer allowances may be claimed to generate a tax refund or to offset other sources of taxable income that are not subject to adequate withholding.

Employers can use one of two methods in calculating the amount of FIT to be withheld: the wage bracket method or the percentage method.

The Wage Bracket Method

To use the wage bracket method do the following:

1. Find the proper table for the employee's *marital status* as shown on his or her Form W-4, and for the *correct payroll period*. Tables are available for employees who are paid weekly, biweekly, semimonthly, monthly, and daily or on a miscellaneous basis. Table 6.6 is for *single persons* paid *weekly*. Table 6.7 is for *married persons* paid *weekly*.
2. Find the intersection of the amount of wages being paid and the number of withholding allowances claimed on the Form W-4. The number at the intersection is the amount of FIT to be withheld.

EXAMPLE   Use the tables to find the FIT withholding for Edward Jones, who earned $465 this week. Edward's Form W-4 shows that he is married and claims four withholding allowances.

Solution   Using Table 6.7 for married persons paid weekly, find the correct line for the amount of pay ($465) on that table. The two leftmost columns are headed:

"At least"   "But less than"

The correct line is "At least" 460, "But less than" 470. Go across that line until it intersects with the column headed by "And the number of withholding allowances claimed is 4." The amount of income tax to be withheld is "18" at the intersection. So, the tax to be withheld is $18.

The Percentage Method

Instead of using the wage bracket tables to determine how much income tax to withhold, a percentage computation based on Table 6.8, Percentage Method—Amount for One Withholding Allowance, and Table 6.9, Tables for Percentage Method of Withholding (For Wages Paid in July–Dec 2001) can be used. This method is generally used when a company uses a computer to process its payroll records and it does not wish to store a complete payroll table. Use the following steps to determine the income tax to withhold when using the percentage method:

1. Multiply one withholding allowance (see Table 6.8) by the number of allowances the employee claims.
2. Subtract that amount from the employee's wages.
3. Determine the amount to withhold from Table 6.9

EXAMPLE   Use the percentage method to find the FIT withholding for Edward Jones, who earned $465 this week. Edward's Form W-4 shows that he is married and claims four withholding allowances.

Solution   *Step 1.* $ 55.77 From Table 6.8 for weekly payroll period, one withholding allowance.

$\times$ 4 From Form W-4, withholding allowances claimed

$223.08 Withholding allowance

TABLE 6.6

SINGLE Persons—WEEKLY Payroll Period

(For Wages Paid in July–Dec 2001)

If the wages are—		And the number of withholding allowances claimed is—										
At least	But less than	0	1	2	3	4	5	6	7	8	9	10
		The amount of income tax to be withheld is—										
$0	$55	0	0	0	0	0	0	0	0	0	0	0
55	60	1	0	0	0	0	0	0	0	0	0	0
60	65	2	0	0	0	0	0	0	0	0	0	0
65	70	2	0	0	0	0	0	0	0	0	0	0
70	75	3	0	0	0	0	0	0	0	0	0	0
75	80	4	0	0	0	0	0	0	0	0	0	0
80	85	5	0	0	0	0	0	0	0	0	0	0
85	90	5	0	0	0	0	0	0	0	0	0	0
90	95	6	0	0	0	0	0	0	0	0	0	0
95	100	7	0	0	0	0	0	0	0	0	0	0
100	105	8	0	0	0	0	0	0	0	0	0	0
105	110	8	0	0	0	0	0	0	0	0	0	0
110	115	9	1	0	0	0	0	0	0	0	0	0
115	120	10	2	0	0	0	0	0	0	0	0	0
120	125	11	2	0	0	0	0	0	0	0	0	0
125	130	11	3	0	0	0	0	0	0	0	0	0
130	135	12	4	0	0	0	0	0	0	0	0	0
135	140	13	5	0	0	0	0	0	0	0	0	0
140	145	14	5	0	0	0	0	0	0	0	0	0
145	150	14	6	0	0	0	0	0	0	0	0	0
150	155	15	7	0	0	0	0	0	0	0	0	0
155	160	16	8	0	0	0	0	0	0	0	0	0
160	165	17	8	0	0	0	0	0	0	0	0	0
165	170	17	9	1	0	0	0	0	0	0	0	0
170	175	18	10	2	0	0	0	0	0	0	0	0
175	180	19	11	2	0	0	0	0	0	0	0	0
180	185	20	11	3	0	0	0	0	0	0	0	0
185	190	20	12	4	0	0	0	0	0	0	0	0
190	195	21	13	5	0	0	0	0	0	0	0	0
195	200	22	14	5	0	0	0	0	0	0	0	0
200	210	23	15	6	0	0	0	0	0	0	0	0
210	220	25	16	8	0	0	0	0	0	0	0	0
220	230	26	18	9	1	0	0	0	0	0	0	0
230	240	28	19	11	3	0	0	0	0	0	0	0
240	250	29	21	12	4	0	0	0	0	0	0	0
250	260	31	22	14	6	0	0	0	0	0	0	0
260	270	32	24	15	7	0	0	0	0	0	0	0
270	280	34	25	17	9	0	0	0	0	0	0	0
280	290	35	27	18	10	2	0	0	0	0	0	0
290	300	37	28	20	12	3	0	0	0	0	0	0
300	310	38	30	21	13	5	0	0	0	0	0	0
310	320	40	31	23	15	6	0	0	0	0	0	0
320	330	41	33	24	16	8	0	0	0	0	0	0
330	340	43	34	26	18	9	1	0	0	0	0	0
340	350	44	36	27	19	11	2	0	0	0	0	0
350	360	46	37	29	21	12	4	0	0	0	0	0
360	370	47	39	30	22	14	5	0	0	0	0	0
370	380	49	40	32	24	15	7	0	0	0	0	0
380	390	50	42	33	25	17	8	0	0	0	0	0
390	400	52	43	35	27	18	10	1	0	0	0	0
400	410	53	45	36	28	20	11	3	0	0	0	0
410	420	55	46	38	30	21	13	4	0	0	0	0
420	430	56	48	39	31	23	14	6	0	0	0	0
430	440	58	49	41	33	24	16	7	0	0	0	0
440	450	59	51	42	34	26	17	9	1	0	0	0
450	460	61	52	44	36	27	19	10	2	0	0	0
460	470	62	54	45	37	29	20	12	4	0	0	0
470	480	64	55	47	39	30	22	13	5	0	0	0
480	490	65	57	48	40	32	23	15	7	0	0	0
490	500	67	58	50	42	33	25	16	8	0	0	0
500	510	68	60	51	43	35	26	18	10	1	0	0
510	520	70	61	53	45	36	28	19	11	3	0	0
520	530	71	63	54	46	38	29	21	13	4	0	0
530	540	73	64	56	48	39	31	22	14	6	0	0
540	550	74	66	57	49	41	32	24	16	7	0	0
550	560	76	67	59	51	42	34	25	17	9	0	0
560	570	79	69	60	52	44	35	27	19	10	2	0
570	580	81	70	62	54	45	37	28	20	12	3	0
580	590	84	72	63	55	47	38	30	22	13	5	0
590	600	87	73	65	57	48	40	31	23	15	6	0

SINGLE Persons—WEEKLY Payroll Period
(For Wages Paid in July–Dec 2001)

If the wages are—		And the number of withholding allowances claimed is—										
At least	But less than	0	1	2	3	4	5	6	7	8	9	10
		The amount of income tax to be withheld is—										
$600	$610	89	75	66	58	50	41	33	25	16	8	0
610	620	92	77	68	60	51	43	34	26	18	9	1
620	630	95	80	69	61	53	44	36	28	19	11	2
630	640	98	83	71	63	54	46	37	29	21	12	4
640	650	100	85	72	64	56	47	39	31	22	14	5
650	660	103	88	74	66	57	49	40	32	24	15	7
660	670	106	91	76	67	59	50	42	34	25	17	8
670	680	108	93	78	69	60	52	43	35	27	18	10
680	690	111	96	81	70	62	53	45	37	28	20	11
690	700	114	99	84	72	63	55	46	38	30	21	13
700	710	116	101	86	73	65	56	48	40	31	23	14
710	720	119	104	89	75	66	58	49	41	33	24	16
720	730	122	107	92	77	68	59	51	43	34	26	17
730	740	125	110	94	79	69	61	52	44	36	27	19
740	750	127	112	97	82	71	62	54	46	37	29	20
750	760	130	115	100	85	72	64	55	47	39	30	22
760	770	133	118	103	88	74	65	57	49	40	32	23
770	780	135	120	105	90	75	67	58	50	42	33	25
780	790	138	123	108	93	78	68	60	52	43	35	26
790	800	141	126	111	96	81	70	61	53	45	36	28
800	810	143	128	113	98	83	71	63	55	46	38	29
810	820	146	131	116	101	86	73	64	56	48	39	31
820	830	149	134	119	104	89	74	66	58	49	41	32
830	840	152	137	121	106	91	76	67	59	51	42	34
840	850	154	139	124	109	94	79	69	61	52	44	35
850	860	157	142	127	112	97	82	70	62	54	45	37
860	870	160	145	130	115	99	84	72	64	55	47	38
870	880	162	147	132	117	102	87	73	65	57	48	40
880	890	165	150	135	120	105	90	75	67	58	50	41
890	900	168	153	138	123	108	92	77	68	60	51	43
900	910	170	155	140	125	110	95	80	70	61	53	44
910	920	173	158	143	128	113	98	83	71	63	54	46
920	930	176	161	146	131	116	101	86	73	64	56	47
930	940	179	164	148	133	118	103	88	74	66	57	49
940	950	181	166	151	136	121	106	91	76	67	59	50
950	960	184	169	154	139	124	109	94	79	69	60	52
960	970	187	172	157	142	126	111	96	81	70	62	53
970	980	189	174	159	144	129	114	99	84	72	63	55
980	990	192	177	162	147	132	117	102	87	73	65	56
990	1,000	195	180	165	150	135	119	104	89	75	66	58
1,000	1,010	197	182	167	152	137	122	107	92	77	68	59
1,010	1,020	200	185	170	155	140	125	110	95	80	69	61
1,020	1,030	203	188	173	158	143	128	113	97	82	71	62
1,030	1,040	206	191	175	160	145	130	115	100	85	72	64
1,040	1,050	208	193	178	163	148	133	118	103	88	74	65
1,050	1,060	211	196	181	166	151	136	121	106	91	75	67
1,060	1,070	214	199	184	169	153	138	123	108	93	78	68
1,070	1,080	216	201	186	171	156	141	126	111	96	81	70
1,080	1,090	219	204	189	174	159	144	129	114	99	84	71
1,090	1,100	222	207	192	177	162	146	131	116	101	86	73
1,100	1,110	224	209	194	179	164	149	134	119	104	89	74
1,110	1,120	227	212	197	182	167	152	137	122	107	92	77
1,120	1,130	230	215	200	185	170	155	140	124	109	94	79
1,130	1,140	233	218	202	187	172	157	142	127	112	97	82
1,140	1,150	235	220	205	190	175	160	145	130	115	100	85
1,150	1,160	238	223	208	193	178	163	148	133	118	102	87
1,160	1,170	241	226	211	196	180	165	150	135	120	105	90
1,170	1,180	243	228	213	198	183	168	153	138	123	108	93
1,180	1,190	246	231	216	201	186	171	156	141	126	111	95
1,190	1,200	249	234	219	204	189	173	158	143	128	113	98
1,200	1,210	252	236	221	206	191	176	161	146	131	116	101
1,210	1,220	255	239	224	209	194	179	164	149	134	119	104
1,220	1,230	258	242	227	212	197	182	167	151	136	121	106
1,230	1,240	261	245	229	214	199	184	169	154	139	124	109
1,240	1,250	264	247	232	217	202	187	172	157	142	127	112

$1,250 and over   Use Table 1(a) for a **SINGLE person** on page 3. Also see the instructions on page 2.

Note: TABLE HANDBOOK to accompany *Business Mathematics*, contains more detailed tables.

TABLE 6.7

MARRIED Persons—WEEKLY Payroll Period

(For Wages Paid in July–Dec 2001)

If the wages are—		And the number of withholding allowances claimed is—										
At least	But less than	0	1	2	3	4	5	6	7	8	9	10
		The amount of income tax to be withheld is—										
$0	$125	0	0	0	0	0	0	0	0	0	0	0
125	130	1	0	0	0	0	0	0	0	0	0	0
130	135	1	0	0	0	0	0	0	0	0	0	0
135	140	2	0	0	0	0	0	0	0	0	0	0
140	145	3	0	0	0	0	0	0	0	0	0	0
145	150	4	0	0	0	0	0	0	0	0	0	0
150	155	4	0	0	0	0	0	0	0	0	0	0
155	160	5	0	0	0	0	0	0	0	0	0	0
160	165	6	0	0	0	0	0	0	0	0	0	0
165	170	7	0	0	0	0	0	0	0	0	0	0
170	175	7	0	0	0	0	0	0	0	0	0	0
175	180	8	0	0	0	0	0	0	0	0	0	0
180	185	9	0	0	0	0	0	0	0	0	0	0
185	190	10	1	0	0	0	0	0	0	0	0	0
190	195	10	2	0	0	0	0	0	0	0	0	0
195	200	11	3	0	0	0	0	0	0	0	0	0
200	210	12	4	0	0	0	0	0	0	0	0	0
210	220	14	5	0	0	0	0	0	0	0	0	0
220	230	15	7	0	0	0	0	0	0	0	0	0
230	240	17	8	0	0	0	0	0	0	0	0	0
240	250	18	10	1	0	0	0	0	0	0	0	0
250	260	20	11	3	0	0	0	0	0	0	0	0
260	270	21	13	4	0	0	0	0	0	0	0	0
270	280	23	14	6	0	0	0	0	0	0	0	0
280	290	24	16	7	0	0	0	0	0	0	0	0
290	300	26	17	9	1	0	0	0	0	0	0	0
300	310	27	19	10	2	0	0	0	0	0	0	0
310	320	29	20	12	4	0	0	0	0	0	0	0
320	330	30	22	13	5	0	0	0	0	0	0	0
330	340	32	23	15	7	0	0	0	0	0	0	0
340	350	33	25	16	8	0	0	0	0	0	0	0
350	360	35	26	18	10	1	0	0	0	0	0	0
360	370	36	28	19	11	3	0	0	0	0	0	0
370	380	38	29	21	13	4	0	0	0	0	0	0
380	390	39	31	22	14	6	0	0	0	0	0	0
390	400	41	32	24	16	7	0	0	0	0	0	0
400	410	42	34	25	17	9	0	0	0	0	0	0
410	420	44	35	27	19	10	2	0	0	0	0	0
420	430	45	37	28	20	12	3	0	0	0	0	0
430	440	47	38	30	22	13	5	0	0	0	0	0
440	450	48	40	31	23	15	6	0	0	0	0	0
450	460	50	41	33	25	16	8	0	0	0	0	0
460	470	51	43	34	26	18	9	1	0	0	0	0
470	480	53	44	36	28	19	11	2	0	0	0	0
480	490	54	46	37	29	21	12	4	0	0	0	0
490	500	56	47	39	31	22	14	5	0	0	0	0
500	510	57	49	40	32	24	15	7	0	0	0	0
510	520	59	50	42	34	25	17	8	0	0	0	0
520	530	60	52	43	35	27	18	10	2	0	0	0
530	540	62	53	45	37	28	20	11	3	0	0	0
540	550	63	55	46	38	30	21	13	5	0	0	0
550	560	65	56	48	40	31	23	14	6	0	0	0
560	570	66	58	49	41	33	24	16	8	0	0	0
570	580	68	59	51	43	34	26	17	9	1	0	0
580	590	69	61	52	44	36	27	19	11	2	0	0
590	600	71	62	54	46	37	29	20	12	4	0	0
600	610	72	64	55	47	39	30	22	14	5	0	0
610	620	74	65	57	49	40	32	23	15	7	0	0
620	630	75	67	58	50	42	33	25	17	8	0	0
630	640	77	68	60	52	43	35	26	18	10	1	0
640	650	78	70	61	53	45	36	28	20	11	3	0
650	660	80	71	63	55	46	38	29	21	13	4	0
660	670	81	73	64	56	48	39	31	23	14	6	0
670	680	83	74	66	58	49	41	32	24	16	7	0
680	690	84	76	67	59	51	42	34	26	17	9	0
690	700	86	77	69	61	52	44	35	27	19	10	2
700	710	87	79	70	62	54	45	37	29	20	12	3
710	720	89	80	72	64	55	47	38	30	22	13	5
720	730	90	82	73	65	57	48	40	32	23	15	6
730	740	92	83	75	67	58	50	41	33	25	16	8

MARRIED Persons—WEEKLY Payroll Period

(For Wages Paid in July–Dec 2001)

If the wages are—		And the number of withholding allowances claimed is—										
At least	But less than	0	1	2	3	4	5	6	7	8	9	10
		The amount of income tax to be withheld is—										
$740	$750	93	85	76	68	60	51	43	35	26	18	9
750	760	95	86	78	70	61	53	44	36	28	19	11
760	770	96	88	79	71	63	54	46	38	29	21	12
770	780	98	89	81	73	64	56	47	39	31	22	14
780	790	99	91	82	74	66	57	49	41	32	24	15
790	800	101	92	84	76	67	59	50	42	34	25	17
800	810	102	94	85	77	69	60	52	44	35	27	18
810	820	104	95	87	79	70	62	53	45	37	28	20
820	830	105	97	88	80	72	63	55	47	38	30	21
830	840	107	98	90	82	73	65	56	48	40	31	23
840	850	108	100	91	83	75	66	58	50	41	33	24
850	860	110	101	93	85	76	68	59	51	43	34	26
860	870	111	103	94	86	78	69	61	53	44	36	27
870	880	113	104	96	88	79	71	62	54	46	37	29
880	890	114	106	97	89	81	72	64	56	47	39	30
890	900	116	107	99	91	82	74	65	57	49	40	32
900	910	117	109	100	92	84	75	67	59	50	42	33
910	920	119	110	102	94	85	77	68	60	52	43	35
920	930	120	112	103	95	87	78	70	62	53	45	36
930	940	122	113	105	97	88	80	71	63	55	46	38
940	950	123	115	106	98	90	81	73	65	56	48	39
950	960	125	116	108	100	91	83	74	66	58	49	41
960	970	127	118	109	101	93	84	76	68	59	51	42
970	980	129	119	111	103	94	86	77	69	61	52	44
980	990	132	121	112	104	96	87	79	71	62	54	45
990	1,000	135	122	114	106	97	89	80	72	64	55	47
1,000	1,010	138	124	115	107	99	90	82	74	65	57	48
1,010	1,020	140	125	117	109	100	92	83	75	67	58	50
1,020	1,030	143	128	118	110	102	93	85	77	68	60	51
1,030	1,040	146	131	120	112	103	95	86	78	70	61	53
1,040	1,050	148	133	121	113	105	96	88	80	71	63	54
1,050	1,060	151	136	123	115	106	98	89	81	73	64	56
1,060	1,070	154	139	124	116	108	99	91	83	74	66	57
1,070	1,080	156	141	126	118	109	101	92	84	76	67	59
1,080	1,090	159	144	129	119	111	102	94	86	77	69	60
1,090	1,100	162	147	132	121	112	104	95	87	79	70	62
1,100	1,110	165	150	134	122	114	105	97	89	80	72	63
1,110	1,120	167	152	137	124	115	107	98	90	82	73	65
1,120	1,130	170	155	140	125	117	108	100	92	83	75	66
1,130	1,140	173	158	143	128	118	110	101	93	85	76	68
1,140	1,150	175	160	145	130	120	111	103	95	86	78	69
1,150	1,160	178	163	148	133	121	113	104	96	88	79	71
1,160	1,170	181	166	151	136	123	114	106	98	89	81	72
1,170	1,180	183	168	153	138	124	116	107	99	91	82	74
1,180	1,190	186	171	156	141	126	117	109	101	92	84	75
1,190	1,200	189	174	159	144	129	119	110	102	94	85	77
1,200	1,210	192	177	161	146	131	120	112	104	95	87	78
1,210	1,220	194	179	164	149	134	122	113	105	97	88	80
1,220	1,230	197	182	167	152	137	123	115	107	98	90	81
1,230	1,240	200	185	170	155	139	125	116	108	100	91	83
1,240	1,250	202	187	172	157	142	127	118	110	101	93	84
1,250	1,260	205	190	175	160	145	130	119	111	103	94	86
1,260	1,270	208	193	178	163	148	133	121	113	104	96	87
1,270	1,280	210	195	180	165	150	135	122	114	106	97	89
1,280	1,290	213	198	183	168	153	138	124	116	107	99	90
1,290	1,300	216	201	186	171	156	141	126	117	109	100	92
1,300	1,310	219	204	188	173	158	143	128	119	110	102	93
1,310	1,320	221	206	191	176	161	146	131	120	112	103	95
1,320	1,330	224	209	194	179	164	149	134	122	113	105	96
1,330	1,340	227	212	197	182	166	151	136	123	115	106	98
1,340	1,350	229	214	199	184	169	154	139	125	116	108	99
1,350	1,360	232	217	202	187	172	157	142	127	118	109	101
1,360	1,370	235	220	205	190	175	160	144	129	119	111	102
1,370	1,380	237	222	207	192	177	162	147	132	121	112	104
1,380	1,390	240	225	210	195	180	165	150	135	122	114	105
1,390	1,400	243	228	213	198	183	168	153	137	124	115	107

$1,400 and over Use Table 1(b) for a **MARRIED person** on page 3. Also see the instructions on page 2.

Note: TABLE HANDBOOK to accompany *Business Mathematics*, contains more detailed tables.

TABLE 6.8

Payroll Period	One Withholding Allowance
Weekly	$55.77
Biweekly	111.54
Semimonthly	120.83
Monthly	241.67
Quarterly	725.00
Semiannually	1,450.00
Annually	2,900.00
Daily or miscellaneous (each day of the payroll period	11.15

Step 2. $ 465.00 Employee's weekly wages
−223.08 From step 1, the withholding allowance
$241.92 Amount subject to withholding

Step 3. $ 241.92 From step 2
−124.00 From Table 6.9, Married person portion of
       Table 1—WEEKLY Payroll Period
$117.92 Excess "Over—$124 But not over—$960."
    15% From Table 6.9, Married person portion of
       Table 1—WEEKLY Payroll Period
$ 17.69 Tax to be withheld

55.77 ☒ 4 ═ 223.08 ⊬ ⊞ 465 ═ 241.92 ⊟ 124 ☒ 15% ═ 17.69

6.10 Practice Problems

Solve the following problems using both the wage bracket method and the percentage method:

1. Alfred Derbowski is single and claims one withholding allowance. His weekly payroll check is for a gross amount of $845. How much FIT will be withheld?

2. A business pays one of its single employees a gross amount of $399.50 weekly. How much will be withheld for FIT if she claims three withholding allowances on her Form W-4.

3. Suki Hsing is paid weekly. She earned $954 during this payroll period. She is married, but does not claim any withholding allowances. How much will be withheld for FIT?

4. A vice president of the Caper Corporation is paid $3,365.38 weekly. He is married and claims five withholding allowances. How much FIT will be withheld?

6.10 Solutions to Practice Problems

1. Wage bracket method: $139 FIT withheld
   Percentage method: $845.00 $ 789.53 $237.53 $ 75.15
                    − 55.47   −552.00   ☒ 27%   + 64.13
                    $789.53 $ 237.53 $ 64.13 $ 139.28   FIT withheld

2. Wage bracket method: $27 FIT withheld
   Percentage method: $ 55.77 $ 399.50 $232.19 $181.19
                    ☒   3   − 167.31   − 51.00   ☒ 15%
                    $167.31 $ 232.19 $ 181.19 $ 27.18 FIT withheld

3. Wage bracket method: $125 FIT withheld
   Percentage method: $ 954 $830.00
                    −124   ☒ 15%
                    $ 830 $124.50 FIT withheld

4. Wage bracket method: Wages exceed $1,400 weekly. Therefore, the wage bracket method cannot be used, and you must use the percentage method.
   $ 55.77 $3,365.38 $ 3,086.53 $1,063.53 $ 412.41
   ☒   5   − 278.85   −2,023.00   ☒   30%   +319.06
   $278.85 $3,086.53 $ 1,063.53 $ 319.06 $ 731.47 FIT withheld

TABLE 6.9

Tables for Percentage Method of Withholding
(For Wages Paid in July–Dec 2001)

TABLE 1—WEEKLY Payroll Period

(a) SINGLE person (including head of household)—

If the amount of wages (after subtracting withholding allowances) is: The amount of income tax to withhold is:

Not over $51 . . . . . . $0

Over—	But not over—		of excess over—
$51	—$552	. . 15%	—51
$552	—$1,196	. . $75.15 plus 27%	—552
$1,196	—$2,662	. . $249.03 plus 30%	—1,196
$2,662	—$5,750	. . $688.83 plus 35%	—2,662
$5,750	. . . . . .	$1,769.63 plus 38.6%	—5,750

(b) MARRIED person—

If the amount of wages (after subtracting withholding allowances) is: The amount of income tax to withhold is:

Not over $124 . . . . . $0

Over—	But not over—		of excess over—
$124	—$960	. . 15%	—$124
$960	—$2,023	. . $125.40 plus 27%	—$960
$2,023	—$3,292	. . $412.41 plus 30%	—$2,023
$3,292	—$5,809	. . $793.11 plus 35%	—$3,292
$5,809	. . . . . .	$1,674.06 plus 38.6%	—$5,809

TABLE 2—BIWEEKLY Payroll Period

(a) SINGLE person (including head of household)—

If the amount of wages (after subtracting withholding allowances) is: The amount of income tax to withhold is:

Not over $102 . . . . . $0

Over—	But not over—		of excess over—
$102	—$1,104	. . 15%	—$102
$1,104	—$2,392	. . $150.30 plus 27%	—$1,104
$2,392	—$5,323	. . $498.06 plus 30%	—$2,392
$5,323	—$11,500	. . $1,377.36 plus 35%	—$5,323
$11,500	. . . . . .	$3,539.31 plus 38.6%	—$11,500

(b) MARRIED person—

If the amount of wages (after subtracting withholding allowances) is: The amount of income tax to withhold is:

Not over $248 . . . . . $0

Over—	But not over—		of excess over—
$248	—$1,919	. . 15%	—$248
$1,919	—$4,046	. . $250.65 plus 27%	—$1,919
$4,046	—$6,585	. . $824.94 plus 30%	—$4,046
$6,585	—$11,617	. . $1,586.64 plus 35%	—$6,585
$11,617	. . . . . .	$3,347.84 plus 38.6%	—$11,617

TABLE 3—SEMIMONTHLY Payroll Period

(a) SINGLE person (including head of household)—

If the amount of wages (after subtracting withholding allowances) is: The amount of income tax to withhold is:

Not over $110 . . . . . $0

Over—	But not over—		of excess over—
$110	—$1,196	. . 15%	—$110
$1,196	—$2,592	. . $162.90 plus 27%	—$1,196
$2,592	—$5,767	. . $539.82 plus 30%	—$2,592
$5,767	—$12,458	. . $1,492.32 plus 35%	—$5,767
$12,458	. . . . . .	$3,834.17 plus 38.6%	—$12,458

(b) MARRIED person—

If the amount of wages (after subtracting withholding allowances) is: The amount of income tax to withhold is:

Not over $269 . . . . . $0

Over—	But not over—		of excess over—
$269	—$2,079	. . 15%	—$269
$2,079	—$4,383	. . $271.50 plus 27%	—$2,079
$4,383	—$7,133	. . $893.58 plus 30%	—$4,383
$7,133	—$12,585	. . $1,718.58 plus 35%	—$7,133
$12,585	. . . . . .	$3,626.78 plus 38.6%	—$12,585

TABLE 4—MONTHLY Payroll Period

(a) SINGLE person (including head of household)—

If the amount of wages (after subtracting withholding allowances) is: The amount of income tax to withhold is:

Not over $221 . . . . . $0

Over—	But not over—		of excess over—
$221	—$2,392	. . 15%	—$221
$2,392	—$5,183	. . $325.65 plus 27%	—$2,392
$5,183	—$11,533	. . $1,079.22 plus 30%	—$5,183
$11,533	—$24,917	. . $2,984.22 plus 35%	—$11,533
$24,917	. . . . . .	$7,668.62 plus 38.6%	—$24,917

(b) MARRIED person—

If the amount of wages (after subtracting withholding allowances) is: The amount of income tax to withhold is:

Not over $538 . . . . . $0

Over—	But not over—		of excess over—
$538	—$4,158	. . 15%	—$538
$4,158	—$8,767	. . $543.00 plus 27%	—$4,158
$8,767	—$14,267	. . $1,787.43 plus 30%	—$8,767
$14,267	—$25,171	. . $3,437.43 plus 35%	—$14,267
$25,171	. . . . . .	$7,253.83 plus 38.6%	—$25,171

Filing the Employer's Quarterly Federal Tax Return (Form 941)

As just discussed, all employers who are subject to income tax withholding or Social Security and Medicare taxes must calculate and withhold their employees' portion of Social Security and Medicare (the employer must also match those amounts) and federal income tax. Each quarter the employer must file Form 941, Employer's Quarterly Federal Tax Return (see Table 6.10).

Depositing Taxes: Federal Tax Deposit (FTD) Coupon (Form 8109)

Employers must deposit income tax withheld and both the employer and employee Social Security and Medicare taxes by mailing or delivering a check, money order, or cash to an authorized financial institution or Federal Reserve bank, using Form 8109, Federal Tax Deposit Coupon (see Table 6.11). The Internal Revenue Service (IRS) notifies employers each November whether they are monthly or semiweekly depositors for the coming calendar year. The deposit schedule is determined from the total taxes reported on Form 941 in a four-quarter "look-back period." However, if the total accumulated tax reaches $100,000 or more on any day during a deposit period, it must be deposited by the next banking day, whether an employer is a monthly or semiweekly depositor.

EXCEL Spreadsheet Application Spreadsheet Application 2 at the end of this chapter is a continuation of Application 1. It calculates net pay.

6.11 Calculating Net Pay

After making the calculations that have been discussed in this chapter to this point, the deductions (involuntary and voluntary) must be subtracted from the gross pay to determine the employees' net pay:

$$\text{Net pay} = \text{gross pay} - \text{deductions}$$

TABLE 6.11

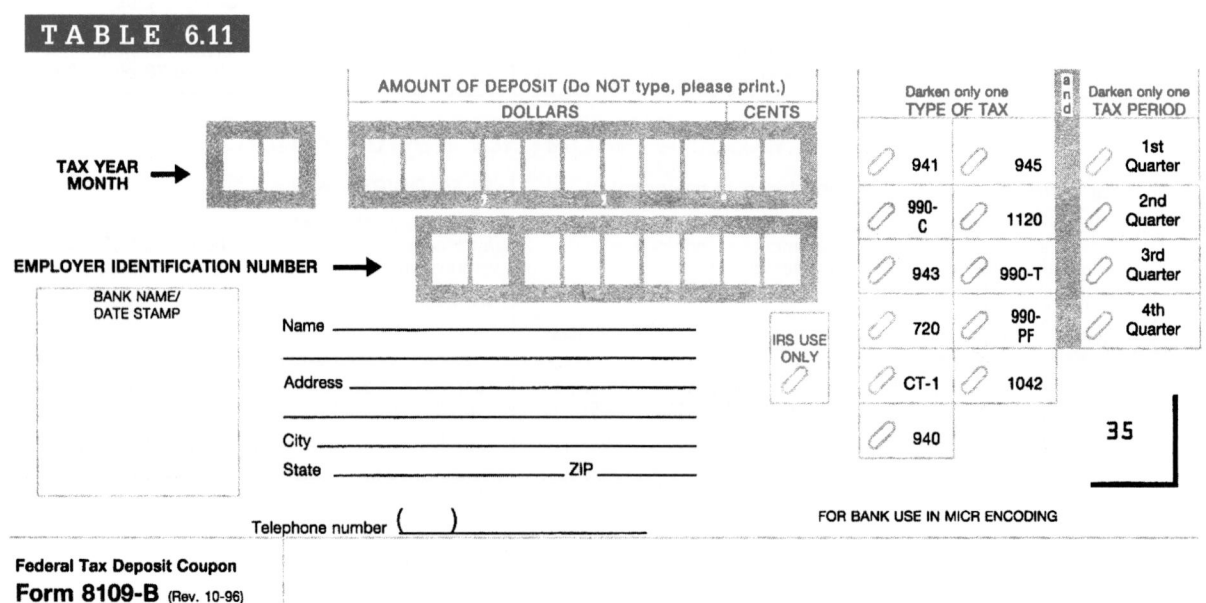

Federal Tax Deposit Coupon
Form 8109-B (Rev. 10-96)

Form **941**
(Rev. January 2001) (O)
Department of the Treasury
Internal Revenue Service

Employer's Quarterly Federal Tax Return

▶ **See separate instructions for information on completing this return.**
Please type or print.

Enter state code for state in which deposits were made **only** if different from state in address to the right ▶ ⬚ (see page 2 of instructions).

Name (as distinguished from trade name)	Date quarter ended
Trade name, if any	Employer identification number
Address (number and street)	City, state, and ZIP code

OMB No. 1545-0029

| T |
| FF |
| FD |
| FP |
| I |
| T |

If address is different from prior return, check here ▶ ⬚

IRS Use

| 1 1 1 1 1 1 1 1 1 1 | 2 | 3 3 3 3 3 3 3 | 4 4 4 | 5 5 5 |
| 6 | 7 | 8 8 8 8 8 8 8 8 | 9 9 9 9 9 | 10 10 10 10 10 10 10 10 10 |

If you do not have to file returns in the future, check here ▶ ⬚ and enter date final wages paid ▶

If you are a seasonal employer, see **Seasonal employers** on page 1 of the instructions and check here ▶ ⬚

1	Number of employees in the pay period that includes March 12th . ▶	**1**		
2	Total wages and tips, plus other compensation		**2**	
3	Total income tax withheld from wages, tips, and sick pay		**3**	
4	Adjustment of withheld income tax for preceding quarters of calendar year		**4**	
5	Adjusted total of income tax withheld (line 3 as adjusted by line 4—see instructions) . . .		**5**	
6	Taxable social security wages	**6a**	× 12.4% (.124) = **6b**	
	Taxable social security tips	**6c**	× 12.4% (.124) = **6d**	
7	Taxable Medicare wages and tips . . .	**7a**	× 2.9% (.029) = **7b**	
8	Total social security and Medicare taxes (add lines 6b, 6d, and 7b). Check here if wages are not subject to social security and/or Medicare tax . . . . ▶ ⬚		**8**	
9	Adjustment of social security and Medicare taxes (see instructions for required explanation) Sick Pay $ _____ ± Fractions of Cents $ _____ ± Other $ _____ =		**9**	
10	Adjusted total of social security and Medicare taxes (line 8 as adjusted by line 9—see instructions)		**10**	
11	**Total taxes** (add lines 5 and 10)		**11**	
12	Advance earned income credit (EIC) payments made to employees		**12**	
13	Net taxes (subtract line 12 from line 11). **If $2,500 or more, this must equal line 17, column (d) below (or line D of Schedule B (Form 941))**		**13**	
14	Total deposits for quarter, including overpayment applied from a prior quarter.		**14**	
15	**Balance due** (subtract line 14 from line 13). See instructions		**15**	
16	**Overpayment.** If line 14 is more than line 13, enter excess here ▶ $ _____ and check if to be: ⬚ Applied to next return **or** ⬚ Refunded.			

● **All filers:** If line 13 is less than $2,500, you need not complete line 17 or Schedule B (Form 941).
● **Semiweekly schedule depositors:** Complete Schedule B (Form 941) and check here . . . . ▶ ⬚
● **Monthly schedule depositors:** Complete line 17, columns (a) through (d), and check here. . . . . ▶ ⬚

17	**Monthly Summary of Federal Tax Liability.** Do not complete if you were a semiweekly schedule depositor.		
(a) First month liability	(b) Second month liability	(c) Third month liability	(d) Total liability for quarter

Sign Here

Under penalties of perjury, I declare that I have examined this return, including accompanying schedules and statements, and to the best of my knowledge and belief, it is true, correct, and complete.

Signature ▶   Print Your Name and Title ▶   Date ▶

For Privacy Act and Paperwork Reduction Act Notice, see back of Payment Voucher.   Cat. No. 17001Z   Form **941** (Rev. 1-2001)

Note: TABLE HANDBOOK to accompany *Business Math*, contains more detailed tables.

All of these calculations are recorded in a payroll register as presented earlier in this chapter.

EXAMPLE

John Jacobs is married and has two children. He claims four withholding allowances. He is paid $12.33 per hour. Overtime is all time in excess of 40 hours per week. Prior to being paid for last week, John had earned $6,411.60 this year. Last week John worked 52 hours. The state income tax withholding is calculated at 10% of the FIT withholding. Life and health insurance is partially paid by the employer. The employer pays a total of $46.13 per week. Any premium over that is deducted from the employee's gross pay. Weekly life and health insurance premiums are as follows:

Employee: $31.15
Spouse: $34.61
Each child: $14.42

John has authorized a checkoff (a deduction to pay union dues) of $17.31 per week. Twenty-five dollars per week is deducted to be put into John's credit union savings account.

Determine the following :

Gross pay	State income tax
Social Security tax	Life and health insurance deduction
Medicare tax	Net pay
FIT (by wage bracket method)	

Solution

Gross Pay

$12.33 × 40 = $493.20
$12.33 × 1.5 × 12 =   221.94
                    $715.14 ← *Gross pay*

Social Security Tax

$715.14
× 6.2%
$ 44.34

Medicare Tax

$715.14
× 1.45%
$ 10.37

FIT

$55 ← *Wage bracket method (Table 6.7)*

State Income Tax

$55.00
× 10%
$ 5.50

Life and Health Insurance

Employee $31.15
Spouse: $34.61
Children: +$28.84 ($14.42 each)
Total: $94.60
Employer: −$46.13
          $48.47 ← *Deducted*

Total Deductions

$44.34 + 10.37 + 55 + 5.50 + 48.47 + 17.31 + 25 = $205.99

Net Pay

$ 715.14
−205.99
$ 509.15

12.33 ⊠ 40 ▣ STO 12.33 ⊠ 1.5 ⊠ 12 ⊞ RCL ▣ STO ⊠ 6.2% ▣
⁺∕₋ ⊞ RCL ▣ STO 715.14 ⊠ 1.45 % ▣ ⁺∕₋ ⊞ RCL ▣ ▣ − 55 = STO 55
⊠ 10 % ▣ ⁺∕₋ ⊞ RCL ▣ STO 31.15 ⊞ 34.61 ⊞ 14.42 ⊞ 14.42 −
46.13 ▣ ⁺∕₋ ⊞ RCL − 17.31 − 25 ▣ 509.15.

6.11 Practice Problems

1. Calculate the weekly net pay for a salaried employee who earns $28,600 annually. Use the FIT wage bracket method for federal income tax. The employee is single and claims three withholding allowances. In addition to FIT and FICA taxes, the employee pays state income tax of 6% of gross earnings, has $30 deducted for a United Way contribution, and pays $36 toward health insurance protection.

2. Sonja Henry has earned $78,775 prior to November's paycheck. She earns $1,825 weekly. Use the percentage method to calculate her FIT withholding. Sonja is married and claims five withholding allowances. Other deductions include $4.50 for life and disability insurance, $44.50 for health insurance, $125 for an employee stock option plan (ESOP), and state income tax of 8.75% of gross income. Calculate her net pay for the month.

3. James Glover's gross sales were $22,890 one week in January. Returns were $540. His commission rate is 7.5% of net sales. Calculate his FIT withholding using the percentage method. James is married and claims three withholding allowances. His employer withholds 1.8% of gross pay for state income tax and a monthly $250 voluntary deduction for a 401(k) account. Determine his net pay.

4. Martin wires circuits using this differential piecework schedule:

1–50 boards	$2.00 each
51–100 boards	$2.50 each
101–200 boards	$3.50 each
All boards over 200	$5.00 each

   During a one-week period, he wired 230 circuits. Prior earnings for the year were $29,000. Martin is single and claims one withholding allowance. Use the wage bracket method to calculate FIT withholding. Deductions other than FIT, Social Security, and Medicare are as follows: union dues, $17.50; state income tax at 12% of the FIT; American Cancer Society, $15; insurance, $45; and government savings bonds, $35. Calculate his net pay.

6.11 Solutions to Practice Problems[1]

1.
Gross Pay

$28,600 ÷ 52 = $550

Social Security Tax	*Medicare Tax*	*FIT*
$550.00	$550.00	$51 ← Wage
× 6.2%	× 1.45%	bracket method
$ 34.10	$ 7.98	(Table 6.6)

State Income Tax	*United Way Contribution*	*Health Insurance*
$550	$30	$36
× 6%		
$ 33		

Total Deductions	*Net Pay*
$34.10 + 7.98 + 51 + 33 + 30 + 36 = $192.08	$ 550.00
	−192.08
	$ 357.92

2.
Gross Pay
$1,825

---

[1]Appendix B provides information for calculating the federal (FUTA) and state (SUTA) unemployment taxes.

	Social Security Tax		Medicare Tax	

$$
\begin{array}{ll}
\$\ 80,400 & \$1,625.00 \\
-78,775 & \times\ \ \ \ 6.2\% \\
\hline
\$\ \ \ 1,625 & \$\ \ 100.75
\end{array}
\qquad
\begin{array}{l}
\$1,825.00 \\
\times\ \ \ \ 1.45\% \\
\hline
\$\ \ \ \ 26.46
\end{array}
$$

FIT

$$
\begin{array}{ccccc}
\text{(Table 6.8)} & & \text{(Table 6.9)} & & \\
\$\ 55.77 & \$1,825.00 & \$1,546.15 & \$\ 586.15 & \$\ \ 125.40 \\
\times\ \ \ \ \ 5 & -\ \ 278.85 & -\ \ 960.00 & \times\ \ \ \ 27\% & +\ 158.26 \\
\hline
\$278.85 & \$1,546.15 & \$\ \ 586.15 & \$\ 158.26 & \$\ \ 283.66
\end{array}
$$

State Income Tax	Life and Disability Insurance	Health Insurance

$$
\begin{array}{l}
\$1,825.00 \\
\times\ \ \ \ 8.75\% \\
\hline
\$\ \ 159.69
\end{array}
\qquad
\$4.50
\qquad\qquad
\$44.50
$$

ESOP
$125

Total Deductions

$$\$100.75 + 26.46 + 283.66 + 159.69 + 4.50 + 44.50 + 125 = \$744.56$$

Net Pay

$$\$1,825 - \$744.56 = \$1,080.44$$

3.   *Gross Pay*

$$
\begin{array}{ll}
\$22,890 & \$22,350.00 \\
-\ \ \ 540 & \times\ \ \ \ 7.5\% \\
\hline
\$22,350 & \$\ 1,676.25
\end{array}
$$

Social Security Tax	Medicare Tax

$$
\begin{array}{l}
\$1,676.25 \\
\times\ \ \ \ 6.2\% \\
\hline
\$\ \ 103.93
\end{array}
\qquad\qquad
\begin{array}{l}
\$1,676.25 \\
\times\ \ \ \ 1.45\% \\
\hline
\$\ \ \ \ 24.31
\end{array}
$$

FIT

$$
\begin{array}{ccccc}
\text{(Table 6.8)} & & \text{(Table 6.9)} & & \\
\$\ 55.77 & \$1,676.25 & \$1,508.94 & \$548.94 & \$\ 125.40 \\
\times\ \ \ \ \ 3 & -\ \ 167.31 & -\ \ 960.00 & \times\ \ \ \ 27\% & +148.21 \\
\hline
\$167.31 & \$1,508.94 & \$\ \ 548.94 & \$148.21 & \$\ 273.61
\end{array}
$$

State Income Tax	401(k) Account

$$
\begin{array}{l}
\$1,676.25 \\
\times\ \ \ \ 1.8\% \\
\hline
\$\ \ \ \ 30.17
\end{array}
\qquad\qquad
\$250
$$

Total Deductions

$$\$103.93 + 24.31 + 273.61 + 30.17 + 250 = \$682.02$$

Net Pay

$$\$1,676.25 - 682.02 = \$994.23$$

4.   *Gross Pay*

$$
\begin{array}{lll}
50 \times \$2 & = \$100 \\
50 \times \$2.50 & = \$125 \\
100 \times \$3.50 & = \$350 \\
30 \times \$5 & = \underline{\$150} \\
& \ \ \ \$725
\end{array}
$$

	Social Security Tax	Medicare Tax	FIT
	$725.00	$725.00	$107 (Table 6.6)
	× 6.2%	× 1.45%	
	$ 44.95	$ 10.51	

	State Income Tax	Insurance	Union Dues	American Cancer Society
	$107.00	$45	$17.50	$15
	× 12%			
	$ 12.84			

Government Savings Bonds
$35

Total Deductions

$44.95 + 10.51 + 107 + 12.84 + 45 + 17.50 + 15 + 35 = $287.80

Net Pay

$725 − 287.80 = $437.20

QUICK REFERENCE SUMMARY AND REVIEW

Page	Section Topic	Learning Concepts	Examples and Solutions
168	**6.1** Calculating the Gross Pay of Salaried Employees	The salaried employee agrees to a certain amount of money usually on an annual basis.	An annual salary of $17,550 will be paid biweekly. What is the gross amount of each paycheck? $17,550 ÷ 26 = $675
170	**6.2** Calculating the Gross Pay for Employees Paid an Hourly Wage: Overtime for Over 40 Hours per Week	Standard Method: Multiply the regular rate of pay by 40 hours or less and add the product of any hours over 40 times 1.5 times the regular rate of pay. Overtime Premium Method: Multiply the regular rate of pay by all hours worked and add the product of .5 times the hours over 40 times the regular rate of pay (the *overtime Premium*).	50 hours worked at $12 per hour Standard Method 40 × $12 = $480 10 (1.5 × $12) = 180 $660 Overtime Premium Method 50 × $12 = $600 10 (.5 × $12) = 60 $660
171	**6.3** Calculating the Gross Pay for Employees Paid an Hourly Wage: Other Methods of Computing Overtime	Overtime may be paid on a basis more favorable to the employee, such as any hours over eight hours per day; double time for weekend and holidays, shift differentials.	An employee worked as follows: M T W H F S 8 10 6 9 8 3 Employees are paid time-and-one-half for anything over eight hours per day and double time for weekends. Their regular pay rate is $12 per hour. 38 × $12 = $456 3 (1.5 × $12) = 54 3 (2 × $12) = 72 $582
174	**6.4** Calculating Straight Piecework Wages	Workers are paid according to the number of units produced.	Workers are paid $.50 per unit produced. One worker produced 32 units one day. Determine gross pay. $.50 × 32 = $16

Page	Section Topic	Learning Concepts	Examples and Solutions
175	**6.5** Calculating Differential Piecework Wages	The wage rate workers are paid increases per item as higher levels of productivity are reached.	Calculate the pay for producing 270 units given the following: 0–50 $.50 each 50–100 .75 each 101–200 1.00 each over 200 1.50 each $50 \times \$\ .50 = \$\ 25$ $50 \times \$\ .75 = \ 37.50$ $100 \times \$1.00 = \ 100$ $70 \times \$1.50 = \underline{\ 105}$ $\$267.50$
176	**6.6** Calculating Single-Rate Straight Commissions	Workers are paid a set amount per item sold, or, more commonly, a percent of the net sales.	The commission rate is 5%. The net sales are $18,000. Find the amount of commissions. $\$18,000 \times 5\% = \$900$
178	**6.7** Calculating Variable-Rate Straight Commissions	The commission rate increases as higher sales levels are reached.	Given the following schedule, calculate the commissions for sales of $21,000: 0–$ 5,000 4% $5,001–$15,000 6% all over $15,000 8% $\$\ 5,000 \times 4\% = \$\ 200$ $10,000 \times 6\% = \ 600$ $6,000 \times 8\% = \underline{\ 480}$ $\$1,280$
179	**6.8** Calculating Salary Plus Commissions	The salary provides a stable, known amount employees can depend on, and compensates for required nonselling activities.	What are gross earnings on sales of $25,000 if an employee is paid a salary of $500 per month plus 3% commissions on sales over $5,000? $\begin{array}{r} \$\ 25,000 \\ -\ \ 5,000 \\ \hline \$\ 20,000 \times 3\% = \$600 \end{array}$ $\$600 + 500 = \$1,100$
180	**6.9** Calculating the FICA Deduction	FICA (Federal Insurance Contributions Act) presently requires two deductions: one for Social Security at 6.2% of the first $80,400 of earnings, and the other for Medicare at 1.45% on all earnings.	An employee had gross earnings of $800 this week. Calculate the Social Security and Medicare deductions. $\begin{array}{cc} \underline{SS} & \underline{Medicare} \\ \$800.00 & \$800.00 \\ \times\ \ 6.2\% & \times\ \ 1.45\% \\ \hline \$\ 49.60 & \$\ 11.60 \end{array}$

Page	Section Topic	Learning Concepts	Examples and Solutions
184	**6.10** Calculating the Federal Income Tax (FIT) Withholding	The income tax to be withheld depends on wages paid, marital status, and withholding allowances. Tables are used for either of two methods of finding the FIT deduction: the wage bracket method and the percentage method.	Calculate the FIT withholding on weekly earnings of $500 for a married employee claiming four withholding allowances.

Wage Bracket Method From Table 6.7

$24

Percentage Method from Table 6.8

$ 55.77 ⟵ one allowance
$\times$ 4
$223.08

From Table 6.9

$ 500.00 $ 276.92
−223.08   −124.00
$ 276.92 $ 152.92

$152.92
$\times$ 15%
$ 22.94

Page	Section Topic	Learning Concepts	Examples and Solutions
192	**6.11** Calculating Net Pay	Net pay is found by subtracting all voluntary and involuntary deductions from the gross pay.	Find the net pay from the following information:

gross pay, $2,000;

FIT withheld, $162;

Social Security $124;

Medicare, $29;

health insurance, $128.

$162 $2,000
124   − 443
29      $1,557
128
$443

SURFING THE INTERNET

For Further Information on the topics covered in this chapter, check out the following sites:

http://www.ssa.gov/employer_info/employer_guide.htm#detax

http://www.tns.lcs.mit.edu/uscode/TITLE_26/Subtitle_A/toc.html

Answers to odd-numbered problems are given in Appendix A.

6.1

Calculate the gross pay per period in the following problems:

1. Jose Sierra is paid an annual salary of $287,500 as a utility infielder for a professional baseball team. He is paid weekly. Find his weekly gross income.
$287,500 ÷ 52 = $5,528.85

2. Suki Aiko has a contract calling for $52,000 annually. Calculate her semimonthly gross pay.
$52,000 ÷ 24 = $2,166.67

3. Opal VanDemeter will be paid biweekly. Her contract is for $24,050 annually. How much is her biweekly gross pay?
$24,050 ÷ 26 = $925

4. An annual contract of $37,980 will be paid monthly. Determine the monthly gross pay.
$37,980 ÷ 12 = $3,165

6.2

Calculate the following hourly wage problems assuming that all employees are paid time-and-one-half for all time over 40 hours per week:

5. Marie Higgins's payroll register is as follows:

	Hours Worked		Total Hours			Gross Earnings		
Employee	S M T W H F S	Reg.	O.T.	Reg Rate	Reg.	O.T.	Total
Higgins, M	– 9 9 8 7 9 8	40	10	$9.33	$373.20	$139.95	$513.15

Calculate her gross pay and fill out the payroll register.
$9.33 × 40 = $373.20
$9.33 × (1.5 × 10) = 139.95
$513.15

6. Jim Smith's payroll register is as follows:

	Hours Worked		Total Hours			Gross Earnings		
Employee	S M T W H F S	Reg.	O.T.	Reg Rate	Reg.	O.T.	Total
Smith, Jim	– 8 9 9 8 9 5	40	8	$6.92	$276.80	$ 83.04	$359.84

Calculate his gross pay and fill out the payroll register.
$6.92 × 40 = $276.80
$6.92 × (1.5 × 8) = 83.04
$359.84

7. Jennifer Holtzer works as a ticket seller at a movie theater. She is paid $5.75 per hour. Last week she worked 46 hours. Calculate her gross pay using the overtime premium method.
$5.75 × 46 = $264.50
$5.75 × (.5 × 6) = 17.25
$281.75

8. Use the overtime premium method to calculate the gross pay for an employee earning $12.50 per hour for 55 hours.
$12.50 × 55 = $687.50
$12.50 × (.5 × 15) = 93.75
$781.25

6.3

Calculate the following gross payroll using the standard method and the overtime premium method:

9. Overtime is anything over eight hours per day and double time for weekends and holidays.

	Hours Worked	Total Hours		Reg	Gross Earnings		
Employee	S M T W H F S	Reg.	O.T. 1.5 2	Rate	Reg.	O.T. Standard	Total
Iberi, Joe	– 8 8 9 9 9 4	40	3 4	$8.50	$340.00	$106.25	$446.25

Standard Method		Overtime Premium Method	
$8.50 × 40	= $340.00	$8.50 × 47	= $399.50
$8.50 × (1.5 × 3) =	38.25	$8.50 × (.5 × 3)=	12.75
$8.50 × (2 × 4) =	68.00	$8.50 × 4 =	34.00
	$446.25		$446.25

10. Overtime is anything over eight hours per day and double time for weekends and holidays. Monday is Memorial Day, a holiday.

	Hours Worked	Total Hours		Reg	Gross Earnings		
Employee	S M T W H F S	Reg.	O.T. 1.5 2	Rate	Reg.	O.T. Premium	Total
Smith, Jan	– 8 8 9 9 9 4	32	3 12	$8.50	$399.50	$114.75	$514.25

Standard Method		Overtime Premium Method	
$8.50 × 32	= $272.00	$8.50 × 47	=$399.50
$8.50 × (1.5 × 3) =	38.25	$8.50 × (.5 × 3) =	12.75
$8.50 × (2 × 12) =	204.00	$8.50 × 12 =	102.00
	$514.25		$514.25

11. Michelle works in a hospital. Her contract calls for $12.30 per hour. Overtime is time-and-one-half for all hours over eight hours per day, and for all hours from 11 P.M. until 7 A.M. Holidays are paid at double time. Monday is July 4th. Michelle's schedule for last week follows:

M	7 A.M.–3 P.M.
T	11 P.M.–7 A.M.
W	11 P.M.–7 A.M.
H	off
F	3 P.M.–11 P.M.
S	3 P.M.–11 P.M.

	Regular Hours	O.T. 1.5×	Hours 2×
M	8 hours		8
T	8 hours	8	
W	8 hours	8	
H	0 hours		
F	8 hours	8	
S	8 hours	8	
	40	16	16	8

Standard Method		Overtime Premium Method	
$12.30 × 16	= $196.80	$12.30 × 40	= $492.00
$12.30 × (1.5 × 16) =	295.20	$12.30 × (.5 × 16) =	98.40
$12.30 × (2 × 8)	= 196.80	$12.30 × 8 =	98.40
	$688.80		$688.80

12. Overtime is defined as all time before 8 A.M. and after 5 P.M. Lunch is one hour per day at no pay for all days that employees work more than 4 hours (to be taken at the end of the 4th hour). Lana Reeves earns $7.50 per hour. Last week she worked the following:

M	7:00 A.M.–5:30 P.M.
T	8:00 A.M.–6:30 P.M.
W	8:00 A.M.–5:00 P.M.
H	8:00 A.M.–5:00 P.M.
F	1:00 P.M.–9:00 P.M.
S	1:00 P.M.–5:00 P.M.

		Regular hours	O.T.
M	9.5 hours	8	1.5
T	9.5 hours	8	1.5
W	8 hours	8	
H	8 hours	8	
F	7 hours	4	3
S	4 hours	4	
	46	40	6

Standard Method		Overtime Premium Method	
$7.50 × 40	= $300.00	$7.50 × 46 = $345.00	
$7.50 × (1.5 × 6) =	67.50	$7.50 × (.5 × 6) =	22.50
	$367.50		$367.50

6.4

Solve the following straight piecework wage problems:

13. A factory worker is paid $.25 for each attaché case he machine stitches. In a one-week period the worker stitched 260 cases. Find his gross pay.

    260 × $.25 = $65

14. Ramona Gonzalez is paid $.15 per basket of peaches loaded. She loaded 64 today. How much are her gross earnings?

    64 × $.15 = $9.60

15. Stanislav Gladonka shovels dirt and gravel into a sluice to find precious metals. The pay is $1 per 1,000 pounds of material shoveled. He loaded 8 tons (2,000 pounds per ton). Calculate his gross pay.

    2,000 × 8 = 16,000   16 × $1 = $16

16. Margarita Sanchez works in a millinery. She is paid $1.50 for every fashionable bonnet she crafts. In one week she produced 318 acceptable bonnets. Calculate her gross pay.

    318 × $1.50 = $ 477

6.5

Calculate the differential piecework wages in the following problems:

17. Kronask Bros., Inc., pays some of its workers on the following differential piecework schedule:

0– 75 units	$.50 each
76–150 units	1.00 each
151–300 units	1.50 each
all units over 300	2.00 each

    Joan completed 280 units in this pay period. What is her gross pay?

    75 × $ .50 = $ 37.50
    75 × 1.00 =   75.00
    130 × 1.50 = 195.00
                 $307.50

18. Use the following differential piecework schedule to determine the gross pay for an employee who reconditioned 482 batteries:

0–100 units	$.20 each
101–250 units	.50 each
251–400 units	.90 each
all units over 400	1.20 each

    100 × $ .20 = $ 20.00
    150 × .50 =   75.00
    150 × .90 =   135.00
    82 × 1.20 =   98.40
                  $328.40

19. O. B. Bently is paid according to the following differential piecework schedule:

0–100 chips	$1.00 each
101–200 chips	1.50 each
201–300 chips	2.00 each
all chips over 300	2.50 each

    O.B. installed 328 computer chips in equipment in one pay period. Calculate his gross pay.

    100 × $1.00 = $100.00
    100 × 1.50 =   150.00
    100 × 2.00 =   200.00
    28 × 2.50 =   70.00
                  $520.00

20. Marquette Desdemona sews precut clothing patterns and is paid by the following schedule:

0–10 units	$2.00 each
11–25 units	$3.00 each
26–40 units	$4.50 each
all units over 40	$5.50 each

    Marquette completed 54 dresses last week. Calculate her gross pay.

    10 × $ 2.00 = $ 20.00
    15 × 3.00 =   45.00
    15 × 4.50 =   67.50
    14 × 5.50 =   77.00
                  $209.50

6.6

Calculate the following single-rate straight commission problems:

21. Nora Jones had net sales of $31,500. Her commission rate is 4.2%. Calculate her gross pay.

    $31,500 × 4.2% = $1,323

22. Mark Novetski sold $9,450 worth of tools. Customers returned $375 worth. The commission rate is 12%. Calculate Mark's gross pay.

    $9,450
    − 375
    $9,075 × 12% = $1,089

23. Lee Minor had annual sales of $394,200. During the year customers returned $5,946 worth of merchandise. Lee's average commission rate was 7.65%. Calculate his gross pay.

    $394,200 − $5,946 = $388,254
    $388,254 × 7.65% = $29,701.43

24. Georgia Paul sold $994 worth of knives. She is paid a commission of 25% of net sales. There were no returns this week. Calculate her gross pay.

    $994 × 25% = $248.50

6.7

Calculate the gross pay in each of the following variable-rate straight commission problems:

25. Alfred Gamoricca is paid according to the following variable-rate commission schedule:

0–$ 5,000	3%
$5,001–10,000	5%
10,001–20,000	7%
20,001 and over	10%

Alfred had net sales of $22,500. Calculate his gross pay.

$ 5,000 × 3% = $ 150.00
$ 5,000 × 5% = 250.00
$10,000 × 7% = 700.00
$ 2,500 × 10% = 250.00
$1,350.00

26. Robert White sells photocopying machines. His company pays him on a variable-rate commission schedule. He had total sales of $44,950 last month, and customer returns totaled $594. Use the following schedule to calculate his commissions:

the first $ 5,000	4.0%
$ 5,001–15,000	5.5%
15,001–25,000	7.5%
25,001 and over	10.0%

$44,950 total sales $ 5,000 × 4% = $ 200.00
− 594 sales returns $10,000 × 5.5% = 550.00
$44,356 net sales $10,000 × 7.5% = 750.00
$19,356 × 10% = 1,935.60
$3,435.60

27. Todd Richie sells for United Forest Products. His sales last week were $9,275. Returns were $350. Calculate his commissions using the following schedule:

0–$ 2,000	5.0%
$ 2,001–5,000	7.5%
5,001–10,000	10.0%
all over 10,000	12.5%

$9,275 total sales $ 2,000 × 5% = $100.00
− 350 sales returns $ 3,000 × 7.5% = 225.00
$8,925 net sales $ 3,925 × 10% = 392.50
$717.50

28. Tran Luang sells industrial fasteners. He had sales of $75,000 last month. Sales returns were $12,500. Calculate his commissions using the following variable rate schedule:

the first $12,000	2.0%
$12,001–25,000	3.5%
25,001–40,000	5.0%
40,001–60,000	7.5%
all over 60,000	10.0%

$ 75,000 total sales $12,000 × 2% = $ 240.00
−12,500 sales returns $13,000 × 3.5% = 455.00
$ 62,500 net sales $15,000 × 5% = 750.00
$20,000 × 7.5% = 1,500.00
$ 2,500 × 10% = 250.00
$3,195.00

6.8

Calculate the following salary plus commission problems:

29. Nelson Brodski is the district sales manager for Avionics Tech Corp. He receives a salary of $1,000 weekly and a 1.5% commission on all sales in his district. Last week sales were $34,800. What is his weekly gross pay?

$34,800 × 1.5% = $ 522 Commission
+ 1,000 Salary
$ 1,522 Gross pay

30. Hydesburg Discount Pharmacy pays Missy Poltser $500 plus 3.5% on all sales over $8,000 each pay period. During the last semimonthly pay period Missy had sales of $15,775. Calculate her gross pay.

$15,775 $7,775 × 3.5% = $ 272.13 Commission
− 8,000   + 500.00 Salary
$ 7,775 $ 772.13 Gross pay

31. Julia Johnstone receives a $300 monthly salary plus commissions of 5% on all sales in her department. Last month's departmental sales were $44,000. What was Julia's gross pay?

$44,000 × 5% = $2,200.00 Commission
+ 300.00 Salary
$2,500.00 Gross pay

32. Blake distributors pays Jason $800 plus the following commission rates on his sales of various categories:

Sales Items	Commission Rate	Jason's Sales
Software	6.0%	$3,000
Printers	3.5%	1,940
Computers	2.5%	1,245
Supplies	3.0%	990
Furniture	7.5%	4,750

Calculate Jason's gross pay.

$ 3,000 × 6% = $ 180.00
$ 1,940 × 3.5% = 67.90
$ 1,245 × 2.5% = 31.13
$ 990 × 3% = 29.70
$ 4,750 × 7.5% = 356.25
$ 664.98
+ 800.00
$1,464.98

6.9

Calculate the FICA (Social Security and Medicare) deductions by using the applicable rates in the following problems:

33. An employee had earnings of $44,745 prior to this paycheck for $2,885. Calculate the FICA deductions for this paycheck.

Social Security Tax	Medicare Tax
$ 2,885 Gross earnings	$ 2,885 Gross earnings
× 6.2% SS tax rate	× 1.45% Medicare tax rate
$178.87 SS tax withheld	$ 41.83 Medicare tax withheld

34. Ann Pearson earned $22,000 prior to this month's check for $1,440. Calculate the Social Security and Medicare deductions for this month.

Social Security Tax	Medicare Tax
$ 1,440 Gross earnings	$ 1,440 Gross earnings
× 6.2% SS tax rate	× 1.45% Medicare tax rate
$ 89.28 SS tax withheld	$ 20.88 Medicare tax withheld

35. Gerald Johansen is paid on a biweekly basis. He is paid $17.55 per hour. Overtime is at time-and-one-half for all hours over 8 hours per day. Last week he worked 40 hours at the regular rate and 6 hours at the overtime rate. This week he worked 37 hours at the regular rate and five hours at the overtime rate. Gerald's prior earnings were $30,610. Calculate the FICA deductions for this biweekly paycheck.

$17.55 × 40 = $702.00 $17.55 × 37 = $649.35
$17.55 × (1.5 × 6) = 157.95 $17.55 × (1.5 × 5) = 131.63
                     $859.95 $780.98

$ 859.95
+ 780.98
$1,640.93

Social Security Tax	Medicare Tax
$1,640.93 Gross earnings	$1,640.93 Gross earnings
× 6.2% SS tax rate	× 1.45% Medicare tax rate
$ 101.74 SS tax withheld	$ 23.79 Medicare tax withheld

36. Nigel VonDyke is an investment banker who works on commissions. His net bond sales in February were $38,750,000. His commission rate is 0.2% of net sales. January's commission check was for $37,375. Calculate the deductions for Social Security and Medicare in February.

$38,750,000	$ 80,400 Total earnings subject to SS tax.
× .2%	− 37,375 Earnings by beginning of the month
$ 77,500	$ 43,025 Earnings subject to SS tax.

Social Security Tax	Medicare Tax
$ 43,025.00 Taxable earnings	$77,500.00 Gross earnings
× 6.2% SS Tax rate	× 1.45% Medicare tax rate
$ 2,667.55 SS tax withheld	$ 1,123.75 Medicare tax withheld

6.10

Solve the following federal income tax (FIT) withholding problems using both the wage bracket method and the percentage method:

37. Damon Lloyd is married and claims three withholding allowances. His weekly paycheck is for a gross amount of $458. Calculate the FIT withholding.

Wage bracket method: $25 withheld

Percentage Method:

$ 55.77	$ 458.00	$ 290.69	$166.69
× 3	− 167.31	− 124.00	× 15%
$167.31	$ 290.69	$ 166.69	$ 25.00 FIT withheld

38. Mert Cardinal is paid $645 gross each week. He is single and claims one withholding allowance. Calculate the amount of FIT to be withheld.

Wage bracket method: $85 withheld

Percentage method:

$ 645.00	$ 589.23	$ 37.23	$ 75.15
− 55.77	−552.00	× 27%	+ 10.05
$ 589.23	$ 37.23	$ 10.05	$ 85.20

39. Corrina Luper is a single mother claiming four withholding allowances. She is paid a gross salary of $420 weekly. Calculate the amount of FIT to be withheld.

Wage bracket method: $21 withheld

Percentage method:

$ 55.77	$ 420.00	$195.92	$145.92
× 4	− 223.08	− 51.00	× 15%
$223.08	$ 195.92	$145.92	$ 21.89 FIT

40. Mildred Quinn is married and claims no withholding allowances. She is paid weekly. This pay period her gross pay is $609. Calculate the amount of FIT to be withheld.

Wage bracket method: $72 withheld

Percentage method:

$ 609	$485.00
− 124	× 15%
$ 485	$ 72.75

6.11

Calculate the following problems to find net pay:

41. George earns $66,600 annually. He is paid semimonthly. He is married and claims four withholding allowances. Use the percentage method to calculate the FIT withholding. His prior earnings were $58,275. Deductions other than those for FICA and FIT are as follows: insurance, $84.35; state income tax at 2.5% of the gross pay; voluntary 401(k) retirement annuity, $250; contributions, $50. Calculate the net pay for George's next check.

$$\frac{\$66,600}{24} = \$2,775 \text{ Gross pay}$$

$120.83	$2,775.00	$ 2,291.68	$212.68	$271.50
× 4	− 483.32	− 2,079.00	× 27%	+ 57.42
$483.32	$2,291.68	$ 212.68	$ 57.42	$328.92 FIT withheld

$2,775.00	$2775.00	$2,775.00		$2,775.00
× 6.2%	× 1.45%	× 2.5%		− 910.59
$ 172.05	$ 40.24	$ 69.38 State tax		$1,864.41 Net pay
SS	Medicare	40.24 Medicare		

40.24 Medicare
328.92 FIT
172.05 SS
250.00 401(k) Retirement
50.00 Contributions
$ 910.59 Total deductions

42. Stubine's Furniture pays Helen a salary of $900 monthly plus commissions for net sales above $5,000 during the month at a rate of 4.5%. Helen's sales this month were $21,794. Prior earnings for the year were $54,330. She is single and claims one withholding allowance. Use the percentage method to calculate the FIT withholding. Other deductions are as follows: state income tax at 15% of the FIT withholding; health insurance, $154; life and disability insurance, $27.50; union dues, $45; credit union deduction, $150.

$21,794.00	$ 900.00 Salary	$1,655.73	$1,655.73
− 5,000.00	+ 755.73 Commission	× 6.2%	× 1.45%
$16,794.00	$1,655.73 Gross income	$ 102.66 SS	$ 24.01 Medicare
× 4.5%			
$ 755.73 Commission			

$1,655.73	$1,414.06	$1,193.06	$178.96
− 241.67	− 221.00	× 15%	× 15%
$1,414.06	$1,193.06	178.96 FIT	26.84 SIT

$ 24.01 Medicare $ 1,655.73 Gross income
102.66 SS   − 708.97 Total deductions
154.00 Health insurance $ 946.76 Net income
27.50 Life insurance
45.00 Union dues
150.00 Credit union
178.96 FIT
+ 26.84 State income tax
$ 708.97 Total deductions

43. Larry Brown is paid $8.50 per hour and time-and one-half for all hours over 40 hours in a week. Larry worked 44 hours last week. His prior annual earnings are $4,597. Larry is single and claims three withholding allowances. Use the wage bracket method to calculate the FIT withholding. State income tax is 2% of gross pay, Larry has $25 deducted every payday to buy government bonds. Other fringe beneits are paid by the company. Find Larry's net pay.

$8.50 × 40 = $340
$8.50 × (1.5 × 4) 51
     $391 Gross income

	$391.00	$391.00
	× 6.2%	×1.45%
	$ 24.24 SS	$ 5.67 Medicare

$ 24.24 SS
5.67 Medicare

$391.00	27.00 FIT
× 2%	7.82 State income tax
$ 7.82 State income tax	25.00 Government bonds
	$89.73 Total deductions

$391.00
− 89.73
$301.27 Net pay

44. Lamonte Greer has earned $12,992 prior to this week's paycheck. He is paid $2 for each metal plate he etches during the day. His company provides a standard production quota of 30 units daily. All units above the 30 are at $1\frac{1}{2}$ times the regular rate. Last week Lamonte completed the following :

M 32 units   H 30 units

T 30 units   F 33 units

W 35 units

Lamonte is married and claims 4 withholding allowances. Use the wage bracket method to calculate his FIT withholding. His state income tax is calculated by multiplying the gross income, less $40 per withholding allowance, by 1.5%. Insurance is $38 weekly, union dues are $12.50 weekly, and a contribution of $25 to the American Heart Association will be deducted this week. Calculate Lamonte's net pay for the week.

Quota production: 150 × $2 = $300
Over quota: 10 × (1.5 × $2) = $ 30
                          $330 Gross income

Total	Reg	Ovrt
32	30	2
30	30	
35	30	5
30	30	
33	30	3
160	150	10

$330.00 $ 330.00
× 6.2%   × 1.45%
$ 20.46 SS $ 4.79 Medicare

$ 20.46 SS
4.79 Medicare
2.55 State income tax
0.00 FIT
38.00 Insurance
12.50 Union dues
+ 25.00 American Heart Association
$103.30 Total deductions

$ 40 $ 330 $170.00
× 4   − 160   × 1.5%
$160 $ 170 $ 2.55

$ 330.00
− 103.30
$ 226.70 Net pay

CHAPTER REVIEW PROBLEMS

Answers to odd-numbered problems are given in Appendix A.

Drill Problems

Find the gross pay for the salaried employees in the following problems:

	Employee	Annual Salary	Pay Period	Gross Pay
1.	Aaron, Z.	$ 25,695	Semimonthly	$1,070.63
2.	Broadly, Y.	148,934	Biweekly	5,728.23
3.	Clemson, X.	49,720	Monthly	4,143.33
4.	Danforth, W.	30,234	Weekly	581.42

Find the gross pay for the hourly wage employees in the following problems (Overtime is paid at time-and-one-half for all hours over 40 in one week).

	Employee	Hours Worked S M T W H F S	Total Hours	Regular Rate	Gross Pay
5.	Allen, Z.	9 6 9 8 7 4	43	$ 5.68	$252.76
6.	Barskie, Y.	8 8 8 8 8 4	44	6.08	279.68
7.	Cleveland, X.	6 8 5 4 3 2	28	6.94	194.32
8.	Douglas, W.	4 9 10 8 10 9	50	7.24	398.20

Find the gross pay for the hourly wage employees in the following problems (Overtime is paid at time-and-one-half for all hours over 8 per day and double time for weekends.)

	Employee	Hours Worked S M T W H F S	Total Hours	Regular Rate	Gross Pay
9.	Franks, U.	9 8 7 9 4	37	$ 7.25	$304.50
10.	Grant, T.	8 8 8 8 4	36	6.50	260.00
11.	Hoskins, S.	6 12 8 8 2	36	8.95	358.00
12.	Iricoati, R.	4 9 10 8 10 9	50	9.20	524.40

Find the gross pay for the piecework wage employees in the following problems:

	Employee	Daily Production S M T W H F S	Total Units	Piece Rate	Gross Pay
13.	Adams, A.	85 76 47 23 99	330	$ .76	$250.80
14.	Boskey, B.	11 9 20 18 14 4	76	2.14	162.64
15.	Carson, C.	47 52 41 47 50	237	.95	225.15
16.	Davida, D.	45 40 35 65 23 40	248	1.20	297.60

Use the following differential piecework schedule to calculate the gross pay for the employees in the following problems:

1 – 20 pieces	$2.50
21 – 40 pieces	$2.75
41 – 60 pieces	$3.25
over 60 pieces	$4.00

	Employee	Daily Production S M T W H F S	Total Units	Gross Pay
17.	Anthony Ohhi	10 12 9 15 14 5	65	$190.00
18.	Bill Willy	11 9 18 14 4	56	157.00
19.	Carla May	17 12 21 17 10	77	238.00
20.	Doris Night	5 10 12 10 13	50	137.50

Find the gross pay for the single-rate straight commission employees in the following problems:

	Employee	Gross Sales	Sales Returns	Commission Rate	Gross Pay
21.	Arnsbarg, A.	$ 38,215	$ 294	3.5%	$1,327.24
22.	Bailey, B.	127,390	1,943	2.0%	2,508.94
23.	Cheatum, C.	29,420	29	5.0%	1,469.55
24.					1,350.65

Use the following variable-rate schedule to calculate the commissions for the employees in the following problems:

first $ 3,000	4%
$3,001 – $ 6,000	6%
$6,001 – $11,000	8%
$11,001 and over	10%

	Employee	Gross Sales	Sales Returns	Gross Rate
25.	Fraley, F.	$ 8,510	$125	$ 490.80
26.	Garret, G.	7,545	45	420.00
27.	Hochkin, H.	19,420	320	1,510.00
28.	Irving, I.	10,995	55	695.20

Federick's Apparel Shop pays its salespeople a salary plus commission. The reliance on salary depends on the salesperson's experience and personal preference. Calculate the gross pay for each of the salespersons in the following problems:

	Employee	Net Sales	Salary	Commission Rate	Gross Pay
29.	Kewter, K.	$18,515	$ 100	5.0%	$1,025.75
30.	Lopez, L.	7,500	500	1.5%	612.50
31.	Msung, M.	12,420	250	3.5%	684.70
32.	Nebrini, N.	6,095	500	1.5%	591.43

Calculate the FICA tax deductions (Social Security tax and Medicare tax) for the employees in the following problems:

	Employee	Prior Earning	Current Pay	Social Security Tax Deduction	Medicare Tax Deduction
33.	Zarley, A.	$44,038	$2,300	$142.60	$33.35
34.	Young, B.	7,500	500	31.00	7.25
35.	Xsing, C.	52,390	4,550	282.10	65.98
36.	Webber, D.	78,770	1,875	101.06	27.19

Calculate the Federal Income tax (FIT) deduction using the wage bracket method for the employees in the following problems:

	Employee	Withholding Allowances	Marital Status	Payroll Period	Gross Pay	FIT Deduction
37.	Utley, F.	4	Married	Weekly	$595	$ 37
38.	Tyler, G.	1	Single	Weekly	845	139
39.	Smiley, H.	3	Single	Weekly	290	12
40.	Rogers, I.	0	Married	Weekly	715	89

Calculate the Federal Income tax (FIT) deduction using the percentage method for the employees in the following problems:

	Employee	Withholding Allowances	Marital Status	Payroll Period	Gross Pay	FIT Deduction
41.	Peters, K.	5	Single	Monthly	1,525	$ 14.35
42.	Otter, L.	1	Married	Biweekly	3,440	631.20
43.	Nasalio, M.	3	Married	Monthly	3,000	260.55
44.	Myers, N.	4	Single	Semimo.	14,550	4,444.70

Calculate the FICA Social Security and Medicare deductions, the FIT deduction using the wage bracket method, the state income tax deduction at 10% of the FIT, and the net income for the employees in the following problems. (The payroll period is weekly.)

	Employee	Withholding Allowances	Marital Status	Gross Pay	Prior Earnings
45.	Kant, P.	3	Married	$775	$ 7,390
46.	Joplin, Q.	0	Single	940	20,775
47.	Ionerst, R.	4	Married	600	56,000
48.	Haskill, S.	1	Single	495	1,980

	Social Security	Medicare	Federal Income Tax	State Income Tax	Other Deductions	Net Income
45.	$48.05	$11.24	$ 73	$ 7.30	$ 75	$560.41
46.	58.28	13.63	181	18.10	180	488.99
47.	37.20	8.70	39	3.90	90	441.19
48.	30.69	7.18	58	5.80	100	293.33

Word Problems

49. Ruth Spearing is paid $8.25 per hour. Overtime is paid at time-and-one-half for all hours over 40 hours per week. Last week she worked 61 hours. How much was her gross pay?

$8.25 × 40 = $330.00
$8.25 × (1.5 × 21) = 259.88
$589.88

50. Paul Boyer has a contract with Stephen's Manufacturing that pays him $90,000. He is paid on a biweekly basis. How much is his gross pay for each check?

$\frac{\$90,000}{26} = \$3,461.54$

51. Herman's regular rate of pay is $8.38 per hour. Last week he worked the following hours: Monday, 9 hours; Tuesday, 7 hours; Wednesday, 10 hours; Thursday, 9 hours; Friday, 8 hours. His union contract specifies that overtime is all hours over eight hours per day and is paid at the rate of two times the regular rate of pay. Determine his gross pay.

Hours Worked				
Total	Reg	OT		
9	8	1	$8.38 × 39 = $326.82
7	7	0	$8.38 × (2 × 4) = 67.04
10	8	2	$393.86
9	8	1	
8	8	0	
43	39	4	

52. Sloan Carlson is paid $3 regular pay for every dress she puts a collar and cuffs on, and time-and-one-half for weekends and holidays. Last week she produced the following:

M	T	W	H	F	S
14	9	12	11	13	6

Calculate her gross pay for the week.

14 + 9 + 12 + 11 + 13 = 59 Regular units
6 × 1.5 = 9 Overtime units
68 × $3 = $204.00 Gross pay

53. A salesman is paid a 7% commission on net sales. During March he sold $18,000 worth of goods. Sales returns amounted to $75. How much were his gross earnings?

$18,000 - 75 = $17,925 \qquad $17,925 \times 7\% = $1,254.75

54. Arnold Swartz had net sales of $12,000. Use the following variable commission schedule to calculate his gross earnings:

first $5,000	2%
$5,001– 11,000	6%
$11,001 and over	10%

$5,000 \times 2\% = $100
$6,000 \times 6\% = 360
$1,000 \times 10\% = \underline{100}
$560

55. Laurie H. Werth Publications pays its sales representatives $400 to perform nonselling activities, plus a commission rate of 4% on net sales. Last month Charise Fontinette's net sales were $41,985. Calculate her gross pay.

$41,985 \times 4\% = $1,679.40
\underline{+400.00}
$2,079.40

56. An employee's gross pay is $800. As of last week her total earnings for the year were $33,000. Compute her FICA deductions for Social Security and Medicare.

Social Security Tax	Medicare Tax
800 Gross earnings	800 Gross earnings
$\underline{\times 6.2\%}$ SS tax rate	$\underline{\times 1.45\%}$ Medicare tax rate
49.60 SS tax withheld	11.60 Medicare tax withheld

57. Fletcher Smith is paid $13.45 per hour for a 40-hour week. One week he worked 48 hours. Overtime is at time-and-one-half for all hours over 40 hours per week. Fletcher is single and claims one withholding allowance. Use the wage bracket method to calculate his FIT deduction.

$13.45 \times 40 \qquad = $538.00 \qquad\qquad $91 FIT
$13.45 \times (1.5 \times 8) = \underline{+161.40}
$699.40 Gross earnings

58. The Exclusive Carpet Company pays Joan Davidson an annual salary of $54,000. She is paid monthly. Joan is married and claims four withholding allowances. Use the percentage method to figure her FIT withholding. Her state income tax is 2.5% of her gross income less $250 for each withholding allowance. Exclusive Carpet deducts a total of $144 for life, health, and disability insurance. Joan has $150 deducted and paid directly into a savings program. Calculate her net pay.

$\dfrac{$54,000}{12} = $4,500.00$ \qquad $4,500.00
$\underline{\times6.2\%}$ \qquad $\underline{\times1.45\%}$
279.00 SS \qquad 65.25 Medicare

$241.67 \qquad $4,500.00 \qquad $3,533.32
$\underline{\times4}$ \qquad $\underline{-966.68}$ \qquad $\underline{-538.00}$
$966.68 \qquad $3,533.32 \qquad $2,995.32

$2,995.32 \qquad\qquad\qquad $250 \qquad $4,500
$\underline{\times15\%}$ \qquad\qquad\qquad $\underline{\times4}$ \qquad $\underline{-1,000}$
449.30 FIT withheld \qquad $1,000 \qquad $3,500

$3,500.00 \qquad Deductions \qquad (total $1,175.05):
$\underline{\times2.5\%}$ \qquad $449.30 FIT \qquad\qquad 87.50 SIT
$87.50 \qquad 279.00 SS \qquad 144.00 Insurance
 65.25 Medicare \qquad 150.00 Savings

$4,500.00
$\underline{-1,175.05}$
$3,324.95 Net Pay

59. Sally Zapata is paid $7.74 per hour for a 40-hour week. Overtime is at one-and-one-half times the regular rate. Last week she worked 43 hours. What was her gross pay for the week?

$7.74 \times 40 \qquad = $309.60
$7.74 \times (1.5 \times 3) = \underline{34.83}
$344.43

60. Jim is a plumber who works irregular hours. His union contract defines overtime as all time before 8:00 A.M. and all time after 5:00 P.M. He is paid time-and-one-half for overtime and double time for weekends and holidays. According to his contract, if he is called out on a job, he cannot be paid for less than one half of a day (four hours). His regular rate of pay is $14.50 per hour. Last year he worked the following schedule in one week during July:

Monday, July 2	9 A.M.– 7 P.M.
Tuesday, July 3	9 A.M.– 11 A.M.
Wednesday, July 4	8 A.M.– 5 P.M. (holiday)
Thursday, July 5	7 A.M.– 5 P.M.
Friday, July 6	8 A.M.– 6 P.M.
Saturday, July 7	8 A.M.– 12 noon

Jim takes off one hour each day from 12 noon to 1 P.M.for lunch. He is not paid for that hour. Compute his gross pay for the week.

		Regular Hours	O.T. 1.5X	2X
M	9 hours	7	2	
T	4 hours	4		
W	8 hours			8
H	9 hours	8	1	
F	9 hours	8	1	
S	4 hours			4
	43	27	4	12

$14.50 \times 27 \qquad = $391.50
$14.50 \times (1.5 \times 4) = 87.00
$14.50 \times (2 \times 12) = \underline{+348.00}
$826.50

61. The differential piecework rate at Arkansas Instrument is as follows:

1 – 500 pieces		$ .10
501 – 1,000 pieces		.15
1,001 – 1,500 pieces		.20
1,501 and over pieces		.25

Bob Pettis produced 1,628 pieces during the pay period. What was his gross pay for the period?

$500 \times \$.10 = \$\ 50.00$
$500 \times\ .15 = \quad 75.00$
$500 \times\ .20 = \quad 100.00$
$128 \times\ .25 = \quad\underline{\ 32.00}$
$\qquad\qquad\qquad \$257.00$

62. A clerk at Sears is paid a 9% commission rate on sales of large appliances. Last week she sold eight washing machines at $398 each. What was her gross pay for the week?

$\$398 \times 8 = \$3,184$
$\$3,184 \times 9\% = \$286.56$

63. The Wilhelm Company pays its salespeople by the following graduated commission system:

first $ 5,000	3%
$ 5,001 – $13,000	5%
$13,001 – $22,000	7%
$22,001 and over	9%

Calculate the gross earnings for Adolf, who had net sales of $15,600.

$\$5,000 \times 3\% = \$150.00$
$8,000 \times 5\% = \quad 400.00$
$2,600 \times 7\% = \quad\underline{\ 182.00}$
$\qquad\qquad\qquad \$732.00$

64. Katrinka Letterman had sales for the month of May totaling $86,000. Sales returns were $1,625. Homerach Corp. pays its sales representatives a $250 salary plus a 3.5% commission rate on net sales over $12,500. Find Katrinka's gross pay.

$\$86,000 - \$1,625 = \$84,375 \qquad \$84,375 - 12,500 = \$71,875$
$\$71,875 \times 3.5\% = \$2,515.63 \qquad \$2,515.63 + 250 = \$2,765.63$ Gross pay

65 Gail Callaway's paycheck for this weekly period was for a gross amount of $790. Gail is single and claims three withholding allowances. Determine her FIT deduction using the wage bracket method.

$96 FIT

66. Last month Samuel van de Geijn sold $31,944 worth of office equipment. Returns were $534. Samuel's commission rate is 6.5% of net sales. He is married and claims one withholding allowance. His annual earnings prior to this month were $76,995. The group medical insurance program costs $79.66 per month. The state income tax withholding is 12.5% of the FIT withholding. He has $50 deducted from his check as a contribution to the Muscular Dystrophy Association. Calculate his net pay.

$\$31,944$ $\$\ 31,410$ $\$2,041.65$ $\$2,041.65$
$\underline{-\quad 534}$ $\underline{\times\quad 6.5\%}$ $\underline{\times\quad 6.2\%}$ $\underline{\times\quad 1.45\%}$
$\$31,410$ $\$2,041.65$ Gross pay $\$\ 126.58$ SS $\$\quad 29.60$ Medicare

$\$2,041.65$ $\$1,799.98$ $\$1,261.98$ Deductions
$\underline{-\ 241.67}$ $\underline{-\ 538.00}$ $\underline{\times\quad 15\%}$ $126.58 SS
$\$1,799.98$ $\$1,261.98$ $\$\ 189.30$ FIT $\quad 29.60$ Medicare
                                                         $\quad 189.30$ FIT
$\$\quad 189.30$ $\quad 23.66$ SIT
$\underline{\times\quad 12.5\%}$ $\quad 79.66$ Insurance
$\$\quad 23.66$ SIT $\underline{\quad 50.00}$ Contributions
                                                         $498.80 Total deductions

$\$ 2,041.65$
$\underline{-\ 498.80}$
$\$ 1,542.85$ Net pay

67. Mohammed G. Ali has an annual employment contract for a salary of $135,096. He is paid weekly. Determine the amount of gross pay Mohammed will receive each week.

$\dfrac{\$135,096}{52} = \$2,598$

68. John Stacey worked 52.75 hours last week. His regular wage is $9.36. Overtime is time-and-one-half for any time over 40 hours per week. Calculate John's gross pay for the week.

$\$9.36 \times 40 \qquad\qquad = \$\ 374.40$
$\$9.36 \times (1.5 \times 12.75) = \underline{+\ 179.01}$
$\qquad\qquad\qquad\qquad\qquad \$\ 553.41$

69. Jacques is a lumberjack. He is paid $11.50 per hour for regular time and double time for weekends and holidays. For overtime, he is paid time-and-one-half. It is defined by his contract as all time in excess of eight hours per day. He is not paid for the one-hour break he takes after working four consecutive hours. His hours for one week last year were as follows:

			Regular Hours	O.T. 1.5X	Hours 2X
Monday, Dec.30	9 A.M.– 8 P.M.	M — 10 hours	8	2	
Tuesday, Dec.31	9 A.M.– 7 P.M.	T — 9 hours	8	1	
Wednesday, Jan.1	9 A.M.– 6 P.M. (holiday)	W — 8 hours			8
Thursday, Jan.2	8 A.M.– 8 P.M.	H — 11 hours	8	3	
Friday, Jan.3	10 A.M.– 7 P.M.	F — 8 hours	8		
Saturday, Jan.4	9 A.M.– 6 P.M.	S — 8 hours			8
		54	32	6	16

How much was his gross pay for the week?

$\$11.50 \times 32 \qquad\quad = \$368.00$
$\$11.50 \times (1.5 \times 6) = \quad 103.50$
$\$11.50 \times (2 \times 16) = \underline{\quad 368.00}$
$\qquad\qquad\qquad\qquad\quad \$839.50$

70. Richard owns a plumbing business. He draws a biweekly salary of $12,900 gross. Calculate the amount he must pay for Social Security and Medicare each payday before reaching the limit for Social Security.

$12,900.00
× 6.2%
$ 799.80 SS

$12,900.00
× 1.45%
$ 187.05 Medicare

71. Roberta Gonzalez is a district sales manager. She receives a salary of $3,000 in each semimonthly pay period. In addition, she receives an override commission of 1.5% on all sales in her district. In the last pay period her salespeople had sales of $92,920 with no sales returns. How much was Roberta's gross pay?

$92,920 × 1.5% = $ 1,393.80 Commission
                  + 3,000.00 Salary
                  $ 4,393.80 Gross pay

72. Marshall Reeves is paid $.98 for each piece of clothing he finishes with fancy stitching. He is paid weekly. Last week he finished 629 pieces of clothing. Determine his gross pay for the week.

$ .98
×   629
$616.42

✓ ENRICHMENT PROBLEMS

73. Alpine Investments pays its agents on the following variable-rate commission schedule:

first $ 30,000	.50%
over $ 30,000 – $ 60,000	1.00%
over $ 60,000 – $110,000	1.75%
over $110,000 – $200,000	3.00%
over $200,000	4.50%

Susan Chen had investment sales totaling $212,934.42 for the month. She had prior earnings of $78,539.96, is married, and claims five withholding allowances. Use the percentage method to calculate her FIT withholding. State income tax is 4.3% of gross salary less $250 for each withholding allowance. Susan has $275 per month deducted to buy shares in a common stock mutual fund. Calculate her net pay.

$30,000 × .50% = $ 150.00
$30,000 × 1.00% =   300.00
$50,000 × 1.75%   875.00
$90,000 × 3.00%   2,700.00
$12,934.42 × 4.50% =   582.05
                    $4,607.05 Gross pay
$241.67 × 5 = $1,208.35

$ 80,400.00
− 78,539.96
$ 1,860.04

$1,860.04
× 6.2%
$ 115.32 SS

$4,607.05
× 1.45%
$ 66.80 Medicare

$ 4,607.05
− 1,208.35
$ 3,398.70

$ 3,398.70
− 538.00
$ 2,860.70

$2,860.70
× 15%
$ 429.11 FIT

$ 250
×   5
$1,250

$ 4,607.05
− 1,250.00
$ 3,357.05
×   4.3%
$ 144.35 SIT

$ 115.32 SS tax
   66.80 Medicare tax
  429.11 FIT
  275.00 Mutual fund
+ 144.35 SIT
$1,030.58 Total deductions

$ 4,607.05
− 1,030.58
$ 3,576.47 Net pay

74. Mickey "Majestic" Marberry is an entertainer under contract to MCI Recording Company, Inc., calling for a yearly salary of $2,389,000 to be paid biweekly. He is married and claims eight withholding allowances. This is the first paycheck of the year. Use the percentage method to calculate the FIT withholding for the pay period. The state income tax withholding is 8.5% of the FIT withholding. Mickey has $5,000 deducted from each paycheck to be divided among several urban youth groups attempting to end violence in the streets. All other benefits are paid for by MCI. Determine Mickey's net pay.

$2,389,000
---------- = $91,884.62 Gross earnings
    26

$80,400.00
× 6.2%
$ 4,984.80 SS tax

$91,884.62
× 1.45%
$ 1,332.33 Medicare

$111.54
×   8
$892.32

$91,884.62
− 892.32
$90,992.30

$ 90,992.30
− 11,617.00
$ 79,375.30

$79,375.30
× 38.6%
$30,638.87

$30,638.87
+ 3,347.84
$33,986.71 FIT

$33,986.71
× 8.5%
$ 2,888.87 SIT

$ 4,984.80 SS tax
  1,332.33 Medicare tax
 33,986.71 FIT
  2,888.87 SIT
  5,000.00 Urban youths
$48,192.71 Total deductions

$ 91,884.62
− 48,192.71
$ 43,691.91 Net pay

75. Dean Morris is an hourly employee. He works in a factory that has three shifts: the day shift from 8:00 A.M. to 4:00 P.M., the night shift from 4:00 P.M. to 12:00 midnight, and a swing shift from 10:00 A.M. to 2:00 P.M. and 6:00 P.M. to 10:00 P.M. The day and night shift pay is $16.98 per hour. The swing shift premium is at time-and-one-half as is overtime which is anything over eight hours per day. Weekend and holiday work is at double time. Dean is paid weekly. One weekly pay period appears here:

Monday, July 4	8 A.M.–	4 P.M. (holiday)
Tuesday, July 5	4 P.M. –	12:45 A.M.
Wednesday, July 6	8 A.M. –	4:30 P.M.
Thursday, July 7	10 A.M. –	2 P.M. and 6 P.M. – 10 P.M.
Friday, July 8	8 A.M. –	4 P.M.

Prior earnings for the year were $41,980.34. Dean is single and claims one withholding allowance. Use the wage bracket method to calculate his FIT withholding. Other deductions are as follows: insurance, $35.92; state income tax, $33.21: union dues, $27.50. Calculate Dean's net pay.

	Regular Hours	O.T. 1.5X	Hours 2X
M 8 hours (holiday)			8
T 8.75 hours	8	.75	
W 8.5 hours	8	.5	
H 8 hours		8	
F 8 hours	8		
41.25 hours	24	9.25	8
	× 1	× 1.5	× 2
	24	+ 13.875	+ 16 = 53.875

$ 16.98 $ 914.80 $914.80
× 53.875   × 1.45%   × 6.2%
$ 914.80 Gross pay $ 13.26 Medicare $ 56.72 SS

$158.00 FIT $ 914.80
56.72 SS   − 324.61
13.26 Medicare $ 590.19 Net pay
33.21 SIT
35.92 Insurance
+ 27.50 Union dues
$324.61 Total deductions

CRITICAL THINKING GROUP PROJECT

Ygacious Office Supply has 15 employees. Their names, titles, and payroll information is shown here:

Employee	Title	Status	Allowance	Salary or Wage
Sylvia Ygacious	President	Married	3	$114,000 annually
José Ygacious	VP of personnel	Single	2	76,020 annually
Manuel Ygacious	VP of production	Married	4	67,800 annually
Teresa Martinez	Office manager	Married	0	31,800 annually
Harvey Farhat	Sales manager	Single	3	30,000 annually
Stanley Gooden	Sales representative	Married	1	150 + weekly
Alice Kazalani	Sales representative	Married	4	150 + weekly
Patti Jakes	Sales representative	Single	1	125 + weekly
Morty Quevada	Secretary	Single	0	8.75 per hour
Jennifer Washington	Secretary	Single	1	7.70 per hour
Ethel Moorehouse	Clerk/typist	Married	5	5.15 per hour
Suzy Montoya	Production worker	Married	3	See Following Piecework Schedule
Jasper Oglethorpe	Production worker	Single	1	
Mable Cheeks	Production worker	Married	7	
Ricky Estrada	Production worker	Single	0	

Sylvia, José, and Manuel receive monthly paychecks. Teresa and Harvey are paid semimonthly. Stanley, Alice, and Patti are paid a weekly salary plus commission using a variable commission schedule. Morty, Jennifer, and Ethel receive a biweekly hourly wage. The production workers, Suzy, Jasper, Mable, and Ricky, are all paid weekly on a differential piecework system.

Differential Piecework Schedule		Variable Commission Schedule	
0 – 50 units	$ .75 each	0.00 – $ 5,000.00	3.0%
51 – 100 units	1.25 each	5,000.01 – 10,000.00	4.5%
Over 100 units	2.00 each	Over 10,000.00	6.0%

For the week of January 1 to January 8, Suzy produced 185 units, Jasper produced 175 units, Mable produced 200 units, and Ricky produced 150 units.

For the week of January 1 to January 8, Stanley had net sales of $9,250, Alice had net sales of $12,975, and Patti had net sales of $8,090.

For the biweekly period of January 1 to January 15, the daily hours worked by the employees paid on an hourly basis were as follows:

	Jan. 1 Monday	Jan. 2 Tuesday	Jan. 3 Wednesday	Jan. 4 Thursday	Jan. 5 Friday	Jan. 6 Saturday	Jan. 7 Sunday
Morty	8	7	8	8	9	3	
Jennifer	8	8	8	10	5	5	
Ethel	9	8	8	9	8		

	Jan. 8 Monday	Jan. 9 Tuesday	Jan. 10 Wednesday	Jan. 11 Thursday	Jan. 12 Friday	Jan. 13 Saturday	Jan. 14 Sunday
Morty	8	7	10	7	8	2	
Jennifer	8	7	9	11	8	3	
Ethel	8	9	8	8	8	1	

Overtime is anything over eight hours per day at time-and-one-half the regular rate and double time on weekends and holidays. January 1, New Year's Day, is a paid holiday.

1. Calculate the gross pay for Sylvia, José, and Manuel in January.

2. Calculate the gross pay for Teresa and Harvey for each of the pay periods in January.

3. Calculate the gross pay for Suzi, Jasper, Mable, and Ricky for the first week in January.

4. Calculate the gross pay for Stanley, Alice, and Patti for the first week in January.

5. Calculate the gross pay for Morty, Jennifer, and Ethel for the first biweekly period in January.

6. Calculate the Social Security, Medicare, and federal income tax deduction for each employee in questions 1 through 5. Use the percentage method to calculate the federal income tax.

7. The state income tax is 10% of the federal income tax, and insurance costs are $1,800 per year (calculated for each employee's pay period). Calculate the net pay for each employee.

Employee	Gross pay	Pay Period	Status	Allowance	Social security	Medicare	FIT	SIT	Insurance	Net Pay
Sylvia Ygacious	$9,500.00	Mo	M	3	$589.00	$137.75	$1,789.83	$178.98	$150.00	$6,654.44
José Ygacious	6,335.00	Mo	S	2	392.77	91.86	1,279.82	127.98	150.00	4,292.57
Manuel Ygacious	5,650.00	Mo	M	4	350.30	81.93	684.83	68.48	150.00	4,314.46
Teresa Martinez	1,325.00	Mo	M	0	82.15	19.21	118.05	11.81	150.00	943.78
Harvey Farhat	1,250.00	Mo	S	3	77.50	18.13	45.60	4.56	150.00	954.21
Stanley Gooden	498.00	Wk	M	1	30.88	7.22	47.73	4.77	34.62	372.78
Alice Kazalani	703.50	Wk	M	4	43.62	10.20	53.46	5.35	34.62	556.25
Patti Jakes	414.05	Wk	S	1	25.67	6.00	46.09	4.61	34.62	297.06
Morty Quevada	870.63	Biwk	S	0	53.98	12.62	115.29	11.53	69.23	607.98
Jennifer Washington	827.75	Biwk	S	1	51.32	12.00	92.13	9.21	69.23	593.86
Ethel Moorehouse	481.53	Biwk	M	5	29.85	6.98	0.00	0.00	69.23	375.47
Suzy Montoya	270.00	Wk	M	3	16.74	3.92	0.00	0.00	34.62	214.72
Jasper Oglethorpe	250.00	Wk	S	1	15.50	3.63	21.48	2.15	34.62	172.62
Mable Cheeks	300.00	Wk	M	7	18.60	4.35	0.00	0.00	34.62	242.43
Ricky Estrada	200.00	Wk	S	0	12.40	2.90	22.35	2.24	34.62	125.49

SELF-TESTING EXERCISES

Answers to all exercises are given in Appendix A.

1. What is the difference between the terms *wage* and *salary*? **W**
A wage is the payment for the use of human services. A salary is a special kind of contractual wage usually agreed upon on an annual basis.

2. Although the wage bracket method is much simpler to use when calculating the FIT by hand, it is important to understand the percentage method also. Why? **W**
Most employers use computers to figure payroll. Computers can be more easily programmed to calculate FIT deductions using the percentage method instead of the wage bracket method.

3. Jerrell Watts works in a pajama factory. He is paid for completed pajama tops according to the following differential piecework schedule:

1 – 100 tops	$ .75 each
101 – 150 tops	1.00 each
over 150 tops	1.25 each

Jerrell completed 200 pajama tops. How much was his gross pay?
100 × $ .75 = $75.00
50 × 1.00 = 50.00
50 × 1.25 = 62.50
$187.50

4. Patti Spencer is under contract to the Fabulous Ice Dancers Troupe. Her contract is for $127,500 annually and calls for biweekly payments. Find the gross pay for each paycheck.
$$\frac{\$127,500}{26} = \$4,903.85$$

5. Jan had annual earnings of $16,300 so far this year. She earned $685 gross for the current semimonthly pay period. How much will be deducted for Social Security and Medicare?
$ 685.00 $ 685.00
× 6.2%   × 1.45%
$ 42.47 SS $ 9.93 Medicare

6. Larry is a construction worker who is called to work at irregular hours. His union contract defines overtime as all time before 7:00 A.M. and all time after 6:00 P.M. If Larry is called out on a job, he cannot be paid for less than a half day (four hours). He is paid double time for all overtime and all weekends. He is paid triple time for all holidays. Larry is not paid for the 30-minute lunch he takes every day in which he works more than four hours. Larry's regular hourly wage is $20.84 per hour. One week in February he worked the following hours:

			Regular Hours	O.T. 2X	Hours 3X
Sunday, Feb. 20	7:00 A.M. – 3:30 P.M.	S 8 hours		8	
Monday, Feb. 21	8:00 A.M. – 11:30 A.M. (President's Day)	M 4 hours			4
Tuesday, Feb. 22	9:30 A.M. – 7:00 P.M.	T 9 hours	8	1	
Wednesday, Feb.23	6:30 A.M. – 3:30 P.M.	W 8.5 hours	8	.5	
Thursday, Feb. 24	7:30 A.M. – 4:00 P.M.	H 8 hours	8		
Friday, Feb. 25	7:30 A.M. – 6:00 P.M.	F 10 hours	10		
Saturday, Feb. 26	8:00 A.M. – 4:30 P.M.	S 8 hours		8	
		45.5 hours	34	17.5	4

Calculate his gross earnings.
$20.84 × 34 = $ 708.56
20.84 × (2 × 17.5) = 729.40
20.84 × (3 × 4) = 250.08
$1,688.04

7. Paul Schlumberger worked 49 hours last week. His regular wage rate is $7.52 per hour. Overtime is all time in excess of 40 hours in a week at time-and-one-half. How much is his gross pay for the week?

$7.52 × 40 = $ 300.80
$7.52 × (1.5 × 9) + 101.52
$ 402.32

8. Benjamin Kuipers is paid a salary of $300 plus a 4% commission rate on all net sales over $3,500 each month. Last month his gross sales were $49,750 with sales returns of $841. Benjamin had prior annual earnings of $58,395. He is married and claims three withholding allowances. Use the percentage method to compute Benjamin's FIT tax. The group medical insurance is $134.65 per month. The state income tax is $16.50. His union dues are 2% of his gross earnings. Calculate Benjamin's net pay.

$49,750 $ 48,909 $45,409.00 $1,816.36 $2,116.36 $2,116.36
− 841   − 3,500   ×   4%   + 300.00   ×   6.2%   × 1.45%
$48,909 $ 45,409 $ 1,816.36 $2,116.36 Gross pay $ 131.21 SS $ 30.69 Medicare

$241.67 $2,116.36 $1,391.35 $853.35 $2,116.36
×   3   − 725.01   − 538.00   × 15%   ×   2%
$725.01 $1,391.35 $ 853.35 $128.00 FIT $ 42.33 Union dues

$131.21 SS
  30.69 Medicare
 128.00 FIT $2,116.36
 134.65 Medical insurance − 483.38
  16.50 State income tax $1,632.98 Net pay
  42.33 Union dues
$483.38 Total deductions

9. Mervin's union contract defines overtime as all time worked in excess of eight hours per day. It is calculated at $1\frac{1}{2}$ times the regular rate of pay. Find Mervin's gross pay for the week.

Employee	Hours Worked S M T W H F S	Total Hours Reg.	O.T.	Reg Rate	Gross Earnings Reg.	O.T.	Total
Jones, M	− 9 9 8 7 9 −	39	3	$6.25	$243.75	$28.13	$271.88

Hours Worked
    Total Reg. Ovtm
M   9   8   1 $6.25 × 39   = $243.75
T   9   8   1 $6.25 × (1.5 × 3) =   28.13
W   8   8 $271.88
H   7   7
F   9   8   1
    42   39   3

10. Margaret Lam works in a factory that pays a piecework wage of $.40 for each toy truck produced. One week Margaret produced 428 toy trucks. How much was her gross pay?

428 × $.40 = $171.20

11. Jerry DeWitt is a sales representative. His company pays commissions according to the following variable-rate schedule:

        first $ 1,000   2.0%
over $ 1,000 – $ 4,000   3.5%
over $ 4,000 – $10,000   5.0%
        over $10,000   7.5%

Last month Jerry had total sales of $10,572.59. Sales returns were $794.29. Calculate Jerry's commissions for the month.

$10,572.59 $1,000.00 × 2%   = $ 20.00
− 794.29   3,000.00 × 3.5%   = 105.00
$ 9,778.30   5,778.30 × 5%   = 288.92
                                 $413.92

12. Xue Liao is married, claims three withholding allowances, receives an annual salary of $63,960, and is paid weekly. Use the wage bracket method to determine the amount of federal income tax to be withheld from each of Xue's paychecks.

$\frac{\$63,960}{52}$ = $1,230 $155 FIT tax withheld

13. Rebecca Oliver sells cleaning supplies and equipment and is paid a commission rate of 8% on net sales. During the last month, Becky had sales of $29,578.21. Customers returned $104.48 worth. Her prior earnings for the year were $78,374.11. Becky is single and claims four withholding allowances. Use the percentage method to calculate the FIT withholding deduction. Her state income tax rate is 6% of the gross pay less $225 for each withholding allowance. Group medical and dental insurance of $78.33 is deducted from each paycheck. Becky also has $300 deducted and automatically deposited into her credit union savings account. Calculate her net pay.

$29,578.21	$29,473.73	$241.67	$2,357.90	$1,391.22	$1,170.22
− 104.48	× 8%	× 4	− 966.68	− 221.00	× 15%
$29,473.73	$2,357.90 Gross pay	$966.68	$1,391.22	$1,170.22	$175.53 FIT

$80,400.00	$2,025.89	$2,357.90	$225	$2,357.90	$1,457.90
− 78,374.11	× 6.2%	× 1.45%	× 4	− 900.00	× 6%
$2,025.89	$125.61 SS	$34.19 Medicare	$900	$1,457.90	$87.47 SIT

$ 175.53 FIT
125.61 SS
34.19 Medicare
87.47 SIT
78.33 Medical insurance
+ 300.00 Savings
$ 801.13 Total deductions

$2,357.90
− 801.13
$1,556.77 Net pay

EXCEL SPREADSHEET APPLICATION FOR CHAPTER 6

APPLICATION 1

Application 1 is a spreadsheet program to determine the gross earnings of hourly workers. You will need to input the names of the employees, the hours worked during the week, and the pay rate. The remaining information will be automatically calculated and entered on the spreadsheet form. When you load Ch6App1 on your spreadsheet application's disk, you will see a screen that looks like the one shown here:

Springfield Department Store
2617 Main Street
Box 219
Springfield, Maryland 58109
Telephone 301-555-2158   FAX 301-555-3498

PAYROLL REGISTER

Employee	Daily Hours Worked							Total Hours		Pay Rate	Gross Earnings		
	S	M	T	W	T	F	S	Reg	O.T.		Reg.	O.T.	Total
								0.00	0.00		$0.00	$0.00	$0.00
								0.00	0.00		$0.00	$0.00	$0.00
								0.00	0.00		$0.00	$0.00	$0.00
								0.00	0.00		$0.00	$0.00	$0.00
								0.00	0.00		$0.00	$0.00	$0.00
								0.00	0.00		$0.00	$0.00	$0.00
								0.00	0.00		$0.00	$0.00	$0.00
								0.00	0.00		$0.00	$0.00	$0.00
								0.00	0.00		$0.00	$0.00	$0.00
								0.00	0.00		$0.00	$0.00	$0.00
								0.00	0.00		$0.00	$0.00	$0.00
								0.00	0.00		$0.00	$0.00	$0.00
								0.00	0.00		$0.00	$0.00	$0.00
								0.00	0.00		$0.00	$0.00	$0.00
TOTALS	0.00	0.00	0.00	0.00									

Enter the following information:

Employee	S	Daily Hours Worked M	T	W	T	F	S	Pay Rate
Johnson, Susan		8	8.5	8	8.75	8.25	4	$ 8.25
Haverson, John		8	8	8.5	8	9	6.5	$ 9.60
Vorhees, George		8.75	9	8.5	8	10.75		$ 6.88
Yolanders, Wilma		8.5	7.5	8	9	8	5	$12.79
Unsled, Louise	2.5	8	7.75	8.5	8	8		$ 5.90
March, Todd		8	9	10.5	8	6.75	6	$11.30
Flanders, Claire		8	8	8	8	8		$ 9.32
North, Quinten	4	9	9.5	8	8.25	8	3.25	$ 8.50
Aberson, Steven		7	5	4	6	4.75		$ 5.00
Uvalde, Paco		8	8	8	8	8	3.75	$ 7.30
Blubaker, Paul		8.5	9.75	8	8.25	8	6.5	$14.38
Marigold, Rita			9.5	10.5	8.5	8	8.25	$11.11
Foster, Hortense	3	4	8	6	4.75	4	5.5	$ 5.00
Fong, Lee	8	8	8	8	8	2.5		$10.35

Answer the following questions after you have completed the spreadsheet:

1. What were the total number of hours worked by all employees on Tuesday?
2. How many total hours were worked by Todd March? How many of those were overtime?
3. How much did Hortense Foster earn in total?
4. How much was Paul Blubaker's overtime pay?
5. What was the Springfield Department Store's total payroll for the week?
6. What was the total overtime pay for the week?
7. How many hours of overtime did Quinten North have during the week?

GROUP REPORT

FOR CHAPTER 6 APPLICATION 1

Switch the hours worked each day by Steven Aberson with those of Paul Blubaker. What is the difference in total payroll? Write a report to the store manager describing the results of the switch and make recommendations based on your findings. Would other information be needed before making a decision to switch Aberson's and Blubaker's hours permanently? What information, and how would your group recommend it be gathered?

APPLICATION 2

Application 2 is a continuation of the spreadsheet from Application 1. You will need to input the names of the employees, the code for marital status, the code for insurance coverage, the number of exemptions claimed by the employee, and from Application 1 the total gross earnings for each employee. The remaining information will be automatically calculated and entered on the spreadsheet form. When you open the file on Ch6App2 from your spreadsheet application's disk, it will look like the one shown here:

Springfield Department Store

2617 Main Street
Box 219
Springfield, Maryland 58109
Telephone: 301-555-2158   FAX: 301-555-3498

PAYROLL DEDUCTIONS

Employee	Marital Status	Insur.	# of Exmpt.	Total Gross Earnings	F.I.T.	S.I.T.	FICA	Medicare	Ins. Deduct.	Total Deduct.	Total Net Earnings
					($10.65)	($1.07)	$0.00	$0.00	#VALUE!	#VALUE!	#VALUE!
					(10.65)	(1.07)	0.00	0.00	#VALUE!	#VALUE!	#VALUE!
					(10.65)	(1.07)	0.00	0.00	#VALUE!	#VALUE!	#VALUE!
					(10.65)	(1.07)	0.00	0.00	#VALUE!	#VALUE!	#VALUE!
					(10.65)	(1.07)	0.00	0.00	#VALUE!	#VALUE!	#VALUE!
					(10.65)	(1.07)	0.00	0.00	#VALUE!	#VALUE!	#VALUE!
					(10.65)	(1.07)	0.00	0.00	#VALUE!	#VALUE!	#VALUE!
					(10.65)	(1.07)	0.00	0.00	#VALUE!	#VALUE!	#VALUE!
					(10.65)	(1.07)	0.00	0.00	#VALUE!	#VALUE!	#VALUE!
					(10.65)	(1.07)	0.00	0.00	#VALUE!	#VALUE!	#VALUE!
					(10.65)	(1.07)	0.00	0.00	#VALUE!	#VALUE!	#VALUE!
					(10.65)	(1.07)	0.00	0.00	#VALUE!	#VALUE!	#VALUE!
					(10.65)	(1.07)	0.00	0.00	#VALUE!	#VALUE!	#VALUE!
					(10.65)	(1.07)	0.00	0.00	#VALUE!	#VALUE!	#VALUE!
TOTALS				$0.00	($149.10)	($14.91)	$0.00	$0.00	#VALUE!	#VALUE!	#VALUE!

Enter the following information:

Employee	Marital Status	Insurance	Number of Exemptions
Johnson, Susan	Married	Employee & Spous	2
Haverson, John	Married	Employee & Spouse	3
Vorhees, George	Single	Employee	1
Yolanders, Wilma	Married	Employee & Children	4
Unsled, Louise	Single	Employee	0
March, Todd	Married	Family	2
Flanders, Claire	Single	Employee & Children	0
North, Quinten	Single	Employee	3
Aberson, Steven	Single	Employee & Children	1
Uvalde, Paco	Married	Employee & Spouse	2
Blubaker, Paul	Married	Family	5
Marigold, Rita	Married	Family	2
Foster, Hortense	Single	Employee	0
Fong, Lee	Married	Family	3

Marital status will be entered by number: 1 if the employee is single, and 2 if married. Insurance coverage will also be entered by code as follows (You do not need to enter the amount. That will be done automatically.):

Code	Coverage	Cost
1	for employee only	$ 0.00
2	for employee and spouse	25.00
3	for employee and children	37.50
4	for entire family	52.00

After completing the spreadsheet for Application 2, answer the following questions:

1. What amount is deducted from George Vorhees' pay this week for federal income tax?

2. What is the amount deducted from Rita Marigold's pay for state income tax?

3. What amount is deducted from Steven Aberson's pay for FICA?

4. What amount is deducted from Susan Johnson's pay for Medicare?

5. What are Claire Flanders' total net earnings for the week?

6. How much is deducted from Lee Fong's pay for insurance?

7. What is the total payroll deduction for the Springfield Department Store for the week?

8. What is the total amount deducted from Paco Uvalde's gross earnings?

GROUP REPORT

FOR CHAPTER 6 APPLICATION 2

1. Several of the employees have elected to not claim any withholding allowance exemptions. Your group has been asked to assess the difference in net pay to those employees if they were to claim one withholding allowance exemption for themselves.

2. Claire Flanders is paying for insurance for herself and her children. That means she could qualify for at least two withholding allowance exemptions. Substitute two exemptions for her, and record the difference it will make in her net pay.

3. Write a memo to each of the affected employees advising them of the results of your findings.

7 MARKETING APPLICATIONS
BUYING

TRADE LOADING VS. NO LOADING

Once upon a time American business chiefs took for granted that if manufacturers could sell in very large quantities, great economies would always result from the large-scale production. They produced and sold to retailers in huge shipments at big discount prices.

The term for the practice is *trade loading*. In fact, in recent years, Americans have discovered that this often causes everybody to lose money in the long run.

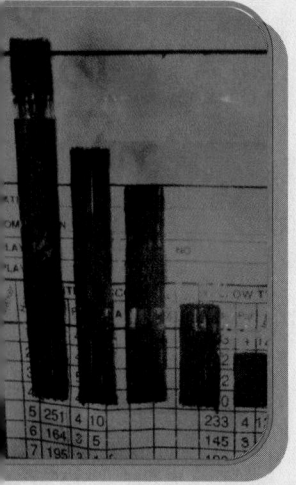

Consider this unappetizing fact: The average grocery product takes 84 days to travel from factory floor to the retail shelf. Products sitting on retailers' shelves or in warehouses too often become stale and have to be discarded. In the end American consumers pay as much as $400 billion too much for groceries every year as a result of spoilage.

Procter & Gamble's chief executive calls trade loading a "monstrosity" and vows to change the practice. Many others agree.

In recent business history the idea of just-in-time management, or "no loading," has caught on. Shipments are made in small regular amounts with smaller discounts, and profits have actually increased. Factories run on normal shifts reducing overtime pay. Wholesalers' inventories are reduced, saving storage and handling costs. Retailers reduce inventories, freeing up cash for other investments. Consumers get fresher goods at lower prices. Everybody wins.

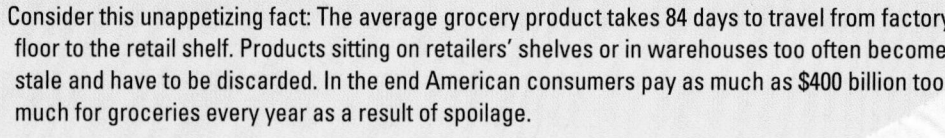

Chapter Glossary

Discounts. Reductions from the list price of a good; they are part of the "pricing package."

List price. The suggested retail price to the consumer.

Trade discounts. Reductions from the list price of a good based on factors such as the buyer's position in the seller's channel of distribution, the season of the year, the condition of the economy, and the competition.

Net cost. List price less discounts.

Complement of a percent. The percent obtained by subtracting another percent from 100%, or, stated another way, the percent that has to be added to another to get 100%.

Net cost equivalent rate. The complement of the trade discount percent.

Single equivalent discount rate. The complement of the net cost equivalent rate.

Cash discount. A reduction of merchandise amount allowed only if payment is made within a specified time period. Cash discounts are offered by sellers to encourage early payment of bills.

Invoice. A bill; a printed record of sales and purchases.

Ordinary dating. Offering cash discounts with the due dates being counted from the date of the invoice.

Sliding scale cash discounts. Offering more than one cash discount. For example, a 4% discount might be offered if payment is made

within 10 days, and a 2% discount might be offered if payment is not made in 10 days, but is made between 11 and 20 days.

AS OF dating. Postdating cash discount terms to start at some date after the invoice date.

ROG dating. Receipt-of-goods (ROG) dating means that the discount period does not begin until after the buyer has received the merchandise ordered.

EOM dating. End-of-month (EOM) dating means that the discount period does not start until the end of the month in which the invoice is dated. For example, an invoice dated 6/8 EOM means that the discount period starts in July. For invoices dated after the 25th of the month, it is common business practice to extend the period for another month. For example, an invoice dated 6/26 means that the discount period starts in August.

Proximo (prox.) dating. The abbreviation *prox.* for the Latin term proximo means "next month." EOM dating and prox. dating result in identical discount periods.

A major function of marketing is distributing products. Manufacturers buy raw materials and component parts from producers, alter them in some way that makes them more marketable, and then sell the final goods to other manufacturers, wholesalers, retailers, or even final consumers.

Wholesalers buy large quantities and provide a sales force, warehouse facilities, delivery services, and other services. Then they sell their assortment of products in smaller quantities to other businesses, usually retailers.

Retailers buy an assortment of finished products from manufacturers and wholesalers. They make a profit by selling to consumers at prices higher than those they paid. Some of the more common channels of distribution are shown in Figure 7.1.

Figure 7.1
Channels of Distribution

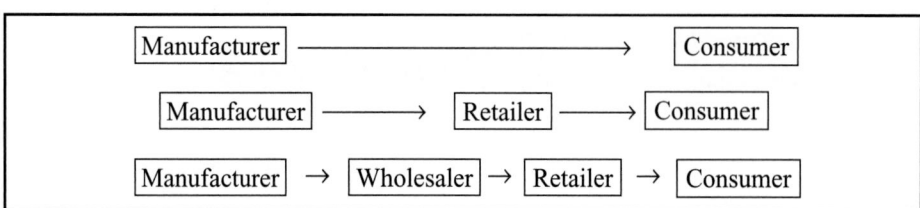

Business buyers and sellers must make several decisions on the discounts that they will offer or take. **Discounts** are offered as part of the "pricing package." Owners or managers charged with the responsibility of buying products must take into account their suppliers' discount policies when making buying decisions.

Each type of discount has a specific purpose. The purpose for, and effects of, offering and accepting discounts must be understood if realistic buying policies are to be followed. In most industries a traditional discount policy exists and usually must be followed if a firm expects to be competitive. The two types of discounts discussed in this chapter are trade discounts and cash discounts.

LEARNING UNIT 1
TRADE DISCOUNTS

 **Excel Spreadsheet Application** Spreadsheet Application 1 at the end of this chapter illustrates a trade discount conversion spreadsheet to find the Springfield Department Store's net cost for merchandise ordered from a wholesale distributor.

Manufacturers provide wholesalers with catalogs. Manufacturers and wholesalers, in turn, often provide retailers with catalogs. The catalogs are often in a loose-leaf format so that one page at a time can be changed. They may contain a large number of different products and thousands of pages. They are often quite elaborate and very expensive to produce and distribute. Printing new catalogs every time a price changes or products are added or deleted might be prohibitively expensive. Instead, the prices in the catalog are the suggested retail prices to the consumer, usually referred to as the **list price**. A discount sheet itemizing the discount rates for all articles in the catalog is then provided to potential buyers. **Trade discounts**, the business term for these rates, vary widely according to such factors as the buyer's position in the seller's channel of distribution (wholesalers receive a larger discount than retailers), the season of the year, the condition of the economy, whether a product is being discontinued, attempts to encourage large quantity purchases, and the severity of competition. When any of these considerations changes enough to affect prices, the seller prepares and distributes a new discount sheet to buyers. All discount rates apply to the list price in the catalog.

7.1 | Calculating the Net Cost with a Single Trade Discount

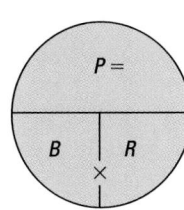

$P =$

B | R

$\times$

This is an application of the percentage formula,
$P = B \times R$

To find the amount of discount, the list price is multiplied by the trade discount. The discount is then subtracted from the list price to arrive at the **net cost** to the buyer. The formulas are:

> Discount = list price × discount rate
> Net cost = list price − discount

EXAMPLE   A retailer bought an emergency first aid kit that had a list price of $23.95. The trade discount was 40%. Find the net cost to the retailer.

Solution   Discount = list price × discount rate
          = $23.95 × 40% = $9.58
      Net cost = list price − discount
          = $23.95 − 9.58
          = $14.37

The *complement method* is another way often used when you only need to know the net cost. It uses the complements of percents. The **complement of a percent** is the difference you get by subtracting that percent from 100%. Stated another way, the complement is the percent that has to be added to another to get 100%. Thus, for example, the complement of 40% is 60%:

$$100\% - 40\% = 60\%$$

or,

$$40\% + 60\% = 100\%$$

If the discount rate is 40%, it represents the amount you *do not* pay; the complement, 60%, represents the amount you *do* pay. This is called the **net cost equivalent rate**. Table 7.1 shows some of the more common net cost equivalent rates of single discounts.

TABLE 7.1   NET COST EQUIVALENT RATES FOR SINGLE DISCOUNTS

Percent Discount	Net Cost Equivalent Percent	Decimal Discount	Net Cost Equivalent Decimal
5%	95%	.05	.95
10%	90%	.10	.90
15%	85%	.15	.85
20%	80%	.20	.80
25%	75%	.25	.75
30%	70%	.30	.70
35%	65%	.35	.65
40%	60%	.40	.60
45%	55%	.45	.55
50%	50%	.50	.50

Solution   You can solve the problem in the previous example using the complement method:

	Amount	Percent	
List price	$23.95	100%	←*Base is always 100%.*
− discount		40%	←*Discount rate given*
= net cost		60%	←*Net cost equivalent rate* (100% − 40% = 60%)

You know the base amount, the list price, so multiply it by the net cost equivalent rate (the complement):

$$\text{Net cost} = \text{list price} \times \text{net cost equivalent}$$
$$= \$23.95 \times 60\%$$
$$= \$14.37$$

$$\boxed{\$23.95 \;\ominus\; 40\ \%\; \equiv\; \$14.37}$$

7.1 Practice Problems

Calculate the net cost in the following problems:

1. A store received a trade discount of 45% from a wholesaler for a dress that had listed for $37. Find the net cost.
2. A cookbook holder is listed at $7 in the Madison Mfg. Co. catalog. The trade discount is 28%. Find the net cost.
3. Fromholtz bought a coffee table with a list price of $259. The trade discount was 50%. Find the net cost to Fromholtz.
4. A paper rack was listed at $44. The trade discount was 25%. Find the net cost.

7.1 Solutions to Practice Problems

1. $100\% - 45\% = 55\%$
   Net cost = list price × net equivalent cost
   $= \$37 \times 55\% = \$20.35$
2. $100\% - 28\% = 72\%$
   Net cost = list price × net equivalent cost
   $= \$7 \times 72\% = \$5.04$
3. $100\% - 50\% = 50\%$
   Net cost = list price × net equivalent cost
   $= \$259 \times 50\% = \$129.50$
4. $100\% - 25\% = 75\%$
   Net cost = list price × net equivalent cost
   $= \$44 \times 75\% = \$33$

7.2 Calculating the Net Cost with a Series Trade Discount

Series trade discounts are given for a variety of reasons. For example, the original discount may have been 30%. In an attempt to stimulate slow sales, the distributor may offer a second discount of 15%. The series trade discount would now be written 30/15. Notice that the percent sign has been eliminated, but it is still understood that the numbers in the series trade discount are percents. If the business qualifies for a quantity discount, an additional discount of, for example, 5% would be given. The series trade discount would now be 30/15/5. Figure 7.2 shows a partial, typical discount sheet that illustrates how single trade discounts, a series of two discounts, and a series of three discounts can occur.

Three ways of solving series trade discount problems are possible. The first example demonstrates the method for using discounts separately. The following steps are used:

1. Find the first discount by multiplying the list price by the first discount percent.
2. Subtract that discount from the list price.
3. Multiply the answer in step 2 by the second discount percent to find the second discount.
4. Subtract that discount from the answer obtained in step 2.

5. If a third discount percent is given, multiply it by the balance remaining after the preceding discount has been subtracted.

6. Subtract the discount from step 5 from the amount in step 4.

Never add the individual discounts together in a series discount. A series discount of 30/15 is *not* 45%.

Figure 7.2
Trade Discount Sheet

JACKSON HOSPITAL SUPPLY COMPANY
3458 West 28th Street
Jackson, Mississippi 39205
Telephone (800) 288-8888

CONFIDENTIAL DISTRIBUTOR DISCOUNT SCHEDULE

Page	Description	Discount(s)
38	Pharmaseal plastic disposable wash basin	30%
38	Pharmaseal reusable stainless steel wash basin	30%, 15%

Additional Discounts

These additional volume discounts are available only on single orders shipped at the same time to a single destination.

1. Orders totaling $300, an additional 5%
2. Orders totaling $500, an additional 7.5%
3. Orders totaling $750, an additional 10%

E X A M P L E   A hospital ordered 10 Pharmaseal stainless steel wash basins. The list price is $12 each. Trade discounts are 30/15. Find the net cost.

Solution

30% Discount		15% Discount	
$12.00	$12.00	→$8.40	$8.40
× 30%	− 3.60	× 15%	− 1.26
$ 3.60	$ 8.40	$1.26	$7.14

Net cost = $7.14 × 10 = $71.40

Obviously, taking each discount separately is a tedious and lengthy process. It is *not* the preferred method for most people charged with finding the net cost using series trade discounts.

A second method uses the complements of the discounts. The complements of the individual discounts are then multiplied together to find the net cost equivalent rate. It is usually stated in decimal fraction form.

Do not round the net cost equivalent rate. Doing so will result in incorrect answers. After you multiply the list price by the net cost equivalent rate, you can round to the nearest cent. Using the previous example again, we get:

Solution

100%	100%	*Find the complements of the two discounts.*
− 30%	− 15%	
70% ×	85% = .595	*Find the net cost equivalent rate by multiplying the complements together (.7 × .85 = .595).*

Note: For convenience, the conversion from percent to decimal will not be shown in solutions. However, remember that step when you are solving problems.

Find the total list price of the merchandise and multiply by the cost equivalent rate.

$$(10 \times \$12) \times .595 = \$120 \times .595 = \$71.40$$

10 ✕ 12 ⊟ 30 % ⊟ 15 % ═ 71.40

TABLE 7.2 NET COST EQUIVALENT RATES WITH SERIES DISCOUNTS

	5%	10%	15%	20%	25%	30%	35%	40%
5	.9025	.855	.8075	.76	.7125	.665	.6175	.57
5/5	.857375	.81225	.767125	.722	.676875	.63175	.585525	.5415
10	.855	.81	.765	.72	.675	.63	.585	.54
10/5	.81225	.7695	.72675	.684	.64125	.5985	.55575	.513
10/10	.7695	.729	.6885	.648	.6075	.567	.5265	.486
15	.8075	.765	.7225	.68	.6375	.595	.5525	.51
15/5	.767125	.72675	.686375	.646	.605625	.56525	.524875	.4845
15/10	.72675	.6885	.65025	.612	.57375	.5355	.49725	.459
15/15	.686375	.65025	.614125	.578	.541875	.50575	.469625	.4335
20	.76	.72	.68	.64	.6	.56	.52	.48
20/5	.722	.684	.646	.608	.57	.532	.494	.456
20/10	.684	.648	.612	.576	.54	.504	.468	.432
20/15	.646	.612	.578	.544	.51	.476	.442	.408
20/20	.608	.576	.544	.512	.48	.448	.416	.384
25	.7125	.675	.6375	.6	.5625	.525	.4875	.45
25/5	.676875	.64125	.605625	.57	.534375	.49875	.463125	.4275
25/10	.64125	.6075	.57375	.54	.50625	.4725	.43875	.405
25/15	.605625	.57375	.541875	.51	.478125	.44625	.414375	.3825
25/20	.57	.54	.51	.48	.45	.42	.39	.36
25/25	.534375	.50625	.478125	.45	.421875	.39375	.365625	.3375
30	.665	.63	.595	.56	.525	.49	.455	.42
40	.57	.54	.51	.48	.45	.42	.39	.36

When using series trade discounts, the complement of the net cost equivalent rate is called the **single equivalent discount rate**. Thus, 100% = 1, and then the single equivalent discount rate is $1.000 - .595 = .405$. If all you need is the discount, you can multiply the list price by the single equivalent discount rate to find the discount.

The third method involves the use of a table. People who work with series trade discounts on a regular basis often use a table such as Table 7.2. Using the previous example yet again with a list price of $12 and trade discounts of 30/15, we arrive at the following solution:

Solution In the leftmost column of Table 7.2 find 30. Go across to the intersection with the column headed by 15%. The net cost equivalent rate at the intersection is .595. Multiply the list price by the net cost equivalent rate:

$$\text{Net cost} = \text{list price} \times \text{net cost equivalent rate}$$
$$= (\$12 \times 10) \times .595$$
$$= \$7.14$$

You should note that the *sequence of discounts does not matter*. The net cost equivalent rate at the intersection of 30/15 is the some as the net cost equivalent rate at the intersection of 15/30.

You may also come across a series of three or more trade discounts. If you do, the equivalent rate is found the same way. The solutions will be the net cost equivalent rates. They are solved first without the table, then with the table.

EXAMPLE The list price of a deluxe sofa is $1,350. The series discounts are 25/10/5. Calculate the net cost.

Solution

100%		100%		100%		$1,350.00
− 25%		− 10%		− 5%		× .64125
75%	×	90%	×	95% = .64125		$ 865.69

$$1{,}350 \; \boxed{-} \; 25 \; \boxed{\%} \; \boxed{-} \; 10 \; \boxed{\%} \; \boxed{-} \; 5 \; \boxed{\%} \; \boxed{=} \; 865.69$$

Solution   From Table 7.2, find the discounts 25/10/5. The sequence does not matter, so you could find 10/5 in the leftmost column and go across to the column headed by 25%, or you could find 25/10 in the leftmost column and go across to the column headed by 5%. In either case, you will find the net cost equivalent rate at the intersection of .64125. Multiply the list price by that net cost equivalent rate:

$$\$1{,}350 \times .64125 = \$865.69$$

7.2 Practice Problems

1. A retailer is going to buy a hair dryer. The wholesaler lists it at $54. Trade discounts are 20/15/10. Find the net cost.

2. The list price for a TV stand is $64. Trade discounts are 10/20/5. Calculate the net cost.

3. Yemen Department Store has ordered women's shoes listing for $135. The trade discounts are 20/20. What is the net cost?

4. A trade discount of 44% is given for a picture frame. The frame lists for $38.98. Find the net cost.

7.2 Solutions to Practice Problems

1.
```
   100%        100%        100%         $54.00
  - 20%       - 15%       - 10%        × .612
   80%   ×     85%   ×     90% = .612   $33.05
```

2.
```
   100%        100%        100%         $64.00
  - 10%       - 20%       -  5%        × .684
   90%   ×     80%   ×     95% = .684   $43.78
```

3.
```
   100%        100%                     $135.00
  - 20%       - 20%                    ×  .64
   80%   ×     80% = .64                $86.40
```

4.
```
   100%                                 $38.98
  - 44%                                ×  .56
   56%                                  $21.83
```

LEARNING UNIT 2
CASH DISCOUNTS

A **cash discount** is offered by sellers to encourage early payment of bills. Competition in an industry usually requires that sellers grant customers time (usually 30 days) to pay for merchandise. However, sellers need a continuous inflow of cash for their operations. The faster a customer pays, the less money sellers have to borrow, or find through other means.

To find the net payment due on an invoice, start with the list price when it is given. Subtract any trade discount(s) first, and then the cash discount. The formula is

> Net payment = list price − trade discount(s) − cash discount.

The cash discount is shown on an invoice as a part of the terms of sale. Many businesses today use computerized systems that compute the amount of the discount and eliminate the need for the buyer to make calculations. Nevertheless, it is important to understand cash discounts even when they are computerized, and many companies do not include the discount amount.

An **invoice** is a bill. It provides a printed record of sales and purchases. To a seller, it is a *sales invoice*, while to a buyer it is a *purchase invoice*. The invoice serves several purposes:

1. It identifies the buyer and the seller.
2. It is dated (the invoice date).

Figure 7.3
Sample Invoice

RAYMOND FRUIT DISTRIBUTOR
P.O. BOX 94867
CHICAGO, IL 60609

SOLD TO	Hammori Grocery 3491 N. Walton Ave. Springfield, IL 66492	Invoice no.	DGT 39568

		Customer order no.	Q12095P

		Invoice date	6/3/02
Terms	2/10, n/30	Shipped on	6/2/02
		Shipped by	NFC Trucking

Product Number	Order Qty.	Product Description	Qty. Shpd.	Unit Price	Total Amount	
Lm2952	3 cs	Lemons, Ca lg.	3 cs	23.59	70.77	
Li3294	2 cs	Limes, Ca std.	2 cs	18.43	36.86	
Or9382	6 cs	Oranges, Ca.	6 cs	38.18	229.08	
Ap39854	2 cs	Apples, Ca Delicious	2 cs	13.65	27.30	
Ct3948	3 cs	Cantaloupe, Ca	3 cs	29.44	88.32	

MEMO					
			Tax %	8%	Subtotal $ 452.33
					Tax amount 36.19
					Freight 27.85
			TOTAL INVOICE Please pay this amount		$ 516.37

3. It gives the date of shipment.

4. It gives product information, the catalog number or code, and a description of the product.

5. It gives the quantity of each product shipped.

6. It lists the unit price and the extended price (price × quantity).

7. It provides the total amount for the merchandise shipped.

8. It gives the amount of any taxes and/or the cost of freight.

9. It shows the total invoice amount.

10. It gives the terms of sale (how much time the buyer has to pay the invoice and the discount that may be taken if it is paid early).

A sample of an invoice is given in Figure 7.3.

Excel Spreadsheet Application Spreadsheet Application 2 at the end of this chapter requires the preparation of an invoice to the Springfield Department Store.

The invoice will always be net of any trade discounts. That is, the trade discounts would be calculated and subtracted from the list price before the invoice is prepared. *Cash discounts are never taken on taxes, freight charges, insurance, or returned goods.* Thus, these charges must be subtracted before cash discounts are taken. However, all but returned goods must be added back after the discount has been taken to find the total amount due.

Determining Cash Discount Due Dates

Cash discount and credit terms are generally shown in abbreviated form such as 2/10, n/30 which is interpreted as follows:

2/10, n/30

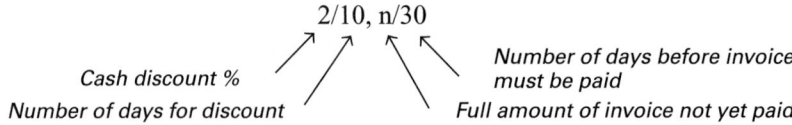

Cash discount %

Number of days for discount

Number of days before invoice must be paid

Full amount of invoice not yet paid

These terms are read, "two ten, net 30," and mean that the invoice must be paid within 10 days from the date of the invoice to receive a 2% discount. Any unpaid amount after the 10 days must be paid within 30 days from the date of the invoice or it will be subject to interest charges.

The invoice date on the sample invoice, Figure 7.3, is 6/3 (June 3). To take the 2% discount, it would have to be paid on or before June 13. The net amount of the invoice is due if it is paid on June 14 through July 3. Starting July 4, the net amount would be subject to interest charges.

It is rather easy to find the due dates for a month with 30 days such as June. But not all months have 30 days. Some have 31 days, and February has 28, unless it is leap year in which case February has 29 days. Leap year occurs every four years, in the years evenly divisible by four. Thus, the years 2000, 2004, and 2008 are leap years.

Four commonly used methods to calculate due dates are (1) the *days-in-a-month rhyme*, (2) the *knuckle method*, (3) the *alternating month method*, and (4) the *days-in-a-year calendar method*.

Days-in-a-Month Rhyme   Perhaps you already know this rhyme:

Thirty days hath September,

April, June, and November.

February has 28 alone.

All the rest have 31;

Excepting leap year—that's the time,

When February's days are 29.

Knuckle Method   If you have not memorized the rhyme method, and you do not have a calendar or table, use your knuckles. First, make a fist. Move from a knuckle to the space between knuckles. Start with the knuckle of your little finger—it represents January. When you are on a knuckle, the month being represented has 31 days. Next, you go to the space between your little finger and your ring finger—it represents February. When you are between knuckles, the month represented has fewer than 31 days. All months represented by the spaces have 30 days except for February. Use only the knuckles on your fingers, not on your thumb. See Figure 7.4.

Alternating Month Method   The days in a month alternate from 31 to fewer than 31 days until you reach the month of July. At that point, you must start over with August having 31 days. Then the alternating begins again. The only two consecutive calendar months that have 31 days in them are July and August. Otherwise, they alternate as demonstrated here:

Month	Number of Days in the Month
January	31
February	(less than 31)—28 or 29
March	31
April	(less than 31)—30
May	31
June	(less than 31)—30
July	31 } The only two consecutive calendar year
August	31 } months that have 31 days in them.
September	(less than 31)—30
October	31
November	(less than 31)—30
December	31

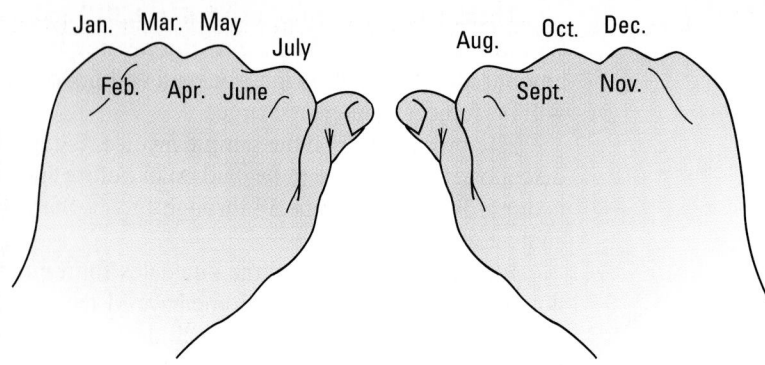

Figure 7.4
Knuckle Dating Method

Be careful when going from a date in one year to a date in another year. Be certain you begin over with January having 31 days when changing years.

Days-in-a-Year Calendar Method   The exact days-in-a-year calendar excludes leap year. To illustrate its use, find 45 days from June 3 using Table 7.3.
    Find June 3 in Table 7.3. You will find that it is the 154th day of the year. Next, add 45 days to 154 days. Your sum is the 199th day of the year. Find day 199 in Table 7.3. You find it at the intersection of July 18. Forty-five days from June 3 is July 18.

From Table 7.3:   June 3 is day   154
$$\underline{+\ 45}\text{ days}$$
is day   199
From Table 7.3: day 199 is July 18

7.3   Cash Discounts When an Ordinary Dating Method Is Used

In the sample invoice, terms of 2/10, n/30 were given, and the invoice was dated June 3. The **ordinary dating** method is the most commonly used method for determining cash discounts. Using it, due dates are counted from the date of the invoice. In counting the days to the discount due date or to the net due date, start with the day after the invoice is dated. In the sample invoice, counting started on June 4. The first day is never counted. An easy way to find due dates when they fall in the same month is to add the number of days given to the invoice date: June 3 + 10 = June 13. When they fall in another month, find the number of days remaining in the current month by subtracting the invoice date from the number of days in the month. Then find the number of days needed in the next month to equal the due date:

30 Days in June	30 Days allowed for net payment
− 3 Date of invoice	− 27 Days in June
27 Days remaining in June	3 Days needed in July

Therefore, the net payment is due July 3.
    The sample invoice shown in Figure 7.3 will be used to illustrate how the amount due on an invoice is calculated.

E X A M P L E   The sample invoice is for $516.37. Terms are 2/10, n/30. The total invoice amount includes merchandise, $452.33; tax, $36.19; and freight, $27.85. If the invoice is paid in full on June 12, what amount must be paid?

Solution   The invoice is paid within the discount period, so a 2% discount can be taken on the merchandise. Discounts cannot be taken on tax, freight, insurance, or returned goods. The discount is taken on merchandise and then the tax and freight are added in to find the total payment:

1. Merchandise cost × discount rate = discount
    ↑   ↑   ↑
   $452.33   ×   2%   = $9.05

TABLE 7.3   EXACT NUMBER OF DAYS-IN-A-YEAR CALENDAR (EXCLUDING LEAP YEAR)

Day of Month	Jan.	Feb.	Mar.	Apr.	May.	June	July	Aug.	Sept.	Oct.	Nov.	Dec.	Day of Month
1	1	32	60	91	121	152	182	213	244	274	305	335	1
2	2	33	61	92	122	153	183	214	245	275	306	336	2
3	3	34	62	93	123	154	184	215	246	276	307	337	3
4	4	35	63	94	124	155	185	216	247	277	308	338	4
5	5	36	64	95	125	156	186	217	248	278	309	339	5
6	6	37	65	96	126	157	187	218	249	279	310	340	6
7	7	38	66	97	127	158	188	219	250	280	311	341	7
8	8	39	67	98	128	159	189	220	251	281	312	342	8
9	9	40	68	99	129	160	190	221	252	282	313	343	9
10	10	41	69	100	130	161	191	222	253	283	314	344	10
11	11	42	70	101	131	162	192	223	254	284	315	345	11
12	12	43	71	102	132	163	193	224	255	285	316	346	12
13	13	44	72	103	133	164	194	225	256	286	317	347	13
14	14	45	73	104	134	165	195	226	257	287	318	348	14
15	15	46	74	105	135	166	196	227	258	288	319	349	15
16	16	47	75	106	136	167	197	228	259	289	320	350	16
17	17	48	76	107	137	168	198	229	260	290	321	351	17
18	18	49	77	108	138	169	199	230	261	291	322	352	18
19	19	50	78	109	139	170	200	231	262	292	323	353	19
20	20	51	79	110	140	171	201	232	263	293	324	354	20
21	21	52	80	111	141	172	202	233	264	294	325	355	21
22	22	53	81	112	142	173	203	234	265	295	326	356	22
23	23	54	82	113	143	174	204	235	266	296	327	357	23
24	24	55	83	114	144	175	205	236	267	297	328	358	24
25	25	56	84	115	145	176	206	237	268	298	329	359	25
26	26	57	85	116	146	177	207	238	269	299	330	360	26
27	27	58	86	117	147	178	208	239	270	300	331	361	27
28	28	59	87	118	148	179	209	240	271	301	332	362	28
29	29	—	88	119	149	180	210	241	272	302	333	363	29
30	30	—	89	120	150	181	211	242	273	303	334	364	30
31	31	—	90	—	151	—	212	243	—	304	—	365	31

2. Subtract the discount from the total merchandise cost:

$$\$452.33 - \$9.05 = \$443.28 \quad \textit{Merchandise payment}$$

3. Add merchandise payment, taxes, and freight:

$$\$443.28 + 36.19 + 27.85 = \$507.32 \quad \textit{Net amount due}$$

> 452.33 ⊟ 2 % ⊞ 36.19 ⊞ 27.85 ⊜ 507.32

The complement method can also be used to calculate the merchandise payment:

$$
\begin{aligned}
\text{Merchandise payment} &= \text{merchandise cost} \times \text{payment rate} \\
&= \$452.33 \times (100\% - 2\%) \\
&= \$452.33 \times 98\% \\
&= \$443.28
\end{aligned}
$$

The complement can almost always be calculated in your head, and it is the required method when partial payments are made. Partial payments will be covered later in the chapter.

Sometimes a seller will offer more than one chance for the buyer to take a discount. This ordinary dating method is referred to as the sliding scale method because it uses **sliding scale cash discounts**. In the sliding scale method, even though several discounts are listed, only one at most is taken, depending on when the payment is made.

EXAMPLE An invoice for $2,844 is dated October 27. The terms are 5/10, 3/20, 1/30, n/45. Find the due dates and the amounts due on each date.

Solution The term 5/10 means that a 5% discount will be given if payment is made within 10 days of October 27; 3/20 indicates that a 3% discount will be given if payment is made between the 11th day and the 20th day after October 27; 1/30 means that a 1% discount will be given if payment is made between the 21st day and the 30th day after October 27; and n/45 means that the net payment is due between the 30th and the 45th day after October 27.

Oct.   31 days   10 days allowed
        −27   − 4
        4 days left in Oct.   6 days needed in Nov.

Due date for 5% discount: Nov. 6
Amount due: $2,844 × 95% = $2,701.80

Oct.   31 days   20 days allowed
        − 27   − 4
        4 days left in Oct.   16 days needed in Nov.

Due date for 3% discount: between Nov. 7 and Nov. 16
Amount due: $2,844 × 97% = $2,758.68

Oct.   31 days   30 days allowed
        − 27   − 4
        4 days left in Oct.   26 days needed in Nov.

Due date for 1% discount: between Nov. 17 and Nov. 26
Amount due: $2,844 × 99% = $2,815.56

Oct.   31 days   Nov. 30 day   45 days allowed
        − 27   + 4   − 34
        4 days left in Oct. 34 days in Oct.   11 days needed
                             and Nov.   in Dec.

Due date for net payment: between Nov. 28 and Dec. 11

With any dating method, if no net payment date is given, it is assumed to be 20 days after the last discount date is due. Some businesses consider a "payment made" only after it has been received. Most, however, consider the payment made when it is mailed (as evidenced by the postmark).

7.3 Practice Problems

1. An invoice for $924.35 dated April 30 had terms of 2/10, n/30. Find the amount that will be paid if payment is made on May 8.

2. Jonathan Custom Tailor's purchased several bolts of material that cost a total of $4,287. When it arrived, one bolt, costing $178, was soiled. It will be returned for full credit. Freight charges to be paid by Jonathan were $44.32, and insurance cost $12.05. Terms were 3/10, n/30 and the invoice was dated November 15. Payment in full was made on November 25. What amount was paid?

3. An invoice dated January 14 for $1,550 had a sliding scale cash discount of 3/10, 1/15, n/30. Merchandise costs were $1,402. The difference was freight, insurance, and taxes. Payment in full was made on January 28. Find the amount paid.

4. Light and Bright sells lighting fixtures. One fixture sold for $58.95 each. An order for 50 of the fixtures was placed. An invoice dated March 25 was received with terms of 5/10, 2/20, n/60. The invoice showed that all of the fixtures ordered were shipped and billed. The total invoice amount was $3,179.95. How much was paid if it was paid in full on April 3?

7.3 Solutions to Practice Problems

1. $924.35 × 98% = $905.86
2. $4,287 − 178 = $4,109
   $4,109 × 97% = $3,985.73
   $3,985.73 + 44.32 + 12.05 = $4,042.10
3. $1,550 − 1,402 = $148
   $1,402 × 99% = $1,387.98
   $1,387.98 + 148 = $1,535.98
4. $58.95 × 50 = $2,947.50
   $3,179.95 − 2,947.50 = $232.45
   $2,947.50 × 95% = $2,800.13
   $2,800.13 + 232.45 = $3,032.58

7.4 Cash Discounts When Other Dating Methods Are Used

Although it is the most popular form of dating used for cash discounts, ordinary dating is by no means the only method. In this section we will look at three other dating methods.

1. Postdating (AS OF), method,
2. Receipt-of-goods (ROG) method
3. End-of-month (EOM) method (Another dating method producing the same result is called *proximo*, abbreviated *prox.*)

Postdating (AS OF), Method

Occasionally, a seller will postdate an invoice to give the buyer a little more time to take a discount, or to pay the net amount. The postdate is shown after the invoice date and is often labeled **AS OF**.

EXAMPLE   An invoice was dated February 25 AS OF March 1. The invoice was for $394.10, with terms of 3/10. What is the due date if a discount is taken? What is the net payment due date if the discount is not taken? What is the payment amount if the invoice is paid on March 10?

Solution   Because the terms start on March 1, the due date for taking the discount is March 1 + 10 days, or March 11. Since it is not stated in the terms, the due date for the net payment is assumed to be 20 days after the discount due date; thus, March 11 + 20 days, or March 31.

Since payment was made before March 11 (on March 10), the 3% discount can be taken:

$$\$394.10 × 3\% = \$11.82 \quad \$394.10 − \$11.82 = \$382.28$$

Using the complement method:

$$\$394.10 × 97\% = \$382.28$$

Receipt-of-Goods (ROG) Method

Goods sometimes take a lengthy time to arrive at the destination after shipment. For example, an importer might order merchandise from Hong Kong. It is shipped on an ocean freighter on the same day the invoice is prepared and mailed to the importer. The invoice might well arrive weeks before the goods. If the ordinary dating method is used, the time start's as of the invoice date.

ROG dating allows the buyer to receive the goods and inspect them to make certain that the right merchandise was shipped and that it arrived undamaged. The discount period and the net payment period begins when delivery is made. The seller knows when the buyer received the shipment because a shipping receipt (a bill of lading) is dated and signed when delivery is made and a copy is sent to the seller.

EXAMPLE   An invoice for $13,078 with terms of 4/15 ROG was dated May 4. The goods were received June 17. Determine the due date for the discount and for the net payment, and find the amount paid if payment in full was made on June 30.

Solution

June has 30 days	15 allowed for discount
terms started -17	-13
13 days left	2 days needed in July

The discount due date is July 2.

Since the terms do not indicate the net payment due date, it is assumed to be 20 days after the discount due date. Therefore, July 2 + 20 = July 22, the net payment due date.

Payment on June 30 is within the discount period. The 4% discount can be taken:

$$\$13{,}078 \times 4\% = \$523.12 \qquad \$13{,}078 - \$523.12 = \$12{,}554.88$$

Using the complement method:

$$\$13{,}078 \times 96\% = \$12{,}554.88$$

End-of-Month (EOM) Method

End-of-month dating is similar to **proximo dating**, and the results are exactly the same. Proximo means "in the following month," so invoices with terms of EOM or **prox**. (abbreviation for proximo) are due in the following month. For example, an invoice with terms of 1/10 EOM dated July 15 has a discount due date of August 10, and a net payment due date of 20 days later, which would be August 30.

EOM dating is intended to provide more lengthy terms than normal. As a business courtesy, common business practice is to allow invoices dated after the 25th of a month to be treated as though they were dated on the 1st of the following month, effectively granting a month's extension on the invoice terms. For example, an invoice with terms of 1/10 EOM dated July 26 would allow a discount due date of September 10 because the invoice would be treated as though it had been dated on the 1st of the following month, August 1. The net payment due date would be assumed to be 20 days later, September 30.

EXAMPLE   An invoice for $33,349.29 dated November 18 with terms of 1/10 prox. was paid on December 9. Find the due dates for the discount and the net payment, and the amount paid.

Solution   The discount due date is 10 days after the end of the month of November, December 10. The net payment due date is 20 days after the discount due date, December 10 + 20 = December 30.

Payment was made within the discount due date, so the discount can be taken. Using the complement method:

$$\$33{,}349.29 \times 99\% = \$33{,}015.80$$

EXAMPLE   An invoice of $5,950 dated May 27 with terms of 3/10 EOM was paid on July 10. Find the discount and net payment due dates and the amount paid.

Solution   The invoice is dated after the 25th of May. Therefore, it is treated as though it was dated June 1. The discount due date is 10 days after the end of June, or July 10.

The net payment due date is 20 days after the discount due date, July 10 + 20 = July 30. Payment was made within the discount due date, so the discount can be taken. Using the complement method:

$$\$5,950 \times 97\% = \$5,771.50$$

7.4 Practice Problems

1. An invoice for $929.10 dated April 17 with terms of 2/10 AS OF April 25 was paid on May 5. Find the amount paid.

2. An invoice for $339.83 dated August 12 with terms of 4/15 ROG was paid June 4. The merchandise arrived on the buyer's premises on May 20. How much was paid?

3. An invoice for $22,938.33 dated January 3 with terms of 1.5/10 EOM was paid on February 10. Find the amount paid.

4. An invoice for $3,382 dated May 28 with terms of 3/10 EOM was paid on July 8. Calculate the amount paid.

7.4 Solutions to Practice Problems

1. $929.10 × 98% = $910.52   2. $339.83 × 96% = $326.24
3. $22,938.33 × 98.5% = $22,594.26   4. $3,382 × 97% = $3,280.54

7.5 Partial Payments

When a buyer does not have enough cash, or cannot borrow enough to pay the entire amount of an invoice within the discount period, a partial payment may be made. Discounts are allowed on partial payments. After all, the purpose of a discount is to encourage early payment of bills, and some payment is better than none.

The principal consideration is that a business firm will receive credit for paying more than it actually pays. The payment is a part of the base, or a percentage. Since the percentage is the amount actually paid, the rate you use must be the percent paid (the rate and the percentage must represent the same thing). The percent paid is the complement of the discount percent. The percentage formula for finding the base can be applied:

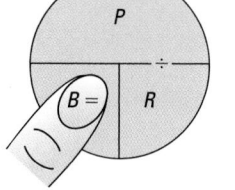

$$(\text{credit received}) \ B = \frac{P\ (\text{amount paid})}{R\ (\%\ \text{paid})}$$

The difference between the amount paid and the credit received is the discount, and the amount still owed is the difference between the invoice amount and the credit received.

EXAMPLE   An invoice for $7,550 dated March 15 had terms of 2/10, n/30. On March 25, $5,000 was paid. Find (1) the credit to be received, (2) the discount, and (3) the amount still owed.

Solution   (1) Credit received $= \dfrac{\text{Amount paid}}{\%\ \text{paid}}$

$$= \frac{\$5,000}{98\%}$$

$$= \$5,102.04$$

(2) Discount = credit received − amount paid
$$= \$5,102.04 - 5,000$$
$$= \$102.04$$

(3) Amount still owed = invoice amount − credit received
$$\$7,550 - 5,102.04 = \$2,447.96$$

$$5,000 \div 98\ \%\ \boxed{+/-}\ +\ 7,550\ =\ 2,447.96$$

7.5 Practice Problems

In the following partial payment problems, find (1) the credit received, (2) the discount, and (3) the amount still owed.

1. An invoice for $3,199.34 dated February 9 had terms of 3/10 EOM. $2,500 was paid on March 8. Find the credit received, the discount, and the amount still owed.

2. An invoice for $12,884 dated September 1 had terms of 5/10 ROG. The merchandise was received on September 29. On October 8, $9,500 was paid. Find the credit received, the discount, and the amount still owed.

3. An invoice for $2,342 dated April 5 had terms of 2/10 AS OF April 10. On April 20, $2,000 was paid. Find the credit received, the discount, and the amount still owed.

4. An invoice for $59,404 dated November 15 had terms of 5/10, 3/20, n/30. On November 24, $40,000 was paid, and on December 2, another $12,500 was paid. Calculate the credit received, the discount, and the amount still owed after each payment.

7.5 Solutions to Practice Problems

1. (1) Credit received $= \dfrac{\$2,500}{97\%} = \$2,577.32$

   (2) Discount = $2,577.32 − 2,500 = $77.32
   (3) Amount still owed = $3,199.34 − 2,577.32 = $622.02

2. (1) Credit received $= \dfrac{\$9,500}{95\%} = \$10,000$

   (2) Discount = $10,000 − 9,500 = $500
   (3) Amount still owed = $12,884 − 10,000 = $2,884

3. (1) Credit received $= \dfrac{\$2,000}{98\%} = \$2,040.82$

   (2) Discount = $2,040.82 − 2,000 = $40.82
   (3) Amount still owed = $2,342 − 2,040.82 = $301.18

4. After first payment of $40,000:

   (1) Credit received $= \dfrac{\$40,000}{95\%} = \$42,105.26$

   (2) Discount = $42,105.26 − 40,000 = $2,105.26
   (3) Amount still owed = $59,404 − 42,105.26 = $17,298.74
   After second payment of $12,500:

   (1) Credit received $= \dfrac{\$12,500}{97\%} = \$13,157.90$

   (2) Discount = $13,157.90 − 12,500 = $657.90
   (3) Amount still owed = $17,298.74 − 13,157.90 = $4,140.84

Page	Section Topic	Learning Concepts	Examples and Solutions
225	**7.1** Calculating the Net Cost with a Single Trade Discount	A single trade discount is a discount off the list price to determine a seller's merchandise cost. Frequently, the complement of the discount (called the net cost equivalent rate) is used.	A chair lists for $50. The trade discount is 35%. Find the net cost. $$\$50 \times 35\% = \$17.50$$ $$\$50 - 17.50 = \$32.50$$ Or, using the complement: $$100\% - 35\% = 65\%$$ $$\$50 \times 65\% = \$32.50$$
226	**7.2** Calculating the Net Cost with a Series Trade Discount	A variety of reasons can lead to a seller offering more than one discount. Unless a table is being used, the complement method is the preferred way to calculate the net cost. Each discount is subtracted from 100%, and the complements are multiplied to find the net cost equivalent. It should not be rounded. The list price is then multiplied by the net cost equivalent to find the net cost. The discounts are never added together.	The list price for a computer mouse is $30 and trade discounts are 15/10/5. Find the net cost. $$\begin{array}{ccc} 100\% & 100\% & 100\% \\ -15\% & -10\% & -5\% \\ \hline 85\% \times & 90\% \times & 95\% = .72675 \end{array}$$ $$\$30 \times .72675 = \$21.80$$
232	**7.3** Cash Discounts When an Ordinary Dating Method Is Used	Cash discounts are given to encourage early payment of bills. An ordinary dating method means that the time in the discount period is counted from the invoice date. The complement method can be used to calculate the net invoice payment.	An invoice for $5,000 dated May 3 with terms of 2/10, n/30, was paid on May 12. Find the net payment $$100\% - 2\% = 98\%$$ $$\$5,000 \times 98\% = \$4,900$$
		Cash discounts cannot be taken on anything except the cost of merchandise. Discounts cannot be taken on freight, taxes, insurance, or returned goods. Sliding scale discounts allow a business that did not pay any or all of the invoice within the first discount period to have another chance.	An invoice for $597 dated June 20 with terms of 2/10, 1/20, n/30 was paid on July 2. Find the amount of payment. The due date for the first discount (2/10) is June 30. The invoice was paid on July 2, after the 2% discount had passed, but within the 1% discount period (July 1 through July 11): $$100\% - 1\% = 99\%$$ $$\$597 \times 99\% = \$591.03$$
235	**7.4** Cash Discounts When Other Dating Methods Are Used	Postdating (AS OF) method: The due dates for taking a cash discount begin after the invoice date, the AS OF date.	An invoice for $954 dated March 24 with terms of 3/10 AS OF April 1 was paid on April 10. Find the amount paid. $$\$954 \times 97\% = \$925.38$$
		Receipt-of-goods (ROG) dating method: The ROG method is most often used when a slow method of transportation is used. The invoice is dated and mailed. If the invoice date were used, the bill might have to be paid before the merchandise arrived.	An invoice for $1,937 dated August 2 had terms of 2/10 ROG. The merchandise was received on September 6. The invoice was paid on September 15. Find the amount paid. $$\$1,937 \times 98\% = \$1,898.26$$

Page	Section Topic	Learning Concepts	Examples and Solutions
		End-of-month (EOM) dating method: The EOM method gives a longer period to take discounts. The due dates do not begin until the end of the month in which the invoice is dated.	An invoice for $299 dated May 9 with terms of 4/10 EOM was paid on June 10. Find the amount paid. $299 × 96% = $287.04
		As a courtesy, when an invoice is dated after the 25th of a month, it is treated as though it was dated in the following month. Thus, an invoice dated May 27 would not be due until July.	An invoice for $775 dated May 27 with terms of 2/10 EOM was paid on July 10. Find the amount paid. $775 × 98% = $759.50
237	7.5 Partial Payments	When a buyer cannot pay the entire amount of an invoice, part of it may be paid, and the discount rate can be taken on that portion. It is necessary to find the amount of credit received, the amount of the discount, and the amount still owed.	An invoice for $21,540 dated October 12 had terms of 3/10, n/30. On October 20, $15,000 was paid. Find the credit received, the discount, and the amount still owed. Credit received: $15,000 ÷ 97% = $15,463.92 Amount of discount: $15,463.92 − 15,000 = $463.92 Amount still owed: $21,540 − 15,463.92 = $6,076.08

SURFING THE INTERNET

For further information on the topics covered in this chapter, check out the following sites:

http://www.plasticmodels.com/khelp.htm

www.toolkit.cch.com/text/P06_4236.asp

ADDITIONAL PRACTICE PROBLEMS

Answers to odd-numbered problems are given in appendix A.

7.1

Calculate the net cost in the following single trade discount problems:

1. Thomas Value Shopping ordered 50 electric fans that list for $17.95 each. The trade discount is 35%. Find the net cost.
100% − 35% = 65% $11.67 × 50 = $583.50
$17.95 × 65% = $11.67

2. Tyrone Lee, the purchasing agent for a department store, has found a distributor offering a 40% trade discount on bath towels. The towels list for $155.40 per dozen. Tyrone placed an order for 12 dozen. What was his net cost?
100% − 40% = 60% $155.40 × 60% = $93.24
$93.24 × 12 = $1,118.88

3. Wicker chairs in one distributor's catalog list for $44.98. The trade discount is 45%. What is the net cost?
100% − 45% = 55%
$44.98 × 55% = $24.74

4. Marge's Antiques' buyer, Jan Schmit, has found a rolltop desk in a dealer's catalog that lists for $5,475. The trade discount is 30%. Find the net cost.
100% − 30% = 70%
$5,475 × 70% = $3,832.50

7.2

Calculate the net cost for the following series trade discount problems:

5. Nicholas Toy Company allows trade discounts of 30/20/4 to wholesalers. How much will a wholesaler pay for an order that lists for $8,000?

100%		100%		100%
− 30%		− 20%		− 4%
70%	×	80%	×	96% = .5376 × $8,000 = $4,300.80

6. An agent purchased merchandise listing for $100,000 to export to the European market. Trade discounts offered by the manufacturer were 40/10/10. Find the agent's net cost.

100%		100%		100%
− 40%		− 10%		− 10%
60%	×	90%	×	90% = .486 × $100,000 = $48,600

7. Alonzo's White Goods allows trade discounts of 40/10/5 to its retail customers that buy in quantities of $5,000 or more. K. B. Enterprises placed the following order:

Quantity	Description	List Price	Total
10 dz.	King-size sheets	$196/dz.	$ 1,960
15 dz.	Queen-size sheets	$168/dz.	2,520
6 dz.	Regular-size sheets	$120/dz.	720
4 dz.	Twin-size sheets	$ 96/dz.	384
			$ 5,584

Find the net cost to K. B. Enterprises.

100%		100%		100%
− 40%		− 10%		− 5%
60%	×	90%	×	95% = .513 × $5,584 = $2,864.59

8. Charlie Huan, the buyer for Huan's Computer Center, is deciding between two distributors of color ink jet cartridges for HP printers. Utley's Office Supply lists the cartridges for $26.77 each and offers trade discounts of 10/10/5. PPE/Micro Center lists the cartridges for $28.89 and offers trade discounts of 15/20. What is the net cost from each distributor?

100%		100%		100%
− 10%		− 10%		− 5%
90%	×	90%	×	95% = .7695 × $26.77 = $20.60 (Utley)

100%		100%
− 15%		− 20%
85%	×	80% = .68 × $28.89 = $19.65 (PPE/Micro Center)

7.3.

Find the discount, net payment dates, and net cost when the ordinary dating method is being used for cash discounts in the following problems:

9. An invoice for $598 dated August 12 with terms of 2/10, n/30 was paid on August 21.

Due date for 2% discount: between 8/12 and 8/22
Due date for net payment: between 8/23 and 9/11
$598 × 98% = $586.04

10. An invoice for $399.44 dated May 2 with terms of 3/15, n/45 was paid on May 17.

Due date for 3% discount: between 5/2 and 5/17
Due date for net payment: between 5/18 and 6/16
$399.44 × 97% = $387.46

11. An invoice for $33,930 dated April 27 with terms of 4/10, n/60 was paid on May 7.

Due date for 4% discount: between 4/27 and 5/7
Due date for net payment: between 5/8 and 6/26
$33,930 × 96% = $32,572.80

12. An invoice for $22,195 dated January 4 with terms of 3/10, 1/25, n/45 was paid on January 28.

Due date for 3% discount: between 1/4 and 1/14
Due date for 1% discount: between 1/15 and 1/29
Due date for net payment: between 1/30 and 2/18
$22,195 × 99% = $21,973.05

7.4

Find the discount, net payment dates, and net cost when other dating methods are being used in the following cash discount problems:

13. An invoice for $777.77 dated July 8 with terms of 2/10 AS OF July 15 was paid on July 24.

Due date for 2% discount: between 7/8 and 7/25
Due date for net payment: between 7/26 and 8/14
$777.77 × 98% = $762.21

14. An invoice for $881.39 dated June 15 had terms of 3/10 ROG. The buyer received the goods on July 8. Payment was made on July 15.

Due date for 3% discount: between 7/8 and 7/18
Due date for net payment: between 7/19 and 8/7
$881.39 × 97% = $854.95

15. An invoice for $1,028.50 dated November 9 with terms of 1.5/10 EOM was paid on December 10.

Due date for 1.5% discount: between 11/9 and 12/10
Due date for net payment: between 12/11 and 12/30
$1,028.50 × 98.5% = $1,013.07

16. An invoice for $103,284 dated February 26 with terms of 5/10, EOM, n/60 was paid on March 9.

Due date for 5% discount: between 2/26 and 4/10
Due date for net payment: between 4/11 and 5/30
$103,284 × 95% = $98,119.80

7.5

Find the credit received, the discount, the balance owed, and the net payment date in the following partial payment cash discount problems:

17. An invoice for $550 dated January 9 had terms of 3/10, n/30. On January 19, $475 was paid.

Credit received $= \dfrac{\$475}{97\%} = \$489.69$

Discount $= \$489.69 - 475 = \$14.69$
Balance owed $= \$550 - 489.69 = \$60.31$
Net payment date $=$ February 8

18. An invoice for $44,900 dated August 24 had terms of 3/10 AS OF September 1. On September 11, $35,000 was paid.

Credit received $= \dfrac{\$35,000}{97\%} = \$36,082.47$

Discount $= \$36,082.47 - 35,000 = \$1,082.47$
Balance owed $= \$44,900 - 36,082.47 = \$8,817.53$
Net payment date $=$ November 1

19. An invoice for $2,850 dated May 29 had terms of 5/15 EOM. On July 14, $1,500 was paid.

Credit received $= \dfrac{\$1,500}{95\%} = \$1,578.95$

Discount $= \$1,578.95 - \$1,500 = \$78.95$
Balance owed $= \$2,850 - 1,578.95 = \$1,271.05$
Net payment date $=$ July 30

20. An invoice for $78,912 dated December 22 had terms of 4/15, 2/30, n/60. On January 5, $50,000 was paid. On January 20, another $20,000 was paid.

Credit received $= \dfrac{\$50,000}{96\%} = \$52,083.33$

Discount $= \$52,083.33 - 50,000 = \$2,083.33$
Balance owed $= \$78,912 - 52,083.33 = \$26,828.67$
Net payment date $=$ February 20

Credit received $= \dfrac{\$20,000}{98\%} = \$20,408.16$

Discount $= \$20,408.16 - 20,000 = \$408.16$
Balance owed $= \$26,828.67 - 20,408.16 = \$6,420.51$

CHAPTER REVIEW PROBLEMS

Answers to odd-numbered problems are in Appendix A.

Drill Problems

Find the net cost equivalent rate and the net cost in the single trade discount problems 1 through 5.

	Item	List Price	Trade Discount	Net Cost Equivalent Rate	Net Cost
1.	Chair	$ 33.98	40%	60%	$ 20.39
2.	Table	159.49	35%	65%	103.67
3.	Sofa	2,938.99	50%	50%	1,469.50
4.	Bed	426.95	45%	55%	234.82
5.	Dresser	194.98	30%	70%	136.49

Find the net cost equivalent rate and the net cost in the series trade discount problems 6 through 15.

	Item	List Price	Trade Discount	Net Cost Equivalent	Net Cost
6.	Bicycle	$ 129.95	30/15	.595	$ 77.32
7.	Tricycle	79.99	25/20	.6	47.99
8.	Scooter	38.98	5/40	.57	22.22
9.	Wagon	26.95	10/35	.585	15.77
10.	Slinky	4.98	20/20	.64	3.19
11.	Doll	54.49	10/15/20	.612	33.35
12.	Playhouse	219.19	30/15/5	.56525	123.90
13.	Top	2.77	15/30/10	.5355	1.48
14.	Yo-yo	1.98	8/8/8	.778688	1.54
15.	Bat	12.97	40/20/5	.456	5.91

Find the discount and net payment due dates for problems 16 through 20.

	Invoice Date	Terms	Date Goods Received	Discount Due	Net Payment Due Date
16.	August 24	2/10, n/30		Sept. 3	Sept. 23
17.	September 8	3/10 ROG	October 23	Nov. 2	Nov. 22
18.	March 6	1/10 EOM		Apr. 10	Apr. 30
19.	May 29	3/15 EOM		July 15	July 30
20.	June 4	2/15, n/45		June 19	July 19

Find the net payment for problems 21 through 40.

	Invoice Date	Terms	Date Payment Made	Amount of Invoice	Net Payment
21.	January 18	2/10, n/30	January 27	$ 1,398.28	$ 1,370.31
22.	November 8	3/10, n/30	December 8	330.67	330.67
23.	July 27	1/10, n/30	August 26	789.01	789.01
24.	February 25	3/15, n/45	March 10	542.90	526.61
25.	June 2	2/10, n/30	June 12	19,330.50	18,943.89
26.	May 20	2/10, 1/20	May 30	720.87	706.45
27.	March 19	3/15, 1/25	April 3	4,021.15	3,900.52
28.	April 9	5/5, 2/10	April 14	503.29	478.13
29.	August 30	2/10, 1/20	September 17	95.14	94.19
30.	October 20	3/10, 1.5/30	December 1	2,066.75	2,066.75
31.	September 9	2/10 AS OF October 1	October 11	7,000.00	6,860.00
32.	November 21	3/10 AS OF December 1	December 9	440.34	427.13
33.	July 3	2/10 AS OF July 15	July 31	68,220.00	68,220.00
34.	February 26	4/10 AS OF March 1	March 11	845.09	811.29
35.	January 2	1/10 AS OF January 10	January 20	4,433.93	4,389.59
36.	April 17	2/10 EOM	May 10	277.90	223.34
37.	October 2	2/10 prox.	November 9	21,900.57	21,462.56
38.	May 28	3/10 EOM	July 10	710.56	689.24
39.	August 30	1.5/10 prox.	October 10	2,907.45	2,863.84
40.	January 18	2.5/10 EOM	February 8	409.60	399.36

Find the net payment for the receipt of goods cash discount problems 41 through 45.

	Invoice Date	Terms	Goods Received	Date Payment Made	Amount of Invoice	Amount of Payment
41.	05-03	2/10 ROG	06-01	06-11	$ 1,009.45	$ 989.26
42.	12-15	3/10 ROG	12-30	01-30	999.23	999.23
43.	10-23	3/10 ROG	11-29	12-09	401.83	389.78
44.	01-29	1/10 ROG	02-15	02-23	4,103.75	4,062.71
45.	07-30	2/15 ROG	08-25	09-09	50,857.21	49,840.07

If the invoice is paid in time to take the cash discount, find the net payment amount for problems 46 through 50.

	Item	List Price	Trade Discounts	Cash Discount Terms	Net Payment
46.	Shirt	$ 44.95	45%	2/10, n/30	$ 24.23
47.	Dress	240.00	10/35	2/10, n/30	137.59
48.	Slacks	90.00	15/15/15	3/15 ROG	53.61
49.	Blouse	59.98	20/30	2/10 EOM	32.92
50.	Skirt	74.49	30/20/5	4/10, n/45	38.04

Find the credit received, the discount, and the balance owed in the partial payment problems 51 through 55.

	Invoice Amount	Invoice Date	Terms	Payment Date	Partial Payment	Credit Received	Discount Amount	Balance Owed
51.	$1,937.45	July 8	2/10, n/30	July 18	$1,500	$ 1,530.61	$ 30.61	$ 406.84
52.	$ 441.89	October 30	3/10 EOM	Dec. 10	$ 375	386.60	11.60	55.29
53.	$5,104.32	May 23	4/10, 2/20	June 11	$3,500	3,571.43	71.43	1,532.89
54.	$9,301.07	December 12	2/10 prox.	Jan. 10	$7,000	7,142.86	142.86	2,158.21
55.	$ 662.95	July 1	4/15, n/60	July 15	$ 500	520.83	20.83	142.12

Word Problems

56. A boat is listed by Lake Craft, Inc., at $8,989.99. The trade discount is 34%. Find the net cost.
100% − 34% = 66%
66% × $8,989.99 = $5,933.39

57. Trade discounts are given as 35/10/5. Find the net cost equivalent rate and the single discount equivalent rate.

100%   100%   100%   1.00000
− 35%   −10%   −5%   − .55575
  65% × 90% × 95% = .55575 Net cost   .44425 Single discount
                              equivalent   equivalent

58. Toy soldier sets list for $9.99. Trade discounts are 25/15. Find the net cost.
100%   100%
− 25%   − 15%
  75% ×   85% = .6375 × $9.99 = $6.37

59. A table lists for $748. Trade discounts are 15/15/10. Find the net cost.
100%   100%   100%
− 15%   − 15%   − 10%
  85% ×   85% ×   90% = .65025 × $748 = $486.39

60. An invoice is dated June 12. Terms are 2/10, n/30. Find the discount and net payment due dates.

12   30 days in June   30 net days
+ 10   − 12   −18
June 22 = last day for 18 days   12 days needed in
    the discount   July. July 12 =
                                      net payment
                                      due date

61. An invoice dated May 23 for $2,912.87 with terms of 1.5/1, n/30 was paid on May 31. Find the amount paid.
100%
− 1.5%
98.5% × $2,912.87 =$2,869.18

62. An invoice dated September 9 for $698.44 with terms of 4/10, 2/20 is paid on September 28. Find the amount paid.
100%
− 2%
98% × $698.44 = $684.47

63. An invoice dated June 14 for $539.50 with terms of 3/10 AS OF July 1 was paid on July 10. Find the amount paid.
100%
− 3%
97% × $539.50 = $523.32

64. An invoice dated March 2 for $30,759.80 with terms of 1/10 EOM was paid on March 30. Find the discount and net payment due dates, and the amount paid.
Due date for 1% discount: between March 2 and April 10
Net payment due date: between April 11 and April 30
100%
− 1%
99% × $30,759.80 = $30,452.20

65. An invoice dated August 30 for $298.54 with terms of 3/10 EOM was paid on October 10. Find the amount paid.
100%
− 3%
97% × $298.54 = $289.58

66. An invoice dated February 4 for $883.01 with terms of 2/15 ROG was paid on April 3. The merchandise was received on March 20. Find the amount paid.

100%
− 2%
98% × $883.01 = $865.35

67. An invoice dated November 17 for $13,945.90 had terms of 2.5/10 ROG. The merchandise was received on December 2. On December 12, $10,000 was paid. Find the amount of credit received, the discount, and the amount still owed.

100%0 $\dfrac{\$10,000}{97.5\%} = \$10,256.41 = $ credit received
− 2.5%
97.5%

$10,256.41 − $10,000 = $256.41 = discount
$13,945.90 − $10,256.41 = $3,689.49 = balance owed

68. Find the net payment required on an invoice that has the following features:

Merchandise cost ...$2,598.20	Terms ...2/10, n/30
Insurance 9.94	Dated ....May 19
Freight 56.38	Paid .....May 29
Taxes 142.90	

100% $2,546.24
− 2%   9.94
98% × $2,598.20 = $2,546.24 56.38
                   + 142.90
                   $2,755.46

69. An invoice to PRC Industries dated August 8 listed the following information:

MERCHANDISE:

2 dozen baseball gloves, model W2000	$820.32 per dz.
1 dozen baseball gloves, model W2500	$556.32 per dz.
20 baseball bats, model L290	$ 54.65 each
6 dozen baseballs, model Raw300	$131.40 per dz.

OTHER CHARGES:

freight	$ 59.24
insurance	16.04
tax	4.5% of merchandise total

TERMS:

4/15 ROG

PRC Industries received the merchandise on August 27. The invoice was paid in full on September 11. Find the amount paid.

100%   2 × $820.32 = $1,640.64
− 4%   1 × 556.32 =   556.32
96%   20 ×   54.65 = 1,093.00
          6 × 131.40 = + 788.40
                   $4,078.36 × 96% = $3,915.23
                                  59.24
$4,078.36   16.04
× 4.5%   → + 183.53
$ 183.53 $4,174.04

70. An invoice dated March 22 for a total of $719.38 with terms of 3/10 AS OF April 1 was paid on April 11. Freight charges were $83.08, and $28.68 worth of merchandise was soiled and had to be returned for full credit. Find the amount of the net payment.

100% $719.38
− 3%   − 28.68
97% $690.70 × 97% = $669.98
                     + 83.08
                     $753.06

71. An invoice dated October 22 for $80,000 had terms of 3/10, 1/20, n/30. On November 1, $50,000 was paid. On November 11, the remainder was paid. Find the credit received, the discount, and the amount remaining to be paid after the $50,000 payment. Also, find the amount that was paid on November 11.

100% $\dfrac{\$50,000}{97\%} = \$51,546.39 = $ credit received
− 3%
97%

$51,546.39 − $50,000 = $1,546.39 discount
$80,000 − $51,546.39 = $28,453.61 balance owed
100%
− 1%
99% × $28,453.61 = $28,169.07 balance owed on Nov. 11

72. An invoice dated December 18 for $7,900.08 had terms of 2/10 prox. Freight of $55.76, taxes of $158, and insurance of $33.79 are included in the $7,900.08 total. Find the discount and the net payment due dates, and the amount that would be paid if the invoice was paid within the discount period.

Discount due date: January 10   Net invoice due date: January 30

$ 55.76 $7,900.08   100% $7,652.53 $7,499.48
 158.00   − 247.55   − 2%   × 98%   + 247.55
+ 33.79 $7,652.53   98% $7,499.48 $7,747.03
$247.55

73. The KV Corporation lists its king-size brand of low-phosphate detergent at $158.16 per case. Trade discounts are 20/15/5. Yoshita Convenience Groceries ordered 25 cases. KV's cash discount terms are 2/10, n/30. The invoice was dated July 8. Freight charges were $29.99. Payment in full was made on July 18. How much was paid?

$$\begin{array}{cccc} \$\ 158.16 & 100\% & 100\% & 100\% \\ \times \quad 25 & -20\% & -15\% & -5\% \\ \hline \$3,954.00 & 80\% \ \times & 85\% \ \times & 95\% = .646 \times \$3,954 = \$2,554.28 \end{array}$$

$$\begin{array}{ll} 100\% & \$2,503.19 \\ -2\% & +\ 29.99 \\ \hline 98\% \times \$2,554.28 = \$2,503.19 & \$2,533.18 \ \text{Payment in full} \end{array}$$

74. An agent purchased merchandise listing for $120,000 to export to the Asian market. Trade discounts offered by the manufacturer were 30/20. The invoice dated August 14 had terms of 4/15 EOM. On September 15, $50,000 was paid. Find the credit received, the discount, and the amount still owed.

$$\begin{array}{ll} 100\% & 100\% \\ -30\% & -20\% \\ \hline 70\% \quad \times & 80\% = .56 \times \$120,000 = \$67,200 \ \text{Net merchandise cost} \end{array}$$

$$\begin{array}{l} 100\% \\ -4\% \qquad\qquad \dfrac{\$50,000}{96\%} = \$52,083.33 \ \text{Credit received} \\ \hline 96\% \end{array}$$

$$\$52,083.33 - 50,000 = \$2,083.33 \ \text{Discount}$$

$$\$67,200 - 52,083.33 = \$15,116.67 \ \text{Balance Owed}$$

75. Teddy Bear's Lair placed an order with a Taiwanese firm for 12 cases of four-foot tall teddies. Each case contained six bears. Each bear listed for $125. Trade discounts were 15/15/15. An invoice dated May 4 had terms of 2/10 ROG. It included freight charges of $88.28, insurance of $19.96, and taxes at 4% of the total merchandise cost. The bears were received by the Lair on July 8, and payment of $4,500 was made on July 18. Find the amount still owed.

$$\begin{array}{l} 12 \\ \times 6 \\ \hline 72 \times \$125 = \$9,000 \ \text{Total list price} \end{array}$$

$$\begin{array}{cccc} 100\% & 100\% & 100\% \\ -15\% & -15\% & -5\% \\ \hline 85\% \ \times & 85\% \ \times & 85\% = .614125 \times \$9,000 = \$5,527.13 \ \text{Net cost} \end{array}$$

$$\begin{array}{llll} \$5,527.13 & 100\% & \dfrac{\$4,500}{98\%} = \$4,591.84 \ \text{Credit for paying} & \$\ 5,527.13 \\ \times \quad 4\% & -2\% & & -\ 4,591.84 \\ \hline \$\ 221.09 \ \text{Taxes} & 98\% & & \$\quad 935.29 \ \text{Merchandise cost still owed} \end{array}$$

$$\begin{array}{l} \$\ 935.29 \ \text{Merchandise} \\ \quad 88.28 \ \text{Freight} \\ \quad 19.96 \ \text{Insurance} \\ +\ 221.09 \ \text{Taxes} \\ \hline \$1,264.62 \ \text{Total amount still owed} \end{array}$$

CRITICAL THINKING GROUP PROJECT

Geraldine Kastanza, the buyer for the Yucanduit Indoor Fitness Center has prepared her shopping list for new items needed by the center. She has narrowed her decision to buy all of the equipment from either Victory Wholesale Fitness Supplies or Jacksonville Equipment and Supplies. She has conducted a vendor analysis of the two wholesalers and will incorporate those results into her buying decision. The quantity and description of her list of proposed purchases, the list prices from the two wholesalers, and the trade and cash discounts allowed by each wholesaler are listed below. The cash discount is shown only once, but it would be taken on the total value of the merchandise.

		Victory Wholesale			Jacksonville Equipment		
Qty	Description	List Price	Trade Discount	Cash Discount	List Price	Trade Discount	Cash Discount
4	BMI home gym	$ 950	30, 15	2/10 EOM	$ 938	20, 20	3/15 , n/30
6	Precor treadmill	888	25, 8		850	20, 15	
3	CSA ski machine	1,250	25, 12		1,150	20, 15	
10	DP exercise bike	750	30, 10		735	25, 17	
5	CSA stair climber	1,500	20, 25		1,450	25, 12	

Additional Discounts

These additional volume discounts are available only on single orders shipped at the same time to a single destination.

Victory Wholesale Fitness Supplies	Jacksonville Equipment and Supplies
Orders totaling: 1. $5,000, an additional 5% 2. $7,500, an additional 7.5% 3. $15,000, an additional 10% 4. $25,000, an additional 12.5%	Orders totaling: 1. $10,000, an additional 8% 2. $20,000, an additional 12% 3. $30,000, an additional 15%

In conducting the vendor analysis, two additional factors need to be considered. Backorders and merchandise damaged in shipment can be annoying, and costly. The following facts have been determined about Victory and Jacksonville:

Victory backorders an average of 2% of all orders.

Jacksonville backorders an average of 1.4% of all orders.

Victory shipments totaling $307,986 have resulted in $7,390 of damaged merchandise having to be returned for credit.

Jacksonville shipments totaling $115,048 have resulted in $3,450 of damaged merchandise having to be returned for credit.

It can be assumed that the same percent of backorders and damaged merchandise will result on the current order. The cost of backorders and damaged merchandise returns to Yucanduit are as follows:

Victory Wholesale

One employee who earns $7 per hour will spend 2.5 hours tracking backorders.

One employee who earns $8.50 per hour will spend 2 hours on the phone arranging for damaged merchandise to be returned. Another employee who earns $10.50 per hour in the accounts receivable department will spend 15 minutes recording returns.

One employee who earns $9.90 per hour will spend 10 minutes calculating and recording the adjustment to the invoice as a result of the deduction of the charge for the returned goods.

Jacksonville Equipment

One employee who earns $7 per hour will spend 4 hours tracking backorders.

One employee who earns $8.50 per hour will spend 2.5 hours on the phone arranging for damaged merchandise to be returned.

One employee who earns $10.50 per hour in the accounts receivable department will spend 10 minutes recording returns.

One employee who earns $9.90 per hour will spend 20 minutes calculating and recording the adjustment to the invoice as a result of the deduction of the charge for the returned goods.

Answer the following questions:

1. In addition to the monetary costs associated with backorders and damaged merchandise that has to be returned for credit, are there any other problems they cause that are important in making a buying decision?
   Student answers may vary, but they should mention the lost opportunity cost associated with not having merchandise available when customers want it.

2. What is the net cost of each piece of exercise equipment from Victory Wholesale Fitness Supplies?
   Home gym $ 565.25   Exercise bike $ 472.50   Treadmill $ 612.72
   Stair climber $ 900.00   Ski machine $ 825.00

3. What is the total cost of each piece of exercise equipment from Victory Wholesale Fitness Supplies?
   Home gym $2,261.00   Exercise bike $ 4,725.00   Treadmill $3,676.32
   Stair climber $4,500.00   Ski machine $2,475.00

4. What is the total cost of the order, before and after the additional volume discount, if the merchandise is purchased from Victory and there is no defective merchandise or backorders?
   Before volume discount; $17,637.32   After volume discount; $15,873.59

5. Using the information on the expected backorders from Victory, what would be the estimated dollar value of goods backordered?
   $352.75

6. Using the information on the expected damaged merchandise, what would be the estimated dollar value of damaged merchandise from Victory?
   $380.88

7. What will be the total cost of the order, before and after the additional volume discount and after deducting the amount that can be expected for backorders and damaged merchandise, if the merchandise is purchased from Victory?
   Before volume discount; $16,903.69   After volume discount; $15,213.32

8. What is the net payment that would have to be made to Victory Wholesale Fitness Supplies when payment is made within the cash discount period assuming no backorders or damaged merchandise? Taking into consideration the amount of expected backorders and damaged merchandise, what would the net payment be?
   Without damaged merchandise or backorders; $15,556.12   Considering damage and backorders; $14,909.05

9. What amounts should be added to the net payment to Victory for comparison purposes because of the additional costs associated with backorders and damaged merchandise returns?
   Backorder cost; $17.50   Damaged merchandise return cost; $22.93

10. Since the damaged merchandise will have to be replaced and the backorders will eventually be shipped, the additional costs should be added to the net payment without damaged merchandise or backorders for comparison purposes. What would be the comparison payment for Victory?
    $15,596.55

11. What is the net cost of each piece of exercise equipment from Jacksonville Equipment and Supplies?
    Home gym $600.32   Exercise bike $457.54   Treadmill $ 578.00
    Stair climber $ 957.00   Ski machine $ 782.00

12. What is the total cost of each piece of exercise equipment from Jacksonville Equipment and Supplies?
    Home gym $2,401.28   Exercise bike $4,575.40   Treadmill $ 3,468.00
    Stair climber $4,785.00   Ski machine $2,346.00

13. What is the total cost of the order, before and after the additional volume discount, if the merchandise is purchased from Jacksonville and there is no defective merchandise or backorders?
    Before volume discount; $17,575.68   After volume discount; $16,169.63

14. Using the information on the expected backorders from Jacksonville, what would be the estimated dollar value of goods backordered?
$226.37

15. Using the information on the expected damaged merchandise, what would be the estimated dollar value of damaged merchandise from Jacksonville?
$484.89

16. What will be the total cost of the order, before and after the additional volume discount and after deducting the amount that can be expected for backorders and damaged merchandise, if the merchandise is purchased from Jacksonville?
Before volume discount; $16,864.42   After volume discount; $15,515.27

17. What is the net payment that would have to be made to Jacksonville Equipment and Supplies when payment is made within the cash discount period assuming no backorders or damaged merchandise? Taking into consideration the amount of expected backorders and damaged merchandise, what would the net payment be?
Without damaged merchandise or backorders; $15,684.54   Considering damage and backorders; $15,049.81

18. What amounts should be added to the net payment to Jacksonville for comparison purposes because of the additional costs associated with backorders and damaged merchandise returns?
Backorder cost; $28   Damaged merchandise return cost; $26.30

19. Since the damaged merchandise will have to be replaced and the backorders will eventually be shipped, the additional costs should be added to the net payment without damaged merchandise or backorders for comparison purposes. What would be the comparison payment for Jacksonville?
$15,710.84

20. From which company should Geraldine order this equipment based on the information given and the calculations you have made?
Victory Wholesale Fitness Supplies

21. Is there any additional information you would like to have before making the final purchasing decision?
Student answers will vary, but they could include wanting to know delivery time and reliability, the frequency with which the sales representatives from both wholesalers call on Yucanduit, how helpful the sales representatives are, the breadth and depth of the product lines handled by both companies, and so forth.

SELF-TESTING EXERCISES

Answers to all exercises are in Appendix A

1. What is the purpose for giving trade discounts? **W**
   Trade discounts are reductions from the list price of merchandise based on factors such as the buyer's position in a seller's channel of distribution, the season of the year, condition of the economy, and the competition.

2. Why do sellers allow cash discounts? **W**
   Cash discounts are reductions of merchandise payments allowed only if payment is made within a specified time period. They are offered to encourage early payment of bills.

3. The Irving Company of the Bronx, New York, ordered merchandise listing for $420. The trade discount is 30%. How much will the Irving Company's net cost be?
   ```
    100%
   - 30%
    70% × $420 = $294
   ```

4. Swanson Department Store purchased furniture listing for $75,000. Trade discounts were 20/15. What is the net cost?
   ```
    100%      100%
   - 20%     - 15%
    80%  ×    85% = .68 × $75,000 = $51,000
   ```

5. Candy lists for $15.95 per box. Trade discounts are 20/8/6. Find the net cost.
   ```
    100%      100%     100%
   - 20%     - 8%     - 6%
    80%  ×    92%  ×   94% = .69184 × $15.95 = $11.03
   ```

6. Trade discounts are 10/15/5. Determine the net cost equivalent rate and the single discount equivalent rate.
   ```
    100%      100%      100%          1.00000
   - 10%     - 15%     - 5%          -.72675
    90%  ×    85%  ×    95% = .72675 Net    .27325 Single
                              cost           discount
                              equivalent     equivalent
   ```

7. An invoice is dated January 8 and has terms of 2/15, n/45. Find the discount and the net payment due dates.
   ```
    08 January starting date
   + 15 days in discount term
    23 of January is last date for discount

    31              45 net days
   - 8             -23 days in January
    23 days in Jan.  Feb. 22 = net payment due date
   ```

8. An invoice for $5,920.18 dated March 20 with terms of 2/10, n/30 is paid on March 30. Find the net payment.
   ```
    100%
   - 2%
    98% × $5,920.18 = $5,801.78
   ```

9. An invoice for $875.75 dated June 22 with terms of 5/10, 3/20 is paid on July 20. Find the net payment.
$875.75 (Payment was not made within the discount period.)

10. An invoice for $1,038.10 dated May 18 with terms of 3/10 AS OF June 1 is paid on June 11. Find the net payment.
100%
− 3%
97% × $1,038.10 = $1,006.96

11. An invoice for $22,779.55 dated February 22 had terms of 2/10 ROG. The merchandise was received on March 25. Payment was made on April 5. How much was paid?
$22,779.55 (Payment was not made within the discount period)

12. An invoice for $3,209.48 dated September 5 had terms of 3/10 EOM. It was paid on October 10. Find the amount of payment.
100%
− 3%
97% × $3,209.48 = $3,113.20

13. An invoice for $921.83 dated December 29 had terms of 2/10 prox. Find the due dates for the discount and the net payment. If it was paid within the discount period, how much was paid?
Discount due date: Feb.10   Net payment due date: Mar. 2

100%
− 2%
98% × $921.83 = $903.39

14. An invoice for $81,634.67 dated July 1 had terms of 2/10, n/30. On July 11, $65,000 was paid. Find the credit received, the discount, and the amount still owed.

100% $65,000
− 2%   ———— = $66,326.53 Credit received
98%   98%

$66,326.53 − $65,000 = $1,326.53 Discount

$81,634.67 − 66,326.53 = $15,308.14 Balance owed

15. An invoice for $39,104.69 dated March 30 had terms of 2/10, 1/15. On April 7, $15,000 was paid, and on April 15, $20,000 more was paid. For each payment, find the amount of credit, the discount, and the amount still owed.

100% $15,000
− 2%   ———— = $15,306.12 Credit received
98%   98%

$15,306.12 − 15,000 = $306.12 Discount

$39,104.69 − 15,306.12 = $23,798.57 Balance owed

100% $20,000
− 1%   ———— = $20,202.02 Credit received
99%   99%

$20,202.02 − 20,000 = $202.02 Discount

$23,798.57 − 20,202.02 = $3,596.55 Balance owed

16. Novell Inc. listed an examination table for $895. Trade discounts were 15/10/5. Mercy Clinic Hospital of Minneapolis ordered 28 of them for its new wing. The invoice dated November 28 had terms of 2/10, n/45. Payment in full was made on December 8. What amount was paid?

$ 895   100%   100%   100%
×   28   − 15%   − 10%   − 5%
$25,060   85% ×   90% ×   95% = .72675 × $25,060
                                      = $18,212.36

100%
− 2%
98% × $18,212.36 = $17,848.11

17. Mission Valley Distributor listed orange juice for $14.16 per case. Trade discounts were 20/5. San Jose Food Fun ordered 50 cases. The invoice dated August 6 had terms of 3/10 EOM. It was for a total of $568.32, which included freight charges. The invoice was paid in full on September 10. Find the amount paid.

100%   100% $ 14.16
−20%   − 5%   × 50
80% ×   95% = .76 × $708.00 = $538.08 Merchandise cost

$568.32 − $538.08   = $30.24
 total   merchandise   Freight charge
invoice   cost

100%
− 3%
97% × $538.08 = $521.94   + $30.24 = $552.18
                 Merchandise   Freight   Invoice
                 net payment   net payment

APPLICATION 1

Springfield has received a catalog from Mason's Wholesale Sporting Goods and has decided to place an order. Mason's catalog shows the list price of the catalog items, but the company is offering a variety of trade discounts. In Application 1 you will use the trade discount conversion spreadsheet to find the price the Springfield Department Store will pay (net cost on the spreadsheet). When you open the spreadsheet application, Ch07App1, from your disk, it will appear as shown here:

Springfield Department Store

2617 Main Street
Box 219
Springfield, Maryland 58109
Telephone: 301-555-2158   FAX: 301-555-3498

Trade Discount Conversion Spreadsheet

Catalog Prices From:

Catalog Number	Product Description	List Price	Trade Discounts			Net Cost Equivalent	Net Cost
			1st Disc.	2nd Disc.	3rd Disc.		
						1	$0.00
						1	$0.00
						1	$0.00
						1	$0.00
						1	$0.00
						1	$0.00
						1	$0.00
						1	$0.00
						1	$0.00
						1	$0.00
						1	$0.00
						1	$0.00

Enter the following information:

1. In cell B10, enter Mason's Wholesale Sporting Goods.
2. In cell B11, enter 12852 Fifth Avenue.
3. In cell B12, enter Chicago, Illinois 60609.
4. In cells A17 through F28 enter the following:

Catalog Number	Production Description	List Price	Trade Discounts
Tn22898	Head rackets, 12 per cs	$3,180.00	30, 25, 10
Gl39388	Wilson 1200 irons, 2-PW	249.95	20, 20, 15
Gl38577	Wilson pro-lite golf bag	129.49	20, 25, 5
Gl33948	Golf glove, m/lg, rh, 12 per crtn	155.76	15, 20, 15
Bs29393	Spaulding inf glove, 12 per cs	1,264.68	40, 20, 15
Bs34958	Bike baseball cleats	59.95	15, 15, 10
Sk33987	Head skis	312.75	30, 30, 5

Catalog Number	Production Description	List Price	Trade Discounts
Wt33389	300-lb freeweight set	59.99	25, 15, 10
Wt58773	Weight-lifting machine, 200 lb	389.95	15, 15, 15
Cl58766	Tennis shorts, men's med, per dz	294.00	20, 15, 20
Cl22856	Tennis shirts, patterns, med, per dz	356.28	15, 20, 25
Cl33199	Tennis dresses, sz 9, per dz	479.88	10, 20, 15

Answer the following questions after you have completed the spreadsheet:

1. What is the net equivalent cost for Head skis?

2. What is the net cost for Head rackets per case?

3. What is the net cost for golf gloves per carton?

4. What is the net equivalent cost for Wilson pro-lite golf bags?

5. What is the net cost for tennis dresses, sz 9, per dozen?

GROUP REPORT

FOR CHAPTER 7 APPLICATION 1

The Springfield Department Store has received a revised list of trade discounts from Mason's Wholesale Sporting Goods. The base price for merchandise remains the list price of the catalog items.

1. Substitute the new trade discounts into the Trade Discount Conversion Spreadsheet to find the new price the Springfield Department Store will pay.

Catalog Number	Product Description	Trade Discounts
Tn22898	Head rackets, 12 per cs	30, 25, 5
Gl39388	Wilson 1200 irons, 2-PW	20, 28, 15
Gl38577	Wilson prolite golf bag	25, 25, 5
Gl33948	Golf glove, m/lg, rh, 12 per crtn	14, 22, 12
Bs29393	Spaulding inf glove, 12 per cs	37, 20, 16
Bs34958	Bike baseball cleats	11, 17, 11
Sk33987	Head skis	30, 20, 15
Wt33389	300-lb freeweight set	22, 10, 12
Wt58773	Weight-lifting machine, 200 lb	15, 10, 15
Cl58766	Tennis shorts, men's med, per dz	20, 15, 5
Cl22856	Tennis shirts, patterns, med, per dz	14, 24, 22
Cl33199	Tennis dresses, sz 9, per dz	10, 20, 5

2. Write a memo to Paul Cheffield, the head buyer for Springfield, describing the changes.

3. Give your collective opinion on the direction of prices for sporting goods and your recommended action.

APPLICATION 2

Springfield recently sent a purchase order to Mason's Wholesale Sporting Goods ordering the items from its catalog for which the net costs were calculated in Application 1. In this application you will prepare Mason's invoice to Springfield. When you open Ch07App2, you will have Mason's spreadsheet invoice. It will appear as shown here:

Mason's Wholesale Sporting Goods

12852 Fifth Avenue
Chicago, Illinois 60609
Telephone: 312-387-7362   FAX: 312-387-3220

SOLD TO: INVOICE NO.:
                                                                            Invoice Date:
                                                                            Shipped On:
                                                                            Shipped By:
                                                                            TERMS:

CUSTOMER ORDER NO.: SG3495720MAS

Catalog Number	Order Qty.	Product Description	Qty. Shpd.	Unit Price	Total Item Cost	Sales Tax	Insurance	Total Cost
					$0.00	$0.00	$0.00	$0.00
					$0.00	$0.00	$0.00	$0.00
					$0.00	$0.00	$0.00	$0.00
					$0.00	$0.00	$0.00	$0.00
					$0.00	$0.00	$0.00	$0.00
					$0.00	$0.00	$0.00	$0.00
					$0.00	$0.00	$0.00	$0.00
					$0.00	$0.00	$0.00	$0.00
					$0.00	$0.00	$0.00	$0.00
					$0.00	$0.00	$0.00	$0.00
					$0.00	$0.00	$0.00	$0.00
					$0.00	$0.00	$0.00	$0.00
TOTALS					$0.00	$0.00	$0.00	$0.00
FREIGHT								
PLEASE PAY THIS AMOUNT								$0.00

Enter the following information:

1. In cells B7 through B10, enter:

   Springfield Department Store

   2617 Main Street

   Box 219

   Springfield, Maryland 58109

2. In cells G6 through G10, enter:

   FLR23398

   8/23/03

   8/23/03

   Illinois Express Lines

   2/10, n/30

3. Beginning in cell A18, and ending in cell D29, enter:

Catalog Number	Order Qty.	Product Description	Qty. Shpd.
Tn22898	6 cs	Head rackets, 12 per cs.	6
Gl39388	24 sets	Wilson 1200 irons, 2-PW	24
Gl38577	48 ea	Wilson pro-lite golf bags	45
Gl33948	20 crtn	Golf glove, m/lg, rh	20
Bs29393	6 cs	Spaulding inf glove	6
Bs34958	24 pr	Bike baseball cleats	24
Sk33987	30 pr	Head Skis	24
Wt33389	20 cs	300-lb free-weight sets,	20
Wt58773	15 ea	Weight-lifting machine, 200 lb	15
Cl58766	20 dz	Tennis shorts, men's med	20
Cl22856	15 dz	Tennis shirts, pattern, med	12
Cl33199	18 dz	Tennis dresses, sz 9	18

4. Beginning in cell E18 and continuing through cell E29, enter the prices (net cost) that you arrived at in the trade discount conversion spreadsheet in Application 1.

5. In cell I31, enter 297.30.

After entering all of the information, answer the following questions for Application 2:

1. Which products were backordered? (A backorder results if the quantity shipped is less than the quantity ordered.)

2. What is the total amount that Springfield must pay?

3. What is the total item cost for Head skis?

4. What is the sales tax for Wilson 1200 irons, 2-PW?

5. How much of the cost of insurance is allocated to tennis dresses?

6. What is the total amount of the invoice before the freight is added?

7. What is the total amount due for the weight-lifting machines, 200 lb?

8. What is the total item cost for all merchandise ordered by Springfield?

GROUP REPORT

FOR CHAPTER 7 APPLICATION 2

Your group should substitute the price list change that Mason's sent to Springfield for which the net costs were calculated in the Group Report for Application 1. Write a report describing the differences between the two invoices. Be sure to explain all changes in the invoice. Send the report to Paul Cheffield.

8 MARKETING APPLICATIONS
SELLING

SOMETIMES IT TAKES MORE THAN A LOWER PRICE

When they arrive at service stations in Japan, motorists are welcomed by a corps of uniformed attendants shouting greetings. The smiling cheerful pack guides cars into position, wipes their windows, empties their ashtrays, checks tire pressure, and pumps the gasoline. On leaving, the driver is aided by attendants who halt traffic to escort cars back onto the road. Such meticulous care employs some 400,000 ashtray emptiers.

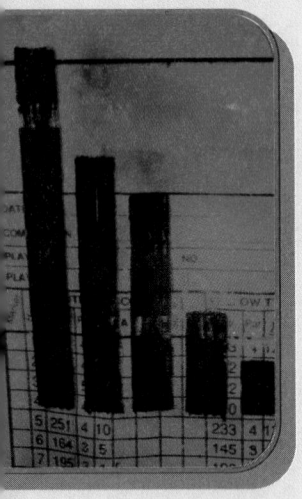

The land where even the elevator ladies bow is known for such pampering, but everything has a price. At $3.31 a gallon, Japanese consumers pay about two and one half times as much as U.S. consumers for their motor fuel. But a radical notion has been suggested for the Japanese: Can't consumers pump their own gas as they do in just about all of the United States except Oregon?

Self-service stations are illegal in Japan because it is believed they are a fire hazard in such a crowded country where most of the buildings are made of wood.

The Japanese government has rigorously striven to deregulate the economy, and the laws that prohibit consumers pumping their own gas are a symbol of what critics say are the numerous and pointless restrictions that make consumers' prices so high. The move is often portrayed as being in the interests of consumers, who would enjoy lower prices.

The trouble is that Japanese drivers do not clamor for the opportunity to gas up their own cars. According to the Japan Automobile Federation, the Japanese equivalent to the American Automobile Association, most licensed drivers in Japan would find self-service too difficult and just don't want it. Apparently price is not the major consideration. Japanese drivers prefer to be pampered and would rather pay than pump.

Chapter Glossary

Markup. The amount a seller adds to the cost of merchandise to arrive at the selling price.

Selling price. The amount a business firm charges customers for merchandise.

Cost. The amount a business pays for merchandise.

Markup percent. The rate used to determine the amount that will be added to the cost of merchandise. It can be based on either cost or the selling price.

Average markup percent. The markup rate a business needs to achieve on all merchandise sold over a period of time, usually one year.

Total planned purchases. The amount a buyer budgets for a business firm to purchase during a period of time.

Purchases to date. The portion of the total planned purchases a buyer has already purchased.

Balance to buy. The portion of the total planned purchases a buyer has remaining to buy.

Perishables. Merchandise that must be sold rapidly before it spoils and becomes unsalable.

Markup on perishables. The amount that must be added to the total cost of perishables to arrive at the selling price after spoilage has been considered.

Markdown. A reduction in the selling price.

Markdown percent. The markdown amount divided by the original selling price.

Student Objectives

Upon completion of this chapter, you should be able to:

1. Calculate the markup.
2. Calculate the markup percent based on either the cost or the selling price.
3. Use a formula to convert a markup percent based on cost to a markup percent based on the selling price.
4. Use a formula to convert a markup percent based on the selling price to a markup percent based on cost.
5. Find the selling price when the cost and the markup percent on cost are known.
6. Find the cost when the selling price and the markup percent on cost are known.
7. Find the selling price when the cost and the markup percent on the selling price are known.
8. Find the cost when the selling price and the markup percent on the selling price are known.
9. Find the markup percent on the balance to buy to attain the desired average markup.
10. Find the markup percent on cost for perishables.
11. Find the markdown and markdown percent based on the original selling price.
12. Find the selling price after a series of markdowns and markups.

S uccess or failure in business ultimately depends on how well a firm markets its products to satisfy the wants of its customers. Marketing involves many considerations, but in a recent survey price was determined to be the most important marketing variable in the minds of customers. But setting prices is not a simple exercise. Prices must be set high enough to cover costs and other expenses plus return a reasonable profit, but low enough to be competitive and attract an adequate number of customers.

LEARNING UNIT 1
MARKUPS AND MARKUP PERCENTS

Several procedures are used to determine a selling price, and markup percent is one of the most important. Many business firms base their markup percent on cost. Manufacturers, wholesalers, some retailers, and many services use cost as the base. This is particularly true of small businesses in each of these categories. Many, however, do so without knowing why, and actually use industry or trade averages that have been based on the selling price. In fact, one study showed inadequate knowledge of markup percents as the third leading cause of small business failure.

8.1 Calculating the Markup

Markup is the amount a seller adds to the cost of merchandise to arrive at the **selling price**, which is the amount the customer will pay for the merchandise. The amount added must be enough to (1) cover the **cost** of the good (the amount the retailer paid for the good); (2) cover operating expenses such as utilities, salaries, rent, and supplies; and (3) provide for a reasonable profit. The formula is

$$\text{Markup} = \text{selling price} - \text{cost.}$$

It is more useful to write the relationship:

Selling price ← *Price retailer charges customers*
− cost ← *Amount retailer pays for the good*
= markup ← *Gross profit, or the amount added to cost to arrive at the selling price*

EXAMPLE A retail store buys clocks for $8 each and sells them for $12 each. How much is the markup on each clock?

Solution
Selling price $12
− cost 8
= markup $ 4

8.1 Practice Problems

Calculate the markup:

1. A clothing store buys men's suits for $176 and sells them for $325. How much is the markup on each suit?

2. A computer is purchased by Computer Universe for $595 from its supplier. It will be sold for $1,295. How much is the markup?

3. Gerhart's Fine Furniture ordered a sofa from the manufacturer and paid $929. Gerhart's will mark it up and sell it for $1,161.25. How much is the markup?

4. A case of paper is bought by Ozark Office Supply from a wholesaler for $8.59. It will be sold for $14.98. Find the markup.

1.	Selling price	$325		2.	Selling price	$1,295
−	cost	176		−	cost	595
=	markup	$149		=	markup	$ 700
3.	Selling price	$1,161.25		4.	Selling price	$14.98
−	cost	929.00		−	cost	8.59
=	markup	$ 232.25		=	markup	$ 6.39

8.2 Calculating the Markup Percent

Businesses use **markup percents** to determine the price to charge customers. Thus, properly determining the markup percent to use and what to base it on is critical. Business firms getting started have to use markup percents that are close to industry averages or some other already established standard. Unfortunately, the markup percent used by another business firm or an average of all businesses may not fit the needs of the new business. As time goes by, firms establish historical records and can begin to use the markup percent that is best for them as indicated by their own past experiences. This presupposes that a business continually evaluates its financial data to determine the "best" present course of action.

Although most retailers base their markup percent on the selling price, a few base it on the cost. Both are merely applied uses of the percentage problems covered in Chapter 5.

Markup Percent Based on Cost

The percentage formula for finding a rate is

$$\text{Rate} = \frac{\text{percentage}}{\text{base}}.$$

In markup percent problems, *the markup percent is the rate*. The base could be either the cost or the selling price, but *this section defines the base as the cost. The percentage is the markup*. To find the markup percent based on cost, the formula is

$$\text{Markup percent} = \frac{\text{markup}}{\text{cost}}.$$

EXAMPLE

A retail store buys clocks for $8 each and sells them for $12 each. How much is the markup percent on cost for each clock?

Solution

	Selling price	$12
−	cost	8
=	markup	$ 4

$$\text{Markup percent} = \frac{\text{markup}}{\text{cost}}$$

$$\text{Markup percent} = \frac{\$4}{\$8} = \frac{1}{2}$$

$$\text{Markup percent} = 50\%$$

Markup Percent Based on the Selling Price

When the markup percent is based on the selling price, it becomes the base in the formula instead of the cost. To find the markup percent based on selling price, the formula is

$$\text{Markup percent} = \frac{\text{markup}}{\text{selling price}}.$$

The previous example will again be used to demonstrate the difference between choosing to base the markup percent on the cost or the selling price.

EXAMPLE A retail store buys clocks for $8 each and sells them for $12 each. What is the markup percent on the selling price for each clock?

Solution

Selling price $12
$-$ cost   8
$=$ markup $ 4

$$\text{Markup percent} = \frac{\text{markup}}{\text{selling price}}$$

$$\text{Markup percent} = \frac{\$4}{\$12} = \frac{1}{3}$$

$$\text{Markup percent} = 33\frac{1}{3}\%$$

Notice that the only difference between the two previous examples is in the words that appear after *markup percent*. In the first example those words are *on cost*. That phrase indicates that the base is cost. In the second example the words after *markup percent* are *on the selling price*. That phrase indicates that the base is the selling price.

A major reason most retailers base their markup percent on the selling price is that a vertical analysis of the income statement (discussed in Chapter 16) shows the percent relationship of product costs and other expenses to the sales dollar. Therefore, using the markup percent on the selling price allows instant comparison of the pricing formula to the analytical results of the income statement conducted at the end of an accounting cycle (which is usually one year).

Markup percents can be converted from one base to another. Two formulas are used for that purpose, as discussed next.

Formula for Converting a Markup Percent on the Selling Price to a Markup Percent on Cost

To convert a markup percent on the selling price to a markup percent on cost, the following formula can be used:

$$\text{Markup percent on cost} = \frac{\text{markup percent on selling price}}{100\% - \text{markup percent on selling price}}$$

EXAMPLE Convert a 20% markup on the selling price to a markup percent on cost.

Solution

$$\text{Markup percent on cost} = \frac{\text{markup percent on selling price}}{100\% - \text{markup percent on selling price}}$$

$$= \frac{20\%}{100\% - 20\%} = \frac{20\%}{80\%} = 25\%$$

Formula for Converting a Markup Percent on Cost to a Markup Percent on the Selling Price

To convert a markup percent on cost to a markup percent on the selling price, the following formula can be used:

$$\text{Markup percent on selling price} = \frac{\text{markup percent on cost}}{100\% + \text{markup percent on cost}}$$

EXAMPLE   Convert a 25% markup on cost to a markup percent on the selling price.

Solution   Markup percent on selling price $= \dfrac{\text{markup percent on cost}}{100\% + \text{markup percent on cost}}$

$= \dfrac{25\%}{100\% + 25\%} = \dfrac{25\%}{125\%} = 20\%$

Table 8.1 provides several of the equivalent markup percents. The markup percent on cost will always be larger than the markup percent on the selling price because the cost (which is the divisor when markup percent is based on cost) is always smaller than the selling price (when dividing, the smaller the divisor the larger the quotient).

TABLE 8.1   EQUIVALENT MARKUPS

Markup Percent on The Selling Price	Markup Percent on Cost
15%	17.6%
20%	25.0%
25%	33.3%
30%	42.9%
35%	53.8%
40%	66.7%
45%	81.8%
50%	100.0%
55%	122.2%

8.2 Practice Problems

Calculate the markup percent in the following problems:

1. A clothing store buys men's suits for $176 and sells them for $325. How much is the markup percent on cost for each suit?

2. A computer is purchased by Computer Universe for $595 from its supplier. It will be sold for $1,295. What is the markup percent on cost? Use the appropriate formula to convert the markup percent on cost to the markup percent on the selling price.

3. Gerhart's Fine Furniture ordered a sofa from the manufacturer and paid $929. Gerhart's will mark it up and sell it for $1,161.25. Determine the markup percent on the selling price.

4. A case of paper is bought by Ozark Office Supply from a wholesaler for $8.59. It will be sold for $14.98. How much is the markup percent on the selling price?

8.2 Solutions to Practice Problems

1.
Selling price $325
−   cost   176
=   markup $149

Markup percent $= \dfrac{\text{markup}}{\text{cost}} = \dfrac{\$149}{\$176} = .847$

Markup percent $= 84.7\%$

2.
Selling price $1,295
−   cost   595
=   markup $ 700

Markup percent $= \dfrac{\text{markup}}{\text{cost}} = \dfrac{\$700}{\$595} = 1.176$

Markup percent $= 117.6\%$

Markup percent on selling price $= \dfrac{\text{markup percent on cost}}{100\% + \text{markup percent on cost}}$

Markup percent on selling price $= \dfrac{117.6\%}{100\% + 117.6\%} = \dfrac{117.6\%}{217.6\%} = 54.0\%$

3. Selling price $\quad$ $1,161.25

$\quad\quad -$ $\quad$ cost $\quad\quad$ 929.00

$\quad\quad =$ $\quad$ markup $\quad$ $ 232.25

Markup percent $= \dfrac{\text{markup}}{\text{selling price}} = \dfrac{\$\,232.25}{\$1,161.25}$

$\quad\quad\quad\quad\quad\quad\quad = .2 = 20\%$

4. Selling price $\quad$ $14.98

$\quad\quad -$ $\quad$ cost $\quad\quad$ 8.59

$\quad\quad =$ $\quad$ markup $\quad$ $ 6.39

Markup percent $= \dfrac{\text{markup}}{\text{selling price}} = \dfrac{\$\,6.39}{\$14.98}$

$\quad\quad\quad\quad\quad\quad\quad = .427 = 42.7\%$

When a business firm uses markups to set (or help set) its prices, the first decision to be made is whether to base the markup percent on cost or on the selling price.

 **EXCEL Spreadsheet Application** In Spreadsheet Application 1 at the end of this chapter you will use an Excel spreadsheet program to set selling prices for individual items received from a supplier.

LEARNING UNIT 2
FINDING THE UNKNOWNS IN RETAILING WHEN THE BASE IS COST

Once a business firm has determined the markup percent it needs to use, and has decided to base that markup percent on cost, it can solve for the cost, selling price, or markup. Usually, two of the three will be unknown. It must be understood that *cost is the base and will be represented by 100%.*

8.3 **Finding the Selling Price When the Cost and the Markup Percent on Cost Are Known**

EXAMPLE $\quad$ Moss Electronics paid $24 for an electric clock. It uses a standard markup percent of 75% on cost for most items. Find the selling price for the clock.

Solution $\quad\quad$ Selling price $=$ cost $\times$ (100% + markup percent on cost)

$\quad\quad\quad\quad\quad\quad$ Selling price $=$ $24 $\times$ (100% + 75%)

$\quad\quad\quad\quad\quad\quad$ Selling price $=$ $24 $\times$ 175%

$\quad\quad\quad\quad\quad\quad$ Selling price $=$ $42

Alternate Solution $\quad$ When cost is the base, it is usually easier to change the standard formula:

$$\text{Markup} = \text{selling price} - \text{cost, or}$$

Selling price		Cost
$-$ $\quad$ cost	to	$+$ $\quad$ markup
$=$ $\quad$ markup		$=$ selling price

The base is usually the top item in the formula and always is represented by 100%. Follow these steps:

1. Expand the formula to include columns for the amount and the percent and fill in the known amounts (including 100% for the cost percent):

	Amount	*Percent*
Cost	$24	100% ← Base is 100%
$+$ $\quad$ markup		75%
$=$ selling price		

2. Make the easy calculation. In this example, the easy calculation is adding the cost percent, 100%, to the markup percent, 75%: 100% + 75% = 175%.

	Amount	Percent
Cost	$24	100%
+ markup		75%
= selling price		175% ← 100% + 75%

3. Since the base amount (cost = $24) is known, multiply it by the desired unknown's percent. In this example, the desired unknown is the selling price and the selling price percent is 175%. Thus, $24 × 175% = $42.

	Amount	Percent
Cost	$24	100%
+ markup		75%
= selling price	$42	175%

$24 × 175%

A simple guideline to help solve markup problems is to remember this: *If the base is given in the problem* (as it was in this problem, a $24 cost), *multiply it by the percent of the desired unknown amount.* (In this example, the desired unknown amount is the selling price, and its percent is 175%.) *The product is your answer* (in this example, the selling price, $42).

While the first solution might seem to be much easier than the alternate solution, closer inspection will show that they are exactly the same. The alternate solution is more systematic and consistent. It also allows problem-solving without having to memorize a number of formulas.

8.3 Practice Problems

Find the selling price when you are given the cost and the markup percent based on cost in each of the following problems:

1. A retailer's markup percent is 60% on cost. A stool was bought for $18. Find the selling price.

2. Cozy Inn Motel estimates its costs at $25 per room. The markup percent desired by management is 80% on cost. How much will guests at the motel pay?

3. Calculate the selling price for a suit costing the retail clothing store $180 if the markup percent is 70% on cost.

4. Find the selling price for a dozen eggs that cost a grocery store $.60 if the markup percent is 30% on cost.

8.3 Solutions to Practice Problems

1. Selling price = cost × (100% + markup percent)
= $18 × (100% + 60%)
= $18 × 160%
= $28.80

2. Selling price = cost × (100% + markup percent)
= $25 × (100% + 80%)
= $25 × 180%
= $45

3. Selling price = cost × (100% + markup percent)
= $180 × (100% + 70%)
= $180 × 170%
= $306

4. Selling price = cost × (100% + markup percent)
= $.60 × (100% + 30%)
= $.60 × 130%
= $.78

Finding the Cost When the Selling Price and the Markup Percent on Cost Are Known

E X A M P L E   Mark Ever's Discount Book Store has a markup percent of 85% on cost. One paperback book is selling for $4.75. How much did it cost?

Solution

$$\text{Cost} = \frac{\text{selling price}}{100\% + \text{markup percent on cost}}$$

$$= \frac{\$4.75}{185\%} = \$2.57$$

Alternate Solution

1. Prepare the format using the formula

> Cost + markup = selling price

and fill in the known amounts (including 100% for the cost percent):

	Amount	*Percent*
Cost		*100%* ← Base is 100%
+ markup		*85%*
= selling price	$4.75	

2. Make the easy calculation. In this example, the easy calculation is to add the cost percent, 100%, to the markup percent, 85%: 100% + 85% = 185%.

	Amount	*Percent*
Cost		*100%*
+ markup		*85%*
= selling price	$4.75	*185%* ← 100% + 85%

3. Since the base amount (cost) is not known, divide the known amount (in this example, the selling price, $4.75) by its percent (in this example, the selling price percent, 185%) to find the cost.

$$\$4.75 \div 185\% = \$2.57$$

$4.75 ÷ 185%

	Amount	*Percent*
Cost	$2.57	*100%*
+ markup		*85%*
= selling price	$4.75	*185%*

To help solve markup problems, keep in mind that *if the base is not given in the problem* (as in this problem), *divide the known amount* (in this example, the known amount is the selling price, $4.75) *by its percent* (in this example, 185%). *The quotient is the base* (in this example, the cost, $2.57).

8.4 Practice Problems

Find the cost when given the selling price and the markup percent based on cost in each of the following problems:

1. A retailer has a markup percent of 55% on cost. A lamp has a selling price of $78. Find the cost.

2. Dominici's Hardware marks hand tools up 100% on cost. A power drill sells for $54. What is Dominici's cost?

3. Find the cost for a toy that retails for $18 when it has been marked up 88% on cost.

4. Karl's Home Cookin' charges $6.95 for chicken-fried steak. The manager attempts to maintain a markup percent of 125% on cost. Calculate the cost.

8.4 Solutions to Practice Problems

1. $\text{Cost} = \dfrac{\text{selling price}}{100\% + \text{markup percent on cost}}$

$= \dfrac{\$78}{100\% + 55\%} = \dfrac{\$78}{155\%} = \$50.32$

2. $\text{Cost} = \dfrac{\text{selling price}}{100\% + \text{markup percent on cost}}$

$= \dfrac{\$54}{100\% + 100\%} = \dfrac{\$54}{200\%} = \$27$

3. $\text{Cost} = \dfrac{\text{selling price}}{100\% + \text{markup percent on cost}}$

$= \dfrac{\$18}{100\% + 88\%} = \dfrac{\$18}{188\%} = \$9.57$

4. $\text{Cost} = \dfrac{\text{selling price}}{100\% + \text{markup percent on cost}}$

$= \dfrac{\$6.95}{100\% + 125\%} = \dfrac{\$6.95}{225\%} = \$3.09$

LEARNING UNIT 3
FINDING THE UNKNOWNS IN RETAILING WHEN THE BASE IS THE SELLING PRICE

When a firm makes a decision to base its markup percent on the selling price, it must recognize that *the selling price will then be represented by 100%.*

8.5. Finding the Selling Price When the Cost Is Known and the Markup Percent Is on the Selling Price

When the markup percent is based on the selling price, the formulas are

$$\text{Selling price} = \dfrac{\text{cost}}{100\% - \text{markup percent}}$$

$$\text{Cost} = \text{selling price} \times (100\% - \text{markup percent})$$

EXAMPLE   Find the selling price for a suitcase that cost the retailer $84 and is marked up 30% on the selling price.

Solution $\text{Selling price} = \dfrac{\text{cost}}{100\% - \text{markup percent on selling price}}$

$= \dfrac{\$84}{100\% - 30\%}$

$= \dfrac{\$84}{70\%}$

$= \$120$

Alternate Solution   The basic formula,

> Markup = selling price − cost,

is more convenient to use in the following form:

> Selling price
> −   cost   *Placing the base at the top of the*
> =   markup   *format makes solving the problem*
> *more convenient.*

The problem can be solved as follows:

1. Prepare the format using the formula

> Selling price − cost = markup

and fill in the know amounts (including 100% for the selling price percent):

	Amount	*Percent*
Selling price		*100%* ← Base is 100%
− cost	$84	
= markup		30%

2. Make the easy calculation. In this example, the easy calculation is to subtract the markup percent, 30%, from the selling price percent, 100%: 100% − 30% = 70%.

	Amount	*Percent*
Selling price		*100%*
− cost	$84	*70%* ← 100% − 30%
= markup		30%

3. Since the base amount (the selling price) is not known, divide the known amount (in this example, the cost, $84) by its percent (in this example, the cost percent, 70%) to find the selling price.

$84 ÷ 70% = $120

$84 ÷ 70%

	Amount	*Percent*
Selling price	$120	*100%*
− cost	$ 84	*70%*
= markup		30%

A simple guideline to help solve markup problems is *if the base is not given in the problem* (as in this problem), *divide the known amount* (in this example, the known amount is the cost, $84) *by its percent* (in this example, 70%). *The quotient is the base* (in this example, the selling price, $120).

8.5 Practice Problems

1. Find the selling price of a model car that cost the dealer $6 and will carry a 40% markup on the selling price.
2. Jonesborough's Furniture pays $65 for a coffee table. Its markup on furniture is 60% on the selling price. What is the selling price to Jonesborough's customers?
3. Washington Whitley's Auto Parts store sells automobile accessories. One style of slip-on seat cover cost Mr. Whitley $39.98. He has decided to mark them up 25% on the selling price to attract new customers. Determine the selling price.

4. Angelina's Fashions and Accessories just purchased an exclusive line of blouses. The store paid $1,026 for one dozen of the blouses. This exclusive will be marked up 55% on the selling price. Find the selling price for each blouse.

8.5 Solutions to Practice Problems

1. Selling price $= \dfrac{\text{cost}}{100\% - \text{markup percent on selling price}}$

$= \dfrac{\$6}{100\% - 40\%}$ Selling price $= \dfrac{\$6}{60\%} = \$10$

2. Selling price $= \dfrac{\text{cost}}{100\% - \text{markup percent on selling price}}$

$= \dfrac{\$65}{100\% - 60\%}$ Selling price $= \dfrac{\$65}{40\%} = \$162.50$

3. Selling price $= \dfrac{\text{cost}}{100\% - \text{markup percent on selling price}}$

$= \dfrac{\$39.98}{100\% - 25\%}$ Selling price $= \dfrac{\$39.98}{75\%} = \$53.31$

4. $\$1,026 \div 12 = \$85.50$

Selling price $= \dfrac{\text{cost}}{100\% - \text{markup percent on selling price}}$

$= \dfrac{\$85.50}{100\% - 55\%} = \dfrac{\$85.50}{45\%} = \$190$

8.6 Finding the Cost When the Selling Price and the Markup Percent on the Selling Price Are Known

When the markup percent is based on the selling price, the formulas are

$$\text{Selling Price} = \dfrac{\text{cost}}{100\% - \text{markup percent}}$$

$$\text{Cost} = \text{selling price} \times (100\% - \text{markup percent})$$

EXAMPLE   Find the cost to a retailer for a hat it sells for $39.99 and marks up 45% on the selling price.

Solution   Cost = selling price × (100% − markup percent on selling price)
= $39.99 × (100% − 45%)
= $39.99 × 55%
= $21.99

Alternate Solution   1. Prepare the format using the following formula:

$$\text{Selling price} - \text{cost} = \text{markup}$$

and fill in the known amounts (including 100% for the selling price percent):

	Amount	Percent
Selling price	$39.99	100% ← Base is 100%
− cost		
= markup		45%

2. Make the easy calculation. In this example, the easy calculation is subtracting the markup percent, 45%, from the selling price percent, 100%: 100% − 45% = 55%.

	Amount	Percent
Selling price	$39.99	100%
− cost		55% ← 100% − 45%
= markup		45%

3. Since the base amount, the selling price, is known (in this example, $39.99), multiply it by the cost percent (in this example, 55%) to find the cost amount: $39.99 × 55% = $21.99.

	Amount	Percent
Selling price	$39.99	100%
− cost	21.99	55%
= markup		45%

$39.99 × 55%

A simple guideline to help solve markup problems is to remember this: *If the base is given in the problem* (as it was in this problem, $39.99, the selling price), *multiply it by the percent of the desired unknown amount* (in this example, the desired unknown amount is the cost and its percent is 55%). *The product is the answer* (in this example, the cost amount, $21.99).

8.6 Practice Problems

1. Find the cost for a box of diskettes that are sold for $7.29 and are marked up 50% on the selling price.
2. Kiki's Business Forms Service has found that it must charge customers $4.25 per hour for preparing business letters to achieve the desired 43% markup on retail. How much is the hourly cost for the service?
3. Calculate the cost for a computer that has a selling price of $720. The markup percent is 35% on the selling price.
4. A set of golf clubs sell for $370. The Par Golf Shop has a markup percent of 58% on the selling price. How much do the clubs cost the golf shop?

8.6 Solutions to Practice Problems

1. Cost = selling price × (100% − markup percent on selling price)
   = $7.29 × (100% − 50%)
   = $7.29 × 50%
   = $3.65

2. Cost = selling price × (100% − markup percent on selling price)
   = $4.25 × (100% − 43%)
   = $4.25 × 57%
   = $2.42

3. Cost = selling price × (100% − markup percent on selling price)
   = $720 × (100% − 35%)
   = $720 × 65%
   = $468

4. Cost = selling price × (100% − markup percent on selling price)
   = $370 × (100% − 58%)
   = $370 × 42%
   = $155.40

LEARNING UNIT 4
AVERAGE MARKUP

The markup problems so far have been on single items, but retailers do not ordinarily buy one item at a time. Some items, such as expensive luxury goods, do not have a large market or much competition. Such goods have higher markups than staple necessity goods, which have a large market and a great deal of competition. The same retailer may sell both types of goods.

Retailers attempt to maintain an **average markup percent** for a department or for the entire store. They must determine the percent of markup necessary to cover the cost of goods sold, pay the operating expenses, and provide a reasonable profit. Prices charged for merchandise must sometimes be adjusted to return the needed markup percent. Buyers work from a budget. They have specific dollar amounts to spend, and they must keep accurate records of expenditures. Also, when buyers purchase merchandise, they must take care to assure that they maintain the necessary average markup.

Merchandise is typically bought in different quantities, at various costs, and at different times. The markup percent used may be based on either the cost or the selling price depending on the preference of the retailer. The following procedure is used:

1. The total budget is determined and recorded as **total planned purchases**. Those amounts are recorded at both the selling price and at cost.

2. When purchases are made, they are accumulated (added to other purchases) and collectively called **purchases to date**. They are recorded at the selling price and at cost. Each total is then subtracted from the selling price and the cost of the total planned purchases. The difference is called the **balance to buy**.

3. The *markup percent on the balance to buy* is calculated. This calculation yields the markup percent that will be required on the remaining purchases during the year if the retailer is to achieve the desired average annual markup.

EXCEL Spreadsheet Application In Spreadsheet Application 2 at the end of this chapter you will use an Excel spreadsheet form to help the Springfield Department Store keep track of the cost, selling price, markup, and markup percent of their purchases.

8.7 Finding the Markup Percent of the Balance to Buy to Determine the Desired Average Markup Percent

EXAMPLE | A department store marks all merchandise up on the selling price. The buyer for the women's department plans to buy clothes that will sell for $20,000. The desired annual average markup for the department is 60%. The early purchases costing $4,500 will be marked up 25% to attract customers to the store. What markup percent will be required for the balance to buy to achieve the desired annual average markup percent?

Solution | The parts of the problem should be organized in the following format:

	Selling Price	− Cost	= Markup	Markup Percent
Total planned purchases	$20,000			60%
− purchases to date		$4,500		25%
= balance to buy				

Chapter 8 Marketing Applications: Selling   269

Note: All columns except the markup percent column are additive. The markup percent of balance to buy *cannot* be found by subtracting purchases to date from total planned purchases.

All the information on the *balance to buy* line must be calculated. To do that, the selling price and cost columns must be filled in completely.

Proceed one line at a time. First calculate the cost amount for total planned purchases with the markup percent based on the selling price:

$$\begin{aligned}
\text{Cost} &= \text{selling price} \times (100\% - \text{markup percent on selling price}) \\
&= \$20,000 \times (100\% - 60\%) \\
&= \$20,000 \times 40\% \\
&= \$8,000
\end{aligned}$$

After entering the $8,000 cost on the total planned purchases line, the format appears as follows:

	Selling Price	− Cost	= Markup	Markup Percent
Total planned purchases	$20,000	*$8,000*		60%
− purchases to date		4,500		25%
= balance to buy				

On the purchases to date line, the selling price amount should be shown. It is found as follows:

$$\begin{aligned}
\text{Selling price} &= \frac{\text{cost}}{100\% - \text{markup percent on selling price}} \\
&= \frac{\$4,500}{100\% - 25\%} \\
&= \frac{\$4,500}{75\%} = \$6,000
\end{aligned}$$

After entering the $6,000 selling price on the purchases to date line, the format appears as follows:

	Selling Price	− Cost	= Markup	Markup Percent
Total planned purchases	$20,000	*$8,000*		60%
− purchases to date	*6,000*	4,500		25%
= balance to buy				

The selling price and cost columns on the balance to buy line can then be determined by subtracting as follows:

Selling Price	Cost
$20,000 − 6,000 = $14,000	$8,000 − 4,500 = $3,500

After entering the $14,000 selling price and the $3,500 cost on the balance to buy line, your format should look like this:

	Selling Price	− Cost	= Markup	Markup Percent
Total planned purchases	$20,000	*$8,000*		60%
− purchases to date	*6,000*	4,500		25%
= balance to buy	*$14,000*	*$3,500*		

The markup on the balance to buy line can be calculated by subtracting the $3,500 cost from the $14,000 selling price on the balance to buy line:

$$\$14,000 - 3,500 = \$10,500$$

After entering the $10,500 markup on the balance to buy line, the format appears as follows:

	Selling Price	− Cost	= Markup	Markup Percent
Total planned purchases	$20,000	$8,000		60%
− purchases to date	6,000	4,500		25%
= balance to buy	$14,000	$3,500	$10,500	

The markup percent on the balance to buy line can then be calculated. The markup percent is based on the selling price, so using only information from the balance to buy line:

$$\text{Markup percent on the selling price} = \frac{\text{markup}}{\text{selling price}}$$
$$= \frac{\$10,500}{\$14,000} = 75\%$$

After entering the markup percent of 75% on the balance to buy line, the finished format appears:

	Selling Price	− Cost	= Markup	Markup Percent
Total planned purchases	$20,000	$8,000		60%
− purchases to date	6,000	4,500		25%
= balance to buy	$14,000	$3,500	$10,500	75%

Note that not all of the information (in the markup column) has to be calculated. However if the markup for the total planned purchases and the purchases to date are calculated, it will provide a check for the balance to buy markup.

8.7 Practice Problems

1. A buyer planned to buy merchandise costing $50,000 for a department store, to be marked up 50% on the selling price. He bought merchandise yesterday and today for a total cost of $20,000. It will be sold for $35,000. Find the markup percent on the selling price for the remaining purchases to achieve the desired average markup percent.

2. The buyer for Pisonici's Hardware plans to buy goods costing $36,000 to sell for $60,000. She went to a trade show and bought various lighting fixture items costing $16,000 that will be marked up 20% on the selling price. What markup percent on the selling price will she need to set on the remaining purchases in order to achieve the desired average markup percent?

3. McClean Micro Electronics Center wants to achieve an average markup percent of 70%. The company always bases its markup percent on the cost. Sales forecasts indicate that software purchases costing $80,000 need to be made to meet the expected demand. To date, the head buyer has purchased software programs costing $30,000 that have been marked up to sell for $48,000. What will the markup percent have to be for the remaining purchases in order to achieve the desired average markup percent?

4. Barney's Shoes attempts to maintain an average markup percent of 60% on cost. Barney Oldfoot plans to purchase oxfords for the winter season that will sell for $20,000. He has so far made purchases costing $4,000 that will sell for $6,400. Calculate the markup percent on cost required for the remaining purchases.

8.7 Solutions to Practice Problems

1. After entering the information given in the problem, the format appears as follows:

	Selling Price	− Cost	= Markup	Markup Percent
Total planned purchases		$50,000		50% (SP)
− purchases to date	$35,000	20,000		
= balance to buy	$	$	$	

The calculations to complete the necessary information to solve the problem can then be made:

Selling price of the total planned purchases:

$$\text{Selling price} = \frac{\text{cost}}{100\% - \text{markup percent on selling price}}$$

$$= \frac{\$50,000}{100\% - 50\%}$$

$$= \frac{\$50,000}{50\%} = \$100,000$$

Selling Price of the Balance to Buy	*Cost of the Balance to Buy*	*Markup of the Balance to Buy*
$ 100,000	$50,000	$65,000
− 35,000	− 20,000	− 30,000
$65,000	$30,000	$35,000

Markup percent on the selling price for the balance to buy:

$$\text{Markup percent on the selling price} = \frac{\text{markup}}{\text{selling price}}$$

$$= \frac{\$35,000}{\$65,000} = 53.8\%$$

After all the calculations have been entered into the format, it appears as follows:

	Selling Price	− Cost	= Markup	Markup Percent
Total planned purchases	*$100,000*	$50,000		50% (SP)
− purchases to date	35,000	20,000		
= balance to buy	$ 65,000	$30,000	$35,000	53.8% (SP)

2. After entering the information given in the problem, the format appears as follows:

	Selling Price	− Cost	= Markup	Markup Percent
Total planned purchases	$60,000	$36,000		
− purchases to date	$	16,000		20% (SP)
= balance to buy	$	$	$	

The calculations to complete the necessary information to solve the problem can then be made:

Selling price of the purchases to date:

$$\text{Selling price} = \frac{\text{cost}}{100\% - \text{markup percent on selling price}}$$

$$= \frac{\$16,000}{100\% - 20\%}$$

$$= \frac{\$16,000}{80\%} = \$20,000$$

Selling Price of the Balance to Buy	Cost of the Balance to Buy	Markup of the Balance to Buy
$60,000	$36,000	$40,000
− 20,000	− 16,000	− 20,000
$40,000	$20,000	$20,000

Markup percent on the selling price for the balance to buy:

$$\text{Markup percent on the selling price} = \frac{\text{markup}}{\text{selling price}}$$

$$= \frac{\$20,000}{\$40,000} = 50\%$$

After all the calculations have been entered into the format, it appears as follows:

	Selling Price	− Cost	= Markup	Markup Percent
Total planned purchases	$60,000	$36,000		
− purchases to date	20,000	16,000		20% (SP)
= balance to buy	$40,000	$20,000	$20,000	50% (SP)

3. After entering the information given in the problem, the format appears as follows:

	Selling Price	− Cost	= Markup	Markup Percent
Total planned purchases		$80,000		70% (C)
− purchases to date	$48,000	30,000		
= balance to buy	$	$	$	

The calculations to complete the necessary information to solve the problem can then be made:

Selling price of the purchases to date:

$$\text{Selling price} = \text{cost} \times (100\% + \text{markup percent on cost})$$
$$= \$80,000 \times (100\% + 70\%)$$
$$= \$80,000 \times 170\%$$
$$= \$136,000$$

Selling Price of the Balance to Buy	Cost of the Balance to Buy:	Markup of the Balance to Buy
$136,000	$80,000	$88,000
−48,000	−30,000	−50,000
$ 88,000	$50,000	$38,000

Markup percent on the selling price for the balance to buy:

$$\text{Markup percent on cost} = \frac{markup}{cost}$$

$$\text{Markup percent on the selling price} = \frac{\$38,000}{\$50,000}$$

$$\text{Markup percent on the selling price} = 76\%$$

After all the calculations have been entered into the format, it appears as follows:

	Selling Price	− Cost	= Markup	Markup Percent
Total planned purchases	$136,000	$80,000		70% (C)
− purchases to date	48,000	30,000		
= balance to buy	$ 88,000	$50,000	$38,000	76% (C)

4. After entering the information given in the problem, the format appears as follows:

	Selling Price	− Cost	= Markup	Markup Percent
Total planned purchases	$20,000			60% (C)
− purchases to date	6,400	$4,000		
= balance to buy	$	$	$	

The calculations to complete the information can then be made:

Selling price of the purchases to date:

$$\text{Cost} = \frac{\text{selling price}}{(100\% + \text{markup percent on cost})}$$

$$= \frac{\$20,000}{(100\% + 60\%)}$$

$$= \frac{\$20,000}{160\%}$$

$$= \$12,500$$

Selling Price of the Balance to Buy	Cost of the Balance to Buy	Markup of the Balance to Buy
$20,000	$12,500	$13,600
− 6,400	− 4,000	− 8,500
$13,600	$ 8,500	$ 5,100

Markup percent on cost for the balance to buy:

$$\text{Markup percent on cost} = \frac{markup}{cost}$$

$$\text{Cost} = \frac{\$ 5,100}{\$ 8,500}$$

$$\text{Cost} = 60\%$$

After all the calculations have been entered into the format, it appears as follows:

	Selling Price	− Cost	= Markup	Markup Percent
Total planned purchases	$20,000	$12,500		60% (C)
− purchases to date	6,400	4,000		
= balance to buy	$13,600	$ 8,500	$5,100	60% (C)

Prices must be adjusted when a business firm expects to have losses due to circumstances such as spoilage, breakage, employee theft, and shoplifting. Most often, these possibilities are assumed to be an inevitable part of doing business, and the markup percent used is high enough to cover them. Firms must make conscientious efforts to adjust the price to cover such contingencies. The following discussion is about perishables and illustrates the type of adjustment owners and managers find necessary.

8.8 Finding the Selling Price per Unit for Perishables

To find the per unit selling price for **perishables** (merchandise that must be sold rapidly before it spoils and becomes unsalable), you work with total product costs and sales instead of unit costs and sales. The **markup on perishables** is the amount that must be added to the total cost of perishables to arrive at the selling price after spoilage has been considered.

EXAMPLE   The Robard Donut Shop bakes 50 dozen donuts each day. On average, 7.5% are not sold and are given to a local charity. Jackson Robard needs to have a 65% markup percent on cost to cover costs and make a reasonable profit. The donuts cost $3.50 per dozen to make. How much should Robard charge per donut?

Solution   To determine the price of each donut, the following steps must be taken:

Step 1. Find the total cost (*TC*) of the daily production:

$$TC = 50 \text{ dozen} \times \$3.50 \text{ per dozen} = \$175$$

Step 2. Find the total sales (*TS*) necessary to make the 65% markup on cost:

$$TS = TC \times (100\% + \text{markup percent on cost})$$

$$TS = \$175 \times (100\% + 65\%)$$
$$TS = \$175 \times 165\%$$
$$TS = \$288.75$$

Step 3. Find the total number of dozens expected to be sold:

50 dozen $\times$ 7.5% = 3.75 dozen   *Not expected to be sold*
50 dozen $-$ 3.75 dozen = 46.25 dozen   *Expected to be sold*

Step 4. Find the price that has to be charged for each dozen donuts that the owner expects to sell:

$$\text{Price per dozen} = \frac{\text{total sales (TS)}}{\text{number expected to be sold}}$$

$$\text{Price per dozen} = \frac{\$288.75}{46.25} = \$6.24$$

Step 5. Find the price per donut expected to be sold:

$$\text{Price per donut} = \frac{\text{price per dozen}}{12}$$

$$\text{Price per donut} = \frac{\$6.24}{12} = \$.52$$

Why bake 50 dozen donuts when only 46.25 dozen are expected to be sold? The answer to that is to make certain the needs and wants of customers are met. Ideally, the last customer of the day would buy the last donut. But it is unlikely to turn out that way. It is better to bake a few too many donuts and have satisfied, happy customers, than to risk baking too few donuts and disappointing some customers.

---

1. Trent's Cafeteria prepares enough food to feed 1,500 people each day Sunday through Thursday, and 2,500 people on Friday and Saturday. Past experience has shown that, on average, (1) about 5% of the food will be left over and will not be salable and (2) $2.50 is the cost to produce each meal. A markup percent on cost of 70% is needed. What should be the average price for a meal?

2. Leonard Hoffman grows fruit and vegetables to sell at his booth at the Farmer's Market. This weekend Leonard is going to feature 200 pounds of his prize avocados. He calculates his cost to be $.20 per pound. His markup percent will be 60% on cost. Leonard estimates that shipment damage will result in 3.5% of the crop being unsalable. How much should Leonard charge for each pound of avocados?

3. Cynthia Wong owns an ice cream parlor. She knows that 7% of the ice cream she buys will be lost. Some will melt, some will be dropped, and some will be given away for taste samples. She paid $1.72 per gallon for 500 gallons. Cynthia repackages the ice cream into quart containers (four quarts in a gallon). She needs a 125% markup on cost. Calculate the selling price for each quart.

4. Samuel Freeman sells fruit at a stand by a major highway. He just bought 250 pounds of peaches for $.12 per pound. He wants to mark the salable peaches up 100% on cost. Samuel expects to lose 6% of his purchase to spoilage, damage, and shoplifting. Determine Samuel's selling price for each pound of peaches.

8.8 Solutions to Practice Problems

1. Total meals served = $(5 \times 1,500) + (2 \times 2,500) = 12,500$
   $TC = 12,500 \times \$2.50 = \$31,250$
   $TS = \$31,250 \times (100\% + 70\%) = \$31,250 \times 170\% = \$53,125$
   Meals not salable = $12,500 \times 5\% = 625$
   Meals sold = $12,500 - 625 = 11,875$
   Price per meal $= \dfrac{\$53,125}{11,875} = \$4.47$

2. $TC = 200 \times \$.20 = \$40$
   $TS = \$40 \times (100\% + 60\%) = \$40 \times 160\% = \$64$
   Unsalable avocados = $200 \times 3.5\% = 7$
   Salable avocados = $200 - 7 = 193$
   Price per pound $= \dfrac{\$64}{193} = \$.33$

3. $TC = 500 \times \$1.72 = \$860$
   $TS = \$860 \times (100\% + 125\%) = \$860 \times 225\% = \$1,935$
   Lost ice cream = $500 \times 7\% = 35$
   Salable ice cream = $500 - 35 = 465$
   Number of quarts = $465 \times 4 = 1,860$
   Price per quart $= \dfrac{\$1,935}{1,860} = \$1.04$

4. $TC = 250 \times \$.12 = \$30$
   $TS = \$30 \times (100\% + 100\%) = \$30 \times 200\% = \$60$
   Lost peaches = $250 \times 6\% = 15$
   Salable peaches = $250 - 15 = 235$
   Price per pound $= \dfrac{\$60}{235} = \$.26$

LEARNING UNIT 6
MARKDOWNS

Markdowns are reductions from the original selling price. Markdowns result from a variety of causes such as seasonal changes, old or dated merchandise, competition, special promotions, and style changes.

8.9 Finding the Markdowns, Markdown Percents, and Selling Price after a Markdown or Series of Markdowns and Markups

A markdown can be calculated by finding the difference between the original price and the sale price. The **markdown percent** can then be calculated by dividing the markdown by the original selling price.

EXAMPLE   A retailer reduced the selling price for a cordless telephone from $128 to $96. Find the markdown and the markdown percent.

Solution   Find the markdown by subtracting the new selling price from the original selling price:

$$\$128 - 96 = \$32$$

Find the markdown percent by dividing the markdown by the original selling price:

$$\text{Markdown percent} = \frac{\text{markdown}}{\text{original selling price}} = \frac{\$32}{\$128} = 25\%$$

Frequently a retailer will decide that merchandise is to be marked down a certain percent and the sale price is to be determined after the markdown percent is calculated.

EXAMPLE   A retailer has decided to mark men's leather accessories down 25% from the original selling price. A billfold originally sold for $25. Find its sales price.

SOLUTION   Find the markdown by multiplying the original selling price by the markdown percent. (This is an application of the percentage formula.)

$$
\begin{array}{ccccc}
P & = & B & \times & R \\
\downarrow & & \downarrow & & \downarrow
\end{array}
$$

$$\text{Markdown} = \text{original selling price} \times \text{markdown percent}$$

$$= \$25 \times 25\% = \$6.25$$

Find the sales price by subtracting the markdown from the original selling price:

$$\$25 - 6.25 = \$18.75$$

Alternative Solution   Use the formula for finding an amount after a reduction:

$$100\% - 25\% = 75\%$$
$$\$25 \times 75\% = \$18.75$$

When business firms mark down merchandise, they often must make a series of markdowns before a product sells. Occasionally, a product will be marked up again between markdowns or after a sale ends. When a series of markdowns and markups is used, the markdown percent or the markup percent will be based on the *previous selling price*.

EXAMPLE   Kromer's Department Store had a one-week-long preholiday sale with a markdown percent of 25% off selected items. At the end of the week, merchandise that was not sold was marked back up 20%. After the holiday, every item in the store was put on sale at 1/3 off. Calculate the final price for a pair of jeans that had an original selling price of $26.95.

SOLUTION   *For the preholiday sale:*

Markdown = original selling price × markdown percent

= $26.95 × 25% = $6.74

New selling price = original selling price − markdown

= $26.95 − 6.74 = $20.21

For the price after the preholiday sale:

Markup = previous selling price × markup percent
= $20.21 × 20% = $4.04
New selling price = $20.21 + 4.04 = $24.25

For the price during the after-holiday sale:

Markdown = previous selling price × markdown percent

= $24.25 × 1/3 = $8.08
New selling price = $24.25 − 8.08 = $16.17

8.9 Practice Problems

1. With cold weather approaching, Bimble's Department Store is putting its swimsuits on sale. One suit originally sold for $60. It has been marked down 25%. Find the sale price.
2. A retailer has reduced the price of the one item of merchandise in his store from $95 to $50. Find the markdown percent.
3. The Rite Stitch Sewing Center had a sewing machine originally priced at $479. An area department store has the same brand on sale for $425. Rite Stitch's management decided to meet the competition's price. What was the necessary markdown percent?
4. In attempting to find the "right" price for one brand of blender, originally priced at $54.25, Cranston's went through a series of adjustments:
   5/25 - marked it down 20%
   7/30 - marked it down a further 15%
   8/25 - marked it up 10%
Find the final selling price for the blender.

8.9 Solutions to Practice Problems

1. $60 × 25% = $15

   $60 − 15 = $45

2. $95 − 50 = $45

   Markdown percent = $\dfrac{\$45}{\$95}$ = 47.4%

3. $479 − 425 = $54

   Markdown percent = $\dfrac{\$\,54}{\$479}$ = 11.3%

4. 5/25 $54.25 × 20% = $10.85

   $54.25 − 10.85 = $43.40

   7/30 $43.40 × 15% = $6.51
   $43.40 − 6.51 = $36.89

   8/25 $36.89 × 10% = $3.69
   $36.89 + 3.69 = $40.58

Page	Section Topic	Learning Concepts	Examples & Solution
258	**8.1** Calculating the Markup	The markup is the amount added to the cost of a good to arrive at the selling price.	A chair costing $189 will be sold for $329. How much is the amount of markup? $329 − 189 = $140
259	**8.2** Calculating the Markup Percent	**1.** When based on the cost, the amount of markup is divided by the cost amount. **2.** When based on the selling price, the amount of markup is divided by the selling price.	Selling price $90 − cost 60 = markup $30 **1.** $\dfrac{\text{Markup}}{\text{cost}} = \dfrac{\$30}{\$60} = 50\%$ **2.** $\dfrac{\text{Markup}}{\text{selling price}} = \dfrac{\$30}{\$90}$ $= 33\ 1/3\%$
		Converting markup percent ($M\%$) on selling price (SP) to markup percent ($M\%$) on cost (C).	35% on selling price $\dfrac{M\% \text{ on } SP}{100\% - (M\% \text{ on } SP)}$ $\dfrac{35\%}{100\% - 35\%} = \dfrac{35\%}{65\%}$ $= 53.8\%$
		Converting markup percent ($M\%$) on cost (C) to markup percent ($M\%$) on selling price (SP)	80% on cost $\dfrac{M\% \text{ on } C}{100\% + (M\% \text{ on } C)}$ $\dfrac{80\%}{100\% + 80\%} = \dfrac{80\%}{180\%}$ $= 44.4\%$
262	**8.3** Finding the Selling Price When the Cost and the Markup Percent on Cost Are Known	Use the following formula: $SP = C \times (100\% + M\% \text{ on } C)$	A company paid $50 for a toy. It will be marked up 70% on cost. What is the selling price? $SP = \$50 \times (100\% + 70\%)$ $= \$50 \times 170\%$ $= \$85$

		Use the following format:
		
		              Amount Percent
		    C
		$+\ M$
		$=\ SP$
		
		If the base is given, multiply it by the percent of the desired unknown amount. The product is the answer.
			A company paid $50 for a toy. It will be marked up 70% on cost. What is the selling price?
			
			            Amount Percent
			    C $50 *100%*
			$+\ M$ 70%
			$=\ SP$ 170%
			
			The base (C) is 100%
			
			$SP\% = 100\% + 70\% = 170\%$
			
			The desired unknown amount is the selling price. Its percent is 170%. Multiply the base amount ($50) by the percent of the desired unknown amount (170%):
			
			$\$50 \times 170\% = \$85$

Page	Section Topic	Learning Concepts	Examples & Solution
264	**8.4** Finding the Cost When the Selling Price and the Markup Percent on Cost Are Known	Use the following formula: $$C = \frac{SP}{100\% + M\% \text{ on } C}$$ Use the following format: $$\begin{array}{lcc} & \text{Amount} & \text{Percent} \\ C & & \\ + M & & \\ \hline = SP & & \end{array}$$ If the base is *not* given in the problem, divide the known amount by its percent. The quotient is the base.	A recliner sells for $472.50. It has been marked up 75% on cost. Find the cost? $$C = \frac{\$472.50}{100\% + 75\%}$$ $$= \frac{\$472.50}{175\%}$$ $$= \$270$$ A recliner sells for $472.50. It has been marked up 75% on cost. Find the cost. $$\begin{array}{lcc} & \text{Amount} & \text{Percent} \\ C & & 100\% \\ + M & & 75\% \\ \hline = SP & \$472.50 & 175\% \end{array}$$ The base (C) is 100% $$SP\% = 100\% + 75\% = 175\%$$ SP is known. Since it is not the base, divide it by its percent to find the base: $$\$472.50 \div 175\% = \$270$$
265	**8.5** Finding the Selling Price When the Cost Is Known and the Markup Percent Is on the Selling Price	Use the following formula: $$SP = \frac{C}{100\% - M\% \text{ on } SP}$$ Use the following format: $$\begin{array}{lcc} & \text{Amount} & \text{Percent} \\ SP & & \\ - C & & \\ \hline = M & & \end{array}$$ If the base is *not* given in the problem, divide the known amount by its percent. The quotient will be the base.	A pair of shoes cost $75. They were marked up 45% on the selling price. How much should the selling price be? $$SP = \frac{\$75}{100\% - 45\%}$$ $$SP = \frac{\$75}{55\%} = \$136.36$$ A pair of shoes cost $75. They were marked up 45% on the selling price. How much should the selling price be? $$\begin{array}{lcc} & \text{Amount} & \text{Percent} \\ SP & & 100\% \\ - C & \$75 & 55\% \\ \hline = M & & 45\% \end{array}$$ The base (SP) is 100% $$C\% = 100\% - 45\% = 55\%$$ C is known and it is not the base, so divide it by its percent to find the base: $$SP = \frac{\$75}{55\%} = \$136.36$$

QUICK REFERENCE **SUMMARY AND REVIEW**

Page	Section Topic	Learning Concepts	Examples & Solution

267	**8.6** Finding the Cost When the the Selling Price and the Markup Percent on the Selling Price Are Known	Use the following formula:
		
		$C = SP \times (100\% - M\% \text{ on } SP)$
		
		Use the following format:
		
		              Amount Percent
		SP
		$- C$ _____
		$= M$
		
		If the base is given in the problem, multiply it by the percent of the unknown amount. The product is the answer.
			Find the cost for a refrigerator that sells for $795 and has been marked up 40% on the selling price.
			
			$C = \$795 \times 100\% - 40\%$
			$C = \$795 \times 60\%$
			$C = \$477$
			
			Find the cost for a refrigerator that sells for $795 and has been marked up 40% on the selling price.
			
			           Amount Percent
			SP $\$795$ 100%
			$- C$ 60%
			$= M$ 40%
			
			The base (SP) is 100%
			
			$C\% = 100\% - 40\% = 60\%$
			
			SP is known and it is the base, so multiply SP by the cost percent to find the cost:
			
			$C = \$795 \times 60\% = \$477$

269	**8.7** Finding the Markup Percent of the Balance to Buy to Determine the Desired Average Markup Percent	An average markup must be determined over the long run for a firm to survive. Buyers work from a budget, and every purchase is recorded and subtracted from the total planned purchases. The difference is the balance to buy. By keeping careful records, business people always know where they stand and the markup percent necessary to achieve long-term success.	A buyer is working from a sales forecast that predicts her department will sell $50,000 worth of new merchandise in the coming month. The store needs to have an average 46% markup on the selling price. The buyer has already made $8,000 worth of purchases, which she plans to sell for $13,000. What markup percent must remaining purchases have to achieve the goal of 46% average markup on all merchandise? TPP = total planned purchases PTD = purchases to date BTB = balance to buy SP = selling price C = cost M = markup $M\%$ = markup percent Enter the information from the problem: SP $- C$ $= M$ $M\%$ TPP $\$50,000$ 46% $- PTD$ 13,000 8,000 $= BTB$ Calculate the C for the TPP: $C = SP \times (100\% - M\%)$ $C = \$50,000 \times (100\% - 46\%)$ $C = \$50,000 \times 54\%$ $C = \$27,000$

Chapter 8 Marketing Applications: Selling   281

Page	Section Topic	Learning Concepts	Examples & Solution

Calculate the *SP*, *C*, and *M* for the *BTB*:

	SP	−	C	=	M	M%
TPP	$50,000		$27,000			
− PTD	13,000		8,000			
BTB	$37,000		$19,000	=	$18,000	

Calculate the *M*% for the *BTB*:

$$M\% \text{ on } SP = \frac{M}{SP} = \frac{\$18,000}{\$37,000} = 48.6\%$$

| 275 | **8.8** Finding the Selling Price per Unit for Perishables | 1. Find the total cost (*TC*).

2. Find the total sales (*TS*) needed to determine the desired markup percent.

3. Find the total number expected to be sold.

4. Find the price that has to be charged for each unit expected to be sold. | A bakery prepares 60 dozen chocolate chip cookies. The cost is $.35 per dozen. The bakery wants a 130% markup on cost. It is expected that two dozen will be broken or will otherwise become unsalable. Find the selling price per dozen.

1. *TC* = $.35 × 60
     = $21

2. *TS* = *C* × (100% + *M*%)
     = $21 × (100% + 130%)
     = $21 × 230%
     = $48.30

3. Expected to be sold:
     60 dozen − 2 dozen = 58

4. Price per dozen:
     $48.30 ÷ 58 = $.83 |
| 277 | **8.9** Finding the Markdowns, Markdown Percents, and Selling Price after a Markdown or Series of Markdowns and Markups | *MD* = markdown

MD% = markdown percent

SP = original selling price

NSP = new *SP*

MD = *SP* × *MD*%

$MD\% = \dfrac{MD}{SP}$

NSP = *SP* − *MD* | Find the sale price for an item selling for $45 when it is marked down 40%.

MD = *SP* × *MD*%
MD = $45 × 40%
MD = $18
$45 − 18 = $27 |

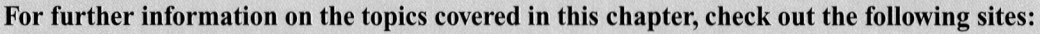

SURFING THE INTERNET

For further information on the topics covered in this chapter, check out the following sites:

http://www.eat2k.org/research/lohr_park.html

http://www.grossprofit.com/solutions_prod_high1.html

http://www.abovetheweather.com/home.asp

8.1

Calculate the markup in the following problems:

1. Juan Valendez paid $8 apiece for billfolds and sold them for $15.95. Determine the markup.

	Selling price	$15.95
−	cost	8.00
=	markup	$ 7.95

2. Sutagamo Department Store paid $3.50 per pair for designer hose. It sells the hose for $6.98. How much is the markup?

	Selling price	$6.98
−	cost	3.50
=	markup	$3.48

3. Nancy Matlin, a buyer for Bright Toys, paid $49.75 for a toy riding truck and sold it for $99.99. Find the markup.

	Selling price	$99.99
−	cost	49.75
=	markup	$50.24

4. Louise's Hats & Gloves bought 6 dozen pairs of fashionable, elbow-length gloves for $576. They were sold for $12.49 per pair. Find the markup per pair.

$6 \times 12 = 72$ pairs

$\dfrac{\$576}{72} = \$8$ cost each

	Selling price	$12.49
−	cost	8.00
=	markup	$ 4.49

8.2

Calculate the markup percent on cost or on the selling price in the following problems:

5. Wahoo McDaniels' Indian Jewelry Shop bought a handmade turquoise ring for $37.50. It will be sold for $75. Find the markup percent on cost.

	Selling price	$75.00
−	cost	37.50
=	markup	$37.50

$\dfrac{\$37.50}{\$37.50} = 1 = 100\%$

6. Naomi Jackson owns a small curio shop. She has been told by her wholesaler that a set of figurines is normally marked up 60% on cost. Naomi marks her merchandise up on the selling price. Use the formula for converting a markup percent on the cost to a markup percent on the selling price to find her markup percent.

$\text{Markup percent on selling price} = \dfrac{\text{markup percent on cost}}{100\% + \text{markup percent on cost}}$

$= \dfrac{60\%}{100\% + 60\%} = \dfrac{60\%}{160\%} = 37.5\%$

7. Eric Getzelbaum is a buyer. He recently bought television sets for $270 each. He plans to sell the sets for $525. Calculate the markup percent on the selling price.

	Selling price	$525
−	cost	270
=	markup	$255

$\dfrac{\$255}{\$525} = .486 = 48.6\%$

8. Sloan Overstreet has just opened a boutique. She paid $90 for an evening dress that she plans to sell for $180. Calculate the markup percent on the selling price. Sloan is unsure; she may want her markup percent to be based on cost. Use the conversion formula to find the markup percent on cost.

	Selling price	$180
−	cost	90
=	markup	$ 90

$\dfrac{\$90}{\$180} = 50\%$ on selling price

$\text{Markup percent on cost} = \dfrac{\text{markup percent on selling price}}{100\% - \text{markup percent on cost}}$

$= \dfrac{50\%}{100\% - 50\%} = \dfrac{50\%}{50\%} = 1 = 100\%$

8.3

Find the selling price when given the cost and the markup percent on cost in the following problems:

9. A desk cost $235. The markup percent on cost is 75%. Find the selling price.

Selling price = cost × (100% + markup percent)
= $235 × (100% + 75%)
= $235 × 175% = $411.25

10. Oglethorpe Hotel Group has novelty shops in its hotels. A hat bearing the Oglethorpe logo cost $2.75. It will be marked up 125% on cost. Find the selling price.

Selling price = cost × (100% + markup percent)
= $2.75 × (100% + 125%)
= $2.75 × 225% = $6.19

11. Gretta Garbraunski runs the gift shop in a hospital. Her markup percent on cost for merchandise is 80%. How much should she charge for a stuffed animal that cost her $7.14?

Selling price = cost × (100% + markup percent)
= $7.14 × (100% + 80%)
= $7.14 × 180% = $12.85

12. A shirt cost a retailer $13.50. It will have a 68% markup on cost. How much will the selling price be?

Selling price = cost × (100% + markup percent)
= $13.50 × (100% + 68%)
= $13.50 × 168% = $22.68

8.4

Find the cost when the selling price and the markup percent on cost are given in the following problems:

13. A factory outlet store sells women's slips for $14.50. It marks women's clothing up 55% on the cost. Find the cost.

$$\text{Cost} = \frac{\text{selling price}}{100\% + \text{markup percent on cost}} = \frac{\$14.50}{100\% + 55\%}$$
$$= \frac{\$14.50}{155\%} = \$9.35$$

14. Universal Lifetime Learning Center sells encyclopedias for $595. They have been marked up 130% on cost. Calculate the cost.

$$\text{Cost} = \frac{\text{selling price}}{100\% + \text{markup percent on cost}} = \frac{\$595}{100\% + 130\%}$$
$$= \frac{\$595}{230\%} = \$258.70$$

15. A set of external computer speakers sells for $49.95. The markup percent is 60% on cost. Find the cost.

$$\text{Cost} = \frac{\text{selling price}}{100\% + \text{markup percent on cost}} = \frac{\$49.95}{100\% + 60\%}$$
$$= \frac{\$49.95}{160\%} = \$31.22$$

16. Mitsuchi Electronics sells one model of clock radios for $24.79 after marking them up 70% on cost. Find the cost.

$$\text{Cost} = \frac{\text{selling price}}{100\% + \text{markup percent on cost}} = \frac{\$24.79}{100\% + 70\%}$$
$$= \frac{\$24.79}{170\%} = \$14.58$$

8.5

Find the selling price when the cost is known and the markup percent is on the selling price in the following problems:

17. Find the selling price for a set of dishes that cost $290 and are marked up 45% on the selling price.

$$\text{Selling price} = \frac{\text{cost}}{100\% - \text{markup percent on selling price}}$$
$$= \frac{\$290}{100\% - 45\%} = \frac{290}{55\%} = \$527.27$$

18. Marilyn Jolly purchased a cardiovascular workout machine for $450. She plans to mark it up 50% on the selling price. Find the selling price.

$$\text{Selling price} = \frac{\text{cost}}{100\% - \text{markup percent on selling price}}$$
$$= \frac{\$450}{100\% - 50\%} = \frac{\$450}{50\%} = \$900$$

19. Truly Beautiful Hair sells wigs that have been marked up 60% on the selling price. Find the selling price of one model that cost $115.

$$\text{Selling price} = \frac{\text{cost}}{100\% - \text{markup percent on selling price}}$$
$$= \frac{\$115}{100\% - \$60\%} = \frac{\$115}{40\%} = \$287.50$$

20. Justin Orlando is a boot buyer for the Western Connection. He recently purchased a snakeskin boot for $152. He will mark it up 40% on the selling price. Find the selling price.

$$\text{Selling price} = \frac{\text{cost}}{100\% - \text{markup percent on selling price}}$$
$$= \frac{\$152}{100\% - 40\%} = \frac{\$152}{60\%} = \$253.33$$

8.6

Find the cost when the selling price and the markup percent on the selling price are given in the following problems:

21. Find the cost of a printer that sells for $349 and is marked up 35% on the selling price.

Cost = selling price × (100% − markup percent on selling price)
= $349 (100% − 35%) = $349 × 65% = $226.85

22. Mickey Retelini owns Mickey's Fine Art Studio. He routinely marks paintings up 66% on the selling price. He is offering a painting by a local artist for $3,500. How much did he pay for it?

Cost = selling price × (100% − markup percent on selling price)
= $3,500 (100% − 66%) = $3,500 × 34% = $1,190

23. Star LaBlanc buys hairstyling supplies. She marks them up 55% on the selling price. One brand of hair spray has been marked to sell for $3.89. How much did the hair spray cost?

Cost = selling price × (100% − markup percent on selling price)
= $3.89 (100% − 55%) = $3.89 × 45% = $1.75

24. Palmer Jones sells a set of knives for $66. He marked them up 77% on the selling price. Find the cost.

Cost = selling price × (100% − markup percent on selling price)
= $66 (100% − 77%) = $66 × 23% = $15.18

8.7

Find the markup percent on the balance to buy to attain the desired average markup percent in the following problems. (Round monetary amounts to the nearest dollar.)

25. The budget for a department store this month requires that merchandise costing $450,000 be purchased. The store wants to maintain an average markup percent of 40% on the selling price. To date, purchases costing $28,000 have been made, which will sell for $40,000. What will be the markup percent on the selling price for the balance to buy to attain the desired average markup percent?

	Selling Price	− Cost	= Markup	Markup Percent
Total planned purchases	$750,000	$450,000		40% (*SP*)
− Purchases to date	$ 40,000	$ 28,000		
= balance to buy	$710,000	$422,000	$288,000	40.6%

Selling Price of Total Planned Purchases	Selling Price of Balance to Buy	Cost of Balance to Buy
$\dfrac{\$450,000}{100\% - 40\%} = \$750,000$	$750,000 −40,000 / $710,000	$450,000 − 28,000 / $422,000

$$\frac{\$450,000}{100\% - 40\%} = \$750,000$$

Selling Price of Balance to Buy
$750,000
− 40,000
$710,000

Cost of Balance to Buy
$450,000
− 28,000
$422,000

Markup on Balance to Buy
$710,000
− 422,000
$288,000

Markup Percent on Balance to Buy
$\dfrac{\$288,000}{\$710,000} = 40.6\%$

26. The bedroom department of a store has a budget to spend a total of $32,000 for merchandise. Voss Linen Collection marks soft goods up 65% on cost. In the past two days, buyers have made purchases costing $12,000, which will be sold for $20,000. Find the markup percent on cost for the balance to buy.

	Selling Price	− Cost	= Markup	Markup Percent
Total planned purchases	$52,800	$32,000		65% (*C*)
− Purchases to date	20,000	$12,000		
= balance to buy	32,800	20,000	$12,800	64%

Selling Price of Total Planned Purchases	Selling Price of Balance to Buy	Cost of Balance to Buy
$32,000 × 100% + 65% = $52,800	$52,800 −20,000 $32,800	$32,000 −12,000 $20,000

Markup on Balance to Buy
$32,800
−20,000
12,800

Markup Percent on Balance to Buy
$\dfrac{\$12,800}{20,000} = 64\%$

27. Myer's Fast Foods plans to buy paper products costing $44,000 to be sold for $85,000. Purchases to date have cost Myer's $8,000. Those purchases will be marked up 45% on the selling price. Find the markup percent on the selling price for the balance to buy that will be necessary to achieve the desired average markup percent.

	Selling Price	− Cost	= Markup	Markup Percent
Total planned purchases	$85,000	$44,000		
− Purchases to Date	14,545	8,000		45% (*SP*)
= balance to buy	$70,455	$36,000	$34,455	48.9%

Selling Price of Purchases to Date	Selling Price of Balance to Buy	Cost of Balance to Buy
$\dfrac{\$8,000}{100\% - 45\%} = \$14,545$	$85,000 −14,545 $70,455	$44,000 − 8,000 $36,000

Markup on Balance to Buy
$70,455
−36,000
$34,455

Markup Percent on Balance to Buy
$\dfrac{\$34,455}{\$70,455} = 48.9\%$

28. Lisa Stewart is a buyer for Folger's. She has been told to buy merchandise that will sell for $100,000 after being marked up 100% on cost. She began making purchases today and bought merchandise costing $24,000 that will be marked up 70% on cost for promotional purposes. What markup percent on cost will be required for the balance to buy to achieve the desired average markup percent?

	Selling Price	− Cost	= Markup	Markup Percent
Total planned purchases	$100,000	$50,000		100% (*C*)
− Purchases to date	40,800	24,000		70% (*C*)
= balance to buy	$ 59,200	$26,000	$33,200	127.7%

Cost of Total Planned Purchases	Selling Price of Purchases to Date	Selling Price of Balance to Buy
$\dfrac{\$100,000}{100\% + 100\%} = \$50,000$	$24,000 × 170% (100% + *M*%) $40,800	$100,000 − 40,800 $ 59,200

Cost of Balance to Buy
$50,000
−24,000
$26,000

Markup on Balance to Buy
$59,200
−26,000
$33,200

Markup Percent on Balance to Buy
$\dfrac{\$33,200}{\$26,000} = 127.7\%$

8.8

Find the selling price per unit for perishables in the following problems:

29. Quail's Bakery baked 20 dozen eclairs at a cost of $6.40 per dozen. The average waste is 10% of the total production. Quail's marks its goods up 70% on cost. Find the selling price needed for each eclair to attain that markup percent.

$TC = 20 \times \$6.40 = \$128$
$TS = \$128 (100\% + 70\%) = \$217.60$
Waste $= 20 \times 10\% = 2$
Eclairs sold $= 20 - 2 = 18$

Selling price per dozen $= \dfrac{\$217.60}{18} = \$12.09$

Selling price per eclair $= \dfrac{\$12.09}{12} = \$1.01$

30. The local drugstore decided to sell egg salad sandwiches. Enough egg salad is prepared each day to make 400 sandwiches at a cost of $1.50 per sandwich. It is expected that 8% of the egg salad will become unsalable. A markup percent of 120% on cost is needed. How much should be the price of each sandwich?

$TC = 400 \times \$1.50 = \$600$
$TS = \$600 (100\% + 120\%) = \$1,320$
Waste $= 400 \times 8\% = 32$
Sandwiches sold $= 400 - 32 = 368$

Selling price $= \dfrac{\$1,320}{368} = \$3.59$

31. Bread costs $.58 per loaf to bake. Six thousand loaves are baked with the expectation that 12% will not be sold. The desired markup percent on cost is 88%. Find the selling price per loaf.

$TC = 6,000 \times \$.58 = \$3,480$
$TS = \$3,400 \, (100\% + 88\%) = \$6,542.40$
Waste $= 6,000 \times 12\% = 720$
Loaves sold $= 6,000 - 720 = 5,280$
Selling price $= \dfrac{\$6,542.40}{5,280} = \$1.24$

32. A Czechoslovakian pastry (kolache) costs $.50 each to prepare. Fifty dozen will be baked, and it is expected that 6% will be lost due to spoilage. The Czech bakery wants to maintain a markup percent of 75% on cost. How much is the selling price for each kolache?

$TC = (50 \times 12) \, \$.50 = 600 \times \$.50 = \$300$
$TS = \$300 \, (100\% + 75\%) = \$525$
Waste $= 600 \times 6\% = 36$
Kolache dozens sold $= 600 - 36 = 564$
Selling price $= \dfrac{\$525}{564} = \$.93$ each

8.9

Find the markdown, markdown percent, and/or new selling price in the following problems:

33. Jodhpurs (breeches worn while horseback riding) originally sold for $147. When the tack shop went out of business at the riding stable, the breeches were marked down 1/3. What was the new selling price?

$\$147 \times 1/3 = \$49$
$\$147 - 49 = \$98$

34. Management has decided to reduce the price of a sport coat from $275 to $214.50. What is the markdown percent?

$\$275 - 214.50 = \$60.50$ amount of markdown
Markdown percent $= \dfrac{\text{markdown}}{\text{original price}} = \dfrac{\$60.50}{\$275} = 22\%$

35. Kent's Sporting Goods sells clothing for all sports. Chuck Kent was told by a wholesaler that one name-brand tennis dress was going out of style. Chuck has been selling the style for $59.95 but marked them down 20%. The following weekend, the dress was worn in competition by the winner of the French Open. Chuck immediately advertised that fact and marked the dress up 30%. Find the final selling price.

$\$59.95 \times 20\% = \$11.99$
$\$59.95 - 11.99 = \$47.96$
$\$47.96 \times 30\% = \$14.39$
$\$47.96 + 14.39 = \$62.35$

36. Julianna's Catering Service had been charging $15 per person for a package service for 12 or less. However, a new caterer advertised the same basic service for $12. Find the markdown percent necessary to meet the competitive price.

$\$15 - \$12 = \$3$ markdown
$\dfrac{\$3}{\$15} = 20\%$

<table>
<tr><td>

**CHAPTER REVIEW
PROBLEMS**

</td><td>

Answers to odd-numbered problems are given in Appendix A.

</td></tr>
</table>

Drill Problems

Calculate the markup in problems 1 through 5.

	Selling Price	Cost	Markup
1.	$ 95	$ 50	$ 45
2.	934	584	350
3.	720	248	472
4.	34	17	17
5.	3	1.75	1.25

Complete the following table, filling in the amounts for all of the unknowns in problems 6 through 15:

	Base	Selling Price	Cost	Markup	Markup Percent
6.	Selling price	$84	$54	$30	35.7%
7.	Cost	3.08	2.10	.98	46.7%
8.	Selling price	.98	.36	.62	63.3%
9.	Selling price	63	39	24	38.1%
10.	Cost	12	5	7	140%

11.	Cost	35	17.50	17.50	100%
12.	Selling price	21.60	10.45	11.15	51.6%
13.	Selling price	9.80	4.90	4.90	50%
14.	Selling price	595	358	237	39.8%
15.	Cost	105.46	64.93	40.53	62.4%

Use either the formula for converting a markup percent on cost to a markup percent on the selling price, or the formula for converting a markup percent on the selling price to a markup percent on cost in problems 16 through 20.

	Markup Percent on Cost	Markup Percent on Selling Price
16.	50%	$33\frac{1}{3}$%
17.	$233\frac{1}{3}$%	70%
18.	25%	20%
19.	40%	28.6%
20.	$566\frac{2}{3}$%	85%

Complete the following table, filling in the amounts for all of the unknowns in problems 21 through 28:

	Base	Selling Price	Cost	Markup	Markup Percent
21.	Cost	$128	$80	$48	60%
22.	Cost	9.90	6	3.90	65%
23.	Cost	750	500	250	50%
24.	Cost	48	24	24	100%
25.	Cost	60	35.29	24.71	70%
26.	Cost	8.20	3.73	4.47	120%
27.	Cost	.59	.32	.27	85%
28.	Cost	490	227.91	262.09	115%

Complete the following table, filling in the amounts for all of the unknowns in problems 29 through 36:

	Base	Selling Price	Cost	Markup	Markup Percent
29.	Selling price	$66.67	$40	$26.67	40%
30.	Selling price	19.23	12.50	6.73	35%
31.	Selling price	1,600	800	800	50%
32.	Selling price	8.36	4.60	3.76	45%
33.	Selling price	20	9.60	10.40	52%
34.	Selling price	36.90	14.76	22.14	60%
35.	Selling price	.79	.41	.38	48%
36.	Selling price	268	187.60	80.40	30%

Complete the following table, filling in the amounts for all of the unknowns in problems 37 through 42:

	Base	Selling Price	Cost	Markup	Markup Percent
37.	Cost	$27.03	$15.90	$11.13	70%
38.	Selling price	1.33	.60	.73	55%
39.	Cost	16.17	9.24	6.93	75%
40.	Selling price	45	22.50	22.50	50%
41.	Selling price	7.42	4.16	3.26	44%
42.	Cost	1.99	1.18	.81	68%

In problems 43 through 46, find the markup percent for the balance to buy. All markup percents are based on the selling price.

43.

	Selling Price	− Cost	= Markup	Markup Percent
Total planned purchases	$360,000			40% (SP)
− purchases to date	40,000	$30,000		
= balance to buy	$_____	$_____	$_____	____% (SP)

Cost of *TPP*

$SP \times (100\% - M\%)$
$360,000 \times 60\% = \$216,000$

Selling Price of Balance to Buy
$360,000
−40,000
$320,000

Cost of Balance to Buy
$216,000
−30,000
$186,000

Markup of Balance to Buy
$320,000
−186,000
$134,000

Markup Percent of Balance to Buy
$M\% = \dfrac{\$134,000}{\$320,000} = 41.9\%$

44.

	Selling Price	− Cost	= Markup	Markup Percent
Total planned purchases	$150,000	$80,000		
− purchases to date		6,000		50% (SP)
= balance to buy	$_____	$_____	$_____	____% (SP)

Selling Price of Purchases to Date

$SP = \dfrac{cost}{(100\% - M\%)}$

$SP = \dfrac{\$6,000}{50\%} = \$12,000$

Selling Price of Balance to Buy
$150,000
− 12,000
$138,000

Cost of Balance to Buy
$80,000
− 6,000
$74,000

Markup of Balance to Buy
$138,000
−74,000
$ 64,000

Markup Percent of Balance to Buy
$M\% = \dfrac{\$64,000}{\$138,000} = 46.4\%$

45.

	Selling Price	− Cost	= Markup	Markup Percent
Total planned purchases		$210,000		30% (SP)
− purchases to date	$100,000	50,000		
= balance to buy	$_____	$_____	$_____	____% (SP)

Selling Price of Total Planned Purchases

$SP = \dfrac{cost}{(100\% - M\%)}$

$SP = \dfrac{\$210,000}{70\%} = \$300,000$

Selling Price of Balance to Buy
$300,000
−100,000
$200,000

Cost of Balance to Buy
$210,000
− 50,000
$160,000

Markup of Balance to Buy
$200,000
−160,000
$ 40,000

Markup Percent of Balance to Buy
$M\% = \dfrac{\$ 40,000}{\$200,000} = 20\%$

46.

	Selling Price	− Cost	= Markup	Markup Percent
Total planned purchases	$68,000	$40,000		
− purchases to date	13,000			42% (*SP*)
= balance to buy	$_____	$_____	$_____	____% (*SP*)

Cost of Purchases to Date	Selling Price of Balance to Buy	Cost of Balance to Buy
	$68,000	$40,000
SP × (100% − *M*%)	−13,000	−7,540
$13,000 × 58% = $7,540	$55,000	$32,460

Markup of Balance to Buy	Markup Percent of Balance to Buy
$55,000	
−32,460	$M\% = \dfrac{\$22{,}540}{\$55{,}000} = 41.0\%$
$22,540	

In problems 47 through 50, find the markup percent for the balance to buy. All markup percents are based on cost (round to the nearest dollar if necessary.)

47.

	Selling Price	− Cost	= Markup	Markup Percent
Total planned purchases	$140,000	$_____		80% (*C*)
− purchases to date	70,000	35,000		
= balance to buy	$_____	$_____	$_____	____% (*C*)

Cost of *TPP*	Selling Price of Balance to Buy	Cost of Balance to Buy
$C = \dfrac{SP}{100\% + M\%}$	$140,000	$77,778
	−70,000	−35,000
$= \dfrac{\$140{,}000}{180\%} = \$77{,}778$	70,000	$42,778

Markup of Balance to Buy	Markup Percent of Balance to Buy
$70,000	
−42,778	$\dfrac{\$27{,}222}{\$42{,}778} = 63.6\%$
$27,222	

48.

	Selling Price	− Cost	= Markup	Markup Percent
Total planned purchases	$90,000	$60,000		
− purchases to date		10,000		100% (*C*)
= balance to buy	$_____	$_____	$_____	____% (*C*)

Selling Price of Purchases to Date	Selling Price of Balance to Buy	Cost of Balance to Buy
SP = Cost × (100% + *M*%)	$90,000	$60,000
= $10,000 × 200%	−20,000	−10,000
= $20,000	$70,000	$50,000

Markup of Balance to Buy	Markup Percent of Balance to buy
$70,000	
−50,000	$\dfrac{\$20{,}000}{\$50{,}000} = 40\%$
$20,000	

49.

	Selling Price	− Cost	= Markup	Markup Percent
Total planned purchases		$800,000		60% (C)
− purchases to date	$ 60,000	35,000		
= balance to buy	$_____	$_____	$_____	____% (C)

Selling Price of
Total Planned Purchase
$SP = \text{cost} \times (100\% + M\%)$
$= \$800,000 \times 160\%$
$= \$1,280,000$

Selling Price of
Balance to Buy
$1,280,000
−   60,000
$1,220,000

Cost of
Balance to Buy
$800,000
−   35,000
$765,000

Markup of
Balance to Buy
$1,220,000
−   765,000
$ 455,000

Markup Percent
of Balance to Buy
$\dfrac{\$455,000}{\$765,000} = 59.5\%$

50.

	Selling Price	− Cost	= Markup	Markup Percent
Total planned purchases	$44,000	$20,000		
− purchases to date	6,600			120% (C)
= balance to buy	$_____	$_____	$_____	____% (C)

Cost of
Purchases to Date
$C = \dfrac{\text{selling price}}{M\% + 100\%}$
$= \dfrac{\$6,600}{220\%} = \$3,000$

Selling Price of
Balance to Buy
$44,000
−   6,600
$37,400

Cost of
Balance to Buy
$20,000
−   3,000
$17,000

Markup of
Balance to Buy
$37,400
−17,000
$20,400

Markup Percent
of Balance to Buy
$\dfrac{\$20,400}{\$17,000} = 120\%$

Find the selling price on cost for the perishables in problems 51 through 54.

51.

Number Produced	Cost Per Unit	Desired Markup Percent	Total Cost	Total Sales	Unsalable	Selling Price
25 dozen	$2.15	100%	$_____	$_____	10%	$____(dz)

$TC = 25 \times \$2.15 = \$53.75$
$TS = \$53.75(100\% + 100\%) = \$107.50$
Unsalable $= 25 \times 10\% = 2.5$ dozen
Salable $= 25 - 2.5 = 22.5$ dozen
Price per dozen $= \dfrac{\$107.50}{22.5} = \$4.78$

52.

Number Produced	Cost Per Unit	Desired Markup Percent	Total Cost	Total Sales	Unsalable	Selling Price
3,000	$.75	85%	$_____	$_____	5%	$____(ea)

$TC = 3,000 \times \$.75 = \$2,250$
$TS = \$2,250(100\% + 85\%) = \$4,162.50$
Unsalable $= 3,000 \times 5\% = 150$
Salable $= 3,000 - 150 = 2,850$
Price $= \dfrac{\$4,162.50}{2,850} = \$1.46$

53.

Number Produced	Cost Per Unit	Desired Markup Percent	Total Cost	Total Sales	Unsalable	Selling Price
12 dozen	$6.50	70%	$_____	$_____	1 dozen	$____(ea)

$TC = 12 \times 12 = 144$ units $144 \times \$6.50 = \$936$
$TS = \$936 (100\% + 70\%) = \$1,591.20$
Unsalable = 1 dozen, or 12 units
Salable = 144 − 12 = 132 units
Price of each $= \dfrac{\$1,591.20}{132} = \$12.05$

54.

Number Produced	Cost Per Unit	Desired Markup Percent	Total Cost	Total Sales	Unsalable	Selling Price
2,000	$2.50	120%	$_____	$_____	100	$____(ea)

$TC = 2,000 \times \$2.50 = \$5,000$
$TS = \$5,000 (100\% + 120\%) = \$11,000$
Unsalable = 100
Salable = 2,000 − 100 = 1,900
Price $= \dfrac{\$11,000}{1,900} = \$5.79$

Fill in the blanks in the markdown problems 55 through 58.

	Original Selling Price	Markdown Percent	Markdown	New Selling Price
55.	$ 100	50%	$ 50	$ 50
56.	34	20%	6.80	27.20
57.	9.98	10%	1	8.98
58.	2,545	30%	763.50	1,781.50

Word Problems

59. Find the markup on a chair that cost $90 and is priced to sell for $160.

Selling price $160
−   cost   90
=   markup $ 70

60. Calculate the markup percent on cost for a pair of scissors that costs $8 and sells for $14.

Selling price $14
−   cost   8
=   markup $ 6 $\dfrac{\$6}{\$8} = 75\%$

61. Calculate the markup percent on the selling price for a dress that costs $129 and sells for $258.

Selling price $258
−   cost   129
=   markup $129 $\dfrac{\$129}{\$258} = 50\%$

62. A table costs $74. It is to be marked up 88% on the cost. How much is the selling price?

100% $ 74
+88%   ×188%
188% Selling price percent $139.12 Selling price

63. Determine the cost of a trombone that sells for $698 and is marked up 80% on cost.

100%
+80%
180% Selling price percent $\dfrac{\$698}{180\%} = \$387.78$ Cost

64. Find the cost of a book that sells for $54 and is marked up 45% on the selling price.

100% $ 54
− 45%   × 55%
55% Cost percent $ 29.70 Cost

65. Compute the selling price of a disc holder that cost $4.35 and will be marked up 60% on the selling price.

100%
−60%
40% Cost percent $\dfrac{\$4.35}{40\%} = \$10.88$ Selling price

66. Abrocrombie's budget this month is to buy goods that will sell for $240,000 and will be marked up 50% on the selling price. The buyers have purchased $100,000 worth of merchandise that will be sold for $178,000. What markup percent on the balance to buy will be required to attain the desired 50% average markup?

	Selling Price	− Cost	= Markup	Markup Percent
Total planned purchases − purchases to date = balance to buy				

Cost of *TPP*
$C = SP(100\% − M\%)$
$\quad = \$240,000 \times 50\%$
$\quad = \$120,000$

Selling price of Balance to Buy	Cost of Balance to Buy	Markup of Balance to Buy
$240,000	$120,000	$62,000
−178,000	−100,000	−20,000
$62,000	$20,000	$42,000

Markup Percent
of Balance to Buy
$M\% = \dfrac{\$42,000}{\$62,000} = 67.7\%$

67. Jorge Baakan was given a budget to buy merchandise costing $80,000. He has made purchases costing $16,000 that will be sold for $28,000. The average markup needed is 80% on cost. What markup percent on the balance to buy will be necessary to meet this goal?

	Selling Price	− Cost	= Markup	Markup Percent
Total planned purchases − purchases to date = balance to buy				

Selling Price of
Total Planned Purchases
$SP = C(100\% + M\%)$

$SP = 80,000 \times 180\%$
$\quad = 144,000$

Selling Price of Balance to Buy	Cost of Balance to Buy	Markup of Balance to Buy
$144,000	$80,000	$116,000
−28,000	−16,000	−64,000
$116,000	$64,000	$52,000

Markup percent
of balance to buy
$M\% = \dfrac{\$52,000}{\$64,000} = 81.3\%$

68. Vivian Tanner owns a diner. She has enough dessert prepared to serve 600 customers. The average number of unsalable desserts is expected to be 8% of the total prepared. Each dessert costs $.95. Vivian desires a markup percent of 105% on cost. How much will be the price of each dessert?
$TC = 600 \times \$.95 = \$570$
$TS = \$570\,(100\% + 105\%) = \$1,168.50$
Waste $= 600 \times 8\% = 48$
Desserts sold $= 600 − 48 = 552$
Selling price $= \dfrac{\$1,168.50}{552} = \$2.12$

69. Susan Winters manages a jewelry store. She recently lowered the selling price of a bracelet from $84 to $71.40. Find the markdown percent.

$84.00
−71.40
$12.60

$\dfrac{\$12.60}{\$84} = 15\%$

70. A bedspread originally sold for $99. It is to be marked down 15%. What will the new selling price be?

$ 99	$99.00
×15%	−14.85
$14.85	$84.15

71. A computer software program has been marked up 70% on cost. The store has changed its markup policy and is now marking all software up on the selling price. Find the markup percent on the selling price for future orders of the software.

$\dfrac{70\%}{100\% + 70\%} = 41.2\%$

72. Stumanhaufer Haberdashery has always marked up merchandise on cost. A tie wholesaler has suggested that to be competitive, new tie purchases should be marked up 25% on the selling price. What should the markup percent on cost be?

$$\frac{25\%}{100\% - 25\%} = 33\frac{1}{3}\%$$

73. Find the selling price for an automobile that cost $15,900 and has been marked up 70% on cost.

100%	C%	$15,900
+70%	M%	×170%
170%	SP%	$27,030

74. Getty Variety Store sells one brand of flashlight for $8.29. It has been marked up 65% on cost. Find the cost.

100%	C%
+65%	M%
165%	SP%

$$\frac{\$8.29}{165\%} = \$5.02 \text{ cost}$$

75. A pair of women's shorts sells for $22.50. The markup percent is 38% on the selling price. How much did the shorts cost?

100%	SP%	$22.50
−38%	M%	×62%
62%	C%	$13.95

76. Get and Go Convenience Store pays $1.98 for a magazine it marks up 60% on the selling price. What is the selling price for the magazine?

100%	SP%
−60%	M%
40%	C%

$$\frac{\$1.98}{40\%} = \$4.95$$

77. Calculate the markup percent on cost for a CD player that cost $195 and is being sold for $398. Use the formula to convert the markup percent on cost to a markup percent on the selling price.

$398
−195
$203

$$\frac{\$203}{\$195} = 104\% \text{ on cost} \qquad \frac{104\%}{100\% + 104\%} = 51\% \text{ on selling price}$$

78. Find the markup percent on the selling price for a lawnmower costing $275 that has been marked to sell for $498. Use the formula to convert the markup percent on the selling price to a markup percent on cost.

$498
−275
$223

$$\frac{\$223}{\$498} = 44.8\% \text{ on selling price} \qquad \frac{44.8\%}{100\% - 44.8\%} = 81.2\% \text{ on cost}$$

79. Jordan's Shoe Store has a patent leather loafer that sells for $129 and is marked up 80% on the cost. Find the cost.

100%	C%
+ 80%	M%
180%	SP%

$$\frac{\$129}{180\%} = \$71.67$$

80. Laymont's Recliners has a model that cost $133. It will be marked up 100% on cost. Find the selling price.

100%	C%	$133
+100%	M%	×200%
200%	SP%	$266

81. Jacques sells underwater diving equipment. A snorkel that cost $14.95 will be marked up 55% on the selling price. Find the selling price.

100%	SP%
−55%	M%
45%	C%

$$\frac{\$14.95}{45\%} = \$33.22$$

82. A basketball is marked up 42% on the selling price. It is sold for $24.95. How much did it cost?

100%	SP%	$24.95
−42%	M%	× 58%
58%	C%	$14.47

83. Pizza Place buys and prepares ingredients for 200 medium pepperoni pizzas at a cost of $3.79 each. It will lose 12 pizzas to spillage, sampling, slow sales, and other assorted causes. A markup percent of 90% on cost is required. What will each pizza need to be sold for to reach the needed markup percent?

$TC = 200 \times \$3.79 = \$758$
$TS = \$758 (100\% + 90\%) = \$1,440.20$
Pizzas sold $= 200 - 12 = 188$
Selling price $= \dfrac{\$1,440.20}{188} = \$7.66$

✓ ENRICHMENT
PROBLEMS

84. The Bridal Boutique has a budget to purchase gowns costing $55,000 that will be marked up 56% on the selling price. To date, the buyer has spent $10,000 for gowns that will be used in a special promotion and only marked up 40% on the selling price. Find the balance to buy markup percent on the selling price that will now be necessary to average 56%. (Round all answers to the nearest dollar.)

	Selling Price	− Cost	= Markup	Markup Percent
Total planned purchases				
− purchases to date				
= balance to buy				

Selling Price
of *TPP*

$$SP = \frac{cost}{100\% - M\%}$$

$$= \frac{\$55,000}{44\%} = \$125,000$$

Selling Price of
Purchases to Date

$$SP = \frac{cost}{100\% - M\%}$$

$$= \frac{\$10,000}{60\%} = \$16,667$$

Selling Price of
Balance to Buy

$125,000$
$\underline{-16,667}$
$\$108,333$

Cost of
Balance to Buy
$\$55,000$
$\underline{-10,000}$
$\$45,000$

Markup of
Balance to Buy
$\$108,333$
$\underline{-45,000}$
$\$ 63,333$

Markup Percent
of Balance to Buy

$$M\% = \frac{M}{SP} = \frac{\$ 63,333}{\$108,333} = 58.5\%$$

85. The Tack Shop sells horse equipment. It has a budget to reach total saddle sales of $28,000 at an average markup percent of 112% on cost. Julia Maplethorpe placed orders for saddles costing $4,000 that will be marked up 120% on cost. Find the markup percent on the balance to buy that will result in reaching the desired average markup percent. (Round all answers to the nearest dollar.)

	Selling Price	− Cost	= Markup	Markup Percent
Total planned purchases				
− purchases to date				
= balance to buy				

Cost of *TPP*

$$SP = \frac{SP}{100\% + M\%}$$

$$= \frac{\$28,000}{212\%} = \$13,208$$

Selling Price of
Purchases to Date

$$SP = cost (100\% + M\%)$$
$$= \$4,000 \times 220\%$$
$$= \$8,800$$

Selling Price of
Balance to Buy

$\$28,000$
$\underline{- 8,800}$
$\$19,200$

Cost of
Balance to Buy
$\$13,208$
$\underline{-4,000}$
$\$ 9,208$

Markup of
Balance to Buy
$\$19,200$
$\underline{-9,208}$
$\$ 9,992$

Markup Percent
of Balance to Buy

$$M\% = \frac{M}{C} = \frac{\$ 9,992}{\$ 9,208} = 108.5\%$$

CRITICAL THINKING GROUP PROJECT

Markol's Department Store has forecast its sales for the women's and men's clothing departments for the spring selling season. Spring sales of women's clothing are forecast to total $890,000, and men's clothing sales are forecast to be $538,500. The inventory of women's clothing that will be available for the spring season cost $57,000 and was originally marked up 45% on the selling price. For the men's clothing department, the inventory cost $32,000 and was marked up 42% on the selling price. Both the men's and women's clothing inventory has been marked down 20%.

Buyers have already purchased women's clothing that cost $112,500. It has been marked up 48% on the selling price. Men's clothing that cost $74,000 has been purchased. Its markup percent is 44% on the selling price.

Markol's wants to maintain a cumulative markup of 55% on the selling price for women's clothing and 47.5% on men's clothing. Calculate the necessary markup percents on the remaining purchases to be made for both men's and women's clothes. (Round all of your answers to the nearest dollar.)

Note: A cumulative markup is similar to an average markup. The only difference is that the beginning inventory is considered in the calculations. To calculate the answer, treat the inventory on hand as you treat the purchases to date.

WOMEN'S CLOTHING

	Selling Price	− Cost	= Markup	Markup Percent
Total planned purchases	$890,000	$400,500		55.0%
− beginning inventory	82,909	57,000		
− purchases to date	216,346	112,500		
= balance to buy	$590,745	$231,000	$359,745	60.9%

MEN'S CLOTHING

	Selling Price	− Cost	= Markup	Markup Percent
Total planned purchases	$538,000	$282,450		47.5%
− beginning inventory	44,138	32,000		
− purchases to date	132,143	74,000		
= balance to buy	$361,719	$176,450	$185,269	51.2%

Answers to all exercises are in Appendix A.

1. Explain why most retailers base the markup percent on the selling price. **W**

   At the end of an accounting cycle, most retailers analyze their income statements. One analysis method is to divide all amounts by net sales. This analysis results in the markup percent on the selling price being calculated on a regular basis. Thus, basing the markup percent on the selling price makes comparisons easier.

2. What are perishables? **W**

   Perishables are merchandise that must be sold rapidly before it spoils and becomes unsalable.

3. Differentiate between the markup percent on an individual item of merchandise and the average markup percent. **W**

   An individual item's markup percent will depend on many factors, including competition, whether the item is a luxury good or a staple good, and the demand for the item. The average markup percent is the markup rate a business needs to average on all merchandise sold over a period of time, usually one year.

4. A knife costs $3.50 and sells for $7. What is the markup percent on the selling price?

$$\begin{array}{r} \$7.00 \\ -3.50 \\ \hline \$3.50 \end{array} \qquad \frac{\$3.50}{\$7.00} = 50\%$$

5. A buyer plans to purchase merchandise costing a total of $50,000 for the upcoming season. This merchandise will be marked up an average of 42% on the selling price. He has so far purchased merchandise costing $10,000 to be used as an enticement for the store's customers. It has been marked up 35% on the selling price. What must the markup percent on the selling price be on the remaining purchases to achieve the desired average markup percent? (Round all answers to the nearest dollar.)

	Selling Price	− Cost	= Markup	Markup Percent
Total planned purchases				
− purchases to date				
= balance to buy				

Selling price of *TPP*
$$SP = \frac{cost}{100\% - M\%}$$
$$= \frac{\$50,000}{58\%} = \$86,207$$

Selling Price of Purchases to Date
$$SP = \frac{cost}{100\% - M\%}$$
$$= \frac{\$10,000}{65\%} = \$15,385$$

Selling Price of Balance to Buy
$$\begin{array}{r} \$86,207 \\ -15,385 \\ \hline \$70,822 \end{array}$$

Cost of Balance to Buy
$$\begin{array}{r} \$50,000 \\ -10,000 \\ \hline \$40,000 \end{array}$$

Markup of Balance to Buy
$$\begin{array}{r} \$70,822 \\ -40,000 \\ \hline \$30,822 \end{array}$$

Markup Percent of Balance to Buy
$$M\% = \frac{M}{SP} = \frac{\$30,822}{\$70,822} = 43.5\%$$

6. A shirt costs $15 and sells for $22. Find the markup percent on cost.

$$\begin{array}{r} \$22 \\ -15 \\ \hline \$\ 7 \end{array} \qquad \frac{\$7}{\$15} = 46.7\%$$

7. A dress sells for $55 and is marked up 30% on the selling price. What is the cost?

$$\begin{array}{r} 100\% \\ -30\% \\ \hline 70\% \end{array} \qquad \begin{array}{r} \$55.00 \\ \times\ 70\% \\ \hline \$38.50 \end{array}$$

8. Stockings are purchased for $122.40 a gross (12 dozen pairs). They are marked up 65% on cost. What is the selling price per pair?

$$12 \times 12 = 144 \text{ pairs} \qquad \frac{\$122.40}{144} = \$.85 \text{ cost per pair}$$

$$\begin{array}{ll} 100\%\ \ C\% & \$\ .85 \\ +65\%\ \ M\% & \times 165\% \\ \hline 165\%\ \ SP\% & \$1.40 \text{ per pair} \end{array}$$

9. Merchandise of $25,000 has been purchased to sell for $40,000. Remaining purchases to be made will cost $50,000. The desired average markup percent on cost is 60%. What must the markup percent on cost be for the remaining purchases? (Remember that the average markup percent is on total purchases to be made.)

	Selling Price	− Cost	= Markup	Markup Percent
Total planned purchases − purchases to date = balance to buy				

Cost of *TPP*	Selling Price of *TPP*	Selling Price of Balance to Buy	Markup of Balance to Buy
$ 50,000	$SP = C(100\% + M\%)$	$120,000	$80,000
+25,000	= $75,000 × 160%	−40,000	−50,000
$ 75,000	= $120,000	$ 80,000	$30,000

Markup percent
of Balance to Buy
$\frac{\$30,000}{\$50,000} = 60\%$

10. A retailer has been using a 48% markup on the selling price. If it changes to marking merchandise up on the cost, what will its markup percent be?

$\frac{48\%}{100\% - 48\%} = 92.3\%$

11. A chair costs $56 and sells for $75.60. Find the markup percent on cost.

$75.60
−56.00
$19.60

$\frac{\$19.60}{\$56.00} = 35\%$

12. Candy sells for $17.50 per box and is marked up 50% on cost. How much is the cost?

100%   C%
+50%   M%
150%   SP%

$\frac{\$17.50}{150\%} = \$11.67$

13. Fudge costs $1.88 per pound to make. Fran Micovich mixes up 50 pounds to be sold at her booth in the mall. She usually cannot sell 5% of her production. Fran wants a markup percent on cost of 135%. How much should she charge per pound?

$TC = 50 \times \$1.88 = \$94$
$TS = \$94(100\% + 135\%) = \$220.90$
Waste = 50 × 5% = 2.5
Fudge sold = 50 − 2.5 = 47.5
Selling price = $\frac{\$220.90}{47.5} = \$4.65$

14. Lipstick costs $1.56 per tube. It is marked up 75% on the selling price. Find the selling price.

100%   SP%
−75%   M%
25%   C%

$\frac{\$1.56}{25\%} = \$6.24$

15. Irwin Coffee sells cleaning equipment that has been marked up 100% on the cost. He is changing the base to the selling price. How much will the markup percent be on the selling price?

$\frac{100\%}{100\% + 100\%} = 50\%$

16. Ties sell for $27.50 each and cost $216 per dozen. How much is the markup percent on the selling price?

$\frac{\$216}{12} = \$18$ Cost

$27.50
−18.00
$ 9.50 Markup

$\frac{\$ 9.50}{\$27.50} = 34.5\%$

17. A wheel cover cost $22 and sells for $49.95. How much is the markup?

$49.95 − 22 = $27.95

18. A broach has been marked up 80% on cost. It sells for $1,575. How much did it cost?

100%   C%
+80%   M%
180%   SP%

$\frac{\$1,575}{180\%} = \$875$

19. Arnolds' Drug Store was selling a cold remedy for $5.89. When sales were too slow, it was marked down 22%. Find the new selling price.

$5.89
×22%
$1.30

$5.89
−1.30
$4.59

20. A new 12 pack of a 12 oz. bottle of sparkling water was originally priced at $13.20. Slow sales resulted in a markdown percent of 15%. Later, an advertising campaign was successful and the price was marked up an additional 7.5%. Recently, a promotion has resulted in another 20% markdown. Find the final selling price for the 12 pack.

$13.20 × 15% = $1.98
$13.20 − 1.98 = $11.22
$11.22 × 7.5% = $ .84
$11.22 + .84 = $12.06
$12.06 × 20% = $2.41
$12.06 − 2.41 = $9.65

APPLICATION 1

In Chapter 7, Application 2, you prepared an invoice to be sent to the Springfield Department Store for a variety of sporting goods purchased from Mason's Wholesale Sporting Goods. That order has been received, and the sporting equipment must be marked up and priced to be sold to customers.

In this application, you will use the spreadsheet form designed by Springfield to determine the selling price of individual items received from a supplier. When you open Ch08App1 from your Excel Spreadsheet Application disk, it will appear as shown here:

Springfield Department Store

2617 Main Street
Box 219
Springfield, Maryland 58109
Telephone: 301-555-2158   FAX: 301-555-3498

PRICE CALCULATIONS

Product Description	Qty. in Cost Unit	Unit Cost	Item Cost	Markup Percent	Base	Item Selling Price
Head rackets			#DIV/0!			#DIV/0!
Wilson 1200 irons, 2-PW			#DIV/0!			#DIV/0!
Wilson pro-lite golf bags			#DIV/0!			#DIV/0!
Golf glove, m/lg, rh			#DIV/0!			#DIV/0!
Spaulding inf glove			#DIV/0!			#DIV/0!
Bike baseball cleats			#DIV/0!			#DIV/0!
Head skis			#DIV/0!			#DIV/0!
300-lb Freeweight set			#DIV/0!			#DIV/0!
Weight-lifting machine, 200 lb			#DIV/0!			#DIV/0!
Tennis shorts, men's med			#DIV/0!			#DIV/0!
Tennis shirts, patterns, med			#DIV/0!			#DIV/0!
Tennis dresses, sz 9			#DIV/0!			#DIV/0!

The markup percent will have to be entered in the proper cell as a decimal fraction. For example, 40% will have to be entered as .40. On the spreadsheet it will appear as a percent.

It would be rare for a department store to base the markup percent on cost for some items and on the selling price for others in the same department (Sporting Goods). In this application, however, both cost and selling price will be used as the base. *The items must be coded 1 if the markup percent is based on cost* (C), *or 2 if it is based on the selling price* (SP).

1. In cells A10 through A21, enter the product description.
2. In cells B10 through B21, enter the quantity in the cost unit. (The cost unit may be per case, per carton, per dozen, etc.)
3. In cells C10 through C21, enter the unit cost.
4. In cells E10 through E21, enter the markup percent.
5. In cells F10 through F21, enter the code for the base.

Product Description	Qty. in Cost Unit	Unit Cost	Markup Percent	Base
Head rackets	12	$1,502.55	40%	SP
Wilson 1200 irons, 2-PW	1	135.97	85%	C
Wilson pro-lite golf bags	1	73.81	50%	SP
Golf glove, m/lg., rh	12	90.03	100%	C
Spaulding inf glove	12	515.99	90%	C
Bike baseball cleats	1	38.99	125%	C
Head skis	1	145.59	60%	SP
300-lb freeweight set	1	34.42	45%	SP
Weight-lifting machine, 200 lb	1	239.48	55%	SP
Tennis shorts, men's med	12	159.94	100%	C
Tennis shirts, patterns, med	12	181.70	100%	C
Tennis dresses, sz 9	12	293.69	115%	C

Answer the following questions after you have completed the spreadsheet:

1. What is the selling price for Head rackets?

2. What is the item cost for golf glove, m/lg, rh?

3. What is the selling price for tennis dresses, sz 9?

4. What is the selling price for Wilson pro-lite golf bags?

5. What is the item cost for Head skis?

6. What is the item cost for Bike baseball cleats?

7. What is the selling price for a 300-lb freeweight set?

GROUP REPORT

FOR CHAPTER 8 APPLICATION 1

The Sporting Goods Department manager, Ms. Cheong, does not fully understand markups. She has asked you to prepare a report based on two changes in the application spreadsheet data.

1. Change the code for Head rackets so that the price will be based on cost.

2. Change the code on Wilson 1200 irons so that the price will be based on the selling price.

3. Note the resulting changes in the selling price and explain them in your report.

4. Make any recommendations your group feels are indicated by the data in the application spreadsheet for the Sporting Goods Department.

EXCEL SPREADSHEET APPLICATION FOR CHAPTER 8

APPLICATION 2

The head buyer and her assistants are currently engaged in a buying trip at the New York Trade Center. Merchandise is to be bought for several departments in the store. A marketing research project, combined with sophisticated forecasting techniques, has resulted in a sales projection for the next season of $750,000. The buyers have been busy. They plan to complete their purchases today, the fifth day of the buying trip. They are using a spreadsheet program to help them keep track of the cost, selling price, markup, and markup percent of their purchases. All markup percents will be based on the selling price. When you open the Ch08App2 spreadsheet from your computer spreadsheet applications disk, you will see the form shown here:

Springfield Department Store

2617 Main Street
Box 219
Springfield, Maryland 58109
Telephone: 301-555-2158   FAX: 301-555-3498

AVERAGE MARKUP FORM

	Selling price		Cost	Markup	Markup %	Base
Total Planned Purchases			$0.00	$0.00		
- Purchases to Date						
1st Purchase	$0.00			$0.00		
2nd Purchase	$0.00			$0.00		
3rd Purchase	$0.00			$0.00		
4th Purchase	$0.00			$0.00		
5th Purchase	#DIV/0!	$0.00	$0.00	$0.00		
Balance to Buy		$0.00	$0.00	$0.00	#DIV/0!	

As you enter each day's cost of purchases and the markup percent to be applied to those purchases, you should notice the changes on the balance to buy line of the spreadsheet.

Enter the following information:

1. In cell C11, enter the sales forecast figure of 750000.

2. In cell G11, enter .45 (45%), the desired markup percent that management has determined will be necessary to cover cost and make a reasonable profit.

3.

	In Cell	Cost	In Cell	Markup percent
1st Purchase	D13	75000	G13	.40 (40%)
2nd Purchase	D14	95000	G14	.45 (45%)
3rd Purchase	D15	65000	G15	.50 (50%)
4th Purchase	D16	90000	G16	.41 (41%)

4. In cells H11, H13 thru H16, and H18, enter SP (selling price).

Answer the following questions after you have completed the spreadsheet:

1. What is the selling price of the balance to buy?

2. What is the cost of the balance to buy?

3. What is the markup of the balance to buy?

4. What will be the required markup percent of the balance to buy?

GROUP REPORT

FOR CHAPTER 8 APPLICATION 2

Make the following changes and write a report conveying the results to the store manager:

1. Change the markup percent of each purchase to 55%.

2. Change the markup percent of each purchase to 40%.

*Hint:*The results of the changes your group made should indicate the problem with marking merchandise up too high or too low for a prolonged period.

9 DEMAND DEPOSITS (CHECKING ACCOUNTS) AND BANK RECONCLIATION

CAR AND ONION GIVEAWAYS TO LURE NEW CUSTOMERS

Years ago financial institutions used giveaways to attract business. New depositors could expect a waffle iron or some other goody to persuade them to bank at Second National instead of Third National. The practice has been renewed. Recent promotions include a trip to Hawaii, a $5,000 online shopping spree, and a one-year lease on a new Volkswagen Beetle. The reason banks offer such great consumer promotions—and not the traditional toaster—for opening a new account is simple. They find themselves in heated competition with not just their traditional rivals for consumer dollars, but also other kinds of institutions, such as the Internet and brokerage houses.

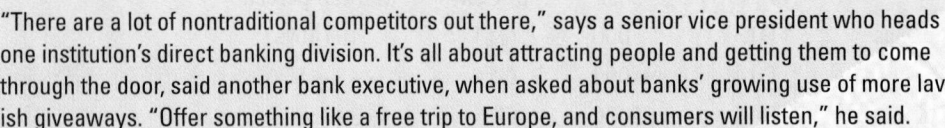

"There are a lot of nontraditional competitors out there," says a senior vice president who heads one institution's direct banking division. It's all about attracting people and getting them to come through the door, said another bank executive, when asked about banks' growing use of more lavish giveaways. "Offer something like a free trip to Europe, and consumers will listen," he said.

But how about onions? If your bank statement doesn't make you cry, the great onion giveaway at Comerica Bank in San Francisco might. Comerica's three Peninsula branches tried serving up 40,000 pounds of Washington State's famous sweet onions one week. Local high school football players and wrestlers hauled heavy bags of onions off a semitrailer truck and created tall and smelly stacks in the middle of Comerica banks. Within minutes, the strong aroma forced bank employees to crank up the air conditioners. "In the Palo Alto branch, we park underneath the building—that's two floors down and you could still smell it," according to the branch manager.

The onion giveaway was started by bank Founder Carl Schmitt, who came from Walla Walla, Washington, where the well-known sweet white onions are grown. Longtime customers remember that Schmitt used to bring back sacks of onions for a few loyal clients from his annual trips to Walla Walla. But demand grew and eventually he was ordering thousands of pounds for everyone at his three branches.

Some customers said they once feared that Comerica, the 10th largest commercial bank in California, would drop the quaint family business tradition after Schmitt retired. "When we acquired the bank, we invited all the customers to come down and ask us any question. . . . But the main question we kept getting was, 'Will you still do the onions?'" the new Comerica California president said. "Our bank is very relationship oriented. We want to feel small even though we're big," he said. "That's why we kept the tradition."

Receiving merchandise up front may cost as much as a point of interest on a deposit, and the depositor will have to report the value of the gift as taxable income. But for some depositors it's what's up front that counts.

Chapter Glossary

Money. Anything that serves as a medium of exchange. The money supply is comprised of currency plus accounts upon which checks can be written.

Currency. Paper money and coins.

Demand deposit. Commonly referred to as a checking account; allows a depositor to require a financial institution to pay a specified sum on demand.

Negotiable order of withdrawal (NOW). A special kind of checking account that earns interest for the depositor.

Electronic funds transfer (EFT). Automatic teller machines (ATMs), automatic payroll deposit systems, and automatic transfers of funds are all forms of EFT.

Check. An order instructing the financial institution on which it is drawn to pay a given sum to a specified person or firm immediately as long as it does not exceed the amount in the checking account.

Check register. A depositor's record of checking account activity; used to keep an accurate record of the balance on deposit.

Endorsement. The signature on the back of a negotiable instrument (a check) to transfer funds to another party.

Bank statement. A bank's listing of all amounts added to or subtracted from a checking account.

Bank reconciliation. A comparison between a bank statement and a check register to reflect the correct balance.

Student Objectives

Upon completion of this chapter, you should be able to:

1. Discuss the features and advantages of demand deposits (checking accounts).

2. Describe the newer innovations in checking: the electronic funds transfer (EFT) and automatic teller machines (ATMs).

3. Differentiate among checking accounts, negotiable orders of withdrawal (NOW accounts), and super NOW accounts.

4. Identify the important features and characteristics of a check, an endorsement, a check register, and a deposit ticket.

5. Write a check.

6. Keep a check register.

7. Use common types of endorsements to endorse checks properly.

8. Prepare a deposit ticket.

9. Explain the purpose of reconciling the bank statement with the check register.

10. Reconcile a bank statement with a check register.

A although an estimated one third of all Americans continues to deal almost exclusively with cash, demand deposits (checking accounts) offer the advantages of convenience and safety and account for the bulk of all spending.

LEARNING UNIT 1
DEMAND DEPOSIT (CHECKING ACCOUNT) ESSENTIALS

Money, by definition, is anything that serves as a medium of exchange. The money supply is comprised of **currency** (coins and paper money) and **demand deposits**. Traveler's checks, **negotiable order of withdrawal (NOW) accounts**, super NOW accounts, and credit union share draft accounts are all specialized checking accounts. Checks can be written on the deposits in such accounts to pay debts at any time of day. Altogether, such check-writing accounts comprise approximately 72% of the money supply.

Many commercial banks, mutual banks, credit unions, and savings and loan institutions also allow customers who need funds on weekends, at night, or at other times when the institution is closed to make deposits or withdrawals using automatic teller machines (ATMs). This is the most common form of **electronic funds transfer (EFT)**. EFTs also enable automatic payroll deposit systems, payment of bills by telephone, and automatic transfers of funds. You can, for example, transfer $1,000 from New York City to Los Angeles within a few hours if necessary.

Checks allow buyers to make large purchases without carrying large amounts of cash. Sellers gain a measure of safety because the checks they receive are valuable only to them and can be exchanged only by them for cash.

Checks and Checking Accounts

A **check** is an order instructing the financial institution on which it is drawn to pay a given sum to a specified person or firm immediately so long as it does not exceed the amount in the checking account. Americans write billions of checks each year, more than 1,000 per second. Nearly 95% of the dollar value of all financial transactions in the United States are conducted with checks rather than with currency.

NOW and super NOW accounts are special interest-bearing checking accounts. A super NOW account offers a higher rate of interest, but requires that a sizable minimum balance be kept in the account. Both permit immediate payment upon request.

9.1 Elements of a Checking Account

Reading and Writing Checks
Most business firms use checks for their convenience and safety features, and because checks make record-keeping easier. The features of a check are shown in Figure 9.1.

Payee. The person or company to whom the check is payable (Data Source Co.).

Date. The date the check is written (July 5, 2002).

Preprinted check number. Checks are numbered in sequence so that it is easy to determine whether or not a particular check has been cashed. If it has not, it may have been lost or stolen. The number is preprinted both at the top and at the bottom of the check (No. 4685).

Code number. Identification code for the bank (48–1530).
2530

Amount of check. Written in both verbal and numeric form. If different, the verbal form will be honored by the bank ($159.95 and One hundred fifty-nine and 95/100 Dollars).

Drawer. The party that signs the check; also called the maker. The drawer's signature must be that of someone authorized to write checks on the account. The bank

Figure 9.1
Features of a Check

Charles D. Jones or **Mary E. Jones**   No. 4685
2603 Oak Street
Milville, Ohio 87655   July 5,   20 02   48-1530
                                                     2530

PAY TO THE
ORDER OF _____ Data Source Co. _____ | $ 159.95

One hundred fifty-nine and 95/100 ——————————— DOLLARS

$N NATIONAL BANK
$B OF ANY CITY

FOR _____   *Charles D. Jones*

253015300   ⑈222 318 8⑈ 4685   0000000015995

has a signature card on file with the authorized signature(s). Some companies require more than one signature as a measure of internal control (Charles D. Jones).

Magnetic ink imprints. At the bottom of the check the bank number (253015300) and Charles D. and Mary E. Jones's account number (222 318 8) are preprinted with magnetic ink for computer processing. In addition, the amount of the check (159.95) is imprinted in magnetic ink when the bank processes the check.

Drawee. The bank that is ordered to make payment is the drawee (National Bank of Any City).

EXCEL Spreadsheet Application Spreadsheet Application 1 at the end of this chapter is a check register for the Springfield Department Store.

Check Register

A bank records all transactions and sends a monthly statement to each depositor. Good business practice requires that each depositor also keep accurate records. Banks can and do make errors. More important, however, is the fact that there is a lapse between the time the statement is prepared and mailed by the bank and its receipt by the depositor. During that lapse, many transactions may have been made, resulting in either a larger or a smaller balance than the one shown on the bank statement. Obviously, it is also important that the depositor know the amount on deposit at any given time between bank statements. Thus, all depositors should keep a check register, such as the one illustrated in Figure 9.2.

		RECORD ALL CHARGES OR CREDITS THAT AFFECT YOUR ACCOUNT							
NUMBER	**DATE**	**DESCRIPTION OF TRANSACTION**	**PAYMENT/DEBIT (−)**		**√ T**	**DEPOSIT/CREDIT (+)**		**Balance** $ 1,201	18
4683	7/4	Sean O'Grady	149	03				1,052	15
4684	7/4	Fireworks A Plenty	381	39				670	76
	7/5	Deposit				154	35	825	11
4685	7/5	Data Source Co.	159	95				665	16

Figure 9.2
Check Register

Common Types of Endorsements

Before any of the checks written by Charles or Mary Jones can be cashed or deposited, they must be endorsed. An **endorsement** transfers ownership of the check when the payee signs it on the back. The most common types of endorsements are shown and explained in Figure 9.3.

Figure 9.3
Types of Endorsements

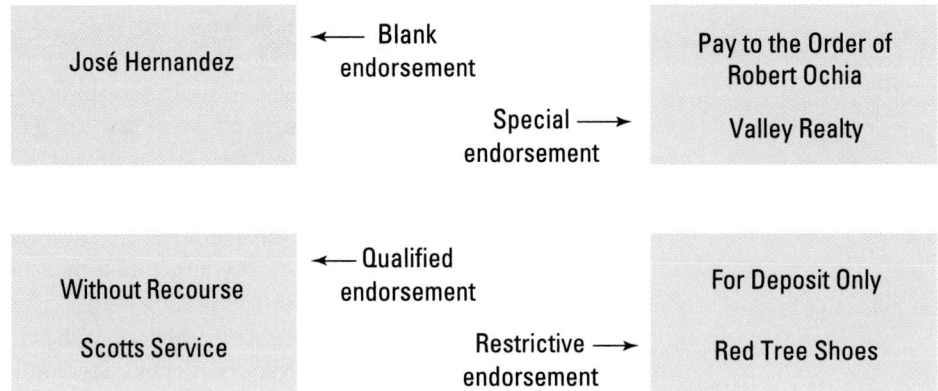

Figure 9.4
Deposit Ticket

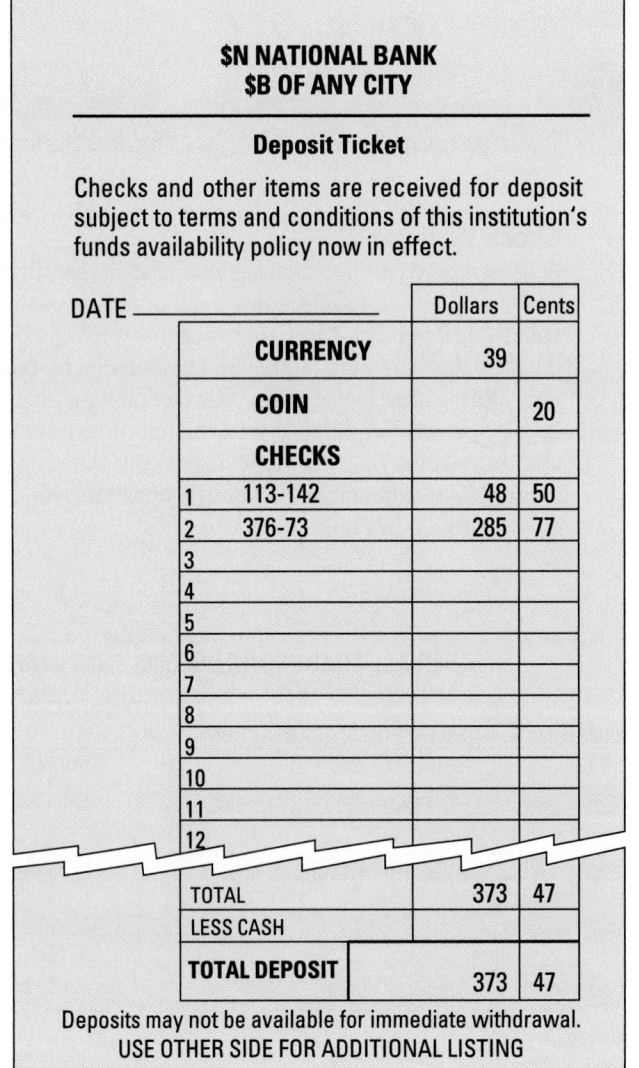

Blank endorsement. Only the payee's signature on the back of the check is required. This makes it payable to the bearer (anyone who has possession of the check). Thus, it is not very safe and should not be used if the check is to be mailed.

Special endorsement. This endorsement specifies the person or company to whom the check is payable. Only the one specified after the words "Pay to the Order of" can further the negotiability of the check. (In the example, that would be Robert Ochia).

Qualified endorsement. The qualification "Without Recourse" will limit the endorser's liability in the event the instrument is not backed by sufficient funds. Therefore, the endorser is not guaranteeing payment of the check.

Restrictive endorsement. A restrictive endorsement limits the negotiability of the check. "For Deposit Only" is a common restrictive endorsement and it means that the check can only be deposited to the indicated account; it cannot be cashed. Such an endorsement can be very helpful if the check is lost or stolen.

Deposit Ticket

After checks have been properly endorsed, they can be cashed or deposited. Deposits can be composed of currency (paper money and coins) or checks. Figure 9.4 shows a typical deposit ticket. Once the deposit has been made, the bank will increase (credit) Charles and Mary Jones's account balance. The deposit should also be recorded in the check register.

9.1 Practice Problems

Complete the following checks using the following information:

Payee (Payable to)	Date	Check no.	Amount of Check	Payer (Signer)
1. José Hernandez	4/2/02	115	$4,865.00	Mary E. Jones
2. Log Cabin Realty	4/3/02	116	381.80	Charles D. Jones
3. Stop & Go	4/4/02	117	8.49	Mary E. Jones
4. Red Tree Shoes	4/4/02	118	28.95	Mary E. Jones
5. Ling Woo	4/5/02	119	128.25	Charles D. Jones

1.

Charles D. Jones or **Mary E. Jones**   **No. 115**
2603 Oak Street
Milville, Ohio 87655   _____ 20 _____   48-1530
                                                                              2530

PAY TO THE
ORDER OF _____ | $

_____ DOLLARS

        $N NATIONAL BANK
        $B OF ANY CITY
FOR _____   _____

253015300   ⑈222 318 8⑈ 0115   0000000000000

2.

Charles D. Jones or Mary E. Jones
2603 Oak Street
Milville, Ohio 87655

No. 116

_____ 20 _____

48-1530
2530

PAY TO THE
ORDER OF _____ ⌐ $ ▢

_____ DOLLARS

$N NATIONAL BANK
$B OF ANY CITY

FOR _____   _____

253015300   ⌐222 318 8⌐ 0116   0000000000000

3.

Charles D. Jones or Mary E. Jones
2603 Oak Street
Milville, Ohio 87655

No. 117

_____ 20 _____

48-1530
2530

PAY TO THE
ORDER OF _____ ⌐ $ ▢

_____ DOLLARS

$N NATIONAL BANK
$B OF ANY CITY

FOR _____   _____

253015300   ⌐222 318 8⌐ 0117   0000000000000

4.

Charles D. Jones or Mary E. Jones
2603 Oak Street
Milville, Ohio 87655

No. 118

_____ 20 _____

48-1530
2530

PAY TO THE
ORDER OF _____ ⌐ $ ▢

_____ DOLLARS

$N NATIONAL BANK
$B OF ANY CITY

FOR _____   _____

253015300   ⌐222 318 8⌐ 0118   0000000000000

5.

Charles D. Jones or **Mary E. Jones** **No. 119**
2603 Oak Street
Milville, Ohio 87655 48-1530
20______ 2530

PAY TO THE
ORDER OF ________________________________ $

____ DOLLARS

$N NATIONAL BANK
$B OF ANY CITY

FOR ____________________ ____________________

253015300 ⑆222 318 8⑆ 0119 0000000000000

6. Charles Jones made a deposit on April 5. It consisted of $378 in currency, $3.32 in coins, and the following checks:

#33–394 for $88.30 from Bowater, Inc.

#19–283 for $293.78 from Rodger O. Codger

#287–238 for $2,981.10 from Stanley's Supply

Fill out the following deposit ticket for Charles:

$N NATIONAL BANK
$B OF ANY CITY

Deposit Ticket

Checks and other items are received for deposit subject to terms and conditions of this institution's funds availability policy now in effect.

DATE ________________

	Dollars	Cents
CURRENCY		
COIN		
CHECKS		
1		
2		
3		
4		
5		
6		
7		
8		
9		
10		
11		
12		
TOTAL		
LESS CASH		
TOTAL DEPOSIT		

Deposits may not be available for immediate withdrawal.
USE OTHER SIDE FOR ADDITIONAL LISTING

7. Record all of the transactions in problems 1 through 6 in the following check register (note that the register has a beginning balance):

		RECORD ALL CHARGES OR CREDITS THAT AFFECT YOUR ACCOUNT						
NUMBER	DATE	DESCRIPTION OF TRANSACTION	PAYMENT/DEBIT (−)	✓ T	DEPOSIT/CREDIT (+)		Balance 7,491.57	

8. Endorse the following check backs with your signature using the type of endorsement specified:

a. Blank endorsement

b. Restrictive endorsement

c. Special endorsement

d. Qualified endorsement

9.1 Solutions to Practice Problems

1.

Charles D. Jones or **Mary E. Jones**   No. 115
2603 Oak Street
Milville, Ohio 87655   April 2,   20 02   48-1530
                                                                    2530

PAY TO THE
ORDER OF _____ José Hernandez _____ | $ 4,865.00

Four thousand, eight hundred sixty-five and 00/100 ——————— DOLLARS

        $N NATIONAL BANK
        $B OF ANY CITY

FOR _____   Mary E. Jones _____

253015300   ⑃222 318 8⑃ 0115   0000000000000

2.

Charles D. Jones or Mary E. Jones	No. 116

2603 Oak Street
Milville, Ohio 87655

4/3 20 02

48-1530
2530

PAY TO THE
ORDER OF _____ Log Cabin Realty _____ $ 381.80

Three hundred eighty-one and 80/100 _____ DOLLARS

$N NATIONAL BANK
$B OF ANY CITY

FOR _____

Charles D. Jones

253015300   ⊪222 318 8⊪ 0116   0000000000000

3.

Charles D. Jones or Mary E. Jones	No. 117

2603 Oak Street
Milville, Ohio 87655

April 4, 20 02

48-1530
2530

PAY TO THE
ORDER OF _____ Stop & Go _____ $ 8.49

Eight and 49/100 _____ DOLLARS

$N NATIONAL BANK
$B OF ANY CITY

FOR _____

Mary E. Jones

253015300   ⊪222 318 8⊪ 0117   0000000000000

4.

Charles D. Jones or Mary E. Jones	No. 118

2603 Oak Street
Milville, Ohio 87655

April 4, 20 02

48-1530
2530

PAY TO THE
ORDER OF _____ Red Tree Shoes _____ $ 28.95

Twenty-eight and 95/100 _____ DOLLARS

$N NATIONAL BANK
$B OF ANY CITY

FOR _____

Mary E. Jones

253015300   ⊪222 318 8⊪ 0118   0000000000000

5.

Charles D. Jones or Mary E. Jones	No. 119

2603 Oak Street
Milville, Ohio 87655

4/5 20 02

48-1530
2530

PAY TO THE
ORDER OF _____ Ling Woo _____ $ 128.25

One hundred twenty-eight and 25/100 _____ DOLLARS

$N NATIONAL BANK
$B OF ANY CITY

FOR _____

Charles D. Jones

253015300   ⊪222 318 8⊪ 0119   0000000000000

6.

$N NATIONAL BANK
$B OF ANY CITY

Deposit Ticket

Checks and other items are received for deposit subject to terms and conditions of this institution's funds availability policy now in effect.

DATE _____

		Dollars	Cents
CURRENCY		378	
COIN		3	32
CHECKS			
1	33-394	88	30
2	19-283	293	78
3	287-238	2,981	10
4			
5			
6			
7			
8			
9			
10			
11			
12			
13			
14			
15			
16			
17			
18			
19			
20			
21			
22			
23			
24			
25			
26			
27			
28			
29			
TOTAL		3,744	50
LESS CASH			
TOTAL DEPOSIT		3,744	50

Deposits may not be available for immediate withdrawal.
USE OTHER SIDE FOR ADDITIONAL LISTING

Chapter 9 Demand Deposits (Checking Accounts) and Bank Reconciliation

7.

		RECORD ALL CHARGES OR CREDITS THAT AFFECT YOUR ACCOUNT							
NUMBER	DATE	DESCRIPTION OF TRANSACTION	PAYMENT/DEBIT (−)		✓ T	DEPOSIT/CREDIT (+)		Balance 7,491	57
115	4/2	José Hernandez	4,865	00				2,626	57
116	4/3	Log Cabin Realty	381	80				2,244	77
117	4/4	Stop & Go	8	49				2,236	28
118	4/4	Red Tree Shoes	28	95				2,207	33
119	4/5	Ling Woo	128	25				2,079	08
	4/5	Deposit				3,744	50	5,823	58

8. a. Blank endorsement

> Your Name

b. Restrictive endorsement

> For Deposit Only
> Your Name

c. Special endorsement

> Pay to the Order of Anybody's Name
> Your Name

d. Qualified endorsement

> Without Recourse
> Your Name

9.2 Bank Statement and Bank Reconciliation

Bank Statement

Each month individuals and business firms with checking accounts receive statements from their banks. **Bank statements** list all amounts added to the accounts (deposits) and all amounts subtracted from them (checks, drafts, and bank charges). Statements also include the monthly opening and closing balances. An example of a bank statement is shown in Figure 9.5.

EXCEL Spreadsheet Application Application 2 requires the Springfield Department Store to reconcile its bank statement with the check register.

Bank Reconciliation Statement

For most bank customers, it would be unusual for the bank statement to show an amount in its closing balance that equals the balance in the depositor's check register. The most common reasons for any discrepancy are the following:

1. *Bank service charge.* Banks may charge a fee for handling the depositor's transactions during the month. Generally, the depositor does not know the amount of the service charge until the bank statement is received.

$N NATIONAL BANK
$B OF ANY CITY

1234 Lime Street * Phone 800 555-3456 * Any City, Ohio 87654

Charles D. Jones
or Mary E. Jones
2603 Oak Street
Milville, Ohio 87655

Account No. 222-318-8

Statement Date: 4/12/02
Number of Transactions: 19

On	Your Balance Was	We Added Deposits		We Subtracted Checks	
03/10/02	$2,388.69	No. 3	$2,711.07	No. 16	$1,196.58

YOUR PRESENT BALANCE

$3,903.18

SERVICE CHARGE

$0.00

Checks and Other Debits			Deposits and Other Credits	Date	Balance
				031002	2,388.69
	19.61	22.00		031102	2,347.08
21.00			CM 191.37	031402	2,517.45
100.00				031502	2,417.45
2.81	64.23	74.99		031602	2,275.42
DM 60.00				031702	2,215.42
38.37	25.14			032802	2,151.91
100.00	378.77	15.66	845.66	033102	2,503.14
150.00	24.00			040602	2,329.14
100.00			1,674.04	041102	3,903.18

PLEASE EXAMINE AT ONCE AND REPORT
ANY ERROR IMMEDIATELY

Last amt.
is your
balance

Please Notify Us of Any Change in Address
Use Reverse Side for Reconciling Your Account

Figure 9.5
Bank Statement

2. *Outstanding checks.* Checks written by the depositor were not received by the bank in time to be included on the bank statement.

3. *Deposits in transit.* Since bank processing and mail delivery usually take several days, deposits made after the bank statement closing date will not appear on the statement.

4. *Debit memo (DM).* Loans from the bank, insurance premiums, and, at some banks, utility bills may be automatically deducted from the depositor's checking account balance. These deductions are like checks and are treated in the same way, but the depositor may not know the exact amount or may, as a matter of policy, record them only when they appear in the bank statement. Such deductions are called *drafts* and are frequently recorded by the bank preceded by *DM* which stands for *debit memo.*

5. *NSF (nonsufficient funds) checks.* NSF checks are checks you receive from another party that are deposited into your account but are later returned

Chapter 9 Demand Deposits (Checking Accounts) and Bank Reconciliation

because the party did not have enough money in his or her account to cover the check. You had deposited the check in good faith and recorded it in your check-register. When the check is returned to you by your bank, you should reduce your check register balance. If not, you will need to do so at the time of reconciliation. In addition, your bank might charge you a handling fee, which will be shown as a debit memo (DM).

6. *Credit memo (CM)*. Deposits are sometimes made into an account. For example, a bank might collect a note for its depositor and add it to the account. The depositor might not know the note has been collected until the bank statement is received. EFTs, discussed at the beginning of this chapter, result in deposits such as paychecks being automatically deposited into accounts. These items are often preceded by *CM* which stands for *credit memo*.

7. *Bookkeeping errors*. Sometimes depositors make errors in the check register when recording the amount of a check or deposit. They may also make errors in the addition and subtraction of transactions to arrive at the balance. To correct such errors, depositors must add or subtract from their balance in the reconciliation process.

Since neither the bank statement nor the check register is likely to reflect accurately the exact checking account balance at any one time, that balance needs to be determined. Though neither alone contains all the information necessary to calculate the correct current balance, together they do. The back side of the bank statement provides a worksheet from which you can prepare the formal reconciliation statement. When you receive your the bank statement, you should adjust your check register to reflect the correct balance. An example of a **bank reconciliation statement** is presented in Figure 9.6.

The reconcilation process entails the following steps:

1. Locate all items recorded in the bank statement that do not appear in the check register. If an item reduced the bank statement balance, deduct it from the check register balance. If an item increased the bank statement balance, add it to the check register balance.

2. Locate all items recorded in the check register that do not appear in the bank statement. If an item increased the check register balance, add it to the bank statement balance. If an item reduced the check register balance, deduct it from the bank statement balance.

$N NATIONAL BANK
$B OF ANY CITY

Bank Reconciliation Form

A. Ending Balance
   Bank Statement $ 3,903.18

H. Ending Balance
   Check Register $ 3,945.71

B. List Deposits not
   Shown on Statement $ 325.00
                           $
                           $

I. Deposits and
   Transfers $ 191.37
   (CM) $
                           $

C. Total of Lines B $ 325.00

J. Total of Lines I $ 191.37

D. Add Line C to A $ 4,228.18

K. Add Line J to H $ 4,137.08

E. List All Checks
   Issued but not
   in Statement

Check No.	Check Amount	Check No.	Check Amount
4688	125.66	4691	17.39
4692	8.05		

L. List All Checks &
   Bank Charges not in
   Check Register (DM)

Date	Amount
031702	60.00

F. Total of Column E $ 151.10

M. Total of Column L $ 60.00

G. Subtract F from D $ 4,077.08

N. Subtract M from K $ 4,077.08

THE BALANCES SHOULD AGREE. IF NOT, RECHECK YOUR ENTRIES FROM
THIS STATEMENT AND YOUR CHECK REGISTER. IF NO ERROR IS REPORTED
WITHIN TEN DAYS OF MAILING OF THE STATEMENT, IT WILL BE
CONSIDERED CORRECT. ALL DEPOSITS AND CREDITS ARE SUBJECT TO
FINAL COLLECTION.

Figure 9.6
Bank Reconciliation Statement

E X A M P L E   Prepare a bank reconciliation statement for Ked, Inc., from the following partial bank statement and check register for September 14, 2002:

				BANK STATEMENT		
				Deposits and Other Credits	Date	Balance
	Checks and Other Debits					742.92
3.90	DM 50.00				081202	689.02
29.36				CM 188.17	081802	847.83
8.19	286.01		3.93		082302	549.70
41.27				545.15	083002	1,053.58
			DM 8.00		091002	1,045.58

		RECORD ALL CHARGES OR CREDITS THAT AFFECT YOUR ACCOUNT							
NUMBER	DATE	DESCRIPTION OF TRANSACTION	PAYMENT/DEBIT (−)		√ T	DEPOSIT/CREDIT (+)		Balance	
								742	92
105	8/5	Kerrs International	29	36	X			713	56
106	8/7	Herman's Flowers	41	27	X			672	29
107	8/10	Sugarbaker's	119	28				553	01
108	8/11	Cash	3	90	X			549	11
109	8/15	Leonard's Hardware	286	01	X			263	10
110	8/17	Office Supply Depot	8	19	X			254	91
111	8/22	Donut Shoppe	3	93	X			250	98
112	8/29	Lotsadog	75	00		545	15	721	13
113	9/8	1st Baptist Church	25	00		100	00	796	13

Solution

1. Find all items contained in the bank statement that are not in the check register:
   a. There is a CM $188.17 from the bank for a note it collected for the depositor. It was added to the bank statement. Thus, it should be added to the check register.
   b. Two DMs appear in the bank statement. The first DM is a $50 NSF check. The second DM is the service charge (sometimes abbreviated SC) of $8.00. Both of these items were deducted from the bank statement and, therefore, should be deducted from the check register.
2. Find the items contained in the check register that are not in the bank statement.
   a. There is a $100.00 deposit in transit. It was added to the check register, and should be added to the bank statement balance.
   b. Three checks are in the check register but have not yet appeared in the bank statement. They should be listed separately with numbers. They are #107, $119.28; #112, $75.00; and #113, $25.00. They should be deducted from the bank statement balance.

KED, INC.
Bank Reconciliation Statement
September 15, 2002

Check register balance			$796.13
Add: Collection of note		188.17	
		$ 984.30	
Deduct: NSF check	$50.00		
Service charge	8.00	58.00	
Reconciled balance		$ 926.30	
Bank statement balance		$1,045.58	
Add: Deposit in Transit		100.00	
		$1,145.58	
Deduct: Outstanding checks			
#107	$119.28		
#112	75.00		
#113	25.00	219.28	
Reconciled balance		$ 926.30	

9.2 Practice Problems

Use the information given to reconcile the bank statement with the check register.

1. William Lobo's January 7, 2002, bank statement and register were as follows:

Statement balance	$193.50
Check register balance	$144.05
Outstanding checks	#412, $26.75; #415, $31.20
Service charge	$8.50

2. Eagle's Basketball Shop's March 21, 2002, bank statement and check register were as follows:

Check register balance	$ 9,345
Statement balance	9,450
CM (collection of note)	300
DM (NSF check)	102
DM (service charge)	9
DM (charge for checks)	6
DM (charge for processing NSF check)	3
Deposit in transit (Dated 4/9)	500
Outstanding checks: #178	90
#180	335

3. Kirkpatrick's Apparel Shop is reconciling its bank account. An analysis of the bank statement and check register has revealed the following: the bank statement balance is $16,320; outstanding checks are #385 for $1,380 and #386 for $3,240. A check for $15 was incorrectly recorded for $7.50; the check register has a balance of $12,630; a note was collected by the bank for $1,800 but the bank charged a collection fee of $30; an insurance draft for $52.50 was paid by the bank; and a deposit dated September 4 for $2,640 was in transit. Prepare a bank reconciliation statement on September 8, 2002.

9.2 Solutions to Practice Problems

1.

Bank statement balance		$ 193.50	
Deduct: Outstanding checks			
#412	$ 26.75		
#415	31.20	57.95	
Reconciled balance		$ 135.55	
Check register balance		$ 144.05	
Deduct: Service charge		8.50	
Reconciled balance		$ 135.55	

2.

Bank statement balance		$ 9,450
Add: Deposit in transit (4/9)		500
		$ 9,950
Deduct: Outstanding checks		
#178	$ 90	
#180	335	425
Reconciled balance		$ 9,525
Check register balance		$ 9,345
Add: Collection of note		300
		$ 9,645
Deduct: NSF check	$ 102	
Processing charge	3	
Service charge	9	
Charge for checks	6	120
Reconciled balance		$ 9,525

3.

Kirkpatrick's Apparel Shop
Bank Reconciliation Statement
September 8, 2002

Bank statement balance		$16,320.00
Add: Deposit in transit (Sept. 4)		2,640.00
		$18,960.00
Deduct: Outstanding checks #385	$1,380.00	
#386	3,240.00	4,620.00
Reconciled balance		$14,340.00
Check register balance		$12,630.00
Add: Collection of note	$1,800.00	
Deduct: Collection fee	30.00	1,770.00
		$14,400.00
Deduct: Recording error ($15 − 7.50)	$ 7.50	
Insurance draft	52.50	60.00
Reconciled balance		$14,340.00

QUICK REFERENCE SUMMARY AND REVIEW

Page	Section Topic	Learning Concepts	Examples and Solutions
302	**9.1** Elements of a Checking Account	1. Reading and writing checks 2. Check register 3. Common types of endorsements 4. Deposit ticket	1. See example on page 302. 2. See example on page 303. 3. **a.** *Blank:* not safe; payable to bearer **b.** *Special:* specifies person or company who can further negotiability **c.** *Qualified:* limits the endorser's liability **d.** *Restrictive:* limits negotiability 4. See example on page 305.
311	**9.2** Bank Statement and Bank Reconciliation	1. The bank statement records the activity in a depositor's account. 2. The bank reconciliation statement adjusts the bank statement balance and the check register balance to reflect the correct current balance.	1. See example on page 311. 2. See example on page 311.

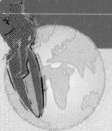

SURFING THE INTERNET

For further information on the topics covered in this chapter, check out the following sites:

http://www.atmwholesale.com/

http://www.howstuffworks.com/atm.htm

http://www.fms.treas.gov/eft/

http://www.flexaccounts.com/Bank_Rcn.html

<table>
<tr><td>ADDITIONAL
PRACTICE
PROBLEMS</td><td>*Answers to odd-numbered problems are given in Appendix A.*</td></tr>
</table>

9.1

Use the following information to write the checks in problems 1 through 5:

Payee	Date	Check No.	Amount of Check	Payer
1. Music Warehouse	2/9/02	689	$398.28	Buddy Allen
2. Town & Country Clothes	2/5/02	690	40.36	Nadia Najinski
3. A & G Warehouse	2/5/02	691	114.75	Thomas Mayer
4. Public Water Co.	2/6/02	692	22.01	Nancy McAutry
5. Martha's Grapes	2/7/02	693	57.99	George Porge

1.

Buddy's Garage 1428 Elm Street Midtowne, Iowa 65432	No. 689 48-1530 2530

2/9 20 02

PAY TO THE
ORDER OF ___Music Warehouse_____ | $ 398.28

Three hundred ninety-eight and 28/100--- DOLLARS

$N NATIONAL BANK
$B OF ANY CITY

FOR _____   *Buddy Allen*

253015300   ⑈222 318 8⑈ 0689   0000000000000

2.

Nadia Najinski Fabrics 6730 Calmont Drive Springdale, Wisconsin 98765	No. 690 48-1530 2530

2/5 20 02

PAY TO THE
ORDER OF ___Town and Country Clothes_____ | $ 40.36

Forty and 36/100--- DOLLARS

$N NATIONAL BANK
$B OF ANY CITY

FOR _____   *Nadia Najinski*

253015300   ⑈222 318 8⑈ 0690   0000000000000

3.

Mayer Productions		No. 691
9275 Sunset		
Hollywood, Calif. 34567	2/5 20 02	48-1530
		2530

PAY TO THE
ORDER OF A & G Warehouse _____ | $ 114.75

One hundred fourteen and 75/100-- DOLLARS

$N NATIONAL BANK
$B OF ANY CITY

FOR _____   *Thomas Mayer* _____

253015300   ⑈222 318 8⑈ 0691   0000000000000

4.

Nancy McAutry		No. 692
892 Wedgemont Circle		
Leafton, Ontario, Canada	2/6 20 02	48-1530
		2530

PAY TO THE
ORDER OF Public Water Co. _____ | $ 22.01

Twenty-two and 01/100--- DOLLARS

$N NATIONAL BANK
$B OF ANY CITY

FOR _____   *Nancy McAutry* _____

253015300   ⑈222 318 8⑈ 0692   0000000000000

5.

Porge Custom Porches		No. 693
8 Fromholz Place		
Anton, South Dakota 38352	2/7 20 02	48-1530
		2530

PAY TO THE
ORDER OF Martha's Grapes _____ | $ 57.99

Fifty-seven and 99/100--- DOLLARS

$N NATIONAL BANK
$B OF ANY CITY

FOR _____   *George Porge* _____

253015300   ⑈222 318 8⑈ 0693   0000000000000

Use the following information to endorse the checks as indicated:

Type of Endorsement	Information for Special Endorsement	Endorser
6. Special	To: Cecile DeLong	Andre Bergstrum
7. Restrictive		Boris Stitch
8. Blank		Margot Spusman
9. Qualified		Michael Anderson
10. Special	To: Stan Lee	Martha T. Jones

6.

Pay to the order of Cecile DeLong Andre Bergstrum

7.

FOR DEPOSIT ONLY Boris Stitch

8.

Margot Spusman

9.

Without Recourse Michael Anderson

10.

Pay to the order of Stan Lee Martha T. Jones

11. The following items are to be deposited. Use them to prepare the deposit ticket that follows:

	Currency	Checks			Coins
No.	Denomination	No.	Amt.	No.	Denomination
6	$ 1 bills	38–1852	$3,385.28	8	Pennies
5	$ 5 bills	38–9562	49.03	3	Nickels
3	$ 10 bills	56–1640	2.72	7	Dimes
7	$ 20 bills	658–3920	112.29	7	Quarters
1	$100 bill	472–4948	46.83		

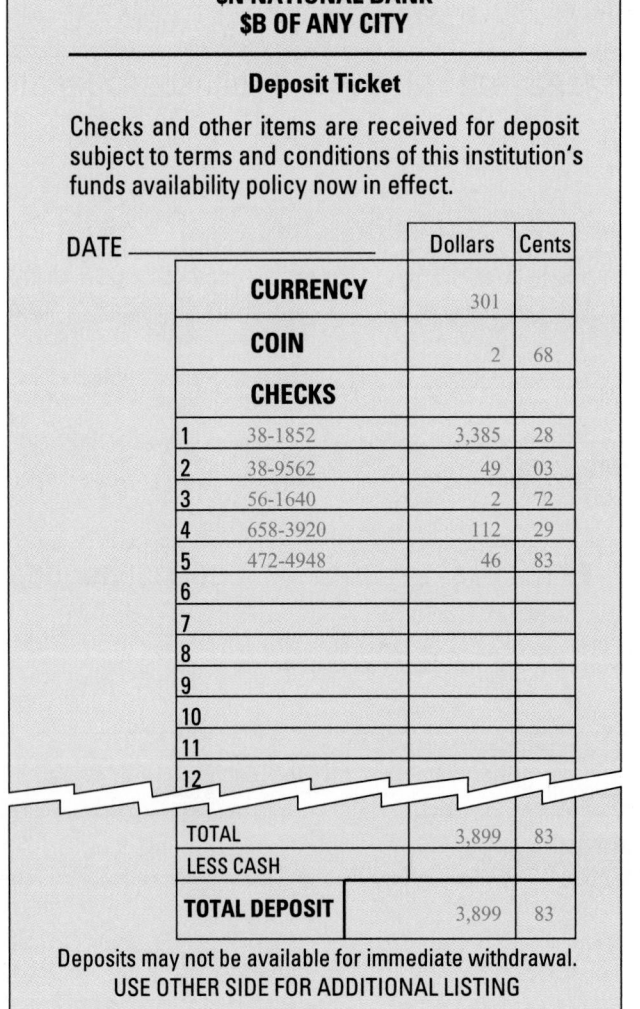

$N NATIONAL BANK
$B OF ANY CITY

Deposit Ticket

Checks and other items are received for deposit subject to terms and conditions of this institution's funds availability policy now in effect.

DATE _____

		Dollars	Cents
	CURRENCY	301	
	COIN	2	68
	CHECKS		
1	38-1852	3,385	28
2	38-9562	49	03
3	56-1640	2	72
4	658-3920	112	29
5	472-4948	46	83
6			
7			
8			
9			
10			
11			
12			
	TOTAL	3,899	83
	LESS CASH		
	TOTAL DEPOSIT	3,899	83

Deposits may not be available for immediate withdrawal.
USE OTHER SIDE FOR ADDITIONAL LISTING

$$6 \times \$ \ \ 1 = \$ \ \ 6$$
$$5 \times \ \ \ 5 = \ \ 25$$
$$3 \times \ \ 10 = \ \ 30$$
$$7 \times \ \ 20 = 140$$
$$1 \times 100 = \underline{100}$$
$$\$301$$

$$8 \times \$.01 = \$ \ .08$$
$$3 \times \ .05 = \ \ .15$$
$$7 \times \ .10 = \ \ .70$$
$$7 \times \ .25 = \underline{1.75}$$
$$\$2.68$$

12. Enter the following information in the check register provided: On 7/29 two checks were written, one to Jumbo Diet Center for $18, and the other to Needham Pharmacy for $12.33. On 8/2 a check was written for $55.98 to Ralph Blanton, and a deposit was made for $53.75. On 8/7 two more checks were written. The first was to Terry Hanratti for $88.34, and the second was to Virginia Thick for $7.13. Another deposit was made on 8/10 for $157.49. The checks were numbered consecutively from #297 through #301. The check register had a beginning balance of $173.19

RECORD ALL CHARGES OR CREDITS THAT AFFECT YOUR ACCOUNT								
NUMBER	DATE	DESCRIPTION OF TRANSACTION	PAYMENT/DEBIT (−)		√ T	DEPOSIT/CREDIT (+)		Balance 173 19
297	7/29	Jumbo Diet Center	18	00				155 19
298	7/29	Needham Pharmacy	12	33				142 86
299	8/2	Ralph Blanton	55	98				86 88
	8/2	Deposit				53	75	140 63
300	8/7	Terry Hanratti	88	34				52 29
301	8/7	Viirginia Thick	7	13				45 16
	8/10	Deposit				157	49	202 65

9.2

13. Using the following information, reconcile Joseph Schmaltz's bank statement with his check register for October 20, 2002:

Statement balance		$671.80
Outstanding checks:	$10.85	
	16.41	
	57.75	
Service charge		11.40
Check register balance		$598.19

JOSEPH SCHMALTZ
Bank Reconciliation Statement
October 20, 2002

Bank statement balance		$671.80
Deduct: Outstanding checks	$10.85	
	16.41	
	57.75	85.01
Reconciled balance		$586.79
Check register balance		$598.19
Deduct: Service charge		11.40
Reconciled balance		$586.79

14. Jack Black received his bank statement on May 18, 2002. The statement balance was $1,371.37. A deposit on May 17 for $123.86 was not recorded on the bank statement. The outstanding checks were for $15.82, $27.83, $33.50, and $137.50. A service charge of $14.70 appeared on the bank statement. The bank returned an uncollectable check in the amount of $66.05. The check register balance was $1,361.33. Reconcile the balances.

JACK BLACK
Bank Reconciliation Statement
May 18, 2002

Bank statement balance		$1,371.37
Add: Deposit in transit (5/17)		123.86
		$1,495.23
Deduct: Outstanding checks	$ 15.82	
	27.83	
	33.50	
	137.50	214.65
Reconciled balance		$1,280.58
Check register balance		$1,361.33
Deduct: Service charge	$ 14.70	
Uncollectable NSF check	66.05	80.75
Reconciled balance		$1,280.58

15. Charles Dickens, Inc., received its bank statement on November 2, 2002. A reconciliation analysis by the bookkeeper found the following differences between the bank statement and the check register:

Not in the Statement		Not in the Register	
a. Four checks:		**a.** Service charge	$ 30.00
#1828	$ 25.00	**b.** Drafts from:	
#1831	82.50	insurance co.	$295.00
#1832	56.65	bank loan	190.00
#1834	23.85		
b. Two deposits:		**c.** Charge for	
made on 2/15	$365.00	check blanks	$ 10.00
made on 2/17	510.00		

In addition, the bookkeeper found that check #1820 had been written for $12.95 but incorrectly recorded in the register as $12.59. The bank statement balance was $2,015.00. The check register balance was $3,227.36. Reconcile the balances.

CHARLES DICKENS, INC.
Bank Reconciliation Statement
November 2, 2002

Bank statement balance			$2,015.00
Add: Deposits in transit (1/15)	$365		
(2/17)	510		875.00
			$2,890.00
Deduct: Outstanding checks	#1828	$25.00	
	#1831	82.50	
	#1832	56.65	
	#1834	23.85	188.00
Reconciled balance			$2,702.00
Check register balance			$3,227.36
Deduct: Service charge		$ 30.00	
Insurance draft		295.00	
Bank loan draft		190.00	
Charge for check blanks		10.00	
Recording error #1820		.36	525.36
Reconciled balance			$2,702.00

Answers to odd-numbered problems are given in Appendix A.

Drill Problems

At the beginning of January, the balance in Juan Valdez's account was $34,980.38 according to his bank statement. The following transactions were made during the month. Calculate the balance after each was recorded in the bank statement.

	Date	Previous Balance	Transaction Deposit	Transaction Check	Ending Balance
1.	1/08	$34,980.38	$2,892.12		$37,872.50
2.	1/15			$381.34	37,491.16
3.	1/24			85.00	37,406.16
4.	1/27			883.25	36,522.91
5.	1/30		55.05	38.01	36,539.95

Use the previous information to do the following:

a. Write checks #484 through #487 for Juan (problems 6 through 9).

b. Fill out deposit tickets for the two deposits (problems 10 and 11).

c. Record all of the information in the check register (problem 12).

(Note that the beginning balance in the check register is not the same as the beginning balance in the bank statement. Give reasons for this situation.)

6. To: Glady's Chemical Supply   For: Moth balls

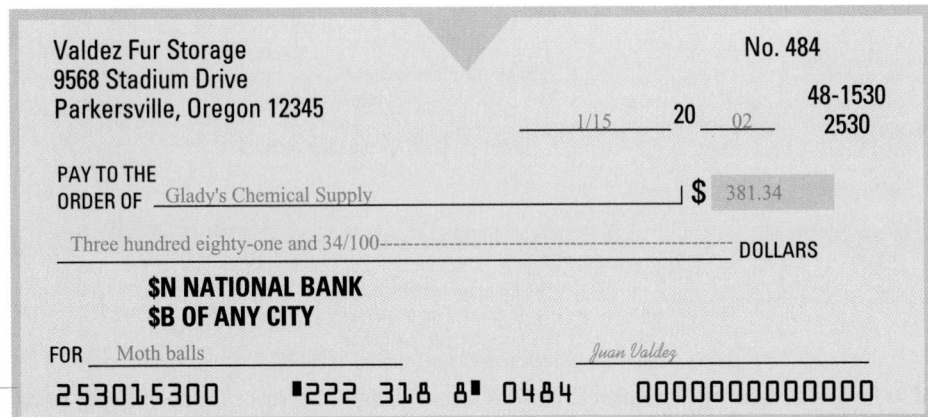

7. To: Parkersville Electric   For: Electricity for October

8. To: Diamond Realty   For: Mortgage Payment

Valdez Fur Storage
9568 Stadium Drive
Parkersville, Oregon 12345

No. 486

48-1530
2530

1/27   20   02

PAY TO THE
ORDER OF   Diamond Realty $ 883.25

Eight hundred eighty-three dollars and 25/100-- DOLLARS

$N NATIONAL BANK
$B OF ANY CITY

FOR   Mortgage payment   _Juan Valdez_

253015300   ⑈222 318 8⑈ 0486   0000000000000

9. To: All-City Restaurant Supply   For: Coffee and mugs

Valdez Fur Storage
9568 Stadium Drive
Parkersville, Oregon 12345

No. 487

48-1530
2530

1/30   20   02

PAY TO THE
ORDER OF   All-City Restaurant Supply $ 38.01

Thirty-eight and 01/100-- DOLLARS

$N NATIONAL BANK
$B OF ANY CITY

FOR   Coffee and mugs   _Juan Valdez_

253015300   ⑈222 318 8⑈ 0487   0000000000000

10.

$N NATIONAL BANK
$B OF ANY CITY
_____

Deposit Ticket

Checks and other items are received for deposit
subject to terms and conditions of this institution's
funds availability policy now in effect.

DATE _____

		Dollars	Cents
	CURRENCY	387	00
	COIN		
	CHECKS		
1	38-3843	387	12
2	36-5671	1,288	00
3	31-9372	830	00
4			
5			
6			
7			
8			
9			
10			
11			
12			
	TOTAL	2,892	12
	LESS CASH		
	TOTAL DEPOSIT	2,892	12

Deposits may not be available for immediate withdrawal.
USE OTHER SIDE FOR ADDITIONAL LISTING

This deposit consists of the following three checks:
38–3843 for $ 387.12
36–5671 for $1,288.00
31–9372 for   830.00
Total checks: $2,505.12

The remainder of the deposit is currency.

$ 2,892.12
− 2,505.12
   387.00

11.

```
┌─────────────────────────────────────┐
│         $N NATIONAL BANK             │
│         $B OF ANY CITY               │
│  ─────────────────────────────────  │
│            Deposit Ticket            │
│                                      │
│  Checks and other items are received │
│  for deposit subject to terms and    │
│  conditions of this institution's    │
│  funds availability policy now in    │
│  effect.                             │
│                                      │
│  DATE _____      Dollars │ Cents  │
│         CURRENCY      29    │  00    │
│         COIN           1    │  05    │
│         CHECKS              │        │
│    1  283-337         25    │  00    │
│    2                        │        │
│    3                        │        │
│    4                        │        │
│    5                        │        │
│    6                        │        │
│    7                        │        │
│    8                        │        │
│    9                        │        │
│   10                        │        │
│   11                        │        │
│   12                        │        │
│                             │        │
│       TOTAL           55    │  05    │
│       LESS CASH             │        │
│       TOTAL DEPOSIT   55    │  05    │
│                                      │
│  Deposits may not be available for   │
│  immediate withdrawal.               │
│  USE OTHER SIDE FOR ADDITIONAL       │
│  LISTING                             │
└─────────────────────────────────────┘
```

This deposit consists of one $25 check, $1.05 in coins, and the remainder in paper currency. (The check number is 283–337.)

$ 25.00
$\underline{+ 1.05}$
$ 26.05

$ 55.05
$\underline{- 26.05}$
$ 29.00

12.

			PAYMENT/DEBIT (−)		✓ T	DEPOSIT/CREDIT (+)		Balance 34,934	94
NUMBER	DATE	DESCRIPTION OF TRANSACTION							
	1/8	Deposit				2,892	12	37,827	06
484	1/15	Glady's Chemical	381	34				37,445	72
485	1/24	Parkersville Electric	85	00				37,360	72
486	1/27	Diamond Realty	883	25				36,477	47
487	1/30	All-City Rest. Sup.	38	01				36,439	46
	1/30	Deposit				55	05	36,494	51

RECORD ALL CHARGES OR CREDITS THAT AFFECT YOUR ACCOUNT

The beginning balance in the check register might be different than the beginning balance in the bank statement for any of several reasons: one or more checks might have been outstanding on the bank statement date, a deposit might have been in transit, a recording error might have been made, and/or the bank may have recorded a debit memo or credit memo.

When checks numbered 484 through 487 were returned to Juan, he checked the endorsement on the back of each check. Juan found that each had used different endorsement types. Endorse each of the following correctly as indicated:

13. Blank Endorsement by Edwena Glady

```
┌─────────────────────────────┐
│                             │
│        Edwena Glady         │
│                             │
└─────────────────────────────┘
```

14. Special Endorsement by Stanley Getts to Boris Herberling

```
┌─────────────────────────────┐
│       Pay to the order of   │
│        Boris Herberling     │
│         Stanley Getts       │
└─────────────────────────────┘
```

Chapter 9 Demand Deposits (Checking Accounts) and Bank Reconciliation

15. Restrictive Endorsement by Roberta Espanosa

```
FOR DEPOSIT ONLY
Roberta Espanosa
```

16. Qualified Endorsement by Theodore Lipps

```
Without Recourse
Theodore Lipps
```

17. Prepare a bank reconciliation for the *Tribunal Law Review Journal* from the following information. The bank statement is dated January 7, 2002.

Check register balance	$58,346.16
Bank statement balance	68,628.62
Outstanding checks (total)	9,549.36
Deposits in transit (total)	4,042.90
Note collected	4,800.00
Bank service charge	24.00

TRIBUNAL LAW REVIEW
Bank Reconciliation Statement
January 7, 2002

Bank statement balance	$68,628.62
Add: Deposits in transit	4,042.90
	$72,671.52
Deduct: Outstanding checks	9,549.36
Reconciled balance	$63,122.16
Check register balance	$58,346.16
Add: Note collected	4,800.00
	$63,146.16
Deduct: Bank service charge	24.00
Reconciled balance	$63,122.16

Word Problems

18. Prepare a bank reconciliation from the following bank statement and check register.

$N NATIONAL BANK
$B OF ANY CITY

1234 Lime Street * Phone 800 555-3456 * Any City, Colo 96544

Sandman Bros.
6845 Maple Ave.
Golden, Colorado 96543

Account No. 691-048-1

Statement Date: 12/12/02
Number of Transactions: 13

On	Your Balance Was	We Added Deposits		We Subtracted Checks	
11/10/02	$385.52	No. 2	$250.00	No. 11	$338.52

YOUR PRESENT BALANCE
$293.00

SERVICE CHARGE
$4.00

Checks and Other Debits			Deposits and Other Credits	Date	Balance
				111002	385.52
19.00	25.00			111102	341.52
32.00	10.50		185.00	111402	484.02
3.15	6.45			111502	474.42
13.90				111902	460.52
44.50	6.02		65.00	112402	475.00
90.00	88.00			120802	202.00
SC 4.00				121202	293.00

PLEASE EXAMINE AT ONCE AND REPORT ANY ERROR IMMEDIATELY

Last amt. is your balance

Please Notify Us of Any Change in Address
Use Reverse Side for Reconciling Your Account

RECORD ALL CHARGES OR CREDITS THAT AFFECT YOUR ACCOUNT

NUMBER	DATE	DESCRIPTION OF TRANSACTION	PAYMENT/DEBIT (−)		✓ T	DEPOSIT/CREDIT (+)		Balance	
								385	52
25	1101	Charley Finley	36	00				349	52
26	1102	Henry Aaron	19	00	X			330	52
27	1105	Reggie Jackson	25	00	X			305	52
28	1107	Louis Apparicio	32	00	X			273	52
29	1108	Salvadore Bando	10	50	X	185	00	448	02
30	1109	Johnny Bench	3	15	X			444	87
31	1112	Brooks Robinson	6	45	X			438	42
32	1116	Jeff Bouroughs	13	90	X			424	52
33	1118	Catfish Hunter	44	50	X			380	02
34	1119	Mark Friedrick	6	02	X	65	00	439	00
35	1123	Toby Harrah	88	00	X			351	00
36	1124	Billy Martin	90	00	X			261	00
37	1125	Muarry Wills	70	02		200	00	390	98
38	1130	Sammy Giaconti	97	98				293	00

Bank statement balance		$293.00	Check register balance	$293.00
Add: Deposit in transit (11/25)		200.00	Deduct: Service charge	4.00
		$493.00	Reconciled balance	$289.00

Deduct: Outstanding checks	#25	$36.00	
	#37	70.02	
	#38	97.98	204.00
Reconciled balance			$289.00

19. First State Bank sent a statement to Forest Hill Golf Club on June 3, 2002. It showed an ending balance of $3,839.23. The bookkeeper for the club found that six checks were outstanding and two deposits were in transit. The checks were #3954 for $382.90, #3958 for $33.45, #3961 for $19.95, #3962 for $55.81, #3963 for $8.15, and #3964 for $50.00. One of the deposits was made on June 1 for $194.50, and the other was for $935.39 made on June 2. In addition, the bank had two DMs, one for the payment of an insurance premium in the amount of $74.50, and the other for payment of a utility bill in the amount of $51.29. There was a bank service charge of $12.75. The balance in the check register was $4,557.40.

Reconcile the statement with the register.

FOREST HILL GOLF CLUB
Bank Reconciliation Statement
June 3, 2002

Bank statement balance			$3,839.23
Add: Deposits in transit (6/1)		$194.50	
(6/2)		935.39	1,129.89
			$4,969.12
Deduct: Outstanding checks	#3954	$382.90	
	#3958	33.45	
	#3961	19.95	
	#3962	55.81	
	#3963	8.15	
	#3964	50.00	550.26
Reconciled balance			$4,418.86
Register balance			$4,557.40
Deduct: Bank service charge		$12.75	
DM insurance		74.50	
DM utility		51.29	138.54
Reconciled balance			$4,418.86

20. On May 3, 2002, Barbells, Inc., received a statement from the Bank of New Jersey. The ending balance was $7,383.02. The balance in the check register was $4,546.83. Total checks outstanding were $3,891.34. There was a DM for an uncollectable check in the amount of $285.65, a DM of $8.00 for handling the uncollectable check, and another DM for a service charge of $11.50. A deposit in transit was for $750.00. Reconcile the statements.

BARBELLS, INC
Bank Reconciliation Statement
May 3, 2002

Bank statement balance		$7,383.02
Add: Deposit in transit		750.00
		$8,133.02
Deduct: Outstanding checks		3,891.34
Reconciled balance		$4,241.68
Register balance		$4,546.83
Deduct: DM Uncollectable check	$285.65	
DM Handling charge	8.00	
DM Service charge	11.50	$ 305.15
Reconciled balance		$4,241.68

21. Lloyd's Bistro had a balance of $28,934.05 in the check register when the bank statement arrived on August 11, 2002, showing a balance of $37,346.21. A comparison showed the following differences:

Checks Outstanding		Deposits in Transit	
No.	Amt.	Date	Amt.
1249	$ 35.00	8/8	$17,985.00
1258	12.50	8/10	4,065.81
1259	110.18		
1260	29,184.29		

DMs		CMs	
Insurance	$1,540.37	Note collection	$2,123.45
Utilities	381.09	EFT for transaction	883.01
Service charge	9.00		

Recording Error in Register
Check #1245 for $127.39 recorded as $172.39
Reconcile the bank statement with the check register.

LLOYD'S BISTRO
Bank Reconciliation Statement
August 11, 2002

Bank statement balance			$37,346.21
Add: Deposits in transit			
	(8/8)	$17,985.00	
	(8/10)	4,065.81	22,050.81
			$59,397.02
Deduct: Outstanding checks			
	#1249	$ 35.00	
	#1258	12.50	
	#1259	110.18	
	#1260	29,184.29	29,341.97
Reconciled balance			$30,055.05
Register balance			$28,934.05
Add: Note collection		$2,123.45	
CM Recording error		45.00	
CM EFT for transaction		883.01	3,051.46
			$31,985.51
Deduct: Insurance		$1,540.37	
DM Utilities		381.09	
DM Service charge		9.00	1,930.46
Reconciled balance			$30,055.05

22. Quality Books and News received its February 12, 2002, bank statement showing an ending balance of $3,485.63. The check register has a balance of $4,383.08. Total outstanding checks are $734.10. One check was recorded in the register as $348.58 but was written for $438.85. The bank collected a $1,000 note for Quality (a CM), and the statement showed two DMs, one for $345.65 to repay a car loan, and the other for $215.00 for building rental. A deposit in transit was for $1,980.63. Reconcile the bank statement with the check register.

QUALITY BOOKS AND NEWS
Bank Reconciliation Statement
February 12, 2002

Bank statement balance		$3,485.63
Add: Deposit in transit		1,980.63
		$5,466.26
Deduct: Outstanding checks		734.10
Reconciled balance		$4,732.16
Register balance		$4,383.08
Add: CM Quality		1,000.00
		$5,383.08
Deduct: Car loan	$345.65	
DM Building rental	215.00	
DM Recording error	90.27	650.92
Reconciled balance		$4,732.16

23. Bledsoe and Co. had a check register balance of $54,505.83. The April 1, 2002, bank statement showed a $52,005.80 balance. It also showed an $82.50 interest income (indicated by a CM), and a DM of $101.48 for payment of a telephone bill. A $660.00 check had been recorded in the register as $550.00. Deposits in transit totaled $22,728.04. Outstanding checks were #573 for $5,500.55, #577 for $11,002.48, and #578 for $3,853.96. Prepare a bank reconciliation for Bledsoe and Co.

BLEDSOE AND CO.
Bank Reconciliation Statement
April 1, 2002

Bank statement balance		$52,005.80
Add: Deposits in transit		22,728.04
		$74,733.84
Deduct: Outstanding checks		
#573	$ 5,500.55	
#577	11,002.48	
#578	3,853.96	20,356.99
Reconciled balance		$54,376.85
Register balance		$54,505.83
Add: CM interest income		82.50
		$54,588.33
Deduct: Recording error	$110.00	
DM telephone bill	101.48	211.48
Reconciled balance		$54,376.85

24. Prepare a bank reconciliation statement for K & G Industries from the following September 23, 2002, bank statement and check register:

BANK STATEMENT					
Checks and Other Debits			**Deposits and Other Credits**	**Date**	**Balance**
					2,021.68
15.60	DM 200.00			081203	2,756.08
117.44			CM 752.68	081803	3,391.32
32.76	1,144.04	15.72		082303	2,198.80
165.08			2,180.60	083003	4,214.32
		DM 32.00		091003	4,182.32

RECORD ALL CHARGES OR CREDITS THAT AFFECT YOUR ACCOUNT							
NUMBER	**DATE**	**DESCRIPTION OF TRANSACTION**	**PAYMENT/DEBIT (−)**		**✓ T**	**DEPOSIT/CREDIT (+)**	**Balance**
							2,021 68
105	8/5	Kirkpatrick Aviator	117	44	X		2,854 24
106	8/7	Herman's Floors	165	08	X		2,689 16
107	8/10	Super Shakers	477	12			2,212 04
108	8/11	Cash	15	60	X		2,196 44
109	8/15	Leonard Shirts	1,144	04	X		1,052 40
110	8/17	Home Supply Depot	32	76	X		1,019 64
111	8/22	Watch Shop Stop	15	72	X		1,003 92
112	8/29	Lots Realty Co.	300	00		2,180 60	2,884 52
113	9/8	1st Baptist Church	100	00		400 00	3,184 52

K & G INDUSTRIES
Bank Reconciliation Statement
September 23, 2002

Bank statement balance			$4,182.32
Add: Deposit in transit			400.00
			$4,582.32
Deduct: Outstanding checks	#107	$477.12	
	#112	300.00	
	#113	100.00	877.12
Reconciled balance			$3,705.20
Register balance			$3,184.52
Add: CM			752.68
			$3,937.20
Deduct: DM	32.00		
DM	200.00		232.00
Reconciled balance			$3,705.20

CRITICAL THINKING GROUP PROJECT

Ken Grady Enterprises had the following check register and bank statement on October 15, 2003:

RECORD ALL CHARGES OR CREDITS THAT AFFECT YOUR ACCOUNT

NUMBER	DATE	DESCRIPTION OF TRANSACTION	PAYMENT/DEBIT (−)		✓ T	DEPOSIT/CREDIT (+)		Balance 79,121	58
7105	9/5	Kelly Morris Vision	317	62				78,803	96
7106	9/7	Hector's Flooring	411	45				78,392	51
7107	9/10	Susan Shadows	165	08				78,227	43
7108	9/11	Caravan Trucks	19	38				78,208	05
7109	9/15	Leo Ardmore Printer	1,101	11				77,106	94
7110	9/17	Hodges' Supplies	20	12				77,086	82
7111	9/22	Weight Watcher Corp	932	76				76,154	06
7112	9/29	Location Finders	7	09				76,146	02
Dep	10/1	Holbrook payment				2,180	60	78,327	57
7113	10/1	1st National Bank	229	42				78,098	15
7114	10/2	Accentuate the Positive	3,485	87				74,612	28
7115	10/2	Life Ins. of America	559	20				74,053	08
7116	10/7	Sydney Sheldon	33	38				74,019	70
7117	10/9	Brenda's Better Way	33,928	94				41,090	76
Dep	10/10	Payment from Linc				330	88	41,421	64
Dep	10/11	Interest income				440	22	41,861	86
7118	10/13	Vernon Spike Ind.	999	73				40,862	13
7119	10/13	Republican Party	27	48				40,834	65
7120	10/13	Data Finder's Co.	229	42				40,605	23
7121	10/13	Eastcoast contractor	481	32				40,123	91
7122	10/14	Quentana Leather	20	15				40,103	76
7123	10/14	Symantha Rogers	491	54				39,612	22
Dep	10/14	Cash from sales				19,093	11	58,705	33
7124	10/14	To payroll account	8,221	07				58,484	26
Dep	10/14	Refund from AALC				229	68	50,713	94
7125	10/14	Meg Tran Cosmetics	98	30				50,615	64
7126	10/14	Ultimate Way Portrait	274	99				50,340	65
7127	10/14	Yousedit Publishing	430	38				49,910	27
Dep	10/14	Payment from WSTS				5,000	00	54,910	27

BANK STATEMENT

Checks and Other Debits			Deposits and Other Credits	Date	Balance 79,121.58
317.62	DM 575.00			091703	78,228.96
411.45	19.38		CM 222.41	092803	78,020.54
932.76	1,101.11	20.12		092903	75,966.55
165.08			2,180.60	093003	77,982.07
DM 72.50				100503	77,909.57
32,928.94	430.38			100703	44,550.25
7.09			330.88	100903	44,874.04
491.54	27.48	229.42	440.22	101003	44,565.82
			19,093.11	101003	63,658.93
8,221.07	999.73	20.15	229.68	101103	54,647.66
274.99				101103	54,372.67

Reconcile the bank statement with the check register.

Ken Grady Enterprises
Bank Reconciliation Statement
September 23, 2003

Bank statement ending balance			$54,372.67
Add: Deposit in transit			5,000.00
			$59,372.67
Deduct: Outstanding checks	#7114	$3,485.87	
	#7115	559.20	
	#7116	33.38	
	#7120	229.42	
	#7121	481.32	
	#7125	98.30	4,887.49
Reconciled balance			$54,485.18
Check register ending balance			$54,910.27
Add: CM			222.41
			$55,132.68
Deduct: DM	$575.00		
DM	72.50		647.50
Reconciled balance			$54,485.18

SELF-TESTING EXERCISES

Answers to all exercises are given in appendix A.

1. Sandman Bros. received a bank statement dated December 12, 2002. The bank statement balance was $293. The check register balance was also $293. The bookkeeper decided that a bank reconciliation statement was unnecessary since the balances agreed. Was the decision right? Why or why not? **W**

   The decision was not right. Outstanding checks, deposits in transit, uncollected notes, bank service charges, etc., could cause either or both balances to be larger or smaller than they might appear.

2. Prepare a bank reconciliation for Arnold Hogg using the following information dated March 7, 2002:

ARNOLD HOGG
Bank Reconciliation Statement
March 7, 2002

Statement balance	$154.80
Check register balance	115.24
Outstanding checks:	$24.96
	21.40
Service charge	6.80

Bank Reconciliation Statement
March 7, 2002

Statement balance		$154.80
Deduct: Outstanding checks	$24.96	
	21.40	46.36
Reconciled balance		$108.44
Register balance		$115.24
Deduct: Service charge		6.80
Reconciled balance		$108.44

3. Write the following check to Mr. James Loftin on 3/24/02 for the amount of $75.23 for a bride doll that was on consignment. The check should be signed with your name. Your name is Joyce Olde.

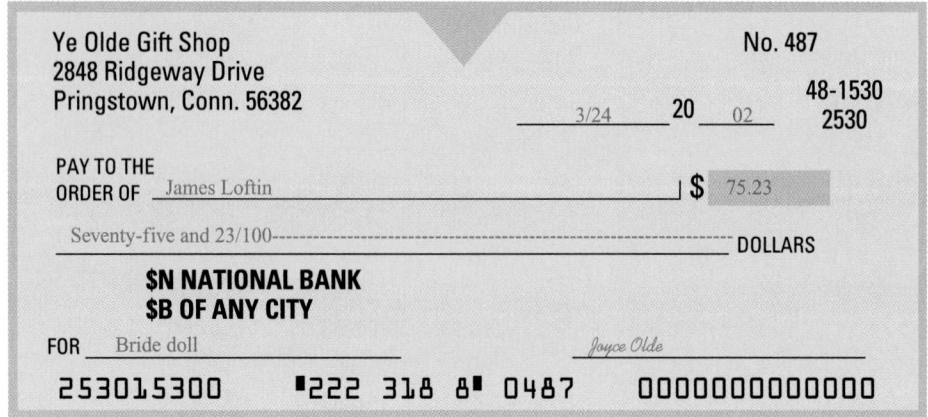

4. Mr. Loftin wants you to sign his name with a restrictive endorsement on the back of the check in Problem 3. Do so in the following space.

```
┌─────────────────────────────┐
│                             │
│     FOR DEPOSIT ONLY        │
│       James Loftin          │
│                             │
└─────────────────────────────┘
```

5. Sam Gioconti made the following deposit:

Checks	Currency	Coin
31–173/1156 for $218.02	1 $100 bill	14 pennies
27–684/3765 for $ 21.75	4 $ 50 bills	7 nickels
	12 $ 20 bills	20 dimes
	10 $ 10 bills	35 quarters
	21 $ 1 bills	

```
$100    $ 50    $ 20    $ 10    $  1
× 1     × 4      12     × 10    × 21
$100 + 200 + 240 + 100 +   21 = $661
```

$$14 \times .01 = \$ .14$$
$$7 \times .05 = .35$$
$$20 \times .10 = 2.00$$
$$35 \times .25 = + 8.75$$
$$\$11.24$$

Record the deposit on the deposit ticket provided here:

$N NATIONAL BANK
$B OF ANY CITY

Deposit Ticket

Checks and other items are received for deposit subject to terms and conditions of this institution's funds availability policy now in effect.

DATE _____

		Dollars	Cents
CURRENCY		661	00
COIN		11	24
CHECKS			
1	31-173	218	02
2	27-684	21	75
3			
4			
5			
6			
7			
8			
9			
10			
11			
12			
TOTAL		912	01
LESS CASH			
TOTAL DEPOSIT		912	01

Deposits may not be available for immediate withdrawal.
USE OTHER SIDE FOR ADDITIONAL LISTING

6. Fill out the following check register given the following information:

Aug. 18	Check #686	to PAY LESS GROCERY	$ 492.59
26	Check #687	to JONES DRUG EMPORIUM	218.20
29	Check #688	to EBONY MAGAZINE	1,550.38
30	Deposit		937.08
Sept. 3	Check #689	to MS. AFRICAN-AMERICAN CONTEST	5,000.00
8	Deposit		3,250.50
11	Check #690	to SEVENTEEN MAGAZINE	2,500.00
15	Deposit		6,350.00

RECORD ALL CHARGES OR CREDITS THAT AFFECT YOUR ACCOUNT								
NUMBER	DATE	DESCRIPTION OF TRANSACTION	PAYMENT/DEBIT (−)		√ T	DEPOSIT/CREDIT (+)		Balance 12,321 29
686	8/18	Pay Less Grocery	492	59				11,828 70
687	8/26	Jones Drug Emporium	218	20				11,610 50
688	8/29	Ebony Magazine	1,550	38				10,060 12
	8/30					937	08	10,902 20
689	9/3	Ms. Afri-Amer. Cont.	5,000	00				5,902 20
	9/8					3,250	50	9,247 70
690	9/11	Seventeen Magazine	2,500	00				6,747 70
	9/15					6,350	00	13,002 70

7. Lucky Lady Truck Stop received a bank statement in the mail on January 17, 2003. The ending balance was $7,284.39. The balance in the check register was $5,291.17. Total outstanding checks were $3,393.44, and the deposits in transit totaled $2,257.92. The statement balance included two CMs totaling $850.75 and one DM for $35.05. One check written for $328.00 had been recorded in the register as $382.00. The bank service charge was $12.00. Reconcile the balances.

LUCKY LADY TRUCK STOP
Bank Reconciliation Statement
January 17, 2003

Bank statement balance		$7,284.39
Add: Deposits in transit		2,257.92
		$9,542.31
Deduct: Outstanding checks		3,393.44
Reconciled balance		$6,148.87
Register balance		$5,291.17
Add: CMs	850.75	
Recording error	54.00	904.75
		$6,195.92
Deduct: DM	35.05	
Service charge	12.00	47.05
Reconciled balance		$6,148.87

8. Skyway Lounge had a balance of $45,246.46 in its check register. The bank statement dated 3/24/02 showed an ending balance of $40,990.56. Following are the differences in the two balances:

1. Checks not recorded in bank statement were: #73, $28.50; #77, $22.75; #79, $114.70; #80, $12.56; #81, $1,940.27; and #82, $338.34.

2. Deposits in transit were $205.10 on 3/22 and $5,421.08 on 3/23.

3. A check for $45.10 was recorded as $45.01.

4. The bank collected a note for $513.04.

5. The bank paid drafts as follows: on 3/12 to Federal Savings for payment of a loan, $123.11; on 3/20 to Blue Note Recording Studios for monthly royalty fee, $500.00; and on 3/21 to Mutual Benefit Fire Insurance Co., $219.23.

6. An uncollectable check due to NSF was returned. It was for $710.45.

7. The bank charge for handling the NSF check was $8.00.

8. The bank charge for collecting the note was $15.00.

9. The bank service charge was $24.00.

Reconcile the balances.

SKYWAY LOUNGE
Bank Reconciliation Statement
March 24, 2002

Bank statement balance			$40,990.56
Add: Deposits in transit (3/22)		$ 205.10	
(3/23)		5,421.08	5,626.18
			$46,616.74
Deduct: Outstanding checks #73		$ 28.50	
	#77	22.75	
	#79	114.70	
	#80	12.56	
	#81	1,940.27	
	#82	338.34	2,457.12
Reconciled balance			$44,159.62
Register balance			$45,246.46
Add: CM			513.04
			$45,759.50
Deduct: Recording error		$ .09	
DMs Federal Savings		123.11	
Blue Note Recording		500.00	
Mutual Benefit		219.23	
Uncollectable check		710.45	
Handling charge		8.00	
Collection charge		15.00	
Service charge		24.00	1,599.88
Reconciled balance			$44,159.62

APPLICATION 1

Application 1 is a check register for the first 15 days of September for the Springfield Department Store. Enter the date, the beginning balance, whether the transaction is a check (by entering the check number) or a deposit, the transaction description, and the check or deposit amount (in the proper column). The spreadsheet program will automatically calculate the balance for you. When you enter Ch09App1 from your computer spreadsheet applications disk, you will see the form shown here:

Springfield Department Store

2617 Main Street
Box 219
Springfield, Maryland 58109
Telephone: 301-555-2158   FAX: 301-555-3498

CHECK REGISTER

Date	Chk # or Deposit	Transaction Description	Check Amount	Deposit Amount	Balance
					$0.00
					$0.00
					$0.00
					$0.00
					$0.00
					$0.00
					$0.00
					$0.00
					$0.00
					$0.00
					$0.00
					$0.00
					$0.00
					$0.00
					$0.00
					$0.00
					$0.00
					$0.00
					$0.00
					$0.00
					$0.00
					$0.00
					$0.00
					$0.00
					$0.00
					$0.00
					$0.00
					$0.00
					$0.00
					$0.00
					$0.00
					$0.00

Enter the following information:

1. In cell A13, the date 9/1/02.
2. In cell C13, the beginning balance.
3. In cell F13, $23,912.29.
4. In cells A14 through E45, the following information:

Date	Check # or Deposit	Transaction Description	Check Amount	Deposit Amount
9/2/02	Deposit	Daily receipts		$ 38,912.99
9/2/02	6745	Mason's Wholesale Sporting Goods	$ 42,199.31	
9/2/02	6746	Mitchell's Supply	478.92	
9/2/02	6747	Nexus Computers	11,847.33	
9/3/02	Deposit	Daily receipts		33,674.03
9/3/02	6748	Power & Light	4,567.21	
9/3/02	6749	Water dept.	2,854.50	
9/3/02	6750	Bell Telephone	5,274.11	
9/3/02	6751	West Distributors	14,832.94	
9/6/02	Deposit	Weekend receipts		156,285.17
9/6/02	6752	Great Falls Bedding	25,875.09	
9/6/02	6753	Ysplanz Furniture	38,194.55	
9/6/02	6754	USA Insurance	7,392.82	
9/7/02	Deposit	Daily receipts		29,476.45
9/7/02	6755	GMAC	22,487.01	
9/7/02	6756	MacDougal Hardware Supplier	10,457.84	
9/7/02	6757	Morganchild Realty	54,022.91	
9/8/02	Deposit	Daily receipts		40,172.66
9/8/02	6758	Overhead Door Repair	832.55	
9/8/02	6759	Ralph's Market	48,091.65	
9/9/02	Deposit	Daily receipts		35,913.90
9/9/02	6760	Utley Brokers	53,987.22	
9/10/02	Deposit	Daily receipts		42,987.87
9/10/02	6761	I. W. B.	138.48	
9/10/02	6762	Teddy's Carpet Cleaners	739.13	
9/13/02	Deposit	Weekend receipts		133,094.19
9/13/02	6763	Egwaite Enterprises	58,902.44	
9/14/02	Deposit	Daily Receipts		41,908.75
9/15/02	Deposit	Daily Receipts		37,493.33
9/15/02	Deposit	Transfer from savings		97,123.49
9/15/02	6764	Jones Bros. remodeling	82,573.88	
9/15/02	6765 - 6818	Payroll	187,301.27	

Answer the following questions after you have completed the spreadsheet:

1. What was the final check register balance on September 15?
2. What was the amount due and the balance after the entry for Ysplanz Furniture?
3. What was the balance after the Overhead Door Repair invoice was paid?
4. What will the balance be after check #6762 clears?
5. What transaction results in the balance of $14,444.99?

APPLICATION 2

Springfield needs to prepare a bank reconciliation statement for July 2002. After receiving the bank statement for July and comparing it to the check register, several entries need to be made. Using your spreadsheet applications disk, open Ch09App2. Your computer screen will appear as follows:

	A	B	C	D	E	F	G	H
1				SPRINGFIELD DEPARTMENT STORE				
2				2617 Main Street				
3				Box 219				
4				Springfield, Maryland 58109				
5				Telephone 301-555-2158 Fax 301-555-3496				
6								
7				BANK RECONCILIATION STATEMENT				
8								
9								
10		BANK STATEMENT			CHECKBOOK REGISTER			
11				*Amount*				*Amount*
12	*ENDING BALANCE*				*ENDING BALANCE*			
13		Date	Amount				Date	Amount
14	Deposits Not				Credit Deposits			
15	Shown on Statement:				and Transfers			
16								
17								
18								
19								
20	TOTAL DEPOSITS			$0.00	TOTAL DEP & TRANS			$0.00
21	BALANCE + DEPOSITS			$0.00	BALANCE + DEP + TRANS			$0.00
22								
23		Number	Amount				Date	Amount
24	Checks Issued but				Debit Checks and			
25	Not on Statement:				Bank Charges:			
26								
27					Insurance Draft			
28					Utilities Draft			
29					Bank Service Charge			
30								
31								
32								
33								
34								
35								
36								
37								
38								
39	TOTAL CHECKS			$0.00	TOTAL CKS & BK CHG			$0.00
40	*RECONCILED BALANCE*			*$0.00*	*RECONCILED BALANCE*			*$0.00*

Enter the following information:

1. The ending balance from the bank statement is $37,937.93 (cell D12).
2. The ending balance from the checkbook register is $30,606.68 (cell H12).

3. Deposits not shown on statement:

DATE		AMOUNT	
7/27/02	cell B16	$ 7,236.45	cell C16
7/28/02	cell B17	$52,399.34	cell C17
7/29/02	cell B18	$33,983.22	cell C18
7/30/02	cell B19	$ 8,229.96	cell C19

4. Credit deposits and transfers:

DATE		AMOUNT	
7/19/02	cell F16	$2,834.39	cell G16
7/20/02	cell F17	$ 398.02	cell G17

5. Checks issued but not on statement:

NUMBER		AMOUNT	
7409	cell B26	$ 3,778.92	cell C26
7412	cell B27	$ 847.99	cell C27
7418	cell B28	$14,926.03	cell C28
7419	cell B29	$ 29.56	cell C29
7420	cell B30	$ 2,298.45	cell C30
7421	cell B31	$ 9,153.83	cell C31
7422	cell B32	$44,917.75	cell C32
7424	cell B33	$ 11.73	cell C33
7425	cell B34	$ 2,202.50	cell C34
7426	cell B35	$10,337.39	cell C35
7427	cell B36	$ 19.48	cell C36
7428	cell B37	$22,519.87	cell C37

6. Description of debit checks and bank charges:

Insurance draft	cell E27
Utilities draft	cell E28
Bank service charge	cell E29

7. Debit checks and bank charges:

DATE		AMOUNT	
7/21/02	cell F27	$3,754.29	cell G27
7/30/02	cell F28	$1,276.05	cell G28
7/31/02	cell F29	$ 66.35	cell G29

Answer the following questions after you have completed the spreadsheet:

1. What is the amount of the total deposits entered in the bank statement?
2. What is the amount of the credit deposits and transfers entered in the check register?
3. What is the amount of total checks entered in the bank statement?
4. What is the amount of total debit checks and transfers entered in the check register?
5. What is the amount of the bank statement ending balance and deposits?
6. What is the amount of the check register ending balance, deposits, and transfers?
7. What is the reconciled balance?

GROUP REPORT

FOR CHAPTER 9 APPLICATION 2

Send a memo to the manager of the accounting department that explains the items in the bank reconciliation statement. An explanation is not necessary for each item in the statement. However, each section should be explained, and if the items in a section vary, the reason for their inclusion should be explained.

10 BANKING APPLICATIONS
SIMPLE INTEREST

HIGH, LOW, AND RELEVANT

"What is the interest rate on the old mortgage?" That was a very legitimate counterquestion to Al's aging neighbor's question, "Should I pay off my mortgage?" The answer was 5.25%. Is 5.25% a high mortgage rate? Today five and a quarter sounds really good, but in 1955 mortgages all over town were going for 4.5%.

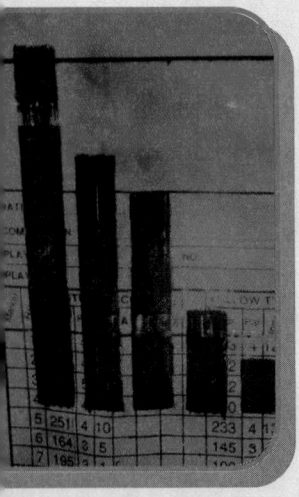

In 1985 Mr. Chan, a newly naturalized American from Cambodia, bought a house and paid a 12% rate. This may sound as though the mortgage company had taken advantage of Mr. Chan, but in 1985, 16% was not unusual. In recent years economists and market analysts have debated the Federal Reserve's attempts to control the economy through interest rate increases and decreases. People who oppose high rates say the nation will not have enough investment (spending for capital goods) if rates are too high, and that will cause unemployment. Those who favor higher rates fear that low rates encourage too little foreign investment, and that can cause a decrease in the value of American money.

But what do *high* and *low* mean? In 1932, the worst year of the Great Depression, Harry's factory had not operated for six months because nobody had any money to buy his product. He was told that the local bank would lend to a qualified customer for $1\frac{1}{2}\%$. Even at that rate Harry couldn't borrow since he had few customers for his product. Even if he had wanted to, a banker probably would not have lent regardless of the interest rate.

Sandra discovered that her firm could earn $1 million this week if it made a $2 million investment today, but not if she waited. She had inside information that the 9% rate today would be 8% next week. Sandra will borrow today anyway, regardless of the interest rate.

Beatrice heard that tomorrow the bank will pay 3.5% instead of 3% on savings accounts. Beatrice's company shut down a year ago, and since then she has been living on state unemployment benefits. She will not increase her savings; she is spending all she receives.

High or low? It is relative.

Chapter Glossary

Interest. The amount charged for the use of borrowed money.

Principal. The amount of money borrowed or invested.

Rate of interest. The percent charged for a loan or earned on an investment *each year*.

Time in a loan period. The time taken to repay the principal with interest, written in years or a fraction of a year.

Ordinary (banker's) interest. Interest calculated on the basis of an assumed 360-day year.

Exact interest. Interest calculated on the basis of a 365-day year (366 days in a leap year).

Usury. An exorbitant amount or rate of interest.

Maturity value. The total amount to be paid or received by the due date of a loan or an investment. It is the sum of the principal and interest.

U.S. Rule. The most often used method of calculating the amount of a partial payment that will be applied to the principal and interest. Interest is the dollar charge on the principal (a loan or an investment) for a definite period of time at a specific annual rate. Every business and every person at some time earns or pays interest.

LEARNING UNIT 1
FINDING THE INTEREST

Every person has a stake in interest. Many people will spend more money on interest charges during their lives than on all the goods and services they will buy. If that is a little frightening, it suggests the beginning of understanding the importance of knowledge about interest.

The formula for calculating interest is

$$\text{Interest} = \text{principal} \times \text{rate} \times \text{time.}$$

It is usually written

$$I = PRT$$

where

- I = **interest**, the amount charged or paid for the use of money or compensation to savers for the act of saving,
- P = **principal**, the amount of money borrowed or invested—the *face value* of a loan or an investment,
- R = **rate of interest**, the percent charged for a loan or the percent earned on an investment *each year*, and
- T = **time**, the time taken to repay the principal with interest, written in terms of years or a fraction of a year.

Time in an interest problem is always written in terms of years or a fraction of a year. It is often stated in different time periods. In the next three sections time will be stated in years, months, and days.

10.1 Calculating Interest When Time Is Stated in Years

When you hear or read that a rate of interest is 10%, that means that the *annual* rate of interest is 10%. Time has to be written in years or as a fraction of a year because money borrowed, saved, or invested for longer or shorter periods than exactly one year will have a real rate that is higher or lower than 10%. That is why items in the formula must always be stated in the same terms. When time is stated in years, the calculations are straightforward and relatively simple. There are three possibilities: time will be exactly one year, more than one year, or less than one year.

EXAMPLE Adams Wholesalers borrowed $8,000 for one year at a rate of 7%. How much interest must Adams pay?

Solution $I = PRT$
$I = \$8,000 \times 7\% \times 1$ *Time is always written in years or fractions of a year.*
$I = \$560$

EXAMPLE Hoover Department Store borrowed $250,000 for two years at a rate of 8.5%. Find the interest that will be paid.

Solution $I = PRT$
$I = \$250,000 \times 8.5\% \times 2$ *Time is stated and written in years, 2 years.*
$I = \$42,500$

EXAMPLE   Driscal Drugs borrowed $28,000 for half a year at a 9.2% rate. Find the interest that will be paid.

Solution $I = PRT$

$I = \$28,000 \times 9.2\% \times \dfrac{1}{2}$ *Time is written as stated, half a year.*

$I = \$1,288$

10.1 Practice Problems

Calculate the interest in the following problems:
1. Liu's Bakery borrowed $2,000 for one year at 12%. Find the interest Liu's had to pay.
2. The National Bank of Springfield made a loan of $50,000 for a quarter of a year at 9%. Find the interest earned.
3. Faverhousen Steel borrowed $12,500 for four years at $6\frac{1}{4}\%$. Determine the interest to be paid.
4. Lionel invested in a $10,000 government treasury bond for half a year at 7%. Find the interest to be earned.

10.1 Solutions to Practice Problems

1. $I = PRT$

   $= \$2,000 \times 12\% \times 1$

   $= \$240$

2. $I = PRT$

   $= \$50,000 \times 9\% \times \dfrac{1}{4}$

   $= \$1,125$

3. $I = PRT$

   $= \$12,500 \times 4 \times 6\frac{1}{4}\%$

   $= \$3,125$

4. $I = PRT$

   $= \$10,000 \times 7\% \times \dfrac{1}{2}$

   $= \$350$

10.2 Calculating Interest When Time Is Stated in Months

If time is not stated in years, it must be converted into yearly terms before the interest formula can be used. When time is stated in months, it must be converted to years by dividing the number of months in the time period by 12 (the number of months in a year).

EXAMPLE   Calculate the interest on a loan of $25,000 at 6% for two months.

Solution $I = PRT$

$= \$25,000 \times 6\% \times \dfrac{2}{12}$ *Divide the 2 months in the loan by 12 months in a year.*

$= \$250$

$$25,000 \;\boxtimes\; 6\;\% \;\boxtimes\; 2 \;\div\; 12 = 250$$

Even if the number of months in the loan period exceeds one year, it is still divided by 12 (the number of months in a year).

EXAMPLE   Calculate the interest on a loan of $14,000 at 5% for 36 months.

Solution $I = PRT$

$= \$14,000 \times 5\% \times \dfrac{36}{12}$ *36 months is 3 years, or 36 divided by 12.*

$= \$2,100$

1. A retailer wants to borrow $40,000 for four months at 12%. Find the amount of interest the retailer will pay.
2. Calculate the interest that will be paid on a note of $250,000 at 10% for one month.
3. Vereen Discount Carpet needs to borrow $66,000. The bank has offered a rate of 9% for 30 months. Find the interest that will be paid.
4. Morganstall National Bank has invested $2,500,000 in a short-term note paying 12% in 8 months. How much interest will Morganstall earn?

10.2 Solutions to Practice Problems

1. $I = PRT$

   $= \$40,000 \times 12\% \times \dfrac{4}{12}$

   $= \$1,600$

2. $I = PRT$

   $= \$250,000 \times 10\% \times \dfrac{1}{12}$

   $= \$2,083.33$

3. $I = PRT$

   $= \$66,000 \times 9\% \times \dfrac{30}{12}$

   $= \$14,850$

4. $I = PRT$

   $= \$2,500,000 \times 12\% \times \dfrac{8}{12}$

   $= \$200,000$

10.3 Calculating Interest When Time Is Stated in Days

EXCEL Spreadsheet Application
Spreadsheet Application 1 at the end of this chapter is a spreadsheet program that the Springfield Department Store uses to make calculations on simple interest loans.

When time is stated in days, two methods are commonly used to calculate the time:

1. *Ordinary interest*. Ordinary interest is the term used when interest is calculated assuming a year has 360 days. This is also referred to as **banker's interest**. *Unless otherwise stated, always use banker's interest to calculate the time in interest problems.*
2. *Exact interest*. Exact interest is the term used when interest is being calculated using a 365-day year.

Use the same methods of calculating the exact number of days in the loan or investment period as were used to find invoice due dates. Those methods were discussed in Chapter 7.

Table 10.1 for finding the exact number of days from the beginning of the year to any date (excluding leap year) has been reprinted in this chapter, for convenience. To find the number of days in a loan period using the table:

Find the number of days for a loan that was made on March 8 and was due on September 24.

1. September 24 is the 267th day of the year:
   a. Find 24 in the leftmost column of Table 10.1.
   b. Go across that row until it intersects with the column headed by September.
   c. The number at that intersection is 267, meaning that September 24 is the 267th day of the year.
2. March 8 is the 67th day of the year:
   a. Find 8 in the leftmost column of Table 10.1.
   b. Go across that row until it intersects with the column headed by March.

TABLE 10.1   EXACT NUMBER OF DAYS FROM BEGINNING OF YEAR TO ANY DATE

Day of Month	Jan.	Feb.	Mar.	Apr.	May	June	July	Aug.	Sept.	Oct.	Nov.	Dec.	Day of Month
1	1	32	60	91	121	152	182	213	244	274	305	335	1
2	2	33	61	92	122	153	183	214	245	275	306	336	2
3	3	34	62	93	123	154	184	215	246	276	307	337	3
4	4	35	63	94	124	155	185	216	247	277	308	338	4
5	5	36	64	95	125	156	186	217	248	278	309	339	5
6	6	37	65	96	126	157	187	218	249	279	310	340	6
7	7	38	66	97	127	158	188	219	250	280	311	341	7
8	8	39	67	98	128	159	189	220	251	281	312	342	8
9	9	40	68	99	129	160	190	221	252	282	313	343	9
10	10	41	69	100	130	161	191	222	253	283	314	344	10
11	11	42	70	101	131	162	192	223	254	284	315	345	11
12	12	43	71	102	132	163	193	224	255	285	316	346	12
13	13	44	72	103	133	164	194	225	256	286	317	347	13
14	14	45	73	104	134	165	195	226	257	287	318	348	14
15	15	46	74	105	135	166	196	227	258	288	319	349	15
16	16	47	75	106	136	167	197	228	259	289	320	350	16
17	17	48	76	107	137	168	198	229	260	290	321	351	17
18	18	49	77	108	138	169	199	230	261	291	322	352	18
19	19	50	78	109	139	170	200	231	262	292	323	353	19
20	20	51	79	110	140	171	201	232	263	293	324	354	20
21	21	52	80	111	141	172	202	233	264	294	325	355	21
22	22	53	81	112	142	173	203	234	265	295	326	356	22
23	23	54	82	113	143	174	204	235	266	296	327	357	23
24	24	55	83	114	144	175	205	236	267	297	328	358	24
25	25	56	84	115	145	176	206	237	268	298	329	359	25
26	26	57	85	116	146	177	207	238	269	299	330	360	26
27	27	58	86	117	147	178	208	239	270	300	331	361	27
28	28	59	87	118	148	179	209	240	271	301	332	362	28
29	29	—	88	119	149	180	210	241	272	302	333	363	29
30	30	—	89	120	150	181	211	242	273	303	334	364	30
31	31	—	90	—	151	—	212	243	—	304	—	365	31

   c. The number at that intersection is 67, meaning that March 8 is the 67th day of the year.

3. Subtract the day of the year the note was made from the day of the year the note is due to find the number of days in the loan period:

$$\begin{array}{r} 267 \\ -\ 67 \\ \hline 200 \text{ days in the loan period} \end{array}$$

Whether ordinary or exact interest is used, 360 or 365 will be the denominator in the fractional part of a year. The numerator will be the exact number of days in a loan or investment period. When time is stated in days, the two possible time fractions are as follows:

<table>
<tr><td align="center">Ordinary Interest</td><td align="center">Exact Interest</td></tr>
<tr><td align="center">exact number of days</td><td align="center">exact number of days</td></tr>
<tr><td align="center">360</td><td align="center">365</td></tr>
</table>

EXAMPLE   A loan of $1,500,000 at 12% was dated on March 8. It was due on September 24. Determine the amount of interest using (1) the ordinary (banker's) interest method and (2) the exact interest method.

Solution   Calculate the exact time in the loan period: The loan was dated on March 8. March has 31 days in it; therefore,

31 days − 8 days = 23 days in March
30 days in April
31 days in May
30 days in June
31 days in July   *The only two consecutive calendar*
31 days in August   *months with 31 days Loan due date*
24 days in September

Total   200 days in the loan period

The ordinary (banker's) interest method assumes 360 days in a year:

$$I = PRT$$

$$= \$1,500,000 \times 12\% \times \frac{200}{360}$$

$$= \$100,000$$

The exact interest method uses 365 days in a year:

$$I = PRT$$

$$= \$1,500,000 \times 12\% \times \frac{200}{365}$$

$$= \$98,630.14$$

The banker's interest method results in a larger amount of interest during the same time period. The conventional reason given for using a 360-day year is that it makes calculations easier. However, with the widespread use of tables, calculators, and computers, that claim has lost its credibility. The real reason for using a 360-day year is that it provides banks and other financial institutions with larger interest returns with the same rate. Oregon's attorney general filed suit against lenders citing **usury** violations. The banks were at the top of the state's allowable interest rates and were basing the interest on 360 days. By dividing 365 by 360, the state showed that the actual rates were higher than the stated rates(called the nominal rate). Instead of 10% the rate was actually 10.139%, and 12% was actually 12.167%. Oregon's banks now use 365-day years. That ruling may well set a trend.

10.3 Practice Problems

1. A loan of $35,000 at 8% dated April 30 was due on May 30. Use the ordinary interest method to calculate the interest.

2. Bill's Place, a local fitness center, borrowed $75,000 on September 29 to renovate the interior. The bank's rate is 7.5%, and the note comes due on December 28. Calculate the interest using the exact interest method.

3. Lionel Standifer borrowed $210,000 at 9% for 120 days to start a business. Find the interest charge using both the ordinary and exact interest methods.

4. A certificate of deposit (CD) for $500,000 had an interest rate of 4.9% for 180 days. Calculate the interest.

10.3 Solutions to Practice Problems

1. $I = PRT$ April has 30 days

$$= \$35,000 \times 8\% \times \frac{30}{360}$$ − 30 days   *Date of note*

$$= \$233.33$$ 0 days in April

          + 30 days in May   *Due date*

          Total   30 days

344 **Chapter 10** Banking Applications: Simple Interest

2. $I = PRT$

$\quad = \$75,000 \times 7.5\% \times \dfrac{90}{365}$

$\quad = \$1,386.99$

September has 30 days
$\quad\quad\quad\quad\quad \underline{-\ 29 \text{ days}}$ *Date of note*
$\quad\quad\quad\quad\quad\quad 1 \text{ day in Sept.}$
$\quad\quad\quad\quad\quad\quad 31 \text{ days in Oct.}$
$\quad\quad\quad\quad\quad\quad 30 \text{ days in Nov.}$
$\quad\quad\quad\quad\quad \underline{+\ 28 \text{ days in Dec.}}$ *Due date*
Total$\quad\quad\quad 90 \text{ days}$

3. $I = PRT$ $\quad\quad\quad\quad\quad\quad\quad\quad\quad\quad I = PRT$

$\quad\quad$ *Ordinary* $\quad\quad\quad\quad\quad\quad\quad\quad\quad$ *Exact*

$\quad = \$210,000 \times 9\% \times \dfrac{120}{360}$ $\quad\quad = \$210,000 \times 9\% \times \dfrac{120}{365}$

$\quad = \$6,300$ $\quad\quad\quad\quad\quad\quad\quad\quad\quad = \$6,213.70$

4. Since the problem did not state the method of calculation, the ordinary interest method is used.

$I = PRT$

$\quad = \$500,000 \times 4.9\% \times \dfrac{180}{360}$

$\quad = \$12,250$

10.4 Calculating the Maturity Value

The **maturity value** is the total value of a loan or an investment. The total value is the principal plus the interest. The maturity value is the amount to be paid by the due date, which is referred to as the maturity date. The formula for calculating the maturity value is

$$\text{Maturity value} = \text{principal} + \text{interest}$$
$$MV = P + I$$

or, if all you really need to know is the maturity value, it can also be found by using the following formula

$$\text{Maturity value} = \text{principal}(1 + \text{Rate} \times \text{Time})$$
$$MV = P[(1 + (RT)]$$

When using a calculator to make this calculation, be aware that if your calculator is arithmetic (not algebraic), it does the calculations in sequence instead of by mathematical priority. To be safe, multiply RT first, add 1, and then multiply by P. When using a calculator, do not round the intermediate answer before multiplying the principal. In this section, the intermediate answers will not be rounded.

If time is stated in days, it will always be based on ordinary interest (360 days) if not otherwise stated. If the exact interest method is to be used, the time will be based on a 365-day year.

E X A M P L E   Find the maturity value of a $60,000 note at 6% for 120 days.

Solution   To solve this problem by the first formula, $MV = P + I$, first calculate the interest:

$\quad\quad I = PRT$ $\quad\quad\quad\quad\quad\quad\quad\quad MV = P + I$

$\quad\quad = \$60,000 \times 6\% \times \dfrac{120}{360}$ $\quad\quad\quad = \$60,000 + \$1,200$

$\quad\quad\quad\quad\quad\quad\quad\quad\quad\quad\quad\quad\quad\quad = \$61,200$

$\quad\quad = \$1,200$

To solve using the second formula:

$$MV = P(1 + RT)$$
$$= \$60{,}000\left[1 + \left(6\% \times \frac{120}{360}\right)\right]$$
$$= \$60{,}000(1.02)$$
$$= \$61{,}200$$

10.4 Practice Problems

1. Find the maturity value of a $30,000 loan at 8% for 60 days.
2. Find the maturity value of a $950 loan at 10% for 180 days.
3. Determine the maturity value of a 7%, $250,000 note dated July 21 and due October 9. Use the exact interest method.
4. Calculate the maturity value of a 13% loan of $50,000 dated May 3 and due July 12.

10.4 Solutions to Practice Problems

1. $MV = P(1 + RT)$

$$= \$30{,}000\left[1 + \left(8\% \times \frac{60}{360}\right)\right]$$
$$= \$30{,}000 \times 1.0133333$$
$$= \$30{,}400$$

2. $MV = P(1 + RT)$

$$= \$950\left[1 + \left(10\% \times \frac{180}{360}\right)\right]$$
$$= \$950 \times 1.05$$
$$= \$997.50$$

3. $MV = P(1 + RT)$

$$= \$250{,}000\left[1 + \left(7\% \times \frac{80}{365}\right)\right]$$
$$= \$250{,}000 \times 1.0153425$$
$$= \$253{,}835.62$$

July	31 days	
	−21 days	Date of note
	10 days	
Aug.	31 days	
Sept.	30 days	
Oct.	+ 9 days	Due date of note
Total	80 days	

4. $MV = P(1 + RT)$

$$= \$50{,}000\left[1 + \left(13\% \times \frac{70}{360}\right)\right]$$
$$= \$50{,}000 \times 1.0252778$$
$$= \$51{,}263.89$$

May	31 days	
	− 3 days	Date of loan
	28 days	
June	30 days	
July	+12 days	Due date of loan
Total	70 days	

10.5 Cash Discounts and Simple Interest

Chapter 7 discussed cash discounts. Cash discounts are given by a seller to encourage early payment of debts. The topic to be addressed in this section is, when a buyer does not have enough cash available to pay a bill early and take advantage of a cash discount, should the buyer borrow the money and pay the debt?

EXAMPLE Kravitz Car and Plane Models received a $21,000 invoice with terms of 3/10, n/30. Kravitz does not have the cash to pay the invoice at the end of 10 days and take advantage of the 3% discount. However, a bank has agreed to lend the necessary funds at 9.9% for the 20 days the bill has to be paid early. Should Kravitz borrow the money?

Solution Based solely on financial considerations, follow these steps:

1. Find the net cost of the invoice if the discount is taken. (Use the complement method, 100% − 3% = 97%.)

$$\$21{,}000 \times 97\% = \$20{,}370$$

2. Find the amount of the discount.

$$\$21{,}000 - 20{,}370 = \$630$$

3. Determine the amount of interest.

$$I = PRT$$
$$= \$20{,}370 \times 9.9\% \times \frac{20}{360}$$
$$= \$112.04$$

4. Compare the two and find the difference.

$$\$630 \text{ discount} - \$112.04 \text{ interest} = \$517.96$$

5. It would definitely be financially advantageous to borrow the money and pay the invoice within the cash discount period.

Considerations other than purely financial are often important and impact borrowing decisions. For example, banks often have minimum amounts that they will loan. Paperwork costs often dictate these minimums. Also, if the savings from borrowing to pay the cash discount is small, the time necessary to find a lending source and make the arrangements, travel time and cost, and other considerations may make it impractical to pursue a loan. The questions in the problems for this section should be answered on a financial basis only.

10.5 Practice Problems

1. An $800 invoice had terms of 1/10, n/30. Funds can be borrowed at 11% to pay the invoice within the discount period. Find the amount of the discount and the amount of interest. Should the money be borrowed?
2. A $6,000 invoice had terms of 2/10, n/30. Funds can be borrowed at 13% to pay the invoice within the discount period. Find the amount of the discount and the amount of interest. Should the money be borrowed?
3. A $24,000 invoice had terms of 3/15, n/45. Funds can be borrowed at 12.5% to pay the invoice within the discount period. Find the amount of the discount and the amount of interest. Should the money be borrowed?
4. A $795 invoice had terms of 1/10, n/60. Funds can be borrowed at 12.2% to pay the invoice within the discount period. Find the amount of the discount and the amount of interest. Should the money be borrowed?

10.5 Solutions to Practice Problems

1. $800 \times 99\% = \$792$ Net cost
   $800 - 792 = \$8$ Discount
   $$\$792 \times 11\% \times \frac{20}{360} = \$4.84 \quad \text{Interest}$$
   Yes, the money should be borrowed.

2. $6,000 \times 98\% = \$5{,}880$ Net cost
   $6,000 - 5{,}880 = \$120$ Discount
   $$\$5{,}880 \times 13\% \times \frac{20}{360} = \$42.47 \quad \text{Interest}$$
   Yes, the money should be borrowed.

3. $24,000 \times 97\% = \$23{,}280$ Net cost
   $24,000 - 23{,}280 = \$720$ Discount
   $$\$23{,}280 \times 12.5\% \times \frac{30}{360} = \$242.50 \quad \text{Interest}$$
   Yes, the money should be borrowed.

4. $795 \times 99\% = \$787.05$ Net cost
   $795 - \$787.05 = \$7.95$ Discount
   $$\$787.05 \times 12.2\% \times \frac{50}{360} = \$13.34 \quad \text{Interest}$$
   No, the money should not be borrowed.

USING THE SIMPLE INTEREST FORMULA TO FIND THE PRINCIPAL, RATE, OR TIME

To this point, all problems were solved for interest given the principal, rate, and time. *Unless otherwise stated, always use ordinary interest (360-day years)*. There are times when the interest is known, and one of the other figures needs to be determined. This section of the chapter will describe how to find the principal, rate, or time.

The formula $I = PRT$ can be rewritten to find each of the other unknowns. The four possible formulas are as follows:

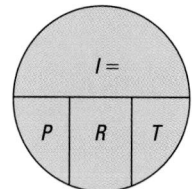

$$I = PRT, \quad P = \frac{I}{RT}, \quad R = \frac{I}{PT}, \quad \text{and } T = \frac{I}{PR}$$

The unknown is isolated (by itself) on the left side of the formula. If the interest (I) is known, it is always divided by the product of the other two known values. Remembering that may be easier than memorizing those three formulas. Having covered Chapter 4, Solving for the Unknowns in Formulas and Equations, the unknown can be determined using the techniques discussed in that chapter.

Two other methods that may help you rapidly remember the formulas are:

Always write the format:

$$\frac{I}{P}$$
$$\times$$
$$R$$
$$\times$$
$$T$$

Interest is always on top. When the known amounts are placed in the format, one will be blank. If I is blank, multiply PRT. However, if I is known, divide it by the product of the other two known amounts.

Cover the unknown amount with your finger to find its formula. To find the formula for interest (I), cover the I with your finger. The formula is $I = PRT$. To find the formula for principal (P), cover the P with your finger. The formula is $P = \dfrac{I}{RT}$. Cover R to find the formula for rate, and cover T to find the formula for time.

Use the circle sketch:

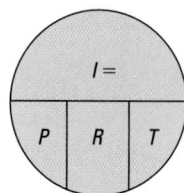

10.6 ## Calculating the Principal

When interest, rate, and time, are known, the principal can be found using the following formula:

$$P = \frac{I}{RT}$$

E X A M P L E Calculate the principal of an 8% note that earned $160 in 60 days.

Solution

$$P = \frac{I}{RT}$$

$$P = \frac{\$160}{8\% \times \dfrac{60}{360}}$$

Here, there is a fraction in the denominator of a fraction.

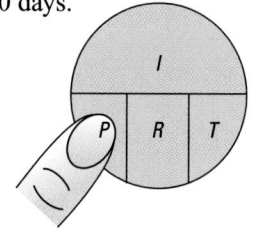

When a common **fraction is in the denominator of a common fraction such as that above, it will be inverted (turned upside down). When that is done, the following is the result:**

$$P = \frac{\$160}{8\%} \times \frac{360}{60} = \frac{\$160 \times 360}{8\% \times 60} = \$12,000$$

$$160 \times 360 \div 8 \% \div 60 = 12,000*$$

10.6 Practice Problems

1. Find the amount that would earn $56 interest at 8% in 90 days.
2. Thatcher Real Estate paid $95 interest after 180 days on a note for 12%. How much was borrowed?
3. Calculate the principal on a 75-day note with an interest rate of 13.9% if the interest due is $245.
4. An 8.5% loan required a payment of $23 interest after 45 days. Find the principal.

10.6 Solutions to Practice Problems

1. $P = \dfrac{I}{RT}$

   $= \dfrac{\$56}{8\% \times \dfrac{90}{360}}$

   $= \$2,800$

2. $P = \dfrac{I}{RT}$

   $= \dfrac{\$95}{12\% \times \dfrac{180}{360}}$

   $= \$1,583.33$

3. $P = \dfrac{I}{RT}$

   $= \dfrac{\$245}{13.9\% \times \dfrac{75}{360}}$

   $= \$8,460.43$

4. $P = \dfrac{I}{RT}$

   $= \dfrac{\$23}{8.5\% \times \dfrac{45}{360}}$

   $= \$2,164.71$

10.7 Calculating the Rate

When determining the rate of interest, the following formula is used:

$$R = \frac{I}{PT}$$

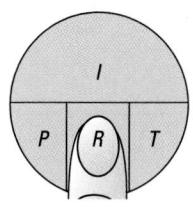

The answer will be the annual rate of interest stated in decimal fraction form. It must be converted to a percent.

---

*The sequence of operation in multiplication does not matter. That is, 2 × 3 is the same as 3 × 2. Also, $\dfrac{8 \times 4}{16 \times 2}$ can be solved by multiplying 8 × 4 = 32 and 16 × 2 = 32, then dividing 32 by 32 = 1. It could also be solved by dividing 8 by 16 = .5, multiplying .5 × 4 = 2, and then dividing 2 by 2 = 1.

EXAMPLE   Calculate the rate of interest for a $16,000 note that earned $240 in 60 days.

Solution

$$R = \frac{I}{PT}$$

$$= \frac{\$240}{\$16,000 \times \dfrac{60}{360}}$$

$$= 9\%$$

Again, when you invert the $\frac{60}{360}$, the 360 will be in the numerator to be multiplied by $240 ($240 × 360). Then, that product will be divided by $16,000 and by 60 (86,400 ÷ 16,000 ÷ 60 = .09 = 9%).

240 ✕ 360 ÷ 16,000 ÷ 60 = .09

10.7 Practice Problems

1. Find the rate if a $45,000 loan cost $1,350 interest in 120 days.
2. Bath and Bedroom paid $75 interest after 72 days on a note of $3,125. Find the rate.
3. Calculate the rate if a $250,000 note earned $2,500 interest in 45 days.
4. A loan of $87,500 cost $11,375 interest after 24 months. Find the interest rate.

10.7 Solutions to Practice Problems

1. $R = \dfrac{I}{PT}$

$$= \frac{\$1,350}{\$45,000 \times \dfrac{120}{360}}$$

$$= 9\%$$

2. $R = \dfrac{I}{PT}$

$$= \frac{\$75}{\$3,125 \times \dfrac{72}{360}}$$

$$= 12\%$$

3. $R = \dfrac{I}{PT}$

$$= \frac{\$2,500}{\$250,000 \times \dfrac{45}{360}}$$

$$= 8\%$$

4. $R = \dfrac{I}{PT}$

$$= \frac{\$11,375}{\$87,500 \times \dfrac{24}{12}}$$

$$= 6.5\%$$

10.8 Calculating the Time

The formula for calculating the time is

$$T = \frac{I}{PR}$$

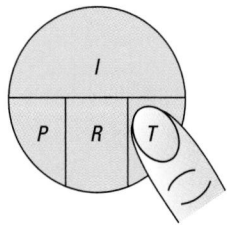

Calculating the time, however, presents an additional problem. *The formula for the time is stated in years.* To find the time in any other time period, most often stated in months or days, an adjustment must be made. If the time is stated in months, multiply the answer from the previous formula by 12 (12 months in a year); if in days, multiply by 360 or 365 depending on whether it is ordinary or exact interest. As usual, if not otherwise specifically indicated, always use the ordinary interest method when time is in days.

EXAMPLE Find the time, stated in years, it will take a $6,000 loan to earn $480 interest at a 6% rate.

Solution

$$T = \frac{I}{PR}$$

$$= \frac{\$480}{\$6,000 \times 6\%}$$

$$= 1.333 \text{ years or } 1\frac{1}{3} \text{ years}$$

| 480 ÷ 6,000 ÷ 6 % = 1.333 |

EXAMPLE Find the time, stated in months, it will take $6,000 to earn $480 interest at a 6% rate.

Solution

$$T = \frac{I}{PR} \times 12$$ *Multiply by 12 because there are 12 months in a year.*

$$= \frac{\$480}{\$6,000 \times 6\%} \times 12$$

$$= 16 \text{ months}$$

| 480 × 12 ÷ 6,000 ÷ 6 % = 16 |

EXAMPLE Find the number of days, using the ordinary interest method, it will take a loan of $6,000 to earn interest of $480 at a 6% rate.

Solution

$$T = \frac{I}{PR} \times 360$$ *Multiply by 360 because there are 360 days in a year using ordinary interest.*

$$= \frac{\$480}{\$6,000 \times 6\%} \times 360$$

$$= 480 \text{ days}$$

| 480 × 360 ÷ 6,000 ÷ 6 % = 480 |

EXAMPLE Find the number of days, using the exact interest method, it will take a $6,000 loan to earn $480 interest at a 6% rate.

Solution

$$T = \frac{I}{PR} \times 365$$ *Multiply by 365 because there are 365 days in a year using exact interest.*

$$= \frac{\$480}{\$6,000 \times 6\%} \times 365$$

$$= 487 \text{ days (rounded to the nearest day)}$$

| 480 × 365 ÷ 6,000 ÷ 6 % = 487 | *(rounded to the nearest day)*

1. How many days will it take a $15,000 note to earn $500 interest at an 8% rate?
2. How many months will it take a $240,000 note to earn $12,000 interest at a 10% rate?
3. Using the exact time method, calculate the number of days it will take a $5,000 loan to earn $150 interest at 15%.
4. How long, in years, will it take $84,000 to earn $4,200 interest at a rate of 5%?

10.8 Solutions to Practice Problems

1. $T = \dfrac{I}{PR} \times 360$

$= \dfrac{\$500}{\$15,000 \times 8\%} \times 360$

$= 150$ days

2. $T = \dfrac{I}{PR} \times 12$

$= \dfrac{\$12,000}{\$240,000 \times 10\%} \times 12$

$= 6$ months

3. $T = \dfrac{I}{PR} \times 365$

$= \dfrac{\$150}{\$5,000 \times 15\%} \times 365$

$= 73$ days

4. $T = \dfrac{I}{PR}$

$= \dfrac{\$4,200}{\$84,000 \times 5\%}$

$= 1$ year

LEARNING UNIT 3
PARTIAL PAYMENTS

EXCEL Spreadsheet Application The Springfield Department Store sometimes makes partial payments to pay off its loans. Spreadsheet Application 2 at the end of this chapter is a spreadsheet form that has been designed to make those calculations.

The recipient of a simple interest-bearing loan may desire to make payments instead of paying off the entire loan at maturity.

10.9 Partial Payment on a Loan

The primary reason to make partial payments is to reduce the amount of interest that must be paid. Another reason for making partial payments is that the maker of the note does not have enough money available to pay off the loan on the maturity date, and has negotiated a partial payment and a loan extension on the balance.

While there are other methods of calculating the amount of a partial payment that will be applied to interest and principal, by far the most commonly used method is called the **U.S. Rule**. The U.S. Rule originated with the Supreme Court in *Story vs. Livingston, 1839*, and has been adopted by many states. It is the method used in most courts or legal proceedings when conflict arises regarding partial payments. The U.S. Rule states that partial payments will first be applied to accumulated interest. The remainder of the payment will be applied to the principal, resulting in a new face value for the loan.

EXAMPLE Peter Newhart, owner of Newhart's Hair Cutting Shop, borrowed $100,000 at 15.9% for 90 days to open a second shop. Business was better than expected, and Peter decided that it would be better to make three payments. The first, after 30 days, was for $30,000. The second was 30 days later (60 days from the note's origination) for $40,000. Determine the allocation of each payment and the amount due at maturity.

Solution Calculate the allocation of the $30,000 payment after 30 days.

Step 1. Find the interest due after 30 days:

$$I = PRT$$
$$= \$100{,}000 \times 15.9\% \times \frac{30}{360}$$
$$= \$1{,}325$$

Step 2. Find the amount allocated to principal:

$$\$30{,}000 - 1{,}325 = \$28{,}675$$

Step 3. Find the amount still owed:

$$\$100{,}000 - 28{,}675 = \$71{,}325 \qquad \textit{New face value of note}$$

Step 4. Find the interest due after another 30 days:

$$I = PRT$$
$$= \$71{,}325 \times 15.9\% \times \frac{30}{360}$$
$$= \$945.06$$

Step 5. Find the amount allocated to principal:

$$\$40{,}000 - 945.06 = \$39{,}054.94$$

Step 6. Find the amount still owed:

$$\$71{,}325 - 39{,}054.94 = \$32{,}270.06 \qquad \textit{New face value of note}$$

Step 7. Find the amount due at maturity:

$$I = PRT$$
$$= \$32{,}270.06 \times 15.9\% \times \frac{30}{360}$$
$$= \$427.58$$
$$MV = P + I$$
$$= \$32{,}270.06 + 427.58 = \$32{,}697.64$$

To determine the amount of interest saved by making partial payments:

1. Calculate the interest that would have been due without any partial payments:

$$I = PRT$$
$$= \$100{,}000 \times 15.9\% \times \frac{90}{360}$$

2. Add the amounts of interest paid during the period with the partial payments:

$$\begin{array}{r} \$1{,}325.00 \\ 945.06 \\ +\ \ 427.58 \\ \hline \$2{,}697.64 \end{array}$$

3. Find the difference:

$$\begin{array}{r} \$3{,}975.00 \\ -\ 2{,}697.64 \\ \hline \$1{,}277.36 \end{array}$$

1. A partial payment of $7,500 was made after 80 days on a 10%, $12,000, 120-day note. Find the total amount due on the maturity date.

2. On June 15, $80,000 was borrowed at 7.5%. The maturity date is September 13. On July 25, a $50,000 partial payment was made. Another $15,000 was paid on August 14. What was the total amount due on the maturity date?

3. On March 2, $20,000 was borrowed at 9% for 180 days. On May 1 and June 30, partial payments of $7,000 each were made. Calculate the total amount due on the maturity date.

4. A partial payment of $75,000 was made after 40 days on an 8.9%, $200,000, 60-day note. Find the total amount due on the maturity date.

10.9 Solutions to Practice Problems

1. $I = PRT$

$$= \$12,000 \times 10\% \times \frac{80}{360}$$

$$= \$266.67$$

$7,500.00	$12,000.00
− 266.67	− 7,233.33
$7,233.33	$4,766.67

Applied to principal   New face value

$I = PRT$

$$= \$4,766.67 \times 10\% \times \frac{40}{360}$$

$$= \$52.96$$

$4,766.67
+ 52.96
$4,819.63

Maturity value

2. $I = PRT$

$$= \$80,000 \times 7.5\% \times \frac{40}{360}$$

$$= \$666.67$$

$50,000.00	$80,000.00
− 666.67	−49,333.33
$49,333.33	$30,666.67

Applied to principal   New face value

$I = PRT$

$$= \$30,666.67 \times 7.5\% \times \frac{20}{360}$$

$$= \$127.78$$

$15,000.00	$30,666.67
− 127.78	− 14,872.22
$14,872.22	$15,794.45

Applied to principal   New face value

$I = PRT$

$$= \$15,794.45 \times 7.5\% \times \frac{30}{360}$$

$$= \$98.72$$

$15,794.45
+ 98.72
$15,893.17

Maturity value

3. $I = PRT$

$$= \$20,000 \times 9\% \times \frac{60}{360}$$

$$= \$300$$

$7,000	$20,000
− 300	− 6,700
$6,700	$13,300

Applied to principal   New face value

$I = PRT$

$$= \$13,300 \times 9\% \times \frac{60}{360}$$

$$= \$199.50$$

$7,000.00	$13,300.00
− 199.50	− 6,800.50
$6,800.50	$ 6,499.50

Applied to principal   New face value

$$I = PRT$$
$$= \$6{,}499.50 \times 9\% \times \frac{60}{360}$$
$$= \$97.49$$

$$\begin{array}{r} \$6{,}499.50 \\ +\ \ \ \ 97.49 \\ \hline \$6{,}596.99 \end{array}$$
↑
Maturity value

4. $I = PRT$
$$= \$200{,}000 \times 8.9\% \times \frac{40}{360}$$
$$= \$1{,}977.78$$

$$\begin{array}{r} \$75{,}000.00 \\ -\ \ 1{,}977.78 \\ \hline \$73{,}022.22 \end{array}$$
↑
Applied to
principal

$$\begin{array}{r} \$200{,}000.00 \\ -\ 73{,}022.22 \\ \hline \$126{,}977.78 \end{array}$$
↑
New face
value

$$I = PRT$$
$$= \$126{,}977.78 \times 8.9\% \times \frac{20}{360}$$
$$= \$627.83$$

$$\begin{array}{r} \$126{,}977.78 \\ +\ \ \ \ 627.83 \\ \hline \$127{,}605.61 \end{array}$$
↑
Maturity value

QUICK REFERENCE SUMMARY AND REVIEW

Page	Section Topic	Learning Concepts	Examples and Solutions
340	**10.1** Calculating Interest When Time Is Stated in Years	Use the formula $$I = PRT$$ and multiply by time as stated (in years).	Calculate the interest on a loan of \$3,000 at 12% for two years. $$I = PRT$$ $$= \$3{,}000 \times 12\% \times 2$$ $$= \$720$$
341	**10.2** Calculating Interest When Time Is Stated in Months	Use the formula $$I = PRT$$ and adjust the time so that the months are stated in annual terms by dividing the number of months in the loan or investment period by 12 (the number of months in one year).	Calculate the interest on a loan of \$7,000 at 8% for four months. $$I = PRT$$ $$= \$7{,}000 \times 8\% \times \frac{4}{12}$$ $$= \$186.67$$
342	**10.3** Calculating Interest When Time Is Stated In Days	Use the formula $$I = PRT$$ and adjust the time so that the days are stated in annual terms by dividing the number of days in the loan or investment period by: (1) 360 if ordinary interest is the method being used (also called banker's interest), or (2) 365 if exact interest is the method being used. Unless otherwise stated, ordinary interest will always be used (360 days in a year).	Calculate the interest on a loan of \$5,000 at 9% for 90 days. Use (1) the ordinary interest method, and (2) the exact interest method. **1.** $I = PRT$ $$= \$5{,}000 \times 9\% \times \frac{90}{360}$$ $$= \$112.50$$ **2.** $I = PRT$ $$= \$5{,}000 \times 9\% \times \frac{90}{365}$$ $$= \$110.96$$

Page	Section Topic	Learning Concepts	Examples and Solutions
345	**10.4** Calculating the Maturity Value	The maturity value is the total value of a loan or investment. It can be found by **1.** adding the principal and the interest together: $MV = P + I$, or **2.** using the formula $MV = P(1 + RT)$.	Find the maturity value of a $10,000 note at 11% for 180 days. **1.** $I = PRT$ $\quad = \$10,000 \times 11\% \times \dfrac{180}{360}$ $\quad = \$550$ $MV = P + I$ $\quad\quad = \$10,000 + 550$ $\quad\quad = \$10,550$ or, **2.** $MV = P(1 + RT)$ $\quad\quad = \$10,000\left[1 + \left(11\% \times \dfrac{180}{360}\right)\right]$ $\quad\quad = \$10,000(1.055)$ $\quad\quad = \$10,550$
346	**10.5** Cash Discounts and Simple Interest	If a buyer does not have enough cash to pay an invoice within the cash discount period, should the money be borrowed? It is necessary to find the net cost of the invoice, the amount of the discount, and the amount of interest that will have to be paid if the money is borrowed.	An invoice for $20,000 dated October 12 had terms of 3/10, n/30. On October 22, not enough cash is available to pay the invoice. A bank will lend the required amount at 13% for 20 days. Should the money be borrowed? Net cost of invoice: $\quad = \$20,000 \times 97\%$ $\quad = \$19,400$ Amount of discount: $\quad = \$20,000 - 19,400$ $\quad = \$600$ Amount of interest: $\quad I = PRT$ $\quad\quad = \$19,400 \times 13\% \times \dfrac{20}{360}$ $\quad\quad = \$140.11$ Yes, the money should be borrowed.
348	**10.6** Calculating the Principal	Use the following formula: $$P = \dfrac{I}{RT}.$$	Find the principal for a loan at 10% that requires the payment of $45 interest in 80 days. $$P = \dfrac{I}{RT}$$ $$= \dfrac{\$45}{10\% \times \dfrac{80}{360}}$$ $$= \$2,025$$

Page	Section Topic	Learning Concepts	Examples and Solutions
349	**10.7** Calculating the Rate	Use the following formula: $$R = \frac{I}{PT}.$$ Your answer is the annual rate of interest stated in decimal fraction form. It should be converted to a percent.	Calculate the rate of interest on a loan of $30,000 for 60 days that requires the payment of $450 interest. $$R = \frac{I}{PT}$$ $$= \frac{\$450}{\$30,000 \times \frac{60}{360}}$$ $$= 9\%$$
350	**10.8** Calculating the Time	Use the following formula: $$T = \frac{I}{PR}.$$ The answer will be the time in years. If another time period is needed (months or days), an adjustment will have to be made. If time is in months, multiply by 12. If time is in days and the ordinary interest method is used, multiply by 360. If time is in days and the exact interest method is used, multiply by 365.	A note for $15,000 at 8% will earn interest of $300. Find the time stated in 1. Years 2. Months 3. Days—ordinary 4. Days—exact 1. $T = \frac{I}{PR}$ $$= \frac{\$300}{\$15,000 \times 8\%} = .25 \text{ years}$$ 2. $.25 \times 12 = 3$ months 3. $.25 \times 360 = 90$ days 4. $.25 \times 365 = 91$ days (to the nearest day)
352	**10.9** Partial Payment On a Loan	A borrower may want to make one or more partial payments on a loan instead of paying the entire maturity value in one payment at the maturity date. This will save money on interest. The most common method for determining the allocation of the payment to interest and principal is the U.S. Rule, which states that partial payments will first be applied to accumulated interest. The reminder will be applied to the principal, resulting in a face value for the loan.	A partial payment of $25,000 was made after 50 days on a 14%, $50,000, 120-day loan. Find the total amount due on the maturity date. $I = PRT$ $= \$50,000 \times 14\% \times \frac{50}{360}$ $= \$972.22$ $\begin{array}{r} \$\,25,000.00 \\ -\quad 972.22 \\ \hline \$\,24,027.78 \end{array}$ *Applied to principal* $\begin{array}{r} \$\,50,000.00 \\ -24,027.78 \\ \hline \$\,25,972.22 \end{array}$ *New face value* $I = PRT$ $= \$25,972.22 \times 14\% \times \frac{70}{360}$ $= \$707.02$ $MV = P + I$ $= \$25,972.22 + 707.02$ $= \$26,679.24$

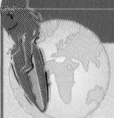
ADDITIONAL
PRACTICE
PROBLEMS

Answers to odd-numbered problems are given in Appendix A.

10.1

Calculate the interest when time is stated in years for the following problems:

1. Determine the interest on a loan of $2,000 at 8% for two years.

$$I = PRT$$
$$= \$2,000 \times 8\% \times 2$$
$$= \$320$$

2. Burns, Inc., charges 12% on past due invoice payments. J. & R. Upholstering's account was one fourth of a year overdue when payment was made. How much interest will be due on the $12,500 invoice?

$$I = PRT$$
$$= \$12,500 \times 12\% \times \frac{1}{4}$$
$$= \$375$$

3. Tinker's Tots has a 4.5%, $50,000 note coming due after $1\frac{1}{2}$ years. How much interest will it receive?

$$I = PRT$$
$$= \$50,000 \times 4.5\% \times 1\frac{1}{2}$$
$$= \$3,375$$

4. Warmer's Television & Electronic Repairs borrowed $66,000 at 10.5% for $\frac{1}{6}$ year. What amount of interest will have to be paid?

$$I = PRT$$
$$= \$66,000 \times 10.5\% \times \frac{1}{6}$$
$$= \$1,155$$

10.2

Calculate the interest when time is stated in months for the following problems:

5. Calculate the amount of interest on a loan of $300 at 12% for four months.

$$I = PRT$$
$$= \$300 \times 12\% \times \frac{4}{12}$$
$$= \$12$$

6. Calculate the interest on a loan of $1,500 at 12% for seven months.

$$I = PRT$$
$$= \$1,500 \times 12\% \times \frac{7}{12}$$
$$= \$105$$

7. Al Obaydi's Costume Creations borrowed $130,000 at 6% for two months. Calculate the interest that will be paid.

$$I = PRT$$
$$= \$130,000 \times 6\% \times \frac{2}{12}$$
$$= \$1,300$$

8. Manhattan Savings and Loan Association pays $4\frac{3}{4}$% on savings accounts. If Alan Sneed left $10,000 in his savings account for nine months, how much interest did his money earn?

$$I = PRT$$
$$= \$10,000 \times 4\frac{3}{4}\% \times \frac{9}{12}$$
$$= \$356.25$$

10.3

Find the interest when time is stated in days for the following problems:

9. A loan of $100,000 at 9.9% was made on April 16; it was due on August 16. Determine the amount of interest using (1) ordinary interest and (2) exact interest.

$$I = PRT$$
$$= \$100,000 \times 9.9\% \times \frac{122}{360}$$
$$= \$3,355 \text{ Ordinary interest}$$

$$I = PRT$$
$$= \$100,000 \times 9.9\% \times \frac{122}{365}$$
$$= \$3,309.04 \text{ Exact interest}$$

Apr. 30 − 16 = 14	
May	31
June	30
July	31
Aug.	16
Total days	122

10. Minnie's Plumbing Company borrowed $750 on July 26, to be repaid on October 26 with interest calculated at 16%. Determine the amount of interest using (1) ordinary interest and (2) exact interest.

$I = PRT$

$= \$750 \times 16\% \times \dfrac{92}{360}$

$= \$30.67$ Ordinary interest

$I = PRT$

$= \$750 \times 16\% \times \dfrac{92}{365}$

$= \$30.25$ Exact interest

July 31 − 26 =	5
Aug.	31
Sept.	30
Oct.	26
Total days	92

11. A note of $32,000 at 5.9% dated April 27 was due on June 26. Find the amount of interest using (1) ordinary interest and (2) exact interest.

$I = PRT$

$= \$32,000 \times 5.9\% \times \dfrac{60}{360}$

$= \$314.67$ Ordinary interest

$I = PRT$

$= \$32,000 \times 5.9\% \times \dfrac{60}{365}$

$= \$310.36$ Exact interest

Apr. 30 − 27 =	3
May	31
June	26
Total days	60

12. Staterhorn Cabinet Makers borrowed $18,000 at 9.5% on January 28. The note is due on May 28. Calculate the interest using (1) ordinary interest and (2) exact interest.

$I = PRT$

$= \$18,000 \times 9.5\% \times \dfrac{120}{360}$

$= \$570$ Ordinary interest

$I = PRT$

$= \$18,000 \times 9.5\% \times \dfrac{120}{365}$

$= \$562.19$ Exact interest

Jan. 31 − 28 =	3
Feb.	28
Mar.	31
Apr.	30
May	28
Total days	120

10.4

Calculate the maturity value in the following problems:

13. Find the maturity value of a $60,000 loan at 10% for 120 days.

$MV = P[1 + (RT)]$

$= \$60,000 \left[1 + \left(10\% \times \dfrac{120}{360} \right) \right]$

$= \$60,000 \times 1.0333333$

$= \$62,000$

14. Find the maturity value of a $750 note at 9.75% that is dated March 24 and is due on June 5. Use the exact interest method.

$MV = P[(1 + (RT)]$

$= \$750 \left[1 + \left(9.75\% \times \dfrac{73}{365} \right) \right]$

$= \$750 \times 1.0195$

$= \$764.63$

Mar. 31 − 24 =	7
Apr.	30
May	31
June	5
Total days	73

15. Calculate the maturity value of a $2,500 loan at 8.9% dated June 15 and due July 30.

$MV = P[1 + (RT)]$

$= \$2,500 \left[1 + \left(8.9\% \times \dfrac{45}{360} \right) \right]$

$= \$2,500 \times 1.01125$

$= \$2,527.81$

June 30 − 15 =	15
July	30
Total days	45

16. Determine the maturity value of a 7.5%, 120-day loan for $200,000.

$MV = P[1 + (RT)]$

$= \$200,000 \left[1 + \left(7.5\% \times \dfrac{120}{360} \right) \right]$

$= \$200,000 \times 1.025$

$= \$205,000$

10.5

Find the cash discount and loan interest in the following problems and determine if the money should be borrowed:

17. An invoice for $10,000 dated February 26 had terms of 2/10, n/30. The funds to pay the invoice within the discount period can be borrowed at 9%. Find the amounts of the discount and interest. Should the money be borrowed?

$\$10,000 \times 98\% = \$9,800$ Net payment

$\$10,000 − 9,800 = \$200$ Discount

$\$9,800 \times 9\% \times \dfrac{20}{360} = \$49$ Interest

Yes, the money should be borrowed.

18. An invoice for $1,550 had terms of 3/10, n/30. A bank will lend the necessary amount to pay the invoice within the discount period at 10.9%. Determine the discount and interest. Should the money be borrowed?

$\$1,550 \times 97\% = \$1,503.50$ Net payment

$\$1,550 − 1,503.50 = \$46.50$ Discount

$\$1,503.50 \times 10.9\% \times \dfrac{20}{360} = \$9.10$ Interest

Yes, the money should be borrowed.

19. An invoice for $28,500 dated March 29 had terms of 5/15 EOM. A bank will lend the amount necessary to pay the invoice within the discount period at 9.5%. Calculate the discount and interest. Should the money be borrowed?

$\$28,500 \times 95\% = \$27,075$ Net cost

$\$28,500 − 27,075 = \$1,425$ Discount

$\$27,075 \times 9.5\% \times \dfrac{15}{360} = \$107.17$ Interest

Yes, the money should be borrowed.

20. An invoice for $44,000 had terms of 1/10, n/30. AS OF September 1. Funds can be borrowed at 14% to pay the discount within the discount period. Calculate the discount and interest. Should the money be borrowed?

$\$44,000 \times 99\% = \$43,560$ Net payment

$\$44,000 − 43,560 = \$440$ Discount

$\$43,560 \times 14\% \times \dfrac{20}{360} = \$338.80$ Interest

Yes, the money should be borrowed.

10.6

Calculate the principal in the following problems:

21. Find the principal of a note that earned $57 interest at a rate of 12% for 90 days.

$$P = \frac{I}{RT}$$

$$= \frac{\$57}{12\% \times \dfrac{90}{360}}$$

$$= \$1,900$$

22. A. R. Jones, Inc., earned $66 interest in 180 days at 5.5% in its NOW account at the bank. How much money was in the account before the interest was added?

$$P = \frac{I}{RT}$$

$$= \frac{\$66}{5.5\% \times \dfrac{180}{360}}$$

$$= \$2,400$$

23. Mortgage Guarantee Corporation charges a 3% rate of interest on payments that arrive late each month. In June the firm billed $587 in late-payment fees. Calculate the total amount of payments that arrived late.

$$P = \frac{I}{RT}$$

$$= \frac{\$587}{3\% \times \dfrac{30}{360}} \qquad \text{A time of } \frac{1}{12} \text{ could also be used.}$$

$$= \$234,800$$

24. Mary Guzman uses her company credit card to make office supply purchases. The bill this month showed interest charges of $45. The interest rate charged by the bank that issued the card is 10.9%. Find the principal amount on which the interest charges were based.

$$P = \frac{I}{RT}$$

$$= \frac{\$45}{10.9\% \times \dfrac{1}{12}}$$

$$= \$4,954.13$$

10.7

Calculate the rate of interest in the following problems:

25. Calculate the rate of interest on a loan of $2,500 for 90 days if the interest paid was $62.50.

$$R = \frac{I}{PT}$$

$$= \frac{\$62.50}{\$2,500 \times \dfrac{90}{360}}$$

$$= 10\%$$

26. Use the exact interest method to find the rate of interest on a note of $45,000 for 146 days that earned interest of $1,710.

$$R = \frac{I}{PT}$$

$$= \frac{\$1,710}{\$45,000 \times \dfrac{146}{365}}$$

$$= 9.5\%$$

27. Johnson Plumbing & Heating borrowed $125,000 for four months to purchase and equip two new vans. At maturity, Johnson will have to repay a total of $130,083.34. Find the rate of interest.

$$\begin{array}{rl} \$\ 130,083.34 & MV \\ -\ 125,000.00 & -P \\ \hline \$\ \ \ \ 5,083.34 & I \end{array}$$

$$R = \frac{I}{PT}$$

$$= \frac{\$5,083.34}{\$125,000 \times \dfrac{4}{12}}$$

$$= 12.2\%$$

28. Mountaintop Ski Resort purchased five $10,000, 90-day corporate bonds. At maturity, the bonds will be redeemed for a total of $50,937.50. Find the interest rate.

$$\begin{array}{rr} \$10,000 & \$50,937.50 \\ \times\ \ \ \ \ \ 5 & -50,000.00 \\ \hline \$50,000 & \$\ \ \ \ 937.50 \end{array}$$

$$R = \frac{I}{PT}$$

$$= \frac{\$937.50}{\$50,000 \times \dfrac{90}{360}}$$

$$= 7.5\%$$

10.8

Calculate the time in the following problems. (Round off to the nearest day if necessary.)

29. Find the number of days in a loan period when a note of $3,500 earns $70 interest at 12%.

$$T = \frac{I}{PR} \times 360$$

$$= \frac{\$70}{\$3,500 \times 12\%}$$

$$= 60 \text{ days}$$

30. Determine the number of days, using the exact interest method, it will take a note of $7,100 to earn $140 interest at 8%.

$$T = \frac{I}{PR} \times 365$$

$$= \frac{\$140}{\$7,100 \times 8\%} \times 365$$

$$= 90 \text{ days}$$

31. Janson's Jewelry received a check for $61,320 in full payment of a loan for $60,000 at 12%. Determine the number of days in the loan period.

$$\begin{array}{r} \$61,320 \\ -60,000 \\ \hline \$1,320 \end{array}$$

$$T = \frac{I}{PR} \times 360$$

$$= \frac{\$1,320}{\$60,000 \times 12\%} \times 360$$

$$= 66 \text{ days}$$

32. Calculate the number of months in a loan period for $4,250 to earn $255 interest at 9%.

$$T = \frac{I}{PR} \times 12$$

$$= \frac{\$255}{\$4,250 \times 9\%} \times 12$$

$$= 8 \text{ months}$$

10.9

Calculate the total amount due at the maturity date after one or more partial payments have been made in the following problems:

33. A partial payment of $10,000 was made after 50 days on an 11%, $34,000, 90-day loan. Find the total amount due on the maturity date.

$$I = PRT$$

$$= \$34,000 \times 11\% \times \frac{50}{360}$$

$$= \$519.44$$

$$\begin{array}{r} \$10,000.00 \\ - \ \ \ 519.44 \\ \hline \$9,480.56 \end{array}$$
↑ Applied to principal

$$\begin{array}{r} \$34,000.00 \\ - \ 9,480.56 \\ \hline \$24,519.44 \end{array}$$
↑ New face value

$$I = PRT$$

$$= \$24,519.44 \times 11\% \times \frac{40}{360}$$

$$= \$299.68$$

$$\begin{array}{r} \$24,519.44 \\ + \ \ \ 299.68 \\ \hline \$24,819.12 \end{array}$$
↑ Maturity value

34. On May 9, $135,000 was borrowed at 9.9%. The maturity date is October 6. On July 8 and again on August 27, partial payments of $45,000 were made. What was the total amount due on the maturity date?

1. May 31 − 9 = 22		2. May 31 − 9 = 22		3. July 31 − 8 = 23	
June	30	June	30	Aug. 27	27
July	31	July	8		50
Aug.	31		60		
Sept.	30				
Oct.	6				
	150				

Days to maturity — Days to 1st payment — Days between 1st & 2nd payment

4. 150 − 60 − 50 = 40 *Days from 2nd payment to maturity*

5. $I = PRT$

$$= \$135,000 \times 9.9\% \times \frac{60}{360}$$

$$= \$2,227.50$$

$$\begin{array}{r} \$45,000.00 \\ - \ 2,227.50 \\ \hline \$42,772.50 \end{array}$$
↑ Applied to principal

$$\begin{array}{r} \$135,000.00 \\ - \ 42,772.50 \\ \hline \$ \ 92,227.50 \end{array}$$
↑ New face value

6. $I = PRT$

$$= \$92,227.50 \times 9.9\% \times \frac{50}{360}$$

$$= \$1,412.81$$

$$\begin{array}{r} \$45,000.00 \\ - \ 1,268.13 \\ \hline \$43,731.87 \end{array}$$
↑ Applied to principal

$$\begin{array}{r} \$92,227.50 \\ - \ 43,731.87 \\ \hline \$48,495.63 \end{array}$$
↑ New face value

7. $I = PRT$

$$= \$48,495.63 \times 9.9\% \times \frac{40}{360}$$

$$= \$533.45$$

$$\begin{array}{r} \$48,495.63 \\ + \ \ \ 533.45 \\ \hline \$49,029.08 \end{array}$$
↑ Maturity value

35. On January 6, $5,000 was borrowed at 10% for 180 days. On February 15, a $2,000 payment was made, and on April 16, a $1,500 payment was made. Calculate the amount due at maturity.

Jan. 31 − 6 = 25		Feb. 28 − 15 = 13	
Feb.	15	Mar.	31
	40	Apr.	16
			60

Days to 1st payment — Days between 1st and 2nd payment

180 − 40 − 60 = 80 *Days from 2nd payment to maturity*

$$I = PRT$$

$$= \$5,000 \times 10\% \times \frac{40}{360}$$

$$= \$55.56$$

$$\begin{array}{r} \$2,000.00 \\ - \ \ \ 55.56 \\ \hline \$1,944.44 \end{array}$$
↑ Applied to principal

$$\begin{array}{r} \$5,000.00 \\ -1,944.44 \\ \hline \$3,055.56 \end{array}$$
↑ New face value

$$I = PRT$$

$$= \$3,055.56 \times 10\% \times \frac{60}{360}$$

$$= \$50.93$$

$$\begin{array}{r} \$1,500.00 \\ - \ \ \ 50.93 \\ \hline \$1,449.07 \end{array}$$
↑ Applied to principal

$$\begin{array}{r} \$3,055.56 \\ -1,449.07 \\ \hline \$1,606.49 \end{array}$$
↑ New face value

$$I = PRT$$

$$= \$1,606.49 \times 10\% \times \frac{80}{360}$$

$$= \$35.70$$

$$\begin{array}{r} \$1,606.49 \\ + \ \ \ 35.70 \\ \hline \$1,642.19 \end{array}$$
↑ Maturity value

36. Partial payments of $12,500 and $10,000 were made on June 5 and August 4, respectively, on a $30,000 loan at 8.25%. The loan was taken out on May 6 and comes due on October 3. Find the amount due at maturity.

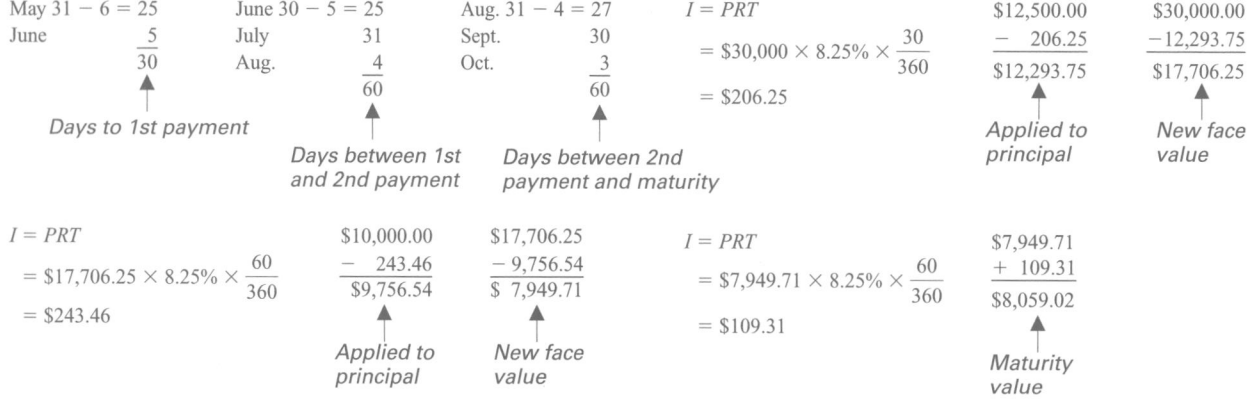

Answers to odd-numbered problems are given in Appendix A.

CHAPTER REVIEW PROBLEMS

Drill Problems

Find the interest when time is stated in years for the following problems:

	Principal	Rate of Interest	Time	Interest
1.	$ 35,000	18.9%	1 year	$ 6,615
2.	2,400	9%	$\frac{1}{6}$ year	36
3.	1,500	10%	$\frac{1}{3}$ year	50
4.	500,000	6.5%	$\frac{1}{2}$ year	16,250

Find the interest when the time is stated in months for the following problems:

	Principal	Rate of Interest	Time	Interest
5.	$250,000	7%	8 months	$ 11,666.67
6.	600	13.9%	6 months	41.70
7.	1,300	6.5%	2 months	14.08
8.	9,750	9%	18 months	1,316.25

Find the interest when the time is stated in days using the ordinary time method in the following problems:

	Principal	Rate of Interest	Time	Interest
9.	$ 10,000	9%	May 10–July 9	$ 150
10.	3,900	12%	September 5–December 14	130
11.	200,000	8%	March 21–September 17	8,000
12.	880	12.5%	July 4–August 3	9.17

Days in problems 9 through 12:

9.		10.		11.		12.	
May 31 − 10 = 21		Sept. 30 − 5 = 25		Mar. 31 − 21 = 10		July 31 − 4 = 27	
June	30	Oct.	31	Apr.	30	Aug.	3
July	9	Nov.	30	May	31		30
	60	Dec	14	June	30		
			100	July	31		
				Aug.	31		
				Sept.	17		
					180		

Find the interest when the time is stated in days using the exact time method in the following problems:

	Principal	Rate of Interest	Time	Interest
13.	$185,000	8%	January 2–March 16	$ 2,960
14.	1,825	11.5%	June 12–September 20	57.50
15.	39,000	10%	February 16–March 28	427.40
16.	730	13%	October 4–December 18	19.50

Days in problems 13 through 16:

13.		14.		15.		16.	
Jan. 31 − 2 = 29		June 30 − 12 = 18		Feb. 28 − 16 = 12		Oct. 31 − 4 = 27	
Feb.	28	July	31	Mar.	28	Nov.	30
Mar.	16	Aug.	31		40	Dec.	18
	73	Sep.	20				75
			100				

Find the maturity value in the following problems:

	Principal	Rate of Interest	Time	Maturity Value
17.	$ 6,000	8.8%	May 3–August 1	$ 6,132
18.	11,500	10.5%	July 22–August 31	11,634.17
19.	150,000	6.9%	January 17–May 17	153,450
20.	975	13%	September 1–November 30	1,006.69

Days in problems 17 through 20:

17.		18.		19.		20.	
May 31 − 3 = 28		July 31 − 22 = 9		Jan. 31 − 17 = 14		Sept. 30 − 1 = 29	
June	30	Aug.	31	Feb.	28	Oct.	31
July	31		40	Mar.	31	Nov.	30
Aug.	1			Apr.	30		90
	90			May	17		
					120		

In problems 21 through 24, find the net payment and the discount given various invoice terms. Compare the discount that would be lost if the invoice could not be paid within the discount period with the interest a bank would charge to borrow the net payment amount.

	Invoice Terms	Amount of Invoice	Net Payment	Discount	Rate to Borrow	Interest
21.	2/10, n/30	$ 1,398.28	$ 1,370.31	27.97	11.5%	$ 8.75
22.	3/10, n/30	330.67	320.75	9.92	13.9%	2.48
23.	1/30, n/60	789.01	781.12	7.89	10%	6.51
24.	3/15, n/45	542.90	526.61	16.29	12%	5.27

Find the principal in the following problems (round your answer to the nearest dollar when necessary):

	Principal	Rate of Interest	Time	Interest
25.	$ 6,400	10%	90 days	$ 160
26.	12,000	9%	July 20–October 8	240
27.	5,625	8%	8 months	300
28.	220,000	4.5%	April 30–September 2 (exact interest method)	3,390.41

Days in problems 26 and 28:

	26.		28.	
	July 31 − 20 = 11		Apr. 30 − 30 = 0	
	Aug.	31	May	31
	Sept.	30	June	30
	Oct.	8	July	31
		80	Aug.	31
			Sept.	2
				125

Find the rate in the following problems:

	Principal	Rate of Interest	Time	Interest
29.	$ 2,460	10%	60 days	$ 41
30.	15,000	6.67%	2.4 months	200
31.	360,000	10%	August 4–November 20	10,800
32.	2,000	6.5%	July 15–December 12 (exact interest method)	53.42

Days in problems 31 and 32:

	31.		32.	
	Aug. 31 − 4 = 27		July 31 − 15 = 16	
	Sept.	30	Aug.	31
	Oct.	31	Sept.	30
	Nov.	20	Oct.	31
		108	Nov.	30
			Dec.	12
				150

Using the ordinary interest method, find the time in the following problems. (Round to the nearest day when necessary.)

	Principal	Rate of Interest	Time	Interest
33.	$ 3,000	6%	80 days	$ 40
34.	6,500	9%	44 days	71.50
35.	175,000	4.25%	180 days	3,718.75
36.	2,000	13.9%	50 days	38.61

Using the exact interest method, find the time in the following problems. (Round to the nearest day when necessary.)

	Principal	Rate of Interest	Time	Interest
37.	$ 14,500	5%	73 days	$ 145
38.	780	7%	180 days	26.93
39.	160,000	5.9%	240 days	6,207.12
40.	33,300	10.3%	30 days	281.91

Chapter 10 Banking Applications: Simple Interest

Find the time in months in the following problems:

	Principal	Rate of Interest	Time	Interest
41.	$ 500	11%	__9_ months	$ 41.25
42.	880	5.6%	__3_ months	12.32
43.	8,250	3.9%	__8_ months	214.50
44.	55,300	8.3%	__6_ months	2,294.95

Find the total amount due at maturity in the following partial payment problems:

	Principal	Rate	Time	Partial Payment After	Partial Payment Amount	Amount Due at Maturity
45.	$ 6,900	6.9%	180 days	50 days	$ 4,000	$ 3,040.04
46.	770	12.5%	150 days	45 days	500	292.31
47.	38,000	9.2%	240 days	100 days	15,000	24,828.74
48.	75,000	8%	120 days	60 days	25,000	51,680

Word Problems

49. Calculate the interest on a $21,000, 8%, half-year note.

$I = PRT$

$= \$21,000 \times 8\% \times \dfrac{1}{2}$

$= \$840$

50. Calculate the interest on an $835, 10%, four-month note.

$I = PRT$

$= \$835 \times 10\% \times \dfrac{4}{12}$

$= \$27.83$

51. Calculate the interest on a $5,500, 7%, 100-day note.

$I = PRT$

$= \$5,500 \times 7\% \times \dfrac{100}{360}$

$= \$106.94$

52. Find the interest on a $40,200, 11% note dated November 23 and due January 2.

Nov. 30 − 23 = 7
Dec.   31
Jan.   _2_
           40

$I = PRT$

$= \$40,200 \times 11\% \times \dfrac{40}{360}$

$= \$491.33$

53. Use the exact interest method to find the interest on a $36,500, 9% note dated April 19 and due September 16.

Apr. 30 − 19 = 11
May   31
June   30
July   31
Aug.   31
Sept.   _16_
           150

$I = PRT$

$= \$36,500 \times 9\% \times \dfrac{150}{365}$

$= \$1,350$

54. Use the exact interest method to find the interest on a $900, 12% note dated September 28 and due November 12.

Sept. 30 − 28 = 2
Oct.   31
Nov.   _12_
          45

$I = PRT$

$= \$900 \times 12\% \times \dfrac{46}{365}$

$= \$13.32$

55. Calculate the maturity value of a $50,775, 9.9%, 200-day note.

$M = P[1 + (RT)]$

$= \$50,775 \times \left[1 + \left(9.9\% \times \dfrac{200}{360}\right)\right]$

$= \$50,775 \times 1.055$

$= \$53,567.63$

56. An invoice dated March 2 for $30,000 had terms of 1/10 EOM. Sufficient cash to pay the invoice within the discount period is unavailable. A bank has agreed to a 14.9% simple interest loan for the amount necessary to pay the invoice within the discount period, to be due on the net payment date. Determine the due dates for the discount and the net payment, the amount of the discount, the net payment, and the interest. Compare the discount and interest and determine if the money should be borrowed.

Discount due date: April 10
Net payment date: April 30

$30,000 \times 99\% = \$29,700$ Net payment
$30,000 − 29,700 = \$300$ Discount

$\$29,700 \times 14.9\% \times \dfrac{20}{360} = \$245.85$ Interest

Yes, the money should be borrowed.

57. Determine the principal (to the nearest dollar) of a 12.2%, 150-day note that earned $177.92 interest.

$$P = \frac{I}{RT}$$

$$= \frac{\$177.92}{12.2\% \times \dfrac{150}{360}}$$

$$= \$3,500$$

58. Calculate the rate of interest on a $25,000, 180-day note that will pay $1,062.50 interest at maturity.

$$R = \frac{I}{PT}$$

$$= \frac{\$1,062.50}{\$25,000 \times \dfrac{180}{360}}$$

$$= 8.5\%$$

59. Calculate the rate of interest on a $420,000, 45-day loan that will require a payment of $2,835 interest at maturity.

$$R = \frac{I}{PT}$$

$$= \frac{\$2,835}{\$420,000 \times \dfrac{45}{360}}$$

$$= 5.4\%$$

60. Find the number of days (round your answer to the nearest day) it takes a $43,000, 6% note to earn $1,620 interest.

$$T = \frac{I}{PR} \times 360$$

$$= \frac{\$1,620}{\$43,000 \times 6\%} \times 360$$

$$= 226 \text{ days}$$

61. How many months will it take a note for $124,000 at 4.9% to earn $1,519 interest?

$$T = \frac{I}{PR} \times 12$$

$$= \frac{\$1,519}{\$124,000 \times 4.9\%} \times 12$$

$$= 3 \text{ months}$$

62. In years, calculate the time it will take for a simple interest loan of $3,600 at 9.25% to earn $832.50 interest.

$$T = \frac{I}{PR} \times 1$$

$$= \frac{\$832.50}{\$3,600 \times 9.25\%} \times 1$$

$$= 2.5 \text{ years}$$

63. Determine the interest earned on an investment of $50,000 at 11% signed on July 16 that matures on November 18.

July 31 − 16 = 15		$I = PRT$
Aug.	31	
Sept.	30	$= \$50,000 \times 11\% \times \dfrac{125}{360}$
Oct.	31	
Nov.	18	$= \$1,909.72$
	125	

64. In the month of April, Januch Sitting Services received late fee payments of $2,100. Januch charges a 1.5% interest rate on late payments. How much was the total amount of late payments?

$$P = \frac{I}{RT}$$

$$= \frac{\$2,100}{1.5\% \times \dfrac{1}{12}}$$

$$= \$1,680,000$$

65. Use the exact interest method to calculate the face value of a 12.3% loan that required an interest payment of $48.19 after 110 days (Round to the nearest dollar.)

$$P = \frac{I}{RT}$$

$$= \frac{\$48.19}{12.3\% \times \dfrac{110}{365}}$$

$$= \$1,300.03 = \$1,300$$

66. A $22,200 note earned interest of $499.50 in 90 days. Find the interest rate.

$$R = \frac{I}{PT}$$

$$= \frac{\$499.50}{\$22,200 \times \dfrac{90}{360}}$$

$$= 9\%$$

67. How many days does it take a $90,000 loan to accumulate interest of $4,500 at 4.5%?

$$T = \frac{I}{PR} \times 360$$

$$= \frac{\$4,500}{\$90,000 \times 4.5\%} \times 360$$

$$= 400 \text{ days}$$

68. A loan of $25,000 at 12.4% for 200 days was taken out on January 25. Two partial payments were made: on March 31, $10,000 was paid, and on June 24, another $8,000 was paid. Calculate the amount due at maturity.

Jan. 31 − 25 = 6	Mar. 31 − 31 = 0
Feb.	28	Apr.	30
Mar.	31	May	31
	65	June	24
			85

Days to 1st payment

Days between 1st and 2nd payment

Days between payment and maturity: 200 − 65 − 85 = 50

$I = PRT$

$$= \$25,000 \times 12.4\% \times \frac{65}{360}$$

$$= \$559.72$$

	$10,000.00	$25,000.00
	− 559.72	− 9,440.28
	$9,440.28	$15,559.72

Applied to principal   *New face value*

$I = PRT$

$$= \$15,559.72 \times 12.4\% \times \frac{85}{360}$$

$$= \$455.55$$

	$8,000.00	15,559.72
	− 455.55	− 7,544.45
	$7,544.45	$8,015.27

Applied to principal   *New face value*

$I = PRT$

$$= \$8,015.27 \times 12.4\% \times \frac{50}{360}$$

$$= \$138.04$$

$8,015.27
+ 138.04
$8,153.31

Maturity value

69. TOYS, Inc., received an invoice for $27,500 worth of merchandise dated February 2. Special terms of 5/10, n/90 had been granted to encourage the purchase of toys early in the year. TOYS did not have enough cash to pay the invoice within the discount period. Its bank was willing to provide a loan for the necessary amount at a 12.3% interest rate. Calculate the discount that could be taken and compare it to the interest the bank would charge. Should the money be borrowed?

$27,500 × 95% = $26,125   Net payment
$27,500 − 26,125 = $1,375   Discount

$$\$26,125 \times 12.3\% \times \frac{80}{360} = \$714.08 \qquad \text{Interest}$$

Yes, the money should be borrowed.

CRITICAL THINKING GROUP PROJECT

Le Pharmacy has been open for four years. Mr. Le is looking for ways to increase his profits. His accountant has suggested that he should begin taking the cash discounts that his suppliers are offering. Mr. Le has gone through his invoices for the past four years and has put together the following information:

Annual Invoice Totals

1st year	$436,985
2nd year	$504,008
3rd year	$793,774
4th year	$756,330

An analysis of the invoices disclosed that two thirds of them offered cash discount terms of 2/10, n/30. The remaining third offered terms of 1.5/10, n/30.

Mr. Le had been waiting the entire 30 days to pay the invoices. However, he had all of his excess cash invested at 9%. At the end of each month he would withdraw enough to pay the monthly bills.

1. Add the annual invoice totals and divide that sum by 4 to arrive at the average annual invoice amount.
   $622,774.25

2. Divide the average annual invoice amount from problem 1 by 12 to find the average monthly invoice amount.
   $51,897.85

3. Find the average amount of cash discount that could be taken at 2% if those invoices were paid within the discount period.
   $691.97

4. What average monthly net payment amount would be required to pay the 2% cash discount invoices within the discount period?
   $33,906.60

5. Find the average amount of cash discount that could be taken at 1.5% if those invoices were paid within the discount period.
$259.49

6. What average monthly net payment amount would be required to pay the 1.5% cash discount invoices within the discount period?
$17,039.79

7. If Mr. Le withdrew the amount necessary to pay the 2% cash discount invoices on the 10th day (20 days early), how much interest would he lose on his investment?
$169.53

8. If Mr. Le withdrew the amount necessary to pay the 1.5% cash discount invoices on the 10th day (20 days early), how much interest would he lose on his investment?
$85.20

9. What is the average total monthly savings Mr. Le can realize by paying the invoices within the cash discount period?
$696.73

10. On average, how much would paying the invoices within the discount period add to annual profits?
$8,360.76

11. Should Mr. Le pay his invoices within the discount period?
Yes

| SELF-TESTING EXERCISES | *Answers to all exercises are given in Appendix A.* |

1. What is generally given as the reason for using 360-day years when calculating interest? Is the reason valid today? Why or why not? What is the trend? Why? **W**

The reason given is that it is easier to calculate and for consumers to understand. Given today's advances in technology that allows the use of computerized tables and calculators for determining the interest, the reason loses its validity. Because of a court case in Oregon and pressure brought by consumer protection groups, the trend is toward using the exact number of days in a year (365 days or 366 days in leap years).

2. Describe the U.S. Rule as it pertains to partial payments. **W**

The U.S. Rule assumes that the interest that has accrued during the time that a note was written, or since the last payment was made, is paid first. Thus, the interest is calculated and subtracted from the payment. The remainder of the partial payment is then applied to the principal of the note.

3. Find the simple rate of interest for a $420, six-month note that requires a $450 payment at maturity.

$$R = \frac{I}{PT}$$

$$\begin{array}{r} \$450 \\ -\ 420 \\ \hline \$30 \end{array}$$

$$= \frac{\$30}{\$420 \times \dfrac{6}{12}}$$

$$= 14.3\%$$

4. Determine the exact number of days between July 7 and October 20.

July 31 − 7 =	24
Aug.	31
Sept.	30
Oct.	20
Total days	105

5. Ceiling Street, Inc., purchased $25,000 worth of three-month, $5\frac{1}{2}$% government securities. How much interest will the company earn?

$$I = PRT$$

$$= \$25,000 \times 5\frac{1}{2}\% \times \frac{3}{12}$$

$$= \$343.75$$

6. Determine the principal of a loan that earns $12 in 30 days at 16%.

$$P = \frac{I}{RT}$$

$$= \frac{\$12}{16\% \times \dfrac{30}{360}}$$

$$= \$900$$

7. Using exact time, determine the amount of principal when 6.6% bonds earn $33 interest between January 1 and March 2.

Jan. .31 − 1 =	30
Feb.	28
Mar.	2
	60

$$P = \frac{I}{RT}$$

$$= \frac{\$33}{6.6\% \times \dfrac{60}{360}}$$

$$= \$3,000$$

8. How many months will it take an investment of $6,750 in 12% corporate bonds to earn interest of $101.25.

$$T = \frac{I}{PR} \times 12$$

$$= \frac{\$101.25}{\$6,750 \times 12\%} \times 12$$

$$= 1.5 \text{ months}$$

9. What rate of interest is required for $16,000 to earn $700 interest in 72 days?

$$R = \frac{I}{PT}$$

$$= \frac{\$700}{\$16,000 \times \frac{72}{360}}$$

$$= 21.9\%$$

10. The Bank of Cicero made a loan of $2,950 at 8% on June 21. Using exact time, find the interest if the loan was to be repaid on September 1.

June 30 − 21 =	9
July	31
Aug.	31
Sept.	1
	72

$$I = PRT$$

$$= \$2,950 \times 8\% \times \frac{72}{365}$$

$$= \$46.55$$

11. Determine the number of days it will take $1,500 to earn $45 at a 9% interest rate.

$$T = \frac{I}{PR} \times 360$$

$$= \frac{\$45}{\$1,500 \times 9\%} \times 360$$

$$= 120 \text{ days}$$

12. Determine the principal on a note that earns $50 in four months at 12%.

$$P = \frac{I}{RT}$$

$$= \frac{\$50}{12\% \times \frac{4}{12}}$$

$$= \$1,250$$

13. Sam Lattimer made a deposit in the Bank of Alaska on April 11. Sam had earned $44 interest when he withdrew his savings on June 23 to prospect for gas and oil. Find the amount deposited if the bank calculates interest on an exact time basis at a rate of 10%.

Apr. 30 − 11 =	19
May	31
June	23
	73

$$P = \frac{I}{RT}$$

$$= \frac{\$44}{10\% \times \frac{73}{365}}$$

$$= \$2,200$$

14. An invoice for $38,000 dated March 30 had terms of 2/10, n/45. Money was not available to pay within the discount period. A bank will lend the necessary amount at 12.5%. Calculate both the amount of the discount and the amount of the bank's interest charge. Should the money be borrowed?

$38,000 × 98% = $37,240 Net Payment
$38,000 − 37,240 = $760 Discount

$$\$37,240 \times 12.5\% \times \frac{35}{360} = \$452.57 \text{ Interest}$$

Yes, the money should be borrowed.

15. Find the maturity value for a $72,000 loan at 6.4% for 75 days.

$$MV = P[1 + (RT)]$$

$$= \$72,000\left[1 + \left(6.4\% \times \frac{75}{360}\right)\right]$$

$$= \$72,960$$

16. Yolanda Mzyrkwicz borrowed $34,000 at 11.6% for 120 days. She made two partial payments of $12,000 each after 40 and 80 days. How much is the total payment due at maturity?

$$I = PRT$$

$$= \$34,000 \times 11.6\% \times \frac{40}{360}$$

$$= \$438.22$$

$12,000.00
−   438.22
$11,561.78

Applied to principal

$34,000.00
−11,561.78
$22,438.22

New face value

$$I = PRT$$

$$= \$10,727.42 \times 11.6\% \times \frac{40}{360}$$

$$= \$138.26$$

$10,727.42
+   138.26
$10,865.68

Maturity value

$$I = PRT$$

$$= \$22,438.22 \times 11.6\% \times \frac{40}{360}$$

$$= \$289.20$$

$12,000.00
−   289.20
$11,710.80

Applied to principal

$22,438.22
−11,710.80
$10,727.42

New face value

17. Find the time in years for an investment of $20,000 to earn $2,400 interest at 6%.

$$T = \frac{I}{PR} \times 1$$

$$= \frac{\$2,400}{\$20,000 \times 6\%} \times 1$$

$$= 1\frac{1}{3} \text{ years, or } 1.333 \text{ years}$$

18. Calculate the interest that will have to be paid for a loan of $954 at 9.75% for a third of a year. (Round to the nearest dollar.)

$$I = PRT$$

$$= \$954 \times 9.75\% \times \frac{1}{3}$$

$$= \$31$$

19. How many days will it take for an $85,000 investment at 4.7% to earn $1,997.50 in interest?

$$T = \frac{I}{PR} \times 360$$

$$= \frac{\$1,997.50}{\$85,000 \times 4.7\%} \times 360$$

$$= 180 \text{ days}$$

20. Find the rate of interest on a 146-day, $27,900 exact interest note that earns $658.44 in interest?

$$R = \frac{I}{PT}$$

$$= \frac{\$658.44}{\$27,900 \times \frac{146}{365}}$$

$$= 5.9\%$$

APPLICATION 1

Application 1 is a spreadsheet program that Springfield uses to make calculations on simple interest loans. Springfield has provided several such loans to businesses in town. When you load Ch10App1 on your computer spreadsheet applications disk, you will see a screen that looks like the one shown here:

Springfield Department Store

2617 Main Street
Box 219
Springfield, Maryland 58109
Telephone: 301-555-2158   FAX: 301-555-3498

SIMPLE INTEREST CALCULATIONS

COMPANY	LOAN AMOUNT	RATE	360 OR 365 DAY YEARS	DAYS IN LOAN	INTEREST	MATURITY VALUE
					$0.00	$0.00
					$0.00	$0.00
				#DIV/0!		$0.00
				#DIV/0!		$0.00
			#DIV/0!			$0.00
	#DIV/0!					#DIV/0!
TOTAL	#DIV/0!				$0.00	#DIV/0!

You must enter a code to indicate if the loan is based on ordinary interest (360-day year) or exact interest (365-day year). *If it is 360 days, enter 1; if it is 365 days, enter 2.*

Enter the following information:

Company	Cell
B. J. Jamison Company	A12
Hasburg Toys	A13
Springfield Hardware	A14
Tina's Fashions	A15
Red Onion Cafe	A16
Computer Universe	A17

Loan Amount	Cell	Rate	Cell	360 or 365 Day Years	Cell	Days in Loan	Cell
$8,374.90	B12	9%	C12	360	D12	120	E12
19,384.07	B13	13.3%	C13	365	D13	75	E13
39,345.30	B14	9.75%	C14	360	D14		
7,393.11	B15	12.5%	C15	365	D15		
2,946.89	B16			360	D16	90	E16
		8.8%	C17	365	D17	220	E17

Interest	Cell
$2,610.72	F14
$184.83	F15
$82.88	F16
$3,976.08	F17

Answer the following questions after you have completed the spreadsheet:

1. What is the interest due at maturity on the B. J. Jamison Company loan?
2. What is the interest due at maturity on the Hasburg Toys loan?
3. What is the number of days to maturity using ordinary interest for the Springfield Hardware loan?
4. What is the number of days to maturity using exact interest for the Tina's Fashions loan?
5. What is the rate for the loan to the Red Onion Cafe?
6. What is the amount of the loan to Computer Universe?
7. What is the maturity value for the Hasburg Toys loan?
8. What is the total simple interest that will be earned at maturity on the loans made by the Springfield Department Store?
9. What is the total maturity value on all loans made by the Springfield Department Store?
10. What is the total amount of all loans made by the Springfield Department Store?

GROUP REPORT

FOR CHAPTER 10 APPLICATION 1

Change the code for the days in the year from 365 days to 360 days, and vice versa. Record all of the changes and write a report describing the changes. Also, make recommendations in your report for how many days in a year Springfield should use on its future loans.

EXCEL SPREADSHEET APPLICATION FOR CHAPTER 10

APPLICATION 2

Springfield took out a series of simple interest loans to finance a second store and purchase its inventory. The loans were for various lengths of time ranging from 90 to 240 days. Management has decided to pay each of the loans by making three partial payments instead of one lump sum payment. A spreadsheet form has been designed to make the calculations. It will show the following information:

1. The amount of interest that would have to be paid if no partial payments were made
2. The amount of each of the three partial payments for each loan
3. The number of days from the issue date of the loans that have passed before the partial payment is made
4. The new face value of each loan after each partial payment (Amount Still Owed) (The third payment will pay the loan in full, so the Amount of 3rd Payment is the amount of the Amount Still Owed column after the 2nd payment plus the accrued interest since that date)
5. The interest saved by making early payments for each loan
6. Totals for the amount of the loans, the interest to maturity without partial payments, the amount of each payment, and the interest saved

When you select Ch10App2 from your spreadsheet applications disk, you will see the following spreadsheet:
Enter the following information:

Amount of Loan	Cell	Rate	Cell	Time of Loan (Days)	Cell
$75,000	A13	.1475	B13	150	C13
$125,000	A14	.125	B14	240	C14
$127,500	A15	.122	B15	180	C15
$162,750	A16	.098	B16	120	C16
$200,000	A17	.085	B17	90	C17

Springfield Department Store

2617 Main Street
Box 219
Springfield, Maryland 58109
Telephone: 301-555-2158   FAX: 301-555-3498

PARTIAL PAYMENTS ON SIMPLE INTEREST LOANS

Amount of Loan	Rate	Time of Loan (Days)	Interest to Maturity W/O Payment	Amount of 1st Payment	Made After (Days)	Amount Still Owed
			$0.00			$0.00
			$0.00			$0.00
			$0.00			$0.00
			$0.00			$0.00
			$0.00			$0.00
$0.00			$0.00	$0.00		$0.00

Amount of Loan (Repeated)	Amount of 2nd Payment	Made After (Days)	Amount Still Owed	Amount of 3rd Payment	Made After (Days)	Interest Saved By Making Early Payments
$0.00			$0.00	$0.00		$0.00
$0.00			$0.00	$0.00		$0.00
$0.00			$0.00	$0.00		$0.00
$0.00			$0.00	$0.00		$0.00
$0.00			$0.00	$0.00		$0.00
$0.00	$0.00		$0.00	$0.00		$0.00

Amount of 1st Payment	Cell	Made After (Days)	Cell	Amount of 2nd Payment	Cell
$25,000	E13	50	F13	$25,000	B26
$40,000	E14	60	F14	$45,000	B27
$45,000	E15	60	F15	$42,500	B28
$50,000	E16	40	F16	$60,000	B29
$70,000	E17	30	F17	$65,000	B30

Made After (Days)	Cell
150	F26
240	F27
180	F28
120	F29
90	F30

Answer the following questions after you have completed the spreadsheet:

1. What is the total amount of interest that will be saved by making partial payments?

2. What amount is still owed on the $125,000 loan after the first partial payment?

3. What amount is still owed on the $162,750 loan after the second partial payment?

4. What is the amount of the third payment for the $75,000 loan?

5. How much interest is saved on the $127,500 loan by making partial payments?

6. What is the total amount borrowed by the Springfield Department Store?

7. What is the total interest to maturity if partial payments are not made?

8. After making the partial payments, what amount of interest was paid on the $125,000 note? (Subtract the interest saved by making early payments from the interest to maturity without partial payments.)

GROUP REPORT

FOR CHAPTER 10 APPLICATION 2

1. In the application, apply each partial payment to the loan bearing the highest interest rate until that loan has been paid in full. Make additional partial payments to the next highest interest rate, and so on. How much interest would be saved?

2. If partial payments were made in this manner, how much more interest would be saved than in Application 1?

3. As a group, write a report to the store manager describing the transactions that took place in this application. Discuss the desirability of paying loans off early, or of making partial payments.

11 BANKING APPLICATIONS
PROMISSORY NOTES AND DISCOUNTING

TRUTH IN LENDING

Jerry opened his junk mail from a lending company in another state. The flyer promised, "Because you are a public school teacher, no credit check is necessary. Just fill in the amount and sign. Your money will be in the mail immediately."

With the flyer was a strange repayment table with terms such as, "Loan amount $2,753.84; a payment of only $91.69 semimonthly for only 38 months." Since this was the year 1968, one year before the passage of the so-called Truth-in-Lending Act, nowhere did the advertisement suggest that the loan would exceed a whopping 90% annual percentage rate (APR).

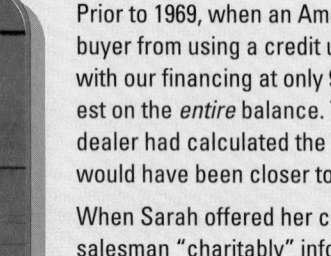

Prior to 1969, when an American shopped for a new car, the salesperson would discourage the buyer from using a credit union with a claim such as, "Your credit union charges 12%. Why not go with our financing at only 9%?" The trouble was, the 9% was calculated as so-called simple interest on the *entire* balance. The credit union charged a true rate of 12% on the *unpaid* balance. If the dealer had calculated the interest rate by the same method used by the credit union, the rate would have been closer to 17%.

When Sarah offered her credit card to put the bill on "revolving credit," the department store salesman "charitably" informed her that the $1,000 refrigerator should be put on the "easy pay" account because that plan's rate is only 9%.

Following an hour or so filling out forms, the unwary consumer was handed a bill for a one-year note reading:

Principal	$1,000	
Interest	90	(9% × $1,000)
Service charge	+ 50	
Total	$1,140	DELIVERY NEXT THURSDAY

Arriving at home Sarah found a letter informing her that her recently deceased rich aunt had left her a bundle of money. Sarah believed that the smart move would be to save interest costs by immediately paying off all her debts. She hurried back to the department store and was told the payoff would be $1,050, not $1,000. The $50 was not interest, the store claimed, but a "service charge" for the privilege of opening her account.

All of these schemes ended with the 1969 Truth-in-Lending Act. According to the law, all lenders must state their rates in standardized APR terms, and any charge in excess of principal is interest regardless of the name given it. Competition is greater since the mail order moneylender, the car dealer's bank, the department store, and other financial institutions must be more truthful.

Chapter Glossary

Promissory note. A written promise to pay a certain sum of money by a specific future date.

Negotiable instrument. A legal document, such as a promissory note, that can be transferred to a third party.

Discount. Interest collected in advance, as is done with a simple discount bank note.

Proceeds. The actual dollar amount that the borrower receives. For example, if $2,000 is borrowed on a "discounted" note with interest calculated at $40, the borrower will receive only $1,960 at the time of the loan.

Maturity value. The amount due on the maturity date. For simple interest notes, the maturity value is calculated as principal plus interest. For simple discount notes, the maturity value is the face value of the note because the interest was deducted in advance.

Simple discount note. A loan from which the discount (interest) is taken at the beginning of the loan period, before the proceeds are given to the borrower.

True rate of interest. The effective rate that must be disclosed to a borrower according to the Truth-in-Lending Act as calculated by using the proceeds as the principal.

W hen a business, a government, or an individual borrows money, the borrower signs a **promissory note,** a legal document that is a promise to pay a certain sum of money by a specific future date. The document is usually interest bearing; that is, the borrower is required to pay principal and interest at maturity. Usually such legal documents are **negotiable instruments**.

LEARNING UNIT 1
PROMISSORY NOTES

Some promissory notes are non-interest-bearing. The borrower pays back only the amount borrowed at maturity. Most notes, however, are interest bearing. Figure 11.1 is an example of an interest-bearing note.

The promissory note in Figure 11.1 is in a form that meets the criteria set forth by the Uniform Commercial Code (UCC):

1. *It is in writing* and *signed by the maker* of the promissory note (Yvonne Bonner).
2. *It contains an unconditional promise to pay a certain sum of money at a fixed or determinable future time.*

A **discount** is interest taken in advance. The interest is calculated on the face value of the note. Unlike simple interest, *the discount is subtracted from the face value of the note to find the proceeds.* The **proceeds** are the amount the borrower actually receives from the lender. *The borrower only gets the use of the proceeds, which then become the principal of the loan.*

11.1 **Calculating the Amount of the Discount and Proceeds for Simple Discount Notes**

EXCEL Spreadsheet Application 1 Application 1 at the end of this chapter is a spreadsheet form designed to calculate the interest and maturity value of promissory notes and the discount, proceeds, and true rate when those notes are discounted.

$50,000	Columbia, Missouri __June 24,__ 20 _02_
120 days	After date, for value received, _I_ promise to pay to
	First Columbia State Bank
	Fifty thousand and 00/100 — — — — — — — — — — — — — — — DOLLARS
	with interest at _8.9%_ per annum
	Payable at First Columbia State Bank
	No. _4510_ *Yvonne Bonner* (Seal)
	Due _October 22, 2002_ (Seal)

Figure 11.1
Promissory Note

Since the passage of the Truth-in-Lending Act in 1969 (see the vignette at the beginning of this chapter), requiring that true interest rates be disclosed, the use of simple discount notes is not as common as it once was, particularly by banks. It is still practiced with some types of business loans, especially in international financial transactions.

Simple discount is found by using the formula

$$B = MDT$$

where

B = bank discount (interest taken in advance)
M = maturity value (amount to be repaid at the end of the loan period)
D = discount rate (interest rate for interest taken in advance)
T = time in the loan period (in years)

Proceeds can then be found by subtracting the bank discount from the maturity value:

$$P = M - B$$

A comparison of the simple discount with the simple interest described in Chapter 10 will highlight the differences. Simple interest is found by using the formula

$$I = PRT$$

where

I = interest
P = principal (face value of a loan)
R = interest rate
T = time in the loan period (in years)

The interest is added to the principal to find the maturity value

$$M = P + I$$

which is the amount the borrower must pay the lender at the end of the loan period.

EXAMPLE Two notes exist: One is a 60-day note for $20,000 discounted at 9%, and the other is a 60-day note for $20,000 with a 9% simple interest rate. Find the following:

1. Interest owed on each note
2. Amount received by the borrower for each note
3. Maturity value of each note

Solution **Simple Discount Note** **Simple Interest Note**

Step 1. Interest (discount) owed:

$B = MDT$ $\quad\quad\quad\quad\quad\quad\quad\quad$ $I = PRT$

$= \$20,000 \times 9\% \times \dfrac{60}{360}$ $\quad\quad$ $= \$20,000 \times 9\% \times \dfrac{60}{360}$

$= \$300$ $\quad\quad\quad\quad\quad\quad\quad\quad$ $= \$300$

Step 2. Amount received by the borrower for each note:

$P = M - D$ $\quad\quad\quad\quad\quad\quad\quad$ Principal = face value

$\quad = \$20,000 - 300$ $\quad\quad\quad\quad\quad\quad$ $= \$20,000$

$\quad = \$19,700$

Step 3: Maturity value of each note:

Maturity value = face value

$$M = P + I$$
$$= \$20,000 + 300$$
$$= \$20,300$$

$$= \$20,000$$

Table 11.1 summarizes and highlights the differences between simple interest and simple discount.

11.1 Practice Problems

Calculate the discount and the proceeds for the following problems:

1. Ms. Willifred Thorndyke signed a $75,000 note discounted at 12% for 90 days. Find the discount and the proceeds.
2. The Madison National Bank made a loan of $50,000 for three months with a discount rate of 9%. Find the discount and the proceeds.
3. Mier Hoffman Cosmetics borrowed $18,500 for four months discounted at $7\frac{1}{4}$%. Determine the discount and the proceeds.
4. Li Chiu signed a $30,000 note for 150 days at a discount rate of 5.7%. Find the discount and the proceeds.

11.1 Solutions to Practice Problems

1. $B = MDT$

$$= \$75,000 \times 12\% \times \frac{90}{360}$$
$$= \$2,250$$

$P = M - B$
$$= \$75,000 - 2,250$$
$$= \$72,750$$

2. $B = MDT$

$$= \$50,000 \times 9\% \times \frac{3}{12}$$
$$= \$1,125$$

$P = M - B$
$$= \$50,000 - 1,125$$
$$= \$48,875$$

3. $B = MDT$

$$= \$18,500 \times 7\frac{1}{4}\% \times \frac{4}{12}$$
$$= \$447.08$$

$P = M - B$
$$= \$18,500 - 447.08$$
$$= \$18,052.92$$

4. $B = MDT$

$$= \$30,000 \times 5.7\% \times \frac{150}{360}$$
$$= \$712.50$$

$P = M - B$
$$= \$30,000 - 712.50$$
$$= \$29,287.50$$

TABLE 11.1 COMPARISON OF SIMPLE INTEREST AND SIMPLE DISCOUNT

Simple Interest Note (Chapter 10)	Simple Discount Note
1. A simple interest note is for a short period of time, usually less than one year (in this example, 60 days).	1. A simple discount note is for a short period of time, usually less than one year (in this example, 60 days).
2. The face value is the principal, the amount the borrower receives (in this example, $20,000).	2. The face value is the maturity value, not the amount the borrower receives (in this example, $20,000).
3. The interest is based on the principal, or face value the amount that the borrower actually receives (in this example, $300).	3. The interest is based on the face value, but the face value is the maturity value, not the amount the borrower actually receives (in this example, $300).
4. The borrower receives the full amount of the principal, or the face value of the note (in this example, $20,000).	4. The borrower receives the proceeds, the maturity value less the discount (in this example, $19,700).
5. The maturity value is the face value of the note plus accumulated interest at maturity (in this example, $20,300).	5. The maturity value is the face value of the note (in this example, $20,000).
6. Used frequently.	6. Used infrequently because the true rate of interest must now be disclosed. Used where legislation does not apply, for example, for personal loans from friends and family.

11.2 Calculating the True (Effective) Interest Rate

As mentioned earlier, the Truth-in-Lending Act requires the lender to disclose the **true rate of interest**. Because different ways of calculating interest caused confusion, the true rate of interest allows almost all lenders' terms to be compared. Interest rates are stated in annual terms. They are calculated on the basis of the amount of money a borrower has the use of for a given period of time. That is,

$$R = \frac{I}{PT}$$

When a note is discounted, the amount of money the borrower has the use of is the proceeds. The formula for simple interest can be rewritten

$$R = \frac{B}{PT}$$

where R is the true rate, B is the amount of the discount, P is amount of the proceeds, and T is the time in the discount period.

The true rate of interest is frequently called the effective rate of interest.

EXAMPLE   Calculate the true rate of interest on a $20,000 note discounted at 9% for 60 days.

Solution   *Step 1.* Find the amount of the discount:

$$B = MDT$$
$$= \$20,000 \times 9\% \times \frac{60}{360}$$
$$= \$300$$

Step 2. Find the amount of the proceeds:

$$P = M - B$$
$$= \$20,000 - 300$$
$$= \$19,700$$

Step 3. Find the true rate of interest:

$$R = \frac{B}{PT}$$
$$= \frac{\$300}{\$19,700 \times \dfrac{60}{360}}$$
$$= 9.14\%$$

300 ✕ 360 ÷ 19,700 ÷ 60 ═ .09137

In the preceding example the true rate of interest is 9.14%, to the nearest hundredth of a percent. The federal regulations under the Truth-in-Lending Act require that a rate be disclosed to the nearest quarter of a percent. Thus, the lender in this example would have to tell the borrower that the rate is 9.25% (the closest $\frac{1}{4}$%).

11.2 Practice Problems

Calculate the true interest rate for the following simple discount problems. (Round answers to the nearest $\frac{1}{4}$%.)

1. Find the true interest rate for a $40,000 note for four months discounted at 12%.

2. Calculate the true interest rate for a $200,000 note that will be discounted at 7.5% for 240 days.

3. Mr. James of James Wholesale Appliances signed an $80,000 note on March 21 at a discount rate of 11%. It will come due on September 17. Find the true rate of interest.

4. MarDavis Enterprises borrowed $2,500,000 at a discount rate of 6.9% for 150 days. Calculate the true rate of interest.

11.2 Solutions to Practice Problems

1. $B = MDT$

$\quad = \$40,000 \times 12\% \times \dfrac{4}{12}$

$\quad = \$1,600$

$R = \dfrac{B}{PT}$

$\quad = \dfrac{\$1,600}{\$38,400 \times \dfrac{4}{12}}$

$\quad = 12.5\%$

$P = M - B$

$\quad = \$40,000 - 1,600$

$\quad = \$38,400$

2. $B = MDT$

$\quad = \$200,000 \times 7.5\% \times \dfrac{240}{360}$

$\quad = \$10,000$

$R = \dfrac{B}{PT}$

$\quad = \dfrac{\$10,000}{\$190,000 \times \dfrac{240}{360}}$

$\quad = 7.89\% = 8.00\%$ rounded to the nearest $\dfrac{1}{4}\%$

$P = M - B$

$\quad = \$200,000 - 10,000$

$\quad = \$190,000$

3. $B = MDT$

$\quad = \$80,000 \times 11\% \times \dfrac{180}{360}$

$\quad = \$4,400$

$R = \dfrac{B}{PT}$

$\quad = \dfrac{\$4,400}{\$75,600 \times \dfrac{180}{360}}$

$\quad = 11.64\% = 11.75\%$ rounded to the nearest $\dfrac{1}{4}\%$

$P = M - B$

$\quad = \$80,000 - 4,400$

$\quad = \$75,600$

4. $B = MDT$

$\quad = \$2,500,000 \times 6.9\% \times \dfrac{150}{360}$

$\quad = \$71,875$

$R = \dfrac{B}{PT}$

$\quad = \dfrac{\$71,875}{\$2,428,125 \times \dfrac{150}{360}}$

$\quad = 7.10\% = 7.00\%$ rounded to the nearest $\dfrac{1}{4}\%$

$P = M - B$

$\quad = \$2,500,000 - 71,875$

$\quad = \$2,428,125 = \$2,428,125$

EXCEL Spreadsheet Application 2 This spreadsheet form calculates the
interest and discount information for treasury bills.

The U.S. federal government frequently borrows money to fund its activities. When
short-term borrowing is necessary, the government sells U.S. Treasury bills (usually
called T-bills). T-bills are short-term promissory notes in the form of securities issued
by the U.S. government.

T-bills are sold in $10,000 denominations (the face value and the maturity value).
The interest rates fluctuate according to supply and demand. T-bills are generally considered to be one of the safest and most liquid financial securities because they are
backed by the resources of the U.S. government.

T-bills are sold with maturity dates of 13 weeks (one quarter, or 91 days),
26 weeks (two quarters, or 182 days), or 52 weeks (one year). A buyer's purchase price
is the discounted price (the proceeds). He or she receives the face value at maturity.

EXAMPLE   A 4.25%, 26-week T-bill was sold. Find (1) the maturity value, (2) the amount of the
discount (interest paid), (3) the purchase price (proceeds), and (4) the true rate of interest (round to the nearest hundredth of a percent).

Solution   *Step 1.* The maturity value and the face value of T-bills is always $10,000.

Step 2. Amount of the discount:

$$B = MDT$$
$$= \$10,000 \times 4.25\% \times \frac{26}{52}$$
$$= \$212.50$$

Step 3. Purchase price (proceeds):

$$P = M - B$$
$$= \$10,000 - 212.50$$
$$= \$9,787.50$$

Step 4. True rate of interest:

$$R = \frac{B}{PT}$$
$$= \frac{\$212.50}{\$9,787.50 \times \frac{26}{52}}$$
$$= 4.34\% \text{ to the nearest hundredth of a percent}$$

**11.3
Practice
Problems**

*Solve the following T-bill problems. (Round the true rate of interest to the nearest hundredth of
a percent.)*

1. The First Bank of Boston purchased $3 million of 13-week T-bills at a rate of 4.5%. Find the
total maturity value, the amount of the discount, the purchase price, and the true rate of
interest.

2. Jerry Tark received an out-of-court settlement on a personal liability suit amounting to
$150,000. He is thinking about buying U.S. T-bills with the money. Jerry does not know too
much about them, but he has learned that one year T-bills can be bought at a rate of 5.3%.
Give him the information he needs to make a decision: find the total maturity value, the
amount of interest he will earn, the purchase price, and the true rate of interest.

3. The Metropolitan Mutual Fund has a balanced fund that mixes stocks, bonds, and money market investments to take advantage of varying market conditions. The fund manager has decided to place $10 million in 13-week T-bills paying 4.75%. Find the amount of the discount, the purchase price, and the true rate of interest.

4. A $10 billion, 26-week T-bill refunding sale at 5.5% has just been completed. Find the amount of the discount, the proceeds, and the true rate of interest.

11.3 Solutions to Practice Problems

1. The total maturity value is the same as the total face value, $3,000,000.

Amount of the discount:

$B = MDT$

$= \$3,000,000 \times 4.5\% \times \dfrac{13}{52}$

$= \$33,750$

Purchase price (proceeds):

$P = M - B$

$= \$3,000,000 - 33,750$

$= \$2,966,250$

True rate of interest:

$R = \dfrac{B}{PT}$

$= \dfrac{\$33,750}{\$2,966,250 \times \dfrac{13}{52}}$

$= 4.55\%$ to the nearest hundredth of a percent

2. The total maturity value is the same as the total face value, $150,000.

Amount of the interest (discount):

$B = MDT$

$= \$150,000 \times 5.3\% \times 1$

$= \$7,950$

Purchase price (proceeds):

$P = M - B$

$= \$150,000 - 7,950$

$= \$142,050$

True rate of interest:

$R = \dfrac{B}{PT}$

$= \dfrac{\$7,950}{\$142,050 \times 1}$

$= 5.60\%$ to the nearest hundredth of a percent

3. Amount of the discount:

$B = MDT$

$= \$10,000,000 \times 4.75\% \times \dfrac{13}{52}$

$= \$118,750$

Purchase price (proceeds):

$P = M - B$

$= \$10,000,000 - 118,750$

$= \$9,881,250$

True rate of interest:

$R = \dfrac{B}{PT}$

$= \dfrac{\$118,750}{\$9,881,250 \times \dfrac{13}{52}}$

$= 4.81\%$ to the nearest hundredth of a percent

4. Amount of the discount:

$B = MDT$

$= \$10 \text{ billion} \times 5.5\% \times \dfrac{26}{52}$

$= \$275,000,000, \text{ or } \$.275 \text{ billion}$

Proceeds:

$P = M - B$

$= \$10 \text{ billion} - .275 \text{ billion}$

$= \$9.725 \text{ billion}$

$(\$9,725,000,000)$

True rate of interest:

$$R = \frac{B}{PT}$$

$$= \frac{\$.275 \text{ billion}}{\$9.725 \text{ billion} \times \frac{26}{52}}$$

$$= 5.66\% \text{ to the nearest hundredth of a percent.}$$

11.4 Calculating the Maturity Value Necessary to Provide a Needed Amount of Proceeds

A borrower usually needs a certain amount of money, say, $4,000, to buy a used car. If a loan is going to be discounted, however, it is the proceeds that will have to amount to $4,000. Thus, the actual amount borrowed (the maturity value, or the face value of the loan) will be more than $4,000. The formula to calculate the maturity value is

$$M = \frac{P}{1 - (DT)}$$

EXAMPLE   Find the amount that needs to be borrowed (maturity value) if $80,000 is needed (proceeds) to buy a new chemistry machine. The note will be discounted at 8% for 120 days.

Solution

$$M = \frac{P}{1 - (DT)}$$

$$= \frac{\$80,000}{1 - \left(8\% \times \frac{120}{360}\right)}$$

$$= \frac{\$80,000}{1 - .027} \text{ Rounded to the nearest thousandth}$$

$$= \frac{\$80,000}{.973}$$

$$= \$82,219.94$$

11.4 Practice Problems

1. Find the maturity value if $20,000 is needed and a note will be discounted at 8% for 60 days.

2. Sam Desmond needs $6,500 to buy a new conference table and chairs for his business. He can borrow the needed funds at a discount rate of 9.2% for four months. How much will the face value of the loan have to be?

3. Determine the maturity value of a note dated June 21, due September 29, and discounted at 7% if the borrower needs $250,000.

4. Calculate the face value of a note discounted at 7% if $50,000 in proceeds were needed. The note was signed on May 3 and is due on July 12.

11.4 Solutions to Practice Problems

1. $M = \dfrac{P}{1 - (DT)}$

$$= \frac{\$20,000}{1 - \left(8\% \times \frac{60}{360}\right)}$$

2. $M = \dfrac{P}{1 - (DT)}$

$$= \frac{\$6,500}{1 - \left(9.2\% \times \frac{4}{12}\right)}$$

$$= \frac{\$20,000}{1 - .013}$$

Rounded to the nearest thousandth

$$= \frac{\$20,000}{.987}$$

$$= \$20,263.43$$

$$= \frac{\$6,500}{1 - .031}$$

Rounded to the nearest thousandth

$$= \frac{\$6,500}{.969}$$

$$= \$6,707.95$$

3. $M = \dfrac{P}{1 - (DT)}$

$$= \frac{\$250,000}{1 - \left(7\% \times \dfrac{100}{360}\right)}$$

$$= \frac{\$250,000}{1 - .019}$$

Rounded to the nearest thousandth

$$= \frac{\$250,000}{.981}$$

$$= \$254,842$$

4. $M = \dfrac{P}{1 - (DT)}$

$$= \frac{\$50,000}{1 - \left(7\% \times \dfrac{70}{360}\right)}$$

$$= \frac{\$50,000}{1 - .014}$$

Rounded to the nearest thousandth

$$= \frac{\$50,000}{.986}$$

$$= \$50,709.94$$

LEARNING UNIT 2
DISCOUNTING INTEREST-BEARING NOTES

Businesses sometimes accept a simple interest or simple discount note instead of a cash payment for the sale of merchandise. This practice is particularly common for sellers of seasonal goods, such as lawn tables and chairs, snowmobiles, ski equipment, and toys. Goods may be delivered to buyers months before payment is expected. In such cases, promissory notes are often signed by buyers to affirm the debt.

Frequently, money is needed before a promissory note comes due. If a note is negotiable, it can be sold to a bank or other financial institution. Financial institutions called factors often discount accounts receivable. The business then receives the proceeds—the maturity value of the note less a fee. The fee is called the bank discount. The bank receives the full maturity value from the maker of the note when it comes due. If the maker of the note does not pay, the bank usually has the recourse to collect from the seller of the note. In this way the bank is protected from loss. This should not be confused with borrowing money using a promissory note (or account receivable) as collateral for a loan. When a bank accepts promissory notes or accounts receivable as collateral, it makes either a simple interest loan or a simple discount loan.

11.5 **Calculating the Amount of Discount and Proceeds When Discounting an Interest-Bearing Note**

Discounting an interest-bearing note, as this process is called, is handled exactly like discounting a simple discount note. If the promissory note is *non-interest-bearing*, the maturity value is the same as the face value of the note. If the note is *interest-bearing*, the interest and maturity value must be calculated. The amount of the discount depends on the discount rate and the number of days the bank has to wait for its money, which is called the discount period.

The steps for discounting an interest-bearing note are as follows:

1. Find the interest for the note ($I = PRT$).
2. Find the maturity value of the note ($M = P + I$).

3. Find the amount of time in the discount period.
4. Find the amount of the discount ($B = MDT$).
5. Find the amount of the proceeds ($P = M - B$).

EXAMPLE   Johnsonville Furniture received a $28,000, 9%, 150-day promissory note dated March 16. The note was discounted the same day, March 16, at Johnsonville's bank. The bank discount rate was 13.5%. Calculate the amount of the discount and the proceeds.

Solution   *Step 1.* Find the interest for the note:

$$I = PRT$$
$$= \$28,000 \times 9\% \times \frac{150}{360}$$
$$= \$1,050$$

Step 2. Find the maturity value of the note:

$$M = P + I$$
$$= \$28,000 + 1,050$$
$$= \$29,050$$

Step 3. Find the time in the discount period: Since the note was discounted on the same day it was dated, the discount period is also 150 days.

Step 4. Find the amount of the discount:

$$B = MDT$$
$$= \$29,050 \times 13.5\% \times \frac{150}{360}$$
$$= \$1,634.06$$

Step 5. Find the amount of the proceeds:

$$P = M - B$$
$$= \$29,050 - 1,634.06$$
$$= \$27,415.94$$

Although a promissory note might be discounted on the same day it was dated and signed by the maker, it is much more likely that it would be discounted at some future date. That would reduce the time in the discount period, and the bank would have to wait less time to receive repayment of its money.

EXAMPLE   Johnsonville Furniture received a $28,000, 9%, 150-day promissory note dated March 16. The note was discounted on May 5 at Johnsonville's bank. The bank discount rate was 13.5%. Calculate the amount of the discount and the proceeds.

Solution   *Step 1.* Find the interest for the note:

$$I = PRT$$
$$= \$28,000 \times 9\% \times \frac{150}{360}$$
$$= \$1,050$$

Step 2. Find the maturity value of the note:

$$M = P + I$$
$$= \$28,000 + 1,050$$
$$= \$29,050$$

Step 3. Find the time in the discount period:

The note was discounted on May 5. The bank will receive payment of the note on August 13 (150 days from the date the note was signed and dated on March 16). The time between May 5 and August 13 is 100 days. See below:

Time in the Promissory Note

Mar.	31 days
	−16 days
	15 days
Apr.	30 days
May	31 days
June	30 days
July	31 days
Aug.	+13 days
	150 days

Time in the Discount Period

May	31 days
	−5 days
	26 days
June	30 days
July	31 days
Aug.	+13 days
	100 days

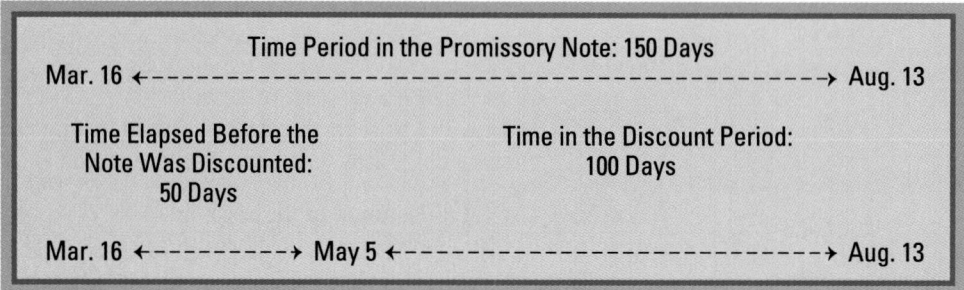

Sometimes it is easier to subtract the time elapsed before the note was discounted (50 days) from the total time in the promissory note (150 days) to find the time in the discount period (100 days):

Time elapsed before note was discounted:

Mar.	31 days
	−16 days
	15 days
Apr.	30 days
May	+ 5 days
	50 days

Promissory note:	150 days
− elapsed time:	− 50 days
discount period:	100 days

Step 4. Find the amount of the discount:

$$B = MDT$$
$$= \$29{,}050 \times 13.5\% \times \frac{100}{360}$$
$$= \$1{,}089.38$$

Step 5. Find the amount of the proceeds:

$$P = M - B$$
$$= \$29{,}050 - 1{,}089.38$$
$$= \$27{,}960.62$$

11.5
Practice
Problems

Calculate the discount and the proceeds for the following interest-bearing promissory notes:

1. Quintana Electric Company accepted an $18,000, 4.5%, 120-day promissory note dated September 3. The note was discounted on October 13. The discount rate was 9.2%. Calculate the amount of the discount and the proceeds.

2. The firm of Su Wong and Ty Hufon accepted a $40,000, 6.7% promissory note dated April 27 and due August 25. The note was discounted on June 2 at a discount rate of 9.2%. Calculate the amount of the discount and the proceeds.

3. A $350,000, 5¾%, 180-day promissory note was discounted 50 days after it was signed and dated at a discount rate of 8%. Calculate the amount of the discount and the proceeds.

4. Akito Ski Equipment Corporation received a $2,950, 10%, 200-day promissory note dated March 18. The note was discounted on June 26. The discount rate was 12.9%. Calculate the amount of the discount and the proceeds.

11.5 Solutions to Practice Problems

1. *Step 1.* Find the interest for the note:

$$I = PRT$$
$$= \$18,000 \times 4.5\% \times \frac{120}{360}$$
$$= \$270$$

Step 2. Find the maturity value of the note:

$$M = P + I$$
$$= \$18,000 + 270$$
$$= \$18,270$$

Step 3. Find the time in the discount period:

Sept.	30 days		
	− 3 days		
	27 days		120 days in note
Oct.	+13 days		− 40
	40 days before discounting		80 days in discount period

Step 4. Find the amount of the discount:

$$B = MDT$$
$$= \$18,270 \times 9.2\% \times \frac{80}{360}$$
$$= \$373.52$$

Step 5. Find the amount of the proceeds:

$$P = M - B$$
$$= \$18,270 - 373.52$$
$$= \$17,896.48$$

2. *Step 1.* Find the interest for the note:

$$I = PRT$$
$$= \$40,000 \times 6.7\% \times \frac{120}{360}$$
$$= \$893.33$$

Apr.	30
	− 27
	3
May	31
June	30
July	31
Aug.	+ 25
	120 days in note

Step 2. Find the maturity value of the note:

$$M = P + I$$
$$= \$40,000 + 893.33$$
$$= \$40,893.33$$

Step 3. Find the time in the discount period:

Apr.   30 days
       − 27 days
         3 days
May   31 days
June + 2 days
    36 days before discounting

120 days in note
− 36
84 days in discount period

Step 4. Find the amount of the discount:

$$B = MDT$$
$$= \$40,893.33 \times 9.2\% \times \frac{84}{360}$$
$$= \$877.84$$

Step 5. Find the amount of the proceeds:

$$P = M - B$$
$$= \$40,893.33 - 877.84$$
$$= \$40,015.49$$

3. *Step 1.* Find the interest for the note:

$$I = PRT$$
$$= \$350,000 \times 5.75\% \times \frac{180}{360}$$
$$= \$10,062.50$$

Step 2. Find the maturity value of the note:

$$M = P + I$$
$$= \$350,000 + 10,062.50$$
$$= \$360,062.50$$

Step 3. Find the time in the discount period:

180 days in the note
− 50 days before discounting
130 days in discount period

Step 4. Find the amount of the discount:

$$B = MDT$$
$$= \$360,062.50 \times 8\% \times \frac{130}{360}$$
$$= \$10,401.81$$

Step 5. Find the amount of the proceeds:

$$P = M - B$$
$$= \$360,062.50 - 10,401.81$$
$$= \$349,660.69$$

4. *Step 1.* Find the interest for the note:

$$I = PRT$$
$$= \$2,950 \times 10\% \times \frac{200}{360}$$
$$= \$163.89$$

Step 2. Find the maturity value of the note:

$$M = P + I$$
$$= \$2,950 + 163.89$$
$$= \$3,113.89$$

Step 3. Find the time in the discount period:

Mar.   31 days
       − 18 days
         13 days
Apr.   30 days
May   31 days
June + 26 days
    100 days before discounting

200 days in note
− 100 days
100 days in discount period

Step 4. Find the amount of the discount:

$$B = MDT$$
$$= \$3,113.89 \times 12.9\% \times \frac{100}{360}$$
$$= \$111.58$$

Step 5. Find the amount of the proceeds:

$$P = M - B$$
$$= \$3,113.89 - 111.58$$
$$= \$3,002.31$$

Chapter 11 Banking Applications: Promissory Notes and Discounting

Page	Section Topic	Learning Concepts	Examples and Solutions
376	**11.1** Calculating the Amount of the Discount and Proceeds for Simple Discount Notes	Use the formula $B = MDT$ to find the amount of the discount, and then use the formula $P = M - B$ to find the proceeds where B = bank discount M = maturity value or face value of the note D = discount rate T = time in the discount period P = proceeds, the amount the borrower receives	Calculate the discount and the proceeds on $3,000 discounted at 12% for 120 days. $B = MDT$ $= \$3,000 \times 12\% \times \dfrac{120}{360}$ $= \$120$ $P = M - B$ $= \$3,000 - 120$ $= \$2,880$
379	**11.2** Calculating the True (Effective) Interest Rate	Use the formula $R = \dfrac{B}{PT}$ where R = true rate of interest B = bank discount P = proceeds T = time in discount period The true rate is used to compare all interest rates. It is found by dividing the amount of interest (no matter what it is called) on an annual basis (T) by the amount of money a borrower actually has to use. The Truth-in-Lending Act requires rounding to the nearest $\frac{1}{4}\%$.	Calculate the true rate of interest on $7,000 discounted at 8% for four months. $B = MDT$ $= \$7,000 \times 8\% \times \dfrac{4}{12}$ $= \$186.67$ $P = M - B$ $= \$7,000 - 186.67$ $= \$6,813.33$ $R = \dfrac{B}{PT}$ $= \dfrac{\$186.67}{\$6,813.33 \times \dfrac{4}{12}}$ $= 8.22\%$ $= 8.25\%$ to nearest $\frac{1}{4}\%$
381	**11.3** Discounting Treasury Bills	Sold in $10,000 denominations, T-bills are sold for short-term government financing. One of the safest of all investments, they are sold with maturity dates of 13 weeks, 26 weeks, or 1 year. A buyer's purchase price is the proceeds, with the maturity value (the $10,000 face value) paid to the buyer at maturity. Unless otherwise stated, ordinary interest will always be used (360 days in a year).	Calculate the amount of discount, the purchase price, and the true rate of interest for the purchase of a $10,000 T-bill for 26 weeks at 6%. $B = MDT$ $= \$10,000 \times 6\% \times \dfrac{26}{52}$ $= \$300$ $P = M - B$ $= \$10,000 - 300$ $= \$9,700$ $R = \dfrac{B}{PT}$ $= \dfrac{\$300}{\$9,700 \times \dfrac{26}{52}}$ $= 6.19\%$

Page	Section Topic	Learning Concepts	Examples and Solutions
383	**11.4** Calculating the Maturity Value Necessary to Provide a Needed Amount of Proceeds	Borrowers usually need a specific amount of cash. If a loan is to be discounted, the borrower will receive the proceeds, not the face value of the loan. The face value is the maturity value of a discounted note. The formula to find the maturity value (amount to be borrowed) to receive the needed proceeds is $$M = \frac{P}{1 - (DT)}$$	Calculate the maturity value of a 150-day loan that will be discounted at 13% if $10,000 in cash is needed. $$M = \frac{P}{1 - (DT)}$$ $$= \frac{\$10,000}{1 - \left(13\% \times \frac{150}{360}\right)}$$ $$= \frac{\$10,000}{1 - .054}$$ $$= \frac{\$10,000}{.946}$$ $$= \$10,570.83$$
384	**11.5** Calculating the Amount of Discount and Proceeds When Discounting an Interest-Bearing Note	A seller accepts a promissory note from a customer as evidence of debt for goods delivered now, but for which payment is not due immediately (usually not for several months). Before the note comes to maturity, the seller needs cash. The note will be discounted by a bank. Discounting a note means the bank buys it and charges a fee, called a discount. The seller receives the proceeds, the maturity value less the discount. At maturity, the bank collects the maturity value of the note from the maker (the buyer) of the note.	A seller accepts a 9%, 200-day, simple interest promissory note in payment for an $80,000 invoice dated May 8. On August 4 the note is discounted at a bank that charges a discount fee of 14%. Calculate the amount of proceeds that were received. **1.** Find interest: $$I = PRT$$ $$= 80,000 \times 9\% \times \frac{200}{360}$$ $$= \$4,000$$ **2.** Find maturity value: $$M = P + I$$ $$= \$80,000 + 4,000$$ $$= \$84,000$$ **3.** Find time in discount period: May 31 days − 8 days 23 days June 30 days July 31 days Aug. + 4 days 88 days before discount 200 days − 88 days 112 days in discount period **4.** Find discount: $$B = MDT$$ $$= \$84,000 \times 14\% \times \frac{112}{360}$$ $$= \$3,658.67$$ **5.** Find proceeds: $$P = M - B$$ $$= \$84,000 - 3,658.67$$ $$= \$80,341.33$$

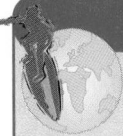

SURFING THE INTERNET

For further information on the topics covered in this chapter, check out the following sites:

http://invest-faq.com/articles/bonds-value-treas-bill.html

http://www.e-analytics.com/fued14.htm

http://www.creditbusiness.net/disc.htm

ADDITIONAL
PRACTICE
PROBLEMS

Answers to odd-numbered problems are given in Appendix A.

11.1

Calculate the discount and the proceeds in the following problems.

1. Margaret Zipple-Eberhart signed a $95,000 note discounted at 10% for 180 days. Find the discount and the proceeds.

$B = MDT$

$= \$95,000 \times 10\% \times \dfrac{180}{360}$

$= \$4,750$

$P = M - B$

$= \$95,000 - 4,750$

$= \$90,250$

2. The Sacramento City Bank made a loan of $500,000 for a third of a year with a discount rate of 8.5%. Find the discount and the proceeds.

$B = MDT$

$= \$500,000 \times 8.5\% \times \dfrac{1}{3}$

$= \$14,166.67$

$P = M - B$

$= \$500,000 - 14,166.67$

$= \$485,833.33$

3. The Morningstar Coffee Shop borrowed $8,850 for nine months discounted at $9\frac{1}{4}$%. Determine the discount and the proceeds.

$B = MDT$

$= \$8,850 \times 9\frac{1}{4}\% \times \dfrac{9}{12}$

$= \$613.97$

$P = M - B$

$= \$8,850 - 613.97$

$= \$8,236.03$

4. Ling Duc Chou signed a $125,000 note for 150 days at a discount rate of 11.5%. Find the discount and the proceeds.

$B = MDT$

$= \$125,000 \times 11.5\% \times \dfrac{150}{360}$

$= \$5,989.58$

$P = M - B$

$= \$125,000 - 5,989.58$

$= \$119,010.42$

11.2

Calculate the true interest rate in the following problems.

5. Find the true interest rate for a $20,000 note for five months discounted at 13%.

$B = MDT$

$= \$20,000 \times 13\% \times \dfrac{5}{12}$

$= \$18,916.67$

$P = M - B$

$= \$20,000 - 1,083.33$

$= \$1,083.33$

$R = \dfrac{B}{PT}$

$= \dfrac{\$1,083.33}{\$18,916.67 \times \dfrac{5}{12}}$

$= 13.75\%$

6. Calculate the true interest rate for a $1,200,000 note that will be discounted at 6.5% for 120 days.

$B = MDT$

$= \$1,200,000 \times 6.5\% \times \dfrac{120}{360}$

$= \$26,000$

$P = M - B$

$= \$1,200,000 - 26,000$

$= \$1,174,000$

$R = \dfrac{B}{PT}$

$= \dfrac{\$26,000}{\$1,174,000 \times \dfrac{120}{360}}$

$= 6.75\%$

7. Lynnanne Black, owner of Black Antiques, signed a $5,890 note on June 12 at a discount rate of 11%. It will come due on September 20. What is the true rate of interest?

June 30 − 12 =	18
July	31
Aug.	31
Sept.	20
	100

$B = MDT$

$= \$5,890 \times 11\% \times \dfrac{100}{360}$

$= \$179.97$

$P = M - B$

$= \$5,890 - 179.97$

$= \$5,710.03$

$R = \dfrac{B}{PT}$

$= \dfrac{\$179.97}{\$5,710.03 \times \dfrac{100}{360}}$

$= 11.25\%$

8. Value Pak Industries borrowed $200,000 at a discount rate of 9.9% for 150 days. Calculate the true rate of interest.

$B = MDT$

$= \$200,000 \times 9.9\% \times \dfrac{150}{360}$

$= \$8,250$

$P = M - B$

$= \$200,000 - 8,250$

$= \$191,750$

$R = \dfrac{B}{PT}$

$= \dfrac{\$8,250}{\$191,750 \times \dfrac{150}{360}}$

$= 10.25\%$

11.3

Solve the following T-bill problems. (Round the true rate of interest to the nearest hundredth of a percent.)

9. The International Bank of Brussels bought $500,000 of 26-week T-bills at a rate of 5%. Find the total maturity value, the amount of the discount, the purchase price, and the true rate of interest.

Amount of
the discount:

$B = MDT$

$= \$500,000 \times 5\% \times \dfrac{26}{52}$

$= \$12,500$

True rate of interest:

$R = \dfrac{B}{PT}$

$= \dfrac{\$12,500}{\$487,500 \times \dfrac{26}{52}}$

$= 5.13\%$ to the nearest hundredth of a percent

Purchase
price (proceeds):

$P = M - B$

$= \$500,000 - 12,500$

$= \$487,500$

10. Melissa Buskirk received an inheritance of $100,000 with which she bought U.S. T-bills with a one-year maturity date, at a rate of 5.58%. Find the amount of interest Melissa will earn, the purchase price, and the true rate of interest.

Amount of
the discount:

$B = MDT$

$= \$100,000 \times 5.58\% \times 1$

$= \$5,580$

True rate of interest:

$R = \dfrac{B}{PT}$

$= \dfrac{\$5,580}{\$94,420 \times 1}$

$= 5.91\%$ to the nearest hundredth of a percent

Purchase
price (proceeds):

$P = M - B$

$= \$100,000 - 5,580$

$= \$94,420$

11. The Washington State Bank has decided to place $150,000,000 in 13-week T-bills paying 4.75%. Find the amount of the discount, the purchase price, and the true rate of interest.

Amount of
the discount:

$B = MDT$

$= \$150,000,000 \times 4.75\% \times \dfrac{13}{52}$

$= \$1,781,250$

True rate of interest:

$R = \dfrac{B}{PT}$

$= \dfrac{\$1,781,250}{\$148,218,750 \times \dfrac{13}{52}}$

$= 4.81\%$ to the nearest hundredth of a percent

Purchase
price (proceeds):

$P = M - B$

$= \$150,000,000 - 1,781,250$

$= \$148,218,750$

12. A $5.2 billion, 13-week T-bill refunding sale at 6.23% has just been completed. Find the amount of the discount, the proceeds, and the true rate of interest.

Amount of
the discount:

$B = MDT$

$= \$5,200,000,000 \times 6.23\% \times \dfrac{13}{52}$

$= \$5,119,010,000$

True rate of interest:

$R = \dfrac{B}{PT}$

$= \dfrac{\$80,990,000}{\$5,119,010,000 \times \dfrac{13}{52}}$

$= 6.33\%$ to the nearest hundredth of a percent

Purchase
price (proceeds):

$P = M - B$

$= \$5,200,000,000 - 80,990,000$

$= \$80,990,000$

11.4

Calculate the maturity value in each of the following simple discount problems:

13. Find the maturity value if $15,000 is needed and a note will be discounted at 11.8% for 75 days.

$M = \dfrac{P}{1 - (DT)}$

$= \dfrac{\$15,000}{1 - \left(11.8\% \times \dfrac{75}{360}\right)}$

$= \dfrac{\$15,000}{1 - .025}$

      ↑

Rounded to the nearest thousandth

$= \dfrac{\$15,000}{.975}$

$= \$15,384.62$

14. Nora Donahue needs $6,500 to buy a new conference table and chairs for her business. She can borrow the needed funds at a discount rate of 13% for three months. What will the face value of the loan have to be?

$M = \dfrac{P}{1 - (DT)}$

$= \dfrac{\$6,500}{1 - \left(13\% \times \dfrac{3}{12}\right)}$

$= \dfrac{\$6,500}{1 - .033}$

      ↑

Rounded to the nearest thousandth

$= \dfrac{\$6,500}{.967}$

$= \$6,721.82$

Using the calculator:

11.8 % × 75 ÷ 360 = ⅟x + 1 = STO
15,000 ÷ RCL = 15,378.04

Using the calculator:

13 % × 3 ÷ 12 = ⅟x + 1 = STO
6,500 ÷ RCL = 6,718.35

Chapter 11 Banking Applications: Promissory Notes and Discounting

15. Determine the maturity value of a note dated April 21, due August 19, and discounted at 10.4% if the borrower needs $750.

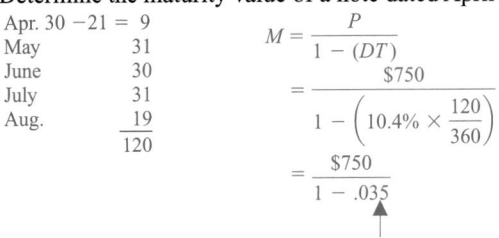

Apr. 30 −21 = 9
May 31
June 30
July 31
Aug. 19
         120

$$M = \frac{P}{1 - (DT)}$$

$$= \frac{\$750}{1 - \left(10.4\% \times \dfrac{120}{360}\right)}$$

$$= \frac{\$750}{1 - .035}$$

↑ *Rounded to the nearest thousandth*

$$= \frac{\$750}{.965}$$

$$= \$777.20$$

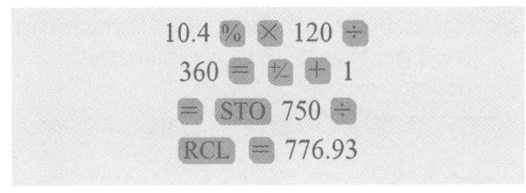

Using the calculator:

10.4 % ✕ 120 ÷
360 = ⅟ₓ + 1
= STO 750 ÷
RCL = 776.93

16. Calculate the face value of a note discounted at 9.5% if $260,000 in proceeds were needed. The note was signed on May 26 and is due on October 29.

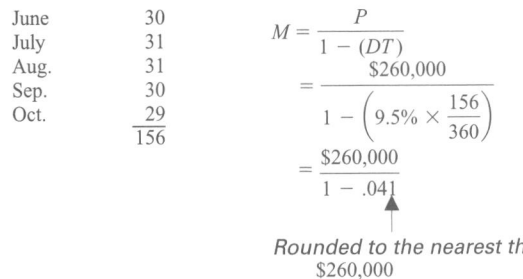

June 30
July 31
Aug. 31
Sep. 30
Oct. 29
       156

$$M = \frac{P}{1 - (DT)}$$

$$= \frac{\$260,000}{1 - \left(9.5\% \times \dfrac{156}{360}\right)}$$

$$= \frac{\$260,000}{1 - .041}$$

↑ *Rounded to the nearest thousandth*

$$= \frac{\$260,000}{.959}$$

$$= \$271,115.75$$

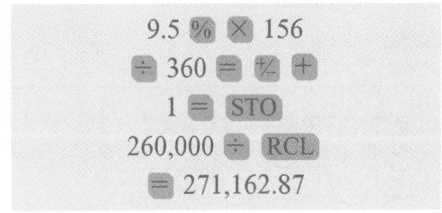

Using the calculator:

9.5 % ✕ 156
÷ 360 = ⅟ₓ +
1 = STO
260,000 ÷ RCL
= 271,162.87

11.5

Calculate the discount and the proceeds for the following interest-bearing promissory notes.

17. Enrique Ochoa Glassworks Company accepted an $8,000, 9%, 90-day promissory note dated July 13. The note was discounted July 18. The discount rate was 13%. Calculate the amount of the discount and the proceeds.

Step 1. Find the interest for the note:
$I = PRT$

$$= \$8,000 \times 9\% \times \frac{90}{360}$$

$$= \$180$$

Step 2. Find the maturity value of the note:
$M = P + I$
$= \$8,000 + 180$
$= \$8,180$

Step 3. Find the time in the discount period:
July 18 days
− 13 days
    5 days
90 − 5 = 85 days

Step 4. Find the amount of the discount:
$B = MDT$

$$= \$8,180 \times 13\% \times \frac{85}{360}$$

$$= \$251.08$$

Step 5. Find the amount of the proceeds:
$P = M - B$
$= \$8,180 - 251.08$
$= \$7,928.92$

18. The dental supply firm of Dixon and Simmons accepted a $150,000, 6.5% promissory note dated August 2 and due January 9. The note was discounted on October 1 at a discount rate of 9.9%. Calculate the amount of the discount and the proceeds.

Step 1. Find the interest for the note:

Aug. 31 − 2 = 29
Sept. 30
Oct. 31
Nov. 30
Dec. 31
Jan. 9
       160

$I = PRT$

$$= \$150,000 \times 6.5\% \times \frac{160}{360}$$

$$= \$4,333.33$$

Step 2. Find the maturity value of the note:
$M = P + I$
$= \$150,000 + 4,333.33$
$= \$154,333.33$

Step 3. Find the time in the discount period:

Aug.31 − 2 = 29
Sept. 30
Oct. 1
       60

160 days in note
− 60 days prior to discount
100 days in discount period

Step 4. Find the amount of the discount:
$B = MDT$

$$= \$154,333.33 \times 9.9\% \times \frac{100}{360}$$

$$= \$4,244.17$$

Step 5. Find the amount of the proceeds:
$P = M - B$
$= \$154,333.33 - 4,244.17$
$= \$150,089.16$

19. A $170,000, $8\frac{3}{4}\%$, 240-day promissory note was discounted 75 days after it was signed and dated, at a discount rate of 12%. Calculate the amount of the discount and the proceeds.

Step 1. Find the interest for the note:
$I = PRT$

$$= \$170,000 \times 8\frac{3}{4}\% \times \frac{240}{360}$$

$$= \$9,916.67$$

Step 2. Find the maturity value of the note:
$M = P + I$
$= \$170,000 + 9,916.67$
$= \$179,916.67$

Step 3. Find the time in the discount period:
240 days
− 75
165 days

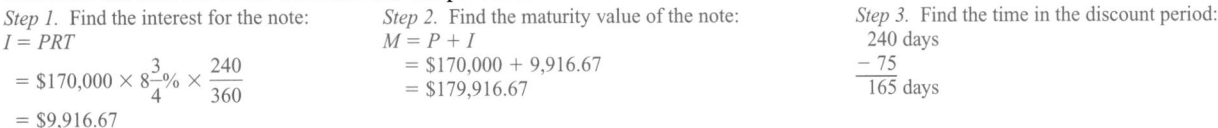

Step 4. Find the amount of the discount:
$B = MDT$

$= \$179{,}916.67 \times 12\% \times \dfrac{165}{360}$

$= \$9{,}895.42$

Step 5. Find the amount of the proceeds:
$P = M - B$

$= \$179{,}916.67 - 9{,}895.42$

$= \$170{,}021.25$

20. Tahereh Bolhassani, owner of the Olympic Gymnastic Equipment Corporation, received a $29,250, 11%, 120-day promissory note dated May 1. The note was discounted on June 5. The discount rate was 14.5%. Calculate the amount of the discount and the proceeds.

Step 1. Find the interest for the note:
$I = PRT$

$= \$29{,}250 \times 11\% \times \dfrac{120}{360}$

$= \$1{,}072.50$

Step 2. Find the maturity value of the note:
$M = P + I$

$= \$29{,}250 + 1{,}072.50$

$= \$30{,}322.50$

Step 3. Find the time in the discount period:

May	31 days	
	− 1 days	240 days in note
	30 days	− 35 days
June	5 days	205 days in discount period
	35 days	

Step 4. Find the amount of the discount:
$B = MDT$

$= \$30{,}322.50 \times 14.5\% \times \dfrac{205}{360}$

$= \$2{,}503.71$

Step 5. Find the amount of the proceeds:
$P = M - B$

$= \$30{,}322.50 - 2{,}503.71$

$= \$27{,}818.79$

CHAPTER REVIEW PROBLEMS

Answers to odd-numbered problems are given in Appendix A.

Drill Problems

Find the discount and the proceeds in the following problems:

	Amount Borrowed	Discount Rate	Time	Discount	Proceeds
1.	$ 35,000	18.9%	1 year	$ 6,615	$ 28,385
2.	2,400	9%	60 days	36	2,364
3.	1,500	10%	4 months	50	1,450
4.	500,000	6.5%	180 days	16,250	483,750

Find the discount, proceeds, and true rate of interest (rounded to the nearest $\frac{1}{4}$%) in the following problems:

	Amount Borrowed	Stated Rate	Time	Discount	Proceeds	True Rate
5.	$250,000	7%	8 months	$ 11,666.67	$ 238,333.33	7.25%
6.	600	13.9%	90 days	20.85	579.15	14.50%
7.	1,300	6.5%	200 days	46.94	1,253.06	6.75%
8.	9,750	9%	5 months	365.63	9,384.37	9.25%

Solve the following T-bill problems. Find the amount of the discount, the purchase price, and the true rate of interest (rounded to the nearest hundredth of a percent).

	Face Value	Stated Rate	Time	Discount	Purchase Price	True Rate
9.	$170,000	5.6%	1 year	$ 9,520	$ 160,480	5.93%
10.	10,000	6.9%	13 weeks	172.50	9,827.50	7.02%
11.	40,000	6.5%	26 weeks	1,300	38,700	6.72%
12.	950,000	5.47%	26 weeks	25,982.50	924,017.50	5.62%

Find the maturity value for the simple discount notes in the following problems (your answers may vary slightly due to the rounding of intermediate steps).

	Amount Borrowed (Maturity Value)	Discount Rate	Time	Proceeds
13.	$ 10,152.28	9%	May 10–July 9	$ 10,000
14.	4,034.48	12%	September 5–December 14	3,900
or	4,033.09			
15.	208,333.33	8%	March 21–September 17	200,000
16.	889.26	12.5%	July 4–August 3	880
or	888.89			

Calculations for the time:

13.	14.	15.	16.
May 31 − 10 = 21	Sept. 30 − 5 = 25	Mar. 31 − 21 = 10	Jul 31 − 4 = 27
June 30	Oct. 31	Apr. 30	Aug. 3
July 9	Nov. 30	May 31	30
60	Dec. 14	June 30	
	100	July 31	
		Aug. 31	
		Sept. 17	
		180	

In the following, each of the promissory notes is to be discounted at a rate and on the date given. Fill in all of the blanks (round the true rate to the nearest $\frac{1}{4}$%).

17.

```
$18,000                                    Raton, New Mexico    May 9      20 02

150 days                 After date, for value received,  I  promise to pay to

   Interstate Bank of Raton

   Eighteen thousand and 00/100------------------------------- DOLLARS

with interest at   9%   per annum

Payable at   Interstate Bank of Raton

No.   1920                             John W. Piner           (Seal)

Due   October 6, 2002                                         (Seal)
```

Amount of Interest	Maturity Value	Date of Discount	Discount Rate	Bank Discount	Proceeds	True Rate
$ 675	$ 18,675	July 8	13%	$ 606.94	$18,068.06	13.50%

Discount period: May 31 − 9 = 22
                   June   30   150 days − 60 days = 90 days
                   July   8
                                60

18.

```
$17,500                          Morgantown, Pennsylvania  January 20  20 02

100 days                 After date, for value received,  I  promise to pay to

  Wilson Canning Company

  Seventeen thousand, five hundred and 00/100 - - - - - - - - - - - - - - - - DOLLARS

with interest at  11%  per annum

Payable at  First State Bank of Morgantown

No.  1139                              Helen Wilmont            (Seal)

Due  April 30, 2002              _____(Seal)
```

Amount of Interest	Maturity Value	Date of Discount	Discount Rate	Bank Discount	Proceeds	True Rate
$ 534.72	$18,034.72	Feb. 9	14%	$ 561.08	$ 17,473.64	14.50%

Jan. 31 − 20 = 11   100 days − 20 days = 80 days
Feb.   9
               ――
               20

19.

```
$1,000                           Abbotsville, Wisconsin  June 19   20 02

  210 days                 After date, for value received,  we  promise to pay to

  Kool Kontry Koner

  One thousand and 00/100 - - - - - - - - - - - - - - - - - - - - - - - - - DOLLARS

with interest at  6.9%  per annum

Payable at  Abbotsville, Wisconsin

No.  9373                              Sigmond Freed            (Seal)

Due  January 15, 2003                  Charlie Freed            (Seal)
```

Amount of Interest	Maturity Value	Date of Discount	Discount Rate	Bank Discount	Proceeds	True Rate
$ 40.25	$ 1,040.25	Sept. 17	9%	$ 31.21	$ 1,009.04	9.25%

June 30 − 19 = 11
July   31   210 days − 90 days = 120 days
Aug.   31
Sept.   17
            ――
            90

20.

```
$145,000                          Pineview, Arizona     April 29   20 02

  100 days           After date, for value received,  I  promise to pay to

  Universal Lawn Furniture

    One hundred forty-five thousand and 00/100 --------------------- DOLLARS

with interest at  7%  per annum

Payable at  Pineview, Arizona

No.  1920                              Penelope Joiner              (Seal)

Due  August 7, 2002                    _____ (Seal)
```

Amount of Interest	Maturity Value	Date of Discount	Discount Rate	Bank Discount	Proceeds	True Rate
$ 2,819.44	$147,819.44	July 17	11%	$ 948.51	$ 146,870.93	11.00%

July 31 − 17 = 14
Aug.   7
              ───
              21 days

21.

```
$72,500                          Carlisle, Oklahoma  September 14    20 02

  270 days          After date, for value received,  we  promise to pay to

  Carlisle National Bank

    Seventy-two thousand, five hundred ------------------------- DOLLARS

with interest at   8%  per annum

Payable at  Carlisle National Bank

No.  9840                              Victoria Ionez              (Seal)

Due  June 11, 2003                     Madeline Ferigomo           (Seal)
```

Amount of Interest	Maturity Value	Date of Discount	Discount Rate	Bank Discount	Proceeds	True Rate
$ 4,350	$ 76,850	Dec. 4	15%	$ 6,051.94	$70,798.06	16.25%

Dec. 31 − 4 = 27
Jan.   31
Feb.   28   →147
Mar.   31   May 31
Apr.   30   Jun 11
             ───   ───
             147   189 days in discount period

22.

```
 $3,000                          Chicago, Illinois    June 11   20 02

  90 days                 After date, for value received,  I  promise to pay to

  Commerce Bank of Chicago

  Three thousand and 00/100 – – – – – – – – – – – – – – – – – – – – – – – – – –  DOLLARS

 with interest at  11.3%  per annum

 Payable at   Commerce Bank of Chicago

 No.  3009                              Mau Tai Jung            (Seal)

 Due  September 9, 2002                                          (Seal)
```

Amount of Interest	Maturity Value	Date of Discount	Discount Rate	Bank Discount	Proceeds	True Rate
$ 84.75	$ 3,084.75	July 31	14.4%	$ 49.36	$ 3,035.39	14.75%

June 30 − 11 = 19
July   31   90 days − 50 days = 40 days
          ‾‾‾‾
            50

23. *(Round your answers to the nearest dollar)*

```
 $1,659,000                      New York, New York    March 1   20 02

  100 days               After date, for value received,  I  promise to pay to

  Queens Commercial Credit Association

  One million, six hundred ninety-five thousand and 00/100 – – – – – – – – – – – – –  DOLLARS

 with interest at  7.9%  per annum

 Payable at   New York, New York

 No.  2095                              Clayton Minifield        (Seal)

 Due  June 9, 2002                                              (Seal)
```

Amount of Interest	Maturity Value	Date of Discount	Discount Rate	Bank Discount	Proceeds	True Rate
$ 37,196	$1,732,196	March 29	11.5%	$ 39,841	$1,692,355	11.75%

Mar. 29 − 1 = 28 days   100 − 28 = 72 days

24.

$27,750   Ipstansia, Utah   November 7 20 02

120 days   After date, for value received, _I_ promise to pay to

Ipstansia Federal Bank

Twenty-seven thousand, seven hundred fifty and 00/100 ------------- DOLLARS

with interest at _6.35%_ per annum

Payable at _Ipstansia Federal Bank_

No. _917_   _Wanda Freeman_   (Seal)

Due _March 7, 2003_   (Seal)

Amount of Interest	Maturity Value	Date of Discount	Discount Rate	Bank Discount	Proceeds	True Rate
$587.38	$ 28,337.38	Nov. 27	13.2%	$ 1,039.04	$ 27,298.34	13.75%

Nov. 27 − 7 = 20   120 days − 20 days = 100 days

Word Problems

25. Calculate the discount and the proceeds on a simple discount note of $21,000 with an 8% discount rate for half a year.

$B = MDT$

$$= \$21{,}000 \times 8\% \times \frac{1}{2}$$

$$= \$840$$

$P = M - B$

$$= \$21{,}000 - 840$$

$$= \$20{,}160$$

26. Calculate the true rate of interest on an $650, 10%, four month simple discount note.

$B = MDT$

$$= \$650 \times 10\% \times \frac{4}{12}$$

$$= \$21.67$$

$P = M - B$

$$= \$650 - 21.67$$

$$= \$628.33$$

$R = \dfrac{B}{PT}$

$$= \frac{\$21.67}{\$628.33 \times \dfrac{4}{12}}$$

$$= 10.3\%$$

27. The First National Bank in Tempe, Arizona, purchased $5 million worth of 13-week T-bills at a rate of 5.45%. Find the amount of the discount, the purchase price, and the true rate of interest (rounded to the nearest hundredth of a percent).

$B = MDT$

$$= \$5{,}000{,}000 \times 5.45\% \times \frac{13}{52}$$

$$= \$68{,}125$$

True rate of interest:

$R = \dfrac{B}{PT}$

$$= \frac{\$68{,}125}{\$4{,}931{,}875 \times \dfrac{13}{52}}$$

$$= 5.53\% \text{ to the nearest hundredth of a percent}$$

$P = M - B$

$$= \$5{,}000{,}000 - 68{,}125$$

$$= \$4{,}931{,}875$$

28. The Ypsilanti Department Store needs $26,500 to buy a new computer system. It can borrow the needed funds at a 6.3% discount rate for 150 days. Find the maturity value of the loan.

$M = \dfrac{P}{1 - (DT)}$

$$= \frac{\$26{,}500}{1 - \left(6.3\% \times \dfrac{150}{360}\right)}$$

$$= \frac{\$26{,}500}{1 - .026}$$

Rounded to the nearest thousandth

$$= \frac{\$26{,}500}{.974}$$

$$= \$27{,}207.39$$

Using the calculator:

6.3 % ✕ 150 ÷ 360

= ½ + 1 = STO

26,500 ÷ RCL = 27,214.38

29. Calculate the true rate of interest on a $9,365, 10%, eight month simple discount note. (Round to the nearest $\frac{1}{4}$%)

$B = MDT$

   $= \$9,365 \times 10\% \times \dfrac{8}{12}$

   $= \$624.33$

$P = M - B$

   $= \$9,365 - 624.33$

   $= \$8,740.67$

$R = \dfrac{B}{PT}$

  $= \dfrac{\$624.33}{\$8,740.67 \times \dfrac{8}{12}}$

  $= 10.75\%$

30. Jamie Dupont purchased a 26-week T-bill at a rate of 6.25%. Find the amount of the discount, the purchase price, and the true rate of interest (rounded to the nearest hundredth of a percent).

$B = MDT$

   $= \$10,000 \times 6.25\% \times \dfrac{26}{52}$

   $= \$312.50$

$P = M - B$

   $= \$10,000 - 312.50$

   $= \$9,687.50$

True rate of interest:

$R = \dfrac{B}{PT}$

  $= \dfrac{\$312.50}{\$9.687.50 \times \dfrac{26}{52}}$

  $= 6.45\%$ to the nearest hundredth of a percent

31. Stephanie McMichaels needs $74,059 to renovate her boutique. She can borrow the needed funds at a discount rate of 14.7% for 200 days. Calculate the maturity value of the loan.

$M = \dfrac{P}{1 - (DT)}$

  $= \dfrac{\$74,059}{1 - \left(14.7\% \times \dfrac{200}{360}\right)}$

  $= \dfrac{\$74,059}{1 - (.082)}$

Rounded to the nearest thousandth

  $= \dfrac{\$74,059}{.918}$

  $= \$ 80,674.29$

Using the calculator:

14.7 % × 200 ÷ 360

= % + 1 = STO

74,059 ÷ RCL = 80,645.01

32. "Moose" Mosenburger, owner of the Sporting Goods Emporium, accepted the following note in payment for merchandise:

$154,370 _____   Derry, New Hampshire __April 19__ 20 _02_

__150 days__ _____After date, for value received, __I__ promise to pay to

__Derry Savings and Loan__ _____

____One hundred fifty-four thousand, three hundred seventy -------------- DOLLARS

with interest at __7.9%__ per annum

Payable at __Derry Savings and Loan__ _____

No. __9328__   *Vito Paglionuchi* _____(Seal)

Due__ September 16, 2002__ _____ _____(Seal)

"Moose" needed money and discounted the note at his bank on July 23. The bank's discount rate was 16.5%. Determine the proceeds.

Step 1. Find the interest for the note:

$I = PRT$

  $= \$154,370 \times 7.9\% \times \dfrac{150}{360}$

  $= \$5,081.35$

Step 2. Find the maturity value of the note:

$M = P + I$

  $= \$154,370 + 5,081.35$

  $= \$159,451.35$

Step 3. Find the time in the discount period:

July 31 − 23 =	8
Aug.	31
Sept.	16
	55

Step 4. Find the amount of the discount:

$B = MDT$

  $= \$159,451.35 \times 16.5\% \times \dfrac{55}{360}$

  $= \$4,019.50$

Step 5. Find the amount of the proceeds:

$P = M - B$

  $= \$159,451.35 - 4,019.50$

  $= \$155,431.85$

33. Martha Jones signed a 100-day simple discount note for $21,500 that carried a discount rate of 15.6%. Calculate the discount and the proceeds.

$B = MDT$

$\quad = \$21,500 \times 15.6\% \times \dfrac{100}{360}$

$\quad = \$931.67$

$P = M - B$

$\quad = \$21,500 - 931.67$

$\quad = \$20,568.33$

34. Leonard Stepnowski needs $64,267 to pay for building materials and supplies. He can borrow the needed funds at a discount rate of 8.25% for 180 days. Calculate the maturity value of the loan.

$M = \dfrac{P}{1 - (DT)}$

$\quad = \dfrac{\$64,267}{1 - \left(8.25\% \times \dfrac{180}{360}\right)}$

$\quad = \dfrac{\$64,267}{1 - .041}$

Rounded to the nearest thousandth

$\quad = \dfrac{\$64,267}{.959}$

$\quad = \$67,014.60$

Using the calculator:

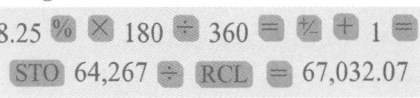

8.25 % × 180 ÷ 360 = %⁺ + 1 =

STO 64,267 ÷ RCL = 67,032.07

35. Smart Shop's chief executive officer accepted the following note in payment for merchandise:

$67,120   Denver, Colorado ___July 11___ 20 _02_

_210 days_____After date, for value received, ___I___ promise to pay to

_Colorado Savings Association_____

Sixty-seven thousand, one hundred twenty and 00/100 – – – – – – – – – – – – – – – DOLLARS

with interest at _10.2%_ per annum

Payable at _Colorado Savings Association_

No. _8377_   _____Susan Martinez_____(Seal)

Due _February 6, 2003_____   _____(Seal)

Smart Shop needed money to meet its December 1 payroll. The note was discounted at the Denver Federal Savings Bank on December 1, and the funds were deposited into Smart Shop's payroll account. Denver Federal's discount rate was 14%. Determine the proceeds.

Step 1. Find the interest for the note:

$I = PRT$

$\quad = \$67,120 \times 10.2\% \times \dfrac{210}{360}$

$\quad = \$3,993.64$

Step 2. Find the maturity value of the note:

$M = P + I$

$\quad = \$67,120 + 3,993.64$

$\quad = \$71,113.64$

Step 3. Find the time in the discount period:

Dec 31 − 1 =   30
Jan.   31
Feb.   6
                 ‾‾‾‾‾
                67 days

Step 4. Find the amount of the discount:

$B = MDT$

$\quad = \$71,113.64 \times 14\% \times \dfrac{67}{360}$

$\quad = \$1,852.91$

Step 5. Find the amount of the proceeds:

$P = M - B$

$\quad = \$71,113.64 - 1,852.91$

$\quad = \$69,260.74$

36. Calculate the true rate of interest on a $39,400, 12.5%, 180-day simple discount note (rounded to the nearest $\frac{1}{4}$%).

$B = MDT$

$\quad = \$39,400 \times 12.5\% \times \dfrac{180}{360}$

$\quad = \$2,462.50$

$P = M - B$

$\quad = \$39,400 - 2,462.50$

$\quad = \$36,937.50$

$R = \dfrac{B}{PT}$

$\quad = \dfrac{\$2,462.50}{\$36,937.50 \times \dfrac{180}{360}}$

$\quad = 13.25\%$

37. Captain Hobart's diner in Portland was paid for supplies with the following note:

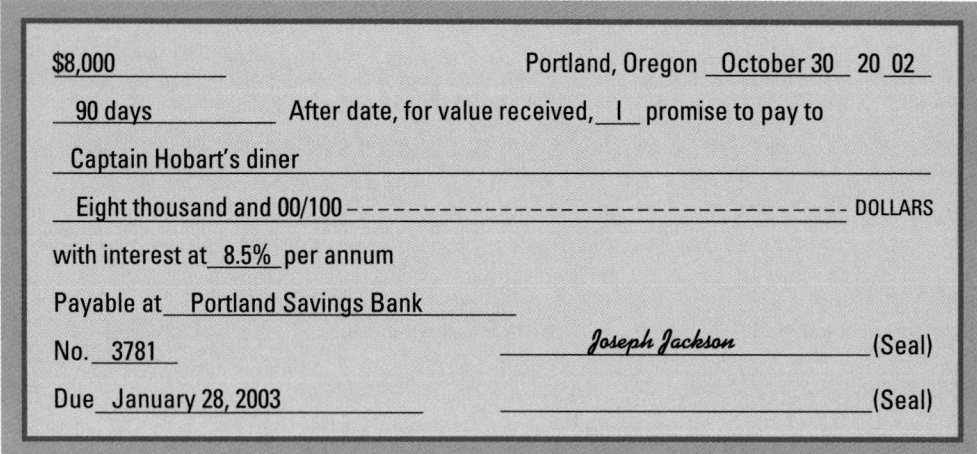

$8,000   Portland, Oregon October 30 20 02

90 days   After date, for value received, I promise to pay to

Captain Hobart's diner

Eight thousand and 00/100 — DOLLARS

with interest at 8.5% per annum

Payable at Portland Savings Bank

No. 3781   *Joseph Jackson*   (Seal)

Due January 28, 2003   (Seal)

The note was discounted on December 3. The bank's discount rate was 12.5%. Determine the proceeds. To pay the note, Joseph Jackson borrowed the money from his bank with a simple discount note at 13% for three months. Find the true rate of interest Mr. Jackson must pay (rounded to the nearest $\frac{1}{4}$%).

First, determine the proceeds received by Captain Hobart's diner.

Step 1. Find the interest for the note:
$$I = PRT$$
$$= \$8,000 \times 8.5\% \times \frac{90}{360}$$
$$= \$170$$

Step 2. Find the maturity value of the note:
$$M = P + I$$
$$= \$8,000 + 170$$
$$= \$8,170$$

Step 3. Find the time in the discount period:
Dec. 31 − 3 = 28
Jan.   28
                  56 days

Step 4. Find the amount of the discount:
$$B = MDT$$
$$= \$8,170 \times 12.5\% \times \frac{56}{360}$$
$$= \$158.86$$

Step 5. Find the amount of the proceeds:
$$P = M - B$$
$$= \$8,170 - 158.86$$
$$= \$8,011.14$$

Next, find the true rate for Mr. Jackson's note (Mr. Jackson needs proceeds equal to the maturity value of the note he signed, $8,170).

Step 1. Find the maturity value of Mr. Jackson's discount:
$$M = \frac{P}{1 - (DT)}$$
$$= \frac{\$8,170}{1 - \left(13\% \times \frac{3}{12}\right)}$$
$$= \frac{\$8,170}{1 - .0325}$$
$$= \frac{\$8,170}{.9675}$$
$$= \$8,444.44 \text{ (or, without a calculator, \$8,440.08)}$$

Step 2. Find the amount of the discount:
$$B = M - P$$
$$= \$8,444.44 - \$8,170$$
$$= \$274.44 \text{ (or \$270.08)}$$

Step 3. Find the true rate:
$$R = \frac{B}{PT}$$
$$= \frac{\$274.44}{\$8,170 \times \frac{3}{12}}$$
$$= 13.50\% \text{ (or 13.25\%)}$$

Using the calculator:

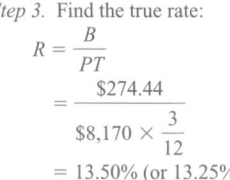

13 % × 3 ÷ 12 = ½ + 1
= STO 8,170 ÷ RCL
= 8,444.44

CRITICAL THINKING GROUP PROJECT

Jairco Baby Dolls, Inc., founded by Janette Cooper, Colleen Peters, and Irene Simiosia, manufactures children's dolls and doll clothes. Stanley's Toy House was allowed to finance an overdue merchandise payment with the following simple interest note:

The note was discounted on August 30. The bank's discount rate was 14.9%.

| $56,500 | Seattle, Washington ___ August 3 ___ 20 _02_ |

___120 days_____After date, for value received, __we__ promise to pay to

Jairco Baby Dolls, Inc._____

___Fifty-six thousand, five hundred and 00/100----------------------- DOLLARS

with interest at __10%__ per annum

Payable at __Seattle State Savings and Loan___

No. _5611_   _Margaret Stanley_____(Seal)

Due_ December 1, 2002_____   _Laverne Kajinsky_____(Seal)

---

1. Calculate the amount of interest Jairco will earn from the simple interest note.
   $1,833.13

2. Calculate the maturity value of the simple interest note.
   $58,383.33

3. Calculate the amount of discount that will be taken by the bank.
   $2,247.27

4. Determine the proceeds from the discounted note.
   $56,136.06

5. Calculate the true rate of interest charged by the bank.
   15.5%

6. The Seattle State Savings and Loan used the payment made on December 1 to help buy six 13-week T-bills at 4.38%. Calculate the amount of the payment required for the T-bills.
   $59,343

7. Determine the additional amount the S & L needed to buy the T-bill in problem 6.
   $959.67

SELF-TESTING EXERCISES

Answers to all exercises are given in Appendix A.

1. Differentiate between discount and interest. **W**
   A discount is interest deducted from the face value of a note on the date the note is originated. The borrower gets the difference between the principal of the note and the discount (called the proceeds). Interest is added to the face value of a note at the end of the loan period. The borrower pays the principal plus the interest (called the maturity value).

2. Why is the true rate of interest higher than the stated **W** (nominal) rate of interest for discounted notes?
   The true rate is found by dividing the discount by the proceeds and time, whereas the stated rate is found by dividing the interest by the principal and time. The true rate is higher because the proceeds are less than the principal.

3. Calculate the discount on a simple discount note of $98,000 with a 7% discount rate for 70 days.
   $B = MDT$

   $$= \$98,000 \times 7\% \times \frac{70}{360}$$

   $$= \$1,333.89$$

4. Calculate the true rate of interest on a $6,950, 12%, nine month simple discount note (rounded to the nearest $\frac{1}{4}$%).
   $B = MDT$

   $$= \$6,950 \times 12\% \times \frac{9}{12}$$

   $$= \$625.50$$

   $P = M - B$

   $$= \$6,950 - 625.50$$

   $$= \$6,324.50$$

   True rate of interest:
   $$R = \frac{B}{PT}$$

   $$= \frac{\$625.50}{\$6,324.50 \times \dfrac{9}{12}}$$

   $$= 13.25\% \text{ to the nearest } \tfrac{1}{4}\%$$

5. The Aleutian Bank of Commerce purchased $60,000 worth of 26-week T-bills at a rate of 5.9%. Find the amount of the purchase price.

$$B = MDT$$
$$= \$60,000 \times 5.9\% \times \frac{26}{52}$$
$$= \$1,770$$

$$P = M - B$$
$$= \$60,000 - 1,770$$
$$= \$58,230$$

6. Morganthal Trust Company needs $54,000 to buy a new office lighting system. It can borrow at a discount rate of 9.2% for 180 days. Find the maturity value of the loan.

$$M = \frac{P}{1 - (DT)}$$

$$= \frac{\$54,000}{1 - \left(9.2\% \times \frac{180}{360}\right)}$$

$$= \frac{\$54,000}{1 - .046}$$

↑ Rounded to the nearest thousandth

$$= \frac{\$54,000}{.954}$$
$$= \$56,603.77$$

Using the calculator:

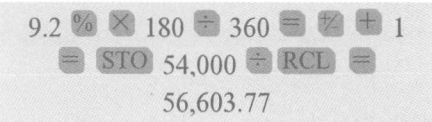

56,603.77

7. Attica Hardware Distributors accepted the following note from a customer in payment for merchandise:

$8,000 _____   Athens, Greece _____ April 8 20 02

 120 days _____   After date, for value received,_I__promise to pay to

  Attica Hardware Distributors _____

   Eight thousand and 00/100 --------------------------------------- DOLLARS

with interest at __8.4%__ per annum

Payable at __West Palm Beach State Bank___

No.__6910__   *Jonathon Wright*_____(Seal)

Due__August 6, 2002_____   _____(Seal)

On June 17 Attica Hardware Distributors discounted the note at the West Palm Beach State Bank at a rate of 12%. Determine the proceeds.

Step 1. Find the interest for the note:
$$I = PRT$$
$$= \$8,000 \times 8.4\% \times \frac{120}{360}$$
$$= \$224$$

Step 2. Find the maturity value of the note:
$$M = P + I$$
$$= \$8,000 + 224$$
$$= \$8,224$$

Step 3. Find the time in the discount period:

Apr.	30 days	
	− 8 days	120 days in note
	22 days	− 70
May	31 days	50 days in discount period
June	17 days	
	70 days	

Step 4. Find the amount of the discount:
$$B = MDT$$
$$= \$8,224 \times 12\% \times \frac{50}{360}$$
$$= \$137.07$$

Step 5. Find the amount of the proceeds:
$$P = M - B$$
$$= \$8,224 - 137.07$$
$$= \$8,086.93$$

8. Calculate the proceeds on a $1,500, 6.4%, 180-day simple discount note.

$$B = MDT$$
$$= \$1,500 \times 6.4\% \times \frac{180}{360}$$
$$= \$48$$

$$P = M - B$$
$$= \$1,500 - 48$$
$$= \$1,452$$

9. Calculate the true rate of interest on a $25,000, 11%, 150-day simple discount note (rounded to the nearest $\frac{1}{4}$%).

$B = MDT$

$\quad = \$25,000 \times 11\% \times \dfrac{150}{360}$

$\quad = \$1,145.83$

$P = M - B$

$\quad = \$25,000 - 1,145.83$

$\quad = \$23,854.17$

True rate of interest:

$R = \dfrac{B}{PT}$

$\quad = \dfrac{\$1,145.83}{\$23,854.17 \times \dfrac{150}{360}}$

$\quad = 11.50\%$ to the nearest $\frac{1}{4}$%

10. Jeremy Jones purchased a one year T-bill at a rate of 6.10%. Find the true rate of interest (rounded to the nearest hundredth of a percent).

$B = MDT$

$\quad = \$10,000 \times 6.10\% \times 1$

$\quad = \$610$

$P = M - B$

$\quad = \$10,000 - 610$

$\quad = \$9,390$

True rate of interest:

$R = \dfrac{B}{PT}$

$\quad = \dfrac{\$610}{\$9,390 \times 1}$

$\quad = 6.50\%$ to the nearest hundredth of a percent

11. Gina Lorry needs $20,000 to purchase additional store fixtures. She can borrow at a discount rate of 14% for 100 days. Calculate the maturity value of the loan.

$M = \dfrac{P}{1 - (DT)}$

$\quad = \dfrac{\$20,000}{1 - \left(14\% \times \dfrac{100}{360}\right)}$

$\quad = \dfrac{\$20,000}{1 - .039}$

Rounded to the nearest thousandth

$\quad = \dfrac{\$20,000}{.961}$

$\quad = \$20,811.66$

Using the calculator:

14 % ✕ 100 ÷ 360 = ⅟ₓ +

1 = STO 20,000 ÷ RCL =

20,809.25

12. The Madison Motel and Restaurant Suppliers accepted the following note in payment for merchandise:

$10,000	North Park, Wisconsin ___September 26__ 20 _02_
90 days	After date, for value received, _I_ promise to pay to
Madison Motel and Restaurant Suppliers	
Ten thousand and 00/100 ------------------------------------ DOLLARS	
with interest at _9.9%_ per annum	
Payable at _Madison, Wisconsin_	
No. _4908_	_Manuel Fernandez_ (Seal)
Due _December 25, 2002_	_____ (Seal)

The note was discounted on November 5. The bank's discount rate was 14.5%. Determine the proceeds.

Step 1. Find the interest for the note:

$I = PRT$

$\quad = \$10,000 \times 9.9\% \times \dfrac{90}{360}$

$\quad = \$247.50$

Step 2. Find the maturity value of the note:

$M = P + I$

$\quad = \$10,000 + 247.50$

$\quad = \$10,247.50$

Step 3. Find the time in the discount period:

Nov. 30 − 5 = 25

Dec. $\dfrac{25}{50}$

Step 4. Find the amount of the discount:

$B = MDT$

$\quad = \$10,247.50 \times 14.5\% \times \dfrac{50}{360}$

$\quad = \$206.37$

Step 5. Find the amount of the proceeds:

$P = M - B$

$\quad = \$10,247.50 - 206.37$

$\quad = \$10,041.13$

APPLICATION 1

The Springfield Department Store has discounted several promissory notes. A spreadsheet form has been designed to calculate the interest and maturity value of the promissory notes when the face value, rate, and time are known. The spreadsheet also calculates the discount, proceeds, and true rate when the stated discount rate and the time in the discount period are known. When you insert your spreadsheet applications disk and load Ch11App1, your screen will look like the one shown here:

Springfield Department Store

2617 Main Street
Box 219
Springfield, Maryland 58109
Telephone: 301-555-2158   FAX: 301-555-3498

DISCOUNTING PROMISORY NOTES

| PROMISORY NOTES | | | | | DISCOUNT SCHEDULE | | | | |
Face Value	Rate	Time (Days)	Interest	Maturity Value	Stated Rate	Time (Days)	Discount	Proceeds	True Rate
			$0.00	$0.00			$0.00	$0.00	#DIV/0!
			$0.00	$0.00			$0.00	$0.00	#DIV/0!
			$0.00	$0.00			$0.00	$0.00	#DIV/0!
			$0.00	$0.00			$0.00	$0.00	#DIV/0!
			$0.00	$0.00			$0.00	$0.00	#DIV/0!
			$0.00	$0.00			$0.00	$0.00	#DIV/0!

Enter the following information :

Face Value	Cell	Rate	Cell	Time	Cell	Stated Rate	Cell	Time	Cell
$ 794.75	A13	.16	B13	30	C13	.125	G13	12	H13
$ 1,050.00	A14	.145	B14	90	C14	.13	G14	60	H14
$ 4,429.05	A15	.1375	B15	120	C15	.1175	G15	55	H15
$14,923.64	A16	.1525	B16	150	C16	.12	G16	100	H16
$28,846.76	A17	.0975	B17	180	C17	.1025	G17	75	H17
$58,500.00	A18	.075	B18	240	C18	.0975	G18	196	H18

Answer the following questions after you have completed the spreadsheet:

1. What is the interest on the $794.75 promissory note?

2. What are the proceeds on the discounted $1,050 promissory note?

3. What is the maturity value on the $4,429.05 promissory note?

4. What is the true rate on the discounted $58,500 promissory note?

5. What is the amount of the discount on the discounted $28,846.76 promissory note?

6. Which promissory note's true discount rate is the highest compared to the stated discount rate of all the discounted notes?

7. What is the amount of proceeds for the discounted $28,846.76 promissory note?

8. What is the maturity value for the $1,050 promissory note?

9. What is the interest on the $58,500 promissory note?

10. What is the amount of discount for the discounted $4,429.05 promissory note?

GROUP REPORT

FOR CHAPTER 11 APPLICATION 1

1. Substitute various amounts of time in the discount period and note the effect of time on the true rate of interest.
2. Write a report to the store manager describing the effects of time on the true rate and make recommendations about future discounted notes.

EXCEL SPREADSHEET APPLICATION FOR CHAPTER 11

APPLICATION 2

The Springfield Department Store invests some of its short-term capital in treasury bills. The bills are of varying durations: 13 weeks, 26 weeks, or 52 weeks. A spreadsheet form has been developed to calculate the following:

1. Total maturity value
2. Total discount
3. Total purchase price (proceeds)
4. True rate
5. Average rate of all bonds purchased
6. Average true rate of all bonds purchased

When you open Ch11App2 from your computer spreadsheet applications disk, you will see the following form:

Springfield Department Store

2617 Main Street
Box 219
Springfield, Maryland 58109
Telephone: 301-555-2158   FAX: 301-555-3498

TREASURY BILLS

Purchase Date	Maturity Value	Rate	Weeks to Maturity	Number Purchased	Total at Maturity	Total Discount	Total Purchase Price	True Rate
					$0	$0.00	$0.00	#DIV/0!
					$0	$0.00	$0.00	#DIV/0!
					$0	$0.00	$0.00	#DIV/0!
					$0	$0.00	$0.00	#DIV/0!
					$0	$0.00	$0.00	#DIV/0!
					$0	$0.00	$0.00	#DIV/0!
					$0	$0.00	$0.00	#DIV/0!
					$0	$0.00	$0.00	#DIV/0!
					$0	$0.00	$0.00	#DIV/0!
	Avg. #DIV/0!		Totals	0	$0	$0.00	$0.00	Avg. #DIV/0!

Enter the following information:

Purchase Date	Cell	Maturity Value	Cell	Rate	Cell	Weeks to Maturity	Cell	Number Purchased	Cell
Jan. 1	A12	$10,000	B12	.0575	C12	26	D12	12	E12
Apr. 1	A13	$10,000	B13	.0525	C13	13	D13	6	E13
Apr. 1	A14	$10,000	B14	.07	C14	52	D14	8	E14
July 1	A15	$10,000	B15	.065	C15	13	D15	5	E15
July 1	A16	$10,000	B16	.0725	C16	26	D16	5	E16
July 1	A17	$10,000	B17	.0775	C17	52	D17	3	E17
Oct. 1	A18	$10,000	B18	.0575	C18	13	D18	7	E18
Oct. 1	A19	$10,000	B19	.0625	C19	26	D19	5	E19
Oct. 1	A20	$10,000	B20	.075	C20	52	D20	8	E20

Answer the following questions after you have completed the spreadsheet:

1. What is the total at maturity for the April 1, 7%, 52-week T-bill?
2. What is the total discount for the October 1, 5.75%, 13-week T-bill?
3. What is the total purchase price for the January 1, 5.75%, 26-week T-bill?
4. What is the total number of T-bills purchased during the year?
5. What is the average rate for the T-bill purchases?
6. What is the true rate of the April 1, 5.25% T-bill?
7. What is the total discount for the July 1, 7.75% T-bill?
8. What is the average true rate for the T-bills purchased during the year?

GROUP REPORT

FOR CHAPTER 11 APPLICATION 2

1. Substitute 52-week maturities for all notes that are for shorter maturity periods and record the true rates of interest.
2. Substitute 13-week maturities for all notes that are for longer maturity periods and record the true rates of interest.
3. Substitute 26-week maturities for all notes having longer or shorter maturity periods and record the true rates of interest.
4. Write a report to the store manager describing the results of the preceding items 1, 2, and 3 and make appropriate recommendations about future T-bill purchases.

12

INSTALLMENT BUYING, CHARGE ACCOUNTS, AND CREDIT CARD APPLICATIONS

PLASTIC CARDS AND MONEY

Bank cards such as VISA and MasterCard have become so important in our economy that many consumers view them as money. Not only can Americans travel or make major purchases without having to risk the danger of carrying hundreds or thousands of dollars in cash, but also, sometimes it is almost impossible to rent a car, stay in certain hotels, or transact business without them.

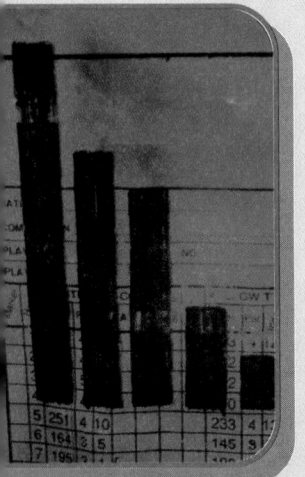

Are credit cards money? you ask. The answer is no—at least not literally. They are ID cards that enable people to buy a large range of goods and services without having to pay immediately. The bank that issues a credit card actually pays the merchant. The consumer repays the bank for the principal plus interest usually through an arrangement of installments. But credit cards *are* money in a sense. Economists teach that the money supply is composed of all the currency plus checking accounts in banks. When a bank makes a loan, it creates either a checking account or currency. A credit card represents preapproved credit.

At the time the credit card is used, a new account entry is created, which is something like a checking account. A credit card merely relieves consumers and bankers of the chore of making new loans every time credit is used. Credit card use poses a real danger to many people in a market society. The banker's real goal is to have consumers run up large balances and pay high interest rates on accounts for many years. That is the chief reason they will extend a credit line of $3,000 or $4,000 so easily—too easily, many critics believe.

Debit cards free people of the need to carry currency or even to depend on checkbooks. With the insertion of a plastic debit card into a terminal, a checking account is automatically debited to pay for merchandise. Since it represents a checking account, a debit card is considered money.

Money still serves its function as a medium of exchange. But anything as crude as a coin, paper currency, or even checks will eventually be discarded in favor of computer records that automatically balance out each person's in-payments and out-payments over the whole of her or his lifetime. Debit cards literally are money and should not be confused with credit cards.

Chapter Glossary

Installment buying. When the consumer agrees to borrow a certain amount and make regular periodic (usually monthly) payments until the loan has been completely repaid.

Annual percentage rate (APR). The true rate of interest which must be disclosed to all borrowers.

Payment periods. The frequency of periods: 12 when payments are monthly, 52 when payments are weekly, 4 when payments are quarterly.

Amount financed. The total cash price of the item(s) being charged, less any down payment.

Finance charge. All charges in excess of the amount financed.

Finance charge rebate. The amount of interest not yet earned by a lender when a loan is paid off before maturity. It is deducted from the total remaining to be paid when the loan is paid off early.

Rule of 78. A method used to calculate the finance charge rebate and the amount required to pay a loan off early. It is called the Rule of 78 because the sum of the years digits for one year $(1 + 2 + 3 + 4 + \ldots + 11 + 12)$ totals 78.

Revolving charge account. A charge account that may never be paid off in total. MasterCard, VISA, Discover, retail store charge cards, and some oil company charge cards use this method of extending credit.

Open-end credit. A type of credit in which several loans or merchandise charges may be made before any one of them is paid off. There are no fixed number of payments. It may never be paid off.

Unpaid balance method. A method of calculating the finance charge. The finance charge is calculated on the amount due at the end of the previous month. No purchases, payments, or returns during the current month are used in calculations.

Average daily balance method. A method of calculating the finance charge. Most revolving charge accounts use this method. Each transaction amount is added to or subtracted from the previous unpaid balance. The resulting balance is found at the end of each day during a billing cycle. The daily balances are totaled at the end of the billing cycle and divided by the number of days in the billing cycle. The finance charge is then calculated by multiplying the average daily balance by the monthly finance rate.

$\Large A$lmost everyone uses credit. It is virtually impossible to pay cash for everything. When buying cars, clothing, furniture, appliances, and certainly homes, credit is used. Loans are often necessary because of medical emergencies, accidents, repairs, and educational expenses. Americans today borrow from commercial banks, loan companies, credit unions, and pawnbrokers. Similarly, people are buying goods in retail establishments—ranging from large department stores to small specialized outlets—at an ever-increasing rate with the use of credit cards and other credit arrangements.

Businesses encourage the use of their charge accounts and credit cards. They also usually accept all, or most, major credit cards. They do it to attract customers, to be competitive, and to earn a substantial and important part of their total revenue (from the interest earned).

This chapter should help you decide if credit is a good idea for your next purchase. Should you use the charge account at the department store or borrow the money at your bank or credit union? Or, should you use a major credit card?

Two commonly used methods of buying on credit are installment buying and open-end credit.

LEARNING UNIT 1
INSTALLMENT BUYING

Installment buying is agreeing to borrow a certain amount and make regular, periodic payments until the loan has been completely repaid. When a consumer buys a new car, payments will be made periodically, usually monthly. For example, a buyer may finance a $14,000 car by paying $350 each month for 48 months until the $14,000 plus interest has been repaid. The total monthly payment will include both principal and interest. That means that the new car buyer has the use of the total amount borrowed (the principal) for only one month.

The true interest rate is higher than it would be if the money borrowed was used for the full length of the loan. The Truth-in-Lending Act was discussed in Chapter 11. Remember that it required all lenders to disclose the true (or effective) *annual* interest rate being charged, rounded to the nearest 1/4%. The true annual rate is often referred to as the **annual percentage rate (APR).** It can be estimated with the use of a formula. It can be determined more accurately by using APR tables. Most consumers do not have tables available, so the use of a formula can sometimes be helpful to make reasonable comparisons.

12.1 Using the Formula to Estimate the Annual Percentage Rate (APR)

The formula used to estimate the APR is

$$APR = \frac{2 \times \text{number of payment periods in 1 year} \times \text{finance charge}}{\text{amount financed} \times (\text{total number of payments} + 1)}.$$

1. *Number of **payment periods** in 1 year* does not refer to the length of the loan. It refers to the *frequency* of pay periods. For example, if payments are made weekly, the number of payment periods in 1 year is 52; if payments are monthly it is 12; if payments are quarterly, the number is 4.

2. *Amount financed* is the total cash price of the item being charged less any down payment:

$$\text{Amount financed} = \text{cash price} - \text{down payment}$$

3. *Finance charge* refers to all charges in excess of the amount financed:

Finance charge = total amount to be repaid − amount financed
↑
Number of payments × amount of each payment

Our first example will be to estimate the APR for the purchase of a television set with no down payment.

E X A M P L E   Use the formula to estimate the APR (rounded to the nearest 1/4%) for Marilyn Romero, who wants to buy a color television set costing $395. The store will finance it for $18.85 per month for two years.

Solution

$$APR = \frac{2 \times \text{number of payment periods in 1 year} \times \text{finance charge}}{\text{amount financed} \times (\text{total number of payments} + 1)}$$

Number of payment periods in 1 year = 12   *(monthly payments, 12 months in 1 year)*

Amount financed = $395   *(no down payment)*

Total number of payments = 24   *(2 years × 12 months per year)*

Finance charge = (number of payments × amount of each payment)
    − amount financed
= (24 × $18.85) − $395
= $452.40 − 395
= $57.40

$$APR = \frac{2 \times 12 \times \$57.40}{\$395 \times (24 + 1)}$$
= 13.95%
= 14%   *(rounded to nearest 1/4%)*

2 ⊠ 12 ⊠ 57.40 ⊟ 395 ⊟ 25 ⊟ 0.139 = 14%   *(rounded)*

The next example is for a new car purchase in which a trade-in is being allowed for the down payment.

E X A M P L E   Use the formula to estimate the APR (rounded to the nearest 1/4%) for John Summer, who wants to finance a car. John and the dealer have agreed on a negotiated price of $14,950. Taxes, title, and license charges will be an additional $1,141.50, which will also be financed. The dealer has offered a $3,500 trade-in on John's old car, which will be used for the down payment. The dealer has offered to finance the loan for $330.60 per month for four years.

Solution

$$APR = \frac{2 \times \text{number of payment periods in 1 year} \times \text{finance charge}}{\text{amount financed} \times (\text{total number of payments} + 1)}$$

Number of payment periods in 1 year = 12   *(monthly payment 12 months in 1 year)*

Amount financed = $14,950 + $1,141.50 − $3,500
      ↑   ↑   ↑
     For car   *tax, title*   *Trade-in*
            and, license *(down payment)*

= $12,591.50

Total number of payments = 48   *(4 years × 12 months per year)*

$$\text{Finance charge} = (\text{number of payments} \times \text{amount of each payment}) - \text{amount financed}$$
$$= (48 \times \$330.60) - \$12{,}591.50$$
$$= \$15{,}868.80 - 12{,}591.50$$
$$= \$3{,}277.30$$
$$\text{APR} = \frac{2 \times 12 \times \$3{,}277.30}{\$12{,}591.50 \times (48 + 1)}$$
$$= 12.75\% \quad \textit{(rounded to nearest 1/4\%)}$$

2 ⊠ 12 ⊠ 3,277.30 ÷ 12,591.50 ÷ 49 ▤ .1275

Use the formula to estimate the APR for the following problems.

1. William Bennett bought a new bedroom suite. The cash price was $2,999. William agreed to pay the furniture store $274.28 each month for one year. Use the formula to estimate the APR.

2. Jordan Erin financed a $7,250 boat, paying 10% down and $241.05 each month for three years. Use the formula to estimate the APR.

3. Brandi Thomas bought a pickup truck for $18,397, including tax, title, and license. Brandi traded her old VW van in for $937. Payments were $371.62 each month for five years. Use the formula to estimate the APR.

4. Siegfried purchased a $1,295 refrigerator for $18.68 per week for one and one half years. Use the formula to estimate the APR.

12.1 Solutions to Practice Problems

1. $\text{APR} = \dfrac{2 \times \text{number of payment periods in 1 year} \times \text{finance charge}}{\text{amount financed} \times (\text{total number of payments} + 1)}$

   Number of payment periods in 1 year = 12   *(monthly payments, 12 months in 1 year)*
   Amount financed = $2,999
   Total number of payments = 12   *(1 year × 12 months per year)*
   Finance charge = (number of payments × amount of each payment) − amount financed
   $$= (12 \times \$274.28) - \$2{,}999$$
   $$= \$3{,}291.36 - 2{,}999$$
   $$= \$292.36$$

   $$\text{APR} = \frac{2 \times 12 \times \$292.36}{\$2{,}999 \times (12 + 1)}$$
   $$= 18.0\% \quad \textit{(rounded to nearest 1/4\%)}$$

2. $\text{APR} = \dfrac{2 \times \text{number of payment periods in 1 year} \times \text{finance charge}}{\text{amount financed} \times (\text{total number of payments} + 1)}$

   Number of payment periods in 1 year = 12   *(monthly payments, 12 months in 1 year)*
   Amount financed = $7,250 − ($7,250 × 10%)
           ↑   ↑
     For boat   Down payment (10% of cash price)
   $$= \$7{,}250 - 725$$
   $$= \$6{,}525$$

   Total number of payments = 36   *(3 years × 12 months per year)*
   Finance charge = (number of payments × amount of each payment) − amount financed
   $$= (36 \times \$241.05) - \$6{,}525$$
   $$= \$8{,}677.80 - 6{,}525$$
   $$= \$2{,}152.80$$

   $$\text{APR} = \frac{2 \times 12 \times \$2{,}152.80}{\$6{,}525 \times (36 + 1)}$$
   $$= 21.5\% \quad \textit{(rounded to nearest 1/4\%)}$$

3. $\text{APR} = \dfrac{2 \times \text{number of payment periods in 1 year} \times \text{finance charge}}{\text{amount financed} \times (\text{total number of payments} + 1)}$

Number of payment periods in 1 year = 12   (monthly payments, 12 months in 1 year)

Amount financed = $18,397 − $937

$$\underset{Car}{\uparrow} \qquad \underset{Down\ payment}{\uparrow}$$

= $17,460

Total number of payments = 60   (5 years × 12 months per year)

Finance charge = (number of payments × amount of each payment) − amount financed

$$= (60 \times \$371.62) - \$17,460$$
$$= \$22,297.20 - 17,460$$
$$= \$4,837.20$$

$$\text{APR} = \frac{2 \times 12 \times \$4,837.20}{\$17,460 \times (36 + 1)}$$

$$= 11.0\% \quad \textit{(rounded to nearest 1/4\%)}$$

4. $$\text{APR} = \frac{2 \times \text{number of payment periods in 1 year} \times \text{finance charge}}{\text{amount financed} \times (\text{total number of payments} + 1)}$$

Number of payment periods in 1 year = 52   (weekly payments, 52 weeks in 1 year)

Amount financed = $1,295

Total number of payments = 78   (1.5 years × 52 weeks per year)

Finance charge = (number of payments × amount of each payment) − amount financed

$$= (78 \times \$18.68) - \$1,295$$
$$= \$1,457.04 - 1,295$$
$$= \$162.04$$

$$\text{APR} = \frac{2 \times 52 \times \$162.04}{\$1,295 \times (78 + 1)}$$

$$= 16.5\% \quad \textit{(rounded to nearest 1/4\%)}$$

12.2 Using the Table to Find the Annual Percentage Rate (APR)

The formula is helpful when an APR table is not available. With a table, however, you can more accurately find the APR to the nearest 1/4%. Table 12.1 is a portion of an APR table based on monthly payments. The tables are per $100 of the amount financed. The table is used as follows:

Step 1. Find the table factor (the number to look up in Table 12.1) using the formula:

$$\text{Table factor} = \frac{\text{finance charge} \times 100}{\text{amount financed}}.$$

Step 2. In Table 12.1, go down the leftmost column to the proper number of payments.

Step 3. Go across the row found in step 2 until you are as close as possible to the table factor found in step 1. Look at the top of that column to find the APR to the nearest 1/4%.

TABLE 12.1 ANNUAL PERCENTAGE RATE TABLE (MONTHLY PAYMENTS)

No. of Payments	10.00%	10.25%	10.50%	10.75%	11.00%	11.25%	11.50%	11.75%
1	0.83	0.85	0.87	0.90	0.92	0.94	0.96	0.98
2	1.25	1.28	1.31	1.35	1.38	1.41	1.44	1.47
3	1.67	1.71	1.76	1.80	1.84	1.88	1.92	1.96
4	2.09	2.14	2.20	2.25	2.30	2.35	2.41	2.46
5	2.51	2.58	2.64	2.70	2.77	2.83	2.89	2.96
6	2.94	3.01	3.08	3.16	3.23	3.31	3.38	3.45
7	3.36	3.45	3.53	3.62	3.70	3.78	3.87	3.95
8	3.79	3.88	3.98	4.07	4.17	4.26	4.36	4.46
9	4.21	4.32	4.43	4.53	4.64	4.75	4.85	4.96
10	4.64	4.76	4.88	4.99	5.11	5.23	5.35	5.46
11	5.07	5.20	5.33	5.45	5.58	5.71	5.85	5.97
12	5.50	5.64	5.78	5.92	6.06	6.20	6.34	6.48
13	5.93	6.08	6.23	6.38	6.53	6.68	6.84	6.99
14	6.36	6.52	6.69	6.85	7.01	7.17	7.34	7.50
15	6.80	6.97	7.14	7.32	7.49	7.66	7.84	8.01
16	7.23	7.41	7.60	7.78	7.97	8.15	8.34	8.53
17	7.67	7.86	8.06	8.25	8.45	8.65	8.84	9.04
18	8.10	8.31	8.52	8.73	8.93	9.14	9.35	9.56
19	8.54	8.76	8.98	9.20	9.42	9.64	9.86	10.08
20	8.98	9.21	9.44	9.67	9.90	10.13	10.37	10.60
21	9.42	9.66	9.90	10.15	10.39	10.63	10.88	11.12
22	9.86	10.12	10.37	10.62	10.88	11.13	11.39	11.64
23	10.30	10.57	10.84	11.10	11.37	11.63	11.90	12.17
24	10.75	11.02	11.30	11.58	11.86	12.14	12.42	12.70
25	11.19	11.48	11.77	12.06	12.35	12.64	12.93	13.22
26	11.64	11.94	12.24	12.54	12.85	13.15	13.45	13.75
27	12.09	12.40	12.71	13.03	13.34	13.66	13.97	14.29
28	12.53	12.86	13.18	13.51	13.84	14.16	14.49	14.82
29	12.98	13.32	13.66	14.00	14.33	14.67	15.01	15.35
30	13.43	13.78	14.13	14.48	14.83	15.19	15.54	15.89
31	13.89	14.25	14.61	14.97	15.33	15.70	16.06	16.43
32	14.34	14.71	15.09	15.46	15.84	16.21	16.59	16.97
33	14.79	15.18	15.57	15.95	16.34	16.73	17.12	17.51
34	15.25	15.65	16.04	16.44	16.85	17.25	17.65	18.05
35	15.70	16.11	16.53	16.94	17.35	17.77	18.18	18.60
36	16.16	16.58	17.01	17.43	17.86	18.29	18.71	19.14
37	16.62	17.06	17.49	17.93	18.37	18.81	19.25	19.69
38	17.08	17.53	17.98	18.43	18.88	19.33	19.78	20.24
39	17.54	18.00	18.46	18.93	19.39	19.86	20.32	20.79
40	18.00	18.48	18.95	19.43	19.90	20.38	20.86	21.34
41	18.47	18.95	19.44	19.93	20.42	20.91	21.40	21.89
42	18.93	19.43	19.93	20.43	20.93	21.44	21.94	22.45
43	19.40	19.91	20.42	20.94	21.45	21.97	22.49	23.01
44	19.86	20.39	20.91	21.44	21.97	22.50	23.03	23.57
45	20.33	20.87	21.41	21.95	22.49	23.03	23.58	24.12
46	20.80	21.35	21.90	22.46	23.01	23.57	24.13	24.69
47	21.27	21.83	22.40	22.97	23.53	24.10	24.68	25.25
48	21.74	22.32	22.90	23.48	24.06	24.64	25.23	25.81
49	22.21	22.80	23.39	23.99	24.58	25.18	25.78	26.38
50	22.69	23.29	23.89	24.50	25.11	25.72	26.33	26.94
51	23.16	23.78	24.40	25.02	25.64	26.26	26.89	27.52
52	23.64	24.27	24.90	25.53	26.17	26.81	27.45	28.09
53	24.11	24.76	25.40	26.05	26.70	27.35	28.00	28.66
54	24.59	25.25	25.91	26.57	27.23	27.90	28.56	29.23
55	25.07	25.74	26.41	27.09	27.77	28.44	29.13	29.81
56	25.55	26.23	26.92	27.61	28.30	28.99	29.69	30.39
57	26.03	26.73	27.43	28.13	28.84	29.54	30.25	30.97
58	26.51	27.23	27.94	28.66	29.37	30.10	30.82	31.55
59	27.00	27.72	28.45	29.18	29.91	30.65	31.39	32.13
60	27.48	28.22	28.96	29.71	30.45	31.20	31.96	32.71

TABLE 12.1 *(Continued)*

No. of 12.00%	12.25%	12.50%	12.75%	13.00%	13.25%	13.50%	13.75%
1.00	1.02	1.04	1.06	1.08	1.10	1.12	1.15
1.50	1.53	1.57	1.60	1.63	1.66	1.69	1.72
2.01	2.05	2.09	2.13	2.17	2.22	2.26	2.30
2.51	2.57	2.62	2.67	2.72	2.78	2.83	2.88
3.02	3.08	3.15	3.21	3.27	3.34	3.40	3.46
3.53	3.60	3.68	3.75	3.83	3.90	3.97	4.05
4.04	4.12	4.21	4.29	4.38	4.47	4.55	4.64
4.55	4.65	4.74	4.84	4.94	5.03	5.13	5.22
5.07	5.17	5.28	5.39	5.49	5.60	5.71	5.82
5.58	5.70	5.82	5.94	6.05	6.17	6.29	6.41
6.10	6.23	6.36	6.49	6.62	6.75	6.88	7.01
6.62	6.76	6.90	7.04	7.18	7.32	7.46	7.60
7.14	7.29	7.44	7.59	7.75	7.90	8.05	8.20
7.66	7.82	7.99	8.15	8.31	8.48	8.64	8.81
8.19	8.36	8.53	8.71	8.88	9.06	9.23	9.41
8.71	8.90	9.08	9.27	9.46	9.64	9.83	10.02
9.24	9.44	9.63	9.83	10.03	10.23	10.43	10.63
9.77	9.98	10.19	10.40	10.61	10.82	11.03	11.24
10.30	10.52	10.74	10.96	11.18	11.41	11.63	11.85
10.83	11.06	11.30	11.53	11.76	12.00	12.23	12.46
11.36	11.61	11.85	12.10	12.34	12.59	12.84	13.08
11.90	12.16	12.41	12.67	12.93	13.19	13.44	13.70
12.44	12.71	12.97	13.24	13.51	13.78	14.05	14.32
12.98	13.26	13.54	13.82	14.10	14.38	14.66	14.95
13.52	13.81	14.10	14.40	14.69	14.98	15.28	15.57
14.06	14.36	14.67	14.97	15.28	15.59	15.89	16.20
14.60	14.92	15.24	15.56	15.87	16.19	16.51	16.83
15.15	15.48	15.81	16.14	16.47	16.80	17.13	17.46
15.70	16.04	16.38	16.72	17.07	17.41	17.75	18.10
16.24	16.60	16.95	17.31	17.66	18.02	18.38	18.74
16.79	17.16	17.53	17.90	18.27	18.63	19.00	19.38
17.35	17.73	18.11	18.49	18.87	19.25	19.93	20.02
17.90	18.29	18.69	19.08	19.47	19.87	20.26	20.66
18.46	18.86	19.27	19.67	20.08	20.49	20.90	21.31
19.01	19.43	19.85	20.27	20.69	21.11	21.53	21.95
19.57	20.00	20.43	20.87	21.30	21.73	22.17	22.60
20.13	20.58	21.02	21.46	21.91	22.36	22.81	23.25
20.69	21.15	21.61	22.07	22.52	22.99	23.45	23.91
21.26	21.73	22.20	22.67	23.14	23.61	24.09	24.56
21.82	22.30	22.79	23.27	23.76	24.25	24.73	25.22
22.39	22.88	23.38	23.88	24.38	24.88	25.38	25.88
22.96	23.47	23.98	24.49	25.00	25.51	26.03	26.55
23.53	24.05	24.57	25.10	25.62	26.15	26.68	27.21
24.10	24.64	25.17	25.71	26.25	26.79	27.03	27.88
24.67	25.22	25.77	26.32	26.88	27.43	27.99	28.55
25.25	25.81	26.37	26.95	27.51	28.08	28.65	29.22
25.82	26.40	26.98	27.56	28.14	28.72	29.31	29.89
26.40	26.99	27.58	28.18	28.77	29.37	29.97	30.57
26.98	27.59	28.19	28.80	29.41	30.02	30.63	31.24
27.56	28.18	28.80	29.42	30.04	30.67	31.29	31.92
28.15	28.78	29.41	30.05	30.68	31.32	31.96	32.60
28.73	29.38	30.02	30.67	31.32	31.98	32.63	33.29
29.32	29.98	30.64	31.30	31.97	32.63	33.30	33.97
29.91	30.58	31.25	31.93	32.61	33.29	33.98	34.66
30.50	31.18	31.87	32.56	33.26	33.95	34.65	35.35
31.09	31.79	32.49	33.20	33.91	34.62	35.33	36.04
31.68	32.39	33.11	33.83	34.56	35.28	36.01	36.74
32.27	33.00	33.74	34.47	35.21	35.95	36.69	37.43
32.87	33.61	34.36	35.11	35.86	36.62	37.37	38.13
33.47	34.23	34.99	35.75	36.52	37.29	38.06	38.83

Note: The Table Handbook that accompanies *Business Mathematics* contains more detailed tables.

EXAMPLE   Find the APR for a consumer who financed $3,000 worth of bathroom fixtures, agreeing to pay $101.08 monthly for three years.

Solution   *Step 1.*   Find the table factor:

Amount financed = $3,000
Total number of payments = 36   *(3 years × 12 months per year)*
Finance charge = (number of payments × amount of each payment) − amount financed
$$= (36 \times \$101.08) - \$3,000$$
$$= \$3,638.88 - 3,000$$
$$= \$638.88$$

$$\text{Table factor} = \frac{\text{finance charge} \times 100}{\text{amount financed}}$$

$$= \frac{\$638.88 \times 100}{\$3,000}$$

$$= 21.30 \qquad \textit{(rounded to the nearest hundredth)}$$

638.88 ☒ 100 ÷ 3,000 ☰ 21.30

Step 2.   Go to the correct number of payments in Table 12.1.

Total number of payments = 36   *(3 years × 12 months per year)*

Step 3.   Go across row 36 to 21.30. Look at the top of that column to find the APR to the nearest 1/4%; 13% is the APR at the top of the column.

Frequently, the exact amount of the table factor found by using the formula will not be found in Table 12.1, and you must use the factor in the table that is closest. For example, if you were looking for a factor of 21.35, it falls between 21.30 and 21.73 (the closest two amounts found on row 36 in Table 12.1). However, since it is closest to 21.30, that is the column you would use.

12.2 Practice Problems

Use Table 12.1 to find the APR for the following problems. (Round to the nearest 1/4%.)

1. William Bennett bought a new bedroom suite. The cash price was $2,999. William agreed to pay the furniture store $268.91 each month for one year. Find the APR using the APR table, 12.1.

2. Jordan Erin financed a $7,250 boat, paying 10% down and $217.50 each month for three years. Find the APR using the APR table, 12.1.

3. Brandi Thomas bought a pickup truck for $18,397, including tax, title, and license. Brandi traded her old VW van in for $937. Payments were $371.62 each month for five years. Find the APR using the APR table, 12.1.

4. Siegfried purchased a $1,295 refrigerator for $78.67 per month for one and a half years. Find the APR using the APR table, 12.1.

12.2 Solutions to Practice Problems

1. *Step 1.*   Find the table factor:

Amount financed = $2,999
Total number of payments = 12   *(1 year × 12 months per year)*
Finance charge = (number of payments × amount of each payment) − amount financed
$$= (12 \times \$268.91) - \$2,999$$
$$= \$3,226.92 - 2,999$$
$$= \$227.92$$

$$\text{Table factor} = \frac{\text{finance charge} \times 100}{\text{amount financed}}$$

$$= \frac{\$227.92 \times 100}{\$2,999}$$

$$= 7.60 \qquad \textit{(Rounded to the nearest hundredth)}$$

Step 2. Go to the correct number of payments in Table 12.1.

Total number of payments = 12   *(1 year × 12 months per year)*

Step 3. Go across row 12 to 7.60. Look at the top of that column to find the APR to the nearest 1/4%; 13.75% is the APR at the top of the column.

2. *Step 1.* Find the table factor:

Amount financed = $7,250 − ($7,250 × 10%)
$$= \$7,250 - 725$$
$$= \$6,525$$

Total number of payments = 36   *(3 years × 12 months per year)*

Finance charge = (number of payments × amount of each payment) − amount financed
$$= (36 \times \$217.50) - \$6,525$$
$$= \$7,830 - 6,525$$
$$= \$1,305$$

$$\text{Table factor} = \frac{\text{finance charge} \times 100}{\text{amount financed}}$$
$$= \frac{\$1,305 \times 100}{\$6,525}$$
$$= 20.00$$

Step 2. Go to the correct number of payments in Table 12.1.

Total number of payments = 36   *(3 years × 12 months per year)*

Step 3. Go across row 36 to 20.00. Look at the top of that column to find the APR to the nearest 1/4%; 12.25% is the APR at the top of the column.

3. *Step 1.* Find the table factor:

Amount financed = $18,397 − 937
$$= \$17,460$$

Total number of payments = 60   *(5 years × 12 months per year)*

Finance charge = (number of payments × amount of each payment) − amount financed
$$= (60 \times \$371.62) - \$17,460$$
$$= \$22,297.20 - 17,460$$
$$= \$4,837.20$$

$$\text{Table factor} = \frac{\text{finance charge} \times 100}{\text{amount financed}}$$
$$= \frac{\$4,837.20 \times 100}{\$17,460}$$
$$= 27.70 \qquad \textit{(Rounded to the nearest hundredth)}$$

Step 2. Go to the correct number of payments in Table 12.1.

Total number of payments = 60   *(5 years × 12 months per year)*

Step 3. Go across row 60 to 27.48. Look at the top of that column to find the APR to the nearest 1/4%; 10.0% is the APR at the top of the column.

4. *Step 1.* Find the table factor:

Amount financed = $1,295

Total number of payments = 18   *(1.5 years × 12 months per year)*

Finance charge = (number of payments × amount of each payment) − amount financed
$$= (18 \times \$78.67) - \$1,295$$
$$= \$1,416.06 - 1,295$$
$$= \$121.06$$

$$\text{Table factor} = \frac{\text{Finance charge} \times \$100}{\text{amount financed}}$$
$$= \frac{\$121.06 \times 100}{\$1,295}$$
$$= 9.35 \qquad \textit{(Rounded to the nearest hundredth)}$$

Step 2. Go to the correct number of payments in Table 12.1.

Total number of payments = 18   *(1.5 years × 12 months per year)*

12.3 Paying Installment Loans Off Early: The Rule of 78

EXCEL Spreadsheet Application Spreadsheet Application 2 at the end of this chapter applies the Rule of 78 to Springfield's commercial customer loans that are being paid off early.

Loans are often paid off early to save finance charges and to escape regular monthly payments. One method used to calculate the **finance charge rebate** (unearned interest) and the amount required to pay a loan off early is called the **Rule of 78.** It is used by many lenders when the installment contract calls for monthly payments. Under the Rule of 78, the numbers of the periods in an installment loan contract are totaled. That is:

Month

1	
2	
3	
4	The fact that adding the digits 1 through 12 totals 78 in a 12-month contract
5	is how the method got its name. Finance charges are then allocated among
6	the months by writing the numbers 1 through 12 in reverse order and placing
7	each over 78 in a common fraction. For example, the first month's finance
8	charge would be $\frac{12}{78}$ of the total charge, the second month is would be $\frac{11}{78}$, and
9	so forth, until the twelfth month, which would be $\frac{1}{78}$ of the total finance
10	charges.
11	
+ 12	
78	

A shortcut to adding all of the digits is to use the sum of the digits formula: $\frac{n(n + 1)}{2}$ where n is the largest number in the sequence of numbers being added. Therefore, adding months 1 through 12 would be:

$$\frac{12(12 + 1)}{2} = \frac{12 \times 13}{2} = 78$$

All contracts are not for one year, of course, but the principle remains the same. The rebate is calculated by multiplying the total finance charge by a fraction whose numerator is the sum of the number of payments remaining, $\frac{n(n + 1)}{2}$, and whose denominator is the sum of the total number of payments, $\frac{N(N + 1)}{2}$:

$$\text{Finance charge rebate} = \text{total finance charge} \times \frac{n(n + 1)/2}{N(N + 1)/2}$$

E X A M P L E   John Elliott purchased a used pickup truck for $8,500. He put $500 down and agreed to repay the remainder in monthly payments of $263.33 for 36 months. With 10 payments remaining, John decides to pay off the loan in full. Find the amount of the finance charge rebate and the amount necessary to repay the loan in full.

Solution   *Step 1.* Find the total finance charge:

Finance charge = (number of payments × amount of each payment) − amount financed
= (36 × $263.33) − ($8,500 − $500)
= $9,479.88 − 8,000
= $1,479.88

Step 2. Find the amount of the finance charge rebate:

$$\text{Finance charge rebate} = \text{total finance charge} \times \frac{n(n+1)/2}{N(N+1)/2}$$

$$= \$1{,}479.88 \times \frac{10(10+1)/2}{36(36+1)/2}$$

$$= \$1{,}479.88 \times \frac{55}{666}$$

$$= \$122.21$$

Step 3. Find the amount necessary to repay the loan in full:

John had 10 payments remaining. Therefore, before the finance charge rebate, he still owed:

$$\text{Loan balance} = \text{number of payments remaining} \times \text{monthly payment}$$
$$= 10 \times \$263.33$$
$$= \$2{,}633.30$$

But, John will save \$122.21 by paying the loan off early (see step 2). Thus:

$$\text{Amount necessary to repay the loan} = \text{loan balance} - \text{rebate}$$
$$= \$2{,}633.30 - 122.21$$
$$= \$2{,}511.09$$

Table 12.2 is a rebate fraction table. It can be used to find the fraction of the total finance charge that is unearned when a consumer pays off an installment loan early. For example, a 24-month loan is being paid off with 9 months remaining:

45	The value in Table 12.2 that represents the sum of the digits for 9 months (it will be your numerator).
300	The value in Table 12.2 that represents the sum of the digits for 24 months (it will be your denominator).

The fraction is $\frac{45}{300}$.

12.3 Practice Problems

Find the finance charge rebate and the amount necessary to repay the loan in the following problems:

1. Wilson Jefferson financed a VCR that cost \$395. The payments were \$36.66 per month for one year. After three months, Wilson decided to pay the entire balance off. Determine the finance charge rebate and the payoff amount.

2. "Moms" Maybury borrowed \$800 on an 18-month installment contract. Her contract called for payments of \$49.72. With 11 payments remaining, she decided to pay the loan off in full. Find the finance charge rebate and the payoff amount.

3. Sean McDougal purchased a new travel trailer for \$28,940. He traded his old van in and used the \$6,295 he received for the down payment. The finance terms then called for payments of \$454.16 each month for five years. With 30 months to go on the contract, Sean decides to pay it off. Calculate the amount of the finance charge rebate and the payoff amount.

4. Maria Sanchez-Trujillo bought a new washer and dryer for a total of \$1,024. The department store opened an installment loan account for her, requiring a 15% down payment and 30 equal monthly payments of \$37.03 each. Maria made the payments for one year. She then decided to pay off the loan in full. Find the finance charge rebate and the payoff amount.

TABLE 12.2   REBATE FRACTION TABLE BASED ON THE RULE OF 78

Months to go	Sum of Digits	Months to Go	Sum of Digits
1	1	31	496
2	3	32	528
3	6	33	561
4	10	34	595
5	15	35	630
6	21	36	666
7	28	37	703
8	36	38	741
9	45	39	780
10	55	40	820
11	66	41	861
12	78	42	903
13	91	43	946
14	105	44	990
15	120	45	1,035
16	136	46	1,081
17	153	47	1,128
18	171	48	1,176
19	190	49	1,225
20	210	50	1,275
21	231	51	1,326
22	253	52	1,378
23	276	53	1,431
24	300	54	1,485
25	325	55	1,540
26	351	56	1,596
27	378	57	1,653
28	406	58	1,711
29	435	59	1,770
30	465	60	1,830

Note:The Table Handbook that accompanies *Business Mathematics* contains more detailed tables.

12.3 Solutions to Practice Problems

1. *Step 1.* Find the total finance charge:

Finance charge = (number of payments × amount of each payment) − amount financed
= (12 × $36.66) − $395
= $439.92 − 395
= $44.92

Step 2. Find the amount of finance charge rebate:

$$\text{Finance charge rebate} = \text{total finance charge} \times \frac{n(n+1)/2}{N(N+1)/2}$$

$$= \$44.92 \times \frac{9(9+1)/2}{12(12+1)/2}$$

$$= \$44.92 \times \frac{45}{78}$$

$$= \$25.92$$

Step 3. Find the amount necessary to repay the loan in full:

$$\text{Loan balance} = \text{number of payments remaining} \times \text{monthly payment}$$
$$= 9 \times \$36.66$$
$$= \$329.94$$

$$\text{Amount necessary to repay the loan} = \text{loan balance} - \text{rebate}$$
$$= \$329.94 - 25.92$$
$$= \$304.02$$

2. *Step 1.* Find the total finance charge:

$$\text{Finance charge} = (\text{number of payments} \times \text{amount of each payment}) - \text{amount financed}$$
$$= (18 \times \$49.72) - \$800$$
$$= \$894.96 - 800$$
$$= \$94.96$$

Step 2. Find the amount of finance charge rebate:

$$\text{Finance charge rebate} = \text{total finance charge} \times \frac{n(n+1)/2}{N(N+1)/2}$$
$$= \$94.96 \times \frac{11(11+1)/2}{18(18+1)/2}$$
$$= \$94.96 \times \frac{66}{171}$$
$$= \$36.65$$

Step 3: Find the amount necessary to repay the loan in full:

$$\text{Loan balance} = \text{number of payments remaining} \times \text{monthly payment}$$
$$= 11 \times \$49.72$$
$$= \$546.92$$

$$\text{Amount necessary to repay the loan} = \text{loan balance} - \text{rebate}$$
$$= \$546.92 - 36.65$$
$$= \$510.27$$

3. *Step 1.* Find the total finance charge:

$$\text{Finance charge} = (\text{number of payments} \times \text{amount of each payment}) - \text{amount financed}$$
$$= (60 \times \$454.16) - (\$28,940 - \$6,295)$$
$$= \$27,249.60 - 22,645$$
$$= \$4,604.60$$

Step 2. Find the amount of finance charge rebate:

$$\text{Finance charge rebate} = \text{total finance charge} \times \frac{n(n+1)/2}{N(N+1)/2}$$
$$= \$4,604.60 \times \frac{30(30+1)/2}{60(60+1)/2}$$
$$= \$4,604.60 \times \frac{465}{1,830}$$
$$= \$1,170.02$$

Step 3. Find the amount necessary to repay the loan in full:

$$\text{Loan balance} = \text{number of payments remaining} \times \text{monthly payment}$$
$$= 30 \times 454.16$$
$$= \$13,624.80$$

$$\text{Amount necessary to repay the loan} = \text{loan balance} - \text{rebate}$$
$$= \$13,624.80 - 1,170.02$$
$$= \$12,454.78$$

4. *Step 1.* Find the total finance charge:

Finance charge = (number of payments × amount of each payment) − amount financed
= (30 × $37.03) − [$1,024 − (15% × $1,024)]
= $1,110.90 − [$1,024 − $153.60]
= $1,110.90 − 870.40
= $240.50

Step 2. Find the amount of finance charge rebate:

$$\text{Finance charge rebate} = \text{total finance charge} \times \frac{n(n+1)/2}{N(N+1)/2}$$

$$= \$240.50 \times \frac{18(18+1)/2}{30(30+1)/2}$$

$$= \$240.50 \times \frac{171}{465}$$

$$= \$88.44$$

Step 3. Find the amount necessary to repay the loan in full:

Loan balance = number of payments remaining × monthly payment
= 18 × $37.03
= $666.54

Amount necessary to repay the loan = loan balance − rebate
= $666.54 − 88.44
= $578.10

A consumer may make several purchases during a month and charge all of them. Generally, a minimum payment is required each month. Since this type of charge account may never be paid off, it is called a **revolving charge account.**

LEARNING UNIT 2
OPEN-END CREDIT

Open-end credit has no fixed number of payments. MasterCard, VISA, Discover, and some oil company charge cards use this method of extending credit. Some of them also require an annual fee, and many allow a 25-day grace period for paying without an interest charge.

Finance charges on open-end credit accounts are usually calculated in one of two ways: the **unpaid balance method** or the **average daily balance method** used by most companies with credit card accounts.

12.4 Calculating the Finance Charge Using the Unpaid Balance Method

When the unpaid balance method is used, the finance charge is calculated on the amount due at the *end of the previous month.* No purchases, payments, or returns during the current month are used in calculations.

E X A M P L E   Kenneth Whatley's charge card had a $394.38 balance at the end of July. The bank's charge for its credit card use is 1.5% per month (1.5% × 12 = 18% APR) on the unpaid balance. Following is a summary of the transactions for August, September, and October:

	Total Purchases	Returns	Payments
August	$ 93.49		$ 50.00
September	139.63	$ 18.03	50.00
October	85.17		75.00

Calculate the balance at the end of each month by filling in the following summary form.

Solution

Month	Unpaid Balance at Beginning of Month	Finance Charge	Purchases During Month	Returns	Payments	Unpaid Balance at End of Month
August	$ 394.38	$ 5.92	$ 93.49		$ 50.00	$ 443.79
September	443.79	6.66	139.63	$ 18.03	50.00	522.05
October	522.05	7.83	85.17		75.00	540.05

August:

    Finance charge: $394.38 \times 1.5\% = \$5.92$

    Unpaid balance: $394.38 + 5.92 + 93.49 - 50.00 = \$443.79$

September:

    Finance charge: $443.79 \times 1.5\% = \$6.66$

    Unpaid balance: $443.79 + 6.66 + 139.63 - 18.03 - 50.00 = \$522.05$

October:

    Finance charge: $522.05 \times 1.5\% = \$7.83$

    Unpaid Balance: $522.05 + 7.83 + 85.17 - 75.00 = \$540.05$

12.4 Practice Problems

Calculate the finance charge and the balance at the end of each month using the unpaid balance method for the following problems:

1. Shakeitha Howard's charge card had a $510.50 balance at the end of April. The bank's charge for its credit card use is 1.6% per month on the unpaid balance. Following is a summary of the transactions for May and June:

	Total Purchases	Returns	Payments
May	$ 39.01	$ 123.04	$ 30.00
June	129.63		50.00

Calculate the balance at the end of each month.

2. Naomi Hutchison's charge card had a $264.10 balance at the end of January. The bank's charge for its credit card use is 1.25% per month on the unpaid balance. Following is a summary of the transactions for February, March, and April:

	Total Purchases	Returns	Payments
February	$ 201.39		$ 100.00
March	9.72	$ 38.54	100.00
April	39.47		100.00

Calculate the balance at the end of each month.

3. Xiaoming Zhou's charge card had a $993.81 balance at the end of June. The bank's charge for its credit card use is 1.075% per month on the unpaid balance. Following is a summary of the transactions for July, August, and September:

	Total Purchases	Returns	Payments
July	$ 391.76	$ 44.45	$ 250.00
August	39.10		250.00
September	180.75	22.90	250.00

Calculate the balance at the end of each month.

4. Cynthia McAnally's charge card had a $218.42 balance at the end of November. The bank's charge for its credit card use is 1.8% per month on the unpaid balance. Following is a summary of the transactions for December and January:

	Total Purchases	Returns	Payments
December	$ 31.20	$ 12.48	$ 50.00
January	119.54		25.00

Calculate the balance at the end of each month.

12.4 Solutions to Practice Problems

1.

Month	Unpaid Balance at Beginning of Month	Finance Charge	Purchases During Month	Returns	Payments	Unpaid Balance at End of Month
May	$ 510.50	$ 8.17	$ 39.01	$123.04	$ 30.00	$ 404.64
June	404.64	6.47	129.63		50.00	490.74

May:

    Finance charge: $510.50 \times 1.6\% = \$8.17$

    Unpaid balance: $\$510.50 + 8.17 + 39.01 - 123.04 - 30.00 = \$404.64$

June:

    Finance charge: $\$404.64 \times 1.6\% = \$6.47$

    Unpaid balance: $\$404.64 + 6.47 + 129.63 - 50.00 = \$490.74$

2.

Month	Unpaid Balance at Beginning of Month	Finance Charge	Purchases During Month	Returns	Payments	Unpaid Balance at End of Month
February	$ 264.10	$ 3.30	$ 201.39	$	$ 100.00	$ 368.79
March	368.79	4.61	9.72	38.54	100.00	244.58
April	244.58	3.06	39.47		100.00	187.11

February:

    Finance charge: $\$264.10 \times 1.25\% = \$3.30$

    Unpaid balance: $\$264.10 + 3.30 + 201.39 - 100.00 = \$368.79$

March:

    Finance charge: $\$368.79 \times 1.25\% = \$4.61$

    Unpaid balance: $\$368.79 + 4.61 + 9.72 - 38.54 - 100.00 = \$244.58$

April:

    Finance charge: $\$244.58 \times 1.25\% = \$3.06$

    Unpaid balance: $\$244.58 + 3.06 + 39.47 - 100.00 = \$187.11$

3.

Month	Unpaid Balance at Beginning of Month	Finance Charge	Purchases During Month	Returns	Payments	Unpaid Balance at End of Month
July	$ 993.81	$ 10.68	$ 391.76	$ 44.45	$ 250.00	$1,101.80
August	1,101.80	11.84	39.10		250.00	902.74
September	902.74	9.70	180.75	22.90	250.00	820.29

July:

    Finance charge: $\$993.81 \times 1.075\% = \$10.68$

    Unpaid balance: $\$993.81 + 10.68 + 391.76 - 44.45 - 250.00 = \$1,101.80$

August:

    Finance charge: $\$1,101.80 \times 1.075\% = \$11.84$

    Unpaid balance: $\$1,101.80 + 11.84 + 39.10 - 250.00 = \$902.74$

September:

    Finance charge: $\$902.74 \times 1.075\% = \$9.70$

    Unpaid balance: $\$902.74 + 9.70 + 180.75 - 22.90 - 250.00 = \$820.29$

4.

Month	Unpaid Balance at Beginning of Month	Finance Charge	Purchases During Month	Returns	Payments	Unpaid Balance at End of Month
December	$ 218.42	$ 3.93	$ 31.20	$ 12.48	$ 50.00	$ 191.07
January	191.07	3.44	119.54		25.00	289.05

December:

    Finance charge: $218.42 \times 1.8\% = \$3.93$

    Unpaid balance: $\$218.42 + 3.93 + 31.20 - 12.48 - 50.00 = \$191.07$

January:

    Finance charge: $\$191.07 \times 1.8\% = \$3.44$

    Unpaid balance: $\$191.07 + 3.44 + 119.54 - 25.00 = \$289.05$

12.5   Calculating the Finance Charge Using the Average Daily Balance Method

EXCEL Spreadsheet Application The credit card the Springfield Department Store issues calculates monthly interest charges using the average daily balance method. Springfield uses Spreadsheet Application 1 shown at the end of this chapter to record credit card transactions.

Today most revolving charge accounts use the average daily balance method. The balance is found at the end of each day during a billing cycle:

Daily balance = previous balance + purchases + cash advances − credit on returns − payments

The amounts of each day's balances are added together and then divided by the total number of days in the billing cycle:

$$\text{Average daily balance} = \frac{\text{total daily balances}}{\text{days in billing cycle}}$$

The finance charge is then calculated by multiplying the average daily balance by the monthly finance rate:

Finance charge = average daily balance × monthly finance rate

---

EXAMPLE   Armando Palos had an ending balance of $494.34 at the end of his last billing cycle on April 8. His bank charge card's monthly finance rate was 1.75%. During the next billing cycle, the following transactions took place:

Date	Description	Transaction Amount	Unpaid Balance
April 8	Billing date		$494.34
April 11	Purchase	$ 183.49	
April 17	Payment	250.00	
April 22	Purchase	23.91	
April 24	Returns	14.56	
May 2	Cash advance	100.00	
May 8	Billing date		

Calculate his finance charge for the cycle using the average daily balance method.

Solution

Date	Description	Transaction Amount	Unpaid Balance	Number of Days Before Balance Changes	Extended Balance
April 8	Billing date		$ 494.34	× 3 =	$ 1,483.03
April 11	Purchase	$ 183.49	677.83	× 6 =	4,066.98
April 17	Payment	250.00	427.83	× 5 =	2,139.15
April 22	Purchase	23.91	451.74	× 2 =	903.48
April 24	Returns	14.56	437.18	× 8 =	3,497.44
May 2	Cash advance	100.00	537.18	× 6 =	3,223.08
May 8	Billing date				
			Totals	30	$15,313.16

Average daily balance = $15,313.16 ÷ 30 = $510.44
Finance charge for billing cycle = $510.44 × 1.75% = $8.93

Step 1. Each transaction amount is added to or subtracted from the previous unpaid balance. Thus, the first transaction, a purchase of $183.49, was added to the previous unpaid balance of $494.34:

$$\$494.34 + 183.49 = \$677.83$$

Step 2. Instead of listing the previous unpaid balance for each date before the unpaid balance changes, such as:

April 8 $494.34
April 9   494.34
April 10   494.34

the date of the previous transaction is subtracted from the new transaction date to find the number of days before the unpaid balance changes. Thus, the unpaid balance of $494.34 on April 8 remained the same for three days until the next transaction occurred on April 11:

April 11
− April   8
3 days

Step 3. The number of days an unpaid balance remained unchanged is then multiplied by the unpaid balance to find the extended balance:

$$3 \times \$494.34 = \$1,483.02$$

Step 4. That process (steps 2 and 3) is continued through the billing cycle after each transaction.

Step 5. At the end of the billing cycle, totals are found for the number of days and the extended balance.

Step 6. The total extended balance is then divided by the total number of days in the billing cycle to find the average daily balance:

$$\text{Average daily balance} = \$15,313.16 \div 30 = \$510.44$$

Step 7. The average daily balance is then multiplied by the monthly finance rate to find the month's finance charge:

$$\text{Finance charge} = \$510.44 \times 1.75\%$$
$$= \$8.93$$

Calculate the billing cycle finance charge for the following installment credit accounts using the average daily balance method.

1. Christy Vernon had an ending balance of $491.04 at the end of her last billing cycle on March 3. Her bank charge card's monthly finance rate was 1.5%. During the next billing cycle, the following transactions took place. Find the finance charge using the average daily balance method.

Date	Description	Transaction Amount	Unpaid Balance
March 3	Billing date		$ 491.04
March 10	Purchase	$ 34.38	
March 15	Payment	150.00	
March 24	Purchase	11.46	
April 3	Billing date		

2. Suzanna Farleigh had an ending balance of $229.15 at the end of her last billing cycle on June 20. Her bank charge card's monthly finance rate was 1.6%. During the next billing cycle, the following transactions took place. Find the finance charge using the average daily balance method.

Date	Description	Tansaction Amount	Unpaid Balance
June 20	Billing date		$ 229.15
July 2	Purchase	$ 25.88	
July 10	Cash advance	50.00	
July 12	Purchase	23.91	
July 15	Payment	20.00	
July 20	Billing date		

3. Dean Young had an ending balance of $239.93 at the end of his last billing cycle on May 1. His bank charge card's monthly finance rate was 1.33%. During the next billing cycle, the following transactions took place. Find the finance charge using the average daily balance method.

Date	Description	Transaction Amount	Unpaid Balance
May 1	Billing date		$ 239.93
May 8	Purchase	$ 192.47	
May 10	Purchase	39.03	
May 24	Payment	75.00	
May 30	Purchase	289.30	
June 1	Billing date		

4. Jeen Hee Chung had an ending balance of $482.39 at the end of his last billing cycle on January 25. His bank charge card's monthly finance rate was 1.25%. During the next billing cycle, the following transactions took place. Find the finance charge using the average daily balance method.

Date	Description	Transaction Amount	Unpaid Balance
January 25	Billing date		$ 482.39
January 26	Payment	$ 100.00	
January 31	Cash advance	60.00	
February 19	Payment	100.00	
February 23	Purchase	9.25	
February 25	Billing date		

12.5 Solutions to Practice Problems

1.

Date	Description	Transaction Amount	Unpaid Balance	Number of Days Before Balance Changes	Extended Balance
March 3	Billing date		$ 491.04	7	$ 3,437.28
March 10	Purchase	$ 34.38	525.42	5	2,627.10
March 15	Payment	150.00	375.42	9	3,378.78
March 24	Purchase	11.46	386.88	10	3,868.80
April 3	Billing date				
			Totals	31	$13,311.96

Average daily balance = $13,311.96 ÷ 31 = $429.42

Finance charge for billing cycle = $429.42 × 1.5% = $6.44

2.

Date	Description	Transaction Amount	Unpaid Balance	Number of Days Before Balance Changes	Extended Balance
June 20	Billing date		$ 229.15	12	$ 2,749.80
July 2	Purchase	$ 25.88	255.03	8	2,040.24
July 10	Cash advance	50.00	305.03	2	610.06
July 12	Purchase	23.91	328.94	3	986.82
July 15	Payment	20.00	308.94	5	1,544.70
July 20	Billing date				
			Totals	30	$ 7,931.62

Average daily balance = $7,931.62 ÷ 30 = $264.39

Finance charge for billing cycle = $264.39 × 1.6% = $4.23

3.

Date	Description	Transaction Amount	Unpaid Balance	Number of Days Before Balance Changes	Extended Balance
May 1	Billing date		$ 239.93	7	$ 1,679.51
May 8	Purchase	$ 192.47	432.40	2	864.80
May 10	Purchase	39.03	471.43	14	6,600.02
May 24	Payment	75.00	396.43	6	2,378.58
May 30	Purchase	289.30	685.73	2	1,371.46
June 1	Billing date				
			Totals	31	$12,894.37

Average daily balance = $12,894.37 ÷ 31 = $415.95
Finance charge for billing cycle = $415.95 × 1.33% = $5.53

4.

Date	Description	Transaction Amount	Unpaid Balance	Number of Days Before Balance Changes	Extended Balance
January 25	Billing date		$ 482.39	1	$ 482.39
January 26	Payment	$ 100.00	382.39	5	1,911.95
January 31	Cash advance	60.00	442.39	19	8,405.41
February 19	Payment	100.00	342.39	4	1,369.56
February 23	Purchase	9.25	351.64	2	703.28
February 25	Billing date		351.64		
		Totals		31	$12,872.59

Average daily balance = $12,872.59 ÷ 31 = $415.24
Finance charge for billing cycle = $415.24 × 1.25% = $5.19

QUICK REFERENCE SUMMARY AND REVIEW

Page	Section Topic	Learning Concepts	Examples and Solutions
412	**12.1** Using the Formula to Estimate the Annual Percentage Rate (APR)	1. Amount financed = cash price − down payment 2. Total finance charge = total of all charges − amount financed 3. APR = $2 \times \dfrac{\text{number of payment periods in 1 year} \times \text{finance charge}}{\text{amount financed} \times (\text{total number of payments} + 1)}$	Use the formula to estimate the APR for a $950 purchase requiring a $50 down payment and 24 monthly payments of $43.36. **1.** $950 − 50 $900 **2.** 24 × $43.36 = $1,040.64 − 900.00 $ 140.64 **3.** $\dfrac{2 \times 12 \times \$140.64}{\$900 \times (24 + 1)} = 15\%$

Page	Section Topic	Learning Concepts	Examples and Solutions
415	**12.2** Using the Table to Find the Annual Percentage Rate (APR)	1. Find the table factor using the following formula: $$\text{Table factor} = \frac{\text{finance charge} \times 100}{\text{amount financed}}$$ 2. Go to the number of payments in Table 12.1. 3. Go across the row found in step 2 until you are as close as possible to the table factor found in step 1. Look at the top of that column to find the APR to the nearest 1/4%.	Find the APR for a consumer who bought merchandise costing $523.98, made a down payment of $50, and will make $43.34 payments each month for one year. 1. Amount financed $= \$523.98 - 50.00 = \$473.98$ Finance charge $=$ $\$43.34 \times 12 = \$520.08$ $\underline{ - 473.98}$ $\$ 46.10$ Table factor $= \dfrac{\$46.10 \times 100}{\$473.98} = 9.73$ 2. Go to 12 payments in Table 12.1. 3. Go across to 9.73; 17.5% heads that column.
420	**12.3** Paying Installment Loans Off Early: The Rule of 78	To pay loans off before maturity, the Rule of 78 is often used. The name comes from the fact that the sum of the months' digits in one year is 78: $$1 + 2 + 3 + \ldots + 11 + 12 = 78$$ The finance charge rebate is Finance charge rebate = total finance charge $\times \frac{n(n+1)/2}{N(N+1)/2}$ where n is the number of payments *remaining* and N is the number of *total payments* in the loan. Amount necessary to repay the loan = loan balance − rebate	An installment loan for $9,000 payable in 36 equal monthly payments of $304 was paid off with 12 payments remaining. Calculate the rebate and the amount necessary to pay off the loan. $$\begin{array}{r}\text{Total payments}\\ \underline{-\ \text{amount financed}}\\ \text{finance charge}\end{array}$$ $\$304 \times 36 = \$10,944$ $\underline{ - 9,000}$ $\$ 1,944$ $n = 12$ $N = 36$ $$\frac{n(n+1)}{2} = \frac{12 \times 13}{2} = 78$$ $$\frac{N(N+1)}{2} = \frac{36 \times 37}{2} = 666$$ $$\$1,944 \times \frac{78}{666} = \$227.68$$ $(\$304 \times 12) - \$227.68 = \$3,648 - 227.68 = \$3,420.32$
424	**12.4** Calculating the Finance Charge Using the Unpaid Balance Method	The finance charge is calculated on the amount due at the end of the previous month. No transactions during the current month are used in calculations.	The balance at the end of May was $700. In June the transactions were: Purchases $295 Payments $400 Returns $ 25 Transactions in July were: Purchases $350 Payments $250 Calculate the balance at the end of June and July. The bank charges 1.8% per month for the use of its credit card.

QUICK REFERENCE SUMMARY AND REVIEW

Page	Section Topic	Learning Concepts	Examples and Solutions

Month	Unpaid Balance at Beginning of Month	Finance Charge	Purchases During Month	Returns	Payments	Unpaid Balance at End of Month
June	$ 700.00	$ 12.60	$ 295.00	$ 25.00	$ 400.00	$ 528.60
July	528.60	10.49	350.00		250.00	639.09

June:
Finance charge: $700 × 1.8\% = \$12.60$
Unpaid balance: $\$700 + 12.60 + 295 - 25 - 400 = \$528.60$

July:
Finance charge: $\$528.60 × 1.8\% = \$10.49$
Unpaid balance: $\$528.60 + 10.49 + 350 - 250 = \$639.09$

427 12.5 Calculating the Finance Charge Using the Average Daily Balance Method

Most charge accounts now use the average daily balance method. The balance is found at the end of each day during a billing cycle. The amounts of each day's balance are added and then divided by the number of days in the billing cycle. The finance charge is then calculated by multiplying the average daily balance by the monthly finance charge.

The balance on June 9, the end of the billing cycle, was $4,593. The monthly finance charge was 1.5%. During the cycle, the following transactions took place:

Date	Description	Transaction Amount	Unpaid Balance
June 9	Billing date		$4,593.00
June 12	Payment	$ 500.00	
June 20	Purchase	43.48	
June 30	Purchase	375.28	
July 5	Purchase	44.54	
July 9	Billing date		

Calculate the finance charge for the cycle.

Date	Description	Transaction Amount	Unpaid Balance	Number of Days Before Balance Changes	Extended Balance
June 9	Billing date		$4,593.00	3	$ 13,779.00
June 12	Payment	$ 500.00	4,093.00	8	32,744.00
June 20	Purchase	43.48	4,136.48	10	41,364.80
June 30	Purchase	375.28	4,511.76	5	22,558.80
July 5	Purchase	44.54	4,556.30	4	18,225.20
July 9	Billing date				
			Totals	30	$128,671.80

Average daily balance = $\$128,671.80 ÷ 30 = \$4,289.06$
Finance charge for billing cycle = $\$4,289.06 × 1.5\% = \$64.34$

ADDITIONAL PRACTICE PROBLEMS

Answers to odd-numbered problems are given in Appendix A.

12.1

Use the formula to estimate the APR for the following problems (rounded to the nearest 1/4%):

1. Rose Monroe bought a new computer. The cash price was $2,549. Rose agreed to pay the retailer $120.48 each month for two years. Use the formula to estimate the APR.

$$APR = \frac{2 \times \text{number of payment periods in 1 year} \times \text{finance charge}}{\text{amount financed} \times (\text{total number of payments} + 1)}$$

$120.48 \times 24 = \$2,891.52$ $\$2,891.52 - 2,549 = \$342.52$
       Total repayment   Interest

$$APR = \frac{2 \times 12 \times \$342.52}{\$2,549 \times (24 + 1)}$$

$= 13.00\%$ (rounded to nearest 1/4 %)

2. Benny Thompson financed a $4,798 motorcycle, paying 15% down and $286.30 each month for 18 months. Use the formula to estimate the APR.

$$APR = \frac{2 \times \text{number of payment periods in 1 year} \times \text{finance charge}}{\text{amount financed} \times (\text{total number of payments} + 1)}$$

$\$4,798 \times 15\% = \$719.70$ $\$4,798 - 719.70 = \$4,078.30$
      Down payment   Amount financed

$\$286.30 \times 18 = \$5,153.40$ $\$5,153.40 - 4,078.30 = \$1,075.10$
      Total repayment   Interest

$$APR = \frac{2 \times 12 \times \$1,075.10}{\$4,078.30 \times (18 + 1)}$$

$= 33.25\%$ (rounded to nearest 1/4 %)

3. Richard Sauceda bought a new camper for his truck. It sold for $2,995. Richard traded his old camper in for $200. Payments were $94.64 each month for three years. Use the formula to estimate the APR.

$$APR = \frac{2 \times \text{number of payment periods in 1 year} \times \text{finance charge}}{\text{amount financed} \times (\text{total number of payments} + 1)}$$

$\$2,995 - 200 = \$2,795$ Amount financed

$\$94.64 \times 36 = \$3,407.04$ $\$3,407.04 - 2,795 = \$612.04$
      Total repayment   Interest

$$APR = \frac{2 \times 12 \times \$612.04}{\$2,795 \times (36 + 1)}$$

$= 14.25\%$ (rounded to nearest 1/4 %)

4. Wayne and Donna Aregood purchased a $12,950 Saturn. Taxes were 5% of the car price, the title fee was $45, and the license was $88.39, all of which were to be financed. Their old car was sold separately and the $1,850 was used as a down payment. The financing arrangements were $292.25 per month for four years. Use the formula to estimate the APR.

$$APR = \frac{2 \times \text{number of payment periods in 1 year} \times \text{finance charge}}{\text{amount financed} \times (\text{total number of payments} + 1)}$$

$\$12,950 \times 5\% = \$647.50$ Taxes

$\$12,950 + 647.50 + 45 + 88.39 - 1,850 = \$11,880.89$ Amount financed

$\$292.25 \times 48 = \$14,028$ $\$14,028 - 11,880.89 = \$2,147.11$
      Total repayment   Interest

$$APR = \frac{2 \times 12 \times \$2,147.11}{\$11,880.89 \times (48 + 1)}$$

$= 8.75\%$ (rounded to nearest 1/4 %)

5. Shiang Mei Hong borrowed $300 from Best Pawnshop using a shotgun and rifle as collateral. The loan was to be repaid with 13 weekly payments of $23.82 each. What is the estimated APR using the formula?

$$APR = \frac{2 \times \text{number of payment periods in 1 year} \times \text{finance charge}}{\text{amount financed} \times (\text{total number of payments} + 1)}$$

$\$23.82 \times 13 = \$309.66$ $309.66 - 300 = \$9.66$
      Total repayment   Interest

$$APR = \frac{2 \times 52 \times \$9.66}{\$309.66 \times (13 + 1)}$$

$= 23.25\%$ (rounded to nearest 1/4 %)

12.2

Use Table 12.1 to find the APR for the following problems. (Round to the nearest 1/4%.)

6. Yolanda Mecedies bought a new desk for her office. The cash price was $492. She agreed to pay the office supply retailer $16.34 each month for three years. Find the APR using the APR table, 12.1.

Finance Charge = (number of payments × amount of each payment) − amount financed

$= (36 \times \$16.34) - \$492$

$= \$588.24 - 492$

$= \$ 96.24$

Table factor $= \dfrac{\text{finance charge} \times \$100}{\text{amount frinanced}}$

$= \dfrac{\$96.24 \times 100}{\$492}$

$= 19.56$ (rounded to the nearest hundredth)

19.56 from table is 12.00% APR.

7. Manuel Cruz bought new dentures for $2,800 from Manhattan Dental Clinic. The monthly payments of $203.90 are to be made for 15 months. What is the APR using the APR table?

Finance Charge = (number of payments × amount of each payment)− amount financed

$= (15 \times \$203.90) - \$2,800$

$= \$3,058.50 - 2,800$

$= \$258.50$

Table factor $= \dfrac{\text{finance charge} \times \$100}{\text{amount financed}}$

$= \dfrac{\$258.50 \times 100}{\$2,800}$

$= 9.23$ (rounded to the nearest hundredth)

9.23 from table is 13.50% APR.

8. Brian Haywood made purchases costing $1,925, which he financed for $50 down and $87.17 per month for two years. Find the APR using the APR table, 12.1.

Amount Financed	Finance Charge
$1,925	$= (24 \times \$87.17) - \$1,875$
− 50	$= \$2,092.08 - 1,875$
$1,875	$= \$217.08$

Table factor $= \dfrac{\text{finance charge} \times \$100}{\text{amount financed}}$

$= \dfrac{\$217.08 \times 100}{\$1,875}$

$= 11.58$ (rounded to the nearest hundredth)

11.58 from table is 10.75% APR.

9. Don Hornrin financed a $2,500 spring wardrobe, paying 10% down and $201.75 each month for one year. Find the APR using the APR table, 12.1

Amount Financed		Finance Charge
$2,500	$2,500	$= (12 \times \$201.75) - \$2,250$
× 10%	− 250	$= \$2,421 - 2,250$
$ 250	$2,250	$= \$171$

Table factor $= \dfrac{\text{finance charge} \times \$100}{\text{amount financed}}$

$= \dfrac{\$171 \times 100}{\$2,250}$

$= 7.60$ (rounded to the nearest hundredth)

7.60 from table is 13.75% APR.

10. Laura Spangler bought new carpet for her home that measured 300 square yards. The carpet sold for $22.50 a square yard installed, and a carpet pad sold for $5.98 per square yard installed. Laura's installment contract called for a 7.5% down payment and $300.66 per month for 30 months. Use the APR table, 12.1, to find the annual APR.

Total Cost			Amount Financed		Finance Charge	
$22.50	$ 5.98	$6,750	$ 8,544	$8,544.00	$ 300.66	
× 300	× 300	+ 1,794	× 7.5%	− 640.80	× 30	
$6,750	$1,794	$8,544	$640.80	$7,903.20	$9,019.80	
					− 7,903.20	
					$1,116.60	

Table factor $= \dfrac{\text{finance charge} \times \$100}{\text{amount financed}}$

$= \dfrac{\$1,116.60 \times 100}{\$7,903.20}$

$= 14.13$ (rounded to the nearest hundredth)

14.13 from table is 10.50% APR

12.3

Find the finance charge rebate and the amount necessary to repay the loan in the following problems.

11. Ruben Flores financed a camcorder that cost $1,455. The payments were $47.27 per month for three years. After 14 months, Wilson decided to pay the entire balance off. Determine the finance charge rebate and the payoff amount.

Finance charge =

(number of payments × amount of each payment)− amount financed

$= (36 \times \$47.27) - \$1,455$

$= \$1,701.72 - 1,455$

$= \$246.72$

Finance charge rebate:

Finance charge rebate = total finance charge $\times \dfrac{\frac{n(n + 1)}{2}}{\frac{N(N + 1)}{2}}$

36 mos. − 14 mos. = 22 mos.

$= \$246.72 \times \dfrac{\frac{22(22 + 1)}{2}}{\frac{36(36 + 1)}{2}}$

$= \$246.72 \times \dfrac{253}{666}$

$= 93.72$

Amount necessary to repay the loan in full:

Loan balance = number of payments remaining × monthly payment

$= 22 \times \$47.27$

$= \$1,039.94$

Amount necessary to repay the loan = loan balance − rebate

$= \$1,039.94 - 93.72$

$= \$946.22$

12. Rockford Willett financed an $875 merchandise purchase. Terms were $50 down and 18 monthly payments of $49.46. With 8 payments remaining, he decided to pay the loan off in full. Find the finance charge rebate and the payoff amount.

Finance charge =
(number of payments × amount of each payment) − amount financed
$$= (18 \times \$49.46) - (\$875 - 50)$$
$$= \$890.28 - 825$$
$$= \$65.28$$

Finance charge rebate:

$$\text{Finance charge rebate} = \text{total finance charge} \times \frac{\frac{n(n+1)}{2}}{\frac{N(N+1)}{2}}$$

$$= \$65.28 \times \frac{\frac{8(8+1)}{2}}{\frac{18(18+1)}{2}}$$

$$= \$65.28 \times \frac{36}{171}$$

$$= \$13.74$$

Amount necessary to repay the loan in full:
Loan balance = number of payments remaining × monthly payment
$$= 8 \times \$49.46$$
$$= \$395.68$$
Amount necessary to repay the loan = loan balance − rebate
$$= \$395.68 \times 13.74$$
$$= \$381.94$$

13. Jerry Cunningham purchased a new entertainment center for $1,500. He made a $100 down payment and financed the remainder with payments of $51.48 each month for 3 years. With 18 months to go on the contract, Jerry decides to pay it off. Calculate the amount of the finance charge rebate and the payoff amount.

Finance charge =
number of payments × amount of each payment) − amount financed
$$= (36 \times \$51.48) - (\$1,500 - 100)$$
$$= \$1,853.28 - 1,400$$
$$= \$453.28$$

Finance charge rebate:

$$\text{Finance charge rebate} = \text{total finance charge} \times \frac{\frac{n(n+1)}{2}}{\frac{N(N+1)}{2}}$$

$$= \$453.28 \times \frac{\frac{18(18+1)}{2}}{\frac{36(36+1)}{2}}$$

$$= \$453.28 \times \frac{171}{666}$$

$$= \$116.38$$

Amount necessary to repay the loan in full:
Loan balance = number of payments remaining × monthly payment
$$= 18 \times \$51.48 = \$926.64$$
Amount necessary to repay the loan = loan balance − rebate
$$= \$926.64 - 116.38$$
$$= \$810.26$$

14. Carolyn Ashford bought new dinnerware for $1,224. The department store opened an installment loan account for her, requiring a 10% down payment and 24 equal monthly payments of $53.55 each. Ms. Ashford made the payments for 10 months. She then decided to pay the loan off in full. Find the finance charge rebate and the payoff amount.

Finance charge =
(number of payments × amount of each payment) − amount financed
$$= (24 \times \$53.55) - (\$1,224 - 122.40)$$
$$= \$1,285.20 - 1,101.60$$
$$= \$183.60$$

Finance charge rebate:

$$\text{Finance charge rebate} = \text{total finance charge} \times \frac{\frac{n(n+1)}{2}}{\frac{N(N+1)}{2}}$$

24 mos. − 10 mos. = 14 mos.

$$= \$183.60 \times \frac{\frac{14(14+1)}{2}}{\frac{24(24+1)}{2}}$$

$$= \$183.60 \times \frac{105}{300}$$

$$= \$64.26$$

Amount necessary to repay the loan in full:
Loan balance = number of payments remaining × monthly payment
$$= 14 \times \$53.55 = \$749.70$$
Amount necessary to repay the loan = loan balance − rebate
$$= \$749.70 - 64.26$$
$$= \$685.44$$

15. Debbie Dorris bought a $2,569 racing bicycle. She paid $100 down and financed the remainder for two and a half years, making monthly payments of $101.43. With nine payments remaining, Debbie decides to pay the bicycle off. Calculate the finance charge rebate and the payoff amount.

Finance charge =
(number of payments × amount of each payment) − amount financed
$$= (30 \times \$101.43) - (\$2,569 - 100)$$
$$= \$3,042.90 - 2,469$$
$$= \$573.90$$

Finance charge rebate:

$$\text{Finance charge rebate} = \text{total finance charge} \times \frac{\frac{n(n+1)}{2}}{\frac{N(N+1)}{2}}$$

$$= \$573.90 \times \frac{\frac{9(9+1)}{2}}{\frac{30(30+1)}{2}}$$

$$= \$573.90 \times \frac{45}{465}$$

$$= \$55.54$$

Amount necessary to repay the loan in full:
Loan balance = number of payments remaining × monthly payment
$$= 9 \times \$101.43$$
$$= \$912.87$$
Amount necessary to repay the loan = loan balance − rebate
$$= \$912.87 - 55.54$$
$$= \$857.33$$

12.4

Calculate the finance charge and the balance at the end of each month using the unpaid balance method for the following problems.

16. Robin Fritzzerd's charge card had a $448.50 balance at the end of April. The bank's charge for its credit card use is 1.3% per month on the unpaid balance. Following is a summary of the transactions for May and June:

	Total Purchases	Returns	Payments
May	$ 203.01	$ 43.28	$ 100.00
June	385.72		75.00

Calculate the balance at the end of each month.

May:
  Finance charge: $448.50 × 1.3% = $5.83
  Unpaid balance: $448.50 + 5.83 + 203.01 − 43.28 − 100 = $514.06
June:
  Finance charge: $514.06 × 1.3% = $6.68
  Unpaid balance: $514.06 + 6.68 + 385.72 − 75 = $831.46

Month	Unpaid Balance at Beginning of Month	Finance Charge	Purchases During Month	Returns	Payments	Unpaid Balance at End of Month
May	$ 448.50	$ 5.83	$203.01	$ 43.28	$100.00	$ 514.06
June	514.06	6.68	385.72		75.00	831.46

17. Mealea Duong's charge card had a $2,333.40 balance at the end of March. The bank's charge for its credit card use is 1.75% per month on the unpaid balance. Following is a summary of the transactions for April, May, and June:

	Total Purchases	Returns	Payments
April	$ 94.29	$	$ 50.00
May	293.47	34.92	100.00
June	58.89		150.00

Calculate the balance at the end of each month.

Month	Unpaid Balance at Beginning of Month	Finance Charge	Purchases During Month	Returns	Payments	Unpaid Balance at End of Month
April	$2,333.40	$ 40.83	$ 94.29	$	$ 50.00	$2,418.52
May	2,418.52	42.32	293.47	34.92	100.00	2,619.39
June	2,619.39	45.84	58.89		150.00	2,574.12

April:
  Finance charge: $2,333.40 × 1.75% = $40.83
  Unpaid balance: $2,333.40 + 40.83 + 94.29 − 50 = $2,418.52
May:
  Finance charge: $2,418.52 × 1.75% = $42.32
  Unpaid balance: $2,418.52 + 42.32 + 293.47 − 34.92 − 100 = $2,619.39
June:
  Finance charge: $2,619.39 × 1.75% = $45.84
  Unpaid balance: $2,619.39 + 45.84 + 58.89 − 150 = $2,574.12

18. Altagarcia Grajeda's charge card had a $230.55 balance at the end of September. The bank's charge for its credit card use is 1.5% per month on the unpaid balance. Following is a summary of the transactions for October, November, and December:

	Total Purchases	Returns	Payments
October	$ 29.54	$ 29.93	$ 50.00
November	385.49		150.00
December	80.38	2.34	100.00

Calculate the balance at the end of each month.

October:
  Finance charge: $230.55 × 1.5% = $3.46
  Unpaid balance: $230.55 + 3.46 + 29.54 − 29.93 − 50 = $183.62
November:
  Finance charge: $183.62 × 1.5% = $2.75
  Unpaid balance: $183.62 + 2.75 + 385.49 − 150 = $421.86
December:
  Finance charge: $421.86 × 1.5% = $6.33
  Unpaid balance: $421.86 + 6.33 + 80.38 − 2.34 − 100 = $406.23

Month	Unpaid Balance at Beginning of Month	Finance Charge	Purchases During Month	Returns	Payments	Unpaid Balance at End of Month
October	$230.55	$3.46	$ 29.54	$29.93	$ 50.00	$ 183.62
November	183.62	2.75	385.49		150.00	421.86
December	421.86	6.33	80.38	2.34	100.00	406.23

19. Roy Heinecke's charge card had a $5,875.42 balance at the end of February. The bank's charge for its credit card use is 1.8% per month on the unpaid balance. Following is a summary of the transactions for March and April:

	Total Purchases	Returns	Payments
March	$ 301.20	$ 52.38	$ 320.00
April	378.29		225.00

Calculate the balance at the end of each month

March:
Finance charge: $5,875.42 × 1.8%
= $105.76
Unpaid balance: $5,875.42 + 105.76
+ 301.20 − 52.38 − 320 = $5,910
April:
Finance charge: $5,910 × 1.8% =
$106.38
Unpaid balance: $5,910 + 106.38
+ 378.29 − 225 = $6,169.67

Month	Unpaid Balance at Beginning of Month	Finance Charge	Purchases During Month	Returns	Payments	Unpaid Balance at End of Month
March	$5,875.42	$105.76	$301.20	$52.38	$320.00	$5,910.00
April	5,910.00	106.38	378.29		225.00	6,169.67

20. Gary House's charge card had a $123.67 balance at the end of June. The bank's charge for its credit card use is 1.15% per month on the unpaid balance. Following is a summary of the transactions for July and August:

	Total Purchases	Returns	Payments
July	$383.06		$123.67
August	348.58	$39.30	250.00

Calculate the balance at the end of each month.

July:
Finance charge: $123.67 × 1.15% =
$1.42
Unpaid balance: $123.67 + 1.42
+ 383.06 − 123.67 = $384.48
August:
Finance charge: $384.48 × 1.15% =
$4.42
Unpaid balance: $384.48 + 4.42
+ 348.58 − 39.50 − 250 = $448.18

Month	Unpaid Balance at Beginning of Month	Finance Charge	Purchases During Month	Returns	Payments	Unpaid Balance at End of Month
July	$123.67	$1.42	$383.06	$	$123.67	$384.48
August	384.48	4.42	348.58	39.30	250.00	448.18

12.5

Calculate the billing cycle finance charge for the following installment credit accounts using the average daily balance method:

21. Morgan Heffer had an ending balance of $395.58 at the end of her last billing cycle on March 8. Her bank charge card's monthly finance rate was 1.6%. If, during the next billing cycle, the following transactions take place, fill in the following table:

Date	Description	Transaction Amount	Unpaid Balance	Number of Days Before Balance Changes	Extended Balance
March 8	Billing date		$395.58	× 2 =	$ 791.16
March 10	Purchase	$75.35	470.93	× 7 =	3,296.51
March 17	Payment	50.00	420.93	× 4 =	1,683.72
March 21	Purchase	26.72	447.65	× 18 =	8,057.70
April 8	Billing date				
	Totals			31	$13,829.09

Average daily balance = $13,829.09 ÷ 31 = $446.10
Finance charge for billing cycle = $446.10 × 1.6% = $7.14

22. Jason Johnson had an ending balance of $2,239.75 at the end of his last billing cycle on April 10. His bank charge card's monthly finance rate was 1.25%. If, during the next billing cycle, the following transactions take place, fill in the following table:

Date	Description	Transaction Amount	Unpaid Balance	Number of Days Before Balance Changes	Extended Balance
April 10	Billing date		$2,239.75	× 2 =	$ 4,479.50
April 12	Purchase	$395.64	2,635.39	× 21 =	55,343.19
May 3	Cash Advance	500.00	3,135.39	× 2 =	6,270.78
May 5	Purchase	49.14	3,184.53	× 4 =	12,738.12
May 9	Payment	350.00	2,834.53	× 1 =	2,834.53
May 10	Billing date				
			Totals	30	$81,666.12

Average daily balance = $81,666.12 ÷ 30 = $2,722.20
Finance charge for billing cycle = $2,722.20 × 1.25% = $34.03

23. Antonio Hinojosa had an ending balance of $491.03 at the end of his last billing cycle on May 4. His bank charge card's monthly finance rate was 1.45%. If, during the next billing cycle, the following transactions take place, fill in the following table:

Date	Description	Transaction Amount	Unpaid Balance	Number of Days Before Balance Changes	Extended Balance
May 4	Billing date		$ 491.03	× 4 =	$1,964.12
May 8	Purchase	$ 39.47	530.50	× 9 =	4,774.50
May 17	Purchase	292.40	822.90	× 6 =	4,937.40
May 23	Payment	50.00	772.90	× 7 =	5,410.30
May 30	Purchase	233.86	1,006.76	× 5 =	5,033.80
June 4	Billing date				
			Totals	31	$22,120.12

Average daily balance = $22,120.12 ÷ 31 = $713.55
Finance charge for billing cycle = $713.55 × 1.45% = $10.35

24. Zack Hurt had an ending balance of $86.96 at the end of his last billing cycle on January 20. His bank charge card's monthly finance rate was 1.0%. If, during the next billing cycle, the following transactions take place, fill in the following table:

Date	Description	Transaction Amount	Unpaid Balance	Number of Days Before Balance Changes	Extended Balance
Jan. 20	Billing date		$ 86.96	× 6 =	$ 521.76
Jan. 26	Payment	$ 50.00	36.96	× 4 =	147.84
Jan. 30	Cash advance	150.00	186.96	× 12 =	2,243.52
Feb. 11	Payment	100.00	86.96	× 2 =	173.92
Feb. 13	Purchase	99.15	186.11	× 7 =	1,302.77
Feb. 20	Billing date				
			Totals	31	$4,389.81

Average daily balance = $ 4,389.81 ÷ 31 = ÷ $141.61
Finance charge for billing cycle = $ 141.61 × 1.0% = $1.42

25. Harold Klotz had an ending balance of $1,861.72 at the end of his last billing cycle on October 5. His bank charge card's monthly finance rate was 0.875%. If, during the next billing cycle, the following transactions take place, fill in the following table:

Date	Description	Transaction Amount	Unpaid Balance	Number of Days Before Balance Changes	Extended Balance
Oct. 5	Billing date		$1,861.72	× 17 =	$31,649.24
Oct. 22	Purchase	$218.49	2,080.21	× 1 =	2,080.21
Oct. 23	Payment	125.00	1,955.21	× 4 =	7,820.84
Oct. 27	Cash advance	350.00	2,305.21	× 4 =	9,220.84
Oct. 31	Purchase	14.86	2,320.07	× 5 =	11,600.35
Nov. 5	Billing date				
			Totals	31	$62,371.48

Average daily balance = $62,371.48 ÷ 31 = $2,011.98

Finance charge for billing cycle = $2,011.98 × 0.875% = $17.60

CHAPTER REVIEW PROBLEMS

Answers to odd-numbered problems are given in Appendix A.

Drill Problems

Use the formula to estimate the APR for problems 1 through 5 (round to the nearest tenth of a percent).

	Cash Price	Down Payment	Payment Frequency	Payments Made for	Payment Amount	Amount Financed	Finance Charge	APR
1.	$1,058	$150	Monthly	2 yrs.	$43.35	$ 908.00	$132.40	14.0%
2.	$ 950	$ 95	Monthly	1 yr.	$79.35	$ 855.00	$ 97.20	21.0%
3.	$2,250	$250	Monthly	30 mos.	$82.17	$2,000.00	$465.10	18.0%
4.	$ 395	$ 25	Weekly	26 wks.	$15.32	$ 370.00	$ 28.32	29.5%
5.	$5,000	$500	Monthly	5 yrs.	$90.06	$4,500.00	$903.60	7.9%

Use Table 12.1 to find the APR to the nearest 1/4% in problems 6 through 10.

	Cash Price	Down Payment	Payment Frequency	Payments Made for	Payment Amount	Amount Financed	Finance Charge	APR
6.	$ 3,283	$ 328	Monthly	2 yrs.	$141.23	$ 2,955.00	$ 434.52	13.50%
7.	$ 495	$ 145	Monthly	10 mos.	$ 36.95	$ 350.00	$ 19.50	12.00%
8.	$12,356	$1,500	Monthly	3.5 yrs.	$308.70	$10,856.00	$2,109.40	10.25%
9.	$ 775	$ 125	Monthly	1 yr.	$ 58.28	$ 650.00	$ 49.36	13.75%
10.	$ 1,000	$ 100	Monthly	18 mos.	$ 54.68	$ 900.00	$ 84.24	11.50%

Find the finance charge rebate and the amount necessary to repay the loan in the following problems:

	Cash Price	Down Payment	Payment Frequency	Payments Made for	Payment Amount	Payments Remaining When Loan is Repaid
11.	$10,000	$3,000	Monthly	5 yrs.	$147.80	20
12.	$ 402	$ 82	Monthly	6 mos.	$ 55.65	3
13.	$ 947	$ 47	Monthly	15 mos.	$ 65.16	8
14.	$ 5,950	$ 600	Monthly	3 yrs.	$171.29	12
15.	$ 1,900	$ 150	Monthly	18 mos.	$111.08	10

	Amount Financed	Finance Charge	$\frac{n(n+1)}{2}$	$\frac{N(N+1)}{2}$	Amount of Rebate	Amount Required to Pay Loan Off
11.	$7,000	$1,868.00	210	1,830	$214.36	$2,741.64
12.	$ 320	$ 13.90	6	21	$ 3.97	162.98
13.	$ 900	$ 77.40	36	120	$ 23.22	498.06
14.	$5,350	$ 816.44	78	666	$ 95.62	1,959.86
15.	$1,750	$ 249.44	55	171	$ 80.23	1,030.57

Calculate the finance charge and the balance at the end of each month using the unpaid balance method for problems 16 through 20 (the monthly finance rate is in parentheses above the Finance Charge in the table).

16.

Month	Unpaid Balance at Beginning of Month	(1.6%) Finance Charge	Purchases During Month	Returns	Payments	Unpaid Balance at End of Month
February	$692.97	$11.09	$119.45	$	$100.00	$723.51
March	723.51	11.58	22.01	18.54	100.00	638.56
April	638.56	10.22	309.78		100.00	858.56

17.

Month	Unpaid Balance at Beginning of Month	(1.5%) Finance Charge	Purchases During Month	Returns	Payments	Unpaid Balance at End of Month
May	$ 119.58	$ 1.79	$1,967.49	$	$119.58	$1,969.28
June	1,969.28	29.54	410.38		300.00	2,109.20
July	2,109.20	31.64	299.54		250.00	2,190.38

18.

Month	Unpaid Balance at Beginning of Month	(1.25%) Finance Charge	Purchases During Month	Returns	Payments	Unpaid Balance at End of Month
February	$395.68	$4.95	$295.23	$18.39	$50.00	$627.47
March	627.47	7.84	29.29	4.10	50.00	610.50
April	610.50	7.63	201.58		75.00	744.71

19.

Month	Unpaid Balance at Beginning of Month	(1.8%) Finance Charge	Purchases During Month	Returns	Payments	Unpaid Balance at End of Month
February	$1,934.78	$34.83	$229.12	$	$450.00	$1,748.73
March	1,748.73	31.48	123.78	284.03	300.00	1,319.96
April	1,319.96	23.76	289.10	24.59	500.00	1,108.23

20.

Month	Unpaid Balance at Beginning of Month	(1.4%) Finance Charge	Purchases During Month	Returns	Payments	Unpaid Balance at End of Month
February	$ 293.59	$ 4.11	$932.48	$	$200.00	$1,030.18
March	1,030.18	14.42	191.49		300.00	936.09
April	936.09	13.11	129.39	44.95	250.00	783.64

Calculate the billing cycle finance charge for the installment credit accounts using the average daily balance method for problems 21 through 25.

21.

Date	Description	Transaction Amount	Unpaid Balance	Number of Days Before Balance Changes	Extended Balance
Jan. 3	Billing date		$ 402.59	× 5	$ 2,012.95
Jan. 8	Payment	$ 50.00	352.59	× 9	3,173.31
Jan. 17	Purchase	302.95	655.54	× 2	1,311.08
Jan. 19	Purchase	48.58	704.12	× 12	8,449.44
Jan. 31	Purchase	387.34	1,091.46	× 3	3,274.38
Feb. 3	Billing date				
			Totals	31	$18,221.16

Average daily balance = $18,221.16 ÷ 31 = $ 587.78
Finance charge for billing cycle = $ 587.78 × 1.5% = $ 8.82

22.

Date	Description	Transaction Amount	Unpaid Balance	Number of Days Before Balance Changes	Extended Balance
June 6	Billing date		$494.57	× 4	$ 1,978.28
June 10	Payment	$300.00	194.57	× 10	1,945.70
June 20	Purchase	329.62	524.19	× 10	5,241.90
June 30	Purchase	303.67	827.86	× 3	2,483.58
July 3	Cash advance	48.30	876.16	× 3	2,628.48
July 6	Billing date				
			Totals	30	$14,277.94

Average daily balance = $14,277.94 ÷ 30 = $ 475.93

Finance charge for billing cycle = $ 475.93 × 1.8% = $ 8.57

23.

Date	Description	Transaction Amount	Unpaid Balance	Number of Days Before Balance Changes	Extended Balance
Apr. 1	Billing date		$3,268.00	× 1	$ 3,268.00
Apr. 2	Purchase	$750.00	4,018.00	× 6	24,108.00
Apr. 8	Purchase	39.68	4,057.68	× 20	81,153.60
Apr. 28	Payment	550.00	3,507.68	× 2	7,015.36
Apr. 30	Purchase	491.30	3,998.98	× 1	3,998.98
May 1	Billing date				
			Totals	30	$119,543.94

Average daily balance = $119,543.94 ÷ 30 = $ 3,984.80

Finance charge for billing cycle = $3,984.80 × 1.25% = $ 49.81

24.

Date	Description	Transaction Amount	Unpaid Balance	Number of Days Before Balance Changes	Extended Balance
Aug. 5	Billing date		$494.17	× 7	$ 3,459.19
Aug. 12	Payment	$ 50.00	444.17	× 10	4,441.70
Aug. 22	Purchase	34.02	478.19	× 4	1,912.76
Aug. 26	Purchase	204.98	683.17	× 2	1,366.34
Aug. 28	Purchase	22.58	705.75	× 8	5,646.00
Sept. 5	Billing date				
			Totals	31	$16,825.99

Average daily balance = $ 16,825.99 ÷ 31 = $ 542.77

Finance charge for billing cycle = $ 542.77 × 1.4% = $ 7.60

25.

Date	Description	Transaction Amount	Unpaid Balance	Number of Days Before Balance Changes	Extended Balance
Apr. 5	Billing date		$ 349.84	× 17	$ 5,947.28
Apr. 22	Cash advance	$ 250.00	599.84	× 3	1,799.52
Apr. 25	Purchase	199.43	799.27	× 5	3,996.35
Apr. 30	Purchase	3,485.84	4,285.11	× 4	17,140.44
May 4	Payment	600.00	3,685.11	× 1	3,685.11
May 5	Billing date				
		Totals		30	$32,568.70

Average daily balance = $ 32,568.70 ÷ 30 = $ 1,085.62
Finance charge for billing cycle = $1,085.62 × 1.125% = $ 12.21

Word Problems

26. Find the APR using both the table and the formula for a consumer who bought merchandise priced at $5,395. Sales tax is an additional 7.3%. A down payment of 10% of the total price plus tax is required. The remainder will be financed by paying $175.55 monthly for three years. (Round your answer to the nearest 1/4%.)

$5,395 × 7.3% = $ 393.84   Sales tax $5,788.84   Total
 + 5,395.00   Merchandise   × 10%   Down payment %
 $5,788.84   Total charge $ 578.88   Down payment

$5,788.84 − 578.88 = $5,209.96   Amount financed

($175.55 × 36)   −   5,209.96   = $1,109.84
Total payment amount   Amount financed   Finance charge

$$\text{APR} = \frac{2 \times \text{number of payment periods in 1 year} \times \text{finance charge}}{\text{amount financed} \times (\text{total number of payments} + 1)}$$

$$\text{APR} = \frac{2 \times 12 \times \$1,109.84}{\$5,209.96 (36 + 1)}$$

$\phantom{\text{APR}}$ = 13.75%   (rounded to nearest 1/4%)

$$\text{Table factor} = \frac{\text{finance charge} \times \$100}{\text{amount financed}}$$

$$= \frac{\$1,109.84 \times 100}{\$5,209.96}$$

 = 21.30 (rounded to the nearest hundredth)

21.30 from table is 13.00% APR.

27. Red Johnson purchased a motorboat for $4,300. He paid $300 down and agreed to repay the remainder in monthly installments of $200.80 for 24 months. With 10 payments remaining, Red decides to pay the loan off in full. Find the amount of the finance charge rebate and the amount necessary to repay the loan in full.

Finance charge =
(number of payments × amount of each payment) − amount financed
 = (24 × $200.80) − ($4,300 − 300)
 = $4,819.20 − 4,000
 = $819.20

Finance charge rebate:

$$\text{Finance charge rebate} = \text{total finance charge} \times \frac{\frac{n(n + 1)}{2}}{\frac{N(N + 1)}{2}}$$

$$= \$819.20 \times \frac{\frac{10(10 + 1)}{2}}{\frac{24(24 + 1)}{2}}$$

$$= \$819.20 \times \frac{55}{300}$$

 = $150.19

Amount necessary to repay the loan in full:
Loan balance = number of payments remaining × monthly payment
 = 10 × $200.80
 = $2,008

Amount necessary to repay the loan = loan balance − rebate
 = $2,008 − 150.19
 = $1,857.81

28. Priscilla Preistly's charge card had a $591.60 balance at the end of December. The bank's charge for its credit card use is 1.2% per month on the unpaid balance. Following is a summary of the transactions for January, February, and March:

	Total Purchases	Returns	Payments
January	$284.95	$22.49	$150.00
February	333.13	83.58	150.00
March	73.20		75.00

Calculate the balance at the end of each month.

Month	Unpaid Balance at Beginning of Month	(1.2%) Finance Charge	Purchases During Month	Returns	Payments	Unpaid Balance at End of Month
January	$591.60	$7.10	$284.95	$22.49	$150.00	$711.16
February	711.16	8.53	333.13	83.58	150.00	819.24
March	819.24	9.83	73.20		75.00	827.27

29. Noel Repaldo had an ending balance of $630.58 at the end of his last billing cycle on September 12. His bank charge card's monthly finance rate was 0.85%. During the next billing cycle, the following transactions took place:

Date	Description	Transaction Amount	Unpaid Balance
September 12	Billing date		$630.58
September 15	Purchase	$573.29	
September 26	Payment	400.00	
September 27	Purchase	110.45	
September 30	Returns	22.06	
October 5	Cash advance	200.00	
October 12	Billing date		

Calculate his finance charge for the cycle using the average daily balance method.

Unpaid Balance	Number of Days Before Balance Changes	Extended Balance
$ 630.58	× 3	$ 1,891.74
1,203.87	× 11	13,242.57
803.87	× 1	803.87
914.32	× 3	2,742.96
892.26	× 5	4,461.30
1,092.26	× 7	7,645.82
Totals	30	$30,788.26

Average daily balance = $30,788.26 ÷ 30 = $1,026.28

Finance charge for billing cycle = $1,026.28 × .85% = $8.72

30. Susan Williams had a swimming pool built on her property for $7,800. She made a down payment of $300 and financed the rest for payments of $286.20 per month for 30 months. Find the APR using both the formula and the table (round both to the nearest 1/4 %).

$7,800
− 300
$7,500   Amount financed

($286.20 × 30) − 7,500 = $1,086

Total payment amount   Amount financed   Finance charge

$$APR = \frac{2 \times \text{number of payment periods in 1 year} \times \text{finance charge}}{\text{amount financed} \times (\text{total number of payments} + 1)}$$

$$APR = \frac{2 \times 12 \times \$1,086}{\$7,500 (30 + 1)}$$

= 11.25% (rounded to nearest 1/4%)

$$\text{Table factor} = \frac{\text{finance charge} \times \$100}{\text{amount financed}}$$

$$= \frac{\$1,086 \times 100}{\$7,500}$$

= 14.48   (rounded to the nearest hundredth)

14.48 from table is 10.75% APR

31. Benito Martinez's charge card had a $295.07 balance at the end of March. The bank's charge for its credit card use is 0.825% per month on the unpaid balance. Following is a summary of the transactions for April, May, and June:

	Total Purchases	Returns	Payments
April	$ 47.57		$50.00
May	77.25	$13.56	50.00
June	192.74		50.00

Calculate the balance at the end of each month.

Month	Unpaid Balance at Beginning of Month	(.825%) Finance Charge	Purchases During Month	Returns	Payments	Unpaid Balance at End of Month
April	$295.07	$2.43	$ 47.57		$50.00	$295.07
May	295.07	2.43	77.25	$13.56	50.00	311.19
June	311.19	2.57	192.74		50.00	456.50

32. Lanna Ngurski had an ending balance of $473.11 at the end of his last billing cycle on June 2. His bank charge card's monthly finance rate was 1.35%. During the next billing cycle, the following transactions took place:

Date	Description	Transaction Amount	Unpaid Balance
June 2	Billing date		$473.11
June 8	Purchase	$ 39.72	
June 12	Purchase	91.35	
June 25	Cash advance	250.00	
June 27	Payment	75.00	
July 1	Purchases	30.67	
July 2	Billing date		

Calculate his finance charge for the cycle using the average daily balance method.

Unpaid Balance	Number of Days Before Balance Changes	Extended Balance
$473.11	× 6	$ 2,838.66
512.83	× 4	2,051.32
604.18	× 13	7,854.34
854.18	× 2	1,708.36
779.18	× 4	3,116.72
809.85	× 1	809.85
Totals	30	$18,379.25

Average daily balance = $18,379.25 ÷ 30 = $612.64
Finance charge for billing cycle = $ 612.64 × 1.35% = $8.27

33. Mary Urestes and an automobile dealer have agreed on a negotiated price of $24,385 for a Buick that Mary wants to buy. Taxes will be an additional 5.5%, the title fee is $50, and the license fee is $112, all of which will also be financed. She has accepted the dealer's offer for a $4,850 trade-in on her old car that will be used for the down payment. The finance terms are for $452.18 per month for five years. Find the APR using both the formula and the table (round both to the nearest 1/4%).

$24,385 × 5.5% = $ 1,341.18 Taxes $25,888.18 Total
        24,385.00 Buick price   − 4,850.00 Down payment
            50.00 Title fee $21,038.18 Amount financed
        + 112.00 License
        $25,888.18 Total

$452.18 × 60 = $27,130.80   Total payment

$27,130.80   −   21,038.18   = $6,092.62
Total payment amount   Amount financed   Finance charge

$$\text{APR} = \frac{2 \times \text{number of payment periods in 1 year} \times \text{finance charge}}{\text{amount financed} \times (\text{total number of payments} + 1)}$$

$$\text{APR} = \frac{2 \times 12 \times \$6,092.62}{\$21,038.18 \,(60 + 1)}$$

= 11.50% (rounded to nearest 1/4%)

$$\text{Table factor} = \frac{\text{finance charge} \times \$100}{\text{amount financed}}$$

$$= \frac{\$6,092.62 \times 100}{\$21,038.18}$$

= 28.96   (rounded to the nearest hundredth)

28.96 from table is 10.50% APR.

34. Yul Bernstein paid $1,000 down and financed the balance of the $10,000 price for a used sports car by agreeing to make monthly payments of $294.65 for three years. Find the APR using both the formula and the table (round both to the nearest 1/4%). With 15 payments remaining, Yul has decided to pay the loan off in full. Find the amount of the finance charge rebate and the amount necessary to repay the loan in full.

$294.65 × 36 = $10,607.40   Total payment

$10,607.40   −   ($10,000 − 1,000)   = $1,607.40
Total payment amount   Amount financed   Finance charge

$$\text{APR} = \frac{2 \times \text{number of payment periods in 1 year} \times \text{finance charge}}{\text{amount financed} \times (\text{total number of payments} + 1)}$$

$$\text{APR} = \frac{2 \times 12 \times \$1,607.40}{\$9,000 \,(36 + 1)}$$

= 11.50% rounded to nearest 1/4%)

$$\text{Table factor} = \frac{\text{finance charge} \times \$100}{\text{amount financed}}$$

$$= \frac{\$1,607.40 \times 100}{\$9,000}$$

= 17.86   (rounded to the nearest hundredth)

17.86 from table is 11.00% APR.

Finance charge rebate:

$$\text{Finance charge rebate} = \text{Total finance charge} \times \frac{\dfrac{n(n + 1)}{2}}{\dfrac{N(N + 1)}{2}}$$

$$= \$1,607.40 \times \frac{\dfrac{15(15 + 1)}{2}}{\dfrac{36(36 + 1)}{2}}$$

$$= \$1,607.40 \times \frac{120}{666}$$

$$= \$289.62$$

Amount necessary to repay the loan in full:
Loan balance = number of payments remaining × monthly payment
        = 15 × $294.65
        = $4,419.75
Amount necessary to repay the loan = loan balance − rebate
        = $4,419.75 − 289.62
        = $4,130.13

CRITICAL THINKING GROUP PROJECT

As a fringe benefit, Frank Younger and Associates provides its president with a new automobile every three years and its three vice presidents with a new automobile every five years. The successful bid for this year's purchases came from the fleet manager at Ito's Toyota/Lexus Autoland. The president's new automobile will be a Lexus, priced at $44,500. The vice presidents will receive identical Avalons, each priced at $28,750. Tax, title, and license will also be financed. For each automobile, taxes will be an additional 6.2%, and the title fee is $50. The license fee is $173 for the Lexus and $146 for each of the Avalons.

Ito's will accept the present automobiles as a down payment. The three-year-old Cadillac Frank Younger has been driving has a trade-in value of $12,900. The vice presidents' automobiles have the following trade-in values:

Wilma Feinstein, VP of Finance, a Buick Roadmaster $8,200

Jesus Fernandez, VP of Marketing, a Dodge Intrepid $9,150

Marilu McGregor, VP of Human Resources, a Mercury Cougar $5,700

The Toyota Motor Credit Corporation will finance all of the automobiles at an annual percentage rate of 10.5%. Each automobile will be financed for the number of years it is expected to be used in the business.

1. Find the total amount to be financed for each of the automobiles.

Frank Younger's Lexus:

$44,500	$44,500	$47,482
× 6.2%	2,759	− 12,900
$ 2,759	50	$34,582 Amount to be financed
	+ 173	
	$47,482	

Wilma Feinstein's Avalon:

$28,750.00	$28,750.00	$30,728.50
× 6.2%	1,782.50	− 8,200.00
$ 1,782.50	50.00	$22,528.50
	146.00	
	$30,728.50	

Jesus Fernandez's Avalon: $30,728.50   Marilu McGregor's Avalon: $30,728.50
                          − 9,150.00   − 5,700.00
                          $21,578.50 $25,028.50

2. Find the monthly payment amount for each of the automobiles. (*Hint:* Use the table factor found at the proper intersection of rate and time. Then, solve for the finance charge in the formula. Add the finance charge and the amount financed. Lastly, find the monthly payment by dividing the total payment by the number of months over which financing has been arranged.)

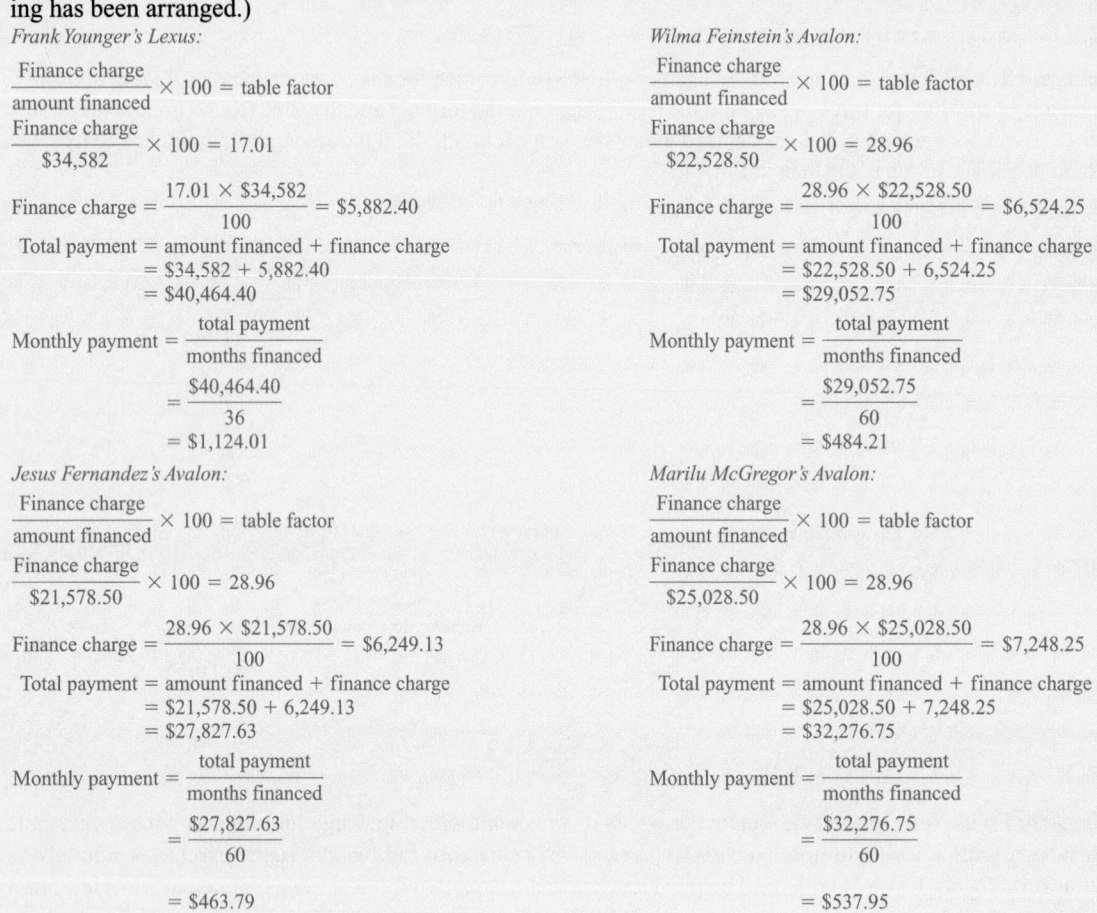

Frank Younger's Lexus:

$$\frac{\text{Finance charge}}{\text{amount financed}} \times 100 = \text{table factor}$$

$$\frac{\text{Finance charge}}{\$34,582} \times 100 = 17.01$$

$$\text{Finance charge} = \frac{17.01 \times \$34,582}{100} = \$5,882.40$$

Total payment = amount financed + finance charge
            = $34,582 + 5,882.40
            = $40,464.40

$$\text{Monthly payment} = \frac{\text{total payment}}{\text{months financed}}$$

$$= \frac{\$40,464.40}{36}$$

$$= \$1,124.01$$

Wilma Feinstein's Avalon:

$$\frac{\text{Finance charge}}{\text{amount financed}} \times 100 = \text{table factor}$$

$$\frac{\text{Finance charge}}{\$22,528.50} \times 100 = 28.96$$

$$\text{Finance charge} = \frac{28.96 \times \$22,528.50}{100} = \$6,524.25$$

Total payment = amount financed + finance charge
            = $22,528.50 + 6,524.25
            = $29,052.75

$$\text{Monthly payment} = \frac{\text{total payment}}{\text{months financed}}$$

$$= \frac{\$29,052.75}{60}$$

$$= \$484.21$$

Jesus Fernandez's Avalon:

$$\frac{\text{Finance charge}}{\text{amount financed}} \times 100 = \text{table factor}$$

$$\frac{\text{Finance charge}}{\$21,578.50} \times 100 = 28.96$$

$$\text{Finance charge} = \frac{28.96 \times \$21,578.50}{100} = \$6,249.13$$

Total payment = amount financed + finance charge
            = $21,578.50 + 6,249.13
            = $27,827.63

$$\text{Monthly payment} = \frac{\text{total payment}}{\text{months financed}}$$

$$= \frac{\$27,827.63}{60}$$

$$= \$463.79$$

Marilu McGregor's Avalon:

$$\frac{\text{Finance charge}}{\text{amount financed}} \times 100 = \text{table factor}$$

$$\frac{\text{Finance charge}}{\$25,028.50} \times 100 = 28.96$$

$$\text{Finance charge} = \frac{28.96 \times \$25,028.50}{100} = \$7,248.25$$

Total payment = amount financed + finance charge
            = $25,028.50 + 7,248.25
            = $32,276.75

$$\text{Monthly payment} = \frac{\text{total payment}}{\text{months financed}}$$

$$= \frac{\$32,276.75}{60}$$

$$= \$537.95$$

SELF-TESTING EXERCISES	*Answers to all exercises are given in Appendix A.*

1. Explain the Rule of 78.

The Rule of 78 is a method used to calculate the finance charge rebate and the amount required to pay a loan off early. It is called the Rule of 78 because the sum of the years' digits for one year (1 + 2 + 3 + . . . + 11 + 12) totals 78.

2. Several methods of extending credit exist. What is open-end credit?

When open-end credit is being used, several loans or merchandise charges may be made before any one of them is paid off. No fixed number of payments is established. It may never be paid off.

Use the following information to solve problems 3, 4, and 5:

George Ripley bought roofing materials that had a cash price of $3,950. He paid $250 down and financed the remainder, agreeing to make monthly payments of $227.37 for 18 months.

3. Use the formula to estimate the APR (to the nearest 1/4%).

$227.37 \times 18 = \$4,092.66$ Total payment

$$\underset{\text{Total payment amount}}{\$4,092.66} - \underset{\text{Amount financed}}{(\$3,950 - 250)} = \underset{\text{Finance charge}}{\$392.66}$$

$$\text{APR} = \frac{2 \times \text{number of payment periods in 1 year} \times \text{Finance charge}}{\text{amount financed} \times (\text{total number of payments} + 1)}$$

$$\text{APR} = \frac{2 \times 12 \times \$392.66}{\$3,700 \, (18 + 1)}$$

$= 13.50\%$ (rounded to nearest 1/4%)

4. Use Table 12.1 to find the APR (to the nearest 1/4%).

$$\text{Table factor} = \frac{\text{finance charge} \times \$100}{\text{amount financed}}$$

$$= \frac{\$392.66 \times 100}{\$3,700}$$

$= 10.61$ (rounded to the nearest hundredth)

10.61 from table is 13.00% APR.

5. With nine payments remaining, George has decided to pay the loan off in full. Find the amount of the finance charge rebate and the amount necessary to repay the loan in full.

Finance charge rebate:

$$\text{Finance charge rebate} = \text{total finance charge} \times \frac{\dfrac{n(n+1)}{2}}{\dfrac{N(N+1)}{2}}$$

$$= \$392.66 \times \frac{\dfrac{9(9+1)}{2}}{\dfrac{18(18+1)}{2}}$$

$$= \$392.66 \times \frac{45}{171}$$

$$= \$103.33$$

Amount necessary to repay the loan in full:

Loan balance = number of payments remaining × monthly payment

$= 9 \times \$227.37$

$= \$2,046.33$

Amount necessary to repay the loan = loan balance − rebate

$= \$2,046.33 - 103.33$

$= \$1,943$

6. Pamello Cellard's charge card had a $1,568.91 balance at the end of February. The bank's charge for its credit card use is 1.5% per month on the unpaid balance. Following is a summary of the transactions for March, April, and May:

	Total Purchases	Returns	Payments
March	$394.46		$250.00
April	396.29	$29.49	175.00
May	22.90		400.00

Calculate the balance at the end of each month.

Month	Unpaid Balance at Beginning of Month	(1.5%) Finance Charge	Purchases During Month	Returns	Payments	Unpaid Balance at End of Month
March	$1,568.91	$23.53	$394.46	$	$250.00	$1,736.90
April	1,736.90	26.05	396.29	29.49	175.00	1,954.75
May	1,954.75	29.32	22.90		400.00	1,606.97

7. Marilyn Montgomery had a balance of $306.78 at the end of her last billing cycle on November 18. Her bank charge card's monthly finance rate was 1.15%. During the next billing cycle, the following transactions took place:

Date	Description	Transaction Amount	Unpaid Balance
November 18	Billing date		$306.78
November 19	Purchase	$599.21	
November 22	Purchase	92.45	
November 30	Cash advance	500.00	
December 15	Payment	350.00	
December 16	Purchases	335.36	
December 18	Billing date		

Calculate her finance charge for the cycle using the average daily balance method.

Unpaid Balance	Number of Days Before Balance Changes	Extended Balance
$ 306.78	× 1	$ 306.78
905.99	× 3	2,717.97
998.44	× 8	7,987.52
1,498.44	× 15	22,476.60
1,148.44	× 1	1,148.44
1,483.80	× 2	2,967.60
Totals	30	$37,604.91

Average daily balance = $37,604.91 ÷ 30 = $1,253.50
Finance charge for billing cycle = $1,253.50 × 1.15% = $14.42

Use the following information to solve problems 8, 9, and 10:

Martha Blake bought a riding lawnmower that had a cash price of $2,443. She paid 5% down and financed the remainder, making monthly payments of $111.16 for 24 months.

8. Use the formula to estimate the APR (to the nearest 1/4%).

$111.16 × 24 = $2,667.84   Total payment

$$\begin{array}{cccc}
\$2,667.84 & - & (\$2,443 \times 95\%) & = & \$346.99 \\
\text{Total payment amount} & & \text{Amount financed} & & \text{Finance charge}
\end{array}$$

$$\text{APR} = \frac{2 \times \text{number of payment periods in 1 year} \times \text{finance charge}}{\text{amount financed} \times (\text{total number of payments} + 1)}$$

$$\text{APR} = \frac{2 \times 12 \times \$346.99}{\$2,320.85 (24 + 1)}$$

= 14.25%   (rounded to nearest 1/4%)

9. Use Table 12.1 to find the APR to the nearest 1/4%.

$$\text{Table factor} = \frac{\text{finance charge} \times \$100}{\text{amount financed}}$$

$$= \frac{\$346.99 \times 100}{\$2,320.85}$$

= 14.95   (rounded to the nearest hundredth)

14.95 from table is 13.75% APR.

10. With seven payments remaining, Martha has decided to pay the loan off in full. Find the amount of the finance charge rebate and the amount necessary to repay the loan in full.

Finance charge rebate:

$$\text{Finance charge rebate} = \text{total finance charge} \times \frac{\frac{n(n + 1)}{2}}{\frac{N(N + 1)}{2}}$$

$$= \$346.99 \times \frac{\frac{7(7 + 1)}{2}}{\frac{24(24 + 1)}{2}}$$

$$= \$346.99 \times \frac{28}{300}$$

= $32.39

Amount necessary to repay the loan in full:

Loan balance = number of payments remaining × monthly payment

= 7 × $111.16

= $778.12

Amount necessary to repay the loan = loan balance − rebate

= $778.12 − 32.39

= $745.73

11. Abdul Hameed Karim's charge card had a $438.35 balance at the end of April. The bank's charge for its credit card use is 1.67% per month on the unpaid balance. Following is a summary of the transactions for May, June, and July:

	Total Purchases	Returns	Payments
May	$112.09	$ 12.99	$50.00
June	129.36		50.00
July	382.33	293.25	50.00

Calculate the balance at the end of each month.

Month	Unpaid Balance at Beginning of Month	(1.67%) Finance Charge	Purchases During Month	Returns	Payments	Unpaid Balance at End of Month
March	$438.35	$7.32	$112.09	$ 12.99	$50.00	$494.77
April	494.77	8.26	129.36		50.00	582.39
May	582.39	9.73	382.33	293.25	50.00	631.20

12. Jonathan Kaszynski had a balance of $992.29 at the end of his last billing cycle on July 8. His bank charge card's monthly finance rate was 1.35%. During the next billing cycle, the following transactions took place:

Date	Description	Transaction Amount	Unpaid Balance
July 8	Billing date		$992.29
July 12	Payment	$75.00	
July 13	Purchase	22.84	
July 25	Purchase	56.33	
July 30	Purchase	39.40	
August 4	Cash advance	25.00	
August 8	Billing date		

Calculate his finance charge for the cycle using the average daily balance method.

Unpaid Balance	Number of Days Before Balance Changes	Extended Balance
$ 992.29	× 4	$ 3,969.16
917.29	× 1	917.29
940.13	× 12	11,281.56
996.46	× 5	4,982.30
1,035.86	× 5	5,179.30
1,060.86	× 4	4,243.44
Totals	31	$30,573.05

Average daily balance = $30,573.05 ÷ 31 = $986.23
Finance charge for billing cycle = $986.23 × 1.35% = $13.31

APPLICATION 1

The Springfield Department Store enters customer's charge card transactions on a spreadsheet form. It starts with a billing date balance. When a customer charges merchandise, receives credit for returns, or makes a payment, it is recorded on the form. Springfield's customary annual interest rate is 18.9% on the average daily balance. When you open Ch12App1 on your computer spreadsheet application's disc, the following form will be shown:

Springfield Department Store
2617 Main Street
Box 219
Springfield, Maryland 58109
Telephone: 301-555-2158   FAX: 301-555-3498

CALCULATION OF FINANCE CHARGES USING THE AVERAGE DAILY BALANCE METHOD

DAY IN BILLING CYCLE	TRANSACTION DESCRIPTION	TRANSACTION AMOUNT Debit (+)	Credit (-)	UNPAID BALANCE	DAY IN BILLING CYCLE	TRANSACTION DESCRIPTION	TRANSACTION AMOUNT Debit(+)	Credit (-)	UNPAID BALANCE
1					17				$0.00
2				$0.00	18				$0.00
3				$0.00	19				$0.00
4				$0.00	20				$0.00
5				$0.00	21				$0.00
6				$0.00	22				$0.00
7				$0.00	23				$0.00
8				$0.00	24				$0.00
9				$0.00	25				$0.00
10				$0.00	26				$0.00
11				$0.00	27				$0.00
12				$0.00	28				$0.00
13				$0.00	29				$0.00
14				$0.00	30				$0.00
15				$0.00	31				$0.00
16				$0.00					
				$0.00					$0.00

Total Daily Unpaid Balances in Billing Cycle		$0.00
Days in the Billing Cycle		
Average Daily Balance		#DIV/0!

Annual Interest Rate		
Monthly Interest Rate		0.000%
Total Billing Cycle Finance Charge		#DIV/0!

Enter the following information:

Transaction Description	Cell	Transaction Amount Debit(+)	Credit(−)	Cell	UNPAID Balance	Cell
Billing date	B13				$7,839.57	E13
Purchase	B18	$375.90		C18		
Purchase	B21	$ 44.59		C21		
Purchase	B23	$290.22		C23		
Purchase	B24	$229.18		C24		
Payment	B28		$750	D28		
Purchase	G15	$ 50		H15		
Purchase	G19	$ 32.99		H19		
Purchase	G20	$129.46		H20		
Purchase	G24	$395.75		H24		
Purchase	G26	$ 18.58		H26		

Also, enter 31 in cell E32 and .189 in cell J31.
Answer the following questions after you have completed the spreadsheet:

1. What is the unpaid balance on day 12 of the billing cycle?
2. After the customer made a payment of $750, what is the unpaid balance?
3. What is the unpaid balance at the end of the billing cycle (day 31)?
4. What is the total daily unpaid balances in the billing cycle?
5. What is the average daily balance?
6. What is the monthly interest rate?
7. What is the total billing cycle finance charge?

GROUP REPORT

FOR CHAPTER 12 APPLICATION 1

Frequently, credit cards will be offered to preapproved prospective customers at low introductory rates. Some of Springfield's managers have suggested offering a 6.9% annual introductory rate to a select group of people in the community that have very good credit ratings.

1. Change the annual rate of interest from 18.9% to 6.9%.
2. What would the finance charge savings be to the sample customers' accounts in this application?
3. Write a report to the store manager that discusses the advantages and disadvantages of the introductory offer.

APPLICATION 2

The Springfield Department Store makes installment loans to some of its commercial customers. Several of those customers elect to pay their contracts off early. Springfield uses the Rule of 78 to determine the amount required to repay loans. The rate of interest on installment loans varies according to market fluctuations. When you open Ch12App2, you will see the form shown here:

Springfield Department Store
2617 Main Street
Box 219
Springfield, Maryland 58109
Telephone: 301-555-2158   FAX: 301-555-3498

PAYING LOANS OFF EARLY USING THE RULE OF 78

Installment Loan Amount	Amt. of Each Payment	Total # of Payments for Loan	Total Payment Amount	Total Finance Charge	Number of Payments Remaining	Amount of Rebate	Loan Balance	Amount to Repay Loan
			$0.00	$0.00		#DIV/0!	$0.00	#DIV/0!
			$0.00	$0.00		#DIV/0!	$0.00	#DIV/0!
			$0.00	$0.00		#DIV/0!	$0.00	#DIV/0!
			$0.00	$0.00		#DIV/0!	$0.00	#DIV/0!
			$0.00	$0.00		#DIV/0!	$0.00	#DIV/0!
			$0.00	$0.00		#DIV/0!	$0.00	#DIV/0!
			$0.00	$0.00		#DIV/0!	$0.00	#DIV/0!
			$0.00	$0.00		#DIV/0!	$0.00	#DIV/0!

Enter the following information:

Loan Amount	Cell	Installment Amount of Each Payment	Cell	Total Number of Payments for Loan	Cell	Number of Payments Remaining	Cell
$35,000	A13	$ 468.13	B13	120	C13	38	F13
$ 9,844.56	A14	$ 238.72	B14	60	C14	40	F14
$ 738.09	A15	$ 37.10	B15	24	C15	9	F15
$56,812.55	A16	$ 632.21	B16	180	C16	72	F16
$47,928.73	A17	$1,314.50	B17	48	C17	20	F17
$17,495.88	A18	$ 306.73	B18	96	C18	48	F18
$26,000	A19	$ 291.82	B19	144	C19	27	F19
$18,743.30	A20	$ 328.89	B20	78	C20	9	F20

Answer the following questions after you have completed the spreadsheet:

1. What amount will be required to pay the $35,000 loan off with 38 payments remaining?

2. What would be the total finance charge on the $56,812.55 loan if it was not paid off early?

3. What amount was saved by paying the $56,812.55 loan off with 72 payments remaining (the amount of rebate)?

4. What is the amount needed to repay the $18,743.30 loan with nine payments remaining?

5. What is the loan balance with 27 payments remaining on the $26,000 loan?

6. What is the amount of rebate when the $26,000 loan is paid off with 27 payments remaining?

7. On the $9,844.56 loan, what is the total payment amount?

8. What is the total finance charge on the $738.09 loan?

9. What is the amount saved (rebate) if the $47,928.73 loan is paid off with 20 payments remaining?

10. What amount is required to repay the $17,495.88 loan with 48 payments remaining?

GROUP REPORT

FOR CHAPTER 12 APPLICATION 2

1. Change the payoff time so that there are only five payments remaining when the loan is repaid.

2. Change the payoff time so that only five payments have been made when the loan is repaid.

3. Write a report to the store manager describing the results of each transaction.

13

FINANCIAL APPLICATIONS
FUTURE VALUE AND PRESENT VALUE AT COMPOUND INTEREST

INSTEAD OF USING CREDIT

Some people like to pay cash for what, to them, sound like good reasons. Mortimer Snyde remembers his youth in Relfs Bluff, Arkansas, during the 1930s. He remembers the bank failures everywhere from Bentonville to Pine Bluff. A sensible man who once lost all the money in his checking account, Mortimer vowed to always pay his bills with nice, green cash. He passed this tradition on to his kids, who, in turn, taught the lesson to their children.

Although the Snyde descendants have prospered, as have so many of their fellow Arkansans in recent years, they are still a cautious family who pay cash and never use credit. The Snydes put aside money in savings accounts to pay for expensive things in the future. The trouble is, how much cash does someone need to bank to have the necessary amount when it comes time to buy a new asset for the farm or an appliance for their modern new house designed by famed architect E. Fay Jones from the state's university at Fayetteville.

Five years from now Lance Snyde, Mortimer's great grandson, wants to buy a Jeep that will cost $15,000 to climb the hills up north around Harrison. Pulaski County National Bank in Little Rock pays 6% on its certificate of deposit accounts. Lance needs to withdraw some money from his mattress and deposit it today to have the necessary amount five years from now. Since he aced the business math course at Westark Community College at Fort Smith, Lance knows how to work it out. He places $11,208.87 in the CD account and, sure enough, five years later the account will contain $15,000 to pay cash to the car dealer.

Chapter Glossary

Compound interest. Interest paid or received on the principal and previously accumulated interest.

Future value. The amount an investment will be worth at the end of some future period of time when interest is compounded. Often referred to as the *compounded amount* or the *maturity value.*

Period rate. The annual interest rate divided by the number of compounding periods in one year.

Constant rate. The period rate plus 100%.

Passbook savings account. A savings account from which money can be withdrawn at any time without penalty. Interest is compounded daily but credited to the account at the end of each quarter.

Certificate of deposit. A savings account in which depositors agree to deposit at least a minimum amount and leave it on deposit for a fixed period of time.

Nominal rate. The stated rate of interest.

Effective rate. The actual or true rate of interest found by dividing the amount of interest earned or paid in one year by the principal.

Yield. Another name for the effective rate.

Present value. The amount of money that must be invested today to return a known fixed future value at a specified compound interest rate.

Student Objectives

Upon completion of this chapter, you should be able to:

1. Calculate the future value and the compound interest without tables.
2. Calculate the future value and the compound interest with tables.
3. Calculate the future value and the interest with daily compounding for passbook savings accounts and certificates of deposit.
4. Calculate the effective rate of interest.
5. Calculate the present value and the compound interest with tables.

$\Large\mathsf{T}$he previous three chapters described various applications of simple interest, which is paid at the end of a given period of time or deducted at the beginning of a loan period.

Interest payments are not always withdrawn in every period in which they are earned, however. If not withdrawn, interest is added to the principal and the next period's interest is calculated on the new principal (the old principal plus interest paid in the previous period).

LEARNING UNIT 1
FUTURE VALUE

Compound interest is accumulated at regular intervals over the life of a loan or investment. The interest is paid on the principal in the first period (like simple interest). That interest is then added to the principal, which means that the next period in which interest is paid, it will be paid on the larger amount. Thus, interest is earned on the principal and on the interest earned in prior periods. The amount an investment will be worth at the end of some future period of time when interest is compounded is called the **future value,** the **compounded amount,** or the **maturity value.**

13.1 Calculating the Future Value and the Compound Interest without Tables

Several methods can be used to calculate the future value and the interest earned without tables. Some of those methods are in many respects preferable to the methods shown for using tables if students have access to calculators and if the instructor allows students to use them. Other methods can be used without calculators and are instructive in the principles involved in calculating the future value.

The first method uses the simple interest formula ($I = PRT$) in each of the periods interest is paid. Interest is usually compounded daily, monthly, quarterly, semiannually, or annually. The number of interest payment periods in each year for each method is shown in Table 13.1.

TABLE 13.1   NUMBER OF INTEREST PAYMENT PERIODS IN ONE YEAR

Compounding Periods in One Year		Time in $I = PRT$*
Daily	365	1/365
Monthly	12	1/12
Quarterly	4	1/4
Semiannually	2	1/2
Annually	1	

*Time in the interest formula is 1 over the number of compounding periods in one year for each period's calculation (for example, if interest is to be compounded monthly, time in $I=PRT$ will be 1/12).

EXAMPLE   Calculate the future value and the interest earned on an investment of $10,000 for two years when interest is compounded semiannually at 10%.

Solution   The simple interest formula ($I = PRT$) will have to be used four times, once for each interest payment (2 years × 2 semiannual payments per year = 4 periods).
1st semiannual period:

Principal	$10,000.00
Interest for period ($10,000 × 10 % × $\frac{1}{2}$)	+ 500.00
Principal at end of first period	$10,500.00

2nd semiannual period:

Principal at end of first period	$10,500.00
Interest for period ($10,500 × 10 % × $\frac{1}{2}$)	+ 525.00
Principal at end of second period	$11,025.00

3rd semiannual period:

Principal at end of second period	$11,025.00
Interest for period ($11,025 × 10% × $\frac{1}{2}$)	+ 551.25
Principal at end of third period	$11,576.25

4th semiannual period:

Principal at end of third period	$11,576.25
Interest for period ($11,576.25 × 10% × $\frac{1}{2}$)	+ 578.81
Principal at end of fourth period	$12,155.06

The *future* value at the end of two years is $12,155.06.
The interest earned at the end of two years is:

Future value	$12,155.06
− original principal	10,000.00
interest	$ 2,155.06

The second method is a shortcut for the first method. Before an explanation, two terms need to be defined: period rate and constant rate.

The **period rate** is the rate of interest to apply to each compounding period. Since interest rates are stated in annual terms, calculate the period rate as shown here:

$$\text{Period rate} = \frac{\text{annual interest rate}}{\text{compounding periods in 1 year}}$$

In each interest payment period the interest is calculated and then added to the principal used for that period. Then it is added to the principal to find a new principal for the next period's calculations. The principal (or new principal) is the base. The base can be represented by 100%. Thus, the new principal can be represented by a **constant rate**, which is calculated as:

$$\text{Constant rate} = 100\% + \text{period rate.}$$

At each interest period, multiply the principal (or new principal) by the constant rate to find the next period's new principal.

EXAMPLE   Calculate the future value and the interest earned on a $10,000 investment for two years when interest is compounded semiannually at 10%.

Solution   The interest will have to be calculated four times, once for each interest payment (2 years × 2 semiannual payments per year = 4 periods). The constant rate will be:

$$100\% + \frac{\text{annual interest rate}}{\text{compounding periods in 1 year}} = 100\% + \frac{10\%}{2} = 105\%$$

1st semiannual period: Principal $10,000.00
                $\times$ (Period rate + 100%) $\times$ 105%
                Principal at end of first period $10,500.00
2nd semiannual period: $\times$ (Period rate + 100%) $\times$ 105%
                Principal at end of second period $11,025.00
3rd semiannual period: $\times$ (Period rate + 100%) $\times$ 105%
                Principal at end of third period $11,576.25
4th semiannual period: $\times$ (Period rate + 100%) $\times$ 105%
                Principal at end of fourth period $12,155.06

The future value at the end of two years is $12,155.06.

    1.05 $\times$ 10,000 = = = = 12,155.06   *(using constant features)*

The interest earned at the end of two years is:
        Future value $12,155.06
        $-$ original principal   10,000.00.
        interest $ 2,155.06

13.1 Practice Problems

Calculate the future value and the interest in the following compound interest problems:

1. A $4,000 note earned 6% compounded annually for three years. Calculate the future value and the interest earned.

2. Joyce Aranda put $50,000 into an investment paying 4% compounded quarterly. Calculate the future value and amount of interest that will be earned at the end of the first year.

3. Arthur Wilson wants to know how much interest he will earn in two years on $8,000 earning 9% compounded semiannually.

4. Quintin McDaniel's $28,000 investment is earning 6% compounded monthly. Calculate the future value and the amount of interest after six months.

13.1 Solutions to Practice Problems

1. The interest must be calculated three times, once for each interest payment (3 years $\times$ 1 payment per year = 3 periods). The constant rate is

$$100\% + \frac{\text{annual interest rate}}{\text{compounding periods in 1 year}} = 100\% + \frac{6\%}{1} = 106\%.$$

1st annual period: Principal $ 4,000.00
                $\times$ (Period rate + 100%) $\times$ 106%
                Principal at end of first period $ 4,240.00
2nd annual period: $\times$ (Period rate + 100%) $\times$ 106%
                Principal at end of second period $ 4,494.40
3rd annual period: $\times$ (Period rate + 100%) $\times$ 106%
                Principal at end of third period $ 4,764.06

The future value at the end of three years is $4,764.06.
The interest earned at the end of three years is:
        Future value $ 4,764.06
        $-$ original principal   4,000.00
        interest $ 764.06

2. The interest must be calculated four times, once for each interest payment (1 year $\times$ 4 payments per year = 4 periods). The constant rate is

$$100\% + \frac{\text{annual interest rate}}{\text{compounding periods in 1 year}} = 100\% + \frac{4\%}{4} = 101\%.$$

1st quarter:	Principal	$50,000.00
	× (Period rate + 100%)	× 101%
	Principal at end of first period	$50,500.00
2nd quarter:	× (Period rate + 100%)	× 101%
	Principal at end of second period	$51,005.00
3rd quarter:	× (Period rate + 100%)	× 101%
	Principal at end of third period	$51,515.05
4th quarter:	× (Period rate + 100%)	× 101%
	Principal at end of fourth period	$52,030.20

The future value at the end of one year is $52,030.20.

The interest earned at the end of 1 year is

	Future value	$52,030.20
	− original principal	50,000.00
	interest	$ 2,030.20

3. The interest must be calculated four times, once for each interest payment (2 years × 2 payments per year = 4 periods). The constant rate is

$$100\% + \frac{\text{annual interest rate}}{\text{compounding periods in 1 year}} = 100\% + \frac{9\%}{2} = 104.5\%.$$

1st semiannual period:	Principal	$ 8,000.00
	× (Period rate + 100%)	× 104.5%
	Principal at end of first period	$ 8,360.00
2nd semiannual period:	× (Period rate + 100%)	× 104.5%
	Principal at end of second period	$ 8,736.20
3rd semiannual period:	× (Period rate + 100%)	× 104.5%
	Principal at end of third period	$ 9,129.33
4th semiannual period:	× (Period rate + 100%)	× 104.5%
	Principal at end of fourth period	$ 9,540.15

The future value at the end of two years is $9,540.15.

The interest earned at the end of two years is:

	Future value	$9,540.15
	− original principal	8,000.00
	interest	$1,540.15

4. The interest must be calculated six times, once for each interest payment (six monthly payment periods). The constant rate is

$$100\% + \frac{\text{annual interest rate}}{\text{compounding periods in 1 year}} = 100\% + \frac{6\%}{12} = 100.5\%.$$

1st month:	Principal	$28,000.00
	× (Period rate + 100%)	× 100.5%
	Principal at end of first period	$28,140.00
2nd month:	× (Period rate + 100%)	× 100.5%
	Principal at end of second period	$28,280.70
3rd month:	× (Period rate + 100%)	× 100.5%
	Principal at end of third period	$28,422.10
4th month:	× (Period rate + 100%)	× 100.5%
	Principal at end of fourth period	$28,564.21
5th month:	× (Period rate + 100%)	× 100.5%
	Principal at end of fifth period	$28,707.04
6th month:	× (Period rate + 100%)	× 100.5%
	Principal at end of sixth period	$28,850.57

The future value at the end of six months is $28,850.57.

The interest earned at the end of six months is:

	Future value	$28,850.57
	− original principal	28,000.00
	interest	$ 850.57

13.2 Calculating the Future Value and the Compound Interest with Tables

Many calculations are done today using financial calculators, and some people use them to solve all future value problems (see the calculator box that follows). However, most people prefer to use tables, especially for calculations involving a large number of interest payment periods.

To use Table 13.2, Future Value of $1 at Compound Interest, follow these steps:

1. Find the period interest rate:

$$\text{Period rate} = \frac{\text{annual interest rate}}{\text{compounding periods in 1 year}}$$

2. Find the number of periods:

$$\text{Periods} = \text{years} \times \text{compounding periods in 1 year}$$

3. In Table 13.2, find the future value of $1 at compound interest at the intersection of the period rate and the periods.
4. Find the future value of the investment:

$$\text{Future value} = \text{future value of } \$1 \times \text{principal}$$

5. If the amount of interest earned is needed:

$$\text{Interest earned} = \text{future value} - \text{principal}$$

EXAMPLE   Find the future value and the interest for an investment of $32,000 in an account paying 10% compounded quarterly for 12 years.

Solution   *Step 1.*   Find the period interest rate:

$$\text{Period rate} = \frac{\text{annual interest rate}}{\text{compounding periods in 1 year}}$$
$$= \frac{10\%}{4} = 2.5\%$$

Step 2. Find the number of periods:

$$\text{Periods} = \text{years} \times \text{compounding periods in 1 year}$$
$$= 12 \times 4 = 48$$

Step 3. In Table 13.2, find the future value of $1 at compound interest at the intersection of 2.5% and 48 periods: 3.271490
Step 4. Find the future value of the investment:

$$\text{Future value} = \text{future value of } \$1 \times \text{principal}$$
$$= 3.271490 \times \$32,000$$
$$= \$104,687.68$$

Step 5. Find amount of interest earned:

$$\text{Interest earned} = \text{future value} - \text{principal}$$
$$= \$104,687.68 - 32,000 = \$72,687.68$$

| N | %i | PMT | PV | FV |

Using the preceding example, you can solve future value problems in the following way:

N	Total number of compounding periods in the problem
	Enter 48 (12 years × 4 quarters per year = 48 periods).

%i	Percent interest per compounding (payment) period
	Enter 2.5 (10% annual rate ÷ 4 quarters per year = 2.5).
	Note: Do not enter .025.

PMT	Amount of the regular payment (annuities only)
	Not used for future value problems.

PV	Amount of the present value or principal
	Enter 32,000.

FV	Future value amount:
	Enter 2nd FV .

The display on the calculator is the future value, $104,687.66.

(The difference in the answers is due to rounding.) If you do not have a financial calculator, but you have a Yˣ key, you can solve future value problems rather easily on your calculator following these steps:

1. Find the period interest rate: 10% ÷ 4 = .025.
2. Add 100% to the period rate: 100% + .025 = 1.025.
3. Find the number of compounding periods: 4 × 12 = 48.
4. Enter 1.025 Yˣ 48 × 32,000 = 104,687.66.

In both previous examples, the present value (PV), $32,000, can be subtracted from the future value (FV), $104,687.66, to find the interest (I), $72,687.66.

13.2 Practice Problems

Use Table 13.2 to find the future value and the interest in the following problems:

1. Henry Zapata put $10,000 into a pension fund for his retirement at age 55. Henry is now 37 years old. The fund guarantees a return of 6% compounded semiannually. Find the guaranteed future value and interest for the investment.

2. The DDC Corporation invested $100,000 in a certificate of deposit paying 12% compounded monthly for four years with the First International Bank of San Francisco. Calculate the future value and the interest to be earned.

3. Mona Petersen established a college trust fund when her granddaughter was born by depositing $25,000 in a fund paying 8% compounded annually. Find the value of the fund and the interest earned after 18 years.

4. Find the future value and interest for $1,500 deposited at 10% compounded quarterly for 10 years.

13.2 Solutions to Practice Problems

1. Period rate $= \dfrac{6\%}{2} = 3\%$ Periods $= (55 - 37) \times 2 = 36$

 Future value $= \$10,000 \times 2.898278 = \$28,982.78$
   Intersection of 3% and 36 periods
   from Table 13.2
 Interest $= \$28,982.78 - 10,000 = \$18,982.78$

2. Period rate $= \dfrac{12\%}{12} = 1\%$ Periods $= 4 \times 12 = 48$

 Future value $= \$100,000 \times 1.612226 = \$161,222.60$
 Intersection of 1% and 48 periods
 from Table 13.2
 Interest $= \$161,222.60 - 100,000 = \$61,222.60$

TABLE 13.2   FUTURE VALUE OF $1 AT COMPOUND INTEREST

$$i\% = \frac{\text{annual interest rate}}{\text{compounding periods per year}}, \; n = \text{compounding periods per year} \times \text{number of years}$$

n	0.5%	$\frac{2}{3}$%	0.75%	1%	1.5%	2%	2.5%	3%	4%
1	1.005000	1.006667	1.007500	1.010000	1.015000	1.020000	1.025000	1.030000	1.040000
2	1.010025	1.013378	1.015056	1.020100	1.030225	1.040400	1.050625	1.060900	1.081600
3	1.015075	1.020134	1.022669	1.030301	1.045678	1.061208	1.076891	1.092727	1.124864
4	1.020151	1.026935	1.030339	1.040604	1.061364	1.082432	1.103813	1.125509	1.169859
5	1.025251	1.033781	1.038067	1.051010	1.077284	1.104081	1.131408	1.159274	1.216653
6	1.030378	1.040673	1.045852	1.061520	1.093443	1.126162	1.159693	1.194052	1.265319
7	1.035529	1.047610	1.053696	1.072135	1.109845	1.148686	1.188686	1.229874	1.315932
8	1.040707	1.054595	1.061599	1.082857	1.126493	1.171659	1.218403	1.266770	1.368569
9	1.045911	1.061625	1.069561	1.093685	1.143390	1.195093	1.248863	1.304773	1.423312
10	1.051140	1.068703	1.077583	1.104622	1.160541	1.218994	1.280085	1.343916	1.480244
11	1.056396	1.075827	1.085664	1.115668	1.177949	1.243374	1.312087	1.384234	1.539454
12	1.061678	1.083000	1.093807	1.126825	1.195618	1.268242	1.344889	1.425761	1.601032
13	1.066986	1.090220	1.102010	1.138093	1.213552	1.293607	1.378511	1.468534	1.665074
14	1.072321	1.097488	1.110276	1.149474	1.231756	1.319479	1.412974	1.512590	1.731676
15	1.077683	1.104804	1.118603	1.160969	1.250232	1.345868	1.448298	1.557967	1.800944
16	1.083071	1.112170	1.126992	1.172579	1.268986	1.372786	1.484506	1.604706	1.872981
17	1.088487	1.119584	1.135445	1.184304	1.288020	1.400241	1.521618	1.652848	1.947900
18	1.093929	1.127048	1.143960	1.196147	1.307341	1.428246	1.559659	1.702433	2.025817
19	1.099399	1.134562	1.152540	1.208109	1.326951	1.456811	1.598650	1.753506	2.106849
20	1.104896	1.142125	1.161184	1.220190	1.346855	1.485947	1.638616	1.806111	2.191123
21	1.110420	1.149740	1.169893	1.232392	1.367058	1.515666	1.679582	1.860295	2.278768
22	1.115972	1.157404	1.178667	1.244716	1.387564	1.545980	1.721571	1.916103	2.369919
23	1.121552	1.165120	1.187507	1.257163	1.408377	1.576899	1.764611	1.973587	2.464716
24	1.127160	1.172888	1.196414	1.269735	1.429503	1.608437	1.808726	2.032794	2.563304
36	1.196681	1.270237	1.308645	1.430769	1.709140	2.039887	2.432535	2.898278	4.103933
48	1.270489	1.375666	1.431405	1.612226	2.043478	2.587070	3.271490	4.132252	6.570528
60	1.348850	1.489846	1.565681	1.816697	2.443220	3.281031	4.399790	5.891603	10.519627
120	1.819397	2.219640	2.451357	3.300387	5.969323	10.765163	19.358150	34.710987	1.10662561

n	5%	6%	7%	8%	9%	10%	11%	12%	13%
1	1.050000	1.060000	1.070000	1.080000	1.090000	1.100000	1.110000	1.120000	1.130000
2	1.102500	1.123600	1.144900	1.166400	1.188100	1.210000	1.232100	1.254400	1.276900
3	1.157625	1.191016	1.225043	1.259712	1.295029	1.331000	1.367631	1.404928	1.442897
4	1.215506	1.262477	1.310796	1.360489	1.411582	1.464100	1.518070	1.573519	1.630474
5	1.276282	1.338226	1.402552	1.469328	1.538624	1.610510	1.685058	1.762342	1.842435
6	1.340096	1.418519	1.500730	1.586874	1.677100	1.771561	1.870415	1.973823	2.081952
7	1.407100	1.503630	1.605781	1.713824	1.828039	1.948717	2.076160	2.210681	2.352605
8	1.477455	1.593848	1.718186	1.850930	1.992563	2.143589	2.304538	2.475963	2.658444
9	1.551328	1.689479	1.838459	1.999005	2.171893	2.357948	2.558037	2.773079	3.004042
10	1.628895	1.790848	1.967151	2.158925	2.367364	2.593742	2.839421	3.105848	3.394567
11	1.710339	1.898299	2.104852	2.331639	2.580426	2.853117	3.151757	3.478550	3.835861
12	1.795856	2.012196	2.252192	2.518170	2.812665	3.138428	3.498451	3.895976	4.334523
13	1.885649	2.132928	2.409845	2.719624	3.065805	3.452271	3.883280	4.363493	4.898011
14	1.979932	2.260904	2.578534	2.937194	3.341727	3.797498	4.310441	4.887112	5.534753
15	2.078928	2.396558	2.759032	3.172169	3.642482	4.177248	4.784589	5.473566	6.254270
16	2.182875	2.540352	2.952164	3.425943	3.970306	4.594973	5.310894	6.130394	7.067326
17	2.292018	2.692773	3.158815	3.700018	4.327633	5.054470	5.895093	6.866041	7.986078
18	2.406619	2.854339	3.379932	3.996019	4.717120	5.559917	6.543553	7.689966	9.024268
19	2.526950	3.025600	3.616528	4.315701	5.141661	6.115909	7.263344	8.612762	10.197423
20	2.653298	3.207135	3.869684	4.660957	5.604411	6.727500	8.062312	9.646293	11.523088
21	2.785963	3.399564	4.140562	5.033834	6.108808	7.400250	8.949166	10.803848	13.021089
22	2.925261	3.603537	4.430402	5.436540	6.658600	8.140275	9.933574	12.100310	14.713831
23	3.071524	3.819750	4.740530	5.871464	7.257874	8.954302	11.026267	13.552347	16.626629
24	3.225100	4.048935	5.072367	6.341181	7.911083	9.849733	12.239157	15.178629	18.788091
36	5.791816	8.147252	11.423942	15.968172	22.251225	30.912681	42.818085	59.135574	81.437412
48	10.401270	16.393872	25.728907	40.210573	62.585237	97.017234	149.796954	230.390776	352.992345
60	18.679186	32.987691	57.946427	101.257064	176.031292	304.481640	524.057242	897.596933	1530.053473

Note: The Table Handbook that accompanies Business Mathematics contains more detailed tables.

3. Period rate $= \dfrac{8\%}{1} = 8\%$ Periods $= 18 \times 1 = 18$

Future value $= \$25,000 \times 3.996019 = \$99,900.48$

Intersection of 8% and 18 periods from Table 13.2

Interest $= \$99,900.48 - 25,000 = \$74,900.48$

4. Period rate $= \dfrac{10\%}{4} = 2.5\%$ Periods $= 15 \times 4 = 60$

Future value $= \$1,500 \times 4.399790 = \$6,599.69$

Intersection of 2.5% and 60 periods from Table 13.2

Interest $= \$6,599.69 - 1,500 = \$5,099.69$

13.3   Calculating the Future Value and the Compound Interest with Daily Compounding

Passbook Savings Accounts

Many banks and savings and loan associations offer **passbook savings accounts** for which interest is compounded daily. Some compound continuously. Computers are almost always used to make the computations. Even though the interest is compounded daily, it is normally only credited to the customer's account quarterly. Customers can withdraw from passbook savings accounts without penalty. The quarters begin on January 1, April 1, July 1, and October 1.

Rates vary from bank to bank and over time. A typical rate would be $5\frac{1}{4}\%$. Table 13.3 shows the daily future value of $1 compounded daily at $5\frac{1}{4}\%$, on a 365-day basis. For crediting purposes each month is assumed to have only 30 days in it. Since interest is credited on a quarterly basis, compounding tables usually go only to 90 days.

Certificates of Deposit

Some accounts require that depositors agree to deposit at least a minimum amount and leave it on deposit for a fixed period of time. For example, a **certificate of deposit** (CD) might be for 180 days (two quarters) or for two years. Early withdrawal will result in a substantial loss of interest. Because of the minimum deposit requirement and the penalty for early withdrawal, the interest rates are usually higher than for passbook savings accounts. Daily compounding tables are available for quarters, such as Table 13.4 at $5\frac{1}{2}\%$, and for years, such as Table 13.5 for a selected number of years at various rates.

The formulas to calculate the future value and the interest for all of the problems involving daily compounding are as follows:

> Future value $=$ future value of \$1 $\times$ principal
> Interest $=$ future value $-$ principal

EXAMPLE   Julie Lindy opened a passbook savings account paying $5\frac{1}{4}\%$ on April 1, depositing \$800. On May 4 Julie withdrew \$200, and on June 18 she deposited \$1,000. Calculate the value of the account and the interest earned at the end of the quarter.

Solution   Only \$600 (\$800 $-$ 200) was in the account for the full 90 days. The \$200 was in the account for 34 days. The \$1,000 was in the account for 12 days.

$$
\begin{array}{ll}
\$ \; 600 \times 1.013028415 = \$ \; 607.82 & \textit{(90 days)} \\
\$ \; 200 \times 1.004902035 = \$ \; 200.98 & \textit{(34 days)} \\
\$1,000 \times 1.001727394 = \$1,001.73 & \textit{(12 days)}
\end{array}
$$

Interest		*Future Value*

$$
\begin{array}{rl}
\$ \; 607.82 - \quad 600 = \$ \; 7.82 \\
200.98 - \quad 200 = \quad .98 \\
\underline{1,001.73 - 1,000 = \quad 1.73} \\
\$10.53
\end{array}
$$

     $\$800 - 200 + 1,000 + 10.53 = \$1,610.53$

TABLE 13.3 DAILY FUTURE VALUE OF $1 COMPOUNDED DAILY AT $5\frac{1}{4}$%, 365-DAY BASIS

Number of Days n	Value of $(1 + i)^n$	n	Value of $(1 + i)^n$	n	Value of $(1 + i)^n$	n	Value of $(1 + i)^n$	n	Value of $(1 + i)^n$
1	1.000143836	19	1.002736417	37	1.005335720	55	1.007941760	73	1.010554556
2	1.000287692	20	1.002880647	38	1.005480323	56	1.008086738	74	1.010699909
3	1.000431569	21	1.003024897	39	1.005624947	57	1.008231737	75	1.010845284
4	1.000575467	22	1.003169167	40	1.005769591	58	1.008376756	76	1.010990679
5	1.000719385	23	1.003313459	41	1.005914257	59	1.008521797	77	1.011136096
6	1.000863324	24	1.003457771	42	1.006058943	60	1.008666858	78	1.011281533
7	1.001007284	25	1.003602104	43	1.006203650	61	1.008811940	79	1.011426992
8	1.001151264	26	1.003746458	44	1.006348378	62	1.008957043	80	1.011711971
9	1.001295266	27	1.003890832	45	1.006493127	63	1.009102167	81	1.011717971
10	1.001439288	28	1.004035227	46	1.006637896	64	1.009247312	82	1.011863492
11	1.001583330	29	1.004179643	47	1.006782687	65	1.009392478	83	1.012009034
12	1.001727394	30	1.004324080	48	1.006927498	66	1.009537665	84	1.012154597
13	1.001871478	31	1.004468538	49	1.007072330	67	1.009682872	85	1.012300181
14	1.002015582	32	1.004613016	50	1.007217183	68	1.009828100	86	1.012445786
15	1.002159708	33	1.004757515	51	1.007362057	69	1.009973350	87	1.012591412
16	1.002303854	34	1.004902035	52	1.007506951	70	1.010118620	88	1.012737058
17	1.002448021	35	1.005046576	53	1.007651867	71	1.010263911	89	1.012882726
18	1.002592209	36	1.005191137	54	1.007968030	72	1.010409223	90	1.013028415

Note: The Table Handbook that accompanies Business Mathematics contains more detailed tables.

TABLE 13.4 INTEREST BY QUARTER AT $5\frac{1}{2}$% COMPOUNDED DAILY

Number of Quarters	Future Value of $1
1	1.0136530
2	1.0274924
3	1.0415207
4	1.0557405

TABLE 13.5 FUTURE VALUE OF $1 COMPOUNDED DAILY (365-DAY BASIS)

n	6%	7%	8%	9%	10%	11%	12%	13%	14%
1	1.061831	1.072501	1.083277	1.094162	1.105156	1.116259	1.127474	1.138802	1.140000
2	1.127486	1.150258	1.173490	1.197190	1.221369	1.246035	1.271198	1.296869	1.299600
3	1.197199	1.233653	1.271215	1.309920	1.349803	1.390898	1.433243	1.476877	1.481544
4	1.271224	1.323094	1.377079	1.433265	1.491742	1.552603	1.615945	1.681870	1.688960
5	1.349825	1.419019	1.491758	1.568224	1.648607	1.733107	1.821937	1.915316	1.925415
6	1.433286	1.521899	1.615988	1.715891	1.821967	1.934597	2.054187	2.181165	2.194976
7	1.521908	1.632238	1.750564	1.877463	2.013557	2.159512	2.316043	2.483914	2.502269
8	1.616010	1.750577	1.896346	2.054248	2.225294	2.410576	2.611279	2.828686	2.852586
9	1.715930	1.877496	2.054269	2.247680	2.459296	2.690828	2.944150	3.221312	3.251949
10	1.822028	2.013616	2.225343	2.459326	2.717904	3.003661	3.319453	3.668436	3.707221

Note: The Table Handbook that accompanies Business Mathematics contains more detailed tables.

EXAMPLE   How much will $15,000 in a 180-day (two quarters), $5\frac{1}{2}$% certificate of deposit be worth at maturity? How much interest will be earned?

Solution   Using Table 13.4, the amount for two quarters is 1.0274924.

$$
\begin{aligned}
\text{Future value} &= \$15,000 \times 1.0274924 \\
&= \$15,412.39 \\
\text{Interest} &= \$15,412.39 - 15,000 \\
&= \$412.39
\end{aligned}
$$

EXAMPLE   Estella Peron invested $50,000 in a five year, 6% certificate of deposit compounded daily. Calculate the value of the certificate at maturity and the interest Estella earned.

Solution   Using Table 13.5, the amount for five years is 1.3498255.

$$
\begin{aligned}
\text{Future value} &= \$50,000 \times 1.3498255 \\
&= \$67,491.28 \\
\text{Interest} &= \$67,491.28 - 50,000 \\
&= \$17,491.28
\end{aligned}
$$

13.3 Practice Problems

Use Tables 13.3, 13.4, or 13.5 to find the future value and the interest in the following daily compounding problems. (Remember that each month is assumed to have 30 days.)

1. On July 1 Maxine Roberts had a passbook savings account balance of $6,250. Two deposits were made during the quarter: July 24, $350 and September 2, $500. The account pays $5\frac{1}{4}$% compounded daily. Calculate the value of the account at the end of the quarter and the interest earned during the quarter.

2. Calculate the maturity value and interest earned for a $20,000, $5\frac{1}{2}$%, 270-day (three quarter) certificate of deposit that is compounded daily.

3. Mark Calveccia invested $80,000 in a three-year certificate of deposit paying 8% compounded daily. Find the maturity value and the interest earned at maturity.

4. Maria's Casual Shoes has a passbook savings account that pays interest at $5\frac{1}{4}$% compounded daily. On January 1 the balance was $3,800. During the quarter, the following account transactions were made:

Date	Transaction	Amount
January 18	Deposit	$1,200
February 6	Deposit	$ 500
March 11	Withdrawal	$ 750

Calculate the value at the end of the quarter and the interest earned during the quarter.

13.3 Solutions to Practice Problems

1. $6,250 × 1.013028415 = $6,331.43   *(for entire quarter or 90 days)*
$ 350 × 1.009537665 = $ 353.34   *(for 6 more days in July + 30 days in August +*
+$ 500 × 1.009537665 = $ 502.02   *30 days in September = 66 days)*
$7,100 × 1.009537665 = $7,186.79   ← *(for 28 days in September)*

Account balance, end of quarter = $7,186.79
Interest earned = $7,186.79 − 7,100 = $86.79

2. Maturity value = $20,000 × 1.0415207
  = $20,830.41
Interest = $20,830.41 − 20,000
  = $830.41

3. Maturity value = $80,000 × 1.271215
= $101,697.20
Interest = $101,697.20 − 80,000
= $21,697.20

4. $3,800 was in the account for the full 90 days.
$1,200 draws interest for 53 days to March 11 (12 days in January, 30 days in February, and 11 days in March).
$500 draws interest for 35 days to March 11 (24 days in February and 11 days in March).
$950 ($1,200 + 500 − 750) draws interest for 19 days in March.
$3,800 × 1.013028415 = $3,849.51
$1,200 × 1.007651867 = $1,209.18
$500 × 1.005046576 = $502.52
$950 × 1.002736417 = $952.60

Interest Earned

$ 3,849.51 $ 1,209.18 $ 502.52 $ 952.60
− 3,800.00   − 1,200.00   − 500.00   − 950.00
$ 49.51 + $ 9.18 + $ 2.52 + $ 2.60 = $63.81

Account Value

$3,800 + 1.200 + 500 − 750 + 63.81 = $4,813.81

13.4 Calculating the Effective Rate of Interest

Obviously, the more times interest is compounded during a year, the greater the amount of interest earned even at the same stated interest rate. The stated rate of interest is called the **nominal rate**. As shown in other chapters, however, the **effective rate** is the actual or true rate. The effective rate is a way of comparing rates of interest stated in different ways or for different time periods during a year. Many financial institutions refer to the effective rate as the **yield.** To calculate the effective rate (yield), use the following formula:

$$\text{Effective interest rate} = \frac{\text{interest for 1 year}}{\text{principal}}$$

For comparisons when the nominal rate is stated, but no principal has been invested, you can use $1. All of the tables give the value of $1 compounded at various rates and periods.

Table 13.6 compares a 12% nominal rate of interest for various compounding periods.

TABLE 13.6 COMPARISON OF EFFECTIVE INTEREST RATES FOR VARIOUS COMPOUNDING PERIODS DURING A YEAR AT A NOMINAL 12% RATE

Principal	Nominal Rate of Interest	Compounding Period	Value at Year's End	Interest	Effective Rate
$1,000	12%	Annually	$1,120.00	$120.00	12.00%
1,000	12%	Semiannually	1,123.60	123.60	12.36%
1,000	12%	Quarterly	1,125.51	125.51	12.55%
1,000	12%	Monthly	1,126.83	126.83	12.68%
1,000	12%	Daily	1,127.47	127.47	12.75%

Note: The Table Handbook that accompanies Business Mathematics contains more detailed tables.

This illustration should once again indicate how important it is to compare the effective rates of one financial institution to another. The stated rates can be misleading or at least not tell the whole story.

EXAMPLE A bank is advertising that it pays 8% compounded quarterly on 30-month CDs. Determine the effective interest rate (rounded to the nearest hundredth of a percent) on a $25,000 investment.

Solution The effective rate is calculated by finding the interest for one year and dividing it by the principal. The fact that the CD is for 30 months is irrelevant for this problem.

$$\text{Period rate} = \frac{8\%}{4} = 2\% \qquad \text{Periods} = 1 \text{ year} \times 4 = 4$$

Table value at intersection of 4 periods and 2%:
1.082432 (from Table 13.2)

$$\text{Value at end of one year} = \$25,000 \times 1.082432$$
$$= \$27,060.80$$

$$\text{Interest for one year} = \$27,060.80 - 25,000$$
$$= \$2,060.80$$

$$\text{Effective interest rate} = \frac{\text{interest for 1 year}}{\text{principal}}$$
$$= \frac{\$2,060.80}{\$25,000}$$
$$= 8.24\%$$

A shortcut for solving effective rate with compound interest problems using tables is to subtract 1 from the value found in the table at the intersection of the period rate and the number of periods for one year and convert the difference to a percent:

1.082432	*From Table 13.2 — rate representing maturity value*
− 1.000000	*Rate representing principal*
.082432	*Rate representing interest*

.082432 = 8.24%

13.4 Practice Problems

Calculate the effective rate of interest for the following problems:

1. Calculate the effective rate of interest for $8,000 invested at 10% compounded semiannually.

2. Susanne Jacobson placed $900 in an account paying 4% compounded quarterly. Determine the effective interest rate.

3. A bank is advertising that it pays $5\frac{1}{2}\%$ compounded daily. What is the effective rate?

4. Mark Irwin deposited $40,000 in a savings account paying 6% compounded monthly. Determine the effective rate the savings account is paying.

13.4 Solutions to Practice Problems

1. $\text{Period rate} = \dfrac{10\%}{2} = 5\% \qquad \text{Periods} = 1 \text{ year} \times 2 = 2$

Table value at intersection of 2 periods and 5%:
1.102500 (from Table 13.2)
1.102500 − 1 = .102500 = 10.25%

2. Period rate $= \dfrac{4\%}{4} = 1\%$ Periods = 1 year $\times$ 4 = 4

Table value at intersection of 4 periods and 1%:
1.040604 (from Table 13.2)
1.040604 $-$ 1 = .040604 = 4.06%

3. Period rate $= 5\frac{1}{2}\%$ compounded daily

Table value for 4 quarters (1 year) at $5\frac{1}{2}\%$ compounded
daily: 1.0557405 (from Table 13.4)
1.0557405 $-$ 1 = .0557405 = 5.57%

4. Period rate $= \dfrac{6\%}{12} = .5\%$ Periods = 1 year $\times$ 12 = 12

Table value at intersection of 12 periods and .5%:
1.061678 (from Table 13.2)
1.061678 $-$ 1 = .061678 = 6.17%

LEARNING UNIT 2
PRESENT VALUE

The **present value** is technically the amount of money that must be invested today to return a known fixed future value at a specified compound interest rate. Present value may be calculated for a variety of reasons. It may be to start a business, put a child through college, purchase new machinery or equipment, save for a vacation, or determine the amount to be set aside for a definite retirement income.

The present value is always less than the future value. Money invested today (the present value) will be "put to work" earning interest, which will be added to the present value.

13.5   Calculating the Present Value and the Compound Interest with Tables

To determine the present value of money, a present value table is usually used. The calculator can be used if preferred (see the following box). Solutions can also be found with the use of a calculator as shown in the calculator box. Table 13.7 gives the present value of $1 at compound interest for various rates and periods. To use the table, follow these steps:

1. Find the period interest rate:

$$\text{Period rate} = \frac{\text{annual interest rate}}{\text{compounding periods in 1 year}}$$

2. Find the number of periods:

Periods = years $\times$ compounding periods in 1 year

3. In Table 13.7, find the present value of $1 at compound interest at the intersection of the period rate and the periods.
4. Find the present value to be invested:

Present value = present value of $1 $\times$ future value

5. If the amount of interest earned is needed:

Interest earned = future value $-$ present value

E X A M P L E   Alex was hired by John Smith with an agreement that John will sell the business to Alex in five years for $180,000. To have the amount needed, how much will Alex have to invest today at 8% compounded quarterly, and how much interest will he earn?

TABLE 13.7   PRESENT VALUE OF $1 AT COMPOUND INTEREST

n = number of periods; i = interest rate per period

n \ i	1%	1½%	2%	2½%	3%	4%	5%	6%	8%	10%	12%
1	.99010	.98522	.98039	.97561	.97087	.96154	.95238	.94340	.92593	.90909	.89286
2	.98030	.97066	.96117	.95181	.94260	.92456	.90703	.89000	.85734	.82645	.79719
3	.97059	.95632	.94232	.92860	.91514	.88900	.86384	.83962	.79383	.75131	.71178
4	.96098	.94218	.92385	.90595	.88849	.85480	.82270	.79209	.73503	.68301	.63552
5	.95147	.92826	.90573	.88385	.86261	.82193	.78353	.74726	.68058	.62092	.56743
6	.94205	.91454	.88797	.86230	.83748	.79031	.74622	.70496	.63017	.56447	.50663
7	.93272	.90103	.87056	.84127	.81309	.75992	.71068	.66506	.58349	.51316	.45235
8	.92348	.88771	.85349	.82075	.78941	.73069	.67684	.62741	.54027	.46651	.40388
9	.91434	.87459	.83676	.80073	.76642	.70259	.64461	.59190	.50025	.42410	.36061
10	.90529	.86167	.82035	.78120	.74409	.67556	.61391	.55839	.46319	.38554	.32197
11	.89632	.84893	.80426	.76214	.72242	.64958	.58468	.52679	.42888	.35049	.28748
12	.88745	.83639	.78849	.74356	.70138	.62460	.55684	.49697	.39711	.31863	.25668
13	.87866	.82403	.77303	.72542	.68095	.60057	.53032	.46884	.36770	.28966	.22917
14	.86996	.81185	.75788	.70773	.66112	.57748	.50507	.44230	.34036	.26333	.20462
15	.86135	.79985	.74301	.69047	.64186	.55526	.48102	.41727	.31524	.23939	.18270
16	.85282	.78803	.72845	.67362	.62317	.53391	.45811	.39365	.29189	.21763	.16312
17	.84438	.77639	.71416	.65720	.60502	.51337	.43630	.37136	.27027	.19784	.14564
18	.83602	.76491	.70016	.64117	.58739	.49363	.41552	.35034	.25025	.17986	.13004
19	.82774	.75361	.68643	.62553	.57029	.47464	.39573	.33051	.23171	.16351	.11611
20	.81954	.74247	.67297	.61027	.55368	.45639	.37689	.31180	.21455	.14864	.10367
21	.81143	.73150	.65978	.59539	.53755	.43883	.35894	.29416	.19866	.13513	.09256
22	.80340	.72069	.64684	.58086	.52189	.42196	.34185	.27751	.18394	.12285	.08264
23	.79544	.71004	.63416	.56670	.50669	.40573	.32557	.26180	.17032	.11168	.07379
24	.78757	.69954	.62172	.55288	.49193	.39012	.31007	.24698	.15770	.10153	.06588
25	.77977	.68921	.60953	.53939	.47761	.37512	.29530	.23300	.14602	.09230	.05882
26	.77205	.67902	.59758	.52623	.46369	.36069	.28124	.21981	.13520	.08391	.05252
27	.76440	.66899	.58586	.51340	.45019	.34682	.26785	.20737	.12519	.07628	.04689
28	.75684	.65910	.57437	.50088	.43708	.33348	.25509	.19563	.11591	.06934	.04187
29	.74934	.64936	.56311	.48866	.42435	.32065	.24295	.18456	.10733	.06304	.03738
30	.74192	.63976	.55207	.47674	.41199	.30832	.23138	.17411	.09938	.05731	.03338
31	.73458	.63031	.54125	.46511	.39999	.29646	.22036	.16425	.09202	.05210	.02980
32	.72730	.62099	.53063	.45377	.38834	.28506	.20987	.15496	.08520	.04736	.02661
33	.72010	.61182	.52023	.44270	.37703	.27409	.19987	.14619	.07889	.04306	.02376
34	.71297	.60277	.51003	.43191	.36604	.26355	.19035	.13791	.07305	.03914	.02121
35	.70591	.59387	.50003	.42137	.35538	.25342	.18129	.13011	.06763	.03558	.01894
36	.69892	.58509	.49022	.41109	.34503	.24367	.17266	.12274	.06262	.03235	.01691
37	.69200	.57644	.48061	.40107	.33498	.23430	.16444	.11579	.05799	.02941	.01510
38	.68515	.56792	.47119	.39128	.32523	.22529	.15661	.10924	.05369	.02673	.01348
39	.67837	.55953	.46195	.38174	.31575	.21662	.14915	.10306	.04971	.02430	.01204
40	.67165	.55126	.45289	.37243	.30656	.20829	.14205	.09722	.04603	.02209	.01075
41	.66500	.54312	.44401	.36335	.29763	.20028	.13528	.09172	.04262	.02009	.00960
42	.65842	.53509	.43530	.35448	.28896	.19257	.12884	.08653	.03946	.01826	.00857
43	.65190	.52718	.42677	.34584	.28054	.18517	.12270	.08163	.03654	.01660	.00765
44	.64545	.51939	.41840	.33740	.27237	.17085	.11686	.07701	.03383	.01509	.00683
45	.63905	.51171	.41020	.32917	.26444	.17120	.11130	.07265	.03133	.01372	.00610
46	.63273	.50415	.40215	.32115	.25674	.16461	.10600	.06854	.02901	.01247	.00544
47	.62646	.49670	.39427	.31331	.24926	.15828	.10095	.06466	.02686	.01134	.00486
48	.62026	.48936	.38654	.30567	.24200	.15219	.09614	.06100	.02487	.01031	.00434
49	.61412	.48213	.37896	.29822	.23495	.14634	.09156	.05755	.02303	.00937	.00388
50	.60804	.47500	.37153	.29094	.22811	.14071	.08720	.05429	.02132	.00852	.00346

Note: The Table Handbook that accompanies *Business Mathematics* contains more detailed tables.

Step 1. Find the period interest rate:

$$\text{Period rate} = \frac{\text{annual interest rate}}{\text{compounding periods in 1 year}} = \frac{8\%}{4} = 2\%$$

Step 2. Find the number of periods:

$$\text{Periods} = \text{years} \times \text{compounding periods in 1 year} = 5 \times 4 = 20$$

Step 3. In Table 13.7, find the present value of $1 at compound interest at the intersection of the 2% period rate and the 20 periods: .67297.

Step 4. Find the present value to be invested:

$$\text{Present value} = \text{present value of }\$1 \times \text{future value}$$
$$= .67297 \times \$180,000$$
$$= \$121,134.60$$

Step 5. If the amount of interest earned is needed:

$$\text{Interest earned} = \text{future value} - \text{present value}$$
$$= \$180,000 - 121,134.60 = \$58,865.40$$

N	Total number of compounding periods in the problem Enter 20 (5 years × 4 quarters per year = 20 periods).
%i	Percent interest per compounding (payment) period Enter 2 (8% annual rate ÷ 4 quarters per year = 2). *Note: Do not enter .02.*
PMT	*Amount of the regular payment (annuities only)* *Not used for present value problems*
FV	Amount of the future value (or amount needed in the future) Enter 180,000. Future value amount
PV	Enter 2nd PV.

This display on the calculator is the present value, $121,134.84 (the difference in the answers is due to rounding).

If you do not have a financial calculator, but you have a Yˣ key and a 1/x key, you can solve future value problems on your calculator by following these steps:

1. Find the period interest rate: 8% ÷ 4 = .02.
2. Add 100% to the period rate: 100% + .02 = 1.02.
3. Find the number of compounding periods: 4 × 5 = 20.
4. Enter 1.02 Yˣ 20 = 1/x × 180,000 = 121,134.84.

In both examples, the present value (*PV*), $121,134.84, can be subtracted from the future value (*FV*), $180,000, to find the interest (*I*), $58,865.16.

13.5 Practice Problems

Use Table 13.7 to calculate the present value and the interest earned for the following problems:

1. Bill and Janet Sievers have a baby girl. Recent news stories have estimated the cost of an education at a good private college will have escalated to $150,000 by the time their baby is college age in 18 years. A financial advisor recommends an investment that will return 8% compounded semiannually. How much will Bill and Janet need to invest now?

2. Oscherwitz Nursery plans to add a new greenhouse in three years. The total amount needed for the project is estimated to be $65,000. Oscherwitz can invest at 5% compounded annually. How much will have to be invested now?

3. Angela Dawson-Spelling wants to take a family vacation to Tahiti to celebrate her parents' 25th wedding anniversary in four years. She has checked with several travel agencies and has determined that the total vacation package cost will be $12,500. She can invest at 10% compounded quarterly. Calculate the amount she needs to invest now.

4. Suliman Subuh received an inheritance recently. He wants to splurge and buy some frivolous things. But first, he wants to take care of his future retirement needs. Suliman is 30 years old now and would like to retire at 55. He wants $650,000 available when he reaches age 55. He can get 10% compounded semiannually. How much will he have to invest now?

13.5 Solutions to Practice Problems

1. Period rate $= \dfrac{8\%}{2} = 4\%$ Periods $= 18$ years $\times 2 = 36$

   Table 13.7 value at intersection of 4% and 36 periods $= .24367$
   Present value $= .24367 \times \$150,000 = \$36,550.50$
   Interest earned $= \$150,000 - 36,550.50 = \$113,449.50$

2. Period rate $= \dfrac{5\%}{1} = 5\%$ Periods $= 3$ years $\times 1 = 3$

   Table 13.7 value at intersection of 5% and 3 periods $= .86384$
   Present value $= .86384 \times \$65,000 = \$56,149.60$
   Interest earned $= \$65,000 - 56,149.60 = \$8,850.40$

3. Period rate $= \dfrac{10\%}{4} = 2.5\%$ Periods $= 4$ years $\times 4 = 16$

   Table 13.7 value at intersection of 2.5% and 16 periods $= .67362$
   Present value $= .67362 \times \$12,500 = \$8,420.25$
   Interest earned $= \$12,500 - 8,420.25 = \$4,079.75$

4. Period rate $= \dfrac{10\%}{2} = 5\%$ Periods $= 25$ years $\times 2 = 50$

   Table 13.7 value at intersection of 5% and 50 periods $= .08720$
   Present value $= .08720 \times \$650,000 = \$56,680$
   Interest earned $= \$650,000 - 56,680 = \$593,320$

QUICK REFERENCE SUMMARY AND REVIEW

Page	Section Topic	Learning Concepts	Examples and Solutions
458	13.1 Calculating the Future Value and the Compound Interest without Tables	The compound interest is the amount of interest earned on principal and on previously earned interest that has been added to the principal. The compound interest can be calculated by using the simple interest formula, $I = PRT$, for each period interest is paid, adding it to the old principal to arrive at the new principal for the next period's calculations. A shortcut method uses a constant rate for each interest payment period. The constant rate is found by adding 100% to the period rate: Period rate $=$ $\dfrac{\text{annual interest rate}}{\text{Number of periods in 1 year}}$	Calculate the future value and the interest earned on $1,000 at 6% compounded semiannually for 1.5 years. Interest will be calculated for three periods: 1.5 years $\times 2 = 3.$ 1st period: $I = \$1,000 \times 6\% \times \frac{1}{2}$ $= \$30$ 2nd period: $I = \$1,030 \times 6\% \times \frac{1}{2}$ $= \$30.90$ 3rd period: $I = \$1,060.90 \times 6\% \times \frac{1}{2}$ $= \$31.83$ Future value: $\$1,060.90 + 31.83 = \$1,092.73$

Page	Section Topic	Learning Concepts	Examples and Solutions
		It is then multiplied by each interest period's principal (or new principal).	Interest: $1,092.73 − 1,000 = $92.73 $1,000.00 × 1.03 $1,030.00 × 1.03 $1,060.90 × 1.03 $1,092.73 = Future value
462	**13.2** Calculating the Future Value and the Compound Interest with Tables	To use Table 13.2, Future Value of $1 at Compound Interest, follow these steps: 1. Find the period rate. 2. Find the number of periods. 3. Use Table 13.2 to find the intersection of the period rate and the periods. 4. Find the future value by multiplying the future value of $1 found in the Table 13.2 by the principal. 5. If the amount of interest is needed, find it by subtracting the principal from the future value.	Find the future value and the interest for $1,000 compounded semiannually for 1.5 years. $$\text{Period rate} = \frac{6\%}{2} = 3\%$$ Periods = 1.5 × 2 = 3 The table value at the intersection of 3 periods and 3% is 1.092727. 1.092727 × $1,000 = $1,092.73 $1,092.73 − 1,000 = $92.73
465	**13.3** Calculating the Future Value and the Compound Interest with Daily Compounding	Passbook savings accounts pay interest compounded daily. However, interest is credited only every quarter (since banks and savings and loan associations assume 30-day months, a quarter is assumed to have only 90 days). There is no penalty for early withdrawal. Interest rates are generally low. Certificates of deposit require at least a certain minimum deposit, and the money must be left for a specified period. There is a substantial loss of interest if an early withdrawal is made. Several daily compounding tables are available. Table 13.3 is a daily table, Table 13.4 is a quarterly table, and Table 13.5 is an annual table.	Find the interest on $1,000 for (1) 62 days at $5\frac{1}{4}\%$ and (2) for 3 quarters at $5\frac{1}{4}\%$. (3) Also find the interest for 4 years at 6%. (All interest is compounded daily.) 1. In Table 13.3, find the value for 62 days: 1.008957043. Multiply it by $1,000: 1.008957043 × $1,000 $1,008.96 Subtract $1,000 from $1,008.96 to find the interest: $ 1,008.96 − 1,000.00 $8.96 2. Go to Table 13.4. Find the table value for three quarters: 1.0415207. Multiply it by $1,000. 1.0415207 × $1,000 $1,041.52 Subtract $1,000 from $1,041.52: $ 1,041.52 − 1,000.00 $41.52

Page	Section Topic	Learning Concepts	Examples and Solutions
			3. Go to Table 13.5. Find the table factor for 4 years at 6%: 1.271224. Multiply it by $1,000: 1.271224 $\times$ $1,000 $1,271.22 Subtract $1,000 from $1,271.22: $ 1,271.22 $-$ 1,000.00 $27.22
468	**13.4** Calculating the Effective Rate of Interest	The nominal rate is the stated rate. The effective rate is the true or actual rate. The effective rate is also often called the yield. The effective rate is calculated by dividing the interest for one year by the principal. When using tables, a shortcut is to subtract 1 from the table value of the period rate and the number of periods for one year and convert the difference to a percent.	Calculate the effective rate of interest for $1,000 at 10% compounded quarterly. The period rate is: $$\frac{10\%}{4} = 2\frac{1\%}{2}$$ The number of periods: $$1 \times 4 = 4$$ From Table 13.2, the value at the intersection of 4 periods and $2\frac{1}{2}\%$: $$1.103813 - 1 = .103813 = 10.38\%$$

470	**13.5** Calculating the Present Value and the Compound Interest with Tables	The present value is the amount of money that must be invested today to return a known, fixed future value at a specified compound interest rate. To use present value tables, follow these steps:
		
		1. Find the period rate.
		
		2. Find the number of periods.
		
		3. In Table 13.7, find the present value of $1 at compound interest at the intersection of the period rate and the number of periods.
		
		4. Find the present value to be invested by multiplying the table value by the principal.
		
		5. If the interest earned is needed, subtract the present value from the future value.
			Calculate the amount we need to invest today to have $1,000 available in five years at 8% compounded semiannually. The period rate is: $\frac{8\%}{2} = 4\%$.
			
			The number of periods is $5 \times 2 = 10$. Find the table value at the intersection of 4% and 10 periods: .67556.
			Find the present value:
			.67556 $\times$ $1,000
			      = $675.56
			$1,000 $-$ 675.56
			      = $324.44

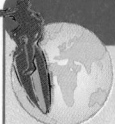
ADDITIONAL PRACTICE PROBLEMS

Answers to odd-numbered problems are given in Appendix A.

13.1

Calculate the future value and the interest without the use of tables for the following compound interest problems:

1. An $18,000 note earned 7% compounded annually for three years. Calculate the future value and the interest earned.

100%	$18,000	Using the calculator:
+ 7%	× 1.07	1.07 ⊗ 18,000 ▣ ▣ ▣ 22,050.77
107% = 1.07	$19,260	
	× 1.07	$22,050.77
	$20,608.20	− 18,000.00
	× 1.07	$ 4,050.77 Interest
	$22,050.77 Future value	

2. Ingrid Slewadenski put $150,000 into an investment paying 8% compounded quarterly. Calculate the future value and the interest that will be earned at the end of the first year.

$\frac{8\%}{4} = 2\%$

100%	1 year
+ 2%	× 4 quarters per year
102% = 1.02	4 compounding periods

$ 150,000	Using the calculator:
× 1.02	1.02 ⊗ 150,000 ▣ ▣ ▣ ▣ 162,364.82
$ 153,000	
× 1.02	$ 162,364.82
$ 156,060	− 150,000.00
× 1.02	$ 12,364.82 Interest
$159,181.20	
× 1.02	
$162,364.82 Future value	

3. Harley Foster wants to know how much interest he will earn in two years on $2,000 earning 6% compounded semiannually.

$\frac{6\%}{2} = 3\%$

100%	2 years
+ 3%	× 2 semiannual periods per year
103% = 1.03	4 compounding periods

$ 2,000	Using the calculator:
× 1.03	1.03 ⊗ 2,000 ▣ ▣ ▣ ▣ 2,251.02
$ 2,060	
× 1.03	$ 2,251.02
$2,121.80	− 2,000.00
× 1.03	$ 251.02 Interest
$2,185.45	
× 1.03	
$2,251.02 Future value	

4. Opal May DeRosen is earning 12% compounded monthly on her investment of $12,000. Calculate the future value and the interest rate after four months.

$\frac{12\%}{12} = 1\%$

100%	
+ 1%	
101% = 1.01	4 compounding periods

$ 12,000	Using the calculator:
× 1.01	1.01 ⊗ 12,000 ▣ ▣ ▣ ▣ 12,487.25
$ 12,120	
× 1.01	$ 12,487.25
$12,241.20	− 12,000.00
× 1.01	$ 487.25 Interest
$12,363.61	
× 1.01	
$12,487.25 Future value	

5. Julia Polk-Evanderer invested $6,000 in an investment that she estimates will earn an average of 5% compounded semiannually. How much will her investment be worth, and how much interest will she have earned, at the end of two years?

$\frac{5\%}{2} = 2.5\%$

100.0%	2 years.
+ 2.5%	× 2 semiannual periods per year
102.5% = 1.025	4 compounding periods

$ 6,000	Using the calculator:
× 1.025	1.025 ⊗ 6,000 ▣ ▣ ▣ ▣ 6,622.88
$ 6,150	
× 1.025	$ 6,622.88
$ 6,303.75	− 6,000.00
× 1.025	$ 622.88 Interest
$ 6,461.34	
× 1.025	
$ 6,622.88 Future value	

13.2

Use Table 13.2 to find the future value and the interest in the following problems:

6. Ester Baldwin put $15,000 into an IRA account for her future needs at age 62. Ester is now 32 years old. The fund guarantees a return of 8% compounded semiannually. How much is the guaranteed future value and interest for the investment?

62	30 years	$\dfrac{8\%}{2} = 4\%$	$ 15,000.00
− 32	× 2 semiannual periods per year		× 10.519627 Table value
30	60 compounding periods		$ 157,794.41 Future value

$157,794.41
− 15,000.00
$142,794.41 Interest

7. Jan Friedman invested $30,000 in a bond paying 6% compounded monthly for four years. Calculate the future value and the interest to be earned.

4 years	$\dfrac{6\%}{12} = .5\%$	$ 30,000.00
× 12 monthly periods per year		× 1.270489 Table value
48 compounding periods		$ 38,114.67 Future value

$ 38,114.67
− 30,000.00
$ 8,114.67 Interest

8. Martha Copurnicus established a college trust fund when her daughter was born by depositing $15,000 in a fund paying 5% compounded semiannually. Find the value of the fund and the interest earned after 18 years.

18 years	$\dfrac{5\%}{2} = 2.5\%$	$ 15,000.00
× 2 semiannual periods per year		× 2.432535 Table value
36 compounding periods		$ 36,488.03 Future value

$ 36,488.03
− 15,000.00
$ 21,488.03 Interest

9. Find the future value and interest for $70,000 deposited at 10% compounded quarterly for 12 years.

12 tears	$\dfrac{10\%}{4} = 2.5\%$	$ 70,000.00
× 4 quarterly periods per year		× 3.271490 Table value
48 compounding periods		$229,004.30 Future value

$229,004.30
− 70,000.00
$159,004.30 Interest

10. Percy Mcbride invested $20,000 at 6% compounded quarterly. Calculate the future value and interest after six years.

6 years	$\dfrac{6\%}{4} = 1.5\%$	$ 20,000.00
× 4 quarterly periods per year		× 1.429503 Table value
24 compounding periods		$ 28,590.06 Future value

$ 28,590.06
− 20,000.00
$ 8,590.06 Interest

13.3

Use Table 13.3, 13.4, or 13.5 to find the future value and the interest in the following daily compounding problems. (Remember that each month is assumed to have 30 days.)

11. On April 1 William James had a passbook savings account balance of $2,000. Two deposits were made during the quarter: May 20, $500 and June 5, $1,500. The account pays $5\frac{1}{4}$% compounded daily. Calculate the value of the account at the end of the quarter and the interest earned during the quarter.

For 90 days, $2,000 × 1.013028415 = $2,026.06 *FV* $26.06 *I*
For 40 days, $ 500 × 1.005769591 = $ 502.88 *FV* $ 2.88 *I*
For 25 days, $1,500 × 1.003602104 = $1,505.40 *FV* $ 5.40 *I*
 $4,034.34 $34.34

12. Calculate the maturity value and interest earned for a $25,000, $5\frac{1}{2}$%, 180-day (two-quarter) certificate of deposit that is compounded daily.

$25,000 × 1.0274924 = $25,687.31 *MV* $25,687.31
− 25,000.00
687.31 Interest

13. Alan Kaplan invested $35,000 in a four-year certificate of deposit paying 7% compounded daily. Find the maturity value and the interest earned at maturity.

$35,000 × 1.323094 = $46,308.29 *MV*

$$\begin{array}{r} \$\ 46,308.29 \\ -\ 35,000.00 \\ \hline \$\ 11,308.29\ \text{Interest} \end{array}$$

14. Margot's Fashion Corner has a passbook savings account that pays interest at $5\frac{1}{2}$% compounded daily. On July 1 the balance in the account was $8,000. During the quarter, the following transactions were made:

Date	Transaction	Amount
July 11	Withdrawal	$1,000
August 6	Deposit	$ 500
August 19	Deposit	$ 800

Calculate the value at the end of the quarter and the interest earned during the quarter.

For 90 days, $7,000 × 1.013028415 = $7,091.20 *FV* $ 91.20 *I*
For 10 days, $1,000 × 1.001439288 = 1,001.44 *FV*   1.44 *I*
For 54 days, $ 500 × 1.007968030 =   503.98 *FV*   3.98 *I*
For 41 days, $ 800 × 1.005914257 =   804.73 *FV*   4.73 *I*
                                              $101.35 *I*

$$\begin{array}{l} \$8,000 - 1,000 + 500 + 800 = \$8,300.00\ P \\ \qquad\qquad\qquad\qquad\quad +\ 101.35\ I \\ \qquad\qquad\qquad\qquad\quad \$8,401.35\ FV \end{array}$$

15. Mark White's Welding routinely estimates its quarterly equipment needs and invests in a one-quarter CD to make the purchases. This quarter's CD rate is $5\frac{1}{2}$% compounded daily. The amount invested in the CD is $7,500. Calculate the amount of the investment at the end of the quarter and the interest earned for the quarter.

$7,500 × 1.013653 = $7,602.40 *FV*

$$\begin{array}{r} \$\ 7,602.40\ FV \\ -\ 7,500.00\ P \\ \hline \$\quad 102.40\ I \end{array}$$

13.4

Calculate the effective interest rate for the following problems (rounded to the nearest hundredth of a percent):

16. Calculate the effective interest rate for $5,000 invested at 8% compounded semiannually.

Table factor for 4%, 2 periods =   1.0816
$$\begin{array}{r} -\ 1.0000 \\ \hline .0816 = 8.16\% \end{array}$$

17. Terri Tatarevich placed $500 in an account paying 6% compounded quarterly. Determine the effective interest rate.

Table factor for 1.5%, 4 periods =   1.061364
$$\begin{array}{r} -\ 1.000000 \\ \hline .061364 = 6.14\% \end{array}$$

18. A bank pays 9% compounded monthly. Find the yield.

Table factor for .75%, 12 periods =   1.093807
$$\begin{array}{r} -\ 1.000000 \\ \hline .093807 = 9.38\% \end{array}$$

19. Yung Lee deposited $10,000 in a savings account paying 5% compounded semiannually. Determine the effective rate the savings account is paying.

Table factor for 2.5%, 2 periods =   1.050625
$$\begin{array}{r} -\ 1.000000 \\ \hline .050625 = 5.06\% \end{array}$$

20. Donald Curry's 30-year treasury bond pays 10% compounded quarterly. Calculate the effective rate.

Table factor for 2.5%, 4 periods =   1.103813
$$\begin{array}{r} -\ 1.000000 \\ \hline .103813 = 10.38\% \end{array}$$

13.5

Use Table 13.7 to calculate the present value and the interest earned for the following problems:

21. Lionel's Ice Cream Parlor has a five-year plan to replace its refrigeration system at an estimated cost of $25,000. An investment that will return 8% compounded semiannually is available. How much will have to be invested now?

5 years
×2 semiannual periods per year
10 compounding periods

$\dfrac{8\%}{2} = 4\%$ $25,000.00
              × .67556 Table value
              $16,889.00 Present value

22. Klopper Brothers Distribution wants to establish a pension plan that will have $750,000 available in 25 years for their employees. The brothers can invest at 8% compounded annually. How much will the initial investment need to be?

25 years
×1 annual periods per year
25 compounding periods

$\dfrac{8\%}{1} = 8\%$ $750,000.00
              ×   .14602 Table value
              $109,515.00 Present value

23. John De La Porte wants a Mercedes. Right now he has enough money to afford a less expensive car. It has been suggested that he might invest the money he has now, drive his old car for another five years, and let the compound interest he will earn make up the difference for the car of his dreams. He estimates he will need $58,000 in five years. He can invest at 10% compounded quarterly. How much will he have to invest now?

5 years
$\times$ 4 quarterly periods per year
20 compounding periods

$\dfrac{10\%}{4} = 2.5\%$

$58,000.00
$\times$ .61027 Table value
$35,395.66 Present value

24. Angie Quinonez wants to start a business in four years. She will need $45,000 in cash at that time. How much must she invest now if she can earn 12% compounded monthly?

4 years
$\times$ 12 quarterly periods per year
48 compounding periods

$\dfrac{12\%}{12} = 1\%$

$45,000.00
$\times$ .62026 Table value
$27,911.70 Present value

25. Estrada Enterprises anticipates upgrading its computer system in five years. Determine the lump sum amount that will have to be invested now at 6% compounded semiannually to have the $80,000 it is estimated will be needed.

5 years
$\times$ 2 semiannual periods per year
10 compounding periods

$\dfrac{6\%}{2} = 3\%$

$80,000.00
$\times$ .74409 Table value
$59,527.20 Present value

CHAPTER REVIEW PROBLEMS

Answers to odd-numbered problems are given in Appendix A.

Drill Problems

Fill in all of the missing information for problems 1 through 30. Note that you do not need to find some of the information for some problems. When that is the case, a broken line (——) is drawn across the blank (for example, in problem 5). (Round to the nearest cent and the nearest hundredth of a percent.)

	Present Value (Amount of Investment)	Nominal Annual Rate	Compounding Frequency	Investment Length	Effective Annual Rate	Period Rate	Number of Compounding Periods	Future Value	Amount of Compound Interest
1.	$12,000	8%	Annually	3 years	8.00 %	8%	3	$15,116.54	$3,116.54
2.	4,000	4%	Semiannually	2 years	4.04%	2%	4	4,329.73	329.73
3.	34,000	6%	Quarterly	1 year	6.14%	1.5%	4	36,086.38	2,086.38
4.	450	12%	Monthly	4 months	12.68%	1%	4	468.27	18.27
5.	5,000	$5\frac{1}{4}$%	Daily	16 days	——		16	5,011.52	11.52

	Present Value (Amount of Investment)	Nominal Annual Rate	Compounding Frequency	Investment Length	Effective Annual Rate	Period Rate	Number of Compounding Periods	Future Value	Amount of Compound Interest
6.	$25,000	4%	Quarterly	12 years	4.06%	1%	48	$40,305.65	$15,305.65
7.	3,500	8%	Annually	36 years	8%	8%	36	77,879.29	74,379.29
8.	75,000	10%	Semiannually	6 years	10.25%	5%	12	134,689.20	59,689.20
9.	2,000	$5\frac{1}{2}$%	Daily	3 quarters	——	——	3	2,083.04	83.04
10.	47,500	8%	Monthly	4 years	8.30%	2/3%	48	65,344.14	17,844.14

Present Value (Amount of Investment)	Nominal Annual Rate	Compounding Frequency	Investment Length	Effective Annual Rate	Period Rate	Number of Compounding Periods	Future Value	Amount of Compound Interest
11. $ 4,529.75	5%	Semiannually	2 years	5.06%	2.5%	4	$ 5,000	$470.25
12. 815.36	10%	Quarterly	1 year	10.38%	2.5%	4	900	84.64
13. 839.62	6%	Annually	3 years	6%	6%	3	1,000	160.38
14. 21,352.98	12%	Monthly	3 months	12.68%	1%	3	22,000	647.02
15. 1,185.47				8.16%	4%	6	1,500	314.53

Present Value (Amount of Investment)	Nominal Annual Rate	Compounding Frequency	Investment Length	Effective Annual Rate	Period Rate	Number of Compounding Periods	Future Value	Amount of Compound Interest
16. $ 39,063.75	5%	Annually	40 years	5%	5%	40	$275,000	$235,936.25
17. 8,180.20	10%	Semiannually	22 years	10.25%	5%	44	70,000	61,819.80
18. 11,487.40	8%	Quarterly	7 years	8.24%	2%	28	20,000	8,512.60
19. 21,709.10	12%	Monthly	4 years	12.68%	1%	48	35,000	13,290.90
20. 241,897.50	3%	Annually	21 years	3%	3%	21	450,000	208,102.50

Present Value (Amount of Investment)	Nominal Annual Rate	Compounding Frequency	Investment Length	Effective Annual Rate	Period Rate	Number of Compounding Periods	Future Value	Amount of Compound Interest
21. $ 88,849	3%	Annually	4 years	3 %	3%	4	$ 100,000	$ 11,151
22. 1,250	5%	Semiannually	30 years	5.06%	2.5%	60	5,499.74	4,249.75
23. 500,000	9%	Daily	3 years	—	—	3	654,960	154,960
24. 1,644.36	10%	Quarterly	9 years	10.38%	2.5%	36	4,000	2,355.64
25. 23,500	8%	Semiannually	7 years	8.16%	4%	14	40,694.39	17,194.39

Present Value (Amount of Investment)	Nominal Annual Rate	Compounding Frequency	Investment Length	Effective Annual Rate	Period Rate	Number of Compounding Periods	Future Value	Amount of Compound Interest
26. $84,595.20	6%	Annually	6 years	6%	6%	6	$120,000	$ 35,404.80
27. 40,000	6%	Semiannually	6 years	6.09%	3%	12	57,030.40	17,030.40
28. 402.24	6%	Quarterly	6 years	6.14%	1.5%	24	575	172.76
29. 145,000	$5\frac{1}{4}$%	Daily	78 days	—	—	78	146,635.82	1,635.82
30. 75,000	6%	Monthly	10 years	6.17%	.5%	120	136,454.78	61,454.78

Word Problems

31. Calculate the future value of a $9,500 lump sum investment at 8% compounded semiannually for 18 years.

18 years
× 2 semiannual periods per year
36 compounding periods

$\dfrac{8\%}{2} = 4\%$

$ 9,500.00 PV
× 4.103933 Table value
$ 38,987.36 FV

32. Find effective rate for an investment of $88,000 at 12% compounded monthly for five years.

$\dfrac{12\%}{12} = 1\%$ 12 periods in one year   In table, intersection of 1%.

12 periods is   1.126825

          $-$ 1.000000

             .126825 = 12.68%

33. Miles Smith invested $15,000 in a one-year (four-quarter), $5\frac{1}{2}$% CD that was compounded daily. Determine its value and the amount of interest earned at the end of the year.

$15,000 × 1.0557405 = $15,836.11 FV $ 15,836.11 FV

                                 $-$ 15,000.00 PV

                              $ 836.11 I

34. Nicole Lateur invested $35,000 in a three-year certificate of deposit at 8% compounded daily to finance the opening of a second Nicole's Bookstore. Calculate the future value and the interest that will be earned.

$35,000 × 1.271215 = $44,492.53 FV $ 44,492.53 FV

                                 $-$ 35,000.00 PV

                              $ 9,492.53 I

35. Thomas Reynolds wants to accumulate $2,500 at 6% compounded quarterly to pay for new office furniture in two years. How much must he invest now?

$\dfrac{6\%}{4} = 1.5\%$ 2 × 4 = 8 periods $2,500 × .88771 = $2,219.28

36. A doctor serving his residency at St. Paul Hospital has estimated that he will need $144,000 in 4 years to open his own office. Determine how much he will have to invest now at 10% compounded semiannually.

$\dfrac{10\%}{2} = 5\%$ 4 × 2 = 8 periods $144,000 × .67684 = $97,464.96

37. Sandusky Corporation has negotiated a long-term agreement with the First International State Bank to establish a retirement fund for company employees. A lump sum deposit of $250,000 is to be compounded monthly for 10 years at 8%. How much will be in the fund at maturity, and how much interest will be earned?

$\dfrac{8\%}{12} = \dfrac{2}{3}\%$ 10 × 12 = 120 periods $ 250,000 $ 554,910

                                      × 2.21964 $-$ 250,000

                                      $ 554,910 FV $ 304,910 I

38. Determine the effective interest rate on $9,000 invested at 5% compounded semiannually for 12 years.

$\dfrac{5\%}{2} = 2.5\%$ 1 × 2 = 2 periods in 1 year   1.050625

                                         $-$ 1.000000

                                           .050625 = 5.06%

39. Calculate the future value and the interest earned for a $60,000, 90-day certificate of deposit at $5\frac{1}{2}$% compounded daily.

$60,000 × 1.013653 = $60,819.18 FV $ 60,819.18

                                 $-$ 60,000.00

                              $ 819.18 I

40. Susan Lightfoot, presently a dance instructor, wants to open her own studio in six years. She estimates she will need $25,000 then. How much will she have to invest now at 8% compounded quarterly?

$\dfrac{8\%}{4} = 2\%$ 6 × 4 = 24 periods $25,000 × .62172 = $15,543 PV

41. Sarah Milistrom opened a passbook savings account by depositing $5,000 on May 6. On June 3 she deposited another $750. At the end of the quarter, how much interest will she have earned and what will her passbook account balance be?

The $5,000 will draw interest for 54 days (24 days in May and 30 days in June): $5,000 × 1.00796803 = $5,039.84

The $750 will draw interest for 27 days: $750 × 1.003890832 = $ 752.92

                                                     Account balance $5,792.76

$ 5,792.76 FV

$-$ 5,750.00 PV

$ 42.76 I

42. Marcus Urestes invested $15,000 in a corporate bond fund that he estimates will return an average of 10% compounded quarterly. Calculate his future value and interest earned at the end of nine years.

$\dfrac{10\%}{4} = 2.5\%$ 9 × 4 = 36 periods $ 15,000 $ 36,488.03

                                          × 2.432535 $-$ 15,000.00

                                      $ 36,488.03 FV $ 21,488.03 I

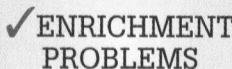

43. Determine the ending balance of a passbook savings account that had a $50,000 balance on April 1 and was compounded daily at $5\frac{1}{4}$%. During the quarter, the following transactions occurred: April 10th, $10,000 was deposited; May 2nd, $5,000 was withdrawn; June 5th, $2,500 was deposited.

$50,000 drew interest for 90- days: $50,000 × 1.013028415 = $50,651.42

$10,000 drew interest for 22 days (20 days in April and 2 days in May): $10,000 × 1.003169167 = $10,031.69

$5,000 ($10,000 − 5,000) drew interest for 58 days (28 days in May and 30 days in June): $ 5,000 × 1.008376756 = $ 5,041.88

$2,500 drew interest for 25 days: $ 2,500 × 1.003602104 = $ 2,509.01

Interest earned:

$651.42 + 31.69 + 41.88 + 9.01 = $734

Ending balance:

$50,000 + 10,000 − 5,000 + 2,500 + 734 = $58,234

44. Madison Forsythe, Inc., plans to build a store instead of leasing in 10 years. The plans call for a total building cost of $750,000. He can invest in one opportunity that he estimates will return an average of 11% compounded daily. Since it is a little risky, Madison is only going to invest $150,000 in it. Another, safer, investment plan will guarantee a return of 6% compounded quarterly. Calculate how much he will have to put into the 6% investment to reach his goal.

Calculate the FV of $150,000 at 11% compounded daily:

$ 150,000
× 3.003661
$450,549.15

Calculate how much more needs to be earned:

$ 750,000.00
− $450,549.15
$ 299,450.85

Find the amount that will have to be invested at 6%:

$299,450.85
× .55126
$165,075.28

CRITICAL THINKING GROUP PROJECT

Quinton Elliott received a $50,000 graduation gift from his Mother. Quinton has decided to work for a corporation for five years and then go into business for himself. He has been investigating the various investment opportunities, and has gathered the following information:

Company	Investment Type	Interest Rate	Compounding Frequency	Risk
Salt Lake City Bank	CD	6.00%	Daily	Low
Morganthal National	CD	6.00%	Quarterly	Low
Utah State Bank	CD	7.00%	Annually	Low
Janus Funds	Bond fund	8.00%	Semiannually	Medium
Lyman Mutual Funds	Stock fund	9.00%	Monthly	High

The risk factor is important to Quinton. The rates that are shown in the illustration are the expected returns. However, the risk factor can influence the return. Low risk means that it is a virtual certainty that the investment will pay the rate stated, and no principal will be lost. Medium risk means that the rate may fluctuate and some of the principal could be lost. High risk means that the rate may fluctuate a greater amount than with the medium risk investment, and although unlikely, all or most of the principal could be lost.

1. Calculate the expected future value of each of the investments.

Salt Lake City Bank.	$67,491.25
Morganthal National	67,342.75
Utah State Bank	70,127.60
Janus Funds	74,012.20
Lyman Mutual Funds	78,284.05

2. What further information would you advise Quinton to obtain before he makes a final decision on the investment?

Student answers will vary, but they could include the need for information on penalties for early withdrawal of funds, and whether the banks provide any other incentives such as free checking, overdraft protection, and so on.

3. What would your recommendation be? Why?

Student answers will vary, but the reason(s) for their recommendation is the important thing. It should be logical and consistent with their recommendation.

1. Distinguish between the period rate and the constant rate.
   The period rate is the annual interest rate divided by the number of compounding periods in one year. The constant rate is the period rate plus 100%.

2. Define *present value* and give two other names frequently used in place of *present value*.
   Present value is the amount an investment will be worth at the end of some future period of time when interest is compounded. It is also called the compounded amount or the maturity value.

3. Without using tables, find the future value and the interest earned by a $20,000 investment compounded annually at 9% for three years.

   9% + 100% = 109% = 1.09

$ 20,000	$ 25,900.58
× 1.09	− 20,000.00
$ 21,800	$ 5,900.58 *I*
× 1.09	
$ 23,762	
× 1.09	
$25,900.58 *FV*	

4. Find the future value and the interest for a $45,000 investment at 6% compounded monthly for 20 months.

   $\frac{6\%}{12} = .5\%$

1.104896	$ 49,720.32
× $45,000.00	− 45,000.00
$ 49,720.32	$ 4,720.32

5. Find the future value and the interest for a $12,000 investment at 8% compounded semiannually for 30 years.

   $\frac{8\%}{2} = 4\%$

30	10.519627	$126,235.52	
× 2	× $12,000.00	− 12,000.00	
60 periods	$ 126,235.52	$114,235.52	

6. Calculate the ending quarterly balance of a $5\frac{1}{4}\%$ passbook savings account given the following:

   Beginning balance April 1 $2,500

   Deposit   May 5   600

   Deposit   May 29   1,400

   $2,500 earned interest for the entire 90 days: $2,500 × 1.013028415 = $2,532.57

   $600 earned interest for 55 days (25 days in May and 30 days in June): $600 × 1.007941760 = $604.77

   $1,400 earned interest for 31 days (1 day in May and 30 days in June): $1,400 × 1.004468538 = $1,406.26

   Interest earned:
$ 2,532.57	$ 604.77	$ 1,406.26
− 2,500.00	− 600.00	− 1,400.00
$ 32.57 + $	4.77 + $	6.26 = $43.60

   Future value: $2,500 + 600 + 1,400 + 43.58 = $4,543.58

7. Determine the value of a $6,000 investment at $5\frac{1}{2}\%$ compounded daily for 180 days.

   $6,000 × 1.0274924 = $6,164.95

8. Manny Ortega invested $50,000 in a five-year certificate of deposit paying 7% compounded daily. Calculate the interest earned and the value at maturity.

   $50,000 × 1.419019 = $70,950.95 *FV*

$ 70,950.95
− 50,000.00
$ 20,950.95 *I*

9. Determine the effective rate of interest of a $3,000 investment at 10% compounded quarterly for seven years.

   $\frac{10\%}{4} = 2.5\%$ 1 × 4 = 4

1.103813
−1.000000
.103813 = 10.38%

10. May Kimberling received an insurance settlement, a portion of which she wants to invest to start a florist shop in six years. At 6% compounded quarterly, how much would she have to invest now to have $75,000 then?

    $\frac{6\%}{4} = 1.5\%$ 6 × 4 = 24 periods

$75,000.00
× .69954
$52,465.50

APPLICATION 1

Springfield has set up a form to find the future value of various investments it has made. For example, the first entry in the form is a $400,000, four-year money market certificate that is expected to return 4.95% compounded semiannually. When you open Ch13App1 from your computer spreadsheet applications disk, you will see the form shown here:

Springfield Department Store

2617 Main Street
Box 219
Springfield, Maryland 58109
Telephone: 301-555-2158   FAX: 301-555-3498

CALCULATING FUTURE VALUE AND COMPOUND INTEREST AMOUNTS

Financial Institution	Present Value	Annual Rate	Compounding Periods per Yr	No. of Years	Future Value	Amount of Compound Int.
					#DIV/0!	#DIV/0!
					#DIV/0!	#DIV/0!
					#DIV/0!	#DIV/0!
					#DIV/0!	#DIV/0!
					#DIV/0!	#DIV/0!
					#DIV/0!	#DIV/0!
					#DIV/0!	#DIV/0!

Enter the following information:

Financial Institution	Cell	Present Value	Cell	Annual Rate	Cell
Bank of New Orleans	A12	$ 400,000	B12	.0495	C12
Gibraltar National	A13	$ 1,934,000	B13	.059	C13
Chase Manhattan	A14	$38,104,000	B14	.0725	C14
Bank of America	A15	$ 250,000	B15	.085	C15
U.S. Federal Savings	A16	$ 3,000,000	B16	.0575	C16
Morgan National	A17	$15,050,000	B17	.0625	C17
Louisianna State Bank	A18	$ 2,745,930	B18	.055	C18

Compounding Periods per Year	Cell	Number of Years	Cell
2	D12	4	E12
365	D13	9	E13
12	D14	3	E14
12	D15	7	E15
4	D16	1.5	E16
365	D17	12	E17
1	D18	8	E18

Answer the following questions after you have completed the spreadsheet:

1. What is the future value of the $400,000 investment?

2. What is the amount of compound interest earned by the $38,104,000 investment?

3. What is the amount of the future value of the $2,745,930 investment?

4. What is the amount of the compound interest earned by the $250,000 investment?

5. What is the amount of the compound interest earned by the $1,934,000 investment?

6. What is the amount of the future value of the $15,050,000 investment?

7. What is the amount of the future value of the $3,000,000 investment?

8. What is the amount of the compound interest earned by the $15,050,000 investment?

GROUP REPORT

FOR CHAPTER 13 APPLICATION 1

Springfield's board of directors is considering various programs that would allow employee participation in a retirement program. The store manager has asked your group to make recommendations.

1. Determine the difference in the amount of interest earned if the compounding periods per year changed from 12 to 365 (monthly to daily compounding).

2. Find the amount of money each member of your group could accumulate by his or her 65th birthday if today each of you could put $5,000 in an account paying 8.5% compounded monthly (remember to alter the number of years so it would reflect the number of years left until each person's 65th birthday).

3. Some members of the board are suggesting that the decision be deferred for 5 to 10 years. Calculate the difference it would make in the future value if you waited 5 or 10 years to put that $5,000 into the same investment.

4. Write a report to the store manager providing the results of your findings and make recommendations based on them.

EXCEL SPREADSHEET APPLICATION FOR CHAPTER 13

APPLICATION 2

Springfield has set up a form to find the present value of various investments it plans to make for future purchases. For example, the first entry in the form is for a planned new store that has an estimated cost of $3,500,000 in five years. That much money can be invested in the Fidelity Small Cap Fund today at an estimated return of 9.8% compounded quarterly (four times per year). When you open Ch13App2 from your computer spreadsheet applications disk, you will see the form shown here:

Springfield Department Store

2617 Main Street
Box 219
Springfield, Maryland 58109
Telephone: 301-555-2158   FAX: 301-555-3498

CALCULATING PRESENT VALUE AND COMPOUND INTEREST AMOUNTS

Financial Institution	Present Value	Annual Rate	Compounding Periods per Yr	No. of Years	Future Value	Amount of Compound Int.
Fidelity Small Cap	#DIV/0!					#DIV/0!
PBHG Emerging Growth	#DIV/0!					#DIV/0!
Janus Mercury	#DIV/0!					#DIV/0!
Harbor International	#DIV/0!					#DIV/0!
Twentieth Century Vista	#DIV/0!					#DIV/0!
Oberweis Emerging Growth	#DIV/0!					#DIV/0!
Manhattan Fund	#DIV/0!					#DIV/0!

Enter the following information:

Financial Institution	Cell	Annual Rate	Cell
Fidelity Small Cap	A12	.098	C12
PBHG Emerging Growth	A13	.0875	C13
Janus Mercury	A14	.125	C14
Harbor International	A15	.10	C15
Twentieth Century Vista	A16	.0915	C16
Oberweise Emerging Growth	A17	.085	C17
Manhattan Fund	A18	.1175	C18

Compounding Periods per Year	Cell	Number of Years	Cell	Future Value	Cell
4	D12	5	E12	$3,500,000	F12
12	D13	7	E13	$ 45,000	F13
2	D14	3	E14	$ 215,000	F14
1	D15	9	E15	$ 30,000	F15
12	D16	10	E16	$2,125,000	F16
365	D17	4	E17	$ 50,900	F17
4	D18	2.5	E18	$ 25,000	F18

Answer the following questions after you have completed the spreadsheet. Once the questions are answered, you may want to vary the data inputs to see the results. For example, you might want to see the amount of money you would have to put into an account today that is paying 8.5% compounded daily to accumulate the future value amount you estimate you will need in five years to buy a new car.

1. What is the present value of the $45,000 needed in seven years?

2. What is the amount of compound interest earned by the investment needed to accumulate the $3,500,000 in five years?

3. What is the present value of the $50,900 needed in four years?

4. What is the amount of the compound interest earned by the investment needed to accumulate the $25,000 in two and a half years?

5. What is the amount of the compound interest earned by the investment needed to accumulate the $215,000 in three years?

6. What is the present value of the $2,125,000 needed in 10 years?

7. What is the present value of the $30,000 needed in nine years?

8. What is the amount of the compound interest earned by the investment needed to accumulate the $45,000 needed in seven years?

GROUP REPORT

FOR CHAPTER 13 APPLICATION 2

The Springfield Employee Association, an elected group that represents employee points of view, publishes an employee newsletter each month. It has asked your group to provide a report for publication that would help employees realize goals for their children's future educational needs.

It has been estimated that the average total cost of providing four years of college five years from now will be $80,000 at the state university. In 10 years, the same four years of college will cost $125,000, and in 15 years, it will cost $200,000.

1. Determine the amounts of money that will have to be put into an account today at 10% compounded daily (365 times per year) to accumulate the amounts needed for an education 5, 10, and 15 years from today.

2. Write a report for the newsletter describing your group's findings.

Chapter 13 Financial Applications: Future Value and Present Value at Compound Interest

14

FINANCIAL APPLICATIONS
ANNUITIES AND SINKING FUNDS

SAVING FOR RETIREMENT

We Americans really like to spend money. Since spending is the opposite of saving, we are often accused of not saving enough to provide ample funds to satisfy the needs of business for the purchase of new plants and equipment.

According to some authorities, saving has increased lately. The reason is that more people are thinking about retirement. Although all economists agree that the Social Security Trust Fund is fundamentally sound, almost no worker has ever believed that it will pay enough to provide a comfortable life in retirement. Americans live longer and want to enjoy it more, so they are placing far more money into private retirement accounts.

The favorite vehicle for savers is the 401(k) plan. Named for the section of the tax code that permits it, 401(k) accounts allow workers to divert 15% of their income, up to $9,500 per year, into a retirement account. The account's principal and interest are not taxed until the owner starts drawing down the funds at retirement. In many plans, the employer matches the employee's savings, sometimes kicking in as much as 65 cents for each $1 the worker saves.

More than $1 trillion has now been placed in 401(k) plans, and the amount is growing. That is a lot. But in the year 2030 the Social Security Trust Fund will have $12 trillion in it. That means there will be plenty to fill the future investment coffers and enough retirement to go around.

Chapter Glossary

Annuity. A series of payments or incomes made or received at regular intervals.

Ordinary annuity. Investments or payments that are made at the *end* of each period.

Annuity due. Investments or payments that are made at the *beginning* of each period.

Present value of an annuity. The lump sum amount that must be deposited or invested now to provide for the withdrawal of a series of periodic equal payments.

Sinking fund. Regular, periodic investments made at interest to accumulate a known lump sum amount needed by a specific date.

uture value and present value problems solved in Chapter 13 involved a specific, one-time, lump sum deposit (present value) that was left in an account for a specified period of time drawing specific periodic interest. The interest was left on deposit for the entire period, at the end of which a lump sum amount (the future value) was available for withdrawal. The difference between future value and present value is the unknown amount. Figure 14.1 illustrates a future value, and Figure 14.2 illustrates a present value.

An **annuity** is a series of payments or incomes made or received at regular intervals. For example, when workers retire at age 65, they begin receiving regular monthly Social Security checks. That is an annuity. Each month most of us make mortgage or rent payments. That is an annuity. When an annuity is invested, or is received from an investment, it is affected by compound interest. The remainder of this chapter will describe various applications of these *streams* of payments or incomes at compound interest.

LEARNING UNIT 1
ORDINARY ANNUITIES AND ANNUITIES DUE

EXCEL Spreadsheet Application Spreadsheet Application 1 at the end of this chapter was designed by Springfield to compare ordinary annuities with annuities due.

Financial advisors recommend that people make regular, periodic investments. A person might invest $2,000 annually in an IRA account from the day his or her full-time job begins until retirement age is reached. Assuming that period is between ages 25 and 65, the question is, Should the person make the investment at the beginning or the end of each year? The answer: If the investment is made at the beginning of each year, the person has chosen an *ordinary annuity*. If the investment is made at the end of each year, the person has chosen an *annuity due*.

Ordinary annuities are investments or payments that are made at the *end* of each period. **Annuities due** are investments or payments that are made at the *beginning* of each period. The main difference is that an ordinary annuity will not earn interest in the first period because the investment is made at the end of the period. An annuity due

Figure 14.1
Future Value at Compound Interest

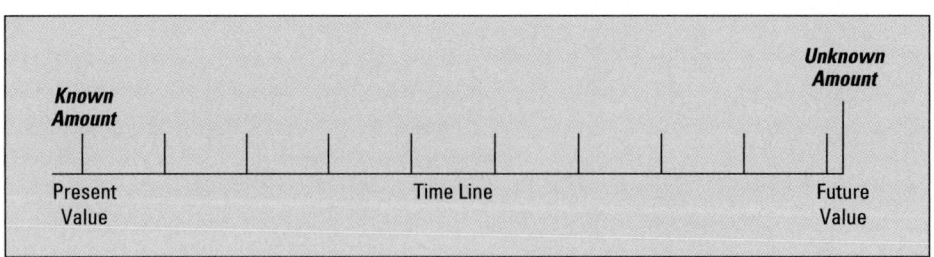

Figure 14.2
Present Value at Compound Interest

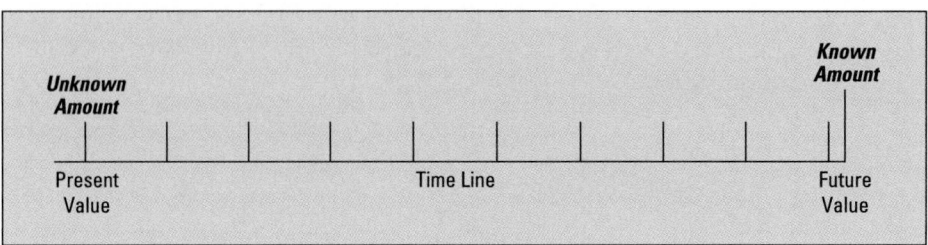

Figure 14.3
Ordinary Annuities and
Annuities Due: A Comparison

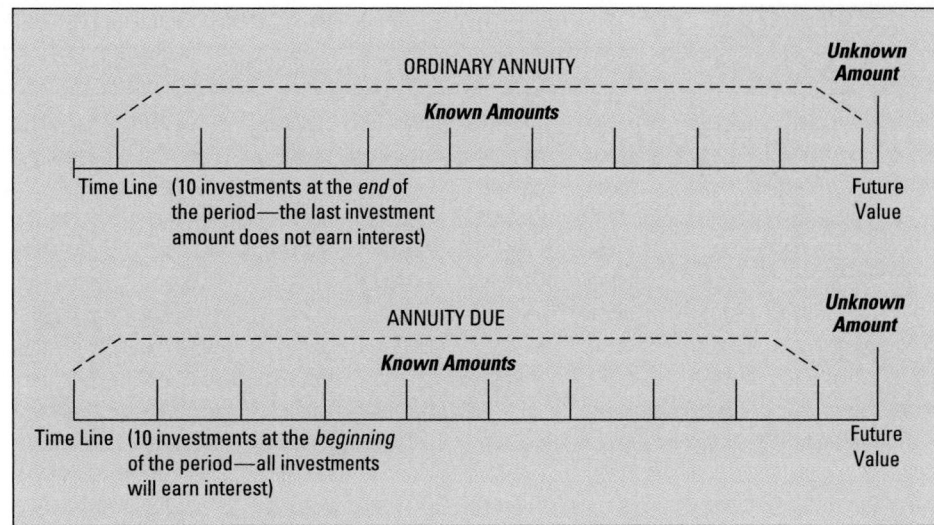

does earn interest in the first period, and that interest will then be compounded over the entire length of the investment period. By the time a person reaches age 65, that makes a significant difference. Figure 14.3 illustrates the characteristics and differences. The known amounts and the unknown amounts should be noted because they show how annuities are distinguished from sinking funds.

14.1 Calculating the Future Value of Ordinary Annuities and Annuities Due

The following steps are used to calculate the future value of ordinary annuities and annuities due:

Step 1. Find the period interest rate:

$$\text{Period rate} = \frac{\text{annual interest rate}}{\text{compounding periods in 1 year}}$$

Step 2. Find the number of periods:
For ordinary annuity:

$$\text{Periods} = \text{years} \times \text{compounding periods in 1 year}$$

For annuity due (one more investment will earn interest):

$$\text{Periods} = (\text{years} \times \text{compounding periods in 1 year}) + 1$$

Step 3. In Table 14.1, find the future value of $1 at compound interest at the intersection of the period rate and the number of periods.

Step 4. Find the future value of the investment:
For ordinary annuity:

$$\text{Future value} = \text{future value of } \$1 \times \text{amount of periodic investment}$$

For annuity due:
By adding 1 to the number of periods, the table factor found gives the principal and the interest for an additional period. The additional interest for that period is

TABLE 14.1 FUTURE VALUE OF A $1 ANNUITY AT COMPOUND INTEREST

i n	1%	1½%	2%	2½%	3%	4%	5%	6%	8%	10%	12%
1	1.00000	1.00000	1.00000	1.00000	1.00000	1.00000	1.00000	1.00000	1.00000	1.00000	1.00000
2	2.01000	2.01500	2.02000	2.02500	2.03000	2.04000	2.05000	2.06000	2.08000	2.10000	2.12000
3	3.03010	3.04522	3.06040	3.07562	3.09090	3.12160	3.15250	3.18360	3.24640	3.31000	3.37440
4	4.06040	4.09090	4.12161	4.15252	4.18363	4.24646	4.31013	4.37462	4.50611	4.64100	4.77933
5	5.10101	5.15227	5.20404	5.25633	5.30914	5.41632	5.52563	5.63709	5.86660	6.10510	6.35285
6	6.15202	6.22955	6.30812	6.38774	6.46841	6.63298	6.80191	6.97532	7.33593	7.71561	8.11519
7	7.21354	7.32299	7.43428	7.54743	7.66246	7.89829	8.14201	8.39384	8.92280	9.48717	10.08901
8	8.28567	8.43284	8.58297	8.73612	8.89234	9.21423	9.54911	9.89747	10.63663	11.43589	12.29969
9	9.36853	9.55933	9.75463	9.95452	10.15911	10.58280	11.02656	11.49132	12.48756	13.57948	14.77566
10	10.46221	10.70272	10.94972	11.20338	11.46388	12.00611	12.57789	13.18079	14.48656	15.93742	17.54874
11	11.56683	11.86326	12.16872	12.48347	12.80780	13.48635	14.20679	14.97164	16.64549	18.53117	20.65458
12	12.68250	13.04121	13.41209	13.79555	14.19203	15.02581	15.91713	16.86994	18.97713	21.38428	24.13313
13	13.80933	14.23683	14.68033	15.14044	15.61779	16.62684	17.71298	18.88214	21.49530	24.52271	28.02911
14	14.94742	15.45038	15.97394	16.51895	17.08632	18.29191	19.59863	21.01507	24.21492	27.97498	32.39260
15	16.09690	16.68214	17.29345	17.93193	18.59891	20.02359	21.57856	23.27597	27.15211	31.77248	37.27971
16	17.25786	17.93237	18.63929	19.38022	20.15688	21.82453	23.65749	25.67253	30.32428	35.94973	42.75328
17	18.43044	19.20136	20.01207	20.86473	21.76159	23.69751	25.84037	28.21288	33.75023	40.54470	48.88367
18	19.61475	20.48938	21.41231	22.38635	23.41444	25.64541	28.13238	30.90565	37.45024	45.59917	55.74971
19	20.81090	21.79672	22.84056	23.94601	25.11687	27.67123	30.53900	33.75999	41.44626	51.15909	63.43968
20	22.01900	23.12367	24.29737	25.54466	26.87037	29.77808	33.06595	36.78559	45.76196	57.27500	72.05244
21	23.23919	24.47052	25.78332	27.18327	28.67649	31.96920	35.71925	39.99273	50.42292	64.00250	81.69874
22	24.47159	25.83758	27.29898	28.86286	30.53678	34.24797	38.50521	43.39229	55.45676	71.40275	92.50258
23	25.71630	27.22514	28.84496	30.58443	32.45288	36.61789	41.43048	46.99583	60.89330	79.54302	104.60289
24	26.97346	28.63352	30.42186	32.34904	34.42647	39.08260	44.50200	50.81558	66.76476	88.49733	118.15524
25	28.24320	30.06302	32.03030	34.15776	36.45926	41.64591	47.72710	54.86451	73.10594	98.34706	133.33387
26	29.52563	31.51397	33.67091	36.01171	38.55304	44.31174	51.11345	59.15638	79.95442	109.18177	150.33393
27	30.82089	32.98668	35.34432	37.91200	40.70963	47.08421	54.66913	63.70577	87.35077	121.09994	169.37401
28	32.12910	34.48148	37.05121	39.85980	42.93092	49.96758	58.40258	68.52811	95.33883	134.20994	190.69889
29	33.45039	35.99870	38.79223	41.85630	45.21885	52.96629	62.32271	73.63980	103.96594	148.63093	214.58275
30	34.78489	37.53868	40.56808	43.90270	47.57542	56.08494	66.43885	79.05819	113.28321	164.49402	241.33268
31	36.13274	39.10176	42.37944	46.00027	50.00268	59.32834	70.76079	84.80168	123.34587	181.94342	271.29261
32	37.49407	40.68829	44.22703	48.15028	52.50276	62.70147	75.29883	90.88978	134.21354	201.13777	304.84772
33	38.86901	42.29861	46.11157	50.35403	55.07784	66.20953	80.06377	97.34316	145.95062	222.25154	342.42945
34	40.25770	43.93309	48.03380	52.61289	57.73018	69.85791	85.06696	104.18375	158.62667	245.47670	384.52098
35	41.66028	45.59209	49.99448	54.92821	60.46208	73.65222	90.32031	111.43478	172.31680	271.02437	431.66350
36	43.07688	47.27597	51.99437	57.30141	63.27594	77.59831	95.83632	119.12087	187.10215	299.12681	484.46312
37	44.50765	48.98511	54.03425	59.73395	66.17422	81.70225	101.62814	127.26812	203.07032	330.03949	543.59869
38	45.95272	50.71989	56.11494	62.22730	69.15945	85.97031	107.70955	135.90421	220.31595	364.04343	609.83053
39	47.41225	52.48068	58.23721	64.78298	72.23423	90.40915	114.09502	145.05846	238.94122	401.44778	684.01020
40	48.88637	54.26789	60.40198	67.40255	75.40126	95.02552	120.79977	154.76197	259.05652	442.59256	767.09142
41	50.37524	56.08191	62.61002	70.08762	78.66330	99.82654	127.83976	165.04768	280.78104	487.85181	860.14239
42	51.87899	57.92314	64.86222	72.83981	82.02320	104.81960	135.23175	175.95054	304.24352	537.63699	964.35948
43	53.39778	59.79199	67.15947	75.66080	85.48389	110.01238	142.99334	187.50758	329.58301	592.40069	1081.08262
44	54.93176	61.68887	69.50266	78.55232	89.04841	115.41228	151.14301	199.75803	356.94965	652.64076	1211.81253
45	56.48107	63.61420	71.89271	81.51613	92.71986	121.02939	159.70016	212.74351	386.50562	718.90484	1358.23003
46	58.04589	65.56841	74.33056	84.55403	96.50146	126.87057	168.68516	226.50812	418.42607	791.79532	1522.21764
47	59.62634	67.55194	76.81718	87.66789	100.39650	132.94539	178.11942	241.09861	452.90015	871.97485	1705.88375
48	61.22261	69.56522	79.35352	90.85958	104.40840	139.26321	188.02539	256.56453	490.13216	960.17234	1911.58980
49	62.83483	71.60870	81.94059	94.13107	108.54065	145.83376	198.42666	272.95840	530.34274	1057.18957	2141.98058
50	64.46318	73.68283	84.57940	97.48435	112.79687	152.66708	209.34800	290.33590	573.77016	1163.90853	2400.01825

n = number of periods in annuity; i = interest per period

earned and needs to be known, but the additional principal payment was not made, so you should subtract 1, as follows:

$$\text{Future value} = (\text{future value of } \$1 - 1) \times \text{amount of periodic investment}$$

EXAMPLE Twenty-five-year-old Jeremy Tannenbaum plans to begin saving for retirement. He is going to buy a $2,000 IRA paying 8% every year until he is 65. He wonders if there is a good enough reason to start now, at the beginning of the year, or if the end of the year will be soon enough. Calculate the future value of both the ordinary annuity and the annuity due. How much more will he have if he invests at the beginning of the year?

Solution *Step 1.* Find the period interest rate:

$$\text{Period rate} = \frac{\text{annual interest rate}}{\text{compounding periods in 1 year}} = \frac{8\%}{1} = 8\%$$

Step 2. Find the number of periods:
For ordinary annuity:

$$\begin{aligned}\text{Periods} &= \text{years} \times \text{compounding periods in 1 year} \\ &= (65 - 25) \times 1 \\ &= 40\end{aligned}$$

For annuity due (one more investment will earn interest):

$$\begin{aligned}\text{Periods} &= (\text{years} \times \text{compounding periods in 1 year}) + 1 \\ &= (40 \times 1) + 1 \\ &= 41\end{aligned}$$

Step 3. In Table 14.1, find the future value of $1 at compound interest at the intersection of the period rate and the periods for 8%:
For ordinary annuity: 259.05652
For annuity due: 280.78104

Step 4. Find the future value of the investment:
For ordinary annuity:

$$\begin{aligned}\text{Future value} &= \text{future value of } \$1 \times \text{amount of periodic investment} \\ &= 259.05652 \times \$2,000 \\ &= \$518,113.04\end{aligned}$$

For annuity due:
By adding 1 to the number of periods, the table factor provided the principal and the interest for an additional period. The amount 1 was subtracted ($1 \times P = P$) (future value of $1 - 1$) because the additional interest but not the additional principal was needed:

$$\begin{aligned}\text{Future value} &= (\text{future value of } \$1 - 1) \times \text{amount of periodic investment} \\ &= (280.78104 - 1) \times \$2,000 \\ &= 279.78104 \times \$2,000 \\ &= \$559,562.08\end{aligned}$$

Step 5. The difference between the ordinary annuity and the annuity due (investing at the beginning rather than at the end of the year):

$$\$559,562 - 518,113 = \$41,449$$

The use of a financial calculator makes these problems rather simple, and is actually an advantage over using a table.

For ordinary annuity:

$$\boxed{40 \;\fbox{N}\; 8 \;\fbox{\%i}\; 2{,}000 \;\fbox{PMT}\; \fbox{2nd}\; \fbox{FV}\; 518{,}113.04}$$

For annuity due:

$$\boxed{40 \;\fbox{N}\; 8 \;\fbox{\%i}\; 2{,}000 \;\fbox{PMT}\; \fbox{due}\; \fbox{FV}\; 559{,}562.09}$$

Remember, for N, you enter the number of compounding periods, and for $\%i$, you enter the period rate.

14.1 Practice Problems

Calculate the future value for both an ordinary annuity and an annuity due in the following annuity problems:

1. Calculate the future value of $4,000 invested at 6% compounded annually for three years (a) at the end of each year and (b) at the beginning of each year.

2. To assure there would be funds to replace his company's truck when it wears out, Milton Myer made periodic $1,500 deposits into an investment that pays 8% compounded quarterly. Find the value of his investment in five years if the deposits are made (a) at the end of each quarter and (b) at the beginning of each quarter.

3. Yoko Hokazono is saving regularly to buy into the family business when she is 35 years old. She wants to know the future value of regular periodic investments of $8,000 earning 10% compounded semiannually for 10 years if money is invested (a) at the end of each six months and (b) at the beginning of each six months.

4. Miller's Chemicals will need to replace some of its laboratory equipment in four years. Toward that goal, $5,000 is invested monthly at 12% compounded monthly. Determine the future value if the deposits are made (a) at the end of each month and (b) at the beginning of each month.

14.1 Solutions to Practice Problems

1. (a) Period rate = 6%   Periods = 3
      Table value = 3.18360   3.18360 × $4,000 = $12,734.40
   (b) Period rate = 6%   Periods = 3 + 1 = 4
      Table value = 4.37462   (4.37462 − 1) × $4,000 = $13,498.48

2. (a) Period rate $= \dfrac{8\%}{4} = 2\%$ Periods = 5 × 4 = 20

      Table value = 24.29737   24.29737 × $1,500 = $36,446.06

   (b) Period rate $= \dfrac{8\%}{4} = 2\%$ Periods = (5 × 4) + 1 = 21

      Table value = 25.78332   (25.7833 − 1) × $1,500 = $37,174.98

3. (a) Period rate $= \dfrac{10\%}{2} = 5\%$ Periods = 10 × 2 = 20

      Table value = 33.06595   33.06595 × $8,000 = $264,527.60

   (b) Period rate $= \dfrac{10\%}{2} = 5\%$ Periods = (10 × 2) + 1 = 21

      Table value = 35.71925   (35.71925 − 1) × $8,000 = $277,754

4. (a) Period rate $= \dfrac{12\%}{12} = 1\%$ Periods = 4 × 12 = 48

      Table value = 61.22261   61.22261 × $5,000 = $306,113.05

   (b) Period rate $= \dfrac{12\%}{12} = 1\%$ Periods = (4 × 12) + 1 = 49

      Table value = 62.83483   (62.83483 − 1) × $5,000 = $309,174.15

LEARNING UNIT 2
PRESENT VALUE OF AN ORDINARY ANNUITY

Unlike finding the future value of a stream of payments, the **present value of an annuity** finds the value of a lump sum amount that must be deposited or invested now to provide for the withdrawal of a series of periodic equal payments.

 14.2 Calculating the Present Value of an Ordinary Annuity

Figure 14.4 illustrates the present value of an ordinary annuity.

To use Table 14.2, Present value of an Ordinary Annuity of $1 at Compound Interest, follow these steps:

Step 1. Find the period interest rate:

$$\text{Period rate} = \frac{\text{annual interest rate}}{\text{compounding periods in 1 year}}$$

Step 2. Find the number of periods:

$$\text{Periods} = \text{years} \times \text{compounding periods in 1 year}$$

Step 3. In Table 14.2, find the present value of an annuity of $1 at compound interest at the intersection of the period rate and the periods.

Step 4. Find the present value of the annuity:

$$\text{Present value} = \text{present value of an annuity of } \$1 \times \text{annuity amount}$$

EXAMPLE   One winner of the state lottery will receive $8 million in $400,000 annual payments for 20 years. To assure the money would be available, the state deposited the necessary lump sum amount today. How much would the state need to deposit in an account paying 7% compounded annually?

Solution   *Step 1.* Find the period interest rate:

$$\text{Period rate} = \frac{\text{annual interest rate}}{\text{compounding periods in 1 year}} = \frac{8\%}{1} = 8\%$$

Step 2. Find the number of periods:

$$\text{Periods} = \text{years} \times \text{compounding periods in 1 year}$$
$$= 20 \times 1 = 20$$

Figure 14.4
Present Value of an Ordinary Annuity

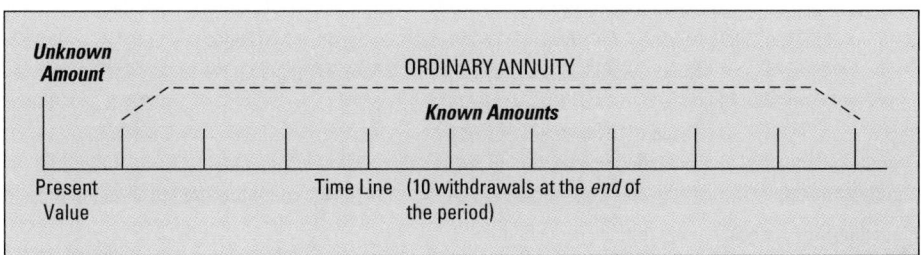

n \ i	1%	1½%	2%	2½%	3%	4%	5%	6%	8%	10%	12%
1	.99010	.98522	.98039	.97561	.97087	.96154	.95238	.94340	.92593	.90909	.89286
2	1.97040	1.95588	1.94156	1.92742	1.91347	1.88609	1.85941	1.83339	1.78326	1.73554	1.69005
3	2.94099	2.91220	2.88388	2.85602	2.82861	2.77509	2.72325	2.67301	2.57710	2.48685	2.40183
4	3.90197	3.85438	3.80773	3.76197	3.71710	3.62990	3.54595	3.46511	3.31213	3.16987	3.03735
5	4.85343	4.78264	4.71346	4.64583	4.57971	4.45182	4.32948	4.21236	3.99271	3.79079	3.60478
6	5.79548	5.69719	5.60143	5.50813	5.41719	5.24214	5.07569	4.91732	4.62288	4.35526	4.11141
7	6.72819	6.59821	6.47199	6.34939	6.23028	6.00205	5.78637	5.58238	5.20637	4.86842	4.56376
8	7.65168	7.48593	7.32548	7.17014	7.01969	6.73274	6.46321	6.20979	5.74664	5.33493	4.96764
9	8.56602	8.36052	8.16224	7.97087	7.78611	7.43533	7.10782	6.80169	6.24689	5.75902	5.32825
10	9.47130	9.22218	8.98259	8.75206	8.53020	8.11090	7.72173	7.36009	6.71008	6.14457	5.65022
11	10.36763	10.07112	9.78685	9.51421	9.25262	8.76048	8.30641	7.88687	7.13896	6.49506	5.93770
12	11.25508	10.90751	10.57534	10.25776	9.95400	9.38507	8.86325	8.38384	7.53608	6.81369	6.19437
13	12.13374	11.73153	11.34837	10.98318	10.63496	9.98565	9.39357	8.85268	7.90378	7.10336	6.42355
14	13.00370	12.54338	12.10625	11.69091	11.29607	10.56312	9.89864	9.29498	8.24424	7.36669	6.62817
15	13.86505	13.34323	12.84926	12.38138	11.93794	11.11839	10.37966	9.71225	8.55948	7.60608	6.81086
16	14.71787	14.13126	13.57771	13.05500	12.56110	11.65230	10.83777	10.10590	8.85137	7.82371	6.97399
17	15.56225	14.90765	14.29187	13.71220	13.16612	12.16567	11.27407	10.47726	9.12164	8.02155	7.11963
18	16.39827	15.67256	14.99203	14.35336	13.75351	12.65930	11.68959	10.82760	9.37189	8.20141	7.24967
19	17.22601	16.42617	15.67846	14.97889	14.32380	13.13394	12.08532	11.15812	9.60360	8.36492	7.36578
20	18.04555	17.16864	16.35143	15.58916	14.87747	13.59033	12.46221	11.46992	9.81815	8.51356	7.46944
21	18.85698	17.90014	17.01121	16.18455	15.41502	14.02916	12.82115	11.76408	10.01680	8.64869	7.56200
22	19.66038	18.62082	17.65805	16.76541	15.93692	14.45112	13.16300	12.04158	10.20074	8.77154	7.64465
23	20.45582	19.33086	18.29220	17.33211	16.44361	14.85684	13.48857	12.30338	10.37106	8.88322	7.71843
24	21.24339	20.03041	18.91393	17.88499	16.93554	15.24696	13.79864	12.55036	10.52876	8.98474	7.78432
25	22.02316	20.71961	19.52346	18.42438	17.41315	15.62208	14.09394	12.78336	10.67478	9.07704	7.84314
26	22.79520	21.39863	20.12104	18.95061	17.87684	15.98277	14.37519	13.00317	10.80998	9.16095	7.89566
27	23.55961	22.06762	20.70690	19.46401	18.32703	16.32959	14.64303	13.21053	10.93516	9.23722	7.94255
28	24.31644	22.72672	21.28127	19.96489	18.76411	16.66306	14.89813	13.40616	11.05108	9.30657	7.98442
29	25.06579	23.37608	21.84438	20.45355	19.18845	16.98371	15.14107	13.59072	11.15841	9.36961	8.02181
30	25.80771	24.01584	22.39646	20.93029	19.60044	17.29203	15.37245	13.76483	11.25778	9.42691	8.05518
31	26.54229	24.64615	22.93770	21.39541	20.00043	17.58849	15.59281	13.92909	11.34980	9.47901	8.08499
32	27.26959	25.26714	23.46833	21.84918	20.38877	17.87355	15.80268	14.08404	11.43500	9.52638	8.11159
33	27.98969	25.87895	23.98856	22.29188	20.76579	18.14765	16.00255	14.23023	11.51389	9.56943	8.13535
34	28.70267	26.48173	24.49859	22.72379	21.13184	18.41120	16.19290	14.36814	11.58693	9.60857	8.15656
35	29.40858	27.07559	24.99862	23.14516	21.48722	18.66461	16.37419	14.49825	11.65457	9.64416	8.17550
36	30.10751	27.66068	25.48884	23.55625	21.83225	18.90828	16.54685	14.62099	11.71719	9.67651	8.19241
37	30.79951	28.23713	25.96945	23.95732	22.16724	19.14258	16.71129	14.73678	11.77518	9.70592	8.20751
38	31.48466	28.80505	26.44064	24.34860	22.49246	19.36786	16.86789	14.84602	11.82887	9.73265	8.22099
39	32.16303	29.36458	26.90259	24.73034	22.80822	19.58448	17.01704	14.94907	11.87858	9.75696	8.23303
40	32.83469	29.91585	27.35548	25.10278	23.11477	19.79277	17.15909	15.04630	11.92461	9.77905	8.24378
41	33.49969	30.45896	27.79949	25.46612	23.41240	19.99305	17.29437	15.13802	11.96723	9.79914	8.25337
42	34.15811	30.99405	28.23479	25.82061	23.70136	20.18563	17.42321	15.22454	12.00670	9.81740	8.26194
43	34.81001	31.52123	28.66156	26.16645	23.98190	20.37079	17.54591	15.30617	12.04324	9.83400	8.26959
44	35.45545	32.04062	29.07996	26.50385	24.25427	20.54884	17.66277	15.38318	12.07704	9.84909	8.27642
45	36.09451	32.55234	29.49016	26.83302	24.51871	20.72004	17.77407	15.45583	12.10840	9.86281	8.28252
46	36.72724	33.05649	29.89231	27.15417	24.77545	20.88465	17.88007	15.52437	12.13741	9.87528	8.28796
47	37.35370	33.55319	30.28658	27.46748	25.02471	21.04294	17.98102	15.58903	12.16427	9.88662	8.29282
48	37.97396	34.04255	30.67312	27.77315	25.26671	21.19513	18.07716	15.65003	12.18914	9.89693	8.29716
49	38.58808	34.52468	31.05208	28.07137	25.50166	21.34147	18.16872	15.70757	12.21216	9.90630	8.30104
50	39.19612	34.99969	31.42361	28.36231	25.72976	21.48218	18.25593	15.76186	12.23348	9.91481	8.30450

n = number of periods; i = interest rate per period

Step 3. In Table 14.2, find the present value of an annuity of $1 at compound interest at the intersection of 8% and 20 periods: 9.81815.

Step 4. Find the present value of the annuity:

Present value = present value of an annuity of $1 × annuity amount
= 9.81815 × $400,000 = $3,927,260

20 [N] 8 [%i] 400,000 [PMT] [2nd] [PV] 3,927,259

14.2 Practice Problems

Use Table 14.2 to find the present value of an annuity in the following problems:

1. Harold Donohoo is establishing an educational trust fund for his daughter. She will start college at the end of this month. Mr. Donohoo wants her to be able to receive $750 each month for four years, from which she will pay her expenses. How much will he have to invest now at 12% compounded monthly?

2. The Ace Manufacturing Company wants to invest in a new machine that is expected to reduce net expenses by $10,000 every six months. The machine will have a seven-year life. Money is currently earning 8% compounded semiannually. Find the most Ace should be willing to pay for the machine.

3. Find the current value of an installment contract that calls for 36 equal monthly payments of $2,575 if the current interest rate is 12% compounded monthly.

4. "Lucky" Smith was a grand-prize winner in a sweepstakes and was offered a choice between $10,000 at the end of each quarter for 12 years or $350,000 now. If she could earn 10% compounded quarterly, which prize is worth more in terms of today's money?

14.2 Solutions to Practice Problems

1. Period rate $= \dfrac{12\%}{12} = 1\%$ Periods $= 4 \times 12 = 48$

   Present value of an annuity = $750 × 37.97396 = $28,480.47
                                                    ↑
   Intersection of 1% and 48 periods from Table 14.2

2. Period rate $= \dfrac{8\%}{2} = 4\%$ Periods $= 7 \times 2 = 14$

   Present value of an annuity = $10,000 × 10.56312 = $105,631.20
                                                      ↑
   Intersection of 4% and 14 periods from Table 14.2

3. Period rate $= \dfrac{12\%}{12} = 1\%$ Periods $= 36$

   Present value of an annuity = $2,575 × 30.10751 = $77,526.84
                                                     ↑
   Intersection of 1% and 36 periods from Table 14.2

4. Period rate $= \dfrac{10\%}{4} = 2.5\%$ Periods $= 12 \times 4 = 48$

   Present value of an annuity = $10,000 × 27.77315 = $277,731.50
                                                      ↑
   Intersection of 2.5% and 48 periods from Table 14.2

   Even though $10,000 × 48 quarters = $480,000 total, it is worth only $277,731.50 in today's money. Thus, $350,000 now is worth more in today's money.

LEARNING UNIT 3
SINKING FUND

EXCEL Spreadsheet Application In Spreadsheet Application 2 at the end of this chapter, Springfield has bond issues to retire and buildings and equipment to replace in the future. Sinking funds have been set up to provide for these eventualities.

Figure 14.5
Sinking Fund

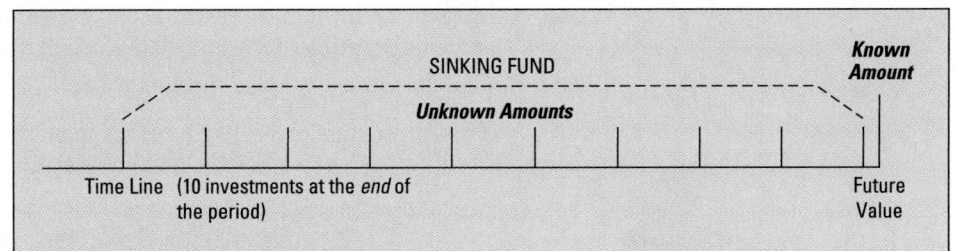

In the discussion of ordinary annuities, the amount of the periodic investments were known, and the goal was to determine the lump sum future value of that annuity. Business firms and individuals often have fixed obligations or needs for lump sum amounts at specified future dates. They need to know how much would have to be invested or saved on a regular periodic basis to accumulate that amount. The resulting accumulation is called a **sinking fund** and is the opposite of an ordinary annuity. Figure 14.5 illustrates the sinking fund.

Sinking funds are used by business firms to determine the amount to save on a regular systematic basis for new or replacement capital investments such as plants, machinery and equipment, furniture and fixtures, and vehicles. Sinking funds are also used to accumulate wealth to retire debt, such as bonds at muturity.

14.3 Calculating a Sinking Fund

A sinking fund table is used to determine the periodic amount to be invested on a regular basis to accumulate a known, lump sum future value. Table 14.3 shows the amount that must be invested at regular periods to accumulate $1 at compound interest. To use the table, follow these steps:

Step 1. Find the period interest rate:

$$\text{Period rate} = \frac{\text{annual interest rate}}{\text{compounding periods in 1 year}}$$

Step 2. Find the number of periods:

$$\text{Periods} = \text{years} \times \text{compounding periods in 1 year}$$

Step 3. In Table 14.3, find the amount that needs to be invested to accumulate $1 at compound interest at the intersection of the period rate and the number of periods.

Step 4. Find the periodic amount to be invested:

$$\text{Investment amount} = \text{amount to accumulate } \$1 \times \text{future value}$$

EXAMPLE   Alex was employed by John Smith with an agreement that John will sell the business to Alex in five years for $180,000. To have the amount needed, how much does Alex need to invest quarterly at 8% compounded quarterly?

Solution   *Step 1.* Find the period interest rate:

$$\text{Period rate} = \frac{\text{annual interest rate}}{\text{compounding periods in 1 year}} = \frac{8\%}{4} = 2\%$$

TABLE 14.3   SINKING FUND TABLE

n \ i	1%	1½%	2%	2½%	3%	4%	5%	6%	8%	10%	12%
1	1.00000	1.00000	1.00000	1.00000	1.00000	1.00000	1.00000	1.00000	1.00000	1.00000	1.00000
2	.49751	.49628	.49505	.49383	.49261	.49020	.48780	.48544	.48077	.47619	.47170
3	.33002	.32838	.32675	.32514	.32353	.32035	.31721	.31411	.30803	.30211	.29635
4	.24628	.24444	.24262	.24082	.23903	.23549	.23201	.22859	.22192	.21547	.20923
5	.19604	.19409	.19216	.19025	.18835	.18463	.18097	.17740	.17046	.16380	.15741
6	.16255	.16053	.15853	.15655	.15460	.15076	.14702	.14336	.13632	.12961	.12323
7	.13863	.13656	.13451	.13250	.13051	.12661	.12282	.11914	.11207	.10541	.09912
8	.12069	.11858	.11651	.11447	.11246	.10853	.10472	.10104	.09401	.08744	.08130
9	.10674	.10461	.10252	.10046	.09843	.09449	.09069	.08702	.08008	.07364	.06768
10	.09558	.09343	.09133	.08926	.08723	.08329	.07950	.07587	.06903	.06275	.05698
11	.08645	.08429	.08218	.08011	.07808	.07415	.07039	.06679	.06008	.05396	.04842
12	.07885	.07668	.07456	.07249	.07046	.06655	.06283	.05928	.05270	.04676	.04144
13	.07241	.07024	.06812	.06605	.06403	.06014	.05646	.05296	.04652	.04078	.03568
14	.06690	.06472	.06260	.06054	.05853	.05467	.05102	.04758	.04130	.03575	.03087
15	.06212	.05994	.05783	.05577	.05377	.04994	.04634	.04296	.03683	.03147	.02682
16	.05794	.05577	.05365	.05160	.04961	.04582	.04227	.03895	.03298	.02782	.02339
17	.05426	.05208	.04997	.04793	.04595	.04220	.03870	.03544	.02963	.02466	.02046
18	.05098	.04881	.04670	.04467	.04271	.03899	.03555	.03236	.02670	.02193	.01794
19	.04805	.04588	.04378	.04176	.03981	.03614	.03275	.02962	.02413	.01955	.01576
20	.04542	.04325	.04116	.03915	.03722	.03358	.03024	.02718	.02185	.01746	.01388
21	.04303	.04087	.03878	.03679	.03487	.03128	.02800	.02500	.01983	.01562	.01224
22	.04086	.03870	.03663	.03465	.03275	.02920	.02597	.02305	.01803	.01401	.01081
23	.03889	.03673	.03467	.03270	.03081	.02731	.02414	.02128	.01642	.01257	.00956
24	.03707	.03492	.03287	.03091	.02905	.02559	.02247	.01968	.01498	.01130	.00846
25	.03541	.03326	.03122	.02928	.02743	.02401	.02095	.01823	.01368	.01017	.00750
26	.03387	.03173	.02970	.02777	.02594	.02257	.01956	.01690	.01251	.00916	.00665
27	.03245	.03032	.02829	.02638	.02456	.02124	.01829	.01570	.01145	.00826	.00590
28	.03112	.02900	.02699	.02509	.02329	.02001	.01712	.01459	.01049	.00745	.00524
29	.02990	.02778	.02578	.02389	.02211	.01888	.01605	.01358	.00962	.00673	.00466
30	.02875	.02664	.02465	.02278	.02102	.01783	.01505	.01265	.00883	.00608	.00414
31	.02768	.02557	.02360	.02174	.02000	.01686	.01413	.01179	.00811	.00550	.00369
32	.02667	.02458	.02261	.02077	.01905	.01595	.01328	.01100	.00745	.00497	.00328
33	.02573	.02364	.02169	.01986	.01816	.01510	.01249	.01027	.00685	.00450	.00292
34	.02484	.02276	.02082	.01901	.01732	.01431	.01176	.00960	.00630	.00407	.00260
35	.02400	.02193	.02000	.01821	.01654	.01358	.01107	.00897	.00580	.00369	.00232
36	.02321	.02115	.01923	.01745	.01580	.01289	.01043	.00839	.00534	.00334	.00206
37	.02247	.02041	.01851	.01674	.01511	.01224	.00984	.00786	.00492	.00303	.00184
38	.02176	.01972	.01782	.01607	.01446	.01163	.00928	.00736	.00454	.00275	.00164
39	.02109	.01905	.01717	.01544	.01384	.01106	.00876	.00689	.00419	.00249	.00146
40	.02046	.01843	.01656	.01484	.01326	.01052	.00828	.00646	.00386	.00226	.00130
41	.01985	.01783	.01597	.01427	.01271	.01002	.00782	.00606	.00356	.00205	.00116
42	.01928	.01726	.01542	.01373	.01219	.00954	.00739	.00568	.00329	.00186	.00104
43	.01873	.01672	.01489	.01322	.01170	.00909	.00699	.00533	.00303	.00169	.00092
44	.01820	.01621	.01439	.01273	.01123	.00866	.00662	.00501	.00280	.00153	.00083
45	.01771	.01572	.01391	.01227	.01079	.00826	.00626	.00470	.00259	.00139	.00074
46	.01723	.01525	.01345	.01183	.01036	.00788	.00593	.00441	.00239	.00126	.00066
47	.01677	.01480	.01302	.01141	.00996	.00752	.00561	.00415	.00221	.00115	.00059
48	.01633	.01437	.01260	.01101	.00958	.00718	.00532	.00390	.00204	.00104	.00052
49	.01591	.01396	.01220	.01062	.00921	.00686	.00504	.00366	.00189	.00095	.00047
50	.01551	.01357	.01182	.01026	.00887	.00655	.00478	.00344	.00174	.00086	.00042

n = number of periods in annuity; i = interest per period

Step 2. Find the number of periods:

Periods = years × compounding periods in 1 year
= 5 × 4 = 20

Step 3. In Table 14.3, find the amount that needs to be invested to accumulate $1 at compound interest at the intersection of 2% and 20 periods: .04116.

Step 4. Find the periodic amount to be invested:

Investment amount = amount to accumulate $1 × future value
= .04116 × $180,000
= $7,408.80

5 ⊠ 4 = Ⓝ 8 ÷ 4 = %i 180,000 FV 2nd PMT 7,408.21

14.3 Practice Problems

Use Table 14.3 to calculate the following sinking fund problems:

1. Peyton Industries sold bonds having a face value of $10 million due in 20 years. The company's indenture contract requires management to set aside a sinking fund at the end of each year until the maturity date. Funds can be invested at 6% compounded annually. How much must be set aside each year?

2. The Shamrock Motel wants to build a new $2,500,000 unit in five years. Management started a sinking fund to accumulate the amount needed. It is estimated that it will receive 8% interest compounded semiannually. How much will need to be invested every six months?

3. Krazinski Manufacturing just purchased a machine with an expected life of 12 years. Company policy is to start a sinking fund to replace machinery at the end of its expected life. The machine cost $85,000 and is expected to have a scrap value at the end of its usable life of $7,500. Calculate the amount that will be invested quarterly in an account paying 8% compounded quarterly.

4. James McLaughlin is 25 years old. He has talked to a financial advisor who recommended that he accumulate a retirement estate of $1 million. The advisor further recommended that James make regular monthly deposits into a mutual fund. While it is not guaranteed, James has found a fund that has averaged 12% compounded annually. How much will James have to save annually to accumulate the $1 million by age 55?

14.3 Solutions to Practice Problems

1. Period rate = $\dfrac{6\%}{1}$ = 6%   Periods = 20 years × 1 = 20

   Table 14.3 value at intersection of 6% and 20 periods = .02718
   Investment amount = .02718 × $10,000,000 = $271,800

2. Period rate = $\dfrac{8\%}{2}$ = 4%   Periods = 5 years × 2 = 10

   Table 14.3 value at intersection of 4% and 10 periods = .08329
   Investment amount = .08329 × $2,500,000 = $208,225

3. Period rate = $\dfrac{8\%}{4}$ = 2%   Periods = 12 years × 4 = 48

   Table 14.3 value at intersection of 2% and 48 periods = .01260
   Investment amount = .01260 × ($85,000 − 7,500)
                     = .01260 × $77,500 = $976.50

4. Period rate = $\dfrac{12\%}{1}$ = 12%   Periods = (55 − 25) 30 years × 1 = 30

   Table 14.3 value at intersection of 12% and 30 periods = .00414
   Investment amount = .00414 × $1,000,000 = $4,140

Page	Section Topic	Learning Concepts	Examples and Solutions
491	**14.1** Calculating the Future Value of Ordinary Annuities and Annuities Due	Annuities are investments or payments made at regular periodic intervals. An ordinary annuity is made at the beginning of each period. An annuity due is made at the end of each period.	Find the future value of $1,000 invested annually for 10 years at 6% compounded annually (a) at the end of each year and (b) at the beginning of each year. (a) From Table 14.1, at the intersection of 6% and 10 periods the future value of $1 is 13.18079. $13.18079 \times \$1,000 = \$13,180.79$ (b) From Table 14.1, at the intersection of 6% and 11 periods the future value of $1 is 14.97164. $(14.97164 - 1) \times \$1,000 = \$13,971.64$
495	**14.2** Calculating the Present Value of an Ordinary Annuity	This calculates the lump sum amount that must be invested now to provide for the withdrawal of a steady stream of periodic equal payments.	How much would have to be invested now at 8% compounded quarterly to allow for $6,000 quarterly withdrawals for eight years? $$\frac{8\%}{4} = 2\% \qquad 8 \times 4 = 32$$ From Table 14.2, at the intersection of 2% and 32 periods: 23.46833. $23.46833 \times \$6,000 = \$140,809.98$
498	**14.3** Calculating a Sinking Fund	A sinking fund is a periodic accumulation of funds invested at compound interest to repay a known fixed future obligation or provide funds for a specific future need.	How much would have to be invested monthly at 12% compounded monthly to accumulate $20,000 in four years? $$\frac{12\%}{12} = 1\% \qquad 4 \times 12 = 48$$ From Table 14.3, at the intersection of 1% and 48 periods: .01633 $.01633 \times \$20,000 = \$326.60$

SURFING THE INTERNET

For further information on the topics covered in this chapter, check out the following sites:

http://www.nysscpa.org/cpajournal/old/14476955.htm

http://web.utk.edu/~jwachowi/annuity2.html

14.1

Use Table 14.1 to calculate the future value for both an ordinary annuity and an annuity due in the following annuity problems:

1. Calculate the future value of $5,000 invested at 8% compounded annually for seven years (a) at the end of each year and (b) at the beginning of each year.
(a) 8.92280 × $5,000 = $44,614
(b) (10.63663 − 1) × $5,000 = 9.63663 × $5,000 = $48,183.15

2. Karl Walker made semiannual deposits of $1,500 into an investment paying 6% compounded semiannually to purchase machinery for his company. Find the value of his investment in eight years if the deposits are made (a) at the end of each six months and (b) at the beginning of each six months.

(a) $\frac{6\%}{2}$ = 3%

8	20.15688	(b) 3%
×2	×$1,500.00	
16	$30,235.32	16 + 1 = 17

21.76159
−1.00000
20.76159
×$1,500.00
$31,142.39

3. Leena Rodriquez is saving regularly to buy a new building for her business. She wants to know the future value of regular quarterly investments of $2,500 earning 8% compounded quarterly for 10 years if money is invested (a) at the end of each quarter and (b) at the beginning of each quarter.

(a) $\frac{8\%}{4}$ = 2%

10	60.40198	(b) 2%
×4	×$2,500.00	
40	$151,004.95	40 + 1 = 41

62.61002
−1.00000
61.61002
×$2,500.00
$154,025.05

4. Running Bear Indian Jewelry, Inc., will replace its rock and gem cutting equipment in 3.5 years. A new fund has been established in which $3,500 is invested monthly. It is believed that the investment will average a 12% rate compounded monthly. Determine the future value if the investment deposits are made (a) at the end of each month and (b) at the beginning of each month.

(a) $\frac{12\%}{12}$ = 1%

3.5	51.87899	(b) 1%
×12	×$3,500.00	
42	$181,576.47	42 + 1 = 43

53.39778
−1.00000
52.39778
×$3,500.00
$183,392.23

5. Peggy Giroux is planning to invest $550 every six months in a mutual fund that she estimates will earn an average 8% compounded semiannually. How much will her investment be worth at the end of 20 years if the money is placed into the account (a) at the end of each 6 months and (b) at the beginning of each 6 months?

(a) $\frac{8\%}{2}$ = 4%

20	95.02552	(b) 4%
× 2	×$550.00	
40	$52,264.04	40 + 1 = 41

99.82654
−1.00000
98.82654
×$550.00
$ 54,354.60

14.2

Use Table 14.2 to find the present value of an annuity in the following problems:

6. Mattie Jean is setting up an educational fund for her granddaughter who is starting college at the end of this year. Ms. Jean wants her granddaughter to receive $12,000 each year for the six years it will take her granddaughter to complete a master's degree. How much must Mattie Jean invest now at 10% compounded annually?

$\frac{10\%}{1}$ = 10%

6	$12,000.00
×1	×4.35526
6	$52,263.12

7. An analysis of new equipment on the market has established that its use will result in a $15,000 saving every six months. The machine has a 12-year usable life expectancy. Money is currently earning 6% compounded semiannually. Find the highest price that should be paid for the new equipment.

$\frac{6\%}{2}$ = 3%

12	$ 15,000.00
× 2	×16.93554
24	$254,033.10

8. Find the present value of a contract that requires monthly payments of $595 for 50 months if the interest rate is 12% compounded monthly.

$$\frac{12\%}{12} = 1\% \quad 50 \quad \begin{array}{r} \$595.00 \\ \times 39.19612 \\ \hline \$23,321.69 \end{array}$$

9. DMA Corporation wants to hire Arthur Goldburg as its CEO. The current CEO has another four years on her contract, however. She is willing to step down if DMA will pay her $25,000 monthly for the remainder of the contract period. Find the lump sum amount that DMA needs to deposit now at 12% compounded monthly to take care of this contract.

$$\frac{12\%}{12} = 1\% \quad \begin{array}{r} 4 \\ \times 12 \\ \hline 48 \end{array} \quad \begin{array}{r} \$25,000.00 \\ \times 37.97396 \\ \hline \$949,349.00 \end{array}$$

10. A $1,000, 25-year bond pays $45 interest every six months. Current market interest rates are 8% compounded semiannually. What is the present value of the interest annuity? How much is the maximum that should be paid for the bond? *Hint: Use the present value of $1 table to find the present value of the bond's face value ($1,000) and add it to the present value of the interest annuity.*

$$\frac{8\%}{2} = 4\% \quad \begin{array}{r} 25 \\ \times 2 \\ \hline 50 \end{array} \quad \begin{array}{r} \$45.00 \\ \times 21.48218 \\ \hline \$966.70 \end{array} \quad \begin{array}{r} \$1,000.00 \\ \times .14071 \\ \hline \$140.71 \end{array} \quad \begin{array}{r} \$966.70 \\ +140.71 \\ \hline \$1,107.41 \end{array}$$

14.3

Use Table 14.3 to calculate the following sinking fund problems:

11. Four years from now Jackson Manufacturing plans to buy a new blood analyzer. Management has decided to create a sinking fund to pay for the analyzer, which it expects will cost $72,500. Calculate the amount of each annual payment if funds can be invested at 5% compounded annually.

$$\frac{5\%}{1} = 5\% \quad \begin{array}{r} 4 \\ \times 1 \\ \hline 4 \end{array} \quad \begin{array}{r} \$72,500.00 \\ \times .23201 \\ \hline \$16,820.73 \end{array}$$

12. Prime Beef Distributors plans to build a new $15,500,000 plant in seven years. Management set up a sinking fund to accumulate the amount needed at 8% interest compounded semiannually. How much must be invested every six months?

$$\frac{8\%}{2} = 4\% \quad \begin{array}{r} 7 \\ \times 2 \\ \hline 14 \end{array} \quad \begin{array}{r} \$15,500,000 \\ \times .05467 \\ \hline \$847,385 \end{array}$$

13. First United Methodist Church sold $640,000 worth of bonds to obtain the financing needed to build a new chapel. The elders voted to set up a sinking fund to repay the bonds at maturity in 10 years. Calculate the amount that will be invested quarterly in an account paying 12% compounded quarterly.

$$\frac{12\%}{4} = 3\% \quad \begin{array}{r} 10 \\ \times 4 \\ \hline 40 \end{array} \quad \begin{array}{r} \$640,000.00 \\ \times .01326 \\ \hline \$8,486.40 \end{array}$$

14. Muhammad Saquib Ariz fishes for a living. He will need $700,000 to buy and outfit a second boat in five years. Mr. Ariz believes that he can earn 16% compounded quarterly in a stock mutual fund. How much will he have to invest quarterly?

$$\frac{16\%}{4} = 4\% \quad \begin{array}{r} 5 \\ \times 4 \\ \hline 20 \end{array} \quad \begin{array}{r} \$700,000 \\ \times .03358 \\ \hline \$23,506 \end{array}$$

15. Naseer Bajwa wants to send his son to college in 15 years. He wants to start a sinking fund so that he will have enough available for his son to receive $3,500 every six months for four years. One investment opportunity will pay 10% compounded semiannually for as long as his money is accumulated and at least some of it remains on deposit. How much will each of his semiannual deposits need to be? (Use present value of annuity tables to find the amount necessary in 15 years. Then use the sinking fund tables.)

Amount needed in 15 years will be the present value of $3,500 every six months for four years at 10% compounded semiannually:

$$\frac{10\%}{2} = 5\% \quad \begin{array}{r} 4 \\ \times 2 \\ \hline 8 \end{array} \quad \begin{array}{r} \$3,500.00 \\ \times 6.46321 \\ \hline \$22,621.24 \end{array}$$

Semiannual deposits necessary to accumulate the $22,621.24 is a sinking fund:

$$\frac{10\%}{2} = 5\% \quad \begin{array}{r} 15 \\ \times 2 \\ \hline 30 \end{array} \quad \begin{array}{r} \$22,621.24 \\ \times .01505 \\ \hline \$340.45 \end{array}$$

Drill Problems

Fill in all of the missing information for the ordinary annuity or annuity due in problems 1 through 10. (Round to the nearest cent and the nearest hundredth of a percent.)

	Amount of Annuity	Nominal Annual Rate	Annuity Deposits and Compounding Frequency	Investment Length	Deposit at Beginning or End of the Period
1.	$2,000	10%	Annually	12 years	End
2.	4,000	5%	Semiannually	6 years	Beginning
3.	500	6%	Quarterly	11 years	Beginning
4.	450	18%	Monthly	4 years	End
5.	300	8%	Annually	30 years	End
6.	750	12%	Semiannually	4 years	End
7.	290	10%	Quarterly	3 years	Beginning
8.	2,000	12%	Monthly	3 years	Beginning
9.	850	6%	Quarterly	7 years	End
10.	225	16%	Semiannually	14 years	Beginning

	Ordinary or Annuity Due	Period Rate	Number of Compounding Periods	Future Value	Amount of Compound Interest
1.	Ordinary	10 %	12	$42,768.56	$18,768.56
2.	Due	2.5%	13	56,561.76	8,561.76
3.	Due	1.5%	45	31,307.10	9,307.10
4.	Ordinary	1.5%	48	31,304.35	9,704.35
5.	Ordinary	8 %	30	33,984.96	24,984.96
6.	Ordinary	6 %	8	7,423.10	1,423.10
7.	Due	2.5%	13	4,100.73	620.73
8.	Due	1 %	37	87,015.30	15,015.30
9.	Ordinary	1.5%	28	29,309.26	5,509.26
10.	Due	8 %	29	23,167.34	16,867.34

Fill in all of the missing information for the present value of an ordinary annuity in problems 11 through 20. (Round to the nearest cent and the nearest hundredth of a percent.)

	Amount of Annuity	Nominal Annual Rate	Annuity Deposits and Compounding Frequency	Investment Length
11.	$ 300	10%	Annually	16 years
12.	1,000	5%	Semiannually	9 years
13.	800	8%	Quarterly	11 years
14.	350	12%	Monthly	3.5 years
15.	1,230	6%	Annually	25 years

16.	975	8%	Semiannually	4 years
17.	449	10%	Quarterly	6 years
18.	1,000	12%	Monthly	4 years
19.	775	6%	Quarterly	4 years
20.	3,000	10%	Semiannually	6 years

	Period Rate	Compounding Periods	Present Value	Amount of Compound Interest
11.	10 %	16	$ 2,347.11	$ 2,452.89
12.	2.5%	18	14,353.36	3,646.64
13.	2 %	44	23,263.97	11,936.03
14.	1 %	42	11,955.34	2,744.66
15.	6 %	25	15,723.53	15,026.47
16.	4 %	8	6,564.42	1,235.58
17.	2.5%	24	8,030.36	2,745.64
18.	1 %	48	37,973.96	10,026.04
19.	1.5%	16	10,951.73	1,448.27
20.	5 %	12	26,589.75	9,410.25

Fill in all of the missing information for the sinking fund problems 21 through 30. (Round to the nearest cent and the nearest hundredth of a percent.)

	Amount of Annuity	Nominal Annual Rate	Annuity Deposits and Compounding Frequency	Investment Length
21.	$787,050	12%	Annually	5 years
22.	14,888	6%	Semiannually	10 years
23.	101.75	8%	Quarterly	8 years
24.	765.93	12%	Monthly	3 years
25.	33.17	10%	Annually	20 years
26.	17.55	8%	Semiannually	9 years
27.	324.38	6%	Quarterly	5 years
28.	39,517.50	18%	Monthly	4 years
29.	1,619.40	8%	Quarterly	7 years
30.	151.16	12%	Semiannually	6 years

	Period Rate	Compounding Periods	Future Value	Amount of Compound Interest
21.	12 %	5	$5,000,000	$1,064,750
22.	3 %	20	400,000	102,240
23.	2 %	32	4,500	1,244
24.	1 %	36	33,000	5,426.52
25.	10 %	20	1,900	1,236.60
26.	4 %	18	450	134.10
27.	1.5%	20	7,500	1,012.40
28.	1.5%	48	2,750,000	853,160
29.	2 %	28	60,000	14,656.80
30.	6 %	12	2,550	736.08

Word Problems

31. Calculate the future value of a $950 investment at the end of each six months at 6% compounded semiannually for 15 years.

$$\frac{6\%}{2} = 3\%$$

15	$ 950.00
×2	×47.57542
30	$45,196.65

32. Find the future value of a $625 investment at the beginning of each month at 12% compounded monthly for four years.

$$\frac{12\%}{12} = 1\%$$

4		62.83483	$625.00
×12		−1.00000	×61.83483
48 + 1 = 49		61.83483	$38,646.77

33. Determine the amount that would have to be saved quarterly to accumulate a $50,000 balance at the end of 12 years if interest is compounded quarterly at 8%.

$$\frac{8\%}{4} = 2\%$$

12	$50,000.00
×4	×.01260
48	$630.00

34. Determine the present value necessary for $30,000 to be withdrawn at the end of each year for six years from an account paying 8% compounded annually.

$$\frac{8\%}{1} = 8\%$$

6	$30,000.00
×1	×4.62288
6	$138,686.40

35. John Devereaux invested $1,050 at the beginning of each quarter in an account paying 10% compounded quarterly to finance the replacement of data processing equipment in four years. How much will be available at the end of the four years?

$$\frac{10\%}{4} = 2.5\%$$

4		20.86473	$1,050.00
×4		−1.00000	×19.86473
16 + 1 = 17		19.86473	$20,857.97

36. David Mays wants his son's business to have every chance to succeed. His son is underfinanced, so David is going to set up a trust fund that will pay $15,000 into the business every quarter for five years. How much is the lump sum amount he will need to deposit now into a fund paying 6% compounded quarterly?

$$\frac{6\%}{4} = 1.5\%$$

5	$15,000.00
×4	×17.16864
20	$257,529.60

37. Rowanda Rex is presently working as a dentist in a dental clinic. She wants to fund her own office in 10 years. She has estimated that the cost of start-up will be $500,000. How much will Rowanda need to deposit into an investment every six months that will average 10% compounded semiannually?

$$\frac{10\%}{2} = 5\%$$

10	$500,000.00
×2	× .03024
20	$ 15,120.00

38. Bronis and Renee Krukulski are looking at an investment plan to assure their travel plans at retirement. They believe they can afford $2,000 every six months until they retire in 20 years. Their investment advisor is urging them to invest now, at the beginning of the year, but they are inclined to start at the end of six months. If the plan averages an 8% return compounded semiannually, how much more will they have if they invest at the beginning of the year?

End of Six Months

$$\frac{8\%}{2} = 4\%$$

20		95.02552
×2		× $2,000.00
40		$190,051.04

Beginning of Six Months

4%		99.82654
		−1.00000
		98.82654
40 + 1 = 41		× $2,000.00
		$197,653.08

$197,653.08
−190,051.04
$ 7,602.04

39. International Investments Company is setting up a sinking fund to retire a $300 million bond issue at maturity in 30 years. Management will deposit the necessary amount annually in a fund paying 6% compounded annually. How much will the annual deposit be?

$$\frac{6\%}{1} = 6\%$$

30	$300,000,000
×1	× .01265
30	$ 3,795,000

40. Find the value of an investment of $250 made at the beginning of each year for 15 years at 4% compounded annually.

$$\frac{4\%}{1} = 4\%$$

15		21.82453	$ 250.00
×1		−1.00000	×20.82453
15 + 1 = 16		20.82453	$ 5,206.13

41. How much will John have if he invests $500 at the end of each year for 30 years in an annuity carrying a 12% annual compound interest?

$$\frac{12\%}{1} = 12\%$$

30	$ 500.00
×1	×241.33268
30	$120,666.34

42. How much must Jones and Brown, Inc., deposit every six months at 8% compounded semiannually to have $20,000 available six years from now?

$$\frac{8\%}{2} = 4\%$$

6	$ 20,000
×2	×.06655
12	$1,331

43. Jackson, Inc., wants to invest in a new machine that will reduce the company's expenses by $5,000 monthly for the next four years. Money is currently earning 12% compounded monthly. Find the maximum amount Jackson, Inc., should be willing to pay for the machine.

$$\frac{12\%}{12} = 1\%$$

12	$ 5,000.00
×4	× 37.97396
48	$189,869.80

The following problems will require the use of more than one financial application. At least one of the applications will use the concepts presented in this chapter. The other applications will come from either Chapter 13 or this chapter.

44. Pedro Quintana is 30 years old and wants to retire at 60. He wants to have enough money saved so that at that time he will be able to withdraw $20,000 every six months for at least 25 years. He believes that when he is 60 he will be able to earn 6% compounded semiannually. Pedro wants to begin saving toward his goal now. Between now and when he retires he can earn 8% compounded annually. How much will he have to invest annually to reach his goal?

Amount needed in 30 years will be the present value of $20,000 every six months for 25 years at 6% compounded semiannually:

$$\frac{6\%}{2} = 3\%$$

	25	$ 20,000.00
	×2	× 25.72976
	50	$514,595.20

Annual deposits necessary to accumulate the $514,595.20 is a sinking fund problem:

$$\frac{8\%}{1} = 8\%$$

	30	$514,595.20
	×1	× .00883
	30	$ 4,543.88

45. The financial manager of Sang Hyun Moon Corp. is making plans to replace machinery in five years. The machinery costs $78,500 now. However, the cost of the machinery will increase at the inflation rate which is 5% compounded annually. How much will the corporation's management have to deposit annually to accumulate the necessary funds if it can earn 10% compounded annually?

Cost of machinery in five years will be the future value of $78,500 compounded annually for 5 years at 5%.

$$\frac{5\%}{1} = 5\%$$

	5	$ 78,500.00
	×1	× 1.276282
	5	$100,188.14

Annual deposit needed to accumulate $100,188.14 in five years at 10% compounded annually is a sinking fund problem:

$$\frac{10\%}{1} = 10\%$$

	5	$100,188.14
	×1	× .16380
	5	$ 16,410.82

46. Beginning when he was 20 years old, Monty Fieldstrom placed $250 at the end of each month into an investment that earned 8% compounded quarterly for 10 years. He then stopped making deposits and transferred the entire account balance into another investment account earning 10% compounded semiannually. It remained in that account until Monty was 60 years old. How much was in the account?

Savings for the first 10 years is a future value of an annuity at 8% compounded quarterly:

$$\frac{8\%}{4} = 2\%$$

	10	$ 250.00
	×4	× 60.40198
	40	$15,100.50

Amount that $15,100.50 will grow to in 30 years (age 60 − 30) at 10% compounded semiannually is a future value problem:

$$\frac{10\%}{2} = 5\%$$

	30	$ 15,100.50
	×2	× 18.679186
	60	$282,065.05

47. A $10,000 bond with 15 years remaining to maturity carried a simple interest rate of 12% paid semiannually. The current market interest rate is 8% compounded semiannually. Determine the maximum amount an investor should be willing to pay for the bond today.

Semiannual interest of bond:

$$\$10,000 \times 12\% \times \frac{1}{2} = \$600$$

Present value of the $10,000 bond at the current interest rate:

$$\frac{8\%}{2} = 4\%$$

	15	$10,000.00
	×2	× .30832
	30	$ 3,083.20

Present value of bond interest annuity at current interest rate:

$$\frac{8\%}{2} = 4\%$$

	15	$ 600.00
	×2	×17.29203
	30	$10,375.22

Maximum amount that should be paid for the bond today:

$10,375.22
+3,083.20
$13,458.42

48. Yassar Mostafa lost a lawsuit after an accident he was responsible for resulted in the loss of a family's earning power. He is required to pay the family $50,000 every six months until the oldest child, now 12, reaches 25. The payments then drop to $37,500 every six months until the youngest child, now 3 years old, reaches age 25. The court decreed that Yassar is to deposit immediately enough money into an account to guarantee the payment. The account will pay 6% compounded semiannually. How much will have to be deposited?

To find the present value of the $50,000 annuity at 6% compounded semiannually for 13 years, use the present value of an ordinary annuity table:

$$\frac{6\%}{2} = 3\%$$

	13	$ 50,000
	×2	×17.87684
	26	$ 893,842

The $515,756.63 must be available in 13 years. A present value table (from Chapter 13) will be used to determine how much must be deposited now:

$$\frac{6\%}{2} = 3\%$$

	13	$515,756.63
	×2	× .46369
	26	$239,151.19

To determine the amount that will have to be available in 13 years after the oldest child reaches age 25 for payments until the youngest child reaches age 25 (a total of 9 years), use the present value of an ordinary annuity table:

$$\frac{6\%}{2} = 3\%$$

	9	$ 37,500.00
	×2	× 13.75351
	18	$515,756.63

Total amount to be deposited now:

$ 893,842.00
+ 239,151.19
$1,132,993.19

Mercedes Townaires is an investment advisor. Linda Rice is 25 years old and wants to retire at age 58. She wants $7,500 per month from her investments until she can begin receiving Social Security payments at age 62. After that, she wants to receive quarterly payments of $24,000 each until she reaches age 70. From age 70 until age 85, she wants to be able to receive semiannual payments of $30,000 each. No one in her family has ever lived past age 80, so Linda believes that guaranteeing income until she is 85 years old is sufficient. Besides, she believes that if she is still in good health, she can save enough out of the previous year's allotments to be financially secure for life.

Mercedes wants to help Linda achieve her goals. She has developed the following investment strategy:

1. From now until Linda is 58 years old, Mercedes recommends a stock mutual fund that she estimates will average a 10% rate compounded annually.

2. At 58 until age 62, Mercedes recommends a stock growth fund that is expected to return an average of 12% compounded monthly.

3. From age 62 until age 70, Mercedes recommends switching to a government bond fund that she estimates will return 8% compounded quarterly.

4. Finally, Mercedes recommends a conservative strategy of a fixed-rate investment that will average a return of 6% compounded semiannually from age 70 to age 85.

1. Calculate the annual amount Linda will have to invest beginning now at age 25 that continues until she reaches age 58.
   Semiannual receipts of $30,000 for 15 years at 6% compounded semiannually (present value of an ordinary annuity):

   $\frac{6\%}{2} = 3\%$ $15 \times 2 = 30$ Intersection of 30 periods and 3%:   19.60044
   Period withdrawals: $\times$ $30,000
          $588,013.20

   Quarterly receipts of $24,000 for eight years at 8% compounded quarterly (present value of an ordinary annuity):

   $\frac{8\%}{4} = 2\%$ $8 \times 4 = 32$ Intersection of 32 periods and 2%:   23.46833
   Period withdrawals: $\times$ $24,000
          $563,239.92

   Monthly receipts of $7,500 for four years at 12% compounded monthly (present value of an ordinary annuity):

   $\frac{12\%}{12} = 1\%$ $4 \times 12 = 48$ Intersection of 48 periods and 1%:   37.97396
   Period withdrawals: $\times$ $ 7,500
          $284,804.70

   $588,013.20 + 563,239.92 + 284,804.70 = $1,436,057.80

   Annual deposits necessary to accumulate $1,436,057.80 in 33 years at 10% compounded annually (sinking fund):

   $\frac{10\%}{1} = 10\%$ $1 \times 33 = 33$ Intersection of 33 periods and 10%:   .00450
   Period withdrawals: $\times$$1,436,057.80
        $ 6,462.26

2. Calculate the total amount Linda will have invested by age 58.
   $6,462.26 \times 33 = $213,254.58   Total invested

3. Calculate the total amount Linda will have received from her investments at age 85.
   $48 \times $7,500 \;\; = $ 360,000
   $32 \times $24,000 = $ 768,000
   $30 \times $30,000 = $ 900,000
          $2,028,000   Total receipts

4. Calculate the amount of interest Linda will earn from her investments.
   $2,028,000.00
   $- 213,254.58$
   $1,814,745.42   Total interest earned

1. How are present value of $1 at compound interest and **W**
present value of an ordinary annuity of $1 at compound
interest similar, and how are they different?
Both require the calculation of a lump sum amount to be placed in a
compound interest account. The present value amount is to be kept on
deposit until some future date when a known lump sum amount will
be available for withdrawal. On the other hand, the present value of
an annuity is to be used up by known periodic withdrawals until, at a
future date, the account will be empty.

2. Can you think of and relate a way that you can check **W**
your answers to either sinking fund problems or future
value of ordinary annuity problems?
Future value of ordinary annuity problems can be checked by using
sinking fund tables. Sinking fund problems can be checked by using
future value of ordinary annuity tables.

3. Find the value of $900 deposits made at the end of each
year for 14 years at an interest rate of 5% compounded
annually.

$$\frac{5\%}{1} = 5\%$$

	14	$ 900.00
	×1	×19.59863
	14	$17,638.77

4. Find the value of $2,000 deposits made at the beginning of
each quarter for five years at 6% compounded quarterly.

$$\frac{6\%}{4} = 1.5\%$$

	5	24.47052	$ 2,000.00
	×4	−1.00000	×23.47052
	20 + 1 = 21	23.47052	$46,941.04

5. A machine will save a company $2,500 each month in
expenses, and has a life expectancy of four years. The
market interest rate is 12% compounded monthly. What
should be the highest price paid for the machine?

$$\frac{12\%}{12} = 1\%$$

	4	$ 2,500.00
	×12	×37.97396
	48	$94,934.90

6. A $700,000 debt must be repaid in 12 years. How much
will need to be deposited every six months in an account
paying 10% compounded semiannually?

$$\frac{10\%}{2} = 5\%$$

	12	$700,000.00
	×2	× .02247
	24	$ 15,729.00

7. Bill wants to buy a Lexus in five years. He estimates that
it will cost $55,000. He can make quarterly deposits in an
investment paying 8% compounded quarterly. How much
would each deposit have to be?

$$\frac{8\%}{4} = 2\%$$

	5	$ 55,000.00
	×4	× .04116
	20	$ 2,263.80

8. Tom Terrific started a monthly investment plan $3\frac{1}{2}$ years
ago. He invests $350 at the beginning of each month in an
account that pays 12% compounded monthly. How much
does the account contain now?

$$\frac{12\%}{12} = 1\%$$

	3.5	53.39778	$ 350.00
	×12	−1.00000	×52.39778
	42 + 1 = 43	52.39778	$18,339.22

9. Earnesto Gonzales put $2,500 at the end of each quarter in
a mutual fund account that averaged earning 6%
compounded quarterly. He quit making deposits after
eight years, but transferred the entire account to an
investment paying 12% compounded semiannually for
another 18 years. Now, 26 years later, Earnesto is 60 years
old. How much does he have in his account if he decides
to retire early? How much interest has he earned so far?

Saving $2,500 quarterly is
a future value of an annuity
at 6% compounded quarterly:

Amount that $101,720.73 will
grow to in 18 years at 12%
compounded semiannually is a
future value problem:

$$\frac{6\%}{4} = 1.5\%$$

	8	$ 2,500.00
	×4	×40.68829
	32	$101,720.73

$$\frac{12\%}{2} = 6\%$$

	18	$101,720.73
	×2	×8.147252
	36	$828,744.42

Interest earned:

$ 2,500	Deposit amount
× 32	Number of quarters
$80,000	Total investment

$828,744.42	Future value
−80,000.00	Total investment
$748,744.42	Interest earned

Bonus credit:

10. Earnesto (in exercise 9) wants to receive payments every
six months for 25 years when he reaches age 60. He
believes he can place his money in a relatively risk-free
investment paying 8% compounded semiannually. How
much would each payment from the account be?
If the stream of payments was known, we could use the present value
of an annuity table to determine the amount of the lump sum present
value amount needed:
Present value = annuity × table factor (at intersection of 4% and 50
periods)

Thus,

$$\text{Annuity} = \frac{\text{present value}}{\text{table factor}}$$
$$= \frac{\$828,744.42}{21.48218}$$
$$= \$38,578.23 \text{ every six months}$$

APPLICATION 1

The Springfield Department Store has developed a worksheet that compares ordinary annuities and annuities due. You will see the following worksheet when you open Ch14App1 from your spreadsheet applications disk:

Springfield Department Store
2617 Main Street
Box 219
Springfield, Maryland 58109
Telephone: 301-555-2158   FAX: 301-555-3498

COMPARING ORDINARY ANNUITIES AND ANNUITIES DUE

Amount of Annuity	Payments Per Year	Number of Years	Total Payments	Annual Rate	Period Rate	Future Value of: Ordinary Annuity	Future Value of: Annuity Due	Interest on: Ordinary Annuity	Interest on: Annuity Due
			0		#DIV/0!	#DIV/0!	#DIV/0!	#DIV/0!	#DIV/0!
			0		#DIV/0!	#DIV/0!	#DIV/0!	#DIV/0!	#DIV/0!
			0		#DIV/0!	#DIV/0!	#DIV/0!	#DIV/0!	#DIV/0!
			0		#DIV/0!	#DIV/0!	#DIV/0!	#DIV/0!	#DIV/0!
			0		#DIV/0!	#DIV/0!	#DIV/0!	#DIV/0!	#DIV/0!
			0		#DIV/0!	#DIV/0!	#DIV/0!	#DIV/0!	#DIV/0!
			0		#DIV/0!	#DIV/0!	#DIV/0!	#DIV/0!	#DIV/0!
			0		#DIV/0!	#DIV/0!	#DIV/0!	#DIV/0!	#DIV/0!
			0		#DIV/0!	#DIV/0!	#DIV/0!	#DIV/0!	#DIV/0!

Enter the following information:

Amount of Annuity	Cell	Payments per Year	Cell	Number of Years	Cell	Annual Rate	Cell
$ 500.00	A13	12	B13	10	C13	.08	E13
275.00	A14	4	B14	5	C14	.075	E14
498.56	A15	2	B15	20	C15	.09	E15
451.07	A16	12	B16	7	C16	.1225	E16
2,650.00	A17	1	B17	3	C17	.1075	E17
335.04	A18	2	B18	15	C18	.113	E18
6,159.55	A19	12	B19	2	C19	.085	E19
5,675.75	A20	4	B20	5	C20	.069	E20
10,500.00	A21	4	B21	30	C21	.0775	E21

Answer the following questions after you have completed the spreadsheet. After answering the questions, you might want to alter the data to find information important or interesting to you. For example, you might want to see how much you would have in an account when you reach age 60 if you save $300 per month. You could use one of the interest rates given in the worksheet, or you could enter an interest rate you think is more realistic. (Interest rates do fluctuate. By the time you work with this spreadsheet, the interest rates in the market may have changed.)

1. What is the future value of an ordinary annuity when $500 is deposited monthly for 10 years at a rate of 8%?

2. What is the future value of an annuity due when $335.04 is invested semiannually for 15 years at 11.3%?

3. What is the amount of interest earned on an annuity due when $2,650 is invested annually for three years at 10.75%?

4. What is the period rate of a 7.75% annual rate when compounding takes place quarterly?

5. How many total monthly payments will be made on a $451.07 annuity at 12.25% for seven years?

6. What is the future value of an ordinary annuity when $498.56 is invested semiannually for 20 years at 9%?

7. What is the future value of an annuity due when $10,500 is invested quarterly for 30 years at 7.75%?

GROUP REPORT

FOR CHAPTER 14 APPLICATION 1

Write a report to the store manager describing the findings in the spreadsheet comparing ordinary annuities with annuities due. Make any recommendations that would be helpful to future decision-making.

EXCEL SPREADSHEET APPLICATION FOR CHAPTER 14

APPLICATION 2

The Springfield Department Store has bond issues to retire and buildings and equipment to replace in the future. For example, it is anticipated that their main store in downtown Springfield will need to be replaced in 20 years. Management has estimated the cost of replacement to be $7,542,934.30. A sinking fund has been set up assuming an annual rate of 7.55% can be earned over the 20 years. When you open Ch14App2 from your computer spreadsheet application's disk, you will see the form shown here:

Springfield Department Store
2617 Main Street
Box 219
Springfield, Maryland 58109
Telephone: 301-555-2158   FAX: 301-555-3498

SINKING FUND WORKSHEET

Amount of Payment	Payments Per Year	Number of Years	Total Payments	Annual Rate	Period Rate	Amount Needed in the Future	Interest Earned
#DIV/0!			0		#DIV/0!		#DIV/0!
#DIV/0!			0		#DIV/0!		#DIV/0!
#DIV/0!			0		#DIV/0!		#DIV/0!
#DIV/0!			0		#DIV/0!		#DIV/0!
#DIV/0!			0		#DIV/0!		#DIV/0!
#DIV/0!			0		#DIV/0!		#DIV/0!
#DIV/0!			0		#DIV/0!		#DIV/0!
#DIV/0!			0		#DIV/0!		#DIV/0!
#DIV/0!			0		#DIV/0!		#DIV/0!

Enter the following information:

Payments per Year	Cell	Number of Years	Cell	Annual Rate	Cell	Amount Needed in the Future	Cell
12	B13	10	C13	.0675	E13	$ 50,000.00	G13
12	B14	6	C14	.055	E14	75,000.00	G14
2	B15	8	C15	.07	E15	295,000.00	G15
12	B16	5	C16	.054	E16	398,500.00	G16
1	B17	13	C17	.096	E17	1,943,390.00	G17
4	B18	15	C18	.069	E18	2,295,729.47	G18
12	B19	20	C19	.0755	E19	7,542,934.30	G19
4	B20	12	C20	.105	E20	19,396,729.00	G20
12	B21	30	C21	.098	E21	25,000,000.00	G21

Answer the following questions after you have completed the spreadsheet. After answering the questions, you may want to vary the data to reflect amounts that are meaningful to you. For example, you may want to know how much you will have to save monthly to have $1 million available when you reach age 65. You can use one of the annual rates of interest or select one that is closer to the current market rate.

1. What is the amount of payment (or investment) that Springfield will have to make monthly for 10 years to have $50,000 available at an annual rate of 6.75%?

2. What is the period rate necessary for $11,540.49 monthly payments to grow to $25,000,000 in 30 years?

3. What amount of interest will be earned by $5,800.18 being invested (amount of payment) monthly at 5.4% for 5 years when the future value needed is $398,500?

4. How many total payments will be required for $81,377.71 to grow to $1,943,390 at 9.6%?

5. What is the amount of payment necessary for a 10.5% investment of $206,257.60 quarterly to grow to $19,396,729 in 12 years?

6. What amount of interest is earned when $22,119.07 is invested at 6.9% quarterly for 15 years?

7. What amount of interest will be earned by investing enough every 6 months for 8 years at 7% compounded semiannually to earn $295,000?

8. What is the amount of payment (or investment) that will have to be made quarterly for 12 years at 10.5% to earn $19,396,729?

GROUP REPORT

FOR CHAPTER 14 APPLICATION 2

The cost of education continues to escalate. The Springfield Department Store management would like to provide five $10,000 scholarships to children of employees. Your group has been asked to determine how much must be saved monthly for three years in an investment that will earn an average of 8.9% compounded monthly.

Another alternative is to offer one $10,000 scholarship for five consecutive years, starting at the end of the first year. Separate monthly deposit investment accounts could be started now to provide the money as follows: (a) one year at 7% compounded monthly, (b) two years at 7.5% compounded quarterly, (c) three years at 7.9% compounded monthly, (d) four years at 9% compounded semiannually, and (e) five years at 9.25% compounded quarterly. Write a report to the Benefits Office of the Human Resources Department with the results and your recommendations.

15

REAL ESTATE APPLICATIONS
MORTGAGES

HOW EXPENSIVE?

Perhaps the most expensive house for sale in the United States is the Rhinelander mansion owned by clothing magnate Ralph Lauren. What makes a house expensive? Certainly in this case it isn't its newness. Gertrude Rhinelander Waldo, a wealthy New Yorker, commissioned it in 1895. Finished in 1898, it cost her the exorbitant price of $500,000. In 1989 it sold for $43 million. The asking price today is $46 million.

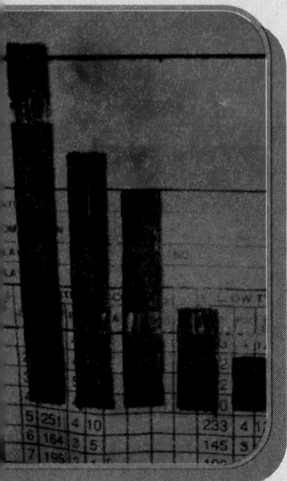

An old refrain among realtors is that there are three considerations in valuing real estate: location, location, and location. The four-story French chateau is located at the corner of Madison Avenue and 72d Street in New York City. That is probably the most expensive shopping district in the nation, if not the whole world.

If anyone is really interested, a 10%, 30-year mortgage would cost $403,680 per month. But at 9%, the monthly payment will only be $370,130. Over the life of the mortgage the buyer paying 9% can save $49,266,000 in interest by opting for a 15-year loan instead of a 30-year loan.

Any takers in this class?

Chapter Glossary

Mortgage. A loan secured by real estate.

Real estate. (real property) Land, buildings, and other improvements attached to land.

Fixed rate mortgage. A mortgage with an interest rate that does not change.

Graduated payment mortgage. A mortgage in which the monthly payments get larger over time with the assumption that the buyer's income will increase during that time.

Adjustable rate. A mortgage rate that changes over time if current mortgage interest rates change (This is sometimes called a variable rate mortgage).

Balloon mortgage. A series of payments ending in a one-time payment that retires the loan in full.

Home-equity loan. A credit line in which a borrower pledges equity in a home as collateral.

Conventional loan. Basic type of mortgage between a lender and borrower.

FHA Loan. A mortgage loan that must be approved and guaranteed by the U.S. Federal Housing Administration.

VA loan. A mortgage loan available to qualified veterans that must be approved and guaranteed by the U.S. Veterans Administration.

Amortization Schedule. A loan repayment schedule showing interest and principal portions of each payment, and the unpaid balance.

Student Objectives

Upon completion of this chapter, you should be able to:

1. Find the size of a monthly mortgage payment using tables.
2. Appreciate the effect of time on the amount of interest on a mortgage.
3. Appreciate the effect of interest rates on the amount of interest on a mortgage.
4. Construct a loan repayment schedule.

B uildings are almost always sold through an arrangement of a down payment and a long-term loan, or **mortgage**, for the balance. A mortgage is a loan secured by **real estate**. In the contemporary world there are several types of mortgages. No particular one is right for every home, and each has good features and bad. Some of the major types with their good and bad points are listed in Figure 15.1.

Type	Good Points	Bad Points
Fixed Rate	A monthly principal and interest payment that will not change. Interest rate cannot be raised.	Owner is locked in to an interest rate that does not change if other interest rates fall.
Graduated Payment	Easy to qualify for and has low payments for young buyers with low incomes.	Monthly payments get larger over time and, if owner's income does not grow, can result in financial difficulty.
Adjustable Rate	Lower initial interest rate than fixed. Rate might go down if other interest rates fall resulting in a smaller monthly payment.	Interest rate could increase resulting in higher monthly payments if other interest rates rise.
Balloon Note	Useful if the current rates are high and the buyer expects them to fall because the payment would fall.	Rates might rise and refinancing might raise the payment. If refinancing is not possible, owner could lose the property.
Home Equity	Easy line of credit in most states. Interest, unlike for most other loans, is tax deductible.	Owner can lose the home if the debt is not repaid.
Conventional	More freedom to choose length of mortgage time. Less government regulation.	Interest rates are usually higher than for FHA and VA loans.
FHA	Interest rates are usually lower than those of conventional loans.	Can be financed for only 15 or 30 years and are government regulated.
VA	Interest rates are the lowest of any mortgage rates.	Can be financed for only 15 or 30 years and are available only for veterans.

Figure 15.1
Types of Mortgages

LEARNING UNIT 1
MONTHLY PAYMENT AMOUNT

Mortgages are usually paid in monthly installments, each of which includes interest on the unpaid balance and a payment on the principal. Rarely does anyone attempt to compute the size of a mortgage payment without a table. Most real estate agents use a table such as Table 15.1 to determine a payment's size.

TABLE 15.1   MONTHLY PAYMENT PER $1,000 MORTGAGE

Rate	15 years	20 years	25 years	30 years
7%	$ 8.99	$ 7.75	$ 7.07	$ 6.21
8%	9.56	8.36	7.72	7.34
9%	10.14	9.00	8.39	8.05
10%	10.75	9.65	9.09	8.78
11%	11.37	10.32	9.80	9.52
12%	12.00	11.01	10.53	10.29
13%	12.65	11.72	11.28	11.06
14%	13.32	12.44	12.04	11.85
15%	14.00	13.17	12.81	12.64
16%	14.69	13.91	13.59	13.45

Note: The *Table Handbook* that accompanies *Business Mathematics* contains more detailed tables.

15.1   Finding the Payment Size Using Per $1,000 Tables

To use Table 15.1, multiply the number of thousands in the principal of a mortgage by the amount per thousand in the appropriate percent and years cell in the table.

The table is the monthly payment for principal plus interest, which is probably not an entire house payment. A house payment usually includes a contribution into a fund called an escrow account, which is used to pay property taxes and insurance premiums when they come due.

EXAMPLE   June and Danny Ford bought a house for $79,000. The interest rate is 10% and the mortgage term is for 30 years. They were required to pay down $9,000. How much will the monthly mortgage payment be?

Solution   *Step 1.* Find the total amount of the mortgage:

$$\begin{array}{r} \$79{,}000 \\ -\ 9{,}000 \\ \hline \$70{,}000 \end{array}$$

Step 2. From Table 15.1, find the monthly payment per thousand for 30 years at 10%: $8.78.

Step 3. Divide the amount of the mortgage by $1,000:

$$\frac{\$70{,}000}{\$\,1{,}000} = 70$$

Step 4. Multiply:

$$\begin{array}{rl} \$\quad\ 70 & \textit{thousand} \\ \times\ \ 8.78 & \textit{per thousand} \\ \hline \$614.60 & \textit{Monthly payment} \end{array}$$

15.1 Practice Problems

1. Martin and Nancy Starr bought a house for $129,000. The interest rate is 14% and the mortgage term is for 15 years. They were required to pay down $29,000. How much will the monthly mortgage payment be?
2. The Jay and Gertrude Washington family purchased a $96,000 home by making a 15% down payment and signing a 30-year mortgage at 12%. Find the monthly payment.

3. Soy and Siem Tsao moved in across the street from the Washingtons. Their house cost $97,000 with a 19% down payment. Mr. and Mrs. Tsao found 30-year mortgage money at 9%. How much will their monthly payment be?

4. Linda and Jerry Randall live next door to the Washingtons. Their house cost $107,000 and they paid down 20%. Since their 30-year mortgage is older than the Washingtons' or Tsaos', the rate is lower. It is 7%. Determine the Randalls' monthly payment.

15.1 Solutions to Practice Problems

1.
$129,000	Price			100	thousand
− 29,000	Down	$\frac{\$100,000}{\$1,000} = 100$		× $13.32	per thousand
$100,000	Principal			$ 1,332	Payment

2.
$ 96,000	Price	$ 96,000		81.6	thousand
× 15%		− 14,400	$\frac{\$81,600}{\$1,000} = 81.6$	× $10.29	per thousand
$ 14,400	Down	$ 81,600	Principal	$ 839.66	Payment

3.
$ 97,000	Price	$ 97,000		78.57	thousand
× 19%		− 18,430	$\frac{\$78,570}{\$1,000} = 78.57$	× $ 8.05	per thousand
$18,430	Down	$ 78,570	Principal	$ 632.49	Payment

4.
$107,000	Price	$107,000		85.6	thousand
× 20%		− 21,400	$\frac{\$85,600}{\$1,000} = 85.6$	× $6.21	per thousand
$21,400	Down	$ 85,600	Principal	$ 531.58	Payment

LEARNING UNIT 2
EFFECT OF TIME AND INTEREST RATE ON PAYMENT SIZE AND TOTAL INTEREST

The real amount of the cost (interest) for a home mortgage loan is often surprising to people who are not aware of the workings of such loans. Depending on the interest rate and length of the loan, the interest portion is typically greater than the principal.

15.2 Effect of Time on the Amount of Interest

To determine the amount of interest, find the payment size in a mortgage table, multiply that figure by the number of monthly payments, and subtract the original principal.

E X A M P L E   Kate and Al Redd bought a new house for $90,000 with a 15% down payment. The interest rate is 10% and the mortgage term is for 30 years. How much will be the total interest cost of the mortgage?

Solution   *Step 1.* Multiply the cost by the down payment percent.

$90,000
× .15
$13,500   *Down payment*

Step 2. Subtract the down payment from the purchase price:

$ 90,000
−13,500
$ 76,500   *Principal*

Step 3. Find the monthly mortgage payment ($8.78 per thousand) in the mortgage table and multiply by the number of thousands:

76.5   *thousand*
× $8.78   *per thousand*
$671.67   *Monthly payment*

Step 4. Multiply that figure by the number of payments in 30 years.

$$
\begin{array}{rr}
& 30 \text{ years} \\
\times\ & 12 \text{ months} \\
\hline
& 360 \text{ payments}
\end{array}
\qquad
\begin{array}{rr}
\$ & 671.67 \\
\times\ & 360 \\
\hline
\$241,801.20 & \quad Total
\end{array}
$$

Step 5. Subtract the principal from the total amount paid:

$$
\begin{array}{rl}
& \$241,801.20 \\
- & 76,500.00 \\
\hline
& \$165,301.20 \quad Interest
\end{array}
$$

---

1. Frank and Wilma Furche bought a dairy for $80,000 with a 10% down payment. How much interest will they pay at a 10% rate if the loan is for 25 years?

2. Moshe and Mae Greenburg bought a small grocery for $90,000 with 10% down at 7% for 30 years. How much interest will they pay? How much could they save with a 25-year mortgage at 7%?

3. Julia and Jesse James bought a new house for $110,000 with 5% down and 9% interest. How much interest will they pay if the loan is for 30 years? How much could they have saved with a 15-year mortgage at 9%?

4. Charlie Green bought a building for his wife Katie's doll business. It cost $225,000 with a 12% mortgage over 25 years and 10% down. How much interest will Charlie pay? How much more would it cost if he had financed for 30 years?

15.2 Solutions to Practice Problems

1.

$$
\begin{array}{rl}
& \$80,000 \\
\times & 10\% \\
\hline
\$ & 8,000 \text{ Down}
\end{array}
\qquad
\begin{array}{rl}
& \$80,000 \\
- & 8,000 \\
\hline
& \$72,000 \text{ Principal}
\end{array}
\qquad
\frac{\$72,000}{\$\ 1,000} =
\begin{array}{l}
72 \text{ thousand} \\
\times\ \$9.09 \text{ per thousand} \\
\hline
\$654.48 \text{ Monthly payment}
\end{array}
$$

$$
\begin{array}{rl}
& 5 \text{ years} \\
\times & 12 \text{ months} \\
\hline
& 300 \text{ payments}
\end{array}
\qquad
\begin{array}{rl}
\$ & 654.48 \\
\times & 300 \text{ payments} \\
\hline
& \$196,344 \text{ Total}
\end{array}
\qquad
\begin{array}{rl}
& \$196,344 \\
- & 72,000 \\
\hline
& \$124,344 \text{ Interest}
\end{array}
$$

2. 30-year mortgage:

$$
\begin{array}{rl}
& \$90,000 \\
\times & 10\% \\
\hline
\$ & 9,000 \text{ Down}
\end{array}
\quad
\begin{array}{rl}
& \$90,000 \\
- & 9,000 \\
\hline
& \$81,000 \text{ Principal}
\end{array}
\quad
\frac{\$81,000}{\$\ 1,000} =
\begin{array}{l}
81 \text{ thousand} \\
\times\ \$6.21 \text{ per thousand} \\
\hline
\$503.01 \text{ Monthly payment}
\end{array}
\quad
\begin{array}{rl}
& 30 \text{ years} \\
\times & 12 \text{ months} \\
\hline
& 360 \text{ payments}
\end{array}
$$

$$
\begin{array}{rl}
\$ & 503.01 \\
\times & 360 \text{ payments} \\
\hline
& \$181,083.60 \text{ Total}
\end{array}
\qquad
\begin{array}{rl}
& \$181,083.60 \\
- & 81,000 \\
\hline
& \$100,083.60 \text{ Interest}
\end{array}
$$

25-year mortgage:

$$
\begin{array}{l}
81 \text{ thousand} \\
\times\ \$7.07 \text{ per thousand} \\
\hline
\$572.67 \text{ Monthly payment}
\end{array}
\quad
\begin{array}{rl}
& 25 \text{ years} \\
\times & 12 \text{ months} \\
\hline
& 300 \text{ payments}
\end{array}
\quad
\begin{array}{rl}
\$ & 572.67 \\
\times & 300 \text{ payments} \\
\hline
& \$171,801 \text{ Interest}
\end{array}
\quad
\begin{array}{rl}
& \$171,801 \\
- & 81,000 \\
\hline
\$ & 90,801 \text{ Total}
\end{array}
$$

$$
\begin{array}{rl}
& \$100,083.60 \text{ Interest for 30 years} \\
- & 90,801.00 \text{ Interest for 25 years} \\
\hline
\$ & 9,282.60 \text{ Savings}
\end{array}
$$

3. 30-year mortgage:

$$
\begin{array}{rl}
& \$110,000 \\
\times & 5\% \\
\hline
\$ & 5,500 \text{ Down}
\end{array}
\quad
\begin{array}{rl}
& \$110,000 \\
- & 5,500 \\
\hline
& \$104,500 \text{ Principal}
\end{array}
\quad
\begin{array}{l}
104.5 \text{ thousand} \\
\times\ \$8.05 \text{ per thousand} \\
\hline
\$841.23 \text{ Monthly payment}
\end{array}
\quad
\begin{array}{rl}
& 30 \text{ years} \\
\times & 12 \text{ months} \\
\hline
& 360 \text{ payments}
\end{array}
$$

$$
\begin{array}{rl}
\$ & 841.23 \\
\times & 360 \text{ payments} \\
\hline
& \$302,842.80 \text{ Total}
\end{array}
\qquad
\begin{array}{rl}
& \$ 302,842.80 \\
- & 104,500.00 \\
\hline
& \$ 198,342.80 \text{ Interest}
\end{array}
$$

15-year mortgage:

104.5 thousand	15 years
× $10.14 per thousand	× 12 months
$1,059.63 Monthly payment	180 payments

$ 1,059.63	$ 190,733.40
× 180 payments	− 104,500.00
$190,733.40 Total	$ 86,233.40 Interest

$198,342.80 Interest for 30 years
− 86,233.40 Interest for 15 years
$112,109.40 Savings

4. 25-year mortgage:

$225,000	$225,000		$202,500		202.5 thousand
× 10%	− 22,500		$1,000	=	× $10.53 per thousand
$ 22,500 Down	$202,500 Principal				$2,132.33 Monthly payment

25 years	$ 2,132.33	$ 639,699.00
× 12 months	× 300 payments	− 202,500.00
300 payments	$639,699.00 Total	$ 437,199.00 Interest

30-year mortgage:

202.5 thousand	30 years	$ 2,083.73
× $10.29 per thousand	× 12 months	× 360 payments
$2,083.73 Monthly payment	360 payments	$750,142.80 Interest

$ 750,142.80	$ 547,642.80 Interest on 30-year loan
− 202,500.00	− 437,199.00 Interest on 25-year loan
$ 547,642.80 Interest	$ 110,443.80 More

15.3 Effect of Interest Rates on Payment Size

Because most mortgages are for extended lengths of time, the effect of interest rate changes is much greater than for other purchases. If a buyer is considering whether to buy a new car over a period of four years, a one-point increase in interest rates will probably add only a few dollars to a monthly payment. When buying a house over 25 to 30 years, an increase of one point might add hundreds of dollars to a monthly payment.

EXAMPLE   George and Kathy Torres bought a new house for $120,000. They paid 10% down and 12% interest rate for 30 years. If they had bought it last month, the rate would have been 11%. How much more is their total interest for having waited a month?

Solution   *Step 1.* Multiply the cost by the down payment percent:

$120,000
× 10%
$ 12,000   *Down payment*

Step 2. Subtract the down payment from the purchase price:

$120,000
− 12,000
$108,000   *Principal*

Step 3. Find the monthly mortgage payment at 12% ($10.29 per thousand) in the mortgage table and multiply by the number of thousands:

108   *thousand*
× $10.29   *per thousand*
$1,111.32   *Monthly payment*

Step 4. Multiply that figure by the number of payments in 30 years:

$$
\begin{array}{r}
\$ \quad 1,111.32 \\
\times \quad\quad 360 \\
\hline
\$400,075.20 \quad\quad \textit{Total}
\end{array}
$$

Step 5. Subtract the principal from the total amount paid:

$$
\begin{array}{r}
\$ \ 400,075.20 \\
- \ 108,000.00 \\
\hline
\$ \ 292,075.20 \quad\quad \textit{Interest at 12\%}
\end{array}
$$

Step 6. Find the monthly mortgage payment at 11% ($9.52 per thousand) in the mortgage table and multiply by the number of thousands:

$$
\begin{array}{r}
108 \quad\quad \textit{thousand} \\
\times \ \$9.52 \quad\quad \textit{per thousand} \\
\hline
\$1,028.16 \quad\quad \textit{Monthly payment}
\end{array}
$$

Step 7. Multiply that figure by the number of payments in 30 years:

$$
\begin{array}{r}
\$ \quad 1,028.16 \\
\times \quad\quad 360 \\
\hline
\$370,137.60 \quad\quad \textit{Total}
\end{array}
$$

Step 8. Subtract the principal from the total amount paid:

$$
\begin{array}{r}
\$ \ 370,137.60 \\
- \ 108,000.00 \\
\hline
\$ \ 262,137.60 \quad\quad \textit{Interest at 11\%}
\end{array}
$$

Step 9. Subtract interest at 11% from interest at 12%:

$$
\begin{array}{r}
\$ \ 292,075.20 \quad\quad \textit{Interest at 12\%} \\
- \ 262,137.60 \quad\quad \textit{Interest at 11\%} \\
\hline
\$ \quad 29,937.60 \quad\quad \textit{More}
\end{array}
$$

15.3 Practice Problems

1. Two builders offer similar new homes for $90,000 each, financed over 30 years with 15% down. The Edwards Company can acquire 9% financing. The Biery Company houses finance at 10%. How much more interest would it cost to buy a Biery house than an Edwards house?

2. Jack and Jill Schwarz are in the market for a new flower shop. The building on Waits Street costs $75,000 and can be financed at 9%. The one on Everest Avenue costs $85,000 and will finance at 8%. Both buildings require 10% down with 20-year mortgages. Find the difference between the total interest costs.

3. Six years ago, Sung and Minya Chan bought a grocery for $55,000 at 14% financed over 25 years with 5% down. Interest rates have declined to 11% since then. How much total interest would the Chans have saved if they had waited six years?

4. Eloy and Juanita Gomez bought a toy store with a $120,000 mortgage for 30 years at 10% with a 20% down payment. They could have financed it for 8% if they had waited one year. How much more is the total interest for the privilege of buying earlier?

15.3 Solutions to Practice Problems

1.

$$
\begin{array}{lll}
\$90,000 & \$\ 90,000 & 76.5 \ \text{thousand} \\
\times \ 15\% & -\ 13,500 & \times \ \$8.05 \ (9\%) \\
\hline
\$13,500 \ \text{Down} & \$\ 76,500 \ \text{Principal} & \$615.83 \ \text{Monthly payment}
\end{array}
$$

$$
\begin{array}{ll}
\$ \quad 615.83 & \$221,698.80 \\
\times \quad\quad 360 \ \text{payments} & -\ 76,500.00 \\
\hline
\$221,698.80 \ \text{Total} & \$145,198.80 \ \text{Interest at 9\%}
\end{array}
$$

```
              76.5  thousand
            × $ 8.78  (10%)
            $ 671.67  Monthly payment

          $      671.67              $241,801.20
          ×        360  payments    − 76,500.00
          $241,801.20  Total        $165,301.20  Interest at 10%

          $  165,301.20
          − 145,198.80
          $    20,102.40  Extra cost of buying a Biery house instead of an Edwards house
```

2.
```
   $75,000              $75,000                 67.5  thousand
   ×  10%               − 7,500               × $9.00  (9%)
   $ 7,500  Down        $67,500  Principal     $607.50  Monthly payment

   $      607.50              $145,800.00
   ×        240  payments    − 67,500.00
   $145,800.00  Total        $ 78,300.00  Interest on Waits St.

   $85,000              $85,000                 76.5  thousand
   ×  10%               − 8,500               × $8.36  (8%)
   $ 8,500  Down        $76,500  Principal     $639.54  Monthly payment

   $      639.54              $ 153,489.60
   ×        240  payments    − 76,500.00
   $153,489.60  Total        $ 76,989.60  Interest on Everest Ave.

   $  78,300.00
   − 76,989.60
   $   1,310.40  Extra cost of Waits St. building over
                 Everest Ave. building
```

3.
```
   $55,000              $55,000                 52.25  thousand
   ×   5%               − 2,750               × $12.04  (14%)
   $ 2,750  Down        $52,250  Principal     $ 629.09  Monthly payment

   $      629.09              $188,727.00
   ×        300  payments    − 52,250.00
   $188,727.00  Total        $136,477.00  Interest at 14%

      52.25  thousand       $      512.05              $153,615
   ×$9.80  (11%)            ×        300  payments    − 52,250
   $512.05  Monthly payment  $153,615.00  Total        $101,365  Interest at 11%

   $  136,477
   − 101,365
   $    35,112  Extra cost of buying six years ago instead of today
```

4.
```
   $120,000             $120,000                 96  thousand
   ×   20%              − 24,000               × $8.78  (10%)
   $ 24,000  Down       $ 96,000  Principal     $842.88  Monthly payment

   $      842.88              $303,436.80
   ×        360  payments    − 96,000.00
   $303,436.80  Total        $207,436.80  Interest at 10%

      96  thousand          $      704.64
   ×$7.34  (8%)             ×        360  payments
   $704.64  Monthly payment  $253,670.40  Total

   $253,670.40
   − 96,000.00
   $157,670.40  Interest at 8%

   $ 207,436.80
   − 157,670.40
   $  49,766.40  Extra interest for buying earlier
```

LEARNING UNIT 3
LOAN REPAYMENT (AMORTIZATION) SCHEDULE

Loan repayment schedules, such as that shown in Figure 15.2, are available ordinarily from the mortgage company. The **amortization schedule** is a loan repayment schedule showing interest and principal portions of each payment, and the unpaid balances.

Figure 15.2
Loan Repayment (Amortization) Schedule The First 3 Years of a $1000,000, 30-Year Loan at 8%

Payment Number	Size of Payment	Interest Portion	Principal Portion	Balance of Principal
0	$734.00			$100,000.00
1	$734.00	$666.67	$67.33	$ 99,932.67
2	$734.00	$666.22	$67.78	$ 99,864.88
3	$734.00	$665.77	$68.23	$ 99,796.65
4	$734.00	$665.31	$68.69	$ 99,727.96
5	$734.00	$664.85	$69.15	$ 99,658.81
33	$734.00	$650.71	$83.29	$ 97,523.81
34	$734.00	$650.16	$83.84	$ 97,439.97
35	$734.00	$649.60	$84.40	$ 97,355.57
36	$734.00	$649.04	$84.96	$ 97,270.61

Note: After 36 payments of $734 each ($26,424), $97,270.61 is still owned. Thus only $2,730 of the $26,424 has been applied to the principal of the loan. The rest ($23,694) is interest.

15.4 Preparing a Loan Repayment (Amortization) Schedule

EXCEL Spreadsheet Application In the spreadsheet application at the end of this chapter, Springfield has designed a loan amortization schedule spreadsheet for its last store building mortgage.

A loan repayment schedule is constructed after the amount of the monthly payment is determined from a table. The formulas used to construct a loan repayment schedule are as follows:

1. The interest portion equals the balance of the loan (P) times the interest rate (R) times time (T): $I = P \times R \times \frac{1}{12}$. ($T$ is always $\frac{1 \text{ monthly payment}}{12 \text{ months in a year}}$).
2. The principal portion is the monthly payment minus the interest portion.
3. The balance of the principal is the previous principal balance minus the principal portion.

EXAMPLE Prepare a loan repayment schedule for the first three payments on a $60,000 loan at 12% for 30 years with a 10% down payment.

Solution **Step 1.** Find the down payment and subtract it from the cost of the property:

$$\$60,000 \times 10\% = \$6,000 \text{ Down}$$
$$\$60,000 - 6,000 = \$54,000 \text{ Principal}$$

Step 2. Determine the size of the monthly payment from the 12% mortgage table:

$$\$10.29 \text{ per thousand} \times 54 \text{ thousand} = \$555.66 \text{ Monthly payment}$$

Chapter 15 Real Estate Applications   523

Step 3. Calculate the first payment:

$$\text{Interest portion:} \quad \$54,000.00 \times 12\% \times \frac{1}{12} = \$540$$

Principal portion: $555.66 − 540.00 = $15.66
Balance of principal: $54,000 − 15.66 = $53,984.34

Step 4. Calculate the second payment:

$$\text{Interest portion:} \quad \$53,984.34 \times 12\% \times \frac{1}{12} = \$539.84$$

Principal portion: $555.66 − 539.84 = $15.82
Balance of principal: $53,984.34 − 15.82 = $53,968.52

Step 5. Calculate the third payment:

$$\text{Interest portion:} \quad \$53,968.52 \times 12 \times \frac{1}{12} = \$539.69$$

Principal portion: $555.66 − 539.69 = $15.97
Balance of principal: $53,968.52 − 15.97 = $53,952.55

Step 6. Set up and fill out the schedule:

Payment Number	Size of Payment	Interest Portion	Principal Portion	Balance of Principal
1	$555.66	$540.00	$15.66	$53,984.34
2	555.66	539.84	15.82	53,968.52
3	555.66	539.69	15.97	53,952.55

15.4 Practice Problems

1. Prepare a loan repayment schedule for the first three payments on a $100,000 loan at 8% for 25 years with a 15% down payment.

2. Prepare a loan repayment schedule for the first three payments on a $96,000 loan at 10% for 30 years with a 10% down payment.

3. Prepare a loan repayment schedule for the first three payments on a $240,000 loan at 12% for 15 years with a 20% down payment.

4. Prepare a loan repayment schedule for the first three payments on an $86,000 loan at 14% for 20 years with a 5% down payment.

15.4 Solutions to Practice Problems

1. *First payment:*

$100,000 $100,000   85 thousand
× 15%   − 15,000   × $7.72 (8%)
$ 15,000 Down $ 85,000 Principal $656.20 Monthly payment

$$\$85,000 \times 8\% \times \frac{1}{12} = \$566.67 \quad \text{Interest portion}$$

$ 656.20 $85,000.00
−566.67   −   89.53
$ 89.53 Principal portion $84,910.47 Balance of principal

Second payment:

$$\$84,910.47 \times 8\% \times \frac{1}{12} = \$566.07 \quad \text{Interest portion}$$

$ 656.20 $84,910.47
−566.07   −   90.13
$ 90.13 Principal portion $84,820.34 Balance of principal

Third payment:

$$\$84,820.34 \times 8\% \times \frac{1}{12} = \$565.47 \text{ Interest portion}$$

$$
\begin{array}{ll}
\$\ 656.20 & \$84,820.34 \\
\underline{-565.47} & \underline{-\quad 90.73} \\
\$\ \ 90.73 \text{ Principal portion} & \$84,729.61 \text{ Balance of principal}
\end{array}
$$

Payment Number	Size of Payment	Interest Portion	Principal Portion	Balance of Principal
1	$656.20	$566.67	$89.53	$84,910.47
2	656.20	566.07	90.13	84,820.34
3	656.20	565.47	90.73	84,729.61

2. *First payment:*

$$
\begin{array}{lll}
\$96,000 & \$\ 96,000 & 86.4 \quad \text{thousand} \\
\underline{\times\ \ 10\%} & \underline{-\ \ 9,600} & \underline{\times\ \$8.78}\ (10\%) \\
\$\ 9,600 \text{ Down} & \$\ 86,400 \text{ Principal} & \$758.59 \text{ Monthly payment}
\end{array}
$$

$$\$\ 86,400 \times 10\% \times \frac{1}{12} = \$720.00 \text{ Interest portion}$$

$$
\begin{array}{ll}
\$\ 758.59 & \$86,400.00 \\
\underline{-720.00} & \underline{-\quad 38.59} \\
\$\ \ 38.59 \text{ Principal portion} & \$86,361.41 \text{ Balance of principal}
\end{array}
$$

Second payment:

$$\$86,361.41 \times 10\% \times \frac{1}{12} = \$719.68 \text{ Interest portion}$$

$$
\begin{array}{ll}
\$\ 758.59 & \$86,361.41 \\
\underline{-719.68} & \underline{-\quad 38.91} \\
\$\ \ 38.91 \text{ Principal portion} & \$86,322.50 \text{ Balance of principal}
\end{array}
$$

Third Payment:

$$\$86,322.50 \times 10\% \times \frac{1}{12} = \$719.35 \text{ Interest portion}$$

$$
\begin{array}{ll}
\$\ 758.59 & \$86,322.50 \\
\underline{-719.35} & \underline{-\quad 39.24} \\
\$\ \ 39.24 \text{ Principal portion} & \$86,283.26 \text{ Balance of principal}
\end{array}
$$

Payment Number	Size of Payment	Interest Portion	Principal Portion	Balance of Principal
1	$758.59	$720.00	$38.59	$86,361.41
2	758.59	719.68	38.91	86,322.50
3	758.59	719.35	39.24	86,283.26

3. *First payment:*

$$
\begin{array}{lll}
\$240,000 & \$240,000 & 192 \quad \text{thousand} \\
\underline{\times\ \ \ 20\%} & \underline{-\ 48,000} & \underline{\times\ \$12.00}\ (12\%) \\
\$\ 48,000 \text{ Down} & \$192,000 \text{ Principal} & \$2,304.00 \text{ Monthly payment}
\end{array}
$$

$$\$192,000 \times \frac{1}{12} = \$1,920 \text{ Interest portion}$$

$$
\begin{array}{ll}
\$\ 2,304.00 & \$192,000.00 \\
\underline{-1,920.00} & \underline{-\quad 384.00} \\
\$\ \ \ 384.00 \text{ Principal portion} & \$191,616.00 \text{ Balance of principal}
\end{array}
$$

Second payment:

$$\$191,616.00 \times 12\% \times \frac{1}{12} = \$1,916.16 \text{ Interest portion}$$

$$
\begin{array}{ll}
\$\ 2,304.00 & \$191,616.00 \\
\underline{-1,916.16} & \underline{-\quad 387.84} \\
\$\ \ \ 387.84 \text{ Principal portion} & \$191,228.16 \text{ Balance of principal}
\end{array}
$$

Third payment:

$$\$191,228.16 \times 12\% \times \frac{1}{12} = \$1,912.28 \text{ Interest portion}$$

$ 2,304.00	$191,228.16
−1,912.28	− 391.72
$ 391.72 Principal portion	$190,836.44 Balance of principal

Payment Number	Size of Payment	Interest Portion	Principal Portion	Balance of Principal
1	$2,304.00	$1,920.00	$384.00	$191,616.00
2	2,304.00	1,916.16	387.84	191,228.16
3	2,304.00	1,912.28	391.72	190,836.44

4. *First Payment:*

$ 86,000	$ 86,000	81.7 thousand
× 5%	− 4,300	× $12.44 (14%)
$ 4,300 Down	$ 81,700 Principal	$1,016.35 Monthly payment

$$\$81,700.00 \times 14\% \times \frac{1}{12} = \$953.17 \text{ Interest portion}$$

$1,016.35	$81,700.00
− 953.17	− 63.18
$ 63.18 Principal portion	$81,636.82 Balance of principal

Second payment:

$$\$81,636.82 \times 14\% \times \frac{1}{12} = \$952.43 \text{ Interest portion}$$

$1,016.35	$81,636.82
− 952.43	− 63.92
$ 63.92 Principal portion	$81,572.90 Balance of principal

Third payment:

$$\$81,572.90 \times 14\% \times \frac{1}{12} = \$951.68 \text{ Interest portion}$$

$1,016.35	$ 81,572.90
− 951.68	− 64.67
$ 64.67 Principal portion	$ 81,508.23 Balance of principal

Payment Number	Size of Payment	Interest Portion	Principal Portion	Balance of Principal
1	$1,016.35	$953.17	$63.18	$81,636.82
2	1,016.35	952.43	63.92	81,572.90
3	1,016.35	951.68	64.67	81,508.23

QUICK REFERENCE SUMMARY AND REVIEW

Page	Section Topic	Learning Concepts	Examples and Solutions
517	**15.1** Finding the Payment Size Using Per $1,000 Tables	Determining monthly mortgage payments using Table 15.1. Divide the amount of the mortgage by 1,000. Multiply that amount by the monthly payment per thousand found in the table.	Mr. and Mrs. Dooley bought a store for $86,000 with a $6,000 down payment. The interest rate is 11% and the term is 25 years. Using Table 15.1, find the monthly payment. To do so, first find the total amount of the mortgage: $86,000 − 6,000 $80,000

Page	Section Topic	Learning Concepts	Examples and Solutions
			Find the payment per thousand for 25 years at 11% ($9.80). Then multiply: $$\begin{array}{r} 80 \text{ thousand} \\ \times\ \$9.80 \text{ per thousand} \\ \hline \$784 \text{ Monthly payment} \end{array}$$
518	**15.2** Effect of Time on the Amount of Interest	To understand the importance of time in a mortgage, find the monthly mortgage payment using Table 15.1. Multiply that figure by the total number of payments. From that figure subtract the principal. The result is the total interest.	Donna and Lloyd bought a TV shop for $120,000. The interest rate is 10% and the mortgage term is thirty years. How much will the total cost of the mortgage be? How much is the interest? First, find the payment per thousand for 30 years at 10% ($8.78). The monthly payment is 120 × $8.78 = $1,053.60. Multiply by the number of payments in 30 years: $$360 \times \$1,053.60 = \$379,296.00 \text{ Total cost}$$ Subtract: $$\$379,296.40 - 120,000$$ $$= \$259,296.00 \text{ Total interest}$$
520	**15.3** Effect of Interest Rates on Payment Size	To illustrate the importance of interest rates on a mortgage, using Table 15.1, find the size of the monthly payments for a mortgage at two different interest rates. By subtracting the smaller from the larger, the cost of a higher interest rate can be determined.	Kim and Frank bought a curio store for $95,000. The interest rate is 11% and the mortgage term is 25 years. If they had bought it last month, the rate would have been 10%. How much more is their payment for having waited a month? Find the payment per thousand for 25 years at 11% ($ 9.80). Then multiply: $$\begin{array}{r} 95 \text{ thousand} \\ \times\ \$9.80 \text{ per thousand} \\ \hline \$931.00 \text{ Monthly payment} \end{array}$$ Find the payment per thousand for 25 years at 10% ($ 9.09). Multiply: $$\begin{array}{r} 95 \text{ thousand} \\ \times\ \$9.09 \text{ per thousand} \\ \hline \$ 863.55 \text{ Monthly payment} \end{array}$$ Subtract: $$\begin{array}{r} \$ 931.00 \\ -\ 863.55 \\ \hline \$ \ \$67.45 \text{ More} \end{array}$$

Page	Section Topic	Learning Concepts	Examples and Solutions
523	**15.4** Preparing a Loan Repayment (Amortization) Schedule	The importance of interest is highlighted by understanding how a mortgage is repaid. Find the principal by subtracting the down payment from the purchase price. Using Table 15.1, find the monthly payment size. The monthly interest portion is found by the following formula: $$I = PRT\left(\text{time is always } \frac{1}{12}\right)$$ The monthly principal portion is found by subtracting the interest portion from the monthly payment. The balance of the principal is found by subtracting the monthly principal portion from the previous balance. The process is repeated until the loan amortization schedule is complete.	Prepare a loan repayment schedule for the first three payments on a $70,000 loan at 9% for 30 years. Determine the size of the payment: 70 thousand $\times$ $8.05 per thousand $563.50 Monthly payment $I = PRT$ $I = \$70,000 \times 9\% \times \dfrac{1}{12} = \$525$ $563.50 - 525 = \$38.50$ $70,000 - 38.50 = \$69,961.50$ $I = \$69,961.50 \times 9\% \times \dfrac{1}{12} = \$524.71$ $563.50 - 524.71 = \$38.79$ $69,961.50 - 38.79 = \$69,922.71$ $I = \$69,922.71 \times 9\% \times \dfrac{1}{12} = \$524.42$ $563.50 - 524.42 = \$39.08$ $69,922.71 - 39.08 = \$69,883.63$

Repayment Schedule

Payment Number	Size of Payment	Interest Portion	Principal Portion	Balance of Principal
1	$563.50	$525.00	$38.50	$69,961.50
2	563.50	524.71	38.79	69,922.71
3	563.50	524.42	39.08	69,883.63

SURFING THE INTERNET

For further information on the topics covered in this chapter, check out the following sites:

http://www.1mortgageloancalculators.com/

http://www.mortgageratesusa.com/

ADDITIONAL PRACTICE PROBLEMS

Answers to odd-numbered problems are in Appendix A.

15.1

1. Bryan and Martha Clutz bought a furniture store for $130,000. The down payment was 20%, the interest rate was 13%, and the mortgage term is 15 years. How much will the monthly mortgage payment be?

   $130,000 Price $130,000
   $\times$ 20% $-$ 26,000
   $ 26,000 Down $104,000

   $\dfrac{\$104,000}{\$1,000} = 104$ 104 thousand
                $\times$ $12.65 per thousand
                $1,315.60 Payment

2. Kay and Clayton Brown bought a $200,000 bookstore by making a 20% down payment and signing a 30-year mortgage at 10%. Find the monthly payment.

   $200,000 Price $200,000
   $\times$ 20% $-$ 40,000
   $ 40,000 Down $160,000

   $\dfrac{\$160,000}{\$1,000} = 160$ 160 thousand
                $\times$ $8.78 per thousand
                $1,404.80 Payment

3. Bernie and Liz Tamayo moved in across the street from the Browns. Their house cost $210,000 with a 15% down payment. Mr. and Mrs. Tamayo found 25-year mortgage money at 8%. How much will their payment be?

$210,000 Price $210,000
×   15%   − 31,500
$ 31,500 Down $178,500

$$\frac{\$178,500}{\$1,000} = 178.5$$

178.5   thousand
× $7.72   per thousand
$1,378.02   Payment

4. Nolan and Rose Richardson bought a ranch in Arkansas. It cost $1,221,000 and they paid down 20%. The 30-year mortgage rate is 8%. Determine their monthly payment.

$1,221,000 Price $1,221,000
×   20%   − 244,200
$ 244,200 Down $ 976,800

$$\frac{\$976,800}{\$1,000} = 976.8$$

976.8   thousand
× $7.34   per thousand
$7,169.71   Payment

15.2

5. Brian and Brenda Sanchez purchased a $200,000 building in upstate New York to start a tourist business. They paid 25% down and signed a mortgage at 10% for 15 years. Find the monthly payment.

$200,000 Price $200,000
×   25%   − 50,000
$ 50,000 Down $150,000

$$\frac{\$150,000}{\$1,000} = 150$$

150   thousand
× $10.75   per thousand
$1,612.50   Payment

6. Mr. and Mrs. Tom Dooley bought an old store in a small town for $90,000 with 10% down. How much total interest will they pay each month at a 10% rate if the loan is for 30 years?

$90,000 $90,000
× 10%   − 9,000
$ 9,000 Down $81,000 Principal

$$\frac{\$81,000}{\$1,000} =$$
81 thousand   30   years
× $8.78 per thousand   × 12   months
$711.18 Monthly payment   360   Payments

711.18 $256,024.80
×   360   − 81,000.00
$256,024.80   Total $175,024.80   Interest

7. Tiffany and Dan Jackson bought a building for $90,000 at 7% for 30 years with 5% down. How much interest will they pay? How much could they save with a 25-year mortgage?

$90,000 $ 90,000 $85,500
×   5%   − 4,500
$ 4,500 Down $ 85,500 Principal

$$\frac{\$85,500}{\$1,000} =$$
85.5 thousand $ 30   years
× $6.21 per thousand   × 12 months
$530.96 Monthly payment   360 Payments

$ 530.96 $191,145.60
×   360   − 85,500.00
$191,145.60   Total $105,645.60   Interest (30-year mortgage)

85.5   thousand   25   years $ 604.49
× $7.07   per thousand   × 12   months   ×   300
$604.49   Monthly payment   300   Payments $181,347.00   Total

$181,347.00 $105,645.60
− 85,500.00   − 95,847.00
$ 95,847.00   Interest (25-year mortgage) $ 9,798.60   Saving

8. Juan and Mary Mendez bought a new house for $100,000 at 9% with a 15% down payment. How much interest will they pay if the loan is for 30 years? How much could they have saved with a 15-year mortgage?

$100,000 $100,000 $85,000
×   15%   − 15,000
$ 15,000 Down $ 85,000 Principal

$$\frac{\$85,000}{\$1,000} =$$
85 thousand   30 years
× $8.05 per thousand   × 12 months
$ 684.25 Monthly payment   360 Payments

$ 684.25 $246,330.00
×   360   − 85,000.00
$246,330.00   Total $161,330.00   Interest (30-year mortgage)

85   thousand   15   years $ 861.90
× $10.14   per thousand   × 12   months   ×   180
$ 861.90   Monthly payment   180   payments $155,142.00   Total

$155,142.00 $161,330.00
− 85,000.00   − 70,142.00
$ 70,142.00   Interest (15-year mortgage) $ 91,188.00   Savings

9. Terri and Jorge Veblen paid $125,000 for a ranch with 10% down at 12% for 25 years. How much interest will they pay? How much more would it cost if they had financed for 30 years?

$$
\begin{array}{ll}
\$\ 125,000 \\
\underline{\times\quad 10\%} \\
\$\quad 12,500 \ \text{Down}
\end{array}
\qquad
\begin{array}{ll}
\$125,000 \\
\underline{-\ 12,500} \\
\$112,500 \ \text{Principal}
\end{array}
\qquad
\frac{\$112,500}{\$1,000} =
\begin{array}{ll}
112.5 \ \text{thousand} \\
\underline{\times\ \$10.53} \ \text{per thousand} \\
\$\ 1,184.63 \ \text{Monthly payment}
\end{array}
\qquad
\begin{array}{ll}
25 \ \text{years} \\
\underline{-\ 12 \ \text{months}} \\
300 \ \text{Payments}
\end{array}
$$

$$
\begin{array}{ll}
\$\ 1,184.63 \\
\underline{\times\quad\ 300} \\
\$355,389.00 \ \text{Total}
\end{array}
\qquad
\begin{array}{ll}
\$\ 355,389.00 \\
\underline{-\ 112,500.00} \\
\$\ 242,889.00 \ \text{Interest (25-year mortgage)}
\end{array}
$$

$$
\begin{array}{ll}
112.5 \ \text{thousand} \\
\underline{\times\ \$10.29} \ \text{per thousand} \\
\$1,157.63 \ \text{Monthly payment}
\end{array}
\qquad
\begin{array}{ll}
30 \ \text{years} \\
\underline{\times\ 12 \ \text{months}} \\
360 \ \text{Payments}
\end{array}
\qquad
\begin{array}{ll}
\$\ 1,157.63 \\
\underline{\times\qquad 360} \\
\$416,746.80 \ \text{Total}
\end{array}
$$

$$
\begin{array}{ll}
\$\ 416,746.80 \\
\underline{-112,500.00} \\
\$\ 304,246.80 \ \text{Interest (30-year mortgage)}
\end{array}
\qquad
\begin{array}{ll}
\$\ 304,246.80 \\
\underline{-\ 242,889.00} \\
\$\quad 61,357.80 \ \text{Extra}
\end{array}
$$

10. Janice and Patrick Kennedy bought a big house in New Hampshire for $650,000. The down payment was 10% and the mortgage is for 30 years at 12%. How much interest will they pay?

$$
\begin{array}{ll}
\$\ 650,000 \\
\underline{\times\quad 10\%} \\
\$\quad 65,000 \ \text{Down}
\end{array}
\qquad
\begin{array}{ll}
\$650,000 \\
\underline{-\ 65,000} \\
\$585,000 \ \text{Principal}
\end{array}
\qquad
\frac{\$585,000}{\$1,000} =
\begin{array}{ll}
585 \ \text{thousand} \\
\underline{\times\ \$10.29} \ \text{per thousand} \\
\$\ 6,019.65 \ \text{Monthly payment}
\end{array}
\qquad
\begin{array}{ll}
30 \ \text{years} \\
\underline{\times\ 12 \ \text{months}} \\
360 \ \text{Payments}
\end{array}
$$

$$
\begin{array}{ll}
\$\quad 6,019.65 \\
\underline{\times\qquad 360} \\
\$2,167,074.00 \ \text{Total}
\end{array}
\qquad
\begin{array}{ll}
\$2,167,074.00 \\
\underline{-\ 585,000.00} \\
\$1,582,074.00 \ \text{Interest (30-year mortgage)}
\end{array}
$$

11. Tony and Nichele Parry bought a very old Boston house to fix up for resell. The mortgage is for $130,000 for 30 years at 9% with 5% down. If they had taken a 15-year mortgage, how much interest would they have saved?

$$
\begin{array}{ll}
\$\ 130,000 \\
\underline{\times\quad 5\%} \\
\$\quad 6,500 \ \text{Down}
\end{array}
\qquad
\begin{array}{ll}
\$130,000 \\
\underline{-\ 6,500} \\
\$123,500 \ \text{Principal}
\end{array}
\qquad
\frac{\$123,500}{\$1,000} =
\begin{array}{ll}
123.5 \ \text{thousand} \\
\underline{\times\ \$8.05} \ \text{per thousand} \\
\$\ 994.18 \ \text{Monthly payment}
\end{array}
\qquad
\begin{array}{ll}
30 \ \text{years} \\
\underline{\times\ 12 \ \text{months}} \\
360 \ \text{Payments}
\end{array}
$$

$$
\begin{array}{ll}
\$\quad 994.18 \\
\underline{\times\qquad 360} \\
\$357,904.80 \ \text{Total}
\end{array}
\qquad
\begin{array}{ll}
\$\ 357,904.80 \\
\underline{-\ 123,500.00} \\
\$\ 234,404.80 \ \text{Interest (30-year mortgage)}
\end{array}
$$

$$
\begin{array}{ll}
123.5 \ \text{thousand} \\
\underline{\times\ \$10.14} \ \text{per thousand} \\
\$1,252.29 \ \text{Monthly payment}
\end{array}
\qquad
\begin{array}{ll}
15 \ \text{years} \\
\underline{\times\ 12 \ \text{months}} \\
180 \ \text{Payments}
\end{array}
\qquad
\begin{array}{ll}
\$\quad 1,252.29 \\
\underline{\times\qquad\ 180} \\
\$\ 225,412.20 \ \text{Total}
\end{array}
$$

$$
\begin{array}{ll}
\$\ 225,412.20 \\
\underline{-123,500.00} \\
\$\ 101,912.20 \ \text{Interest (15-year mortgage)}
\end{array}
\qquad
\begin{array}{ll}
\$\ 234,404.80 \\
\underline{-\ 101,912.20} \\
\$\ 132,492.60 \ \text{Saving}
\end{array}
$$

15.3

12. Two builders sell similar new homes for $100,000 each, financed over 30 years with 15% down. The Lanier Company can acquire 7% financing. The Johnson Company houses finance at 11%. How much more per month would it cost to buy a Johnson house than a Lanier house?

$$
\begin{array}{ll}
\$100,000 \\
\underline{\times\quad 15\%} \\
\$\ 15,000 \ \text{Down}
\end{array}
\qquad
\begin{array}{ll}
\$\ 100,000 \\
\underline{-\ 15,000} \\
\$\ 85,000 \ \text{Principal}
\end{array}
\qquad
\begin{array}{ll}
85 \ \text{thousand} \\
\underline{\times\ \$6.21} \ (7\%) \\
\$527.85 \ \text{Monthly payment}
\end{array}
$$

$$
\begin{array}{ll}
85 \ \text{thousand} \\
\underline{\times\ \$9.52} \ (11\%) \\
\$809.20 \ \text{Monthly payment}
\end{array}
\qquad
\begin{array}{ll}
\$\ 809.20 \\
\underline{-\ 527.85} \\
\$\ 281.35 \ \text{More}
\end{array}
$$

13. Jim and Dolly Madison are in the market for a new home. The house on Nell Street costs $85,000 and can be financed at 10% for 30 years. The one on Cottonwood Trail costs $95,000 and will finance at 8% for 20 years. Both require 15% down. Find the difference between the monthly payments.

$$
\begin{array}{ll}
\$\ 85,000 \\
\underline{\times\quad 15\%} \\
\$\ 12,750 \ \text{Down}
\end{array}
\qquad
\begin{array}{ll}
\$\ 85,000 \\
\underline{-\ 12,750} \\
\$\ 72,250 \ \text{Principal}
\end{array}
\qquad
\begin{array}{ll}
72.25 \ \text{thousand} \\
\underline{\times\ \$8.78} \ \text{per thousand} \\
\$634.36 \ \text{Nell St.}
\end{array}
$$

$$
\begin{array}{ll}
\$\ 95,000 \\
\underline{\times\quad 15\%} \\
\$\ 14,250 \ \text{Down}
\end{array}
\qquad
\begin{array}{ll}
\$\ 95,000 \\
\underline{-\ 14,250} \\
\$\ 80,750 \ \text{Principal}
\end{array}
\qquad
\begin{array}{ll}
80.75 \ \text{thousand} \\
\underline{\times\ \$8.36} \ \text{per thousand} \\
\$675.07 \ \text{Cottonwood Tr.}
\end{array}
$$

$$
\begin{array}{ll}
\$\ 675.07 \\
\underline{-\ 634.36} \\
\$\quad 40.71 \ \text{Difference}
\end{array}
$$

14. Four years ago Maria Velasquez bought a dress shop for $75,000 with 5% down financed at 16% over 25 years. Interest rates have declined to 10% since then. How much could Maria have saved per month if she had waited five years?

$$
\begin{array}{ll}
\$75,000 \\
\underline{\times\quad 5\%} \\
\$\ 3,750 \ \text{Down}
\end{array}
\qquad
\begin{array}{ll}
\$\ 75,000 \\
\underline{-\ 3,750} \\
\$\ 71,250 \ \text{Principal}
\end{array}
\qquad
\begin{array}{ll}
71.25 \ \text{thousand} \\
\underline{\times\ \$13.59} \ (16\%) \\
\$\ 968.29 \ \text{Monthly payment}
\end{array}
$$

$$
\begin{array}{ll}
71.25 \ \text{thousand} \\
\underline{\times\ \$9.09} \ (10\%) \\
\$647.66 \ \text{Monthly payment}
\end{array}
\qquad
\begin{array}{ll}
\$\ 968.29 \\
\underline{-\ 647.66} \\
\$\ 320.63 \ \text{Savings}
\end{array}
$$

15. Ed bought a woodworking shop for $80,000 with 5% down. The mortgage is for 25 years at 11%. He could have financed it for 20 years but wanted a lower payment. How much lower is the payment for the additional five years of credit? How much more did it cost him over the life of the mortgage?

$80,000	$80,000	76.00 thousand	76.00 thousand	$ 784.32
$\times$ 5%	$-$ 4,000	$\times$ $9.80	$\times$ $10.32	$-$ 744.80
$ 4,000 Down	$76,000 Principal	$744.80 Monthly payment	$ 784.32 Monthly payment	$ 39.52 Lower

25	$ 744.80	20	$ 784.32	$ 223,440.00
$\times$ 12	$\times$ 300	$\times$ 12	$\times$ 240	$-$ 188,236.80
300 Total payments	$223,440 Total cost for 25 years	240	$188,236.80 Total cost for 20 years	$ 35,203.20 Additional

16. Mildred has been trying to sell her house for four years. The price is $100,000 with 10% down. In that time, interest rates declined from 14% to 7%. How much difference would that make in a monthly payment on a 25-year mortgage? How much less will it cost in total over the life of the mortgage?

$100,000	$100,000	90 thousand	90 thousand
$\times$ 10%	$-$ 10,000	$\times$ $12.04 (14%)	$\times$ $7.07 (7%)
$ 10,000 Down	$ 90,000 Principal	$1,083.60 Monthly payment	$636.30 Monthly payment

$1,083.60	25	$ 447.30
$-$ 636.30	$\times$ 12	$\times$ 300
$ 447.30 Less monthly	300 Months	$134,190 Less total

15.4

17. Prepare a loan repayment schedule for the first three payments on a $110,000 loan with 15% down at 12% for 30 years.

First payment:

$$I = PRT = \$93,500 \times 12\% \times \frac{1}{12} = \$935 \text{ Interest portion}$$

$110,000	$110,000	93.5 thousand	$ 962.12	$93,500.00
$\times$ 15%	$-$ 16,500	$\times$ $10.29 (12%)	$-$ 935.00	$-$ 27.12
$ 16,500 Down	$ 93,500 Principal	$ 962.12 Monthly payment	$ 27.12 Principal portion	$93,472.88 Balance of principal

Second payment:

$$\$93,472.88 \times 12\% \times \frac{1}{12} = \$934.73 \text{ Interest portion}$$

Third Payment:

$$\$93,445.49 \times 12\% \times \frac{1}{12} = \$934.46 \text{ Interest portion}$$

$ 962.12	$93,472.88	$ 962.12	$93,445.49
$-$ 934.73	$-$ 27.39	$-$ 934.46	$-$ 27.66
$ 27.39 Principal portion	$93,445.49 Balance of principal	$ 27.66 Principal portion	$93,417.83 Balance of principal

Payment Number	Size of Payment	Interest Portion	Principal Portion	Balance of Principal
1	$962.12	$935.00	$27.12	$93,472.88
2	962.12	934.73	27.39	93,445.49
3	962.12	934.46	27.66	93,417.83

18. Prepare a loan repayment schedule for the first three payments on a $100,000 loan with 5% down at 7% for 20 years.

First payment:

$$I = PRT = \$95,000 \times 7\% \times \frac{1}{12} = \$554.17 \text{ Interest portion}$$

$100,000	$100,000	95 thousand	$ 736.25	$95,000.00
$\times$ 5%	$-$ 5,000	$\times$ $7.75 (7%)	$-$ 554.17	$-$ 182.08
$ 5,000 Down	$ 95,000 Principal	$736.25 Monthly payment	$ 182.08 Principal portion	$94,817.92 Balance of principal

Second Payment:

$$\$94,817.92 \times 7\% \times \frac{1}{12} = \$553.10 \text{ Interest portion}$$

Third Payment:

$$\$94,634.77 \times 7\% \times \frac{1}{12} = \$552.04 \text{ Interest portion}$$

$ 736.25	$94,817.92	$ 736.25	$94,634.77
$-$ 553.10	$-$ 183.15	$-$ 552.04	$-$ 184.21
$ 183.15 Principal portion	$94,634.77 Balance of principal	$ 184.21 Principal portion	$94,450.56 Balance of principal

Payment Number	Size of Payment	Interest Portion	Principal Portion	Balance of Principal
1	$736.25	$554.17	$182.08	$94,817.92
2	736.25	553.10	183.15	94,634.77
3	736.25	552.04	184.21	94,450.56

19. Prepare a loan repayment schedule for the first three payments on a $90,000 loan with a 10% down payment at 16% for 25 years.

First payment:

$$I = PRT = \$81,000 \times 16\% \times \frac{1}{12} = \$1,080 \text{ Interest portion}$$

$90,000	$90,000	81 thousand	$ 1,100.79	$81,000.00
× 10%	− 9,000	× $13.59 (16%)	− 1,080.00	− 20.79
$ 9,000 Down	$81,000 Principal	$1,100.79 Monthly payment	$ 20.79 Principal portion	$80,979.21 Balance of principal

Second payment:

$$\$80,979.21 \times 16\% \times \frac{1}{12} = \$1,079.72 \text{ Interest portion}$$

$ 1,100.79	$80,979.21
− 1,079.72	− 21.07
$ 21.07 Principal portion	$80,958.14 Balance of principal

Third payment:

$$\$80,958.14 \times 16\% \times \frac{1}{12} = \$1,079.44 \text{ Interest portion}$$

$ 1,100.79	$80,958.14
− 1,079.44	− 21.35
$ 21.35 Principal portion	$80,936.79 Balance of principal

Payment Number	Size of Payment	Interest Portion	Principal Portion	Balance of Principal
1	$1,100.79	$1,080.00	$ 20.79	$80,979.21
2	1,100.79	1,079.72	21.07	80,958.14
3	1,100.79	1,079.44	21.35	80,936.79

20. Prepare a loan repayment schedule for the first three payments on a $145,000 loan at 10% with 15% down for 15 years.

First payment:

$$I = PRT = \$123,250 \times 10\% \times \frac{1}{12} = \$1,027.08 \text{ Interest portion}$$

$145,000	$145,000	123.25 thousand	$ 1,324.94	$123,250.00
× 15%	− 21,750	× $10.75 (10%)	− 1,027.08	− 297.86
$ 21,750 Down	$123,250 Principal	$1,324.94 Monthly payment	$ 297.86 Principal portion	$122,952.14 Balance of principal

Second payment:

$$\$122,952.14 \times 10\% \times \frac{1}{12} = \$1,024.60 \text{ Interest portion}$$

$ 1,324.94	$122,952.14
− 1,024.60	− 300.34
$ 300.34 Principal portion	$122,651.80 Balance of principal

Third payment:

$$\$122,651.80 \times 10\% \times \frac{1}{12} = \$1,022.10 \text{ Interest portion}$$

$ 1,324.94	$122,651.80
− 1,022.10	− 302.84
$ 302.84 Principal portion	$122,348.96 Balance of principal

Payment Number	Size of Payment	Interest Portion	Principal Portion	Balance of Principal
1	$1,324.94	$1,027.08	$297.86	$122,952.14
2	1,324.94	1,024.60	300.34	122,651.80
3	1,324.94	1,022.10	302.84	122,348.96

21. Prepare a loan repayment schedule for the first three payments on a $180,000 loan with 10% down at 9% for 30 years.

First payment:

$$I = PRT = \$162,000 \times 9\% \times \frac{1}{12} = \$1,215 \text{ Interest portion}$$

$180,000	$180,000	$ 162 thousand	$ 1,304.10	$162,000.00
× 10%	− 18,000	× 8.05 (9%)	− 1,215.00	− 89.10
$ 18,000 Down	$162,000 Principal	$1,304.10 Monthly payment	$ 89.10 Principal portion	$161,910.90 Balance of principal

Second payment:

$$\$161,910.90 \times 9\% \times \frac{1}{12} = \$1,214.33 \text{ Interest portion}$$

$ 1,304.10	$161,910.90
− 1,214.33	− 89.77
$ 89.77 Principal portion	$161,821.13 Balance of principal

Third payment:

$$\$161,821.13 \times 9\% \times \frac{1}{12} = \$1,213.66 \text{ Interest portion}$$

$ 1,304.10	$161,821.13
− 1,213.66	− 90.44
$ 90.44 Principal portion	$161,730.69 Balance of principal

Payment Number	Size of Payment	Interest Portion	Principal Portion	Balance of Principal
1	$1,304.10	$1,215.00	$89.10	$161,910.90
2	1,304.10	1,214.33	89.77	161,821.13
3	1,304.10	1,213.66	90.44	161,730.69

Answers to odd-numbered problems are given in Appendix A.

Drill Problems

Find the monthly payment using the Payment Per $1,000 Table (15.1)

	Amount	Time (years)	Rate	Monthly Payment
1.	$90,000	30	10%	$ 790.20
2.	90,000	25	10%	818.10
3.	90,000	30	11%	856.80
4.	90,000	25	11%	882.00
5.	135,000	15	16%	1,983.15
6.	135,000	15	7%	1,213.65
7.	135,000	30	16%	1,815.75
8.	135,000	30	8%	990.90
9.	75,000	15	7%	674.25
10.	75,000	30	7%	465.75
11.	250,000	15	10%	2,687.50
12.	250,000	25	10%	2,272.50
13.	250,000	30	10%	2,195.00
14.	95,000	30	10%	834.10
15.	85,000	30	15%	1,074.40
16.	85,000	30	7%	527.85
17.	65,000	15	16%	954.85
18.	100,000	15	7%	899.00
19.	350,000	30	12%	3,601.50
20.	350,000	30	11%	3,332.00

Word Problems

21. Linda and Don Miller bought a used $900,000 office building with a 10% down payment. How much total interest will they pay at a 10% rate if the loan is for 25 years?

$900,000
×   10%
$ 90,000 Down

$900,000
− 90,000
$810,000 Principal

$\dfrac{\$810,000}{\$1,000}$ =   810   thousand
× $9.09   per thousand
$7,362.90   Monthly payment

25 years
× 12 months
300 Payments

$ 7,362.90
×   300
$2,208,870 Total

$2,208,870
− 810,000
$1,398,870 Interest

22. Ron and Sarah Goldstein bought a barber shop for $90,000 at 7% for 30 years with 15% down. How much interest will they pay? How much could they save with a 25-year mortgage?

$90,000
×   15%
$13,500 Down

$ 90,000
− 13,500
$ 76,500 Principal

76.5 thousand
× $7.07 per thousand
$540.86 Monthly payment

25 years
× 12 months
300 Payments

$ 540.86
×   300
$162,258 Total

$\dfrac{\$76,500}{1,000}$ =   76.5   thousand
× $6.21   per thousand
$ 475.07   Monthly payment

30 years
× 12 months
360 Payments

$162,258
− 76,500
$ 85,758   Interest (25-year mortgage)

$ 94,525
− 85,758
$ 8,767   Savings

$ 475.07
×   360
$171,025.20   Total

$171,025.20
− 76,500.00
$ 94,525.20   Interest (30-year mortgage)

23. Linda and John Washburn bought a laundry for $210,000 at 9% with 10% down. How much interest will they pay if the loan is for 30 years? How much could they have saved with a 15-year mortgage?

$210,000
× 10%
‾‾‾‾‾‾‾‾
$ 21,000 Down

$210,000
− 21,000
‾‾‾‾‾‾‾‾
$189,000 Principal

189 thousand
× $10.14 per thousand
‾‾‾‾‾‾‾‾
$1,916.46 Monthly payment

15 years
× 12 months
‾‾‾‾‾‾‾‾
180 Payments

$ 1,916.46
× 180
‾‾‾‾‾‾‾‾
$344,962.80 Total

$189,000
‾‾‾‾‾‾ =
$1,000

189 thousand
× $8.05 per thousand
‾‾‾‾‾‾‾‾
$1,521.45 Monthly payment

30 years
× 12 months
‾‾‾‾‾‾‾‾
360 Payments

$ 344,962.80
− 189,000.00
‾‾‾‾‾‾‾‾
$ 155,962.80 Interest (15-year mortgage)

$ 358,722.00
− 155,962.80
‾‾‾‾‾‾‾‾
$ 202,759.20 Saving

$ 1,521.45
× 360
‾‾‾‾‾‾‾‾
$547,722.00 Total

$ 547,722.00
− 189,000.00
‾‾‾‾‾‾‾‾
$ 358,722.00 Interest (30-year mortgage)

24. Ed and Sherrie Morginstein bought a house for $125,000 with a 10% down payment and 12% mortgage over 25 years. How much interest will they pay? How much more would it cost if they had financed for 30 years?

$125,000
× 10%
‾‾‾‾‾‾‾‾
$ 12,500 Down

$125,000
− 12,500
‾‾‾‾‾‾‾‾
$112,500 Principal

$112,500
‾‾‾‾‾‾ = $ 112.5 thousand
$1,000   × 10.53 per thousand
‾‾‾‾‾‾‾‾
$1,184.63 Monthly payment

25 years
× 12 months
‾‾‾‾‾‾‾‾
300 Payments

$ 1,184.63
× 300
‾‾‾‾‾‾‾‾
$355,389.00 Total

$ 355,389.00
− 112,500.00
‾‾‾‾‾‾‾‾
$ 242,889.00 Interest (25-year mortgage)

$ 416,746.80
− 112,500.00
‾‾‾‾‾‾‾‾
$ 304,246.80 Interest (30-year mortgage)

$ 304,246.80
− 242,889.00
‾‾‾‾‾‾‾‾
$ 61,357.80 More

112.5 thousand
× $10.29 per thousand
‾‾‾‾‾‾‾‾
$1,157.63 Monthly payment

30 years
× 12 months
‾‾‾‾‾‾‾‾
360 payments

$ 1,157.63
× 360
‾‾‾‾‾‾‾‾
$416,746.80 Total

25. Cynthia and Travis Gifford bought a magic shop in California for $250,000 with 10% down. The mortgage is for 30 years at 11%. How much interest will they pay?

$250,000
× 10%
‾‾‾‾‾‾‾‾
$ 25,000 Down

$250,000
− 25,000
‾‾‾‾‾‾‾‾
$225,000 Principal

$225,000
‾‾‾‾‾‾ =
$1,000

225 thousand
× $9.52 per thousand
‾‾‾‾‾‾‾‾
$2,142 Monthly payment

30 years
× 12 months
‾‾‾‾‾‾‾‾
360 Payments

$ 2,142
× 360
‾‾‾‾‾‾‾‾
$771,120 Total

$ 771,120
− 225,000
‾‾‾‾‾‾‾‾
$ 546,120 Interest

26. Mr. and Mrs. Stubbs bought a very old house in a small Mississippi town. The mortgage is for $70,000 for 30 years at 11% with 5% down. If they take a 15-year mortgage, how much interest could they save?

$70,000
× 5%
‾‾‾‾‾‾‾‾
$ 3,500 Down

$70,000
− 3,500
‾‾‾‾‾‾‾‾
$66,500 Principal

$ 66,500
‾‾‾‾‾‾ =
$1,000

66.5 thousand
× $9.52 per thousand
‾‾‾‾‾‾‾‾
$633.08 Monthly payment

30 years
× 12 months
‾‾‾‾‾‾‾‾
360 Payments

$ 633.08
× 360
‾‾‾‾‾‾‾‾
$227,908.80 Total

$227,908.80
× 66,500.00
‾‾‾‾‾‾‾‾
$161,408.80 Interest (30-year mortgage)

66.5 thousand
× $11.37 per thousand
‾‾‾‾‾‾‾‾
$ 756.11 Monthly payment

15 years
× 12 months
‾‾‾‾‾‾‾‾
180 Payments

$ 756.11
× 180
‾‾‾‾‾‾‾‾
$136,099.80 Total

$136,099.80
− 66,500.00
‾‾‾‾‾‾‾‾
$ 69,599.80 Interest (15-year mortgage)

$161,408.80
− 66,599.80
‾‾‾‾‾‾‾‾
$ 91,809.00 Saving

27. Two builders offer similar new homes for $110,000 each, financed over 30 years with 15% down. The Snyder Company can acquire 15% financing. The Jacobs Company houses finance at 14%. How much more per month would it cost to buy a Snyder house than a Jacobs house?

$110,000
× 15%
‾‾‾‾‾‾‾‾
$ 16,500 Down

$110,000
− 16,500
‾‾‾‾‾‾‾‾
$ 93,500 Principal

93.5 thousand
× $12.64 per thousand
‾‾‾‾‾‾‾‾
$1,181.84 Snyder Co.

93.5 thousand
× $11.85 per thousand
‾‾‾‾‾‾‾‾
$1,107.98 Jacobs Co.

$ 1,181.84
− 1,107.98
‾‾‾‾‾‾‾‾
$ 73.86 Difference

28. Al and Sherry Stone are in the market for a new home. The house on Oxford Drive costs $395,000 and can be financed at 9% for 30 years with 20% down. The one on Rosemont Avenue costs $390,000 and will finance at 8% for 20 years with 15% down. Find the difference between the monthly payments.

$395,000
× 20%
‾‾‾‾‾‾‾‾
$ 79,000 Down

$395,000
− 79,000
‾‾‾‾‾‾‾‾
$316,000 Principal

316 thousand
× $8.05 per thousand
‾‾‾‾‾‾‾‾
$2,543.80 Oxford Dr.

$390,000
× 15%
‾‾‾‾‾‾‾‾
$ 58,500 Down

$390,000
− 58,500
‾‾‾‾‾‾‾‾
$331,500 Principal

331.5 thousand
× $ 8.36 per thousand
‾‾‾‾‾‾‾‾
$2,771.34 Rosemont Ave.

$ 2,771.34
− 2,543.80
‾‾‾‾‾‾‾‾
$ 227.54 Difference

29. Two years ago, Ms. Sandi Nguyen bought a diner for $85,000 at 10% interest with 10% down financed over 25 years. Interest rates are now 14%. How much did Ms. Nguyen save monthly by buying promptly?

$$
\begin{array}{ll}
\$\ 85{,}000 & \$\ 85{,}000 \\
\underline{\times\quad 10\%} & \underline{-\ \ 8{,}500} \\
\$\ \ 8{,}500\ \ \text{Down} & \$76{,}500\ \ \text{Principal}
\end{array}
$$

76.5 thousand
$\underline{\times\ \$9.09}$ per thousand
$\$695.39$ Monthly payment 2 years ago

76.5 thousand
$\underline{\times\ \$12.04}$ per thousand
$\$\ 921.06$ Monthly payment today

$$
\begin{array}{l}
\$\ 921.06 \\
\underline{-\ 695.39} \\
\$\ 225.67\ \ \text{Saving}
\end{array}
$$

30. Bill and Heather Malone bought a warehouse with a $110,000 mortgage for 30 years at 10% with 5% down. They could have financed it for 25 years but wanted a lower payment. How much lower is the payment for the additional five years of financing?

$$
\begin{array}{ll}
\$110{,}000 & \$110{,}000 \\
\underline{\times\quad 5\%} & \underline{-\ \ 5{,}500} \\
\$\ \ 5{,}500\ \ \text{Down} & \$104{,}500\ \ \text{Principal}
\end{array}
$$

104.5 thousand
$\underline{\times\ \$8.78}$ per thousand
$\$917.51$ Monthly payment (30-year mortgage)

104.5 thousand
$\underline{\times\ \$9.09}$ per thousand
$\$\ 949.91$ Monthly payment (25-year mortgage)

$$
\begin{array}{l}
\$\ 949.91 \\
\underline{-\ 917.51} \\
\$\ \ 32.40\ \ \text{Lower}
\end{array}
$$

31. Jennifer Jones has been trying to sell her beauty shop for four years. The price is $80,000 with 20% down. In that time, interest rates declined from 14% to 7%. How much difference does that make in a monthly payment on a 30-year mortgage?

$$
\begin{array}{ll}
\$\ 80{,}000 & \$\ 80{,}000 \\
\underline{\times\quad 20\%} & \underline{-\ 16{,}000} \\
\$\ 16{,}000\ \ \text{Down} & \$\ 64{,}000\ \ \text{Principal}
\end{array}
$$

64 thousand
$\underline{\times\ \$11.85}$ per thousand (14%)
$\$\ 758.40$ Monthly payment

64 thousand
$\underline{\times\ \$6.21}$ per thousand (7%)
$\$\ 397.44$ Monthly payment

$$
\begin{array}{l}
\$\ 758.40 \\
\underline{-\ 397.44} \\
\$\ 360.96\ \ \text{Difference}
\end{array}
$$

32. Al and Anne Gore are in the market for a new home. The house on University Drive costs $210,000 and can be financed at 9% for 30 years. The one on Wedgwood Drive costs $200,000 and will finance at 8% for 20 years. Both require 10% down. Find the difference between the monthly payments.

$$
\begin{array}{ll}
\$210{,}000 & \$210{,}000 \\
\underline{\times\quad 10\%} & \underline{-\ 21{,}000} \\
\$\ 21{,}000\ \ \text{Down} & \$189{,}000\ \ \text{Principal}
\end{array}
$$

189 thousand
$\underline{\times\ \$8.05}$ per thousand
$\$1{,}521.45$ University Dr.

$$
\begin{array}{ll}
\$200{,}000 & \$200{,}000 \\
\underline{\times\quad 10\%} & \underline{-\ 20{,}000} \\
\$\ 20{,}000\ \ \text{Down} & \$180{,}000\ \ \text{Principal}
\end{array}
$$

180 thousand
$\underline{\times\ \$8.36}$ per thousand
$\$1{,}504.80$ Wedgwood Dr.

$$
\begin{array}{l}
\$\ 1{,}521.45 \\
\underline{-\ 1{,}504.80} \\
\$\ \ \ \ \ 16.65\ \ \text{Difference}
\end{array}
$$

33. Prepare a loan repayment schedule for the first three payments on a $200,000 loan at 12% for 30 years with 5% down.

First payment:

$$
\begin{array}{ll}
\$200{,}000 & \$200{,}000 \\
\underline{\times\quad 5\%} & \underline{-\ 10{,}000} \\
\$\ 10{,}000\ \ \text{Down} & \$190{,}000\ \ \text{Principal}
\end{array}
$$

190 thousand
$\underline{\times\ \$10.29}$ (12%)
$\$\ 1{,}955.10$ Monthly payment

$$I = PRT = \$190{,}000 \times 12\% \times \frac{1}{12} = \$1{,}900 \text{ Interest portion}$$

$$
\begin{array}{l}
\$\ 1{,}955.10 \\
\underline{-\ 1{,}900.00} \\
\$\ \ \ \ \ 55.10\ \ \text{Principal portion}
\end{array}
$$

$$
\begin{array}{l}
\$190{,}000.00 \\
\underline{-\ \ \ \ \ \ 55.10} \\
\$189{,}944.90\ \ \text{Balance of principal}
\end{array}
$$

Second payment:

$$\$189{,}944.90 \times 12\% \times \frac{1}{12} = \$1{,}899.45 \text{ Interest portion}$$

$$
\begin{array}{l}
\$\ 1{,}955.10 \\
\underline{-\ 1{,}899.45} \\
\$\ \ \ \ \ 55.65\ \ \text{Principal portion}
\end{array}
$$

$$
\begin{array}{l}
\$189{,}944.90 \\
\underline{-\ \ \ \ \ \ 55.65} \\
\$189{,}889.25\ \ \text{Balance of principal}
\end{array}
$$

Third payment:

$$\$189{,}889.25 \times 12\% \times \frac{1}{12} = \$1{,}898.89 \text{ Interest portion}$$

$$
\begin{array}{l}
\$\ 1{,}955.10 \\
\underline{-\ 1{,}898.89} \\
\$\ \ \ \ \ 56.21\ \ \text{Principal portion}
\end{array}
$$

$$
\begin{array}{l}
\$189{,}889.25 \\
\underline{-\ \ \ \ \ \ 56.21} \\
\$189{,}833.04\ \ \text{Balance of principal}
\end{array}
$$

Payment Number	Size of Payment	Interest Portion	Principal Portion	Balance of Principal
1	$1,955.10	$1,900.00	$55.10	$189,944.90
2	1,955.10	1,899.45	55.65	189,889.25
3	1,955.10	1,898.89	56.21	189,833.04

34. Prepare a loan repayment schedule for the first three payments on a $200,000 loan at 10% for 30 years with 10% down.

First payment:

$$I = PRT = \$180,000 \times 10\% \times \frac{1}{12} = \$1,500 \text{ Interest portion}$$

$$
\begin{array}{ll}
\$200,000 & \$200,000 \\
\times\ \underline{\quad 10\%} & -\ \underline{\quad 20,000} \\
\$\ 20,000\ \text{Down} & \$180,000\ \text{Principal}
\end{array}
\qquad
\begin{array}{l}
180\ \text{thousand} \\
\times\ \underline{\$8.78}\ \ 10\% \\
\$1,580.40\ \text{Monthly payment}
\end{array}
$$

$$
\begin{array}{ll}
\$\ 1,580.40 & \$180,000.00 \\
-\ \underline{1,500.00} & -\ \underline{\quad\quad 80.40} \\
\$\quad\ 80.40\ \text{Principal portion} & \$179,919.60\ \text{Balance of principal}
\end{array}
$$

Second payment:

$$\$179,919.60 \times 10\% \times \frac{1}{12} = \$1,499.33 \text{ Interest portion}$$

$$
\begin{array}{ll}
\$\ 1,580.40 & \$179,919.60 \\
-\ \underline{1,499.33} & -\ \underline{\quad\quad 81.07} \\
\$\quad\ 81.07\ \text{Principal portion} & \$179,838.53\ \text{Balance of principal}
\end{array}
$$

Third payment:

$$\$179,838.53 \times 10\% \times \frac{1}{12} = \$1,498.65 \text{ Interest portion}$$

$$
\begin{array}{ll}
\$\ 1,580.40 & \$179,838.53 \\
-\ \underline{1,498.65} & -\ \underline{\quad\quad 81.75} \\
\$\quad\ 81.75\ \text{Principal portion} & \$179,756.78\ \text{Balance of principal}
\end{array}
$$

Payment Number	Size of Payment	Interest Portion	Principal Portion	Balance of Principal
1	$1,580.40	$1,500.00	$80.40	$179.919.60
2	1,580.40	1,499.33	81.07	179,838.53
3	1,580.40	1,498.65	81.75	179,756.78

35. Prepare a loan repayment schedule for the first three payments on a $200,000 loan at 7% for 30 years with 15% down.

First payment:

$$I = PRT = \$170,000 \times 7\% \times \frac{1}{12} = \$991.67 \text{ Interest portion}$$

$$
\begin{array}{ll}
\$200,000 & \$200,000 \\
\times\ \underline{\quad 15\%} & -\ \underline{\quad 30,000} \\
\$\ 30,000\ \text{Down} & \$170,000\ \text{Principal}
\end{array}
\qquad
\begin{array}{l}
170\ \text{thousand} \\
\times\ \underline{\$6.21}\ \ (7\%) \\
\$\ 1,055.70\ \text{Monthly payment}
\end{array}
$$

$$
\begin{array}{ll}
\$1,055.70 & \$170,000.00 \\
-\ \underline{\quad 991.67} & -\ \underline{\quad\quad 64.03} \\
\$\quad\ 64.03\ \text{Principal portion} & \$169,935.97\ \text{Balance of principal}
\end{array}
$$

Second Payment:

$$\$169,935.97 \times 7\% \times \frac{1}{12} = \$991.29 \text{ Interest portion}$$

$$
\begin{array}{ll}
\$1,055.70 & \$169,935.97 \\
-\ \underline{\quad 991.29} & -\ \underline{\quad\quad 64.41} \\
\$\quad\ 64.41\ \text{Principal portion} & \$169,871.56\ \text{Balance of principal}
\end{array}
$$

Third Payment:

$$\$169,871.56 \times 7\% \times \frac{1}{12} = \$990.92 \text{ Interest portion}$$

$$
\begin{array}{ll}
\$1,055.70 & \$169,871.56 \\
-\ \underline{\quad 990.92} & -\ \underline{\quad\quad 64.78} \\
\$\quad\ 64.78\ \text{Principal portion} & \$169,806.78\ \text{Balance of principal}
\end{array}
$$

Payment Number	Size of Payment	Interest Portion	Principal Portion	Balance of Principal
1	$1,055.70	$991.67	$64.03	$169,935.97
2	1,055.70	991.29	64.41	169,871.56
3	1,055.70	990.92	64.78	169,806.78

36. Prepare a loan repayment schedule for the first three payments on a $100,000 loan at 15% for 30 years with 10% down.

First payment:

$$I = PRT = \$90,000 \times 15\% \times \frac{1}{12} = \$1,125 \text{ Interest portion}$$

$$
\begin{array}{ll}
\$100,000 & \$100,000 \\
\times\ \underline{\quad 10\%} & -\ \underline{\quad 10,000} \\
\$\ 10,000\ \text{Down} & \$\ 90,000\ \text{Principal}
\end{array}
\qquad
\begin{array}{l}
90\ \text{thousand} \\
\times\ \underline{\$12.64}\ \ (15\%) \\
\$1,137.60\ \text{Monthly payment}
\end{array}
$$

$$
\begin{array}{ll}
\$\ 1,137.60 & \$90,000.00 \\
-\ \underline{1,125.00} & -\ \underline{\quad\ 12.60} \\
\$\quad\ 12.60\ \text{Principal portion} & \$89,987.40\ \text{Balance of principal}
\end{array}
$$

Second payment:

$$\$89,987.40 \times 15\% \times \frac{1}{12} = \$1,124.84 \text{ Interest portion}$$

$$
\begin{array}{ll}
\$\ 1,137.60 & \$89,987.40 \\
-\ \underline{1,124.84} & -\ \underline{\quad\ 12.76} \\
\$\quad\ 12.76\ \text{Principal portion} & \$89,974.64\ \text{Balance of principal}
\end{array}
$$

Third payment:

$$\$89,974.64 \times 15\% \times \frac{1}{12} = \$1,124.68 \text{ Interest portion}$$

$$
\begin{array}{ll}
\$\ 1,137.60 & \$89,974.64 \\
-\ \underline{1,124.68} & -\ \underline{\quad\ 12.92} \\
\$\quad\ 12.92\ \text{Principal portion} & \$89,961.72\ \text{Balance of principal}
\end{array}
$$

Payment Number	Size of Payment	Interest Portion	Principal Portion	Balance of Principal
1	$1,137.60	$1,125.00	$12.60	$89,987.40
2	1,137.60	1,124.84	12.76	89,974.64
3	1,137.60	1,124.68	12.92	89,961.72

37. Prepare a loan repayment schedule for the first three payments on an $80,000 loan at 14% for 25 years with 25% down.

First payment:

$$I = PRT = \$60,000 \times 14\% \times \frac{1}{12} = \$700 \text{ Interest portion}$$

$ 80,000	$ 80,000	60 thousand
× 25%	− 20,000	× $12.04 (14%)
$ 20,000 Down	$ 60,000 Principal	$ 722.40 Monthly payment

$ 722.40	$60,000.00
− 700.00	− 22.40
$ 22.40 Principal portion	$59,977.60 Balance of principal

Second payment:

$$\$59,977.60 \times 14\% \times \frac{1}{12} = \$699.74 \text{ Interest portion}$$

$ 722.40	$59,977.60
− 699.74	− 22.66
$ 22.66 Principal portion	$59,954.94 Balance of principal

Third payment:

$$\$59,954.94 \times 14\% \times \frac{1}{12} = \$699.47 \text{ Interest portion}$$

$ 722.40	$59,954.94
− 699.47	− 22.93
$ 22.93 Principal portion	$59,932.01 Balance of principal

Payment Number	Size of Payment	Interest Portion	Principal Portion	Balance of Principal
1	$722.40	$700.00	$22.40	$59,977.60
2	722.40	699.74	22.66	59,954.94
3	722.40	699.47	22.93	59,932.01

38. Prepare a loan repayment schedule for the first three payments on an $800,000 loan at 16% for 20 years with 20% down.

First payment:

$$I = PRT = \$640,000 \times 16\% \times \frac{1}{12} = \$8,533.33 \text{ Interest portion}$$

$800,000	$ 800,000	640 thousand
× 20%	− 160,000	× $13.91 (16%)
$160,000 Down	$ 640,000 Principal	$ 8,902.40 Monthly payment

$ 8,902.40	$640,000.00
− 8,533.33	− 369.07
$ 369.07 Principal portion	$639,630.93 Balance of principal

Second payment:

$$\$639,630.93 \times 16\% \times \frac{1}{12} = \$8,528.41 \text{ Interest portion}$$

$ 8,902.40	$639,630.93
− 8,528.41	− 373.99
$ 373.99 Principal portion	$639,256.94 Balance of principal

Third payment:

$$\$639,256.94 \times 16\% \times \frac{1}{12} = \$8,523.43 \text{ Interest portion}$$

$ 8,902.40	$639,256.94
− 8,523.43	− 378.97
$ 378.97 Principal portion	$638,877.97 Balance of principal

Payment Number	Size of Payment	Interest Portion	Principal Portion	Balance of Principal
1	$8,902.40	$8,533.33	$369.07	$639,630.93
2	8,902.40	8,528.41	373.99	639,256.94
3	8,902.40	8,523.43	378.97	638,877.97

39. Mollie and Bill Ivins bought a building for $240,000 with 10% down. The interest rate is 9% and the mortgage term is for 30 years. If they had bought it last year, the rate would have been 12%. How much less is their monthly payment because they waited a year? How much will they save over 30 years? Prepare a loan repayment schedule for the first three payments.

$240,000
× 10%
$ 24,000 Down

$240,000
− 24,000
$216,000 Principal

$$\frac{\$216,000}{\$1,000} = 216$$

216 thousand
× $8.05 per thousand (9%)
$1,738.80 Monthly Payment

216 thousand
× $10.29 per thousand (12%)
$2,222.64 Monthly payment

$ 2,222.64
− 1,738.80
$ 483.84 Less per month

30
× 12
360

$ 483.84
× 360
$174,182.40 Less in total

First payment:

$$I = PRT = \$216,000 \times 9\% \times \frac{1}{12} = \$1,620 \text{ Interest portion}$$

$ 1,738.80
− 1,620.00
$ 118.80 Principal portion

$216,000.00
− 118.80
$215,881.20 Balance of principal

Third payment:

$$\$215,951.40 \times 9\% \times \frac{1}{12} = \$1,618.21 \text{ Interest portion}$$

Second payment:

$$\$215,881.20 \times 9\% \times \frac{1}{12} = \$1,619.11 \text{ Interest portion}$$

$1,738.80
− 1,619.11
$ 119.69 Principal portion

$215,881.20
− 119.69
$215,761.51 Balance of principal

$1,738.80
− 1,618.21
$ 120.59 Principal portion

$215,761.51
− 120.59
$215,640.92 Balance of principal

Payment Number	Size of Payment	Interest Portion	Principal Portion	Balance of Principal
1	$1,738.80	$1,620.00	$118.80	$215,881.20
2	1,738.80	1,619.11	119.69	215,761.51
3	1,738.80	1,618.21	120.59	215,640.92

CRITICAL THINKING GROUP PROJECT

Harry Zumwaldt and his sister Harriet are looking for office space. One building that seems appropriate has a selling price of $275,000. The owner wants a 7.5% down payment. Two mortgage companies are willing to finance the balance. Jarvis Mortgages will finance for 30 years at 9%. Mellon Mortgage Company will finance the balance for a maximum of 20 years at 9%. Harry and Harriet know that the monthly payment will also include a property tax escrow of $8.80 per $1,000 of the appraised valuation. They estimate that the county will appraise the building at $250,000. Another escrow will have to be set up to pay the insurance premium on the building and its contents. The building would be insured for 80% of the selling price, and the contents for $70,000. Their agent has given them a preliminary figure of $.50 per $100 for the structure, and $.35 per $100 for its contents.

1. Calculate the monthly payment on principal and interest if the building is financed through Jarvis Mortgages.
$2,047.72

2. Calculate the monthly payment on principal and interest if the building is financed through the Mellon Mortgage Company.
$2,289.38

3. What would be the monthly amount required for the tax escrow?
$183.33

4. What would be the monthly amount required for the insurance escrow?
$91.67 for the building; $20.42 for its contents; a total of $112.09

5. Determine the total monthly mortgage payment if the financing is done through Jarvis Mortgages.
$2,343.14

6. Determine the total monthly mortgage payment if the financing is done through the Mellon Mortgage Company.
$2,584.80

7. Calculate the total amount of interest that would be paid if the financing is through Jarvis Mortgages.
$482,804.20

8. Calculate the total amount of interest that would be paid if the financing is through the Mellon Mortgage Company.
$295,076.20

9. How much in interest payments would be saved by financing through the Mellon Mortgage Company?
$187,728

SELF-TESTING
EXERCISES

Answers to all exercises are given in Appendix A

1. Why would a person prefer to have a fixed-rate mortgage? **W**

The interest part of the monthly payment cannot be raised on a fixed-rate mortgage if market interest rates rise.

2. Who can get a VA loan? **W**

Only persons who are quaified veterans are eligible for VA loans.

3. Mr. and Mrs. John Cantalope bought an auto repair shop for $89,000. The interest rate is 10% and the mortgage term is for 30 years with 10% down. Using Table 15.1, determine how much the monthly mortgage payment will be.

```
  $89,000              $89,000
×    10%             −   8,900
$  8,900  Down       $80,100  Principal
```

```
$80,100         80.1   thousand
───────  =    × $8.78  per thousand
$1,000        $703.28  Monthly payment
```

4. Stacy and Mildred Turnipseed bought a service station for $100,000. The interest rate is 12% and the mortgage term is for 30 years. They were required to pay down 10%. Using Table 15.1, determine the size of the monthly mortgage payment.

```
 $100,000             $100,000
×     10%            −  10,000
$  10,000  Down      $ 90,000  Principal
```

```
$90,000          90   thousand
───────  =    × $10.29  per thousand
$1,000         $926.10  Monthly payment
```

5. Marcus and Paula Smith bought an electronics store for $230,000. The interest rate is 9% and the mortgage term is for 30 years with 5% down. Find the monthly mortgage payment using Table 15.1.

```
 $230,000             $230,000
×      5%            −  11,500
$  11,500  Down      $218,500  Principal
```

```
$218,500          218.5   thousand
────────  =     × $8.05   per thousand
$1,000          $1,758.93  Monthly payment
```

6. Mr. and Mrs. Clodfelter bought a new house for $90,000 with 15% down. The interest rate is 14% and the mortgage term is for 30 years. Find the monthly mortgage payment using Table 15.1.

```
 $ 90,000             $ 90,000
×     15%            −  13,500
$ 13,500  Down       $ 76,500  Principal
```

```
$76,500          76.5   thousand
───────  =     × $11.85  per thousand
$1,000          $ 906.53  Monthly payment
```

7. Joe and Marla Louis bought an old store for $100,000 with 10% down. The interest rate is 10% and the mortgage term is for 25 years. How much will be the total interest cost of the mortgage?

```
 $100,000             $100,000
×     10%            −  10,000
$  10,000  Down      $ 90,000  Principal
```

```
$90,000         90   thousand        25  years
───────  =    × $9.09  per thousand  × 12  months
$1,000        $818.10  Monthly payment  300  Payments
```

```
$     818.10          $245,430.00
×        300         −  90,000.00
$245,430.00  Total   $155,430.00  Interest
```

8. Ray and Tipper Bradly bought a small bakery for $120,000 with 10% down. The interest rate is 12% and the mortgage term is for 30 years. How much will be the total interest cost of the mortgage?

```
 $120,000             $120,000
×     10%            −  12,000
$  12,000  Down      $108,000  Principal
```

```
$108,000          108   thousand        30  years
────────  =     × $10.29  per thousand  × 12  months
$1,000          $1,111.32  Monthly payment  360  Payments
```

```
$   1,111.32          $ 400,075.20
×        360         −  108,000.00
$400,075.20  Total   $ 292,075.20  Interest
```

9. Dick and Marylou Hancock bought a donut shop for $220,000 with 5% down. The interest rate is 12% and the mortgage term is for 30 years. If they had bought it last month, the rate would have been 11%. How much more is their monthly payment for having waited a month?

$220,000		$220,000	
× 5%		− 11,000	
$ 11,000	Down	$209,000	Principal

$$\frac{\$209,000}{\$1,000} = \begin{array}{l} 209 \text{ thousand} \\ \times \ \$10.29 \text{ per thousand (12\%)} \\ \hline \$2,150.61 \text{ Monthly payment} \end{array}$$

209 thousand	$ 2,150.61
× $9.52 per thousand (11%)	− 1,989.68
$1,989.68 Monthly payment	$ 160.93 More

10. Mike and Jean Moncrief bought a new house for $87,500 with 7.5% down. The interest rate is 16% and the mortgage term is for 20 years. If they had bought it last year, the rate would have been 13%. How much more is their monthly payment for having waited a year?

$87,500.00		$87,500.00	
× 7.5%		− 6,562.50	
$ 6,562.50	Down	$80,937.50	Principal

$$\frac{\$80,937.50}{\$1,000} = \begin{array}{l} 80.9375 \text{ thousand} \\ \times \ \$13.91 \text{ per thousand (16\%)} \\ \hline \$1,125.84 \text{ Monthly payment} \end{array}$$

80.9375 thousand	$1,125.84
× $11.72 per thousand (13%)	− 948.59
$ 948.59 Monthly payment	$ 177.25 More

11. Prepare a loan repayment schedule for the first three payments on a $60,000 house with a 5% down payment at 12% for 30 years.

First Payment:

$$I = PRT = \$57,000 \times 12\% \times \frac{1}{12} = \$570 \text{ Interest portion}$$

$60,000		$60,000		57 thousand	
× 5%		− 3,000		× $10.29 (12%)	
$ 3,000	Down	$57,000	Principal	$ 586.53	Monthly payment

$ 586.53		$ 57,000.00	
− 570.00		− 16.53	
$ 16.53	Principal portion	$ 56,983.47	Balance of principal

Second payment:

$$\$56,983.47 \times 12\% \times \frac{1}{12} = \$569.84 \text{ Interest portion}$$

$ 586.53		$56,983.47	
− 569.83		− 16.70	
$ 16.70	Principal portion	$56,966.77	Balance of principal

Third payment:

$$\$56,966.77 \times 12\% \times \frac{1}{12} = \$569.67 \text{ Interest portion}$$

$ 586.53		$56,966.77	
− 569.67		− 16.86	
$ 16.86	Principal portion	$56,949.91	Balance of principal

Payment Number	Size of Payment	Interest Portion	Principal Portion	Balance of Principal
1	$586.53	$570.00	$16.53	$56,983.47
2	586.53	569.83	16.70	56,966.77
3	586.53	569.67	16.86	56,949.91

12. Prepare a loan repayment schedule for the first three payments on a $100,000 loan at 9% for 30 years. The down payment is 10%.

First payment:

$$I = PRT = \$90,000 \times 9\% \times \frac{1}{12} = \$675 \text{ Interest portion}$$

$100,000		$100,000		90 thousand	
× 10%		− 10,000		× $8.05 (9%)	
$ 10,000	Down	$ 90,000	Principal	$724.50	Monthly payment

$ 724.50		$90,000.00	
− 675.00		− 49.50	
$ 49.50	Principal portion	$89,950.50	Balance of principal

Second Payment:

$$\$89,950.50 \times 9\% \times \frac{1}{12} = \$674.63 \text{ Interest portion}$$

$ 724.50		$89,950.50	
− 674.63		− 49.87	
$ 49.87	Principal portion	$89,900.63	Balance of principal

Third payment:

$$\$89,900.63 \times 9\% \times \frac{1}{12} = \$674.25 \text{ Interest portion}$$

$ 724.50		$89,900.63	
− 674.25		− 50.25	
$ 50.25	Principal portion	$89,850.38	Balance of principal

Payment Number	Size of Payment	Interest Portion	Principal Portion	Balance of Principal
1	$724.50	$675.00	$49.50	$89,950.50
2	724.50	674.63	49.87	89,900.63
3	724.50	674.25	50.25	89,850.38

The Springfield Department Store mortgaged its last store building for $2,000,000 at 9.25% for 20 years. The loan amortization schedule designed by Springfield is shown as Ch15App1 on your computer spreadsheet application disk. In part, it appears as shown here:

Springfield Department Store

2617 Main Street
Box 219
Springfield, Maryland 58109
Telephone: 301-555-2158   FAX: 301-555-3498

LOAN REPAYMENT (AMORTIZATION) SCHEDULE FOR 1ST 20 YEARS OF LOAN

Payment Number	Size of Payment	Interest Portion	Principal Portion	Balance of Principal
0				$0.00
1	#DIV/0!	#NUM!	#NUM!	#NUM!
2	#DIV/0!	#NUM!	#NUM!	#NUM!
3	#DIV/0!	#NUM!	#NUM!	#NUM!
4	#DIV/0!	#NUM!	#NUM!	#NUM!

MORTGAGE INFORMATION

Annual Int. Rate	Amount to Be Financed	For No. of Years

Summary for length of Loan

Interest Portion	Principal Portion	Total Mfg. Cost
#DIV/0!	$0.00	#DIV/0!

Enter the following information:

Annual Int. Rate: Cell F8, 9.25%   Amount to Be Financed: Cell G8, $2,000,000   For No. of Years: Cell H8, 20

Answer the following questions after you have completed the worksheet. It might be interesting for you to vary the annual interest rate, amount to be financed, and/or number of years. For example, you might change the number of years to 30 and observe the differences in the size of payment, total interest, and total mortgage costs.

1. What is the size of payment?

2. What is the interest portion after the first payment?

3. What is the principal portion after the first payment?

4. What is the interest portion after the 240th payment?

5. What is the principal portion after the 240th payment?

6. What is the summary amount of interest?

7. What is the summary amount of principal?

8. What is the total cost of the mortgage (principal + interest)?

Note: The spreadsheet program is set up for 20 years. If you put more than 20 years in the block for number of years, the calculations will be seen for only the first 240 payments (20 × 12 = 240). However, the summary figures will be for the entire number of years entered.

If the number of years entered is less than 20, the size of the payment will be shown for the entire 240 periods even though fewer would actually be made. However, none of the other calculations will be carried past the proper number of periods. The summary information will be for the correct number of payment periods entered.

GROUP REPORT

The store manager wants your group's recommendation on the following mortgage options:

1. $2,500,000 mortgage at 8.25% for 30 years
2. $2,750,000 mortgage at 8% for 25 years
3. $2,225,000 mortgage at 8.5% for 30 years
4. $3,000,000 mortgage at 7.25% for 20 years

In the report your group prepares, point out all of the advantages and disadvantages of each alternative given. Be specific about what your group is recommending and why.

16

ACCOUNTING APPLICATIONS
READING, ANALYZING, AND INTERPRETING ACCOUNTING FINANCIAL STATEMENTS

IT'S ONLY MONEY

"Parting," Shakespeare wrote, "is such sweet sorrow." Maybe just sweet.

General Motors finally said goodbye to Electronic Data Systems. After trying for at least a year to find a way to profitably separate from its subsidiary, GM decided on a stock swap that left EDS in the hands of its shareholders.

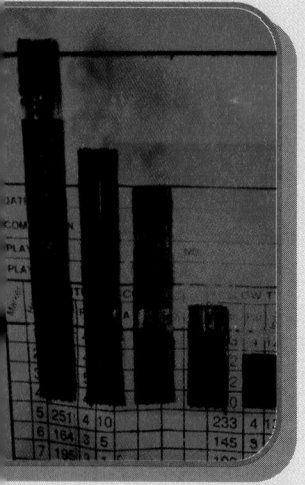

GM bought the computer software company from Ross Perot in 1984. As part of that deal, Mr. Perot joined GM's board of directors, where he criticized the company's management so much they got angry enough to buy out his interest in 1986. Mr. Perot claimed EDS's worth was $2.5 billion and demanded $742.8 million for his part. Many observers of the time believed Mr. Perot had been intentionally obnoxious to agitate GM management into buying him out for more than EDS was really worth.

GM, being the world's biggest carmaker, never showed much interest in the computer business and, in 1995, contributed its EDS shares to the company's underfunded pension plan. The pension plan is certainly not underfunded now. When EDS was turned over, its estimated worth was more than $21 billion—an 840% increase in nine years.

An important question is, Whose accountants read, analyzed, and interpreted the accounting financial statements right in 1986? A better question is, Who came out ahead in the deal when Mr. Perot left GM and then when the stock was swapped in 1995? Maybe everybody won. Mr. Perot was set free to be a gadfly who goads politicians instead of businessmen, the GM boardroom became a much more sanguine place, and GM pensioners are more secure and can relax.

When you have as much as Ross Perot, it's only money anyway.

Chapter Glossary

Balance sheet. A document that indicates the worth or the financial condition of a business on a given date.

Accounting equation. The basic equation is Assets = liabilities + owner's equity.

Current assets. Cash and other items that are expected to be converted into cash or used up in the short term, usually in one year or less.

Plant and equipment assets. Building, property, and equipment assets acquired to use in production rather than for resale that are expected to last longer than one year.

Intangible assets. Assets without physical substance that have value as a result of the rights and benefits that the owner derives from them.

Current liabilities. Debts or obligations due within one year.

Long-term liabilities. Debts or obligations not due for a relatively long period of time, usually more than one year.

Common stock. Representations of ownership in a corporation. Owners of common stock are called stockholders.

Preferred stock. A class of stock that has preferential rights to dividends over common stock. Holders are owners of the business just as are common stockholders but usually do not have voting rights in the affairs of the enterprise.

Retained earnings. The amount of prior earnings that have been kept or retained in a corporation instead of being distributed to the stockholders.

Vertical analysis. Dividing each balance sheet item by total assets, or dividing each income statement item by net sales.

Horizontal analysis. Finding the amount of change between two or more years' financial statement entries and dividing by the earlier year's amount to find the percent of change.

Income statement. A summary of all actual or potential inflows of revenue and outflows of costs and expenses during an accounting period.

Basic income statement. The basic formula is Net income (net loss) = revenues − expenses.

Revenues. An inflow of income earned by a business.

Gross sales. Total earned sales, cash or credit.

Sales returns. Merchandise sold to, but returned by, customers.

Sales allowances. Reductions in price granted to customers for various reasons such as damaged or defective merchandise.

Net sales. The value of sales revenue after the value of all returned goods and discounts has been deducted.

Beginning inventory. The amount of merchandise a firm has available to sell to customers at the beginning of an accounting period.

Purchases. The cost of merchandise bought to be resold to customers during an accounting period.

Goods available for sale. The total amount paid for the goods a business had available to sell to customers during an accounting period.

Ending inventory. The amount of merchandise a firm has available to sell to customers at the end of an accounting period.

Cost of goods sold. The amount paid for all the merchandise a firm sold during an accounting period.

Gross profit. The return to a firm for its production; determined by finding the difference between net sales and the cost of goods sold.

Operating expenses. The expenses incurred in running a business or in attempting to sell merchandise.

Net income before taxes. The difference between the gross profit and the operating expenses before paying taxes.

Taxes. The payments made to governments by corporations because they are "legal persons." Proprietorships and partnerships pay taxes as personal income tax on profits.

Net income after taxes. The amount remaining after all expenses have been deducted from the total revenue. If the total expenses are more than the total revenue, a *net loss* will result.

Ratio. The relationship of one number to another.

Current ratio. The measure of a firm's ability to pay its current debts as they mature.

Acid-test ratio. The measure of a firm's ability to meet its current debt on short notice.

Earnings per share. The measure of the amount of profit earned for each share of common stock outstanding.

Return on sales. The measure of a company's profitability.

Return on equity. The measure of returns being received by owners on their investment.

Inventory turnover ratio. The measure of the number of times merchandise moves through a business in an accounting cycle.

Debt to owner's equity ratio. The measure of the extent to which the operations of a firm are financed by borrowed funds.

Debt to total assets ratio. The measure of the extent to which the assets are financed by borrowed funds.

B usiness students often have a goal of someday starting firms of their own. Entrepreneurs take risks, and many are not successful. One of the principal reasons for small business failure is inadequate understanding of accounting principles.

All business firms must keep good records. To be successful, those firms must analyze and interpret their records. Owners and managers can then take action to correct any deficiencies before problems become too serious. Moreover, many other parties are interested in the financial condition of a business. Potential investors, creditors, governmental agencies, and employees are just a few.

The two financial statements prepared and analyzed by virtually all business firms are the **balance sheet** and the **income statement**. The balance sheet is considered first.

LEARNING UNIT 1
BALANCE SHEET

EXCEL Spreadsheet Application Spreadsheet Application 1 at the end of this chapter was designed by Springfield to perform vertical and horizontal analyses on its comparative balance sheets.

A balance sheet indicates the worth or the financial condition of a business enterprise on a given date. It is a formal presentation of the basic accounting equation and answers questions such as the following:

How much does this business own? (Assets)

How much does this business owe? (Liabilities)

How much is this business worth? (Owner's equity)

The basic **accounting equation** is:

$$\text{Assets} = \text{liabilities} + \text{owner's equity.}$$

Since things of value held by the business (assets) must be owned by either the creditors (liabilities) or the owners (owner's equity), the two sides of the equation must always be equal.

A small business would have a relatively simple balance sheet such as that in Figure 16.1. To make it easier to follow the discussion of the items in the balance sheet, each major segment is lettered. Instead of trying to memorize the items, try to identify the similarities of each category. As work with balance sheets progresses, the elements are more easily seen within their correct categories.

Figure 16.1.
BALANCE SHEET

KNIVES AND THINGS
BALANCE SHEET
DECEMBER 31, 20XX

ASSETS		
a. Current assets		
Cash	$ 6,500	
Accounts receivable	33,850	
Merchandise inventory	9,900	
Prepaid expenses	7,500	
Total current assets		$ 57,750
b. Plant and Equipment		
Furniture	60,000	
Equipment	30,250	
Total plant and equipment assets		$ 90,250
c. Intangible assets		
Goodwill	$ 1,000	
Trademark	1,000	
Total intangible assets		$ 2,000
Total assets		$150,000
LIABILITIES		
d. Current liabilities		
Accounts payable	$ 8,500	
Salaries payable	19,000	
Total current liabilities		$ 27,500
e. Long-term liabilities		
Mortgages payable	$40,300	
Long-term notes payable	12,200	
Total long-term liabilities		$ 52,500
Total liabilities		$ 80,000
OWNER'S EQUITY		
f. Common stock (30,000 shares		
outstanding at $1 par)	$30,000	
g. Retained earnings	40,000	
Total owner's equity		$ 70,000
Total liabilities and owner's equity		$150,000

Current Assets

Current assets are cash and other items expected to be converted into cash or used up in the short term, usually one year or less. Some examples follow:

Cash	To Be Converted Into Cash	To Be Used Up
Checking accounts	Accounts receivable	Prepaid rent
Currency	Notes receivable	Prepaid insurance
	Merchandise Inventory	

Plant and Equipment Assets

Plant and equipment assets are assets used either directly or indirectly by a business to produce other goods and services to sell. Their purchase is called an *investment*; they are not for resale themselves, and they are expected to last longer than one year. Because they physically wear out or become technically obsolete, most plant and equipment assets decrease in value over time. Allocation of the decrease in value is called depreciation (see Chapter 17).

Depreciation is accumulated over the years and is deducted as a separate amount from the assets that are subject to depreciation. Land does not ordinarily lose value over time and is not depreciable. Examples of plant and equipment assets are as follows:

Land	Office equipment
Machinery	Furniture
Vehicles	Fixtures
Operating equipment	Buildings

Intangible Assets

Intangible assets are not physical. They have value because of the rights and benefits that the owner derives from them. Examples are as follows:

Goodwill	Trademarks
Patents	Copyrights

Current Liabilities

Current liabilities are debts or obligations due within one year. Current liabilities normally are paid from existing current assets or by creating other current liabilities. Examples are amounts owed to banks, suppliers of goods, employees, and government agencies. On a balance sheet they are labeled as follows:

Notes payable	Salaries payable
Accounts payable	Taxes payable

Long-Term Liabilities

Long-term liabilities are debts or obligations not expected to come due sooner than one year. Cash borrowed by issuing bonds or signing long-term notes or mortgages are all long-term liabilities. On the balance sheet they are labeled as follows:

Bonds payable	Mortgages payable
Long-term notes payable	

Common Stock

Common stock represents ownership in a corporation, and the people who own shares of common stock are called stockholders or shareholders. A corporation may also issue **preferred stock**, so called because it has preferential rights to dividends over common stock. The holders of preferred stock are owners of a corporation just as are common stockholders. However, preferred stockholders usually do not have voting rights in the affairs of the enterprise. Stock as an item appears only if a firm is organized as a corporation. If a firm is a sole proprietorship or a partnership, each owner's individual investment in the firm is listed separately.

Retained Earnings

Retained earnings is the amount of earnings of prior years that have been kept or retained in the business and not distributed to the stockholders.

16.1 Vertical Analysis of a Balance Sheet

Financial statement analysis is often more meaningful when the information from the current accounting period is compared to the information from one or more previous accounting periods. An abnormally large percent increase or decrease should alert the reader of the financial statement that a more detailed analysis should be performed.

Problems can then be identified and appropriate corrective action taken before they become even more serious.

A **vertical analysis** of the balance sheet is done by dividing each item by the total assets. Be certain to change the base (total assets) when changing years.

EXAMPLE Perform a vertical analysis of the following comparative balance sheet for the Magic Slope Ski Shop:

Magic Slope Ski Shop
Comparative Balance Sheet—December 31, 2002 and 2003

	2002 Amount	2002 %	2003 Amount	2003 %
Assets				
Current assets				
Cash	$ 9,200	8.6%	$ 11,800	10.9%
Accounts receivable	21,200	19.9%	22,400	20.7%
Merchandise inventory	26,000	24.4%	26,400	24.4%
Total current assets	$ 56,400	52.9%	$ 60,600	56.0%
Plant and equipment				
Land	$ 4,000	3.8%	$ 4,000	3.7%
Building	28,600	26.8%	28,000	25.9%
Equipment	17,600	16.5%	15,600	14.4%
Total plant and equipment	$ 50,200	47.1%	$ 47,600	44.0%
Total assets	$106,600	100.0%	$108,200	100.0%
Liabilities and Owner's Equity				
Current liabilities				
Accounts payable	$ 17,900	16.8%	$ 17,000	15.7%
Notes payable	9,000	8.4%	10,000	9.2%
Taxes payable	3,500	3.3%	4,000	3.7%
Total current liabilities	$ 30,400	28.5%	$ 31,000	28.7%
Long-term liabilities				
Bonds payable	$ 20,000	18.8%	$ 20,000	18.5%
Total liabilities	$ 50,400	47.3%	$ 51,000	47.1%
Owner's equity				
Preferred stock	$ 15,000	14.1%	$ 15,000	13.9%
Common stock	30,000	28.1%	30,000	27.7%
Retained earnings	11,200	10.5%	12,200	11.3%
Total owner's equity	$ 56,200	52.7%	$ 57,200	52.9%
Total liabilities and owner's equity	$106,600	100.0%	$108,200	100.0%

Solution The vertical analysis is performed by dividing each component of the balance sheet by the total assets. Total liabilities and owner's equity is the same figure as total assets. For example, cash in 2002 is $9,200. Total assets in 2002 is $106,600. Thus

$$\frac{\text{Cash (2002)}}{\text{total assets (2002)}} = \frac{\$9,200}{\$106,600} = 8.6\%.$$

Likewise, in 2003, cash is $11,800 and total assets $108,200. Thus

$$\frac{\text{Cash (2003)}}{\text{total assets (2003)}} = \frac{\$11,800}{\$108,200} = 10.9\%.$$

All other calculations are done the same way, and the results are shown in the comparative balance sheet.

$$9,200 \div 106,600 = .086$$

Perform a vertical analysis on the following partial comparative balance sheet:

Baskets Galore
Comparative Balance Sheet—December 31, 2002 and 2003

	2002		2003	
	Amount	%	Amount	%
Assets				
Current assets				
1. Cash	$ 19,500		$ 21,800	
2. Accounts receivable	11,000		15,600	
3. Merchandise inventory	36,500		46,600	
4. Total current assets	$ 67,000		$ 84,000	
.	.	.	.	.
.	.	.	.	.
Total assets	$348,000		$366,000	

16.1 Solutions to Practice Problems

1. $\dfrac{\text{Cash (2002)}}{\text{total assets (2002)}} = \dfrac{\$19,500}{\$348,000} = 5.6\%$

   $\dfrac{\text{Cash (2003)}}{\text{total assets (2003)}} = \dfrac{\$ 21,800}{\$366,000} = 6.0\%$

2. $\dfrac{\text{Accounts receivable (2002)}}{\text{total assets (2002)}} = \dfrac{\$11,000}{\$348,000} = 3.2\%$

   $\dfrac{\text{Accounts receivable (2003)}}{\text{total assets (2003)}} = \dfrac{\$15,600}{\$366,000} = 4.3\%$

3. $\dfrac{\text{Merchandise inventory (2002)}}{\text{total assets (2002)}} = \dfrac{\$36,500}{\$348,000} = 10.5\%$

   $\dfrac{\text{Merchandise inventory (2003)}}{\text{total assets (2003)}} = \dfrac{\$46,600}{\$366,000} = 12.7\%$

4. $\dfrac{\text{Total current assets (2002)}}{\text{total assets (2002)}} = \dfrac{\$67,000}{\$348,000} = 19.3\%$

   $\dfrac{\text{Total current assets (2003)}}{\text{total assets (2003)}} = \dfrac{\$84,000}{\$366,000} = 23.0\%$

16.2 Horizontal Analysis of a Balance Sheet

The **horizontal analysis** of a comparative balance sheet finds the amount and percent of increase or decrease between each item in previous years' and the current year's business. When finding the percents, always use the earlier year as the base.

EXAMPLE Perform a horizontal analysis of the following comparative balance sheet for the Magic Slope Ski Shop:

Magic Slope Ski Shop
Comparative Balance Sheet—December 31, 2002 and 2003

	2002	2003	Increase (Decrease) Amount	%
		Assets		
Current assets				
Cash	$ 9,200	$ 11,800	$ 2,600	28.3%
Accounts receivable	21,200	22,400	1,200	5.7%
Merchandise inventory	26,000	26,400	400	1.5%
Total current assets	$ 56,400	$ 60,600	$ 4,200	7.4%
Plant and equipment				
Land	$ 4,000	$ 4,000	$ 0	0%
Building	28,600	28,000	(600)	(2.1%)
Equipment	17,600	15,600	(2,000)	(11.4%)
Total plant and equipment	$ 50,200	$ 47,600	$(2,600)	(5.2%)
Total assets	$106,600	$108,200	$ 1,600	1.5%
		Liabilities and Owner's Equity		
Current liabilities				
Accounts payable	$ 17,900	$ 17,000	$ (900)	(5.0%)
Notes payable	9,000	10,000	1,000	11.1%
Taxes payable	3,500	4,000	500	14.3%
Total current liabilities	$ 30,400	$ 31,000	$ 600	(2.0%)
Long-term liabilities				
Bonds payable	$ 20,000	$ 20,000	$ 0	0%
Total liabilities	$ 50,400	$ 51,000	$ 600	1.2%
Owner's equity				
Preferred stock	$ 15,000	$ 15,000	$ 0	0%
Common stock	30,000	30,000	0	0%
Retained earnings	11,200	12,200	1,000	8.9%
Total owner's equity	$ 56,200	$ 57,200	$ 1,000	1.8%
Total liabilities and owner's equity	$106,600	$108,200	$ 1,600	1.5%

Solution   The *amount* of increase or decrease is the difference between each of the items in 2002 and 2003. The difference is then divided by the earlier year's amount, 2002 in this illustration, to find the *percent* of increase or decrease. For example, a horizontal analysis of cash gives the following result:

$11,800 ←——2003 cash amount
− 9,200 ←——2002 cash amount
$ 2,600 ←——Amount increase

$$\frac{\$2,600 \text{ Increase}}{\$9,200 \text{ 2002 cash}} = 28.3\% \quad \text{Percent increase}$$

All of the remaining balance sheet figures are handled in the same way until every category has been calculated. If the difference is a decrease (in this case from 2002 to 2003), it is so indicated by putting parentheses around both the amount difference and the percent difference.

Each of the amounts for the Magic Slope Ski Shop have been analyzed horizontally, and the results are reported in the comparative balance sheet.

Perform a horizontal analysis on the following partial comparative balance sheet:

Lincoln's Bookstop
Comparative Balance Sheet—December 31, 2002 and 2003

	2002	2003	Increase (Decrease) Amount	%
		Liabilities and Owner's Equity		
Current liabilities				
1. Accounts payable	$ 7,400	$ 7,000	$	%
2. Notes payable	1,000	1,500		%
3. Taxes payable	1,700	2,000		%
4. Total current liabilities	$10,100	$10,500		%
Long-term liabilities				
5. Bonds payable	$10,000	$10,000	$	%
Total liabilities and owner's equity	$52,000	$61,000	$	%

16.2 Solutions to Practice Problems

1. $\quad$
$$\frac{\$7,000 \quad \text{2003 accounts payable} \quad (\$440) \quad \text{Decrease (5.4\%)}}{-\ 7,400 \quad \text{2002 accounts payable} \quad \$7,400 \quad \text{2002 accounts payable}} = (5.4\%)$$
$\quad\quad$ (400) $\quad$ Amount decrease

2. $\quad$
$$\frac{\$1,500 \quad \text{2003 notes payable} \quad \$500 \quad \text{Increase (50\%)}}{-\ 1,000 \quad \text{2002 notes payable} \quad \$1,000 \quad \text{2002 notes payable}} = 50\%$$
$\quad\quad$ 500 $\quad$ Amount increase

3. $\quad$
$$\frac{\$2,000 \quad \text{2003 taxes payable} \quad \$300 \quad \text{Increase (17.6\%)}}{-\ 1,700 \quad \text{2002 taxes payable} \quad \$1,700 \quad \text{2002 taxes payable}} = 17.6\%$$
$\quad\quad$ 300 $\quad$ Amount increase

4. $\quad$
$$\frac{\$10,500 \quad \text{2003 total current liabilities} \quad \$400 \quad \text{Increase (4.0\%)}}{-10,100 \quad \text{2002 total current liabilities} \quad \$10,100 \quad \text{2002 total current liabilities}} = 4.0\%$$
$\quad\quad$ 400 $\quad$ Amount increase

5. No change from 2002 to 2003

LEARNING UNIT 2
INCOME STATEMENT

EXCEL Spreadsheet Application Spreadsheet Application 2 was designed by Springfield to perform vertical and horizontal analyses on its comparative income statements.

A balance sheet records the financial position of a company on a specific date. An **income statement** is a summary of all actual or potential inflows of revenue (income) and outflows of costs and expenses during an accounting period. *Profit* is made if the revenues, the inflows from selling the product or service, are greater than the outflows, the costs and expenses incurred while offering the product or service. A firm that has expenses greater than its revenues suffers a *loss*. The form of an income statement varies according to the type of business. However, the **basic income statement** formula is always the same:

> Net income (net loss) = revenues − expenses

That formula can be expanded to reflect the basic income statement format as shown in Figure 16.2, for Jan and Steve's business, Knives and Things.

Figure 16.2
INCOME STATEMENT

KNIVES AND THINGS
Income Statement for the Year Ending December 31, 20XX

1.	Revenues:		
2.	Gross sales		$150,000
3.	Deduct: Sales returns	$ 1,000	
4.	Sales allowances	600	1,600
5.	Net sales		$148,400
	Cost of goods sold:		
6.	Beginning inventory (Jan. 1)	$ 6,800	
7.	Purchases	69,880	
8.	Goods available for sale	$ 76,680	
9.	Ending inventory (Dec. 31)	$ 9,900	
10.	Cost of goods sold		66,780
11.	Gross profit		$ 81,620
12.	Operating expenses		67,620
13.	Net income before taxes		$ 14,000
14.	Taxes		8,000
15.	Net income after taxes		$ 6,000

The following is a brief discussion of each of the major items found in the Knives and Things income statement, Figure 16.2. Each item is numbered to coordinate the comparison.

1. ***Revenue***. The major source of income earned by a business enterprise. Usually the income is from sales, but it could be from other sources, for example, interest income or rental fees.

2. ***Gross sales***. Total earned sales, cash or credit.

3. ***Sales returns***. Merchandise sold to, and returned by, customers.

4. ***Sales allowances***. Reductions in price granted to customers for various reasons, typically because of damaged or defective merchandise.

5. ***Net sales***. The value of sales revenue after the value of all returned goods and discounts have been deducted.

6. ***Beginning Inventory (January 1)***. The amount of merchandise a business enterprise has available to sell to customers at the beginning of an accounting period.

7. ***Purchases***. The cost of merchandise bought to be resold to customers during an accounting period. The purchases are added to the beginning inventory to find the goods available for sale.

8. ***Goods available for sale***. The total amount paid for goods a business enterprise had available to sell to customers during an accounting period.

9. ***Ending Inventory (December 31)***. The amount of merchandise a business enterprise has available to sell to customers at the end of an accounting period. This amount is subtracted from the goods available for sale to find the cost of goods sold.

10. ***Cost of goods sold***. The amount paid for all the merchandise a company sold during an accounting period.

11. ***Gross profit***. The difference found by subtracting the cost of goods sold from net sales.

12. ***Operating expenses***. The expenses incurred in running the business or in attempting to sell merchandise.

13. ***Net income before taxes***. The difference between the gross profit and the operating expenses before paying taxes. It is the amount earned (or lost) by a

business enterprise during an accounting period before paying taxes, and in sometimes referred to as operating profit.

14. **Taxes.** The payments made to governments by corporations because they are "legal persons." Proprietorships and partnerships pay taxes as personal income tax on profits.

15. **Net income after taxes.** The amount remaining after all expenses (including taxes) have been deducted from the total revenue. If the total expenses are more than the total revenues, a *net loss* results.

In summary, to find net income, follow these steps:

Step 1. Calculate net sales:

$$\text{Net sales} = \text{gross sales} - \text{sales returns} - \text{sales allowances}$$

Step 2. Calculate the cost of goods sold:

$$\text{Goods available for sale} = \text{beginning inventory} + \text{purchases}$$
$$\text{Cost of goods sold} = \text{goods available for sale} - \text{ending inventory}$$

Step 3. Calculate the gross profit:

$$\text{Gross profit} = \text{net sales} - \text{cost of goods sold}$$

Step 4. Calculate the net income:

$$\text{Net income} = \text{gross profit} - \text{operating expenses}$$

16.3 Vertical Analysis of an Income Statement

A vertical analysis of an income statement is performed just as it is for the balance sheet, except that *the base is net sales*. Each item in the income statement is divided by the same year's net sales.

Business firms can then compare the rates obtained in the vertical analysis with their own past performance, with the rates of similar companies within their geographic area, or with industry-wide rates to help determine their competitive position and progress. Some of the sources are Dun and Bradstreet, the Mail-Me-Monday Barometer (Accounting Corporation), and the National Retail Merchants Association.

EXAMPLE   Perform a vertical analysis on the following comparative income statement:

Motor City Garage, Incorporated
Comparative Income Statement
for the Years Ending December 31, 2002 and 2003

	2002 Amount	2002 %	2003 Amount	2003 %
Sales	$123,000	102.5%	$137,500	102.6%
Deduct: Sales returns	3,000	2.5%	3,500	2.6%
Net sales	$120,000	100.0%	$134,000	100.0%
Deduct: Cost of goods sold	50,000	41.7%	60,000	44.8%
Gross profit	$ 70,000	58.3%	$ 74,000	55.2%
Deduct: Operating expenses	34,000	28.3%	50,000	37.3%
Net income	$ 36,000	30.0%	$ 24,000	17.9%

Solution Each component in the income statement is divided by the net sales in the same year. For example, the cost of goods sold in 2002 as a percent of net sales in 2002 is

$$\frac{\text{Cost of goods sold (2002)}}{\text{net sales (2002)}} = \frac{\$50,000}{\$120,000} = 41.7\%.$$

The cost of goods sold in 2003 as a percent of the net sales in 2003 is

$$\frac{\text{Cost of goods sold (2003)}}{\text{net sales (2003)}} = \frac{\$60,000}{\$134,000} = 44.8\%.$$

The remaining calculations are performed the same way. The results are shown in the comparative income statement.

16.3 Practice Problems

Perform a vertical analysis on the following partial comparative income statement:

Bruce's Men's Store
Comparative Income Statement
for the Years Ending December 31, 2002 and 2003

	2002 Amount	%	2003 Amount	%
1. Sales	$192,500		$208,250	
2. Deduct: Sales returns	4,000	___	6,250	___
3. Net sales	$188,500		$202,000	
4. Deduct: Cost of goods sold	95,000	___	111,500	___

16.3 Solutions to Practice Problems

1. $\dfrac{\text{Sales (2002)}}{\text{net sales (2002)}} = \dfrac{\$192,500}{\$188,500} = 102.1\%$

   $\dfrac{\text{Sales (2003)}}{\text{net sales (2003)}} = \dfrac{\$208,250}{\$202,000} = 103.1\%$

2. $\dfrac{\text{Sales returns (2002)}}{\text{net sales (2002)}} = \dfrac{\$4,000}{\$188,500} = 2.1\%$

   $\dfrac{\text{Sales returns (2003)}}{\text{net sales (2003)}} = \dfrac{\$6,250}{\$202,000} = 3.1\%$

3. $\dfrac{\text{Net sales (2002)}}{\text{net sales (2002)}} = \dfrac{\$188,500}{\$188,500} = 100\%$

   $\dfrac{\text{Net sales (2003)}}{\text{net sales (2003)}} = \dfrac{\$202,000}{\$202,000} = 100\%$

4. $\dfrac{\text{Cost of goods sold (2002)}}{\text{net sales (2002)}} = \dfrac{\$95,000}{\$188,500} = 50.4\%$

   $\dfrac{\text{Cost of goods sold (2003)}}{\text{net sales (2003)}} = \dfrac{\$111,500}{\$202,000} = 55.2\%$

16.4 **Horizontal Analysis of an Income Statement**

A horizontal analysis of an income statement is performed just as it is for a balance sheet. The change (increase or decrease) is found between each component part in a base year and a comparison year. *The base year is the earlier year* in the comparison. The change is then divided by the base year to determine the percent change. Any unusual changes, such as a sizable percent decline in the beginning inventory, from period to period should be brought to management's attention for further analysis and/or action. When the amounts being compared are positive in each year, or when the base year is positive, percent changes can be calculated. Sometimes income statement amounts are not positive. Obviously, a firm cannot have a net loss in income. *If the base year is zero or negative, the percent change cannot be calculated.* Each of these possibilities is illustrated in the following examples.

When the base year and the comparison year are positive and the change is positive:

EXAMPLE Calculate the amount and percent change in the following portion of a comparative income statement:

	2002	2003	Increase (Decrease) Amount	%
Net income	$10,000	$15,000	$5,000	50.0%

Solution The difference between a $10,000 profit in 2002 and a $15,000 profit in 2003 is an increase of $5,000. Divide the increase by the base year (2003):

$$\frac{\$5,000}{\$10,000} = 50\% \text{ increase}$$

When the base year and the comparison year are positive and the change is negative:

EXAMPLE Calculate the amount and percent change in the following portion of a comparative income statement:

	2002	2003	Increase (Decrease) Amount	%
Net income	$15,000	$10,000	($5,000)	(33.3%)

Solution The difference between a $15,000 profit in 2002 and a $10,000 profit in 2003 is a decrease of $5,000. Divide the decrease by the base year (2002):

$$\frac{(\$5,000)}{\$15,000} = (33.3\%) \text{ decrease}$$

When the base year is positive, but the comparison year is negative:

EXAMPLE Calculate the amount and percent change in the following portion of a comparative income statement:

	2002	2003	Increase (Decrease) Amount	%
Net income	$15,000	($10,000)	($25,000)	(166.7%)

Solution The difference between a $15,000 profit in 2002 and a $10,000 loss in 2003 is a decrease of $25,000. Divide the decrease by the base year (2002):

$$\frac{(\$25,000)}{\$15,000} = (166.7\%) \text{ decrease}$$

When the base year is zero and the comparison year is positive:

EXAMPLE   Calculate the amount and percent change in the following portion of a comparative income statement:

	2002	2003	Increase (Decrease) Amount	%
Net income	$0	$1,000	*$1,000*	—

Solution   The difference between a net income of $0 in 2002 and $1,000 in 2003 is an increase of $1,000. The percent increase, however, need not be calculated because anything divided by zero is infinite and has no application in this type of problem.

When the base year is negative and the comparison year is positive:

EXAMPLE   Calculate the amount and percent change in the following portion of a comparative income statement:

	2002	2003	Increase (Decrease) Amount	%
Net income	($15,000)	$10,000	*$25,000*	—

Solution   The difference between a $15,000 loss in 2002 and a $10,000 profit in 2003 is an increase of $25,000. Dividing the increase of $25,000 by the negative $15,000 base year (2002) amount would result in a negative percent increase. Since that is impossible, the percent increase is not calculated.

When the base year and the comparison year are both negative and the change is positive:

EXAMPLE   Calculate the amount and percent change in the following portion of a comparative income statement:

	2002	2003	Increase (Decrease) Amount	%
Net income	($15,000)	($10,000)	*$5,000*	—

Solution   The difference between a $15,000 loss in 2002 and a $10,000 loss in 2003 is an increase of $5,000. Dividing the increase by the negative base year (2002) would result in a negative increase. That is clearly not possible, so the percent change cannot be calculated.

When the base year and the comparison year are both negative and the change is negative:

EXAMPLE   Calculate the amount and percent change in the following portion of a comparative income statement:

	2002	2003	Increase (Decrease) Amount	%
Net income	($10,000)	($15,000)	($5,000)	—

Solution   The difference between a $10,000 loss in 2002 and a $15,000 loss in 2003 is a decrease of $5,000. Dividing the decrease by the negative base year (2002) would result in a positive decrease. Since that is not possible, the percent change cannot be calculated.

16.4 Practice Problems

Perform a horizontal analysis on the following partial comparative income statement:

Bruce's Men's Store
Comparative Income Statement
for the Years Ending December 31, 2002 and 2003

	2002	2003	Increase (Decrease) Amount	%
1. Sales	$192,500	$208,250	$_____	_____%
2. Deduct: Sales returns	$ 4,000	$ 6,250	$_____	_____%
3. Net sales	$188,500	$202,000	$_____	_____%
4. Deduct: Cost of goods sold	$ 95,000	$111,500	$_____	_____%

16.4 Solutions to Practice Problems

1.
$$
\begin{array}{r} \$208,250 \\ -192,500 \\ \hline \$\ 15,750 \end{array} \quad \frac{\$15,750}{\$192,500} = 8.2\%
$$

2.
$$
\begin{array}{r} \$6,250 \\ -4,000 \\ \hline \$2,250 \end{array} \quad \frac{\$2,250}{\$4,000} = 56.3\%
$$

3.
$$
\begin{array}{r} \$202,000 \\ -188,500 \\ \hline \$\ 13,500 \end{array} \quad \frac{\$13,500}{\$188,500} = 7.2\%
$$

4.
$$
\begin{array}{r} \$111,500 \\ -95,000 \\ \hline \$\ 16,500 \end{array} \quad \frac{\$16,500}{\$95,000} = 17.4\%
$$

LEARNING UNIT 3
FINANCIAL RATIO ANALYSIS

The vertical and horizontal analyses of a balance sheet and an income statement provide managers with valuable problem-solving tools. Ratios are another tool accountants and financial officers use. A **ratio** is the relationship of one number to another. Ratios are used by bankers to decide on loans, by investors to help decide on reasonable purchase prices, and by management to help identify a company's strengths and weaknesses. Ratios are useful to make comparisons of such things as current financial results to those of previous periods, firms of similar size, or firms in the same industry. A ratio that differs significantly from that of previous periods or from industry averages can indicate that a financial problem needs attention. Some basic sources of useful ratios for industry comparison are the U.S. Department of Commerce, the Small Business Administration, bankers, accounting firms, and newspaper and magazine articles.

Many ratios are used for decision-making. Table 16.1 provides a summary of a variety of them. The management of each firm must decide which ratios are best for it, and the selection varies widely.

Ratios are generally written as 2 : 1. The colon (:) is the sign used to denote the word *to*. Thus, the ratio would be read, "2 to 1". Two exceptions should be noted: If the ratio is less than 1, it is frequently written as a percent, and the inventory turnover ratio is usually written as having turned a certain number of times, for example, 6 times rather than 6 : 1.

TABLE 16.1 FINANCIAL RATIOS

Ratio	Formula	What It Measures	Satisfactory Result
LIQUIDITY RATIOS (Measure a firm's ability to meet its short-term obligations)			
Current ratio	$\dfrac{\text{Current assets}}{\text{Current liabilities}}$	Measures a firm's ability to pay its current debts as they mature	2 : 1
Acid-test ratio	$\dfrac{\text{Quick assets}}{\text{Current liabilities}}$	Measures a firm's ability to meet its current debt on short notice	1 : 1
PROFITABILITY RATIOS (Measure the overall financial performance of a firm)			
Earnings per share	$\dfrac{\text{Net income after taxes}}{\text{Number of common stock shares outstanding}}$	Measures the amount of profit earned for each share of common stock outstanding	Compared to past earnings per share and to industry averages
Return on sales	$\dfrac{\text{Net income after taxes}}{\text{Net sales}}$	Measures company profitability	Compared with profit forecast—past performance and industry averages
Return on equity	$\dfrac{\text{Net income after taxes}}{\text{Total owner's equity}}$	Measures returns being received by owners on their investment	Compared with past performance and industry averages
ACTIVITY RATIO (Measures the effectiveness of a firm's use of its resources)			
Inventory turnover ratio	$\dfrac{\text{Cost of goods sold}}{\text{Average inventory (valued at cost)}}$	Measures the number of times merchandise moves through a business in an accounting cycle	Compared to industry averages
DEBT RATIOS (Measure the extent to which a firm relies on debt financing)			
Debt to owner's equity ratio	$\dfrac{\text{Total liabilities}}{\text{Total owner's equity}}$	Measures the extent to which the operations of a firm are financed by borrowed funds	Compared to management expectations, past performance, and industry averages
Debt to total assets ratio	$\dfrac{\text{Total liabilities}}{\text{Total assets}}$	Measures the extent to which the assets are financed by borrowed funds	Compared to management expectations, past performance, and industry averages

Each ratio in Table 16.1 is calculated here using the balance sheet for Knives and Things illustrated in Figure 16.1 and the income statement for Knives and Things illustrated in Figure 16.2 presented earlier in the chapter.

$$\text{Current ratio} = \frac{\text{current assets}}{\text{current liabilities}} = \frac{\$57,750}{\$27,500} = 2.1:1$$

This is probably satisfactory since the rule of thumb is 2 : 1; however, a comparison to other firms in the same industry, of the same size, and in the same geographic location, if available, would be more meaningful for this and all other ratios.

$$\text{Acid-test ratio} = \frac{\text{quick assets}}{\text{current liabilities}} = \frac{\$40,350}{\$27,500} = 1.467:1$$

Quick assets are cash, readily marketable securities, and receivables. They would *not* include merchandise inventory or prepaid expenses.

$$\text{Earnings per share} = \frac{\text{net income after taxes}}{\text{common stock outstanding}} = \frac{\$6,000}{30,000} = \$.20$$

$$\text{Return on sales} = \frac{\text{net income after taxes}}{\text{net sales}} = \frac{\$6,000}{\$148,400} = 4.0\%$$

$$\text{Return on equity} = \frac{\text{net income after taxes}}{\text{total owner's equity}} = \frac{\$6,000}{\$70,000} = 8.6\%$$

$$\text{Inventory turnover ratio} = \frac{\text{cost of goods sold}}{\text{average inventory (valued at cost)}} = \frac{\$66,780}{\dfrac{\$6,800 + \$9,900}{2}}$$
$$= \frac{\$66,780}{\$8,350} = 7.998 \text{ times}$$

$$\text{Debt to owner's equity ratio} = \frac{\text{total liabilities}}{\text{total owner's equity}} = \frac{\$80,000}{\$70,000}$$
$$= 1.14:1$$

$$\text{Debt to total assets ratio} = \frac{\text{total liabilities}}{\text{total assets}} = \frac{\$80,000}{\$150,000} = 53.3\%$$

16.5 Practice Problems

Solve the following financial ratio problems using the following balance sheet and income statement for the Lorical Lawn Furniture Company:

LORICAL LAWN FURNITURE COMPANY
BALANCE SHEET
DECEMBER 31, 20XX

ASSETS

Current assets

Cash	$ 16,000	
Accounts receivable	85,000	
Merchandise inventory	25,000	
Prepaid expenses	19,000	
Total current assets		$145,000

Plant and equipment

Land	$ 62,000	
Buildings	150,000	
Fixtures	13,000	
Total plant and equipment assets		$225,000

Intangible assets

Goodwill	$ 10,000	
Trademark	25,000	
Total intangible assets		$ 35,000
Total assets		$405,000

LIABILITIES

Current liabilities

Accounts payable	$ 21,000	
Salaries payable	48,000	
Total current liabilities		$ 69,000

Long-term liabilities

Mortgages payable	$101,000	
Long-term notes payable	31,000	
Total long-term liabilities		$132,000
Total liabilities		$201,000

OWNER'S EQUITY

Common stock (150,000 shares outstanding at $1 par)	$150,000	
Retained earnings	54,000	
Total owner's equity		$204,000
Total liabilities and owner's equity		$405,000

LORICAL LAWN FURNITURE COMPANY
Income Statement for the Year Ending December 31, 20XX

Revenues:

Gross sales			$375,000
Deduct: Sales returns		$ 3,000	
Sales allowances		2,000	5,000
Net sales			$370,000
Cost of goods sold:			
Beginning inventory (Jan. 1)		$ 17,000	
Purchases		175,000	
Goods available for sale		$192,000	
Ending inventory (Dec. 31)		25,000	
Cost of goods sold			167,000
Gross profit			$203,000
Operating expenses			169,000
Net income before taxes			$ 34,000
Taxes			9,000
Net income after taxes			$ 25,000

1. Calculate the current ratio.
2. Calculate the acid-test ratio.
3. Calculate the earnings per share.
4. Calculate the return on sales.
5. Calculate the return on equity.

16.5 Solutions to Practice Problems

1. Current ratio $= \dfrac{\text{current assets}}{\text{current liabilities}} = \dfrac{\$145{,}000}{\$69{,}000} = 2.101 : 1$

2. Acid-test ratio $= \dfrac{\text{quick assets}}{\text{current liabilities}} = \dfrac{\$101{,}000}{\$69{,}000} = 1.464 : 1$

3. Earnings per share $= \dfrac{\text{net income after taxes}}{\text{common stock outstanding}} = \dfrac{\$25{,}000}{150{,}000} = \$.17$

4. Return on sales $= \dfrac{\text{net income after taxes}}{\text{net sales}} = \dfrac{\$25{,}000}{\$370{,}000} = 6.8\%$

5. Return on equity $= \dfrac{\text{net income after taxes}}{\text{total owner's equity}} = \dfrac{\$25{,}000}{\$204{,}000} = 12.3\%$

QUICK REFERENCE SUMMARY AND REVIEW

Page	Section Topic	Learning Concepts	Examples and Solutions
546	**16.1** Vertical Analysis of a Balance Sheet	For a given year, each item in the balance sheet is divided by the total assets.	Cash in 2002 is $9,000 and total assets are $360,000. Conduct a vertical analysis on cash. $$\dfrac{\$9{,}000}{\$360{,}000} = 2.5\%$$
548	**16.2** Horizontal Analysis of a Balance Sheet	The change from one year to another in a comparative balance sheet is divided by the earlier year's business to find the percent of change. A decrease is shown by placing both the difference and the percent in parentheses ( ).	Cash is $8,000 in 2002 and $9,000 in 2003. Conduct a horizontal analysis of cash. $9,000 − 8,000 $1,000 Increase $$\dfrac{\$1{,}000}{\$8{,}000} = 12.5\% \text{ Increase}$$
552	**16.3** Vertical Analysis of an Income Statement	Each item in the income statement is divided by the same year's net sales.	Conduct a vertical analysis of the cost of goods sold, $40,000, when net sales are $100,000. $$\dfrac{\$40{,}000}{\$100{,}000} = 40\%$$
553	**16.4** Horizontal Analysis of an Income Statement	The change from one year to another is calculated. It is then divided by the earlier year's amount. A decrease is indicated by putting the change and the percent in parentheses. If the base year is zero or negative, the percent change cannot be calculated.	Conduct a horizontal analysis of net sales when they are $300,000 in 2002 and $275,000 in 2003. $300,000 − 275,000 ($ 25,000) Decrease $$\dfrac{\$25{,}000}{\$300{,}000} = (8.3\%) \text{ Decrease}$$

Page	Section Topic	Learning Concepts	Examples and Solutions
557	**16.5** Calculating Financial Ratios	A ratio is the relationship of one number to another. Eight ratios were presented in the chapter:	Use the following information to calculate each of the ratios: current assets, $90,000; current liabilities, $45,000; beginning inventory, $36,000 ending inventory, $40,000; prepaid expenses, $5,000; net income after taxes, $10,000; total owner's equity, $50,000; net sales, $180,000; number of common stock shares outstanding, 25,000; cost of goods sold, $100,000; total liabilities, $75,000.

$$\text{Current ratio} = \frac{\text{current assets}}{\text{current liabilities}}$$
$$= \frac{\$90,000}{\$45,000} = 2:1$$

$$\text{Acid-test ratio} = \frac{\text{quick assets}}{\text{current liabilities}}$$
$$= \frac{\$45,000}{\$45,000} = 1:1$$

$$\text{Earnings per share} = \frac{\text{net income after taxes}}{\text{common stock outstanding}}$$
$$= \frac{\$10,000}{25,000} = \$.40$$

$$\text{Return on sales} = \frac{\text{net income after taxes}}{\text{net sales}}$$
$$= \frac{\$110,000}{\$180,000} = 5.6\%$$

$$\text{Return on equity} = \frac{\text{net income after taxes}}{\text{total owner's equity}}$$
$$= \frac{\$10,000}{\$50,000} = 20\%$$

$$\text{Inventory turnover} = \frac{\text{cost of goods sold}}{\text{average inventory}}$$
$$= \frac{\$100,000}{\$38,000} = 2.632 \text{ times}$$

$$\text{Debt to owner's equity} = \frac{\text{total liabilities}}{\text{total owner's equity}}$$
$$= \frac{\$75,000}{\$50,000} = 1.5:1$$

$$\text{Debt to total assets} = \frac{\text{total liabilities}}{\text{total assets}}$$
$$= \frac{\$\,75,000}{\$125,000} = 60\%$$

SURFING THE INTERNET

For further information on the topics covered in this chapter, check out the following sites:

http://www.moorheadmgmt.com/resources.htm

http://www.lib.sfu.ca/kiosk/mbodnar/ratioan.htm

http://invest-faq.com/articles/analy-roe-vs-roc.html

Answers to odd-numbered problems are given in Appendix A.

16.1

Conduct a vertical analysis of the following partial balance sheet for Time Lauris:

Time Lauris
Comparative Balance Sheet—December 31, 2002 and 2003

	2002 Amount	2002 %	2003 Amount	2003 %
		Assets		
Current assets				
1. Cash	$ 20,000	6.5%	$ 30,000	9.7%
2. Accounts receivable	100,000	32.5%	90,000	29.0%
3. Merchandise inventory	38,000	12.3%	50,000	16.1%
4. Total current assets	$158,000	51.3%	$170,000	54.8%
Plant and equipment				
5. Land	$ 35,000	11.4%	$ 35,000	11.3%
6. Building	80,000	26.0%	75,000	24.2%
7. Equipment	35,000	11.4%	30,000	9.7%
8. Total plant and equipment	$150,000	48.7%	$140,000	45.2%
9. Total assets	$308,000	100.0%	$310,000	100.0%

16.2

Conduct a horizontal analysis of the following partial balance sheet for Time Lauris:

Time Lauris
Comparative Balance Sheet—December 31, 2002 and 2003

	2002	2003	Increase (Decrease) Amount	%
		Liabilities and Owners Equity		
Current liabilities				
10. Accounts payable	$ 17,000	$ 20,000	$ 3,000	17.6 %
11. Notes payable	12,000	11,000	(1,000)	(8.3)%
12. Taxes payable	8,000	3,000	(5,000)	(62.5)%
13. Total current liabilities	$ 37,000	$ 34,000	$(3,000)	(8.1)%
Long-term liabilities				
14. Bonds payable	$ 50,000	$ 50,000	$ 0	0%
15. Total liabilities	$ 87,000	$ 84,000	$(3,000)	(3.4)%
Owner's equity				
16. Common stock	$150,000	$150,000	$ 0	0 %
17. Preferred stock	50,000	45,000	(5,000)	(10.0)%
18. Retained earnings	21,000	31,000	10,000	47.6%
19. Total owner's equity	$221,000	$226,000	$ 5,000	2.3%
20. Total liabilities and owner's equity	$308,000	$310,000	$ 2,000	.6%

16.3

Conduct a vertical analysis of the follwing partial income statement for Suzanne's Party Place:

Suzanne's Party Place
Comparative Income Statement
for the Years Ending December 31, 2002 and 2003

	2002 Amount	%	2003 Amount	%
21. Sales	$544,000	105.2%	$612,000	104.3%
22. Deduct: Sales returns	27,000	5.2%	25,000	4.3%
23. Net sales	$517,000	100.0%	$587,000	100.0%
24. Deduct: Cost of goods sold	192,000	37.1%	237,000	40.4%
25. Gross profit	$325,000	62.9%	$350,000	59.6%
26. Deduct: Operating expenses	270,000	52.2%	274,000	46.7%
27. Net income	$ 55,000	10.6%	$ 76,000	12.9%

16.4

Conduct a horizontal analysis of the following partial income statement for Suzanne's Party Place:

Suzanne's Party Place
Comparative Income Statement
for the Years Ending December 31, 2002 and 2003

	2002	2003	Increase (Decrease) Amount	%
28. Sales	$544,000	$612,000	$68,000	12.5%
29. Deduct: sales returns	27,000	25,000	(2,000)	(7.4)%
30. Net sales	$517,000	$587,000	$70,000	13.5%
31. Deduct: Cost of goods sold	192,000	237,000	45,000	23.4%
32. Gross profit	$325,000	$350,000	25,000	7.7%
33. Deduct: Operating expenses	270,000	274,000	4,000	1.5%
34. Net income	$ 55,000	76,000	$21,000	38.2%

16.5

To solve problems 35 through 42 for the specified financial ratio, use the following account balance information:

Current assets	$200,000	Cost of goods sold	$350,000
Merchanise inventory	90,000	Beginning inventory	82,000
Prepaid expenses	10,000	Ending inventory	90,000
Current liabilities	100,000	Total owner's equity	300,000
Net income after taxes	60,000	Total liabilities	400,000
Net sales	750,000	Total assets	700,000
Common stock outstanding	187,500 (shares)		

35. Calculate the current ratio.

$$\text{Current ratio} = \frac{\text{current assets}}{\text{current liabilities}} = \frac{\$200,000}{\$100,000} = 2:1$$

36. Calculate the acid-test ratio.

$$\text{Acid-test ratio} = \frac{\text{quick assets}}{\text{current liabilities}} = \frac{\$100,000}{\$100,000} = 1:1$$

37. Calculate the earnings per share.

$$\text{Earnings per share} = \frac{\text{net income after taxes}}{\text{common stock outstanding}} = \frac{\$60,000}{187,500} = \$.32$$

38. Calculate the return on sales.

$$\text{Return on sales} = \frac{\text{net income after taxes}}{\text{net sales}} = \frac{\$ 60,000}{\$750,000} = 8\%$$

39. Calculate the return on equity.

$$\text{Return on equity} = \frac{\text{net income after taxes}}{\text{total owner's equity}} = \frac{\$ 60,000}{\$300,000} = 20\%$$

40. Calculate the inventory turnover ratio.

$$\text{Inventory turnover ratio} = \frac{\text{cost of goods sold}}{\text{average inventory}} = \frac{\$350,000}{\dfrac{\$82,000 + \$90,000}{2}}$$

$$= \frac{\$350,000}{\$ 86,000} = 4.070 \text{ times}$$

41. Calculate the debt to owner's equity ratio.

$$\text{Debt to owner's equity ratio} = \frac{\text{total liabilities}}{\text{total owner's equity}} = \frac{\$400,000}{\$300,000}$$
$$= 1.333 : 1, \text{ or } 133.3\%$$

42. Calculate the debt to total assets.

$$\text{Debt to total assets} = \frac{\text{total liabilities}}{\text{total assets}} = \frac{\$400,000}{\$700,000} = 57.1\%$$

| CHAPTER REVIEW PROBLEMS | *Answers to odd-numbered problems are given in Appendix A.* |

Drill Problems

Conduct a vertical analysis of the following comparative balance sheet for the Mattress Mart:

The Mattress Mart
Comparative Balance Sheet - December 31, 2002 and 2003

	2002 Amount	%	2003 Amount	%
Assets				
Current assets				
1. Cash	$ 16,100	8.7%	$ 15,300	10.9%
2. Accounts receivable	37,100	20.0%	29,100	20.7%
3. Merchandise inventory	45,500	24.5%	34,300	24.4%
4. Total current assets	$ 98,700	53.2%	$ 78,700	56.0%
Plant and Equipment				
5. Land	$ 7,000	3.8%	$ 5,200	3.7%
6. Building	50,000	26.9%	36,400	25.9%
7. Equipment	30,000	16.2%	20,300	14.4%
8. Total plant and equipment	$ 87,000	46.8%	$ 61,900	44.0%
9. Total assets	$185,700	100.0%	$140,600	100.0%
Liabilities and Owner's Equity				
Current liabilities				
10. Accounts payable	$ 30,200	16.3%	$ 22,100	15.7%
11. Notes payable	15,800	8.5%	13,000	9.2%
12. Taxes payable	6,000	3.2%	5,200	3.7%
13. Total current liabilities	$ 52,000	28.0%	$ 40,300	28.7%
Long-term liabilities				
14. Bonds payable	$ 35,000	18.8%	$ 35,000	24.9%
15. Total liabilities	$ 87,000	46.8%	$ 75,300	53.6%
Owner's equity				
16. Preferred stock	$ 26,000	14.0%	$ 19,500	13.9%
17. Common stock	52,100	28.1%	39,000	27.7%
18. Retained earnings	20,600	11.1%	6,800	4.8%
19. Total owner's equity	$ 98,700	53.2%	$ 65,300	46.4%
20. Total liabilities and owner's equity	$185,700	100.0%	$140,600	100.0%

Conduct a horizontal analysis of the following comparative balance sheet for The Mattress Mart:

The Mattress Mart
Comparative Balance Sheet—December 31, 2002 and 2003

	2002 Amount	2003 Amount	Increase (Decrease) Amount	%
Assets				
Current assets				
21. Cash	$ 16,100	$ 15,300	$ (800)	(5.0)%
22. Accounts receivable	37,100	29,100	(8,000)	(21.6)%
23. Merchandise inventory	45,500	34,300	(11,200)	(24.6)%
24. Total current assets	$ 98,700	$ 78,700	$(20,000)	(20.3)%
Plant and equipment				
25. Land	$ 7,000	$ 5,200	$ (1,800)	(25.7)%
26. Building	50,000	36,400	(13,600)	(27.2)%
27. Equipment	30,000	20,300	(9,700)	(32.3)%
28. Total plant and equipment	$ 87,000	$ 61,900	$(25,100)	(28.9)%
29. Total assets	$185,700	$140,600	$(45,100)	(24.3)%
Liabilities and Owner's Equity				
Current liabilities				
30. Accounts payable	$ 30,200	$ 22,100	$ (8,100)	(26.8)%
31. Notes payable	15,800	13,000	(2,800)	(17.7)%
32. Taxes payable	6,000	5,200	(800)	(13.3)%
33. Total current liabilities	$ 52,000	$ 40,300	$(11,700)	(22.5)%
Long-term liabilities				
34. Bonds payable	$ 35,000	$ 35,000	$ 0	0%
35. Total liabilities	$ 87,000	$ 75,300	$(11,700)	(13.4)%
Owner's equity				
36. Common stock	$ 52,100	$ 39,000	$(13,100)	(25.1)%
37. Preferred stock	26,000	19,500	(6,500)	(25.0)%
38. Retained earnings	20,600	6,800	(13,800)	(67.0)%
39. Total owner's equity	$ 98,700	$ 65,300	$(33,400)	(33.8)%
40. Total liabilities and owner's equity	$185,700	$140,600	$(45,100)	(24.3)%

Conduct a vertical analysis of the following comparative income statement for the Mattress Mart:

The Mattress Mart
Comparative Income Statement
for the Years Ending December 31, 2002 and 2003

	2002	%	2003	%
Revenues:				
41. Gross sales	$495,000	101.2%	$445,500	101.6%
42. Sales returns	4,500	.9%	5,400	1.2%
43. Sales allowances	1,500	.3%	1,600	.4%
44. Net sales	$489,000	100.0%	$438,500	100.0%
Cost of goods sold:				
45. Beginning Inventory (Jan. 1)	$ 38,500	7.9%	$ 45,500	10.4%
46. Purchases	301,000	61.6%	268,100	61.1%
47. Goods available for sale	$339,500	69.4%	$313,600	71.5%
48. Ending Inventory (Dec. 31)	45,500	9.3%	34,300	7.8%
49. Cost of goods sold	$294,000	60.1%	$279,300	63.7%
50. Gross profit	$195,000	39.9%	$159,200	36.3%
51. Operating expenses	100,000	20.4%	110,000	25.1%
52. Net income before taxes	$ 95,000	19.4%	$ 49,200	11.2%
53. Taxes	27,000	5.5%	14,000	3.2%
54. Net income after taxes	$ 68,000	13.9%	$ 35,200	8.0%

Conduct a horizontal analysis of the comparative income statement for The Mattress Mart:

The Mattress Mart
Comparative Income Statement
for the Years Ending December 31, 2002 and 2003

			Increase (Decrease)	
	2002	2003	Amount	%
Revenues:				
55. Gross sales	$495,000	$445,500	$(49,500)	(10.0)%
56. Sales returns	4,500	5,400	900	20.0%
57. Sales allowances	1,500	1,600	100	6.7%
58. Net sales	$489,000	$438,500	$(50,500)	(10.3)%
Cost of goods sold:				
59. Beginning inventory (Jan. 1)	$ 38,500	$ 45,500	$ 7,000	18.2%
60. Purchases	301,000	268,100	(32,900)	(10.9)%
61. Goods available for sale	$339,500	$313,600	$(25,900)	(7.6)%
62. Ending inventory (Dec. 31)	45,500	34,300	(11,200)	(24.6)%
63. Cost of goods sold	$294,000	$279,300	$(14,700)	(5.0)%
64. Gross profit	$195,000	$159,200	$(35,800)	(18.4)%
65. Operating expenses	100,000	110,000	10,000	10.0%
66. Net income before taxes	$ 95,000	$ 49,200	$(45,800)	(48.2)%
67. Taxes	27,000	14,000	(13,000)	(48.1)%
68. Net income after taxes	$ 68,000	$ 35,200	$(32,800)	(48.2)%

Use the balance sheet and the income statement for The Mattress Mart to solve problems 69 through 76 for both 2002 and 2003 (round to the nearest hundred).

69. Calculate the current ratio.

2002

$$\text{Current ratio} = \frac{\text{current assets}}{\text{current liabilities}} = \frac{\$98,700}{\$52,000} = 1.90:1$$

2003

$$= \frac{\text{current assets}}{\text{current liabilities}} = \frac{\$78,700}{\$40,300} = 1.95:1$$

70. Calculate the acid-test ratio.

2002

$$\text{Acid-test ratio} = \frac{\text{quick assets}}{\text{current liabilities}} = \frac{\$53,200}{\$52,000} = 1.02:1$$

2003

$$= \frac{\text{quick assets}}{\text{current liabilities}} = \frac{\$44,400}{\$40,300} = 1.10:1$$

71. Calculate the return on sales.

<u>2002</u>

$$\text{Return on sales} = \frac{\text{net income after taxes}}{\text{net sales}} = \frac{\$68,000}{\$489,000} = 13.9\%$$

<u>2003</u>

$$= \frac{\text{net income after taxes}}{\text{net sales}} = \frac{\$35,200}{\$438,500} = 8.0\%$$

72. Calculate the return on equity.

<u>2002</u>

$$\text{Return on equity} = \frac{\text{net income after taxes}}{\text{total owner's equity}} = \frac{\$68,000}{\$98,700} = 68.9\%$$

<u>2003</u>

$$= \frac{\text{net income after taxes}}{\text{total owner's equity}} = \frac{\$35,200}{\$65,300} = 53.9\%$$

73. Calculate the inventory turnover ratio.

<u>2002</u>

$$\text{Inventory turnover ratio} = \frac{\text{cost of goods sold}}{\substack{\text{average inventory} \\ \text{(valued at cost)}}} = \frac{\$294,000}{\dfrac{\$38,500 + \$45,500}{2}}$$

$$= \frac{\$294,000}{\$42,000} = 7 \text{ times}$$

<u>2003</u>

$$\text{Inventory turnover ratio} = \frac{\text{cost of goods sold}}{\substack{\text{average inventory} \\ \text{(valued at cost)}}} = \frac{\$279,300}{\dfrac{\$45,500 + \$34,300}{2}}$$

$$= \frac{\$279,300}{\$39,900} = 7 \text{ times}$$

74. Calculate the debt to owner's equity ratio.

<u>2002</u>

$$\text{Debt to owner's equity ratio} = \frac{\text{total liabilities}}{\text{total owner's equity}} \quad \frac{\$87,000}{\$98,700}$$

$$= .88 : 1$$

<u>2003</u>

$$= \frac{\text{total liabilities}}{\text{total owner's equity}} \quad \frac{\$75,300}{\$65,300}$$

$$= 1.15 : 1$$

75. Calculate the debt to total assets.

<u>2002</u>

$$\text{Debt to total assets} = \frac{\text{total liabilities}}{\text{total assets}} = \frac{\$87,000}{\$185,700} = 46.8\%$$

<u>2003</u>

$$= \frac{\text{total liabilities}}{\text{total assets}} = \frac{\$75,300}{\$140,600} = 53.6\%$$

Word Problems

Use the following account balances for the Yirwomic Company to solve problems 76 and 77.(Round to the nearest hundred.)

Accounts receivable	$47,000
Accounts payable	32,000
Notes receivable	13,000
Notes payable	18,000
Merchandise inventory	30,000
Taxes payable	7,000
Prepaid insurance	1,000

76. Calculate the current ratio.

$$\text{Current ratio} = \frac{\text{current assets}}{\text{current liabilities}} = \frac{\$91,000}{\$57,000} = 1.60 : 1$$

77. Calculate the acid-test ratio for the Yirwomic Company.

$$\text{Acid-test ratio} = \frac{\text{quick assets}}{\text{current liabilities}} = \frac{\$60,000}{\$57,000} = 1.05 : 1$$

Use the following account balances for the Loo Corporation to solve problems 78 through 82:

Net income after taxes	$ 250,000
Common stock outstanding	200,000 shares
Net sales	$1,600,000
Total owner's equity	$1,400,000
Total liabilities	$ 700,000
Total assets	$2,100,000

78. Calculate the earnings per share.

$$\text{Earnings per share} = \frac{\text{net income after taxes}}{\text{common stock outstanding}} = \frac{\$250,000}{200,000} = \$1.25$$

79. Calculate the return on sales.

$$\text{Return on sales} = \frac{\text{net income after taxes}}{\text{net sales}} = \frac{\$250,000}{\$1,600,000} = 15.6\%$$

80. Calculate the return on equity.

$$\text{Return on equity} = \frac{\text{net income after taxes}}{\text{total owner's equity}} = \frac{\$250,000}{\$1,400,000} = 17.9\%$$

81. Calculate the debt to owner's equity.

$$\text{Debt to owner's equity ratio} = \frac{\text{total liabilities}}{\text{total owner's equity}} = \frac{\$700,000}{\$1,400,000}$$

$$= .50 : 1$$

82. Calculate the debt to total assets.

$$\text{Debt to total assets} = \frac{\text{total liabilities}}{\text{total assets}} = \frac{\$700,000}{\$2,100,000} = 33.3\%$$

83. Use the following account balances to calculate the inventory turnover ratio for the Grinder Shop:

Beginning Inventory (Jan. 2002)	$ 23,000
Purchases	275,000
Ending Inventory (Dec. 2002)	27,000

$$\text{Inventory turnover ratio} = \frac{\text{cost of goods sold}}{\substack{\text{average inventory} \\ \text{(valued at cost)}}} = \frac{\$271,000}{\dfrac{\$23,000 + \$27,000}{2}}$$

$$= \frac{\$271,000}{\$25,000} = 10.84 \text{ times}$$

84. Conduct a vertical analysis of accounts receivable given the following:

	2002	2003
Accounts receivable	$ 83,000	$ 90,000
Total assets	$450,000	$460,000

2002
$$\frac{\$83,000}{\$450,000} = 18.4\%$$

2003
$$\frac{\$90,000}{\$460,000} = 19.6\%$$

85. Conduct a vertical analysis of purchases given the following:

	2002	2003
Purchases	$212,000	$226,000
Net sales	$365,000	$370,000

2002
$$\frac{\$212,000}{\$365,000} = 58.1\%$$

2003
$$\frac{\$226,000}{\$370,000} = 61.1\%$$

86. Conduct a horizontal analysis of cash given the following:

	2002	2003
Cash	$44,000	$39,000

$$\frac{\$\ 44,000}{-\ 39,000}$$
$$(\$\ 5,000)\ \text{Decrease}$$

$$\frac{\$5,000}{\$44,000} = (11.4\%)\ \text{Decrease}$$

87. Conduct a horizontal analysis of advertising given the following:

	2002	2003
Advertising	$280,000	$320,000

$$\frac{\$\ 320,000}{-\ 280,000}$$
$$\$\ 40,000\ \text{Increase}$$

$$\frac{\$40,000}{\$280,000} = 14.3\%\ \text{Increase}$$

88. Two account balances from the Harcourt Bit Company's comparative balance sheet for December 31, 2002 and 2003 are (1) cash: 2002, $4,650; 2003, $5,895 and (2) accounts payable: 2002, $24,000; 2003, $18,000. Perform a horizontal analysis of these two account balances.

Cash

$$\frac{\$\ 5,895}{-\ 4,650}$$
$$\$\ 1,245\ \text{Increase}$$

$$\frac{\$1,245}{\$4,650} = 26.77\%\ \text{Increase}$$

Accounts payable

$$\frac{\$\ 24,000}{-\ 18,000)}$$
$$(\$\ 6,000\ \text{Decrease}$$

$$\frac{(\$6,000)}{\$24,000} = (25\%)\ \text{Decrease}$$

Use the following account balances for the Weinstein Corporation to solve problems 89 and 90. (Round to the nearest hundred.)

Accounts receivable	$222,000
Accounts payable	162,000
Notes receivable	55,000
Notes payable	18,000
Merchandise inventory	130,000
Taxes payable	23,500
Prepaid insurance	8,000

89. Calculate the current ratio.

$$\text{Current ratio} = \frac{\text{current assets}}{\text{current liabilities}} = \frac{\$415,000}{\$203,500} = 2.04:1$$

90. Calculate the acid-test ratio.

$$\text{Acid-test ratio} = \frac{\text{quick assets}}{\text{current liabilities}} = \frac{\$277,000}{\$203,500} = 1.36:1$$

Use the following account balances for the Nolan Manufacturing Company to solve problems 92 through 95. (Round to the nearest hundred.)

Net income after taxes	$ 60,000
Common stock outstanding	100,000 shares
Net sales	$600,000
Total owner's equity	$400,000
Total liabilities	$150,000
Total assets	$550,000

91. Calculate the earnings per share.

$$\text{Earnings per share} = \frac{\text{net income after taxes}}{\text{common stock outstanding}} = \frac{\$60,000}{100,000} = \$.60$$

92. Calculate the return on sales.

$$\text{Return on sales} = \frac{\text{net income after taxes}}{\text{net sales}} = \frac{\$60,000}{\$600,000} = 10\%$$

93. Calculate the return on equity.

$$\text{Return on equity} = \frac{\text{net income after taxes}}{\text{total owner's equity}} = \frac{\$60,000}{\$400,000} = 15\%$$

94. Calculate the debt to owner's equity.

$$\text{Debt to owner's equity ratio} = \frac{\text{total liabilities}}{\text{total owner's equity}} = \frac{\$150,000}{\$400,000} = .38:1$$

95. Calculate the debt to total assets.

$$\text{Debt to total assets} = \frac{\text{total liabilities}}{\text{total assets}} = \frac{\$150,000}{\$550,000} = 27.3\%$$

96. Use the following account balances to calculate the inventory turnover ratio for the Grinder Shop:

Beginning Inventory (Jan. 2002)	$ 65,000
Purchases	475,000
Ending Inventory (Dec. 2002)	55,000

$$\text{Inventory turnover ratio} = \frac{\text{cost of goods sold}}{\text{average inventory (valued at cost)}} = \frac{\$485,000}{\frac{\$65,000 + \$55,000}{2}}$$

$$= \frac{\$485,000}{\$60,000} = 8.08\ \text{times}$$

97. From the following, prepare a partial comparative income statement for Smith Hardware and analyze it both vertically and horizontally:

	2002	2003
Net sales	$650,000	$600,000
Net profit	80,000	75,000
Gross margin	360,000	350,000
Sales returns	20,000	70,000

SMITH HARDWARE
Comparative Income Statement
For the Years Ending December 31, 2002 and 2003

	VERTICAL ANALYSIS				HORIZONTAL ANALYSIS Increase or (Decrease)	
	2002		2003			
	Amount	%	Amount	%	Amount	%
Gross sales	$670,000	103.1%	$670,000	111.7%	$ 0	0 %
Sales returns	20,000	3.1%	70,000	11.7%	50,000	250.0%
Net sales	$650,000	100.0%	$600,000	100.0%	$ (50,000)	(7.7)%
Cost of goods sold	290,000	44.6%	250,000	41.7%	(40,000)	(13.8)%
Gross margin	$360,000	55.4%	$350,000	58.3%	$ (10,000)	(2.8)%
Operating expenses	280,000	43.1%	275,000	45.8%	(5,000)	(1.8)%
Net profit	$ 80,000	12.3%	$ 75,000	12.5%	$ (5,000)	(6.3)%

CRITICAL THINKING GROUP PROJECT

Use the following income statement and balance sheet to solve all of the project problems:

YVONNE'S GIFTS
Comparative Income Statement
For the Years Ending December 31, 2002 and 2003

	VERTICAL ANALYSIS				HORIZONTAL ANALYSIS Increase or (Decrease)	
	2002		2003			
	Amount	%	Amount	%	Amount	%
Sales	$371,000	%	$398,000	%	$	%
Sales returns	7,000	%	8,000	%		%
Net sales	$364,000	%	$390,000	%		%
Cost of goods sold						
Inventory, 1/1	$ 11,000	%	$ 12,000	%		%
Purchases	170,000	%	175,000	%		%
Freight-in	5,500	%	6,000	%		%
Goods available for sale	$186,500	%	$193,000	%		%
Inventory, 12/31	12,000	%	15,000	%		%
Cost of goods sold	$174,500	%	$178,000	%		%
Gross Income	$189,500	%	$212,000	%		%
Operating expenses						
Salaries	$ 40,000	%	$ 45,000	%		%
Advertising	22,500	%	20,000	%		%
Depreciation	18,000	%	16,000	%		%
Supplies	10,000	%	12,000	%		%
Total operating expenses	$ 90,500	%	$ 93,000	%		%
Net income before taxes	$ 99,000	%	$119,000	%		%
Taxes	33,000	%	39,000	%		%
Net income after taxes	$ 66,000	%	$ 80,000	%		%

YVONNE'S GIFTS
Comparative Balance Sheet
December 31, 2002 and 2003

| | VERTICAL ANALYSIS | | | | HORIZONTAL ANALYSIS Increase or (Decrease) | |
| | 2002 | | 2003 | | | |
	Amount	%	Amount	%	Amount	%
Current assets						
Cash	$ 42,000	%	$ 60,000	%	$	%
Accounts receivable	144,000	%	165,000	%		%
Notes receivable	24,000	%	22,500	%		%
Inventory	54,000	%	82,500	%		%
Prepaid expenses	6,000	%	10,500	%		%
Total	$270,000	%	$340,500	%		%
Plant assets						
Land	$180,000	%	$200,000	%		%
Building	112,500	%	100,000	%		%
Furniture	30,000	%	28,000	%		%
Equipment	82,500	%	90,500	%		%
Total	$405,000	%	$418,500	%		%
Intangible assets						
Goodwill	$ 39,000	%	$ 50,000	%		
Trademark	16,000	%	15,000	%		%
Total	$ 55,000	%	$ 65,000	%		%
Total assets	$730,000	%	$824,000	%		%
Current liabilities						
Accounts payable	$ 31,000	%	$ 25,000	%		%
Notes payable	7,000	%	5,000	%		%
Taxes payable	14,000	%	19,500	%		%
Payroll payable	89,000	%	95,000	%		%
Total	$141,000	%	$144,500	%		%
Long-term liabilities						
Bonds payable	$125,000	%	$150,000	%		%
Mortgage payable	55,000	%	54,000	%		%
Total	$180,000	%	$204,000	%		%
Total liabilities	$321,000	%	$348,500	%		%
Owner's equity						
Common stock	$250,000	%	$250,000	%		%
Retained earnings	159,000	%	225,500	%		%
Total	$409,000	%	$475,500	%		%
Total liabilities and equities	$730,000	%	$824,000	%		%

1. Conduct a vertical analysis of the income statement. (See item 2 for answer.)

2. Conduct a horizontal analysis of the income statement.

YVONNE'S GIFTS
Comparative Income Statement
For the Years Ending
December 31, 2002 and 2003

| VERTICAL ANALYSIS | | HORIZONTAL ANALYSIS | |
2002 %	2003 %	Increase or (Decrease) Amount	%
101.9%	102.1%	$27,000	7.3%
1.9%	2.1%	1,000	14.3%
100.0%	100.0%	$26,000	7.1%
3.0%	3.1%	1,000	9.1%
46.7%	44.9%	5,000	2.9%
1.5%	1.5%	500	9.1%
51.2%	49.5%	$ 6,500	3.5%
3.3%	3.8%	3,000	25.0%
47.9%	45.6%	3,500	2.0%
52.1%	54.4%	$22,500	11.9%
11.0%	11.5%	$ 5,000	12.5%
6.2%	5.1%	(2,500)	(11.1%)
4.9%	4.1%	(2,000)	(11.1%)
2.7%	3.1%	2,000	20.0%
24.9%	23.8%	$ 2,500	27.6%
27.2%	30.5%	$20,000	20.2%
9.1%	10.0%	6,000	18.2%
18.1%	20.5%	$14,000	21.2%

3. Conduct a vertical analysis of the balance sheet. (See items 4 for answer.)

4. Conduct a horizontal analysis of the balance sheet.

YVONNE'S GIFTS
Comparative Balance Sheet
December 31, 2002 and 2003

| VERTICAL ANALYSIS | | HORIZONTAL ANALYSIS | |
2002 %	2003 %	(Decrease) Amount	%
5.8%	7.3%	$18,000	42.9%
19.7%	20.0%	21,000	14.6%
3.3%	2.7%	(1,500)	(6.3%)
7.4%	10.0%	28,500	52.8%
.8%	1.3%	4,500	75.0%
37.0%	41.3%	$70,500	26.1%
24.7%	24.3%	$20,000	11.1%
14.4%	12.1%	(12,500)	(11.1%)
4.1%	3.4%	(2,000)	(6.7%)
11.3%	11.0%	8,000	9.7%
55.5%	50.8%	$13,500	3.3%
5.3%	6.1%	$11,000	28.2%
2.2%	1.8%	(1,000)	(6.3%)
7.5%	7.9%	$10,000	18.2%
100.0%	100.0%	$47,000	8.5%
4.2%	3.0%	$(6,000)	(19.4%)
1.0%	.6%	(2,000)	(28.6%)
1.9%	2.4%	5,500	39.3%
12.2%	11.5%	6,000	6.7%
19.3%	17.5%	$ 3,500	2.5%
17.1%	18.2%	$25,000	20.0%
7.5%	6.6%	(1,000)	(1.8%)
24.7%	24.8%	$24,000	13.3%
44.0%	42.3%	$27,500	8.6%
34.2%	30.3%	$ 0	0%
21.8%	27.4%	$66,500	41.8%
56.0%	57.7%	$66,500	16.3%
100.0%	100.0%	$47,000	8.5%

5. Calculate the current ratio for 2002 and 2003.

2002
$$\text{Current ratio} = \frac{\text{current assets}}{\text{current liabilities}} = \frac{\$270,000}{\$141,000} = 1.91:1$$

2003
$$\text{Current ratio} = \frac{\text{current assets}}{\text{current liabilities}} = \frac{\$340,500}{\$144,500} = 2.36:1$$

6. Calculate the acid-test ratio.

2002

$$\text{Acid-test ratio} = \frac{\text{quick assets}}{\text{current liabilities}} = \frac{\$210,000}{\$141,000} = 1.49:1$$

2003

$$\text{Acid-test ratio} = \frac{\text{quick assets}}{\text{current liabilities}} = \frac{\$247,500}{\$144,500} = 1.71:1$$

7. Calculate the earnings per share (250,000 shares).

2002

$$\text{Earnings per share} = \frac{\text{net income after taxes}}{\text{common stock outstanding}} = \frac{\$66,000}{250,000} = \$.26$$

2003

$$\text{Earnings per share} = \frac{\text{net income after taxes}}{\text{common stock outstanding}} = \frac{\$80,000}{250,000} = \$.32$$

8. Calculate the return on sales.

2002

$$\text{Return on sales} = \frac{\text{net income after taxes}}{\text{net sales}} = \frac{\$66,000}{\$364,000} = 18.1\%$$

2003

$$\text{Return on sales} = \frac{\text{net income after taxes}}{\text{net sales}} = \frac{\$80,000}{\$390,000} = 20.5\%$$

9. Calculate the return on equity.

2002

$$\text{Return on equity} = \frac{\text{net income after taxes}}{\text{total owner's equity}} = \frac{\$66,000}{\$409,000} = 16.1\%$$

2003

$$\text{Return on equity} = \frac{\text{net income after taxes}}{\text{total owner's equity}} = \frac{\$80,000}{\$475,500} = 16.8$$

10. Calculate the inventory turnover ratio.

2002

$$\text{Inventory turnover ratio} = \frac{\text{cost of goods sold}}{\substack{\text{average inventory}\\ \text{(valued at cost)}}} = \frac{\$174,500}{\frac{\$11,000 + \$12,000}{2}}$$

$$= \frac{\$174,500}{\$11,500} = 15.17 \text{ times}$$

2003

$$\text{Inventory turnover ratio} = \frac{\text{cost of goods sold}}{\substack{\text{average inventory}\\ \text{(valued at cost)}}} = \frac{\$178,000}{\frac{\$12,000 + \$15,000}{2}}$$

$$= \frac{\$178,000}{\$13,500} = 13.19 \text{ times}$$

11. Calculate the debt to owner's equity ratio.

2002

$$\text{Debt to owner's equity ratio} = \frac{\text{total liabilities}}{\text{total owner's equity}} = \frac{\$321,000}{\$409,000}$$
$$= .78:1$$

2003

$$\text{Debt to owner's equity ratio} = \frac{\text{total liabilities}}{\text{total owner's equity}} = \frac{\$348,500}{\$475,500}$$
$$= .73:1$$

12. Calculate the debt to total assets.

2002

$$\text{Debt to total assets} = \frac{\text{total liabilities}}{\text{total assets}} = \frac{\$321,000}{\$730,000} = 44.0\%$$

2003

$$\text{Debt to total assets} = \frac{\text{total liabilities}}{\text{total assets}} = \frac{\$348,500}{\$824,000} = 42.3\%$$

13. Based on your analysis of the income statement and the balance sheet, would you be willing to make a $100,000 loan to Yvonne's Gifts? Why or why not?

Student answers will vary, but they should be logically argued based on the analysis presented in problems 1 through 12.

14. Based on your analysis of the income statement and the balance sheet, would you be willing to buy shares of common stock in Yvonne's Gifts?

Student answers will vary, but they should be logically argued based on the analysis presented in problems 1 through 12.

15. Based on your analysis of the income statement and the balance sheet, would you be willing to buy bonds issued by Yvonne's Gifts?

Student answers will vary, but they should be logically argued based on the analysis presented in problems 1 through 12.

SELF-TESTING EXERCISES

Answers to all exercises are given in Appendix A.

1. Why are financial statements analyzed? **W**

Financial statement analysis provides management with information necessary to determine areas of deficiency that need correction before problems become too critical. In addition, it provides other interested parties with needed information to make funding, investing, lending, or taxing decisions.

2. Which financial ratio described in this chapter would be calculated by performing a vertical analysis of the balance sheet? Which ratio would be calculated by a vertical analysis of the income statement? What is the purpose of these two ratios? **W**

The debt to total assets ratio would be calculated as a result of a vertical analysis of the balance sheet. Its purpose is to measure the extent to which the assets are financed by borrowed funds.

The return on sales ratio would be calculated as a result of a vertical analysis of the income statement. Its purpose is to measure company profitability.

Use the following balance sheet and income statement for Dennis Drugs to answer all of the questions that follow:

DENNIS DRUGS
Comparative Income Statement
For the Years Ending December 31, 2002 and 2003

| | VERTICAL ANALYSIS | | | | HORIZONTAL ANALYSIS Increase or (Decrease) | |
| | 2002 | | 2003 | | | |
	Amount	%	Amount	%	Amount	%
Sales	$275,000	101.9%	$295,000	102.1%	$20,000	7.3%
Sales returns	5,000	1.9%	6,000	2.1%	1,000	20 %
Net sales	$270,000	100.0%	$289,000	100.0%	$19,000	7.0%
Cost of goods sold						
Inventory, 1/1	$ 8,000	3.0%	$ 9,000	3.1%	$ 1,000	12.5%
Purchases	126,500	46.9%	130,000	45.0%	3,500	2.8%
Freight-in	4,000	1.5%	5,000	1.7%	1,000	25 %
Goods available for sale	$138,500	51.3%	$144,000	49.8%	$ 5,500	2.7%
Inventory, 12/31	9,000	3.3%	11,000	3.8%	2,000	22.2%
Cost of goods sold	$129,500	48.0%	$133,000	46.0%	$ 3,500	2.7%
Gross income	$140,500	52.0%	$156,000	54.0%	$15,500	11.0%
Operating expenses						
Salaries	$ 44,500	16.5%	$ 50,000	17.3%	$ 5,500	12.4%
Advertising	25,000	9.3%	22,000	7.6%	3,000	12 %
Depreciation	20,000	7.4%	18,000	6.2%	2,000	10 %
Supplies	11,000	4.1%	13,000	4.5%	2,000	18.2%
Total operating expenses	$100,500	37.2%	$103,000	35.6%	$ 2,500	2.5%
Net income before taxes	$ 40,000	14.8%	$ 53,000	18.3%	$13,000	32.5%
Taxes	12,000	4.4%	18,000	6.2%	6,000	50 %
Net income after taxes	$ 28,000	10.4%	$ 35,000	12.1%	$ 7,000	25 %

3. Conduct a vertical analysis of the income statement.
4. Conduct a horizontal analysis of the income statement.

DENNIS DRUGS
Comparative Balance Sheet
December 31, 2002 and 2003

	VERTICAL ANALYSIS				HORIZONTAL ANALYSIS Increase or (Decrease)	
	2002		2003			
	Amount	%	Amount	%	Amount	%
Current assets						
Cash	$ 7,000	2.0%	$ 8,000	2.2%	$ 1,000	14.3%
Accounts receivable	24,000	6.7%	22,000	5.9%	(2,000)	(8.3)%
Notes receivable	4,000	1.1%	3,000	.8%	(1,000)	(25)%
Inventory	9,000	2.5%	11,000	3.0%	2,000	22.2%
Prepaid expenses	1,000	.3%	1,500	.4%	500	50 %
Total	$ 45,000	12.6%	$ 45,500	12.3%	$ 500	1.1%
Plant assets						
Land	$120,000	33.6%	$120,000	32.4%	$ 0	0 %
Building	75,000	21.0%	70,000	18.9%	(5,000)	(6.7)%
Furniture	20,000	5.6%	28,000	7.6%	8,000	40%
Equipment	55,000	15.4%	60,000	16.2%	5,000	9.1%
Total	$270,000	75.6%	$278,000	75.0%	$ 8,000	3.0%
Intangible assets						
Goodwill	$ 30,000	8.4%	$ 35,000	9.4%	$ 5,000	16.7%
Trademark	12,000	3.4%	12,000	3.2%	0	0%
Total	$ 42,000	11.8%	$ 47,000	12.7%	$ 5,000	11.9%
Total assets	$357,000	100.0%	$370,500	100.0%	$13,500	3.8%
Current liabilities						
Accounts payable	$ 19,000	5.3%	$ 23,000	6.2%	$ 4,000	21.1%
Notes payable	4,000	1.1%	5,000	1.3%	1,000	25 %
Taxes payable	8,000	2.2%	9,500	2.6%	1,500	18.8%
Payroll payable	48,000	13.4%	45,000	12.1%	(3,000)	(6.3)%
Total	$ 79,000	22.1%	$ 82,500	22.3%	$ 3,500	4.4%
Long-term liabilities						
Bonds payable	$ 50,000	14.0%	$ 50,000	13.5%	$ 0	0 %
Mortgage payable	22,000	6.2%	18,000	4.9%	(4,000)	(18.2)%
Total	$ 72,000	20.2%	$ 68,000	18.4%	(4,000)	(5.6)%
Total liabilities	$151,000	42.3%	$150,500	40.6%	$ (500)	(.3)%
Owner's equity						
Common stock	$150,000	42.0%	$150,000	40.5%	$ 0	0 %
Retained earnings	56,000	15.7%	70,000	18.9%	14,000	25 %
Total	$206,000	57.7%	$220,000	59.4%	$14,000	6.8%
Total liabilities and owner's equity	$357,000	100.0%	$370,500	100.0%	$13,500	3.8%

5. Conduct a vertical analysis of the balance sheet.
6. Conduct a horizontal analysis of the balance sheet.
7. Calculate the current ratio for 2002 and 2003.

$$\underline{2002}$$

$$\text{Current ratio} = \frac{\text{current assets}}{\text{current liabilities}} = \frac{\$45,000}{\$79,000} = .57:1 \qquad \underline{2003} \qquad \text{Current ratio} = \frac{\text{current assets}}{\text{current liabilities}} = \frac{\$45,500}{\$82,500} = .55:1$$

8. Calculate the acid test ratio.

$$\underline{2002}$$

$$\text{Acid-test ratio} = \frac{\text{quick assets}}{\text{current liabilities}} = \frac{\$35,000}{\$79,000} = .44:1 \qquad \underline{2003} \qquad \text{Acid-test ratio} = \frac{\text{quick assets}}{\text{current liabilities}} = \frac{\$33,000}{\$82,500} = .40:1$$

9. Calculate the earnings per share (150,000 shares).

<u>2002</u>

$$\text{Earnings per share} = \frac{\text{net income after taxes}}{\text{common stock outstanding}} = \frac{\$28,000}{150,000} = \$.19$$

<u>2003</u>

$$\text{Earnings per share} = \frac{\text{net income after taxes}}{\text{common stock outstanding}} = \frac{\$45,000}{150,000} = \$.30$$

10. Calculate the return on sales.

<u>2002</u>

$$\text{Return on sales} = \frac{\text{net income after taxes}}{\text{net sales}} = \frac{\$28,000}{\$270,000} = 10.4\%$$

<u>2003</u>

$$\text{Return on sales} = \frac{\text{net income after taxes}}{\text{net sales}} = \frac{\$35,000}{\$289,000} = 12.1\%$$

11. Calculate the return on equity.

<u>2002</u>

$$\text{Return on equity} = \frac{\text{net income after taxes}}{\text{total owner's equity}} = \frac{\$35,000}{\$206,000} = 13.6\%$$

<u>2003</u>

$$\text{Return on equity} = \frac{\text{net income after taxes}}{\text{total owner's equity}} = \frac{\$35,000}{\$220,000} = 15.9\%$$

12. Calculate the inventory turnover ratio.

<u>2002</u>

$$\text{Inventory turnover ratio} = \frac{\text{cost of goods sold}}{\substack{\text{average inventory} \\ \text{(valued at cost)}}} = \frac{\$129,500}{\frac{\$8,000 + \$9,000}{2}}$$

$$= \frac{\$129,500}{\$8,500} = 15.24 \text{ times}$$

<u>2003</u>

$$\text{Inventory turnover ratio} = \frac{\text{cost of goods sold}}{\substack{\text{average inventory} \\ \text{(valued at cost)}}} = \frac{\$133,000}{\frac{\$9,000 + \$11,000}{2}}$$

$$= \frac{\$133,000}{\$10.000} = 13.3 \text{ times}$$

13. Calculate the debt to owner's equity ratio.

<u>2002</u>

$$\text{Debt to owner's equity ratio} = \frac{\text{total liabilities}}{\text{total owner's equity}} = \frac{\$151,000}{\$206,000}$$
$$= .73 : 1$$

<u>2003</u>

$$\text{Debt to owner's equity ratio} = \frac{\text{total liabilities}}{\text{total owner's equity}} = \frac{\$150,500}{\$220,000}$$
$$= .68 : 1$$

14. Calculate the debt to total assets.

<u>2002</u>

$$\text{Debt to total assets} = \frac{\text{total liabilities}}{\text{total assets}} = \frac{\$151,000}{\$357,000} = 42.3\%$$

<u>2003</u>

$$\text{Debt to total assets} = \frac{\text{total liabilities}}{\text{total assets}} = \frac{\$150,500}{\$370,500} = 40.6\%$$

APPLICATION 1

The Springfield Department Store has designed a spreadsheet to perform vertical and horizontal analyses on its comparative balance sheets. Enter the data for the comparative balance sheet into form Ch16App1 shown here:

Springfield Department Store

2617 Main Street
Box 219
Springfield, Maryland 58109
Telephone: 301-555-2158   FAX: 301-555-3498

BALANCE SHEET ANALYSIS

COMPARATIVE BALANCE SHEET DECEMBER 31, 2002 AND 2003

| | VERTICAL ANALYSIS | | | | HORIZONTAL ANLYS | |
| | 2002 | | 2003 | | Increase (Decrease) | |
	Amount	%	Amount	%	Amount	%
ASSETS						
Current assets						
Cash		#DIV/0!		#DIV/0!	$0	#DIV/0!
Accounts receivable		#DIV/0!		#DIV/0!	$0	#DIV/0!
Merchandise inventory		#DIV/0!		#DIV/0!	$0	#DIV/0!
Total current assets	$0	#DIV/0!	$0	#DIV/0!	$0	#DIV/0!
Plant & equipment						
Land		#DIV/0!		#DIV/0!	$0	#DIV/0!
Buildings		#DIV/0!		#DIV/0!	$0	#DIV/0!
Furniture & fixtures		#DIV/0!		#DIV/0!	$0	#DIV/0!
Equipment		#DIV/0!		#DIV/0!	$0	#DIV/0!
Total plant & equipment	$0	#DIV/0!	$0	#DIV/0!	$0	#DIV/0!
Intangible assets						
Goodwill		#DIV/0!		#DIV/0!	$0	#DIV/0!
Trademark		#DIV/0!		#DIV/0!	$0	#DIV/0!
Total intangible assets	$0	#DIV/0!	$0	#DIV/0!	$0	#DIV/0!
TOTAL ASSETS	$0	#DIV/0!	$0	#DIV/0!	$0	#DIV/0!
LIABILITIES & OWNER'S EQUITY						
LIABILITIES						
Current liabilities						
Accounts payable		#DIV/0!		#DIV/0!	$0	#DIV/0!
Notes payable		#DIV/0!		#DIV/0!	$0	#DIV/0!
Taxes payable		#DIV/0!		#DIV/0!	$0	#DIV/0!
Salaries payable		#DIV/0!		#DIV/0!	$0	#DIV/0!
Total current liabilities	$0	#DIV/0!	$0	#DIV/0!	$0	#DIV/0!
Long-term liabilities						
Bonds, due 2013		#DIV/0!		#DIV/0!	$0	#DIV/0!
Mortgage		#DIV/0!		#DIV/0!	$0	#DIV/0!
Total long-term liabilities	$0	#DIV/0!	$0	#DIV/0!	$0	#DIV/0!
TOTAL LIABILITIES	$0	#DIV/0!	$0	#DIV/0!	$0	#DIV/0!
OWNER'S EQUITY						
Common stock		#DIV/0!		#DIV/0!	$0	#DIV/0!
Preferred stock		#DIV/0!		#DIV/0!	$0	#DIV/0!
Retained earnings		#DIV/0!		#DIV/0!	$0	#DIV/0!
Total owner's equity	$0	#DIV/0!	$0	#DIV/0!	$0	#DIV/0!
TOTAL LIABILITIES & OWNER'S EQUITY	$0	#DIV/0!	$0	#DIV/0!	$0	#DIV/0!

Enter the following information:

Cell	Amount	Cell	Amount	Cell	Amount	Cell	Amount
B16	$ 17,020	B23	$178,950	B36	$ 36,190	B43	$620,000
B17	$169,245	B24	$ 88,325	B37	$ 77,500	B47	$650,000
B18	$223,903	B27	$500,000	B38	$ 53,213	B48	$225,000
B21	$195,000	B28	$125,000	B41	$400,000	B49	$293,637
B22	$535,000	B35	$ 76,903	B42	$220,000		

Cell	Amount	Cell	Amount	Cell	Amount	Cell	Amount
D16	$ 20,385	D23	$193,200	D36	$ 30,985	D43	$585,000
D17	$172,004	D24	$ 93,163	D37	$ 69,290	D47	$650,000
D18	$235,982	D27	$500,000	D38	$ 58,209	D48	$225,000
D21	$195,000	D28	$125,000	D41	$400,000	D49	$335,758
D22	$493,000	D35	$ 73,492	D42	$185,000		

Answer the following questions after you have completed the spreadsheet:

1. What is the percent of equipment to total assets in both 2002 and 2003?
2. What is the amount of change and the percent of increase (or decrease) for accounts receivable?
3. What is the percent of taxes payable to total assets in both 2002 and 2003?
4. What is the amount of change and the percent of increase (or decrease) for retained earnings?
5. What is the amount of change and the percent of increase (or decrease) for total plant and equipment?
6. What is the percent of accounts payable to total assets in both 2002 and 2003?
7. What is the percent of accounts receivable to total assets in both 2002 and 2003?
8. What is the amount of change and the percent of increase (or decrease) for salaries payable?

GROUP REPORT

FOR CHAPTER 16 APPLICATION 1

Write a report to the chief financial officer (CFO) describing the results of the analyses performed on the balance sheet. Point out the areas or specific accounts that would require further analysis to head off any potential financial crises. Make any recommendations in which your group believes the CFO should be interested.

APPLICATION 2

The Springfield Department Store also has designed a spreadsheet to perform vertical and horizontal analyses on its comparative income statements. Enter the data for the comparative income statement into form Ch16App2 shown here:

Springfield Department Store

2617 Main Street
Box 219
Springfield, Maryland 58109
Telephone: 301-555-2158   FAX: 301-555-3498

INCOME STATEMENT ANALYSIS

COMPARATIVE INCOME STATEMENTS FOR 2002 AND 2003

| | VERTICAL ANALYSIS | | | | HORIZONTAL ANALYSIS | |
| | 2002 | | 2003 | | Increase (Decrease) | |
	Amount	%	Amount	%	Amount	%
Gross sales		#DIV/0!		#DIV/0!	$0	#DIV/0!
Sales returns		#DIV/0!		#DIV/0!	$0	#DIV/0!
Sales allowances		#DIV/0!		#DIV/0!	$0	#DIV/0!
Net sales	$0	#DIV/0!	$0	#DIV/0!	$0	#DIV/0!
Cost of goods sold						
Inventory, January 1		#DIV/0!		#DIV/0!	$0	#DIV/0!
Purchases		#DIV/0!		#DIV/0!	$0	#DIV/0!
Goods available for sale	$0	#DIV/0!	$0	#DIV/0!	$0	#DIV/0!
Inventory, December 31		#DIV/0!		#DIV/0!	$0	#DIV/0!
Cost of goods sold	$0	#DIV/0!	$0	#DIV/0!	$0	#DIV/0!
Gross profit	$0	#DIV/0!	$0	#DIV/0!	$0	#DIV/0!
Operating expenses						
Administrative salaries		#DIV/0!		#DIV/0!	$0	#DIV/0!
Wages		#DIV/0!		#DIV/0!	$0	#DIV/0!
Rent		#DIV/0!		#DIV/0!	$0	#DIV/0!
Advertising		#DIV/0!		#DIV/0!	$0	#DIV/0!
Utilities		#DIV/0!		#DIV/0!	$0	#DIV/0!
Taxes, payroll		#DIV/0!		#DIV/0!	$0	#DIV/0!
Depreciation		#DIV/0!		#DIV/0!	$0	#DIV/0!
Insurance		#DIV/0!		#DIV/0!	$0	#DIV/0!
Office supplies		#DIV/0!		#DIV/0!	$0	#DIV/0!
Miscellaneous expenses		#DIV/0!		#DIV/0!	$0	#DIV/0!
Total operating expenses	$0	#DIV/0!	$0	#DIV/0!	$0	#DIV/0!
Net profit before taxes	$0	#DIV/0!	$0	#DIV/0!	$0	#DIV/0!
Corporate income tax		#DIV/0!		#DIV/0!	$0	#DIV/0!
Net profit after taxes	**$0**	**#DIV/0!**	**$0**	**#DIV/0!**	**$0**	**#DIV/0!**

Enter the following information:

Cell	Amount	Cell	Amount	Cell	Amount	Cell	Amount
B14	$11,985,766	B22	$ 223,903	B30	$173,048	B35	$ 45,928
B15	$ 214,466	B26	$ 669,720	B31	$192,938	B38	$186,083
B16	$ 155,986	B27	$1,885,000	B32	$373,829		
B19	$ 216,984	B28	$ 125,000	B33	$ 25,906		
B20	$ 6,861,739	B29	$ 735,000	B34	$128,045		

Cell	Amount	Cell	Amount	Cell	Amount	Cell	Amount
D14	$12,439,085	D22	$ 235,982	D30	$167,093	D35	$ 51,124
D15	$ 227,739	D26	$ 690,433	D31	$221,604	D38	$180,950
D16	$ 134,876	D27	$2,147,886	D32	$318,375		
D19	$ 223,903	D28	$ 125,000	D33	$ 29,567		
D20	$ 6,998,145	D29	$ 813,512	D34	$124,486		

Answer the following questions after you have completed the spreadsheet:

1. What is the percent of purchases to net sales in both 2002 and 2003?
2. What is the amount of change and the percent of increase (or decrease) for sales returns?
3. What is the percent of advertising to net sales in both 2002 and 2003?
4. What is the amount of change and the percent of increase (or decrease) for insurance?
5. What is the amount of change and the percent of increase (or decrease) for gross profit?
6. What is the percent of total operating expenses to net sales in both 2002 and 2003?
7. What is the percent of net profit after taxes to net sales in both 2002 and 2003?
8. What is the amount of change and the percent of increase (or decrease) for wages?

GROUP REPORT

FOR CHAPTER 16 APPLICATION 2

Your group will use the information from the spreadsheet to prepare a report to the chief financial officer (CFO). Discuss the results of both the vertical and horizontal analyses. Make any recommendations that would be helpful to the CFO.

17

ACCOUNTING APPLICATIONS
DEPRECIATION

HONESTY MAY BE THE BEST POLICY FOR PROFIT

U.S. West, Inc., is a giant Colorado-based Bell holding communications company serving 25 million customers in 14 western states. A few years ago management became fed up with what amounted to reporting phony earnings. The company substituted shorter depreciation schedules on its Security and Exchange Commission statements.

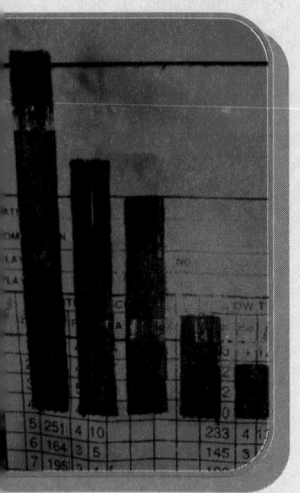

In one fell swoop U.S. West had reduced the number of years for depreciation by 43%. The move caused a $5.4 billion pretax charge against the company's earnings (about $7.45 loss per share). So impressed were stock market investors with the company's honesty, they began bidding up U.S. West's stock. In the first day it rose 4%. Since the new schedules better represented U.S. West's real finances, Wall Street rewarded the company's integrity. The accounting change actually added 23 cents per share to the company's yearly earnings, which amounted to $2.95 per share.

U.S. West must still use the old schedules in its regulatory filings, but in the markets, the company showed that honesty is not only the best ethical policy. It may also be the most profitable policy.

Chapter Glossary

Depreciation. The process of allocating the cost of plant and equipment assets as an expense to those periods during which the asset contributes to the revenue-producing process.

Straight-line depreciation. A depreciation method in which it is assumed that the asset loses an equal amount of value during each year of its estimated usable life.

Original Cost. The amount paid for an asset plus any freight or installation costs that are incurred.

Resale value. The residual, salvage, or trade-in value of a plant and equipment asset at the end of its usable life.

Usable life. The estimated number of years or production units a plant and equipment asset will be used and depreciated.

Sum-of-the-years'-digits depreciation. An accelerated method in which depreciation is allocated each year on a fractional basis in which the denominator is the sum of the years of the asset's estimated usable life.

Units-of-production depreciation. A method that bases depreciation on the amount of production in each year of the asset's estimated total usable life.

Declining-balance depreciation. An accelerated depreciation method in which a constant percent is multiplied by the declining book value.

Book value. The value of an asset after accumulated depreciation has been deducted.

Modified accelerated cost recovery system (MACRS). An accelerated depreciation method using IRS schedules for tax reporting.

Student Objectives

Upon completion of this chapter, you should be able to:

1. Calculate depreciation using the straight-line method.
2. Calculate partial-year depreciation using the straight-line method.
3. Calculate depreciation using the sum-of-the-years'-digits method.
4. Calculate depreciation using the units-of-production method.
5. Calculate depreciation using the declining-balance method.
6. Calculate depreciation using the modified accelerated cost recovery system (MACRS).

$\boxed{\text{M}}$ost business assets do not keep their original worth. Just as clothing or a personal car wears out or becomes less useful because of style or technological improvements, so do equipment and buildings.

Current expenses, those that are expected to be incurred in one year or less, are deducted by a business firm from its total revenue to determine total profit and for tax purposes. Plant and equipment assets, those that last more than one year, have their estimated decline in value allocated over their expected life. The amount deducted, or written off, each year is called **depreciation**. Since nobody knows for certain how long an asset will be productive or how much money can be realized by selling or trading in a used asset, the amount of depreciation taken is an estimate.

Today, depreciation for financial accounting is usually accounted for differently from tax accounting purposes.

LEARNING UNIT 1
DEPRECIATION FOR FINANCIAL ACCOUNTING

Several methods are used for financial accounting. The most common are the straight-line, sum-of-the-years'-digits, units-of-production, and declining-balance methods.

17.1 Straight-Line Depreciation

Straight-line depreciation is the easiest and most commonly used depreciation method. Using the method requires knowing the following:

1. *Original cost.* The amount paid for an asset plus any freight or installation costs that are incurred.
2. *Resale Value.* The estimated amount for which the asset can be sold at the end of its usable life (also called *salvage value, trade-in value, residual value,* or *scrap value*).
3. *Usable life.* The estimated number of years an asset will be used and depreciated.

To find the amount of yearly depreciation using the straight-line method, use the formula

$$\text{Yearly depreciation} = \frac{\text{cost} - \text{resale value}}{\text{usable life}}.$$

EXAMPLE   Using the straight-line method, find the yearly depreciation expense for a $3,500 power saw that is expected to be in service for five years and have a $500 resale value.

Solution

$$\text{Yearly depreciation} = \frac{\text{cost} - \text{resale value}}{\text{usable life}}.$$

$$= \frac{\$3,500 - \$500}{5}$$

$$= \frac{\$3,000}{5} = \$600$$

3,500 ⊟ 500 ÷ 5 ⊜ 600

1. Idlefast, Inc., bought a truck for $24,800 plus $284 freight. Company records indicate that trucks of this type last an average of three years and can be traded in for $1,600. Determine the yearly amount of depreciation using the straight-line method.

2. Wilson Plate Glass purchased a stamping machine for $8,595. When the machine arrived, Wilson had to pay $215 freight. Installation and preparation costs were $75. If the machine is expected to be used for 12 years and have a junk value of $1,250, find the yearly depreciation using the straight-line method.

3. Tarrant Bank bought a new computer for $7,000. Delivery cost was $40, and installation was $260. Experience indicates that the equipment will last 10 years and can be sold for $250. Find the yearly depreciation using the straight-line method.

4. Goodwrench Garage purchased a hydraulic lift for $6,500. Installment costs were $2,500. It is expected to last eight years and have a junk value of $200. Find the yearly depreciation using the straight-line method.

17.1 Solutions to Practice Problems

1. $24,800 + 284 = $25,084$ Cost

$$\text{Yearly depreciation} = \frac{\text{cost} - \text{resale value}}{\text{usable life}}.$$

$$= \frac{\$25,084 - 1,600}{3}$$

$$= \frac{\$23,484}{3} = \$7,828$$

2. $8,595 + 215 + 75 = $8,885$ Cost

$$\text{Yearly depreciation} = \frac{\text{cost} - \text{resale value}}{\text{usable life}}$$

$$= \frac{\$8,885 - 1,250}{12}$$

$$= \frac{\$7,635}{12} = \$636.25$$

3. $7,000 + 40 + 260 = $7,300$ Cost

$$\text{Yearly depreciation} = \frac{\text{cost} - \text{resale value}}{\text{usable life}}$$

$$= \frac{\$7,300 - 250}{10}$$

$$= \frac{\$7,050}{10} = \$705$$

4. $6,500 + 2,500 = $9,000$ Cost

$$\text{Yearly depreciation} = \frac{\text{cost} - \text{resale value}}{\text{usable life}}$$

$$= \frac{\$9,000 - 200}{8}$$

$$= \frac{\$8,800}{8} = \$1,100$$

17.2 Partial-Year Depreciation Using the Straight-Line Method

In most coverage of the subject of depreciation it is assumed that assets are purchased at the beginning of the accounting year, but that is rarely the case. Most assets must be depreciated for a part of the first year and for a part of the last accounting year of their usable life. See the Excel Spreadsheet Application 1 at the end of this chapter for an example of the use of a partial-year depreciation using each depreciation method. The one exception to using partial-year depreciation occurs when using the units-of-production method.

A firm is entitled to include a full month's depreciation if the asset was in operation during 15 days or more of that month. For example, if a firm placed a new asset into use on April 15 or earlier that month, the asset could be depreciated for all of April. If the asset is placed in use on April 16 or later in the month, the asset cannot be depreciated in April. The depreciation period would begin in May. Partial-year depreciation will be illustrated using the straight-line method.

EXAMPLE   Using the straight-line method, find the first year's depreciation expense for a $3,500 saw that is expected to be used for five years and have a $500 resale value. The machine was purchased on April 12.

Solution   Step 1.   Find the straight-line depreciation:

$$\frac{\$3,500 - 500}{5} = \$600 \text{ Yearly straight-line depreciation}$$

Step 2. Calculate depreciation for the first year:

$$\frac{\text{Yearly straight-line depreciation} \times (12 - \text{months previous})}{\text{number of months in a year}}$$

$\$600 \times \dfrac{12 - 3}{12}$ *The machine was purchased on April 12, so it can be depreciated for April. That means there were three months in the calendar year—January, February, and March—previous to the month depreciation began.*

$\$600 \times \dfrac{9}{12} = \$450$ *First-year depreciation*

Step 3. Calculate depreciation for the last year:

$$\frac{\text{Yearly straight-line depreciation} \times (12 - \text{months remaining})}{\text{number of months in a year}}$$

$\$600 \times \dfrac{12 - 9}{12}$ *Since depreciation began in April, there are nine months remaining in the calendar year that will not be depreciated. That leaves three months that must be depreciated in the sixth year: 12 − 9 = 3.*

$\$600 \times \dfrac{3}{12} = \$150$ *Sixth-year depreciation*

Step 4. Show the full depreciation schedule. Depreciation for the full five years would be illustrated as follows:

Year	Annual Depreciation	× Part of Year	= Depreciation
1	$600	$\dfrac{9}{12}$	$ 450
2	600	1	600
3	600	1	600
4	600	1	600
5	600	1	600
6	600	$\dfrac{3}{12}$	150
Total		5	$3,000

If the asset had been bought five days or more later, the time fraction would have been

$$\frac{12-4}{12} = \frac{8}{12}$$

and the solution would then have been as follows:

$$\$600 \times \frac{8}{12} = \$400 \text{ First-year depreciation}$$

$$\$600 \times \frac{4}{12} = \$200 \text{ Sixth-year depreciation}$$

17.2 Practice Problems

1. Minnie's Fried Pies bought a delivery van on May 6. It cost $14,600 plus $30 delivery charge. Company records indicate it will last four years and can be traded in for $6,000. Determine each year's depreciation using the straight-line method.

2. Monty's Stables purchased a saddle for $800 on February 24. To make it fit a very large horse, certain changes had to be made that cost $82. The saddle is expected to be used six years and then sold to a "greenhorn" for $75. Calculate each year's depreciation using the straight-line method.

3. Barb's Grocery bought a new cash register for $700. Delivery cost was $20, and installation was $150. Experience indicates that the machine will be obsolete in 10 years and that the old one can be sold for $50. Calculate each year's depreciation using the straight-line method if the cash register was bought on July 6.

4. Budget House Leveling Co. purchased a concrete mixer for $1,500 that cost $60 to assemble. It is expected to last five years and have a junk value of $50. Determine each year's depreciation using the straight-line method if the mixer was purchased May 7.

17.2 Solutions to Practice Problems

1. $14,600 + 30 − 6,000 = $8,630 Total depreciation

$$\frac{\$8,630}{4} = \$2,157.50 \text{ Annual depreciation}$$

Year × Annual Depreciation × Full or Part of Year = Depreciation

Year	Annual Depreciation	Full or Part of Year	Depreciation
1	$2,157.50	$\frac{8}{12}$	$1,438.33
2	2,157.50	1	2,157.50
3	2,157.50	1	2,157.50
4	2,157.50	1	2,157.50
5	2,157.50	$\frac{4}{12}$	719.17
Total		4	$8,630.00

2. $800 + 82 − 75 = $807 Total depreciation

$$\frac{\$807}{6} = \$134.50 \text{ Annual depreciation}$$

Year × Annual Depreciation × Full or Part of Year = Depreciation

Year	Annual Depreciation	Full or Part of Year	Depreciation
1	$134.50	$\frac{10}{12}$	$112.08
2	134.50	1	134.50
3	134.50	1	134.50
4	134.50	1	134.50
5	134.50	1	134.50
6	134.50	1	134.50
7	134.50	$\frac{2}{12}$	22.42
Total		6	$807.00

3. $700 + 20 + 150 - 50 = \$820$ Total depreciation

$$\frac{\$820}{10} = \$82 \text{ Annual depreciation}$$

Year × Annual Depreciation × Full or Part of Year = Depreciation

Year	Annual Depreciation	Full or Part of Year	Depreciation
1	82	$\frac{6}{12}$	$ 41
2	82	1	82
3	82	1	82
4	82	1	82
5	82	1	82
6	82	1	82
7	82	1	82
8	82	1	82
9	82	1	82
10	82	1	82
11	82	$\frac{6}{12}$	41
Total		10	$820

4. $1,500 + 60 - 50 = \$1,510$ Total depreciation

$$\frac{\$1,510}{5} = \$302 \text{ Annual depreciation}$$

Year × Annual Depreciation × Full or Part of Year = Depreciation

Year	Annual Depreciation	Full or Part of Year	Depreciation
1	$302	$\frac{8}{12}$	$ 201.33
2	302	1	302.00
3	302	1	302.00
4	302	1	302.00
5	302	1	302.00
6	302	$\frac{4}{12}$	100.67
Total		5	$1,510.00

17.3 Sum-of-the-Years'-Digits Depreciation

A primary reason for using the straight-line depreciation method is that it is easy. However, as everyone who has bought a new car knows, assets typically lose more of their value in the first year and less in each succeeding year. Because of inflation and the fact that money can earn interest, the asset is more valuable now than it will be in the future. Most business firms find it expedient to use a method of depreciation that reflects an accelerated pattern, allowing them to save more in taxes now and take advantage of cheaper money in the future.

The **sum-of-the-years'-digits depreciation** method is such a method, but it is more involved than straight-line depreciation.

E X A M P L E   Find the yearly depreciation expense for a $3,500 power saw expected to be used for five years and have a resale value of $500 using the sum-of-the-years'-digits method.

Solution   *Step 1.* List the digits of the asset's usable life in reverse order: 5, 4, 3, 2, 1.

Step 2. Add the digits to find the denominator for all calculations:
$5 + 4 + 3 + 2 + 1 = 15$.

Step 3. Place each year's digit over the denominator:

$$\frac{5}{15}, \frac{4}{15}, \frac{3}{15}, \frac{2}{15}, \frac{1}{15}$$

Step 4. Subtract the resale value from the asset's original cost: $\$3,500 - 500 = \$3,000$, which is the total depreciation.

Step 5. Multiply the result by the rate for each successive year:

Year	Digits in Reverse	Rate	× Total Depreciation	= Yearly Depreciation
1	5	$\frac{5}{15}$	$3,000	$1,000
2	4	$\frac{4}{15}$	3,000	800
3	3	$\frac{3}{15}$	3,000	600
4	2	$\frac{2}{15}$	3,000	400
5	1	$\frac{1}{15}$	3,000	200
Total	15	$\frac{15}{15}$	$3,000	$3,000

Note: If an asset's life is long, adding the digits can be tedious and time consuming. The sum-of-the-digits formula can be used to simplify the calculation for the denominator. The sum-of-the-digits formula is

$$\frac{\text{Largest number in the series (largest number in the series } + 1)}{2}$$

or

$$\frac{n(n + 1)}{2}.$$

3,000 [STO] [×] 5 [÷] 15 [=] 1,000

[RCL] [×] 4 [÷] 15 [=] 800

[RCL] [×] 3 [÷] 15 [=] 600

[RCL] [×] 2 [÷] 15 [=] 400

[RCL] [×] 1 [÷] 15 [=] 200

E X A M P L E   Find the sum of the digits from 1 through 30.

Solution
$$\frac{30(30 + 1)}{2} = 465$$

1. Harold's Machine Shop bought a new lathe for $4,000. The shop estimates that it will replace the lathe in four years and sell the old one for $400. Find the yearly depreciation using the sum-of-the-years'-digits method.

2. José's Cal-Mex Bar and Grill bought a new soft drink dispenser for $2,225. The vendor charged $275 to install the machine. José estimates it will last six years and can then be sold to a local junkyard for $150. Find the yearly depreciation using the sum-of-the-years'-digits method.

3. Bruce's Beauty Salon estimates that hair dryers have a five-year usable life. This year the new dryers cost $9,500. Estimates are that the old ones can be sold for $500. Find the yearly depreciation using the sum-of-the-years'-digits method.

4. Using the sum-of-the-years'-digits method, determine the estimated depreciation for the sixth year of a building with a usable life of 25 years. The building cost $2,000,000 and has a residual value of $800,000.

17.3 Solutions to Practice Problems

1. $4 + 3 + 2 + 1 = 10$, or $\dfrac{4 \times 5}{2} = 10$

$$\$4,000 - 400 = \$3,600 \text{ Total depreciation}$$

Year	Digit	Rate	×	Total Depreciation	=	Yearly Depreciation
1	4	$\dfrac{4}{10}$		$3,600		$1,440
2	3	$\dfrac{3}{10}$		3,600		1,080
3	2	$\dfrac{2}{10}$		3,600		720
4	1	$\dfrac{1}{10}$		3,600		360
Total	10	$\dfrac{10}{10}$		3,600		$3,600

2. $6 + 5 + 4 + 3 + 2 + 1 = 21$, or $\dfrac{6 \times 7}{2} = 21$

$$\$2,225 + 275 - 150 = \$2,350 \text{ Total depreciation}$$

Year	Digit	Rate	×	Total Depreciation	=	Yearly Depreciation
1	6	$\dfrac{6}{21}$		$2,350		$ 671.43
2	5	$\dfrac{5}{21}$		2,350		559.52
3	4	$\dfrac{4}{21}$		2,350		447.62
4	3	$\dfrac{3}{21}$		2,350		335.71
5	2	$\dfrac{2}{21}$		2,350		223.81
6	1	$\dfrac{1}{21}$		2,350		111.90
Total	21	$\dfrac{21}{21}$		$2,350		$2,349.99

The total yearly depreciation does not add to exactly $2,350 due to rounding. In practice, the remaining $.01 would be taken in the last year, making the ⟶ sixth year's depreciation $111.91.

3. $5 + 4 + 3 + 2 + 1 = 15$, or $\dfrac{5 \times 6}{2} = 15$

$\$9,500 - 500 = \$9,000$ Total depreciation

Year	Digit	Rate	×	Total Depreciation	=	Yearly Depreciation
1	5	$\dfrac{5}{15}$		$9,000		$3,000
2	4	$\dfrac{4}{15}$		9,000		2,400
3	3	$\dfrac{3}{15}$		9,000		1,800
4	2	$\dfrac{2}{15}$		9,000		1,200
5	1	$\dfrac{1}{15}$		9,000		600
Total	15	$\dfrac{15}{15}$		$9,000		$9,000

4. $\$2,000,000 - 800,000 = \$1,200,000$ Total depreciation

$$\frac{n(n + 1)}{2}$$

$$\frac{25(25 + 1)}{2} = 325$$

Year	Digit	Rate	×	Total Depreciation	=	Yearly Depreciation
1	25	$\dfrac{25}{325}$				
2	24	$\dfrac{24}{325}$				
3	23	$\dfrac{23}{325}$				
4	22	$\dfrac{22}{325}$				
5	21	$\dfrac{21}{325}$				
6	20	$\dfrac{20}{325}$		$1,200,000		$73,846.15

17.4 Units-of-Production Depreciation

To depreciate machinery and equipment, sometimes the expenses and revenues for the period are matched to the actual number of units produced. Units can be any reasonable measurement, such as hours, miles driven, or units produced. **Units-of-production depreciation** is then calculated on the basis of an estimated number of units the asset will produce during its life, rather than on the estimated number of years it can be used. To calculate depreciation using the units-of-production method, follow these steps

Step 1. Calculate the cost of the equipment per unit of production:

$$\text{Cost per unit of production} = \frac{\text{cost} - \text{resale value}}{\text{total units}}$$

Step 2. Multiply the cost per unit of production by the number of units produced in a year.

EXAMPLE A power saw cost $3,500. The buyer estimated it could be sold for $500 salvage after cutting lumber for 6,000 houses. The saw produced as follows: first year, 1,300 houses; second year, 1,950 houses; third year, 1,400 houses; fourth year, 1,100 houses; and fifth year, 250 houses. Calculate the yearly depreciation using the units-of-production method.

Solution

$$\text{Cost per unit} = \frac{\text{cost} - \text{resale value}}{\text{total units}}$$

$$\text{Cost per unit} = \frac{\$3,500 - 500}{6,000} = \$.50$$

Year	Yearly Production	×	Cost per Unit of Production	=	Depreciation
1	1,300		$.50		$ 650
2	1,950		.50		975
3	1,400		.50		700
4	1,100		.50		550
5	250		.50		125
Total	6,000				$3,000

.50 ⊠ 1,300 ⊟ 650

1,950 ⊟ 975

1,400 ⊟ 700

1,100 ⊟ 550

250 ⊟ 125

17.4 Practice Problems

1. Mendez electronics bought a delivery truck for $16,000. The truck is expected to be worn out when it has been driven 100,000 miles. It is estimated that such trucks can be sold to a salvage yard for $200. Using the units-of-production method, determine the depreciation over the truck's life if it was driven 23,000 miles the first year, 12,000 the second year, 25,000 the third year, 28,000 the fourth year, and 12,000 the fifth year.

2. A new generator cost the City of Muleshoe Electric Utility company $224,000. It is estimated that such generators last 40,000 hours and can be sold as junk for $4,000. Using the units-of-production method, determine the depreciation over the generator's life if it runs 8,520 hours the first year, 7,670 the second year, 8,200 the third year, 8,700 the fourth year, and 6,910 the fifth year.

3. Marvin's Plastic Products bought a new stamping machine for $20,000. The machine is expected to be worn out and need to be replaced after it has produced 500,000 parts. Marvin's estimates it can be scrapped for $2,000. Using the units-of-production method, determine the depreciation over the machine's life if it produces 180,620 parts the first year, 199,760 the second year, and 119,620 the third year.

4. Rashaan's Waffle Shop depreciates cooking equipment using the units-of-production method. The estimated production use of a waffle iron is 135,000 waffles. New waffle irons

cost $2,200, and Roshaan estimates they can be sold as junk for $25. How much can a waffle iron be depreciated each year if it cooked 36,410 waffles the first year, 56,640 the second year, and 41,950 the third year?

17.4 Solutions to Practice Problems

1.
$$\text{Cost per unit} = \frac{\text{cost} - \text{resale value}}{\text{total units}}$$
$$= \frac{\$16,000 - 200}{100,000}$$
$$= \frac{\$15,800}{100,000} = \$.158$$

Year	Yearly Production	×	Cost per Unit of Production	=	Depreciation
1	23,000		$.158		$ 3,634
2	12,000		.158		1,896
3	25,000		.158		3,950
4	28,000		.158		4,424
5	12,000		.158		1,896
Total	100,000				$15,800

2.
$$\text{Cost per unit} = \frac{\text{Cost} - \text{resale value}}{\text{total units}}$$
$$= \frac{\$224,000 - 4,000}{40,000}$$
$$= \frac{\$220,000}{40,000} = \$5.50$$

Year	Yearly Production	×	Cost per Unit of Production	=	Depreciation
1	8,520		$5.50		$ 46,860
2	7,670		5.50		42,185
3	8,200		5.50		45,100
4	8,700		5.50		47,850
5	6,910		5.50		38,005
Total	40,000				$220,000

3.
$$\text{Cost per unit} = \frac{\text{cost} - \text{resale value}}{\text{total units}}$$
$$= \frac{\$20,000 - 2,000}{500,000}$$
$$= \frac{\$18,000}{500,000} = \$.036$$

Year	Yearly Production	×	Cost per Unit of Production	=	Depreciation
1	180,620		$.036		$ 6,502.32
2	199,760		.036		7,191.36
3	119,620		.036		4,306.32
Total	500,000				$18,000.00

4.
$$\text{Cost per unit} = \frac{\text{cost} - \text{resale value}}{\text{total units}}$$
$$= \frac{\$2,200 - 25}{135,000}$$
$$= \frac{\$2,175}{135,000} = \$.016111$$

Carry out six places to minimize rounding error, or leave the entire amount in the calculator and use it as a constant.

Year	Yearly Production	×	Cost per Unit of Production	=	Depreciation
1	36,410		$.016111		$ 586.61
2	56,640		.016111		912.53
3	41,950		.016111		675.86
Total	135,000				$2,175.00

17.5 Declining-Balance Depreciation

The **declining-balance depreciation** method is another accelerated method that calculates the most depreciation in the first year and less in each succeeding year. Like the other methods, the maximum depreciation is the total cost less the estimated resale or salvage value.

Unlike the other methods, you do not subtract the resale value to find the base. The base for the first year is the total cost of the asset. In each succeeding year, the base is the **book value** of the asset. The book value declines from year to year by the amount of the previous period's depreciation, causing the annual depreciation to decline. That gives the method its name.

There are three common declining-balance rates:

200% declining balance (declining balance at twice the straight-line rate)
150% declining balance (declining balance at $1\frac{1}{2}$ times the straight-line rate)
125% declining balance (declining balance at $1\frac{1}{4}$ times the straight-line rate)

To compute the depreciation using the declining-balance method, follow these steps:

Step 1. Find the total allowable depreciation:

> Allowable depreciation = cost − resale value

Step 2. Calculate the declining-balance rate:

> Declining-balance rate = straight-line rate × allowable declining-balance rate

Note: The straight-line rate can be determined by simply placing 1 in the numerator position and the years of usable life in the denominator position of a common fraction. For example, an asset with a 5-year usable life has a straight-line rate of 1/5, and an asset with a 12-year usable life has a straight-line rate of 1/12.

Step 3. Multiply the original cost by the rate found in step 2. The answer will be the amount of depreciation for the first year of the asset's life.

Step 4. Accumulate the depreciation by adding the current year's depreciation to the previous total, and deduct it from the original cost of the asset to find the book value.

Step 5. Multiply the book value for the second year by the declining-balance rate. The product is the depreciation for the second year.

Step 6. Repeat steps 4 and 5 in succeeding years until all allowable depreciation (found in step 1) has been taken or until the last year's depreciation is to be calculated. *The last year's depreciation is the difference between the allowable depreciation and the amount of depreciation taken in the previous years.*

EXAMPLE A power saw cost $3,500. Resale value is estimated at $500 after its five years of usable life. Calculate the annual depreciation using the declining-balance method at 200%, 150%, and 125% of the straight-line rate.

Solution　*Step 1.*　Find the total allowable depreciation:

Allowable depreciation = cost − resale value

$$\$3,500 - 500 = \$3,000$$

Step 2.　Calculate the declining-balance rate:

Declining-balance rate = straight-line rate × allowable declining-balance rate
200% declining-balance rate = 1/5 × 200% = 40%
150% declining-balance rate = 1/5 × 150% = 30%
125% declining-balance rate = 1/5 × 125% = 25%

Steps 3, 4, 5, and 6.　These steps, making the calculations, are shown in the following charts. After calculating the amount of depreciation for each year, that amount must be subtracted from the previous year's balance to determine the book value as shown.

200% Declining Balance

Year	Balance (Book Value) × Rate	=	Yearly Depreciation	Total Depreciation	Allowable Depreciation
1	$3,500	40%	$1,400	$1,400	$3,000
2	2,100	40%	840	2,240	3,000
3	1,260	40%	504	2,744	3,000
4*	756		256	3,000	3,000
5	500		0	3,000	3,000

*$756 × 40% = $302.40. However, at the end of the third year $2,744 of the allowable $3,000 had been taken, which left only $256 ($3,000 − 2,744 = $256). There is no allowable depreciation left after the fourth year, and none can be taken in the fifth year.

150% Declining Balance

Year	Balance (Book Value) × Rate	=	Yearly Depreciation	Total Depreciation	Allowable Depreciation
1	$3,500.00	30%	$1,050.00	$1,050.00	$3,000.00
2	2,450.00	30%	735.00	1,785.00	3,000.00
3	1,715.00	30%	514.50	2,299.50	3,000.00
4	1,200.50	30%	360.15	2,659.65	3,000.00
5*	840.35		340.35	3,000.00	3,000.00
	500.00				

*At the end of the fourth year $2,659.65 of the allowable $3,000 had been taken, which left $340.35 ($3,000 − 2,659.65 = $340.35). All of the remaining allowable depreciation can be taken in the fifth year.

125% Declining Balance

Year	Balance (Book Value) × Rate	=	Yearly Depreciation	Total Depreciation	Allowable Depreciation
1	$3,500.00	25%	$875.00	$ 875.00	$3,000.00
2	2,625.00	25%	656.25	1,531.25	3,000.00
3	1,968.75	25%	492.19	2,023.44	3,000.00
4	1,476.56	25%	369.14	2,392.58	3,000.00
5*	1,107.42		607.42	3,000.00	3,000.00
	500.00				

*At the end of the fourth year $2,392.58 of the allowable $3,000 had been taken, which left $607.42 ($3,000 − 2,392.58 = $607.42). All of the remaining allowable depreciation can be taken in the fifth year.

1. Goop Oil Corporation purchased 10 new computers for $210,000. The firm estimates a three-year usable life and a residual value of $10,000. Find the depreciation for each year using the declining-balance method at 200% of the straight-line rate.

2. Bimble's Grocery chain depreciates cash registers using the declining-balance method at 150% of the straight-line rate. Calculate the yearly depreciation for $120,000 worth of cash registers that are estimated to have a $5,000 resale value and a five-year usable life expectancy.

3. A peanut mill bought a new drying machine for $60,000. The machine is estimated to last four years and be worth $4,000 as junk. Find the yearly depreciation using the declining-balance method at 125% of the straight-line rate.

4. East Indiana Pipe Co. purchased a clay crusher for $30,320. It is estimated to have a scrap value of $820 and a four-year usable life. Determine the yearly depreciation using the declining-balance method at 200%, 150%, and 125% of the straight-line rate.

17.5 Solutions to Practice Problems

1. Find the total depreciation: $210,000 - 10,000 = $200,000.

    Find the straight-line rate: $\frac{1}{3}$.

    Determine the yearly percent of depreciation:

$$200\% \text{ declining balance} = \frac{1}{3} \times 200\% = \frac{2}{3} = 66\frac{2\%}{3}$$

Year	Balance (Book Value)	× Rate =	Yearly Depreciation	Total Depreciation	Allowable Depreciation
1	$210,000.00	2/3	$140,000.00	$140,000.00	$200,000.00
2	70,000.00	2/3	46,666.67	186,666.67	200,000.00
3	23,333.33		13,333.33	200,000.00	200,000.00
	10,000.00				

2. Find the total depreciation: $120,000 - 5,000 = $115,000.

    Find the straight-line rate: $\frac{1}{5}$.

    Determine the yearly percent of depreciation:

$$150\% \text{ declining balance} = \frac{1}{5} \times 150\% = 30\%$$

Year	Balance (Book Value)	× Rate =	Yearly Depreciation	Total Depreciation	Allowable Depreciation
1	$120,000.00	30%	$36,000.00	$ 36,000.00	$115,000.00
2	84,000.00	30%	25,200.00	61,200.00	115,000.00
3	58,800.00	30%	17,640.00	78,840.00	115,000.00
4	41,160.00	30%	12,348.00	91,188.00	115,000.00
5	28,812.00		23,812.00	115,000.00	115,000.00
	5,000.00				

3. Find the total depreciation: $60,000 - 4,000 = $56,000.

    Find the straight-line rate $= \frac{1}{4}$.

    Determine the yearly percent of depreciation:

$$125\% \text{ declining balance} = \frac{1}{4} \times 125\% = 31.25\%$$

Year	Balance (Book Value)	× Rate =	Yearly Depreciation	Total Depreciation	Allowable Depreciation
1	$60,000.00	31.25%	$18,750.00	$18,750.00	$56,000.00
2	41,250.00	31.25%	12,890.63	31,640.63	56,000.00
3	28,359.37	31.25%	8,862.30	40,502.93	56,000.00
4	19,497.07		15,497.07	56,000.00	56,000.00
	4,000.00				

4. Find the total depreciation: $30,320 - 820 = $29,500.

Find the straight-line rate $= \dfrac{1}{4}$

200% Declining Balance

$$200\% \text{ declining balance} = \dfrac{1}{4} \times 200\% = \dfrac{1}{2} = 50\%$$

Year	Balance (Book Value)	× Rate =	Yearly Depreciation	Total Depreciation	Allowable Depreciation
1	$60,000.00	50%	$30,000.00	$30,000.00	$56,000.00
2	30,000.00	50%	15,000.00	45,000.00	56,000.00
3	15,000.00	50%	7,500.00	52,500.00	56,000.00
4	7,500.00		3,500.00	56,000.00	56,000.00
	4,000.00				

150% Declining Balance

$$150\% \text{ declining balance} = \dfrac{1}{4} \times 150\% = 37.5\%$$

Year	Balance (Book Value)	× Rate =	Yearly Depreciation	Total Depreciation	Allowable Depreciation
1	$60,000.00	37.5%	$22,500.00	$22,500.00	$56,000.00
2	37,500.00	37.5%	14,062.50	36,562.50	56,000.00
3	23,437.50	37.5%	8,789.06	45,351.56	56,000.00
4	14,648.44		10,648.44	56,000.00	56,000.00
	4,000.00				

125% Declining Balance

$$125\% \text{ declining balance} = \dfrac{1}{4} \times 125\% = 31.25\%$$

Year	Balance (Book Value)	× Rate =	Yearly Depreciation	Total Depreciation	Allowable Depreciation
1	$60,000.00	31.25%	$18,750.00	$18,750.00	$56,000.00
2	41,250.00	31.25%	12,890.63	31,640.63	56,000.00
3	28,359.37	31.25%	8,862.30	40,502.93	56,000.00
4	19,497.07		15,497.07	56,000.00	56,000.00
	4,000.00				

EXCEL Spreadsheet Applications The spreadsheet for Application 1 at the end of this chapter compares various depreciation methods that could be used to depreciate a new computer, while Application 2 is a comparison of the various possible methods to depreciate Springfield's new building.

LEARNING UNIT 2
DEPRECIATION FOR TAX ACCOUNTING

The concept of depreciation and the methods of calculating it changed profoundly with the passage of the Economic Recovery Act in 1981. Before the Act, the amount of depreciation charged to an asset each year was supposed to approximate the amount by which its value decreased and reflected a "using up" of the asset. Business firms were never allowed to depreciate assets below a reasonable estimate of their actual market value.

With the 1981 Economic Recovery Act the term *depreciation* was replaced by the concept of *cost recovery*. Cost recovery has little connection to the actual current value of an asset or the actual length of its usable life, and no distinction is made between new and used property.

Assets are placed into designated categories. Each year a business firm is allowed to recover a certain percentage of the original cost until the entire cost has been claimed as an operating expense.

17.6 Modified Accelerated Cost Recovery System (MACRS)

The original method was called the *accelerated cost recovery system (ACRS)*. It was revised in 1986 as the **modified accelerated cost recovery system (MACRS)**. Since many state governments do not allow the use of MACRS, business firms often keep one set of financial statements for financial purposes and state income tax and another set for federal income tax purposes.

Recovery Periods

The recovery period is the length of time over which an asset can be depreciated. The recovery period for IRS purposes is often shorter than the usable life used for financial accounting purposes. Under MACRS, assets are placed in one of eight recovery periods. The IRS publishes charts that dictate the recovery for various assets.

Examples of the assets for each recovery period are shown in Table 17.1, which is only a portion of the tables from IRS Publication 534.

TABLE 17.1   RECOVERY PERIODS

Recovery Period @ 200% Straight Line Rate	Examples of Assets
3 years	1. tractors to be used over the road
	2. racehorses more than 2 years old and other horses over 12 years old when placed in service
	3. all specialized tools used in manufacturing rubber, plastic, or glass products; and fabricated metal; or motor vehicles
	4. containers and handling devices for food and beverages
5 years	1. computers and peripheral equipment
	2. office equipment (not furniture)
	3. airplanes except commercial ones
	4. Automobiles, taxis, buses, trucks
	5. breeding animals and dairy cattle
	6. oil and gas drilling equipment
	7. general construction equipment
	8. cloth and clothing manufacturing equipment
	9. timber cutting and handling equipment
	10. manufacture of chemical products tools
	11. ship- and boat-building tools
	12. broadcasting equipment
7 years	1. office furniture and fixtures
	2. railroad cars and locomotives
	3. agriculture equipment, grain bins, cotton gins
	4. mining equipment

Recovery Period @ 200% Straight Line Rate	Examples of Assets
	5. oil and gas exploration equipment
	6. manufacture of tobacco products equipment
	7. sawmill equipment
	8. pulp and paper products equipment
	9. machinery and equipment to manufacture rubber, plastic, glass, stone and clay, and fabricated metal products
	10. machinery and equipment to manufacture airplanes, ships, locomotives, and motor vehicles
10 years	1. water transportation equipment
	2. petroleum refining equipment
	3. most food products processing equipment
	4. dry docks for ship building

Recovery Period @ 150% Straight Line Rate	Examples of Assets
15 years	1. land improvements such as sidewalks, roads, fences, canals, bridges, shrubbery
	2. industrial electricity producing equipment
	3. pole lines, cable, aerial wire, underground conduits
	4. municipal wastewater equipment
20 years	1. farm buildings
	2. municipal water treatment plants

Recovery Period @ 100% Straight Line Rate	Examples of Assets
27.5 years	Rental houses and apartments
31.5 years	Office buildings, retail stores, warehouses, hotels

Table 17.2 depicts the depreciation rates for each year of an asset's recovery period. Two things should be noted about the table. First, the numbers are percents even though the percent sign has been left off. Second, the table uses the half-year convention. It is assumed the asset is purchased at the end of June. Thus, the first and the last year of the asset's usable life recovers half of that year's depreciation value. That is why an asset having a three-year cost recovery period has depreciation remaining to be taken in the fourth year.

TABLE 17.2   MACRS DEPRECIATION RATES

Year	Recovery Percent for the Class of an Asset					
	3 yrs.	5 yrs.	7 yrs.	10 yrs.	15 yrs.	20 yrs.
1	33.33	20.00	14.29	10.00	5.00	3.750
2	44.45	32.00	24.49	18.00	9.50	7.219
3	14.81	19.20	17.49	14.40	8.55	6.677
4	7.41	11.52	12.49	11.52	7.70	6.177
5		11.52	8.93	9.22	6.93	5.713
6		5.76	8.92	7.37	6.23	5.285
7			8.93	6.55	5.90	4.888
8			4.46	6.55	5.90	4.522
9				6.56	5.91	4.462
10				6.55	5.90	4.461
11				3.28	5.91	4.461
12					5.90	4.461
13					5.91	4.461
14					5.90	4.461
15					5.91	4.461
16					2.95	4.461
17						4.461
18						4.461
19						4.461
20						4.461
21						2.231

EXAMPLE   A power saw cost $3,500. The buyer estimated it could be sold for $500 salvage after its estimated five years of usable life. Calculate the third year's depreciation using the MACRS method.

Solution   *Step 1.* Since a saw comes under the heading of general construction equipment, the recovery period from Table 17.1 is five years.

Step 2. From Table 17.2, find the depreciation rate in the third year of recovery (19.20%).

Step 3. Multiply the rate by the full cost of the property:

$$
\begin{array}{r}
\$\ 3,500 \\
\underline{\times\ 19.2\%} \\
\$\ \ \ \ 672
\end{array}
$$

From Table 17.1 and Table 17.2

Third-year depreciation

**17.6
Practice
Problems**

Use Tables 17.1 and 17.2 to solve the following problems:

1. The Northern Atlantic Railroad bought $7,100,000 worth of new railroad cars. Determine the sixth year's depreciation using the MACRS method.

2. Mack's Big Grocery Outlet replaced its computer system with a $445,000 new system. How much can the company depreciate the new computer system each year using the MACRS method?

3. Last year West Arizona Sheet Metal Co. paid $29,720 for a new delivery truck. How much can West Arizona depreciate the truck the second year using the MACRS method?

4. Nuckolls Nebraska Water Co. bought a water treatment plant six years ago for $1,256,400. Using the MACRS method, how much can it be depreciated in the seventh year?

17.6 Solutions to Practice Problems

1. $7,100,000
   <u>$\times$ 8.92%</u>   From Table 17.1 and Table 17.2
   $ 633,320   Sixth-year depreciation

2. $ 445,000
   <u>$\times$ 20.00%</u>   From Table 17.1 and Table 17.2
   $ 89,000   First-year depreciation
   $ 445,000
   <u>$\times$ 32.00%</u>   From Table 17.1 and Table 17.2
   $ 142,400   Second-year depreciation
   $ 445,000
   <u>$\times$ 19.20%</u>   From Table 17.1 and Table 17.2
   $ 85,440   Third-year depreciation
   $ 445,000
   <u>$\times$ 11.52%</u>   From Table 17.1 and Table 17.2
   $ 51,264   Fourth-year depreciation
   $ 445,000
   <u>$\times$ 11.52%</u>   From Table 17.1 and Table 17.2
   $ 51,264   Fifth-year depreciation
   $ 445,000
   <u>$\times$ 5.76%</u>   From Table 17.1 and Table 17.2
   $ 25,632   Sixth-year depreciation

3. $29,720.00
   <u>$\times$ 32%</u>   From Table 17.1 and Table 17.2
   $ 9,510.40   Second-year depreciation

4. $1,256,400.00
   <u>$\times$ 4.888%</u>   From Table 17.1 and Table 17.2
   $ 61,412.80   Seventh-year depreciation

QUICK REFERENCE SUMMARY AND REVIEW

Page	Section Topic	Learning Concepts	Examples and Solutions
582	**17.1** Straight-Line Depreciation	To find the yearly depreciation using the straight-line method, subtract the resale value from the cost and divide by the number of years.	Find the yearly depreciation for a $2,600 planer with an estimated nine-year life and an estimated $400 resale value. $$\frac{\$2,600 - 400}{9} = \$244.44$$
583	**17.2** Partial-Year Depreciation Using the Straight-Line Method	To find the partial-year depreciation for the first year, determine the annual straight-line depreciation. Then, multiply the annual depreciation by $\frac{12 - \text{months previous}}{12}$. For the last year, multiply by $\frac{12 - \text{months remaining}}{12}$.	Find the first year's depreciation for a $2,600 planer purchased on April 9 that will last nine years and have a $400 resale value. $$\$244.44 \times \frac{12 - 3}{12}$$ $$= \$244.44 \times \frac{9}{12}$$ $$= \$183.33$$

Page	Section Topic	Learning Concepts	Examples and Solutions
586	**17.3** Sum-of-the-Years'-Digits Depreciation	List the digits of an asset's usable life in reverse order. Add the digits to find the denominator for all calculations. Place each year's digit over the denominator. Subtract the resale value from the asset's original cost. Multiply each year's rate by the total depreciation to find the yearly depreciation.	Find the yearly depreciation for a $3,000 planer that is expected to be used four years and will have a $600 resale value using the sum-of-the-years'-digits method. $4 + 3 + 2 + 1 = 10$ $3,000 − 600 =$ $2,400 Total depreciation

Year	Digit	Rate	×	Total Depreciation	=	Yearly Depreciation
1	4	$\frac{4}{10}$		$2,400		$ 960
2	3	$\frac{3}{10}$		2,400		720
3	2	$\frac{2}{10}$		2,400		480
4	1	$\frac{1}{10}$		2,400		240
Total	10	$\frac{10}{10}$		$2,400		$2,400

Page	Section Topic	Learning Concepts	Examples and Solutions
589	**17.4** Units-of-Production Depreciation	Calculate the cost of the equipment per unit of production. Multiply the cost per unit of production by the number produced in a year to find that year's depreciation.	A machine cost $1,800. Estimated salvage value is $200 after its 2,000 units of estimated usable life. It produced 840 units in the first year, 644 units in the second year, and 516 units in the third year. Calculate the yearly depreciation using the units-of-production method. $\frac{\text{Cost − resale value}}{\text{total units}}$ $\frac{\$1,800 − 200}{2,000} = \$.80$

Year	Yearly Production	×	Cost per Unit of Production	=	Yearly Depreciation
1	840		$.80		$ 672.00
2	644		.80		515.20
3	516		.80		412.80
Total	2,000				$1,600.00

Page	Section Topic	Learning Concepts	Examples and Solutions
592	**17.5** Declining-Balance Depreciation	Find the allowable depreciation. Find the straight-line rate. Determine the declining-balance rate. Multiply the total cost of the asset by the declining-balance rate for the first year's depreciation. Subtract the depreciation from the asset's cost to find the book value. Multiply the book value by the declining-balance rate. Subtract the accumulated depreciation from the asset cost to find the subsequent year's base. For the last year, subtract the accumulated depreciation from the allowable depreciation.	An asset cost $2,400. Estimated salvage value is $300 after three years of estimated usable life. Calculate the annual depreciation using the declining-balance method at 200%, 150%, and 125% of the straight-line rate. $$\$2,400 - 300 = \$2,100$$ $$\frac{1}{3} = \text{straight-line rate}$$ $$200\% \text{ declining balance} = \frac{1}{3} \times 200\%$$ $$= \frac{2}{3} = 66\frac{2\%}{3}$$

Year	Balance (Book Value)	×	Rate	=	Yearly Depreciation	Total Depreciation	Allowable Depreciation
1	$2,400		$\frac{2}{3}$		$1,600	$1,600	$2,100
2*	800		$\frac{2}{3}$		500	2,100	2,100
3	300				0	0	2,100

*At the end of the first year $1,600 of the allowable $2,100 had been taken, which left only $500 ($2,100 − 1,600 = $500). There is no allowable remaining depreciation after the second year, and none can be taken in the third year.

$$150\% \text{ declining balance} = \frac{1}{3} \times 150\% = 50\%$$

Year	Balance (Book Value)	×	Rate	=	Yearly Depreciation	Total Depreciation	Allowable Depreciation
1	$2,400.00		50%		$1,200.00	$1,200.00	$2,100.00
2	1,200.00		50%		600.00	1,800.00	2,100.00
3*	600.00 300.00				300.00	2,100.00	2,100.00

*At the end of the second year $1,800 of the allowable $2,100 had been taken, which left $300 ($2,100 − 1,800 = $300.00). All of the remaining allowable depreciation can be taken in the third year.

$$125\% \text{ declining balance} = \frac{1}{3} \times 125\% = 41\frac{2\%}{3}$$

Year	Balance (Book Value)	×	Rate	=	Yearly Depreciation	Total Depreciation	Allowable Depreciation
1	$2,400.00		$41\frac{2\%}{3}$		$1,000.00	$1,000.00	$2,100.00
2	1,400.00		$41\frac{2\%}{3}$		583.33	1,583.33	2,100.00
3*	816.67 300.00				516.67	2,100.00	2,100.00

*At the end of the second year $1,583.33 of the allowable $2,100 had been taken, which left $516.67 ($2,100 − 1,583.33 = $516.67). All of the remaining allowable depreciation can be taken in the third year.

Page	Section Topic	Learning Concepts	Examples and Solutions
596	**17.6** Modified Accelerated Cost Recovery System (MACRS)	Find the recovery period in Table 17.1. Find the depreciation rate in Table 17.2 for the year in question. Multiply the rate by the full cost of the property.	A new desk cost $1,400. Estimated salvage value is $300 after the end of estimated usable life. Calculate the fourth year's depreciation using the MACRS method. Since a desk is office furniture, the recovery period from Table 17.1 is seven years. From Table 17.2 the depreciation rate is 12.49%.

$$\begin{array}{r} \$\quad 1,400 \\ \times\ \underline{12.49\%} \\ \$\quad 174.86 \end{array}\ \text{Fourth-year depreciation}$$

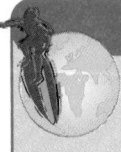

SURFING THE INTERNET

For further information on the topics covered in this chapter, check out the following sites:

http://www.irs.gov/prod/forms_pubs/pubs/p946ch03.htm

http://www.xrefer.com/entry/589161

http://www.allianceonline.org/faqs.html

ADDITIONAL PRACTICE PROBLEMS

Answers to odd-numbered problems are given in Appendix A.

17.1

1. Bradford Sales, Inc., bought a car for $18,200, which the dealer charged $35 to deliver. The company records indicate that the car will last an estimated three years and can be traded in for an estimated $1,200. Determine the yearly amount of depreciation using the straight-line method.

$18,200 + 35 = $18,235 Cost

$$\text{Yearly depreciation} = \frac{\text{cost} - \text{resale value}}{\text{usable life}}$$
$$= \frac{\$18,235 - 1,200}{3}$$
$$= \frac{\$17,035}{3} = \$5,678.33$$

2. Mervin's Sweet Tooth Candies purchased a set of pots for $397.95. When the pots arrived, the company paid $18.50 delivery. The pots' estimated usable life will be eight years, and the estimated junk value is $20. How much is the yearly depreciation using the straight-line method?

$397.95 + 18.50 = $416.45 Cost

$$\text{Yearly depreciation} = \frac{\text{cost} - \text{resale value}}{\text{usable life}}$$
$$= \frac{\$416.45 - 20}{8}$$
$$= \frac{\$396.45}{8} = \$49.56$$

3. The County Employees Credit Union bought new printers for $6,435. The company that sold them charged a $47 delivery fee. Experience indicates the printers will last an estimated five years and that the old ones can be sold for an estimated $187. Find the amount of the yearly depreciation using the straight-line method.

$6,435 + 47 = $6,482 cost

$$\text{Yearly depreciation} = \frac{\text{cost} - \text{resale value}}{\text{usable life}}$$
$$= \frac{\$6,482 - 187}{5}$$
$$= \frac{\$6,295}{5} = \$1,295$$

4. Mr. George's Chicken Shack bought $5,600 of cooking equipment. Installment was $525. The equipment is expected to last 18 years and have a $600 junk value. Find the yearly depreciation using the straight-line method.

$5,600 + 525 = $6,125 cost

$$\text{Yearly depreciation} = \frac{\text{cost} - \text{resale value}}{\text{usable life}}$$
$$= \frac{\$6,125 - 600}{18}$$
$$= \frac{\$5,525}{18} = \$306.94$$

5. Miller's Tire Shop bought a new mounting machine for $1,700. Delivery cost was $20, and installation was $160. It is estimated such machines will probably last 10 years and can be sold as junk for $50. Find the amount of the yearly depreciation using the straight-line method.

$1,700 + 20 + 160 = $1,880$ cost

$$\text{Yearly depreciation} = \frac{\text{cost} - \text{resale value}}{\text{usable life}}$$
$$= \frac{\$1,880 - 50}{10}$$
$$= \frac{\$1,830}{10} = \$183$$

17.2

6. Jane's Plumbing Co. bought a new pickup truck on June 8. It cost $18,400 plus $160 for window tinting. The company estimates that the truck will probably last five years and have a trade-in value of $3,000. Determine the yearly depreciation using the straight-line method.

$18,400 + 160 − 3,000 = $15,560$ Total depreciation

$\frac{\$15,560}{5} = \$3,112$ Annual depreciation

Year ×	Annual Depreciation	× Full or Part of Year	= Depreciation
1	$3,112	$\frac{7}{12}$	$1,815.33
2	3,112	1	3,112.00
3	3,112	1	3,112.00
4	3,112	1	3,112.00
5	3,112	1	3,112.00
6	3,112	$\frac{5}{12}$	1,296.67

7. Murray's Downtown Meat Market bought a slicing machine for $600 on March 27. The machine is estimated to have a six-year usable life and a junk value of $40. Calculate each year's depreciation using the straight-line method.

$600 − 40 = 560 Total depreciation

$\frac{\$560}{6} = \$93.33$ Annual depreciation

Year ×	Annual Depreciation	× Full or Part of Year	= Depreciation
1	$93.33	$\frac{9}{12}$	$70.00
2	93.33	1	93.33
3	93.33	1	93.33
4	93.33	1	93.33
5	93.33	1	93.33
6	93.33	1	93.33
7	93.33	$\frac{3}{12}$	23.33

8. Bob's Grain Co. bought a new motor for $800. The delivery cost was $50, and installation was $300. Estimates indicate the motor will be worn out in 10 years and that the old one can be sold for $10. Calculate the first and last years' depreciation using the straight-line method if the motor was bought on November 16.

$800 + 50 + 300 − 10 = $1,140$ Total depreciation

$\frac{\$1,140}{10} = \$114$ Annual depreciation

Year ×	Annual Depreciation	× Full or Part of Year	= Depreciation
1	$114	$\frac{1}{12}$	$ 9.50
11	114	$\frac{11}{12}$	104.50

9. Ben's Boiler Repair purchased a welding machine for $2,400. It cost $25 to assemble and is expected to last five years. Junk value is estimated to be $200. Determine the yearly depreciation using the straight-line method if the machine was purchased on April 22.

$2,400 + 25 − 200 = $2,225$ Total depreciation

$\frac{\$2,225}{5} = \$445$ Annual depreciation

Year ×	Annual Depreciation	× Full or Part of Year	= Depreciation
1	$445	$\frac{8}{12}$	$296.67
2	445	1	445
3	445	1	445
4	445	1	445
5	445	1	445
6	445	$\frac{4}{12}$	148.33

10. On June 7, Chem's Office Supply Company bought a new machine for moving heavy loads of paper. It cost $12,500. Delivery cost was $40. It is estimated that such machines will last four years and can be resold for $2,000. Determine each year's depreciation using the straight-line method.

$12,500 + 40 − 2,000 = $10,540$ Total depreciation

$\frac{\$10,540}{4} = \$2,635$ Annual depreciation

Year ×	Annual Depreciation	× Full or Part of Year	= Depreciation
1	$2,635	$\frac{7}{12}$	$1,537.08
2	2,635	1	2,635.00
3	2,635	1	2,635.00
4	2,635	1	2,635.00
5	2,635	$\frac{5}{12}$	1,097.92

11. Carter's Peanut Mill bought 10 new dryers at $1,200 each. Company executives estimate dryers will last five years and can be sold for $100 each. Find the total yearly depreciation for all of the dryers using the sum-of-the-years'-digits method.

$5 + 4 + 3 + 2 + 1 = 15$, or $\dfrac{5 \times 6}{2} = 15$

$1,200 - 100 = 1,100$
$1,100 \times 10 = 11,000$ Total depreciation

Year	Digit	Rate	×	Total Depreciation	=	Yearly Depreciation
1	5	$\dfrac{5}{15}$		$11,000		$ 3,666.67
2	4	$\dfrac{4}{15}$		11,000		2,933.33
3	3	$\dfrac{3}{15}$		11,000		2,200.00
4	2	$\dfrac{2}{15}$		11,000		1,466.67
5	1	$\dfrac{1}{15}$		11,000		733.33
						$11,000.00

12. Barney's Bakery bought a bread-mixing machine for $1,800. The installation fee was $125. Barney estimates it will last four years and can then be sold to a local junkyard for $200. Find the yearly depreciation using the sum-of-the-years'-digits method.

$4 + 3 + 2 + 1 = 10$, or $\dfrac{4 \times 5}{2} = 10$

$1,800 + 125 - 200 = 1,725$ Total depreciation

Year	Digit	Rate	×	Total Depreciation	=	Yearly Depreciation
1	4	$\dfrac{4}{10}$		$1,725		$ 690.00
2	3	$\dfrac{3}{10}$		1,725		517.50
3	2	$\dfrac{2}{10}$		1,725		345.00
4	1	$\dfrac{1}{10}$		1,725		172.50
						$1,725.00

13. The usable life of furniture and fixtures at Emmanuel's Makeup Salon is estimated to be three years and cost $12,500. Find the yearly depreciation using the sum-of-the-years'-digits method if the resale value is estimated to be $2,500.

$3 + 2 + 1 = 6$, or $\dfrac{3 \times 4}{2} = 6$

$12,500 - 2,500 = 10,000$ Total depreciation

Year	Digit	Rate	×	Total Depreciation	=	Yearly Depreciation
1	3	$\dfrac{3}{6}$		$10,000		$ 5,000.00
2	2	$\dfrac{2}{6}$		10,000		3,333.33
3	1	$\dfrac{1}{6}$		$10,000		1,666.67
						$10,000.00

14. Using the sum-of-the-years'-digits method, determine depreciation for the ninth year of a building with an estimated usable life of 40 years and a resale value of $50,000. It cost $6,000,000.

$\dfrac{40 \times 41}{2} = 820$

$6,000,000 - 50,000 = 5,950,000$ Total depreciation

Year	Digit	Rate	×	Total Depreciation	=	Yearly Depreciation
1	40					
2	39					
|	|					
|	|					
|	|					
9	32	$\dfrac{32}{820}$	×	$5,950,000	=	$232,195.12

15. Amalgamated Clothing Manufacturers purchased 20 ironing machines for $600 each. It is estimated the machines will last 20 years and have a $25 salvage value each. Calculate the total depreciation for all 20 machines in the eighth year using the sum-of-the-years'-digits method.

$\dfrac{20 \times 21}{2} = 210$ $600 - 25 = 575$

$575 \times 20 = 11,500$ Total depreciation

Year	Digit	Rate	×	Total Depreciation	=	Yearly Depreciation
1	20					
2	19					
|	|					
|	|					
|	|					
8	13	$\dfrac{13}{210}$	×	$11,500	=	$711.90

16. Mario's Curios bought a company car for $17,990. The car is estimated to have a usable life of 90,000 miles. Such cars can be sold to a used car lot for an estimated $800. Using the units-of-production method, determine the depreciation over the car's life if it was driven 25,000 miles the first year; 28,000 the second year; 10,000 the third year; and 27,000 the fourth year.

Cost per unit $= \dfrac{\text{cost} - \text{resale value}}{\text{total units}}$

Cost per unit $= \dfrac{17,990 - 800}{90,000}$

Cost per unit $= \dfrac{17,190}{90,000} = .191$

Year	Yearly Production	× Cost per Unit of Production	= Depreciation
1	25,000	$.191	$ 4,775
2	28,000	.191	5,348
3	10,000	.191	1,910
4	27,000	.191	5,157
Total	90,000		$17,190

17. A new pump cost Western Oil Co. $112,000. Such pumps last an estimated 34,520 hours. Pumps of this type will be used as a trade-in for an estimated $3,000. Using the units-of-production method, determine the depreciation over the pump's life if it runs 7,450 hours the first year; 8,120 the second year; 4,610 the third year; 7,430 the fourth year; and 6,910 the fifth year.

$$\text{Cost per unit} = \frac{\text{cost} - \text{resale value}}{\text{total units}}$$
$$= \frac{\$112,000 - 3,000}{34,520}$$
$$= \frac{\$109,000}{34,520} = \$3.1575898 \quad \text{Answers will be slightly different if you round.)}$$

Year	Yearly Production	×	Cost per Unit of Production	=	Depreciation
1	7,450		$3.1575898		$ 23,524.04
2	8,120		3.1575898		25,639.63
3	4,610		3.1575898		14,556.49
4	7,430		3.1575898		23,460.89
5	6,910		3.1575898		21,818.95
Total	34,520				$109,000.00

19. Charles I, Inc., uses the units-of-production method for depreciation. A $12,000 pipe-cutting machine with an estimated $4,000 residual value produced the following number of units over its estimated 20,000-unit life: first year, 4,200; second year, 3,900; third year, 4,600; fourth year, 3,300; fifth year, 4,000. Determine each year's depreciation.

$$\text{Cost per unit} = \frac{\text{cost} - \text{resale value}}{\text{total units}}$$
$$= \frac{\$12,000 - 4,000}{20,000}$$
$$= \frac{\$8,000}{20,000} = \$.40$$

Year	Yearly Production	×	Cost per Unit of Production	=	Depreciation
1	4,200		$.40		$1,680.00
2	3,900		.40		1,560.00
3	4,600		.40		1,840.00
4	3,300		.40		1,320.00
5	4,000		.40		1,600.00
Total	20,000				$8,000.00

18. Harvey House Delicacies estimates it can sell old mixing machines for $600. New ones cost $8,000. One mixer's expected life was 873 days of actual productive use. It has been used the following number of days: 260 days the first year, 180 days the second year, 313 days the third year, and 120 days the fourth year. Determine the depreciation for each year using the units-of-production method.

$$\text{Cost per unit} = \frac{\text{cost} - \text{resale value}}{\text{total units}}$$
$$= \frac{\$8,000 - 600}{873}$$
$$= \frac{\$7,400}{873} = \$8.4765178$$

Year	Yearly Production	×	Cost per Unit of Production	=	Depreciation
1	260		$8.4765178		$2,203.89
2	180		8.4765178		1,525.77
3	313		8.4765178		2,653.15
4	120		8.4765178		1,017.18
Total	873				$7,399.99

20. A machine with an estimated $3,000 scrap value cost the Berman Co. $24,000. Total production during the life of the machine is an estimated 105,000 units. Using the units-of-production method, how much can the machine be depreciated each year if it produced 27,200; 29,800; 23,500; and 24,500 in consecutive years.

$$\text{Cost per unit} = \frac{\text{cost} - \text{resale value}}{\text{total units}}$$
$$= \frac{\$24,000 - 3,000}{105,000}$$
$$= \frac{\$21,000}{105,000} = \$.20$$

Year	Yearly Production	×	Cost per Unit of Production	=	Depreciation
1	27,200		$.20		$ 5,440.00
2	29,800		.20		5,960.00
3	23,500		.20		4,700.00
4	24,500		.20		4,900.00
Total	105,000				$21,000.00

17.5

21. Old Fido Dog Food Co. purchased six new pressure cookers for $800 each. The firm estimates a usable life of four years and a residual value of $100 apiece. Find the total depreciation for the new cookers in each year using the declining-balance method at 200% of the straight-line rate.

$6 \times (\$800 - 100) = \$700 \times 6 = \$4,200$ Total allowable depreciation
200% Declining Balance
$$\frac{1}{4} \times 200\% = 50\%$$

Year	Balance (Book Value)	× Rate	= Yearly Depreciation	Total Depreciation	Allowable Depreciation
1	$4,800	50%	$2,400	$2,400	$4,200
2	2,400	50%	1,200	3,600	4,200
3	1,200	50%	600	4,200	4,200
4*	600		0	4,200	4,200

*At the end of the third year all of the allowable $4,200 had been taken.

22. Dr. Rosko Brown, D.D.S, depreciates tooth drills using the declining-balance method at 150% of the straight-line rate. Calculate the yearly depreciation for $1,200 worth of drills that have an estimated $400 resale value and a five-year usable life expectancy.

$1,200 - 400 = \$800$ Total allowable depreciation
150% Declining Balance
$$\frac{1}{5} \times 150\% = 30\%$$

Year	Balance (Book Value)	× Rate	= Yearly Depreciation	Total Depreciation	Allowable Depreciation
1	$1,200.00	30%	$360.00	$360.00	$800
2	840.00	30%	252.00	612.00	800
3	588.00	30%	176.40	788.40	800
4*	411.60	30%	11.60	800.00	800
5	400.00		0	800.00	800

*At the end of the third year $788.40 of the allowable $800 had been taken, which left $11.60 ($800 − 788.40 = $11.60) to be taken in the fourth year. No depreciation can be taken in the fifth year.

23. AAA Gutters and Downspouts bought a sheet metal–bending machine for $2,450. The machine is estimated to have a usable life of four years and a salvage value of $50 at a local junkyard. Find the yearly depreciation using the declining-balance method at 125% of the straight-line rate.

$2,450 − 50 = $2,400 Total allowable depreciation

125% Declining Balance

$\frac{1}{4} \times 125\% = 31.25\%$

Year	Balance (Book value)	× Rate =	Yearly Depreciation	Total Depreciation	Allowable Depreciation
1	$2,450.00	31.25%	$ 765.63	$ 765.63	$2,400
2	1,684.37	31.25%	526.37	1,292.00	2,400
3	1,158.00	31.25%	361.88	1,653.88	2,400
4*	796.12		746.12	2,400.00	2,400
	50.00				

*At the end of the fourth year $1,653.88 of the allowable $2,400 had been taken, which left $746.12 ($2,400 − 1,653.88 = $746.12). All of the remaining allowable depreciation can be taken in the fourth year.

24. Block's Roofing Co. spent $1,100 for new ladders for the roofers. At the end of the three-year estimated usable life, Block estimates they can be sold as junk for $100. Find the yearly depreciation using the declining-balance method at 125% of the straight-line rate.

$1,100 − 100 = $1,000 = Total allowable depreciation

200% Declining Balance

$\frac{1}{3} \times 125\% = 41.67\%$

Year	Balance (Book value)	× Rate =	Yearly Depreciation	Total Depreciation	Allowable Depreciation
1	$1,100.00	41.67%	$458.33	$ 458.33	$1,000
2	641.67	41.67%	267.36	725.69	1,000
3	374.31		274.31	1,000.00	1,000
	100.00				

25. The Golden Gloves Youth Center bought $20,000 of gymnastic equipment. It is estimated the equipment can be resold for $2,450 and has a five-year usable life. Calculate the yearly depreciation using the declining-balance method at 150% of the straight-line rate.

$20,000 − 2,450 = $17,550 Total allowable depreciation

150% Declining Balance

$\frac{1}{5} \times 150\% = 30\%$

Year	Balance (Book value)	× Rate =	Yearly Depreciation	Total Depreciation	Allowable Depreciation
1	$20,000	30%	$6,000	$ 6,000	$17,550
2	14,000	30%	4,200	10,200	17,550
3	9,800	30%	2,940	13,140	17,550
4	6,860	30%	2,058	15,198	17,550
5*	4,802		2,352	17,550	17,550

*At the end of the fourth year $15,198.00 of the allowable $17,550 had been taken, which left $2,352 ($17,550 − 15,198 = $2,352). All of the remaining allowable depreciation can be taken in the fifth year.

17.6

26. Classic Plaster, Inc., replaced all of the desk chairs in the office for $960. Determine the fifth year's depreciation using the MACRS method.

$ 960.00
× __8.93%__ From Table 17.1 and Table 17.2
$ 85.73 Fifth-year depreciation

27. Three years ago Airtech Heating Systems replaced two company work vans for $17,260 each. How much can the company depreciate the vans the fourth year using the MACRS method?

$17,260.00 × 2 = $34,520

$ 34,520
× __11.52%__ From Table 17.1 and Table 17.2
$ 3,976.70 Fourth-year depreciation

28. Gorbochev Wheat Farm in Kansas replaced a dilapidated barn with a new one five years ago for $240,500. Using the MACRS method, how much can it be depreciated the sixth year?

$240,500.00
× __5.285%__ From Table 17.1 and Table 17.2
$ 12,710.43 Sixth-year depreciation

29. Burpsy Cola, Inc., purchased $6,000 worth of food-handling equipment in January of this year. How much can Burpsy depreciate the equipment in each year using the MACRS method?

$ 6,000.00
× __33.33%__ From Table 17.1 and Table 17.2
$ 1,999.80 First-year depreciation
$ 6,000.00
× __44.45%__ From Table 17.1 and Table 17.2
$ 2,667.00 Second-year depreciation
$ 6,000.00
× __14.81%__ From Table 17.1 and Table 17.2
$ 888.60 Third-year depreciation
$ 6,000.00
× __7.41%__ From Table 17.1 and Table 17.2
$ 444.60 Fourth-year depreciation

30. Mr. George's Chicken Processing bought some new computers for $23,400. How much can the company depreciate the equipment each year using the MACRS method?

$23,400.00
× 20.00% From Table 17.1 and Table 17.2
$ 4,680.00 First-year depreciation
$23,400.00
× 32.00% From Table 17.1 and Table 17.2
$ 7,488.00 Second-year depreciation
$23,400.00
× 19.20% From Table 17.1 and Table 17.2
$ 4,492.80 Third-year depreciation
$23,400.00
× 11.52% From Table 17.1 and Table 17.2
$ 2,695.68 Fourth-year depreciation
$23,400.00
× 11.52% From Table 17.1 and Table 17.2
$ 2,695.68 Fifth-year depreciation
$23,400.00
× 5.76% From Table 17.1 and Table 17.2
$ 1,347.84 Sixth-year depreciation

> ## CHAPTER REVIEW PROBLEMS

Answers to odd-numbered problems are given in Appendix A.

Drill Problems

Find the yearly depreciation using the straight-line method for the following problems:

	Cost of Asset	Time (years)	Estimated Salvage Value	Depreciation
1.	$ 96,000	10	$ 6,000	$9,000.00
2.	18,000	5	600	3,480.00
3.	3,500	8	50	431.25
4.	220,000	25	18,000	8,080.00
5.	35,000	6	5,000	5,000.00

Find the first and last years' depreciation using the partial-year depreciation straight-line-method for the following problems:

	Cost of Asset	Time (years)	Estimated Salvage Value	Date of Purchase	Depreciation First year	Last year
6.	$36,000	6	$4,000	Feb. 4	$4,888.88	$ 444.44
7.	5,000	3	40	Apr. 20	1,102.22	551.11
8.	16,500	10	1,000	Nov. 12	258.33	1,291.67
9.	3,200	5	600	Jan. 24	476.67	43.33
10.	76,500	8	1,650	June 17	4,678.13	4,678.13

Find the year's depreciation using the sum-of-the-years'-digits method for the following problems:

	Cost of Asset	Time (years)	Estimated Salvage Value	Year of Depreciation	Depreciation
11.	$250,000	6	$50,000	4	$28,571.43
12.	12,600	5	600	3	2,400.00

	Cost of Asset	Estimated Time (years)	Salvage Value	Year of Depreciation	Depreciation
13.	3,000	8	250	5	305.56
14.	95,000	25	7,000	12	3,790.77
15.	5,000	4	700	1	1,720.00

Find the depreciation using the units-of-production method for the following problems:

	Cost of Asset	Estimated Total Units Produced	Salvage Value	Units in Depreciation Year	Depreciation
16.	$ 85,000	250,000	$5,000	29,583	$ 9,466.56
17.	37,600	85,000	1,200	18,420	7,888.09
18.	100,000	158,000	350	43,280	27,296.53
19.	12,250	10,300	400	1,628	1,872.99
20.	2,780	150,000	600	60,000	872.00

Find the indicated depreciation using the declining-balance method for the following problems:

	Cost of Asset	Estimated Years of Usable Live	Salvage Value	Percent of Straight-Line Rate	Year	Depreciation
21.	$18,000	4	$2,000	200%	3rd	$2,250.00
22.	7,600	3	300	150%	2nd	1,900.00
23.	50,000	5	4,500	125%	4th	5,273.44
24.	11,450	5	400	200%	3rd	1,648.80
25.	1,390	6	600	150%	5th	0

Find the indicated depreciation using the MACRS method for the following problems:

	Cost of Asset	Type of Asset	Year	Depreciation
26.	$19,600	Automobile	3rd	$3,763.20
27.	9,800	3-yr.-old racehorse	2nd	4,356.10
28.	46,000	Sidewalks	9th	2,718.60
29.	1,360	Grain bin	4th	169.86
30.	680	Breeding pig	3rd	130.56

Word Problems

31. Melissa Marvin, a real estate broker, bought a new Pontiac to drive only for her business. It cost $28,600. The dealer in Memphis charged her $260 extra for a car phone. She expects to drive it four years and trade it in for $4,000. Find the amount of the yearly depreciation using the straight-line method.

$28,600 + 260 = $28,860 Cost

$$\text{Yearly depreciation} = \frac{\text{cost} - \text{resale value}}{\text{usable life}} \qquad \text{Yearly depreciation} = \frac{\$28,860 - 4,000}{4} \qquad \text{Yearly depreciation} = \frac{\$24,860}{4} = \$6,215$$

Chapter 17 Accounting Applications: Depreciation

32. Aikman Moving Co. bought a moving van for $67,400. The dealer charged Aikman $160 to deliver it from the factory. It has an estimated life of five years. Management estimates it can then be sold for $7,000. Determine the first and last years' depreciation using the partial-year straight-line method if the van was purchased March 8.

$67,400 + 160 - 7,000 = $60,560 Total depreciation

$$\frac{$60,560}{5} = $12,112 \text{ Annual depreciation}$$

Year	×	Annual Depreciation	×	Part of Year	=	Depreciation
1		$12,112		$\frac{10}{12}$		$10,093.33
5		$12,112		$\frac{2}{12}$		$2,018.67

33. Jean Jacque Timber Co. bought a $6,000 saw to cut up logs. Records show it can be traded in after four years of use for an estimated $400. Calculate the depreciation for each year using the sum-of-the-years'-digits method.

$$4 + 3 + 2 + 1 = 10, \text{ or } \frac{4 \times 5}{2} = 10$$

$6,000 - 400 = $5,600 Total depreciation

Year	Digit	Rate	×	Total Depreciation	=	Yearly Depreciation
1	4	$\frac{4}{10}$		$5,600		$2,240
2	3	$\frac{3}{10}$		5,600		1,680
3	2	$\frac{2}{10}$		5,600		1,120
4	1	$\frac{1}{10}$		5,600		560
						$5,600

34. Mack's Sporting Goods Factory bought a leather-stitching machine for $6,600. The machine is expected to be worn out and need to be replaced after it has sewn 250,000 catcher's mitts. It is estimated it can be sold for $200. Using the units-of-production method, determine the depreciation over the machine's life if it produces 67,120 catcher's mitts the first year, 89,530 the second year, and 93,350 the third year.

$$\text{Cost per unit} = \frac{\text{cost} - \text{resale value}}{\text{total units}}$$

$$= \frac{$6,600 - 200}{250,000}$$

$$= \frac{$6,400}{250,000} = $.0256$$

Year	Yearly Production	×	Cost per Unit of Production	=	Depreciation
1	67,120		$.0256		$1,718.27
2	89,530		.0256		2,291.97
3	93,350		.0256		2,389.76
Total	250,000				$6,400.00

35. Buck's Outboard Motor Repair bought a machine for grinding valves for $1,500. Estimates are that it can be sold for scrap in three years for $25. Calculate the yearly depreciation using the declining-balance method at 200%, 150%, and 125% of the straight-line rate.

$1,500 - 25 = $1,475 Total allowable depreciation

200% Declining Balance

$$\frac{1}{3} \times 200\% = 66.67\%$$

Year	Balance (Book Value)	× Rate	= Yearly Depreciation	Total Depreciation	Allowable Depreciation
1	$1,500.00	66.67%	$1,000.00	$1,000.00	$1,475
2*	500.00	66.67%	333.33	1,333.33	1,475
3	166.67		141.67	1,475.00	1,475
	25.00				1,475

*At the end of the second year $1,333.33 of the allowable $1,475 depreciation had been taken, which left $141.67 ($1,475 − 1,333.33 = $141.67). All of the remaining depreciation can be taken in the third year.

150% Declining Balance

$$\frac{1}{3} \times 150\% = 50\%$$

Year	Balance (Book Value)	× Rate	= Yearly Depreciation	Total Depreciation	Allowable Depreciation
1	$1,500.00	50%	$750.00	$ 750.00	$1,475
2	750.00	50%	375.00	1,125.00	1,475
3*	375.00		350.00	1,475.00	1,475
	25.00				

*At the end of the second year $1,125.00 of the allowable $1,475 had been taken, which left $350.00 ($1,475 − 1,125.00 = $350.00). All of the remaining allowable depreciation can be taken in the third year.

125% Declining Balance

$$\frac{1}{3} \times 125\% = 41.67\%$$

Year	Balance (Book Value)	× Rate	= Yearly Depreciation	Total Depreciation	Allowable Depreciation
1	$1,500.00	41.67%	$625.00	$ 625.00	$1,475
2	875.00	41.67%	364.58	989.58	1,475
3*	510.42		485.42	1,475.00	1,475
	25.00				

*At the end of the second year $989.64 of the allowable $1,475 had been taken, which left $485.36 ($1,475 − 989.64 = $485.36). All of the remaining allowable depreciation can be taken in the third year.

36. Last year Reading Railroad bought six new flatcars for $368,000 each. How much can the company depreciate them the first year using the MACRS method?

$6 \times $368,000 = $2,208,000$

$2,208,000.00
× 14.29%   From Table 17.1 and Table 17.2
$ 315,523.20   First-year depreciation

37. General Dynamics purchased $1,820,000 worth of equipment to use in airplane construction. Management estimates it can be sold for scrap metal for $20,000 when it is used up. How much can GD depreciate in the fourth year using the straight-line method, the MACRS method, the sum-of-the-years'-digits method, and the declining-balance method at 200% of the straight-line rate. The equipment has an estimated 15-year usable life.

Straight-Line Method

$$\text{Yearly depreciation} = \frac{\text{cost} - \text{resale value}}{\text{usable life}}$$

$$= \frac{\$1,820,000 - 20,000}{15}$$

$$= \frac{\$1,800,000}{15} = \$120,000$$

MACRS Method

$1,820,000
× 12.49%   From Table 17.1 and Table 17.2 (seven years)
$ 227,318 Fourth-year depreciation

Sum-of-The-Year's-Digits Method

$$\frac{15 \times 16}{2} = 120$$

$1,820,000 − 20,000 = $1,800,000 Total depreciation

Year	Digit	Rate ×	Total Depreciation	=	Yearly Depreciation
1	15				
2	14				
3	13				
4	12	$\frac{12}{120}$	$1,800,000		$180,000.00

200% Declining Balance

$$\frac{1}{15} \times 200\% = 13.33\%$$

Year	Balance (Book Value) ×	Rate	=	Yearly Depreciation	Total Depreciation	Allowable Depreciation
1	$1,820,000.00	13.33%		$242,666.67	$142,666.67	$1,820,000.00
2	1,577,333.33	13.33%		210,311.11	452,977.78	1,820,000.00
3	1,367,022.33	13.33%		182,269.63	635,247.41	1,820,000.00
4	1,184,752.59	13.33%		157,967.01 Fourth-year Depreciation	793,214.42	1,820,000.00

CRITICAL THINKING GROUP PROJECT

Your company, the Weisenhunt Manufacturing Corporation, manufacturers and sells telecommunications equipment. Nationwide, 14 salespeople call on industrial accounts. Each salesperson is provided a new automobile every five years or 100,000 miles, whichever comes sooner. All salespeople were given a new automobile this year with an average cost of $22,500 each. Experience has shown that an average of $2,500 can be expected from a trade-in.

1. Prepare depreciation schedules showing each year's rate of depreciation, annual depreciation, accumulated depreciation, and the book value using each of the following methods:

(a) Straight-line method

Year	Rate	Total Depreciation	Yearly Depreciation	Accumulated Depreciation	Book Value
1	1/5	$280,000	$56,000	$ 56,000	$259,000
2	1/5	$280,000	$56,000	112,000	203,000
3	1/5	280,000	56,000	168,000	147,000
4	1/5	280,000	56,000	224,000	91,000
5	1/5	280,000	56,000	280,000	35,000

(b) Sum-of-the-years'-digits method

Year	Rate	Total Depreciation	Yearly Depreciation	Accumulated Depreciation	Book Value
1	5/15	$280,000	$93,333.33	$ 93,333.33	$221,666.67
2	4/15	280,000	74,666.67	168,000.00	147,000.00
3	3/15	280,000	56,000.00	224,000.00	91,000.00
4	2/15	280,000	37,333.33	261,333.33	53,666.67
5	1/15	280,000	18,666.67	280,000.00	35,000.00

(c) Units-of-production method (Remember, combine the mileage to find the total units of production for all automobiles). The actual miles driven each year were as follows:

First year, 178,000   Fourth year, 280,000
Second year, 360,000   Fifth year, 240,000
Third year, 340,000   Sixth year, 130,000 (only 2,000 can be used this year.)

Year	Rate	Miles Driven	Yearly Depreciation	Accumulated Depreciation	Book Value
1	.2	178,000	$ 35,600	$ 35,600	$279,400
2	.2	360,000	72,000	107,600	207,400
3	.2	340,000	68,000	175,600	139,400
4	.2	280,000	56,000	231,600	83,400
5	.2	240,000	48,000	279,600	35,400
6	.2	2,000	400	280,000	35,000

(d) Declining-balance method at 150% of the straight-line rate

Year	Rate	Beginning Book Value	Yearly Depreciation	Accumulated Depreciation	Ending Book Value
1	.3	$315,000	$94,500	$ 94,500	$220,500
2	.3	220,500	66,150	160,650	154,350
3	.3	154,350	46,305	206,955	108,045
4	.3	108,045	32,413.50	239,368.50	75,631.50
5		75,631.50	40,631.50	280,000	35,000

(e) MACRS method

Year	Rate	Total Cost	Yearly Depreciation	Accumulated Depreciation	Book Value
1	20.00%	$315,000	$ 63,000	$ 63,000	$252,000
2	32.00%	315,000	100,800	163,800	151,200
3	19.20%	315,000	60,480	224,280	90,720
4	11.52%	315,000	36,288	260,568	54,432
5	11.52%	315,000	36,288	296,856	18,144
6	5.76%	315,000	18,144	315,000	0

2. Which method would you recommend that your company use for financial and state income tax purposes? Why?
   Student answers will vary, but the explanation should be logical.

3. For federal income tax purposes, the MACRS will be used. Since depreciation is tax deductible, if you multiply the company's tax rate by the amount of annual depreciation, you will find the amount of tax savings for each year. If Weisenhunt has a tax rate of 37.5%, calculate the amount of tax savings for each year the automobiles are depreciated.

Year	Tax Rate	Depreciation	Tax Savings
1	37.5%	$ 63,000	$ 23,625
2	37.5%	100,800	37,800
3	37.5%	60,480	22,680
4	37.5%	36,288	13,608
5	37.5%	36,288	13,608
6	37.5%	18,144	6,804

4. What is the total amount of tax savings?
   $118,125

5. If one of the financial depreciation methods was used, what would be the total amount of tax savings (again, assuming a tax rate of 37.5%)?
   $105,000

6. How can you account for the difference in the total tax savings when using the financial methods instead of the MACRS?
   The MACRS method allows recovery of the total cost of an asset, while the financial accounting methods require that a reasonable amount be subtracted from the total cost to determine the allowable depreciation amount. Thus, the difference is 37.5% of the trade-in value of $35,000.

1. Why would any business firm want to use the declining
balance at a multiple of the straight-line rate? **W**
Assets typically lose more of their value in the first year and less in
each succeeding year. Since money now is more valuable than money
in the future, an accelerated depreciation method allows business
firms to save more in taxes now and take advantage of cheaper
money in the future.

2. What is the major shortcoming of straight-line
depreciation? **W**
Most assets lose the greatest amount of their original value in the
earliest time of their use. Straight-line depreciation is considered
unrealistic for most assets because it assumes that all assets lose their
value at a constant rate.

3. Cougot's Musical Instruments estimates a six-year usable
life for its furniture that had an original cost of $227,000.
It estimates a residual value of $17,000. Find the yearly
depreciation using the straight-line method.

$$\text{Yearly depreciation} = \frac{\text{cost} - \text{resale value}}{\text{usable life}}$$
$$= \frac{\$227,000 - 17,000}{6}$$
$$= \frac{\$210,000}{6} = \$35,000$$

4. New equipment for Rita's Realty Office cost $8,200. Rita
will depreciate it over an eight-year period using straight-
line depreciation and sell the old furniture to a salvage
store for an estimated $100. How much will the yearly
depreciation be?

$$\text{Yearly depreciation} = \frac{\text{cost} - \text{resale value}}{\text{usable life}}$$
$$= \frac{\$8,200 - 100}{8}$$
$$= \frac{\$8,100}{8} = \$1,012.50$$

5. Alta-Mesa Aluminum Siding Co. bought a power nailing
machine for $7,400. Its usable life is four years, and it is
estimated it can be sold for $50 as junk. Determine the
first and last years' depreciation using the partial-year
straight-line method if it was purchased June 3.

$7,400 - 50 = \$7,350$ Total depreciation
$\dfrac{\$7,350}{4} = \$1,837.50$ Annual depreciation

Year	×	Annual Depreciation	×	Part of Year	=	Depreciation
1		$1,837.50		$\frac{7}{12}$		$1,071.88
4		1,837.50		$\frac{5}{12}$		765.63

6. On March 3, Earth and You Landscape Co. bought a ditch-
digging machine for $3,000. The machine will be
depreciated over six years, and the resale value is
estimated to be $300. Determine the first and last years'
depreciation using the partial-year straight-line method.

$3,000 - 300 = \$2,700$ Total depreciation
$\dfrac{\$2,700}{6} = \$450$ Annual depreciation

Year	×	Annual Depreciation	×	Part of Year	=	Depreciation
1		$450		$\frac{10}{12}$		$375
6		450		$\frac{2}{10}$		75

7. Hytech Cabinet Works bought a $4,200 ShopSmith to
finish cabinets. It is estimated the ShopSmith can be sold
for junk after five years of use for $800. Calculate the
depreciation for each year using the sum-of-the-years'-
digits method.

$5 + 4 + 3 + 2 + 1 = 15$, or $\dfrac{5 \times 6}{2} = 15$

$\$4,200 - 800 = \$3,400$ Total depreciation

Year	Digit	Rate	× Total Depreciation	= Yearly Depreciation
1	5	$\frac{5}{15}$	$3,400	$1,133.33
2	4	$\frac{4}{15}$	3,400	906.67
3	3	$\frac{3}{15}$	3,400	680.00
4	3	$\frac{2}{15}$	3,400	453.33
5	1	$\frac{1}{15}$	3,400	226.67
				$3,400.00

8. Just-State Inspections bought a machine to test engine
emissions for $5,000. It is estimated the machine can be
sold to a salvage yard after four years of use for $600.
Calculate the depreciation for each year using the sum-of-
the-years'-digits method.

$4 + 3 + 2 + 1 = 10$, or $\dfrac{4 \times 5}{2} = 10$

$\$5,000 - 600 = \$4,400$ Total depreciation

Year	Digit	Rate	× Total Depreciation	= Yearly Depreciation
1	4	$\frac{4}{10}$	$4,400	$1,760
2	3	$\frac{3}{10}$	4,400	1,320
3	2	$\frac{2}{10}$	4,400	880
4	1	$\frac{1}{10}$	4,400	440
				$4,400

9. Tech-Engine Rebuilder's bought a milling machine for surfacing fly wheels. It is estimated that the machine, which cost $3,600, will be worn out and need replacing after it has surfaced 50,000 flywheels. The resale value is estimated to be $400. Using the units-of-production method, determine the yearly depreciation if the machine ground 18,718 the first year, 21,440 the second year, and 9,842 the third year.

$$\text{Cost per unit} = \frac{\text{cost} - \text{resale value}}{\text{total units}}$$
$$= \frac{\$3,600 - 400}{50,000}$$
$$= \frac{\$3,200}{50,000} = \$.064$$

Year	Yearly Production	×	Cost per Unit of Production	=	Depreciation
1	18,718		$.064		$1,197.95
2	21,440		.064		1,372.16
3	9,842		.064		629.89
Total	50,000				$3,200.00

10. Bently Air Conditioning and Heating Co. purchased a pickup truck that is expected to be used for 160,000 miles. The truck cost $18,400 and can be traded in for an estimated $250. Using the units-of-production method, determine the yearly depreciation if the truck is driven 57,542 miles the first year, 49,330 the second year, and 53,128 the third year.

$$\text{Cost per unit} = \frac{\text{cost} - \text{resale value}}{\text{total units}}$$
$$= \frac{\$18,400 - 250}{160,000}$$
$$= \frac{\$18,150}{160,000} = \$.1134375$$

Year	Yearly Production	×	Cost per Unit of Production	=	Depreciation
1	57,542		$.1134375		$ 6,527.42
2	49,330		.1134375		5,595.87
3	53,128		.1134375		6,026.71
Total	160,000				$18,150.00

11. The Global Outdoor Sign Co. bought a crane for $27,000. Estimates are that it will be sold for scrap in four years for $1,800. Calculate the yearly depreciation using the declining-balance method at 200% of the straight-line rate.

200% Declining Balance
$27,000 − 1,800 = $25,200 Allowable depreciation

$$\frac{1}{4} \times 200\% = 50\%$$

Year	Balance (Book Value)	×	Rate =	Yearly Depreciation	Total Depreciation	Allowable Depreciation
1	$27,000		50%	$13,500	$ 13,500	$25,200
2	13,500		50%	6,750	20,250	25,200
3	6,750		50%	3,375	23,625	25,200
4	3,375			1,575	25,200	25,200
	1,800					

12. Laidlaw Waste Disposal purchased 20 new dumpsters for $1,200 each. It is estimated they can be sold for scrap metal in three years for $15 each. Calculate the yearly depreciation using the declining-balance method at 150% of the straight-line rate.

150% Declining Balance
$1,200 × 20 = $24,000 Book value
$15 × 20 = $300 Scrap value
$24,000 − 300 = $23,700 Allowable depreciation

$$\frac{1}{3} \times 150\% = 50\%$$

Year	Balance (Book Value)	×	Rate =	Yearly Depreciation	Total Depreciation	Allowable Depreciation
1	$24,000		50%	$12,000.00	$12,000.00	$23,700
2	12,000		50%	6,000.00	18,000.00	23,700
3	6,000			5,700.00	23,700.00	23,700
	300					

13. Last year the Travel Hut Agency paid $1,900 each for nine computers that are estimated to be worth $100 as junk after they are completely depreciated. How much can the company depreciate them the second year using the MACRS method?

$ 1,900 × 9 = $17,100 = Total depreciation
$17,100
× 32% From Table 17.1 and Table 17.2 (five years)
$ 5,472 Second-year depreciation

APPLICATION 1

The Springfield Department Store has prepared a computer spreadsheet program to compare several depreciation methods for its new computer system. From that comparison, management will select the method that best suits its goals. When you open Ch17App1 from your computer spreadsheet applications disk, you will see the form shown here:

Springfield Department Store
2617 Main Street
Box 219
Springfield, Maryland 58109
Telephone: 301-555-2158   FAX: 301-555-3498

DEPRECIATION SCHEDULE

Year	Straight = Line	Sum-of-the Years' = Digits	Declining = Balance 1.5 X SL	Modified Cost Recovery		Asset	Cost	Years of Usable Life	Salvage Value	Month Purchased
1	#DIV/0!	#NUM!	$0.00	$0.00						
2	#DIV/0!	#NUM!	$0.00	$0.00						
3	#DIV/0!	#NUM!	$0.00	$0.00						
4	#DIV/0!	#NUM!	$0.00	$0.00						
5	#DIV/0!	#NUM!	$0.00	$0.00						
6	#DIV/0!	#NUM!	$0.00	$0.00						
TOTAL	#DIV/0!	#NUM!	$0.00	$0.00						

Enter the following information:

Asset	Cell	Cost	Cell	Years of Usable Life	Cell	Salvage Value	Cell	Month Purchased	Cell
Computer	F15	$4,758	G15	5	H15	$450	I15	1	J7

Answer the following questions after you have completed the spreadsheet:

1. What is the depreciation for the first year using each of the depreciation methods?
2. Which method of calculating depreciation ended with a different total amount of depreciation?
3. What is the depreciation for the fifth year using each of the depreciation methods?
4. Which method of calculating depreciation gave the most depreciation in the third year?
5. Which method of calculating depreciation gave the least depreciation in the sixth year?

GROUP REPORT

FOR CHAPTER 17 APPLICATION 1

Springfield has purchased other assets that will be depreciated, as described here:

Asset	Cost	Salvage Value	Usable Life	Month Purchased
Truck	$ 38,000	$ 4,000	4 years	1
Fixtures	175,000	20,000	5 years	1
Furniture	350,000	25,000	5 years	1

Write a report to the store manager describing the results of each depreciation method and make recommendations about which method should be used for each asset, and why.

APPLICATION 2

The Springfield Department Store has developed a computer spreadsheet to evaluate varying depreciation methods for its new retail store. When you open Ch17App2 from your computer spreadsheet applications disk, you will see the form shown here:

Springfield Department Store

2617 Main Street
Box 219
Springfield, Maryland 58109
Telephone: 301-555-2158   FAX: 301-555-3498

DEPRECIATION SCHEDULE

| Year | DEPRECIATION METHOD | | | | Asset | Cost | Years of Usable Life | Salvage Value | Month Purchased |
	Straight - Line	Sum-of-the Years'-Digits	Declining - Balance 1.6 X SL	Modified Cost Recovery					
1	#DIV/0!	#NUM!	#NUM!	$0.00					
2	#DIV/0!	#NUM!	#NUM!	$0.00					
3	#DIV/0!	#NUM!	#NUM!	$0.00					
4	#DIV/0!	#NUM!	#NUM!	$0.00					
5	#DIV/0!	#NUM!	#NUM!	$0.00					
6	#DIV/0!	#NUM!	#NUM!	$0.00					
7	#DIV/0!	#NUM!	#NUM!	$0.00					
8	#DIV/0!	#NUM!	#NUM!	$0.00					
9	#DIV/0!	#NUM!	#NUM!	$0.00					
10	#DIV/0!	#NUM!	#NUM!	$0.00					
11	#DIV/0!	#NUM!	#NUM!	$0.00					
12	#DIV/0!	#NUM!	#NUM!	$0.00					
13	#DIV/0!	#NUM!	#NUM!	$0.00					
14	#DIV/0!	#NUM!	#NUM!	$0.00					
15	#DIV/0!	#NUM!	#NUM!	$0.00					
16	#DIV/0!	#NUM!	#NUM!	$0.00					
17	#DIV/0!	#NUM!	#NUM!	$0.00					
18	#DIV/0!	#NUM!	#NUM!	$0.00					
19	#DIV/0!	#NUM!	#NUM!	$0.00					
20	#DIV/0!	#NUM!	#NUM!	$0.00					
21	#DIV/0!	#NUM!	#NUM!	$0.00					
22	#DIV/0!	#NUM!	#NUM!	$0.00					
23	#DIV/0!	#NUM!	#NUM!	$0.00					
24	#DIV/0!	#NUM!	#NUM!	$0.00					
25	#DIV/0!	#NUM!	#NUM!	$0.00					
26	#DIV/0!	#NUM!	#NUM!	$0.00					
27	#DIV/0!	#NUM!	#NUM!	$0.00					
28	#DIV/0!	#NUM!	#NUM!	$0.00					
29	#DIV/0!	#NUM!	#NUM!	$0.00					
30	#DIV/0!	#NUM!	#NUM!	$0.00					
31				$0.00					
32				$0.00					
TOTAL	#DIV/0!	#NUM!	#NUM!	$0.00					

Enter the following information:

Asset	Cell	Cost	Cell	Years of Usable Life	Cell	Salvage Value	Cell	Month Purchased	Cell
Retail Store	F16	$2,500,000	G16	30	H16	$500,000	I16	1	J16

Answer the following questions after you have completed the spreadsheet:

1. What is the depreciation for the first year using each of the depreciation methods?
2. Which method of calculating depreciation ended with a different total amount of depreciation?
3. What is the depreciation for the 15th year using each of the depreciation methods?
4. Which method of calculating depreciation gave the most depreciation in the 23rd year?
5. Which method of calculating depreciation gave the least depreciation in the 16th year?
6. What is the 27th-year depreciation using each of the depreciation methods?

GROUP REPORT

FOR CHAPTER 17 APPLICATION 2

Springfield could depreciate the store at a more accelerated rate. Change the number of years of usable life to 10 years, 15 years, 20 years, and 25 years. Record the results of each change and include them in your report to the store manager, along with your recommendations for the number of years each asset should be depreciated, and why. (Don't forget to consider legal issues when making your recommendations.)

18

ACCOUNTING APPLICATIONS
INVENTORY AND OVERHEAD

HIGH-TECH INVENTORY FOR LOW-TECH INDUSTRY

By almost anybody's reckoning, auto salvage is a low-tech industry. AAA Small Car World had a lot of parts in stock, each labeled by hand. Paper records were kept in tiny drawers of a filing cabinet rescued when a drugstore threw it away. If a customer wanted an alternator for a Honda, an AAA employee would search the files. Trouble is, there was no way to know if an Acura alternator would also fit a Honda Accord.

For $70,000, owner Ron Sturgeon bought an inventory system using 20 PCs, numerous printers, modems, software packages, and two weeks of training for all the employees.

AAA buys about 100 junk cars a week. Now when cars arrive, an assessor tells the database that, for example, it has a 1998 Nissan Maxima. The database creates a report listing specific parts (such as taillights with chrome bezels) and prints a copy. The assessor walks around the car with the printout, checking off the usable parts. In 15 minutes the computer prints the labels for all the parts along with their prices. The program tracks interchangeable parts such as the Honda alternator that fits an Acura. The 19 salespeople at AAA's six locations use the system simultaneously, selling and invoicing in one step. As salespeople look up parts, the computer checks the number of times each part is requested by a customer, compared with the number of times that part is actually sold. If the part is requested frequently but does not sell, AAA lowers the price. High-tech inventory in a low-tech industry created an $8 million business firm.

Chapter Glossary

Perpetual inventory. Inventory continuously updated by cost-coding with a computer so that each purchase and sale is recorded.

Periodic inventory. Inventory taken at regular intervals by a physical count of items in stock.

Specific identification method. An inventory method in which the inventory value of each individual item is cost-coded. The total inventory value is the sum of the cost of items not sold at the end of a time period.

First-in, first-out (FIFO) method. An inventory method that assumes that items bought first are sold first so that the items still in the inventory are those that were purchased most recently.

Last-in, first-out (LIFO) method. An inventory method that assumes that items bought last are sold first so that the items still in the inventory are those that were purchased earliest.

Weighted-average method. An inventory method in which each item in inventory is valued at the weighted-average unit cost paid during the time interval for that item.

Retail method of estimating inventory. An inventory method used to estimate instead of actually counting the inventory. It uses a ratio of the cost of goods available for sale to the retail value of goods available for sale.

Gross profit method of estimating inventory. An inventory method used to estimate instead of actually counting the inventory. It uses the average rate of gross profit to net sales.

Overhead. Business expenses other than the costs of materials or merchandise, such as administrative salaries, rent, utilities, and advertising.

Inventory is the unsold merchandise a firm has on hand at a specific time. The amount of inventory kept by a firm is important because if it keeps too much, the firm might tie up funds that could be used for something else and might have to pay taxes on it as an asset. If it keeps too little, a firm might not have goods to fill customer orders. That could anger customers and cost future sales. The method of valuing inventory often reflects directly on company profits since the value of inventory is one of the amounts used to determine net income.

LEARNING UNIT 1
INVENTORY VALUATION METHODS

During any time period, a firm may purchase merchandise several times. At the end of each period, the value of the ending inventory must be determined. To value an inventory, the first step is to determine the number of items in inventory. Many large companies keep a **perpetual inventory** that is continuously updated by cost-coding with a computer so that each purchase and sale is recorded. Most firms make a physical count of items in inventory at regular intervals. This is referred to as a **periodic inventory**. Even companies using a perpetual inventory will also conduct a periodic inventory to account for such things as errors, theft, breakage, and spillage. The common periodic methods are specific identification; first-in, first-out (FIFO); last-in, first-out (LIFO); and weighted-average.

18.1 Specific Identification Method

The **specific identification method** is used if individual inventory items can be easily identified and costs do not fluctuate. Each item is cost-coded with numbers or letters, and the inventory value is the sum of the costs of the individual items at the end of an accounting period. This is usually used for big-ticket items such as cars, major appliances, and furniture.

To find the value of inventory using the specific identification method, merely add the value of all the items in inventory.

EXAMPLE   A count of refrigerators in inventory at the Alpine Appliance Store found 24 in stock. Two of them were from the beginning inventory and cost $545 each, 8 were from a May 10 purchase and cost $450 each, and 14 were from a November 12 purchase and cost $500 each. Using the specific identification method, find the value of the inventory.

Solution

$$
\begin{array}{lll}
2 @ \$545 & = & \$\ 1{,}090 \\
8 @ \ \ 450 & = & \ \ 3{,}600 \\
14 @ \ \ 500 & = & + \ 7{,}000 \\
\hline
\text{Total cost} & = & \$11{,}690
\end{array}
$$

2 ✕ 545 ▣ STO 8 ✕ 450 ▣ RCL ▣ STO 14 ✕ 500 ▣ RCL ▣ 11,690

18.1 Practice Problems

1. A count of the $\frac{3}{4}$-inch pipe fittings in inventory at Joyce Plumbing Supply found the store had 160 in stock. Fifty cost $.96 each, 40 cost $.54 each, and 70 cost $1.12 each. Using the specific identification method, find the value of the total inventory.

2. Inventory records show there were 220 saw blades in stock at Big Depot Building Supply. Code numbers on the saw blades show 20 cost $5 each, 60 cost $5.25 each, and 140 cost $5.50 each. Using the specific identification method, find the value of the inventory.

Chapter 18 Accounting Applications: Inventory and Overhead

3. Schwartz toy shop has 63 toy space modules in stock for Christmas. Code numbers on the toys show 20 cost $7.50 each, 18 cost $10.00 each, and 25 cost $12.00 each. Using the specific identification method, find the value of the inventory.

4. Bowling Bike Shop has 121 bicycles in stock. Code numbers indicate 40 cost $197.50 each, 46 cost $220.85 each, and 35 cost $203.60 each. Using the specific identification method, find the value of the inventory.

18.1 Solutions to Practice Problems

1.
50 @ $ .96	=	$ 48.00
40 @ .54	=	21.60
70 @ 1.12	=	+ 78.40
Total cost	=	$148.00

2.
20 @ $5.00	=	$ 100.00
60 @ 5.25	=	315.00
140 @ 5.50	=	+ 770.00
Total cost	=	$1,185.00

3.
20 @ $ 7.50	=	$ 150.00
18 @ 10.00	=	180.00
25 @ 12.00	=	+ 300.00
Total cost	=	$ 630.00

4.
40 @ $197.50	=	$ 7,900.00
46 @ 220.85	=	10,159.10
35 @ 203.60	=	+ 7,126.00
Total cost	=	$ 25,185.10

18.2 First-In, First-Out (FIFO) Method

The **first-in, first-out (FIFO) method** of inventory valuation assumes that the merchandise was sold in the order it was received; that is, the merchandise received first was sold first. For tax purposes, the least possible inventory value is most desirable for the business firm. FIFO would be best to use when the price a firm pays for a product is expected to decline. That happens occasionally, especially with technical products such as pocket calculators, camcorders, personal computers, digital watches, and VCRs.

EXAMPLE Using the FIFO inventory valuation method, find the value of the following inventory of baseballs at Great Game Sporting Goods:

Date of Purchase	Units Purchased	Unit Cost
Feb. 1	30	$5
May. 15	25	6
Sept. 1	40	5
Dec. 6	50	7

A December 31 count of inventory showed there were 55 baseballs in stock.

Solution Step 1. When using the FIFO method, the valuation begins with the last purchase date. Fifty of the 55 units are from the December 6 order. Multiply the number of units by the cost per unit.

Step 2. The remaining units (5) are from the September 1 order, which is the next-to-last purchase date. Multiply 5 by the unit cost of that order.

Step 3. Add the two costs.

From Dec. 6 order:	50 × $7 = $350
From Sept. 1 order:	5 × 5 = + 25
FIFO inventory	55 $375

1. Quality Band Instruments imported the following merchandise for resale: On June 1, six trumpets at $125 each; on September 3, ten trumpets at $110 each; and on November 30, eight trumpets at $115 each; Use the FIFO method to determine the value of the inventory if there are ten trumpets still in the inventory.

2. During a one-month period, Fast Shop Specialty Grocery Store purchased canned green beans as follows:

First order	5 cases @ $12.00 per case
Second order	7 cases @ 12.50 per case
Third order	7 cases @ 12.80 per case
Fourth order	8 cases @ 13.00 per case

The month-end inventory showed 11 cases in inventory. Fast Shop uses the FIFO method to calculate its inventories. Calculate the value of the green bean inventory.

3. Garth Retail Tire Outlet specializes in selling steel-belted radial tires. Purchases are made in large quantities to take advantage of quantity discounts. Purchase records for last year for the best quality tires were as follows:

Feb. 18	200 tires @ $90.00 each
May 7	150 tires @ 94.00 each
Aug. 21	220 tires @ 85.00 each
Nov. 30	180 tires @ 95.00 each

The year-end inventory count showed that 190 tires were in stock. Use the FIFO method to calculate the inventory value.

4. Dilworth Department Store purchases specialty fad items for the Christmas season. Last year it bought the following orders of beanbags:

Mar. 6	20 cases @ $40.00 per case
Apr. 1	50 cases @ 38.00 per case
Apr. 26	50 cases @ 38.00 per case
May 5	70 cases @ 36.00 per case
June 1	100 cases @ 34.00 per case
June 20	100 cases @ 35.00 per case
July 20	200 cases @ 33.00 per case
Aug. 5	100 cases @ 37.00 per case
Sept. 20	4,000 cases @ 30.00 per case

Unfortunately for Dilworth, the fad ended in September. The year-end inventory showed 4,450 cases in stock. Value the inventory using the FIFO method.

18.2 Solutions to Practice Problems

1. From Nov. 30 order: 8 × $115 = $ 920
   From Sept. 3 order: 2 × 110 = + 220
   FIFO inventory: 10 $1,140

2. From fourth order: 8 × $13.00 = $104.00
   From third order: 3 × 12.80 = + 38.40
   FIFO inventory: 11 $142.40

3. From Nov. 30 order: 180 × $95.00 = $17,100
   From Aug. 21 order: 10 × 85.00 = + 850
   FIFO inventory: 190 $17,950

4. From Sept. 20 order: 4,000 × $30.00 = $120,000
   From Aug. 5 order: 100 × 37.00 = 3,700
   From July 20 order: 200 × 33.00 = 6,600
   From June 20 order: 100 × 35.00 = 3,500
   From June 1 order: 50 × 34.00 = + 1,700
   FIFO inventory: 4,450 $135,500

18.3 Last-In, First-Out (LIFO) Method

The **last-in, first-out method** of inventory valuation assumes that the last merchandise received is the first to be sold. While it is unlikely that the last merchandise received would be the first sold, the point is that inventory valuation is a cost flow *assumption* and not necessarily related to actual physical flow. LIFO is an acceptable accounting procedure for assigning costs to inventories.

EXAMPLE

Using the LIFO inventory valuation method, find the value of the following inventory of baseballs at Great Game Sporting Goods:

Date of Purchase	Units Purchased	Unit Cost
Feb. 1	30	$5
May 15	25	6
Sept. 1	40	5
Dec. 6	50	7

On December 31, a count of inventory showed there were 55 baseballs in stock.

Solution

Step 1. When using the LIFO method, valuation begins with the first purchase date. Thirty of the 55 units are from the February 1 order. Multiply the number of units by the cost per unit.

Step 2. The remaining units (25) are from the second purchase date, May 15. Multiply 25 by the unit cost of that order.

Step 3. Add the two total costs.

From Dec. 6 order:	30 × $5 =	$ 150
From Sept. 1 order:	25 × 6 =	+ 150
LIFO inventory:	55	$ 300

18.3 Practice Problems

1. Use the LIFO method to determine the value of 48 units of canned corn at Wee Little Grocery when purchases were as follows:

Feb. 19	25 cases @ $10 per case
Mar. 12	15 cases @ 11 per case
Apr. 14	50 cases @ 10 per case
May 6	30 cases @ 12 per case

2. Using the LIFO method, determine the value of inventory of antifreeze at Big Eastern Auto Parts if there are 15 cases in stock that were purchased as follows:

First purchase	10 cases @ $100 each
Second purchase	12 cases @ 105 each
Third purchase	10 cases @ 110 each

3. Calculate the value of inventory at Moonbeam Corp. using the LIFO method if there are 215 packages of party favors left in inventory on December 31. Purchases were as follows:

Mar. 4	150 packages @ $30 per package
May 8	200 packages @ 31 per package
Sept. 12	175 packages @ 32 per package
Dec. 5	180 packages @ 33 per package

Chapter 18 Accounting Applications: Inventory and Overhead   623

4. Ambassador's Reducing Salon stocks rubbing alcohol to treat tired, aching muscles. Purchases for January and February were as follows:

Jan. 1   4 cases @ $35.00 per case
Jan. 5   5 cases @ 34.00 per case
Jan. 12   9 cases @ 33.50 per case
Feb. 4   1 case @ 37.00 per case
Feb. 12   2 cases @ 36.50 per case
Feb. 25   1 case @ 38.00 per case

Ten cases are in inventory. Value the inventory using the LIFO method.

18.3 Solutions to Practice Problems

1. From Feb. 19 order: 25 × $10 = $250
From Mar. 12 order: 15 × 11 = 165
From Apr. 14 order: 8 × 10 = + 80
LIFO inventory: 48 $495

2. From first purchase: 10 × $100 = $1,000
From second purchase: 5 × 105 = + 525
LIFO inventory: 15 $1,525

3. From Mar. 4 order: 150 × $30 = $ 4,500
From May 8 order: 65 × 31 = + 2,015
LIFO inventory: 215 $ 6,515

4. From Jan. 1 order: 4 × $35.00 = $140.00
From Jan. 5 order: 5 × 34.00 = 170.00
From Jan. 12 order: 1 × 33.50 = + 33.50
LIFO inventory: 10 $343.50

18.4 Weighted-Average Method

EXCEL Spreadsheet Application To determine which inventory valuation method to use, Springfield has designed a comparison spreadsheet found in Spreadsheet Application 1 at the end of this chapter.

The **weighted-average method** of inventory valuation is probably the most accurate method for most business firms. Unless strict controls are enforced on stock rotation, some of the inventory on hand at any given time will likely include units from different purchases.

The name is from the method of having the average price of each unit "weighted" by the number of units purchased on each purchase date.

EXAMPLE   Eagle Pest Control has 55 pints of rat poison in stock. Find the value of the inventory using the weighted-average method if purchases were as follows:

Feb. 1   30 pints @ $5 each
May 15   25 pints @ 6 each
Sept. 1   40 pints @ 5 each
Dec. 6   50 pints @ 8 each

Solution   *Step 1.* For each purchase date, multiply the number of units purchased by the price of each unit to determine the total cost of each purchase. Add the total costs of each purchase to arrive at the total cost of goods purchased during the valuation period. Find the sum of total units purchased during the period.

Feb.   1:   30 pints × $5 = $150
May 15:   25 pints × 6 = 150
Sept. 1:   40 pints × 5 = 200
Dec.   6:   50 pints × 8 = 400
Total: 145 pints $900

Step 2. Divide the total cost of the units purchased during the period by the total number of units purchased during the period to find the weighted-average cost:

$$\frac{\$900}{145} = \$6.21 \text{ (rounded)}$$

Step 3. Multiply the weighted-average cost by the number of units in the inventory at the end of the period:

$$\$6.21 \times 55 = \$341.55 \qquad \textit{Weighted-average inventory}$$

30 ⊞ 25 ⊞ 40 ⊞ 50 ⊜ 145

30 ⊠ 5 ⊜ STO 25 ⊠ 6 ⊞ RCL ⊜ STO 40 ⊠ 5 ⊞ RCL

⊜ STO 50 ⊠ 8 ⊞ RCL ⊜ 900 ÷ 145 ⊜ ⊠ 55 ⊜ 341.38

18.4 Practice Problems

1. Monticello Teleco Station purchased the following cases of oil

Jan.	1	10 cases @ $15 each
Jan.	8	10 cases @ 16 each
Jan.	15	15 cases @ 15 each
Jan.	22	8 cases @ 14 each
Jan.	29	10 cases @ 16 each

   There are 22 cases left in inventory. Find the inventory's value using the weighted-average method.

2. The Brown Bag Gift Shop made the following purchases of gift-wrapping paper:

Jan.	9	200 rolls @ $4.10 each
Feb.	11	175 rolls @ 4.00 each
Mar.	15	215 rolls @ 4.25 each

   There are 280 rolls in stock. Find their value using the weighted-average method.

3. Calculate the weighted-average value of Cheese House's monthly Edam cheese inventory of 250 pounds if purchases for December were as follows:

Dec.	1	185 pounds @ $2.75 per pound
Dec.	15	300 pounds @ 2.70 per pound
Dec.	23	75 pounds @ 2.78 per pound

4. Cowtown Harley Motorcycle Shop has 20 motorcycle mudflap sets in stock. Mudflaps were purchased last year as follows:

Jan.	26	10 sets @ $13.85 per set
Apr.	5	8 sets @ 14.00 per set
Aug.	29	12 sets @ 13.75 per set
Dec.	15	15 sets @ 13.50 per set

   Calculate the value of the inventory using the weighted-average method.

18.4 Solutions to Practice Problems

1.

Jan.	1:	10 cases	×	$15 =	$ 150
Jan.	8:	10 cases	×	16 =	160
Jan.	15:	15 cases	×	15 =	225
Jan.	22:	8 cases	×	14 =	112
Jan.	29:	10 cases	×	16 =	+ 160
Total:		53 cases			$ 807

   $$\frac{\$807}{53} \times 22 = \$334.98 \qquad \textit{Weighted-average inventory}$$

2.
Jan. 9:	200 rolls	×	$4.10	=	$ 820.00
Feb. 11:	175 rolls	×	4.00	=	700.00
Mar. 15:	215 rolls	×	4.25	=	+ 913.75
Total:	590 rolls				$2,433.75

$$\frac{\$2,433.75}{590} \times 280 = \$1,155.00 \quad \text{\textit{Weighted-average inventory}}$$

3.
Dec. 1:	185 pounds	×	$2.75	=	$ 508.75
Dec. 15:	300 pounds	×	2.70	=	810.00
Dec. 23:	75 pounds	×	2.78	=	+ 208.50
Total:	560 pounds				$1,527.25

$$\frac{\$1,527.25}{560} \times 250 = \$681.81 \quad \text{\textit{Weighted-average inventory}}$$

4.
Jan. 26:	10	sets	×	$13.85	=	$ 138.50
Apr. 5:	8	sets	×	14.00	=	112.00
Aug. 29:	12	sets	×	13.75	=	165.00
Dec. 15:	15	sets	×	13.50	=	+ 202.50
Total:	45	sets				$ 618.00

$$\frac{\$618}{45} \times 20 = \$274.67 \quad \text{\textit{Weighted-average inventory}}$$

18.5 Retail Method of Estimating Inventory

EXCEL Spreadsheet Application The Springfield Department Store uses an Excel spreadsheet to estimate its inventory on a quarterly basis for income tax purposes. This can be found in Spreadsheet Application 2 at the end of this chapter.

Business firms often prepare interim reports. Among other considerations, management wants to assess the status of a business as often as monthly, and the Internal Revenue Service requires filing tax returns quarterly. Accurate records are kept on purchases and sales, but the inventory value is usually estimated.

Retail firms often use the **retail method of estimating inventory,** as illustrated in Table 18.1. Retailers know the cost and the retail price of merchandise available for sale during the period. With this information, an estimate of the value of inventory can be made without laboriously counting the merchandise on the shelves.

EXAMPLE During an inventory period, Bailey's Hardware had merchandise available for sale that cost $24,000. It was marked to sell for $40,000. Total sales at retail for the period were $14,000. Find the estimated cost value of the inventory at the end of the period.

TABLE 18.1 RETAIL METHOD OF ESTIMATING INVENTORY

	Cost	Retail
Beginning inventory	$ 5,000	$ 9,500
Purchases	+ 19,000	+ 30,500
Cost of goods available for sale	$ 24,000	$ 40,000
Deduct net sales		− 14,000
Ending inventory at retail		$ 26,000 (*Step 2*)
Ratio of cost of goods available for sale to retail value of goods available for sale		.6 (*Step 1*)
Ending inventory at cost (.6 × 26,000)	$ 15,600 (*Step 3*)	

Solution *Step 1.* Divide the cost of the merchandise available for sale during the inventory period by the retail price of the merchandise:

$$\frac{\text{Cost of merchandise available for sale}}{\text{retail value of merchandise}} = \frac{\$24,000}{\$40,000} = .6$$

Step 2. Subtract the amount sold from the amount available for sale at retail:

Retail value of merchandise available	$ 40,000
− amount sold	− 14,000
= retail value of unsold inventory	$ 26,000

Step 3. Multiply step 1 by step 2:

Ratio of merchandise available at cost to retail value of merchandise	.6
× retail value of unsold inventory	× $26,000
= estimated cost value of inventory	$15,600

18.5 Practice Problems

1. During one accounting period, The Bedroom Shop had waterbeds available for sale that cost $64,000 with a retail value of $128,000. If sales were $48,000, find the estimated cost of the inventory.

2. The total merchandise available for sale at the Ninety-Nine-Cent Store cost $80,000 and had been marked to sell for $120,000. Sales during the period were $45,000. Find the estimated cost of the inventory for the period.

3. Backwoods Sporting Goods had camping equipment available for sale that cost $176,000. Its retail price was $320,000. If sales were $120,000, how much is the estimated cost of the inventory?

4. During an inventory period, Stein Mart Department Store had merchandise available for sale that cost $390,000 and was marked to sell for $520,000. Total sales for the period were $240,000. Find the estimated cost of inventory at the end of the period.

18.5 Solutions to Practice Problems

1. $\dfrac{\text{Cost of merchandise available for sale}}{\text{retail value of merchandise}} = \dfrac{\$ 64,000}{\$128,000} = .5$

Retail value of merchandise	$128,000
− amount sold	− 48,000
= retail value of unsold inventory	$ 80,000
Ratio of merchandise available at cost to retail value of merchandise	.5
× retail value of unsold inventory	× $80,000
= estimated cost value of inventory	$40,000

2. $\dfrac{\text{Cost of merchandise available for sale}}{\text{retail value of merchandise}} = \dfrac{\$80,000}{\$120,000} = .66\frac{2}{3}$

Retail value of merchandise	$120,000
− amount sold	− 45,000
= retail value of unsold inventory	$75,000
Ratio of merchandise available at cost to retail value of merchandise	$.66\frac{2}{3}$
× retail value of unsold inventory	× $75,000
= estimated cost value of inventory	$50,000

3. $\dfrac{\text{Cost of merchandise available for sale}}{\text{retail value of merchandise}} = \dfrac{\$176,000}{\$320,000} = .55$

Retail value of merchandise	$320,000
− amount sold	− 120,000
= retail value of unsold inventory	$200,000
Ratio of merchandise available at cost to retail value of merchandise	.55
× retail value of unsold inventory	× $200,000
= estimated cost value of inventory	$110,000

4. Cost of merchandise available for sale = $\dfrac{\$390,000}{\$520,000}$ = .75

	Retail value of merchandise	$520,000
−	amount sold	− 240,000
=	retail value of unsold inventory	$280,000

	Ratio of merchandise available at cost to retail value of merchandise	.75
×	retail value of unsold inventory	× $280,000
=	estimated cost value of inventory	$210,000

18.6   Gross Profit Method of Estimating Inventory

Successfully operating a business firm requires that profits be calculated periodically during the year. An asset that must be considered is inventory. Counting and calculating the value of the closing inventory is an expensive and time-consuming task. An alternative to a physical count is to estimate the closing inventory using the **gross profit method of estimating inventory** as illustrated in Table 18.2.

EXAMPLE   Walsh's Department Store had a $150,000 opening inventory at cost. During a three-month period $450,000 worth of goods was purchased and $525,000 worth was sold. The store's gross profit rate average is 40% of sales. Estimate the closing inventory using the gross profit method.

Solution   *Step 1.* Find the value of merchandise available for sale:

Opening inventory	$ 150,000 (cost)
+ purchases	+ 450,000 (cost)
= merchandise available for sale	$ 600,000 (cost)

Step 2. Multiply the sales by the store's average gross profit rate:

$$
\begin{array}{r}
\$525,000 \\
\times \quad 40\% \\
\hline
\$210,000
\end{array}
$$

Step 3. Calculate the cost of goods sold:

Sales	$ 525,000
− gross profit (40% of sales)	− 210,000
= cost of goods sold	$ 315,000

Step 4. Subtract the cost of goods sold from the merchandise available for sale:

Merchandise available for sale	$600,000
− cost of goods sold	− 315,000
= closing inventory	$285,000

TABLE 18.2   GROSS PROFIT METHOD OF ESTIMATING INVENTORY

Opening inventory		$150,000
Purchases		+450,000
Merchandise available for sale		$600,000 (*Step 1*)
Estimated gross profit		
Sales	$525,000	$ 525,000
Gross profit rate average	× 40%	
Gross profit estimate		−$210,000
Estimated cost of goods sold		−$315,000 (*Step 2*)
Closing inventory		$285,000 (*Step 3*)

1. The 7 Dollar Store had a $15,000 opening inventory at cost. During a three-month period $55,000 worth of goods was purchased and $75,500 worth was sold. The store's gross profit rate average is 30% of sales. Estimate the closing inventory using the gross profit method.

2. Opening inventory at City View Center was $100,000. Gross profit as a percent of sales averages 35% of sales. Merchandise selling for $600,000 was purchased for $400,000. Estimate the value of the closing inventory using the gross profit method.

3. Rick Grape and Company averages 42% gross profit on sales. The company's opening inventory for this period was $112,000 and purchases were $120,000. If sales were $260,000, how much was the estimated value of the closing inventory using the gross profit method?

4. Trafalger Cards and Gifts burned down so there was no record of the value of inventory. From accounting records management was able to determine that opening inventory was $200,000, purchases were $500,000, sales were $937,500, and gross profit as a percent average of sales was 52%. Calculate the estimated loss of inventory in the fire.

18.6 Solutions to Practice Problems

1.

Opening inventory	$ 15,000	
+ purchases	+ 55,000	
= merchandise available for sale	$ 70,000	
Sales	$ 75,500	$75,500
− gross profit (30% of sales)	− 22,650	× 30%
= cost of goods sold	$ 52,850	$22,650
Merchandise available for sale	$ 70,000	
− cost of goods sold	− 52,850	
= closing inventory	$ 17,150	

2.

Opening inventory	$100,000	
+ purchases	+ 400,000	
= merchandise available for sale	$500,000	
Sales	$600,000	$600,000
− gross profit (35% of sales)	− 210,000	× 35%
= cost of goods sold	$390,000	$210,000
Merchandise available for sale	$500,000	
− cost of goods sold	− 390,000	
= closing inventory	$110,000	

3.

Opening inventory	$112,000	
+ purchases	+ 120,000	
= merchandise available for sale	$232,000	
Sales	$260,000	$260,000
− gross profit (42% of sales)	− 109,200	× 42%
= cost of goods sold	$150,800	$109,200
Merchandise available for sale	$232,000	
− cost of goods sold	− 150,800	
= closing inventory	$ 81,200	

4.

Opening inventory	$200,000	
+ purchases	+ 500,000	
= merchandise available for sale	$700,000	
Sales	$937,500	$937,500
− gross profit (52% of sales)	− 487,500	× 52%
= cost of goods sold	$450,000	$487,500
Merchandise available for sale	$700,000	
− cost of goods sold	− 450,000	
= closing inventory	$250,000	

LEARNING UNIT 2
ALLOCATING OVERHEAD

Beyond the costs of materials and merchandise, business firms cover other costs called operating expenses. Such expenses include salaries, rent, utilities, office supplies, taxes, depreciation, and insurance. Collectively such expenses are called **overhead.**

Overhead contributes to the total cost of merchandise produced or sold by a firm. Managers need to know the profitability of each department and often call on accountants to divide expenses among departments. Several methods of distributing overhead are used.

18.7 Allocating Overhead by Floor Space

For allocating the cost of rent, the amount of *floor space* occupied by a department within a plant is especially relevant.

EXAMPLE Schmerts Automart's average monthly overhead is $124,000. Floor space by square feet within the departments are as follows: new cars, 8,000; used cars, 2,000; trucks, 2,500; repair, 4,500; paint and body, 3,000. Allocate the overhead according to the floor space for each department.

Solution **Step 1.** Find the total floor space by adding each department's amount:

New cars:	8,000
Used cars:	2,000
Trucks:	2,500
Repair:	4,500
Paint and body:	+ 3,000
	20,000 *Total square feet*

Step 2. Determine each department's allocation of overhead:

$$\text{New cars:} \quad \frac{8,000}{20,000} \times \$124,000 = \$\ 49,600$$

$$\text{Used cars:} \quad \frac{2,000}{20,000} \times \ 124,000 = \ \ \ 12,400$$

$$\text{Trucks:} \quad \frac{2,500}{20,000} \times \ 124,000 = \ \ \ 15,500$$

$$\text{Repair:} \quad \frac{4,500}{20,000} \times \ 124,000 = \ \ \ 27,900$$

$$\text{Paint and body:} \quad \frac{3,000}{20,000} \times \ 124,000 = + \ 18,600$$

$$\$124,000 \quad \textit{Total overhead}$$

8,000 ⊞ 2,000 ⊞ 2,500 ⊞ 4,500 ⊞ 3,000 ⊟	
STO 124,000 ÷ RCL ⊟6.2 ⊠ 8,000 ⊟	49,600
2,000 ⊟	12,400
2,500 ⊟	15,500
4,500 ⊟	27,900
3,000 ⊟	18,600

1. Carlo's Food Mart's average monthly overhead is $41,000. Floor space by square feet within the departments is as follows: produce, 5,000; meat, 2,000; dairy, 1,500; canned goods, 2,500; other, 6,000. Allocate the overhead according to the floor space for each department.

2. Bigtown Furniture Sales' average monthly overhead is $200,500. The square feet of floor space occupied by each department is as follows: receiving, 6,000; warehouse, 12,000; display, 15,000; shipping, 4,000. Allocate the overhead according to the floor space for each department.

3. Burford Hardware's average monthly overhead is $96,000. The square feet of floor space occupied by each department is as follows: glass, 4,000; tools, 9,000; electrical, 8,000; plumbing, 3,000. Allocate the overhead according to the floor space for each department.

4. The Wurst Bakery's average monthly overhead is $25,000. Floor space by square feet within the departments is as follows: storage, 1,000; baking, 2,000; display, 1,500; seating, 2,500. Allocate the overhead according to the floor space for each department.

18.7 Solutions to Practice Problems

1.
Produce: 5,000
Meat: 2,000
Dairy: 1,500
Canned goods: 2,500
Other: + 6,000
              17,000 Total square feet

Produce: $\frac{5,000}{17,000} \times \$41,000 = \$12,058.82$

Meat: $\frac{2,000}{17,000} \times 41,000 = 4,823.53$

Dairy: $\frac{1,500}{17,000} \times 41,000 = 3,617.65$

Canned goods: $\frac{2,500}{17,000} \times 41,000 = 6,029.41$

Other: $\frac{6,000}{17,000} \times 41,000 = + 14,470.59$

Total = $41,000.00

2.
Receiving: 6,000
Warehouse: 12,000
Display: 15,000
Shipping: + 4,000
             37,000 Total square feet

Receiving: $\frac{6,000}{37,000} \times \$200,500 = \$32,513.51$

Warehouse: $\frac{12,000}{37,000} \times 200,500 = 65,027.03$

Display: $\frac{15,000}{37,000} \times 200,500 = 81,283.78$

Shipping: $\frac{4,000}{37,000} \times 200,500 = + 21,675.68$

Total = $200,500.00

3.
Glass: 4,000
Tools: 9,000
Electrical: 8,000
Plumbing: + 3,000
             24,000 Total square feet

Glass: $\frac{4,000}{24,000} \times \$96,000 = \$16,000$

$$\text{Tools:} \quad \frac{9,000}{24,000} \times 96,000 = \quad 36,000$$

$$\text{Electrical:} \quad \frac{8,000}{24,000} \times 96,000 = \quad 32,000$$

$$\text{Plumbing:} \quad \frac{3,000}{24,000} \times 96,000 = \underline{+\ 12,000}$$

$$\text{Total} = \quad \$96,000$$

4.
Storage:	1,000
Baking:	2,000
Display:	1,500
Seating:	+ 2,500
	7,000 Total square feet

$$\text{Storage:} \quad \frac{1,000}{7,000} \times \$25,000 = \quad \$\ 3,571.43$$

$$\text{Baking:} \quad \frac{2,000}{7,000} \times \ 25,000 = \quad 7,142.86$$

$$\text{Display:} \quad \frac{1,500}{7,000} \times \ 25,000 = \quad 5,357.14$$

$$\text{Seating:} \quad \frac{2,500}{7,000} \times \ 25,000 = \underline{+\ 8,928.57}$$

$$\text{Total} = \$25,000.00$$

18.8 Allocating Overhead by Total Net Sales

A second method for allocating overhead is by the percent of net sales by each department to total net sales within a plant.

EXAMPLE   Total overhead expenses of Best Buy Shoe Store were $48,000 last year. Net sales by departments for the year were as follows: men, $20,000; boys, $25,000; women, $45,000; girls, $30,000. Allocate the overhead according to the net sales in each department.

Solution   *Step 1.* Find the total net sales by adding the amounts of the departments together:

Men:	$ 20,000
Boys:	25,000
Women:	45,000
Girls:	+ 30,000
	$120,000 Total net sales

Step 2. Determine each department's allocation of overhead.

$$\text{Men:} \quad \frac{\$20,000}{120,000} \times \$48,000 = \$\quad 8,000$$

$$\text{Boys:} \quad \frac{25,000}{120,000} \times \ 48,000 = \quad 10,000$$

$$\text{Women:} \quad \frac{45,000}{120,000} \times \ 48,000 = \quad 18,000$$

$$\text{Girls:} \quad \frac{30,000}{120,000} \times \ 48,000 = \underline{+\ 12,000}$$

$$\text{Total} = \$\ 48,000$$

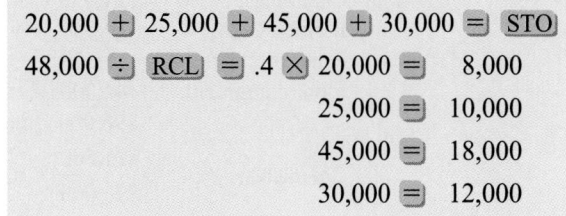

$$20,000 \; \boxed{+} \; 25,000 \; \boxed{+} \; 45,000 \; \boxed{+} \; 30,000 \; \boxed{=} \; \boxed{STO}$$

$$48,000 \; \boxed{\div} \; \boxed{RCL} \; \boxed{=} \; .4 \; \boxed{\times} \; 20,000 \; \boxed{=} \quad 8,000$$

$$25,000 \; \boxed{=} \quad 10,000$$

$$45,000 \; \boxed{=} \quad 18,000$$

$$30,000 \; \boxed{=} \quad 12,000$$

18.8 Practice Problems

1. Goldsmith Jewelers' average monthly overhead is $36,000. Average sales by departments are as follows: jewelry, $100,000; silverware, $50,000; china, $50,000; watch repair, $2,000. Allocate the overhead according to the net sales for each department.

2. The total overhead for Warren's Quick Foods was $9,600 last year. Net sales by departments for the year were as follows: dairy, $4,000; produce, $5,000; canned goods, $9,000; other, $6,000. Allocate the overhead by the net sales in each department.

3. Snow White Janitorial Supply's monthly average overhead is $20,000. Average net sales by departments are as follows: chemicals, $21,500; disinfectants, $19,000; paper products, $11,500; floor equipment, $44,000. Allocate the overhead according to the net sales for each department.

4. The total overhead expenses of Ace Appliance was $14,000 last year. Net sales by departments were as follows: washer, $21,500; television, $8,050; refrigerator, $13,300; dishwasher, $4,200. Allocate the overhead according to the net sales in each department.

18.8 Solutions to Practice Problems

1. Jewelry: $100,000
   Silverware: 50,000
   China: 50,000
   Watch repair: + 2,000
   ─────────────────────────
   $202,000 Total net sales

   Jewelry: $\dfrac{100,000}{202,000} \times \$36,000 = \$17,821.78$

   Silverware: $\dfrac{50,000}{202,000} \times 36,000 = \quad 8,910.89$

   China: $\dfrac{50,000}{202,000} \times 36,000 = \quad 8,910.89$

   Watch repair: $\dfrac{2,000}{202,000} \times 36,000 = + \quad 356.44$

   Total = \$36,000.00

2. Dairy: $4,000
   Produce: 5,000
   Canned goods: 9,000
   Other: + 6,000
   ─────────────────────────
   $24,000 Total net sales

   Dairy: $\dfrac{4,000}{24,000} \times \$9,600 = \$ \; 1,600$

   Produce: $\dfrac{5,000}{24,000} \times 9,600 = \quad 2,600$

   Canned goods: $\dfrac{9,000}{24,000} \times 9,600 = \quad 3,600$

   Other: $\dfrac{6,000}{24,000} \times 9,600 = +2,400$

   Total = \$ 9,600

3. Chemicals: $21,500
Disinfectants: 19,000
Paper products: 11,500
Floor equipment: + 44,000
                $96,000 Total net sales

Chemicals: $\dfrac{\$21,500}{\$96,000} \times \$20,000 = \$4,479.17$

Disinfectants: $\dfrac{\$19,000}{\$96,000} \times 20,000 = 3,958.33$

Paper products: $\dfrac{\$11,500}{\$96,000} \times 20,000 = 2,395.83$

Floor equipment: $\dfrac{\$44,000}{\$96,000} \times 20,000 = + 9,166.67$
                            Total = $20,000.00

4. Washer: $21,500
Refrigerator: 13,300
Television: 8,050
Dishwasher: + 4,200
              $47,050 Total net sales

Washer: $\dfrac{\$21,500}{\$47,050} \times \$14,000 = \$6,397.45$

Refrigerator: $\dfrac{\$13,300}{\$47,050} \times 14,000 = 3,957.49$

Television: $\dfrac{\$8,050}{\$47,050} \times 14,000 = 2,395.32$

Dishwasher: $\dfrac{\$4,200}{\$47,050} \times 14,000 = 1,249.73$
                      Total = $13,999.99

Due to rounding

18.9 Allocating Overhead by Number of Employees in Each Department

A third method for allocating overhead is according to the number of employees in each department within a plant.

E X A M P L E Overhead expenses for Sterling Clothing Store totaled $128,000 last year. The number of employees by departments were as follows: men, 7; boys, 5; women, 9; girls, 6. Allocate the overhead according to the number of employees in each department.

Solution *Step 1.* Find the total number of employees by adding the number in each of the departments together:

              Men: 7
              Boys: 5
              Women: 9
              Girls: + 6
                      27   Total number of employees

Step 2. Determine each department's ratio of number of employees to the total number of employees. Multiply that ratio by the overhead.

Men: $\dfrac{7}{27} \times \$128,000 = \$33,185.19$

Boys: $\dfrac{5}{27} \times 128,000 = 23,703.70$

Women: $\dfrac{9}{27} \times 128,000 = 42,666.67$

$$\text{Girls:} \qquad \frac{6}{27} \times 128{,}000 = \underline{\quad 28{,}444.44 \quad}$$

$$\text{Total} = \$128{,}000.00$$

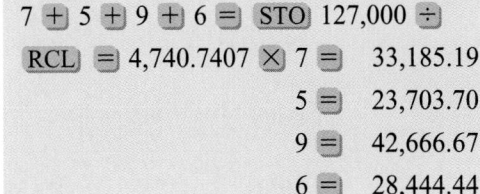

18.9 Practice Problems

1. Sweeny Construction Co. has $47,000 monthly overhead. The number of employees in each part of the company is as follows: foundation, 12; carpentry, 15; bricklaying, 18; drywall, 6. Allocate the overhead according to the number of employees per department.

2. The total overhead expenses of Joshua Motors was $45,000 last month. The number of employees by departments is as follows: new cars, 9; used cars, 6; trucks, 3; repair, 12. Allocate the overhead according to the number of employees in each department.

3. AI-Jai's 24-Hour Grocery's monthly average overhead is $30,000. The number of employees by departments is as follows: produce, 8; dairy, 5; meats, 6; bakery, 12. Allocate the overhead according to the number of employees in each department.

4. Total overhead expenses at Red Barn Furniture was $41,000 last year. The number of employees by departments is as follows: dining, 4; living, 6; kitchen, 8; bedroom, 5. Allocate the overhead according to the number of employees per department.

18.9 Solutions to Practice Problems

1. Foundation: 12
   Carpentry: 15
   Bricklaying: 18
   Drywall: + 6
   $\overline{\qquad}$
   51 Total number of employees

   Foundation: $\dfrac{12}{51} \times \$47{,}000 = \$11{,}058.82$

   Carpentry: $\dfrac{15}{51} \times 47{,}000 = \ 13{,}823.53$

   Bricklaying: $\dfrac{18}{51} \times 47{,}000 = \ 16{,}588.24$

   Drywall: $\dfrac{6}{51} \times 47{,}000 = \underline{+5{,}529.41}$
   $\qquad\qquad\qquad\qquad \text{Total} = \$47{,}000.00$

2. New cars: 9
   Used cars: 6
   Trucks: 3
   Repair: + 12
   $\overline{\qquad}$
   30 Total number of employees

   New cars: $\dfrac{9}{30} \times \$45{,}000 = \$13{,}500$

   Used cars: $\dfrac{6}{30} \times 45{,}000 = \ 9{,}000$

   Trucks: $\dfrac{3}{30} \times 45{,}000 = \ 4{,}500$

   Repair: $\dfrac{12}{30} \times 45{,}000 = \underline{+18{,}000}$
   $\qquad\qquad\qquad\qquad \text{Total} = \$45{,}000$

3. Produce: 8
Dairy: 5
Meats: 6
Bakery: + 12

        31   Total number of employees

Produce: $\dfrac{8}{31} \times \$30{,}000 = \$\ \ 7{,}741.94$

Dairy: $\dfrac{5}{31} \times \ \ 30{,}000 = \ \ \ 4{,}838.71$

Meats: $\dfrac{6}{31} \times \ \ 30{,}000 = \ \ \ 5{,}806.45$

Bakery: $\dfrac{12}{31} \times \ \ 30{,}000 = +11{,}612.90$

                            Total = $ 30,000.00

4. Dining: 4
Living: 6
Kitchen: 8
Bedroom: + 5

        23   Total number of employees

Dining: $\dfrac{4}{23} \times \$41{,}000 = \$\ \ 7{,}130.43$

Living: $\dfrac{6}{23} \times \ \ 41{,}000 = \ \ 10{,}695.65$

Kitchen: $\dfrac{8}{23} \times \ \ 41{,}000 = \ \ 14{,}260.87$

Bedroom: $\dfrac{5}{23} \times \ \ 41{,}000 = +18{,}913.04$

                            Total = $ 40.999.99

                                ↑
                         Due to rounding

QUICK REFERENCE SUMMARY AND REVIEW

Page	Section Topic	Learning Concepts	Examples and Solutions
620	**18.1** Specific Identification Method	To find the value of inventory using the specific identification method, add the values of all cost-coded items in inventory.	A count of hair dryers at Jesse's makeup shop found 14 in stock; 2 were from the first purchase at $12.50 each, 6 were from the second purchase at $13 each, 5 were from the third purchase at $15 each, and 1 was from the fourth purchase at $14.50 each. Find the value of the inventory using the specific identification method.

                                           2 @ $12.50 = $ 25.00
                                           6 @   13.00 =   78.00
                                           5 @   15.00 =   75.00
                                           1 @   14.50 = +114.50
                                                         $ 192.50

Page	Section Topic	Learning Concepts	Examples and Solutions
621	**18.2** First-In, First-Out (FIFO) Method	Using FIFO inventory valuation, begin with the last purchase date in the accounting period. Counting from the last units bought, determine which of the purchases represent the units in the inventory. Multiply the number of units by the cost per unit of the order. Add the products.	Using the FIFO method, find the value of the 12 cases of green beans found in inventory at José's Grocery.

Using the FIFO method, find the value of the 12 cases of green beans found in inventory at José's Grocery.

Dates	Units	Cost
2/1	6	$7
5/12	4	6
9/2	3	9
12/5	8	8

12/5	$8 \times \$8 = \$64$	
9/2	$3 \times 9 = 27$	
5/12	$1 \times 6 = +6$	
FIFO	$= \$97$	

Page	Section Topic	Learning Concepts
623	**18.3** Last-In, First-Out (LIFO) Method.	Using LIFO inventory valuation, begin with the first purchase date. Counting from the first units bought, determine which of the purchases represent the units in the inventory. Multiply the number of units by the cost per unit of the order. Add the products.

Using the LIFO method, find the value of the 12 cases of green beans found in inventory at José's Grocery.

Dates	Units	Cost
2/1	6	$7
5/12	4	6
9/2	3	9
12/5	8	8

2/1	$6 \times \$7 = \$\ 42$	
5/12	$4 \times 6 = 24$	
9/2	$2 \times 9 = + 18$	
	$\$84$	

Page	Section Topic	Learning Concepts
624	**18.4** Weighted-Average Method	**(1)** Multiply the total cost of units by the price of each unit to determine the total cost of each purchase and add the costs of each purchase to find the total purchase cost during the valuation period.

(2) Find the sum of the units purchased during the period.

(3) Divide (1) by (2):

$$\frac{\text{Total purchase cost}}{\text{total units purchased}}$$

to find the weighted average cost per unit.

(4) Multiply the average cost per unit by the number of units left in inventory. |

Archie's electrical supply has 25 boxes of lightbulbs in stock. Purchases were as follows:

Date	Units	Cost
2/1	15	$10
6/16	12	12
10/2	20	10
12/4	25	14

Find the value of the inventory using the weighted-average method.

2/1	$15 \times \$10 = \$150$	
6/16	$12 \times 12 = 144$	
10/2	$20 \times 10 = 200$	
12/4	$25 \times 14 = +350$	
Total	72	$\$844$

(*Step 2*)　　(*Step 1*)

$\dfrac{\$844}{72} = \$11.72$ (*Step 3*)

$\$11.72 \times 25 = \$293$ (*Step 4*)
Weighted average $= \$293$

Page	Section Topic	Learning Concepts	Examples and Solutions
626	**18.5** Retail Method of Estimating Inventory	**(1)** Divide the cost of the merchandise available for sale during the inventory period by the retail price of the merchandise. **(2)** Subtract the amount sold from the amount available for sale at retail. **(3)** Multiply the two figures found in (1) and (2).	During an inventory period, Barney's Sporting Goods had goods available for sale that cost $12,000 and were marked to sell for $20,000. Total sales at retail for the period were $7,000. Find the estimated cost value of the inventory at the end of the period. $\dfrac{\$12,000}{\$20,000} = .6$ *(Step 1)* $\$20,000$ $- \ 7,000$ $\$13,000$ *(Step 2)* $.6$ $\times \ \$13,000$ *(Step 3)* $\$ \ 7,800$
628	**18.6** Gross Profit Method of Estimating Inventory	**(1)** Find the value of merchandise available for sale by adding the opening inventory to purchases. **(2)** Calculate the cost of goods sold by multiplying the gross profit by the profit rate. **(3)** Subtract the estimated gross profit from sales to find the the cost of goods sold. **(4)** Subtract the cost of goods sold from the merchandise available for sale.	Reed's Hardware had $7,500 opening inventory at cost. During a three-month period, $22,500 worth of goods was purchased and $35,850 worth was sold. The store's gross profit rate is 40%. Estimate the closing inventory using the gross profit method. $\$ \ \ 7,500$ $+ \ 22,500$ $\$ \ 30,000$ *(Step 1)* $\$35,850$ $\times \ \ 40\%$ $\$14,340$ *(Step 2)* $\$ \ 35,850$ $- \ 14,340$ $\$ \ 21,510$ *(Step 3)* $\$ \ 30,000$ $- \ 21,510$ $\$ \ \ 8,490$ *(Step 4)*

Page	Section Topic	Learning Concepts	Examples and Solutions
630	**18.7** Allocating Overhead by Floor Space	Find the total floor space by adding the amounts of the departments. Divide each department's space by the floor space, and multiply that by the average overhead.	Morgan's Furniture's average monthly overhead is $6,200. Floor space by square feet within the departments is as follows: kitchen, 4,000; bedroom, 1,000; living room, 1,250; and dining room, 2,250. Allocate the overhead according to the floor space for each department.
632	**18.8** Allocating Overhead by Net Sales.	Find the total net sales by adding the net sales in each department. Divide each department's net sales by the total net sales and multiply that figure by the average overhead.	Morgan's Furniture's average monthly overhead is $6,200. Net sales by departments are as follows: kitchen, $8,500; bedroom, $6,500; living room, $9,000; dining room, $1,000. Allocate the overhead according to the net sales for each department.

Example and Solution for 18.7:

$$\begin{array}{r} 4,000 \\ 1,000 \\ 1,250 \\ + \underline{2,250} \\ 8,500 \end{array} \text{ Total square feet}$$

$$\frac{4,000}{8,500} \times \$6,200 = \$2,917.65$$

$$\frac{1,000}{8,500} \times \$6,200 = \$729.41$$

$$\frac{1,250}{8,500} \times \$6,200 = \$911.76$$

$$\frac{2,250}{8,500} \times \$6,200 = \$1,641.18$$

Example and Solution for 18.8:

$$\begin{array}{r} \$\ 8,500 \\ 6,500 \\ 9,000 \\ + \underline{1,000} \\ \$25,000 \end{array} \text{ Total net sales}$$

$$\frac{\$\ 8,500}{\$25,000} \times \$6,200 = \$2,108.00$$

$$\frac{\$\ 6,500}{\$25,000} \times \$6,200 = \$1,612.00$$

$$\frac{\$\ 9,000}{\$25,000} \times \$6,200 = \$2,232.00$$

$$\frac{\$\ 1,000}{\$25,000} \times \$6,200 = \$\ 248.00$$

Page	Section Topic	Learning Concepts	Examples and Solutions
634	**18.9** Allocating Overhead by Number of Employees in Each Department	Find the total number of employees by adding the number in each department together. Divide the number of employees in each department by the total number of employees and multiply that figure by the average overhead.	Morgan's Furniture's average monthly overhead is $6,200. The number of employees by departments is as follows: kitchen, 5; bedroom, 3; living room, 6; dining room, 2. Allocate the overhead according to the number of employees per department.

$$\begin{array}{r} 5 \\ 3 \\ 6 \\ + \ 2 \\ \hline 16 \ \ \text{Total employees} \end{array}$$

$$\frac{5}{16} \times \$6{,}200 = \$1{,}937.50$$

$$\frac{3}{16} \times \$6{,}200 = \ \ 1{,}162.50$$

$$\frac{6}{16} \times \$6{,}200 = \ \ 2{,}325.00$$

$$\frac{2}{16} \times \$6{,}200 = \ \ \ \ 775.00$$

SURFING THE INTERNET

For further information on the topics covered in this chapter, check out the following sites:

http://www.stern.nyu.edu/~adamodar/New_Home_Page/AccPrimer/inventory.htm

http://www.southware.com/Excelassist/Lessons/ic/costing.html

http://www.aphis.usda.gov/bad/bamanual/bam_ch6.html

ADDITIONAL
PRACTICE
PROBLEMS

Answers to odd-numbered problems are given in Appendix A.

18.1

1. A count of the tires in inventory at Kirby's Tire Co. revealed 320 in stock. One hundred were 16-inch wheels and cost $19.20 each, 80 were 15-inch wheels and cost $16.20 each, and 140 were 14-inch wheels and cost $14.00 each. Using the specific identification method, find the total value of the inventory.

$$\begin{array}{r} 100 \times \$19.20 = \$ \ 1{,}920 \\ 80 \times \ 16.20 = \ \ \ 1{,}296 \\ 140 \times \ 14.00 = + \ 1{,}960 \\ \hline \$ \ 5{,}176 \end{array}$$

2. Inventory reveals there were 110 paint brushes in stock at Dillard Supply Co. Code numbers on the brushes show 10 cost $2.50 each, 30 cost $2.60 each, and 70 cost $2.75 each. Using the specific identification method, find the value of the inventory.

$$\begin{array}{r} 10 \times \$2.50 = \ \$ \ 25.00 \\ 30 \times \ 2.60 = \ \ \ \ 78.00 \\ 70 \times \ 2.75 = + \ 192.50 \\ \hline \$295.50 \end{array}$$

3. Anglin Radiator Shop has 31 new radiators in stock. Code numbers on the radiators show 10 cost $87.50 each, 9 cost $90.00 each, and 12 cost $100.00 each. Using the specific identification method, find the value of the inventory.

$$
\begin{array}{rl}
10 \times \$\,87.50 = & \$\,875 \\
9 \times 90.00 = & 810 \\
12 \times 100.00 = & \underline{+1{,}200} \\
& \$2{,}885
\end{array}
$$

4. Dynamic Ford had 58 new Fords on the lot last Thursday. Twenty of the cars cost $14,860 each, 33 cost $11,760 each, and 5 cost $21,680 each. Using the specific identification method, find the total value of the inventory.

$$
\begin{array}{rl}
20 \times \$14{,}860 = & \$\,297{,}200 \\
33 \times 11{,}760 = & 388{,}080 \\
5 \times 21{,}680 = & \underline{+\,108{,}400} \\
& \$\,793{,}680
\end{array}
$$

5. Art Image uses the specific identification method to keep records of its picture frame inventory. Of the 118 frames in stock, 38 cost $26.40 each, 46 cost $17.30 each, and 34 cost $32.80 each. Find the value of the inventory.

$$
\begin{array}{rl}
38 \times \$26.40 = & \$\,1{,}003.20 \\
46 \times 17.30 = & 795.80 \\
34 \times 32.80 = & \underline{+\,1{,}115.20} \\
& \$\,2{,}914.20
\end{array}
$$

18.2

6. Hopkins Appliance purchased the following microwave ovens to sell: May 2, eight at $115 each; October 4, twelve at $100 each; and December 31, eight at $105 each. Use the FIFO method to determine the value of the inventory if there are twelve microwaves still in the inventory.

$$
\begin{array}{lrl}
\text{Dec. 31:} & 8 \times \$105 = & \$\,840 \\
\text{Oct. 4:} & 4 \times 100 = & \underline{+\,400} \\
& & \$1{,}240
\end{array}
$$

7. During a one-month period, Budget Auto Parts purchased cases of motor oil as follows:

First order	15 cases @	$18.00 per case
Second order	17 cases @	19.50 per case
Third order	17 cases @	15.70 per case
Fourth order	18 cases @	16.00 per case

The month-end inventory showed 23 cases in inventory. Budget uses the FIFO method to calculate inventory. Calculate the value of the motor oil inventory.

$$
\begin{array}{lrl}
\text{Fourth order:} & 18 \times \$16 = & \$288.00 \\
\text{Third order:} & 5 \times 15.70 = & \underline{+\,78.50} \\
& & \$366.50
\end{array}
$$

8. Purchase records for last year showed that Wishing Well China placed the following orders for dishes last year.

Mar. 19	10 sets @	$80.00 per set
June 8	20 sets @	74.00 per set
Sept. 22	10 sets @	86.00 per set
Dec. 30	18 sets @	95.00 per set

The year-end inventory count showed that 24 sets were available for sale. Use the FIFO method to calculate the inventory value.

$$
\begin{array}{lrl}
\text{Dec. 30:} & 18 \times \$95 = & \$1{,}710 \\
\text{Sept. 22:} & 6 \times 86 = & \underline{+\,516} \\
& & \$2{,}226
\end{array}
$$

9. Mabel's Hardware Store uses the FIFO method for valuing inventory. The store bought electric sanders as follows:

Jan. 9	15 sanders @	$12.25 each
Mar. 17	10 sanders @	13.50 each
Apr. 12	12 sanders @	11.25 each
Oct. 6	13 sanders @	13.75 each

An inventory at the end of November showed there are 32 sanders in stock. Use the FIFO method to calculate the inventory value.

$$
\begin{array}{lrl}
\text{Oct. 6:} & 13 \times \$13.75 = & \$178.75 \\
\text{Apr. 12:} & 12 \times 11.25 = & 135.00 \\
\text{Mar. 17:} & 7 \times 13.50 = & \underline{+\,94.50} \\
& & \$408.25
\end{array}
$$

10. Iron Horse Caterers keeps a stock of mushrooms. At the end of March an inventory count showed 15 gallons in stock. Use the FIFO method to value the inventory if the month's purchases were as follows:

Mar. 8	7 @	$36.85 per gallon
Mar. 18	8 @	36.92 per gallon
Mar. 21	4 @	36.20 per gallon
Mar. 26	9 @	37.00 per gallon
Mar. 29	5 @	37.20 per gallon

$$
\begin{array}{llrl}
\text{Mar. 29:} & 5 & \times \$37.20 = & \$\,186.00 \\
\text{Mar. 26:} & 9 & \times 37.00 = & 333.00 \\
\text{Mar. 21:} & 1 & \times 36.20 = & \underline{+\,36.20} \\
& & & \$\,555.20
\end{array}
$$

18.3

11. Use the LIFO method to determine the value of 20 cases of green beans at Murry's Grocery when purchases were as follows:

Jan. 20	10 cases @ $8 per case
Apr. 13	5 cases @ 9 per case
May 15	6 cases @ 10 per case
June 7	4 cases @ 12 per case

Jan. 20: $10 \times \$8 = \$ 80$
Apr. 13: $5 \times 9 = 45$
May 15: $5 \times 10 = + 50$
$\overline{\$175}$

12. Using the LIFO method, determine the value of the 25 cases in the toothpaste inventory at Little West Drug Store given the following purchases record:

First purchase	12 cases @ $80 per case
Second purchase	10 cases @ 75 per case
Third purchase	4 cases @ 70 per case

First purchase: $12 \times \$80 = \$ 960$
Second purchase: $10 \times 75 = 750$
Third purchase: $3 \times 70 = + 210$
$\overline{\$1,920}$

13. Calculate the value of inventory at Slink Corp. using the LIFO method if there are 35 boxes of candy left in inventory on April 31. Purchases were as follows:

Jan. 5	10 boxes @ $10 per box
Feb. 8	22 boxes @ 11 per box
Mar. 12	5 boxes @ 12 per box
Apr. 1	8 boxes @ 10 per box

Jan. 5: $10 \times \$10 = \$100$
Feb. 8: $22 \times 11 = 242$
Mar. 12: $3 \times 12 = + 36$
$\overline{\$378}$

14. Bernie's Cafe stocks canned potatoes for a special dish. Purchases for March and April were as follows:

Mar. 2	2 cases @ $15.00 per case
Mar. 4	3 cases @ 14.00 per case
Mar. 13	4 cases @ 13.50 per case
Apr. 3	2 cases @ 17.00 per case
Apr. 11	1 case @ 16.50 per case
Apr. 26	2 cases @ 18.00 per case

Eleven cases are in inventory. Value the inventory using LIFO.

Mar. 2: $2 \times \$15.00 = \$ 30.00$
Mar. 4: $3 \times 14.00 = 42.00$
Mar. 13: $4 \times 13.50 = 54.00$
Apr. 3: $2 \times 17.00 = + 34.00$
$\overline{\$160.00}$

15. Use the LIFO method to calculate the value of 120 pounds of hamburger meat in inventory at the end of November for Louie's Deli. Louie's purchase record for the month was as follows:

Nov. 1	60 pounds @ $ .99 per pound
Nov. 5	20 pounds @ .97 per pound
Nov. 17	50 pounds @ 1.02 per pound
Nov. 22	40 pounds @ .89 per pound
Nov. 27	80 pounds @ .91 per pound

Nov. 1: $60 \times \$ .99 = \$ 59.40$
Nov. 5: $20 \times .97 = 19.40$
Nov. 17: $40 \times 1.02 = + 40.80$
$\overline{\$119.60}$

18.4

16. Centre Cleaners purchased the following cases of cleaning fluid in February:

Feb. 1	2 cases @ $25 per case
Feb. 7	4 cases @ 26 per case
Feb. 10	5 cases @ 25 per case
Feb. 16	6 cases @ 24 per case
Feb. 28	3 cases @ 27 per case

There are 12 cases left in inventory. Find the inventory's value using the weighted-average method.

Feb. 1: $2 \times \$25 = \$ 50$
Feb. 7: $4 \times 26 = 104$
Feb. 10: $5 \times 25 = 125$
Feb. 16: $6 \times 24 = 144$
Feb. 28: $\underline{3} \times 27 = + 81$
$20 \qquad \overline{\$504}$

$\frac{\$504}{20} \times 12 = \$302.40$

17. Cousin's Wall Coverings purchased the following wallpaper:

Mar. 8	120 rolls @ $9.20 per roll
Apr. 12	110 rolls @ 8.90 per roll
May 16	115 rolls @ 10.25 per roll

There are 215 rolls in stock. Find their value using the weighted-average method.

Mar. 8: $120 \times \$9.20 = \$ 1,104.00$
Apr. 12: $110 \times 8.90 = 979.00$
May 16: $\underline{115} \times 10.25 = + 1,178.75$
$345 \qquad \overline{\$ 3,261.75}$

$\frac{\$3,261.75}{345} \times 215$
$= \$2,032.68$

18. Calculate the weighted-average value of Bogart Landscape Co.'s monthly fertilizer inventory of 340 pounds if purchases for March were as follows:

Mar. 2	285 pounds @	$3.75 per pound
Mar. 16	200 pounds @	3.70 per pound
Mar. 24	80 pounds @	3.79 per pound

Mar. 2: $285 \times \$3.75 = \$1,068.75$
Mar. 16: $200 \times 3.70 = 740.00$
Mar. 24: $\dfrac{80 \times 3.79 = + 303.20}{565}$ $\dfrac{\$2,111.95}{$

$\dfrac{\$2,111.95}{565} \times 340$
$= \$1,270.91$

20. Centerline Supply Co., which uses the weighted-average method of estimating inventory, has 85 gallons of house paint in stock. Find the value of the inventory if the store purchased the paint as follows:

Mar. 12	50 gallons @	$13.30 per gallon
Apr. 14	35 gallons @	14.00 per gallon
May 16	46 gallons @	13.75 per gallon

Mar. 12: $50 \times \$13.30 = \$665.00$
Apr. 14: $35 \times 14.00 = 490.00$
May 16: $\dfrac{46 \times 13.75 = + 632.50}{131}$ $\dfrac{\$1,787.50}{$

$\dfrac{\$1,787.50}{131} \times 85$
$= \$1,159.83$

19. City Camping Equipment Shop has 45 tents in stock. The tents were purchased last year as follows.

Feb. 16	20 tents @	$ 93.85	each
May. 6	8 tents @	104.00	each
July 30	14 tents @	103.75	each
Nov. 16	30 tents @	99.50	each

Calculate the value of the inventory using the weighted-average method.

Feb. 16: $20 \times \$93.85 = \$1,877.00$
May. 6: $8 \times 104.00 = 832.00$
July 30: $14 \times 103.75 = 1,452.50$
Nov. 16: $\dfrac{30 \times 99.50 = + 2,985.00}{72}$ $\dfrac{\$7,146.50}{$

$\dfrac{\$7,146.50}{72} \times 45$
$= \$4,466.56$

18.5

21. The Kitchen Shop had sinks that cost $32,000 available for sale. The retail price is $64,000. If sales were $24,000, find the estimated cost of the inventory.

$\dfrac{\$32,000}{\$64,000} = 50\%$

$\begin{array}{r} \$64,000 \\ -24,000 \\ \hline \$40,000 \end{array}$

$\$40,000 \times 50\% = \$20,000$

22. The total merchandise available for sale at High Priced Everything Store was $160,000 and was marked to sell for $240,000. Sales were $90,000. Find the estimated cost of the inventory for the period.

$\dfrac{\$160,000}{\$240,000} = \dfrac{2}{3}$

$\begin{array}{r} \$240,000 \\ -90,000 \\ \hline \$150,000 \end{array}$

$\$150,000 \times \dfrac{2}{3} = \$100,000$

23. City Sporting Goods had golfing equipment available for sale that cost $8,000. Its retail price was $16,000. If sales were $6,000, how much is the estimated cost of the inventory?

$\dfrac{\$8,000}{\$16,000} = 50\%$

$\begin{array}{r} \$16,000 \\ -6,000 \\ \hline \$10,000 \end{array}$

$\$10,000 \times 50\% = \$5,000$

24. During an inventory period, Canon White Goods had merchandise available for sale that cost $130,000 and was marked to sell for $175,000. Total sales for the period were $80,000. Find the estimated cost of inventory at the end of the period.

$\dfrac{\$130,000}{\$175,000} = 74.3\%$

$\begin{array}{r} \$175,000 \\ -80,000 \\ \hline \$95,000 \end{array}$

$\$95,000 \times 74.3\% = \$70,585$

25. According to a recent inventory, the total merchandise available at the Big Man's Clothing was $63,000 and was marked to sell for $100,000. Sales were $75,000. Find the estimated cost of the inventory for the period.

$\dfrac{\$63,000}{\$100,000} = 63\%$

$\begin{array}{r} \$100,000 \\ -75,000 \\ \hline \$25,000 \end{array}$

$\$25,000 \times 63\% = \$15,750$

18.6

26. Danka Business Systems had a $15,000 opening inventory at cost. During a three-month period $45,000 worth of goods were purchased and $66,150 worth was sold. The store's gross profit rate is 35%. Estimate the closing inventory using the gross profit method.

Opening inventory	$15,000
+ purchases	+ 45,000
Available for sale	$60,000

Sales	$66,150.00	$66,150.00
− gross profit (35% of sales)	− 23,152.50 ←	× 35%
cost of goods sold	$42,997.50	$23,152.50

Available for sale	$60,000.00
− cost of goods sold	− 42,997.50
closing inventory	$17,002.50

27. Opening inventory at Valley Center was $400,000. Gross profit percent is 30% of sales. Sales were $2,000,000, and purchases were $1,600,000. Estimate the value of the closing inventory using the gross profit method.

Opening inventory	$ 400,000
+ purchases	+ 1,600,000
Available for sale	$2,000,000

Sales	$2,000,000	$2,000,000
− gross profit (30% of sales)	− 600,000 ←	× 30%
cost of goods sold	1,400,000	$ 600,000

Available for sale	$2,000,000
− cost of goods sold	− 1,400,000
closing inventory	$ 600,000

28. Gibson Medical Supply makes 46% gross profit on sales. The company's opening inventory for this period was $13,000 and purchases were $21,000. If sales were $16,000, how much was the value of the closing inventory using the gross profit method?

Opening inventory	$ 13,000		
+ purchases	+ 21,000		
available for sale	$ 34,000		

Sales		$16,000	$16,000
− gross profit (46% of sales)		− 7,360 ◄	× 46%
cost of goods sold		$ 8,640	◟ $ 7,360

Available for sale	$34,000
− cost of goods sold	− 8,640
closing inventory	$25,360

29. Spence Pharmacy management determined that opening inventory was $240,000, purchases were $1,100,000, sales were $1,500,000, and gross profit percent was 32%. Calculate the inventory.

Opening inventory	$ 240,000		
+ purchases	+ 1,100,000		
available for sale	$ 1,340,000		

Sales		$1,500,000	$1,500,000
− gross profit (32% of sales)		− 480,000 ◄	× 32%
cost of goods sold		$1,020,000	◟ $ 480,000

Available for sale	$1,340,000
− cost of goods sold	− 1,020,000
closing inventory	$ 320,000

30. The opening inventory at Schult's Plastics was $75,000. Gross profit percent is 35% of sales. Sales were $450,000, and purchases were $300,000. Estimate the value of the closing inventory using the gross profit method.

Opening inventory	$ 75,000		
+ purchases	+ 300,000		
available for sale	$375,000		

Sales		$450,000	$450,000
− gross profit (35% of sales)		− 157,500 ◄	× 35%
cost of goods sold		$292,500	◟ $157,500

Available for sale	$375,000
− cost of goods sold	− 292,500
closing inventory	$82,500

18.7

31. Furniture Warehouse's average monthly overhead is $123,000. Floor space by square feet within the departments is as follows: office, 1,500; kitchen, 6,000; bedroom, 1,500; living, 7,500; bath, 600. Allocate the overhead according to the floor space for each department.

Office:	1,500
Kitchen:	6,000
Bedroom:	1,500
Living:	7,500
Bath:	+ 600
	17,100

Office: $\dfrac{1,500}{17,100} \times \$123,000 = \$10,789.47$

Kitchen: $\dfrac{6,000}{17,100} \times 123,000 = 43,157.90$

Bedroom: $\dfrac{1,500}{17,100} \times 123,000 = 10,789.47$

Living: $\dfrac{7,500}{17,100} \times 123,000 = 53,947.37$

Bath: $\dfrac{600}{17,100} \times 123,000 = + 4,315.79$

Total $= \$123,000.00$

32. Littletown Auto Sales' average monthly overhead is $20,500. The square feet of floor space occupied by each department is as follows: new cars, 9,000; used cars, 6,000; repair, 15,000; paint and body, 4,000. Allocate the overhead according to the floor space for each department.

New cars:	9,000
Used cars:	6,000
Repair:	15,000
Paint and body:	+ 4,000
	34,000

New cars: $\dfrac{9,000}{34,000} \times \$20,500 = \$ 5,426.47$

Used cars: $\dfrac{6,000}{34,000} \times 20,500 = 3,617.65$

Repair: $\dfrac{15,000}{34,000} \times 20,500 = 9,044.12$

Paint and Body: $\dfrac{4,000}{34,000} \times 20,500 = 2,411.76$

Total $= \$20,500.00$

33. Central Town Hardware's average monthly overhead is $16,000. The square feet of floor space occupied by each department is as follows: glass, 5,000; tools, 10,000; electrical, 9,000; plumbing, 4,000. Allocate the overhead according to the floor space for each department.

Glass:	5,000
Tools:	10,000
Electrical:	9,000
Plumbing:	+ 4,000
	28,000

Glass: $\dfrac{5,000}{28,000} \times \$16,000 = \$ 2,857.14$

Tools: $\dfrac{10,000}{28,000} \times 16,000 = 5,714.29$

Electrical: $\dfrac{9,000}{28,000} \times 16,000 = 5,142.86$

Plumbing: $\dfrac{4,000}{28,000} \times 16,000 = + 2,285.71$

Total $= \$20,500.00$

Chapter 18 Accounting Applications: Inventory and Overhead

34. Betty's Best Clothes' average monthly overhead is $12,500. The square feet of floor space occupied by each department is as follows: women, 5,000; men, 3,000; girls, 2,000; boys, 1,950. Allocate the overhead according to the floor space for each department.

Women: 5,000
Men: 3,000
Girls: 2,000
Boys: + 1,950
        11,950

Women: $\dfrac{5,000}{11,950} \times \$12,500 = \$\ 5,230.13$

Men: $\dfrac{3,000}{11,950} \times 12,500 = 3,138.08$

Girls: $\dfrac{2,000}{11,950} \times 12,500 = 2,092.05$

Boys: $\dfrac{1,950}{11,950} \times 12,500 = + 2,039.75$

Total = $\$20,500.00$

35. At The World Down Under Aquarium Supply, floor space is allocated by square feet within the departments as follows: sales, 4,000; custom design, 5,500; maintenance, 1,500; office, 1,500. Monthly average overhead is $22,300. Allocate the overhead according to the floor space for each department.

Sales: 4,000
Custom design: 5,500
Maintenance: 1,500
Office: + 1,500
               12,500

Sales: $\dfrac{4,000}{12,500} \times \$22,300 = \$\ 7,136$

Custom design: $\dfrac{5,500}{12,500} \times 22,300 = 9,812$

Maintenance: $\dfrac{1,500}{12,500} \times 22,300 = 2,676$

Office: $\dfrac{1,500}{12,500} \times 22,300 = + 2,676$

Total = $\$22,300$

18.8

36. Fin & Feather Boat Supply's monthly overhead is $45,000. Average net sales by department are as follows: ski boats, $50,000; party boats, $200,000; fishing boats, $48,000; service, $15,000. Allocate the overhead according to the net sales for each department.

Ski boats: $ 50,000
Party boats: 200,000
Fishing boats: 48,000
Service: + 15,000
                $313,000

Ski boats: $\dfrac{\$50,000}{\$313,000} \times \$45,000 = \$\ 7,188.50$

Party boats: $\dfrac{200,000}{313,000} \times 45,000 = 28,753.99$

Fishing boats: $\dfrac{48,000}{313,000} \times 45,000 = 6,900.96$

Service: $\dfrac{15,000}{313,000} \times 45,000 = + 2,156.55$

Total = $\$45,000.00$

37. The total overhead expenses of Warren's Fast Foods was $8,500 for the past year. The store's net sales by department for the year were as follows: dairy, $3,000; produce, $4,000; meats, $8,000; other, $7,000. Allocate the overhead according to the net sales by each department.

Dairy: $ 3,000
Produce: 4,000
Meats: 8,000
Other: + 7,000
          $22,000

Dairy: $\dfrac{\$3,000}{\$22,000} \times \$8,500 = \$1,159.09$

Produce: $\dfrac{4,000}{22,000} \times 8,500 = 1,545.45$

Meats: $\dfrac{8,000}{22,000} \times 8,500 = 3,090.91$

Other: $\dfrac{7,000}{22,000} \times 8,500 = + 2,704.55$

Total = $\$8,500.00$

38. Adair Optical's monthly average overhead is $40,000. Average net sales by department are as follows: contact lenses, $43,000; exams, $38,000; frames, $88,000; glasses, $23,000. Allocate the overhead according to the net sales for each department.

Lenses: $ 43,000
Exams: 38,000
Frames: 88,000
Glasses: + 23,000
          $192,000

Lenses: $\dfrac{\$43,000}{\$192,000} \times \$40,000 = \$\ 8,958.33$

Exams: $\dfrac{38,000}{192,000} \times 40,000 = 7,916.67$

Frames: $\dfrac{88,000}{192,000} \times 40,000 = 18,333.33$

Glasses: $\dfrac{23,000}{192,000} \times 40,000 = + 4,791.67$

Total = $\$40,000.00$

39. The total overhead expenses for Kelly Appliance were $70,000 for the past year. The store's net sales by department for the year were as follows: washer and dryer, $75,250; refrigerator, $55,500; water heater, $40,250; air conditioning, $21,000. Allocate the overhead according to the net sales by each department.

Washer & dryer: $ 75,250
Refrigerator: 55,500
Water heater: 40,250
Air conditioner: + 21,000
$192,000

Washer & dryer: $\frac{\$75,250}{\$192,000} \times \$70,000 = \$27,434.90$

Refrigerator: $\frac{55,500}{192,000} \times 70,000 = 20,234.38$

Water heater: $\frac{40,250}{192,000} \times 70,000 = 14,674.48$

Air conditioner: $\frac{21,000}{192,000} \times 70,000 = + 7,656.25$

Total = $70,000.01

40. The average monthly overhead expenses of Busy Boy's Appliance Repair are $4,900 for the past year. The company's net sales by department for the year were as follows: television, $3,510; radio, $3,100; microwave, $1,884; other, $980. Allocate the overhead according to the net sales by each department.

Television: $3,510
Radio: 3,100
Microwave: 1,884
Other: + 980
$9,474

Television: $\frac{\$3,510}{\$9,474} \times \$4,900 = \$1,815.39$

Radio: $\frac{3,100}{9,474} \times 4,900 = 1,603.34$

Microwave: $\frac{1,884}{9,474} \times 4,900 = 974.41$

Other: $\frac{980}{9,474} \times 4,900 = + 506.86$

Total = $4,900.00

18.9

41. The total overhead expenses of Mervin's Motors was $15,000 last month. The company's number of employees by department is as follows: new cars, 7; used cars, 4; trucks, 1; repair, 10. Allocate the overhead according to the number of employees by each department.

New cars: 7
Used cars: 4
Trucks: 1
Repair: + 10
22

New cars: $\frac{7}{22} \times \$15,000 = \$ 4,772.73$

Used cars: $\frac{4}{22} \times 15,000 = 2,727.27$

Trucks: $\frac{1}{22} \times 15,000 = 681.82$

Repair: $\frac{10}{22} \times 15,000 = + 6,818.18$

Total = $15,000.00

42. Aardvark's Grocery's monthly average overhead is $4,285. The number of employees by department is as follows: produce, 9; dairy, 5; meats, 8; bakery, 4. Allocate the overhead according to the number of employees for each department.

Produce: 9
Dairy: 5
Meats: 8
Bakery: + 4
26

Produce: $\frac{9}{26} \times \$4,285 = \$1,483.27$

Dairy: $\frac{5}{26} \times 4,285 = 824.04$

Meats: $\frac{8}{26} \times 4,285 = 1,318.46$

Bakery: $\frac{4}{26} \times 4,285 = + 659.23$

Total = $4,285.00

43. The total overhead expenses of Trinity Auto Salvage are $21,000 for the past year. The company's number of employees by department for the year as follows: imports, 5; domestic, 7; trucks, 9; office, 3. Allocate the overhead according to the number of employees by each department.

Imports: 5
Domestic: 7
Trucks: 9
Office: + 3
24

Imports: $\frac{5}{24} \times \$21,000 = \$ 4,375$

Domestic: $\frac{7}{24} \times 21,000 = 6,125$

Trucks: $\frac{9}{24} \times 21,000 = 7,875$

Office: $\frac{3}{24} \times 21,000 = + 2,625$

Total = $21,000

44. Hearne Department Store's monthly average overhead is $127,500. The number of employees by department is as follows: furniture, 15; hardware, 13; housewares, 17; clothing, 19. Allocate the overhead according to the number of employees for each department.

Furniture: 15
Hardware: 13
Housewares: 17
Clothing: + 19
              64

Furniture: $\frac{15}{64} \times \$127,000 = \$\ 29,765.63$

Hardware: $\frac{13}{64} \times 127,000 = \ 25,796.88$

Housewares: $\frac{17}{64} \times 127,000 = \ 33,734.38$

Clothing: $\frac{19}{64} \times 127,000 = +\ 37,703.13$
                              Total = $\overline{\$127,000.02}$

45. Condor Auto Service is divided into departments according to types of repair. Total overhead was $23,000 for the past month. The company's number of employees by department is as follows: transmission, 6; engine, 8; electrical, 4; air conditioning, 4; and suspension, 5. Allocate the overhead according to the number of employees by each department.

Transmission: 6
Engine: 8
Electrical   4
A/C: 4
Suspension: + 5
                27

Transmission: $\frac{6}{27} \times \$23,000 = \$\ 5,111.$

Engine: $\frac{8}{27} \times 23,000 = \ 6,814.81$

Electrical $\frac{4}{27} \times 23,000 = \ 3,407.41$

A/C: $\frac{4}{27} \times 23,000 = \ 3,407.41$

Suspension: $\frac{5}{27} \times 23,000 = +\ 4,259.26$
                            Total = $\overline{\$23,000.00}$

CHAPTER REVIEW PROBLEMS

Answers to odd-numbered problems are given in Appendix A.

Drill Problems

Value the inventory using the LIFO, FIFO, and weighted-average methods in problems 1 through 5.

1. Purchases

	Ending Inventory
4 @ $10.50	7 units
5 @ 12.00	
6 @ 13.00	

LIFO $78.00

FIFO $90.00

W.A. $84.00

LIFO

$4 \times \$10.50 = \$42.00$
$3 \times\ \ \ 12.00 = +36.00$
                    $\overline{\$78.00}$

FIFO

$6 \times \$13.00 = \$78.00$
$1 \times\ \ \ 12.00 = +12.00$
                    $\overline{\$90.00}$

Weighted Average

$\ \ \ 4 \times \$10.50 = \$42.00$
$\ \ \ 5 \times\ \ \ 12.00 = \ \ 60.00$
$\underline{\ \ \ 6} \times\ \ \ 13.00 = +78.00$
$15 \ \ \ \ \ \ \ \ \ \ \ \ \overline{\$180.00}$

$\$180 \div 15 \times 7 = \$84.00$

2. Purchases

	Ending Inventory
6 @ $ 5.00	8 units
3 @ 8.00	
3 @ 10.00	

LIFO $46.00

FIFO $64.00

W.A. $56.00

LIFO

$6 \times \$5.00 = \$30.00$
$2 \times\ \ 8.00 = +16.00$
                  $\overline{\$46.00}$

FIFO

$3 \times \$10.00 = \$30.00$
$3 \times\ \ \ 8.00 = \ \ 24.00$
$2 \times\ \ \ 5.00 = +10.00$
                    $\overline{\$64.00}$

Weighted Average

$\ \ \ 6 \times \$5.00 = \$30.00$
$\ \ \ 3 \times\ \ 8.00 = \ \ 24.00$
$\underline{\ \ \ 3} \times 10.00 = +30.00$
$12 \ \ \ \ \ \ \ \ \ \ \overline{\$84.00}$

$\$84 \div 12 \times 8 = \$56.00$

	Ending		*LIFO*	*FIFO*

3. Purchases

Purchases	Ending Inventory
12 @ $2.00	14 units
8 @ 3.25	
10 @ 4.00	

LIFO $30.50

FIFO $53.00

W.A. $42.00

LIFO

$12 \times \$2.00 = \$24.00$
$2 \times 3.25 = \underline{+ 6.50}$
$\$30.50$

FIFO

$10 \times \$4.00 = \$40.00$
$4 \times 3.25 = \underline{+13.00}$
$\$53.00$

Weighted Average

$12 \times \$2.00 = \$24.00$
$8 \times 3.25 = 26.00$
$\underline{10} \times 4.00 = \underline{+40.00}$
$30 \qquad \$90.00$

$\$ 90 \div 30 \times 14 = \$42.00$

4. Purchases

Purchases	Ending Inventory
5 @ $16.20	10 units
12 @ 16.50	
8 @ 18.25	

LIFO $163.50

FIFO $179.00

W.A. $170.00

LIFO

$5 \times \$16.20 = \$81.00$
$5 \times 16.50 = \underline{+82.50}$
$\$163.50$

FIFO

$8 \times \$18.25 = \$146.00$
$2 \times 16.50 = \underline{+ 33.00}$
$\$179.00$

Weighted Average

$5 \times \$16.20 = \$81.00$
$12 \times 16.50 = 198.00$
$\underline{8} \times 18.25 = \underline{+146.00}$
$25 \qquad \$425.00$

$\$425 \div 25 \times 10 = \$170$

5. Purchases

Purchases	Ending Inventory
6 @ $8.75	13 units
20 @ 9.25	
12 @ 7.45	

LIFO $117.25

FIFO $98.65

W.A. $111.83

LIFO

$6 \times \$8.75 = \$52.50$
$7 \times 9.25 = \underline{+ 64.75}$
$\$117.25$

FIFO

$12 \times \$7.45 = \$89.40$
$1 \times 9.25 = \underline{+ 9.25}$
$\$98.65$

Weighted Average

$6 \times \$8.75 = \$52.50$
$20 \times 9.25 = 185.00$
$\underline{12} \times 7.45 = \underline{+ 89.40}$
$38 \qquad \$326.90$

$\$326.90 \div 38 \times 13 = \$111.83$

Estimate the value of the closing inventory using the gross profit method in problems 6 through 10.

6. Opening inventory: $14,000   Closing inventory: $12,175
Goods purchased: 44,000
Goods sold: 70,500
Profit rate: 35%

Opening inventory	$14,000
+ goods purchased	+ 44,000
goods available for sale	$58,000
Sales	$70,500
− gross profit (35% of sales)	− 24,675
cost of goods sold	$45,825
Goods available for sale	$58,000
− cost of goods sold	− 45,825
closing inventory	$12,175

$70,500
× 35%
$24,675

7. Opening inventory: $18,200   Closing inventory: $25,900
Goods purchased: 57,200
Goods sold: 90,000
Profit rate: 45%

Opening inventory	$18,200
+ goods purchased	+ 57,200
goods available for sale	$75,400
Sales	$90,000
− gross profit (45% of sales)	− 40,500
cost of goods sold	$49,500
Goods available for sale	$75,400
− cost of goods sold	− 49,500
closing inventory	$25,900

$90,000
× 45%
$40,500

8. Opening inventory: $ 6,000   Closing inventory: $14,440
Goods purchased: 19,000
Goods sold: 22,000
Profit rate: 52%

Opening inventory	$6,000
+ goods purchased	+ 19,000
goods available for sale	$25,000
Sales	$22,000
− gross profit (52% of sales)	− 11,440
cost of goods sold	$10,560
Goods available for sale	$25,000
− cost of goods sold	− 10,560
closing inventory	$14,440

$22,000
× 45%
$11,440

9. Opening inventory: $12,600   Closing inventory: $12,780

Goods purchased: 39,900
Goods sold: 66,200
Profit rate: 40%

Opening inventory	$12,600
+ goods purchased	+ 39,900
goods available for sale	$52,500
Sales	$66,200
− gross profit (40% of sales)	− 26,480
cost of goods sold	$39,720
Goods available for sale	$52,500
− cost of goods sold	− 39,720
closing inventory	$12,780

$66,200
$\times$ 40%
$26,480

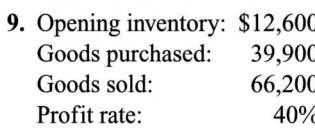
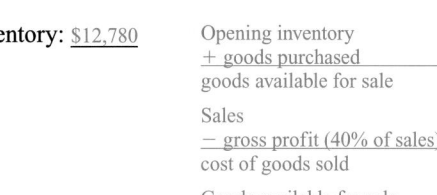
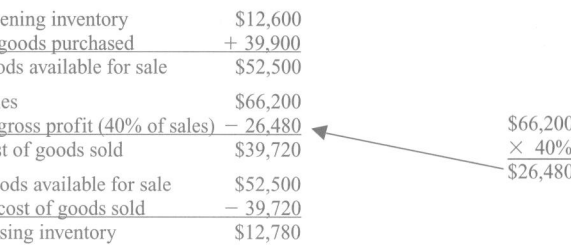

10. Opening inventory: $17,640   Closing inventory: $13,500

Goods purchased: 55,860
Goods sold: 120,000
Profit rate: 50%

Opening inventory	$17,640
+ goods purchased	+ 55,860
goods available for sale	$73,500
Sales	$120,000
− gross profit (50% of sales)	− 60,000
cost of goods sold	$ 60,000
Goods available for sale	$73,500
− cost of goods sold	− 60,000
closing inventory	$13,500

$120,000
$\times$ 50%
$ 60,000

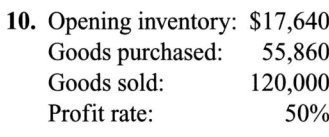
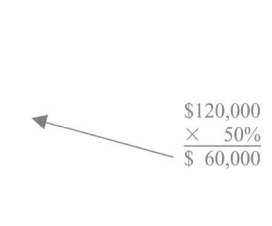

Estimate the value of the inventory using the retail method in problems 11 through 15.

11. Cost of goods available for sale : $31,000
Retail price of goods available for sale: 63,000
Sales: 42,000
Closing inventory: $7,000

$$\frac{\text{Cost of goods available for sale}}{\text{retail price of goods available for sale}} = \frac{\$31,000}{\$63,000} = \frac{1}{3}$$

Retail price of goods available for sale	$63,000
− sales	− 42,000
retail value of closing inventory	$21,000

$\frac{1}{3} \times \$21,000 = \$7,000$

12. Cost of goods available for sale: $43,400
Retail price of goods available for sale: 88,200
Sales: 62,200
Closing inventory: $12,792

$$\frac{\text{Cost of goods available for sale}}{\text{retail price of goods available for sale}} = \frac{\$43,400}{\$88,200} = 49.2\%$$

Retail price of goods available for sale	$88,200
− sales	− 62,200
retail value of closing inventory	$26,000

49.2% $\times$ $26,000 = $12,792

13. Cost of goods available for sale $94,000
Retail price of goods available for sale: 190,000
Sales: 120,000
Closing inventory: $34,650

$$\frac{\text{Cost of goods available for sale}}{\text{retail price of goods available for sale}} = \frac{\$ 94,000}{\$190,000} = 49.5\%$$

Retail price of goods available for sale	$190,000
− sales	− 120,000
retail value of closing inventory	$ 70,000

49.5% $\times$ $70,000 = $34,650

14. Cost of goods available for sale: $56,420
Retail price of goods available for sale: 114,660
Sales: 81,860
Closing inventory: $16,137.60

$$\frac{\text{Cost of goods available for sale}}{\text{retail price of goods available for sale}} = \frac{\$ 56,420}{\$114,660} = 49.2\%$$

Retail price of goods available for sale	$114,660
− sales	− 81,860
retail value of closing inventory	$ 32,800

49.2% $\times$ $32,800 = $16,137.60

15. Cost of goods available for sale: $26,000
Retail price of goods available for sale: 54,000
Sales: 40,000
Closing inventory: $6,734

$$\frac{\text{Cost of goods available for sale}}{\text{retail price of goods available for sale}} = \frac{\$26,000}{\$54,000} = 48.1\%$$

Retail price of goods available for sale	$54,000
− sales	− 40,000
retail value of closing inventory	$14,000

48.1% $\times$ $14,000 = $6,734

Distribute overhead according to floor space in problems 16 through 20.

16.

Department	Floor Space	Total Overhead	Allocation of Overhead	
A	2,500	$60,000	$15,000	2,500
B	500		3,000	500
C	5,000		30,000	5,000
D	2,000		12,000	+2,000
				10,000

A $\dfrac{2,500}{10,000} \times \$60,000 = \$15,000$

B $\dfrac{500}{10,000} \times 60,000 = 3,000$

C $\dfrac{5,000}{10,000} \times 60,000 = 30,000$

D $\dfrac{2,000}{10,000} \times 60,000 = 12,000$

17.

Department	Floor Space	Total Overhead	Allocation of Overhead	
A	3,000	$48,000	$9,000	3,000
B	6,000		18,000	6,000
C	2,000		6,000	2,000
D	4,000		12,000	4,000
E	1,000		3,000	+1,000
				16,000

A $\dfrac{3,000}{16,000} \times \$48,000 = \$9,000$

B $\dfrac{6,000}{16,000} \times 48,000 = 18,000$

C $\dfrac{2,000}{16,000} \times 48,000 = 6,000$

D $\dfrac{4,000}{16,000} \times 48,000 = 12,000$

E $\dfrac{1,000}{16,000} \times 48,000 = 3,000$

18.

Department	Floor Space	Total Overhead	Allocation of Overhead	
A	4,000	$35,000	$14,000	4,000
B	2,000		7,000	2,000
C	2,500		8,750	2,500
D	1,500		5,250	+1,500
				10,000

A $\dfrac{4,000}{10,000} \times \$35,000 = \$14,000$

B $\dfrac{2,000}{10,000} \times 35,000 = 7,000$

C $\dfrac{2,500}{10,000} \times 35,000 = 8,750$

D $\dfrac{1,500}{10,000} \times 35,000 = 5,250$

19.

Department	Floor Space	Total Overhead	Allocation of Overhead	
A	8,000	$60,000	$24,000	8,000
B	2,000		6,000	2,000
C	2,500		7,500	2,500
D	4,500		13,500	4,500
E	3,000		9,000	+3,000
				20,000

A $\dfrac{8,000}{20,000} \times \$60,000 = \$24,000$

B $\dfrac{2,000}{20,000} \times 60,000 = 6,000$

C $\dfrac{2,500}{20,000} \times 60,000 = 7,500$

D $\dfrac{4,500}{20,000} \times 60,000 = 13,500$

E $\dfrac{3,000}{20,000} \times 60,000 = 9,000$

20.

Department	Floor Space	Total Overhead	Allocation of Overhead	
A	4,000	$30,000	$2,857.14	4,000
B	11,000		7,857.14	11,000
C	8,250		5,892.86	8,250
D	12,250		8,750.00	12,250
E	6,500		4,642.86	+6,500
				42,000

A $\dfrac{4,000}{42,000} \times \$30,000 = \$2,857.14$

B $\dfrac{11,000}{42,000} \times 30,000 = 7,857.14$

C $\dfrac{8,250}{42,000} \times 30,000 = 5,892.86$

D $\dfrac{12,250}{42,000} \times 30,000 = 8,750.00$

E $\dfrac{6,500}{42,000} \times 30,000 = 4,642.86$

Distribute overhead according to net sales in problems 21 through 25.

21.

Department	Net Sales	Total Overhead	Allocation of Overhead	
A	$2,000	$4,800	$800	$ 2,000
B	2,500		1,000	2,500
C	4,500		1,800	4,500
D	3,000		1,200	+ 3,000
				$12,000

A $\dfrac{\$ 2,000}{\$12,000} \times \$4,800 = \$ 800.00$

B $\dfrac{2,500}{12,000} \times 4,800 = 1,000.00$

C $\dfrac{4,500}{12,000} \times 4,800 = 1,800.00$

D $\dfrac{3,000}{12,000} \times 4,800 = 1,200.00$

Chapter 18 Accounting Applications: Inventory and Overhead

22.

Department	Net Sales	Total Overhead	Allocation of Overhead	
A	$10,000	$90,000	$12,000	$10,000
B	15,000		18,000	15,000
C	5,000		6,000	5,000
D	25,000		30,000	25,000
E	20,000		24,000	+20,000
				$75,000

A $\frac{\$10,000}{\$75,000} \times \$90,000 = \$12,000$

B $\frac{15,000}{75,000} \times 90,000 = 18,000$

C $\frac{5,000}{75,000} \times 90,000 = 6,000$

D $\frac{25,000}{75,000} \times 90,000 = 30,000$

E $\frac{20,000}{75,000} \times 90,000 = 24,000$

23.

Department	Net Sales	Total Overhead	Allocation of Overhead	
A	$15,000	$20,000	$3,000	$15,000
B	20,000		4,000	20,000
C	12,500		2,500	12,500
D	10,000		2,000	10,000
E	5,000		1,000	5,000
F	37,500		7,500	+37,500
				$100,000

A $\frac{\$15,000}{\$100,000} \times \$20,000 = \$3,000$

B $\frac{20,000}{100,000} \times 20,000 = 4,000$

C $\frac{12,500}{100,000} \times 20,000 = 2,500$

D $\frac{10,000}{100,000} \times 20,000 = 2,000$

E $\frac{5,000}{100,000} \times 20,000 = 1,000$

F $\frac{37,500}{100,000} \times 20,000 = 7,500$

24.

Department	Net Sales	Total Overhead	Allocation of Overhead	
A	$9,000	$5,000	$1,730.77	$9,000
B	7,000		1,346.15	7,000
C	5,500		1,057.69	5,500
D	4,500		865.38	+ 4,500
				$26,000

A $\frac{\$9,000}{\$26,000} \times \$5,000 = \$1,730.77$

B $\frac{7,000}{26,000} \times 5,000 = 1,346.15$

C $\frac{5,500}{26,000} \times 5,000 = 1,057.69$

D $\frac{4,500}{26,000} \times 5,000 = 865.38$

25.

Department	Net Sales	Total Overhead	Allocation of Overhead	
A	$2,000	$15,000	$6,000	$2,000
B	500		1,500	500
C	625		1,875	625
D	1,125		3,375	1,125
E	750		2,250	+ 750
				$5,000

A $\frac{\$2,000}{\$5,000} \times \$15,000 = \$6,000$

B $\frac{500}{5,000} \times 15,000 = 1,500$

C $\frac{625}{5,000} \times 15,000 = 1,875$

D $\frac{1,125}{5,000} \times 15,000 = 3,375$

E $\frac{750}{5,000} \times 15,000 = 2,250$

Distribute overhead according to the number of employees in problems 26 through 30.

26.

Department	Number of Employees	Total Overhead	Allocation of Overhead	
A	10	$72,000	$20,000	10
B	12		24,000	12
C	8		16,000	8
D	6		12,000	+6
				36

A $\frac{10}{36} \times \$72,000 = \$20,000$

B $\frac{12}{36} \times 72,000 = 24,000$

C $\frac{8}{36} \times 72,000 = 16,000$

D $\frac{6}{36} \times 72,000 = 12,000$

27.

Department	Number of Employees	Total Overhead	Allocation of Overhead	
A	9	$140,000	$21,000	9
B	18		42,000	18
C	12		28,000	12
D	6		14,000	6
E	15		35,000	+15
				60

A $\frac{9}{60} \times \$140,000 = \$21,000$

B $\frac{18}{60} \times 140,000 = 42,000$

C $\frac{12}{60} \times 140,000 = 28,000$

D $\frac{6}{60} \times 140,000 = 14,000$

E $\frac{15}{60} \times 140,000 = 35,000$

28.

Department	Number of Employees	Total Overhead	Allocation of Overhead	
A	6	$24,000	$4,800	6
B	10		8,000	10
C	5		4,000	5
D	9		7,200	+9
				30

A $\frac{6}{30} \times \$24,000 = \$4,800$

B $\frac{10}{30} \times 24,000 = 8,000$

C $\frac{5}{30} \times 24,000 = 4,000$

D $\frac{9}{30} \times 24,000 = 7,200$

29.

Department	Number of Employees	Total Overhead	Allocation of Overhead	
A	6	$96,000	$12,000	6
B	12		24,000	12
C	16		32,000	16
D	6		12,000	6
E	8		16,000	+8
				48

A $\frac{6}{48} \times \$96,000 = \$12,000$

B $\frac{12}{48} \times 96,000 = 24,000$

C $\frac{16}{48} \times 96,000 = 32,000$

D $\frac{6}{48} \times 96,000 = 12,000$

E $\frac{8}{48} \times 96,000 = 16,000$

30.

Department	Number of Employees	Total Overhead	Allocation of Overhead	
A	12	$28,000	$5,600.00	12
B	20		9,333.33	20
C	10		4,666.67	10
D	18		8,400.00	+18
				60

A $\frac{12}{60} \times \$28,000 = \$5,600.00$

B $\frac{20}{60} \times 28,000 = 9,333.33$

C $\frac{10}{60} \times 28,000 = 4,666.67$

D $\frac{18}{60} \times 28,000 = 8,400.00$

Word Problems

31. During an inventory period, Cabin Whister Parks, Inc., had merchandise available for sale that cost $113,000 and was marked to sell for $186,000. Total sales for the period were $120,000. Find the estimated cost of inventory at the end of the period.

$\frac{\$113,000}{\$186,000} = 60.8\%$

$\begin{array}{r} \$\ 186,000 \\ -120,000 \\ \hline \$\ 66,000 \end{array}$

$\$66,000 \times 60.8\% = \$40,128$

32. Sparky's Pet Shop sells a new kind of dog collar. Inventory shows 30 in stock. Purchases were 20 at $7.50, 18 at $10, and 25 at $12. Find the value of the inventory by FIFO, LIFO, and weighted-average methods.

LIFO $250.00

FIFO $350.00

W.A. $300.00

LIFO

$\begin{array}{l} 20 \times \$7.50 = \ \$150.00 \\ 10 \times 10.00 = +100.00 \\ \hline \qquad\qquad\quad\ \$250.00 \end{array}$

FIFO

$\begin{array}{l} 25 \times \$12.00 = \$300.00 \\ 5 \times \ 10.00 = + 50.00 \\ \hline \qquad\qquad\quad \$350.00 \end{array}$

Weighted Average

$\begin{array}{l} 20 \times \$7.50 = \ \$150.00 \\ 18 \times 10.00 = \quad 180.00 \\ 25 \times 12.00 = + 300.00 \\ \hline 63 \qquad\qquad \$630.00 \end{array}$

$\$630 \div 63 \times 30 = \$300$

33. Johnson Dental Lab makes 56% gross profit on sales. The lab's opening inventory for this period was $54,000 and purchases were $450,000. If sales were $1,016,500, how much was the value of the closing inventory using the gross profit method?

Opening inventory	$ 54,000
+ purchases	+ 450,000
available for sale	$ 504,000
Sales	$1,016,500
− gross profit (56% of sales)	− 569,240
cost of goods sold	$ 447,260
Available for sale	$ 504,000
− cost of goods sold	− 447,260
closing inventory	$ 56,740

$\begin{array}{r} \$1,016,500 \\ \times \qquad 56\% \\ \hline \$\ 569,240 \end{array}$

34. Jean's Sportswear has made the following wholesale purchases of a new jogging shoe: 12 pairs @ $22; 30 pairs @ $22.50; 18 pairs @ $24.50. An inventory taken last week indicates that 20 pairs are still in stock. Evaluate the cost of the inventory by FIFO, LIFO, and weighted-average methods.

LIFO $444.00

FIFO $486.00

W.A. $460.00

LIFO

$\begin{array}{l} 12 \times \$22.00 = \$ 264.00 \\ 8 \times \ 22.50 = + 180.00 \\ \hline \qquad\qquad\quad\ \$ 444.00 \end{array}$

FIFO

$\begin{array}{l} 18 \times \$24.50 = \$441.00 \\ 2 \times \ 22.50 = + 45.00 \\ \hline \qquad\qquad\quad \$486.00 \end{array}$

Weighted Average

$\begin{array}{l} 12 \times \$22.00 = \$ 264.00 \\ 30 \times \ 22.50 = \quad 675.00 \\ 18 \times \ 24.50 = +441.00 \\ \hline 60 \qquad\qquad\ \ \$1,380.00 \end{array}$

$\$1,380 \div 60 \times 20 = \$460$

35. American Clothing allocates overhead according to total floor space for each department. Determine the overhead to be assigned to each department if total overhead for November was $72,000.

Department	Floor Space
Women	9,000
Girls	4,000
Men	7,500
Boys	6,000
Shoes	2,000
Linens	4,500
Housewares	+ 3,000
Total	36,000

Women: $\dfrac{9,000}{36,000} \times \$72,000 = \$18,000$

Girls: $\dfrac{4,000}{36,000} \times 72,000 = 8,000$

Men: $\dfrac{7,500}{36,000} \times 72,000 = 15,000$

Boys: $\dfrac{6,000}{36,000} \times 72,000 = 12,000$

Shoes: $\dfrac{2,000}{36,000} \times 72,000 = 4,000$

Linens: $\dfrac{4,500}{36,000} \times 72,000 = 9,000$

Housewares: $\dfrac{3,000}{36,000} \times 72,000 = 6,000$

36. Brenda's Furniture Outlet apportions overhead to various departments according to each department's ratio of total net sales. If monthly operating expenses were $30,000, find each department's share of the overhead.

Department	Net Sales
Living	$25,000
Dining	15,000
Bedroom	20,000
Patio	6,000
Kitchen	4,000
Carpets	10,000
Appliances	12,000
TV/electronics	+ 8,000
Total	$100,000

Living: $\dfrac{\$25,000}{\$100,000} \times \$30,000 = \$7,500$

Dining: $\dfrac{15,000}{100,000} \times 30,000 = 4,500$

Bedroom: $\dfrac{20,000}{100,000} \times 30,000 = 6,000$

Patio: $\dfrac{6,000}{100,000} \times 30,000 = 1,800$

Kitchen: $\dfrac{4,000}{100,000} \times 30,000 = 1,200$

Carpets: $\dfrac{10,000}{100,000} \times 30,000 = 3,000$

Appliances: $\dfrac{12,000}{100,000} \times 30,000 = 3,600$

TV/electronics: $\dfrac{8,000}{100,000} \times 30,000 = 2,400$

37. During an inventory period, Worldwide Group, Inc., had merchandise available for sale that cost $188,000 and was marked to sell for $470,000. Total sales for the period were $438,750. Find the estimated cost of inventory at the end of the period.

$\dfrac{\$188,000}{\$470,000} = 40\%$

$\begin{array}{r} \$\ 470,000 \\ -438,750 \\ \hline \$\ \ 31,250 \end{array}$

$\$31,250 \times 40\% = \$12,500$

38. Operating expenses at Sunbelt Office Supply are apportioned according to the total number of employees in each division. If the October overhead was $72,000, determine how much should be charged to each division.

Division	Number of Employees
Office supplies	9
Office furniture	6
Office machines	8
Machine maintenance	10
Accounting	+ 3
Total	36

Office supplies: $\dfrac{9}{36} \times \$72,000 = \$18,000$

Office furniture: $\dfrac{6}{36} \times 72,000 = 12,000$

Office machines: $\dfrac{8}{36} \times 72,000 = 16,000$

Machine maintenance: $\dfrac{10}{36} \times 72,000 = 20,000$

Accounting: $\dfrac{3}{36} \times 72,000 = 6,000$

39. Goldfarb Industries makes 37.5% gross profit on sales. The company's opening inventory for this period was $60,000 and purchases were $480,000. If sales were $773,600, how much was the value of the closing inventory using the gross profit method?

Opening inventory	$ 60,000
+ purchases	+480,000
available for sale	$540,000

Sales	$773,600
− gross profit (37.5% of sales)	−290,100
cost of goods sold	$483,500

$\begin{array}{r} \$773,600 \\ \times\ 37.5\% \\ \hline \$290,100 \end{array}$

Available for sale	$540,000
− cost of goods sold	−483,500
closing inventory	$ 56,500

40. Muligan's Digging Equipment purchased spades last year as follows:

Mar. 3   10 @ $15.00 each
May 2   25 @   19.00 each
July 23   25 @   18.00 each
Sept. 5   30 @   16.00 each
Nov. 4   50 @   14.00 each

Sales last month by products were as follows: shovels, $2,750; pitchforks, $3,250; gloves, $1,800; spades, $3,300. Allocate the $4,750 overhead according to the net sales for each product and find the value of the 37-unit spade inventory using the LIFO, FIFO, and weighted average methods.

Sales
$2,750 + 3,250 + 1,800 + 3,300 = $11,100

Overhead Allocation

Shovels: $\dfrac{\$2,750}{\$11,100} \times \$4,750 = \$1,176.80$

Pitchforks: $\dfrac{3,250}{11,100} \times 4,750 = 1,390.77$

Gloves: $\dfrac{1,800}{11,100} \times 4,750 = 770.27$

Spades: $\dfrac{3,300}{11,100} \times 4,750 = 1,412.16$

Inventory Valuation

LIFO

Mar. 3:	10 × $15 =	$150
May 2:	25 × 19 =	475
July 23:	2 × 18 =	+ 36
		$661

Weighted Average

Mar. 3:	10 × $15 =	$ 150
May 2:	25 × 19 =	475
July 23:	25 × 18 =	450
Sept. 5:	30 × 16 =	480
Nov. 4:	+50 × 14 =	+700
	140	$2,255

FIFO

Nov. 4:   37 × $14 = $518

$2,255 ÷ 140 × 37 = $595.96

CRITICAL THINKING GROUP PROJECT

Symantha's Dog Supplies made the following purcases of doghouses last year:

Feb. 23   12 @ $75.00 each
Mar. 5   15 @   77.50 each
June 14   10 @   79.00 each
Sept. 9   18 @   76.00 each
Dec. 1   25 @   76.80 each

Sales last month by products were as follows: leashes, $1,700; collars, $2,550; bowls, $1,200; toys, $1,800; houses, $1,500; miscellaneous, $3,100.

1. Allocate the $4,000 monthly overhead according to the net sales for each product.

Sales
$1,700 + 2,550 + 1,200 + 1,800 + 1,500 + 3,100 = $11,850

Overhead allocation

Leashes: $\dfrac{\$1,700}{\$11,850} \times \$4,000 = \$573.84$

Collars: $\dfrac{2,250}{11,850} \times 4,000 = 860.76$

Bowls: $\dfrac{1,200}{11,850} \times 4,000 = 405.06$

Toys: $\dfrac{1,800}{11,850} \times 4,000 = 607.59$

Houses: $\dfrac{1,500}{11,850} \times 4,000 = 506.33$

Miscellaneous: $\dfrac{3,100}{11,850} \times 4,000 = 1,046.41$

2. Find the value of the 22-unit doghouse inventory using the LIFO, FIFO, and weighted-average methods.

Inventory Valuation:

LIFO   **FIFO**

Feb. 23:   12 × $75.00 = $ 900   Dec. 1:   22 × $76.80 = $1,689.60
Mar. 5:   10 × 77.50 = + 775
                          $1,675

Weighted Average

Feb. 23:   12 @ $75.00 each = $ 900.00 $\frac{\$6,140.50}{80}$ = $76.76
Mar. 5:   15 @ 77.50 each =   1,162.50
June 14:   10 @ 79.00 each =   790.00   22 × $76.76 = $1,688.72
Sept. 9:   18 @ 76.00 each =   1,368.00
Dec. 1:   25 @ 76.80 each = +1,920.00
           80                 $ 6,140.50

3. Which inventory valuation method would you choose? Why?

Student answers will vary, but the reason(s) for their choices should be logical.

Answers to all exercises are given in Appendix A.

1. Define inventory and briefly discuss its importance to **W** a business firm.

Inventory is the unsold merchandise a firm has available for sale. Because it usually represents a significant investment by a company, having adequate amounts on hand is important. Too much inventory means funds are tied up in an unproductive asset. Too little on hand means that there customer needs may not be satisfied. Lost sales can result.

2. Name the four most common inventory valuation **W** methods used by business.

The four must common methods used to value inventories are specific identification: first-in, first-out (FIFO); last-in, first-out (LIFO); and weighted-average.

3. Morgan's Spas has 30 spas in stock. Code numbers indicate 13 cost $1,197.50 each, 15 cost $1,220.50 each, and 12 cost $2,103.60 each. Using the specific identification method, find the value of the inventory.

13 × $1,197.50 = $ 15,567.50
15 × 1,220.50 =   18,307.50
12 × 2,103.60 = +25,243.20
                 $ 59,118.20

4. Cain Fence Co. purchased corner posts last year as follows:

Jan.   3   18 bundles @ $20.00 per bundle
Apr.   2   22 bundles @ 19.00 per bundle
June 23   21 bundles @ 18.50 per bundle
Oct.   5   40 bundles @ 18.00 per bundle
Nov.   4   28 bundles @ 17.00 per bundle

The year-end inventory showed 76 bundles in stock. Value the inventory using the FIFO, LIFO, and weighted-average methods.

FIFO   **LIFO**

Nov. 4:   28 × $17.00 = $ 476   Jan.   3:   18 × $20   = $ 360.00
Oct. 5:   40 × 18.00 =   720   Apr.   2:   22 × 19   =   418.00
June 23:   8 × 18.50 = + 148   Jun. 23:   21 × 18.50   =   388.50
                        $1,344   Oct.   5:   15 × 18   = + 270.00
                                                                $1,436.50

Weighted Average

Jan.   3:   18 × $20.00 = $ 360.00 $2,362.50 ÷ 129 × 76 = $1,391.86
Apr.   2:   22 × 19.00 =   418.00
June 23:   21 × 18.50 =   388.50
Oct.   5:   40 × 18.00 =   720.00
Nov.   4:   28 × 17.00 = + 476.00
           129              $2,362.50

5. Use the FIFO, LIFO, and weighted-average methods to calculate the value of 20 gallons of honey bought over a four-month period. The purchase record for the period is as follows:

Jan.	3	8 gallons @ $33 per gallon
Feb.	11	6 gallons @ 32 per gallon
Mar.	7	14 gallons @ 31 per gallon
Apr.	1	3 gallons @ 34 per gallon

FIFO

Apr. 1:	$3 \times \$34 = \$102$
Mar. 7:	$14 \times 31 = 434$
Feb. 11:	$3 \times 32 = +96$
	$\overline{\$632}$

LIFO

Jan. 3:	$8 \times \$33 = \$264$
Feb. 11:	$6 \times 32 = 192$
Mar. 7:	$6 \times 31 = +186$
	$\overline{\$642}$

Weighted Average

Jan. 3:	$8 \times \$33 = \$264$
Feb. 11:	$6 \times 32 = 192$
Mar. 7:	$14 \times 31 = 434$
Apr. 1:	$3 \times 34 = +102$
31	$\$992$

$\$992 \div 31 \times 20 = \$640$

6. During its last inventory period, Lakeview Hardware Store had merchandise available for sale that cost $35,000 and was marked to sell for $50,000. Total sales for the period were $30,000. Determine the approximate cost of inventory at the end of the period.

$$\frac{\$35,000}{\$50,000} = 70\%$$

$\$50,000$
$-30,000$
$\$20,000$

$\$20,000 \times 70\% = \$14,000$

7. Green Acres Clothing averages 60% profit on sales. The store's opening inventory for this period was $54,000 and purchases were $540,000. If sales were $1,375,000, how much was the value of the closing inventory using the gross profit method?

$\$54,000$	$\$1,375,000$	$\$1,375,000$	$\$594,000$
$+540,000$	$-825,000$	$\times 60\%$	$-550,000$
$\$594,000$	$\$550,000$	$\$825,000$	$\$44,000$
Goods available for sale	Cost of goods sold		Closing inventory

8. Lucille's Donut Shop's average monthly overhead is $5,000. Floor space by square feet within the departments is as follows: storage, 1,000; baking, 2,000; display, 1,500; seating, 2,500. Allocate the overhead according to the floor space for each area.

$1,000 + 2,000 + 1,500 + 2,500 = 7,000$

Storage: $\dfrac{1,000}{7,000} \times \$5,000 = \$714.29$

Display: $\dfrac{1,500}{7,000} \times 5,000 = 1,071.43$

Baking: $\dfrac{2,000}{7,000} \times 5,000 = 1,428.57$

Seating: $\dfrac{2,500}{7,000} \times 5,000 = 1,785.71$

9. Cleanup Supply Co.'s monthly average overhead is $30,000. Average sales by departments are as follows: disinfectants, $5,000; safety products, $7,000; sanitary supplies, $3,300; repair, $10,000. Allocate the overhead according to the net sales for each department.

$\$5,000 + 7,000 + 3,300 + 10,000 = \$25,300$

Disinfectants: $\dfrac{\$5,000}{\$25,300} \times \$30,000 = \$5,928.85$

Sanitary supplies: $\dfrac{3,300}{25,300} \times 30,000 = 3,913.04$

Safety products: $\dfrac{7,000}{25,300} \times 30,000 = 8,300.40$

Repair: $\dfrac{10,000}{25,300} \times 30,000 = 11,857.71$

10. W. F. Carter Construction Co. has $87,000 monthly overhead. The number of employees involved in each part of the company's line of construction is as follows: offices, 14; apartments, 16; warehouses, 19; stores, 6. Allocate the overhead according to the number of employees for each area of expertise.

$14 + 16 + 19 + 6 = 55$

Offices: $\dfrac{14}{55} \times \$87,000 = \$22,145.46$

Apartments: $\dfrac{16}{55} \times 87,000 = 25,309.09$

Warehouses: $\dfrac{19}{55} \times 87,000 = 30,054.55$

Stores: $\dfrac{6}{55} \times 87,000 = 9,490.91$

 **EXCEL SPREADSHEET APPLICATION FOR CHAPTER 18**

APPLICATION 1

The Automotive Department of the Springfield Department Store decided to handle Ford Taurus auto parts. In determining which inventory valuation method to use, a comparison spreadsheet has been designed. When you run Ch18App1 from your computer spreadsheet application's disk, you will see the following spreadsheet:

Springfield Department Store
2617 Main Street
Box 219
Springfield, Maryland 58109
Telephone: 301-555-2158   FAX: 301-555-3498

INVENTORY VALUATION COMPARISON

Right Front Fender for 1997 Ford Taurus

Date	Qty. Rcvd.	Price per Unit	Total Cost	Inventory 12/31/2002	LIFO Valuation	FIFO Valuation	Weighted-Average Valuation
			$0.00		$0.00	$0.00	#DIV/0!
			$0.00				
			$0.00				
			$0.00				
			$0.00				
			$0.00				
			$0.00				
			$0.00				
			$0.00				
			$0.00				
			$0.00				
TOTALS	0		$0.00				

Enter the following information:

Date	Cell	Quantity Received	Cell	Price per Unit	Cell
1/7/02	A14	24	B14	$239.49	C14
2/20/02	A15	20	B15	240.59	C15
3/28/02	A16	18	B16	241.48	C16
5/2/02	A17	27	B17	228.17	C17
6/9/02	A18	21	B18	244.50	C18
7/17/02	A19	36	B19	239.95	C19
8/30/02	A20	18	B20	245.83	C20
10/5/02	A21	26	B21	245.99	C21
11/1/02	A22	57	B22	233.88	C22
11/26/02	A23	25	B23	246.25	C23
12/15/02	A24	44	B24	235.33	C24
Inventory 12/31/02	E14	59			

Answer the following questions after you have completed the spreadsheet:

1. What is the total quantity received?
2. What is the total cost?
3. What is the LIFO valuation?
4. What is the FIFO valuation?
5. What is the weighted-average valuation?

GROUP REPORT

FOR CHAPTER 18 APPLICATION 1

Springfield sells other parts for the Ford Taurus. The year-end inventory count reveals that there are 27 taillight covers and 33 generators in stock. Your group should use the inventory valuation comparison spreadsheet from Application 1 to record the following two items. Write a report to the store manager with your recommendations for the best valuation method for each of these items.

	Taillight Cover			Generator	
Date	Number	Cost	Date	Number	Cost
01/22/02	75	$44.95	01/18/02	39	$73.99
02/12/02	48	45.55	03/27/02	33	72.77
04/04/02	100	40.50	04/30/02	25	74.64
06/19/02	60	45.95	05/31/02	30	75.23
09/25/02	45	47.95	09/07/02	50	73.98
12/28/02	36	50.05	12/22/02	75	74.98

EXCEL SPREADSHEET APPLICATION FOR CHAPTER 18

APPLICATION 2

Each quarter, for income tax purposes, the Springfield Department Store estimates its inventory using the retail method. A form has been designed that will provide the information on the cost of the ending inventory. It will be shown when you run Ch18App2 from your spreadsheet application's disk. It will look like the form shown here:

	A	B	C	D
1	**Springfield Department Store**			
2	2617 Main Street			
3	Box 219			
4	Springfield, Maryland 58109			
5	Telephone: 301-555-2158 FAX: 301-555-3498			
6				
7	RETAIL METHOD OF ESTIMATING INVENTORY			
8				*Calculation of Inventory at Cost (D18 X D21 = B22)*
9				
10				
11				
12		*Cost*	*Retail*	
13				
14	Beginning inventory			
15	Add: Purchases			
16	Goods available for sale	$0.00	$0.00	
17	Deduct: Net sales			
18	Ending inventory (at retail)		$0.00	$0.00
19	Ratio of cost of goods available			
20	for sale to retail value of			
21	goods available for sale			#DIV/0!
22	Ending inventory (at cost)	#DIV/0!		
23	Cost of goods sold	#DIV/0!		
24				

Enter the following information:

	Cost	Retail
Beginning inventory	$ 37,293	$ 65,098
Add: Purchases	293,582	526,183
Deduct: Net sales		530,283

Answer the following questions after you have completed the spreadsheet:

1. What is the amount of goods available for sale at cost?

2. What is the amount of goods available for sale at retail?

3. What is the ending inventory (at retail)?

4. What is the ratio of cost of goods available for sale to retail value of goods available for sale?

5. What is the ending inventory (at cost)?

6. What is the cost of goods sold?

GROUP REPORT

FOR CHAPTER 18 APPLICATION 2

Write a report to the manager of the accounting department at Springfield discussing reasons that the estimated ending inventory at cost might not be accurate. Think of both internal and external possibilities for any possible inaccuracy in the inventory valuation. Make recommendations to the manager concerning the feasibility of conducting an accurate inventory count quarterly. What would be the advantages and disadvantages?

19 TAX APPLICATIONS
SALES, EXCISE, AND PROPERTY TAXES

A NEW KIND OF NATIONAL TAX

Americans like to believe that those who make up the government budgets and create tax laws are persons of good conscience who would never deceive the U.S. citizenry. Most probably are.

Recently some politicians and pundits have filled the air with ideas they claim will make life better for working men and women everywhere. A notable proposal, supposedly very original say the proposers, is to replace the federal income tax with a 17% national sales tax. Such a tax, so goes the claim, would be much more fair to everybody than a graduated income tax that levies a higher rate on high incomes than on low incomes.

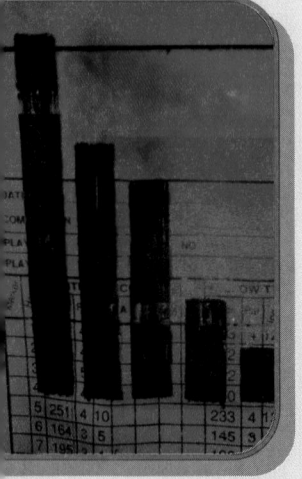

An idea called "the law of diminishing marginal utility" originated in the 19th century and is one of the most universally accepted principles among economists. The law holds roughly that as the amount of a good consumed increases, the marginal utility (including derived satisfaction) of the good tends to diminish. This means that the first unit of anything consumed returns more satisfaction to a consumer than would any additional units that consumer might acquire.

Which pair of shoes is more important—pair number 1 or pair number 300? So it is with money. Mr. Bill Gates, who reportedly is paid more than $1million per day, receives less satisfaction from an additional dollar than a hamburger worker who is paid $50 per day. If both incomes are taxed at the same 17% rate, the pain of paying $8.50 endured by the hamburger flipper is greater than the $170,000 to Mr. Gates. An equitable tax system would necessarily place a higher rate on Mr. Gates's income than on a hamburger worker's.

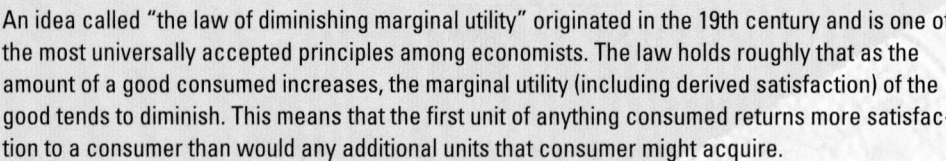

Chapter Glossary

General sales tax. A tax levied on final sales of most goods and services by states, counties, and local governments.

Excise tax. A tax levied on the manufacture or sales of particular goods or services, such as gasoline, alcohol, and cigarettes.

Property tax. A tax on all wealth that has exchange value, such as real property and personal property.

Real property. Land, buildings, and other permanent fixtures.

Personal property. Movable items of exchange value, such as livestock, motor vehicles, business fixtures, household furniture, machinery, tools, corporate stocks and bonds, bank deposits, and accounts receivable.

Fair market value. The estimated worth of property if it were on the market; also called *appraised value* because it is usually determined by a government appraiser.

Assessment rate. A rate set arbitrarily by a taxing authority at some level less than 100%. The rate is multiplied by the fair market value to determine the assessed valuation.

Assessed value. Property value; usually computed as some percent of true market value, which is used as a basis for levying property taxes.

Tax rate. The ratio between the amount of tax and the assessed valuation.

Real estate tax. The amount paid by a real estate owner calculated by multiplying the assessed valuation by the tax rate.

Student Objectives

Upon completion of this chapter, you should be able to:

1. Calculate the sales tax without a table.
2. Calculate the sales tax using a table.
3. Calculate actual sales when sales tax is included.
4. Calculate the excise tax.
5. Calculate property taxes for individual property owners.
6. Find the tax rate for property taxes.

We often take the services of government for granted. Of course these services are not free, so we must pay for them. The more citizens expect from government, the more they must expect to pay.

The power to tax is a right of the sovereign. In an absolute monarchy, the right belonged solely to the individual who was head of the state. In a democracy citizens are the sovereign, so the right resides in the people. In their capacity as rulers, the people delegate the power to chosen representatives. The ability of governments to perform their many functions depends largely on the willingness of citizens to pay taxes.

Because taxes absorb such a sizable portion of business and personal income, the payment of taxes has an influence on the economic decisions of business firms and individuals.

The largest taxes most people pay are the personal income tax and the FICA tax, both of which were covered in Chapter 6. This chapter is concerned with the other taxes that are of great interest to business: sales, excise, and property taxes.

According to the great economist Adam Smith, the classic four principles of taxation are that taxes must be (1) *fair*, based on the ability to pay; (2) *understandable*, with the time of payment and manner of payment clear to the taxpayer; (3) *convenient*, or levied at a time and in a manner that is easiest to pay; and (4) *economical*, or inexpensive to collect.

LEARNING UNIT 1
SALES AND EXCISE TAXES

For most states the greatest amount of revenue comes from a tax levied on *retail* sales. In many states local governments are also allowed to collect such a tax. Sales tax is ordinarily applied only to sales made within the jurisdiction of the taxing body. That means merchandise sold outside the state (such as by mail or through the Internet) is not subject to the tax. The tax is collected on sales within a state regardless of the buyer's place of residence. Rates vary but generally range from 2% in municipalities to 8% in some states.

Because a **general sales tax** based on all sales is widely considered to be regressive, (falling most heavily on those with the least ability to pay), certain items are often exempted from the tax. Such items are food, funerals, prescription medicine, and other items deemed "necessities" by legislators.

Levies on the sale of particular goods are a special kind of sales tax called an **excise tax**. Excises are, of course, levied to produce revenue, but at least one of three possible rationales is behind them. The rationales are benefits received (use), undesirable product (sin), and nonessential goods (luxury). Revenue from the federal tax on replacement tires is used to maintain the interstate highways. People pay for highways when they buy new tires. The very high tax on alcohol, first levied in 1792, is intended to discourage the use of a product considered detrimental to the public health. A tax on jewelry is levied against what is considered a nonessential luxury item.

19.1 Calculating Sales Tax without a Table

A sales tax is a *percentage* of retail sales. Retail sales is a *base*. The amount to be paid is determined by a tax *rate* set by a legislature. Sales tax calculation is, therefore, a good example of a percentage problem.

The formula to determine the amount of sales tax is

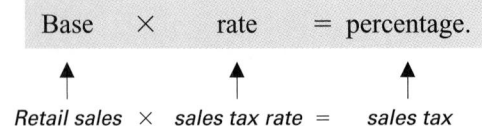

$$\text{Base} \quad \times \quad \text{rate} \quad = \text{percentage.}$$

Retail sales × sales tax rate = sales tax

Schmirtz Variety Store operates in a state that levies a 6% sales tax. Minnie Little bought $47.59 worth of school supplies from the store. How much state sales tax must she pay?

Solution   Multiply the retail sales times the tax rate:

$$\$47.59 \times 6\% = \$2.86$$

The sales tax rate in stores in Mort Henry's state is 7%.
He received this cash register receipt at A & G Grocery:

```
A & G GROCERY
3527 S. EIGHTH ST

BREAD           1.39
MARGARINE       1.55
BROOM           7.95 * T
CHICKEN         3.49
BUBBLE GUM       .79 * T
SALTINES        1.79
BLEACH          2.05 * T
    SUBTOTAL  $
    TAX PAID  _____
    TOTAL     _____

    CASH TEND _____
    CHANGE    _____
```

T means the item is taxable. In many states, most food items purchased in grocery stores are not subject to state sales taxes.

Mort paid with a $20 bill. Find the total, subtotal, tax paid, and change received.

Solution   *Step 1.* Add the costs of the items: $19.01.
Step 2. Add the items subject to the tax: $7.95 + .79 + 2.05 = $10.79.
Step 3. Multiply by the tax rate: $10.79 × 7% = $.76.
Step 4. Add the subtotal to the tax: $19.01 + .76 = $19.77.
Step 5. Subtract from cash tendered: $20.00 − 19.77 = $.23.

```
A & G GROCERY
3527 S. EIGHTH ST

BREAD           1.39
MARGARINE       1.55
BROOM           7.95 * T
CHICKEN         3.49
BUBBLE GUM       .79 * T
SALTINES        1.79
BLEACH          2.05 * T
    SUBTOTAL  $ 19.01
    TAX PAID  $   .76
    TOTAL     $ 19.77

    CASH TEND $ 20.00
    CHANGE    $   .23
```

1. A 7% sales tax is charged on all retail sales in Shaheed Washington's home state. Shaheed bought swimming pool supplies for $86.58. How much sales tax will he pay?

2. Melinda Furche bought a suitcase for $164.75. The state sales tax rate is 4%, and the local sales tax rate is 2%. How much tax will Melinda pay?

3. Joyce Gomez received the following cash register receipt at Kroger Grocery:

```
KROGER GROCERY
4708 W. VICKERY


SPAGHETTI          1.29
COFFEE             3.12
SOFT DRINKS        2.75* T
COOKIES            2.49
CANDY              2.26* T
CORN FLAKES        1.99
LIGHT BULBS        4.25* T

   SUBTOTAL    $ _____
   TAX PAID      _____
   TOTAL         _____

   CASH TEND     _____
   CHANGE        _____
```

Joyce paid with a $20 bill. Find the subtotal, tax paid, and change if the sales tax rate is 6%.

4. Determine the sales tax and total price Joe Martin was charged for an electric calculator marked $12.95 if the tax rate is 5%.

19.1 Solutions to Practice Problems

1. $86.58 × 7% = $6.06

2. 4% + 2% = 6%
   $164.75 × 6% = $9.89

3.
```
KROGER GROCERY
4708 W. VICKERY


SPAGHETTI          1.29
COFFEE             3.12
SOFT DRINKS        2.75* T
COOKIES            2.49
CANDY              2.26* T
CORN FLAKES        1.99
LIGHT BULBS        4.25* T

   SUBTOTAL    $ 18.15
   TAX PAID    $   .56
   TOTAL       $ 18.71

   CASH TEND   $ 20.00
   CHANGE      $  1.29
```

$ 2.75
  2.26
+ 4.25
‾‾‾‾‾‾
$ 9.26   Taxable items

$9.26 × 6% = $ .56

$18.15 Subtotal

$18.15 + .56 = $18.71 Total

$20.00 − 18.71 = $1.29 Change

4. $12.95 × 5% = $.65 Tax
   $12.95 + .65 = $13.60 Total

19.2 **Calculating Sales Tax Using a Table**

Most large retailers use cash registers with built-in computers that automatically calculate the sales tax. Assuming the tax rates are programmed into the machine correctly, an error would be almost impossible. When automatic cash registers are not available, a table such as Table 19.1 is often used to reduce the possibility of error.

TABLE 19.1 $6\frac{1}{4}$% SALES TAX COLLECTION CHART (STATE SALES TAX ONLY RATE = .0625)

Through	Tax	Through	Tax	Through	Tax	Through	Tax	Through	Tax
.07	.00	6.95	.43	13.83	.86	20.71	1.29	27.59	1.72
.23	.01	7.11	.44	13.99	.87	20.87	1.30	27.75	1.73
.39	.02	7.27	.45	14.15	.88	21.03	1.31	27.91	1.74
.55	.03	7.43	.46	14.31	.89	21.19	1.32	28.07	1.75
.71	.04	7.59	.47	14.47	.90	21.35	1.33	28.23	1.76
.87	.05	7.75	.48	14.63	.91	21.51	1.34	28.39	1.77
1.03	.06	7.91	.49	14.79	.92	21.67	1.35	28.55	1.78
1.19	.07	8.07	.50	14.95	.93	21.83	1.36	28.71	1.79
1.35	.08	8.23	.51	14.11	.94	21.99	1.37	28.87	1.80
1.51	.09	8.39	.52	15.27	.95	22.15	1.38	29.03	1.81
1.67	.10	8.55	.53	15.43	.96	22.31	1.39	29.19	1.82
1.83	.11	8.71	.54	15.59	.97	22.47	1.40	29.35	1.83
1.99	.12	8.87	.55	15.75	.98	22.63	1.41	29.51	1.84
2.15	.13	9.03	.56	15.91	.99	22.79	1.42	29.67	1.85
2.31	.14	9.19	.57	16.07	1.00	22.95	1.43	29.83	1.86
2.47	.15	9.35	.58	16.23	1.01	23.11	1.44	29.99	1.87
2.63	.16	9.51	.59	16.39	1.02	23.27	1.45	30.15	1.88
2.79	.17	9.67	.60	16.55	1.03	23.43	1.46	30.31	1.89
2.95	.18	9.83	.61	16.71	1.04	23.59	1.47	30.47	1.90
3.11	.19	9.99	.62	16.87	1.05	23.75	1.48	30.63	1.91
3.27	.20	10.15	.63	17.03	1.06	23.91	1.49	30.79	1.92
3.43	.21	10.31	.64	17.19	1.07	24.07	1.50	30.95	1.93
3.59	.22	10.47	.65	17.35	1.08	24.23	1.51	31.11	1.94
3.75	.23	10.63	.66	17.51	1.09	24.39	1.52	31.27	1.95
3.91	.24	10.79	.67	17.67	1.10	24.55	1.53	31.43	1.96
4.07	.25	10.95	.68	17.83	1.11	24.71	1.54	31.59	1.97
4.23	.26	11.11	.69	17.99	1.12	25.87	1.55	31.75	1.98
4.39	.27	11.27	.70	18.15	1.13	25.03	1.56	31.91	1.99
4.55	.28	11.43	.71	18.31	1.14	25.19	1.57	32.07	2.00
4.71	.29	11.59	.72	18.47	1.15	25.35	1.58	32.23	2.01
4.87	.30	11.75	.73	18.63	1.16	25.51	1.59	32.39	2.02
5.03	.31	11.91	.74	18.79	1.17	25.67	1.60	32.55	2.03
5.19	.32	12.07	.75	18.95	1.18	25.83	1.61	32.71	2.04
5.35	.33	12.23	.76	19.11	1.19	25.99	1.62	32.87	2.05
5.51	.34	12.39	.77	19.27	1.20	26.15	1.63	33.03	2.06
5.67	.35	12.55	.78	19.43	1.21	26.31	1.64	33.19	2.07
5.83	.36	12.71	.79	19.59	1.22	26.47	1.65	33.35	2.08
5.99	.37	12.87	.80	19.75	1.23	26.63	1.66	33.51	2.09
6.15	.38	13.03	.81	19.91	1.24	26.79	1.67	33.67	2.10
6.31	.39	13.19	.82	20.07	1.25	26.95	1.68	33.83	2.11
6.47	.40	13.35	.83	20.23	1.26	27.11	1.69	33.99	2.12
6.63	.41	13.51	.84	20.39	1.27	27.27	1.70	34.15	2.13
6.79	.42	13.67	.85	20.55	1.28	27.43	1.71	34.31	2.14

(continues)

TABLE 19.1 (Continued)

Through	Tax	Through	Tax	Through	Tax		
34.47	2.15	40.07	2.50	45.67	2.85	Sales Over $50	
34.63	2.16	40.23	2.51	45.83	2.86	Amount	Tax
34.79	2.17	40.39	2.52	45.99	2.87	$ 60.00	$ 3.75
34.95	2.18	40.55	2.53	46.15	2.88	$ 70.00	$ 4.38
35.11	2.19	40.71	2.54	46.31	2.89	$ 80.00	$ 5.00
35.27	2.20	40.87	2.55	46.47	2.90	$ 90.00	$ 5.63
35.43	2.21	41.03	2.56	46.63	2.91	$100.00	$ 6.25
35.59	2.22	41.19	2.57	46.79	2.92	$150.00	$ 9.38
35.75	2.23	41.35	2.58	46.95	2.93	$200.00	$12.50
35.91	2.24	41.51	2.59	47.11	2.94	$250.00	$15.63
36.07	2.25	41.67	2.60	47.27	2.95	$300.00	$18.75
36.23	2.26	41.83	2.61	47.43	2.96		
36.39	2.27	41.99	2.62	47.59	2.97	HOW TO FIGURE THE TAX:	
36.55	2.28	42.15	2.63	47.75	2.98		
36.71	2.29	42.31	2.64	47.91	2.99	Example: Sale is $75.95	
36.87	2.30	42.47	2.65	48.07	3.00	Tax on $70.00	$4.38
37.03	2.31	42.63	2.66	48.23	3.01	Tax on $ 5.95	.37
37.19	2.32	42.79	2.67	48.39	3.02	TOTAL TAX	$4.75
37.35	2.33	42.95	2.68	48.55	3.03		
37.51	2.34	43.11	2.69	48.71	3.04		
37.67	2.35	43.27	2.70	48.87	3.05		
37.83	2.36	43.43	2.71	49.03	3.06		
37.99	2.37	43.59	2.72	49.19	3.07		
38.15	2.38	43.75	2.73	49.35	3.08		
38.31	2.39	43.91	2.74	49.51	3.09		
38.47	2.40	44.07	2.75	49.67	3.10		
38.63	2.41	44.23	2.76	49.83	3.11		
38.79	2.42	44.39	2.77	49.99	3.12		
38.95	2.43	44.55	2.78	50.15	3.13		
39.11	2.44	44.71	2.79	50.31	3.14		
39.27	2.45	44.87	2.80	50.47	3.15		
39.43	2.46	45.03	2.81	50.63	3.16		
39.59	2.47	45.19	2.82	50.79	3.17		
39.75	2.48	45.35	2.83	50.95	3.18		
39.91	2.49	45.51	2.84	51.11	3.19		

EXAMPLE Mervin's Department Store operates in a state that levies a $6\frac{1}{4}$% sales tax. Roberto Garza bought $47.58 worth of school clothes from the store. How much state sales tax will Roberto pay?

Solution Find the amount of sales tax in Table 19.1. $47.58 is found between $47.43 and $47.59. The amount of sales tax is the higher amount, $2.97.

19.2 Practice Problems

1. A $6\frac{1}{4}$% sales tax rate is charged on all retail sales in Lee Wilson's home state. Corey bought sporting goods at Lee's store for $15.98. Using Table 19.1, how much sales tax will he pay?

2. The sales tax charged on all retail sales in Elmer Martin's home state is $6\frac{1}{4}$%. Mr. Atkinson bought camping supplies for $39.86 at Elmer's store. Using Table 19.1, how much sales tax will he pay?

3. Rose Richardson bought some cosmetics at a local drugstore for $37.93. The state sales tax rate is $6\frac{1}{4}$%. How much sales tax did Ms. Richardson pay?

4. Danny Dodge bought $50.76 worth of bathroom products at the local Wal-Mart. The state sales tax rate is 6¼%. How much sales tax did Mr. Dodge pay?

19.2 Solutions to Practice Problems

1. $15.98 is found between $15.91 and $16.07. The amount of sales tax is the higher amount, $1.00.
2. $39.86 is found between $39.75 and $39.91. The amount of sales tax is the higher amount, $2.49.
3. $37.93 is found between $37.83 and $37.99. The amount of sales tax is the higher amount, $2.37.
4. $50.76 is found between $50.63 and $50.79. The amount of sales tax is the higher amount, $3.17.

19.3 Calculating Actual Sales When Sales Tax Is Included

Sometimes a manager gets a summary of total sales for the day from a cash register but still does not know what actual sales were because the cash register has included the sales tax. To find the actual sales, the sales tax must be deducted.

EXAMPLE   Martin Murdock manages a Mervin's Department Store. Last night he checked the receipts of one of the cash registers and found $30,000 had been registered into it. The sales tax in Martin's state is 6%. How much were actual sales?

Solution   *Step 1.* Add the sales tax percent to 100%:

$$6\% + 100\% = 106\%$$

Step 2. Divide the amount in cash register receipts by the percent from step 1:

$$\text{Actual sales} = \frac{\$30,000}{106\%} = \$28,301.89$$

19.3 Practice Problems

1. Jason Crunch manages a Toughwrench Auto Parts store. Last night he checked the receipts of the cash register and found $12,000 had been registered into it. The sales tax in Jason's state is 5%. How much were actual sales?
2. Soy Chan operates a restaurant. Yesterday's cash register receipts were $3,100. The sales tax in Soy's state is 7%. How much were actual sales?
3. The sales tax in Corliss Williamson's state is 4%. Receipts at his sports bar yesterday were $1,800. How much were actual sales?
4. The sales tax in Scotty Thurman's state is 5.6%. Receipts at his sporting goods store yesterday were $2,500. How much were actual sales.

19.3 Solutions to Practice Problems

1. $5\% + 100\% = 105\%$

$$\text{Actual sales} = \frac{\$12,000}{105\%} = \$11,428.57$$

2. $7\% + 100\% = 107\%$

$$\text{Actual sales} = \frac{\$3,100}{107\%} = \$2,897.20$$

3. $4\% + 100\% = 104\%$

$$\text{Actual sales} = \frac{\$1,800}{104\%} = \$1,730.77$$

4. $5.6\% + 100\% = 105.6\%$

$$\text{Actual sales} = \frac{\$2,500}{105.6\%} = \$2,367.42$$

EXCEL Spreadsheet Application Springfield wants to estimate its property tax and has designed a spreadsheet form for that purpose, which is found at the end of this chapter.

Property taxes on real estate are the oldest type of tax most Americans pay. Ownership of land being the measure of wealth in early America, and fairness being a principle of all taxation, towns, counties, and school districts all levied against the property of landowners. Property can have two meanings, both subject to property tax. **Real property** consists of land, buildings, and other permanent fixtures. **Personal property** consists of movable items of exchange value, such as livestock, motor vehicles, business fixtures, household furniture, tools, corporate stocks and bonds, bank deposits, and accounts receivable. Property tax, then, is tax on all wealth that has exchange value.

Five terms are found in most problems concerning real estate taxes:

Fair market value. The estimated worth of property if it were placed on the market as determined by a tax appraiser; also called *appraised value*.

Assessment rate. An arbitrary rate set by the taxing authority originally to avoid overtaxing because of human error in appraisal. The market value is multiplied by the assessment rate, which is usually less than 100%, although this will vary from one area to another.

Assessed valuation. A percentage of the true market value determined by multiplying the market value by the assessment rate.

Tax rate. The ratio set between the amount of tax and the assessed valuation. Normally, the tax rate is not stated as a percent. It is stated in dollars-and-cents terms, such as $2.15 per $100 of assessed valuation or $21.50 per $1,000 of assessed valuation.

Real estate tax. The amount paid by a real estate owner calculated by multiplying the assessed valuation by the tax rate.

19.4   Calculating Property Taxes for Individual Property Owners

Individual homeowners or owners of business property may want to know how much taxes on their property will be. Tax rates are stated in terms of percent, dollars per $100, dollars per $1,000, or in mills. A mill is $\frac{1}{10}$ of one cent or $\frac{1}{1,000}$ of a dollar. Thus, 21.20 mills could be written

$$\frac{\$2.12}{\$100} = \frac{\$21.2}{\$1,000} = \frac{21.2}{1,000} = 2.12\%.$$

Writing the rate as stated in a given problem is probably better, but all of the above have the same value. To solve property tax problems, the following format is used (it is, as illustrated, another application of the percentage formula):

Market Value	*MV*	*B*
× assessment rate	× *AR*	× *R*
assessed valuation	*AV*	*P(B)*
× tax rate	× *TR*	× *R*
tax	*T*	*P*

EXAMPLE   Clint McDaniel's house has been appraised at $270,000. The county assessment rate is 60%, and the tax rate is 2.12% of valuation. How much county property tax will Clint have to pay?

Solution   Set up a format as shown here:

MV	$270,000
× AR	× 60%
AV	$162,000

AV	$162,000.00
× TR	× 2.12%
T	$3,434.40

The rate might be quoted by the taxing authority in the following ways:

$\dfrac{\$2.12}{\$100}$ or $\dfrac{\$\ 21.2}{\$1,000}$ or 21.2 mills or $\dfrac{21.2}{1,000}$

270,000 ⊗ 60% ⊗ 2.12% ⊜ 3,434.40

19.4 Practice Problems

1. Stephen Moralis owns a house with a $184,000 market value. The assessment rate is 55%. The county tax rate is $3.80 per $100. How much tax does Stephen pay?

2. Susanne Johanson owns an old house with a market value of $30,000. The city assessed such property at 65% of market value. If the city tax rate is 280 mills, how much city tax does Susanne pay?

3. Bruce Wayne pays $.27 per $100 county tax and $21.40 per $1,000 school tax. His $4,160,000 mansion is assessed at 40% of market value. How much combined county and school taxes does he pay?

4. Ray Biggers' house has a market value of $96,000. The county tax rate is $2.40 per $100 valuation. The assessment rate is 65%. How much county tax does Ray have to pay?

19.4 Solutions to Practice Problems

1.
MV	$184,000
× AR	× 55%
AV	$101,200

AV	$101,200.00
× TR	× .0380
T	$3,845.60

$\dfrac{\$3.80}{\$100} = .0380$

3.
MV	$4,160,000
× AR	× 40%
AV	$1,664,000

AV	$1,664,000
× TR	× .0214
T	$35,609.60

$\dfrac{\$21.40}{\$1,000} = .0214$

AV	$1,664,000
× TR	× .0027
T	$ 4,492.80

$\dfrac{\$.27}{\$100} = .0027$

$35,609.60
+ 4,492.80
$40,102.40 Total tax

2.
MV	$30,000
× AR	× 65%
AV	$19,500

AV	$19,500
× TR	× .280
T	$ 5,460

280 mills $= \dfrac{280}{1,000} = .280$

4.
MV	$96,000
× AR	× 65%
AV	$62,400

AV	$62,400.00
× TR	× .0240
T	$ 1,497.60

$\dfrac{\$2.40}{\$100} = .0240$

19.5 Finding the Tax Rate for Property Taxes

Because owners must pay property taxes, a taxing authority must levy them. Any of the other terms defined in the last section could be an unknown. Usually the taxing authority is concerned with setting the rate to raise needed revenue.

EXAMPLE   Armont, Utah, needs $970,000 from property taxes this year. The market value of the town's property is $172,000,000 and is assessed at 55% for tax purposes. How much will the tax rate per $100 have to be to raise the needed revenue?

Solution   Set up the format as shown:

$$AV = MV \times AR$$
$$AV = \$172,000,000 \times 55\%$$
$$AV = \$94,600,000$$

$$\frac{TR}{\$100} = \frac{T}{AV}$$

$$TR = \frac{T}{AV} \times \$100$$

$$TR = \frac{\$970,000}{\$94,600,000} \times \$100$$ *It might be easier to cancel by 100 before dividing. That way, all the digits will fit into your calculator.*

$$TR = \$1.03$$

An easy way to make the calculation is to divide the tax *(T)* by the assessed valuation *(AV)*. Then, depending on which one of the five common ways to express a tax rate on real estate is being used, move the decimal point as indicated here:

When the Rate Is	After Division	To Finalize the Calculation	Final Answer
Per dollar (decimal)	.0103		.0103
Percent	.0103	Move the decimal point two spaces to the RIGHT (multiply by 100).	1.03%
Per $100	.0103	Move the decimal point two spaces to the RIGHT (multiply by $100).	$1.03
Per $1,000	.0103	Move the decimal point three spaces to the RIGHT (multiply by $1,000).	$10.30
Mills	.0103	Move the decimal point three spaces to the RIGHT (multiply by 1,000).	10.3

19.5 Practice Problems

1. Gotham City needs $86,000,000. The market value of the property is $6,000,000,000 and is assessed at 60% for tax purposes. Find the tax rate per $1,000.

2. The city of Metropolis will spend $9,600,000 this year. The market value of the property in the city is $180,000,000. The property is assessed at 55% of its market value for tax purposes. Find the tax rate per $100 valuation.

3. The market value of the property in Atlantis is $24,000,000,000. For tax purposes, property is appraised at 60% of its market value. If the tax to be raised is $52,782,464, how many mills will the city need to levy?

4. Fayette City needs $8,642,928 next year to meet the town's expenses. What percent will the tax rate need to be if the property is worth $978,000,000 and is taxed at 67% of market value?

19.5 Solutions to Practice Problems

1. $AV = MV \times AR$
   $AV = \$6,000,000,000 \times 60\%$
   $AV = \$3,600,000,000$

   $$TR = \frac{T}{AV}$$

   $$TR = \frac{\$86,000,000}{\$3,600,000,000}$$

   $TR = .02389$ *Since TR is per $1,000, move the decimal point three places to the right.*

   $TR = \$23.89$ per $1,000

2. $AV = MV \times AR$
$AV = \$180{,}000{,}000 \times 55\%$
$AV = \$99{,}000{,}000$

$TR = \dfrac{T}{AV}$

$TR = \dfrac{\$9{,}600{,}000}{\$99{,}000{,}000}$

$TR = .09696$

$TR = \$9.70$ per $\$100$

Since TR is per $100, move the decimal point two places to the right.

3. $AV = MV \times AR$
$AV = \$24{,}000{,}000{,}000 \times 60\%$
$AV = \$14{,}400{,}000{,}000$

$TR = \dfrac{T}{AV}$

$TR = \dfrac{\$52{,}782{,}464}{\$14{,}400{,}000{,}000}$

$TR = .00367$

$TR = 3.67$ mills

Since you are going to move the decimal point three spaces to the right, it might be easier to remove three zeros in the denominator before dividing.
Since TR is per 1,000, move the decimal point three places to the right if you did not first remove three zeros in the denominator before you divided.

4. $AV = MV \times AR$
$AV = \$978{,}000{,}000 \times 67\%$
$AV = \$655{,}260{,}000$

$TR = \dfrac{T}{AV}$

$TR = \dfrac{\$8{,}642{,}928}{\$655{,}260{,}000}$

$TR = .01319$

$TR = 1.3\%$

Since TR is a percent, move the decimal point two places to the right.

QUICK REFERENCE SUMMARY AND REVIEW

Page	Section Topic	Learning Concepts	Examples and Solutions
662	**19.1** Calculating Sales Tax without a Table	A sales tax is a percentage. Retail sales is a base. The amount to be paid is determined by a tax rate set by a taxing authority. Sales tax calculation is a good example of a percentage problem ($P = B \times R$). To find the amount of tax, multiply the amount of retail sales by the tax rate.	The sales tax rate in the state where Joe operates his store is 7%. Rebecca bought $84.63 of taxable merchandise at Joe's store. Find the sales tax. $T = \text{Sales} \times \text{Tax rate}$ $T = \$84.63 \times 7\%$ $T = \$5.92$
665	**19.2** Calculating Sales Tax Using a Table	When automatic cash registers are not available, a table such as Table 19.1 is often used to reduce the possibility of error and speed up calculations when determining the amount of tax.	Mildred's Speciality Shop operates in a state with a $6\frac{1}{4}\%$ sales tax rate. Find the amount of tax on a purchase of $28.93 at Mildred's. From Table 19.1, $28.93 is between $28.87 and $29.03. The amount of the sales tax is the higher amount, $1.81.
667	**19.3** Calculating Actual Sales When Sales Tax Is Included	To find the actual sales over some period of time when there is a sales tax collected, a manager must deduct the amount of sales tax collected over that period of time.	Jenifer manages a Bush Department Store. Last night's receipts were $20,000. The tax rate is 6%. How much were actual sales? $6\% + 100\% = 106\%$ $\dfrac{\$20{,}000}{106\%} = \$18{,}867.93$

Page	Section Topic	Learning Concepts	Examples and Solutions
668	**19.4** Calculating Property Taxes for Individual Property Owners	Homeowners and business property owners need to know how much tax they must pay on their property.	Calculate the tax on Mr. Mayberry's home office if it is appraised at $190,000. The assessment rate is 65%, and the rate is $1.35 per $100 of assessed valuation. $$AV = MV \times AR$$ $$AV = \$190,000 \times 65\%$$ $$AV = \$123,500$$ $$T = AV \times TR$$ $$T = \$123,500 \times \frac{\$1.35}{\$100}$$ $$T = \$1,667.25$$
669	**19.5** Finding the Tax Rate for Property Taxes	Taxing authorities must know what tax rate to set to raise the amount of money needed to pay for government expenses.	Gardner, Massachusetts, needs $194,000 from property taxes. The market value of the town's property is $34,400,000 and is assessed at 55% for tax purposes. Find the tax rate per $100 valuation. $$AV = MV \times AR$$ $$AV = \$34,400,000 \times 55\%$$ $$AV = \$18,920,000$$ $$TR = \frac{T}{AV} \times \$100$$ $$R = \frac{\$194,000}{\$18,920,000} \times \$100$$ $$R = \$1.03$$

SURFING THE INTERNET

For further information on the topics covered in this chapter, check out the following sites:

http://www.assessor.com/under.htm

http://www.orps.state.ny.us/

http://www.state.nd.us/businessreg/oversales.htm

http://www.cnie.org/nle/trans-24.html

ADDITIONAL
PRACTICE
PROBLEMS

Answers to odd-numbered problems are given in Appendix A.

19.1

1. A 5% sales tax is charged on all retail sales in Mike Forman's home state. Mike bought gardening supplies for $97.75. How much sales tax will he pay?

$97.75 × 5% = $4.89

2. Anne Nichols bought a chair for $589.95. The state sales tax rate is 6% and the local sales tax rate is 1%. How much tax will Anne pay?

$589.95 × 7% = $41.30

3. Roberta Novac received the following cash register receipt at Winn-Dixie Grocery:

WINN-DIXIE
5301 Worrell Drive

PEANUT BUTTER	2.59
TEA	1.75
DISH SOAP	2.20* T
CRACKERS	1.49
BLEACH	1.39* T
YELLOW CORN	.99
VACUUM BAGS	3.25* T
SUBTOTAL	$ 13.66
TAX PAID	$ .48
TOTAL	$ 14.14
CASH TEND	$ 15.00
CHANGE	$ .86

$$\begin{array}{r} \$\ 2.20 \\ 1.39 \\ +\ 3.25 \\ \hline \$\ 6.84 \end{array} \text{ Taxable items}$$

$6.85 \times 7\% = \$.48$ Tax

$$\begin{array}{r} \$13.66 \text{ Subtotal} \\ +\ .48 \text{ Tax} \\ \hline \$14.14 \text{ Total} \end{array}$$

$10 + 5 = \$15$
$15 - 14.14 = \$.86$

Roberta paid with a $10 and a $5 bill. Find the subtotal, tax paid, total, and change if the sales tax rate is 7%.

4. Jane Alexander bought a new dishwasher from Sears. It cost $575. Jane's state levies a 6.5% sales tax and the city levies an additional 1% sales tax. How much tax did Jane pay?
$575 \times 7.5\% = \$43.13$

5. Zach Filmore shopped at Wal-Mart and received the following cash register receipt:

WAL*MART
6538 HWY 377

BOXER SHORTS	8.96* T
SWEATPANTS	6.97* T
SWEATSHIRT	5.97* T
CASHEW NUTS	7.42
SUBTOTAL	$ 29.32
TAX PAID	$ 1.40
TOTAL	$ 30.72
CASH TEND	$ 40.00
CHANGE	$ 9.28

$$\begin{array}{r} \$\ 8.96 \\ 6.97 \\ +\ 5.97 \\ \hline \$21.90 \end{array} \text{ Taxable items}$$

$21.90 \times 6.4\% = \$1.40$

$40.00 - 30.72 = \$9.28$

The sales tax rate is 6.4%. Zach paid the clerk with four $10 bills. How much is the subtotal, tax paid, and change?

19.2

6. A $6\frac{1}{4}\%$ sales tax rate is charged on all retail sales in Joe Zilch's home state. Chris bought clothing goods at Joe's store for $75.99. Using Table 19.1, determine how much sales tax he will pay.

For $70.00 → $4.38
For $ 5.99 → + .37
$4.75

7. The sales tax rate charged on all retail sales in Pete Geren's home state is $6\frac{1}{4}\%$. Morgan Fritz bought sporting goods for $79.44 at Pete's store. Use Table 19.1 to determine how much sales tax he will pay.

For $70.00 → $4.38
$9.44 is between 9.35 and 9.51 (use higher tax) → + .59
$4.97

8. Rabbi Korman bought some Kosher pickles at a drive-in grocery for $2.79. The state sales tax rate is $6\frac{1}{4}$%. Use Table 19.1 to determine how much sales tax the good rabbi paid.

$ .17

9. Coach Nutt bought $198.69 worth of footballs at the local discount store. The state sales tax rate is $6\frac{1}{4}$%. Use Table 19.1 to determine how much tax the coach paid.

$150.00 →	$ 9.38
$48.69 is between 48.55 and 48.71 (use higher tax) →	+ 3.04
	$12.42

10. The state sales tax rate in Linda Miller's home state is $6\frac{1}{4}$%. She bought a new Honda for $14,378.50. Find the sales tax using Table 19.1.

From table, $100		→		$6.25
($100 × 100 = $10,000)		→	$6.25 × 100 →	$625.00
($300 × 10 = 3,000)		→	$18.75 × 10 →	187.50
($100 × 10 = 1,000)		→	$ 6.25 × 10 →	62.50
	300	→		18.75
	70	→		4.38
$8.50 is between 8.39 and 8.55 (use higher tax)				+ .53
				$898.66

19.3

11. Kate Torres manages a gift shop. Last night she checked the receipts of the cash register and found $9,000 had been registered into it. The sales tax in Kate's state is 5%. How much were actual sales?

Actual sales = $\dfrac{\text{total receipts}}{100\% + \text{tax rate}}$ $100\% + 5\% = 105\%$

Actual sales = $\dfrac{\$9,000}{105\%}$ = $8,571.43

12. Gene Hunt operates BBQ's restaurant. Yesterday's cash register receipts were $18,400. The sales tax in Gene's state is 6%. How much were actual sales?

Actual sales = $\dfrac{\text{total receipts}}{100\% + \text{tax rate}}$ $100\% + 6\% = 106\%$

Actual sales = $\dfrac{\$18,400}{106\%}$ = $17,358.49

13. The sales tax in Micky Jordon's state is 6%. Receipts at his golf shop yesterday were $1,200. How much were actual sales?

Actual sales = $\dfrac{\text{total receipts}}{100\% + \text{tax rate}}$ $100\% + 6\% = 106\%$

Actual sales = $\dfrac{\$1,200}{106\%}$ = $1,132.08

14. The sales tax in Todd Knight's state is 6.5%. Receipts at his curio shop yesterday were $1,980. How much were actual sales?

Actual sales = $\dfrac{\text{total receipts}}{100\% + \text{tax rate}}$ $100\% + 6.5\% = 106.5\%$

Actual sales = $\dfrac{\$1,980}{106.5\%}$ = $1,859.15

15. The sales tax in Reggie Garret's state is 4.7%. Receipts at his candy store were $8,700 last week. How much were Reggie's actual sales?

Actual sales = $\dfrac{\text{total receipts}}{100\% + \text{tax rate}}$ $100\% + 4.7\% = 104.7\%$

Actual sales = $\dfrac{\$8,700}{104.7\%}$ = $8,309.46

19.4

16. Anne Richards owns a house with a $1,275,000 market value. The assessment rate is 65%. The county tax rate is $2.70 per $100. How much tax does Anne pay?

MV	$1,275,000.00
× *AR*	× 65%
= *AV*	$ 828,750.00
× *TR*	× $2.70/$100
= *T*	$ 22,376.25

17. George Gore lives in an old house with a market value of $23,000,000. The city assesses such property at 55% of market value. If the city tax rate is 125 mills, how much city tax should George pay?

MV	$23,000,000
× *AR*	× 55%
= *AV*	$12,650,000
× *TR*	× 125/1,000
= *T*	$ 1,581,250

18. Clark Kent pays $.89 per $100 county tax and $18.60 per $1,000 school tax. His $150,000 house is assessed at 40% of market value. How much combined county and school taxes does he pay?

MV	$150,000	
$\times AR$	$\times$	40%
$= AV$	$\$$	$60,000$
$\times TR$	$\times 2.75/100$	
$= T$	$\$$	$1,650$

$$\frac{\$.89}{\$100} + \frac{\$18.60}{\$1,000} = \frac{\$.89}{\$100} + \frac{\$1.86}{\$100} = \frac{\$2.75}{\$100}$$

19. Sue Reed's house has a market value of $46,000. The county tax rate is $1.29 per $100 valuation. The assessment rate is 75%. How much county tax does Sue have to pay?

MV	$\$\quad 46,000$
$\times AR$	75%
$= AV$	$\$34,500.00$
$\times TR$	$\$1.29/\$100$
$= T$	$\$\quad 445.05$

20. Clay Henry owns a little house with a market value of $43,000. The county tax rate is $1.18 per $100 valuation. School taxes are $7.40 per $1,000 valuation. The assessment rate is 70%. How much tax does Clay pay?

MV	$\$\quad 43,000$
$\times AR$	$\times\quad 70\%$
$= AV$	$\$30,100.00$
$\times TR$	$\$1.92/\$100$
$= T$	$\$\quad 577.92$

$$\frac{\$1.18}{\$100} + \frac{\$7.40}{\$1,000} = \frac{\$1.18}{\$100} + \frac{\$.74}{100} = \frac{\$1.92}{\$100}$$

19.5

21. Grahamm City needs $46,000,000. The market value of the property is $5,000,000,000, and it is assessed at 40% for tax purposes. Find the tax rate per $1,000.

MV	$\$5,000,000,000$
$\times AR$	$\times\quad 40\%$
$= AV$	$\$2,000,000,000$
$\times TR$	$\times\quad TR/\$1,000$
$= T$	$\$\quad 46,000,000$

$\$5,000,000,000 \times 40\% = \$2,000,000,000$

$\$2,000,000,000 \times \dfrac{TR}{\$1,000} = \$46,000,000$

Cancel by $1,000. $\longrightarrow \$2,000,000 \times TR = \$46,000,000$

Divide both sides by $\dfrac{\$2,000,000}{\$2,000,000} \times TR = \dfrac{\$46,000,000}{\$2,000,000}$
$2,000,000 and cancel.

$TR = \$23$ per $1,000$

22. The city of Monmouth will spend $6,700,000 this year. The market value of the property in the city is $220,000,000. The property is assessed at 65% of its market value for tax purposes. Find the tax rate per $100 valuation.

MV	$\$220,000,000$
$\times AR$	$\times\quad 65\%$
$= AV$	$\$143,000,000$
$\times TR$	$\times\quad TR/\$100$
$= T$	$\$\quad 6,700,000$

$\$220,000,000 \times 65\% = \$143,000,000$

$\$143,000,000 \times \dfrac{TR}{\$100} = \$6,700,000$

Cancel by $100. $\longrightarrow \$1,430,000 \times TR = \$6,700,000$

Divide both sides by $\dfrac{\$1,430,000}{\$1,430,000} \times TR = \dfrac{\$6,700,000}{\$1,430,000}$
$1,430,000 and cancel.

$TR = \$4.69$ per 100

23. The market value of the property in Harmon City is $18,000,000. For tax purposes property is appraised at 60% of its market value. If the tax to be raised is $257,000, how many mills will the city need to levy?

MV	$\$18,000,000$
$\times AR$	$\times\quad 60\%$
$= AV$	$\$10,800,000$
$\times TR$	$\times\quad TR/1,000$
$= T$	$\$\quad 257,000$

$\$18,000,000 \times 60\% = \$10,800,000$

$\$10,800,000 \times \dfrac{TR}{1,000} = \$257,000$

Cancel by $1,000. $\longrightarrow \$10,800 \times TR = \$257,000$

Divide both sides by $\dfrac{\$10,800}{\$10,800} \times TR = \dfrac{\$257,000}{\$10,800}$
$10,800 and cancel.

$TR = 23.80$ mills

24. Evening Shade City needs $5,270,000 next year to meet the town's expenses. What percent will the tax rate need to be if the property is worth $435,000,000 and is taxed at 62% of market value?

MV	$\$435,000,000$
$\times AR$	$\times\quad 62\%$
$= AV$	$\$269,700,000$
$\times TR$	$\times\quad TR$
$= T$	$\$\quad 5,270,000$

$\$435,000,000 \times 62\% = \$269,700,000$

$\$269,700,000 \times TR = \$5,270,000$

Divide both sides by $\dfrac{\$269,700,000}{\$269,700,000} \times TR = \dfrac{\$5,270,000}{\$269,700,000}$
$269,700,000.

$TR = 2.0\%$

25. The market value of the property in Oldsburg is $60,500,000. For tax purposes, property is appraised at 60% of its market value. If the tax to be raised is $1,527,000, how much will the tax rate per thousand need to be?

MV	$\$\ 60,500,000$
$\times AR$	$\times\quad 60\%$
$= AV$	$\$\ 36,300,000$
$\times TR$	$\times\quad TR/\$1,000$
$= T$	$\$\ 1,527,000$

$\$60,500,000 \times 60\% = \$36,300,000$

$\$36,300,000 \times \dfrac{TR}{\$1,000} = \$1,527,000$

Cancel by $1,000. $\longrightarrow \$36,300 \times TR = \$1,527,000$

Divide both sides by $\dfrac{\$36,300}{\$36,300} \times TR = \dfrac{\$1,527,000}{\$36,300}$
$36,300 and cancel.

$TR = \$42.07$ per $1,000$

Drill Problems

Calculate the sales tax in the following problems:

	Sales	Tax Rate	Tax
1.	$273.95	8.5%	$23.29
2.	75.50	7.6%	5.74
3.	12.99	4.3%	.56
4.	189.97	6.4%	12.16
5.	1,278.46	5.9%	75.43

Using Table 19.1, calculate the sales tax in the following problems:

	Sales	Tax
6.	$75.93	$4.75
7.	31.24	1.95
8.	44.44	2.78
9.	67.88	4.24
10.	6.95	.43

Find the actual sales in the following problems:

	Receipts	Rate	Actual Sales
11.	$18,000	4%	$17,307.69
12.	9,000	5%	8,571.43
13.	25,400	7%	23,738.32
14.	4,300	6%	4,056.60
15.	37,300	3%	36,213.59

Find the property tax in the following problems:

	Market Value	Assessment Rate	Tax Rate	Tax
16.	$180,000	60%	$1.25 per $100	$1,350
17.	75,000	55%	$13.4 per $1,000	552.75
18.	560,000	65%	1.02%	3,712.80
19.	235,000	62%	125 mills	18,212.50
20.	98,500	57%	.0104 per dollar	583.91

Find the tax rates in the following problems:

	Market Value	Assessment Rate	Revenue Needed	Tax Rate	Expressed Per
21.	$65,435,000	67%	$1,650,000	$3.76	$100
22.	135,000,000	56%	1,840,000	24.34	$1,000
23.	425,500,000	65%	25,250,000	91.30	mills
24.	58,000,000	60%	2,150,000	6.2%	rate
25.	987,648,000	52%	41,653,000	81.10	$1,000

Word Problems

26. A 6% sales tax rate is charged on all retail sales in Marcus Welborn's home state. Marcus bought building supplies for $97.69. How much sales tax will he pay?

$97.69 × 6% = $5.86

27. Rhonda Birdow bought party supplies for $218.18. The state sales tax rate is 5% and the local sales tax rate is 1%. How much tax will Rhonda pay?

$218.18 × 6% = $13.09

28. Linda Garcia received the following cash register receipt at Save-a-Lot Grocery:

```
SAVE-A-LOT
4708 W. VICKERY

MILK            1.99
BACON           2.69
CANDY           3.85* T
BAKE MIX        1.49
MOP            12.95* T
CHEERIOS        2.99
ROOT BEER       2.25* T
    SUBTOTAL   $ 28.21
    TAX PAID   $  1.33
    TOTAL      $ 29.54

    CASH TEND  $ 30.00
    CHANGE     $   .46
```

Taxable items:
  $3.85 + 12.95 + 2.25 = $19.05
  $19.05 × 7% = $1.33

Find Linda's subtotal, tax paid, and change if the sales tax rate is 7%.

29. Determine the sales tax and the total price Ken Bindel was charged for a clutch that cost $42.95 if the sales tax rate is 6%.

$42.95 × 6% = $2.58 Tax $42.95 + 2.58 = $45.53   Total price

30. Hussein Binmadshel sold some dehumidifying equipment to Custom Woods Inc. The equipment cost $849.75. The state levies a 6% sales tax rate and the city levies an additional 3% sales tax rate. How much tax did Custom Woods pay?

$849.75 × 9% = $76.48

31. A $6\frac{1}{4}$% sales tax rate is charged on all retail sales in Spike Dickes's home state. Clint bought building supplies at Dickes's store for $25.89. Using Table 19.1, determine how much sales tax he will pay.

Between $25.83 and $25.99 (use higher tax): $1.62

32. The sales tax rate charged on all retail sales in Ray Biggers' home state is $6\frac{1}{4}$%. Mr. Nolan bought some cowboy boots for $50.95 at Ray's shoe store. Using Table 19.1, determine how much sales tax he will pay.

$3.18

33. Joan Binder sold perfume at a drugstore for $27.95. The state sales tax rate is $6\frac{1}{4}$%. How much sales tax did the buyer pay?

Between $27.91 and $28.07 (use higher tax): $1.75

34. Ray Ford bought $37.95 worth of hardware from a local Target Store. The state sales tax rate is $6\frac{1}{4}$%. How much tax did Ray pay?

Between $37.83 and $37.99 (use higher tax): $2.37

35. The state sales tax rate in Linda Miller's home state is $6\frac{1}{4}$%. She had her nails manicured for $17.25. How much sales tax was collected?

Between $17.19 and $17.35 (use higher tax): $1.08

36. Mark Spinks manages the Webb Garage Door Co. Yesterday's receipts were for $2,800. The sales tax rate in Mark's state is 6%. How much were actual sales?

Actual sales = $\frac{\$2,800}{106\%}$ = $2,641.51

37. Yesterday's cash register receipts were $4,200 at Grady's Grill. The state sales tax rate in Grady's state is 5%. How much were actual sales?

Actual sales $= \dfrac{\$4,200}{105\%} = \$4,000$

38. Receipts at Montel's plumbing shop yesterday were $800. The sales tax rate in Montel's state is 7%. How much were actual sales?

Actual sales $= \dfrac{\$800}{107\%} = \$747.66$

39. Receipts yesterday at Bryan's sporting goods store were $1,900. The sales tax rate in Bryan's state is 6.5%. How much were actual sales?

Actual sales $= \dfrac{\$1,900}{106.5\%} = \$1,784.04$

40. The sales tax rate in Frank Goldtharp's state is 6%. Receipts at his workout parlor were $8,700 last week. How much were Frank's actual sales?

Actual sales $= \dfrac{\$8,700}{106\%} = \$8,207.55$

41. Manuel Gomez owns a house with a $273,000 market value. The assessment rate is 65%. The county tax rate is $2.70 per $100. How much tax does Manuel pay?

MV	$\$\ 273,000.00$
$\times AR$	$\times\ \ \ \ \ \ 65\%$
$= AV$	$\$\ 177,450.00$
$\times TR$	$\times\ \$2.70/\$100$
$=\ \ T$	$\$\ \ \ \ \ 4,791.15$

42. Vivian Goebel owns an old house with a market value of $36,000. The city assessed such property at 55% of market value. If the city tax rate is $1.90 per $100, how much city tax does Vivian pay?

MV	$\$\ \ 36,000.00$
$\times AR$	$\times\ \ \ \ \ \ \ 55\%$
$= AV$	$\$\ \ 19,800.00$
$\times TR$	$\times\ \$1.90/\$100$
$=\ \ T$	$\$\ \ \ \ \ \ 376.20$

43. Bill Redford pays $.39 per $100 county tax and $22.20 per $1,000 school tax. His $2,380,000 mansion is assessed at 45% of market value. How much combined county and school taxes does Bill pay?

MV	$\$2,380,000.00$
$\times AR$	$\times\ \ \ \ \ \ \ \ \ \ 45\%$
$= AV$	$\$1,071,000.00$
$\times TR$	$\times\ \ \ \$2.61/\$100$
$=\ \ T$	$\$\ \ \ \ 27,953.10$

$\dfrac{\$.39}{\$100} + \dfrac{\$22.20}{\$1,000} = \dfrac{\$.39}{\$100} + \dfrac{\$2.22}{\$100} = \dfrac{\$2.61}{\$100}$

44. Dana Yant's house has a market value of $185,000. The county tax rate is $1.20 per $100 valuation. The assessment rate is 70%. How much county tax does Dana have to pay?

MV	$\$185,000.00$
$\times AR$	$\times\ \ \ \ \ \ \ 70\%$
$= AV$	$\$129,500.00$
$\times TR$	$\times\ \$1.20/\$100$
$=\ \ T$	$\$\ \ \ 1,554.00$

45. Franklin Broyles owns a big house with a market value of $6,293,000. The county tax rate is $1.35 per $100 valuation. School taxes are $5.40 per $1,000 valuation. The assessment rate is 65%. How much tax does Franklin pay?

MV	$\$6,293,000.00$
$\times AR$	$\times\ \ \ \ \ \ \ \ \ \ 65\%$
$= AV$	$\$4,090,450.00$
$\times TR$	$\times\ \ \ \$1.89/\$100$
$=\ \ T$	$\$\ \ \ \ 77,309.51$

$\dfrac{\$1.35}{\$100} + \dfrac{\$5.40}{\$1,000} = \dfrac{\$1.35}{\$100} + \dfrac{\$.54}{\$100} = \dfrac{\$1.89}{\$100}$

46. Garth, Utah, needs $45,000,000. The market value of the property is $8,000,000,000 and is assessed at 70% for tax purposes. Find the tax rate per $1,000.

MV	$\$8,000,000,000$
$\times AR$	$\times\ \ \ \ \ \ \ \ \ \ \ 70\%$
$= AV$	$\$5,600,000,000$
$\times TR$	$\times\ \ \ \ TR/\$1,000$
$=\ \ T$	$\$\ \ \ \ \ 45,000,000$

$\$5,600,000,000 \times \dfrac{TR}{\$1,000} = \$45,000,000$

$\$5,600,000 \times TR = \$45,000,000$

$TR = \dfrac{\$45,000,000}{\$5,600,000} = \$8.04 \text{ per } \$1,000$

47. The market value of the property in Jeremy, Wisconsin, is $18,000,000. For tax purposes property is appraised at 65% of its market value. If the tax to be raised is $64,350, how much will the tax rate per hundred need to be?

MV	$\$18,000,000$
$\times AR$	$\times\ \ \ \ \ \ \ \ 65\%$
$= AV$	$\$11,700,000$
$\times TR$	$\times\ \ \ TR/\$100$
$=\ \ T$	$\$\ \ \ \ \ 64,350$

$\$11,700,000 \times \dfrac{TR}{\$100} = \$64,350$

$\$117,000 \times TR = \$64,350$

$TR = \dfrac{\$64,350}{\$117,000} = \$.55 \text{ per } \$100$

48. The city of Megopolis will spend $8,400,000 this year. The market value of the property in the city is $240,000,000. The property is assessed at 70% of its market value for tax purposes. Find the tax rate per $100 valuation.

MV	$\$240,000,000$
$\times AR$	$\times\ \ \ \ \ \ \ \ \ 70\%$
$= AV$	$\$168,000,000$
$\times TR$	$\times\ \ \ \ TR/\$100$
$=\ \ T$	$\$\ \ \ \ 8,400,000$

$\$168,000,000 \times \dfrac{TR}{\$100} = \$8,400,000$

$\$1,680,000 \times TR = \$8,400,000$

$TR = \dfrac{\$8,400,000}{\$1,680,000} = \$5 \text{ per } \$100$

49. Pine City needs $4,321,510 next year to meet the town's expenses. How much per $1,000 will the tax rate need to be if the property is worth $434,000,000 and is taxed at 59% of market value?

MV	$434,000,000
× *AR*	× 59%
= *AV*	$256,060,000
× *TR*	× *TR*/$1,000
= *T*	$ 4,321,510

$256,060,000 \times \dfrac{TR}{\$1,000} = \$4,321,510$

$256,060 \times TR = \$4,321,510$

$TR = \dfrac{\$4,321,510}{\$256,060} = \$16.88 \text{ per } \$1,000$

50. The market value of the property in Bradley, Missouri, is $65,300,000. For tax purposes, property is appraised at 60% of its market value. If the tax to be raised is $231,400, how much will the tax rate per thousand need to be?

MV	$65,300,000
× *AR*	× 60%
= *AV*	$39,180,000
× *TR*	× *TR*/$1,000
= *T*	$ 231,400

$39,180,000 \times \dfrac{TR}{\$1,000} = \$231,400$

$39,180 \times TR = \$231,400$

$TR = \dfrac{\$231,400}{\$39,180} = \$5.91 \text{ per } \$1,000$

✓ ENRICHMENT PROBLEM

51. The market value of the property in Bennet, Arkansas, is $76,400,000. For tax purposes, property is appraised at 55% of its market value. The property tax rate is now $10 per $1,000. If the total city revenue to be raised from both property and sales tax is $650,000, how much will be needed from a new sales tax to meet the city's needs? The city council has estimated that the taxable sales revenue for the coming year will be $4,596,000. What will the new sales tax rate need to be?

MV	$76,400,000
× *AR*	× 55%
= *AV*	$42,020,000
× *TR*	× 10/$1,000
= *T*	$ 420,200

$650,000	Total revenue needed
− 420,200	Raised from property tax
$229,800	Needed from sales tax

Taxable sales revenue × sales tax rate = sales tax

$\$4,596,000 \times R = \$229,800$

$R = \dfrac{\$229,800}{\$4,596,000} = 5\%$

CRITICAL THINKING GROUP PROJECT

The market value of the property in Alamosa, Colorado, is $82,185,000. For tax purposes, property is assessed at 72% of its appraised value. The local taxing authorities have forecast property tax revenue will raise $5,029,722. That figure represents 80% of the income needs. The other 20% must be raised from sales tax revenue. The forecast for taxable sales revenue for the coming year is $62,871,525.

1. Calculate the property tax rate per $100 of assessed valuation.

MV	$82,185,000
× *AR*	× 72%
= *AV*	$59,173,200
× *TR*	× *R*/$100
= *T*	$ 5,029,722

$59,173,200 \times \dfrac{R}{\$100} = \$5,029,722$

$591,732 \times R = \$5,029,722$

$R = \dfrac{\$5,029,722}{\$591,732} = \$8.50$

2. Calculate the taxing authority's total revenue needs.

Total revenue × % of revenue raised by property tax = property tax

$\text{Total revenue} = \dfrac{\text{property tax}}{\text{\% of revenue raised by property tax}}$

$= \dfrac{\$5,029,722}{80\%}$

$= \$6,287,152.50$

3. Calculate the amount of revenue to be raised by sales tax.

$6,287,152.50		$6,287,152.50
−5,029,722.00	or	× 20%
$1,257,430.50		$1,257,430.50

4. Calculate the sales tax rate necessary to raise the needed revenue from retail sales.

Taxable sales revenue × sales tax rate = sales tax

$\$62,871,525 \times \text{sales tax rate} = \$1,257,430.50$

$R = \dfrac{\$1,257,430.50}{\$62,871,525.00} = 2\%$

1. What is fair market value? **W**

Fair market value is the estimated worth of property if it were on the market. It is often called the appraised value because it is usually determined by a government appraiser.

2. What is a regressive tax? **W**

A regressive tax is a tax that falls most heavily on those with the least ability to pay.

3. Myrtle Smith shopped at Winn-Dixie Grocery. Her cash register receipt was as follows:

```
WINN-DIXIE GROCERY
1429 N. ALTA MEZA


1.25 LB  @  1.49/LB
TOMATOES              1.87
.91 LB  @  .89/LB
GRANNY APPLES         .81
SKILLET            16.99* T
BROOM               6.25* T



  SUBTOTAL      $ 25.92
  TAX PAID      $  1.71
  TOTAL         $ 27.63


  CASH TEND
  CHANGE        $  2.37
```

Taxable items:
$16.99 + 6.25 = $23.24
$23.24 × 7.35% = $1.71
$25.92 × 1.71% = $27.63

Find the subtotal, tax paid, total, and change from Myrtle's payment if the tax rate is 7.35%.

4. Dillon's Department Store operates in a state that levies a $6\frac{1}{4}\%$ sales tax. Kathy Torres bought $46.53 worth of clothes from the store. Using Table 19.1, determine how much state sales tax Kathy paid.

Between $46.47 and $46.63 (use higher tax): $2.91

5. Billy Ray Jones spent $15.67 for nachos during a basketball game. The state tax rate is $6\frac{1}{4}\%$. Using Table 19.1, determine how much tax Billy Ray was charged.

Between $15.59 and $15.75 (use higher tax): $.98

6. Joseph Barton manages a Variety Store. Last night he checked the receipts of one of the cash registers and found $20,000 had been registered into it. The sales tax rate in Joseph's state is 7%. How much were actual sales?

$$\text{Actual sales} = \frac{\$20,000}{107\%} = \$18,691.59$$

7. The sales tax rate in Nolan Dixon's state is 6.5%. Receipts at his card shop were $21,400 last week. How much was the actual amount Nolan received?

$$\text{Actual sales} = \frac{\$21,400}{106.5\%} = \$20,093.90$$

8. Clyde Donaldson owns a house that has been appraised at $340,000. The county assessment rate is 65%. The tax rate is $1.25 per $100 of valuation. How much county tax will Clyde have to pay?

MV	$ 340,000.00
× AR	× 65%
= AV	$ 221,000.00
× TR	× $1.25/$100
= T	$ 2,762.50

9. Dale Brown pays $.64 per $100 county tax and $14.30 per $1,000 school tax. His $340,000 house is assessed at 60% of market value. How much combined county and school taxes does she pay?

MV	$340,000.00
× AR	× 60%
= AV	$204,000.00
× TR	×$2.07/$100
= T	$ 4,222.80

$$\frac{\$.64}{\$100} + \frac{\$14.30}{\$1,000} = \frac{\$.64}{\$100} + \frac{\$1.43}{\$100} = \frac{\$2.07}{\$100}$$

10. Ogdan, Mississippi, needs $430,000 from property taxes this year. The market value of the town's property is $43,000,000 and is assessed at 60% for tax purposes. How much is the tax rate per $100?

MV	$43,000,000
× AR	× 60%
= AV	$25,800,000
× TR	× TR/$100
= T	$ 430,000

$$\$25,800,000 \times \frac{TR}{\$100} = \$430,000$$

$$\$258,000 \times TR = \$430,000$$

$$TR = \frac{\$430,000}{\$258,000} = \$1.67 \text{ per } \$100$$

11. Fort Jones, New Jersey, needs $14,600,000 next year to meet the town's expenses. How much per $1,000 will the tax rate need to be if the property is worth $899,000,000 and is taxed at 55% of market value?

MV	$899,000,000
× AR	× 55%
= AV	$494,450,000
× TR	× TR/$1,000
= T	$ 14,600,000

$$\$494,450,000 \times \frac{TR}{\$1,000} = \$14,600,000$$

$$\$494,450 \times TR = \$14,600,000$$

$$TR = \frac{\$14,600,000}{\$494,450} = \$29.53 \text{ per } \$1,000$$

Springfield wants to estimate its property tax expense for the year 2003. It has developed the spreadsheet form that you will call up when you enter Ch19App1 from your computer spreadsheet application's disk. It will appear as shown here:

Springfield Department Store

2617 Main Street
Box 219
Springfield, Maryland 58109
Telephone: 301-555-2158   FAX: 301-555-3498

PROPERTY TAX ESTIMATE - 2003

Property	County Location	Appraised Value	Assessment Rate	Assessed Valuation	Tax Rate	Tax
				$0.00		$0.00
				$0.00		$0.00
				$0.00		$0.00
				$0.00		$0.00
				$0.00		$0.00
TOTALS		$0		$0.00		$0.00

Enter the following information:

Property	Cell	County Location	Cell	Appraised Value	Cell	Assessment Rate	Cell	Tax Rate	Cell
Store 1	A12	Lincoln	B12	$2,000,000	C12	.7425	C12	$4.28/$100	F12
Store 2	A13	Mariville	B13	$1,495,500	C13	.64	C13	$23.19/$1,000	F13
Store 3	A14	Willowsby	B14	$2,375,250	C14	.775	C14	.0845	F14
Lot 1633	A15	Stanton	B15	$ 147,500	C15	.565	C15	115 mills	F15
Lot 2840	A16	Colfax	B16	$ 205,000	C16	.6775	C16	.104	F16

Answer the following questions after you have completed the spreadsheet:

1. What is the assessed valuation for store 1?
2. What is the tax for store 1?
3. What is the assessed valuation for lot 2840?
4. What is the assessed valuation for store 3?
5. What is the tax for store 2?
6. What is the tax for lot 1633?

GROUP REPORT

Springfield's management has been watching the appropriate political subdivision discussions on the coming year's tax needs. The best estimate of management is that the appraised value of the property will remain the same. However, two of the subdivisions have indicated that they may raise the assessment rates by 10%. The other three subdivisions intend to raise their tax rate by 10%.

Your group has been asked to assess the effects of the changes and to inform the store manager of your findings and conclusions. (Part of your conclusion should focus on the desirability of an increase in the assessment rate versus the tax rate.)

The tax rates are expected to be raised for store 1, store 3, and lot 1633. Store 2 and lot 2840 will have assessment rate increases.

20 INSURANCE APPLICATIONS
LIFE, FIRE, AND AUTO

NO-FAULT INSURANCE—A GREAT IDEA THAT MIGHT NOT BE

Not long ago a new idea to save money appeared on the auto insurance scene. It was called "no-fault" meaning literally that fault in an auto accident would not be a principal consideration when deciding who should pay for damages to the property of a policyholder. Well-intentioned people everywhere believed millions would be saved on attorney's fees and court costs.

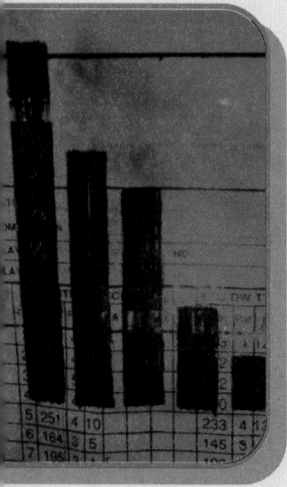

Several variations of no-fault were adopted in some states, and the U.S. Congress even considered making a standard no-fault policy mandatory nationwide.

With **no-fault insurance**, each driver collects for bodily injuries from her or his own insurance company regardless of who is to blame for an accident. Each person's own policy pays for medical expenses, the value of lost wages, and other expenses.

For a while the logic of no-fault was very tempting, and it was a popular idea for reducing insurance costs. Although no-fault promised to save money, the promise was not kept.

It turns out that the savings pertain only to reduced bodily injury premiums. Premiums for property damage, comprehensive damages, and collision on the driver's own car are not reduced by the adoption of no-fault coverage. Since most premiums apply toward those types of insurance, the savings have not been as great as was originally hoped. Rising costs for repairing automobiles and the tendency of victims to sue for large amounts have caused premiums to rise. Since the savings have been so disappointingly low, enthusiasm for the idea has diminished.

Some states now have no-fault insurance, but the rest are not likely to follow them in the experiment. The savings are just not great enough.

Chapter Glossary

No-fault insurance. Injury liability insurance in which damages are paid by each policyholder's own insurance company, regardless of who is at fault in an accident.

Insurance. Any contract made legal by signing an agreement in which a company guarantees to pay the insured for losses incurred. For this guarantee the insured pays premiums to the insurance company.

Premium. The amount paid or to be paid by a policyholder for coverage under an insurance contract.

Beneficiary. The person designated as the recipient of the proceeds of an insurance policy.

Term insurance. A policy that protects the purchaser for a specified period of time. At the end of the specified time, the policy expires and can be converted to another type of policy at a higher rate.

Straight life insurance. A policy requiring payment of a premium each year until the insured dies, at which time the beneficiary collects the stated value of the policy. Straight life has a cash surrender value that can be collected if the insured stops paying the premiums.

Cash surrender value. The value of an insurance policy if the insured decides to liquidate the policy at some point before maturity.

Limited-payment life insurance. A policy requiring payments for a limited number of years after which the policy is paid up and no further premiums are required. Limited-payment life policies have a cash surrender value.

Endowment life insurance. A policy much like a savings account with insurance protection.

It accumulates money with a face value that will be paid to the insured at the end of a specified amount of time. If the insured dies, the money goes to a beneficiary.

Coinsurance. A fire insurance policy requiring coverage of a stipulated percent (usually 80%) of value at the time of a fire to qualify for full reimbursement for damages.

Liability insurance. Standard motor vehicle insurance that provides financial protection when a person or business is held legally responsible for personal injuries or physical damages.

Collision insurance. A policy that pays for damages to a policyholder's vehicle when the insured's vehicle is damaged, either in an accident caused by the insured, or when there is no other responsible person whose liability insurance will pay.

Comprehensive insurance. A policy that pays for damages of any kind to the policyholder's vehicle except those caused by collision.

Student Objectives

Upon completion of this chapter, you should be able to:

1. Calculate a life insurance premium.
2. Calculate the cash value of a life insurance policy.
3. Calculate a fire insurance premium.
4. Calculate the refund due to cancellation of a fire insurance policy.
5. Calculate an insurance company's fire damage liability when there is a coinsurance clause in a policy.
7. Calculate the premium for compulsory coverage on an automobile insurance policy.
8. Calculate the premium for optional coverage on an automobile insurance policy.

LEARNING UNIT 1
LIFE INSURANCE

Insurance is any contract made legal by signing an agreement in which a company guarantees to pay for losses incurred by the insured. For this guarantee the insured pays premiums to the insurance company. A **premium** is the amount paid by a policyholder for coverage. Life insurance is purchased by individuals to protect their loved ones from financial hardship. It is usually used in business to compensate a firm following the death of a person on whose services the firm depends. To become insured, a person's health must be good enough to satisfy the insurance company's guidelines. If the insured person dies while insured, the life insurance pays an agreed-upon sum to a person designated as the **beneficiary**. There are several types of life insurance.

Term Insurance
Term insurance provides protection to beneficiaries for a given period of time, such as 1, 5, 10, or 15 years. The face value is paid only if the insured dies within the given term.

Because term insurance provides only death benefits to a beneficiary, it has the lowest premium. Rates are based on several considerations such as age, sex, and health. Smokers and men pay higher rates than nonsmokers and women because nonsmokers and women are expected to live longer, according to insurance statistics.

Straight Life Insurance
Straight life insurance, which is sometimes called *whole life* or *ordinary life*, provides protection to beneficiaries and a savings account, called a **cash surrender value**, that is payable to the policyholder if the policy is canceled after a certain number of years.

Limited-Payment Life Insurance
Limited-payment life insurance requires the policyholder to make payments for a limited number of years, after which the policy is "paid up" and no further premiums are required. Limited-payment life policies have cash surrender values.

Endowment Life Insurance
Endowment life insurance provides protection to beneficiaries and guarantees payment of the face value of the policy to the policyholder after a specified number of years. Endowment life insurance policies have higher cash values than whole life policies.

20.1 Calculating the Premium for Life Insurance

Table 20.1 is used for determining yearly premiums for four different types of life insurance policies.

Semiannual rate = .51 times the annual rate
Quarterly rate = .26 times the annual rate
Monthly rate = .0875 times the annual rate

To find a premium on a life insurance policy, follow these steps:

Step 1. Determine the status of the premium payer. (Remember to take into account whether the payer is male or female and a smoker or nonsmoker.)
Step 2. Find the person's position in Table 20.1.
Step 3. Multiply the table value by the number of thousands of dollars of life insurance in the problem.

TABLE 20.1		ANNUAL PREMIUM RATES PER $1,000		
Age Issued	10-Year Term	Straight Life	Limited-Payment 20-Year	20-Year Endowment
20	$ 8.44	$16.06	$26.30	$47.08
21	8.66	16.44	26.78	47.15
22	8.87	16.83	27.28	47.28
23	9.09	17.23	27.78	47.31
24	9.31	17.66	28.31	47.40
25	9.53	18.10	28.85	47.49
26	9.75	18.57	29.40	47.60
27	9.97	19.06	29.98	47.71
28	10.18	19.57	30.57	47.84
29	10.51	20.10	31.18	47.98
30	10.73	20.67	31.82	48.14
31	11.08	21.33	32.52	48.35
32	11.43	21.98	33.23	48.56
33	11.78	22.64	33.93	48.78
34	12.12	23.29	34.64	48.99
35	12.47	23.95	35.34	49.20
36	12.95	24.80	36.19	49.54
37	13.43	25.65	37.04	49.89
38	13.91	26.49	37.90	50.23
39	14.39	27.43	38.75	50.58
40	14.87	28.19	39.60	50.92
41	15.48	29.29	40.63	51.44
42	16.09	30.39	41.66	51.97
43	16.71	31.48	42.69	52.49
44	17.32	32.58	43.72	53.02
45	17.93	33.68	44.75	53.54
46	18.67	35.11	46.04	54.35
47	19.41	36.55	47.32	55.16
48	20.15	37.98	48.61	55.96
49	29.89	39.42	49.89	56.77
50	21.63	40.85	51.18	57.58

Note: These are rates for *males.* To find rates for *females,* subtract three years from the age in the table. These are rates for nonsmokers. For smokers, add eight years to the actual age.

EXAMPLE   Joe Biggs is 25 years old, does not smoke, and wants to buy a straight life policy of $120,000. Determine the annual premium he must pay for a straight life policy.

Solution   *Step 1.* Joe is a 25-year-old male nonsmoker.

Step 2. From Table 20.1: Straight life insurance costs $18.10 per thousand.

Step 3. There are 120 thousands in $120,000.

$$\frac{\$120,000}{1,000} = 120$$

$$120 \times \$18.10 = \$2,172 \text{ Annual premium}$$

| 120,000 ÷ 1,000 × 18.10 = 2,172 |

EXAMPLE   Jane Little is 25 years old, smokes, and wants to buy a straight life policy of $120,000. Determine the annual premium she must pay for a straight life policy.

Solution   *Step 1.* Jane is a 25-year-old female smoker.

Step 2. From Table 20.1: Add eight years for a smoker. Subtract three years for a female. The age figure is 30 and the annual premium per thousand is $20.67.

Step 3. There are 120 thousands in $120,000.

$$\frac{\$120,000}{\$1,000} = 120$$
$$120 \times \$20.67 = \$2,480.40 \text{ Annual premium}$$

$$120,000 \div 1,000 \times 20.76 = 2,480.40$$

E X A M P L E   Bill Schwartz is 25 years old, smokes, and wants to buy a straight life policy of $120,000. Determine the premium he must pay for a straight life policy if he pays monthly.

Solution   *Step 1.* Bill is a 25-year-old male smoker.

Step 2. From Table 20.1: Add eight years for a smoker. The figure at 33 is $22.64.

Step 3. There are 120 thousands in $120,000.

$$\frac{\$120,000}{\$1,000} = 120$$
$$120 \times \$22.64 = \$2,716.80 \text{ Annual premium}$$

$$\$2,716.80 \times .0875 \text{ (monthly rate)} = \$237.72 \text{ Monthly premium}$$

$$120,000 \div 1,000 \times 22.64 \times .0875 = 237.72$$

20.1 Practice Problems

1. John Scarborough, a nonsmoker, is 22 years old. He wants to buy $100,000 of life insurance. How much more per year will a limited-payment 20-year policy cost than a straight life policy?

2. Mary Small is 30 years old and does not smoke. She is going to buy $250,000 of limited-payment, 20-year life insurance. How much more will it cost her per year to pay quarterly?

3. Joe Mannix is a 40-year-old heavy smoker. Joe wants to buy an $80,000 straight life policy. How much could he save if he stopped smoking?

4. Lulu Garza is a 29-year-old smoker. She wants to buy a $180,000 straight life insurance policy. How much will her monthly payments be?

20.1 Solutions to Practice Problems

1. *Step 1.* John is a 22-year-old male nonsmoker.

   Step 2. From Table 20.1: Limited-payment, 20-year insurance costs $27.28 per thousand. From Table 20.1: Straight life costs $16.83 per thousand.

   Step 3. There are 100 thousands in $100,000:

$$\frac{\$100,000}{\$1,000} = 100$$

$$100 \times \$27.28 = \$2,728 \text{ Annual premium}$$

$$100 \times \$16.83 = \$1,683 \text{ Annual premium}$$

$$\begin{array}{r} \$\ 2,728 \\ -\ 1,683 \\ \hline \$\ 1,045 \text{ More} \end{array}$$

2. *Step 1.* Mary is a 30-year-old female nonsmoker. Subtract three years from her actual age $(30 - 3 = 27)$.

   Step 2. From Table 20.1: Limited-payment, 20-year life insurance cost per thousand is $29.98.

   Step 3. There are 250 thousands in $250,000:

   $$\frac{\$250,000}{\$1,000} = 250$$

   $250 \times \$29.98 = \$7,495$ Annual premium

   $$
   \begin{array}{rl}
   \$\ 7,495.00 & \\
   \times \quad\quad .26 & \text{Quarterly rate} \\
   \hline
   \$\ 1,948.70 & \text{Quarterly premium} \\
   \times \quad\quad\quad 4 & \text{Four quarters in a year} \\
   \hline
   \$\ 7,994.80 & \text{Annual amount when premiums are paid four times per year} \\
   -\ 7,495.00 & \text{Annual premium paid once per year} \\
   \hline
   \$\quad 299.80 & \text{More}
   \end{array}
   $$

3. *Step 1.* Joe is a 40-year-old male smoker. Add eight years to his actual age:

   $$40 + 8 = 48$$

   Step 2. From Table 20.1: Straight life insurance cost per thousand is $37.98 for a smoker. From Table 20.1: Straight life insurance cost per thousand is $28.19 for a non-smoker.

   Step 3. There are 80 thousands in $80,000:

   $$\frac{\$80,000}{\$1,000} = 80$$

   $80 \times \$37.98 = \$3,038.40$ Annual premium for smoker

   $80 \times \$28.19 = \$2,255.20$ Annual premium for nonsmoker

   $$
   \begin{array}{rl}
   \$\ 3,838.80 & \\
   -\ 2,255.20 & \\
   \hline
   \$\quad 783.20 & \text{Savings}
   \end{array}
   $$

4. *Step 1.* Lulu is a 29-year-old female smoker. Subtract three years from her actual age and add eight years for her being a smoker to that difference:

   $$(29 - 3 = 26 + 8 = 34)$$

   Step 2. From Table 20.1: Straight life insurance cost per thousand is $23.29 for a smoker.

   Step 3. There are 180 thousands in $180,000:

   $$\frac{\$180,000}{\$1,000} = 180$$

   $180 \times \$23.29 = \$4,192.20$ Annual premium

   $$
   \begin{array}{rl}
   \$4,192.20 & \\
   \times \quad .0875 & \\
   \hline
   \$\quad 366.82 & \text{Monthly premium}
   \end{array}
   $$

20.2 Calculating Cash Values of Life Insurance Policies

Table 20.2 is used for determining the cash surrender value of different types of life insurance policies. For cash surrender values there is no difference between males and females or smokers and nonsmokers.

Remember, the cash surrender value is the amount an insurance company must pay a policyholder if the policyholder decides to cash in the policy. The cash surrender

TABLE 20.2   CASH VALUES PER $1,000

	Straight Life End of Year						
Age	1	2	3	5	10	15	20
20			3	26	87	158	239
25			8	34	106	187	277
30			15	45	127	218	318
35		5	22	57	151	253	361
40		11	30	70	176	289	406
45		17	39	85	204	376	451
50		23	49	101	233	365	494
55	1	31	60	118	263	401	533
60	5	38	71	136	291	433	570

	Limited-Payment, 20-Year Life End of Year						
Age	1	2	3	5	10	15	20
20		10	29	70	183	315	468
25		14	35	81	206	351	518
30		18	42	93	231	390	571
35		24	50	106	257	429	625
40		29	58	118	282	467	679
45	3	34	66	131	307	503	731
50	5	39	73	143	329	534	779
55	8	44	80	154	347	559	822
60	10	49	87	164	360	573	860

	Endowment at 65 End of Year						
Age	1	2	3	5	10	15	20
20			14	44	127	223	333
25		5	22	58	157	270	399
30		12	33	76	195	329	481
35		21	47	99	243	405	590
40	2	33	65	130	308	510	746
45	11	51	91	175	405	672	1,000
50	25	81	138	157	581	1,000	
55	53	143	235	430	1,000		

value is also an amount an insurance company will use as collateral for a loan to the policyholder at a very low rate of interest.

EXAMPLE   Pete Calico wishes to surrender his $160,000 straight life policy, which he purchased when he was 20 years old and has held for 10 years. Using Table 20.2, determine the cash surrender value.

Solution   Step 1. Find the straight life table.

Step 2. In Table 20.2: Straight life at age 20 at the end of 10 years has a cash value of $87 per thousand.

Step 3. There are 160 thousands in $160,000:

$$\frac{\$160,000}{\$1,000} = 160$$

Step 4. 160 × $87 = $13,920 Cash surrender value

$$160,000 \div 1,000 \times 87 = 13,920$$

20.2 Practice Problems

1. Find the cash surrender value on a $140,000 limited-payment, 20-year life policy Amy Carter purchased at age 25 and surrendered for cash 10 years later.
2. Jerry Paul bought a $180,000 endowment at 65 policy when he was 20 years old. He is now 35 years old. Find the cash surrender value of the policy.
3. Freddie Stringer owns two life insurance policies. He purchased a $100,000 straight life policy when he was 20 years old and an endowment at 65 policy for $100,000 when he was 30. He is now 40 years old. How much total cash can he receive if he surrenders both policies now?
4. Donna Cooper bought two $200,000 policies 20 years ago when she was 25 years old. One is a straight life policy and the other is a limited-payment, 20-year life policy. How much more is the limited-payment, 20-year life policy now worth than the straight life policy?

20.2 Solutions to Practice Problems

1. *Step 1.* Find the limited-payment, 20-year life table.

    Step 2. In Table 20.2: Limited-payment, 20-year life at age 25 at the end of 10 years has a cash value of $206 per $1,000.

    Step 3. $\dfrac{\$140,000}{\$1,000} = 140$

    Step 4. 140 × $206 = $28,840 Cash surrender value

2. *Step 1.* Find the endowment at 65 table.

    Step 2. In Table 20.2: Endowment at 65 bought at age 20 at the end of 15 years has a cash value of $223 per thousand.

    Step 3. $\dfrac{\$180,000}{\$1,000} = 180$

    Step 4. 180 × $223 = $40,140 Cash surrender value

3. *Step 1.* Find the straight life table.

    Step 2. In Table 20.2: Straight life at age 20 at the end of 20 years has a cash value of $239 per thousand.

    Step 3. $\dfrac{\$100,000}{\$1,000} = 100$

    Step 4. 100 × $239 = $23,900 Cash surrender value

    Step 5. Find the endowment at 65 table.

    Step 6. In Table 20.2: Endowment at 65 at age 30 at the end of 10 years has a cash value of $195 per thousand.

    Step 7. $\dfrac{\$100,000}{\$1,000} = 100$

    Step 8. 100 × $195 = $19,500 Cash surrender value

    Step 9. $23,900 + 19,500 = $43,400 Total cash surrender value

4. *Step 1.* Find the straight life table.

    Step 2. In Table 20.2: Straight life at age 25 at the end of 20 years has a cash value of $277 per thousand.

Step 3. $\dfrac{\$200,000}{\$1,000} = 200$

Step 4. $200 \times \$277 = \$55,400$ Cash surrender value

Step 5. Find the limited-payment, 20-year life table.

Step 6. In Table 20.2: Limited-payment, 20-year life at age 25 at the end of 20 years has a cash value of $518 per thousand.

Step 7. $\dfrac{\$200,000}{\$1,000} = 200$

Step 8. $200 \times \$518 = \$103,600$ Cash surrender value

Step 9. $\$103,600 - \$55,400 = \$48,200$ Difference

LEARNING UNIT 2
FIRE INSURANCE

This unit covers how to calculate the premium for fire insurance, the refund of premium due to cancellation of a policy, and payment for loss incurred as a result of fire.

20.3 Calculating the Premium for Fire Insurance

Insurance rates are usually stated in terms of a dollar value per hundred dollars of insurance. The rates are multiplied by the number of hundreds to be insured to find the premium.

EXAMPLE The rate for insuring a brick building is $.345 per hundred. Determine the annual premium for $25,000 worth of insurance.

Solution Determine the number of hundreds in $25,000.

$$\frac{\$25,000}{\$100} = 250$$

Multiply by the rate per hundred
$250 \times \$.345 = \$86.25$ Annual premium

$$\boxed{25,000 \div 100 \times .345 = 86.25}$$

20.3 Practice Problems

1. Find the annual premium for a $480,000 fire insurance policy if the rate is $.562 per hundred.

2. The rate for fire insurance on a frame building is $.784 per hundred. How much will the annual premium be if the building is insured for $120,000?

3. The rate for fire insurance on a new building is $.465 per hundred. How much will the annual premium be if the building is insured for $1,000,000?

4. The rate for fire insurance on an old building is $1.72 per hundred. How much will the annual premium be to insure it for $200,000?

20.3 Solutions to Practice Problems

1. $\dfrac{\$480,000}{\$100} = 4,800$

   $4,800 \times \$.562 = \$2,697.60$ Annual premium

2. $\dfrac{\$120,000}{\$100} = 1,200$

   $1,200 \times \$.784 = \$940.80$ Annual premium

3. $\dfrac{\$1{,}000{,}000}{\$100} = 10{,}000$

$10{,}000 \times \$.465 = \$4{,}650$ Annual premium

4. $\dfrac{\$200{,}000}{\$100} = 2{,}000$

$2{,}000 \times \$1.72 = \$3{,}440$ Annual premium

20.4 Calculating Fire Insurance Premiums for More than One Year

Typically, insurance is less expensive if the insured pays premiums in advance for a period longer than one year. The rates for longer terms are as follows:

1 year	100% yearly premium
2 years	185% yearly premium
3 years	270% yearly premium
4 years	355% yearly premium
5 years	440% yearly premium

EXAMPLE The rate for fire insurance for a brick building is $.47 per hundred. Calculate the premium to insure the building for $200,000 for one, two, three, four, and five years.

Solution

$\dfrac{\$200{,}000}{\$100} = 2{,}000$

$2{,}000 \times \$.47\ = \$940$ Annual premium

$\$940 \times 185\% = \$1{,}739$ Premium for two years

$\$940 \times 270\% = \$2{,}538$ Premium for three years

$\$940 \times 355\% = \$3{,}337$ Premium for four years

$\$940 \times 440\% = \$4{,}136$ Premium for five years

200,000 ÷ 100 × .47 =	940
1.85 =	1,739
2.70 =	2,538
3.55 =	3,337
4.40 =	4,136

20.4 Practice Problems

1. The fire insurance rate for a run-down building on the old side of a city is $.96 per hundred. How much will the premiums be to insure the building for $125,000 for two years?

2. The fire insurance rate for a new brick and steel building with an automatic sprinkler system is $.27 per hundred. How much will the premium be to insure the building for $275,000 for three years?

3. Fire insurance for a building in a part of town known for arson is $1.82 per hundred. How much will an owner have to pay to insure a dilapidated building for $1,000,000 for four years at a time?

4. Fire insurance in the expensive Ridgelea area across the street from the fire station is $.18 per hundred. How much will it cost Mr. Schnob to insure his business for $500,000 if he pays for five years?

20.4 Solutions to Practice Problems

1. $\dfrac{\$125{,}000}{\$100} = 1{,}250$

$1{,}250 \times \$.96 = \$1{,}200 \times 185\% = \$2{,}220$

2. $\dfrac{\$275,000}{\$100} = 2,750$

$2,750 \times \$.27 = \$742.50 \times 270\% = \$2,004.75$

3. $\dfrac{\$1,000,000}{\$100} = 10,000$

$10,000 \times \$1.82 = \$18,200 \times 355\% = \$64,610$

4. $\dfrac{\$500,000}{\$100} = 5,000$

$5,000 \times \$.18 = \$900 \times 440\% = \$3,960$

20.5 Calculating the Refund Due to Cancellation of a Policy

Insurance companies furnish rate tables such as Table 20.3 for calculating fire insurance rates covering less than one year. The same tables cover the amount of premiums the insurance company has earned in case the policy is canceled by the insured party.

EXAMPLE The Remington Company insured its office building for two years for a premium of $1,725. The term of the policy was from June 8, 2003 (inception), to June 8, 2005 (expiration). On September 20, 2003, the company canceled the policy. Determine the amount of refund due.

Solution *Step 1.* Calculate the exact number of days the policy has been in effect.

June   30 days
     −   8
       22 days in June
       31 days in July
       31 days in August
     + 20 days in September
       104 days the policy was in effect

Step 2. Find the number of days in the first column on the left of Table 20.3 (103–105 days).

Step 3. Move across the table to the correct amount of time indicated on the policy (two years).

Step 4. At the junction of 103–105 days and 2 years is the number 21.1, which is the percent of the premium the insurance company has earned.

Step 5. Multiply the percent of the premium the insurance company has earned by the amount of the premium:

$21.1\% \times \$1,725 = \$363.98$ Amount the insurance company has earned

Step 6. Subtract the amount of the premium the insurance company has earned from the total premium:

$1,725.00
− 363.98
$1,361.02 Refund amount

20.5 Practice Problems

1. A building was insured for $190,000 for three years with a $1,500 premium. The policy was purchased on January 9, 2003, and was canceled on May 18, 2003. Determine the amount of refund due.

2. A building insured for $280,000 cost the owner $1,344 for a three-year policy. The policy was bought on May 12, 2002, and canceled on May 2, 2003. Determine the amount of refund due.

TABLE 20.3 — CANCELLATION OR SHORT RATE TABLE SHOWING PERCENT OF PREMIUM EARNED

Policy in Force (Days)	1 Yr.	2 Yrs.	3 Yrs.	Policy in Force (Days)	1 Yr.	2 Yrs.	3 Yrs.
		Percent of Premium Earned				Percent of Premium Earned	
1	5	2.7	1.9	161–164	55	29.7	20.4
2	6	3.2	2.2	165–167	56	30.3	20.7
3–4	7	3.8	2.6	168–171	57	30.8	21.1
5–6	8	4.3	3.0	172–175	58	31.4	21.5
7–8	9	4.9	3.3	176–178	59	31.9	21.9
9–10	10	5.4	3.7	179–182	60	32.4	22.2
11–12	11	5.9	4.1	183–187	61	33.0	22.6
13–14	12	6.5	4.4	188–191	62	33.5	23.0
15–16	13	7.0	4.8	192–196	63	34.1	23.3
17–18	14	7.6	5.2	197–200	64	34.6	23.7
19–20	15	8.1	5.6	201–205	65	35.1	24.1
21–22	16	8.6	5.9	206–209	66	35.7	24.4
23–25	17	9.2	6.3	210–214	67	36.2	24.8
26–29	18	9.7	6.7	215–218	68	36.8	25.2
30–32	19	10.3	7.0	219–223	69	37.3	25.6
33–36	20	10.8	7.4	224–228	70	37.8	25.9
37–40	21	11.4	7.8	229–232	71	38.4	26.3
41–43	22	11.9	8.1	233–237	72	38.9	26.7
44–47	23	12.4	8.5	238–241	73	39.5	27.0
48–51	24	13.0	8.9	242–246	74	40.0	27.4
52–54	25	13.5	9.3	247–250	75	40.5	27.4
55–58	26	14.1	9.6	251–255	76	41.1	28.1
59–62	27	14.6	10.0	256–260	77	41.6	28.5
63–65	28	15.1	10.4	261–264	78	42.2	28.9
66–69	29	15.4	10.7	265–269	79	42.7	29.3
70–73	30	16.2	11.1	270–273	80	43.2	29.6
74–76	31	16.8	11.5	274–278	81	43.8	30.0
77–80	32	17.3	11.9	279–282	82	44.3	30.4
81–83	33	17.8	12.2	283–287	83	44.9	31.1
84–87	34	18.4	12.6	288–291	84	45.4	31.3
88–91	35	18.9	13.0	292–296	85	45.9	31.5
92–94	36	19.5	13.3	297–301	86	46.5	31.9
95–98	37	20.0	13.7	302–305	87	47.0	32.2
99–102	38	20.5	14.1	306–310	88	47.6	32.6
103–105	39	21.1	14.4	311–314	89	48.1	33.0
106–109	40	21.6	14.8	315–319	90	48.6	33.3
110–113	41	22.2	15.2	320–323	91	49.2	33.7
114–116	42	22.7	15.6	324–328	92	49.7	34.1
117–120	43	23.2	15.9	329–332	93	50.3	34.4
121–124	44	23.8	16.3	333–337	94	50.8	34.8
125–127	45	24.3	16.7	338–342	95	51.4	35.2
128–131	46	24.9	17.0	343–346	96	51.9	35.6
132–135	47	25.4	17.4	347–351	97	52.4	35.9
136–138	48	25.9	17.8	352–355	98	53.0	36.3
139–142	49	26.5	18.1	356–360	99	53.5	36.7
143–146	50	27.0	18.5	361–365	100	54.1	37.0
147–149	51	27.6	18.9				
150–153	52	28.1	19.3				
154–156	53	28.6	19.6				
157–160	54	29.2	20.0				

3. A building is insured for $240,000 for two years at a cost of $1,824. If the owner bought the policy on June 6, 2002, and canceled it on February 4, 2003, how much refund is due?

4. An owner paid $729.60 to insure a building for two years. The policy was for $48,000. Find the amount of refund if the policy was bought on February 4, 2003, and canceled on May 2, 2003.

20.5 Solutions to Practice Problems

1. January   31 days
        $\underline{-\ 9}$
           22 days in January
           28 days in February
           31 days in March
           30 days in April
        $\underline{+\ 18}$ days in May
        129 days the policy was in effect
        128–131 days @ 3 years = 17.0%
        17.0% × $1,500 = $255.00 Earned
        $1,500.00
        $\underline{-\ 255.00}$
        $1,245.00 Refund

2. May 12, 2002, to May 12, 2003 =   365 days
   May 2 to May 12   = $\underline{-\ 10}$ days
                                       355 days
                                       352–355 days @ 3 years = 36.3%
                                       36.3% × $1,344 = $487.87 Earned
                                       $1,344.00
                                       $\underline{-\ 487.87}$
                                       $ 856.13 Refund

3. June   30 days
        $\underline{-\ 6}$
           24 days in June
           31 days in July
           31 days in August
           30 days in September
           31 days in October
           30 days in November
           31 days in December
           31 days in January
        $\underline{+\ 4}$ days in February
        243 days the policy was in effect
        242–246 days @ 2 years = 40.0%
        40.0% × $1,824 = $729.60 Earned
        $1,824.00
        $\underline{-\ 729.60}$
        $1,094.40 Refund

4. February   28 days
        $\underline{-\ 4}$
            24 days in February
            31 days in March
            30 days in April
        $\underline{+\ 4}$ days in May
         89 days the policy was in effect
         88–91 days @ 2 years = 18.9%
         18.9% × $729.60 = $137.89 Earned
        $ 729.60
        $\underline{-\ 137.89}$
        $ 591.71 Refund

20.6 Calculating an Insurance Company's Fire Damage Liability with Coinsurance

 **EXCEL Spreadsheet Application** Springfield's management has designed a spreadsheet shown at the end of this chapter, to analyze its fire insurance coverage and assess any needed changes.

Because a building is almost never entirely destroyed by a fire, insurance companies rarely insure them for 100% of their total worth. Most fire insurance policies contain what is called a coinsurance clause.

Coinsurance requires an insured party to carry coverage of a specified percentage of the total value of property but not more. The specified percentage is typically 80%. Since an insurance company will never pay more than the face value of the insurance policy, a business firm should always carry exactly the right amount of fire insurance but not more. If too much is carried, a firm wastes money on premiums. If too little is carried, a firm risks too much from fire loss. The insurance company's *liability* (the amount it will pay) when an insured party suffers a fire loss is calculated by the following formula:

$$\text{Liability} = \text{loss} \times \frac{\text{amount of policy}}{80\% \times \text{value of property}}$$

EXAMPLE A building worth $400,000 was insured for $240,000 under a policy with an 80% coinsurance clause. A fire caused $200,000 damage. How much will the insurance company pay?

Solution

$$\text{Liability} = \text{loss} \times \frac{\text{amount of policy}}{80\% \times \text{value of property}}$$

$$= \$200,000 \times \frac{\$240,000}{80\% \times \$400,000}$$

$$= \$200,000 \times \frac{\$240,000}{\$320,000}$$

$$= \$150,000$$

200,000 ☒ 240,000 ➗ 80 % ➗ 400,000 ＝ 150,000

20.6 Practice Problems

1. A building worth $540,000 is insured under a policy containing an 80% coinsurance clause for $378,000. A fire caused damages of $216,000. How much will the insurance company pay?

2. A building worth $2,400,000 is insured for $1,500,000 under a policy containing an 80% coinsurance clause. The building had a $1,000,000 fire loss. How much will the insurance company pay?

3. An office building worth $600,000 was insured for $500,000 under a policy containing an 80% coinsurance clause. The building had a $500,000 fire loss. How much will the insurance company pay?

4. An apartment building valued at $560,000 was insured for $448,000 under a policy with an 80% coinsurance clause. How much will the insurance company pay for a $175,000 fire loss?

20.6 Solutions to Practice Problems

1. Liability $= \text{loss} \times \dfrac{\text{amount of policy}}{80\% \text{ of value}}$

$\quad = \$216{,}000 \times \dfrac{\$378{,}000}{80\% \times \$540{,}000}$

$\quad = \$216{,}000 \times \dfrac{\$378{,}000}{\$432{,}000}$

$\quad = \$189{,}000$

2. Liability $= \text{loss} \times \dfrac{\text{amount of policy}}{80\% \text{ of value}}$

$\quad = \$1{,}000{,}000 \times \dfrac{\$1{,}500{,}000}{80\% \times \$2{,}400{,}000}$

$\quad = \$1{,}000{,}000 \times \dfrac{\$1{,}500{,}000}{\$1{,}920{,}000}$

$\quad = \$781{,}250$

3. Liability $= \text{loss} \times \dfrac{\text{amount of policy}}{80\% \text{ of value}}$

$\quad = \$500{,}000 \times \dfrac{\$500{,}000}{80\% \times \$600{,}000}$

$\quad = \$500{,}000 \times \dfrac{\$500{,}000}{\$480{,}000}$

$\quad = \$520{,}833 \quad$ *However, the insurance company will not pay more than the actual loss of $500,000.*

4. Liability $= \text{loss} \times \dfrac{\text{amount of policy}}{80\% \text{ of value}}$

$\quad = \$175{,}000 \times \dfrac{\$448{,}000}{80\% \times \$560{,}000}$

$\quad = \$175{,}000 \times \dfrac{\$448{,}000}{\$448{,}000}$

$\quad = \$175{,}000$

LEARNING UNIT 3
AUTOMOBILE INSURANCE

Automobile owners, whether business firms or private citizens, are required by most states to carry basic liability insurance. Other coverage, such as comprehensive and collision, is optional by law, although coverage may be required by a lender as long as the car has a lien against it.

Liability insurance provides financial protection for the policy holder for damage to another person's automobile or bodily injury to another person.

Minimum liability coverage is now typically quoted as "20/40/15 coverage." This means that the policy will pay up to $20,000 for the bodily injury caused to a single person, or, when more than one person is involved in an accident, a maximum total of $40,000 for the injuries inflicted on all victims. The 15 refers to $15,000 that will be paid for the property damage resulting from a single accident. States may require a higher or lower coverage than 20/40/15. In a suit brought against a policyholder that asks for more than the amount of coverage, the insured must pay any amount awarded above coverage.

Two categories of considerations determine the rates charged for liability insurance. One is the area in which the car is driven, and the other is the age, gender, and driving record of the driver. Rates are usually higher in densely populated areas and lower in less congested ones. If a driver is young, unmarried, and has a record of accidents and speeding tickets, rates will be higher. Table 20.4 contains excerpts of the

TABLE 20.4 DRIVER CLASSIFICATIONS

		Pleasure— less than 3 miles to work each way	Drives to work 3–10 miles each way	Drives to work 10 miles or more each way	Used in business
No young drivers	Only driver is female, age 30–64	90%	100%	130%	140%
	One or more drivers age 65 or over	100%	110%	140%	150%
	All others	100%	115%	140%	150%
Young females	Age 16–19				
	*DT	140%	150%	145%	155%
	No DT	155%	165%	180%	190%
	Age 20–21				
	DT	105%	115%	145%	160%
	No DT	110%	120%	150%	230%
Young married males	Age 16–19				
	DT	160%	170%	200%	210%
	No DT	180%	190%	220%	230%
	Age 20				
	DT	145%	155%	185%	195%
	No DT	150%	160%	190%	200%
	Age 21–23	140%	150%	180%	190%
	Age 24–29	110%	120%	150%	160%
Young unmarried males, not principal driver	Age 16–19				
	DT	205%	215%	245%	255%
	No DT	230%	240%	270%	280%
	Age 20				
	DT	170%	180%	210%	220%
	No DT	205%	215%	245%	255%
	Age 21–23	155%	165%	195%	205%
	Age 24–29	110%	120%	150%	160%
Young unmarried males, principal driver	Age 16–19				
	DT	270%	280%	310%	320%
	No DT	330%	340%	370%	380%
	Age 20				
	DT	255%	265%	295%	305%
	No DT	270%	280%	310%	320%
	Age 21–23	250%	260%	290%	300%
	Age 24–25	190%	200%	230%	240%
	Age 26–29	150%	160%	190%	200%

*DT means the person has completed a certified driver training course.

driver classifications used to determine liability insurance premiums. The percentages are multiplied by the base annual automobile insurance premium.

Table 20.5 shows some typical base annual rates for automobile liability insurance. The total premium cost for two or more vehicles would be reduced by a certain percent when the vehicles are covered under one policy.

20.7 Calculating the Premium for Compulsory Coverage

Use Tables 20.4 and 20.5 to calculate the premium for compulsory insurance coverage.

TABLE 20.5 PREMIUMS FOR LIABILITY AND MEDICAL PAYMENT

Bodily Injury			Property Damage		
Coverage	Rural	Urban	Coverage	Rural	Urban
20/40	$61	$108	$ 15,000	$70	$ 95
25/40	65	113	25,000	69	97
25/50	69	120	50,000	71	101
50/50	72	128	100,000	75	104
50/100	75	134	150,000	79	110
100/100	77	137			
100/200	81	144	Optional Medical Payment		
100/300	83	149			
200/300	90	156	$ 5,000	$41	$44
			10,000	45	51
			15,000	48	56
			20,000	52	60

EXAMPLE   Marshall Bishop is 22 years old and not married. He lives in the country and drives his car 7 miles to work each way. Marshall has passed a driver training program. Determine the cost of 20/40/15 liability and $10,000 additional medical insurance on his car.

Solution   *Step 1.* Using Table 20.4, find the intersection of "Young unmarried males, principal driver, age 21–23," and "Drives to work 3–10 miles each way." The percent is 260% of the base annual automobile insurance premium.

Step 2. Using Table 20.5, under "Bodily Injury" find 20/40 Rural. The figure is $61.

Step 3. Using Table 20.5, under "Property Damage," find "$15,000 Rural." The figure is $70.

Step 4. Using Table 20.5, under "Optional Medical Payment," find "$10,000 Rural." The figure is $45.

Step 5. Add the amounts found in steps 2, 3, and 4:

$$\begin{array}{r} \$\ 61 \\ 70 \\ +\ 45 \\ \hline \$176 \end{array}$$

Step 6. Multiply the sum found in step 5 by the table figure found in step 1:

$$\$176 \times 260\% = \$457.60 \text{ Annual liability insurance premium}$$

20.7 Practice Problems

1. Steven Doorstop is 20 years old, not married, and has never taken driver training. He lives in the country and drives his car eight miles to work each way. Determine the cost of 20/40/15 liability and $15,000 additional medical insurance on his car.

2. Mary Schmirtz is 19 years old and not married. She lives in the country and drives her car nine miles to work each way. She has passed a driver training course. Determine the cost of 20/40/15 liability and $15,000 additional medical insurance on her car.

3. William Miller is 21 years old and married. He lives in a large city and drives his car two miles to work each way. Determine the cost of 25/50/50 liability and $15,000 additional medical insurance on his car.

4. Linda Cole is 46 years old and single. She lives in a rural area and drives her car only on weekends to visit friends. Determine the cost of 100/100/100 liability and $15,000 additional medical insurance on her car.

1. From Table 20.4 = 280%
   From Table 20.5, 20/40 Rural = $61
   From Table 20.5, $15,000 Rural = $70
   From Table 20.5, $15,000 Rural = $48

   $ 61
   70
   + 48
   $179
   $179 × 280% = $501.20

2. From Table 20.4 = 150%
   From Table 20.5, 20/40 Rural = $61
   From Table 20.5, $15,000 Rural = $70
   From Table 20.5, $15,000 Rural = $48

   $ 61
   70
   + 48
   $179
   $179 × 150% = $268.50

3. From Table 20.4 = 140%
   From Table 20.5, 25/50 Urban = $120
   From Table 20.5, $50,000 Urban = $101
   From Table 20.5, $15,000 Urban = $56

   $ 120
   101
   + 56
   $ 277
   $ 277 × 140% = $387.80

4. From Table 20.4 = 90%
   From Table 20.5, Rural = $77
   From Table 20.5, $100,000 Rural = $75
   From Table 20.5, $15,000 Rural = $48

   $ 77
   75
   + 48
   $200
   $200 × 90% = $180

20.8 Calculating the Premium for Optional Coverage

Automobile liability insurance protects a policyholder for damage to another person's car or other property. To protect one's own automobile from the costs of an accident, **collision insurance** is needed. **Comprehensive insurance** covers damage to one's own car from other causes such as fire, theft, vandalism, or acts of nature.

Insurance companies use tables to classify cars according to size, type, age, and cost. Larger and more expensive cars are assigned a higher classification letter because they cost more to repair than small, inexpensive ones. Premiums for older cars are lower than for newer ones because newer ones are more expensive to repair or replace.

Table 20.6 illustrates sample rates for collision and comprehensive insurance. Note that this is only a partial table to demonstrate the method of calculating premiums.

TABLE 20.6   PREMIUMS FOR COMPREHENSIVE AND COLLISION INSURANCE

		Base Annual Premiums			
Model Class	Age of Automobile	$300 Deductible Comprehensive	$500 Deductible Comprehensive	$300 Deductible Collision	$500 Deductible Collision
A–H	1	$ 63	$ 56	$182	$161
	2,3	77	69	165	151
	4	67	60	144	130
I–K	1	116	103	284	249
	2,3	102	91	256	228
	4	84	75	221	196
L–O	1	133	118	326	274
	2,3	119	106	298	259
	4	95	85	252	224
P–S	1	165	147	385	336
	2,3	140	125	350	305
	4	112	100	298	263

EXAMPLE   Harold Schmirtz carries $300 deductible comprehensive and $300 deductible collision insurance on his three-year-old Lincoln. It is in the S model class. Determine the amount Harold must pay for collision and comprehensive insurance.

Solution   *Step 1.* Using Table 20.6, find the intersection of S, 3, and $300 deductible comprehensive. The figure is $140.

Step 2. Using Table 20.6, find the intersection of S, 3, and $300 deductible collision. The figure is $350.

Step 3. Add the two figures:

$$\begin{array}{r} \$\ 140 \\ +\ 350 \\ \hline \$\ 490 \end{array} \text{ \textit{Total premium}}$$

20.8 Practice Problems

1. Anne McDermott carries $300 deductible comprehensive and $300 deductible collision insurance on her two-year-old Ford Thunderbird. It is in the P model class. Determine the amount Anne must pay for collision and comprehensive insurance.

2. Harvey Schwartz carries $300 deductible comprehensive and $500 deductible collision insurance on his new Honda Civic. It is in the B model class. Determine the amount Harold must pay for collision and comprehensive insurance.

3. May Korman carries $500 deductible comprehensive and $300 deductible collision insurance on her new Dodge Neon. It is in the F model class. Determine the amount May must pay for collision and comprehensive insurance.

4. Dr. Charley O'Bannon has $300 deductible comprehensive and $300 deductible collision insurance on his four-year-old Infiniti. The car is very expensive, which puts it in the S model class. Determine the amount Dr. O'Bannon must pay for collision and comprehensive insurance.

20.8 Solutions to Practice Problems

1. From Table 20.6, comprehensive = $\ 140
   From Table 20.6 collision   = +\ 350
                                  ──────
                                   $\ 490

2. From Table 20.6, comprehensive = $\ \ 63
   From Table 20.6, collision   = +\ 161
                                  ──────
                                   $\ 224

3. From Table 20.6, comprehensive = $\ \ 56
   From Table 20.6, collision   = +\ 182
                                  ──────
                                   $\ 238

4. From Table 20.6, comprehensive = $\ 112
   From Table 20.6, collision   = +\ 298
                                  ──────
                                   $\ 410

QUICK REFERENCE SUMMARY AND REVIEW

Page	Section Topic	Learning Concepts	Examples and Solutions
684	**20.1** Calculating the Premium for Life Insurance	Using Table 20.1, find the cost of the premium per thousand for the insured person. Multiply the premium per thousand by the number of thousands being purchased. The table is for nonsmoking males. Add eight years for smokers and deduct three years for females.	Mary is a 26-year-old nonsmoker who wants to buy a $100,000 limited-payment, 20-year life policy. Determine the premium. $$\frac{\$100,000}{\$1,000} = 100 \text{ thousands}$$

Page	Section Topic	Learning Concepts	Examples and Solutions
			Since Mary is a female, subtract 3 years from her actual age ($26 - 3 = 23$).
			From Table 20.1, limited-payment, 20-year life insurance cost per thousand at age 23 is $27.78.
			The total annual premium is $100 \times \$27.78 = \$2,778$.
687	**20.2** Calculating Cash Values of Life Insurance Policies	Use Table 20.2 to determine the cash surrender value per thousand of different types of life insurance policies.	Jayne wishes to surrender her $120,000 limited-payment, 20-year life policy, which she bought five years ago. Jayne is now 40 years old. Determine the cash surrender value.
			From Table 20.2, the cash value is $106 per $1,000. There are 120 thousands in $120,000.
			$$\frac{\$120,000}{\$1,000} = 120$$
			$$120 \times \$106 = \$12,720$$
690	**20.3** Calculating the Premium for Fire Insurance	Fire insurance rates are usually stated in terms of a dollar value per hundred dollars of insurance. The rates are multiplied by the amount to be insured to find the premium.	Find the annual premium for a $300,000 fire insurance policy if the rate is $.687 per hundred.
			$$\frac{\$300,000}{\$100} = 3,000$$
			$$3,000 \times \$.687 = \$2,061$$
691	**20.4** Calculating Fire Insurance Premiums for More than One Year	Fire insurance premiums are usually less expensive if the insured will pay premiums in advance for a period longer than one year: 1 year 100% 2 years 185% 3 years 270% 4 years 355% 5 years 440%	Find the fire insurance premium to insure a building for $250,000 for two years if the rate is $.86 per hundred.
			$$\frac{\$250,000}{\$100} = 2,500$$
			$2,500 \times \$.86 \times 185\% = \$3,977.50$

Page	Section Topic	Learning Concepts	Examples and Solutions
692	**20.5** Calculating the Refund Due to Cancellation of a Policy	Insurance companies furnish Table 20.3 for calculating the amount of premiums the insurance company has earned in case the policy is canceled by the insured party.	A building was insured for $280,000 for three years for a $2,200 premium. The policy was purchased March 8, 2002, and canceled July 17, 2002. Determine the amount of refund due.

$$\begin{array}{rl} 31 & \text{March has 31 days} \\ -\ 8 & \\ \hline 23 & \text{days in March} \\ 30 & \text{days in April} \\ 31 & \text{days in May} \\ 30 & \text{days in June} \\ +\ 17 & \text{days in July} \\ \hline 131 & \text{days the policy was in effect} \end{array}$$

128–131 days @ 3 years = 17.0%

17.0% × $2,200 = $374.00 Earned

$$\begin{array}{rl} \$2,200.00 & \text{Premium} \\ -\ \ \ \ 374.00 & \text{Earned} \\ \hline \$1,826.00 & \text{Refund} \end{array}$$

Page	Section Topic	Learning Concepts	Examples and Solutions
695	**20.6** Calculating an Insurance Company's Fire Damage Liability with Coinsurance	Insurance companies rarely insure buildings for 100% of their total worth because buildings are rarely totally destroyed by fire. Most fire insurance policies contain what is called a coinsurance clause.	A building worth $630,000 is insured under a policy with an 80% coinsurance clause for $441,000. A fire caused damages of $252,000. How much will the insurance company pay?

$$\begin{aligned} \text{Liability} &= \text{loss} \times \frac{\text{amount of policy}}{80\% \text{ of value}} \\ &= \$252,000 \times \frac{\$441,000}{80\% \times \$630,000} \\ &= \$252,000 \times \frac{\$441,000}{\$504,000} \\ &= \$220,500 \end{aligned}$$

Page	Section Topic	Learning Concepts	Examples and Solutions
697	**20.7** Calculating the Premium for Compulsory Coverage	Insurance that covers damage to another person's automobile and bodily injury is required in most states. Use Tables 20.4 and 20.5 to determine premiums	Jane Munroe is 18 years old and drives eight miles to work each way in a rural area. Jane has passed a driver training course. Determine the cost of 20/40/15 liability and $15,000 additional medical insurance on her car.

From Table 20.4 = 150%

From Table 20.5, 20/40 Rural = $61

From Table 20.5, $15,000 Rural = $70

From Table 20.5, $15,000 Rural = $48

$$\begin{array}{rl} \$\ 61 & \text{Bodily injury} \\ 70 & \text{Property damage} \\ +\ 48 & \text{Optional medical payment} \\ \hline \$179 & \text{Total basic} \end{array}$$

$179 × 150% = $268.50

Page	Section Topic	Learning Concepts	Examples and Solutions
699	**20.8** Calculating the Premium for Optional Coverage	To protect one's own automobile, collision insurance is needed. Comprehensive insurance covers damage to one's own car from causes such as fire, theft, vandalism, or acts of nature. Use Table 20.6 to determine premiums.	Dang Ngyuen carries $300 deductible collision insurance on his new Saturn. It is in the B model class. Determine the amount Dang must pay for $300 deductible collision and $300 deductible comprehensive insurance. From Table 20.6, comprehensive = $63 From Table 20.6, collision = $182 $63 + 182 = $245

SURFING THE INTERNET

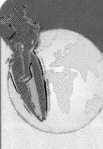

For further information on the topics covered in this chapter, check out the following sites:

http://www.boydins.com/elements.htm

http://www.bajajcapital.com/general_ins/article.html

ADDITIONAL PRACTICE PROBLEMS

Answers to odd-numbered problems are given in Appendix A.

20.1

1. Joe Binge is 29 years old and does not smoke. He is going to buy $500,000 of limited-payment, 20-year life insurance. How much more will it cost him per year to pay quarterly?

500 × $31.18 = $15,590 Annual premium

$15,590.00 × .26 = $ 4,053.40 Quarterly payments
$\underline{\times\qquad 4}$ (4 quarters)
$ 16,213.60 Annual premium paid by quarters
$\underline{- 15,590.00}$ Annual premium
$ 623.60 Difference

2. Jill James is a 39-year-old smoker. Jill wants to buy an $85,000 limited-payment 20-year life policy. How much could she save if she stopped smoking?

85 × $43.72 = $ 3,716.20 Smoker's premium
85 × $36.19 = $\underline{- \$3,076.15}$ Nonsmoker's premium
$ 640.05 Savings

3. Wanda Hill, a nonsmoker, is 25 years old. She wants to buy $200,000 worth of life insurance. How much more per year will a limited-payment, 20-year policy cost instead of straight life?

200 × $27.28 = $ 5,456 Annual premium, limited-payment, 20-year
200 × $16.83 = $\underline{- \$3,366}$ Annual premium, straight life
$ 2,090 More

4. Richard Miers is a 28-year-old smoker. He wants to buy a $350,000 straight life policy. How much will his monthly payments be?

350 × $24.80 × .0875 = $759.50 Monthly payment

5. Robert Black and Mary White are both 38-year-old nonsmokers. Both wish to buy $400,000 of straight life insurance. How much difference is there between their annual premiums?

400 × $26.49 = $ 10,596 Annual premium for Robert
400 × $23.95 = $\underline{- \$9,580}$ Annual premium for Mary
$ 1,016 Difference

20.2

6. Minnie Small bought a $100,000 endowment at 65 policy when she was 25 years old. She is now 45 years old. Find the cash surrender value of the policy.

100 × $399 = $39,900 Cash surrender value

7. Annie Gunner owns two life insurance policies. She purchased a $150,000 straight life policy when she was 25 years old and an endowment at 65 policy for $150,000 when she was 30. She is now 35 years old. How much total cash can she receive if she surrenders both policies now?

150 × $106 = $ 15,900 Cash surrender value for straight life
150 × $ 76 = + $11,400 Cash surrender value for endowment at 65
         $ 27,300 Total cash surrender value

8. Jim Blair bought two $100,000 policies 15 years ago when he was 20 years old. One is a straight life policy and the other is a limited-payment, 20-year life policy. How much more is the limited-payment, 20-year life policy now worth than the straight life policy?

100 × $315 = $ 31,500 Cash surrender value for limited-payment 20-year
100 × $158 = − $15,800 Cash surrender value for straight life
         $ 15,700 Difference.

9. Find the cash surrender value on a $280,000 limited-payment, 20-year life policy Mike Regan purchased at age 35 and surrendered for cash at the end of 10 years.

280 × $257 = $71,960 Cash surrender value

10. George Macho bought two $50,000 policies 10 years ago when he was 25 years old. One is a straight life policy and the other is an endowment at 65 policy. How much less is the straight life policy now worth than the Endowment at 65 policy?

50 × $157 = $ 7,850 Cash surrender value for endowment at 65
50 × $106 = − $5,300 Cash surrender value for straight life
        $ 2,550 Difference

20.3

11. The rate for fire insurance on a new building is $.568 per hundred. How much will the annual premium be if the building is insured for $3,000,000?

$$\frac{\$3,000,000}{\$100} = 30,000$$

30,000 × $.568 = $17,040 Annual premium

12. Find the annual premium for a $640,000 fire insurance policy if the rate is $1.62 per hundred.

$$\frac{\$640,000}{\$100} = 6,400$$

6,400 × $1.62 = $10,368 Annual premium

13. The rate for fire insurance on a frame building is $1.84 per hundred. How much will the annual premium be if the building is insured for $240,000?

$$\frac{\$240,000}{\$100} = 2,400$$

2,400 × $1.84 = $4,416

14. The rate for fire insurance on a new concrete building is $.235 per hundred. How much will the annual premium be if the building is insured for $1,500,000?

$$\frac{\$,1500,000}{\$100} = 15,000$$

15,000 × $.235 = $3,525 Annual premium

15. The rate for fire insurance on an old building is $3.85 per hundred. How much will the annual premium be to insure it for $100,000?

$$\frac{\$100,000}{\$100} = 1,000$$

1,000 × $3.85 = $3,850 Annual premium

16. The rate for fire insurance on a new building with an automatic sprinkler system is $.235 per hundred. How much will the annual premium be if the building is insured for $9,000,000?

$$\frac{\$9,000,000}{\$100} = 90,000$$

90,000 × $.235 = $21,150 Annual premium

20.4

17. The fire insurance rate for a new brick and steel building with an automatic sprinkler system is $.31 per hundred. How much will the premium be to insure the building for $12,000,000 for three years?

$$\frac{\$12,000,000}{\$100} = 120,000$$

120,000 × $.31 = $37,200 × 270% = $100,440

18. The fire insurance rate for an old building is $1.26 per hundred. How much will the premium be to insure the building for $1,200,000 for two years?

$$\frac{\$1,200,000}{\$100} = 12,000$$

12,000 × $1.26 = $15,120 × 185% = $27,972

19. Fire insurance for a building in a part of town known for arson is $2.37 per hundred. How much will an owner have to pay to insure a dilapidated building for $2,000,000 for four years at a time?

$$\frac{\$2,000,000}{\$100} = 20,000$$

20,000 × $2.37 = $47,400 × 355% = $168,270

20. Fire insurance in an expensive section of town near a new fire station is $.23 per hundred. How much will it cost Harvey Ups to insure his $1,400,000 office if he pays every five years?

$$\frac{\$1,400,000}{\$100} = 14,000$$

14,000 × $.23 = $3,220 × 440% = $14,168

21. Fire insurance for a building is $.98 per hundred. How much will an owner have to pay to insure it for $280,000 for four years at a time?

$$\frac{\$280,000}{\$100} = 2,800$$

$2,800 \times \$.98 = \$2,744 \times 355\% = \$9,741.20$

20.5

22. The policy for a building insured for $140,000 for three years cost the owner $672. The policy was bought on July 2, 2002, and canceled on June 8, 2003. Determine the amount of refund due.

July 2, 2002, to July 2, 2003 = 365 days

June 30 − 8 = 22 days
July   +2 days
          24   365 − 24 = 341

35.2% × $672 = $236.54 Earned
$672.00 − 236.54 = $435.46 Refund

23. A building was insured for $380,000 for three years with a $3,200 premium. The policy was purchased on June 8, 2002, and was canceled on October 12, 2002. Find the amount of refund due.

June 30 − 8 =   22 days in June
                31 days in July
                31 days in August
                30 days in September
            + 12 days in October
              126 days the policy was in effect

16.7% × $3,200 = $534.40 Earned
$3,200.00 − 534.40 = $2,665.60 Refund

24. A building was insured for $840,000 for two years at a cost of $3,648. If the owner bought the policy on June 6, 2002, and canceled it on February 4, 2003, how much refund is due?

June   30 days
       − 6
       24 days in June
       31 days in July
       31 days in August
       30 days in September
       31 days in October
       30 days in November
       31 days in December
       31 days in January
     + 4 days in February
       243 days the policy was in effect

40.0% × $3,648 = $1,459.20 Earned
$3,648.00 − 1,459.20 = $2,188.80 Refund

25. An owner paid $2,188.80 to insure a building two years. The policy was for $144,000. Find the amount of refund if the policy was bought on March 5, 2003, and canceled on May 2, 2003.

March   31 days
        − 5
        26 days in March
        30 days in April
      + 2 days in May
        58 days the policy was in effect

14.1% × $2,188.80 = $308.62 Earned
$2,188.80 − 308.62 = $1,880.18 Refund

26. A building is insured for $2,940,000 for two years at a cost of $12,768. If the owner bought the policy on May 3, 2002, and canceled it on March 4, 2003, how much refund is due?

May 3, 2002, to May 3, 2003 = 365 days

March 31 − 4=   27 days
April   30 days   365 days
May   + 3 days   − 60 days
           60 days   305 days

47% × $12,768 = $6,000.96 Earned
$12,768.00 − 6,000.96 = $ 6,767.04 Refund

20.6

27. A building worth $2,880,000 is insured for $1,800,000 under a policy containing an 80% coinsurance clause. The building had a $2,000,000 fire loss. How much will the insurance company pay?

$$\text{Liability} = \$2,000,000 \times \frac{\$1,800,000}{80\% \times \$2,880,000}$$

$$= \$2,000,000 \times \frac{\$1,800,000}{\$2,304,000}$$

$$= \$1,562,500$$

28. A building worth $648,000 is insured under a policy containing an 80% coinsurance clause for $453,600. A fire caused damages of $432,000. How much will the insurance company pay?

$$\text{Liability} = \$432,000 \times \frac{\$453,600}{80\% \times \$648,000}$$

$$= \frac{\$432,000 \times \$453,600}{\$518,400}$$

$$= \$378,000$$

29. An office building worth $7,800,000 was insured for $6,500,000 under a policy containing an 80% coinsurance clause. The building suffered $600,000 worth of fire damage. How much will the insurance company pay?

$$\text{Liability} = \$600,000 \times \frac{\$6,500,000}{80\% \times \$7,800,000}$$ This building is overinsured:

$$= \$600,000 \times \frac{\$6,500,000}{\$6,240,000}$$ $\frac{\$6,500,000}{\$6,240,000} = 104\%$

$$= \$600,000$$ The insurance company will not pay more than the loss.

30. A building valued at $728,000 was insured for $582,000 under a policy with an 80% coinsurance clause. How much will the insurance company pay for a $227,500 fire loss?

$$\text{Liability} = \$227,500 \times \frac{\$582,000}{80\% \times \$728.000}$$

$$= \$227,500 \times \frac{\$582,000}{\$582,400}$$

$$= \$227,343.75$$

31. A building worth $2,016,000 is insured for $1,260,000 under a policy containing an 80% coinsurance clause. The building had a $1,400,000 fire loss. How much will the insurance company pay?

$$\text{Liability} = \$1,400,000 \times \frac{\$1,260,000}{80\% \times \$2,016,000}$$

$$= \$1,400,000 \times \frac{\$1,260,000}{\$1,612,800}$$

$$= \$1,093,750$$

20.7

32. Kathy Wade is 39 years old and not married. She lives in a city and drives her car seven miles to work each way. She has passed a driver training course. Determine the cost of 20/40/15 liability and $15,000 additional medical insurance on her car.
$108 + 95 + 56 = $259 $259 + 100% = $259

33. Bart Maverick is 19 years old, not married, and has passed driver training. He lives in the country and is the principal driver of the car he drives 15 miles to work each way. Determine the cost of 20/40/15 liability and $15,000 additional medical insurance on his car.
$61 + 70 + 48 = $179 $179 × 310% = $554.90

34. Hollie Schnelenberger is 19 years old and unmarried. She lives in a large city and drives her car four miles to work each way. She has passed driver training. Determine the cost of 25/40/50 liability and $15,000 additional medical insurance on her car.
$113 + 101 + 56 = $270
$270 × 150% = $405

35. Mike Pate is 46 years old and single. He lives in a city and drives his car only on weekends. Determine the cost of 100/100/100 liability and $20,000 additional medical insurance on his car.
$137 + 104 + 60 = $301
$301 × 100% = $301

20.8

36. George Farman carries $500 deductible comprehensive and $300 deductible collision insurance on his two-year-old Cadillac DeVille. It is in the P model class. Determine the amount George must pay for collision and comprehensive insurance.
From Table 20.6, comprehensive = $ 125
From Table 20.6, collision =   + 350
                                        $ 475

37. Latanya Smith carries $500 deductible comprehensive and $500 deductible collision insurance on her new Nissan Sentra. It is in the B model class. Determine the amount Latanya must pay for collision and comprehensive insurance.
From Table 20.6, comprehensive = $ 56
From Table 20.6, collision =   + 161
                                        $ 217

38. Kareem Reid carries $500 deductible comprehensive and $300 deductible collision insurance on his four-year-old Chrysler LaBaron. It is in the N model class. Determine the amount Kareem must pay for collision and comprehensive insurance.
From Table 20.6, comprehensive = $ 85
From Table 20.6, collision =   + 252
                                        $ 337

39. Mildred Cook, D.D.S, has $300 deductible comprehensive and $300 deductible collision insurance on her three-year-old Lincoln. It is in the Q model class. Determine the amount Dr. Cook must pay for collision and comprehensive insurance.
From Table 20.6, comprehensive = $ 140
From Table 20.6, collision =   + 350
                                        $ 490

40. Darnell Robinson has $300 deductible comprehensive and $500 deductible collision insurance on his 4 year old Hyundai Excel. It is in the G model class. Determine the amount Darnell must pay for collision and comprehensive insurance.
From Table 20.6, comprehensive = $ 67
From Table 20.6, collision =   + 130
                                        $ 197

| CHAPTER REVIEW PROBLEMS | *Answers to odd-numbered problems are given in Appendix A.* |

Drill Problems

Find the amount of premium per period in the following problems:

	Age Issued	Type of Policy	Amount of Insurance	Gender	Smoker?	Frequency of Payment	Premium period
1.	25	10-year term	$ 10,000	Female	No	Monthly	$ 7.76

2.	42	Straight life	50,000	Male	Yes	Quarterly	531.05
3.	29	Limited - payment, 20-year	25,000	Female	Yes	Annual	866.00
4.	35	20 Year Endowment	100,000	Male	No	Semiannual	2,509.20
5.	20	Straight life	24,000	Female	Yes	Monthly	38.01

Find the cash values in the following problems:

	Age Issued	Type of Policy	Amount of Insurance	Years at Time Surrendered	Cash Value
6.	30	Straight life	$ 30,000	5	$ 1,350
7.	25	20-year, limited-payment life	5,000	15	1,755
8.	45	Endowment at 65	100,000	10	40,500
9.	35	Straight life	5,000,000	2	25,000
10.	20	Endowment at 65	25,000	20	8,325

Find the annual fire insurance premium in the following problems:

	Amount of Insurance	Rate per $100	Annual Premium
11.	$ 290,000	.573	$1,661.70
12.	1,200,000	.466	5,592.00
13.	150,000	1.35	2,025.00
14.	640,000	.387	2,476.80
15.	4,400,000	.219	9,636.00

Find the insurance premium for more than one year in the following problems:

	Amount of Insurance	Rate per $100	Number of Years	Premium
16.	$ 250,000	.97	2	$ 4,486.25
17.	550,000	.38	3	5,643.00
18.	1,000,000	1.44	4	51,120.00
19.	400,000	.19	5	3,344.00
20.	9,550,000	.28	5	117,656.00

Calculate the refund due to cancellation of a fire policy in the following problems:

	Number of Years in Policy	Cost of Policy	Date of Inception	Date Canceled	Refund
21.	2	$1,400	Jan. 9, 2002	Jan. 25, 2003	$ 544.60
22.	3	1,250	May 6, 2002	Jan. 12, 2003	898.75
23.	1	640	Mar. 9, 2002	June 1, 2002	422.40
24.	2	4,425	July 5, 2002	Mar. 3, 2003	2,677.13
25.	3	5,763	Feb. 7, 2002	Apr. 7, 2004	922.08

Calculate the insurance company liability with 80% coinsurance in the following problems:

	Value of Building	Amount of Insurance	Fire Damage	Insurance Company Liability
26.	$ 600,000	$ 480,000	$ 120,000	$ 120,000
27.	1,250,000	700,000	$ 220,000	154,000
28.	4,800,000	3,000,000	$2,000,000	1,562,500
29.	280,000	224,000	$ 65,000	65,000
30.	490,000	390,000	$ 12,000	11,938.78

Using Tables 20.4 and 20.5, calculate the premium for compulsory liability automobile insurance in the following problems (all drivers are principal drivers of the vehicle insured):

	Bodily Injury Coverage	Rural or Urban	Property Damage Coverage	Optional Medical	M or F	Miles to Work	Age	M or S	DT	Annual Premium
31.	20/40	Urban	$ 25,000	$10,000	M	10	35	M	Y	$294.40
32.	25/50	Rural	$ 15,000	5,000	M	2	18	S	N	594
33.	50/50	Urban	$ 50,000	15,000	F	20	17	M	Y	413.25
34.	100/100	Rural	$100,000	$20,000	F	4	61	S	N	204
35.	200/300	Urban	$150,000	0	F	12	43	M	N	345.80

Calculate the annual premium for comprehensive and collision insurance in the following problems:

	Class of Car	Age of Car	Comprehensive Deductible	Collision Deductible	Total Annual Premium
36.	D	3	$300	$300	$242
37.	Q	2	500	500	430
38.	A	1	500	300	238
39.	J	2	300	500	330
40.	N	3	300	300	417

Word Problems

41. Leon Williams, a nonsmoker, is 22 years old. He wants to buy $100,000 of life insurance. How much more per year will it cost Leon to buy a limited-payment, 20-year life policy instead of straight life?

$27.28 × 100 = $ 2,728 Limited-payment, 20-year life
$16.83 × 100 = − $1,683 Straight life
$ 1,045 More

42. Barbara Oline is 30 years old and smokes. She is going to buy $150,000 of limited-payment, 20-year life insurance. How much more will it cost her per year to pay semiannually?

$35.34 × 150 × .51 × 2 = $ 5,407.02 Annual payment
$35.34 × 150   = −5,301.00 Semiannual payment
                         $ 106.02 More

43. Burke Johnson is 40 years old and a nonsmoker. Burke wants to buy an $80,000 straight life policy. How much did he save per year by giving up cigarettes three years ago?

$37.98 × 80 = $ 3,038.40 Smoker's rate
$28.19 × 80 = − 2,255.20 Nonsmoker's rate
              $ 783.20 Savings

44. Bill Torey bought a $250,000 endowment at 65 policy when he was 35 years old. He is now 55 years old. Find the cash surrender value of the policy.

$590 × 250 = $147,500

45. Amy Hill bought two life insurance policies. She purchased a $90,000 straight life policy when she was 20 years old and an endowment at 65 policy for $100,000 when she was 30. She is now 40 years old. How much total cash can she receive if she surrenders both policies now?

$239 × 90 = $ 21,510
$195 × 100 = + 19,500
             $ 41,010

46. Hazel Sweeney bought two $200,000 policies 15 years ago when she was 30 years old. One is a straight life policy and the other is a 20-year, limited-payment policy. How much more is the 20-year, limited-payment policy now worth than the straight life policy?

$390 × 200 = $ 78,000 Cash value of 20-year, limited-payment
$218 × 200 = − 43,600 Cash value of straight life
             $ 34,400 More

47. Find the annual premium for a $400,000 fire insurance policy if the rate is $.893 per hundred.

$.893 × 4,000 = $3,572

48. The rate of fire insurance on a brick building is $.467 per hundred. How much will the annual premium be if the building is insured for $2,500,000?

$.467 × 25,000 = $11,675

49. The rate for fire insurance on a new building is $.122 per hundred. How much will the annual premium be if the building is insured for $6,000,000 for three years?

$.122 × 60,000 × 270% = $19,764

50. A building was insured for $760,000 for two years. How much is the premium if the rate is $.89 per hundred?

$.89 × 7,600 × 185% = $12,513.40

51. An owner insured a building for $520,000 for five years. How much will she pay if the premium is $1.21 per hundred?

$1.21 × 5,200 × 440% = $27,684.80

52. A building is insured for $960,000 at a cost of $5,400 for two years. If the owner bought the policy on June 3, 2002, and canceled it on January 3, 2003, how much refund is due?

June 31 − 3 =	28	$5,400 × 36.8% = $1,987.20 Earned
July	31	
Aug.	31	$5,400 − 1,987.20 = $3,412.80 Refund
Sept.	30	
Oct.	31	
Nov.	30	
Dec.	31	
Jan.	+ 3	
	215	

53. A building was insured for $760,000 for two years with a $2,200 premium. The policy was bought on May 7, 2002, and was canceled on September 17, 2002. Determine the amount of refund due.

May 31 − 7 =	24	$2,200 × 25.4% = $558.80 Earned
June	30	
July	31	$2,200 − 558.80 = $1,641.20 Refund
Aug.	31	
Sep.	+ 17	
	133	

54. A building insured for $280,000 cost the owner $3,800 for a three-year policy. The policy was bought on November 10, 2002, and canceled on November 3, 2003. Determine the amount of refund due.

Nov. 10, 2002, to Nov. 10, 2003 = 365 days
Nov. 3 to Nov. 10 =   − 7 days
                                   358 days

$3,800 × 36.7% = $1,394.60 Earned

$3,800 − 1,394.60 = $2,405.40 Refund

55. A building is insured for $350,000 at a cost of $4,100 for three years. If the owner bought the policy on December 5, 2002, and canceled it on November 5, 2003, how much refund is due?

Dec. 5, 2002, to Dec. 5, 2003 = 365 days
Nov. 30 − 5= 25
Dec.   + 5   − 30 days
            30   335 days

$4,100 × 34.8% = $1,426.80 Earned

$4,100 − 1,426.80 = $2,673.20 Refund

56. A building worth $800,000 is insured under a policy containing an 80% coinsurance clause for $600,000. A fire caused damages of $200,000. How much will the insurance company pay?

$$\text{Liability} = \$200,000 \times \frac{\$600,000}{\$800,000 \times 80\%}$$
$$= \$187,500$$

57. A building worth $7,600,000 is insured for $5,000,000. The policy contains an 80% coinsurance clause. It suffered a $2,000,000 fire loss. How much will the insurance company pay?

$$\text{Liability} = \$2,000,000 \times \frac{\$5,000,000}{\$7,600,000 \times 80\%}$$
$$= \$1,644,736.80$$

58. An office building worth $1,500,000 was insured for $500,000 under a policy containing an 80% coinsurance clause. The building was completely destroyed by fire. How much will the insurance company pay?

Liability = $1,500,000 $\times \dfrac{\$500,000}{\$1,500,000 \times 80\%}$

= $625,000

However, the insurance company will never pay more than the face value of the insurance policy, or $500,000 in this case.

59. An office building worth $900,000 was insured for $850,000 with a policy containing an 80% coinsurance clause. A fire caused $250,000 in damages. How much will the insurance company pay?

Liability = $250,000 $\times \dfrac{\$850,000}{\$900,000 \times 80\%}$

= $295,138.89

However, the insurance company will never pay more than the actual amount of damage, or $250,000 in this case.

60. A building worth $84,000,000 is insured for $48,000,000 under a policy containing an 80% coinsurance clause. The building had a $1,600,000 fire loss. How much will the insurance company pay?

Liability = $1,600,000 $\times \dfrac{\$48,000,000}{\$84,000,000 \times 80\%}$

= $1,142,857.10

61. Randy Buck is 30 years old, not married, and has taken driver training. He lives in a big city and drives his car 17 miles to work each way. Determine the cost of 20/40/15 liability and $15,000 additional medical insurance on his car.

$108 + 95 + 56 = $259 $259 $\times$ 140% = $362.60

62. Neil Rutman is 38 years old and married. He has passed driver training, lives in a city, and drives his car six miles to work each way. Determine the cost of 20/40/15 liability and $15,000 additional medical insurance on his car.

$108 + 95 + 56 = $259 $259 $\times$ 115% = $297.85

63. Leslie's Day Care service insures a van to be driven by the 30-year-old married manager. He lives in the country and drives the van 15 miles each day to pick up and deliver children. Determine the cost of 20/40/15 liability and $10,000 additional medical insurance on the van.

$61 + 70 + 45 = $176 $176 $\times$ 150% = $264

64. Charley Evans is 75 years old and single. He lives in a rural area and drives his car only on weekends to visit friends. Determine the cost of 50/50/50 liability and $10,000 additional medical insurance on his car.

$72 + 71 + 45 = $188 $188 $\times$ 100% = $188

65. Helen Hunt is 25 years old and married. She lives in a large city and drives her car five miles to work each way and took driver education classes last year. Determine the cost of 50/100/25 liability and $15,000 additional medical insurance on her car.

$134 + 97 + 56 = $287 $287 $\times$ 115% = $330.05

66. Greta Thomas has $300 deductible comprehensive and $300 deductible collision insurance on her three-year-old Oldsmobile. It is in the O model class. Determine the amount Greta must pay for collision and comprehensive insurance.

$119 + 298 = $417

67. Brad Renfro carries $300 deductible comprehensive and $300 deductible collision insurance on his new Jeep. It is in the J model class. Determine the amount Brad must pay for collision and comprehensive insurance.

$116 + 284 = $400

68. Cynthia Eaves carries $300 deductible comprehensive and $500 deductible collision insurance on her new Nissan. It is compact enough to be in the G model class. Determine the amount Cynthia must pay for collision and comprehensive insurance.

$63 + 161 = $224

69. Grady McClard has $500 deductible comprehensive and $500 deductible collision insurance on his four-year-old Mitsubishi sports car. It is in the L model class. Find the amount Grady must pay for collision and comprehensive insurance.

$85 + 224 = $309

70. Josephine Cove bought a two-year-old Chevrolet Cavalier. She carries $300 deductible comprehensive and $300 deductible collision insurance on it. Josephine's car is in the A model class. Determine the amount she must pay for collision and comprehensive insurance.

$77 + 165 = $242

✓ ENRICHMENT PROBLEM

71. When nonsmoker Admiral Clay Blowhard was a mere 40-year-old captain, he bought a $100,000 20-year, limited-payment life insurance policy. Five years later he bought a $250,000 straight life policy. When the admiral retired at 60, he cashed in his life insurance policies to use as a down payment on a building that had a $200,000 appraisal value. One month later the building suffered a $90,000 fire loss. His policy was for $140,000 with an 80% coinsurance clause.

Answer the following questions:

a. What were the monthly payments for the life insurance policies?

$39.60 $\times$ 100 $\times$ .0875 = $346.50 Monthly for the limited-payment, 20-year life

$33.68 $\times$ 250 $\times$ .0875 = $736.75 Monthly for the straight life

b. How much did the admiral pay in total for each of the policies he bought?

$346.50 × 12 × 20 = $ 83,160 In 20 years for limited-payment, 20-year life
$736.75 × 12 × 15 = + $132,615 In 15 years for straight life
                         $215,775 Total for both policies

c. How much did he gain or lose on the policies after he cashed them in?

$679 × 100 = $ 67,900 Cash for limited-payment, 20-year life
$376 × 250 = +   94,000 Cash for straight life
                  $161,900 Total surrender value

$215,775 − 161,900 = $53,875 Loss (payment for $350,000 of protection)

d. How much did he owe on the building after applying the cash surrender value from his life insurance policies?

$200,000 − 161,900 = $38,100 Owed on the building after applying the cash surrender value of the life insurance

e. How much did the fire insurance company pay the admiral?

$$\text{Liability} = \$90,000 \times \frac{\$140,000}{\$200,000 \times 80\%} = \$78,750 \text{ Paid by the insurance company}$$

CRITICAL THINKING GROUP PROJECT

Five years ago Ajax Enterprises was formed by Al Jablonski (married, age 40) and Alfredo Xennochi (unmarried, age 28). The partnership acquires small businesses that are in financial difficulty, turns them around with sound management practices, and sells them at a profit.

When the partnership was formed, an office building in downtown Hartford, Connecticut, was purchased for $380,000. It was insured for $300,000 under a policy containing an 80% coinsurance clause. The policy cost $.78 per hundred.

Al and Alfredo both invested their life savings into the business. They were fearful that if either of them died, the creditors might call for immediate settlement of debts since legally the partnership would be dissolved. They decided to shift that risk to a life insurance company by taking out partnership life insurance. Each had his life insured under a 10-year term policy for $500,000 making the other the beneficiary. Al smokes, but Alfredo does not.

Al and Alfredo drive company cars that were purchased new. Al bought a Mercedes, rated N in the model class. Alfredo purchased a Corvette, rated S in the model class. They both will have 100/300/100 liability and property damage coverage with an additional $20,000 medical payment coverage. Both cars will carry $500 deductible collision and $300 deductible comprehensive coverage.

1. Calculate the premium for the fire insurance coverage.

$300,000 ÷ $100 × $.78 = $2,340

2. Calculate the premium for the life insurance for each partner.

Al Jablonski: $500,000 ÷ $1,000 × $20.15 = $10,075
Alfredo Xennochi: $500,000 ÷ $1,000 × $10.18 = $5,090

3. Calculate the premium for the automobile insurance for each partner.

Al Jablonski: 150% ($149 + 104 + 60) + 133 + 274 = $876.50
Alfredo Xennochi: 200% ($149 + 104 + 60) + 165 + 336 = $1,127

4. Property values have increased an average of 5.5% annually for each of the last five years in Hartford. The partners agree that their office building's worth has appreciated a like amount. They are concerned that their fire insurance protection is presently inadequate. Calculate the amount the insurance company would pay if a fire caused $150,000 damage to the building.

Building's present worth = (105.5%)5 × $380,000 = $496,644.80

$$\text{Liability} = \text{loss} \times \frac{\text{Amount of policy}}{80\% \text{ of market value}}$$

$$= \$150,000 \times \frac{\$300,000}{80\% \times \$496,644.80}$$

$$= \$113,260.02$$

5. What would you recommend the partners do about their fire insurance coverage?

Student answers may vary, but probably the best answer is for the partners to increase the fire insurance coverage to 80% of the current worth of the building:

80% × $496,644.80 = $397,315.84

Answers to all exercises are given in Appendix A.

1. Why do insurance companies require a coinsurance clause 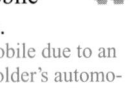 in fire insurance policies?
   Buildings are almost never completely destroyed by a fire so to insure their total value would be to overinsure.

2. Differentiate between comprehensive automobile insurance and collision automobile insurance.
   Collision pays for damages to a policyholder's automobile due to an accident. Comprehensive covers damage to a policyholder's automobile from causes other than accidents covered by collision, such as fire, theft, vandalism, or acts of nature.

3. Dr. Barbara Dossie is buying a $125,000, 20-year endowment policy. She is 36 years old and does not smoke. How much will it cost per year if she decides to pay quarterly?
   $48.78 × 125 × .26 × 4 = $6,341.40

4. Bill Garner bought a $1,000,000 limited-payment, 20-year policy. Bill does not smoke and is 41 years old. Find his semiannual premium payments.
   $40.63 × 1,000 × .51 = $20,721.30

5. Bernice Jones bought a $100,000 straight life policy when she was 20 years old. She is now 30 years old. Find the cash surrender value of the policy.
   $87 × 100 = $8,700

6. Jeff Foxworthy owns two life insurance policies. He purchased a $90,000 straight life policy when he was 25 years old and a limited-payment, 20-year policy for $200,000 when he was 30. He is now 40 years old. How much total cash will Jeff receive if he surrenders both policies now?
   $187 × 90 = $16,830 Straight life policy
   $231 × 200 = + 46,200 20-year, limited-payment policy
                   $63,030

7. The rate for fire insurance on a building is $.687 per hundred. How much will the annual premium be if the building is insured for $350,000?
   $.687 × 3,500 = $2,404.50

8. The rate for fire insurance on an old building is $1.25 per hundred. How much will the annual premium be to insure it for $700,000?
   $1.25 × 7,000 = $8,750.00

9. The fire insurance rate for a new wooden building with a fireproof roof is $.86 per hundred. How much will the premium be to insure the building for $296,000 for three years?
   $.86 × 2,960 × 270% = $6,873.12

10. Fire insurance for a new building made of concrete and steel in a new part of a business district costs $.28 per hundred. How much will it cost to insure it for $7,500,000 for two years?
    $.28 × 75,000 × 185% = $38,850

11. A building insured at $.98 per hundred was insured for $375,000. The owner bought a three-year policy on April 4, 2002. The policy was canceled on May 20, 2003. Determine the amount of refund due.
    April 4, 2002, to April 4, 2003 =   365 days ⟶ 37.0% Earned
    April 30 − 4 =   26 days
    May   + 20 days   → + 46 days ⟶ _8.5% Earned_
                        46   411 days ⟶ 45.5% Earned

    $.98 × 3,750 × 270% = $9,922.50 Total premium

    $9,922.50 × 45.5% = $4,514.74 Earned

    $9,922.50 − 4,514.74 = $5,407.76 Refund

12. A building is insured for $1,500,000 at the rate of $.88 per hundred. The policy is for two years. The owner bought the policy on September 3, 2002, and canceled on September 2, 2003. How much refund is due?
    September 3, 2002, to September 3, 2003 = 365 days
    September 2 to September 3   = −1 day
                                            364 Days ⟶ 54.1% Earned

    $.88 × 15,000 × 185% = $24,420 Total premium

    $24,420 × 54.1% = $13,211.22 Earned

    $24,420 − 13,211.22 = $11,208.78 Refund

13. A building worth $1,010,000 is insured for $840,000 under a policy containing an 80% coinsurance clause. The building had a $290,000 fire loss. How much will the insurance company pay?
    Liability = $290,000 × $\dfrac{\$840,000}{\$1,010,000 \times 80\%}$
    = $301,485.15
    However, the insurance company will never pay more than the amount of fire loss, or in this case, $290,000.

14. An office building worth $560,000 was insured for $445,000 under a policy containing an 80% coinsurance clause. The building had a $122,000 fire loss. How much will the insurance company pay?
    Liability = $122,000 × $\dfrac{\$445,000}{\$560,000 \times 80\%}$
    = $121,183.04

15. Betsy Robin Schwartz is 36 years old and married. She lives in a large city and drives her car 20 miles to work each way. Determine the cost of 50/50/100 liability and $15,000 additional medical insurance on her car.
    $128 + 104 + 56 = $288 $288 × 130% = $374.40

16. Roland Gladden is 37 years old and married. He lives in the city and commutes to and from work by public transportation. He drives his car only on weekends for pleasure. Determine the cost of 20/40/15 liability and $15,000 additional medical insurance on his car.
    $108 + 95 + 56 = $259 $259 × 100% = $259

17. Judith Gallman bought a new Jaguar. She carries $500 deductible comprehensive and $500 deductible collision insurance on it. It is in the S model class. Determine the amount Judith must pay for collision and comprehensive insurance.
$147 + 336 = $483

18. Todd Meridith bought a small two-year-old Chevrolet to drive while in college. He carries $300 deductible comprehensive and $500 deductible collision insurance on it. It is in the D model class. Determine the amount Todd must pay for collision and comprehensive insurance.
$77 + 151 = $228

19. Betty Dove is 26 years old and unmarried. She lives in a large city and drives her three-year-old Mustang convertible, rated in the M model class, 15 miles to work each way. She has never had driver training. Determine the cost of 50/100/50 liability, $15,000 additional medical insurance, $300 deductible comprehensive, and $300 deductible collision.

50/100 50 15,000
↓ ↓ ↓
$134 + 101 + 56 = $291 $291 × 140% = $407.40 Premium for 50/100/50
and $15,000 additional
medical insurance
$407.40 + 119 + 298 = $824.40 Total premium
↑   ↖
Comprehensive   Collision

EXCEL SPREADSHEET APPLICATION FOR CHAPTER 20

The Springfield Department Store's management wants to analyze its fire insurance needs because its coverage hasn't been updated for several years. The fire insurance coverage contains an 80% coinsurance clause. In the following spreadsheet, management has provided columns for the estimated current market value of the insurable property, the estimated market value of its contents, the current insurance coverage, an analysis of the insurance company's liability if that property had an assumed fire loss, the amount of insurance needed for full coverage, and the amount of fire insurance increase needed to bring it up to full coverage. When you enter Ch20App1 from your computer spreadsheet applications disk, you will see the form shown here:

Springfield Department Store
2617 Main Street
Box 219
Springfield, Maryland 58109
Telephone: 301-555-2158   FAX: 301-555-3498

FIRE INSURANCE NEEDS ANALYSIS

Property	Est. Current Market Value	Contents	Insurance Coverage	Assumed Damage	Ins. Co. Liability	Amt Needed for Full Coverage	Increase Needed
					#DIV/0!	$0.00	$0.00
					#DIV/0!	$0.00	$0.00
					#DIV/0!	$0.00	$0.00
					#DIV/0!	$0.00	$0.00
					#DIV/0!	$0.00	$0.00

Enter the following information:

Property	Cell	Est. Current Market Value	Cell	Contents	Cell	Insurance Coverage	Cell
Store 1	A12	$2,000,000	B12	$325,000	C12	$1,450,000	D12
Store 2	A13	1,850,000	B13	275,000	C13	1,200,000	D13
Store 3	A14	2,550,000	B14	375,000	C14	2,000,000	D14
Warehouse	A15	785,000	B15	420,500	C15	750,000	D15
Outlet store	A16	1,250,000	B16	112,750	C16	1,000,000	D16

Assumed Damage	Cell
$500,000	E12
500,000	E13
500,000	E14
250,000	E15
500,000	E16

Answer the following questions after you have completed the spreadsheet:

1. What is the amount of fire insurance needed for full coverage on store 1?
2. What is the amount of increase needed on store 1?
3. In the case of an assumed amount of $500,000 damage on store 3, what is the amount of the insurance company's liability?
4. What is the amount of increase needed on the warehouse?
5. What is the amount needed for full coverage on the outlet store?
6. What is the insurance company's liability now on an assumed $250,000 loss on the warehouse?

GROUP REPORT

Based on the information in the completed spreadsheet, analyze the data as a group and then write a report to the store manager that summarizes your findings. Your report should also contain your insurance recommendations.

21 SECURITIES MARKET APPLICATIONS
STOCKS AND BONDS

WILL BROKERS OFFER DISCOUNTS?

Industry leaders don't like to admit it and brokerage firms don't advertise the fact, but in today's competitive markets, brokers grant customer discounts. The practice goes on everywhere. Twenty percent off posted rates for almost all customers and up to 50% discount for the largest and best customers is not unusual.

Brokers may fear their customers will migrate to firms that offer smaller commission rates, but many wait until asked to lower their own. Brokers follow no hard-and-fast rules when granting discounts, but generally the more individual attention buyers require, the less likely they are to secure a discount. Older, more established brokers are, furthermore, less likely to grant discounts than are young ones trying to build business.

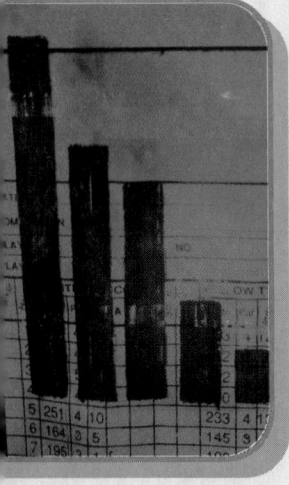

Smaller investors, predictably, have the least negotiating muscle. Investors generating less than $1,000 per year may find that brokers are willing to sacrifice their business rather than lower a commission rate.

Regardless of the size of accounts, buyers should keep track of the amount paid in commissions for all transactions. When asking for discounts, buyers have better negotiating positions when they control the numbers. Buyers also must be willing to take accounts elsewhere if their brokers aren't willing to negotiate or meet their terms.

Chapter Glossary

Stock. A representation of corporate ownership: divided into portions called shares.

Stockholder. The owner or part owner of a corporation.

Dividend. A portion of corporate profits that is returned to the owners.

Bond. A representation of long-term borrowing.

Bondholder. A creditor who owns a bond.

Maturity date. The date by which a bond's face value must be repaid to the bondholder.

Yield. Distributions such as dividends and interest paid by a company on its securities. For comparison purposes, it is divided by the last market price and expressed as a percent.

Price/earnings (P/E) ratio. The measure of a firm's earnings determined by dividing the last market price by the company's primary per share earnings for the most recent four quarters.

Last price. The last price paid for a share of stock during a specific trading day (also known as the *closing price*).

Net change. The amount of change between one day's last price and the last price from the previous working day.

Odd-lot. A transaction usually of fewer than 100 shares of stock.

Round-lot. A transaction usually of exactly 100 shares of stock.

Odd-lot differential. A fee or commission charged for services rendered in purchases of fewer than 100 shares of stock.

Outstanding stock. The amount of stock a corporation has sold of the total that has been authorized.

Par value. A value arbitrarily assigned to stock at the time of its issue.

Noncumulative preferred stock. Stock that pays stockholders dividends that are declared by the corporate board of directors in any given year. If dividends are not declared in any given year, they are lost forever to the stockholder.

Cumulative preferred stock. Stock on which all dividends not declared in previous years plus the current year's dividends must be paid before the holders of common stock are paid any dividends.

Face value. The issue value of bonds, usually $1,000.

Bond discount. The amount for which a bond sells below its face value.

Bond premium. The amount for which a bond sells above its face value.

Student Objectives

Upon completion of this chapter, you should be able to:

1. Read stock and bond quotations from financial newspapers.
2. Determine the cost of stock and bond purchases.
3. Find the receipts from stock and bond sales.
4. Calculate stock dividends for common stockholders.
5. Calculate cash dividends for common stockholders.
6. Calculate cash dividends for noncumulative and cumulative preferred stockholders.
7. Read bond quotations from financial newspapers.
8. Calculate the current yield on a bond issue.
9. Calculate a bond discount or premium.

When creating a business firm, a person must decide on the form of ownership preferred. The three major choices are sole proprietorship (single owner), partnership (two or more owners), and corporation (one or more owners). Advantages and disadvantages are associated with each form of ownership. One major advantage of the corporate form is *limited liability*. Limited liability means that the owner or owners cannot lose more than the amount invested in the business. For this reason, in much of the rest of the world, such organizations are known as "limiteds."

Owners of sole proprietorships and general partners in partnerships have unlimited liability. That means the owners risk losing not just the amount invested in the business, but their personal wealth as well. Today, almost all large and many small and medium-size business firms are incorporated.

Corporations obtain needed funds to purchase plant and equipment assets from two main sources, the sale of stocks and the sale of bonds. While the sale of either provides funds for long-term financing, there are important differences between the two types of securities. The main differences are presented in Table 21.1.

Decisions to purchase or sell stocks or bonds are based on many different goals and objectives. Such decisions are so important that most large organizations have departments that specialize in stock and bond analysis. The chief financial officers within these departments are often corporate vice presidents.

Whether a person has ambitions to be a corporate vice president, an individual stockholder sharing in American business, or simply an observer, it is almost impossible not to become involved in some way with corporate securities. Insurance companies, banks, trust companies, mutual fund companies, and pension funds touch almost everyone in some way. Each is heavily involved with stock and bond investment decisions.

TABLE 21.1 COMPARISON BETWEEN STOCKS AND BONDS

STOCKS	BONDS
1. Shares of **stock** represent ownership. **Stockholders** are owners.	1. **Bonds** represent debt. **Bondholders** are creditors.
2. Cash payments are called **dividends**.	2. Cash payments are called interest.
3. Stockholders receive dividends if any are declared, but no dividends ever have to be paid.	3. A fixed amount of interest must be paid to bondholders each year, and it must be paid before any dividends can be declared.
4. Shares of stock have no maturity date.	4. Bonds have a specified maturity date. The **maturity date** is the date by which a bond's face value must be repaid to the bondholder.
5. There is no promise to pay a certain amount in the future.	5. The face value must be paid on the maturity date.
6. Stockholders of common stock are entitled to vote on corporate matters. Stockholders of preferred stock are usually not entitled to vote.	6. Bondholders are not entitled to vote on corporate matters unless the interest or the face value are not paid when due.
7. If a corporation is liquidated, stockholders are paid last.	7. If a corporation is liquidated, bondholders are paid first.

This chapter discusses reading stock and bond quotes as published in newspapers, buying and selling stocks and bonds, and calculating the distribution of stock dividends and bond interest. For comparison purposes, interest is divided by the last market price and expressed as a percent called the **yield.**

LEARNING UNIT 1
READING STOCK TRANSACTIONS

 Calculating Earnings per Share and Yield Percent

All major newspapers publish stock price quotations on weekdays when the market is open. Each paper's quotations may be slightly different, but the essentials are the same. Most, if not all, papers have a section with explanatory notes to guide you in reading their quotations. An example of stock quotations is shown in Table 21.2.

E X A M P L E A N D S O L U T I O N Looking at the Coca-Cola Company and referring to Table 21.2, beginning at the left and proceeding to the right, stock quotations are read as follows:

1. **YTD % CHG.** This reflects the stock price percent change for the calendar year to date. Coca-Cola has a −21.2. That means that from the beginning of the calendar year until this date in November, Coca-Cola's stock has declined by 21.2%.

2. **52 WEEKS HI, LO.** This column shows the highest and the lowest price for the stock during the preceding 52 weeks plus the current week, but not the latest trading day. The highest price Coca-Cola has sold for in the past 52 weeks is $63.38 per share. The lowest price is $42.37 per share.

3. **STOCK (SYM).** The stock name or abbreviated stock name, followed by its trading symbol. A preferred stock issue is followed by "pf." Coca-Cola is known by the symbol KO. (Not all papers show the symbol.)

4. **DIV.** Dividend distribution. Unless otherwise noted, it is the annual disbursements based on the last monthly, quarterly, semiannual, or annual declaration. (Not all papers show this column.) The last dividend Coca-Cola paid was $.72 per share

5. **YLD %.** Dividends or other distributions paid by a company on its securities divided by the closing (or last) market price and expressed as a percent. (Not all papers show this column.) Coca-Cola's yield percent is 1.5%. Div./last price = $.72/$47.99 = .015 = 1.5%.

6. **PE.** The **price/earnings (P/E) ratio** is determined by dividing the closing (or last) market price of a share of stock by the company's primary per-share earnings for the most recent four quarters. The P/E ratio is often used by investors to judge whether the stock is selling at a bargain price or if it is particularly vulnerable to changing economic conditions. Since the ratio itself is given, it is possible to calculate the most recent *earnings per share* as follows:

$$\frac{\text{Price}}{\text{earnings}} = \text{ratio}.$$

Therefore,

$$\frac{\text{Price}}{\text{Ratio}} = \text{Earnings}.$$

The price used is the day's closing (or last) price. Coca-Cola has a PE ratio of 36. That is, $47.99/earnings = 36. Therefore, earnings = $47.99/36 = $1.33 per share.

TABLE 21.2 STOCK QUOTATIONS

NEW YORK STOCK EXCHANGE COMPOSITE TRANSACTIONS

YTD % CHG	52 WEEKS HI	52 WEEKS LO	STOCK (SYM)	DIV	YLD %	PE	VOL 100S	LAST	NET CHG
– 13.8	27.23	19.63	CitizensComm **CZB** n	.69e	3.1	...	285	21.98	+ 0.43
+ 13.4	49.75	31	CityNtl **CYN**	.74	1.7	15	1598	44	– 0.01
– 20.7	24.94	11.50♣	ClairStrs **CLE**	.16	1.1	15	1137	14.23	– 0.36
+ 29.8	27.54	16.88♣	CLARCOR **CLC**	.48f	1.8	16	168	26.85	– 0.12
+ 21.7	16.55	9.31	ClaytnHms **CMH**	.06f	.4	19	2812	14	– 0.47
– 1.9	68.08	35.20	ClearChanl **CCU**		...	dd	23758	47.51	+ 0.86
– 25.6	28.25	19.40♣	CLECO **CNL** s	.88	4.3	16	2223	20.38	+ 0.21
– 22.2	22.94	13.65	ClvlndClfs **CLF**	.40	2.4	dd	170	16.77	– 0.27
+ 9.4	48.63	28.38	Clorox **CLX**	.84	2.2	31	7465	38.82	– 0.28
– 11.5	29.42	24.08	CMS Engy PEPS	1.81	7.1	...	212	25.55	– 0.20
+ 15.2	42.75	20	Coach **COH**		...	22	2814	33.11	+ 0.16
– 4.0	13.65	7.94♣	Coachmen **COA**	.20	2.0	dd	244	10.08	– 0.12
– 54.3	13.50	4	Coastcast **PAR**	.26e	4.6	cc	73	5.65	+ 0.15
+ 95.6	9.05	3.31	Cobalt **CBZ**	.05	.8	...	15	6.60	+ 0.05
– 21.2	63.38	42.37	CocaCola **KO**	.72	1.5	36	35674	47.99	– 0.32
– 17.5	25.94	17.40	CCFemsa ADR **KOF**	.21e	1.1	...	3761	18.45	– 0.55
– 8.4	23.90	13.46	CocaColaEnt **CCE**	.16	.9	cc	8319	17.40	– 0.50
– 30.7	2.02	0.63	Coeur dAMn **CDE**		...	dd	1318	0.65	– 0.02
+ 67.5	15.22	7.20	ColeNtl A **CNJ**		...	44	243	14.45	– 0.10
▲+ 6.0	32.88	24	ColesMyer **CM**	1.42e	4.3	...	6	33.25	+ 1.75
– 10.5	65.69	48.50	ColgatePalm **CL**	.72	1.2	31	14189	57.79	– 1.05
+ 77.0	8.90	2.88	CollnsAikman **CKC**		...	dd	101	7.41	– 0.19
+ 28.8	14.94	8.25	ColonlBcgp **CNB**	.48	3.5	13	923	13.85	+ 0.08
+ 14.4	31.69	24.44♣	ColonlProp **CLP**	2.52	8.5	16	973	29.82	– 0.29
+ 6.0	25.69	23.88	ClmbsSo A **CSJ**	2.09	8.3	...	49	25.30	+ 0.06
– 96.2	16.95	0.38	Comdisco **CDO**	j	...	dd	5182	0.44	– 0.04
+ 0.6	25.89	24	ComericaCap **CMAZ** n	.32e	1.3	...	308	25.30	– 0.05
– 13.6	65.15	44.02	Comerica **CMA**	1.76	3.4	13	8323	51.30	– 0.03
+ 55.3	4.75	1.70	CmfrtSysUSA **FIX**		...	dd	765	3.30	+ 0.11
+ 10.4	77.90	52	ComrcBcpNJ **CBH**	1.10	1.5	26	1049	75.51	+ 0.51
+ 39.3	40.35	24.44	CommrcGpInc **CGI**	1.20	3.2	11	160	37.85	+ 0.06
+ 32.9	28.90	16	ComrclFed **CFB**	.32	1.2	49	2150	25.83	+ 0.01
+ 44.9	32.95	19.75	CmrclMtls **CMC**	.52	1.6	14	311	32.25	...
+ 30.9	14.25	9.88	CmrclNetRlty **NNN**	1.26	9.4	10	1141	13.34	+ 0.03
+ 19.7	26.80	14.75	Commscope **CTV**		...	20	4711	19.83	+ 0.23
+ 3.7	29.85	22	CmntyBkSys **CBU**	1.08	4.2	13	213	25.67	+ 0.02
– 27.3	37.20	21.25	CmntyHlth **CYH**		...	59	5240	25.43	+ 0.22
+ 45.9	13.30	8.20	EnrgGerCemig ADS **CIG** n		...	...	1416	13.20	– 0.01
– 17.5	10.65	4.71	Copel ADS **ELP**	.41e	5.9	...	3128	6.96	– 0.01
– 28.9	24.89	9.10	CompnhiaSidr **SID** s	17.83e	116.2	...	365	15.35	– 0.05
▼– 0.1	19.45	19.10	CoAnonVen wd **VNT:** n		...	...	21	19.10	– 0.01
– 36.7	25.23	7.26♣	Compaq **CPQ**	.10	1.1	dd	148032	9.52	– 0.42
+ 62.9	39.03	18.13	CptrAssoc **CA**	.08	.3	dd	28994	31.77	+ 0.77
– 18.5	74.94	28.99	CptrSci **CSC**		...	58	7760	49	+ 1.46
– 25.8	7.13	1.30♣	CptrTask **CTG**	.05	1.7	dd	342	2.92	+ 0.07
+ 12.4	13.40	8.50	CompxInt A **CIX**	.50	5.0	14	49	10.05	+ 0.20
– 55.6	**15**	**4.96**	**ComstkRes CRK**		...	**4**	**4031**	**6.55**	**– 0.35**
– 12.7	26.19	17.50♣	ConAgraFoods **CAG**	.94f	4.1	17	6992	22.70	– 0.38
– 27.8	4.13	1.11♣	ConeMills **COE**		...	dd	169	1.85	...
+ 19.9	24.25	17.19	Conectiv **CIV**	.88	3.7	8	1002	24.06	– 0.09
+ 53.4	22.80	12.19	Conectiv A **CIVA**	1.00	5.1	...	61	19.75	+ 0.05
– 8.0	33.35	23.77	Conoco **COC**	.76	2.9	8	19355	26.63	– 0.17
– 67.8	20.24	2.51	Conseco **CNC**		...	dd	82058	4.25	+ 0.01
– 15.8	42.48	18.30	ConsolEngy **CNX**	1.12	4.8	11	4223	23.51	– 0.21
+ 1.1	43.37	31.44	ConEd **ED**	2.20	5.7	13	5694	38.91	+ 0.03
+ 2.7	[illegible]	24	ConEd [illegible]	1.94	7.7	...	[illegible]	[illegible]	+ 0.06
– 13.4	92.50	41	Elan wtA		...	...	48	50.55	– 1.95
– 18.2	68.40	29.50	Elan ADS wt		...	...	11	36	– 0.50
+ 39.6	24.43	13.56	Elcor **ELK**	.20	.8	47	468	23.56	+ 0.02
+ 226.8	8.85	1.13♣	ElderTr **ETT**		...	11	237	8.17	+ 0.03
▲+ 18.4	58.98	48.50	EDS PRIDES **EDSI** n	1.49e	2.5	...	3349	60.35	+ 1.38
▲+ 24.5	70.55	48.56	EDS Cp **EDS**	.60	.8	26	34773	71.88	+ 1.83
– 3.0	5.38	3.45	Elscint **ELT**		...	...	1445	3.70	– 0.10
– 21.2	29.63	19.25	Elsevier **ENL**	.50e	2.2	...	151	23.20	+ 0.06
– 53.4	47.40	10.50	EmbrBrazil ADS **ERJ**	1.20e	6.5	...	4543	18.52	– 0.49
– 71.0	17.63	2.25	EmbrtlPtcp **EMT**	.32e	7.0	...	11987	4.55	+ 0.05
– 32.7	79.75	44.04	EmersnElec **EMR**	1.55f	2.9	22	15563	53.01	+ 0.58
– 21.7	29.75	17.50	EmpDistElec **EDE**	1.28	6.2	17	726	20.60	– 0.24
– 0.7	12.22	7.96	EELChile ADR **EOC**	.05e	.4	...	1195	10.80	– 0.24
+ 84.5	3.05	0.81	EmpIca ADR **ICA**		...	...	426	1.96	+ 0.17
+ 0.1	49.60	37.50	EnbridgeEngy **EEP**	3.50	8.5	43	1521	41.30	+ 0.04
– 5.1	28.88	22.25	Enbridge g **ENB**	1.40g	...	...	83	27.16	+ 0.38
– 67.6	9.80	1.50	EncmpssSvcs **ESR**		...	dd	4645	1.64	+ 0.14
– 10.2	17.80	11	EncoreAcq **EAC** n		...	...	98	13.07	– 0.06
– 6.8	19.75	14.20	Endesa ADS **ELE**	.57e	3.7	...	603	15.56	– 0.35
– 28.3	39.55	25	Enel ADS **EN**	1.10e	4.0	...	313	27.70	– 0.90
– 23.9	40.25	21.50	Energen **EGN**	.70	2.9	11	810	24.50	+ 0.10
– 11.2	27.55	15	EnrgzrHldg **ENR**		...	dd	1431	18.98	– 0.17
+ 1.8	25.62	24.80	EngyEst **ECT** n	.56p	...	...	315	25.49	+ 0.03
– 4.0	22.14	16.96	EngyEast **EAS**	.92	4.9	13	3218	18.90	– 0.11
– 51.1	14.38	6.01	EngyPrtnrs **EPL**		...	dd	548	6.14	– 0.25
+ 2.9	23.50	13.79	EnerplusRes g	6.00eg	...	...	849	15.69	+ 0.33
– 17.2	20.10	11.33	Enersis ADR **ENI**	.15e	1.0	...	1306	14.59	– 0.26
+ 32.3	7.31	3.30	Enesco **ENC**		...	7	523	6.20	– 0.02
+ 36.0	29.20	17.63	Engelhard **EC**	.40	1.4	22	3267	27.71	– 0.16
+ 20.3	9.19	6.88	EnnisBus **EBF**	.62	7.0	11	166	8.87	– 0.27
– 95.1	84.88	3.76	EnronCp **ENE**	.50	12.2	41	684775	4.11	+ 0.10
– 42.5	44.49	12.81	ENSCO **ESV**	.10	.5	12	20186	19.58	+ 0.13
+ 4.1	15.86	4.90	EnterasysNtwk **ETS**		...	...	21518	10.15	+ 0.18
+ 31.0	54.40	25.50	Entercom **ETM**		...	cc	1688	45.10	+ 0.47
– 12.6	44.67	32.56♣	Entergy **ETR**	1.32f	3.6	11	3670	37	+ 0.10
– 23.1	28.86	18.26	EntOil **ETP**	.40e	2.0	...	2	19.60	+ 0.20
+ 56.0	52.60	25	♣EntPdtsPtnr **EPD**	2.50f	5.1	15	429	49.05	+ 0.55
+ 60.9	18.65	11	EntnPropTr **EPR**	1.80	10.2	11	698	17.70	– 0.25
– 38.7	20.50	7	Entravision **EVC**		...	dd	765	11.27	+ 0.17
– 4.2	37.08	13.51	EnzoBiochm **ENZ**	stk	...	91	2636	22.70	+ 0.99
– 41.1	103	28.50	Epcos ADS **EPC**	.93p	...	...	92	49.80	+ 0.30
– 52.9	31.56	7.20	Equant **ENT**		...	...	641	11.98	– 0.02
+ 46.9	27.41	15.80	Equifax **EFX** s	.08	.3	19	3668	24.94	– 0.28
– 1.6	40.49	26	EquitRes **EQT** s	.64	1.9	14	2055	32.84	+ 0.05
+ 7.5	25.25	21.56	EquitResTr **ERE**	1.84	7.3	...	16	25.05	+ 0.15
▲+ 11.4	40	33.70	EqtsSecsTr **XCT** n		...	...	16980	40.55	+ 0.95
+ 20.9	9.97	5.50	EquityInns **ENN**	1.00	13.4	10	529	7.48	+ 0.04
– 9.7	33.50	26.20	EqtyOffcProp **EOP**	2.00f	6.8	18	9860	29.46	– 0.23
▲+ 24.8	12.53	9.38	EquityOne **EQY**	1.08f	8.8	12	143	12.32	– 0.18
+ 1.0	30.45	24.31	EqResdntl **EQR** s	1.73	6.2	23	6901	27.93	– 0.02
+ 40.9	32.65	17.56♣	EscoTech **ESE**	j	...	13	263	29.14	– 1.06
– 6.8	19	15.44	EspirSan **ESF**	.63e	3.8	...	151	16.54	– 0.04
– 12.4	57.75	42.28	EssexProp **ESS**	2.80	5.8	19	511	47.98	– 0.30
– 24.1	45.31	30.30	EsteeLaudr A **EL**	.20	.6	28	11737	33.2[illegible]	[illegible]0.13
– 19.3	83.69	63	EstelauTr II	.11	8.1	[illegible]	2	[illegible]	[illegible]
+ 13.4	39.52	26.44♣	EthanAllen **ETH**	.16	.4	20	2008	37.98	– 0.87
– 39.5	2.44	0.55	EthylCp **EY**	.19j	...	dd	1217	0.87	– 0.02
– 1.5	78.50	46.51	EvrstReGrp **RE**	.28	.4	29	3482	70.55	+ 1.37
...	50.99	26.75	EvergrnRes **EVG**		...	18	944	38.61	– 0.13
– 37.6	71	38.75	Exelon **EXC**	1.69	3.9	13	12099	43.81	+ 0.71
– 88.3	12.30	0.39	Exide **EX**	.08	9.0	...	4181	0.89	– 0.06
+ 17.1	19.35	11.45	ExtndStayAm **ESA**		...	21	1991	15.05	...
+ 70.6	5.35	1.25	Extendicare **EXEA**		...	dd	6	3.60	+ 0.10
– 14.1	47.34	35.01	ExxonMobil **XOM** s	.92	2.5	15	172908	37.35	– 0.42
			-F-F-F-						
+ 1.6	19.50	12.50♣	FBL Fnl A **FFG**	.40	2.3	13	92	17.65	– 0.06
– 26.3	84	45.65	FMC Cp **FMC**		...	dd	2812	52.82	+ 0.63
– 40.5	22.48	10.99	FMC Tech **FTI** n		...	...	2145	13.10	– 0.10
– 22.7	73	51.21	FPL Gp **FPL**	2.24	4.0	13	25553	55.44	+ 0.04
+ 222.7	36.25	5.63	FTI Cnsltng **FCN**		...	28	1227	33.08	– 0.92
– 17.2	47.49	17.80	FactstRsch **FDS**	.16	.5	32	2061	30.70	+ 0.35
+ 10.8	29.25	22	FahnestkVnr **FVH**	.36g	1.3	14	15	26.70	– 0.10
+ 70.0	69.90	27	FairIsaac **FIC** s	.08	.1	29	1025	57.80	+ 0.35
– 29.1	**7.74**	**2.05**	**FairchldCp FA**		...	**dd**	**1730**	**3.90**	**+ 0.24**
+ 63.5	25.35	11.19	FrchldSemi A **FCS**		...	35	9806	23.60	+ 0.57
+ 40.1	23.46	13.98	FairmntHtlRsrt g **FHR** s		...	...	8848	21.51	+ 0.94
– 31.8	10.05	4.85	FalcnPdt **FCP**	.16	3.0	dd	319	5.41	– 0.09
+ 38.7	31.35	18.38	FamilyDlr **FDO**	.24	.8	27	12780	29.73	– 0.81
– 7.0	89.38	72.08♣	FannieMae **FNM**	1.20	1.5	16	21763	80.64	– 0.86
– 28.9	5.60	2.30	Fedders **FJC**	.12	3.6	dd	491	3.29	– 0.12
– 30.9	5.02	1.55	Fedders A **FJA**	.12	4.2	dd	104	2.85	– 0.10
+ 79.6	33.60	16.13	FedAgrMtg A **AGMA**		...	27	2	33	– 0.60
+ 93.6	46.40	18.88	FedAgri C **AGM**		...	...	623	45.26	– 1.07
– 50.7	5.50	0.32	vjFedMogul **FMO**	.01	...	...	5627	1.14	– 0.07
+ 16.4	23.88	18.94	FedlRlty **FRT**	1.92	8.7	15	3366	22.12	– 0.48
+ 6.6	24.63	17	FedlSgnl **FSS**	.78	3.7	19	1054	20.93	+ 0.16
+ 10.1	49.90	26.05	FedDeptStr **FD**		...	15	16841	38.55	– 0.17
– 8.4	21.41	1.10	FedDeptStr wtD		...	...	263	8.70	– 0.11
+ 1.9	32.80	23.31	FedInv B **FII**	.18	.6	21	1573	29.69	– 0.73
+ 13.3	49.85	33.15	FedExCp **FDX**		...	25	12700	45.27	– 0.68
– 30.9	24.94	11.90♣	FelCor **FCH**	2.20	13.3	13	3893	16.55	...
+ 51.7	22.20	12.38	Ferrellgas **FGP**	2.00	10.0	13	706	20	+ 0.09
+ 8.3	25.17	19.41	Ferro **FOE**	.58	2.3	19	1510	24.90	+ 0.10
– 31.5	25.63	14	Fiat ADS **FIA**	.55e	3.3	...	56	16.60	– 0.35
▼– 34.1	14.80	5.05♣	FiberMark **FMK**		...	dd	1089	5.15	...
– 31.8	35.80	17.91	FidNtlFnl **FNF** s	.40b	1.7	7	4098	22.91	– 0.09
– 65.9	**9.38**	**1.80**	**FilaHldg FLH** s		...	**dd**	**379**	**2.60**	**+ 0.22**
+ 12.7	29.75	21.44	FnlFed **FIF**		...	15	180	26.90	+ 0.05
– 15.0	5.53	0.47♣	Finova **FNV**	j	...	...	4105	0.85	– 0.02
– 45.9	35.49	16.30	FstAmCp **FAF**	.28	1.6	8	3889	17.80	+ 0.30
+ 2.0	25.75	24	FstBcp MIPS **FBPC** n	1.85	7.3	...	40	25.50	– 0.05
+ 22.7	30	19.50	FstBcp **FBP**	.52	1.8	12	33	28.98	– 0.22
+ 71.0	33.19	16.06	FstBksAm **FBA**		...	11	6	30.13	– 0.27
+ 20.0	15.10	8.81	FstCmwlthFnl **FCF**	.58	4.8	14	312	12	...
+ 37.1	74.11	47.38	FstData **FDC**	.08	.1	35	12913	72.24	– 0.69
– 11.8	35	26.83♣	FstIndRlty **FR**	2.63	8.8	11	3895	30	+ 0.24
– 1.8	27.20	18	♣FstRepBnk **FRC** s		...	13	570	21.60	...
+ 26[illegible]	[illegible]9	21.69♣	FstTN Ntl **FTN**	1.00f	2.7	16	2258	36.52	– 0.45
[illegible]	[illegible]	2.16	FstUnionRE **FUR**		...	dd	180	2.35	...
[illegible]	[illegible]	[illegible]	[illegible] **FVB**	[illegible]	[illegible]	[illegible]	[illegible]	[illegible]	[illegible]0.04

Source: The Wall Street Journal. (Reprinted by permission.)

7. **VOL 100s.** This column shows the day's unofficial total volume of shares traded, normally quoted in hundreds with two zeros omitted. If the volume number is followed by an f, four zeros have been omitted. Coca-Cola traded 35,674 shares on the sample day. That means, adding the two zeros back in, 3,567,400 shares traded in one day. Assuming that all shares were traded at approximately the price of the last share traded, \$47.99, the total monetary exchange for Coca-Cola was \$47.99 × 3,567,400 = \$171,199,530.
8. **LAST.** The **last price** (frequently called the *closing price*) paid during the day. Coca-Cola closed at 47.99 (\$47.99).
9. **NET CHG.** The amount of change between one day's last price and the last price from the previous working day. Coca-Cola had a **net change** of -0.32, or \$.32 less than it had closed for on the previous working day.

21.1
Practice Problems

Use Table 21.2 to answer the following questions:

1. What are the 52-week hi and lo prices for Clayton Homes?
2. Determine the earnings per share for Clorox.
3. Show the calculations that were used to calculate the yield for Colgate Palmolive common stock.
4. Calculate the previous day's last price for Coach by using the current last price and the net change.

21.1 Solutions to Practice Problems

1. $16.55 hi, $9.31 lo

2. $\dfrac{P}{E} = 31 \qquad \dfrac{\$38.82}{E} = 31 \qquad \dfrac{\$38.82}{31} = \$1.25$

3. $\text{Yield} = \dfrac{\text{dividend}}{\text{last price}} \qquad \text{Yield} = \dfrac{\$.72}{\$57.79} = 1.2\%$

5. $32.11 - .16 = $31.95

LEARNING UNIT 2
BUYING AND SELLING STOCK

The four major stock exchanges in the United States are the New York Stock Exchange, the American Stock Exchange, the Pacific Stock Exchange, and the Midwest Stock Exchange. Most stockbrokers trade on all of these exchanges. A broker acts as an agent, performing various transactions between buyer and seller. For these services, the broker receives either a commission, a set fee based on the dollar value of the stocks, or a flat fee. Because these commissions or fees are negotiable, they vary widely. Fees depend on such things as broker services provided, the dollar amount of the stock transaction, and whether the customer is a regular, valued customer or a first-time customer engaging in a small transaction.

EXCEL Spreadsheet Application Spreadsheet Application 1 at the end of this chapter is a form designed to help Springfield keep track of its common stock transactons.

21.2 ## Calculating Round-Lot, Odd-Lot, and Combination Sales

Shares of stock may be purchased in **odd-lots** or **round-lots**. An odd-lot is usually a transaction of fewer than 100 shares. A round-lot is usually a transaction of exactly 100 shares. For some stock that is traded infrequently, a round-lot is considered to be 10 shares. However, for purposes of this book, a round-lot will be 100 shares. Of course, it is possible for an investor to purchase a combination of a round-lot and an odd-lot of stock, for example, 145 shares. The price is generally higher for an odd-lot because the transaction is handled differently in the exchange. Stock in the exchange is sold only in round-lots. Thus, odd-lots are accumulated by an odd-lot broker until he has a total of 100 shares. The round-lot is then purchased and divided among the odd-lot buyers. The odd-lot broker charges a fee for services rendered. It is called an **odd-lot differential**.

EXAMPLE
Alan T. Smith bought 200 shares of Digital Equipment stock at $75.85 per share. The broker charged a 2% commission rate. Calculate the total purchase price.

Solution

200 × $75.85 = $15,170.00 ⟵ *Multiply the number of*
2% × $15,170 = + 303.40   *shares purchased by the*
    ↑   → $15,473.40   *per share purchase price.*

Multiply the total share cost amount by
the commission rate of 2% and add it to
the total share cost.

EXAMPLE
Harold Locker bought 45 shares of Dayton Hudson at $74.25 per share. The odd-lot differential is an additional 1%, and the broker charged a fee of $25. Calculate the total purchase price.

Solution

45 × $74.25   = $3,341.25 ⟵ *Multiply the number of shares*
1% × $3,341.25 = + 33.41   *purchased by the per share*
  ↑   → $3,374.66   *purchase price.*

Multiply the total share cost
by the amount of the odd-lot
differential rate of 1%
and add it to the total share
cost.

$3,374.66
+ 25.00 ⟵ *Add the fee.*
$3,399.66 ⟵ *Total purchase price*

EXAMPLE
Vivian Corcoran bought 275 shares of Bank One stock at $38.01. An odd-lot differential charge of an additional $.15 per share was made on the odd-lot portion of the purchase. The broker also charged a 2% commission on the total stock price. Determine the total cost of the stock purchase.

Solution

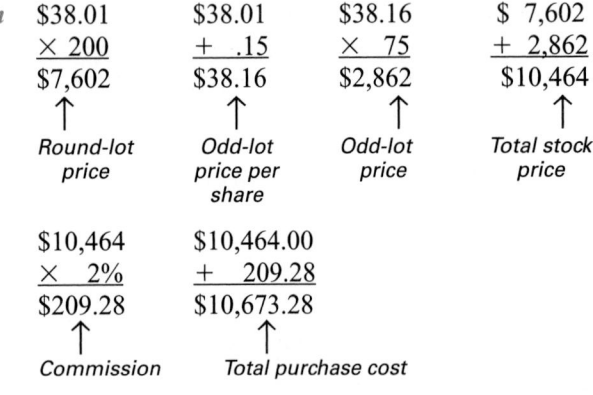

$38.01	$38.01	$38.16	$ 7,602
× 200	+ .15	× 75	+ 2,862
$7,602	$38.16	$2,862	$10,464
↑	↑	↑	↑
Round-lot price	Odd-lot price per share	Odd-lot price	Total stock price

$10,464	$10,464.00
× 2%	+ 209.28
$209.28	$10,673.28
↑	↑
Commission	Total purchase cost

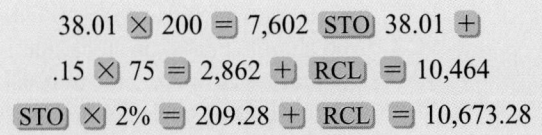

38.01 ⊠ 200 ⊟ 7,602 STO 38.01 ⊞
.15 ⊠ 75 ⊟ 2,862 ⊞ RCL ⊟ 10,464
STO ⊠ 2% ⊟ 209.28 ⊞ RCL ⊟ 10,673.28

Had the transactions in the previous examples been *sales* of stock instead of *purchases*, the calculations would have been the same except that the odd-lot differential and the broker's commission, or fee, would have been *subtracted* from the total stock price.

Solve the following problems on buying and selling stock:

1. Spurrier and Associates charges a 2% commission on stock sales. Alice Terance sold 500 shares of Caterpillar stock at $48.70. Find the amount Ms. Terance will receive.

2. Thomas Hwan purchased 180 shares of EMC stock at $17.85. The odd-lot differential is 1% of the odd-lot portion, and the commission rate is 2.5% of the total stock price. Find the total cost to Mr. Hwan.

3. An investor bought 50 shares of a stock selling at $80.63. The odd-lot differential is $.25 per share, and the commission is 2%. Calculate the total cost of the transaction.

4. Three thousand shares of PepsiCo stock were sold at $48.44. The commission rate is 1.5%. How much did the seller receive?

21.2 Solutions to Practice Problems

1. $48.70 × 500 = $24,350
   $24,350 × 2% = − 487
   _____
                  $23,863

2. $ 17.85 $ 17.85 $1,428.00 $3,227.28
   ×   100   ×   80   ×   1%   ×   2.5%
   _____   _____   _____   _____
   $1,785.00 + $1,428.00 + $ 14.28 = $3,227.28 + $ 80.68 = $3,307.96

3. $80.63 $ 80.88 $4,044.00
   + .25   ×   50   ×   2%
   _____   _____   _____
   $80.88 $4,044.00 + $ 80.88 = $4,124.88

4. $ 48.44 $145,320.00
   ×   3,000   ×   1.5%
   _____   _____
   $145,320.00 − $ 2,179.80 = $143,140.20

LEARNING UNIT 3
PAYING DIVIDENDS

 21.3 ## Calculating Common Stock Dividends

For a business firm to become a corporation, it must be chartered by the state or states in which it does business. The corporate charter provides for the number of shares of stock that can be issued. However, not all stock that has been authorized for issue is always sold. The amount that is sold is called **outstanding stock**. All corporations have *common stock* outstanding, and some have *preferred stock* outstanding.

Stockholders are the owners of a corporation. When corporations earn profits, they either *retain* the profits for future operations and/or expansion or *distribute* the profits to the stockholders in the form of dividends. As the name implies, preferred stock has preference over common stock when dividends are paid. That is, holders of preferred stock are paid the dividends due them before any dividends are paid to holders of common stock. Common stock dividends will be discussed in this section, and preferred stock dividends will be discussed in the following section.

Cash Dividends
When a corporation declares a cash dividend payment, the dividends are distributed proportionately among stockholders of record on the date of declaration. Dividends are normally paid quarterly.

E X A M P L E   Occidental Petroleum declared dividends of $30,000,000 on its common stock to be paid to the shareholders of record on April 1. Fifty million shares of common stock were outstanding on that date. Sam Clement had 1,000 shares of Occidental's stock. How much did Sam receive in dividends?

Solution

$$\frac{\$30{,}000{,}000}{50{,}000{,}000} = \$.60 \text{ per share of stock}$$

1,000 shares × $.60 per share = $600 dividends

$$30{,}000{,}000 \div 50{,}000{,}000 \times 1{,}000 = 600$$

Stock Dividends

Sometimes a corporation that has stock authorized but not issued will declare a stock dividend. The dividend payment will then be made in additional shares of stock to each stockholder of record on the declaration date in proportion to the number of shares held. This declaration is made in accordance with a stated percent, for example, 5%.

E X A M P L E Praxair declared a 5% common stock dividend. Calculate the amount of the dividend paid to a stockholder who owns 1,000 shares of common stock.

Solution 1,000 shares × 5% = 50 shares (dividends to be paid)

21.3 Practice Problems

1. Alcan declared dividends of $3,215,892 on 10 million shares of stock. Prissy McGriff owned 5,000 shares. How much will she receive in dividends? (Round the dividend per share to the nearest cent.)

2. Bear Stearns declared a 2% stock dividend to stockholders of record on January 1. The total common stock outstanding is 55 million shares. What is the total number of common stock dividend shares to be paid?

3. CBS declared a 3.5% stock dividend to stockholders of record. Jonathan had 350 shares. How many dividend shares will he receive? (Round to the nearest whole share.)

4. CSX declared $1.04 per share dividend. Sterno Spangucci owns 570 of the 12 million shares outstanding. How much will Sterno receive, and what is the total amount of dividends declared by CSX?

21.3 Solutions to Practice Problems

1. $\dfrac{\$3{,}215{,}892}{10{,}000{,}000} = \$.32$ $.32 × 5{,}000 = \$1{,}600$

2. $55{,}000{,}000 × 2\% = 1{,}100{,}000$

3. $350 × 3.5\% = 12$

4. $570 × \$1.04 = \$592.80$ Sterno Spangucci's dividends
   $12{,}000{,}000 × \$1.04 = \$12{,}480{,}000$ Total amount of dividends

21.4 Calculating Preferred Stock Dividends

Preferred stock dividends are usually a fixed percent of their par value. The **par value** is a value arbitrarily assigned to stock at the time it is issued and is not an indication of its market value or selling price. When a stock sells at a price above the stated par value, which is most often the case, the difference is called the *premium*. If a stock sells at a price below the par value, the difference is called the *discount*.

Cash Dividends for Noncumulative Preferred Stock

Some preferred stock is **noncumulative**, which means that if dividends are not declared by the corporate board of directors in any given year, the dividends are lost forever to the stockholder.

E X A M P L E   Bolen Sage, Inc., declared preferred stock dividends to be paid to stockholders of record on June 30. The preferred stock has a par value of $100, and dividends are 5% of par value. Calculate the amount of dividends to be paid if there are 200,000 shares of outstanding stock.

Solution   Dividends per share:

$$\$100 \times 5\% = \$5$$

Total dividends to be paid:

$$\$5 \times 200,000 = \$1,000,000$$

$$100 \;\boxed{\times}\; 5\% \;\boxed{\times}\; 200,000 \;\boxed{=}\; 1,000,000$$

Cash Dividends for Cumulative Preferred Stock

Most preferred stock is **cumulative**. If the issuing company's board of directors declares dividends in a given year, the holders of preferred stock must be paid all dividends not declared in previous years plus the current year's dividends before the holders of common stock are paid any dividends.

E X A M P L E   Unisys has 700,000 shares of $100 par, 6% cumulative preferred stock outstanding. No dividends were paid last year. At this year's annual stockholders' meeting it was announced that sufficient dividends had been declared to bring the payment up to date. Compute the total amount of dividends to be paid to preferred stockholders.

Solution   *Step 1.* Calculate the dividends per share:

$$\$100 \times 6\% = \$6$$

Step 2. Calculate the total dividends to be paid per share (last year and this year):

$$\$6 \times 2 = \$12$$

Step 3. Calculate total dividends (last year and this year):

$$700,000 \times \$12 = \$8,400,000$$

$$100 \;\boxed{\times}\; 6\% \;\boxed{\times}\; 2 \;\boxed{\times}\; 700,000 \;\boxed{=}\; 8,400,000$$

Some companies have several issues of stock outstanding. When dividends are declared, the cumulative preferred stockholders must be brought up to date first. If the dividends are sufficient, all preferred stockholders receive dividends for the current year. Assuming there are still some dividends left over, the common stockholders are then paid.

E X A M P L E   WHX Corp. has the following common and preferred stock outstanding: 300,000 shares of $100 par, 5% cumulative preferred; 80,000 shares of $100 par, 7% noncumulative preferred; and 1,000,000 shares of common.

WHX did not declare dividends last year. This year the board declared total dividends of $5,060,000. Calculate the total amount of dividends and the dividends per share for each class of stock.

Solution   *Step 1.* Calculate the cumulative preferred stock dividends:

$$\$100 \times 5\% = \$5 \qquad \textit{Dividends per share}$$
$$2 \times \$5 = \$10 \qquad \textit{Total dividends per share}$$
$$300,000 \times \$10 = \$3,000,000 \qquad \textit{Total dividends to bring the cumulative}$$
$$\textit{preferred up to date}$$

Step 2. Calculate the noncumulative preferred stock dividends:

$100 \times 7\% = \$7$ *Dividends per share*

$\$7 \times 80{,}000 = \$560{,}000$ *Total dividends to bring the noncumulative preferred up to date*

Step 3. Calculate the total preferred stock dividends:

$3,000,000$
$+\ \ 560,000$
$\$3{,}560{,}000$ *Total dividends to be paid to preferred stockholders*

Step 4. Calculate the total dividends to be paid to common stockholders:

$5,060,000$
$-\ 3,560,000$
$\$1{,}500{,}000$ *Total dividends to be paid to common stockholders*

Step 5. Calculate the dividends per share paid to common stockholders:

$$\frac{\$1{,}500{,}000}{1{,}000{,}000} = \$1.50 \quad \textit{Dividends per share}$$

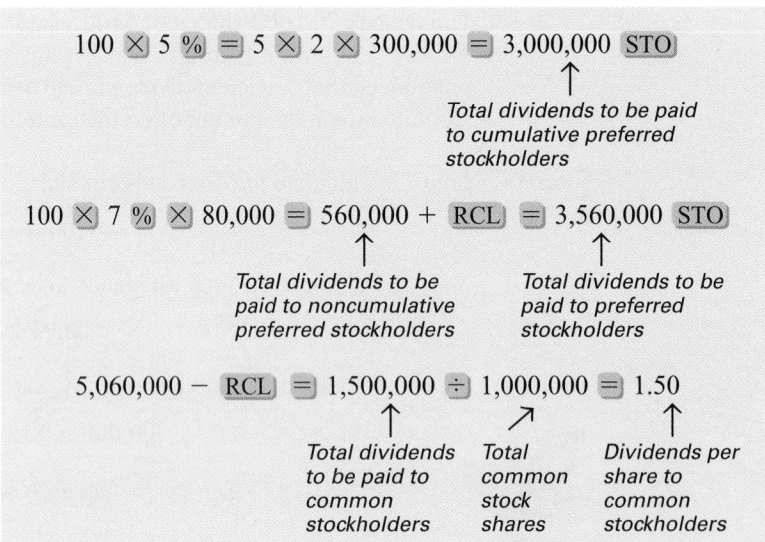

21.4
Practice
Problems

1. Alex Schroeder has 175 shares of noncumulative, $100 par, 5 1/2% preferred stock. He did not receive dividends last year, but the board of directors declared dividends this year sufficient to bring dividends up to date. How much will Mr. Schroeder receive in dividends?

2. Valero Energy has 657,000 shares of cumulative, $100 par, 6% preferred stock outstanding. The stockholders have not received dividends for the previous two years. The board of directors wants to declare dividends sufficient to bring them up to date. Find the minimum amount of dividends that will have to be declared.

3. Cinergy Corp. has the following common and preferred stock outstanding: 200,000 shares of $100 par, 4 1/2% cumulative preferred; 50,000 shares of $100 par, 6 1/2% noncumulative preferred; and 7,000,000 shares of common. Cinergy did not declare dividends last year. This year the board declared total dividends of $37,125,000. Calculate the total amount of dividends and the dividends per share for each class of stock.

4. U.S. Air Group has the following common and preferred stock outstanding: 500,000 shares of $100 par, 5% cumulative preferred; 75,000 shares of $100 par, 8% noncumulative preferred; and 4,500,000 shares of common. U.S. Air has not declared dividends for the two previous years. This year the board declared total dividends of $41,850,000. Calculate the total amount of dividends and the dividends per share for each class of stock.

21.4 Solutions to Practice Problems

1. $5.5\% \times \$100 = \$5.50$ per share
   $\$5.50 \times 175 = \$962.50$ Noncumulative dividends

2. $\$100 \times 6\% = \$6$ $\$6 \times 3 = \$18$ per share
   $\$18 \times 657,000 = \$11,826,000$ Dividends to bring cumulative dividends up to date

3. Calculate the cumulative preferred stock dividends:
   $4.5\% \times \$100 = \$4.50$ Dividends per share
   $2 \times \$4.50 = \$9$ Total dividends per share
   $200,000 \times \$9 = \$1,800,000$ Total dividends to bring the cumulative preferred up to date

   Calculate the noncumulative preferred stock dividends:
   $6.5\% \times \$100 = \$6.50$ Dividends per share
   $\$6.50 \times 50,000 = \$325,000$ Total dividends to bring the noncumulative preferred up to date

   Calculate the total dividends to be paid to preferred stockholders:
   $\$1,800,000$
   $\underline{+\ 325,000}$
   $\$2,125,000$ Total dividends to be paid to preferred stockholders

   Calculate the total dividends to be paid to common stockholders:
   $\$37,125,000$
   $\underline{-\ 2,125,000}$
   $\$35,000,000$ Total dividends to be paid to common stockholders

   Calculate the common stock dividends per share:
   $\dfrac{\$35,000,000}{7,000,000} = \$5$ Common stock dividends per share

4. Calculate the cumulative preferred stock dividends:
   $5\% \times \$100 = \$5$ Dividends per share
   $3 \times \$5 = \$15$ Total dividends per share
   $500,000 \times \$15 = \$7,500,000$ Total dividends to bring the cumulative preferred up to date

   Calculate the noncumulative preferred stock dividends:
   $8\% \times \$100 = \$8$ Dividends per share
   $\$8 \times 75,000 = \$600,000$ Total dividends to bring the noncumulative preferred up to date

   Calculate the total preferred stock dividends:
   $\$7,500,000$
   $\underline{+\ 600,000}$
   $\$8,100,000$ Total dividends to be paid to preferred stockholders

   Calculate the total common stock dividends:
   $\$41,850,000$
   $\underline{-\ 8,100,000}$
   $\$33,750,000$ Total dividends to be paid to common stockholders

   Calculate the common stock dividends per share:
   $\dfrac{\$33,750,000}{4,500,000} = \$7.50$ Dividends per share

LEARNING UNIT 4
BUYING AND SELLING BONDS

Bonds are a major source of corporate and government financing. A bond issued by public or private institutions is bought and sold through security brokers, much like corporate stock. Bonds generally are issued in $1,000 denominations, although the denomination, which is called the **face value,** can be more or less than $1,000.

A corporation needing long-term capital can sell additional stock, or it can sell bonds. Stock issues have several advantages, but one major disadvantage is that when others buy shares of stock, the current owners' percent share of the corporation is diluted. A bond does not represent ownership. A bond represents debt. Bondholders, then, are creditors of a corporation. The major disadvantages of bonds are that (1) the face value has to be paid back to the bondholders at maturity, and (2) interest must be

TABLE 21.3 — VALUE OF EIGHTHS OF 1

1/8	= .125	5/8		= .625
2/8 = 1/4	= .25	6/8 = 3/4		= .75
3/8	= .375	7/8		= .875
4/8 = 1/2	= .5			

paid to the bondholders at regular intervals over the life of the bond (see Table 21.1 for other comparisons).

Bond price quotations are stated in percent terms, as discussed further in the section on reading bond quotations. You might note that the price quotations are stated in eighths. It might be useful to review the value of eighths. They are shown in Table 21.3.

21.5 Reading Bond Quotations

The amount received by the investor at maturity is always the face value. However, a bond's market value commonly fluctuates. This fluctuation may be caused by the financial condition of the issuing company, by fluctuations in the current market interest rate, or by both. Table 21.4 shows a portion of the corporation bonds section from the *Wall Street Journal*.

EXAMPLE   Let's look at the Exxon bond found in Table 21.4:

BONDS	CUR YLD.	VOL.	CLOSE	NET CHG.
Exxon 6s05	5.7	5	106	−1½

Solution   The 6 (next to the company name) means that this bond is paying 6% interest. The 05 is the maturity date. That means that the face value of the bond will mature and be payable in 2005. The current yield (CUR YLD.) is 5.7. That can be found by dividing the annual interest by the closing price of the bond (CLOSE) as shown in the calculations following this explanation. The volume (VOL.) is 5. Volume is in thousands. That means 5,000 bonds were traded. The close is 106. That is the last price an Exxon bond sold for during the day. The 106 is the percent of face value at which the bond is selling. To find the price of the bond, multiply the face value, $1,000, by the quoted rate, 106 (106%): $1,000 × 106% = $1,060. The last column is the net change (NET CHG.). Exxon had a net change of −1½. That means the rate is 1½% lower than it was on the previous trading day. Following are calculations for the annual interest, the closing price in dollars, and the yield:

$$\text{Annual interest} = PRT$$
$$= \$1,000 \times 6\% \times 1$$
$$= \$60$$

$$\text{Closing price} = \text{close} \times \text{face value}$$
$$= 106\% \times \$1,000$$
$$= \$1,060$$

$$\text{Yield} = \frac{\text{annual interest}}{\text{closing price}}$$
$$= \frac{\$60}{\$1,060}$$
$$= .0566 = 5.7\%$$

TABLE 21.4 EXAMPLE OF BOND QUOTATIONS

U.S. EXCHANGE BONDS

Tuesday, November 27, 2001
Quotations as of 4 p.m. Eastern Time

DOW JONES BOND AVERAGES

2000 HIGH	2000 LOW	2001 HIGH	2001 LOW		2001 CLOSE	2001 CHG.	2001 %YLD	2000 CLOSE	2000 CHG.
97.41	93.23	104.66	97.85	20 Bonds	103.56	−0.54	7.17	95.68	+0.03
96.99	90.69	102.87	96.85	10 Utilities	101.24	−0.49	7.05	95.09	+0.36
99.86	95.53	106.89	98.86	10 Industrials	105.88	−0.60	7.30	96.26	−0.30

VOLUME

Total New York	$8,672,000
Corporation Bonds	$8,445,000
Foreign Bonds	$224,000
Amex Bonds	$1,623,000

SALES SINCE JAN. 1

New York

2001	$2,496,262,000
2000	$2,130,779,000
1999	$2,965,789,000

AMEX

2001	$196,197,000
2000	$106,819,000
1999	$166,919,000

DIARIES

New York	DOMESTIC TUE.	DOMESTIC MON.	ALL ISSUES TUE.	ALL ISSUES MON.
Issues Traded	130	139	139	145
Advances	46	44	50	47
Declines	59	72	63	74
Unchanged	25	32	26	24
New highs	5	3	5	3
New lows	3	5	3	5

AMEX	ALL ISSUES TUE.	MON.	FRI.	WED.
Issues Traded	14	14	5	7
Advances	6	8	2	1
Declines	6	2	2	6
Unchanged	2	4	1	0
New highs	1	0	1	0
New lows	0	0	0	

NEW YORK BONDS

Corporation Bonds •

BONDS	CUR YLD.	VOL.	CLOSE	NET CHG.
AES Cp 8s8	8.3	72	96	+1
AMR 9s16	9.2	49	97½	+½
ATT 7⅛02	7.1	25	100 1/16	−3/16
ATT 6½02	6.4	10	101 5/16	+1/16
ATT 6¾04	6.6	1	102⅜	−⅛
ATT 5⅝04	5.6	45	101⅛	...
ATT 7½06	7.1	81	105⅜	+¼
ATT 6s09	6.3	145	95¼	−⅛
ATT 8⅛22	8.0	66	102	+¼
ATT 8⅛24	8.0	31	101¾	−¼
ATT 8.35s25	8.1	37	103¼	−¼
ATT 6½29	7.6	552	85⅞	−¼
ATT 8⅝31	8.3	59	103⅝	...
Aames 10½02	11.0	1	95	−1½
AForP 5s30	8.3	3	60	+3⅞
ARetire 5¾02	cv	16	65	+3
BauschL 7⅛28	8.4	10	84½	...
BellsoT 6¼03	6.1	10	101⅞	...
BellsoT 6⅜04	6.2	15	103⅜	−1⅛
BellsoT 5⅞09	5.8	209	100⅝	−⅜
BellsoT 7⅞32	7.5	58	104⅝	...
BellsoT 7½33	7.3	80	103⅛	−⅛
BellsoT 6¾33	7.0	67	97⅛	−¾
BellsoT 7⅝35	7.4	62	103½	−⅜
vjBethS8.45s05f	...	328	9⅝	−1⅞
Bevrly 9s06	8.8	25	102½	−1
Bluegrn 8¼12	cv	10	66	−4
Bordn 8⅜16	10.0	17	83¾	−¼
BrnSh 9½06	9.3	30	102	−⅞
CallonP 10¼04	10.6	15	96¾	−⅛
Caterplnc 6s07	6.0	110	100⅝	...
Chkpnt 5¼05	cv	23	85	...
ClrkOil 9½04	9.6	75	98½	−⅛
Coeur 6⅜04	cv	50	31	+1
Consec 8⅛03	10.8	209	75⅛	−4⅞
Conseco 10¼02	11.9	1352	86	−2⅞
CrownC 7⅛02	13.3	427	53½	−3 15/32
CypSemi 4s05	cv	2	91	...
DR Hrtn 10s06	9.6	31	104	...
Deere 6.55s28	6.8	30	96⅛	−3⅝
DelcoR 8⅝07	8.6	25	100¾	+¾
DevonE 4.9s08	cv	4	100⅛	−⅞
Dole 7s03	6.9	18	102	+⅞
Dole 7⅞13	7.8	21	100¾	+¼
DukeEn 6¾25	6.7	18	100⅞	+1⅞
DukeEn 7½25	7.3	18	102⅜	−¾
DukeEn 7s33	6.9	12	101	+¼
Exxon 6s05	5.7	5	106	−1½
FUnRE 8⅞03	9.2	20	96⅝	+⅛
FordCr 6⅜08	6.3	5	101¼	+1¼
GBCB 8⅜07	8.7	20	96	−⅛
GMA 8½03	8.2	20	103⅞	...
GMA 6⅛08	6.2	30	99¼	−⅛
GMA zr12	...	12	443	...
GMA zr15	...	9	358	−3⅞
HewlPkd zr17	...	13	47	+1⅞
Hilton 5s06	cv	16	87½	+⅛
Hollngr 9¼06	9.3	330	99	+2
Honywll 9½16	7.5	4	127½	...
HuntPly 11¾04	117.5	25	10	+2
IPap dc5⅛12	5.9	12	87¾	−¾
JPMChse 7½03	7.3	10	103½	...
JPMChse 6½09	6.4	9	102¼	−¼
K&B Hm 9⅜03	9.3	100	101	...
K&B Hm 7¾04	7.7	12	101⅛	−⅛
K&B Hm 9⅝06	9.3	41	104	+½
Koppers 8½04	8.7	20	98	+6
Loews 3⅛07	cv	10	87	+1⅛
LglsLt 9s22	8.3	2	108½	+⅜
Lucent 7¼06	8.2	319	88⅝	...
Lucent 5½08	7.2	70	76½	−1½
Lucent 6½28	9.0	29	72	−¼
Lucent 6.45s29	9.3	68	69¼	−¼
MBNA 8.28s26	8.5	121	97	−2
Malan 9½04	cv	2	92½	−¾
MarO 7s02	6.9	125	101⅛	+1/32
McDnl 7.05s25	7.1	23	99	+3
MSDW 5⅝04	5.5	100	102¼	+⅛
Motrla zr13	...	1	76	+1
NRurU 5½05	5.4	20	101¼	−¼
NatwFS 8s27	7.9	35	100⅞	−2⅛
NETelTel 6⅛06	6.1	35	100½	−¼
NETelTel 6⅜08	6.3	30	101¼	+⅞
NYTel 6s07	6.0	10	100⅜	−¼
NYTel 7⅜11	7.3	10	101¼	−½
NYTel 7⅝23	7.4	5	102½	...
Noram 6s12	cv	35	95	−1
OcciP 10⅛09	8.4	30	120	...
OffDep zr07	...	6	78	+1⅞
OreStl 11s03	11.3	244	97¾	−¼
PhilPt 7.92s23	7.6	6	104½	−1
PhilPt 7.2s23	7.1	5	102	+1
PSvEG 7s24	7.2	25	97⅛	−2⅝
PSEG 5s37	6.8	25	74	+1¼
Quanx 6.88s07	cv	50	101	+¾
RalsP 7¾15	7.2	16	107¼	...
ReynTob 8⅝02	7.8	15	102½	...
ReynTob 7⅝03	7.5	6	102¼	...
ReynTob 8¾04	8.4	10	104½	+⅝
ReynTob 8¾05	8.3	3	105½	+⅛
ReynTob 9¼13	8.7	23	106½	−⅛
Safwy 9.65s04	8.9	21	109	−⅞
Safewy 6.85s04	6.5	5	105¾	...
SalSB 03t	...	20	98⅝	−½
SearsAc 6¾05	6.6	41	102½	−⅞
SvcCorp 6¾08	cv	100	114	−⅞
SilicnGr 5¼04	cv	131	52⅞	+½
Sizeler 8s03	cv	2	100	...
SoCG 6⅞02	6.8	5	101 1/32	+1/32
StdCmcl 07	cv	55	91¾	...
StdPac 8½07	8.6	14	99	−⅜
TVA 6⅞43	6.8	205	102	−1
Tenet 6s05	cv	10	98	−½
TerR 4s19	4.6	28	86⅛	+2⅛
TmeWar 7¾05	7.2	10	108	−1
TmeWar 8.18s07	7.4	9	109⅞	+1⅜
TmeWar 9.15s23	7.9	30	116	+1¾
TolEd 8s03	7.9	1	101	+¾
THilfig 6½03	6.6	115	99	...
US Timb 9⅝07	14.6	10	66	+5
vjUSG 8½05f	...	31	74	+2
UtdAir 10.67s04	13.0	318	82	+1½
Valhi zr07	...	1	58	−2¼
WsteM 4s02	cv	11	100¼	+19/32
Webb 9s06	8.9	10	101½	...
Webb 10¼10	9.6	10	107¼	−¾
WebbDel 9⅜09	9.0	67	104	−1
Weirton 10¾05f	...	149	10	+3¾
XeroxCr 7.2s12	9.5	10	76	−1

Foreign Bonds

BONDS	CUR YLD.	VOL.	CLOSE	NET CHG.
Inco cv04	cv	15	97	+⅝
Inco 7¾16	cv	90	99½	+1¾
SeaCnt 12½04A	15.2	10	82	...
SeaCnt 12½04B	16.2	10	77	−2
SeaCnt 10½03	12.6	9	83	−5
SeaCnt 9½03	11.4	16	83⅛	+⅞
TelMex 4¼04	cv	2	121	+5
TelArg 11⅞04	12.3	21	96⅜	−⅞
TrnMarMx 03	...	130	79½	+2⅜
TrnMarMx 06	cv	28	67½	−2

AMEX BONDS

BONDS	CUR YLD.	VOL.	CLOSE	NET CHG.
ABN C 12¾02	cv	25	99¾	−¾
ABN C 11.25s02	cv	14	95½	+1⅜
ABN T 11½03	cv	55	99½	+½
AdvMd 7¼02	cv	5	99	...
LehNdq100 04	...	1072	99	−½
Leh Prudents04	...	80	94	−1
Leh Prudents06	...	205	104	+¼
LehYeelds 8s03	7.8	3	102½	+2
ThmElec 4s05	cv	6	93½	...
Trump 11¾03f	...	14	71¼	−¾
UBS INTC02	cv	25	96	+½
UBS CSCO 02	cv	10	61	−½
UBS EMC 02	...	59	58¼	+2½
UBS JDSU 02	cv	10	59	−1¼

NASDAQ BONDS

BONDS	CUR YLD.	VOL.	CLOSE	NET CHG.
Agnico 3½04	cv	10	85¾	−3 11/64
Jacobsn 6¾11	cv	28	59	+3
Sys&Comp04	cv	10	88	...

EXPLANATORY NOTES

(For New York and American Bonds)

Yield is Current yield. Volume is in thousands.

cv-Convertible bond. cf-Certificates. **cld**-Called. dc-Deep discount. **ec**-European currency units. **f**-Dealt in flat. **il**-Italian lire. **kd**-Danish kroner. **m**-Matured bonds, negotiability impaired by maturity. **na**-No accrual. **r**-Registered. **rp**-Reduced principal. **st, sd**-Stamped. **t**-Floating rate. **wd**-When distributed. **ww**-With warrants. **x**-Ex interest. **xw**-Without warrants. **zr**-Zero coupon.
vj-In bankruptcy or receivership or being reorganized under the Bankruptcy Act, or securities assumed by such companies.

Source: The Wall Street Journal. (Reprinted with permission.)

21.5
Practice
Problems

Use Table 21.4 to solve the following problems about MBNA:

1. Find the market price of the bond.
2. How many MBNA bonds were traded?
3. What was the previous trading day's closing quote?
4. Show the calculation necessary to find the yield.

21.5 Solutions to Practice Problems

1. $1,000 × 97% = $970
2. 121,000 bonds were traded.
3. 97 + 2 = 99
4. Annual interest = *PRT*
   $$= \$1,000 \times 8.28\% \times 1$$
   $$= \$82.80$$

   Closing price = close × face value
   $$= 97\% \times \$1,000$$
   $$= \$970$$

   $$\text{Yield} = \frac{\text{annual interest}}{\text{closing price}}$$
   $$= \frac{\$82.80}{\$970}$$
   $$= .08536 = 8.5\%$$

21.6 Calculating Bond Discount and Premium

A **bond discount** is the amount for which a bond sells below its face value.

> **EXAMPLE** From Table 21.4, ATT 6½29 closed at 85 7/8. Calculate the amount of the discount.
>
> *Solution* That ATT bond is selling at
>
> $1,000 × 85 7/8% = $858.75
> $1,000 − 858.75 = $141.25   *The difference between the face value and the selling price is the amount of the discount.*

A **bond premium** is the amount for which a bond sells above its face value.

> **EXAMPLE** From Table 21.4, ATT 8 5/8 31 closed at 103 5/8. Calculate the amount of the premium.
>
> *Solution* That ATT bond is selling at
>
> $1,000 × 103 5/8% = $1,036.25
> $1,036.25 − 1,000 = $36.25   *The difference between the selling price and the face value is the amount of the premium.*

21.6
Practice
Problems

Find the premium or discount in the following problems:

1. Find the discount for Conseco 10¼02 that closed at 86.
2. Xerox Corporation's 7.2s12 closed at 76. Find the discount.
3. Bell South's 6 3/8 04 bond closed at 103 3/8. Find the premium.
4. Ford Credit 6 3/8 08 closed at 101¼. Find the premium.

21.6 Solutions to Practice Problems

1. $1,000 × 86% = $860 $1,000 − 860 = $140 Discount

2. $1,000 \times 76\% = \$760$ $\$1,000 - 760 = \$240$ Discount
3. $1,000 \times 103\ 3/8\% = \$1,033.75$ $\$1,033.75 - 1,000 = \$33.75$ Premium
4. $1,000 \times 101\ 1/4\% = \$1,012.50$ $\$1,012.50 - 1,000 = \$12.50$ Premium

EXCEL Spreadsheet Application Spreadsheet Application 2 at the end of this chapter is a form designed to help Springfield keep track of its bond transactions.

21.7 Buying and Selling Bonds

The buyer or seller of bonds must pay a fee to the broker handling the transactions. The fee varies from broker to broker, but a common charge is as follows:

1–49 bonds	$5 each
50 bonds and over	$2.50 each

For this book, problems will assume these charges unless stated otherwise. In addition, since bonds pay interest at specified periods, the amount of accumulated unpaid interest at the date of transaction completion must be added to the market price of the bonds. Bond interest for this purpose is always calculated using ordinary time and interest. That is, 30-day months and 360-day years. The principal is always the face value of the bond (not the market value).

Buying Bonds

EXAMPLE   Calculate the total transaction cost of purchasing ten $1,000 bonds quoted at 104 3/8. The last interest payment was on January 1, and the transaction settlement date is April 1. The interest rate on the bonds is 8 3/4%.

Solution   *Step 1.* Determine the market price:

Market price = face value × number of bonds × quoted percent
$$= \$1,000 \times 10 \times 104.375\%$$
$$= \$10,437.50 \text{ Total market price}$$

Step 2. Determine the accumulated unpaid interest:

$I = PRT$

Time from January 1 to April 1:

January	29 days	$(30 - 1 = 29)$
February	30 days	
March	30 days	
April	+ 1 day	
Total	90 days	

$$I = \$1,000 \times 8.75\% \times \frac{90}{360} = \$21.875 \text{ per bond}$$

$\$21.875 \times 10 \text{ bonds} = \$218.75 \text{ Total interest}$

Step 3. Determine the broker's fee:

Broker's fee = fee per bond × number of bonds
$$= \$5 \times 10$$
$$= \$50 \text{ Total fee}$$

Step 4. Determine the total purchase price by adding the total market price, interest, and broker's fee:

Total purchase price = $10,437.50 + 218.75 + 50
$$= \$10,706.25$$

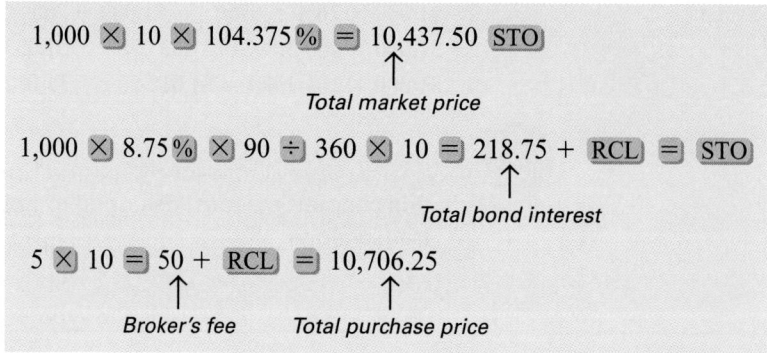

$$1,000 \times 10 \times 104.375\% = 10,437.50 \;\boxed{STO}$$

↑
Total market price

$$1,000 \times 8.75\% \times 90 \div 360 \times 10 = 218.75 + \boxed{RCL} = \boxed{STO}$$

↑
Total bond interest

$$5 \times 10 = 50 + \boxed{RCL} = 10,706.25$$

↑   ↑
Broker's fee   *Total purchase price*

Selling Bonds

EXAMPLE   Calculate the total transaction receipts from selling 60 $1,000 bonds quoted at 92 1/2 on September 13. The last interest payment was on July 1. The interest rate on the bonds is 6%.

Solution   **Step 1**   Determine the market price:

$$\text{Market price} = \text{face value} \times \text{number of bonds} \times \text{quoted percent}$$
$$= \$1,000 \times 60 \times 92.5\%$$
$$= \$55,500 \text{ Total market price}$$

Step 2   Determine the accumulated unpaid interest:

$I = PRT$

Time from July 1 to September 12:

July	29 days (30 − 1 = 29)
August	30 days
September	+ 13 days
Total	72 days

$$I = \$1,000 \times 6\% \times \frac{72}{360} = \$12 \text{ per bond}$$

$$\$12 \times 60 = \$720 \text{ Total interest}$$

Step 3   Determine the broker's fee:

$$\text{Broker's fee} = \text{fee per bond} \times \text{number of bonds}$$
$$= \$2.50 \times 60$$
$$= \$150 \text{ Total fee}$$

Step 4   Determine the total receipts by adding the total market price and interest, and subtracting the broker's fee:

$$\text{Total receipts} = \$55,500 + 720 - 150 = \$56,070$$

$$1,000 \times 60 \times 92.5\% = 55,500 \;\boxed{STO}$$

↑
Total market price

$$1,000 \times 6\% \times 72 \div 360 \times 60 = 720 + \boxed{RCL} = \boxed{STO}$$

↑
Total bond interest

$$2.50 \times 60 = 150 \;\boxed{+/-} + \boxed{RCL} = 56,070$$

↑   ↑
Broker's fee   *Total sales receipts*

Find the purchase price or sales receipts in the following problems:

1. James Utley purchased 3 Ametek 8 1/8% $1,000 bonds quoted at 86. Calculate the total purchase price if the bonds were bought on March 10 and interest was last paid as of December 31.

2. Quinten McDonald sold 10 Philadelphia Electric 9 5/8% bonds at 102 1/2 on October 20. Interest was last paid as of June 30. Find the total receipts.

3. Office Depot sold 100 9 7/8 97 bonds at 98 5/8. The transaction date was April 22 and interest was last paid as of December 31. Calculate the total receipts.

4. Martha Chen bought four 10 1/8 02 bonds at 75 3/8 on June 12. Interest was last paid on December 31. Find the total purchase price.

21.7 Solutions to Practice Problems

1. Determine the market price:

$$\text{Market price} = \text{number of bonds} \times \text{face value} \times \text{quoted percent}$$
$$= 3 \times \$1,000 \times 86\%$$
$$= \$2,580 \text{ Total market price}$$

Determine the accumulated unpaid interest:

$I = PRT$

Time from December 31 to March 10:

January	30 days
February	30 days
March	+ 10 days
Total	70 days

$$I = \$1,000 \times 8.125\% \times \frac{70}{360} = \$15.80 \text{ per bond}$$

$$\$15.80 \times 3 = \$47.40 \text{ Total interest}$$

Determine the broker's fee:

$$\text{Broker's fee} = \text{Number of bonds} \times \text{Fee per bond}$$
$$= 3 \times \$5$$
$$= \$15 \text{ Total fee}$$

Determine the total purchase price by adding the total market price, interest, and broker's fee:

$$\text{Total cost} = \$2,580 + 47.40 + 15$$
$$= \$2,642.40$$

2. Determine the market price:

$$\text{Market price} = \text{number of bonds} \times \text{face value} \times \text{quoted percent}$$
$$= 10 \times \$1,000 \times 102.5\%$$
$$= \$10,250 \text{ Total market price}$$

Determine the accumulated unpaid interest:

$I = PRT$

Time from June 30 to October 20:

July	30 days
August	30 days
September	30 days
October	+ 20 days
Total	110 days

$$I = \$1,000 \times 9.625\% \times \frac{110}{360} = \$29.41 \text{ per bond}$$

$$\$29.41 \times 10 = \$294.10 \text{ Total interest}$$

Determine the broker's fee:

$$\text{Broker's fee} = \text{number of bonds} \times \text{fee per bond}$$
$$= 10 \times \$5$$
$$= \$50 \text{ Total fee}$$

Determine the total sales receipts by adding the total market price and interest, and subtracting the broker's fee:

$$\text{Total receipts} = \$10,250 + 294.10 - 50$$
$$= \$10,494.10$$

3. Determine the market price:

$$\text{Market price} = \text{number of bonds} \times \text{face value} \times \text{quoted percent}$$
$$= 100 \times \$1,000 \times 98.625\%$$
$$= \$98,625 \text{ Total market price}$$

Determine the accumulated unpaid interest:

$I = PRT$

Time from December 31 to April 22:

January	30 days
February	30 days
March	30 days
April	+ 22 days
Total	112 days

$$I = \$1,000 \times 9.875\% \times \frac{112}{360} = \$30.72 \text{ per bond}$$

$\$30.72 \times 100 = \$3,072$ Total interest

Determine the broker's fee:

$$\text{Broker's fee} = \text{number of bonds} \times \text{fee per bond}$$
$$= 100 \times \$2.50$$
$$= \$250 \text{ Total fee}$$

Determine the total sales receipts by adding the total market price and interest, and subtracting the broker's fee:

$$\text{Total receipts} = \$98,625 + 3,072 - 250$$
$$= \$101,447$$

4. Determine the market price:

$$\text{Market price} = \text{number of bonds} \times \text{face value} \times \text{quoted percent}$$
$$= 4 \times \$1,000 \times 75.375\%$$
$$= \$3,015 \text{ Total market price}$$

Determine the accumulated unpaid interest:

$I = PRT$

Time from December 31 to June 12:

January	30 days
February	30 days
March	30 days
April	30 days
May	30 days
June	+ 12 days
Total	162 days

$$I = \$1,000 \times 10.125\% \times \frac{162}{360} = \$45.56 \text{ per bond}$$

$\$45.56 \times 4 = \$182.24$ Total interest

Determine the broker's fee:

$$\text{Broker's fee} = \text{number of bonds} \times \text{fee per bond}$$
$$= 4 \times \$5$$
$$= \$20 \text{ Total fee}$$

Determine the total purchase price by adding the total market price, interest, and broker's fee:

$$\text{Total cost} = \$3,015 + 182.24 + 20$$
$$= \$3,217.24$$

Page	Section Topic	Learning Concepts	Examples and Solutions
719	**21.1** Calculating Earnings per Share and Yield Percent	Stock quotations are found in many sources such as the *Wall Street Journal*. Calculations are made to determine stock yield percent and earnings per share	Given the quote for Newport News, calculate (1) the yield percent and (2) the earnings per share.

YTD YLD %	52 WK HI	LO	STOCK	SYM	DIV	YLD %	PE	VOL 100S	LAST	NET CHG
+28.3	73.85	45.19	NewportNews	NNS	.16	.2	22	31506	66.74	+0.31

(1) $\text{Yield \%} = \dfrac{\text{dividend}}{\text{last price}}$

$\text{Yield \%} = \dfrac{\$.16}{\$66.74}$

$= .2\%$

(2) $\text{Earnings} = \dfrac{\text{last price}}{\text{P/E ratio}}$

$= \dfrac{\$66.74}{22}$

$= \$3.03$

Page	Section Topic	Learning Concepts	Examples and Solutions
721	**21.2** Calculating Round-Lot, Odd-Lot, and Combination Sales	Stocks are transacted in round-lots (100) or odd-lots (less than 100). A fee is charged for odd-lots. Brokers charge a fee or commission for transaction costs. That charge is added to the cost of a stock purchase or subtracted from the receipts in a sale of stock.	Yolanda Septula sold 255 shares of stock at $40.38. An odd-lot differential of $.25 per share is charged on the odd-lot portion. The broker charged a commission of 1.75% on the total stock price. Determine the total receipts.

Round-Lot:

$\begin{array}{r} \$\quad 40.38 \\ \times \quad\quad 200 \\ \hline \$8,076.00 \end{array}$

Odd-Lot:

$\begin{array}{r} \$40.38 \\ -\quad .25 \\ \hline \$40.13 \end{array}$ $\begin{array}{r} \$\quad 40.13 \\ \times \quad\quad 55 \\ \hline \$2,207.15 \end{array}$

Receipts:

$\begin{array}{r} \$\ 8,076.00 \\ +\ 2,207.15 \\ \hline \$10,283.15 \end{array}$

Broker's Commission

$\begin{array}{r} \$10,283.15 \\ \times \quad 1.75\% \\ \hline \$\quad 179.96 \end{array}$

Total Receipts

$\begin{array}{r} \$10,283.15 \\ -\quad 179.96 \\ \hline \$10,103.19 \end{array}$

Page	Section Topic	Learning Concepts	Examples and Solutions
723	**21.3** Calculating Common Stock Dividends	Dividends are paid in either cash or additional shares.	<u>Cash Dividends</u> Dividends of $300,000 were declared to be paid to the stockholders of the 250,000 outstanding shares. Calculate the dividend to be paid for each share of stock.

$\dfrac{\$300,000}{250,000} = \$1.20$

<u>Stock Dividends</u>

A 3% stock dividend was declared. Calculate the dividend to be received by a stockholder owning 17,000 shares.

$17,000 \times 3\% = 510$ dividend shares

QUICK REFERENCE SUMMARY AND REVIEW

Page	Section Topic	Learning Concepts	Examples and Solutions
724	**21.4** Calculating Preferred Stock Dividends	Preferred stock dividends are stated as a percent of par value. The dividends are either *noncumulative* (if a dividend is not declared in a given year, the dividends are never to be paid) or *cumulative* (dividends not paid in previous years and the current year must be paid before common stockholders are paid).	Dividends were declared this year. None were declared last year. The corporation has 20,000 shares of $100 par, 10% noncumulative preferred, and 50,000 shares of $100 par, 8% cumulative pf. Calculate the amount of dividends required to bring the dividend payments up to date. Noncumulative $$\$100 \times 10\% = \$10$$ $$\$10 \times 20,000 = \$200,000$$ Cumulative $$\$100 \times 8\% = \$8$$ $$\$8 \times 2 = \$16$$ $$\$16 \times 50,000 = \$800,000$$ Total $$\begin{array}{r}\$\ 200,000 \\ +\ 800,000 \\ \hline \$1,000,000\end{array}$$
728	**21.5** Reading Bond Quotations	A bond's value fluctuates on the market. At maturity, an investor receives the face value. Calculations are made to find the closing price and the yield of the bond.	BONDS: RJR Nb 8 3/4 04, CUR. YLD. 9.4, VOL. 182, CLOSE 92 5/8, NET CHG. +1/2 Use the quotation above to find the closing price and verify the yield. Annual interest = PRT $$= \$1,000 \times 8\tfrac{3}{4}\% \times 1 = \$87.50$$ Closing price = close × face value $$= 92\ 5/8\% \times \$1,000$$ $$= \$926.25$$ $$\text{Yield} = \frac{\text{annual interest}}{\text{closing price}}$$ $$= \frac{\$87.50}{\$926.25}$$ $$= 9.4\%$$
730	**21.6** Calculating Bond Discount and Premium	A bond selling below its face value is selling at a discount. If it is selling above its face value, it is selling at a premium.	Two different bonds are selling at 95 3/8 and 104 respectively. Find the discount for the first bond and the premium for the second. (1) $95.375\% \times \$1,000 = \$953.75$ $\$1,000 - 953.75 = \$46.25$ Discount (2) $104\% \times \$1,000 = \$1,040$ $\$1,040 - 1,000 = \$40$ Premium

QUICK REFERENCE SUMMARY AND REVIEW

Page	Section Topic	Learning Concepts	Examples and Solutions
731	**21.7** Buying and Selling Bonds	Buyers and sellers of bonds must pay a fee to the broker. The fee varies, but a typical fee is $5 each for 1–49 bonds and $2.50 each for 50 bonds and over. Also, accumulated bond interest must be added to the price of the bond. Time for the interest calculation always assumes 30-day months and 360-day years.	Calculate the sales receipts and the buying costs for five $1,000, 9% bonds quoted at 94 if the last interest payment was on 12/31 and the transaction settlement date is 3/5.

Market Price

$$5 \times \$1,000 \times 94\% = \$4,700$$

Unpaid Interest

$I = PRT$

Jan.	30 days
Feb.	30 days
Mar.	5 days
	65 days

$$= \$1,000 \times 9\% \times \frac{65}{360}$$
$$= \$16.25 \text{ (for each bond)}$$
$$5 \times \$16.25 = \$81.25$$

Broker's Fee

$$5 \times \$5 = \$25$$

Total Purchase Price

$$\$4,700 + 81.25 + 25 = \$4,806.25$$

Total Sales Receipts

$$\$4,700 + 81.25 - 25 = \$4,756.25$$

SURFING THE INTERNET

For further information on the topics covered in this chapter, check out the following sites:

http://www.dailystocks.com/

http://www.fmsbonds.com/bondbasics.html

http://www.teenanalyst.com/stocks/stockquotes.html

ADDITIONAL
PRACTICE
PROBLEMS

Answers to odd-numbered problems are given in Appendix A.

21.1

Use the following quotation to solve problems 1 through 5:

YTD % CHG.	52 WK. HI	52 WK. LO	STOCK	SYM.	DIV.	YLD. %	PE	VOL. 100S	LAST	NET CHG.
16.8	59.75	38.99	PPG Ind	PPG	1.68	3.1	21	4493	54.11	−0.29

1. What are the 52-week hi and lo prices for PPG Ind?
    hi $59.75 low $38.99

2. Determine the earnings per share for PPG Ind.
    Ratio = P/E
    Earnings = price/ratio
    $$= \frac{\$54.11}{21} = \$2.58$$

3. Verify that the yield was calculated correctly for PPG Ind.

$$\text{Yield} = \frac{\text{dividend}}{\text{price}} \qquad \text{Yield} = \frac{\$1.68}{\$54.11} = .031 = 3.1\%$$

4. Calculate the previous day's last price for PPG Ind.

$54.11 + .29 = $54.40

5. How many shares of PPG Ind. were traded?

449,300

21.2

Solve the following problems on buying and selling stock:

6. Newburg Brokerage Co. charges a 1.75% commission on stock sales. Sarah Jones sold 300 shares of New Age stock at $15.38. Find the amount Ms. Jones will receive.

$ 15.38	$ 4,614.00	$4,614.00
× 300	× 1.75%	− 80.75
$ 4,614	$ 80.75	$4,533.25

7. Martin Shwibager purchased 165 shares of Maytag stock at $20.75. The odd-lot differential is 1% of the odd-lot portion and the commission rate is 2% of the total stock price. What is the total cost to Mr. Shwibager?

$ 20.75	$ 20.75	$1,348.75	$1,348.75	$ 2,075.00
× 100	× 65	× 1%	+ 13.49	+ 1,362.24
$2,075.00	$1,348.75	$ 13.49	$1,362.24	$ 3,437.24
↑	↑	↑	↑	↑
Round-lot cost	Odd-lot portion	Odd-lot differential	Odd-lot cost	Total stock cost

$3,437.24	$3,437.24
× 2%	+ 68.74
$ 68.74	$3,505.98
↑	↑
Commission	Total cost

8. An investor bought 40 shares of stock selling at $50.88. The odd-lot differential is $.25 per share; and the commission is 2.3%. Calculate the total cost of the transaction.

$ 50.88	$ 51.13	$2,045.20	$2,045.20
+ .25	× 40	× 2.3%	+ 47.04
$ 51.13	$2,045.20	$ 47.04	$2,092.24
↑	↑	↑	↑
Odd-lot differential	Odd-lot cost	Commission	Total cost

9. Eight thousand shares of ECC Int stock were sold at $10.50. The commission rate is 1.75%. How much did the seller receive?

$ 10.50	$84,000.00	$84,000.00
× 8,000	× 1.75%	− 1,470.00
$84,000.00	$ 1,470.00	$82,530.00

10. Nadine Warabi sold 700 shares of GTE stock at $48.25. The commission was 1.5%. How much did she receive?

$ 48.25	$33,775.00	$33,775.00
× 700	× 1.5%	− 506.63
$33,775.00	$ 506.63	$33,268.37

21.3

Calculate the common stock dividends for the following problems:

11. Corning declared dividends of $18 million on 25 million shares of stock. Orinthal McGarity owned 450 shares. How much will he receive in dividends?

$$\frac{\$18,000,000}{25,000,000} = \$.72 \text{ per share} \qquad 450 \times \$.72 = \$324 \text{ Dividends}$$

12. ChiquitaBrd declared a 2% stock dividend to stockholders of record on January 1. The total common stock outstanding is 44,500,000 shares. What is the total number of common stock dividend shares to be paid?

44,500,000 × 2% = 890,000 shares

13. GATX declared a 5.5% stock dividend to stockholders of record. Juan had 350 shares. How many dividend shares will he receive? (Round your answer to the nearest whole share.)

350 × 5.5% = 19 Shares

14. Hershey declared a dividend of $1.30 per share. Myaki Dage owns 750 of the 12 million shares outstanding. How much will she receive, and what is the total amount of dividends declared?

750 × $1.30 = $975 Myaki will receive
12,000,000 × $1.30 = $15,600.000 Total amount declared

15. Ronald Blair was a stockholder of record with 8,500 shares when IBM declared $1.29 per share cash dividend and 2.5% stock dividends. Calculate the amount of cash and stock dividends he received. (Round the stock dividends to the nearest whole share.)

8,500 × $1.29 = $10,965.00 Cash dividends
8,500 × 2.5% = 213 Stock dividends

21.4

Calculate the preferred stock dividends for the following problems:

16. Alice Johansen has 325 shares of noncumulative, $100 par, $7\frac{1}{2}$% preferred stock. She did not receive dividends last year, but the board of directors declared dividends this year. How much will Alice receive in dividends?

325 × ($100 × $7\frac{1}{2}$%) = $2,437.50 Noncumulative dividends

17. Cooper Ind has 550,000 shares of cumulative, $100 par, 5% preferred stock outstanding. The stockholders have not received dividends for the previous two years. The board of directors wants to declare dividends sufficient to bring them up to date. What is the minimum amount of dividends that will have to be declared?

$100 × 5% = $5 per share per year $5 × 3 = $15 per share to bring them up to date

550,000 × $15 = $8,250,000 Minimum

18. ChaseManh has the following common and preferred stock outstanding:

120,000 shares of $100 par, $6\frac{1}{2}$% cumulative preferred stock

80,000 shares of $100 par, 9 1/2% noncumulative preferred stock

2,000,000 shares of common stock

The company did not declare dividends last year. This year the board declared total dividends of $7,230,000. Calculate the total amount of dividends and the dividends per share for each class of stock.

Cumulative Preferred
$100 × 6.5% = $6.50 $6.50 × 2 = $13 Dividends per share
$13 × 120,000   = $1,560,000 Total dividends

Noncumulative Preferred
$100 × 9.5% = $9.50 per share $9.50 × 80,000 = $760,000 Total dividends

Common Stock

| $1,560,000 | $ 7,230,000 | $4,910,000 = $2.455 |
| + 760,000 | −2,320,000 | 2,000,000   per share |

$2,320,000 to preferred $ 4,910,000 to common
         stockholders   stockholders

19. KeyCorp has the following common and preferred stock outstanding:

250,000 shares of $100 par, 6% cumulative preferred stock

25,000 shares of $100 par, 8% noncumulative preferred stock

5,000,000 shares of common stock

KeyCorp has not declared dividends for the two previous years. This year the board declared total dividends of $9,200,000. Calculate the total amount of dividends and the dividends per share for each class of stock.

Cumulative Preferred
$100 × 6% = $6 $6 × 3 = $18 Dividends per share
$18 × 250,000 = $4,500,000 Total dividends

Noncumulative Preferred
$100 × 8% = $8 per share $8 × 25,000 = $200,000 Total dividends

Common Stock

| $4,500,000 | $ 9,200,000 | $4,500,000 = $.90 |
| + 200,000 | −4,700,000 | 5,000,000   per share |

$4,700,000 to preferred $ 4,500,000 to common
         stockholders   stockholders

20. JP Morgan has the following common and preferred stock outstanding:

250,000 shares of $100 par, 5% cumulative preferred stock

200,000 shares of $100 par, 9% noncumulative preferred stock

15,000,000 shares of common stock

Dividends were not declared last year. This year the board declared total dividends of $49,300,000. Calculate the total amount of dividends and the dividends per share for each class of stock.

Cumulative Preferred
$100 × 5% = $5 $5 × 2 = $10 Dividends per share
$10 × 250,000 = $2,500,000 Total dividends

Noncumulative Preferred
$100 × 9% = $9 per share $9 × 200,000 = $1,800,000 Total dividends

Common Stock

| $2,500,000 | $49,300,000 | $45,000,000 = $3 per |
| +1,800,000 | − 4,300,000 | 15,000,000   share |

$4,300,000 to preferred $45,000,000 to common
         stockholders   stockholders

21.5

Use the following information to solve problems 21 through 25:

Bonds	Cur. Yld.	Vol.	Close	Net Chg.
Lily 8 3/8 06	8.1	59	103	−1/2

21. Find the market price of the bonds.

$1,000 × 103.625% = $1,036.25

22. How many Lily bonds were traded?

59,000

23. What was the previous trading day's closing quote?

103 5/8 + 1/2 = 104 1/8

24. What is the annual amount of interest Lily must pay per bond?

$1,000 × 8.375% = $83.75 Annual interest

25. Show the calculation necessary to find the yield.

From question 24, annual interest = $83.75 = .0808 = 8.1%
From question 21, market price = $1,036.25

21.6

Find the premium or discount in the following problems:

26. Navisstar's 8 5/8 09 $1,000 bond closed at 88. Find the discount.

$1,000 × 88 = $880 $1,000 − 880 = $120 Discount

27. MBNA's 6 1/2 07 $1,000 bond closed at 105 1/4. Find the premium.

$1,000 × 105.25% = $1,052.50 $1,052.50 − 1,000 = $52.50 Premium

28. Chubb's 10 5/8s 11 $1,000 bond closed at 102 7/8. Find the premium.

$1,000 × 102.875% = $1,028.75 $1,028.75 − 1,000 = $28.75 Premium

29. Goodrich's 5 1/8 08 $1,000 bonds closed at 79 1/2. Find the discount.

$1,000 × 79.5% = $795 $1,000 − 795 = $205 Discount

30. CrwnCrfts 8 3/8 17 $1,000 bonds closed at 68 3/4. Find the discount.

$1,000 × 68.75% = $687.50 $1,000 − 687.50 = $312.50 Discount

21.7

Find the purchase price or sales receipts in the following problems:

31. Harvey Spay purchased 8 Citicorp 8 1/4% bonds quoted at 96. Calculate the total purchase price if the bonds were bought on May 14 and interest was last paid as of March 31.

April   30 days $1,000 $8,000.00 × 8.25% × $\frac{44}{360}$ = $80.67 Bond interest
May + 14 days   ×   8
        44 days $8,000
                        Face value
                        of bonds

$8,000 × 96% = $7,680   8 × $5 = $40 $7,680.00
            Market value   Commission   80.67
            of bonds   + 40.00
                                                     $7,800.67 Total purchase price

32. Richard Quick sold 15 GettyPete 7 7/8 10 bonds at 104 1/8 on August 12. Interest was last paid as of June 30. Find the total receipts.

July   30 days $ 1,000 $15,000 × 7.875% × $\frac{42}{360}$ = $137.81 Bond Interest
Aug. + 12 days   ×   15
        42 days $15,000
                     Face value
                     of bonds

$15,000 × 104.125% = $15,618.75   15 × $5 = $75
            Market value   Commission
            of bonds

$15,618.75 + 137.81 − 75 = $15,681.56   Sales receipts

33. Fansteel sold 100 12 7/8 19 bonds at 93 3/8. The transaction date was March 2 and interest was last paid as of December 31. Calculate the total sales receipts.

Jan.   30 days $ 1,000 $100,000 × 12.875% × $\frac{62}{360}$ = $2,217.36 Bond Interest
Feb.   30 days   ×   100
Mar. + 2 days $100,000
        62 Days   Face value
                      of bonds

$100,000 × 93.375% = $93,375   100 × $2.50 = $250
            Market value   Commission
            of bonds

$93,375 + 2,217.36 − 250 = $95,342.36   Sales receipts

34. Morgan Cherry bought four 6 1/4 09 bonds at 65 3/4 on June 2. Interest was last paid on December 31. Find the total purchase price.

Jan.   30 days $1,000 $4,000 × 6.25% × $\frac{152}{360}$ = $105.56 Bond Interest
Feb.   30 days   ×   4
Mar.   30 days $4,000   Face value of bonds
Apr.   30 days
May   30 days
June + 2 days
        152 days

$4,000 × 65.75% = $2,630   Market value of bonds   4 × $5 = $20   Commission
$2,630 + 105.56 + 20 = $2,755.56   Purchase price

35. Lanora Spandow bought 20 9 3/4 15 bonds at 108 5/8. Calculate the total purchase price if the bond transaction date was May 24 and interest was last paid on April 31.

May 24 days $ 1,000 $20,000 × 9.75% × $\frac{24}{360}$ = $130   Bond Interest
                     ×   20 $20,000 × 108.625% = $21,725   Market value of bonds
                     $20,000   Face value of bonds   20 × $5 = $100   Commission
                                                                     $21,725 + 130 + 100 = $21,955   Purchase price

Answers to odd-numbered problems are given in Appendix A.

Drill Problems

Use the information given to calculate the remainder of the information:

	STOCK	DIV.	YLD. %	PE	EARNINGS PER SHARE	LAST	NET CHG.	PREVIOUS CLOSE
1.	Exel	$1.30	$3.5%	10	$3.71	37.12	−0.25	$37.37
2.	IFG	.64	2.8%	6	3.77	22.63	+0.50	22.13
3.	KemperCp	.92	2.4%	8	4.75	38	−1	39
4.	EthylCp	.50	5.0%	14	.71	10	+0.12	9.88
5.	CTS	.40	1.5%	54	.51	27.50	+0.75	26.75

Calculate the sales receipts or the purchase cost of the following transactions:

	SHARES BOUGHT (B) OR SOLD (S)	STOCK QUOTE	ODD-LOT DIFFERENTIAL	BROKER'S COMMISSION	SALES RECEIPTS	PURCHASE COST
6.	1,000 (B)	28.88		2%	$	$29,457.60
7.	280 (S)	7.75	1/8	2.5%	2,106	
8.	55 (S)	83.50	1/4	1.5%	4,510.07	
9.	725 (B)	33.12	1/8	2%		24,495.43
10.	3,000 (S)	13		3%	37,830.00	

Fill in the appropriate blanks in the following common stock cash and stock dividend problems. (Round stock dividends to the nearest whole share.)

	TOTAL SHARES OUTSTANDING	SHARES HAROLD OWNS	TOTAL CASH DIVIDENDS DECLARED	% OF STOCK DIVIDENDS DECLARED
11.	300,000	150	$ 150,000	5.0%
12.	4,400,000	2,000	8,140,000	3.0%
13.	2,750,000	565	2,612,500	3.5%
14.	32,000,000	25,000	76,800,000	7.5%
15.	680,000	1,920	938,400	2.5%
16.	9,500,000	1,500	3,800,000	3.5%

	TOTAL STOCK DIVIDENDS DECLARED	CASH DIV. PER SHARE	HAROLD'S TOTAL CASH DIV.	HAROLD'S TOTAL STOCK DIV.
11.	15,000	$ .50	$ 75.00	8
12.	132,000	1.85	3,700	60
13.	96,250	.95	536.75	20
14.	2,400,000	2.40	60,000	1,875
15.	17,000	1.38	2,649.60	48
16.	332,500	.40	600	53

In the following problems, calculate the dividends per share for each of the three classifications of stock (noncumulative preferred, cumulative preferred, and common stock) for which information is given. The column "Yrs. W/O Div." represents the years in which no dividends were paid, and do not include this year.

	SHARES OF NONCUMULATIVE PREFERRED	PAR VALUE	RATE	SHARES OF CUMULATIVE PREFERRED	PAR VALUE	RATE	YRS W/O DIV.
17.	150,000	$100	6.0%				
18.				325,000	$100	6.5%	1
19.	75,000	100	10%	350,000	100	7.8%	3
20.	200,000	100	8.5%	1,000,000	100	5.0%	0
21.	25,000	100	12%	100,000	100	7.5%	4

	SHARES OF COMMON STOCK	TOTAL AMT. OF DIVIDENDS DECLARED	NONCUM. DIVS. PER SHARE	CUM. DIVS. PER SHARE	COMMON STK. DIV. PER. SH.
17.	700,000	$ 2,700,000	$ 6.00		$2.57
18.	3,400,000	6,945,000		13.00	.80
19.	7,000,000	35,470,000	10.00	31.20	3.40
20.	24,000,000	26,860,000	8.50	5.00	.84
21.	560,000	2,120,000	0.00	21.20	0.00

Fill in the missing information in the following bond quotation problems:

	BOND	ANNUAL INT.	YLD. %	CLOSE	NET CHG.	PREVIOUS CLOSE	CURRENT MKT. PRICE
22.	Mead $6\frac{1}{4}$ 09	$ 62.50	6.6%	$94\frac{7}{8}$	$-\frac{1}{4}$	$95\frac{7}{8}$	$ 948.75
23.	Nynex $12\frac{1}{8}$ 10	121.25	11.8%	$102\frac{1}{2}$	$+\frac{1}{8}$	$102\frac{3}{8}$	1,025.00
24.	Pulte $9\frac{3}{4}$ 12	97.50	9.6%	$101\frac{5}{8}$	$+\frac{3}{8}$	$101\frac{1}{4}$	1,016.25
25.	Digital $7\frac{1}{2}$ 10	75.00	7.1%	$106\frac{3}{8}$	$+ 2$	$104\frac{3}{8}$	1,063.75
26.	Intel 5.9 11	59.00	6.2%	$95\frac{3}{4}$	$-\frac{3}{4}$	$96\frac{1}{2}$	957.50

Calculate the amount of premium or discount in the following problems:

	BOND	CLOSE	PREMIUM	DISCOUNT
27.	Mead $6\frac{1}{4}$ 09	$94\frac{7}{8}$	$	$51.25
28.	Nynex $12\frac{1}{8}$ 10	$102\frac{1}{2}$	25.00	
29.	Pulte $9\frac{3}{4}$ 12	$101\frac{5}{8}$	16.25	
30.	Digital $7\frac{1}{2}$ 10	$106\frac{3}{8}$	63.75	
31.	Intel 5.9 21	$95\frac{3}{4}$		42.50

Calculate the broker's fee, accumulated unpaid interest, current market price, and total purchase cost or total sales receipts in the following problems. Assume the broker's fee to be based on the following:

1–49 bonds $5.00 each
50 bonds and over $2.50 each

	TRANSACTION TYPE	NO.	QUOTE	LAST INT. PAYMENT	TRANSACTION DATE	BROKER'S FEE
32.	Purchase	5	$101\frac{3}{8}$	June 30	July 20	$ 25.00
33.	Sale	10	94	December 31	February 8	50.00
34.	Sale	160	$67\frac{7}{8}$	March 31	June 21	400.00
35.	Purchase	85	$105\frac{3}{4}$	September 30	October 24	212.50
36.	Sale	4	100	December 31	March 25	20.00

	BOND RATE	BOND INTEREST	CURRENT MKT. PRICE	TOTAL PURCHASE COST	TOTAL SALES RECEIPTS
32.	$9\frac{1}{4}$%	$ 25.69	$ 5,068.75	$ 5,119.44	$
33.	$6\frac{3}{8}$%	67.29	9,400.00		9,417.29
34.	$12\frac{1}{2}$%	4,500.00	108,600.00		112,700.00
35.	$8\frac{1}{8}$%	460.42	89,887.50	90,560.42	
36.	7%	66.11	4,000.00		4,046.11

Word Problems

Use the following quotation to solve problems 37 through 41:

52 WK.					YLD.		VOL.		NET
HI	LO	STOCK	SYM.	DIV.	%	PE	100S	LAST	CHG.
29.37	21.38	NICOR	GAS	1.26	5.2	12	638	24.13	+.37

37. What are the 52-week hi and lo prices for NICOR?
hi $29.37 per share   lo $21.38 per share

38. Determine the earnings per share for NICOR.
$$\text{Ratio} = \frac{P}{E} \qquad E = \frac{P}{\text{Ratio}} = \frac{\$24.13}{12} = \$2.01$$

39. Verify that the yield was calculated correctly for NICOR.
$$\frac{\$1.26}{\$24.13} = 5.2\%$$

40. Calculate the previous day's last price for NICOR.
$24.13 − .37 = $23.76

41. How many shares of NICOR were traded?
63,800

42. Quinn & Co., a brokerage firm, charges a 2.5% commission on stock sales. Rachel Todd sold 500 shares of Utley Corp. stock at $35.34. Find the amount Ms. Todd will receive.

$ 35.34	$17,670.00	$17,670.00
× 500	× 2.5%	− 441.75
$17,670.00	$ 441.75	$17,228.25

43. Paula Coniberio purchased 345 shares of GE stock at $78.75. The odd-lot differential is 1% of the odd-lot portion and the commission rate is 2% of the total stock price. What is the total cost to Paula?

$ 78.75	$ 78.75	$3,543.75	$23,625.00
× 300	× 45	× 1%	3,543.75
$23,625.00	$3,543.75	$ 35.44	+ 35.44
			$27,204.19

$27,204.19	$27,204.19
× 2%	+ 544.08
$ 544.08	$27,748.27 Total cost

44. Thomas Fwabzii sold 1,200 shares of PennP&L stock at $25.25. The commission was 1.5%. How much did he receive?

$ 25.25	$30,300.00	$30,300.00
× 1,200	× 1.5%	− 454.50
$30,300.00	$ 454.50	$29,845.50

45. Columbia Electric Utility Co. declared dividends of $8 million on 12 million shares of stock. Roger McMurtry owned 850 shares. How much will he receive in dividends?

$$\frac{\$8,000,000}{12,000,000} = \$.67 \text{ per share}$$

$$\begin{array}{r} 850 \\ \times\ \underline{\$.67} \\ \$569.50 \end{array}$$

46. Prestley Tot's, Inc., declared a dividend of $1.62 per share. Meg Hill owns 230 of the 2,350,000 shares outstanding. How much will she receive, and what is the total amount of dividends declared?

$$\begin{array}{r} \$\ \ \ 1.62 \\ \times\ \underline{\ \ \ 230} \\ \$372.60 \ \ \text{Meg's dividend} \end{array}$$

$$\begin{array}{r} \$\ \ \ \ \ \ 1.62 \\ \times\ \underline{2,350,000} \\ \$\ 3,807,000 \ \ \text{Total} \end{array}$$

47. Williams was a stockholder of record with 205,000 shares when Urgertl Leblanc declared cash dividends of $1.21 per share and 2.5% stock dividends. Calculate the amount of cash and stock dividends Williams received.

$$\begin{array}{r} 205,000 \\ \times\ \underline{\$\ \ \ 1.21} \\ \$248,050 \ \ \text{Cash dividend} \end{array}$$

$$\begin{array}{r} 205,000 \\ \times\ \underline{2.5\%} \\ 5,125 \ \ \text{Stock dividend} \end{array}$$

48. OmniCraft has the following common and preferred stock outstanding:

140,000 shares of $100 par, 7 1/2% cumulative preferred stock

70,000 shares of $100 par, 9 1/2% noncumulative preferred stock

1,500,000 shares of common stock

It did not declare dividends last year. This year the board declared total dividends of $4,250,000. Calculate the total amount of dividends and the dividends per share for each class of stock.

Cumulative Preferred
$100 × 7.5% = $7.50 $7.50 × 2 = $15 Dividends per share
$15 × 140,000 = $2,100,000 Total dividends
Noncumulative Preferred
$100 × 9.5% = $9.50 per share $9.50 × 70,000 = $665,000 Total
Common Stock

$$\begin{array}{r} \$2,100,000 \\ +\ \underline{\ 665,000} \\ \$2,765,000 \ \text{to preferred} \\ \text{stockholders} \end{array}$$

$$\begin{array}{r} \$\ 4,250,000 \\ -\ \underline{\ 2,765,000} \\ \$\ 1,485,000 \ \text{to common} \\ \text{stockholders} \end{array}$$

$$\frac{\$1,485,000}{1,500,000} = \$.99 \text{ per share}$$

49. TaxCo has the following common and preferred stock outstanding:

220,000 shares of $100 par, $5\frac{1}{2}$% cumulative preferred stock

250,000 shares of $100 par, $9\frac{1}{8}$% noncumulative preferred stock

7,000,000 shares of common stock

It has not declared dividends for the two previous years. This year the board declared total dividends of $14,311,250. Calculate the total amount of dividends and the dividends per share for each class of stock.

Cumulative Preferred
$100 × 5.5% = $5.50 $5.50 × 3 = $16.50   Dividends per share
$16.50 × 220,000 = $3,630,000   Total dividends
Noncumulative Preferred
$100 × 9.125% = $9.125   per share
$9.125 × 250,000 = $2,281,250   Total
Common Stock

$$\begin{array}{r} \$\ 3,630,000 \\ +\ \underline{2,281,250} \\ \$\ 5,911,250 \ \text{to preferred} \\ \text{stockholders} \end{array}$$

$$\begin{array}{r} \$14,311,250 \\ -\ \underline{\ 5,911,250} \\ \$\ 8,400,000 \ \text{to common} \\ \text{stockholders} \end{array}$$

$$\frac{\$8,400,000}{7,000,000} = \$1.20 \text{ per share}$$

50. RJR-Nabisco's 6 5/8 04 bond closed at 82. Find the discount.
$1,000 × 82% = $820 $1,000 − 820 = $180 Discount

51. WXYZ's 12 1/2 07 bond closed at 107 3/8. Find the premium.
$1,000 × 107.375% = $1,073.75 $1,073.75 − 1,000 = $73.75 Premium

52. PetrolFuel's 4 07 bonds closed at 68 3/4. Find the discount.
$1,000 × 68.75% = $687.50 $1,000 − 687.50 = $312.50 Discount

53. Gerald Archibald purchased five BkAmer 8 1/4% bonds quoted at 91. Calculate the total purchase price if the bonds were bought on May 2 and interest was last paid as of March 31.

Apr.   30 days
May + 2 days
       32 days

$$\$5,000 \times 8.25\% \times \frac{32}{360} = \$36.67 \text{ Interest}$$

$$\begin{array}{r} \$5,000 \\ \times\ \underline{91\%} \\ \$4,550 \ \text{Market Price} \end{array}$$

$$\begin{array}{r} \$\ 5 \\ \times\ \underline{5} \\ \$25 \ \text{Broker's fee} \end{array}$$

$4,550 + 36.67 + 25 = $4,611.67   Purchase price

54. Sally Goecher bought four 6 1/4 09 bonds at 75 3/8 on June 22. Interest was last paid on December 31. Find the total purchase price.

Jan.   30 days
Feb.   30 days
Mar.   30 days
Apr.   30 days
May   30 days
June + 22
         172 days

$$\$4,000 \times 6.25\% \times \frac{172}{360} = \$119.44 \text{ Interest}$$

$$\begin{array}{r} \$\ \ \ 4,000 \\ \times\ \underline{75.375\%} \\ \$\ \ \ 3,015 \ \text{Market price} \end{array}$$

$$\begin{array}{r} \$\ 5 \\ \times\ \underline{4} \\ \$\ 20 \ \text{Broker's fee} \end{array}$$

$3,015 + 119.44 + 20 = $3,154.44 Purchase price

55. Manny Espanosa sold 25 7 3/8 02 bonds at 104. Calculate the total sales receipts if the bond transaction date was June 2 and interest was last paid on April 30.

May   30 days
June + 2 day
      32 days

$$\$25,000 \times 7.375\% \times \frac{32}{360} = \$163.89 \text{ Interest}$$

$$\begin{array}{r} \$25,000 \\ \times\ \underline{104\%} \\ \$26,000 \ \text{Market price} \end{array}$$

$$\begin{array}{r} \$\ \ 5 \\ \times\ \underline{25} \\ \$125 \ \text{Broker's fee} \end{array}$$

$26,000 + 163.89 − 125 = $26,038.89 Purchase price

56. An investor bought 40 shares of stock selling at $45.86. The odd-lot differential is $.25 per share, and the commission is 3%. Calculate the total cost of the transaction.

$$
\begin{array}{cccc}
\$45.86 & \$\quad 46.11 & \$1,844.40 & \$1,844.40 \\
+\ .25 & \times \qquad 40 & \times \qquad 3\% & +\quad 55.33 \\
\hline
\$46.11 & \$1,844.40 & \$\quad 55.33 & \$1,899.73
\end{array}
$$

57. Eight thousand shares of Tennessee Walkers, Inc., stock was sold at $1.50. The commission rate is 2.5%. How much did the seller receive?

$$
\begin{array}{ccc}
\$\quad 1.50 & \$12,000 & \$12,000 \\
\times\ 8,000 & \times\ 2.5\% & -\quad 300 \\
\hline
\$ 12,000 & \$\quad 300 & \$11,700
\end{array}
$$

58. LCR declared an 8% stock dividend to stockholders of record on January 1. The total common stock outstanding is 1,500,000 shares. What is the total number of common stock dividend shares to be paid?
$1,500,000 \times 8\% = 120,000$ shares

59. CoastWtch declared a 7.5% stock dividend to stockholders of record. Nick had 850 shares. How many dividend shares will he receive? (Round your answer to the nearest whole share.)
$850 \times 7.5\% = 64$ shares

60. Denise Utlander has 405 shares of noncumulative, $100 par, $8\frac{1}{2}\%$ preferred stock. She did not receive dividends last year, but the board of directors declared dividends this year sufficient to bring the dividends up to date. How much will Denise receive in dividends?
$100 \times 8.5\% = \$8.50$ per share $\$8.50 \times 405 = \$3,442.50$

61. Kmart has 500,000 shares of cumulative, $100 par, 8% preferred stock outstanding. The stockholders have not received dividends for the previous three years. The board of directors wants to declare dividends sufficient to bring them up to date. What is the minimum amount of dividends that will have to be declared?
$100 \times 8\% = \$8$ Dividends per share $\$8 \times 4 = \$32$ For four years
$500,000 \times \$32 = \$16,000,000$ Minimum

62. PropMgrsCorp has the following common and preferred stock outstanding:

150,000 shares of $100 par, 7% cumulative preferred stock

100,000 shares of $100 par, 11% noncumulative preferred stock

2,000,000 shares of common stock

Dividends were not declared last year. This year the board declared total dividends of $9,200,000. Calculate the total amount of dividends and the dividends per share for each class of stock.

Cumulative Preferred
$100 \times 7\% = \$7$ $\$7 \times 2 = \$14$ Dividends per share
$14 \times 150,000 = \$2,100,000$ Total dividends
Noncumulative Preferred
$100 \times 11\% = \$11$ per share $\$11 \times 100,000 = \$1,100,000$ Total
Common Stock

$$
\begin{array}{ll}
\$\ 2,100,000 & \$\ 9,200,000 \\
+\ 1,100,000 & -\ 3,200,000 \\
\hline
\$\ 3,200,000 \text{ to preferred} & \$\ 6,000,000 \text{ to common} \\
\qquad\text{stockholders} & \qquad\text{stockholders}
\end{array}
$$

$\dfrac{\$6,000,000}{2,000,000} = \$3$ per share

Use the following information to solve problems 63 through 67:

BONDS	CUR. YLD.	VOL.	CLOSE	NET CHG.
Owen 7 3/8 06	8.8	34	83 7/8	−1/4

63. Find the market price of the bonds.
$1,000 \times 83.875\% = \$838.75$

64. How many Owen bonds were traded?
34,000

65. What was the previous trading day's closing quote?
83 7/8 + 1/4 = 84 1/8

66. Show the calculation necessary to find the yield.
$1,000 \times 7.375\% = \$73.75$ Annual interest
$1,000 \times 83.875\% = \$838.75$ Market value
$\dfrac{\$73.75}{\$838.75} = 8.8\%$

67. What is the annual amount of interest Owen must pay?
$1,000 \times 7.375\% = \$73.75$ Annual interest

68. PershRug's 12 5/8s 21 bond closed at 106 5/8. Find the premium.
$1,000 \times 106.625\% = \$1,066.25$ $\$1,066.25 - 1,000 = \$66.25$ Premium

69. Goodyear's 4 3/4 15 closed at 67 1/2. Find the discount.
$1,000 \times 67.5\% = \$675$ $\$1,000 - 675 = \$325$ Discount

70. Willard Clark sold 25 BalliHigh 9 1/8 10 bonds at 102 1/2 on September 22. Interest was last paid as of June 30. Find the total receipts.

July   30 days $\$25,000 \times 9.125\% \times \dfrac{82}{360} = \$519.62$ Interest
Aug.   30 days
Sept. + 22 days
        82 days

$$
\begin{array}{ll}
\$\ 25,000 & \$\ 5 \\
\times\ 102.5\% & \times\ 25 \\
\hline
\$\ 25,625 \text{ Market price} & \$125 \text{ Broker's fee}
\end{array}
$$

$25,625 + 519.62 - 125 = \$26,019.62$ Total receipts

71. USX bought 100 6 7/8 99 bonds at 73 3/8. The transaction date was April 2 and interest was last paid as of December 31. Calculate the total purchase cost.

Jan. 30 days $\$100,000 \times 6.875\% \times \dfrac{92}{360} = \$1,756.94$ Interest $\$\ 100,000$

Feb. 30 days $\underline{\times\ 73.375\%}$

Mar. 30 days $\$\ \ \ \ \ 73,375$ Market price

Apr. $\underline{+\,2}$ days $100 \times \$2.50 = 250$ Broker's fee

       92 days

$\$73,375 + 1,756.94 + 250 = \$75,381.94$ Total purchase price

---

✓ ENRICHMENT PROBLEM

72. The Brown Investment Group's (BIG) management has agreed to make some additions to and deletions from its portfolio. Their broker charges a 2% commission on stock transactions. Bond transactions are at $3.50 per bond for any number bought or sold. The odd-lot differential is 1% of the total odd-lot portion. On April 4 the following transactions were made:

A. Buy 250 shares of General Electric stock at $55.35 per share. The current dividend is $1.65 per share and the PE ratio is 15.

B. Buy 50 Office Depot $1,000 9% bonds. The last interest payment was made on December 31. The bonds were quoted at $103\frac{5}{8}$

C. Sell 200 shares of Ford Motor stock at $29.25 per share. The current dividend is $1.10 per share and the P/E ratio is 6.5.

  1. For the General Electric and the Ford Motor stock, calculate the following:

    (a) Yield percent

    (b) Per-share earnings

    (c) Total purchase price for the General Electric stock

    (d) Total sales receipts for the Ford Motor stock.

  2. For the Office Depot bonds, calculate the following:

    (e) Premium

    (f) Annual interest

    (g) Current yield

    (h) Total purchase price

  3. Find the net amount (purchase prices − sales receipts) that must be paid to the broker to settle the transactions.

1. General Electric   Ford Motor

(a) $\dfrac{\$1.65}{\$55.35} = 3.0\%$ Yield percent $\dfrac{\$1.10}{\$29.25} = 3.8\%$ Yield percent

(b) Earnings $= \dfrac{P}{\text{Ratio}}$ Earnings $= \dfrac{P}{\text{Ratio}}$

           $= \dfrac{\$55.35}{15}$ $= \dfrac{\$29.25}{6.5}$

           $= \$3.69$ $= \$4.50$

(c) $200 \times \$55.35 = \ \ \ \ \$11,070.00$ (d) $200 \times \$29.25 = \$5,850$

     $50 \times \$55.35 = \ \ \ \ \ \ 2,767.50$ $\$5,850 \times 2\% = \underline{-\ \ 117}$

     $\$2,767.50 \times 1\% = \underline{+\ \ \ \ \ 27.68}$ $\$5,733$

                          $\$13,865.18$ Sales receipts

     $\$13,865.18 \times 2\% = \underline{+\ \ \ 277.30}$

                          $\$14,142.48$

                     Purchase price

2. Office Depot

(e) $\$1,000 \times 103.625\% = \$1,036.25$ $\$1,036.25 - 1,000 = \$36.25$ Premium per bond

     $\$36.25 \times 50 = \$1,812.50$ Total premium

(f) $\$1,000 \times 9\% = \$90$ Annual interest per bond

     $50 \times \$90 = \$4,500$ Total annual interest

(g) $\dfrac{\$90}{\$1,036.25} = 8.7\%$ Current yield

(h) Jan.   30 days $50 \times \$1,000 \times 9\% \times \dfrac{94}{360} = \$1,175$ Interest $\$\ \ 3.50$

     Feb.   30 days $\underline{\times\ \ \ \ \ 50}$

     Mar.   30 days $\$175.00$ Broker's fee

     Apr. $\underline{+\,4}$ days

            94 days $(50 \times \$1,036.25) + 1,175 + 175 = \$53,162.50$ Purchase price

3. Net Amount

     $\$14,142.48 + 53,162.50 - 5,733 = \$61,571.98$ Net amount due broker

You own the Great Experiment, an electronics specialty store. Lately you have been concerned that you have been thinking too much about the present and trying to keep your head above water, and too little about the future and retirement. While you still plan on the profits from your business to be a major contributor to your future, you have decided to diversify your investment exposure. Your first purchase of securities is listed here:

STOCKS

NUMBER PURCHASED	NAME	PRICE	DIV.
150 shares	GTE	39.50	1.88
75 shares	IBM	113.63	1.40
125 shares	KmartF pf	49.98	3.88

BONDS

NUMBER PURCHASED	NAME	QUOTE
10 bonds	CompUSA 9 1/2 20	104
55 bonds	BellsoT 5 7/8 09	97 3/4

Your broker charges a 2.5% commission rate on stock transactions. The odd-lot differential is $.25 per share for stock selling below $50 per share and $.125 per share for stock selling at $50 or above per share. For bonds, the broker's fee is $5 per bond if fewer than 50 are purchased, and $2.50 per bond if 50 or more are purchased.

1. Describe each issue that was purchased. (For example, 150 shares of GTE common stock were purchased for $39.50 per share. GTE is currently paying a dividend of $1.88 per share.)

   150 shares of GTE common stock were purchased for $39.50 per share. GTE is currently paying a dividend of $1.88 per share.
   75 shares of IBM common stock were purchased at $113.63 per share. IBM is currently paying a dividend of $1.40 per share.
   125 shares of Kmart preferred stock were purchased at $49.98 per share. Kmart is currently paying a dividend of $3.88 per share.
   10 CompUSA bonds were purchased at a premium of 104% of their $1,000 face value. The bonds pay a 9.5% interest rate per year and come due in the year 2020.
   55 Bell South Telephone bonds were purchased at a discount of 97.75% of their $1,000 face value. The bonds pay a 5.875% interest rate per year and come due in the year 2009.

2. Calculate the yield for each of the securities purchased.

   GTE: $1.88 ÷ 39.50   = 4.8%
   IBM: $1.40 ÷ 113.63   = 1.2%
   Kmart: $3.88 ÷ 49.98   = 7.8%
   CompUSA: $95 ÷ 1,040   = 9.1%
   BellsoT: $58.75 ÷ 977.50   = 6.0%

   $$\left(\text{Yield} = \frac{\text{dividends or interest}}{\text{purchase price}} \right)$$

3. Compute the cost of each common stock issue before the broker's fee is added.

   GTE: 100 × $39.50 = $ 3,950.00
           50 × ($39.50 + .25) = + 1,987.50
                                    $ 5,937.50
   IBM: 75 × ($113.63 + .125) = $8,531.62

4. Compute the cost of each preferred stock issue before the broker's fee is added.

   Kmart pf: 100 × $49.98 = $4,998.00
                25 × ($49.98 + .25) = + 1,255.75
                                       $6,223.75

5. Calculate the broker's fee for the stock purchases.

   $5,937.50 + 8,531.62 + 6,223.75 = $20,692.87
                                    ×   2.5%
                                    $ 517.32

6. Calculate the total cost of the stock purchases.

   $20,692.87 + 517.32 = $21,210.19

7. Which bond is selling at a premium and what is the amount of the premium per bond?

   CompUSA is selling at $1,040 per bond: $1,040 − 1,000 = $40 Premium

8. Which bond is selling at a discount and what is the amount of the discount per bond?

   BellsoT is selling at $977.50 per bond: $1,000 − 977.50 = $22.50 Discount

9. Calculate the cost of the bond purchases before the broker's fee is added.

10 × 104% × $1,000 = $10,400.00
55 × 97.75% × $1,000 = + 53,762.50
$64,162.50

10. Calculate the broker's fee for the bond purchases.

10 × $5 = $ 50.00
55 × $2.50 = + 137.50
$ 187.50

11. The transaction date was April 27 and interest was last paid as of December 31 on both bond issues. Calculate the amount of accumulated unpaid bond interest.

Jan.   30 days
Feb.   30 days
Mar.   30 days
Apr . + 27 days
Total 117 days

CompUSA: $I = \$1,000 \times 10 \times 9.5\% \times \dfrac{117}{360} = \$308.75$

BellsoT: $I = \$1,000 \times 55 \times 5.875\% \times \dfrac{117}{360} = \$1,050.16$

12. What is the total purchase cost of the bonds?

$64,162.50 + 187.50 + 308.75 + 1,050.16 = $65,708.91

13. What is the total cost of all stock and bond purchases?

$21,210.19 + 65,708.91 = $86,919.10

SELF-TESTING EXERCISES

Answers to all exercises are given in Appendix A.

1. What is the difference between cumulative and noncumulative preferred stock?

If a corporation misses paying dividends in any given year, the holders of noncumulative preferred stock will never receive those dividends. Cumulative preferred stockholders, however, must be paid missed years' dividends and current years' dividends before common stockholders receive any dividends.

2. Differentiate between stocks and bonds.

a. Stocks represent ownership: bonds represent debt.
b. Cash payment for bonds is interest and must be paid each year. Cash payment for stocks is dividends if declared, but dividends never have to be paid.
c. Stock has no maturity date. Bonds do have a maturity date, and the face value of the bonds must be paid to bondholders on that date.
d. Common stockholders have voting rights. Preferred stockholders usually have no voting rights. Bondholders are not entitled to vote unless the interest or the face value are not paid when due.
e. Upon liquidation, stockholders receive payment after bondholders.

Use the following quote to solve problems 3, 4 and 5:

YTD % CHG.	52 WK. HI	LO	STOCK	SYM.	DIV.	YLD. %	PE	VOL. 100S	LAST	NET CHG.
+3.7	39.27	23.33	JBCInd	JBI	1.52		16	750	34.12	+0.87

3. Determine the earnings per share for JBCInd.

$\text{Earnings} = \dfrac{\text{last price}}{\text{ratio}} = \dfrac{\$34.12}{16} = \$2.13$

4. Calculate the yield for JBCInd.

$\text{Yield} = \dfrac{\text{dividend}}{\text{last price}} = \dfrac{\$1.52}{\$34.12} = 4.5\%$

5. Calculate the previous day's last price for JBCInd.

$34.12 − .87 = $33.25

6. Knoblock Investments charges a 2% commission on stock sales. Linda Ten Horse sold 500 shares of John Deere stock at $44.39. Find the amount Ms. Ten Horse will receive.

$44.39 × 500 = $22,195.00
$22,195 × 2% = − 443.90
$21,751.10

7. Taylor Adams purchased 180 shares of RCA stock at $37.75. The odd-lot differential is 1% of the odd-lot portion, and the commission rate is 3% of the total stock price. What is the total cost to Mr. Adams?

$37.75 × 100   = $3,775.00 Round-lot cost
$37.75 × 80   = 3,020.00 Odd-lot cost before differential
$3,020 × 1%   = + 30.20 Odd-lot differential cost
                  $6,825.20 Total stock cost
$6,825.20 × 3% = + 204.76 Commission
                  $7,029.96 Total cost

8. AmerCanCo declared dividends of $7,480,000 on 5.5 million shares of common stock. Jane Pitney owned 2,500 shares. How much will she receive in dividends?

$\dfrac{\$7,480,000}{5,500,000} = \$1.36$ per share

$ 1.36
× 2,500
$ 3,400 Total dividends

9. Merrill Lynch declared a 7% stock dividend to stockholders of record on January 1. The total common stock outstanding is 75,000,000 shares. What is the total number of common stock dividend shares to be paid?
75,000,000 × 7% = 5,250,000

10. NBC declared a 2.5% stock dividend to stockholders of record. Louis had 950 shares. How many dividend shares will he receive? (Round your answer to the nearest whole share.)
950 × 2.5% = 24

11. Stan Booker has 4,100 shares of noncumulative, $100 par, 9 1/2% preferred stock. He did not receive dividends last year, but the board of directors declared dividends this year. How much will Mr. Booker receive in dividends?
$100 × 9.5% = $9.50 per share   4,100 × $9.50 = $38,950

12. Discount Warehouse has 350,000 shares of cumulative, $100 par, 6% preferred stock outstanding. The stockholders have not received dividends for the previous three years. The board of directors want to declare dividends sufficient to bring them up to date. What is the minimum amount of dividends that will have to be declared?
$100 × 6% = $6   Dividends per share per year
$6 × 4 = $24   Total dividends per share
350,000 × $24 = $8,400,000   Minimum

13. FBCN has the following common and preferred stock outstanding:

   100,000 shares of $100 par, 6 1/2% cumulative preferred stock

   250,000 shares of $100 par, 9 1/2% noncumulative preferred stock

   40,000,000 shares of common stock

   It did not declare dividends last year. This year the board declared total dividends of $140,480,000. Calculate the total amount of dividends and the dividends per share for each class of stock.
   Cumulative Preferred
   $100 × 6.5% = $6.50 $6.50 × 2 = $13   Dividends per share
   $13 × 100,000 = $1,300,000   Total dividends
   Noncumulative Preferred
   $100 × 9.5% = $9.50 per share
   $9.50 × 250,000 = $2,375,000 Total
   Common Stock

   $ 1,300,000 $140,480,000 $\frac{\$136,805,000}{40,000,000} = \$3.42$ per share
   + 2,375,000   − 3,675,000
   $ 3,675,000 to preferred $136,805,000 to common
            stockholders   stockholders

Use the following bond quote information to solve problems 14 through 17:

BONDS	CUR. YLD.	VOL.	CLOSE	NET CHG.
MarCorp7 3/8 07		33	76 5/8	−1 1/2

14. Find the market price of the bonds.
$1,000 × 76.625% = $766.25

15. What was the previous trading day's closing quote?
$76\dfrac{5}{8} + 1\dfrac{1}{2} = 78\dfrac{1}{8}$

16. What is the annual amount of interest MarCorp must pay for each bond in the issue?
$1,000 × 7.375% = $73.75

17. Calculate the yield.
$\text{Yield} = \dfrac{\text{interest}}{\text{market price}} = \dfrac{\$73.75}{\$766.25} = 9.6\%$

18. Southwestern Bell's 7 1/8 12 bond closed at 96 3/8. Find the discount.
$1,000 × 96.375% = $963.75 $1,000 − 963.75 = $36.25

19. Geico's 9 7/8 17 bond closed at 107 1/2. Find the premium.
$1,000 × 107.5% = $1,075 $1,075 − 1,000 = $75

20. Jamu Amhadi purchased 90 Ametek 5 1/8% bonds quoted at 76 3/4. Calculate the total purchase price if the bonds were bought on April 4 and interest was last paid as of December 31.

   Jan.   30 days $ 90,000 × 5.125% × $\dfrac{94}{360}$ = $1,204.38   Interest $ 90,000
   Feb.   30 days   × 76.75%
   Mar.   30 days   90 × $2.50 = $225   Broker's fee $ 69,075   Market price
   Apr. + 4 days
        94 days
   $69,075 + 1,204.38 + 225 = $70,504.38   Total purchase price

21. Cliff Brazos sold 15 Vermont Gas Co. 8 5/8% bonds at 103 1/8 on August 12. Interest was last paid as of June 30. Find the total receipts.

   July   30 days $ 15,000 × 8.625% × $\dfrac{42}{360}$ = $150.94   Interest $ 15,000.00
   Aug. + 12 days   × 103.125%
        42 days   15 × $5 = $75   Broker's fee $ 15,468.75   Market price
   $15,468.75 + 150.94 − 75 = $15,544.69   Total receipts

APPLICATION 1

Springfield has designed a form to help it keep track of its common stock transactions. When you open Ch21App1 from your computer spreadsheet applications disk, you will see the form shown here:

Springfield Department Store

2617 Main Street
Box 219
Springfield, Maryland 58109
Telephone: 301-555-2158   FAX: 301-555-3498

COMMON STOCK TRANSACTIONS

Company	Buy (1) or Sell (2)	No. of Shares	Per Share Quote	Odd-lot Differential Rate	Odd-lot Differential Amount	Broker's Commission Rate	Broker's Commission Amount	Receipts From Sale	Cost for Purchase
					$0.00		$0.00	$0.00	$0.00
							$0.00	$0.00	$0.00
					$0.00		$0.00	$0.00	$0.00
							$0.00	$0.00	$0.00
					$0.00		$0.00	$0.00	$0.00
							$0.00	$0.00	$0.00
					$0.00		$0.00	$0.00	$0.00
					$0.00		$0.00	$0.00	$0.00
					$0.00		$0.00	$0.00	$0.00
TOTAL								$0.00	$0.00

Enter the following information:

Company	Cell	Buy (1) or Sell (2)	Cell	No. of Shares	Cell	Per Share Quote	Cell	Odd-Lot Differential Rate	Cell	Broker's Fee	Cell
IBM	A12	1	B12	250	C12	90.75	D12	$.125	E12	$.02	G12
GE	A13	2	B13	300	C13	62.50	D13			$.0175	G13
GM	A14	2	B14	175	C14	44.625	D14	.01	E14	$.02	G14
Exxon	A15	1	B15	500	C15	73.25	D15			$.02	G15
Texaco	A16	1	B16	225	C16	65.375	D16	.01	E16	$.015	G16
Motorola	A17	2	B17	1000	C17	64	D17			$.015	G17
Wal-Mart	A18	1	B18	750	C18	23.875	D18	.25	E18	$.0175	G18
Colgate Pal.	A19	2	B19	180	C19	67.875	D19	.01	E19	$.02	G19
Mattel	A20	1	B20	450	C20	28.125	D20	.125	E20	$.02	G20

Answer the following questions after you have completed the spreadsheet:

1. What was the cost for purchasing 250 shares of IBM?

2. What was the odd-lot differential amount for Mattel?

3. What was the broker's fee for the sale of Motorola?

4. What was the cost for selling GM?
5. What was the broker's fee for selling Colgate Palmolive?
6. What was the odd-lot differential amount on Texaco?
7. What was the amount of receipts from the sale of GE?
8. What was the total cost for purchasing Exxon?
9. What was the broker's fee for the purchase of Wal-Mart stock?

GROUP REPORT

FOR CHAPTER 21 APPLICATION 1

Using today's *Wall Street Journal*, or any other source's daily stock transaction section, change the prices in the spreadsheet to the current prices. Record the changes that have taken place in the value of each stock, and the total changes. Write a report to the store manager describing those changes, and make any recommendations your group thinks are appropriate.

EXCEL SPREADSHEET APPLICATION FOR CHAPTER 21

APPLICATION 2

Springfield has a form for keeping track of its bond transactions. When you open Ch21App2 from your computer spreadsheet application's disk, you will see the following form:

Springfield Department Store
2617 Main Street
Box 219
Springfield, Maryland 58109
Telephone: 301-555-2158 FAX: 301-555-3498

BOND TRANSACTIONS

Company	Buy (1) Sell (2)	No. of Bonds	Quote Per Share	Total Bond Price	Interest				Broker's Fee		Receipts From Sale	Purchase Cost
					Since Paid (Days)	Rate	Amount	Yield	Per Bond	Amount		
				$0.00			$0.00	#DIV/0!		$0.00	$0.00	$0.00
				$0.00			$0.00	#DIV/0!		$0.00	$0.00	$0.00
				$0.00			$0.00	#DIV/0!		$0.00	$0.00	$0.00
				$0.00			$0.00	#DIV/0!		$0.00	$0.00	$0.00
				$0.00			$0.00	#DIV/0!		$0.00	$0.00	$0.00
				$0.00			$0.00	#DIV/0!		$0.00	$0.00	$0.00
				$0.00			$0.00	#DIV/0!		$0.00	$0.00	$0.00
				$0.00			$0.00	#DIV/0!		$0.00	$0.00	$0.00
				$0.00			$0.00	#DIV/0!		$0.00	$0.00	$0.00
TOTAL											$0.00	$0.00

Enter the following information:

Company	Cell	Buy (1) Sell (2)	Cell	No. of Bonds	Cell	Quote Per Share	Cell	Interest Since Paid	Cell
Caterpillar	A13	2	B13	25	C13	90.75	D13	44	F13
Alcon	A14	1	B14	10	C14	101	D14	72	F14
Textron	A15	1	B15	75	C15	73.125	D15	56	F15
Ford Motors	A16	2	B16	50	C16	98.5	D16	104	F16
Ga Pacific	A17	1	B17	20	C17	64.25	D17	25	F17
Phillips	A18	2	B18	10	C18	112.375	D18	55	F18
Sears	A19	2	B19	70	C19	100.625	D19	93	F19
Prctr & Gmbl	A20	1	B20	15	C20	88.875	D20	156	F20
US Steel	A21	1	B21	45	C21	102.5	D21	81	F21

Company	Interest Rate	Cell	Broker's Fee per Bond	Cell
Caterpillar	.0625	G13	$5	I13
Alcon	.1050	G14	5	I14
Textron	.0475	G15	2.50	I15
Ford Motors	.07	G16	2.50	I16
Ga Pacific	.045	G17	5	I17
Phillips	.1125	G18	5	I18
Sears	.0975	G19	2.50	I19
Prctr & Gmbl	.075	G20	5	I20
US Steel	.115	G21	5	I21

Answer the following questions after you have completed the spreadsheet:

1. What were the receipts from the sale of Caterpillar bonds?
2. What was the purchase cost of Textron bonds?
3. What was the total bond price for Phillips?
4. What was the amount of interest that had accumulated since it was last paid on US Steel Bonds?
5. What was the yield on Ford Motors bonds?
6. What was the broker's fee on Ga Pacific bonds?
7. What were the receipts from the sale of Sears bonds?
8. What was the purchase cost for Alcon bonds?
9. What was the yield on Procter & Gamble bonds?

GROUP REPORT

FOR CHAPTER 21 APPLICATION 2

From the New York Stock Exchange Corporate Bond section of the *Wall Street Journal,* or any other sources' financial transaction section, select five bonds that your group agrees are good buys. Enter your choices in the spreadsheet. Write a report informing the store manager of your group's choices, the reasons for your choices, the total purchase cost, and your expectations for future returns. (You might be aided in your report by comparing today's bond interest rates with those you entered in the original spreadsheet application.)

22 STATISTICAL APPLICATIONS

WHAT'S IN A NUMBER

Robert Reich, who was secretary of labor in President Clinton's cabinet, once observed that if he, at four feet ten inches, and basketball star Shaquille O'neal, who is seven feet two, were in an elevator together, the average height of a man in the elevator would be six feet.

George showed the photograph of what he said was last year's pecan crop from his backyard. "It increased 500% this year," he said. Sounds good! Yeah, last year the lone tree produced one pecan. This year it produced five.

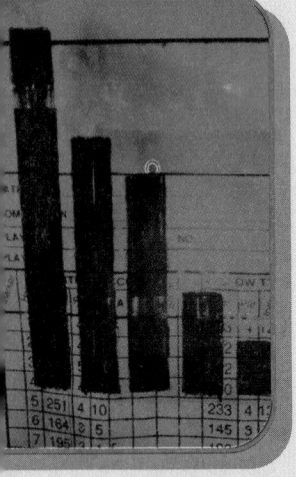

Between 1987 and 1988 New Zealand endured the greatest percent increase in murder of any nation in the world. That suggests New Zealand is a very dangerous place to live. Right? Wrong! All it really means is that in 1988 there were two murders and in 1987 one. New Zealand is one of the safest places on earth to live.

The Japanese death rate is one of the world's lowest, but the birthrate is even lower. Doesn't that mean that the future date at which there will be no Japanese people is mathematically predictable?

And consider the six-foot man who drowned trying to wade across a river that was on average only four feet deep.

Anything can be "proved" with statistics and often "is." That means that opposites can be "proved", which means nothing really can be.

Chapter Glossary

Statistics. The branch of mathematics concerned with collecting, classifying, analyzing, and interpreting data.

Data. Information used in an experiment.

Array. An arrangement of data according to numerical size.

Frequency distribution. An arrangement of data showing the frequency with which each number appears.

Range. The distance between the highest and lowest values in a set of numbers.

Central tendency. A number designed to represent the typical number within a group of numbers.

Mean. The arithmetic average found by dividing the sum of values by the number of values.

Median. The value at the midpoint of a series of numbers arranged in an array.

Mode. The value that occurs most often in a set of numbers.

Graph. A visual representation of data.

Bar graph. Data illustrated as bars to show comparisons of size.

Line graph. A graphical presentation using lines to illustrate data.

Circle graph. A graphical presentation, sometimes called a pie chart, using a circle divided into sections to illustrate data. The circle represents the whole.

Student Objectives

Upon completion of this chapter, you should be able to:

1. Arrange data in an array.
2. Perform a frequency distribution of data.
3. Find the range in data.
4. Calculate the mean, median, and mode.
5. Find the central tendency with class intervals.
6. Construct line graphs, bar graphs, and circle graphs.

Statistics is the branch of mathematics that is concerned with collecting, classifying, analyzing, and interpreting data. **Data** are the pieces of information used in an experiment. The purpose of statistics in business is to arrange data in an order that is useful. Because business judgments depend on definite measurable facts rather than intuition, business managers often need to analyze statistical data accurately.

LEARNING UNIT 1
ARRAY

To use statistical data, the numbers usually must first be arranged in order from smallest to largest or largest to smallest. The arrangement is called an **array**. In this chapter arrays are all arranged from smallest to largest.

A group of data such as 11, 9, 7, 4, 8, 7, 8, 11, 7 can often be made more useful if reordered as 4, 7, 7, 7, 8, 8, 9, 11, 11.

LEARNING UNIT 2
FREQUENCY DISTRIBUTION AND RANGE

The previous arrayed data can be made further useful if arranged in a **frequency distribution** showing how often each value appears.

Value	Frequency
11	2
9	1
8	2
7	3
4	1

The **range**, the distance between the highest and lowest values, is determined by subtracting the lowest value from the highest.

$$
\begin{array}{r}
11 \text{ Largest value} \\
- \ 4 \text{ Smallest value} \\
\hline
7 \text{ Range}
\end{array}
$$

 Arranging an Array, Performing a Frequency Distribution, and Finding the Range

EXAMPLE   Given the data 8, 12, 3, 8, 53, 12, 8, 3, (1) arrange them in an array, (2) perform a frequency distribution, and (3) find the range.

Solution   (1) Array: 3, 3, 8, 8, 8, 12, 12, 53

(2) Frequency Distribution

Value	Frequency
3	2
8	3
12	2
53	1

(3) *Range*

$$
\begin{array}{r}
53 \text{ Highest value} \\
- \ 3 \text{ Lowest value} \\
\hline
50 \text{ Range}
\end{array}
$$

Given the following data, arrange them into an array, perform a frequency distribution, and find the range.

1. 31, 37, 8, 37, 9, 31, 37
2. 87, 42, 112, 37, 42, 87
3. 275, 201, 338, 275, 103, 201, 275
4. 4,389, 2,003, 5,971, 4,389, 5,971, 4,389, 2,003, 4,389

22.1 Solutions to Practice Problems

1. Array: 8, 9, 31, 31, 37, 37, 37

   Frequency Distribution

Value	Frequency
8	1
9	1
31	2
37	3

   Range   37 Highest value
   $\underline{-\ 8}$ Lowest value
   29 Range

2. Array: 37, 42, 42, 87, 87, 112

   Frequency Distribution

Value	Frequency
37	1
42	2
87	2
112	1

   Range   112 Highest value
   $\underline{-\ 37}$ Lowest value
   75 Range

3. Array: 103, 201, 201, 275, 275, 275, 338

   Frequency Distribution

Value	Frequency
103	1
201	2
275	3
338	1

   Range   338 Highest value
   $\underline{-\ 103}$ Lowest value
   235 Range

4. Array: 2,003, 2,003, 4,389, 4,389, 4,389, 4,389, 5,971, 5,971

   Frequency Distribution

Value	Frequency
2,003	2
4,389	4
5,971	2

   Range   5,971 Highest value
   $\underline{-\ 2,003}$ Lowest value
   3,968 Range

LEARNING UNIT 3
MEASURES OF CENTRAL TENDENCY (AVERAGES)

Central tendency is a value that represents a group of values within a range. The three commonly used measures are the mean, the median, and the mode. Each can be useful in certain instances, depending on the data being analyzed and on what is to be determined from the data.

EXCEL Spreadsheet Application Springfield Department Store
developed the form shown in Spreadsheet Application 1 at the end of
this chapter to perform an annual sales analysis.

22.2 Finding the Mean

The most commonly used measure of central tendency is the arithmetic **mean**, usually called the average, which is found by adding the values and dividing the sum by the number of values.

EXAMPLE Given the data 8, 12, 3, 8, 50, 12, 8, 3, find the arithmetic mean.

Solution

$$\text{Arithmetic mean} = \frac{\text{sum of values}}{\text{number of values}}$$

$$
\begin{array}{l}
8 \\
12 \\
3 \\
8 \\
50 \\
12 \\
8 \\
+ 3 \\
\hline
104
\end{array}
$$

Number of values = 8

Sum of values

$$\frac{104}{8} = 13$$

22.2 Practice Problems

1. Big Tex George's oil well produced the following number of barrels in one week: Sunday, 641; Monday, 579; Tuesday, 748; Wednesday, 625; Thursday, 475; Friday, 924; Saturday, 348. Find the arithmetic mean for daily production.

2. Jerry's grades in Economics I last semester were 87, 46, 96, 86, 73, and 54. Find his average grade for the semester.

3. Sister Sarah at St. Sophia's Convent School serves lunch to the children. Last week she served 327 on Monday, 302 on Tuesday, 312 on Wednesday, 298 on Thursday, and 296 on Friday. Find the arithmetic mean for the number of lunches served each day.

4. Mr. Bass of Bass Enterprises buys shopping center space. In each of the months in the first half of last year, he bought the following number of square feet: January, 4, 211; February, 3,812; March, 3,016; April, 3,015; May, 4,547; June, 3,701. Find the average amount bought each month.

12.2 Solutions to Practice Problems

1. $\text{Arithmetic mean} = \dfrac{\text{sum of values}}{\text{number of values}}$

$$
\begin{array}{l}
641 \\
579 \\
748 \\
625 \\
475 \\
924 \\
+ 348 \\
\hline
4,340
\end{array}
$$

Number of values = 7

Sum of values

$$\frac{4,340}{7} = 620$$

2.

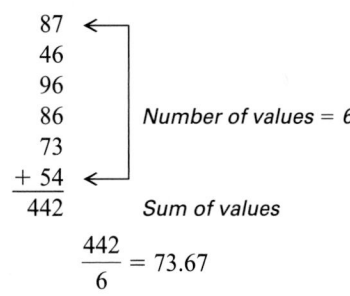

$$\frac{442}{6} = 73.67$$

3.

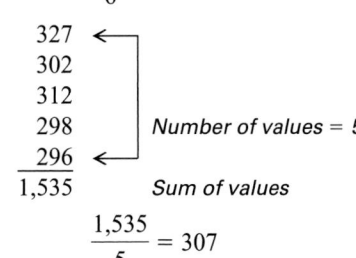

$$\frac{1,535}{5} = 307$$

4.

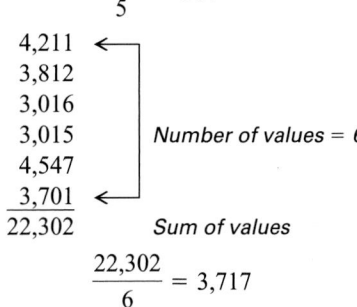

$$\frac{22,302}{6} = 3,717$$

22.3 Finding the Median

The **median** is the midpoint value in an array of data. The midpoint is found by counting the number of values in an array and applying the formula $\frac{n+1}{2}$. If there are an odd number of values, the middle value will be the median. If the array has an even number of values, the median will be the mean of the two middle values.

EXAMPLE   (For an odd number of values) The employees at Schmirk Inc. are paid monthly as follows: $11,000, $8,000, $12,000, $600, $900, $4,000, $1,000. Find the median income.

Solution   *Step 1.* Arrange the data into an array: $600, $900, $1,000, $4,000, $8,000, $11,000, $12,000.

Step 2. Count the number of values (there are seven).

Step 3. The middle value would be in the fourth position counting from either end:

$$\frac{7+1}{2} = 4$$

Step 4. The median is $4,000, the fourth value.

EXAMPLE   (For an even number of values) The employees at Antone's Inc. are paid monthly as follows: $12,000, $9,000, $13,000, $700, $1,000, $6,000, $2,000, $4,000. Find the median income.

Solution   *Step 1.* Arrange the data into an array: $700, $1,000, $2,000, $4,000, $6,000, $9,000, $12,000, $13,000.

Step 2. Count the number of values (there are eight).

Step 3. The middle value would be between the fourth value and the fifth value:

$$\frac{8 + 1}{2} = 4.5$$

Step 4. $4,000 is the fourth value and $6,000 is the fifth value. The median would be the mean of $4,000 and $6,000:

$$\frac{\$4,000 + \$6,000}{2} = \$5,000 \text{ Median}$$

22.3 Practice Problems

1. Students in Dr. Kidd's seminar made the following grades last semester: George, 88; Martha, 93; Rebecca, 80; Melinda, 75; Herman, 99; Jim, 87; Elizabeth, 84. Who made the median grade?

2. Bob's little company had the following revenues for the last half of the last year: July, $25,000; August, $12,000; September, $31,000; October, $9,000; November, $8,000; December, $38,000. Find the median revenue for Bob's little company.

3. Nine students traveled from different directions the following miles to commute to college last month: 220 miles, 540 miles, 330 miles, 660 miles, 450 miles, 860 miles, 475 miles, 660 miles, 475 miles. Find the median mileage traveled.

4. A company attempts to help people reduce their weight. The weight of six new customers are 180 pounds, 320 pounds, 220 pounds, 195 pounds, 320 pounds, 310 pounds. Find the median weight of these people.

22.3 Solutions to Practice Problems

1. *Step 1.* Arrange the data into an array: 75, 80, 84, 87, 88, 93, 99.

   Step 2. Count the number of values (there are seven).

   Step 3. The middle value would be in the fourth position counting from either end:

   $$\frac{7 + 1}{2} = 4$$

   Step 4. The median is 87 (the fourth value from either end of the array).

   Step 5. Jim made 87, so Jim made the median grade.

2. *Step 1.* Arrange the data into an array: $8,000, $9,000, $12,000, $25,000, $31,000, $38,000.

   Step 2. Count the number of values (there are six).

   Step 3. The middle value would be halfway between the third and fourth values counting from either end:

   $$\frac{6 + 1}{2} = 3.5$$

   Step 4. The median values are $12,000 and $25,000, the third and fourth values from either end of the array.

   Step 5. $$\frac{\$12,000 + 25,000}{2} = \$18,500$$

3. *Step 1.* Arrange the data into an array: 220, 330, 450, 475, 475, 540, 660, 660, 860.

   Step 2. Count the number of values (there are nine).

   Step 3. The middle value is in the fifth position counting from either end:

   $$\frac{9 + 1}{2} = 5$$

   Step 4. The median is 475 (the fifth value from either end of the array).

4. *Step 1.* Arrange the data into an array: 180, 195, 220, 310, 320, 320.

Step 2. Count the number of values (there are six).

Step 3. The middle value would be halfway between the third and fourth values counting from either end:

$$\frac{6 + 1}{2} = 3.5$$

Step 4. The median values are 220 and 310, the third and fourth values from either end of the array.

Step 5. $\dfrac{220 + 310}{2} = 265$

22.4 Finding the Mode

The **mode** is the value that occurs the greatest number of times in a series of data. There may be more than one mode. If there are two modes, the data are bimodal, if there are three modes, the data are trimodal, and so on. If no number appears more than once, or if all numbers appear the same number of times, there is no mode.

EXAMPLE   Find the modal output for workers at Zelda's sewing shop in a week; Anita, 7 dresses; Bruce, 10 dresses; Cora, 9 dresses; Diane, 4 dresses; Elane, 12 dresses; Flora, 9 dresses; Gene, 7 dresses; Hanna, 9 dresses.

Solution   Arrange the data into an array and find the frequency distribution.
Array: 4, 7, 7, 9, 9, 9, 10, 12

Value	Frequency
4	1
7	2
9 = mode	3
10	1
12	1

22.4 Practice Problems

1. Find the mode for salaries at Zeke's print shop: Albert, $312; Bennie, $288; Clara, $330; Dora, $270; Emmet, $300; Flora, $312; George, $312.

2. The number of letters received each day at Jesse's office last week was as follows: Monday, 25; Tuesday, 35; Wednesday, 40; Thursday, 35; Friday, 35; Saturday, 10. What number of letters represents the daily mode?

3. Determine the mode for cashiers' hourly wages at Hobb's Supermarket: $6.50, $9.00, $9.00, $9.00, $9.50, $9.50, $9.50, $9.50.

4. Find the mode for daily hours worked at Bruce's factory last week: Monday, 240 hours; Tuesday, 320 hours; Wednesday, 300 hours; Thursday, 220 hours; Friday, 400 hours.

22.4 Solutions to Practice Problems

1.

Values in Array	Frequency
$270	1
288	1
300	1
312 = mode	3
330	1

2.

Values in Array	Frequency
10	1
25	1
35 = mode	3
40	1

3.

Value in Array	Frequency
$6.50	1
9.00	3
9.50 = mode	4

4.

Value in Array	Frequency
220	1
240	1
300	1
320	1
400	1

No number appears more than one time. There is no mode.

22.5 Finding the Central Tendency with Class Intervals

When a large number of values is presented, they may be grouped to show the number of times values occur within size classes. To find the arithmetic mean, the sum of the product is divided by the number of values, as in Section 22.2. The midpoint of each class must first be determined to determine the total product.

E X A M P L E   Last week the workers in a shirt factory produced the following:

Number of Shirts	Number of Workers
Between 76 and 80	3
Between 71 and 75	12
Between 66 and 70	18
Between 61 and 65	9
Between 56 and 60	6
Between 51 and 55	2

Find the arithmetic mean for the number of shirts produced by each worker in the factory, the median production per worker, and the mode.

Solution

Number of Shirts (Class = c)	Number of Workers (Frequency = f)	Midpoint of Class $\left(\dfrac{Low + high}{2} = m\right)$	Total Product (f × m)
76–80	3	78	234
71–75	12	73	876
66–70	18	68	1,224
61–65	9	63	567
56–60	6	58	348
51–55	+ 2	53	+ 106
	50		3,355

$$\frac{3,355}{50} = 67.1 \text{ Mean}$$

$$\frac{50 + 1}{2} = \frac{51}{2} = 25.5 \text{ Middle number of the frequency}$$

Counting from either end, 25.5 will be in frequency 18, which is in the class 66–70. The median is the midpoint of that class (68). Since the 66–70 class appears the most times (18), 68 is the mode.

22.5 Practice Problems

1. The players on a baseball team struck out the following numbers of times during the season: 40–50, 3 times; 30–39, 2 times; 20–29, 8 times; 10–19, 2 times. Find the average (mean) number of strikeouts per player, the median number for the team, and the modal number of strikeouts.

2. Of the workers in a shoe factory, 4 produced between 86 and 90 pairs per week, 13 produced between 81 and 85, 19 produced between 76 and 80, 11 produced between 71 and 75, 6 produced between 66 and 70, and 3 produced between 61 and 65. Find the arithmetic mean for the number of shoes produced by each worker in the factory, the median production per worker, and the mode.

3. Find the mean, median, and mode for the weights of players applying to be on a basketball team, given the following:

Weight Class	Frequency
211–225	3
196–210	12
181–195	28
166–180	14
151–165	2

4. Use the following classes to prepare a frequency distribution: 6–10, 11–15, 16–20, 21–25, 26–30. Find the mean, median, and mode for the following numbers of sports shoes sewn by the 39 workers in a Taiwan factory one day:

21	30	6	27	11	29	30	21	30	15
7	12	21	20	6	8	21	30	24	20
11	26	16	22	19	26	22	26	29	30
26	25	15	21	14	25	24	21	24	

22.5 Solutions to Practice Problems

1.

No. of Strikeouts (Class = c)	No. of Players (Frequency = f)	Midpoint of Class $\left(\dfrac{Low + high}{2} = m\right)$	Product (f × m)
40–50	3	45	135
30–39	2	34.5	69
20–29	8	24.5	196
10–19	+2	14.5	+ 29
	15		429

$$\frac{429}{15} = 28.6 \text{ Mean}$$

$$\frac{15 + 1}{2} = \frac{16}{2} = \text{8th value in the frequency}$$

Counting from either end, the 8th value will fall in the class 20–29. The median is the midpoint of that class (24.5).

Since 20–29 appears the most times (8), 24.5 is the mode.

2.

Number of shoes (Class = c)	Number of workers (Frequency = f)	Midpoint of Class $\left(\dfrac{Low + high}{2} = m\right)$	Product (f × m)
86–90	4	88	352
81–85	13	83	1,079
76–80	19	78	1,482
71–75	11	73	803
66–70	6	68	408
61–65	+ 3	63	189
	56		4,313

$$\frac{4,313}{56} = 77.018 \text{ Mean}$$

$$\frac{56 + 1}{2} = \frac{57}{2} = \text{28.5th value number in the frequency}$$

Counting in the frequency column from either end, the 28.5th value will fall in the class 76–80. The midpoint of that class is 78, the median. Since 76–80 appears the most times(19), 78 is the mode.

3.

Weights (Class = c)	No. of people (Frequency = f)	Midpoint of Class $\left(\dfrac{Low + high}{2} = m\right)$	Product (f × m)
211–225	3	218	654
196–210	12	203	2,436
181–195	28	188	5,264
166–180	14	173	2,422
151–165	+2	158	+ 316
	59		11,092

$$\frac{11,092}{59} = 188 \text{ Mean}$$

$$\frac{59 + 1}{2} = 30\text{th value in the frequency.}$$

Counting from either end, the 30th value will fall in the class 181–195. The midpoint of that class is 188, the median.

Since 181–195 appears the most times (28), 188 is the mode.

4.

Number of shoes (Class = c)	Number of workers (Frequency = f)	Midpoint of Class $\left(\dfrac{Low + high}{2} = m\right)$	Product (f × m)
6–10	4	8	32
11–15	6	13	78
16–20	4	18	72
21–25	13	23	299
26–30	+12	28	+336
	39		817

$$\frac{817}{39} = 20.95 \text{ Mean}$$

$$\frac{39 + 1}{2} = 20\text{th value in the frequency}$$

Counting from either end, the 20th value will fall in the class 21–25. The midpoint of that class is 23, the median.

Since the class interval 21–25 appears the most times (13), 23 is the mode.

LEARNING UNIT 4
STATISTICAL GRAPHS

Data are usually more easily understood if they can be visualized. A **graph** allows readers to visualize complex data in an understandable way. Although a table may contain the same data and be more accurate than a graph, it is not as good for viewing the picture at a glance. The most common types of graphs are bar graphs, line graphs, and circle graphs.

EXCEL Spreadsheet Application Using the spreadsheet and bar graph shown in Spreadsheet Application 2 at the end of this chapter, Springfield projected sales for 2003.

Bar Graphs

Bar graphs are useful to show comparisons among values. Bar graphs, which illustrate the same data as line and circle graphs, are sometimes easier to understand.

EXAMPLE   Illustrate the following data for Scmaltz Food Mart with a bar graph:

Sales By Department

	Bakery	Frozen Food	Grocery	Meat	Produce
2002	$207,000	$250,000	$390,000	$307,000	$148,000
2003	225,000	260,000	422,000	298,000	150,000

Solution *Step 1.* Draw a vertical axis on the left side of the page and a horizontal axis across the bottom.

Step 2. Fill in the vertical line with a convenient scale (in this case, hundreds of thousands of dollars).

Step 3. Fill in the horizontal line with a convenient scale (in this case, the names of the departments).

Step 4. Plot the data.

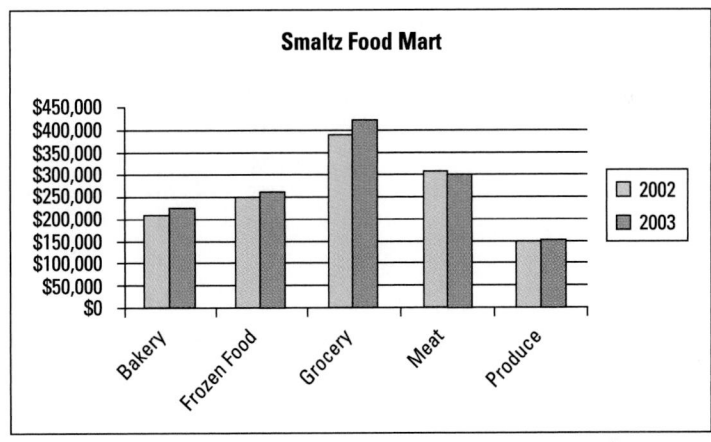

22.6 Practice Problems

1. Draw a bar graph showing a comparison of sales for the month of March for the following salespeople:

Salesperson	Sales in March
Alice	$46,400
Bill	40,800
Carol	43,600
Donald	39,400
Emma	33,800
Gary	36,600

2. Prepare a bar graph for José's Hardware showing the first six months of sales for this year compared to last year.

Month	Last Year	This Year
Jan.	$100,000	$110,000
Feb.	90,000	70,000
Mar.	130,000	135,000
Apr.	145,000	150,000
May	160,000	170,000
June	200,000	190,000

3. Construct a bar graph to illustrate changes in sales for five major oil companies.

Company	Last Year (in billions)	This Year (in billions)
Exxon	$350	$300
Mobil	120	150
Phillips	50	61
Sun Oil	110	90
Texaco	205	220

4. Mary's Used Cars finances for some customers. Others provide their own financing. Use a bar graph to illustrate the car prices Mary financed and those she did not finance.

Price Range	Financed by Mary	Not Financed by Mary
$ 0–1,999	3	3
2,000–3,999	6	1
4,000–5,999	6	4
6,000–7,999	2	1
8,000–9,999	2	2

22.6 Solutions to Practice Problems

1.

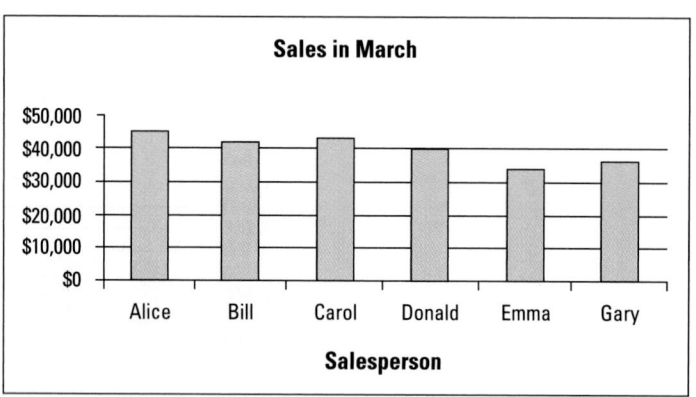

2.

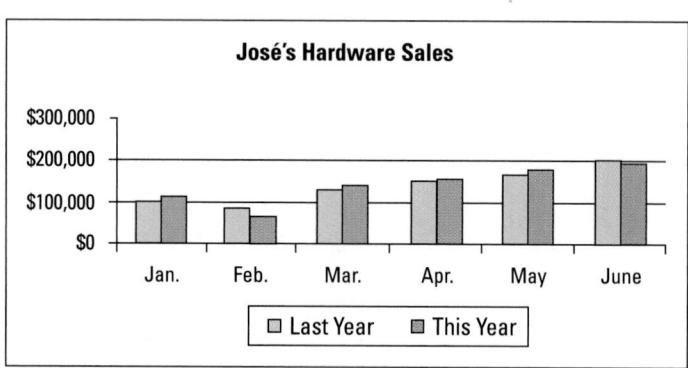

3.

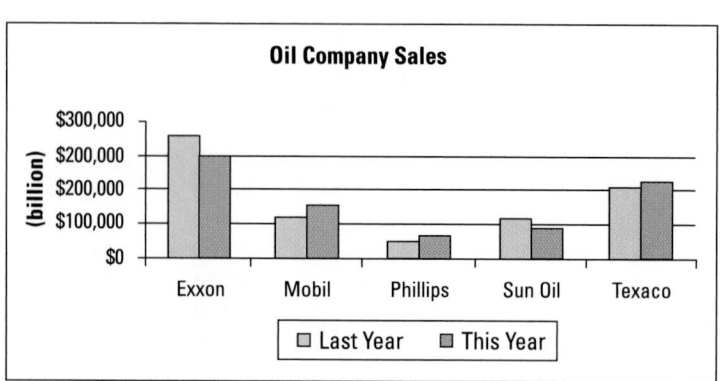

4.

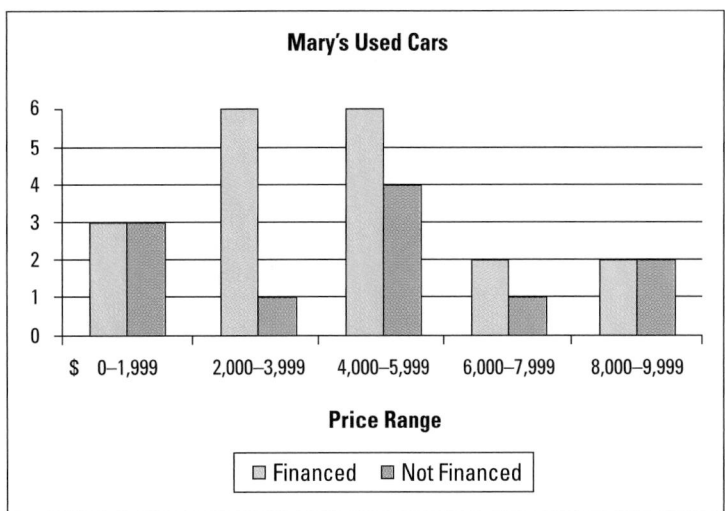

Mary's Used Cars

22.7 Line Graphs

Line graphs are useful for presenting progression in historical data. Equal spaces in the graph represent equal time intervals, such as weeks, months, or years.

EXAMPLE   Prepare a line graph that compares the Brach Company's sales and cost of goods sold over a five-year period using the following data:

Year	Sales	Cost of Goods Sold
1999	$516,000	$380,000
2000	584,000	410,000
2001	620,000	420,000
2002	570,000	390,000
2003	560,000	440,000

Solution   *Step 1.* Draw a vertical axis on the left side of the page and a horizontal axis across the bottom.

Step 2. Fill in the vertical line with a convenient scale (in this case, hundreds of thousands of dollars).

Step 3. Fill in the horizontal line with a convenient scale (in this case, the years from 1999 through 2003).

Step 4. Plot the data and label it.

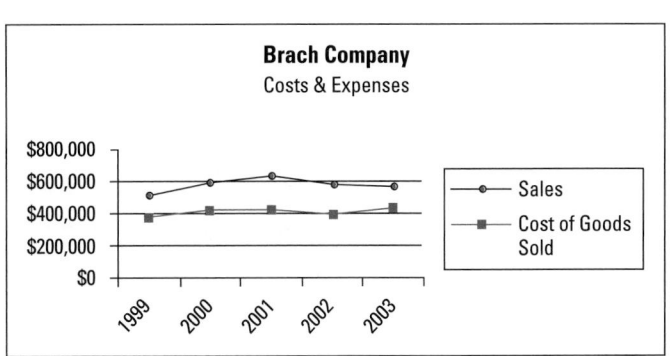

Brach Company
Costs & Expenses

1. Prepare a line graph that compares the monthly value of sales of chlorine at Leslie Pool Supply to the price the company paid for it over the past five-month period. Use the following data:

Month	Sales	Price Paid for Chlorine
Jan.	$2,580	$1,900
Feb.	2,920	2,050
Mar.	3,100	2,100
Apr.	2,850	1,950
May	2,800	2,200

2. Two competing companies had the following sales during the first half of last year:

Month	Babbage Software (in millions)	Software Etc. (in millions)
Jan.	$20	$14
Feb.	14	8
Mar.	11	10
Apr.	14	15
May	11	8
June	13	7

Prepare a line graph that compares the two companies' sales.

3. Herman's Quicopy operates two stores. One is in a suburb and the other is in the middle of a very large city. The city store typically outperforms the suburban store. Using the following data for the final half of last year, compare the two stores with a line graph:

Store	July	Aug.	Sept.	Oct.	Nov.	Dec.
City	$60,000	$70,000	$55,000	$57,500	$67,500	$62,500
Suburb	32,500	27,500	25,000	40,000	42,500	37,500

4. Prepare a line graph comparing the income from residential and commercial accounts for the Craighead County, Ark. Gas Co.

Month	Income from Residential	Income from Commercial
Jan.	$156,000	$100,000
Feb.	148,000	84,000
Mar.	200,000	175,000
Apr.	180,000	140,000
May	204,000	182,000
June	260,000	280,000

22.7 Solutions to Practice Problems
1.

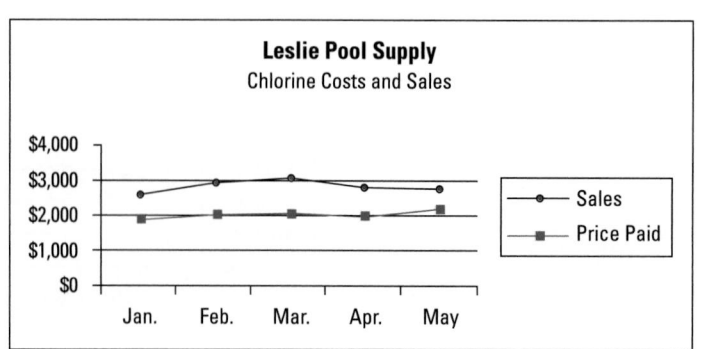

2.

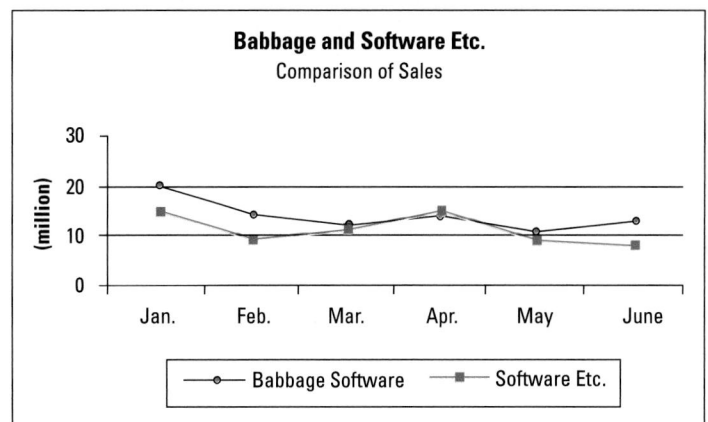

3.

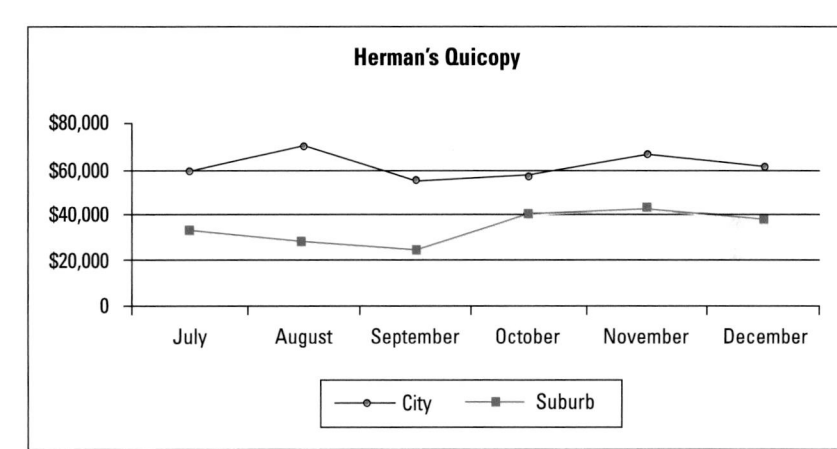

4.

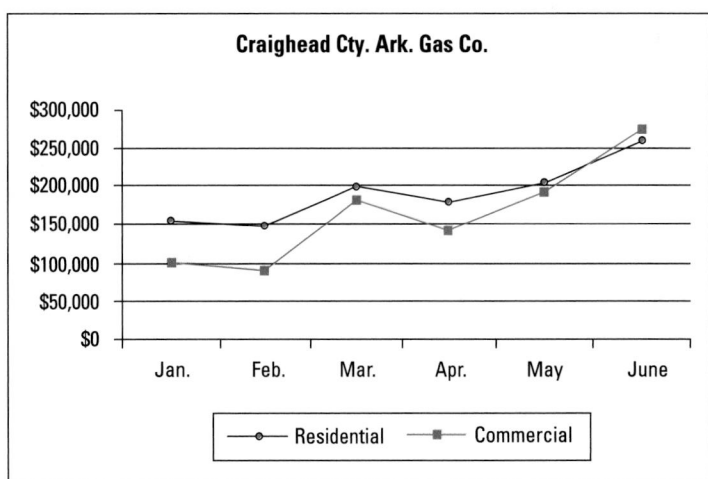

Circle Graphs

Circle graphs are useful for illustrating how data are divided. They are used frequently to show the percentage comparison of component parts and are often highlighted by coloring or shading the sectors differently.

EXAMPLE   Prepare a circle graph to show the major components of U.S. government revenues last
           year, given the following:

Individual Income Tax	Social Security Tax	Corporate Income Tax	Excise Taxes	Other Taxes
45%	35%	10%	5%	5%

Solution   *Step 1.* Draw a circle.

           Step 2. The circle contains 360°. Multiply the percent of each part of the data by 360°.

           Individual income tax: 45% × 360° = 162°
           Social security tax: 35% × 360° = 126°
           Corporate income tax: 10% × 360° =   36°
           Excise taxes: 5% × 360° =   18°
           Other taxes: 5% × 360° =   18°

           Step 3. Using a protractor, divide the circle into sections corresponding to the number
           of degrees each section represents.

           Step 4. Label the parts of the graph.

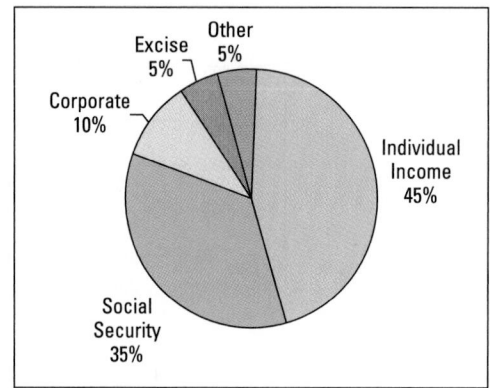

**22.8
Practice
Problems**

1. Prepare a circle graph to illustrate national defense spending of the United States, Russia,
   and all other nations (in billions of dollars).

United States	Russia	All Other Nations Combined
$250	$50	$200

2. Prepare a circle graph showing the breakdown of shoe sales at Rambo's shoe store. The
   sales statistics are as follows:

Women	Men	Girls	Boys
36%	14%	32%	18%

3. Bunko Publishing Co. has the following long-term debt and equity (in millions):

Long-term liabilities	$30
Preferred stock	15
Common stock	25
Retained earnings	20

   Prepare a circle graph to illustrate the situation.

4. A breakdown of the Administrative U.S. Federal Budget reveals expenditures as follows:

Military	$250 billion
Health, labor, education, and welfare	125 billion
Commerce, transportation, and housing	83 billion
Agriculture	4 billion
Other	38 billion

   Construct a circle graph to demonstrate this.

22.8 Solutions to Practice Problems

1.

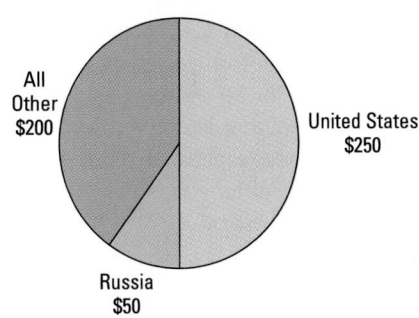

World Defense (in billions)

All Other $200
United States $250
Russia $50

2.

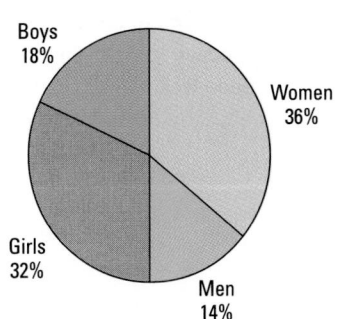

Rambo's Shoe Sales

Boys 18%
Women 36%
Men 14%
Girls 32%

3.

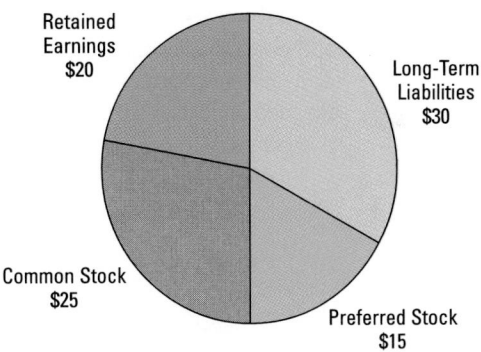

Bunko Publishing Co. Debt and Equity (in millions)

Retained Earnings $20
Long-Term Liabilities $30
Common Stock $25
Preferred Stock $15

4.

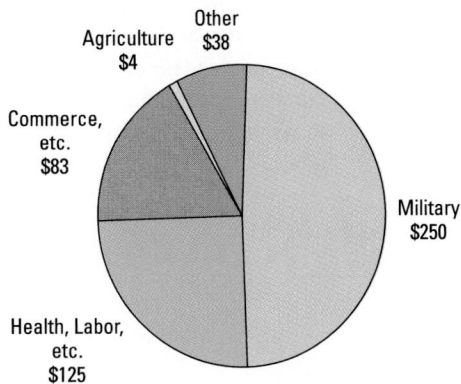

U.S. Federal Budget (in billions)

Agriculture $4
Other $38
Commerce, etc. $83
Military $250
Health, Labor, etc. $125

Page	Section Topic	Learning Concepts	Examples and Solutions
756	**22.1** Arranging an Array, Performing a Frequency Distribution, and Finding the Range	An array is the arrangement of data in order from lowest to highest or highest to lowest. A frequency distribution requires determining the number of times each value appears. The range is the difference between the lowest and highest values.	Arrange 8, 12, 3, 8, 53, 12, 8, 3 in an array, perform a frequency distribution, and find the range. Array: 3, 3, 8, 8, 8, 12, 12, 53 Frequency distribution: 3 appears 2 times, 8 appears 3 times, 12 appears 2 times. Range: $53 - 3 = 50$
758	**22.2** Finding the Mean	The most common measure of central tendency, usually called the average, is found by dividing the sum of the values by the number of values.	Find the arithmetic mean for 8, 12, 3, 8, 53, 12, 8, 3. $$\frac{\text{Sum of values}}{\text{number of values}} = \text{mean}$$ $8 + 12 + 3 + 8 + 53 + 12 + 8 + 3 = 107$ $$\frac{107}{8} = 13.375$$
759	**22.3** Finding the Median	The midpoint of an array is found at the halfway point between the highest and lowest values in the array. If the array has an even number of values, the median is the mean value of the two central values.	Calculate the median in 8, 12, 3, 8, 53, 12, 8, 9. Arrange the data in an array: 3, 8, 8, 8, 9, 12, 12, 53. Midpoint formula: $\frac{8+1}{2} = 4.5$ The midvalue would be the mean value of 8 and 9: $$\frac{8+9}{2} = 8.5 \text{ median}$$
761	**22.4** Finding the Mode	The mode is the value that appears most often in a set of data. If no number appears more than once, or if all data appear the same number of times, there is no mode. If two or more numbers appear the same number of times, there will be more than one mode.	Find the mode in 8, 12, 3, 8, 53, 12, 8, 3. Arrange the data in an array: 3, 3, 8, 8, 8, 12, 12, 53. Perform a frequency distribution: 3 appears 2 times, 8 appears 3 times, 12 appears 2 times, 53 appears 1 time Since 8 appears the most times, it is the mode.

Page	Section Topic	Learning Concepts	Examples and Solutions
762	**22.5** Finding the Central Tendency with Class Intervals	When a large number of values are presented, they may be grouped within class sizes to better portray the information.	Find the mean, median, and mode for the following:

Class = c	Frequency = f	Midpoint of Class $\dfrac{(Low + high)}{2} = m$	Product (f × m)
6–10	4	8	32
11–15	6	13	78
16–20	5	18	90
21–25	11	23	253
26–30	+12	28	+336
	38		789

$$\frac{789}{38} = 20.763 \text{ Mean}$$

$$\frac{38 + 1}{2} = 19.5 \text{ Midpoint}$$

The median is between the 19th and 20th values in the distribution. The number falls in the class 21–25. The midpoint of that class is 23 (median).

Class 26–30 appears most often (12 times). The midpoint of the class is 28 (mode).

Page	Section Topic	Learning Concepts	Examples and Solutions
764	**22.6** Bar Graphs	Bar graphs illustrate differences in data by using a larger or smaller bar to represent a larger or smaller quantity of something. When two or more items are presented with different bars on the same graph, the graph can make a more useful visual comparison than numbers alone can.	Prepare a bar graph comparing the first six months of this year with last year.

Month	This Year (in millions)	Last Year (in millions)
Jan.	$100	$110
Feb.	90	70
Mar.	130	135
Apr.	145	150
May	160	170
June	200	190

Sales Comparison
(in millions)

□ This Year ■ Last Year

Page	Section Topic	Learning Concepts	Examples and Solutions
767	**22.7** Line Graphs	Line graphs are useful for presenting progression in historical data.	Prepare a line graph comparing the first five months of sales this year with last year.

Month	Last Year	This Year
Jan.	$250	$190
Feb.	290	200
Mar.	300	200
Apr.	280	190
May	280	220

Sales Comparison

Page	Section Topic	Learning Concepts	Examples and Solutions
769	**22.8** Circle Graphs	Circle graphs are useful for illustrating how data are divided.	Prepare a circle graph showing how a company's debt and equity are related using the following data (in millions):

Long-term debt	$60
Preferred stock	30
Common stock	50
Retained earnings	40

Debt and Equity (in millions)

SURFING THE INTERNET

For further information on the topics covered in this chapter, check out the following sites:

http://www.wikipedia.com/wiki/Statistics

http://simon.cs.vt.edu/SoSci/Site/MMM/mmm.html

Answers to odd-numbered problems are given in Appendix A.

22.1

Given the following data, arrange them in an array, perform a frequency distribution, and find the range.

1. 62, 74, 16, 74, 18, 62, 74
Array: 16, 18, 62, 62, 74, 74, 74

Frequency Distribution	Value	Frequency
	16	1
	18	1
	62	2
	74	3

Range   74 Highest value
    − 16 Lowest value
    58 Range

2. 174, 84, 224, 74, 84, 174
Array: 74, 84, 84, 174, 174, 224

Frequency Distribution	Value	Frequency
	74	1
	84	2
	174	2
	224	1

Range   224 Highest Value
    − 74 Lowest Value
    150 Range

3. 137, 101, 169, 137, 52, 101, 137
Array: 52, 101, 101, 137, 137, 137, 169

Frequency Distribution	Value	Frequency
	52	1
	101	2
	137	3
	169	1

Range: 169 Highest Value
    − 52 Lowest Value
    117 Range

4. 2,195, 1,002, 2,985, 2,195, 2,985, 2,195, 1,002, 2,195
Array: 1,002, 1,002, 2,195, 2,195, 2,195, 2,195, 2,985, 2,985

Frequency Distribution	Value	Frequency
	1,002	2
	2,195	4
	2,985	2

Range   2,985 Highest value
    − 1,002 Lowest value
    1,983 Range

5. 2, 14, 26, 10, 26, 2, 10
Array: 2, 2, 10, 10, 14, 26, 26

Frequency Distribution	Value	Frequency
	2	2
	10	2
	14	1
	26	2

Range   26 Highest value
    − 2 Lowest value
    24 Range

22.2

6. Lousiana Gas produced the following millions of cubic feet of gas last week: Sunday, 1,923; Monday, 1,737; Tuesday, 2,244; Wednesday, 1,875; Thursday, 1,425; Friday, 2,772; Saturday, 1,044. Find the arithmetic mean for daily production.

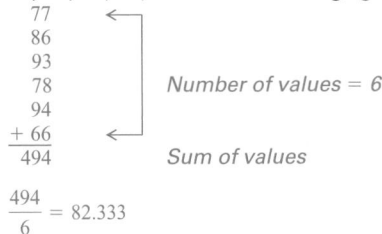

1,923
1,737
2,244
1,875   *Number of values = 7*
1,425
2,772
+ 1,044
13,020   *Sum of values*

$$\frac{13,020}{7} = 1,860$$

7. Juanita's grades in Business Math last semester were 77, 86, 93, 78, 94, 66. Find her average grade for the semester.

77
86
93
78   *Number of values = 6*
94
+ 66
494   *Sum of values*

$$\frac{494}{6} = 82.333$$

8. Gilbert's Dinner serves breakfast. Last Monday he served 109; Tuesday, 102; Wednesday, 104; Thursday, 99; and Friday, 98. Find the arithmetic mean for the number of breakfast meals served each day.

109
102
104   *Number of values = 5*
99
+ 98
512   *Sum of values*

$$\frac{512}{5} = 102.4$$

9. Miller Construction builds houses. In each of the months in the first half of last year Ms. Miller finished construction of the following number of square feet: January, 25,268; February, 22,876; March, 18,100; April, 18,094; May, 27,286; June, 22,206. Find the average number of square feet finished each month.

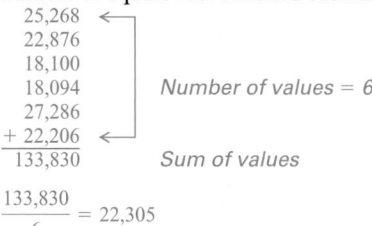

$$\frac{133,830}{6} = 22,305$$

10. Bubba travels between Springdale and Fort Worth regularly for business. The small airline changes prices regularly. In July the round trip fare was $221. In August the price was $257. In September there was a special $99. In October the price went back up to $244. Find the average price Bubba had to pay for travel.

$$\begin{array}{r} \$221 \\ 257 \\ 99 \\ + \ 244 \\ \hline \$821 \end{array} \quad \textit{Number of values = 4}$$

Sum of values

$$\frac{\$821}{4} = \$205.25$$

22.3

11. Mr.Krum's third grade class made the following grades on a test: Betty, 80; Clyde, 75; Donna, 94; Eddie, 96; Florence, 79; Gary, 87; Hanna, 90. Who made the median grade in the class and what was it?

Step 1. Arrange the data into an array:
   75, 79, 80, 87, 90, 94, 96

Step 2. Count the number of values (there are seven).

Step 3. The middle value would be in the fourth position counting from either end:

$$\frac{7 + 1}{2} = 4$$

Step 4. The median is 87 (the fourth value from either end of the array).

Step 5. Gary made the median grade.

12. Brita's Doll shop had the folowing revenues for the first half of the last year: January, $18,000; February, $12,000; March, $28,000; April, $10,000; May, $8,000; June, $27,000. Find the median revenue.

Step 1. Arrange the data into an array:
   $8,000, 10,000, 12,000, 18,000, 27,000, 28,000

Step 2. Count the number of values (there are six).

Step 3. The middle value would be halfway between third and fourth values from either end:

$$\frac{6 + 1}{2} = 3.5$$

Step 4. The median is the mean of $12,000 and $18,000 (the third and fourth value from either end of the array).

Step 5. $\dfrac{\$12,000 + 18,000}{2} = \$15,000$

13. Employees of the Mortz Co. traveled from different directions the folowing miles to commute to work last month: 440 miles, 650 miles, 360 miles, 330 miles, 250 miles, 970 miles. Find the median mileage traveled.

Step 1. Arrange the data into an array:
   250, 330, 360, 440, 650, 970

Step 2. Count the number of values (there are six).

Step 3. The middle value would be halfway between the third and fourth values from either end:

$$\frac{6 + 1}{2} = 3.5$$

Step 4. The median is the mean of 360 and 440 (the third and fourth values from either end of the array).

Step 5. $\dfrac{360 + 440}{2} = 400$

14. An investor bought six different corporate bonds. They pay rates of 5%, 8%, 8%, 11%, 9%, and 12%. Find the median rate of return on the different bonds.

Step 1. Arrange the data into an array:
   5%, 8%, 8%, 9%, 11%, 12%

Step 2. Count the number of values (there are six).

Step 3. The middle value would be halfway between the third and fourth values from either end:

$$\frac{6 + 1}{2} = 3.5$$

Step 4. The median is the mean of 8% and 9% (the third and fourth values from either end of the array).

Step 5. $\dfrac{8\% + 9\%}{2} = 8.5\%$

15. A union negotiated the following hourly pay increases over the past five years: $.70, $.84, $1.32, $.44, $.91. Find the median pay increase for the membership.

Step 1. Arrange the data into an array:
   $.44, $70, $.84, $.91, $1.32

Step 2. Count the number of values (there are five).

Step 3. The middle value would be in the third position counting from either end:

$$\frac{5 + 1}{2} = 3$$

Step 4. The median is $.84 (the third value from either end of the array).

22.4

16. Find the mode for salaries at Martha's plumbing shop: Ann, $325; Bill, $377; Carl, $430; Donna, $360; Ernest, $402; Flora, $402; Gary $170.

Value	Frequency
$170	1
325	1
360	1
377	1
402 = mode	2
430	1

17. The number of telephone calls received each day last week at Colonel Bob's Fried Chicken were as follows: Monday, 35; Tuesday, 30; Wedneday, 55; Thursday, 40; Friday, 40; Saturday, 25. What number of calls represents the daily mode?

Value	Frequency
25	1
30	1
35	1
40 = mode	2
55	1

18. Determine the mode for stockers' hourly wages at Office Barginmarket: $8.50, $8.00, $9.00, $7.00, $5.50, $5.50, $5.50, $5.50.

Value	Frequency
$5.50 = mode	4
7.00	1
8.00	1
8.50	1
9.00	1

19. Find the mode weekly hours worked at the Old Nantucket factory over the last two months: week 1, 1,240 hours; week 2, 1,320 hours; week 3, 1,300 hours; week 4, 1,240 hours; week 5, 1,240 hours; week 6, 1,320 hours; week 7, 1,300 hours; week 8, 1,320 hours.

Value	Frequency	
1,240 = mode	3	
1,300	2	(bimodal)
1,320 = mode	3	

20. A bakery sells several different flavors of cookies by the dozen at different prices. The prices per dozen are $1.87, $3.98, $1.87, $2.96, $1.87, $3.98, $3.98, $3.98, $2.96. Find the modal price.

Value	Frequency
$1.87	3
2.96	2
3.98 = mode	4

22.5

21. A basketball team made the following numbers of points per game during the season: 70–80, 6 times; 60–69, 4 times; 50–59, 6 times; 40–49, 12 times. Find the mean, median, and the mode points per game.

No. of Points (class)	No. of Games (frequency)	Midpoint of Class $\left(\frac{Low + high}{2} = m\right)$	Product (f × m)
70–80	6	75	450
60–69	4	64.5	258
50–59	6	54.5	327
40–49	+ 12	44.5	+ 534
	28		1,569

$$\frac{1,569}{28} = 56.036 \text{ Mean}$$

$$\frac{28 + 1}{2} = 14.5\text{th number in the frequency}$$

Counting from either end, the 14.5th value will fall in the class 50–59. The midpoint of that class is 54.5, the median.

Since 40–49 appears the most times (12), 44.5 is the mode.

22. Of the workers in a dress factory 8 produced between 76 and 80 dresses per week, 10 produced between 71 and 75, 19 produced between 66 and 70, 11 produced between 61 and 65, 5 produced between 56 and 60, and 2 produced between 51 and 55. Find the mean for the number of dresses produced by each worker in the factory, the median production per worker, and the mode.

No. of Dresses (class)	No. of Workers (frequency)	Midpoint of Class $\left(\frac{Low + high}{2} = m\right)$	Product (f × m)
76–80	8	78	624
71–75	10	73	730
66–70	19	68	1,292
61–65	11	63	693
56–60	5	58	290
51–55	+ 2	53	+ 106
	55		3,735

$$\frac{3,735}{55} = 67.73 \text{ Mean}$$

$$\frac{55 + 1}{2} = 28\text{th value in the frequency}$$

Counting from either end, 28 will fall in the class 66–70. The midpoint of that class is 68, the median.
Since 66–70 appears the most times (12), and $\frac{66 + 70}{2} = 68$, 68 is the mode.

23. Find the mean, median, and mode for the weights of linemen on a college football team.

Weight Class	Frequency	Midpoint of Class $\left(\frac{Low + high}{2} = m\right)$	Product (f × m)
311–325	4	318	1,272
296–310	10	303	3,030
281–295	18	288	5,184
266–280	10	273	2,730
251–265	+ 4	258	+ 1,032
	46		13,248

$$\frac{13,248}{46} = 288 \text{ Mean}$$

$$\frac{46 + 1}{2} = 23.5\text{th value in the frequency}$$

Counting from either end, the 23.5th value will fall in the class 281–295. The midpoint of that class is 288, the median.
Since 281–295 appears the most times (18), 288 is the mode.

24. Find the mean, median, and mode for the following numbers of flower pots produced by the 39 workers in a factory in Mexico one day:

31	40	16	37	21	39	40	31	40	25
17	22	31	30	16	18	31	40	34	30
21	36	26	32	29	36	32	36	39	40
36	35	25	31	24	35	34	31	34	

No. of Pots (class)	No. of Workers (frequency)	Midpoint of Class $\left(\frac{Low + high}{2} = m\right)$	Product $(f \times m)$
16–20	4	18	72
21–25	6	23	138
26–30	4	28	112
31–35	13	33	429
36–40	+ 12	38	+ 456
	39		1,207

$$\frac{1,207}{39} = 30.949 \text{ Mean}$$

$$\frac{39 + 1}{2} = 20\text{th number in the frequency}$$

Counting from either end, the 20th value will fall in the class 31–35. The midpoint of that class is 33, the median.

Since 31–35 appears the most times (13), 33 is the mode.

25. Find the mean, median, and mode of the January sales by employees of the Hutcheson Manufacturing Co.

January Sales	Frequency	Midpoint of Class $\left(\frac{Low + high}{2} = m\right)$	Product $(f \times m)$
$30,000–$31,999	5	$30,999.50	$ 154,997.50
28,000– 29,999	39	28,999.50	1,130,980.50
26,000– 27,999	66	26,999.50	1,781,967.00
24,000– 25,999	37	24,999.50	924,981.50
22,000– 23,999	+ 9	22,999.50	+ 206,995.50
	156		$4,199,922.00

$$\frac{\$4,199,922}{156} = \$26,922.58 \text{ Mean}$$

$$\frac{156 + 1}{2} = 78.5\text{th number in the frequency}$$

Counting from either end, the 78.5th value will fall in the class $26,000–$27,999. The midpoint of that class is $26,999,50, the median.

Since $26,000–$27,999 appears the most times (66), $26,999.50 is the mode.

22.6

26. Draw a bar graph showing a comparison of sales for the month of July for the following salespeople at Herman's Computer Mart:

Salesperson	Sales in July
Albert	$37,000
Barbara	30,000
Calvin	34,000
Dolores	20,000
Eddie	24,000
Gary	27,000

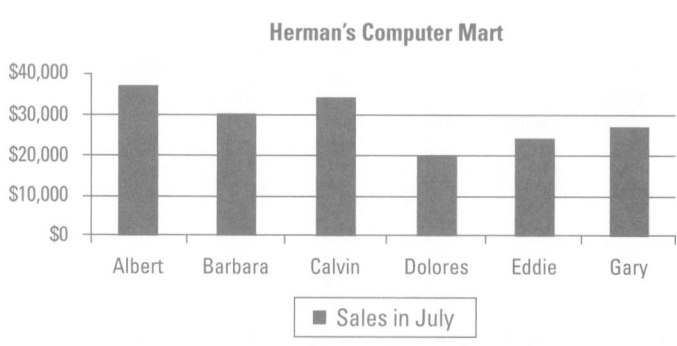

27. Prepare a bar graph for Ben's Cakes' sales for the last six months of this year compared to last year.

Month	Sales Last Year	Sales This Year
July	$200,000	$220,000
Aug.	100,000	80,000
Sept.	240,000	270,000
Oct.	290,000	300,000
Nov.	320,000	340,000
Dec.	300,000	380,000

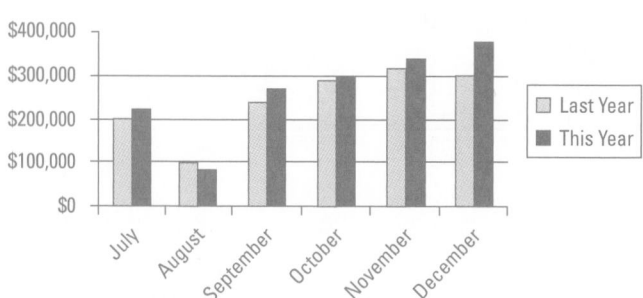

28. Construct a bar graph to illustrate changes in sales for three major auto companies.

Company	Sales Last Year (in billions)	Sales This Year (in billions)
G.M.	$450	$400
Ford	250	260
Chrysler	180	140

Major Auto Companies
Changes in Sales Between Last Year and This Year

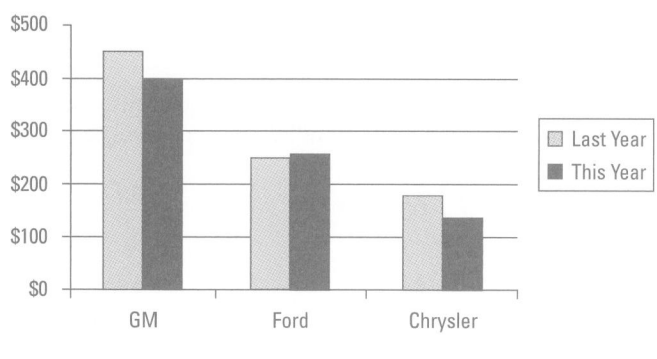

29. Alphonso's Bike Shop sells Blue Streak and Red Speedster brands of bicycles. Use bar graphs to illustrate the number of sales in each category of prices the shop sold last week.

Price Range	Blue Streak	Red Speedster
$100–199	4	4
200–399	7	2
400–499	7	5
600–799	3	2
800–999	3	3

Alphonso's Bike Shop
Number of Sales by Category of Price Ranges and Models

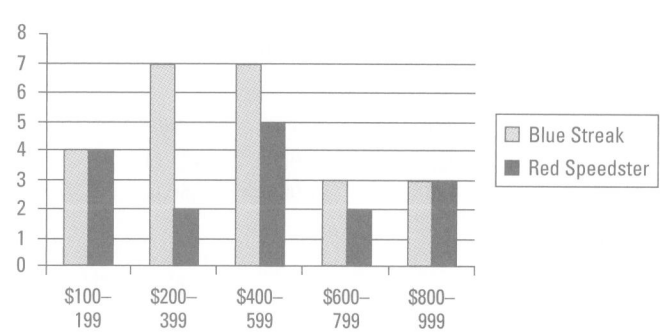

30. The Barton Paper Company had a bad year and lowered the salaries of its top five executives as follows:

Executive	Salary Last Year	Salary This Year
Amilda	$200,000	$180,000
Bob	245,000	300,000
Carolyn	160,000	130,000
Donald	90,000	80,000
Edith	250,000	160,000

Illustrate the salary changes with a bar graph.

Barton Paper Company
Salary Changes of Top Five Executives

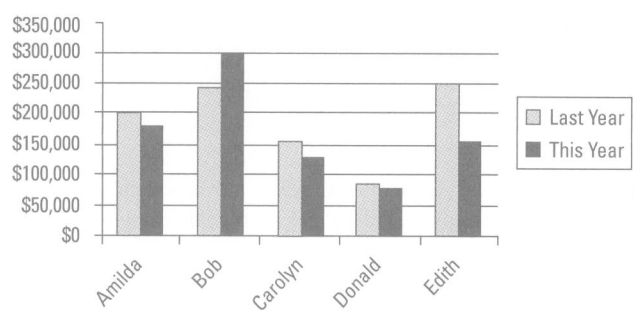

22.7

31. Prepare a line graph that compares the sales with prices Joe paid for food and drinks at Joe's Cafe for the following week:

Day	Sales	Price Paid
Mon.	$1,670	$1,000
Tues.	2,010	1,140
Wed.	2,200	1,200
Thurs.	1,940	1,000
Fri.	1,900	1,300
Sat.	2,000	1,000

Joe's Cafe
Value of Sales Compared to the Price Paid

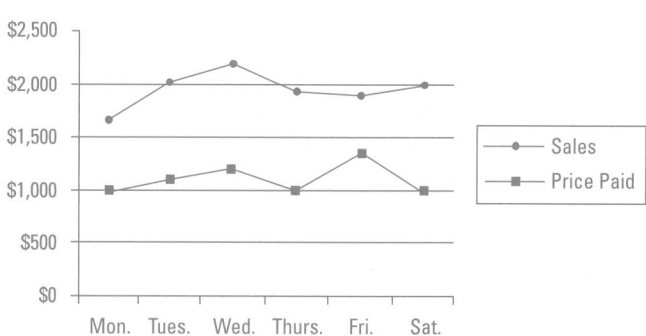

32. Two competing companies had the following sales during the last half of last year:

Month	Sharp's Cleaners (in thousands)	Dullie's Cleaners (in thousands)
July	$10	$25
Aug.	13	17
Sept.	21	15
Oct.	24	18
Nov.	33	14
Dec.	23	17

Prepare a line graph that compares the two companies' sales.

Sharp's and Dullie's Cleaners
Comparison of Sales
(in thousands)

33. Mildred operates two bakeries. The small one is situated in an office building downtown serving a limited group of customers. The large bakery sells to institutions such as churches. Using the following data for the final half of last year, compare the two stores with a line graph:

Store	July	Aug.	Sept.	Oct.	Nov.	Dec.
Small	$30,000	$35,000	$25,000	$30,000	$35,000	$25,000
Large	64,000	54,000	50,000	80,000	84,000	74,000

Mildred's Bakeries
Comparison of Sales for Final Half of Year

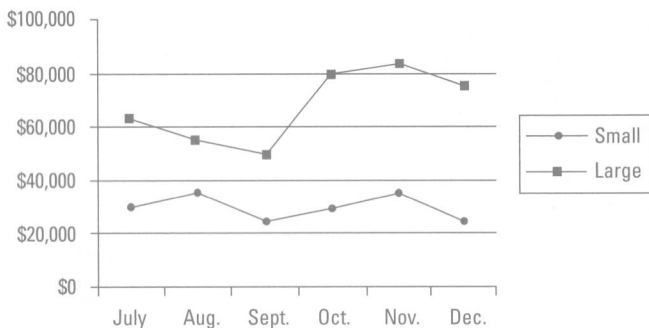

34. One week last September the Dow moved erratically between bull and bear markets. Prepare a line graph to illustrate the closing price of the Dow Jones average on each day.

Day	Dow-Jones Average
Mon.	11,040
Tues.	11,220
Wed.	11,160
Thurs.	11,240
Fri.	11,400

Dow-Jones Average
Closing Price of Dow for a Week

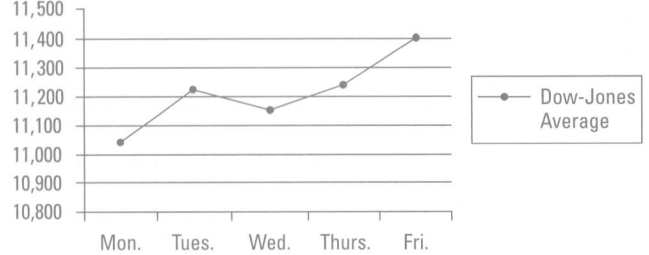

35. Prepare a line graph to illustrate the volume of net sales and net profits of the Nixon Watercraft Company.

Year	Net Sales	Net Profit
1	$165,000	$17,000
2	174,000	17,000
3	171,000	17,300
4	179,000	20,000
5	195,000	21,000
6	200,000	16,300
7	219,000	17,000

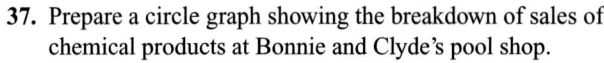

Nixon Watercraft Company
Volume of Net Sales and Net Profits

22.8

36. Prepare a circle graph to show the major components of the Acer Computer Company's income last year.

Computers	Monitors	Printers	Software	Other
60%	20%	10%	5%	5%

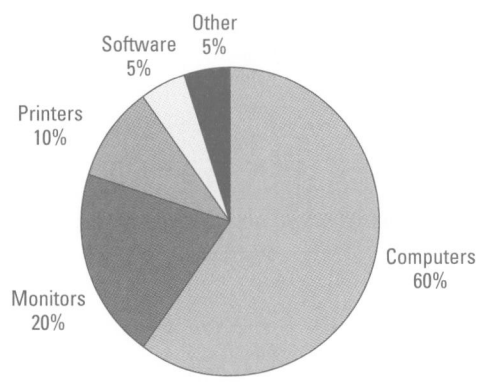

Acer Computer Company
Sales by Major Components

37. Prepare a circle graph showing the breakdown of sales of chemical products at Bonnie and Clyde's pool shop.

Chlorine	Stabilizer	Soda Ash	Acid
45%	10%	20%	25%

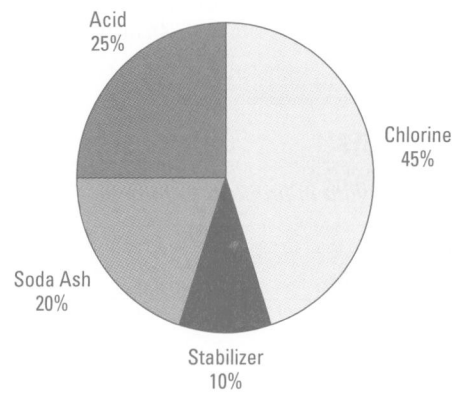

Bonnie and Clyde's Pool Shop
Breakdown by Sales of Chemical Products

38. Texas Steel's balance sheet reveals the following current liabilities situation (in percents):

Accounts payable	33%
Notes payable	17%
Salaries payable	28%
Taxes payable	22%

Prepare a circle graph to illustrate the situation.

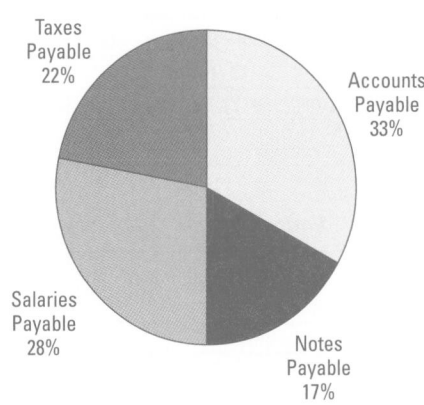

Texas Steel
Debt and Equity Situation

39. State tax money is used to provide many governmental services. Draw a circle graph to demonstrate the relationship of the following services per $100:

Highway building and maintenance	$25
Education	30
State correctional institutions	40
Other	5

40. Jill's White Goods sold the following number of sheets last week:

King-size sheets	$700
Queen-size sheets	200
Full-size sheets	300
Twin-size sheets	100

With a circle graph, show how sales of each type of sheet relate to the total sales in percents.

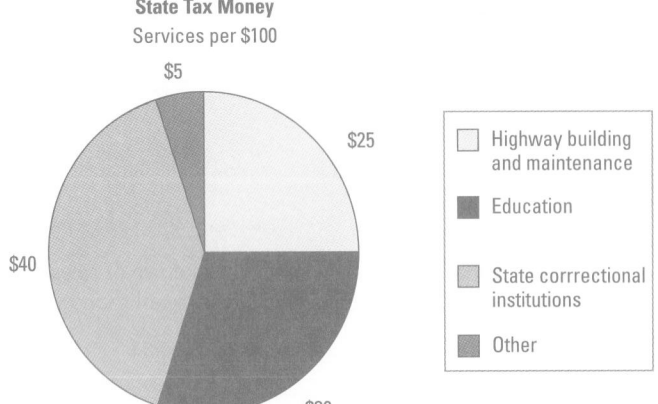

State Tax Money
Services per $100

$5 · $25 · $40 · $30

Highway building and maintenance · Education · State correctional institutions · Other

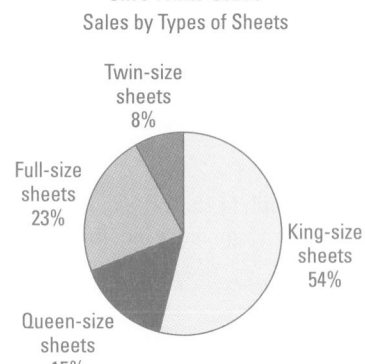

Jill's White Goods
Sales by Types of Sheets

Twin-size sheets 8% · Full-size sheets 23% · King-size sheets 54% · Queen-size sheets 15%

CHAPTER REVIEW PROBLEMS

Answers to odd-numbered problems are given in Appendix A.

Drill Problems

Arrange the raw data in problems 1 through 15 into arrays, perform a frequency distribution, and find the range.

	Raw data	31, 37, 8, 37, 9, 31, 37
1.	Array	8, 9, 31, 31, 37, 37, 37
2.	Frequency	8 (1), 9 (1), 31 (2), 37 (3)
3.	Range	29

	Raw data	87, 42, 112, 37, 42, 87
4.	Array	37, 42, 42, 87, 87, 112
5.	Frequency	37 (1), 42 (2), 87 (2), 112 (1)
6.	Range	75

	Raw data	68, 50, 84, 68, 26 50, 68
7.	Array	26, 50, 50, 68, 68, 68, 84
8.	Frequency	26 (1), 50 (2), 68 (3), 84 (1)
9.	Range	58

	Raw data	1,097, 501, 1,492, 1,097, 1,492, 1,097, 501, 1,097
10.	Array	501, 501, 1,097, 1,097, 1,097, 1,097, 1,492, 1,492
11.	Frequency	501 (2), 1,097 (4), 1,492 (2)
12.	Range	991

	Raw data	6, 42, 78, 30, 78, 6, 30
13.	Array	6, 6, 30, 30, 42, 78, 78
14.	Frequency	6 (2), 30 (2), 42 (1), 78 (2)
15.	Range	72

Find the mean, median, and mode in the following problems:

	Raw Data	22, 23, 27, 21, 22
16.	Mean	23
17.	Median	22
18.	Mode	22

	Raw Data	37, 47, 86, 55, 37, 38
19.	Mean	50
20.	Median	42.5
21.	Mode	37

Word Problems

22. Arko Electric produced the following millions of kilowatts of electricity last week: Sunday, 5,769; Monday, 5,211; Tuesday, 6,732; Wednesday, 5,625; Thursday, 4,275; Friday, 8,166; Saturday, 3,132. Find the arithmetic mean for daily production.

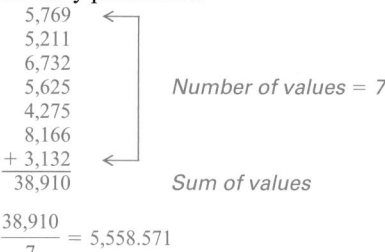

$$\frac{38,910}{7} = 5,558.571$$

23. Josh's grades in accounting last semester were 77, 86, 93, 78, 94, 66. Find his average grade for the semester.

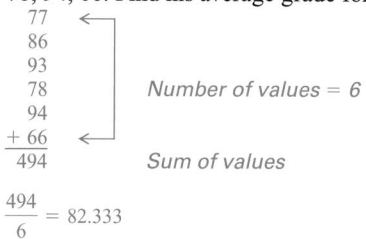

$$\frac{494}{6} = 82.333$$

24. Jan's Cafe serves lunch. Last Monday she served 55; Tuesday, 50; Wednesday, 52; Thursday, 49; and Friday, 49. Find the arithmetic mean for the number of lunches served each day.

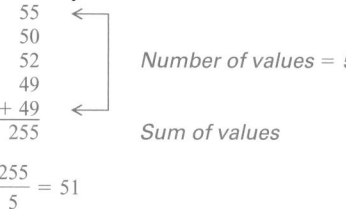

$$\frac{255}{5} = 51$$

25. Monroe Contractors pours concrete. In each of the months in the first half of last year Ms. Monroe's company poured the following number of square feet: January, 12,635; February, 11,438; March, 9,050; April, 9,047; May, 13,643; June, 11,103. Find the average number of square feet poured each month.

```
12,635  ←─┐
11,438     │
 9,050     │
 9,047     ├── Number of values = 6
13,643     │
+ 11,103 ←─┘
66,916      Sum of values
```

$$\frac{66,916}{6} = 11,152.667$$

26. Barbara buys out-of-town newspapers at a bookstore every Sunday. The *Washington Post* costs $3.75, the *Los Angeles Times* costs $3.25, the *Saint Louis Post* costs $2.75, The *New York Times* costs $4.00, and The *Atlanta Journal* costs $2.50. Find the average price Barbara pays for the newspapers.

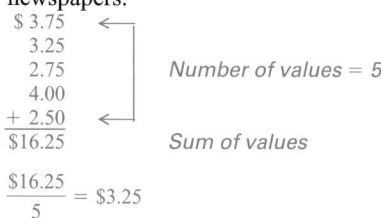

$$\frac{\$16.25}{5} = \$3.25$$

27. Dr. Schoppmeyer's graduate class made the following grades in a seminar: Bob, 90; Cristy, 85; Darrel, 94; Emilda, 97; Frank, 89; Gary, 87; and Helen, 92. Who made the median grade?

Step 1. Arrange the data into an array:
  85, 87, 89, 90, 92, 94, 97

Step 2. Count the number of values (there are seven).

Step 3. The middle value would be in the fourth position counting from either end:

$$\frac{7 + 1}{2} = 4$$

Step 4. The median is Bob's, 90 (the fourth value from either end of the array).

28. Ben's Donut Shop had the following revenues for the first half of last year: January, $6,000; February, $4,000; March, $9,333; April, $3,000; May, $2,000; June, $9,000. Find the median.

Step 1. Arrange the data into an array:
  $2,000, 3,000, 4,000, 6,000, 9,000, 9,333

Step 2. Count the number of values (there are six).

Step 3. The middle value would be halfway between the third and fourth values from either end:

$$\frac{6 + 1}{2} = 3.5$$

Step 4. The median is the mean of $4,000 and $6,000 (the third and fourth values from either end of the array).

Step 5. $\dfrac{\$4,000 + 6,000}{2} = \$5,000$

29. Some employees of Amalgamated Inc. traveled on vacations last summer. They traveled 660 miles, 580 miles, 540 miles, 495 miles, 375 miles, and 1,455 miles. Find the median mileage.

Step 1. Arrange the data into an array:
  375, 495, 540, 580, 660, 1,455

Step 2. Count the number of values (there are six).

Step 3. The middle value would be halfway between the third and fourth values from either end.

$$\frac{6 + 1}{2} = 3.5$$

Step 4. The median is the mean of 540 and 580 (the third and fourth values from either end of the array).

Step 5. $\dfrac{540 + 580}{2} = 560$

30. An investor bought six different corporate bonds. They pay interest rates of 6%, 9%, 9%, 12%, 10%. Find the median rate on the different bonds.

Step 1. Arrange the data into an array:
6%, 9%, 9%, 10%, 12%

Step 2. Count the number of values (there are five).

Step 3. The middle value would be halfway between the third and fourth values from either end.

$$\frac{5 + 1}{2} = 3$$

Step 4. The median value is 9% (the third and fourth value from either end of the array).

31. George's union negotiated the following hourly pay increases over the past four years: $1.70, $.94, $1.02, $.64. Find the median pay increase for the membership.

Step 1. Arrange the data into an array:
$.64, .94, 1.02, 1.70

Step 2. Count the number of values (there are four).

Step 3. The middle value would be halfway between the second and third values from either end:

$$\frac{4 + 1}{2} = 2.5$$

Step 4. The median is the mean of $.94 and $1.02 (the second and third values from either end of the array).

Step 5. $\dfrac{\$.94 + 1.02}{2} = \$.98$

32. Find the modal weekly salary at Marvin's Boutique: Arnold, $422.50; Bell, $490.10; Carl, $559; Doris, $468; Elmer, $522.60; Florence, $522.60; George; $221.

Value	Frequency
$221.00	1
422.50	1
468.00	1
490.10	1
522.60-mode	2
559.00	1

33. The number of customers each day last week at Barney's Rock Shop was as follows: Monday, 48; Tuesday, 36; Wednesday, 66; Thursday, 48; Friday, 48; Saturday, 36. How many customers represent the daily mode?

Value	Frequency
36	2
48-mode	3
66	1

34. Determine the mode for workers' monthly wages at Computer Discount Mart: $1,360, $1,280, $1,440, $1,120, $880, $880, $880, $880, $1,280 $1,440.

Value	Frequency
$ 880-mode	4
1,120	1
1,280	2
1,360	1
1,440	2

35. Find the mode for weekly hours worked at the New Rothschild factory over the last six weeks: week 1, 1,488 hours; week 2, 1,584 hours; week 3, 1,560 hours; week 4, 1,488 hours; week 5, 1,584 hours; week 6, 1,584 hours.

Value	Frequency
$1,488	2
1,584-mode	3
1,560	1

36. A decorator makes several different styles of wedding cakes at different prices. The prices are $57.07, $123.38, $57.97, $91.76, $57.07, $123.38, $92.38, $123.38, $91.76. Find the modal price for wedding cakes.

Value	Frequency
$57.07	2
57.97	1
91.76	2
92.38	1
123.38-mode	3

37. The top running backs of each college of the Southeastern Conference West ran the following number of yards last year: Alabama, 620; Arkansas, 544; Auburn, 550; LSU, 420; Mississippi State, 570; Ole Miss, 550. Find the mean, median, and mode.

Array

420	$\dfrac{3,254}{6} = 542.333$ *Mean*
544	
550	$\dfrac{6 + 1}{2} = 3.5$th *value in the*
550	*frequency*
570	
+ 620	
3,254 *Sum of values*	

Counting from either end, 3.5 is between 550, and 550, so 550 is the median.

Since 550 appears the most times (2), it is also the mode.

38. Of the workers in a dress factory 7 sewed between 76 and 80 dresses per week, 9 sewed between 71 and 75, 18 sewed between 66 and 70, 10 sewed between 61 and 65, 4 sewed between 56 and 60, and 1 sewed between 51 and 55. Find the arithmetic mean for the number of dresses sewn by each worker in the factory, the median production per worker, and the mode.

No. of Dresses (class)	No. of Workers (frequency)	Midpoint of Class $\left(\dfrac{Low + high}{2} = m\right)$	Product (f × m)
76–80	7	78	546
71–75	9	73	657
66–70	18	68	1,224
61–65	10	63	630
56–60	4	58	232
51–55	+ 1	53	+ 53
	49		3,342

$\dfrac{3,342}{49} = 68.204$ *Mean*

$\dfrac{49 + 1}{2} = 25$th *value in the frequency*

Counting from either end, the 25th value will fall in the class 66–70. The midpoint of that class is 68, the median.

Since 66–70 appears the most times (18), 68 is the mode.

39. Find the mean, median, and mode for the weights of customers in a weight-reduction establishment.

Weight Class	Frequency	Midpoint of Class $\left(\dfrac{Low + high}{2} = m\right)$	Product $(f \times m)$
211–225	3	218	654
196–210	14	203	2,842
181–195	12	188	2,256
166–180	9	173	1,557
151–165	+ 3	158	+ 474
	41		7,783

$\dfrac{7,783}{41} = 189.829$ *Mean*

$\dfrac{41 + 1}{2} = 21$st *value in the frequency*

Counting from either end, the 21st value will fall in the class 181–195. The midpoint of that class is 188, the median.

Since 196–210 appears the most times (14), 203 is the mode.

40. Find the mean, median, and mode for the following numbers of toys produced by the 19 workers in a Chinese factory one day:

40 52 21 48 27 51 52 40 52 33
22 29 40 39 21 23 40 52 44

No. of Toys (class)	No. of Workers (frequency)	Midpoint of Class $\left(\dfrac{Low + high}{2} = m\right)$	Product $(f \times m)$
21–25	4	23	92
26–30	2	28	56
31–35	1	33	33
36–40	5	38	190
41–45	1	43	43
46–50	1	48	48
51–55	+5	53	+265
	19		727

$\dfrac{727}{19} = 38.263$ *Mean*

$\dfrac{19 + 1}{2}$ = the median is the 10th *value in the frequency*

Counting from either end, the 10th value will fall in the class 36–40.
The midpoint of that class is 38, the median.

Since 36–40 and 51–55 appear the most times (5), 38 and 53 are the modes; the data are bimodal.

41. Find the mean, median, and mode of the daily January receipts of the Armey Demolition Company's home office and various subsidiaries.

January Receipts	Frequency	Midpoint of Class $\left(\dfrac{Low + high}{2} = m\right)$	Product $(f \times m)$
$130,000–$131,999	4	$130,999.50	$523,998.00
128,000– 129,999	38	128,999.50	4,901,981.00
126,000– 127,999	65	126,999.50	8,254,967.50
124,000– 125,999	36	124,999.50	4,499,982.00
122,000– 123,999	+ 8	122,999.50	+ 983,996.00
	151		$19,164,924.50

$\dfrac{\$19,164,924.50}{151} = \$126,920.03$ *Mean*

$\dfrac{151 + 1}{2} = 76$th *value in the frequency*

Counting from either end, the 76th value will fall in the class $126,000–127,999. The midpoint of that class is $126,999.50, the median.

Since $126,000–127,999 appears the most times (65), $126,999.50 is the mode.

42. Draw a bar graph showing a comparison of sales for the month of June for the following salespeople at Wheely's Inc.:

Salesperson	Sales in June
Allie	$28,000
Bill	21,000
Carol	25,000
Darrel	11,000
Edith	15,000
Connie	18,000

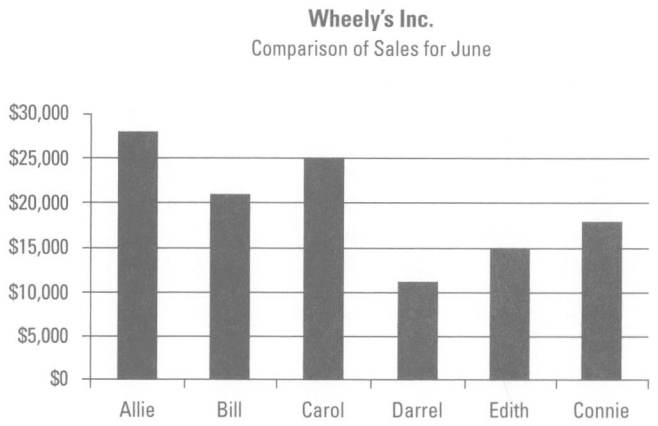

43. Prepare a bar graph for pipe sales at Al's Pipe Shop for the last six months of this year compared to last year.

Month	Last Year	This Year
July	$50,000	$55,000
Aug.	25,000	20,000
Sept.	60,000	70,000
Oct.	70,000	75,000
Nov.	80,000	85,000
Dec.	75,000	95,000

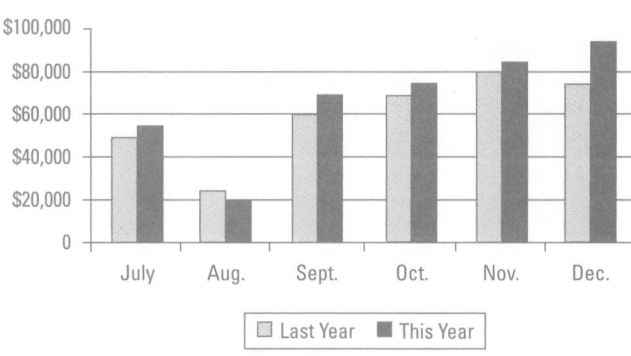

Al's Pipe Shop
Comparison of Sales for Last Six Months Last Year to This Year

44. Construct a bar graph to illustrate changes in sales for three competing steel companies.

Company	Last Year (in billions)	This Year (in billions)
U.S.X.	$50	$54
Bethlehem	25	30
Inland	20	10

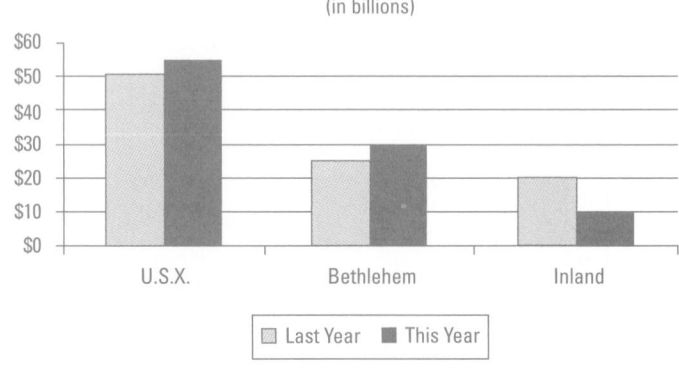

Competing Steel Companies
Changes in Sales from Last Year to This Year
(in billions)

45. Terri's Sporting Goods sells wooden bats and aluminum bats. Use bar graphs to illustrate the categories of prices the shop sold last month.

Price Range	Wooden	Aluminum
$10–19	4	4
20–39	7	2
40–59	7	5
60–79	3	2
80–99	3	3

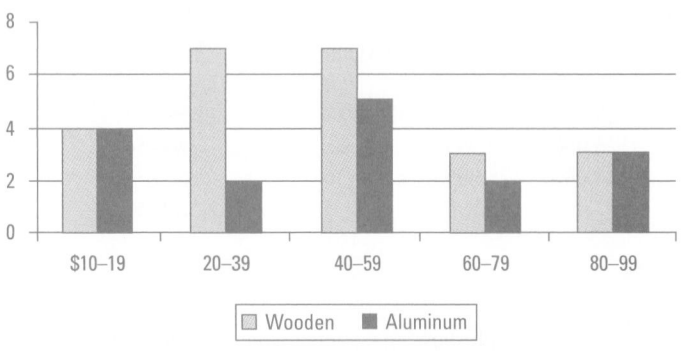

Terri's Sporting Goods
Comparison of Wooden to Aluminum Bat Sales

46. The Geren Company had a bad year and lowered the monthly salaries of its lowest paid workers as follows:

	Monthly Salary	
Worker	Last Year	Salary This Year
Kevin	$1,000	$ 900
Bob	1,500	1,200
Carolyn	800	750
Donald	450	400
Edith	1,300	1,000

Illustrate the salary changes with a bar graph.

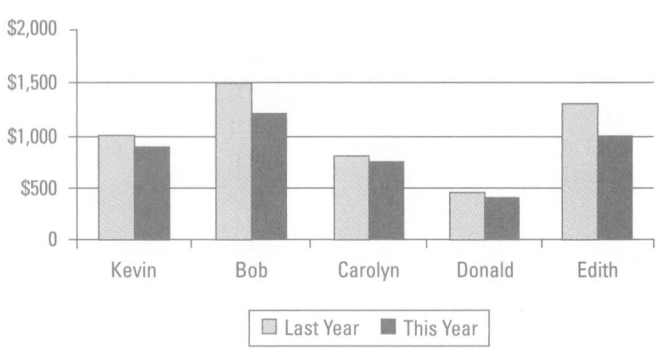

The Geren Company
Lowering Salaries of Lowest Paid Workers

47. Prepare a line graph that compares the weekly sales receipts from toys at Marty's Toy Store to the price Marty paid for the toys from wholesalers.

Day	Sales	Wholesale Costs
Mon.	$3,200	$2,000
Tues.	4,000	2,200
Wed.	4,400	2,400
Thurs.	3,800	2,000
Fri.	4,800	2,600
Sat.	6,000	3,000

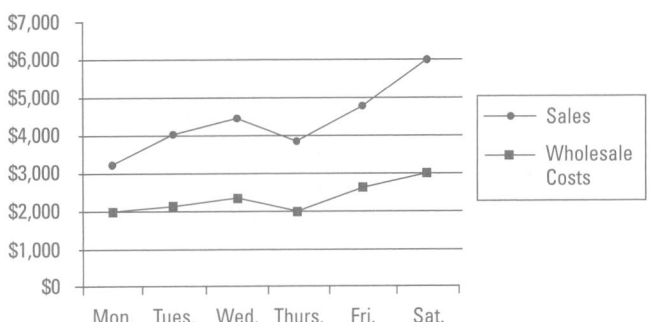

Marty's Toy Store
Weekly Value of Sales and Wholesale Prices

48. Two competing companies had the following sales during the last half of last year:

Month	Slick Used Cars	Good Used Cars
July	30	75
Aug.	39	34
Sept.	42	30
Oct.	48	36
Nov.	66	28
Dec.	46	34

Prepare a line graph that compares the two companies' sales.

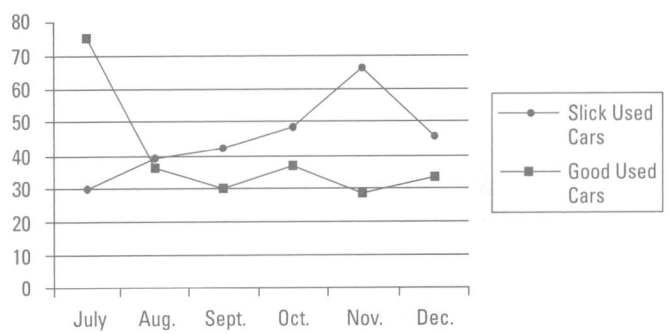

Slick Cars and Good Cars
Comparison of Sales during the Last Half of the Year

49. Gerald operates two plumbing shops. The large one is situated in Detroit and the small one is in Dearborn. Using the following data for the final half of last year, compare sales in the two shops with a line graph:

Shop	July	Aug.	Sept.	Oct.
Dearborn	$10,000	$12,000	$ 8,000	$10,000
Detroit	21,000	18,000	17,000	27,000

Shop	Nov.	Dec.
Dearborn	$12,000	$8,000
Detroit	28,000	25,000

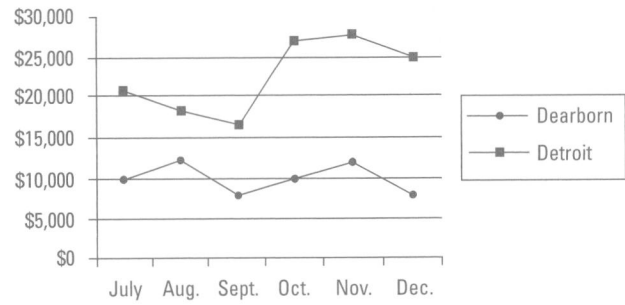

Gerald's Plumbing Shops
Comparison of Sales at Dearborn Shop and Detroit Shop

50. One week last May the Dow moved up and down all week. Prepare a line graph to illustrate the movement.

Day	Dow-Jones Average
Mon.	10,002
Tues.	9,956
Wed.	9,790
Thurs.	10,057
Fri.	9,847

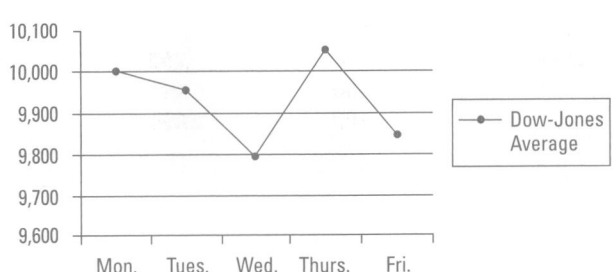

Dow-Jones Average
Movement One Week in May

51. Prepare a line graph to illustrate the volume of sales and net profit of the Falwell Bookban Company.

Year	Net Sales	Net Profit
1	$355,000	$127,000
2	265,000	108,000
3	262,000	128,300
4	168,000	111,000
5	286,000	130,000
6	300,000	107,300
7	308,000	126,000

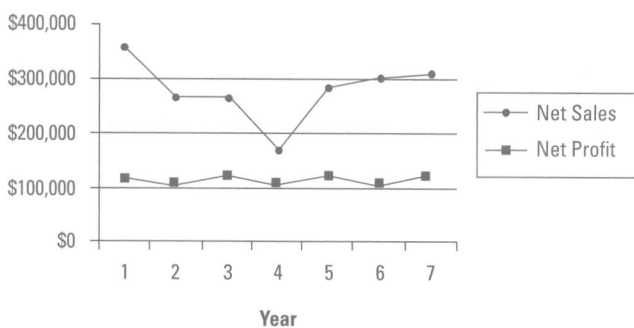

Falwell Bookban Company
Volume of Sales and Net Profit

52. Prepare a circle graph to show the major components of sales at Newt's Bake Shop last year.

Cakes	Donuts	Cookies
30%	60%	10%

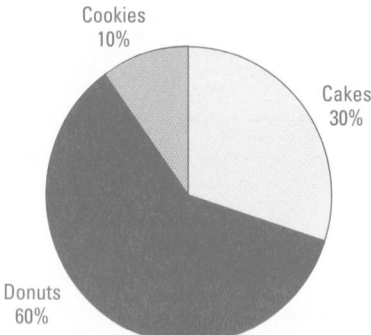

Newt's Bake Shop
Sales by Major Components

53. Prepare a circle graph showing the breakdown of products at Joe's Candy store.

Fudge	Jelly Beans	Peppermint	Caramel
40%	10%	25%	25%

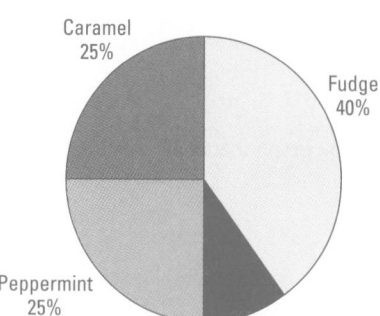

Joe's Candy Store
Breakdown of Products

54. Scott Thurman's Basketball Supply's balance sheet reveals the following long-term debt and equity situation (in millions):

Long-term liabilities	$40
Preferred stock	20
Common stock	30
Retained earnings	10

Prepare a bar graph to illustrate the situation.

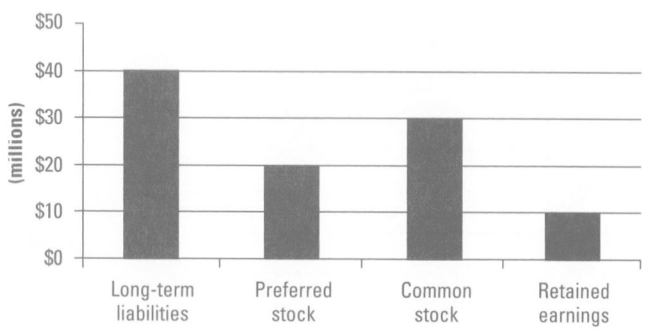

Scott Thurman's Basketball Supply
Long-Term Debt and Equity

55. Federal revenue is spent for many things. Draw a circle graph to demonstrate the relationship of each to the whole.

National defense	22%
Social security	35%
Interest	14%
Social programs	18%
Other	11%

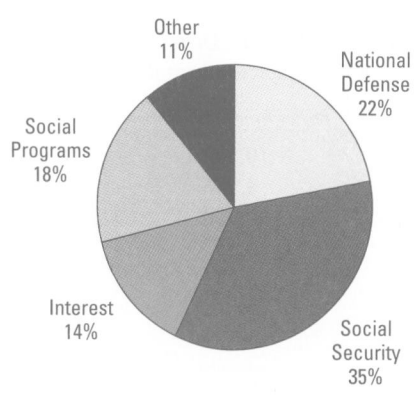

Federal Tax Money
Relationship of Spending

56. John's Wholesale Furniture Outlet sold the following selection of products last week:

Chairs	$21,000
Tables	60,000
Sofas	90,000
Beds	30,000

With a circle graph, show how sales of each type of each item relate to the total sales by percents.

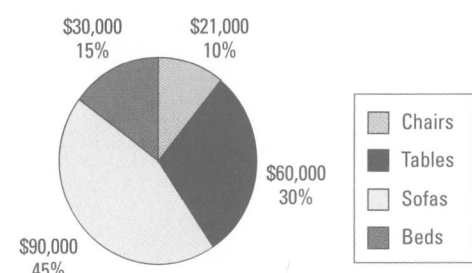

John's Wholesale Furniture Outlet
Relationship of Each Item to Total Sales

$30,000 15% $21,000 10%

Chairs
Tables
Sofas
Beds

$60,000 30%

$90,000 45%

✓ ENRICHMENT PROBLEMS

57. The west gate of the Seven Flags Amusement Park was open 10 hours last Saturday. The turnstile counted the following number of patrons each of those hours:

8:00– 9:00	2,318	1:00–2:00	2,336
9:00–10:00	2,318	2:00–3:00	2,088
10:00–11:00	3,122	3:00–4:00	1,114
11:00–12:00	2,437	4:00–5:00	2,318
12:00– 1:00	2,212	5:00–6:00	2,336

Arrange the data into an array; perform a frequency distribution; and find the mean, median, and mode.

Array: 1,114, 2,088, 2,212, 2,318, 2,318, 2,318, 2,336, 2,336, 2,437, 3,122

Frequency Distribution

Value	Frequency
1,114	1
2,088	1
2,212	1
2,318	3
2,336	2
2,437	1
3,122	1

1,114 ←
2,088
2,212
2,318
2,318
2,318
2,336
2,336
2,437
+ 3,122 ←
——
22,599   *Sum of values*

$$\frac{22,599}{10} = 2,259.9 \quad Mean$$

Number of values = 10 $\frac{10 + 1}{2} = 5.5$th *value in the frequency*

Counting from either end, the 5.5th value will fall between 2,318 and 2,318, which makes that number the median.

Since 2,318 appears the most times (4), it is also the mode.

58. Mildred writes letters to the editor of her local paper regularly. Last year the following numbers of her letters were published by month:

Jan.	2	May	4	Sept.	3
Feb.	3	June	1	Oct.	0
Mar.	4	July	2	Nov.	0
Apr.	0	Aug.	3	Dec.	2

Find the mean, median, and mode and construct a bar graph to illustrate her writing efforts for the year.

0 ←
0
0
1
2
2
2
3
3
3
4
+ 4 ←
——
24   *Sum of values*

$$\frac{24}{12} = 2 \quad Mean$$

Number of values = 12 $\frac{12 + 1}{2} = 6.5$th *value in the frequency*

Counting from either end, the 6.5th value will fall between 2 and 2, which makes 2 the median.
Since 0, 2, and 3 appear the most times (3 each), the data are trimodal.

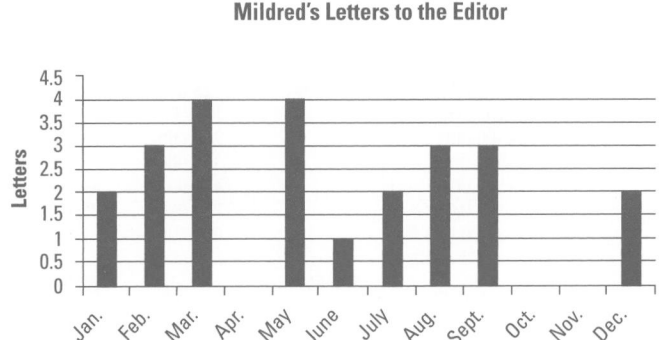

Mildred's Letters to the Editor

Letters

Jan. Feb. Mar. Apr. May June July Aug. Sept. Oct. Nov. Dec.

Following is a comparison of two countries' salary levels for selected categories:

Salary Categories	Number of Workers	
	Country A	Country B
$ 0–15,000	5,000	500,000
15,001–30,000	50,000	20,000
30,001–45,000	100,000	10,000
45,001–60,000	70,000	2,000
60,001–75,000	40,000	1,000
75,001–100,000	10,000	500
100,001–150,000	5,000	100
150,001–200,000	5,000	10
200,001–300,000	4,000	5
300,001–400,000	3,000	2
400,001–500,000	2,000	1
500,001–1,000,000	1,000	1
1,000,001–5,000,000	50	0
5,000,001–10,000,000	5	50

1. Calculate the mean, median, and mode for country A. (Round your answer to the nearest dollar.)

Salary Categories	Workers in Country A	Midpoint of Class	Total Salaries
$ 0–15,000	5,000	$ 7,500	$ 37,500,000
15,001–30,000	50,000	22,500	1,125,000,000
30,001–45,000	100,000	37,500	3,750,000,000
45,001–60,000	70,000	52,500	3,675,000,000
60,001–75,000	40,000	67,500	2,700,000,000
75,001–100,000	10,000	87,500	875,000,000
100,001–150,000	5,000	125,000	625,000,000
150,001–200,000	5,000	175,000	875,000,000
200,001–300,000	4,000	250,000	1,000,000,000
300,001–400,000	3,000	350,000	1,050,000,000
400,001–500,000	2,000	450,000	900,000,000
500,001–1,000,000	1,000	750,000	750,000,000
1,000,001–5,000,000	50	3,000,000	150,000,000
5,000,001–10,000,000	5	7,500,000	37,500,000
	295,055		$17,550,000,000

Mean

$$\frac{\$17,550,000,000}{295,055} = \$59,480$$

Median

$$\frac{295,550 + 1}{2} = \frac{295,551}{2} = 147,775.5 \text{ Middle number of the frequency}$$

Counting from either end, 147,775.5 will be in frequency 100,000, which is in the class $30,001–45,000. The median is the midpoint of that class: $37,500.

Mode

$30,001–45,000 class appears the most times (100,000). The mode is the midpoint of that class: $37,500.

2. Which of the measures of central tendency do you think best represents the average salary for country A?
Student answers may vary, but most will state either the median or the mode.

3. Calculate the mean, median, and mode for country B. (Round your answer to the nearest dollar.)

Salary Categories	Workers in Country B	Midpoint of Class	Total Salaries
$ 0–15,000	500,000	$ 7,500	$3,750,000,000
15,001–30,000	20,000	22,500	450,000,000
30,001–45,000	10,000	37,500	375,000,000
45,001–60,000	2,000	52,500	105,000,000
60,001–75,000	1,000	67,500	67,500,000
75,001–100,000	500	87,500	43,750,000
100,001–150,000	100	125,000	12,500,000
150,001–200,000	10	175,000	1,750,000
200,001–300,000	5	250,000	1,250,000
300,001–400,000	2	350,000	700,000
400,001–500,000	1	450,000	450,000
500,001–1,000,000	1	750,000	750,000
1,000,001–5,000,000	0	3,000,000	0
5,000,001–10,000,000	+ 50	7,500,000	37,500,000
	533,669		$4,846,150,000

Mean

$$\frac{\$4,846,150}{533,669} = \$9,080.82$$

Median

$$\frac{533,669 + 1}{2} = \frac{533,670}{2} = 266,835 \text{ Middle number of the frequency}$$

Counting from either end, 266,835 will be in frequency 500,000, which is in the class $0–15,000. The median is the midpoint of that class: $7,500.

Mode

0–$15,000 class appears the most times (500,000). The mode is the midpoint of that class: $7,500.

4. Which of the measures of central tendency do you think best represents the average salary for country B?
Student answers may vary, but most will state either the median or the mode.

5. What are some of the potential problems with using class intervals to determine measures of central tendency?
Student answers will vary, but should include such criticism as the fact that interval size can produce significant errors. While it is assumed that there will be as many items above as below the midpoint of the class interval, that will not always be the case.

SELF-TESTING EXERCISES

Answers to all exercises are given in Appendix A.

1. What is meant by central tendency? What are the most common?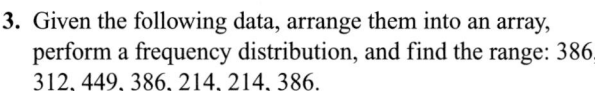
Central tendency is a number designed to represent the typical number within a group of numbers. The most common are the mean, the median, and the mode.

2. Why are statistics important in business?
Statistics in business puts data in an order, which makes them more useful. Because business judgments depend on definite measurable facts rather than on intuition, business managers often need to analyze statistical data accurately.

3. Given the following data, arrange them into an array, perform a frequency distribution, and find the range: 386, 312, 449, 386, 214, 214, 386.
Array: 214, 214, 312, 386, 386, 386, 449

Frequency Distribution	Value	Frequency
	214	2
	312	1
	386	3
	449	1

Range   449 Highest value
         − 214 Lowest value
          235 Range

4. Given the following data, arrange them into an array, perform a frequency distribution, and find the range: 256.8, 463.2, 374.4, 538.8, 463.2, 256.8, 463.2.
Array: 256.8, 256.8, 374.4, 463.2, 463.2, 463.2, 538.8

Frequency Distribution	Value	Frequency
	256.8	2
	374.4	1
	463.2	3
	538.8	1

Range: 538.8 Highest value
         − 256.8 Lowest value
          282.0 Range

5. Arrange into an array; perform a frequency distribution; and find the range, mean, median, and mode: 138, 266, 138, 224, 15, 287.
Array: 15, 138, 138, 224, 266, 287

Frequency Distribution	Value	Frequency	Product
	15	1	15
	138	2	276
	224	1	224
	266	1	266
	287	+ 1	+ 287
		6	1,068

Range: 287 Highest value
         − 15 Lowest value
          272 Range

$\dfrac{1,068}{6} = 178$ Mean

$\dfrac{6 + 1}{2} = 3.5$ Value is the midpoint 181 (median)
Since 138 appears the most times (2), it is the mode.

6. Joe started typing his master's thesis last Saturday. He completed the following numbers of pages per night:

Sat.	2	Wed.	3
Sun.	5	Thurs.	5
Mon.	2	Fri.	4
Tues.	6		

Find the average number of pages per night.

2
5
2
6   *Number of values = 7*
3
5
+ 4
27   *Sum of values*

$\dfrac{27}{7} = 3.857$ pages (mean = average)

7. A gym helps people build their muscles. Six men increased their biceps size as follows:

	Before in inches	After in inches
Albert	7	12
Barney	12	16
Charlie	10	14
Dan	16	18
Elvis	7	15
Floyd	12	17

Determine the average increase in biceps size.

12 − 7 = 5
16 − 12 = 4
14 − 10 = 4   *Number of values = 6*
18 − 16 = 2
15 − 7 = 8
17 − 12 = 5
        28   *Sum of values*

$\dfrac{28}{6} = 4.667$ inches (mean = average)

8. Seven people were on an elevator. Their heights were 69", 80", 72", 62", 64", 66", 79". Find their average height.

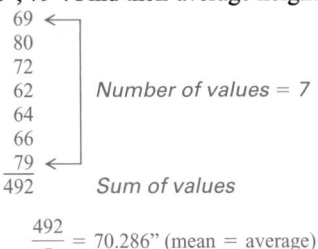

Number of values = 7

$$\frac{492}{7} = 70.286\text{" (mean = average)}$$

9. A Class had the following grades on a test: 87, 98, 65, 65, 87, 91, 79, 80. Find the mean, median, and mode.

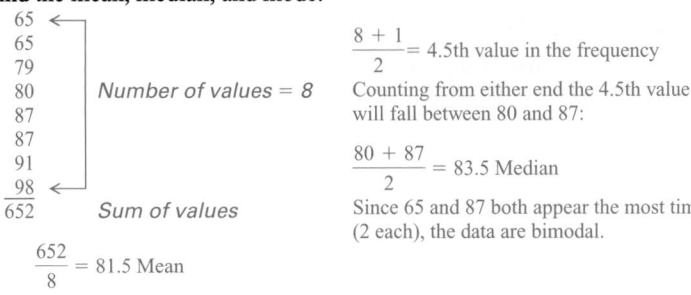

Number of values = 8

Sum of values

$$\frac{652}{8} = 81.5 \text{ Mean}$$

$$\frac{8 + 1}{2} = 4.5\text{th value in the frequency}$$

Counting from either end the 4.5th value will fall between 80 and 87:

$$\frac{80 + 87}{2} = 83.5 \text{ Median}$$

Since 65 and 87 both appear the most times (2 each), the data are bimodal.

10. Find the mean, median, and mode for the February sales by employees of the Gore Poultry Co.

February Sales	Frequency	Midpoint of Class $\frac{Low + high}{2}$ = m	Product $(f \times m)$
$29,000–$30,999	7	$29,999.50	$ 209,996.50
27,000– 28,999	41	27,999.50	1,147,979.50
25,000– 26,999	76	25,999.50	1,975,962.00
23,000– 24,999	48	23,999.50	1,151,976.00
21,000– 22,999	11	21,999.50	241,994.50
	183		$4,727,908.50

$$\frac{\$4,727,908.50}{183} = \$25,835.57 \text{ Mean}$$

$$\frac{183 + 1}{2} = 92\text{nd value in the frequency}$$

Counting from either end, the 92nd value will fall in the class $25,000–26,999. The midpoint of that class is $25,999.50, the median.

Since 25,000–26,999 appears the most times (76), $25,999.50 is the mode.

11. Because of trade negotiations, U.S. exports to Japan increased and then declined. Construct a bar graph to illustrate this in billions of dollars.

Month	U.S. Exports to Japan (in billions)
Nov. 2002	3.25
Dec. 2002	4.00
Jan. 2003	3.40
Feb. 2003	1.75
Mar. 2003	1.25
Apr. 2003	1.00
May 2003	.75
June 2003	1.50
July 2003	1.00

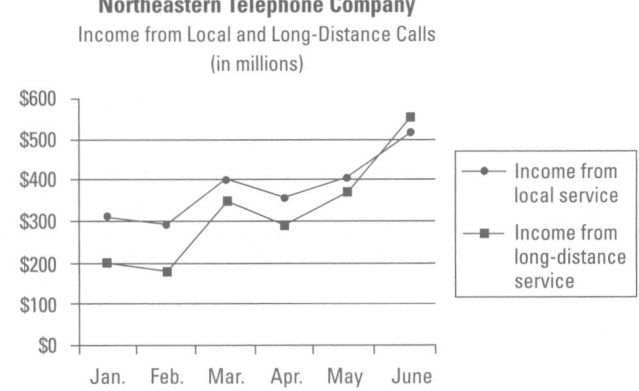

12. Prepare a line graph comparing the income from local and long-distance service for the Northeastern Telephone Co.

Month	Income from Local Service (in $millions)	Income from Long-Distance (in $millions)
Jan	$312	$200
Feb.	296	168
Mar.	400	350
Apr.	360	280
May	408	354
June	520	560

Northeastern Telephone Company
Income from Local and Long-Distance Calls
(in millions)

Income from local service
Income from long-distance service

13. A breakdown of the local junior college budget reveals expenditures as follows:

Faculty salaries	60%
Administrative salaries	30%
Maintenance of facilities	10%

Construct a circle graph to demonstrate this.

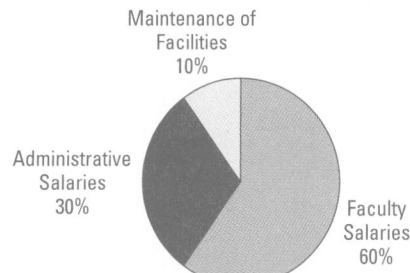

Local Junior College Budget
Expenditures

Maintenance of Facilities 10%

Administrative Salaries 30%

Faculty Salaries 60%

EXCEL SPREADSHEET APPLICATION FOR CHAPTER 22

APPLICATION 1

The Springfield Department Store's management does an annual departmental sales analysis (broken down by months). A form has been developed for that purpose. When you open Ch22App1 from your computer spreadsheet application's disk, you will see the form shown here:

Springfield Department Store
2617 Main Street
Box 219
Springfield, Maryland 58109
Telephone: 301-555-2158   FAX: 301-555-3498

DEPARTMENTAL SALES ANALYSIS

Month	Men's Clothing	Women's Clothing	Children's Clothing	Household Linens	Home Furnishings	Appliances	Automotive	TOTALS
January								$0.00
February								$0.00
March								$0.00
April								$0.00
May								$0.00
June								$0.00
July								$0.00
August								$0.00
September								$0.00
October								$0.00
November								$0.00
December								$0.00
TOTALS	$0.00	$0.00	$0.00	$0.00	$0.00	$0.00	$0.00	$0.00
MEAN	#DIV/0!	#DIV/0!	#DIV/0!	#DIV/0!	#DIV/0!	#DIV/0!	#DIV/0!	$0.00
MEDIAN	#NUM!	#NUM!	#NUM!	#NUM!	#NUM!	#NUM!	#NUM!	$0.00
MODE	#N/A	#N/A	#N/A	#N/A	#N/A	#N/A	#N/A	$0.00
MAXIMUM	$0.00	$0.00	$0.00	$0.00	$0.00	$0.00	$0.00	$0.00
MINIMUM	$0.00	$0.00	$0.00	$0.00	$0.00	$0.00	$0.00	$0.00
RANGE	$0.00	$0.00	$0.00	$0.00	$0.00	$0.00	$0.00	$0.00

Enter the following information:

Month	Column B	Column C	Column D	Column E	Column F	Column G	Column H
January	$100,176.00	$246,321.90	$128,981.70	$88,271.04	$136,813.50	$68,498.80	$71,840.75
February	97,914.59	227,302.49	124,338.20	74,285.10	123,949.20	73,293.48	108,364.91
March	105,294.02	228,339.02	133,293.59	72,194.93	137,242.49	74,394.10	84,405.91
April	104,392.33	254,017.28	124,294.73	83,989.01	124,302.45	84,592.10	94,392.09
May	94,375.24	208,289.07	142,948.22	73,392.28	154,127.08	85,230.02	83,937.65
June	125,928.78	212,329.30	123,992.06	87,873.21	125,431.31	88,439.39	75,991.32
July	109,224.83	218,382.31	121,948.03	83,478.93	127,309.27	89,300.32	108,364.91
August	145,297.58	283,185.04	179,002.86	78,630.01	122,694.13	94,817.77	79,361.49
September	140,375.91	277,910.35	166,946.19	78,308.27	142,918.23	96,810.36	88,037.18
October	154,094.84	298,012.48	281,947.29	88,271.04	124,302.45	99,046.99	94,847.88
November	247,037.55	377,104.96	361,995.83	87,873.21	140,884.71	116,025.15	108,364.91
December	187,935.56	483,659.46	317,492.19	86,018.46	146,054.39	188,293.10	97,123.28

Answer the following questions after you have completed the spreadsheet:

1. What is the mean for sales in the Home Furnishings Department?
2. What is the median for sales in the Men's Clothing Department?
3. What is the mode for sales in the Automotive Department?
4. What is the range of sales in the Children's Clothing Department?
5. What is the annual total sales for the Springfield Department Store?
6. What is the mean for sales in the Women's Clothing Department?
7. What is the median for sales in the Appliances Department?
8. What is the mode for sales in the Household Linens Department?

GROUP REPORT

FOR CHAPTER 22 APPLICATION 1

Write a group report to the store manager reporting your findings from the spreadsheet entries. Assess the meaning of the data. For example, how many of the months were above the mean for the Automotive Department? Which statistical average (the mean, median, or mode) does your group find most useful? Explain the findings and make any recommendations your group believes are appropriate.

EXCEL SPREADSHEET APPLICATION FOR CHAPTER 22

APPLICATION 2

The Springfield Department Store's management has projected sales for 2003 using sales figures for 1999 through 2002. To better visualize the changes in sales for the various departments, a bar graph has also been prepared. When you open Ch22App2 from your computer spreadsheet application's disk, you will see the following spreadsheet and graph:

Springfield Department Store

2617 Main Street
Box 219
Springfield, Maryland 58109
Telephone: 301-555-2158   FAX: 301-555-3498

PROJECTED SALES FOR 2003

| Department | Actual Sales | | | | Projected Sales 2003 |
	1999	2000	2001	2002	
Men's Clothing					$0
Women's Clothing					$0
Children's Clothing					$0
Household Linens					$0
Home Furnishings					$0
Appliances					$0
Automotive					$0
TOTAL	$0	$0	$0	$0	$0

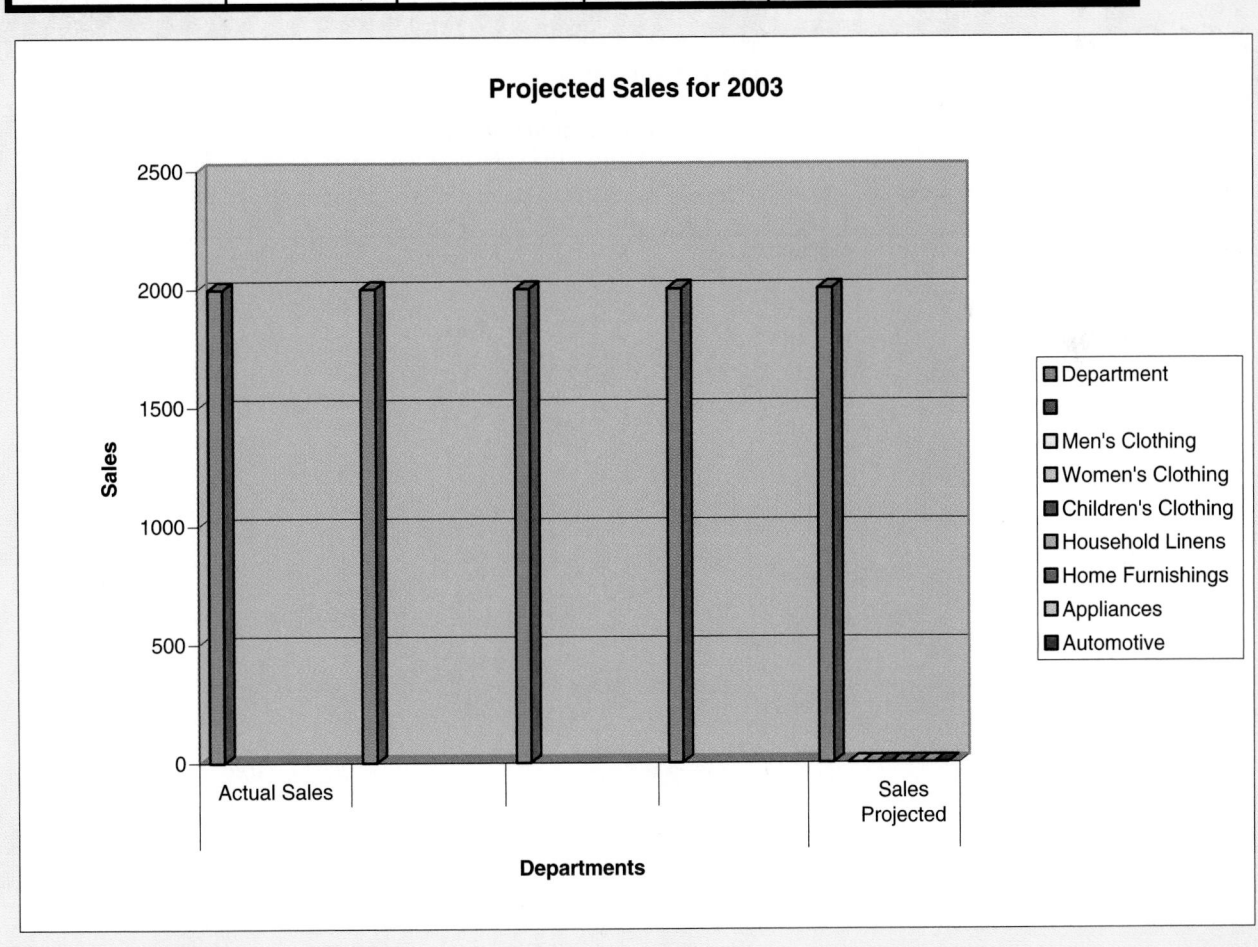

Projected Sales for 2003

Enter the following information:

	Column B	Column C	Column D	Column E
Men's Clothing	$1,194,652	$1,472,923	1,639,287	$1,712,047
Women's Clothing	2,753,647	3,012,846	3,210,378	3,314,854
Children's Clothing	1,774,639	1,983,547	2,087,563	2,207,181
Household Linens	999,162	1,126,192	1,375,490	982,585
Home Furnishings	1,093,327	1,398,573	1,431,543	1,606,029
Appliances	829,382	882,910	992,762	1,158,742
Automotive	771,609	800,217	878,291	1,095,032

Answer the following questions after you have completed the spreadsheet:

1. What are the projected total sales for Springfield for 2003?

2. What are the projected sales for the Women's Clothing Department?

3. What were the total sales for 1999?

4. What are the projected sales for the Appliances Department?

5. What are the projected sales for the Household Linen Department?

GROUP REPORT

FOR CHAPTER 22 APPLICATION 2

Write a group report based on the findings from the spreadsheet. For example, based on the information, what data are important for the store manager to know. Then, write your recommendations for a more successful 2003. For example, are there departments that should be closed? Would more promotions be appropriate for some departments?

23

INTERNATIONAL BUSINESS MATH

SPEEDING AND FINES IN MEXICO

Cruising over the rolling hills and across the plains, Arnold was enjoying his new Corvette as much as his first vacation in a foreign country. Not only was this part of Mexico more beautiful than he could have hoped, certain amenities were everywhere. The people were friendly, the food was great, and about a mile back he saw the speed limit marker proclaiming 100 the legal limit. Moving at 90, although not a real test for such a powerful car, seemed fast to this Kansan who was accustomed to 65 mph back home. So he was astonished when a police cruiser's blinking lights appeared in the rearview mirror.

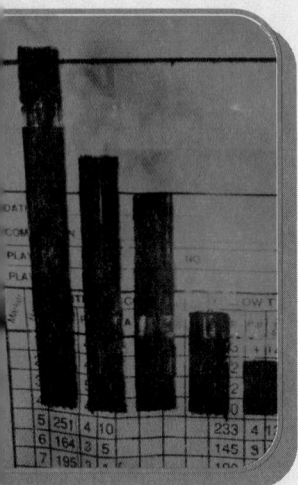

Officer Garcia was exceedingly polite but equally firm as he tried to explain, in imperfect English, the difference between U.S. customary and metric measurement. In most nations 100 on a speed limit marker means kilometers and translates as approximately 62 miles per hour.

Arnold could not be persuaded. He attempted to argue his way out of a citation and found himself trying to explain his plight to unsympathetic Judge Hernandez. Exasperated, the judge finally told the hapless American to pay a fine or spend two days in jail. Having made a D in high school Spanish, Arnold did not understand the judge's words so she wrote it out for him—"$1,000 o 2 dias," which he translated as a thousand dollars or two days in jail. Arnold said he couldn't possibly afford to pay that much and opted for jail.

If he had known that the symbol for peso ($) is the same as the one for dollar ($), and that there were approximately 10 pesos per dollar, he might have converted and discovered that 1,000 pesos would have been about 100 U.S. dollars. Certainly a hundred-dollar fine would be preferable to two days in jail anywhere.

Chapter Glossary

Metric measurement. A standard system of weights and measure used in every industrial nation except the United States.

Meter. A fundamental metric unit of measure, erroneously defined in 1790 as one ten-millionth of the distance from the equator to the North Pole.

Gram. A basic metric unit of weight that is a cube of distilled water at sea level that measures 1 one-hundredth of a meter on each side.

Liter. A basic metric unit of volume that is the amount of space occupied by 1,000 grams.

Kilometer. A basic metric unit of distance that is 1,000 meters.

Kilogram. A common metric unit of weight used in everyday markets to measure foodstuffs; the weight of one liter of distilled water at sea level.

Kilo. An everyday abbreviation for kilogram used by most consumers.

Are. A basic metric unit of area that equals 100 square meters.

Hectare. A unit of area measurement, 100 ares, which is usually used to measure tracts of land.

U.S. customary. A system of weights and measures used in the United States; based on the foot and yard.

Avoirdupois weight. A system of weights and measures based on the pound.

Foreign exchange. The monies of countries that are used to facilitate international trade in goods, services, and financial assets.

Exports. Sales of domestically produced goods and services to foreign buyers.

Imports. Purchases by domestic residents of foreign-produced goods and services.

Exchange rate. The relative price of one national currency in terms of another national currency.

Flexible or **floating exchange rate.** An international monetary arrangement in which exchange rates are determined by supply and demand without government intervention.

Devaluation. A change in a country's exchange rate in which the number of units of a country's money that purchases one unit of another country's currency increases.

Student Objectives

Upon completion of this chapter, you should be able to

1. Move up and down the international metric measurement scale.
2. Solve similar problems using international metric measurement.
3. Convert from U.S. dollars to other currencies.
4. Convert from other currencies to U.S. dollars.
5. Determine what happens when the exchange rates between currencies change.

LEARNING UNIT 1
METRIC MEASUREMENT

An ideal standard of measure must be rigidly defined relative to some unchangeable unit in nature so that it will never change. The French government sponsored a scientific attempt to devise such an ideal in 1790. A faulty estimate of the distance from the North Pole to the equator resulted in a fundamental unit of length, the meter (m), defined as $\frac{1}{10,000,000}$ of that distance. Although the measure was incorrect, the length of a meter, slightly longer than a yard, has not changed. All other units of measure, such as gram and liter, are derived from meter. **Metric measurement** is the standard system of weights and measures used in every industrial nation except the United States.

Metric Terms

The distinct advantage of metric measurement is that it is a decimal system based on algebra instead of geometry. There are three basic units of measure: **meter** for length, **gram** for weight, and **liter** for capacity or volume. Around the world some derived measures are in such general use they are considered to be common units of measure. These are:

Kilometer. A basic metric unit of distance that is 1,000 meters.

Kilogram. A common metric unit of weight used in every day markets to measure foodstuffs which is the weight of one liter of distilled water at sea level.

Kilo. An everyday abbreviation for kilogram used by most consumers.

Are. A basic Metric unit of area that equals 100 square meters.

Hectare. A unit of area measurement, 100 ares, which is usually used to measure tracts of land.

The basic units, meter, gram, and liter, should be regarded as midpoints on a scale. Moving up the scale multiplies the previous unit by 10 at each step. Moving down the scale divides the previous unit by 10 at each step. To move up the scale, merely move the decimal point from left to right one space for each step and to move down the scale, move the decimal point one place from right to left for each step. At each step a Greek or Latin prefix denotes the number of spaces attached to the beginning of the basic unit to indicate how large it is.

Prefix	Symbol	Number $\times$ Basic Unit	
kilo	k	$(10^3$ or $1,000)$	$\times$ basic unit
hecto	h	$(10^2$ or $100)$	$\times$ basic unit
deka	da	$(10^1$ or $10)$	$\times$ basic unit
basic	m, g, l	1	$\times$ basic unit
deci	d	$\left(10^{-1}\ \text{or}\ \dfrac{1}{10}\right)$	$\times$ basic unit
centi	c	$\left(10^{-2}\ \text{or}\ \dfrac{1}{100}\right)$	$\times$ basic unit
milli	m	$\left(10^{-3}\ \text{or}\ \dfrac{1}{1,000}\right)$	$\times$ basic unit

---

23.1 Moving Up and Down the Metric Scale

The basic units of measure with their respective abbreviations are as follows:

Length		Weight		Capacity	
Unit	Symbol	Unit	Symbol	Unit	Symbol
kilometer	km	kilogram	kg	kiloliter	kl
hectometer	hm	hectogram	hg	hectoliter	hl
dekameter	dkm	dekagram	dkg	dekaliter	dkl
meter	m	gram	g	liter	l
decimeter	dm	decigram	dg	deciliter	dl
centimeter	cm	centigram	cg	centiliter	cl
millimeter	mm	milligram	mg	milliliter	ml

To convert from one unit to another, move the decimal point one space for each level on the scale.

EXAMPLE   How many grams are there in three kilograms?

Solution   Begin at three kilograms and move down the scale to grams.

kilogram	3	*Starting point*
hectogram	30	
dekagram	300	
gram	3,000	

When moving down the scale, move the decimal point one place to the **right** for each step taken.

EXAMPLE   How many meters are there in four centimeters?

Solution   Begin at four centimeters and move up the scale to meters.

meter	.04	
decimeter	.4	
decimeter	4	*Starting point*

When moving up the scale, move the decimal point one place to the **left** for each step taken.

EXAMPLE   How many hectoliters are in 700 deciliters?

Solution   Begin at 700 deciliters and move up the scale to hectoliters.

hectoliter	.7	
dekaliter	7	
liter	70	
deciliter	700	*Starting point*

Move the decimal point one place to the **left** for each step taken.

23.1 Practice Problems

Complete the following conversions:
1. 1,000 meter = _____ kilometer(s)
2. .2 gram = _____ decigram(s)
3. 3 hectoliter = _____ liter(s)
4. .001 centigram = _____ milligram(s)

23.1 Solutions to Practice Problems

1.
kilometer	1
hectometer	10
dekameter	100
meter	1,000 *Starting point*

2.
gram	.2 *Starting point*
decigram	2

3.
hectoliter	3 *Starting point*
dekaliter	30
liter	300

4.
centigram	.001 *Starting point*
milligram	.01

23.2   ## Working with Metric Measurement

Solving problems using metric measurement is not different from solving any other problems using base 10 numbering. The following problems are solved much more simply using the metric system of measurement than are similar problems using

U.S. customary (a system of weights and measures used in the United States based on the foot and yard) or **avoirdupois weight** (a system of weights and measures based on the pound).

E X A M P L E   Fort Worth is 56 kilometers from Dallas. Arlington is between the two cities. Arlington is 25 kilometers from Fort Worth. How far is Arlington from Dallas?

Solution
$$\begin{array}{r} 56 \text{ km} \\ - \ 25 \text{ km} \\ \hline 31 \text{ km} \end{array}$$

23.2 Practice Problems

1. A car traveling 86 kilometers per hour will go how far in 12 hours?
2. A board is four meters long. How many pieces eight decimeters long can be cut from the board?
3. Gasoline costs $.45 per liter. How much does a kiloliter cost?
4. A book is three centimeters thick. How many of these books will be in a stack six meters tall?

23.2 Solutions to Practice Problems

1.
$$\begin{array}{r} 86 \text{ km} \\ \times \ 12 \\ \hline 1{,}032 \text{ km} \end{array}$$

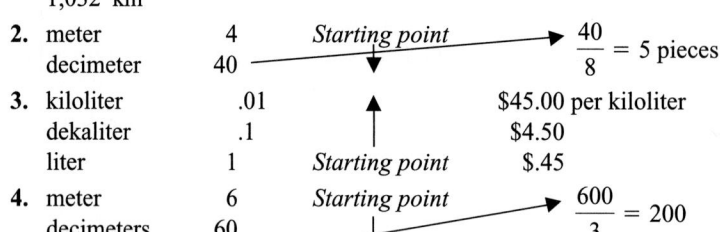

2. meter   4   *Starting point* $\dfrac{40}{8} = 5$ pieces
decimeter   40

3. kiloliter   .01 $45.00 per kiloliter
dekaliter   .1 $4.50
liter   1   *Starting point* $.45

4. meter   6   *Starting point* $\dfrac{600}{3} = 200$
decimeters   60
centimeters   600

23.3 Metric and U.S. (Avoirdupois) Conversion

Metric measurement is common in essentially all of the world except the United States. Americans should accustom themselves to thinking in terms of meters, grams, and liters instead of feet, ounces, and gallons. However, to provide a reference point with which we are already familiar, a few conversions are useful. The equivalents for commonly used metric measure are as follows:

meter	= 39.37 inches
gram	= .0353 ounce
liter	= 1.057 quarts
kilogram (kilo)	= 2.21 pounds
kilometer	= .621 mile

E X A M P L E   1 dekameter = _____ yards

Solution
1 meter   = 30.37 inches
1 dekameter = 10 meters
10×39.37 = 393.7 inches
$\dfrac{393.7}{36}$ = 10.94 yards

(*number of inches in one yard*)

Make the following conversions (carry out the answer to the nearest one hundredth):
1. 240 kilometers = _____ miles
2. 30 quarts = _____ liters
3. An American tourist is buying sugar in a German supermarket. If the sugar weighs two kilos, how many pounds does it weigh?
4. An athletic field is 90 meters long. How many yards long is it?

23.3 Solutions to Practice Problems

1.   240 kilometers
    × .621
    149.04 miles

2. $\dfrac{30 \text{ quarts}}{1.057} = 28.38 \text{ liters}$

3.   2.21 pounds per kilogram
    × 2
    4.42 pounds

4. $39.37 \times 90 = \dfrac{3{,}543.3 \text{ inches}}{36 \text{ inches per yard}} = 98.43 \text{ yards}$

23.4   Approximate Conversion

Converting from metric to U.S. is difficult and not very accurate, and we should not be encouraged to do it. Still, some attempts are inevitable. To help converting when a calculator is not available and complete accuracy is not very important, it is useful to remember the following approximate conversions.

$$\text{meter} = 1\tfrac{1}{10} \text{ yards}$$
$$\text{gram} = \tfrac{1}{30} \text{ ounce}$$
$$\text{liter} = 1 \text{ liquid quart}$$
$$\text{kilogram} = 2 \text{ pounds}$$
$$\text{kilometer} = \tfrac{3}{5} \text{ mile}$$

1. Approximately how many pounds are there in a bag of flour that weighs four kilos?
2. Approximately how many liters are in a four-gallon can of gasoline?
3. Two cities are 50 miles apart. Approximately how many kilometers would that be?
4. A can of soup weighs 300 grams. Approximately how many ounces does it weigh?

23.4 Solutions to Practice Problems

1.   4 kilos
    × 2
    8 pounds

2. 4 liters = 1 gallon
    4 gallon
    × 4
    16 liters

3. $\dfrac{50}{\frac{3}{5}} = 83.33 \text{ kilometers}$

4. $300 \text{ grams} \times \dfrac{1}{30} = 10 \text{ ounces}$

LEARNING UNIT 2
MONETARY CONVERSIONS

When Americans buy oranges from Florida or cars made in Michigan, they want to pay with dollars. Also, the Florida grower and the Michigan manufacturer expect to be paid in dollars since all their expenses are settled in dollars. Within any nation such economic transactions are simple.

Every nation has its own currency. If an American company wishes to buy Indian spices, the company must pay with Indian rupees because Indian merchants use rupees to settle their transactions.

Similarly, the Indian buyer must get some U.S. dollars to buy American-made computers. Americans will accept Indian rupees, Japanese yen, British pounds, or any other foreign currency only if they can be certain the money can be converted into U.S. dollars.

To simplify and promote more trade among the nations of the European Economic Community, 12 of the members of that organization recently switched to a system with a common currency called a euro. The nations of Austria, Belgium, Finland, France, Germany, Greece, Ireland, Italy, Luxembourg, the Netherlands, Portugal, and Spain no longer use their traditional currencies. Other nations will probably join the group in the future.

 **EXCEL Spreadsheet Application** The spreadsheet application at the end of this chapter is a cumulative end-of-the-year report of the products purchased from foreign sources.

Foreign Exchange Rates

Foreign Exchange refers to the monies of countries that are used to facilitate international trade in goods, services, and financial assets. **Exports** (sales of domestically produced goods and services to foreign buyers) and **imports** (purchases by domestic residents of foreign-produced goods and services) between nations with different monetary units present a mathematical issue: how to handle the foreign **exchange rate**, which states the price of a foreign money in terms of each nation's own money.

A recent issue of the *New York Times* quoted the price of British pounds at .7034 and Japanese yen at 124.28. This means that a buyer in Britain would need just over .70 of a pound to buy a U.S. dollar. It means an American buyer would need $1.42 to buy a British pound ($\frac{1}{.7034}$) and less than 1 cent to buy a Japanese yen ($\frac{1}{124.28}$).

Although this might make the yen appear to be a low-valued currency compared to pounds, that is not the case. Over the last few decades the Japanese currency has been one of the world's most stable. Exchange rates are merely that and have no connection to the relative state of economic health or activity of a particular society.

23.5 Converting from U.S. Dollars to Other Currencies

> **EXAMPLE** A U.S. company negotiated the sale of a $25,000,000 airliner to a French airline company. Calculate the price in euros if the exchange rate is quoted as 1 USD = 1.12 EUR.
>
> *Solution* $25,000,000 \times 1.12 = 28,000,000$ euros

23.5 Practice Problems

1. A British company sold $10,333.75 of leather goods to Beautiful British, Inc., in Miami. How much will Beautiful British, Inc., receive in pounds sterling if the exchange rate is 1 USD = .70 GBP?

2. Today there are 124.828 yen per dollar (1 USD = 124.828 JPY). How much will a Japanese carmaker receive for a car that costs $27,000 in New York?

3. A Canadian-made auto part costs $49.95 in Houston. How much will the Canadian company be paid in Canadian currency if the Canadian dollar is being exchanged at 1.572 per U.S. dollar (1 USD = 1.572 CAD)?

4. How much will a Norwegian company receive in Norwegian currency for a $6,800 shipment of fish if the exchange rate is 8.928 kroner per dollar?

23.5 Solutions to Practice Problems
1. $10,333.75 \times .70 = 7,233.63$ pounds
2. $27,000 \times 124.828 = 3,370,380.91$ yen
3. $49.95 \times 1.572 = 78.52$ Canadian dollars
4. $6,800 \times 8.928 = 60,710.40$ kroner

23.6 Converting from Other Currencies to U.S. Dollars

EXAMPLE   A French company bought a shipment of U.S.-made bicycles for 1,384 euros. How much will the U.S. company receive in dollars if the exchange rate is quoted as $.894 per euro (1 EUR = .894 USD)?

Solution   1,384 euros $\times$ $.894 = $1,237.30

23.6 Practice Problems

1. A British company paid 25,000 pounds for canned vegetables from a U.S. company. How much will the U.S. firm receive in dollars if the exchange rate is one pound per $1.4275 (1 GBP = 1.4275 USD)?

2. It costs .008 dollars to buy one yen today. How much will a Japanese importer pay in dollars for a 750,000-yen purchase of Arkansas rice (1 JPY = .008 USD)?

3. A consumer in Amsterdam, Holland, wants a Buick that costs 22,524 euros. At .894 dollars per euro, How much will a New Jersey car dealer receive in dollars for the car (1 EUR = .894 USD)?

4. A company in Israel paid 238,500 new shekels for U.S.-built airliner parts. How much did the U.S. company receive in dollars if the exchange rate is .2362 dollars per new shekel (1 ILS = .2362 USD)?

23.6 Solutions to Practice Problems
1. 25,000 pounds $\times$ 1.4275 = $35,687.50
2. 750,000 yen $\times$ .008 = $6,000
3. 22,524 euros $\times$ .894 = $20,136.46
4. 238,500 $\times$ .2362 = $56,333.70

23.7 Results of Changes in Exchange Rates

Most industrial nations today depend on the economic forces of supply and demand to determine exchange rates by what is termed a **flexible** or **floating exchange rate**. If a nation's economy produces well-made goods at reasonable prices, consumers in other nations will buy them. That will cause the price of the seller nation's currency to rise against the currency of the buyer nation. That raises the prices of the goods to the buyer and should tend to reduce imports. If the price of a nation's currency falls, that makes its goods cheaper to consumers in other nations and should increase its exports.

A **devaluation** is a change in a country's exchange rate in which the number of units of that country's money that purchases one unit of another country's currency increases. Before the advent of floating exchange rates, in most of the world, nations would sometimes devalue their currency. The intent of a nation's devaluation was to make its goods cheaper in other countries and foreign goods more expensive in the domestic economy, an action designed to increase exports and decrease imports.

The Mexican government once declared a moratorium on that nation's money. The peso had declined in value from $.08 to about $.00033 or 3,030 pesos to the dollar. The Mexican government merely moved the decimal point three places. That made a peso worth about $.33 U.S. or about three pesos per dollar. Students should be aware that a change in exchange rates is something that happens every day and is a result of market forces, not a government's action. It is very different from the monetary moratorium the Mexican government declared.

Expanding the converting coverage somewhat, two possibilities when converting from foreign currencies (FC) to U.S. dollars are as follows:

1. U.S. dollar value = FC value × U.S. dollars per 1 FC ←— *Foreign currency exchange rate given in U.S. dollars*

2. U.S. dollar value = $\dfrac{\text{FC value}}{\text{FC per \$1 U.S.}}$ ←— *Foreign currency exchange rate given in foreign currency*

EXAMPLE   A U.S. company has been buying bottled water from a French company for 16,414 euros per month. The exchange rate changed from $.8197 to $.7782 per euro. Determine the effect in dollars to the U.S. company from the change in the valuation of the euro.

Solution   Since the exchange rate is given in U.S. dollars, use

> U.S. dollar value = FC value × U.S. dollars per 1 FC.

Step 1. Find the number of dollars the U.S. company was paying prior to the valuation change:

$$\begin{aligned} \text{U.S. dollar value} &= \text{FC value} \times \text{U.S. dollars per 1 FC} \\ &= 16{,}414 \times \$.8197 \\ &= \$13{,}454.56 \end{aligned}$$

Step 2. Find the number of dollars the U.S. company was paying after the valuation change:

$$\begin{aligned} \text{U.S. dollar value} &= \text{FC value} \times \text{U.S. dollars per 1 FC} \\ &= 16{,}414 \times \$.7782 \\ &= \$12{,}773.38 \end{aligned}$$

Step 3. Find the difference between the dollar amount the U.S. firm paid after the valuation change:

$$\begin{array}{ll} \$\ 13{,}454.56 & \text{←— } \textit{Prior to valuation change} \\ -\ 12{,}773.38 & \text{←— } \textit{After valuation change} \\ \$\qquad 681.18 & \text{←— } \textit{Savings to U.S. firm} \end{array}$$

EXAMPLE   A U.S. company has been buying bottled water from a French company for 16,414 euros per month. The exchange rate changed from 1.2199585 euros to 1.285 euros per dollar. Determine the effect in dollars to the U.S. company from the change in the valuation of the euro.

Solution   Since the exchange rate is given in foreign currency, use

$$\text{U.S. dollar value} = \dfrac{\text{FC value}}{\text{FC per \$1 U.S.}}.$$

Step 1. Find the number of dollars the U.S. company was paying before the valuation change:

$$\text{U.S. dollar value} = \frac{\text{FC value}}{\text{FC per \$1 U.S.}}$$

$$= \frac{16,414}{1.2199585}$$

$$= \$13,454.56$$

Step 2. Find the number of dollars the U.S. company would pay after the valuation change:

$$\text{U.S. dollar value} = \frac{\text{FC value}}{\text{FC per \$1 U.S.}}$$

$$= \frac{16,414}{1.285}$$

$$= \$12,773.38$$

Step 3. Find the difference between the dollar amount the U.S. firm paid after the valuation change:

```
$ 13,454.56  ◄── Prior to valuation change
-12,773.38   ◄── After valuation change
$    681.18  ◄── Savings to U.S. firm
```

23.7
Practice
Problems

1. A British company sells 8,335 pounds worth of soap each month to a U.S. firm. If the exchange rate changed from .6532 pounds per dollar to .7123 pounds per dollar, what effect will the change have on the dollar payment for the U.S. company?

2. The South Korean won changed in price from one won per $.00079 to $.0009365. In U. S. dollars, what will happen to the price of a South Korean–made car that used to sell for 14,400,000 won?

3. Today there are 124 yen per dollar. If the exchange rate changes to 123.675, how much will a Japanese-made computer printer change in price in dollars for a U.S. buyer if it cost 26,000 yen before the change?

4. A U.S. company sells shipments of motor oil to a company in Brazil. The Brazilian company had been paying 8,400 real for each shipment before the change from 1 real equals $.425894 U.S. to one real equals $.4595588 U.S. Find the increace in U.S. dollars to the U.S. company.

23.7. Solutions to Practice Problems

1. $\dfrac{8,335}{.6532} = \$12,760.26$ Before the change

$\dfrac{8,335}{.7132} = \$11,686.76$ After the change

```
$ 12,760.26
-11,686.76
$  1,073.50  Price reduction to the U.S. firm
```

2.
```
  14,400,000              14,400,000
×     .00079            ×   .0009365
$     11,376  Before     $ 13,485.60   After the change
              the change
$ 13,485.60
- 11,376.00
$  2,109.60  Price increase to U.S. customer
```

3. $\dfrac{26{,}000}{124} = \$209.68$ Before the change

$\dfrac{26{,}000}{123.675} = \$210.23$ After the change

$\begin{array}{r} \$\ 210.23 \\ -209.68 \\ \hline \$\qquad .55 \end{array}$ Price increase to U.S. buyer

4.
$\begin{array}{r} 8{,}400.00 \\ \times\ \$.425894 \\ \hline \$\ 3{,}577.51 \end{array}$ Before the change

$\begin{array}{r} 8{,}400.00 \\ \times\ \$.4595588 \\ \hline \$\ 3{,}860.29 \end{array}$ After the change

$\begin{array}{r} \$3{,}860.29 \\ -\ 3{,}577.51 \\ \hline \$\ 282.78 \end{array}$ Price increase to U.S. buyer

QUICK REFERENCE SUMMARY AND REVIEW

Page	Section Topic	Learning Concepts	Examples and Solutions
800	**23.1** Moving up and Down the Metric Scale	Convert from one unit of metric measure to another.	How many meters are in 5 kilometers? kilometers 5 hectometers 50 dekameters 500 meters 5,000
801	**23.2** Working with Metric Measurement	Solving problems with metric is no more difficult than solving problems with U.S. customary (avoirdupois).	Jane's flour canister was full. It holds four kilograms. She used one kilogram to make some bread. How many kilograms were left? 4 − 1 = 3 kilograms
802	**23.3** Metric and U.S. (Avoirdupois) Conversion	Conversion provides a reference point with which we are already familiar.	An American tourist bought flour in a French market. The flour weighs 3 kilos. How many pounds does it weigh? $\begin{array}{r} 2.21 \\ \times\ 3 \\ \hline 6.63 \end{array}$ pounds
803	**23.4** Approximate Conversion	When a calculator is not available and complete accuracy is not very important, approximate conversions can be used.	Approximately how many kilos are there in a package of meat that weighs 6 pounds? $\begin{array}{r} 6 \\ \times\ 2 \\ \hline 12 \end{array}$ kilos
804	**23.5** Converting from U.S. Dollars to Other Currencies	When people from other countries buy and sell goods with Americans, they must know how much they are paying or getting in terms of their own money.	A U.S. department store bought a supply of Mexican flowerpots for $4,650. If pesos are exchanging for 15 pesos per dollar, how many pesos will the Mexican firm be paid? $\begin{array}{r} \$\ 4{,}650 \\ \times\ 15 \\ \hline 69{,}750 \end{array}$ pesos

Page	Section Topic	Learning Concepts	Examples and Solutions
805	**23.6** Converting from Other Currencies to U.S. Dollars	When Americans buy and sell goods with people from other countries, they must know how much they are paying or getting in terms of their own money.	A Pakistani importer bought a supply of U.S. grain for 393,272 rupees. How many dollars will the U.S. exporter receive if rupees are worth $.0327 U.S.? $$\begin{array}{r} 393,272 \\ \times\ \ .0327 \\ \hline \$12,859.99 \end{array}$$
805	**23.7** Results of Changes in Exchange Rates	When a nation's money declines in value against other currencies, its goods become cheaper to foreign buyers and exports increase. When a nation's money rises in value against other currencies, foreign goods become cheaper and its imports increase.	A U.S. company sells $20,000 of potatoes each month in Greece. The euro declined from 1.356 per dollar to 1.473 per dollar. What happened to the price of potatoes in euros? $20,000 \times 1.356 = 27,120$ Euros before decline $20,000 \times 1.473 = 29,460$ Euros after decline $$\begin{array}{r} 29,460 \\ -\ 27,120 \\ \hline 2,340\ \text{Increase in euros} \end{array}$$

SURFING THE INTERNET

For further information on the topic covered in this chapter checkout the following sites:

http://ts.nist.gov/ts/htdocs/200/202/mpo_hom2.htm

http://www.essex1.com/people/speer/metric.html

http://finance.yahoo.com/m3

> ADDITIONAL
> PRACTICE
> PROBLEMS

Answers to odd-numbered problems are given in Appendix A.

23.1

1. How many meters are in 85 decimeters?

meter	8.5	↑
decimeter	85	Starting point

2. How many decigrams are in 76,428 dekagrams?

dekagram	76,428	Starting point
gram	764,280	↓
decigram	7,642,800	

3. How many millimeters are in 574 meters?

meter	574	Starting point
decimeter	5,740	
centimeter	57,400	↓
millimeter	574,000	

4. How many grams are in 71,690 dekagrams?

dekagram	71,690	Starting point
gram	716,900	↓

5. How many centiliters in 19,404 deciliters?

deciliter	19,404	Starting point
centiliter	194,040	↓

23.2

6. A bicyclist rides 24 kilometers per hour in a race. How far will she go in 15 hours?

$15 \times 24 = 360$ kilometers

7. A roll of wire is 18 meters long. How many 9-decimeter pieces can be cut from the roll?

meter	18	Starting point
decimeter	180	↓

$\dfrac{180}{9} = 20$ pieces

8. Milk costs $.60 per liter. How much does a dekaliter cost?

dekaliter $6.00
liter $ .60   ↑ Starting point

9. A truck is loaded with lumber made up of boards two centimeters thick. How many boards tall is in a stack that is two meters tall?

meter   2   Starting point
decimeter   20 $\frac{200}{2} = 100$
centimeter   200   ↓

10. A football player drinks two liters of Gatoraid during each game. How many grams does he drink?

1 liter = 1,000 grams = 1 kilogram

kilogram   2   Starting point
hectogram   20
dekagram   200   ↓
gram   2,000

23.3

11. Linda bought 16 liters of cola. Exactly how many gallons did she buy?

$16 \times 1.057 = 16.192$ quarts

$\frac{16.192}{4} = 4.23$ gallons

12. Martin bought 10 pounds of hamburger meat. Exactly how many kilos did he buy?

$\frac{10}{2.2} = 4.52$ kilos

13. Nurse Maryann administered 246 grams of drugs yesterday. Exactly how many ounces was that?

$\begin{array}{r} 246 \\ \times\ .0353 \\ \hline 8.68 \end{array}$ ounces

23.4

14. Approximately how many liters are in half a gallon of milk?

$\frac{4}{2} = 2$ liters approximately

15. The tops of basketball nets are 10 feet from the floor. Since there are three feet in one yard, approximately how many meters would that be?

$\frac{10}{3} = 3\frac{1}{3}$ yards

$3\frac{1}{3}$ yards $\times 1\frac{1}{10}$

$= \frac{10}{3} \times \frac{11}{10} = \frac{110}{30} = 3\frac{2}{3}$ meters

16. Donya bought four kilos of Italian parmesan. Approximately how many pounds did she buy?

$4 \times 2 = 8$ pounds

23.5

17. When there are 98.56 yen per dollar, how much will a Japanese television set maker receive for a set that costs $450 in Fort Worth, Texas?

$98.56 \times \$450 = 44,352$ yen

18. A British glassmaker sold 50 sets of glasses to an American dealer. How much will the British company receive in pounds if the exchange rate is .7131 and they cost the American company $125 each? (Round to the nearest pound.)

$.7131 \times \$125 \times 50 = 4,457$ pounds

19. The exchange rate between dollars and euros is $1 = 1.32 euros. An American bought a Lamborghini that cost $245,000 in Milan. How much would the car have cost in euros?

$1.32 \times \$245,000 = 323,400$ euros

20. How much will a $4,000 shipment of cheese from Switzerland cost in Swiss francs if the exchange is 4.57 per dollar?

$4.57 \times \$4,000 = 18,280$ Swiss francs

21. French perfume costs $6,995 in Charleston. How much will the French company be paid in euros if they are being exchanged at 1.21 per U.S. dollar?

$1.21 \times \$6,995 = 8,463.95$ euros

23.6

22. Euros are trading today for 1.18 per U.S. dollar. A company in Munich wants an American-made airliner that costs 11,988,527 euros. How much will the German company pay in dollars for the plane?

$11,988,527 \times 1.18 = \$14,146,461$

23. It costs .010032 dollars to buy one yen today. How much will a Japanese importer pay in dollars for a 524,000-yen purchase of U.S.-milled flour?

$.010032 \times 524,000 = \$5,256.77$

24. A Canadian police department buys U.S.-made warning lights for their cars. They paid 36,000 Canadian dollars for them when the exchange rate was $.7231 U.S. How much will the U.S. company receive in U.S. dollars?

36,000 (CAD) × .7231 (USD) = $26,031.60 (U.S.)

25. British Leyland Ltd. bought 475,000 pounds worth of electrical parts from Delco in Michigan. How much will Delco receive in dollars if the exchange rate is 1.6201?

475,000 × 1.6201 = $769,547.50

26. Today it takes 1.23 euros to buy one U.S. dollar. If a German importer pays 25,000,000 euros for U.S.-made transmissions, how much will the U.S. company receive in dollars?

$\frac{25,000,000}{1.23}$ = $20,325,203

23.7

27. The exchange rate between dollars and Saudi Arabian riyal is $.2633 per riyal today. Yesterday it was $.2511 per riyal. A U.S. company has been buying shipments of Saudi-produced oil at 8,460,350 riyal per shipment. What will happen to the price of the oil in dollars?

8,460,350 × .2633 = $2,227,610.16   Before the change
8,460,350 × .2511 = $2,124,393.89   After the change

$ 2,227,610.16
− 2,124,393.89
$ 103,216.27   Price decrease to the U.S. firm

28. A U.S. company sells wheat to a company in Spain. The Spanish company had been paying 1,800,000 euros for each shipment when the exchange was 1.46 euros per dollar. There was a change to 1.23 euros per dollar. Find the result in U.S. dollars to the U.S. company.

$\frac{1,800,000}{1.46}$ = $1,232,876.70   Before the change

$\frac{1,800,000}{1.23}$ = $1,463,414.63   After the change

$ 1,463,414.63
− 1,232,876.70
$ 230,537.93   Price increase to the U.S. firm

29. A Brazilian company sells finished shirts to a U.S. firm each month for 125,000 reals. If the exchange rate changed from 2.213 reals per U.S. dollar to 2.336 reals per dollar, what effect will the change have on the dollar payment to the U.S. company?

$\frac{125,000}{2.213}$ = $56,484.41   Before the change

$\frac{125,000}{2.336}$ = $53,310.27   After the change

$ 56,484.41
− 53,310.27
$ 2,974.14   Price decrease to the U.S. firm

30. Australian dollars changed in price from .5413 per USD to .5244 per USD. In U.S. dollars, what will happen to the price of a shipment of truck parts that used to sell for 4,400,000 Australian dollars?

4,400,000 × .5413 = $ 2,381,720   Before the change
4,400,000 × .5244 = − $2,307,360   After the change
$ 74,360   Price decrease to the U.S. firm

31. Today there are 132.65 yen per dollar. If the exchange rate increases to 133.75, how much will a Japanese-made VCR change in price in yen for a U.S. buyer if it cost $300 before the change?

$300 × 132.65 = 39,795   yen before the change
$300 × 133.75 = 40,125   yen after the change

40,125
− 39,795
330   yen price increase to the U.S. firm

CHAPTER REVIEW PROBLEMS

Answers to odd-numbered problems are given in Appendix A.

Drill Problems

Name each metric unit or indicate the multiple of each given unit

1. 2 deciliters = _____20_____ centiliters
2. 100 dekagrams = 1 _hectogram_
3. 2 millimeters = _____.2_____ centimeters
4. 100 liters = 1 _hectoliter_
5. 3 kilometers = _____3,000_____ meters
6. 4 deciliters = _____.4_____ liters
7. .001 gram = 1 _milligram_
8. .01 hectometer = 1 _dekameter_
9. 5 grams = _____.5_____ dekagrams
10. 2 liters = _____20_____ deciliters

11. 1,000 milligrams = 1 _gram_
12. .001 hectometers = 1 _decimeter_
13. 1 dekameter = _____10_____ meters
14. 100 liters = 1 _hectoliter_
15. .001 gram = 1 _milligram_
16. 1 deciliter = _____.1_____ liter
17. 1 meter = _____100_____ centimeter
18. .1 decagram = 1 _gram_
19. 1,000 meters = 1 _kilometer_
20. 1 milliliter = _____.001_____ liters

Convert the following from foreign currencies to U.S. dollars:

	Foreign Currency	Exchange Rate (U.S. to 1 FC)	Number Foreign	Number Dollars
21.	Australia, dollar	.7435	38	$ 28.25
22.	Brazil, real	1.1765	165	194.12
23.	Britain, pound	1.574	69	108.61
24.	Canada, dollar	.7456	1,290	961.82
25.	Denmark, krone	.1637	15,000	2,455.50
26.	Israel, shekel	.3298	8,674	2,860.69
27.	Japan, yen	.010235	985,000	10,081.48
28.	Mexico, peso	.294118	112,000	32,941.22
29.	Saudi Arab, riyal	.2666	28,000	7,464.80
30.	So. Korea, won	.00125	928,000	1,160.00

Convert the following from U.S. dollars to foreign currencies:

	Foreign Currency	Exchange Rate (FC to 1 U.S.)	Number Foreign	Number Dollars
31.	Australia, dollar	1.345	33.63	$ 25
32.	Brazil, real	.85	67.15	79
33.	Britain, pound	.6353	81.32	128
34.	Canada, dollar	1.3412	887.87	662
35.	Denmark, krone	6.109	109,962	18,000
36.	Israel, shekel	3.032	211,330.40	69,700
37.	Japan, yen	97.7	2,051,700	21,000
38.	Mexico, peso	3.4	33,524	9,860
39.	Saudi Arab, riyal	3.7504	367,539.20	98,000
40.	So. Korea, won	799.8	36,790,800	46,000

Determine the result of a change in exchange rates in the following:

	Foreign Currency	Before	After	Change in Dollars	Number Dollars
41.	Australia, dollar	1.345	1.356	$ .28	$ 25
42.	Brazil, real	.85	.91	4.74	79
43.	Britain, pound	.6353	.6373	.26	128
44.	Canada, dollar	1.3412	1.3513	6.69	662
45.	Denmark, krone	6.109	6.0835	459.00	18,000
46.	Israel, shekel	3.032	3.031	69.70	69,700
47.	Japan, yen	97.7	98.56	18,060	21,000
48.	Mexico, peso	3.4	3.4035	34.51	9,860
49.	Saudi Arab, riyal	3.7504	3.75	39.20	98,000
50.	So. Korea, won	799.8	798.1	78,200	46,000

Word Problems

51. The exchange rate between dollars and euros was 1.22 per dollar. If a U.S. company buys a shipment of electrical parts made in Hamburg for $26,000, how much will the company pay in euros?
$26,000 × 1.22 = 31,720 euros

52. A British company sold $8,700 of Scottish-made beverage goods to an importer in Connecticut. How much will the British company receive in pound sterling if the exchange rate is one dollar = .7122? (Round to the nearest pound.)
$8,700 × .7122 = 6,196 pounds

53. Last week there were 133 yen per dollar. How many yen will a Japanese tire maker receive for a $350,000 shipment in Boston?

$350,000 × 133 = 46,550,000 yen

54. The exchange rate between dollars and euros is 1.31 per dollar. If a U.S. company buys a shipment of Italian-made pasta priced at $25,000, how much will the company pay in euros?

$25,000 × 1.31 = 32,750 euros

55. A Canadian-made truck engine block costs $999.95 U.S. in Philadelphia. How much will the Canadian company be paid in Canadian money if the Canadian dollar is being exchanged at 1.45 per U.S. dollar?

$999.95 × 1.45 = 1,449.93 CAD

56. Greek-grown grapes sold for $5,200 in Atlanta. How much will the Greek exporter receive in euros if there are 1.27 euros per U.S. dollar?

$5,200 × 1.27 = 6,604 euros

57. Euros trade for 1.23 per dollar today. A company in Tilburg, Holland, wants an IBM printer that costs 1,183.24 euros. How much will a dealer in Nashville receive in dollars for the printer?

$\frac{1,183.24}{1.23} = \$961.98$

58. A British importer bought 129,000 pounds worth of Kansas wheat. How much will the firm in Russell receive in dollars if the exchange rate is one pound per $1.68?

129,000 × $1.68 = $216,720

59. It costs .010111 dollars to buy one yen. How much will a Japanese importer pay in dollars for a 62,000-yen purchase of Apple Software?

62,000 yen × $.010111 = $626.88

60. A Mexican buyer wants U.S.-made blue jeans. She paid 82,600 pesos for them when the exchange rate was $.11 U.S. per one Mexican peso. How much will the U.S. exporter receive in U.S. dollars?

$.11 × 82,600 = $9,086

61. A company in India bought some North Dakota grain for 18,950,000 rupees. How much will the company in Bismark receive in dollars if an Indian rupee is worth .0211 dollars?

.0211 × 18,950,000 = $399,845

62. A U.S. exporter sells razor blades to a Japanese barber supplier. The exchange between yen and dollars changed from 134.25 per dollar to 137.67 per dollar. The Japanese firm has been buying $1,500 worth per month. Find the change this makes in yen for the Japanese importer.

$1,500 × 137.67 = 206,505 yen

$1,500 × 134.25 = 201,375 yen

$$\begin{array}{r} 206,505 \\ - 201,375 \\ \hline 5,130 \text{ more yen after} \\ \text{the change} \end{array}$$

63. The exchange rate between euros and U.S. dollars changed from 1.435 to 1.525 euros per dollar. A U.S. company in Salt Lake City has been buying shipments of Italian-made eyeglass frames for 9,500 euros. What will happen to the price of the frames in dollars?

$\frac{9,500}{1.435} = \$6,620.21$ Before the change

$\frac{9,500}{1.525} = \$6,229.51$ After the change

$$\begin{array}{r} \$\ 6,620.21 \\ - 6,229.51 \\ \hline \$\ \ \ \ 390.70 \end{array}$$ Price decrease to the U.S. firm

64. The South Korean won changed in price from one won per $.001115 to $.001470. In U.S. dollars, what will happen to the price of a South Korean–made turbine that sells for 156,380,000 won?

$$\begin{array}{r} 156,380,000 \\ \times \$\ .001115 \\ \hline \$174,363.70 \end{array}$$ Before

$$\begin{array}{r} 156,380,000 \\ \times \$\ .001470 \\ \hline \$229,878.60 \end{array}$$ After

$$\begin{array}{r} \$\ 229,878.60 \\ -174,363.70 \\ \hline \$\ \ 55,514.90 \end{array}$$ Price increase in the U.S.

65. The exchange rate between Israeli shekels and U.S. dollars changed from 2.557 to 2.998 per dollar. A U.S. company has been buying monthly shipments of oil filters made in Israel for 785,000 shekels each month. What will happen to the price of the oil filters in dollars?

$$\frac{785,000}{2.557} = \$307,000.39 \text{ Before the change}$$

$$\frac{785,000}{2.998} = \$261,841.23 \text{ After the change}$$

$$\begin{array}{r} \$\ 307,000.39 \\ -261,841.23 \\ \hline \$\ \ 45,159.16 \end{array} \text{ Price decrease to the U.S. firm}$$

66. A British company sells 11,445 pounds worth of air filters each month to a U.S. firm. If the exchange rate changed from .7114 pounds per dollar to .6121 per dollar, what effect will the change have on the dollar payment by the U.S. company?

$$\frac{11,445}{.7114} = \$16,088.00 \text{ Before the change}$$

$$\frac{11,445}{.6121} = \$18,697.93 \text{ After the change}$$

$$\begin{array}{r} \$\ 18,697.93 \\ -16,088.00 \\ \hline \$\ \ 2,609.93 \end{array} \text{ Price increase to the U.S. firm}$$

CRITICAL THINKING GROUP PROJECT

Several foreign students attend the local university. The tuition is $134 per hour. The foreign exchange rate for five foriegn nations is as follows:

	FC per $1	Dollars per 1 FC
Chile (peso)		$.00243
Ireland (euro)	.6179	
Japan (yen)	109.39	
Norway (krone)		.1563
Switzerland (franc)		.828

Jorge Perez from Chile is taking 14 hours.

Kathleen McNeil from Ireland is taking 15 hours.

Ichikawa Sukumi from Japan is taking 18 hours.

Eric Brewer from Norway is taking 16 hours.

Heidi Borge from Switzerland is taking 12 hours.

1. Calculate the tuition cost in U.S. dollars for each of the students.
Jorge Perez: $134 × 14 = $1,876
Kathleen McNeil: $134 × 15 = $2,010
Ichikawa Sukumi: $134 × 18 = $2,412
Eric Brewer: $134 × 16 = $2,144
Heidi Borge: $134 × 12 = $1,608

2. Calculate the tuition cost for each student in the currency of their homeland.

Jorge Perez: $\dfrac{\$1,876}{.00243} = 772,016.46$ pesos

Kathleen McNeil: $2,010 × .6179 = 1,241.98 euros

Ichikawa Sukumi: $2,412 × 109.39 = 263,848.68 yen

Eric Brewer: $\dfrac{\$2,144}{.1563} = 13,717.21$ krones

Heidi Borge: $\dfrac{\$1,608}{.828} = 1,942.03$ francs

1. 1 hectogram   = __1,000__ decigrams
2. .1 centiliter   = 1 __milliliter__
3. 3 kilometers   = __300__ dekameters
4. 100 decigrams = 1 __dekagram__
5. 64 kiloliters   = __64,000__ liters

6. 86 decimeters   = __8.6__ meters
7. 4.6 hectograms = __460__ grams
8. 216 centigrams = __21,600__ grams
9. 18 meters   = __1.8__ dekameters
10. 3.6 liters   = __3,600__ milliliters

11. A piece of pipe is two meters long. How many pieces five decimeters long can be cut from the piece?

| meter | 2 | Starting point $\frac{20}{5}$ = 4 pieces |
| decimeter | 20 | ↓ |

12. Milk costs $.75 per liter. How much does a kiloliter cost?

kiloliter		$750.00
hectoliter		$ 75.00
dekaliter		$ 7.50
liter	Starting point	$ .75

13. A board is two centimeters thick. How many boards are in a stack three meters tall?

meter	3	Starting point $\frac{300}{2}$ = 150 boards
decimeters	30	↓
centimeters	300	

14. Vanilla extract is sold in .5 liter bottles in Mexico. Exactly how many ounces would that be?

$\frac{1.057}{2}$ = .05285 × 32 ounces per quart = 16.19 ounces

15. The gasoline tank on Herman's Dodge holds 14 gallons. Approximately how many liters will the tank hold?

1 liter = approximately 1 quart
4 quarts = 1 gallon

```
   14
 × 4
   56 liters
```

16. Why do most nations have floating exchange rates today? **W**
Floating exchange rates eliminate the need for government intervention. Instead of governments determining exchange rates, they are determined by the forces of supply and demand.

17. Why would a nation want its currency to be devalued? **W**
When a nation's currency is devalued, it makes the nation's products cheaper in foreign markets and products of other nations more expensive at home. That should increase exports and decrease imports.

18. Today there are 132.78 yen per dollar. How much will a Japanese carmaker receive for a car that costs $39,000 in Denver?
132.78 × $39,000 = 5,178,420 yen

19. A Mexican-made auto part costs $125 in Arlington, Texas. How much will the Mexican company be paid in pesos if the exchange rate is 9 pesos per dollar.?
9 × $125 = 1,125 pesos

20. A florist in St. Petersburg, Florida bought a supply of flowers grown in the Netherlands. The U.S. florist paid the Dutch company $3,200 for the shipment. How much will the Dutch company receive if the exchange rate is 1.272 euros per dollar?
1.272 × $3,200 = 4,070.4 euros

21. When there are 125 yen per dollar, how much will a Japanese television set maker receive for a set that costs $450 in Omaha, Nebraska?
125 × $450 = 56,250 yen

22. A British carmaker sold four $48,000 Jaguars to an American dealer. How much will the British company receive in pounds if the exchange is .6373 pounds per USD?
.6373 × $48,000 × 4 = 122,361.60 pounds

23. A French-made tire costs $89.95 in Atlanta. How much will the French company be paid in euros if it is being exchanged at 1.299 per U.S. dollar?
1.299 × $89.95 = 116.85 euros

At the end of the year, Springfield's management wants a cumulative report of the products purchased from foreign sources. You will see the following form when you open Ch23App1 from your computer spreadsheet application's disk:

Springfield Department Store

2617 Main Street
Box 219
Springfield, Maryland 58109
Telephone: 301-555-2158   FAX: 301-555-3498

MONETARY CONVERSIONS

Product Category	Country Purchased From	Foreign Currency Price	Currency Name	Exchange Rate = $1 U. S.	U. S. Dollar Cost
			#N/A	#N/A	#N/A
			#N/A	#N/A	#N/A
			#N/A	#N/A	#N/A
			#N/A	#N/A	#N/A
			#N/A	#N/A	#N/A
			#N/A	#N/A	#N/A
			#N/A	#N/A	#N/A
			#N/A	#N/A	#N/A
			#N/A	#N/A	#N/A
			#N/A	#N/A	#N/A
			#N/A	#N/A	#N/A
			#N/A	#N/A	#N/A
			#N/A	#N/A	#N/A
TOTAL					#N/A

Enter the following information:

Product Category	Cell	Country Purchased From	Cell	Foreign Currency Price	Cell
Men's clothing	A13	Hong Kong	B13	195,764	C13
Electronic parts	A14	Japan	B14	3,810,239	C14
Women's clothing	A15	France	B15	333,985	C15
Leather goods	A16	Mexico	B16	366,209	C16
Appliances	A17	Taiwan	B17	771,923	C17
Automobile parts	A18	India	B18	98,338	C18
Carpeting	A19	Sweden	B19	145,109	C19
Furniture	A20	Denmark	B20	373,199	C20
Glassware	A21	Ireland	B21	21,908	C21
Figurines	A22	Canada	B22	30,294	C22
Toys	A23	Hong Kong	B23	92,383	C23
Bicycle parts	A24	Chile	B24	9,228	C24
Sporting goods	A25	Japan	B25	937,199	C25

Answer the following questions after you have completed the spreadsheet:

1. What is the name of Denmark's currency?

2. What was the dollar value of the bicycle parts purchased from Chile?

3. What was the dollar value of the glassware purchased from Ireland?

4. What was the dollar value of the toys purchased from Hong Kong?

5. What was the dollar value of the leather goods purchased from Mexico?

6. What was the dollar value of the men's clothing purchased from Hong Kong?

7. What was the dollar value of the appliances purchased from Taiwan?

8. What was the dollar value of the sporting goods purchased from Japan?

9. What was the dollar value of the figurines purchased from Canada?

10. What was the dollar value of the furniture purchased from Denmark?

GROUP REPORT

Inflation has caused a 20% increase in the cost of foreign products. Calculate the changes and enter them into the spreadsheet. Write a report informing the store manager of the results of the price changes. What are your group's recommendations?

APPENDIX A
ANSWERS TO END-OF-CHAPTER PROBLEMS

CHAPTER 1

Chapter 1 Additional Practice Problems

1.1

1. 8,763
3. 49,000,412,000,027
5. Fourteen
7. One hundred twenty

1.2

9. 5,000
11. 577,000,000,000,000

1.3

13. 322
15. 3,830,337

1.4

	Estimated	Actual		Estimated	Actual
17.	810	843	**19.**	640,000	608,441

1.5

21. 3,297
23. 89,332

1.6

	Estimated	Actual		Estimated	Actual
25.	5,000	9,425	**27.**	6,000	5,449

1.7

29. 12,062
31. 73,947,048

1.8

33. 2,95*0*
35. 9,347,2*00,000*

1.9

	Estimated	Actual		Estimated	Actual
37.	2,800	2,592	**39.**	3,000	3,660

1.10

41. 18
43. 1 R79

1.11

45. 248
47. 432

1.12

	Estimated	Actual		Estimated	Actual
49.	66	62	**51.**	75	71 R624

1.13

53.
Actual	Proof
6,931	239
	29)6,931

55.
Actual	Proof
30	$30 \times 70 = 2,100$

1.14

57. 34 Total hours
59. $5 Total cost for all candy bars

Chapter 1 Review Problems

1. 419
3. 394,273
5. 607
7. 126
9. 218,4*00,000*
11. 23
13. 20 R6
15. 9,100
17. 61,000
19. 26,000
21. 700
23. 4,000
25. 15
27. 230,000
29. 315,*000*
  Proof $3,150 \div 9 = 350$
31. 2,000
  Proof $31 \times 2 = 6,2$*00,000*
33. 6,000,6*00,000*
  Proof $60,006 \div 2 = 30,002$
35. $490 $514
37. $1,595
39. $1,105,064
41. $1,400
43. 6,00*0,000,000*
45. $288   yes
47. $300
49. $194
51. 600 dozen on shift 3; 1,000 dozen per day 5,000 dozen per week; 260,000 dozen per year
53. 8,848

Enrichment Problems

54.

	M	T	W	T	F	Totals
Room						$427
Transportation						627
Meals						227
Entertainment						+ 424
Totals:	$306 + 126 + 235 + 526 + 512 = $1,705					

55.

Game 1	27,230
Game 2	9,215
Game 3	6,258
Game 4	5,074
Game 5	44,575
Totals:	3,089 + 699 + 3,615 + 18,961 + 65,988 = 92,352

56.

Golf clubs	$ 6,500
Golf balls	2,150
Golf bags	1,875
Pull carts	3,240
Shirts	800
Sweaters	875
Trousers	360
Blouses	825
Shorts	560
Caps	300
Shoes	1,800
	$19,285

57. $21,941,952 Amount managers received
$2,625 Loss to Michael Schmaltz if he sells his stock

Chapter 1 Self-Testing Exercises

1. Multiplication is essentially a shortcut method of addition. If you have memorized the table, you can avoid the cumbersome addition of a series of addends that have the same value.

2. A number is often rounded off because either it is unnecessary to be perfectly accurate or it is not feasible or convenient to determine the exact number.

3. 62,000,500,826   **4.** 37,123,000   **5.** 871,100   **6.** 400,001,001   **7.** 14,397

8. 37,000   **9.** 87,500,000   **10.** 69,430   **11.** 9,000,000   **12.** 870,000

13.
Actual	Estimated	Proof
3,668	3,700	3,668

14.
Actual	Estimated	Proof
990	967	990

15.
Actual	Estimated	Proof
103,529	104,259	103,529

16.
Actual	Estimated	Proof
325	330	392

17.
Actual	Estimated	Proof
5,265	5,500	5,738

18.
Actual	Estimated	Proof
5,721	5,000	25,194

19.
Actual	Estimated	Proof
4,392	4,200	732

20.
Actual	Estimated	Proof
12,180,000	12,000,000	21,000

21.
Actual	Estimated	Proof
435,000,000	420,000,000	725,000

22.
Actual	Estimated	Proof
11 R3	11	69

23.
Actual	Estimated	Proof
34	30	6,188

24.
Actual	Estimated	Proof
40	42	260,000

25. $17,225   **26.** 3,940   **27.** $710   **28.** 89,399   **29.** 4,960

30. $4,101   **31.** $1 Maria   **32.** 32   **33.** 60   **34.** $605

35. $152   **36.** 1,600   **37.** $718, $555   **38.** $47,600,000

CHAPTER 2

Chapter 2 Additional Practice Problems

2.1

1. nine tenths   **3.** fifty-one thousandths   **5.** .76   **7.** .612

2.2

9. Fifteen and sixty-nine hundredths

11. Two thousand, five hundred seventy-two and two hundred thirty-one thousandths

13. 1.016   **15.** 5,469.0174

2.3

17. 280   **19.** 534.9

2.4

21. 1.0535   **23.** 388.005

2.5

25. *Estimated*	*Actual*	**27.** *Estimated*	*Actual*
8,800	9,218.8701	53.2	51.225

2.6

29. .2638   **31.** 173.86024

2.7

33. *Estimated*	*Actual*	**35.** *Estimated*	*Actual*
.5	.411	4,500	4,499.713

2.8

37. .11058   **39.** .0252

2.9

41. 34.9   **43.** 14,137

2.10

45. *Estimated*	*Actual*	**47.** *Estimated*	*Actual*
40	35.676	150	120.02102

2.11

49. 1.5   **51.** .309

2.12

53. .28   **55.** .034

2.13

57. *Estimated*	*Actual*	**59.** *Estimated*	*Actual*
667	603.101	.667	.593

Chapter 2 Review Problems

1. .2   **3.** .0005   **5.** fourteen thousandths

7. eight thousand, seven hundred sixty-five ten thousandths   **9.** 1.06

11. 3,000,025.0201   **13.** Twenty-three and forty-one hundredths

15. Seventy-eight thousand, forty-six and ninety-one thousand, three hundred eighty-five hundred thousandths

17. .10   **19.** 16.1   **21.** $18.09   **23.** $38.28   **25.** 15.9

27. 7.6181   **29.** 513.9443   **31.** 1.8   1.851   **33.** 13.4   15.572

35. 251.940887   **37.** 138.89306

39. *Estimated*	*Actual*	**41.** *Estimated*	*Actual*
1,700	1,251.59	397	390.1399

43. 298.3176   **45.** .174231   **47.** 462,000   **49.** 88,320

51. *Estimated*	*Actual*	**53.** *Estimated*	*Actual*
210	256.2	24,000	22,686

55. .075   **57.** 1.381   **59.** .03782   **61.** .000432

63. *Estimated*	*Actual*	**65.** *Estimated*	*Actual*
14	21.545	60	48.95

67. $23,740,193.98   **69.** 111

71. *Estimated*	*Actual*	*Estimated*	*Actual*	**73.** *Estimated*	*Actual*
150 min.	160 min.	2.5 hours	2.7 hours	158	177.5

75. $153.60   **77.** 3,874   **79.** 3.571

Enrichment Problems

80. .366   **81.** $51.68   **82.** $1.62

Chapter 2 Self-Testing Exercises

1. A mixed decimal is a whole number combined with a decimal fraction.

2. A decimal fraction is a fraction expressed as a part of a whole in the base 10 system. Thus, the value is stated in ten*ths*, hundred*ths*, thousand*ths*, and so on, depending on the position occupied.

3. .026   **4.** .3479   **5.** 43,000,300,257.41   **6.** 362,300.033

7. 22,976,000.527   **8.** 1.1   **9.** 6,286.249   **10.** 14.99

11. 12,977   **12.** 38.54937

13. *Estimated*	*Actual*	**14.** *Estimated*	*Actual*	**15.** *Estimated*	*Actual*
172	174.11	977	1,001.646	100,259	103,532.003

16. *Estimated*	*Actual*	**17.** *Estimated*	*Actual*	**18.** *Estimated*	*Actual*
4,138	3,855.651	330	325.805	5,500	5,265.36

19. *Estimated*	*Actual*	**20.** *Estimated*	*Actual*	**21.** *Estimated*	*Actual*
20	20.52985	270	270.1121	4,200	4,648.835
22. *Estimated*	*Actual*	**23.** *Estimated*	*Actual*	**24.** *Estimated*	*Actual*
810	820.92444	4,200	4,350	30,000	28,093
25. *Estimated*	*Actual*	**26.** *Estimated*	*Actual*	**27.** *Estimated*	*Actual*
10	10.687	300	313.187	1	1.2
28. *Estimated*	*Actual*	**29.** $17,227.32		**30.** $10.27	
.03	.03				

31. $2.05

32. Maria earned $.20 per hour more than Harry.

33. $2.40

34.
	To Serve 2	*To Serve 16*
	1.25 cup sugar	10 cups sugar
	1 tablespoon malt	8 tablespoons malt

35. $80,186   **36.** $349.42   **37.** $494

38. $4,686.96   **39.** 4 bags   **40.** $68.03

41. $169.25   **42.** 24.4

CHAPTER 3

Chapter 3 Additional Practice Problems

3.1

1. I (numerator is larger than the denominator)
3. I (numerator is larger than the denominator)

3.2

5. 17/6   **7.** 13/3

3.3

9. $3\frac{1}{5}$ **11.** $19\frac{1}{3}$

3.4

13. $\frac{1}{2}$ **15.** $\frac{2}{7}$

3.5

17. $\frac{2}{7}$ **19.** $\frac{1}{4}$

3.6

21. $\frac{12}{20}$ **23.** $\frac{39}{66}$

3.7

25. 120 LCD   **27.** 90 LCD

3.8

29. $\frac{7}{8}$ **31.** $1\frac{3}{4}$

3.9

33. $\frac{7}{15}$ **35.** $\frac{8}{63}$ **37.** $99\frac{3}{16}$

3.10

39. 30   **41.** $21\frac{7}{18}$

3.11

43. $\frac{3}{4}$ **45.** $\frac{35}{57}$

3.12

47. .556   **49.** .029

3.13

51. $\frac{61}{200}$ **53.** $1\frac{4}{5}$

3.14

55. 6   **57.** 11   **59.** 90   **61.** 3   **63.** 10.8

Chapter 3 Review Problems

1. M   **3.** I   **5.** $\frac{109}{25}$ **7.** $\frac{137}{3}$ **9.** $1\frac{5}{7}$

11. $2\frac{81}{122}$ **13.** $192\frac{4}{9}$ **15.** $\frac{1}{8}$ **17.** $\frac{749}{4,000}$ **19.** 212.083

21. 2.143　　　**23.** $\dfrac{5}{6}$　　　**25.** $\dfrac{131}{272}$　　　**27.** $\dfrac{17}{31}$　　　**29.** $\dfrac{5}{7}$

31. 12　　　**33.** 615　　　**35.** $\dfrac{54}{72}, \dfrac{63}{72}, \dfrac{16}{72}, \dfrac{60}{72}$　　　**37.** $\dfrac{120}{315}, \dfrac{35}{315}, \dfrac{63}{315}, \dfrac{18}{315}$

39. $\dfrac{39}{64}$　　　**41.** $18\dfrac{13}{56}$　　　**43.** $\dfrac{1}{12}$　　　**45.** $\dfrac{3}{5}$　　　**47.** $\dfrac{5}{48}$

49. $\dfrac{3}{7}$　　　**51.** 15　　　**53.** 7　　　**55.** 80　　　**57.** 111,000

59. $5\dfrac{1}{3}$　　　**61.** $\dfrac{1}{114}$　　　**63.** 1.2　　　**65.** $\dfrac{1}{3}$　　　**67.** $19\dfrac{15}{16}$

69. 4　　　**71.** $6\dfrac{1}{5}$　　　**73.** $3\dfrac{1}{2}$　　　**75.** $1\dfrac{13}{16}$　　　**77.** $\dfrac{5}{12}$

79. 10,000　　　**81.** $9\dfrac{15}{16}$

Enrichment Problems

83. $990　　　**84.** $75,000 (Robert); $50,000 (John); $25,000 (Mike)

Chapter 3 Self-Testing Exercises

1. The greatest common divisor is the largest number that will divide evenly into both the numerator and the denominator of a fraction, while the least common denominator is the smallest number that is evenly divisible by each denominator of the common fractions being added or subtracted.

2. A prime number is a number that can be divided evenly only by itself and 1.

3. $1\dfrac{1}{2}$　　　**4.** $\dfrac{1}{16}$　　　**5.** $\dfrac{4}{5}$　　　**6.** $\dfrac{3}{8}$　　　**7.** $\dfrac{7}{96}$　　　**8.** $\dfrac{4}{5}$

9. $5\dfrac{7}{8}$　　　**10.** $1\dfrac{199}{399}$　　　**11.** $56\dfrac{11}{16}$　　　**12.** $16\dfrac{1}{7}$　　　**13.** $16\dfrac{16}{21}$　　　**14.** $1\dfrac{3}{4}$

15. .375　　　**16.** .667　　　**17.** .938　　　**18.** 13.833　　　**19.** 216.6　　　**20.** $\dfrac{2}{3}$

21. $\dfrac{5}{8}$　　　**22.** $\dfrac{5}{6}$　　　**23.** $\dfrac{3}{8}$　　　**24.** $\dfrac{23}{100}$　　　**25.** $1\dfrac{1}{5}$　　　**26.** $\dfrac{3}{8}$

27. $2\dfrac{69}{500}$　　　**28.** 125　　　**29.** 201　　　**30.** 36　　　**31.** 200　　　**32.** 600

33. 30 gallons　　　**34.** $22\dfrac{43}{96}$　　　**35.** 85　　　**36.** 8　　　**37.** 56　　　**38.** $292\dfrac{1}{2}$ units

39. 240　　　**40.** 243　　　**41.** $304.50　　　**42.** $\dfrac{13}{18}$　　　**43.** .96

CHAPTER 4

Chapter 4 Additional Practice Problems

4.1

1. 23　　　**3.** 129

4.2

5. 126　　　**7.** 96

4.3

9. 2　　　**11.** −9　　　**13.** 24　　　**15.** 30

4.5

17. 18　　　**19.** 7

4.6

21. 6   **23.** $\dfrac{M}{T}$

4.7

25. 9   **27.** 49.5

4.8

29. 9   **31.** 3

4.9

33. 3   **35.** 4

4.10

37. 3   **39.** 15

4.11 and 4.12

41. 41

43. 11 lots (Stan's sales)   33 lots (Carla's sales)

45. 19 cases at $150 per case = $2,850 for syringes
    5 cases at $60 per case = $ 300 for needles

47. 180 tables, $14,400
    900 chairs, $27,000

Chapter 4 Review Problems

1. 9   **3.** 5   **5.** 156   **7.** −52   **9.** −6   **11.** 23

13. 15   **15.** 25   **17.** 5   **19.** 124   **21.** 135   **23.** 1,428

25. $R + Q$ **27.** RQ **29.** 4   **31.** 102   **33.** 2   **35.** 12

37. 78   **39.** 8   **41.** $1,215,000   **43.** 4 Yvonne   28 Dale

45. $7,200,000 Auto Bright's sales $1,800,000 Competitor's sales

47. 130 for $1,040 Brush sales   **49.** $394.85 Craig's tips   **51.** 3,875   Square feet tile $ 46,500 Tile
    170 for $425 Comb sales $454.35 Alan's tips   9,687.5 Square feet carpet $193,750 Carpet

Enrichment Problems

53. 1,200 men's shoes for $48,000   **54.** 7 Julie   14 Wade
    4,800 women's shoes for $144,000

55.   250 Shirts,   Shirts: $ 6,250
    1,250 Shorts,   Shorts: $18,750

Chapter 4 Self-Testing Exercises

1. Absolute value refers to the value of a number itself without regard to its positive or negative sign.

2. An equation represents the equality between two quantities.

3. −72   **4.** 5   **5.** −1   **6.** −8   **7.** 3   **8.** 11

9. 5   **10.** $\dfrac{3}{25}$ **11.** $P + Z$ **12.** ZH **13.** $\dfrac{RS}{U}$ **14.** $\dfrac{CB}{Z}$

15. 5   **16.** −12   **17.** $4,770 Abe's sales   **18.** $\dfrac{25}{43}$ **19.** .414

20. 16 Coreena's age   **21.** Hardback: 200 for $ 3,500
    Paperback: 1,400 for $8,050

22. 50 dozen pens for $425
    20 dozen pencils for $14.40

23. $12(N - 25) = 72$ **24.** $\dfrac{1}{4} - 15 = 10$ **25.** $200 - 8N = 80$ **26.** $6 + 2N = N + 14$

27. $5 \times (N - 6) = 3(N + 2)$ **28.** $ 50,000 Jim's sales
    $ 96,000 Liz' sales

CHAPTER 5

Chapter 5 Additional Practice Problems

5.1

1. .12   **3.** .00035

5.2

5. 80%   **7.** 88.9%

5.3

9. $\dfrac{12}{125}$ 11. $\dfrac{11}{20,000}$ 13. 87.5%

5.4

15. 50.8%

5.5

17. 12.48   19. $10,800
21. 35%   23. 15%

5.7

25. 1,720   27. $50,000

5.8

29. $42,700   31. 71.5

5.9

33. $50   35. $291.27

5.10

37. $33\dfrac{1}{3}\%$ 39. 22%

5.11

41. 1,750   25%   43. 2%

Chapter 5 Review Problems

1. 1/25   4%   3. 3 9/10   390%   5. .8   80%   7. .121   12.1%
9. 1/8   .125   11. $\dfrac{3}{400}$ .0075   13. $125   15. $240   17. 36%   19. 125%
21. $650   23. $16,000   25. $2,062.50 $812.50   27. $364.23 $22.23
29. $1,581.25   55%   31. $25   10%   33. $3,080 $920   35. $22,498.65 $3,451.35
37. $351.50   74%   39. $.31   4.9%   41. $330 $115.50   43. 1.8   45. $4.88
47. $405,000   49. $2,873   51. 60
53. Rent, 15.68%; Utilities, 4.75%; Coffee, 1.19%; Salaries, 44.69%; Miscellaneous, 33.75%   55. 70%
57. 16.7%   59. 40%   61. 6 pounds   63. $18,360   65. 25,000
67. 104,348,000   69. 400,000   71. $600,000   73. $738.53   75. $3,880,000   77. 33
79. 7.4   81. 277   83. 16,485   85. $31.96   87. 367   89. 9.1%
91. 7.5%   93. 50.5%   95. $3,472,875   97. 82%   99. $33\dfrac{1}{3}\%$ 101. 8.9%
103. 32.1%

Enrichment Problems

105. Total meal would cost $67.68. With $65 he can only tip $6.15, which is a tip of 10.5%.
106. $10,665.91   107. $200,000 3 years ago

Chapter 5 Self-Testing Exercises

1. The three main components are the base, the rate and the percentage. Base can be defined as the starting point, the number to which comparisons are made, or the total amount. Rate can be defined as the percent relationship determined by dividing the percentage by the base. Percentage can be defined as a part of the base.

2. To convert a percent to a decimal fraction, move the decimal point two places to the left and remove the percent sign.

3. 62.5%   4. 5.6%   5. .00575   6. $\dfrac{1}{3}$ 7. $465,000   8. $33\dfrac{1}{3}$

9. $10,000   10. $56,840   11. 22%   12. $319.92 or $320   13. $2,125
14. 7.5%   15. $7.00   16. 8.3%   17. 36   18. 37.5%   19. 12.5%
20. $13,000   21. 42%   22. 92.5%

CHAPTER 6

Chapter 6 Additional Practice Problems

6.1
1. $5,528.85   3. $925

6.2
5. $513.15   7. $281.75

6.3
9. $446.25   11. $688.80

6.4
13. $65   15. $16

6.5
17. $307.50   19. $520.00

6.6
21. $1,323   23. $29,701.43

6.7
25. $1,350.00   27. $717.50

6.8
29. $1,522   31. $2,500.00

6.9
33. $178.87 SS tax withheld $ 41.83 Medicare tax withheld
35. $101.74 SS tax withheld $23.79 Medicare tax withheld

6.10
37. Wage bracket method: $25 withheld
    Percentage method: $25 FIT withheld
39. Wage Bracket Method: $21 withheld
    Percentage method: $21.89 FIT withheld

6.11
41. $1,864.41 Net pay   43. $301.27 Net pay

Chapter 6 Review Problems
1. $1,070.63   3. $4,143.33   5. 43 $252.76   7. 28 $194.32   9. 37 $304.50
11. 36 $358.00   13. 330 $250.80   15. 237 $225.15   17. 65 $190.00
19. 77 $238.00   21. $1,327.24   23. $1,469.55   25. $490.80   27. $1,510.00   29. $1,025.75
31. $684.70   33. $142.60 $33.35   35. $282.10 $65.98   37. $37   39. $12   41. $14.35
43. $260.55   45. $48.05 $11.24 $73 $7.30 $560.41
47. $37.20 $8.70 $39 $3.90 $441.19   49. $589.88   51. $393.86   53. $1,254.75
55. $2,079.40   57. $91 FIT   59. $344.43   61. $257.00   63. $732.00   65. $96 FIT
67. $2,598   69. $839.50   71. $4,393.80 Gross pay

Enrichment Problems
73. $3,576.47 Net pay
74. $43,691.91 Net pay
75. $590.19 Net pay

Chapter 6 Self-Testing Exercises
1. A wage is the payment for the use of human services. A salary is a special kind of contractual wage usually agreed upon on an annual basis.
2. Most employers use computers to figure payroll. Computers can be more easily programmed to calculate FIT deductions using the percentage method instead of the wage bracket method.
3. $187.50   4. $4,903.85   5. $42.47 SS $9.93 Medicare   6. $1,688.04   7. $402.32
8. $1,632.98 Net pay   9. $271.88   10. $171.20   11. $413.92
12. $155 FIT tax withheld   13. $1,556.77 Net pay

CHAPTER 7

Chapter 7 Additional Practice Problems

7.1   ### 7.2

1. $583.50   **3.** $24.74   **5.** $4,300.80   **7.** $2,864.59

7.3

9. Due date for 2% discount 8/12 to 8/22   Due date for net payment 8/23 to 9/11 $586.04
11. Due date for 4% discount 4/27 to 5/7   Due date for net payment 5/8 to 6/26 $32,572.80

7.4

13. Due date for 2% discount 7/8 to 7/25   Due date for net payment 7/26 to 8/14 $762.21
15. Due date for 1.5% discount 11/9 to 12/10   Due date for net payment 12/12 to 12/30 $1,013.07

7.5

17. (1) $489.69   (3) $60.31   **19.** (1) $1,578.95   (3) $1,271.05
    (2) $14.69   (4) February 8   (2) $78.95   (4) July 30

Chapter 7 Review Problems

1. 60% $20.39   **3.** 50% $1,469.50 **5.** 70% $136.49 **7.** .6 $47.99   **9.** .585 $15.77
11. .612 $33.35   **13.** .5355 $1.48   **15.** .456 $5.91   **17.** Nov. 2   Nov. 22   **19.** July 15   July 30
21. $1,370.31   **23.** $789.01   **25.** $18,943.89   **27.** $3,900.52   **29.** $94.19
31. $6,860.00   **33.** $68,220.00   **35.** $4,389.59   **37.** $21,462.56   **39.** $2,863.84
41. $989.26   **43.** $389.78   **45.** 49,840.07   **47.** $137.59   **49.** $32.92
51. $1,530.61 $30.61 $406.84   **53.** $3,571.43 $71.43 $1,532,89
55. $520.83 $20.83 $142.12   **57.** .55575 Net cost equivalent   .44425 Single discount equivalent
59. $486.39   **61.** $2,869.18   **63.** $523.32   **65.** $289.58
67. Credit received, $10,256.41; Discount, $256.41; Balance owed, $3,689.49   **69.** $4,174.04
71. Credit received, $51,546.39 Discount, $1,546.39; Balance owed 11/1, $28,453.61; Balance owed 11/11, $28,169.07

Enrichment Problems

73. $2,533.18   **74.** $52,083.33 Credit received; $2,083.33 Discount; $15,116.67 Balance   **75.** $1,264.62

Chapter 7 Self-Testing Exercises

1. Trade discounts are reductions from the list price of merchandise based on factors such as the buyer's position in the seller's channel of distribution, the season of the year, the condition of the economy, and competition.

2. Cash discounts are reductions of merchandise payments allowed only if payment is made within a specified time period. They are offered to encourage early payment of bills.

3. $294   **4.** $51,000   **5.** $11.03   **6.** .72675 Net cost equivalent   .27325 Single discount equivalent
7. Jan. 23 last day for discount; Feb. 22 Net payment due date
8. $5,801.78   **9.** $875.75   **10.** $1,006.96   **11.** $22,779.55 **12.** $3,113.20   **13.** $903.39
14. Credit received, $66,326.53; Discount, $1,326.53; Balance owed, $15,308.14
15.   *APRIL 7*   *APRIL 15*
    Credit received, $15,306.12;   Credit received, $20,202.02;
    Discount, $306.12;   Discount, $202.02;
    Balance owed, $23,798.57   Balance owed, $3,596.55
16. $17,848.11   **17.** $552.18 Invoice net payment

CHAPTER 8

Chapter 8 Additional Practice Problems

8.1
1. $7.95   **3.** $50.24

8.2
5. $100%   **7.** 48.6%

8.3
9. $411.25   **11.** $12.85

8.4
13. $9.35   **15.** $31.22

8.5
17. $527.27   **19.** $287.50

8.6
21. $226.85   **23.** $1.75

8.7
25. 40.6%   **27.** 48.9%

8.8
29. $1.01   **31.** $1.24

8.9
33. $98   **35.** $62.35

Chapter 8 Review Problems

1. $45   **3.** $472   **5.** $1.25   **7.** $.98   46.7%   **9.** $24   38.1%

11. $17.50   100%   **13.** $9.80   50%   **15.** $105.46   62.4%   **17.** $233\frac{1}{3}$%   **19.** 28.6%

21. $128 $48   **23.** $750 $250   **25.** $35.29 $24.71   **27.** $.32 $.27   **29.** $66.67 $26.67

31. $1,600 $800   **33.** $9.60 $10.40   **35.** $.41 $.38   **37.** $27.03 $11.13

39. $16.17 $6.93   **41.** $4.16 $3.26   **43.** 41.9%   **45.** 20%   **47.** 63.6%

49. 59.5%   **51.** $4.78   **53.** $12.05   **55.** $50 $50   **57.** 10% $1

59. $70   **61.** 50%   **63.** $387.78   **65.** $10.88   **67.** 81.3%

69. 15%   **71.** 41.2%   **73.** $27,030   **75.** $13.95   **77.** 51%

79. $71.67   **81.** $33.22   **83.** $7.66

Enrichment Problems

84. 58.5%   **85.** 108.5%

Chapter 8 Self-Testing Exercises

1. At the end of an accounting cycle, most retailers analyze their income statements. One analysis method is to divide all amounts by net sales. This analysis results in the markup percent on the selling price being calculated on a regular basis. Thus, basing the markup percent on the selling price makes comparisons easier.

2. Perishables are merchandise that must be sold rapidly before it spoils and becomes unsalable.

3. An individual item's markup percent will depend on many factors, including competition, whether the item is a luxury good or a staple good, and the demand for the item. The average markup percent is the markup rate a business needs to average on all merchandise sold over a period of time, usually one year.

4. 50%   **5.** 43.5%   **6.** 46.7%   **7.** $38.50   **8.** $1.40   **9.** 60%   **10.** 92.3%

11. 35%   **12.** $11.67   **13.** $4.65   **14.** $6.24   **15.** 50%   **16.** 34.5%   **17.** $27.95

18. $875   **19.** $4.59   **20.** $9.65

CHAPTER 9

Chapter 9 Additional Practice Problems

9.1.

1.

Buddy's Garage		No. 689
1428 Elm Street		
Midtowne, Iowa 65432	2/9 20 02	48-1530
		2530

PAY TO THE ORDER OF _____ Music Warehouse _____ | $ 398.28

Three hundred ninety-eight and 28/100 _____ DOLLARS

$N NATIONAL BANK
$B OF ANY CITY

FOR _____   *Buddy Allen*

253015300 ⬛222 318 8⬛ 0689   0000000000000

3.

Mayer Productions		No. 691
9275 Sunset		
Hollywood, Calif. 34567	2/5 20 02	48-1530
		2530

PAY TO THE ORDER OF _____ A & G Warehouse _____ | $ 114.75

One hundred fourteen and 75/100 _____ DOLLARS

$N NATIONAL BANK
$B OF ANY CITY

FOR _____   *Thomas Mayer*

253015300 ⬛222 318 8⬛ 0691   0000000000000

5.

Porge Custom Porches		No. 693
8 Fromholz Place		
Anton, South Dakota 38352	2/7 20 02	48-1530
		2530

PAY TO THE ORDER OF _____ Martha's Grapes _____ | $ 57.99

Fifty-seven and 99/100 _____ DOLLARS

$N NATIONAL BANK
$B OF ANY CITY

FOR _____   *George Porge*

253015300 ⬛222 318 8⬛ 0693   0000000000000

7.

FOR DEPOSIT ONLY
BORIS STITCH

9.

Without Recourse
Michael Anderson

11.

$N NATIONAL BANK
$B OF ANY CITY

Deposit Ticket

Checks and other items are received for deposit subject to terms and conditions of this institution's funds availability policy now in effect.

DATE _____

		Dollars	Cents
CURRENCY		301	
COIN		2	68
CHECKS			
1	38-1852	3,385	28
2	38-9562	49	03
3	56-1640	2	72
4	658-3920	112	29
5	472-4948	46	83
6			
7			
8			
9			
10			
11			
12			
13			
14			
15			
16			
17			
18			
19			
20			
21			
22			
23			
24			
25			
26			
27			
28			
29			
TOTAL		3,899	83
LESS CASH			
TOTAL DEPOSIT		3,899	83

Deposits may not be available for immediate withdrawal.
USE OTHER SIDE FOR ADDITIONAL LISTING

$$6 \times \$ \ 1 = \$ \quad 6$$
$$5 \times \quad 5 = \quad 25$$
$$3 \times \quad 10 = \quad 30$$
$$7 \times \quad 20 = \quad 140$$
$$1 \times 100 = \underline{+100}$$
$$\$ \ 301$$

$$8 \times \$.01 = \$ \ .08$$
$$3 \times \ .05 = \quad .15$$
$$7 \times \ .10 = \quad .70$$
$$7 \times \ .25 = \underline{+1.75}$$
$$\$2.68$$

9.2

13.

JOSEPH SCHMALTZ
Bank Reconciliation Statement
October 20, 2002

Bank statement balance		$671.80
Deduct: Outstanding checks	$10.85	
	16.41	
	57.75	85.01
Reconciled Balance		$586.79
Check register balance		$598.19
Deduct: Service charge		11.40
Reconciled balance		$586.79

15.

CHARLES DICKENS, INC.
Bank Reconciliation Statement
November 2, 2002

Bank statement balance			$2,015.00
Add: Deposits in transit (1/15)	$365		
(2/17)	510		875.00
			$2,890.00
Deduct: Outstanding checks #1828	$25.00		
#1831	82.50		
#1832	56.65		
#1834	23.85		188.00
Reconciled statement balance			$2,702.00
Check register balance			$3,227.36
Deduct: Service charge		$ 30.00	
Insurance draft		295.00	
Bank loan draft		190.00	
Charge for check blanks		10.00	
Recording error #1820		.36	525.36
Reconciled balance			$2,702.00

Chapter 9 Review Problems

1. $37,872.50   **3.** $37,406.16   **5.** $36,539.95

7.

Valdez Fur Storage
9568 Stadium Drive
Parkersville, Oregon 12345

No. 485

1/24   20 02   48-1530 / 2530

PAY TO THE ORDER OF Parkersville Electric $ 85.00

Eighty-five and 00/100 — DOLLARS

$N NATIONAL BANK
$B OF ANY CITY

FOR Electricity for Oct.   Juan Valdez

253015300   ⑆222 318 8⑆ 0485   0000000000000

9.

Valdez Fur Storage
9568 Stadium Drive
Parkersville, Oregon 12345

No. 487

1/30   20 02   48-1530 / 2530

PAY TO THE ORDER OF All-City Restaurant Supply $ 38.01

Thirty-eight and 01/100 — DOLLARS

$N NATIONAL BANK
$B OF ANY CITY

FOR Coffee and mugs   Juan Valdez

253015300   ⑆222 318 8⑆ 0487   0000000000000

11.

This deposit consists of one $25 check, $1.05 in coin, and the remainder in paper currency. (The check number is 283-337.)

$N NATIONAL BANK
$B OF ANY CITY

Deposit Ticket

Checks and other items are received for deposit subject to terms and conditions of this institution's funds availability policy now in effect.

DATE _____	Dollars	Cents
CURRENCY	29	00
COIN	1	05
CHECKS		
1 283-337	25	00
2		
3		
4		
5		
6		
7		
8		
9		
10		
11		
12		
13		
14		
15		
16		
17		
18		
19		
20		
21		
22		
23		
24		
25		
26		
27		
28		
29		
TOTAL	55	05
LESS CASH		
TOTAL DEPOSIT	55	05

Deposits may not be available for immediate withdrawal.
USE OTHER SIDE FOR ADDITIONAL LISTING

$ 25.00
+ 1.05
$ 26.05

$ 55.05
− 26.05
$ 29.00

13.

15.

FOR DEPOSIT ONLY
Roberta Espanosa

17. TRIBUNAL LAW REVIEW
Bank Reconciliation Statement
January 7, 2002

Bank statement balance	$68,628.62
Add: Deposits in transit	4,042.90
	$72,671.52
Deduct: Outstanding checks	9,549.36
Reconciled statement balance	$63,122.16
Check register balance	$58,346.16
Add: Note collected	4,800.00
	$63,146.16
Deduct: Bank service charge	24.00
Reconciled balance	$63,122.16

19. FOREST HILL GOLF CLUB
Bank Reconciliation Statement
June 3, 2002

Bank statement balance			$3,839.23
Add: Deposits in transit	(6/1)	$194.50	
	(6/2)	935.39	1,129.89
			$4,969.12
Deduct: Outstanding checks	#3954	$382.90	
	#3958	33.45	
	#3961	19.95	
	#3962	55.81	
	#3963	8.15	
	#3964	50.00	550.26
Reconciled balance			$4,418.86
Register balance			$4,557.40
Deduct: Bank service charge		$ 12.75	
DM insurance		74.50	
DM utility		51.29	138.54
Reconciled register balance			$4,418.86

21. LLOYD'S BISTROL
Bank Reconciliation Statement
August 11, 2002

Bank statement balance			$37,346.21
Add: Deposits in transit	(8/8)	$17,985.00	
	(8/10)	4,065.81	22,050.81
			$59,397.02
Deduct: Outstanding checks			
	#1249	$35.00	
	#1258	12.50	
	#1259	110.18	
	#1260	29,184.29	29,341.97
Reconciled balance			$30,055.05
Register balance			$28,934.05
Add: Note Collection		$2,123.45	
Recording error		45.00	
EFT for transaction		883.01	3,051.46
			$31,985.51
Deduct: Insurance		$1,540.37	
Utilities		381.09	
Service charge		9.00	1,930.46
Reconciled register balance			$30,055.05

23. BLEDSOE AND CO.
Bank Reconciliation Statement
April 1, 2002

Bank statement balance			$52,005.80
Add: Deposits in transit			22,728.04
			$74,733.84
Deduct: Outstanding checks			
	#573	$5,500.55	
	#577	11,002.48	
	#578	3,853.96	20,356.99
Reconciled balance			$54,376.85
Register balance			$54,505.83
Add: Interest income			82.50
			$54,588.33
Deduct: Recording error		$110.00	
Telephone bill		101.48	211.48
Reconciled balance			$54,376.85

Enrichment Problems

24.

K & G IND
Bank Reconciliation Statement
September 23, 2002

Bank statement balance			$4,182.32
Add: Deposit in transit			400.00
			$4,582.32
Deduct: Outstanding checks			
	#107	$477.12	
	#112	300.00	
	#113	100.00	877.12
Reconciled balance			$3,705.20
Register balance			$3,184.52
Add: CM			752.68
			$3,937.20
Deduct: DM	$32.00		
DM	200.00		232.00
Reconciled balance			$3,705.20

Chapter 9 Self-Testing Exercises

1. The decision was not right. Outstanding checks, deposits in transit, uncollected notes, bank service charges, and so forth, could cause both balances to be either larger or smaller than they might appear on the statement and/or the check register.

2. Bank Reconciliation Statement
March 7, 2002

Statement balance		$154.80
Deduct: Outstanding checks	$24.96	
	21.40	46.36
Reconciled balance		$108.44
Register balance		$115.24
Deduct: Service charge		6.80
Reconciled balance		$108.44

3.

```
Ye Olde Gift Shop                          No. 487
2848 Ridgeway Drive
Pringstown, Conn. 56382                        48-1530
                          3/24     20 02        2530

PAY TO THE
ORDER OF ____James Loftin_____  | $ 75.23

Seventy-five and 23/100 _____ DOLLARS
    $N NATIONAL BANK
    $B OF ANY CITY
FOR ___Bride Doll_____      Joyce Olde_____

  253015300      ⑆222 318 8⑆ 0487     0000000000000
```

4.

```
    FOR DEPOSIT ONLY
        James Loftin
```

5.

$$\begin{array}{ccccc}
\$100 & \$\ 50 & \$\ 20 & \$\ 10 & \$\ 1 \\
\underline{\times\ 1} & \underline{\times\ 4} & \underline{\times\ 12} & \underline{\times\ 10} & \underline{\times 21} \\
\$100 & +\ 200 & +\ 240 & +\ 100 & +\ 21 = \$661
\end{array}$$

$$\begin{array}{rl}
14 \times .01 = & \$\quad .14 \\
7 \times .05 = & \quad\ .35 \\
20 \times .10 = & \quad 2.00 \\
35 \times .25 = & \underline{+\ 8.75} \\
& \$11.24
\end{array}$$

$N NATIONAL BANK
$B OF ANY CITY

Deposit Ticket

Checks and other items are received for deposit subject to terms and conditions of this institution's funds availability policy now in effect.

DATE _____

		Dollars	Cents
	CURRENCY	661	01
	COIN	11	24
	CHECKS		
1	31-173	218	02
2	27-684	21	75
3			
4			
5			
6			
7			
8			
9			
10			
11			
12			
13			
14			
15			
16			
17			
18			
19			
20			
21			
22			
23			
24			
25			
26			
27			
28			
29			
TOTAL		912	01
LESS CASH			
TOTAL DEPOSIT		912	01

Deposits may not be available for immediate withdrawal.
USE OTHER SIDE FOR ADDITIONAL LISTING

6.

RECORD ALL CHARGES OR CREDITS THAT AFFECT YOUR ACCOUNT									
NUMBER	DATE	DESCRIPTION OF TRANSACTION	PAYMENT/DEBIT (−)		✓ T	DEPOSIT/CREDIT (+)		Balance 12,321	29
686	8/18	Pay Less Grocery	492	59				11,828	70
687	8/26	Jones Drug Emporium	218	20				11,610	50
688	8/29	Ebony Magazine	1,550	38				10,060	12
	8/30					937	08	10,997	20
689	9/3	Ms. Afri-Amer. Cont.	5,000	00				5,997	20
	9/8					3,250	50	9,247	70
690	9/11	Seventeen Magazine	2,500	00				6,747	70
	9/15					6,350	00	13,097	70

7.

LUCKY LADY TRUCK STOP
Bank Reconciliation Statement
January 17, 2003

Bank statement balance		$7,284.39
Add: Deposits in transit		2,257.92
		$9,542.31
Deduct: Outstanding checks		3,393.44
Reconciled balance		$6,148.87
Register balance		$5,291.17
Add: CMs	$850.75	
Recording error	54.00	$904.75
		$6,195.92
Deduct: DM	$35.05	
Service charge	12.00	47.05
Reconciled balance		$6,148.87

8.

SKYWAY LOUNGE
Bank Reconciliation Statement
March 24, 2002

Bank statement balance			$40,990.56
Add: Deposits in transit	(3/22)	205.10	
	(3/23)	5,421.08	5,626.18
			$46,616.74
Deduct: Outstanding checks	#73	$28.50	
	#77	22.75	
	#79	114.70	
	#80	12.56	
	#81	1,940.27	
	#82	338.34	2,457.12
Reconciled balance			$44,159.62
Register balance			$45,246.46
Add: CM			513.04
			$45,759.50
Deduct: DMs Recording error		.09	
Federal Savings		$123.11	
Blue Note Recording		500.00	
Mutual Benefit		219.23	
Uncollectable check		710.45	
Handling charge		8.00	
Collection charge		15.00	
Service charge		24.00	1,599.88
Reconciled balance			$44,159.62

CHAPTER 10

Chapter 10 Additional Practice Problems

10.1

1. $320 **3.** $3,375

10.2

5. $12 **7.** $1,300

10.3

9. $3,355 Ordinary interest $3,309.04 Exact interest
11. $314.67 Ordinary interest $ 310.36 Exact interest

10.4

13. $62,000 **15.** $2,527.81

10.5

17. $200 discount $49 interest
     Yes, the money should be borrowed.

19. $1,425 discount $107.17 interest
     Yes, the money should be borrowed.

10.6

21. $1,900   **23.** $234,800

10.7

25. 10%   **27.** 12.2%

10.8

29. 60   **31.** 66

10.9

33. $24,819.12   **35.** $1,642.19 Maturity value

Chapter 10 Review Problems

1. $6,615   **3.** $50   **5.** $11,666.67   **7.** $14.08   **9.** $150   **11.** $8,000
13. $2,960   **15.** $427.40   **17.** $6,132   **19.** $153,450   **21.** $1,370.31 $27.97 $8.75
23. $781.12 $7.89 $6.51   **25.** $6,400   **27.** $5,625   **29.** 10%   **31.** 10%
33. 80   **35.** 180   **37.** 73   **39.** 240   **41.** 9   **43.** 8
45. $3,040.04   **47.** $24,828.74   **49.** $840   **51.** $106.94   **53.** $1,350   **55.** $53,567.63
57. $3,500   **59.** 5.4%   **61.** Three months   **63.** $1,909.72   **65.** $1,300   **67.** 400 days

Enrichment Problems

68. $8,153.31   **69.** $1,375 discount $714.08 interest
                           Yes, the money should be borrowed.

Chapter 10 Self-Testing Exercises

1. The reason given is that it is easier to calculate and for consumers to understand. Given today's advances in technology that allows the use of computerized tables and calculators for determining the interest, the reason loses its validity. Because of a court case in Oregon and pressure brought by consumer protection groups, the trend is toward using the exact number of days in a year (365 days or 366 days in leap year).

2. The U.S. Rule assumes that the interest that has accrued during the time that a note was written, or since the last payment was made, is paid first. Thus, the interest is calculated and subtracted from the payment. The remainder of the partial payment is then applied to the principal of the note.

3. 14.3%   **4.** 105   **5.** $343.75
6. $900   **7.** $3,000   **8.** 1.5 months
9. 21.9%   **10.** $46.55   **11.** 120

12. $1,250   **13.** $2,200   **14.** $760 discount $452.57 interest   Yes, the money should be borrowed.
15. $72,960   **16.** $10,865.68   **17.** 1.333 years   **18.** $31   **19.** 180   **20.** 5.9%

CHAPTER 11

Chapter 11 Additional Practice Problems

11.1

1. $4,750 $90,250   **3.** $613.97 $8,236.03

11.2

5. 13.75%   **7.** 11.25%

11.3

9. $ 487,500 Purchase price $ 12,500 Discount   5.13%
11. $148,218,750 Purchase price $1,781,250 Discount   4.81%

11.4

13. $ 15,384.62   **15.** $777.20

11.5

17. $ 251.08 Discount $ 7,928.92 Proceeds
19. $9,895.42 Discount $170,021.25 Proceeds

Chapter 11 Review Problems

1. $6,615 $28,385   **3.** $50 $1,450   **5.** $11,666.67 $238,333.33   7.25%
7. $46.94 $1,253.06   6.75%   **9.** $9,520 $160,480   5.93%
11. $1,300 $38,700   6.72%   **13.** $10,152.28   **15.** $208,333.33
17. $675 $18,675 $606.94 $18,068.06   13.50%
19. $40.25 $1,040.25 $31.21 $1,009.04   9.25%
21. $4,350 $76,850 $6,051.94 $70,798.06   16.25%
23. $37,196 $1,732,196 $39,841 $1,692,355   11.75%
25. $840 Discount $20,160 Proceeds   **27.** $68,125 Discount $4,931,875 Proceeds   5.53%
29. 10.75%   **31.** $ 80,674.29   **33.** $931.67 Discount $20,568.33 Proceeds   **35.** $69,260.74

Enrichment Problem

37. 13.50% (or 13.25%)

Chapter 11 Self-Testing Exercises

1. A discount is interest deducted from the face value of a note on the date the note is originated. The borrower gets the difference between the principal of the note and the discount (called the proceeds). Interest is added to the face value of a note at the end of the loan period. The borrower pays the principal plus the interest (called the maturity value).

2. The true rate is found by dividing the discount by the proceeds and time, whereas the stated rate is found by dividing the interest by the principal and time. The true rate is higher because the proceeds are less than the principal.

3. $1,333.89   **4.** 13.25% to the nearest 1/4%
8. $1,452   **9.** 11.50% to the nearest 1/4%

5. $58,230   **6.** $56,603.77   **7.** $8,086.93
10. 6.50%   **11.** $20,811.66   **12.** $10,041.13

CHAPTER 12

Chapter 12 Additional Practice Problems

12.1

1. 13.00%   **3.** 14.25%   **5.** 23.25%

12.2

7. 13.50% APR   **9.** 13.75% APR

12.3

11. $ 93.72 Rebate $946.22 Payoff
13. $116.38 Rebate $810.26 Payoff
15. $ 55.54 Rebate $857.33 Payoff

12.4

17. April, $2,418,52; May, $2,619.39; June, $2,574.12
19. March, $5,910; April, $6,169.67

12.5

21.

Date	Description	Transaction Amount	Unpaid Balance	Number of Days Before Balance Changes	Extended Balance
March 8	Billing date			× 2 =	$ 791.16
March 10	Purchase		470.93	× 7 =	3,296.51
March 17	Payment		420.93	× 4 =	1,683.72
March 21	Purchase		447.65	× 18 =	8,057.70
April 8	Billing date				
			Totals	31	$13,829.09

Average daily balance = $13,829.09 ÷ 31 = $446.10
Finance charge for billing cycle = $446.10 × 1.6% = $7.14

23.

Date	Description	Transaction Amount	Unpaid Balance	Number of Days Before Balance Changes	Extended Balance
May 4	Billing date			× 4 =	$ 1,964.12
May 8	Purchase	530.50		× 9 =	4,774.50
May 17	Purchase	822.90		× 6 =	4,937.40
May 23	Payment	772.90		× 7 =	5,410.30
May 30	Purchase	1,006.76		× 5 =	5,033.80
June 4	Billing date				
			Totals	31	$22,120.12

Average daily balance = $22,120.12 ÷ 31 = $713.55

Finance charge for billing cycle = $713.55 × 1.45% = $10.35

25.

Date	Description	Transaction Amount	Unpaid Balance	Number of Days Before Balance Changes	Extended Balance
Oct. 5	Billing date			× 17 =	$31,649.24
Oct. 22	Purchase		2,080.21	× 1 =	2,080.21
Oct. 23	Payment		1,955.21	× 4 =	7,820.84
Oct. 27	Cash advance		2,305.21	× 4 =	9,220.84
Oct. 31	Purchase		2,320.07	× 5 =	11,600.35
Nov. 5	Billing date				
			Totals	31	$62,371.48

Average daily balance = $62,371.48 ÷ 31 = $2,011.98

Finance charge for billing cycle = $2,011.98 × 0.875% = $17.60

Chapter 12 Review Problems

1. $908.00 $132.40   14.0%   **3.** $2000.00 $465.10   18.0%

5. $4,500.00 $903.60   7.9%   **7.** $350.00 $19.50   12.00%

9. $650.00 $49.36   13.75%   **11.** $7,000 $1,868.00   210   1,830 $214.36 $2,741.64

13. $900 $77.40   36   120 $23.22 $498.06

15. $1,750 $249.44   55   171 $80.23 $1,030.57

17. May: $1.79, $1,969.28; June: $1,969.28, $29.54, $2,109.20; July: $2,109.20, $31.64, $2,190.38

19. February: $34.83, $1,748.73; March: $1,748.73, $31.48, $1,319.96; April: $1,319.96, $23.76, $1,108.23

21.

Date	Description	Transaction Amount	Unpaid Balance	Number of Days Before Balance Changes	Extended Balance
Jan. 3	Billing date	$		× 5	$2,012.95
Jan. 8	Payment		352.59	× 9	3,173.31
Jan. 17	Purchase		655.59	× 2	1,311.08
Jan. 19	Purchase		704.12	× 12	8,449.44
Jan. 31	Purchase		1,091.46	× 3	3,274.38
Feb. 3	Billing date				
			Totals	31	$18,221.16

Average daily balance = $18,221.16 ÷ 31 = $587.78

Finance charge for billing cycle = $587.78 × 1.5% = $8.82

23.

Date	Description	Transaction Amount	Unpaid Balance	Number of Days Before Balance Changes	Extended Balance
April 1	Billing date	$		× 1	$ 3,268.00
April 2	Purchase		4,018.00	× 6	24,108.00
April 8	Purchase		4,057.68	× 20	81,153.06
April 25	Payment		3,507.68	× 2	7,015.36
April 30	Purchase		3,998.98	× 1	3,998.98
May 1	Billing date				
			Totals	30	$119,543.94

Average daily balance = $119,543.94 ÷ 30 = $3,984.80

Finance charge for billing cycle = $3,984.80 × 1.25% = $49.81

25.

Date	Description	Transaction Amount	Unpaid Balance	Number of Days Before Balance Changes	Extended Balance
April 5	Billing date	$		× 17	$ 5,947.28
April 22	Cash advance		599.84	× 3	1,799.52
April 25	Purchase		799.27	× 5	3,996.35
April 30	Purchase		4,285.11	× 4	17,140.44
May 4	Payment		3,685.11	× 1	3,685.11
May 5	Billing date				
			Totals	30	$32,568.70

Average daily balance = $32,568.70 ÷ 30 = $1,085.62

Finance charge for billing cycle = $1,085.62 × 1.125% = $12.21

27. $150.19 Rebate $1,857.81 Payoff

29.

Unpaid Balance	Number of Days Before Balance Changes	Extended Balance
$ 630.58	× 3	$ 1,891.74
1,203.87	× 11	13,242.57
803.87	× 1	803.87
914.32	× 3	2,742.96
892.26	× 5	4,461.30
1,092.26	× 7	7,645.82
Totals	30	$30,788.26

Average daily balance = $30,788.26 ÷ 30 = $1,026.28

Finance charge for billing cycle = $1,026.28 × .85% = $8.72

31.

Month	Unpaid Balance Beginning of Month	(.825%) Finance Charge	Purchases During Month	Returns	Payments	Unpaid Balance at End of Month
April	$	$ 2.43	$	$		$295.07
May	295.07	2.43				311.19
June	311.19	2.57				456.50

Enrichment Problems

33. 11.50% APR using formula; 10.50% APR using table   **34.** $289.62 Rebate; $4,130.13 Payoff

Chapter 12 Self-Testing Exercises

1. The Rule of 78 is a method used to calculate the finance charge rebate and the amount required to pay a loan off early. It is called the Rule of 78 because the sum of the year's digits for one year $(1 + 2 + 3 + \ldots + 11 + 12)$ totals 78.
2. When open-end credit is being used, several loans or merchandise charges may be made before any one of them is paid off. No fixed number of payments is established. It may never be paid off.
3. 13.50%   **4.** 13.00%   **5.** $103.33 Rebate $1,943 Payoff
6. March: $23.53 $1,736.90
   April: $1,736.90 $26.05 $1,954.75
   May: $1,954.75 $29.32 $1,606.97

7.

Unpaid Balance	Number of Days Before Balance Changes	Extended Balance
$ 306.78	× 1	$ 306.78
905.99	× 3	2,717.97
998.44	× 8	7,987.52
1,498.44	× 15	22,476.60
1,498.44	× 1	1,148.44
1,483.80	× 2	2,967.60
Totals	30	$37,604.91

Average daily balance = $37,604.91 ÷ 30 = $1,253.50
Finance charge for billing cycle = $1,253.50 × 1.15% = $14.42

8. 14.25%   **9.** 13.75% APR   **10.** $32.39 Rebate $745.73 Payoff
11. March: $ 7.32 $494.77
   April: $494.77 $ 8.26 $582.39
   May: $582.39 $ 9.73 $631.20

12.

Unpaid Balance	Number of Days Before Balance Changes	Extended Balance
$ 992.29	× 4	$ 3,969.16
917.29	× 1	917.29
940.13	× 12	11,281.56
996.46	× 5	4,982.30
1,035.86	× 5	5,179.30
1,060.86	× 4	4,243.44
Totals	31	$30,573.05

Average daily balance = $30,573.05 ÷ 31 = $986.23
Finance charge for billing cycle = $ 986.23 × 1.35% = $13.31

CHAPTER 13

Chapter 13 Additional Practice Problems

13.1

1. $22,050.77 Future value $4,050.77 Interest
3. $ 2,251.02 Future value $ 251.02 Interest
5. $ 6,622.88 Future value $ 622.88 Interest

13.2

7. $ 38,114.67 Future value $ 8,114.67 Interest
9. $229,004.30 Future value $159,004.30 Interest

13.3

11. $4,034.34 Future value $34.34 Interest
13. $11,308.29 Interest $46,308.29 Maturity value
15. $7,602.40 Future value $102.40 Interest

13.4

17. 6.14%   **19.** 5.06%

13.5

21. $16,889.00   **23.** $35,395.66   **25.** $59,527.20

Chapter 13 Review Problems

1. 8.00%   8%   3 $15,116.54 $3,116.54
5. 16 $5,011.52 $11.52
9. 3 $2,083.04 $83.04
13. $839.62   6%   6%   3 $160.38
17. $8,180.20   10.25%   5%   44 $61,819.80
19. $21,709.10   12.68%   1%   48 $13,290.90
23. 3 $654,960 $154,960
25. 8.16%   4%   14 $40,694.39 $17,194.39
27. 6.09%   3%   12 $57,030.40 $17,030.40
31. $38,987.36   **33.** $15,836.11 Future value $836.11 Interest
37. $554,910 Future value $304,910 Interest
41. $5,792.76 Account balance $42.76 Interest

3. 6.14%   1.5%   4 $36,086.38 $2,086.38
7. 8%   8%   36 $77,879.29 $74,379.29
11. $4,529.75   5.06%   2.5%   4 $470.25
15. $1,185.47   8.16%   4%   6 $314.53
21. $88,849   3%   3%   4 $11,151
29. 78 $146,635.82 $1,635.82
35. $2,219.28
39. $60,819.18 Future value $819.18 Interest

Enrichment Problems

43. $58,234   **44.** $165,075.28

Chapter 13 Self-Testing Exercises

1. The period rate is the annual interest rate divided by the number of compounding periods in one year. The constant rate is the period rate plus 100%.

2. Present value is the amount an investment will be worth at the end of some future period of time when interest is compounded. It is also called the compounded amount or the maturity value.

3. $25,900.58 Future value $5,900.58 Interest
5. $126,235.52 Future value $114,235.52 Interest
8. $70,950.95 Future value $20,950.95 Interest

4. $49,720.32 Future value $ 4,720.32 Interest
6. $4,543.58 Interest
9. 10.38%
7. $6,164.95
10. $52,465.50

CHAPTER 14

Chapter 14 Additional Practice Problems

14.1

1. (a) $ 44,614   (b) $48,183.15
3. (a) $151,004.95   (b) $154,025.05
5. (a) $ 52,264.04   (b) $54,354.60

14.2

7. $254,033.10
9. $949,349.00

14.3

11. $16,820.73   **13.** $8,486.40   **15.** $340.45

Chapter 14 Review Problems

1. Ordinary   10%   12 $42,768.56 $18,768.56
3. Due   1.5%   45 $31,307.10 $9,307.10
5. Ordinary   8%   30 $33,984.96 $24,984.96

7. Due   2.5%   13 $4,100.73 $620.73

9. Ordinary   1.5%   28 $29,309.26 $5,509.26

11. 10%   16 $2,347.11 $2,452.89   **13.** 2%   44 $23,263.97 $11,936.03

15. 6%   25 $15,723.53 $15,026.47   **17.** 2.5%   24 $8,030.36 $2,745.64

19. 1.5%   16 $10,951.73 $1,448.27   **21.** $787,050   12%   5 $1,064,750

23. $101.75   2%   32 $1,244   **25.** $33.17   10%   20 $1,236.60

27. $324.38   1.5%   20 $1,012.40   **29.** $1,619.40   2%   28 $14,656.80

31. $45,196.65   **33.** $630.00   **35.** $20,857.97   **37.** $15,120.00

39. $3,795,000   **41.** $120,666.34   **43.** $189,869.80

Enrichment Problems

44. $4,543.88   **45.** $16,410.82   **46.** $282,065.05   **47.** $13,458.42   **48.** $1,132,993.19

Chapter 14 Self-Testing Exercises

1. Both require the calculation of a lump sum amount to be placed in a compound interest account. The present value amount is to be kept on deposit until some future date when a known lump sum amount will be available for withdrawal. On the other hand, the present value of an annuity is to be used up by known periodic withdrawals until, at a future date, the account will be empty.

2. Future value of ordinary annuity problems can be checked by using sinking fund tables. Sinking fund problems can be checked by using future value of ordinary annuity tables.

3. $17,638.77   **4.** $46,941.04   **5.** $94,934.90

6. $15,729.00   **7.** $2,263.80   **8.** $18,339.22

9. $828,744.42 Future value $748,744.42 Interest earned

10. $38,578.23 every six months

CHAPTER 15

Chapter 15 Additional Practice Problems

15.1

1. $1,315.60   **3.** $1,378.02   **5.** $1,612.50

15.2

7. $105,645.60 Interest $ 9,798.60 Savings

9. $242,889.00 Interest $61,357.80 Savings

11. $132,492.60 Savings

15.3

13. $40.71   **15.** $39.52 Lower $35,203.20 Additional

15.4

17.

Payment Number	Size of Payment	Interest Portion	Principal Portion	Balance of Principal
1	$962.12	$935.00	$27.12	$93,472.88
2	962.12	934.73	27.39	93,445.49
3	962.12	934.46	27.66	93,417.83

19.

Payment Number	Size of Payment	Interest Portion	Principal Portion	Balance of Principal
1	$1,100.79	$1,080.00	$20.79	$80,979.21
2	1,100.79	1,079.72	21.07	80,958.14
3	1,100.79	1,079.44	21.35	80,936.79

21.

Payment Number	Size of Payment	Interest Portion	Principal Portion	Balance of Principal
1	$1,304.10	$1,215.00	$89.10	$161,910.90
2	1,304.10	1,214.33	89.77	161,821.13
3	1,304.10	1,213.66	90.44	161,730.69

Chapter 15 Review Problems

1. $790.20	**3.** $856.80	**5.** $1,983.15	**7.** $1,815.75	**9.** $674.25
11. $2,687.50	**13.** $2,195.00	**15.** $1,074.40	**17.** $954.85	**19.** $3,601.50
21. $1,398,870	**23.** $358,722 Interest	$202,759.20 Savings	**25.** $546,120	
27. $73.86	**29.** $225.67	**31.** $360.96		

33.

Payment Number	Size of Payment	Interest Portion	Principal Portion	Balance of Principal
1	$1,955.10	$1,900.00	$55.10	$189,944.90
2	1,955.10	1,899.45	55.65	189,889.25
3	1,955.10	1,898.89	56.21	189,833.04

35.

Payment Number	Size of Payment	Interest Portion	Principal Portion	Balance of Principal
1	$1,055.70	$991.67	$64.03	$169,935.97
2	1,055.70	991.29	64.41	169,871.56
3	1,055.70	990.92	64.78	169,806.78

37.

Payment Number	Size of Payment	Interest Portion	Principal Portion	Balance of Principal
1	$722.40	$700.00	$22.40	$59,977.60
2	722.40	699.74	22.66	59,954.94
3	722.40	699.47	22.93	59,932.01

Enrichment Problem

37. $483.84 Savings per month $174,182.40 Total Savings

Payment Number	Size of Payment	Interest Portion	Principal Portion	Balance of Principal
1	$1,738.80	$1,620.00	$118.80	$215,881.20
2	1,738.80	1,619.11	119.69	215,761.51
3	1,738.80	1,618.21	120.59	215,640.92

Chapter 15 Self-Testing Exercises

1. The interest part of the monthly payment cannot be raised on a fixed-rate mortgage if market interest rates rise.
2. Only persons who are qualified veterans are eligible for V.A. loans.

3. $703.28	**4.** $926.10	**5.** $1,758.93	**6.** $906.53
7. $155,430.00	**8.** $292,075.20	**9.** $160.93	**10.** $177.25

11.

Payment Number	Size of Payment	Interest Portion	Principal Portion	Balance of Principal
1	$586.53	$570.00	$16.53	$56,983.47
2	586.53	569.83	16.70	56,966.77
3	586.53	569.67	16.86	56,949.91

12.

Payment Number	Size of Payment	Interest Portion	Principal Portion	Balance of Principal
1	$724.50	$675.00	$49.50	$89,950.50
2	724.50	674.63	49.87	89,900.63
3	724.50	674.25	50.25	89,850.38

CHAPTER 16

Chapter 16 Additional Practice Problems

16.1

	2002	2003
1. Cash	6.5%	9.7%
3. Merchandise inventory	12.3%	16.1%
Plant and Equipment		
5. Land	11.4%	11.3%
7. Equipment	11.4%	9.7%
9. Total assets	100.0%	100.0%

16.2

	2002	2003
11. Notes payable	(1,000)	(8.3)%
13. Total current liabilities	(3,000)	(8.1)%
Long-term liabilities		
15. Total liabilities	$(3,000)	(3.4)%
Owner's equity		
17. Preferred stock	(5,000)	(10.0)%
19. Total owners equity	$5,000	2.3 %

16.3

	2002	2003
21. Sales	105.2%	104.3%
23. Net sales	100.0%	100.0%
25. Gross profit	62.9%	59.6%
27. Net income	10.6%	12.9%

16.4

	2002	2003
29. Deduct: Sales returns	(2,000)	(7.4)%
31. Deduct: Cost of goods sold	45,000	23.4 %
33. Deduct: Operating expenses	4,000	1.5 %

16.5.

35. 2:1
37. $.32
39. 20%
41. 1.333:1, or 133.3%

Chapter 16 Review Problems

	2002	2003
1. Cash	8.7%	10.9%
3. Merchandise inventory	24.5%	24.4%
5. Land	3.8%	3.7%
7. Equipment	16.2%	14.4%
9. Total assets	100.0%	100.0%
11. Notes payable	8.5%	9.2%
13. Total current liabilities	28.0%	28.7%
15. Total liabilities	46.8%	53.6%
17. Common stock	28.1%	27.7%
19. Total owner's equity	53.2%	46.4%
21. Cash	$ (800)	(5.0)%
23. Merchandise inventory	$(11,200)	(24.6)%
Plant and equipment		
25. Land	$(1,800)	(25.7)%
27. Equipment	(9,700)	(32.3)%
29. Total assets	$(45,100)	(24.3)%
Liabilities and Owner's Equity Current liabilities		
31. Notes payable	(2,800)	(17.7)%
33. Total current liabilities	(11,700)	(22.5)%
Long-term liabilities		
35. Total liabilities	$(11,700)	(13.4)%
Owner's equity		
37. Preferred stock	(6,500)	(25.0)%
39. Total owner's equity	$(33,400)	(33.8)%
41. Gross sales	101.2%	101.6%
43. Sales allowances	.3%	.4%
45. Beginning inventory, (Jan. 1)	7.9%	10.4%
47. Goods available for sale	69.4%	71.5%
49. Cost of goods sold	60.1%	63.7%
51. Operating expenses	20.4%	25.1%
53. Taxes	5.5%	3.2%
55. Gross sales	$(49,500)	(10.0)%

	2002	2003
57. Sales allowances	100	6.7%
Cost of goods sold:		
59. Beginning inventory (Jan. 1)	$7,000	18.2%
61. Goods available for sale	$(25,900)	(7.6)%
63. Cost of goods sold	$(14,700)	(5.0)%
65. Operating expenses	10,000	10.0%
67. Taxes	(13,000)	(48.1)%

	2002	2003		2002	2003		2002	2003		2002	2003
69.	1.90 : 1	1.95 : 1	**71.**	13.9%	8.0%	**73.** 7 times	7 times	**75.**	46.8%	53.6%

77. 1.05 : 1   **79.** 15.6%   **81.** .50 : 1   **83.** 10.84 times

	2002	2003				
85.	58.1%	61.1%	**87.** $40,000 increase	14.3% increase	**89.** 2.04 : 1
91. $.60			**93.** 15%		**95.** 27.3%

Enrichment Problem

97.						
Gross sales	$670,000	103.1%	$670,000	111.7%	$ 0	0%
Sales returns	20,000	3.1%	70,000	11.7%	50,000	250.0%
Net sales	$650,000	100.0%	$600,000	100.0%	$(50,000)	(7.7)%
Cost of goods sold	290,000	44.6%	250,000	41.7%	(40,000)	(13.8)%
Gross margin	$360,000	55.4%	$350,000	58.3%	(10,000)	(2.8)%
Operating expenses	280,000	43.1%	275,000	45.8%	(5,000)	(1.8)%
Net Profit	$ 80,000	12.3%	$75,000	12.5%	$(5,000)	(6.3)%

Chapter 16 Self-Testing Exercises

1. Financial statement analysis provides management with information necessary to determine areas of deficiency that need correction before problems become too critical. In addition, it provides other interested parties with needed information to make funding, investing, lending, or taxing decisions.

2. The debt to total assets ratio would be calculated as a result of a vertical analysis of the balance sheet. Its purpose is to measure the extent to which the assets are financed by borrowed funds.

   The return on sales ratio would be calculated as a result of a vertical analysis of the income statement. Its purpose is to measure company profitability.

3. **and 4.**

	2002	2003		
Sales	101.9%	102.1%	$20,000	7.3%
Sales returns	1.9%	2.1%	1,000	20%
Net sales	100.0%	100.0%	$19,000	7.0%
Cost of goods sold				
Inventory, 1/1	3.0%	3.1%	$1,000	12.5%
Purchases	46.9%	45.0%	3,500	2.8%
Freight-in	1.5%	1.7%	1,000	25%
Goods available for sale	51.3%	49.8%	$5,500	2.7%
Inventory, 12/31	3.3%	3.8%	$2,000	22.2%
Cost of goods sold	48.0%	46.0%	$3,500	2.7%
Gross income	52.0%	54.0%	$15,500	11.0%
Operating expenses				
Salaries	16.5%	17.3%	$5,500	12.4%
Advertising	9.3%	7.6%	3,000	12%
Depreciation	7.4%	6.2%	2,000	10%
Supplies	4.1%	4.5%	2,000	18.2%
Total operating expenses	37.2%	35.6%	$2,500	2.5%
Net income before taxes	14.8%	18.3%	$13,000	32.5%
Taxes	4.4%	6.2%	6,000	50%
Net income after taxes	10.4%	12.1%	$ 7,000	25%

5. and 6.

	2002	2003		
Cash	2.0%	2.2%	$1,000	14.3%
Accounts receivable	6.7%	5.9%	(2,000)	(8.3)%
Notes receivable	1.1%	.8%	(1,000)	(25)%
Inventory	2.5%	3.0%	2,000	22.2%
Prepaid expenses	.3%	.4%	500	50%
Total	12.6%	12.3%	$500	1.1%
Plant assets				
Land	33.6%	32.4%	$0	0%
Building	21.0%	18.9%	(5,000)	(6.7)%
Furniture	5.6%	7.6%	8,000	40%
Equipment	15.4%	16.2%	5,000	9.1%
Total	75.6%	75.0%	$8,000	3.0 %
Intangible assets				
Goodwill	8.4%	9.4%	$5,000	16.7%
Trademark	3.4%	3.2%	0	0%
Total	11.8%	12.7%	5,000	11.9%
Total assets	100.0%	100.0%	$13,500	3.8%
Current liabilities				
Accounts payable	5.3%	6.2%	$4,000	21.1%
Notes payable	1.1%	1.3%	1,000	25 %
Taxes payable	2.2%	2.6%	1,500	18.8%
Payroll payable	13.4%	12.1%	(3,000)	(6.3)%
Total	22.1%	22.3%	$3,500	4.4%
Long-term liabilities				
Bonds payable	14.0%	13.5%	$0	0%
Mortgage payable	6.2%	4.9%	(4,000)	(18.2)
Total	20.2%	18.4%	$(4,000)	(5.6)%
Total liabilities	42.3%	40.6%	$ (500)	(.3)%
Owner's equity				
Common stock	42.0%	40.5%	$0	0%
Retained earnings	15.7%	18.9%	14,000	25%
Total	57.7%	59.4%	$14,000	6.8%
Total liabilities and owner's equity	100.0%	100.0%	$13,500	3.8%

	2002	2003		2002	2003		2002	2003		2002	2003
7.	.57 : 1	.55 : 1	**8.**	.44 : 1	.40 : 1	**9.**	$.19	$.30	**10.**	10.4%	12.1%

	2002	2003		2002	2003		2002	2003		2002	2003
11.	13.6%	15.9%	**12.**	15.24 times	13.3 times	**13.**	.73 : 1	.68 : 1	**14.**	42.3%	40.6%

CHAPTER 17

Chapter 17 Additional Practice Problems

17.1

1. $5,678.33   **3.** $1,295   **5.** $183

17.2

7.

Year	Depreciation
1	$70.00
2	93.33
3	93.33
4	93.33
5	93.33
6	93.33
7	23.33

9.

Year	Depreciation
1	$296.67
2	445
3	445
4	445
5	445
6	148.33

17.3

11.

1	$3,666.67
2	2,933.33
3	2,200.00
4	1,466.67
5	733.33

13.

1	$5,000.00
2	3,333.33
3	1,666.67

15. $711.90

17.4

17.

1	$ 23,524.04
2	25,639.63
3	14,556.49
4	23,460.89
5	21,818.95

19.

1	$ 1,680.00
2	1,560.00
3	1,840.00
4	1,320.00
5	1,600.00

17.5

21.

1	$2,400
2	1,200
3	600
4	0

23.

1	$765.63
2	526.37
3	361.88
4	746.12

25.

1	$6,000
2	4,200
3	2,940
4	2,058
5	2,352

17.6

27. $3,976.70

29.

1	$1,999.80
2	2,667.00
3	888.60
4	444.60

Chapter 17 Review Problems

1. $9,000.00 **3.** 431.25 **5.** 5,000.00 **7.** $1,102.22 $551.11 **9.** $476.67 $43.33 **11.** $28,571.43

13. $305.56 **15.** 1,720.00 **17.** $7,888.09 **19.** $1,872.99 **21.** $2,250.00 **23.** $5,273.44

25. $0 **27.** $4,356.10 **29.** $169.86 **31.** $6,215

33.

1	$2,240
2	1,680
3	1,120
4	560

35.

	200%		150%		125%
1	$1,000.00	1	$750.00	1	$625.00
2	333.33	2	375.00	2	364.58
3	141.67	3	350.00	3	485.42

Enrichment Problem

37. $120,000   Straight line
$227,318   Fourth-year depreciation MACRS
$180,000.00   Sum-of-the years digits
$157,967.01   200% Declining Balance

Chapter 17 Self-Testing Exercises

1. Assets typically lose more of their value in the first year and less in each succeeding year. Since money now is more valuable than money in the future, an accelerated depreciation method allows business firms to save more in taxes now and take advantage of cheaper money in the future.

2. Most assets lose the greatest amount of their original value in the earliest time of their use. Straight-line depreciation is considered unrealistic for most assets because it assumes that all assets lose their value at a constant rate.

3. $35,000	**4.** $1,012.50	**5.** 1 $1,071.88	**6.** 1 $375
		4 765.63	6 75

7. 1 $1,133.33	**8.** 1 $1,760	**9.** 1 $1,197.95	**10.** 1 $ 6,527.42
2 906.67	2 1,320	2 1,372.16	2 5,595.87
3 680.00	3 880	3 629.89	3 6,026.71
4 453.33	4 440		
5 226.67			

11. 1 $13,500	**12.** 1 $12,000	**13.** $5,472
2 6,750	2 6,000	
3 3,375	3 5,700	
4 1,575		

CHAPTER 18

Chapter 18 Additional Practice Problems

18.1

1. $5,176   **3.** $2,885   **5.** $2,914.20

18.2

7. $366.50   **9.** $408.25

18.3

11. $175   **13.** $378   **15.** $119.60

18.4

17. $2,032.68   **19.** $4,466.56

18.5

21. $20,000   **23.** $5,000   **25.** $15,750

18.6

27. $600,000   **29.** $320,000

18.7

31. $10,789.47 Office
43,157.90 Kitchen
10,789.47 Bedroom
53,947.37 Living room
4,315.79 Bath

33. $2,857.14 Glass
5,714.29 Tools
5,142.86 Electrical
2,285.71 Plumbing

35. $7,136 Sales
9,812 Custom design
2,676 Maintenance
2,676 Office

18.8

37. $1,159.09 Dairy
1,545.45 Produce
3,090.91 Meats
2,704.55 Other

39. $27,434.90 Washer & dryer
20,234.38 Refrigerator
14,674.48 Water heater
7,656.25 Air conditioner

18.9

41. $4,772.73 New cars
2,727.27 Used cars
681.82 Trucks
6,818.18 Repairs

43. $4,375 Imports
6,125 Domestic
7,875 Trucks
2,625 Office

45. $5,111.11 Transmission
6,814.81 Engine
3,407.41 Electrical
3,407.41 AC
4,259.26 Suspension

Chapter 18 Review Problems

1. LIFO $78.00	**3.** LIFO $30.50	**5.** LIFO $117.25	**7.** $25,900	**9.** $12,780.00
FIFO $90.00	FIFO $53.00	FIFO $ 98.65	**11.** $7,000	**13.** $34,650
W.A. $84.00	W.A. $42.00	W.A. $111.83	**15.** $6,734	

17.	A	$9,000	19.	A	$24,000	21.	A	$ 800.00	23.	A	$ 3,000.00	25.	A	$ 6,000.00
	B	18,000		B	6,000		B	1,000.00		B	4,000.00		B	1,500.00
	C	6,000		C	7,500		C	1,800.00		C	2,500.00		C	1,875.00
	D	12,000		D	13,500		D	1,200.00		D	2,000.00		D	3,375.00
	E	3,000		E	9,000					E	1,000.00		E	2,250.00
										F	7,500.00			

27.	A	$21,000.00	29.	A	$12,000.00	31.	$40,128
	B	42,000.00		B	24,000.00		
	C	28,000.00		C	32,000.00		
	D	14,000.00		D	12,000.00		
	E	35,000.00		E	16,000.00		

33. $56,740

35. $18,000 Women
    8,000 Girls
  15,000 Men
  12,000 Boys
   4,000 Shoes
   9,000 Linens
   6,000 Housewares

37. $12,500

39. $56,500

Enrichment Problem

40.	Shovels	$1,176.80		LIFO	$661
	Pitchforks	1,390.77		FIFO	518
	Gloves	770.27		WA	595.96
	Spades	1,412.16			

Chapter 18 Self-Testing Exercises

1. Inventory is the unsold merchandise a firm has available for sale. Because it usually represents a significant investment by a company, having adequate amounts on hand is important. Too much inventory means funds are tied up in an unproductive asset. Too little on hand means that there will be stock shortages and customer needs may not be satisfied. Lost sales can result.

2. The four must common methods used to value inventories are specific identification; first-in, first-out (FIFO); last-in, first-out (LIFO); and weighted-average.

3. $59,118.20

4.	FIFO	$1,344	5.	FIFO	$632
	LIFO	1,436.50		LIFO	642
	W.A.	2,362.50		W.A.	992

6. $14,000

7. $44,000 Closing inventory

8.	$ 714.29 Storage
	1,428.57 Baking
	1,071.43 Display
	1,785.71 Seating

9.	$ 5,928.85 Disinfectants
	8,300.40 Safety products
	3,913.04 Sanitary supplies
	11,857.71 Repair

10.	$ 22,145.46 Offices
	25,309.09 Apartments
	30,054.55 Warehouses
	9,490.91 Stores

CHAPTER 19

Chapter 19 Additional Practice Problems

19.1

1. $4.89

3.

WINN-DIXIE
5301 Worrell Drive

SUBTOTAL	$ 13.66
TAX PAID	$ .48
TOTAL	$ 14.14
CASH TEND	$ 15.00
CHANGE	$ .86

5.

```
WAL*MART
6538 HWY 377

    SUBTOTAL    $ 29.32
    TAX PAID    $  1.40
    TOTAL       $ 30.72

    CASH TEND   $ 40.00
    CHANGE      $  9.28
```

19.2

7. $4.97   **9.** $12.42

19.3

11. $8,571.43   **13.** $1,132.08
15. $8,309.46

19.4

17. $1,581,250   **19.** $445.05

19.5

21. $23 per $1,000   **23.** 23.80 mills
25. $42.07 per $1,000

Chapter 19 Review Problems

1. $23.29   **3.** $.56   **5.** $75.43   **7.** $1.95   **9.** $4.24   **11.** $17,307.69
13. $23,738.32   **15.** $36,213.59   **17.** $552.75   **19.** $18,212.50   **21.** $3.76   **23.** $91.30
25. $81.10   **27.** $13.09
29. $2.58 Tax $45.53 Total price **31.** $1.62   **33.** $1.75
35. $1.08   **37.** $4,000   **39.** $1,784.04 **41.** $4,791.15   **43.** $27,953.10   **45.** $77,309.51
47. $.55 per $100 **49.** $16.88 per $1,000

Enrichment Problem

51. 5%

Chapter 19 Self-Testing Exercises

1. Fair market value is the estimated worth of property if it were on the market. It is often called the appraised value becuase it is usually determined by a goverment appraiser.

2. A regressive tax is a tax that falls most heavily on those with the least ability to pay.

3.

```
WINN-DIXIE GROCERY
1429 N. ALTA MEZA

    SUBTOTAL    $ 25.92
    TAX PAID    $  1.71
    TOTAL       $ 27.63

    CASH TEND   $ 30.00
    CHANGE      $  2.37
```

4. $2.91   **5.** $.98
6. $18,691.59   **7.** $20,093.90
8. $2,762.50   **9.** $4,222.80
10. $1.67 per $100   **11.** $29.53 per $1,000

CHAPTER 20

Chapter 20 Additional Practice Problems

20.1

1. $623.60   **3.** $2,090   **5.** $1,016

20.2

7. $27,300   **9.** $71,960 Cash surrender value

20.3

11. $17,040   **13.** $4,416   **15.** $3,850

20.4

17. $100,440   **19.** $168,270   **21.** $9,741.20

20.5

23. $2,665.60   **25.** $1,880.18

20.6

27. $1,562,500
29. The insurance company will pay $600,000. It will
not pay more than the loss.   **31.** $1,093,750

20.7

33. $554.90   **35.** $301

20.8

37. $217   **39.** $490

Chapter 20 Review Problems

1. $7.76   **3.** $866.00   **5.** $38.01   **7.** $1,755   **9.** $25,000   **11.** $1,661.70   **13.** $2,025.00
15. $9,636.00   **17.** $5,643.00   **19.** $3,344.00   **21.** $544.60   **23.** $422.40   **25.** $922.08   **27.** $154,000
29. $65,000   **31.** $294.40   **33.** $413.25   **35.** $345.80   **37.** $430   **39.** $330
41. $1,045   **43.** $783.20   **45.** $41,010   **47.** $3,572   **49.** $19,764   **51.** $27,684.80
53. $1,641.20   **55.** $2,673.20   **57.** $1,644,736.80

59. The insurance company will never pay more
than the face amount of damage, or $250,000
in this case.
67. $400   **69.** $309

61. $259 Liability $362.60 Additional medical
63. $176 Liability $264 Additional medical
65. $287 Liability $330.05 Additional medical

Enrichment Problem

71. a. $736.75 SL   b. $83,160 LP   c. $53,875 Loss   d. $38,100   e. $78,750
  346.50 LP   132,615 SL

Chapter 20 Self-Testing Exercises

1. Buildings are almost never completely destroyed by a fire
so to insure their total value would be to overinsure.
3. $6,341.40   **4.** $20,721.30   **5.** $8,700
6. $63,030   **7.** $2,404.50   **8.** $8,750.00
9. $6,873.12   **10.** $38,850   **11.** $5,407.76
12. $11,208.78
13. $290,000. The insurance company will never pay
more than the amount of the actual loss.
16. $259 Liability $259 Additional medical

2. Collision pays for damages to a policyholder's automobile due to an accident. Comprehensive covers
damage to a policyholder's automobile from causes
other than accidents covered by collision, such as
fire, theft, vandalism, or acts of nature.

14. $121,183.04   **15.** $374.40

17. $483   **18.** $228   **19.** $824.40

CHAPTER 21

Chapter 21 Additional Practice Problems

21.1

1. hi $59.75   low $38.99   **3.** 3.1%
5. 449,300

21.2

7. $3,505.98   **9.** $82,530.00

21.3

11. $324   **13.** 19
15. $10,965 Cash dividends
  213 Stock dividends

21.4

17. $8,250,000
19. $18 per share and $4,500,000 Total cumulative preferred stockholders
  $8 per share and $200,000 Total to noncumulative
preferred stockholders
  $.90 per share and $4,500,000 Total to common
stockholders

21.5

21. $1,036.25

23. $104\frac{1}{8}$

25. 8.1%

21.6

27. $52.50   **29.** $205

21.7

31. $7,800.67   **33.** $95,342.36   **35.** $21,955

Chapter 21 Review Problems

1. 3.5% $3.71 $37.37   **3.** 2.4% $4.75 $39   **5.** 1.5% $.51 $26.75   **7.** $2,106
9. $24,495.43   **11.** $15,000 $.50 $75.00   8   **13.** $2,612,500   3.5% $536.75   20
15. 680,000   1,920   17,000 $2,649.60   **17.** $6.00 $2.57

19. $10.00 $31.20 $3.40   **21.** $0.00 $21.20 $0.00   **23.** $121.25 $11.8% $102\frac{3}{8}$ $1,025.00

25. $75.00 $7.1% $104\frac{3}{8}$ $1,063.75   **27.** $51.25   **29.** $16.25

31. $42.50   **33.** $50.00 $67.29 $9,400.00 $9,417.29

35. $212.50 $460.42 $89,887.50 $90,560.42   **37.** High: $29.37 per share   Low: $21.38 Per share
39. 5.2%   **41.** 63,800   **43.** $27,748.27   **45.** $569.50
47. $248,050 Cash dividend   5,125 Stock dividend

49.
	Common Stock	Cumulative Preferred Stock	Noncumulative Preferred Stock
	$1.20 Per share	$16.50 Per share	$9.125 Per share
	$8,400,000 Total	$3,630,000 Total	$2,281,250 Total

51. $73.75   **53.** $4,611.67   **55.** $26,038.89   **57.** $11,700   **59.** 64   **61.** $16,000,000

63. $838.75   **65.** $84\frac{1}{8}$ **67.** $73.75   **69.** $325   **71.** $75,381.94

Enrichment Problem

72.
1. *General Electric*   *Ford Motor*
   (a) 3.0% Yield   3.8% Yield
   (b) $3.69 Earnings $4.50 Earnings
   (c) $14,142.48 Purchase price
   (d) $5,733 Sales receipts
2. *Office Depot*   3. $61,571.98 Net amount due broker
   (e) $1,812.50 Premium
   (f) $90 Annual interest
   (g) 8.7% Current yield
   (h) $53,162.50 Purchase price

Chapter 21 Self-Testing Exercises

1. If a corporation misses paying dividends in any given year, the holders of noncumulative preferred stock will never receive those dividends. Cumulative preferred stockholders, however, must be paid missed years' dividends and current years' dividends before common stockholders receive any dividends.
2. a. Stocks represent ownership; bonds represent debt.
   b. Cash payment for bonds is interest and must be paid each year. Cash payment for stock is dividends if declared, but dividends never have to be paid.
   c. Stock has no maturity date. Bonds do have a maturity date, and the face value of the bonds must be paid to bondholders on that date.
   d. Common stockholders have voting rights. Preferred stockholders usually have no voting rights. Bondholders are not entitled to vote unless the interest or the face value are not paid when due.
   e. Upon liquidation, stockholders receive payment after bondholders.
3. $2.13   4. 4.5%   5. 33.25   6. $21,751.10   7. $7,029.96

8. $3,400   **9.** 5,250,000   **10.** 24   **11.** $38,950   **12.** $8,400,000

13.
Cumulative Preferred	*Noncumulative Preferred*	*Common*
$1,300,000 Total	$2,375,000 Total	$136,805,000 Total
$13 Per share	$9.50 Per share	$3.42 Per share

14. $766.25   **15.** $78\frac{1}{8}$ **16.** $73.75   **17.** 9.6%   **18.** $36.25

19. $75   **20.** $70,504.38   **21.** $15,544.69

CHAPTER 22

Chapter 22 Additional Practice Problems

22.1

1. Array: 16, 18, 62, 62, 74, 74, 74
Frequency Distribution

Value	Frequency
16	1
18	1
62	2
74	3
58	Range

3. Array: 52, 101, 101, 137, 137, 137, 169
Frequency Distribution

Value	Frequency
52	1
101	2
137	3
169	1
117	Range

5. Array: 2, 2, 10, 10, 14, 26, 26
Frequency Distribution

Value	Frequency
2	2
10	2
14	1
26	2
24	Range

22.2

7. 82.333
9. 22,305

22.3

11. Median = 87 Gary made the median grade.
13. Median = 400
15. Median = $.84

22.4

17. 40 = Mode
19. 1,240 and 1,320 (bimodal)

22.5

21. 56.036 Mean
54.5 Median
44.5 Mode

23. 288 Mean
288 Median
288 Mode

25. $26,922.58 Mean
$26,999.50 Median
$26,999.50 Mode

22.6

27.

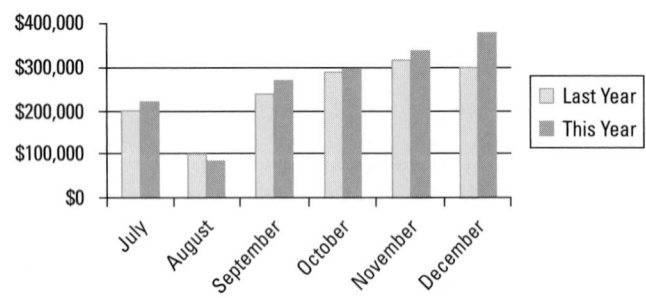

Ben's Cakes
Comparison of Sales Between Last Year and This Year

29.

Alphonso's Bike Shop

Number of Sales by Category of Price Ranges and Models

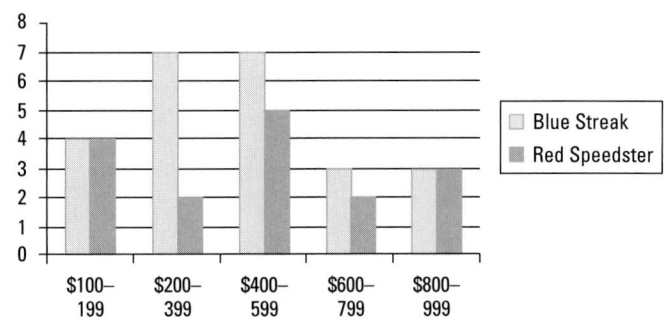

22.7

31.

Joe's Cafe

Value of Sales Compared to the Price Paid

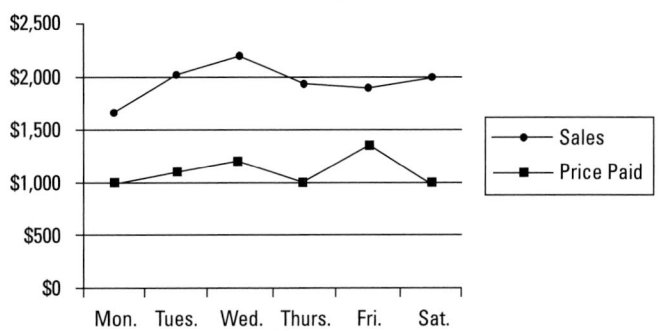

33.

Mildred's Bakeries

Comparison of Sales for Final Half of Year

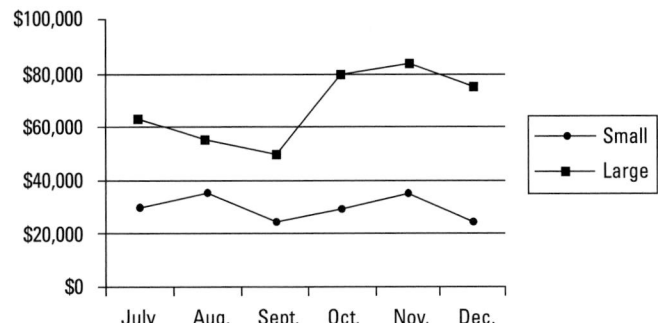

35.

Nixon Watercraft Company

Volume of Net Sales and Net Profits

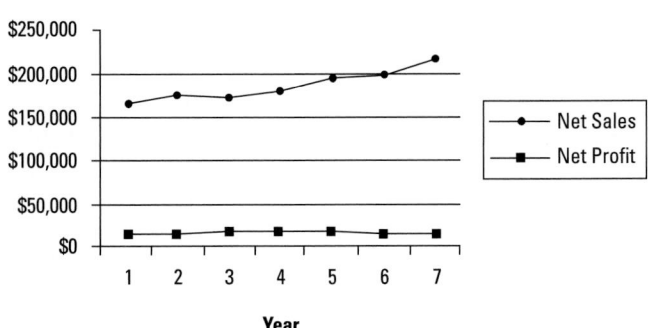

22.8

37.

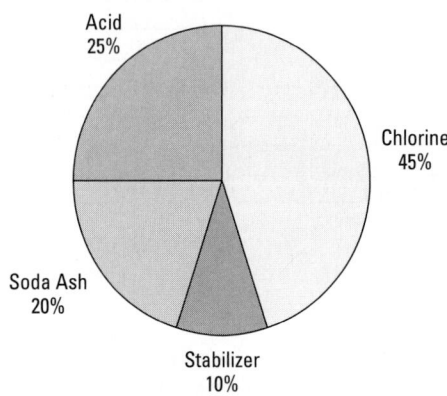

Bonnie and Clyde's Pool Shop
Breakdown by Sales of Chemical Products

Acid 25%
Chlorine 45%
Stabilizer 10%
Soda Ash 20%

39.

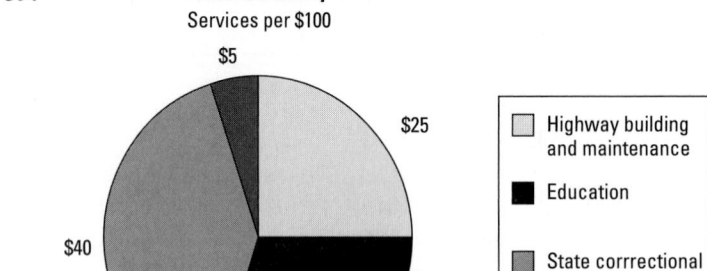

State Tax Money
Services per $100

$5
$25
$40
$30

- ☐ Highway building and maintenance
- ■ Education
- ▨ State corrrectional institutions
- ▣ Other

Chapter 22 Review Problems

1. 8, 9, 31, 31, 37, 37, 37   **3.** 29   **5.** 37 (1), 42 (2), 87 (2), 112 (1)
7. 26, 50, 50, 68, 68, 68, 84   **9.** 58   **11.** 501 (2), 1,097 (4), 1,492 (2)
13. 6, 6, 30, 30, 42, 78, 78   **15.** 72   **17.** 22   **19.** 50
21. 37   **23.** 82.333   **25.** 11,152.667   **27.** Median = 90, Bob's Grade
29. Median = 560   **31.** Median = $.98   **33.** Mode = 48   **35.** Mode = 1,584
37. Mean   = 542.333   **39.** Mean   = 189.829   **41.** Mean   = $126,920.03
    Median = 550   Median = 188   Median = $126,999.50
    Mode   = 550   Mode   = 203   Mode   = $126,999.50

43.

Al's Pipe Shop

Comparison of Sales for Last Six Months Last Year to This Year

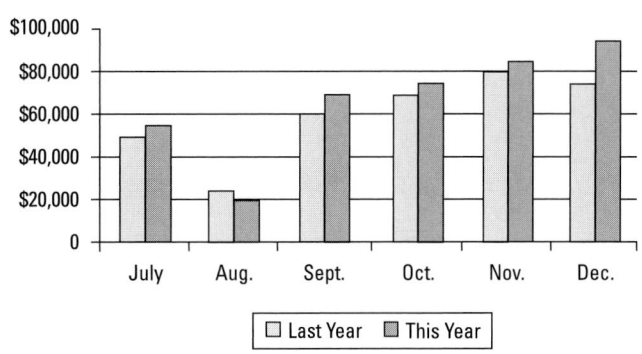

45.

Terri's Sporting Goods

Comparison of Wooden to Aluminum Bat Sales

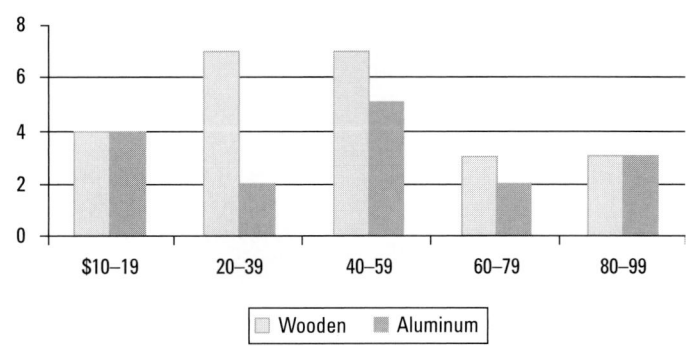

47.

Marty's Toy Store

Weekly Value of Sales and Wholesale Prices

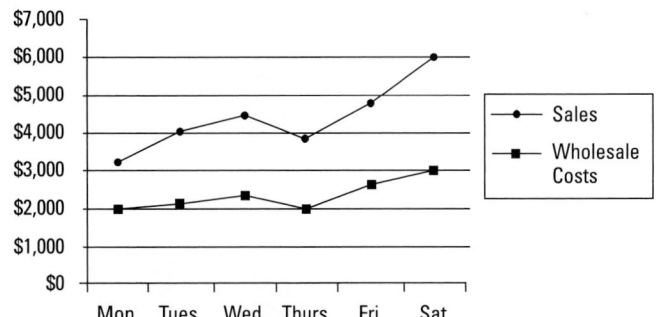

49.

Gerald's Plumbing Shops

Comparison of Sales at Dearborn Shop and Detroit Shop

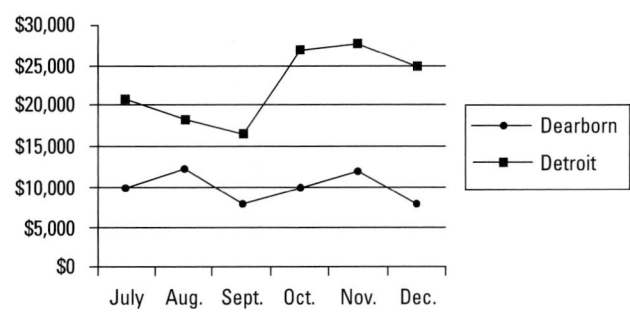

51.

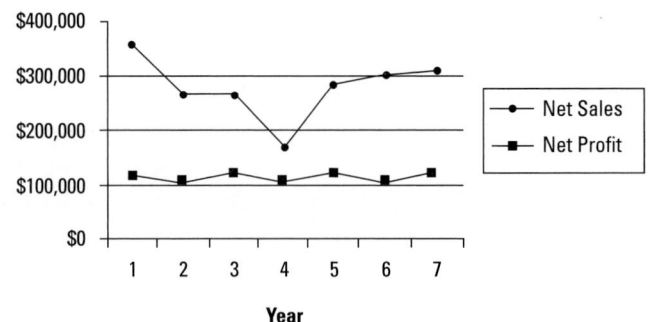

Falwell Bookban Company
Volume of Sales and Net Profit

53.

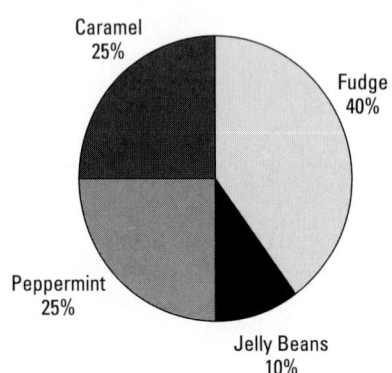

Joe's Candy Store
Breakdown of Products

55.

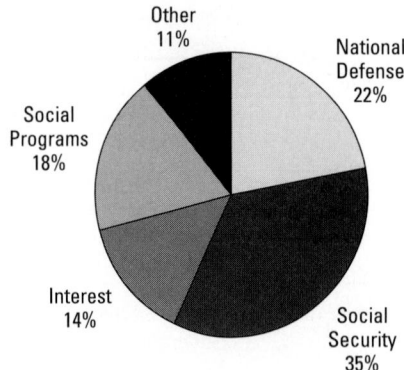

Federal Tax Money
Relationship of Spending

Enrichment Problems

57. Array: 1,114; 2,088; 2,212; 2,318; 2,318; 2,318; 2,336; 2,336; 2,437; 3,122

Frequency Distribution	Value	Frequency
Mean = 2,259.9	1,114	1
Median = 2,318	2,088	1
	2,212	1
Mode = 2,318	2,318	3
	2,336	2
	2,437	1
	3,122	1

58.

Mean 2
Median 2
Mode 0, 2, 3 (Trimodal)

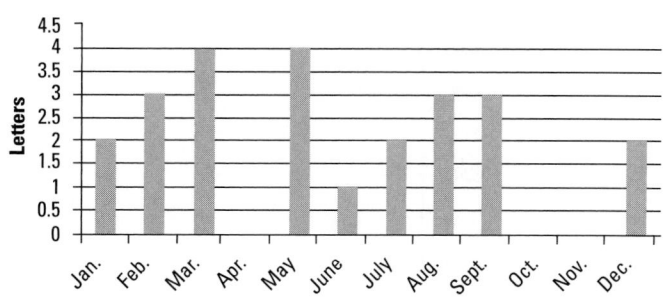

Mildred's Letters to the Editor

Chapter 22 Self-Testing Exercises

1. Central tendency is a number designed to represent the typical number within a group of numbers. The most common are the mean, the median, and the mode.

2. Statistics in business puts data in an order, which makes them more useful. Because business judgments depend on definite measurable facts rather than on intuition, business managers often need to analyze statistical data accurately.

3. Array: 214, 214, 312, 386, 386, 386, 449
Frequency Distribution:

Value	Frequency
214	2
312	1
386	3
449	1

Range = 235

4. Array: 256.8, 256.8, 374.4, 463.2, 463.2, 463.2, 538.8
Frequency Distribution:

Value	Frequency
256.8	2
374.4	1
463.2	3
538.8	1

Range = 282.0

5. Array: 15, 138, 138, 224, 266, 287
Frequency Distribution:

Value	Frequency	Product
15	1	15
138	2	276
224	1	224
266	1	266
287	1	287
	6	1,068

Range = 272
Mean = 178
Median = 181
Mode = 138

6. Mean = 3.857
7. Mean = 4.667
8. Mean = 70.286″
9. Mean = 81.5
Median = 83.5
Mode = 65 and 87 (The data are bimodal.)
10. Mean = $25,835.57
Median = $25,999.50
Mode = $25,999.50

11.

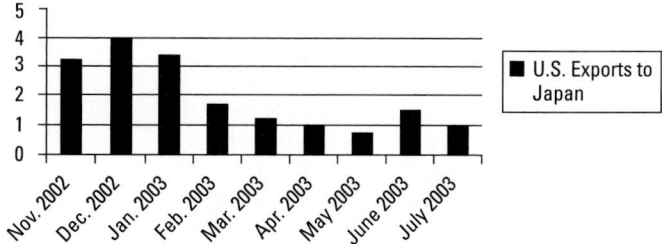

General Agreement on Tariffs and Trade
Increase of Exports to Japan

■ U.S. Exports to Japan

12.

Northeastern Telephone Company
Income from Local and Long-Distance Calls

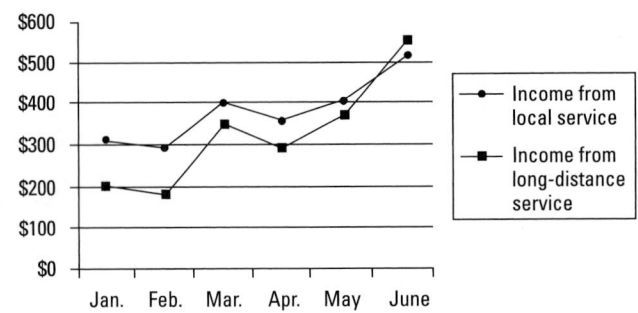

13.

Local Junior College Budget
Expenditures

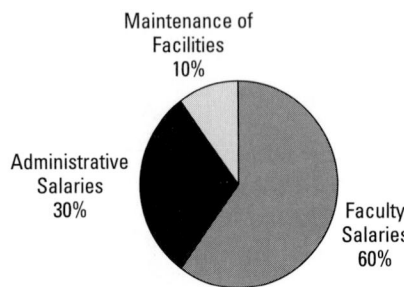

Chapter 23 Additional Practice Problems

23.1

1. 8.5 meters   **3.** 574,000 millimeters   **5.** 194,040 centiliters

23.2

7. 20 pieces
9. 100 boards

23.3

11. 4.23 gallons   **13.** 8.68 ounces

23.4

15. $3\frac{2}{3}$ meters

23.5

17. 44,352 yen
19. 323,400 euros
21. 8,463.95 euros

23.6

23. $5,256.77   **25.** $769,547.50.

23.7

27. $ 103,216.27 Price decrease to the U.S. firm
29. $ 2,974.14 Price decrease to the U.S. firm
31. 330 yen Price increase to the U.S. firm

Chapter 23 Review Problems

1. 20   **3.** .2   **5.** 3,000   **7.** milligram   **9.** .5
11. gram   **13.** 10   **15.** milligram   **17.** 100   **19.** kilometer
21. $28.25   **23.** $108.61   **25.** $2,455.50   **27.** $10,081.48   **29.** $7,464.80
31. $33.63   **33.** $81.32   **35.** $109,962   **37.** $2,051,700   **39.** $367,539.20
41. $.28   **43.** $.26   **45.** $459   **47.** $18,060   **49.** $39.20
51. 31,720 euros **53.** 33,950,000 yen **55.** $1,449.93 Canadian **57.** $961.98   **59.** $626.88
61. $399,845   **63.** $390.70 Price decrease to the U.S. firm

Enrichment Problems

65. $45,159.16 Price decrease to the U.S. firm   **66.** $2,609.93 Price increase to the U.S. firm

Chapter 23 Self-Testing Exercises

1. 1,000	**2.** milliliter	**3.** 300	**4.** dekagram	**5.** 64,000
6. 8.6	**7.** 460	**8.** 21,600	**9.** 1.8	**10.** 3,600
11. 4 pieces	**12.** $750.00	**13.** 150 boards	**14.** 16.19 ounces	**15.** 56 liters

16. Floating exchange rates eliminate the need for government intervention. Instead of governments determining exchange rates, they are determined by the forces of supply and demand.

17. When a nation's currency is devalued, it makes the nation's products cheaper in foreign markets and products of other nations more expensive at home. That should increase exports and decrease imports.

18. 5,178,420 yen   **19.** 1,125 pesos   **20.** 4,070.4 euros   **21.** 56,250 yen

22. 122,361.60 pounds   **23.** 116.85 euros

APPENDIX B FUTA AND SUTA

Additional Practice Problems

1. $228.64
3. SUTA $1,433.97   FUTA $212.44
5. $203.60

Word Problems

7. $198.78

Appendix B Chapter Review Problems

Drill Problems

	SUTA	FUTA
1.	$1,512.00	$224
2.	11,568.69	1,713.88
3.	24,401.00	3,904.16

Appendix B Self-Testing Exercises

	SUTA	FUTA
1.	$1,616.65	$239.50

APPENDIX B
FEDERAL (FUTA) AND STATE (SUTA) UNEMPLOYMENT TAX

Student Objectives

Upon completion of this appendix, you should be able to:

1. Calculate the employer's federal unemployment tax (FUTA).
2. Calculate the employer's state unemployment tax (SUTA).

Chapter Glossary

Federal unemployment tax (FUTA). Federal tax paid by employers to provide for payment of unemployment compensation to workers who have lost their jobs.

State unemployment tax (SUTA). State tax paid by employers to provide for payment of unemployment compensation to workers who have lost their jobs. Usually the SUTA tax is credited toward FUTA.

 Calculating Federal (FUTA) and State (SUTA) Unemployment Tax

The Federal Unemployment Tax Act (FUTA) together with state unemployment systems, provide for payment of unemployment compensation to workers who have lost their jobs. Most employers pay both a federal and state unemployment tax. Only the employer pays this tax, and it is not deducted from the employees' wages. Employers report the federal unemployment tax on Form 940 (see Table B.1).

The FUTA tax rate is 6.2% of the first $7,000 of wages paid during the year to each employee. The $7,000 is the federal wage base. The state wage base may be different. Employers can generally take a credit against the FUTA tax for amounts paid into state unemployment funds. That credit cannot be more than 5.4% of taxable wages, but 5.4% will be credited even if the SUTA tax rate is higher or lower than 5.4%.

If it is over $100, the tax liability must be deposited quarterly by electronic funds transfer or in an authorized financial institution using Form 8109. When making quarterly deposits, the employer multiplies the earnings subject to FUTA by 0.8% (6.2% − 5.4% = .8%). Any difference between the deposited amount and the annual tax due would be made up or refunded at the end of the year when Form 940 is filed.

The standard rate in most states is 5.4%, but the amount an employer pays depends on past employment experience. Employers that fire or lay off fewer employees receive better tax rates. Those with poor employment records pay higher rates. Rates are as low as 1.8% for employers with good employment records, and can be as high as 7% for those with poor records.

EXAMPLE
Marcor, Inc., a small manufacturer, hired six employees. The first quarter and annual earnings of each employee are as follows:

Name	Weekly Earnings	Weeks in Quarter	Quarterly Earnings	Weeks in Year	Annual Earnings
Jones, M.	$200	13	$2,600	52	$10,400
Uristes, U.	250	13	3,250	52	13,000
Yeager, O.	475	13	6,175	52	24,700
Peterson, S.	550	13	7,150	52	28,600

TABLE B.1

Form **940**	**Employer's Annual Federal Unemployment (FUTA) Tax Return**	OMB No. 1545-0028
Department of the Treasury Internal Revenue Service (99)	► See separate Instructions for Form 940 for information on completing this form.	**2000**

		T	
Name (as distinguished from trade name)	Calendar year	FF	
		FD	
Trade name, if any		FP	
		I	
Address and ZIP code	Employer identification number	T	

A Are you required to pay unemployment contributions to only one state? (If "No," skip questions B and C.) . ☐ Yes ☐ No

B Did you pay all state unemployment contributions by January 31, 2001? ((1) If you deposited your total FUTA tax when due, check "Yes" if you paid all state unemployment contributions by February 12, 2001. (2) If a 0% experience rate is granted, check "Yes." (3) If "No," skip question C.) . . . . ☐ Yes ☐ No

C Were all wages that were taxable for FUTA tax also taxable for your state's unemployment tax? . . . . . ☐ Yes ☐ No

If you answered "No" to any of these questions, you must file Form 940. If you answered "Yes" to all the questions, you may file Form 940-EZ, which is a simplified version of Form 940. (Successor employers see **Special credit for successor employers** on page 3 of the instructions.) You can get Form 940-EZ by calling 1-800-TAX-FORM (1-800-829-3676) or from the IRS Web Site at **www.irs.gov.**

If you will not have to file returns in the future, check here (see **Who Must File** in separate instructions), and complete and sign the return . . . . ► ☐

If this is an Amended Return, check here. . . . . ► ☐

Part I	**Computation of Taxable Wages**			
1	Total payments (including payments shown on lines 2 and 3) during the calendar year for services of employees	**1**		
2	Exempt payments. (Explain all exempt payments, attaching additional sheets if necessary.) ► _____ _____	**2**		
3	Payments of more than $7,000 for services. Enter only amounts over the first $7,000 paid to each employee. (See separate instructions.) Do not include any exempt payments from line 2. The $7,000 amount is the Federal wage base. Your state wage base may be different. **Do not use your state wage limitation.**	**3**		
4	Total exempt payments (add lines 2 and 3)	**4**		
5	**Total taxable wages** (subtract line 4 from line 1) . . . . ►	**5**		

Be sure to complete both sides of this form, and sign in the space provided on the back.

For Privacy Act and Paperwork Reduction Act Notice, see separate instructions.   Cat. No. 11234O   Form **940** (2000)

DETACH HERE

Form **940-V**	**Form 940 Payment Voucher**	OMB No. 1545-0028
Department of the Treasury Internal Revenue Service	**Use this voucher only when making a payment with your return.**	**2000**

Complete boxes 1, 2, 3, and 4. Do not send cash, and do not staple your payment to this voucher. Make your check or money order payable to the **"United States Treasury".** Be sure to enter your employer identification number, "Form 940", and "2000" on your payment.

1 Enter the first four letters of your last name (business name if partnership or corporation).	**2** Enter your employer identification number.	**3** Enter the amount of your payment.
		$

Instructions for Box 1

—Individuals (sole proprietors, trusts, and estates)— Enter the first four letters of your last name.

—Corporations and partnerships—Enter the first four characters of your business name (omit "The" if followed by more than one word).

4 Enter your business name (individual name for sole proprietors)

Enter your address

Enter your city, state, and ZIP code

Part II **Tax Due or Refund**

1	Gross FUTA tax. Multiply the wages from Part I, line 5, by .062	**1**
2	Maximum credit. Multiply the wages from Part I, line 5, by .054 . . **2**	

3 Computation of tentative credit (**Note:** *All taxpayers must complete the applicable columns.*)

(a) Name of state	(b) State reporting number(s) as shown on employer's state contribution returns	(c) Taxable payroll (as defined in state act)	(d) State experience rate period		(e) State experience rate	(f) Contributions if rate had been 5.4% (col. (c) x .054)	(g) Contributions payable at experience rate (col. (c) x col. (e))	(h) Additional credit (col. (f) minus col.(g)). If 0 or less, enter -0-.	(i) Contributions paid to state by 940 due date
			From	To					

3a	Totals . . . ▶	
3b	**Total tentative credit** (add line 3a, columns (h) and (i) only—for late payments also see the instructions for Part II, line 6 . . . . ▶	**3b**
4		
5		
6	**Credit:** Enter the smaller of the amount from Part II, line 2 or line 3b; or the amount from the worksheet in the Part II, line 6 instructions	**6**
7	**Total FUTA tax** (subtract line 6 from line 1). If the result is over $100, also complete Part III . .	**7**
8	Total FUTA tax deposited for the year, including any overpayment applied from a prior year . .	**8**
9	**Balance due** (subtract line 8 from line 7). Pay to the "United States Treasury". If you owe more than $100, see **Depositing FUTA Tax** on page 3 of the separate instructions . . . . . . ▶	**9**
10	**Overpayment** (subtract line 7 from line 8). Check if it is to be: ☐ **Applied to next return** or ☐ **Refunded** . . . . ▶	**10**

Part III **Record of Quarterly Federal Unemployment Tax Liability** (Do not include state liability.) **Complete only if line 7 is over $100.** See page 6 of the separate instructions.

Quarter	First (Jan. 1–Mar. 31)	Second (Apr. 1–June 30)	Third (July 1–Sept. 30)	Fourth (Oct. 1–Dec. 31)	Total for year
Liability for quarter					

Under penalties of perjury, I declare that I have examined this return, including accompanying schedules and statements, and, to the best of my knowledge and belief, it is true, correct, and complete, and that no part of any payment made to a state unemployment fund claimed as a credit was, or is to be, deducted from the payments to employees.

Signature ▶   Title (Owner, etc.) ▶   Date ▶

✿

Form **940** (2000)

Name	Weekly Earnings	Weeks in Quarter	Quarterly Earnings	Weeks in Year	Annual Earnings
Yates, W.	625	13	8,125	52	32,500
Taylor, B.	975	13	12,675	52	50,700

The SUTA experience rate for Marcor is 3.9% (also on the first $7,000 of earnings). Calculate: (1) the FUTA deposit required in the first quarter and (2) the SUTA and the FUTA tax liability for the year.

Solution   (1) The solution for the first quarterly FUTA deposit is as follows:

Name	Quarterly Earnings	Exempt Earnings	Taxable Earnings
Jones	$ 2,600	$0	$ 2,600
Uristes	3,250	0	3,250
Yeager	6,175	0	6,175
Peterson	7,150	150	7,000
Yates	8,125	1,125	7,000
Taylor	12,675	5,675	7,000
Total			$33,025

$$\underset{\substack{\text{Total taxable} \\ \text{earnings}}}{\$33,025} \times \underset{\substack{(6.2\% - 5.4\%) \\ \text{FUTA rate} \quad \text{SUTA credit}}}{.8\%} = \underset{\substack{\text{Amount} \\ \text{of deposit}}}{\$264.20}$$

(2) The solution for the SUTA and the FUTA tax liability for the year is as follows:

Name	Annual Earnings	Exempt Earnings	Taxable Earnings
Jones	$10,400	$ 3,400	$ 7,000
Uristes	13,000	6,000	7,000
Yeager	24,700	17,700	7,000
Peterson	28,600	21,600	7,000
Yates	32,500	25,500	7,000
Taylor	50,700	43,700	7,000
Total			$42,000

SUTA: $42,000 \times 3.9\% = \$1,638$

FUTA: $42,000 \times .8\% = 336$ (FUTA = 6.2% − 5.4%)

AppB.1 Practice Problems

1. Determine the FUTA deposit required after the first quarter for a company that has five employees with semimonthly earnings as follows:

Thelma	$1,560	Petrinko	$ 880
Suzanne	935	Juan	1,715
Sabine	1,470		

2. Drebonski Furniture downsized from 12 to 8 employees just prior to the beginning of the year. As a consequence, the state imposed an experience rate of 6.5% for the year. All eight of the employees earned more than $7,000 during the year. Determine both the SUTA and the FUTA taxes for the year.

3. Given the following payroll history for the year, find the amount of the SUTA and the FUTA taxes for a year in which the state experience rate was 5.4%:

Don Lee	$42,500
Suki Itachi	3,900 (hired in November)
Dianna Shumatsu	22,000
Mark Johnston	6,400 (part-time employee)

4. Martin Steinbrenner is very proud of the fact that he has not lost a single employee in the past five years. The state has rewarded his company with a SUTA experience rate of 2.25% this year. Each of the 21 employees earned more than $7,000 this year. Determine both the SUTA and the FUTA taxes for the year.

AppB.1 Solutions to Practice Problems

1.

Name	Semimonthly Earnings	Periods in Quarter	Quarterly Earnings	Taxable Earnings
Thelma	$1,560	6	$ 9,360	$ 7,000
Suzanne	935	6	5,610	5,610
Sabine	1,470	6	8,820	7,000
Petrinko	880	6	5,280	5,280
Juan	1,715	6	10,290	7,000
				$31,890

$31,890 \times .8\% = \$255.12$

2.

SUTA	FUTA
$7,000 \times 8 = \$56,000$	$7,000 \times 8 = \$56,000$
$56,000 \times 6.5\% = \$3,640$	$56,000 \times 6.2\% = \$3,472$
	$56,000 \times 5.4\% = -\ \$3,024$
	$\ \$\ \ 448$

3.

Name	Annual Earnings	Taxable Earnings
Don Lee	$42,500	$ 7,000
Suki Itachi	3,900	3,900
Dianna Shumatsu	22,000	7,000
Mark Johnston	6,400	6,400
		$24,300

$$\underline{SUTA} \qquad\qquad \underline{FUTA}$$

$$\$24,300 \times 5.4\% = \$1,312.20 \quad \$24,300 \times 6.2\% = \$1,506.60$$
$$ \underline{-\ 1,312.20}$$
$$ \$\ \ \ 194.40$$

4.

$$\underline{SUTA} \qquad\qquad\qquad \underline{FUTA}$$

$$\$7,000 \times 21 = \$147,000 \qquad \$7,000 \times 21 = \$147,000$$
$$\$147,000 \times 2.25\% = \$3,307.50 \quad \$147,000 \times 6.2\% = \quad \$9,114$$
$$ \$147,000 \times 5.4\% = \underline{-\ \$7,938}$$
$$ \$1,176$$

QUICK REFERENCE SUMMARY AND REVIEW

Page	Section Topic	Learning Concepts	Examples and Solutions
B-1	AppB.1 Calculating Federal (FUTA) and State (SUTA) Unemployment Tax	Only the employer pays these taxes based on past employment experience. State rates vary, but the federal rate is 6.2% on the first $7,000 of wages to each employee in a year. The state tax can be credited against the federal tax up to 5.4%. These taxes provide unemployment compensation to employees who have lost their jobs.	Calculate the FUTA and SUTA for a company that has 10 employees each earning over $7,000 this year. The state rate is 5.4%

Examples and Solutions continued:

SUTA	FUTA
$70,000	6.2%
× 5.4%	−5.4%
$ 3,780	.8%

$$\begin{aligned}\$70,000 \\ \times \quad .8\% \\ \hline \$\quad\ \ 560\end{aligned}$$

| ADDITIONAL PRACTICE PROBLEMS | *Answers to odd-numbered problems are given in Appendix A.* |

AppB.1

Solve the following Federal Unemployment Tax (FUTA) and State Unemployment Tax (SUTA) problems:

1. Determine the FUTA deposit required after the first quarter for Smythe & Daughter. Smythe has six employees with monthly earnings as follows:

Jenkins, B.	$3,000	Latro, E.	$ 580
Guzman, R.	1,250	Huan, K.	3,575
Adams, P.	970	Pettis, O.	2,060

Name	Monthly Earnings	Quarterly Earnings	Exempt Earnings	Taxable Earnings
Jenkins	$3,000	$9,000	$2,000	$7,000
Guzman	1,250	3,750	0	3,750
Adams	970	2,910	0	2,910
Latro	580	1,740	0	1,740
Huan	3,575	10,725	3,725	7,000
Pettis	2,060	6,180	0	6,180
Total				$28,580

$$\$28,580 \quad \times \quad .8\% \quad = \quad \$228.64$$

Total taxable earnings   (6.2%) FUTA rate   └(5.4%) SUTA credit   Amount of deposit

2. Karborn's Sports Shop laid six employees off and dismissed four others last year. The state imposed an experience rate of 7% for the year. All six of the remaining full-time employees earned more than $7,000 during the year. The two part-time employees earned $4,375, and $6,890 during the year. Determine both the SUTA and the FUTA taxes for the year.

SUTA
FT Employees: $7,000 × 6 = $42,000
PT Employees: $4,375
+ 6,890   +11,265
$11,265 $53,265
$53,265 × 7% = $3,728.55

FUTA
$53,265 × 6.2% = $3,302.43
$53,265 × 5.4% = −2,876.31
$426.12

3. Given the following payroll history for the year, find the amount of the SUTA and the FUTA taxes for a year in which the state experience rate was 5.4%:

		Taxable Earnings
Sue O'Brien	$32,608	$ 7,000
Sky Blue	5,555	5,555
James Rodman	12,300	7,000
Marie Lindstrum	8,250	+ 7,000
		$26,555

SUTA
$26,555 × 5.4% = $1,433.97

FUTA
$26,555 × 6.2% = $1,646.41
− 1,433.97
$ 212.44

4. Martha Urestes, general manager for Richmound Amusement Park, has had an excellent record of employment for several years. The state SUTA experience rate of 3.5% this year is a reflection of that record. All of the 415 employees earned more than $7,000 this year. Determine both the SUTA and the FUTA taxes for the year.

SUTA
$7,000 × 415 = $2,905,000
$2,905,000 × 3.5% = $101,675

FUTA
$7,000 × 415 = $2,905,000
$2,905,000 × 6.2% = $180,110
$2,905,000 × 5.4% = − $156,870
$ 23,240

5. Lordcastle Pawn Shop's year-to-date payroll record for the first quarter was as follows:

Leon Hastings	$32,100
Thomas Jacobs	6,250
Wu Provia	14,900
Jerri Maxwell	5,200

Determine the necessary FUTA tax deposit for the quarter.

Name	Quarterly Earnings	Exempt Earnings	Taxable Earnings
Hastings	$32,100	$25,100	$ 7,000
Jacobs	6,250	0	6,250
Provia	14,900	7,900	7,000
Maxwell	5,200	0	+ 5,200
Total			$25,450

$$\underset{\substack{\text{Total}\\\text{taxable}\\\text{earnings}}}{\$25,450} \times \underset{\substack{(6.2\%\ \llcorner5.4\%)\\\text{FUTA}\quad\text{SUTA}\\\text{rate}\quad\text{credit}}}{.8\%} = \underset{\substack{\text{Amount}\\\text{of deposit}}}{\$203.60}$$

CHAPTER REVIEW PROBLEMS

Answers to odd-numbered problems are given in Appendix A.

Drill Problems

Calculate the FUTA and the SUTA yearly tax liability for the companies in the following problems:

	Employee	SUTA Experience Rate	Annual Payroll	Exempt Earnings	SUTA	FUTA
1.	ARN Corp	5.4%	$ 76,475	$ 48,475	$ 1,512.00	$ 224.00
2.	Autley Inc	4.8%	209,700	156,400	2,558.40	426.40
3.	Beach Bros	5.4%	365,325	151,090	11,568.69	1,713.88
4.	Cost Less	6.3%	122,205	34,520	5,524.16	701.48
5.	Dipway Ltd	5.0%	944,220	456,200	24,401.00	3,904.16

Word Problems

6. Gouda's Clothing Store has eight employees, all who make more than $7,000 per year. The state employment experience rate is 4.4%. Calculate both the SUTA and FUTA taxes for the year.

SUTA

$7,000 × 8 = $56,000 $56,000 × 4.4% = $2,464

FUTA

$56,000 × .8% = $448

7. In the first quarter of the year, company employees had the following earnings:

Jacqueline Henry	$ 296 per week
Matthew Kincaid	$ 992 per week
Harrick Vin	$ 765 per week
Glen Zuckerman	$2,128 per week

Find the quarterly FUTA deposit for Hardaway Quick Shop.

Name	Weekly Earnings	Weeks in Quarter	Quarterly Earnings	Exempt Earnings	Taxable Earnings
Henry	$ 296	13	$ 3,848	$ 0	$ 3,848
Kincaid	992	13	12,896	5,896	7,000
Vin	765	13	9,945	2,945	7,000
Zuckerman	2,128	13	27,664	20,664	+ 7,000
Total					$ 24,848

$$\underset{\substack{\text{Total}\\\text{taxable}\\\text{earnings}}}{\$24,848} \times \underset{\substack{(6.2\%\ \llcorner5.4\%)\\\text{FUTA}\quad\text{SUTA}\\\text{rate}\quad\text{credit}}}{.8\%} = \underset{\substack{\text{Amount}\\\text{of deposit}}}{\$198.78}$$

8. The Automotive Machine Shop has been given an employment experience rating of 6.4% this year. It hires 22 full-time employees, all of whom earned more than $7,000 this year. Eight part-time employees also earned more than $7,000 during the year. Six other part-time employees had the following earnings for the year: $2,908; $1,037; $4,018; $6,991; $2,217; and $5,671. Determine the SUTA and FUTA taxes due for the year.

		SUTA	FUTA
$7,000 × 30 = $210,000		$232,842.00	$232,842.00
	2,908	× 6.4%	× .8%
	1,037	$ 14,901.89	$ 1,862.74
	4,018		
	6,991		
	2,217		
	+ 5,671		
	$232,842		

SELF-TESTING EXERCISES	*Answers to all exercises are given in Appendix A.*

1. Wildwood Equipment Rental Service has a state employment experience rate of 5.4%. The employees and their annual earnings are shown here:

		Taxable Earnings
Williams, Inez	$17,498	$ 7,000
Quintana, Alberto	16,993	7,000
Martin, Cynthia	21,056	7,000
Thompson, Melisa	6,281	6,281
Blake, Trent	2,657	+ 2,657
		$29,938

Calculate the SUTA and FUTA taxes for the year.

SUTA = $29,938 × 5.4% = $1,616.65
FUTA = $29,938 × .8% = $239.50

INDEX

Page numbers followed by *f* and *t* indicate figures and tables, respectively.

Electronic Data Systems, sale of, 542
electronic funds transfer (EFT), 301, 302
employees, per department, overhead
　　　allocation by, 634–636
employer, payroll responsibilities of,
　　　192–197, 192t, 193t
ending inventory, 543, 551
end-of-month (EOM) dating, for cash
　　　discounts, 223, 236–237
endorsement, 301, 304, 304f
endowment life insurance, 683, 684
EOM (end-of-month) dating, for cash
　　　discounts, 223, 236–237
equations
　　brackets in, 113–114
　　conversion of
　　　　with addition, 106–107
　　　　with cross multiplication, 110–111
　　　　with division, 107–109
　　　　with inversion, 109–110
　　　　with multiplication, 107–109
　　　　with subtraction, 106–107
　　definition of, 101
　　formatting for solving, 115–120, 115f
　　parentheses in, 113–114
　　solving, 105
　　　　by combining like unknowns,
　　　　　112–113
　　　　with formatting, 115–120, 115f
　　　　with multiple arithmetic operations,
　　　　　111–112
　　　　for multiple unknowns, 118, 118f
　　writing, 114–115
equipment and plant assets, 543, 545–546
equivalent fractions
　　definition of, 65
　　from raising, 71–72
equivalent markup percents, 261, 261t
eras
　　decimal positional values for, 4t
　　definition of, 3, 4
estimation
　　of annual percentage rate (APR),
　　　412–415
　　of decimal number operations
　　　addition, 41–42
　　　division, 47–48
　　　multiplication, 45
　　　subtraction, 43
　　definition of, 3, 6
　　of inventory
　　　gross profit method for, 619,
　　　　628–629
　　　retail method for, 619, 626–628
　　of whole number operations
　　　addition, 6–7
　　　division, 13
　　　multiplication, 11
　　　subtraction, 8
exact interest, 339, 342
exchange rate, 798
　　changes in, 805–808

definition of, 799, 804
flexible (floating), 799, 805
excise tax, 661, 662
expenses, operating, 544, 551
exports, 799, 804

F

face value, 717, 727
factors, 3, 9
fair market value, 661, 668
Federal Income Tax (FIT)
　　calculating, 184–185, 184t, 186t–189t,
　　　190, 190t, 191t
　　in deductions, 168
　　definition of, 167
　　replacement of, 660
federal unemployment tax (FUTA),
　　　862–866, 863f–864f
FHA loan, 515, 516f
FICA (social security tax)
　　benefits of, 181
　　calculating deduction for, 180–184,
　　　181t
　　definition of, 167
FIFO (first-in, first-out) method, for
　　　inventory, 619, 620–621
finance charge
　　average daily balance method for, 411,
　　　427–431
　　definition of, 411
　　in estimating APR, 412
　　unpaid balance method for, 411,
　　　424–427
finance charge rebate, 411, 420–424,
　　　422t
financial ratio. See ratio
fire insurance
　　cancellation of policy, refund for,
　　　692–694, 693t
　　liability under, with coinsurance,
　　　695–696
　　premium for, 690–691
　　　for more than one year, 691–692
first-in, first-out (FIFO) method, for
　　　inventory, 619, 620–621
FIT. See Federal Income Tax
fixed rate mortgage, 515, 516f
flexible (floating) exchange rate, 799,
　　　805
floor space, overhead allocation by,
　　　630–632
foot measure, origin of, 64
foreign exchange, 799, 804
formatting
　　definition of, 101
　　for problem-solving, 16–19
　　to solve for unknowns, 115–120, 115f
401(k) plan, 488
fractions
　　common (See common fractions)
　　decimal (See decimal fractions)

definition of, 65
　　in equations, 109–111
　　equivalent, 65, 71–72
　　improper (See improper fractions)
　　proper (See proper fractions)
　　reducing, 68–71, 68t
frequency distribution, 755, 756–757
FUTA (federal unemployment tax),
　　　862–866, 863f–864f
future value. See also maturity value
　　of annuity, 490f, 491–494, 492t
　　calculating, 458–461, 458t
　　　with daily compounding, 465–468,
　　　　467t
　　　with tables, 462–465, 464t
　　definition of, 457, 458

G

General Motors, and Electronic Data
　　　Systems, 542
general sales tax, 661, 662
goods available for sale, 543, 551
graduated payment mortgage, 515, 516f
gram, 799, 800
graph
　　bar type, 755, 764–767
　　circle type, 755, 769–771
　　definition of, 755
　　line type, 755, 767–769
greatest common divisor
　　definition of, 65
　　in reducing fractions, 69–71
gross pay, 168
　　deductions from, 180, 180t
　　definition of, 167
　　for hourly wage employees, 169, 169t
　　　with overtime, 170–174
　　for salaried employees, 168–169, 168t,
　　　169t
gross profit, 544, 551
gross profit method, for inventory
　　　estimation, 619, 628–629
gross sales, 543, 551

H

hectare, 799, 800
home-equity loan, 515, 516f
horizontal analysis
　　of balance sheet, 548–550
　　definition of, 543, 548
　　of income statement, 553–556
hourly wage
　　definition of, 167, 169
　　gross pay for, 169, 169t
　　　with overtime, 170–174

I

imports, 799, 804
improper fractions
　　conversion of, to mixed numbers,
　　　67–68